¡Ven conmigo!®

Your passport to proficiency

Pasaporte al mundo

Plan your itinerary for success

What's your **Destination?**

Communication!

¡Ven conmigo! takes

your classroom there.

It's even possible that

"What's next?"

becomes your

students' favorite

question!

Communication
and culture in context

The clear structure of each chapter makes it easy to present, practice, and apply language skills—all in the context of the location where the chapter takes place!

Grammar support and
practice in every lesson

¡Ven conmigo! builds a proven communicative approach on a solid foundation of grammar and vocabulary so students become proficient readers, writers, and speakers of Spanish. With the Cuaderno de gramática, Grammar Tutor, and the CD-ROM and DVD Tutors, students can practice the way they learn best.

Technology that takes you there

Bring the world into your classroom with integrated audio, video, CD-ROM, DVD, and Internet resources that immerse students in authentic language and culture.

Assessment for state and national standards

To help you incorporate standardized test practice, the **Standardized Assessment Tutor** provides reading, writing, and math tests in Spanish that target the skills students need. The **¡Lee conmigo!** Reader and **Reading Strategies and Skills Handbook** offer additional reading practice and reading skills development.

Easy lesson planning for all learning styles

Planning lessons has never been easier with a **Lesson Planner with Substitute Teacher Lesson Plans**, an editable **One-Stop Planner®** CD-ROM, and a **Student Make-Up Assignments with Alternative Quizzes** resource.

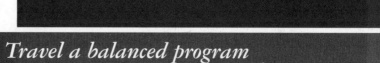

*Travel a balanced program that's **easy to navigate.***

¡El mundo a su alcance!

The *¡Ven conmigo!* family

or ...

Program components

¡Ven conmigo! Levels 1-3

Texts
- Pupil's Edition
- Teacher's Edition

Planning and Presenting
- One-Stop Planner CD-ROM with Test Generator
- Exploratory Guide
- Lesson Planner with Substitute Teacher Lesson Plans
- Student Make-Up Assignments with Alternative Quizzes
- Teaching Transparencies

Native Speakers
- Cuaderno para hispanohablantes

Grammar
- Cuaderno de gramática
- Grammar Tutor for Students of Spanish

Reading and Writing
- Reading Strategies and Skills Handbook
- ¡Lee conmigo! Reader
- Cuaderno de actividades

Listening and Speaking
- Audio CD Program
- Listening Activities
- Activities for Communication
- TPR Storytelling Book (Levels 1 and 2)

Assessment
- Testing Program
- Alternative Assessment Guide
- Student Make-Up Assignments with Alternative Quizzes
- Standardized Assessment Tutor

Technology
- One-Stop Planner CD-ROM with Test Generator
- Audio CD Program
- Interactive CD-ROM Tutor
- Video Program
- Video Guide
- DVD Tutor (Levels 1 and 2)

Internet
- go.hrw.com
- www.hrw.com
- www.hrw.com/passport

ANNOTATED TEACHER'S EDITION

¡Ven conmigo!®

HOLT SPANISH

LEVEL 1

HOLT, RINEHART AND WINSTON

A Harcourt Classroom Education Company

Austin · New York · Orlando · Atlanta · San Francisco · Boston · Dallas · Toronto · London

In the Annotated Teacher's Edition:
Acknowledgments
For permission to reprint copyrighted material, grateful acknowledgment is made to the following sources:
National Standards in Foreign Language Education Project: "National Standards Report" from Standards for Foreign Language Learning: Preparing for the 21st Century. Copyright © 1996 by National Standards in Foreign Language Education Project.

Photography Credits
Abbreviations used: (b) bottom, (c) center, (r) right, (l) left.

All photos belong to Holt, Rinehart & Winston except:

Front Cover: bkgd, Robert Frerck/Odyssey/Chicago; teens, Steve Ewert/HRW Photo; back cover: © Robert Freck/Odyssey/Chicago; frame, ©1998 Image Farm Inc.

15D (bl) Philadelphia Museum of Art/CORBIS; 45D(bl) Joe Viesti/Viesti Collection, Inc.; 77C (br) Rosenthal/HRW; 77D (bl) Miwako Ikeda/International Stock Photography; T78 (br) Laurie Platt Winfrey, Inc., Sor Juana Inés de la Cruz, oil, Miranda, 1651, University of Mexico City.; T78 (bl) Christie's Images/SuperStock; 107D (cl) Sam Dudgeon/HRW; 107D (cr) Sam Dudgeon/HRW; 139D(bl) Nik Wheeler/CORBIS; 139D (br) Beryl Goldberg Photography; 167H (all) Michelle Bridwell/Frontera Fotos; 201D (bl) Suzanne L. Murphy/D. Donne Bryant Photography; 201D (br) Jackson Vereen/FoodPix; 229D (cl) Suzanne Murphy-Larronde; 229D (r) Sam Dudgeon/HRW; 263D (cl) Frank S. Balthis; 291D (cl) Bob Daemmrich Photo, Inc.; 291C (cr) Sam Dudgeon/HRW; 325D (cr) Michelle Bridwell/HRW; 355D (bl) Suzanne Murphy-Larronde.

Art Credits
All art, unless otherwise noted, by Holt, Rinehart & Winston.

Preliminary Chapter: Page T65, Guy Maestracci. Chapter Two: Page 45H, Edson Campos . Chapter Five: Page 139H, Edson Campos. Chapter Twelve: Page 355G, Ignacio Gomez/ Carol Chislovsky Design, Inc.

In the Pupil's Edition:
See pages R45–R48 for acknowledgments.
Copyright © 2000 **CNN** and **CNNfyi.com** are trademarks of Cable News Network LP, LLLP, a Time Warner Company. All rights reserved.
Copyright © 2000 Turner Learning logos are trademarks of Turner Learning, Inc., a Time Warner Company. All rights reserved.

¡VEN CONMIGO! is a trademark licensed to Holt, Rinehart and Winston, registered in the United States of America and/or other jurisdictions.

ONE-STOP PLANNER is a trademark licensed to Holt, Rinehart and Winston, registered in the United States of America and/or other jurisdictions.

Printed in the United States of America
2 3 4 5 6 7   048   05 04 03 02
ISBN 0-03-057324-6

¡Ven conmigo! Level 1
Annotated Teacher's Edition

CONTRIBUTING WRITERS

Dr. Marjorie E. Artzer
Northern Kentucky University
Highland Heights, KY

Dr. Artzer was the principal
writer for Level One.

Jackie Moase-Burke
Language Arts Oakland Schools
Clinton Township, MI

Jo Anne S. Wilson
J. Wilson Associates
Glen Arbor, MI

Ms. Moase-Burke and Ms. Wilson
contributed Teaching Suggestions
and notes for Chapters 1, 2, and 3.

Susan Dennis
Texas A&M University
College Station, TX

Dr. Dennis wrote the Circumlocution
suggestions for Chapters 6–12.

**The following people researched and
wrote culture features:**

Mildred A. Price
Austin, TX

Mary Nichols
Austin, TX

Mariángeles LaPointe
Austin, TX

Amy Propps
Austin, TX

CONSULTANTS

Dr. Audrey L. Heining-Boynton
The University of North Carolina
Chapel Hill, NC

Jo Anne S. Wilson
J. Wilson Associates
Glen Arbor, MI

TEACHER-TO-TEACHER CONTRIBUTORS

Patricia Ahrens
Central Junior High School
West Lawn, PA

Diana Goff
Chaparral High School
Scottsdale, AZ

Norah Jones
Rustburg High School
Rustburg, VA

Mani Hernández
Presentation High School
San Jose, CA

Diane Kalata
Pioneer High School
Ann Arbor, MI

Latanza Garvin
Lexington Catholic High School
Lexington, KY

Shelli Albertson
Shorewood High School
Shorewood, WI

Patricia Wells
C.C. Sweeting Junior High School
Nassau, Bahamas

Linda Hale
Sonoma Valley High School
Sonoma, CA

Kimberly Bromley
Warren Township High School
Gurnee, IL

Susan DiGiandomenico
Wellesley Middle School
Wellesley, MA

Irene Garcia
Travis High School
Austin, TX

Aura Cole
Parkway Central Middle School
Chesterfield, MO

Alisa Glick
Greenwich Country Day School
Greenwich, CT

Bill Heller
Perry High School
Perry, NY

Maritza and Robert Furillo
Franklin Alternative School
Columbus, OH

Jean Schuster
Eagan High School
Eagan, MN

Paula Bernard
Sandy Creek High School
Fayette County, GA

Sarah Voorhees
Saratoga High School
Saratoga, CA

Carolyn Ostermann-Healy
Oakton High School
Vienna, VA

Jeanne Jendrzejewski
LSU Lab School
Baton Rouge, LA

Carol Chadwick
Taipei American School
Taipei, Taiwan

Kristine Conlon
Muscatine High School
Muscatine, IA

Kim Peters
Mooresville High School
Mooresville, IN

PROFESSIONAL ESSAYS

Bringing Standards into the Classroom
Paul Sandrock
Foreign Language Consultant
Department of Public Instruction
Madison, WI

Reading Strategies and Skills
Nancy A. Humbach
Miami University
Oxford, OH

Technology in the Language Classroom
Cindy A. Kendall
Williamston High School
Williamston, MI

*Using Portfolios in the Language
Classroom*
Jo Anne S. Wilson
J. Wilson Associates
Glen Arbor, MI

Teaching Culture
Nancy A. Humbach
Miami University
Oxford, OH

Dorothea Bruschke
Parkway School District
Chesterfield, MO

*Learning Styles and Multi-Modality
Teaching*
Mary B. McGehee
Louisiana State University
Baton Rouge, LA

New Perspectives for Native Speakers
Cecilia Rodríguez-Pino
New Mexico State University
Las Cruces, NM

To the Teacher

Principles and Practices

As nations become increasingly interdependent, the need for effective communication and sensitivity to other cultures becomes more important. Today's youth must be culturally and linguistically prepared to participate in a global society. At Holt, Rinehart and Winston, we believe that proficiency in more than one language is essential to meeting this need.

The primary goal of the Holt, Rinehart and Winston World Languages programs is to help students develop linguistic proficiency and cultural sensitivity. By interweaving language and culture, our programs seek to broaden students' communication skills while at the same time deepening their appreciation of other cultures.

We believe that all students can benefit from foreign language instruction. We recognize that not everyone learns at the same rate or in the same way; nevertheless, we believe that all students should have the opportunity to acquire language proficiency to a degree commensurate with their individual abilities.

Holt, Rinehart and Winston's World Languages programs are designed to accommodate all students by appealing to a variety of learning styles.

We believe that effective language programs should motivate students. Students deserve an answer to the question they often ask: "Why are we doing this?" They need to have goals that are interesting, practical, clearly stated, and attainable.

Holt, Rinehart and Winston's World Languages programs promote success. They present relevant content in manageable increments that encourage students to attain achievable functional objectives.

We believe that proficiency in another language is best nurtured by programs that encourage students to think critically and to take risks when expressing themselves in the language. We also recognize that students should strive for accuracy in communication. While it is imperative that students have a knowledge of the basic structures of the language, it is also important that they go beyond the simple manipulation of forms.

Holt, Rinehart and Winston's World Languages programs reflect a careful progression of activities that guide students from comprehensible input of authentic language through structured practice to creative, personalized expression. This progression, accompanied by consistent re-entry and spiraling of functions, vocabulary, and structures, provides students with the tools and the confidence to express themselves in their new language.

Finally, we believe that a complete program of language instruction should take into account the needs of teachers in today's increasingly demanding classrooms.

At Holt, Rinehart and Winston, we have designed programs that offer practical teacher support and provide resources to meet individual learning and teaching styles.

Contents

Pacing and Planning

Traditional Schedule

Days of instruction: 180

Location Opener	2 days per Location Opener	
	x 6 Location Openers	12 days
Chapter	13 days per chapter	
	x 12 chapters	156 days
		168 days

If you are teaching on a traditional schedule, we suggest following the plan above and spending 13 days per chapter. A complete set of lesson plans in the interleaf provides detailed suggestions for each chapter. For more suggestions, see the **Lesson Planner with Substitute Teacher Lesson Plans.**

Block Schedule

Blocks of instruction: 90

Location Opener	1/2 block per Location Opener	
	x 6 Location Openers	3 blocks
Chapter	7 blocks per chapters	
	x 12 chapters	84 blocks
		87 blocks

If you are teaching on a block schedule, we suggest following the plan above and spending seven blocks per chapter. A complete set of lesson plans in the interleaf provides detailed suggestions for each chapter. For more suggestions, see the **Lesson Planner with Substitute Teacher Lesson Plans.**

 One-Stop Planner CD-ROM

Use the **One-Stop Planner CD-ROM with Test Generator** to aid in lesson planning and pacing.

- Editable lesson plans with direct links to teaching resources
- Printable worksheets from resource books
- Direct launches to the HRW Internet activities
- Video and audio segments
- Test Generator
- Clip Art for vocabulary items

 Pacing Tips

At the beginning of each chapter, you will find a Pacing Tip to help you plan your lessons.

Articulation Across Levels

The following chart shows how topics are repeated across levels in *Ven conmigo!* from the end of Level 1 to the beginning of Level 3.

- In each level, the last chapter is a review chapter.
- In Levels 2 and 3, the first two chapters review the previous level.

LEVEL 1

CHAPTER 12
Review of Level 1

- **gustar** and **encantar**
- **e** to **ie** and **o** to **ue** stem-changing verbs
- Uses of verbs **ser** and **estar**
- Present progressive
- Uses of the preterite
- Verbs followed by an infinitive
- Discussing what you would like to do on vacation
- Making future plans
- Saying where you went and what you did on vacation
- Talking about what you do and like to do every day

LEVEL 2

CHAPTER 1
Review of Level 1

- Adjective agreement
- Future tense with **ir**
- **gustar**
- Indirect object pronouns
- Present tense of regular verbs
- Present tense of **salir, venir, hacer, ver, ir, tener**
- Describing people
- Introducing yourself and others
- Saying what you like and don't like
- Talking about what you and others do

CHAPTER 2

- The verb **estar**
- Preterite of **-ar** verbs
- Present tense of **querer** and **poder**
- Asking for and offering help
- Clothing
- Describing your city or town
- Places around town
- Making suggestions and responding
- Saying if something has already been done
- Talking about how you are feeling

CHAPTER 12
Review of Level 2

- Imperfect tense
- Regular and irregular verbs in the preterite tense
- Subjunctive mood
- Describing places
- Exchanging the latest news
- Saying how you feel about people
- Saying when you're going to do something
- Talking about where you went and what you did
- Telling when something happened

LEVEL 3

CHAPTER 1
Review of Level 2

- Adjectives
- Stem-changing verbs in the present tense
- The present tense
- The preterite
- Question formation
- **saber** vs. **conocer**
- **y** and **o** before vowels
- Asking for information
- Describing yourself and others
- Expressing interest, indifference, and displeasure
- Sports and hobbies

CHAPTER 2

- Informal commands
- Irregular informal commands
- Present progressive
- Reflexive verbs
- The imperfect
- Uses of the imperfect
- Asking for and giving advice
- Parts of the body
- Talking about taking care of yourself

CHAPTER 12
Review of Level 3

- Future tense and **ir a** + infinitive
- Personal **a** before certain pronouns
- Preterite and imperfect
- The past subjunctive
- The subjunctive
- Giving advice and making recommendations about work
- Talking about former jobs and goals
- Talking about future career plans

¡Ven conmigo! Spanish Level 1
Scope and Sequence

FUNCTIONS	GRAMMAR	VOCABULARY	CULTURE	RE-ENTRY
CAPÍTULO PRELIMINAR ¡Adelante!, Pages xxx–11				
• Frases útiles		• Nombres comunes • El alfabeto • Colores y números • Para mejor aprender el español	• El mapa del mundo hispanohablante • El español—¿Por qué? • ¿Sabías...? • ¿Los conoces?	
España CAPÍTULO 1 ¡Mucho gusto!, Pages 16–45				
• Saying hello and goodbye • Introducing people and responding to an introduction • Asking how someone is and saying how you are • Asking and saying how old someone is • Asking where someone is from and saying where you're from • Talking about likes and dislikes	• Spanish punctuation marks • Pronouns **yo** and **tú** • Use of **ser** for origin • Forming questions with **cómo, cuántos, de dónde** • Singular definite articles: **el, la** • Noun gender and agreement	• Numbers 0–30 • Names of some Spanish-speaking countries • Sports • Musical genres • Classes at school • Foods	• Greetings and goodbyes • First names and saint's days • **¿De dónde eres?** • **la distancia interpersonal**	• Accent marks • Numbers 0–30
España CAPÍTULO 2 ¡Organízate!, Pages 46–70				
• Talking about what you want and need • Describing the contents of your room • Talking about what you need and want to do	• Indefinite articles **un, una, unos, unas** • Making nouns plural • Agreement of **mucho** and **cuánto** with nouns • Subject pronouns **él** and **ella** • The three types of infinitives: **-ar, -er, -ir**	• School supplies • The contents of your room • Things you do • Numbers 31–199	• The school day in Spain and Latin America • **¿Qué necesitas para el colegio?** • Apartments in Spain • Spanish currency	• Subject pronouns **yo** and **tú** • Talking about likes and dislikes • Forming questions with **¿cuántos?**

México

CAPÍTULO 3   Nuevas clases, nuevos amigos, *Pages 78–107*

FUNCTIONS	GRAMMAR	VOCABULARY	CULTURE	RE-ENTRY
• Talking about class schedules and sequencing events • Telling time • Telling at what time something happens • Talking about being late or in a hurry • Describing people and things • Talking about things you like and explaining why	• Plural definite articles **los, las** • Using **ser** to tell time • Forms of **ser** • Adjective agreement • Tag questions • Possession with **de**	• School subjects • Words that describe people and things • Free-time activities and things you like • Words that refer to time	• Grade scales • **¿Cómo es un día escolar típico?** • Student course loads • **hora latina** • Entertainment guide	• Present tense of **tener** • Numbers 0–199 • Forming questions • Noun-adjective agreement • Forms of **necesitar, querer**

México

CAPÍTULO 4   ¿Qué haces esta tarde? *Pages 108–135*

FUNCTIONS	GRAMMAR	VOCABULARY	CULTURE	RE-ENTRY
• Talking about what you like to do • Discussing what you and others do during free time • Telling where people and things are • Talking about where you and others go during free time	• Present tense of regular **-ar** verbs • Present tense of **jugar** • The contraction **al** • **con, conmigo, contigo** • Use of **que** • Present tense of **estar** • Subject pronouns • Present tense of **ir** • Use of **el** and **los** with days of the week	• Places in town and their location • The days of the week • Things you like to do • Talking about where you and others go	• Popular sports in Spanish-speaking countries • Use of **tú** and **usted** • **el paseo** • School-sponsored activities	• Subject pronouns: **yo, tú, él, ella** • Present tense of **ser** and **tener** • Telling time

Florida

CAPÍTULO 5   El ritmo de la vida, *Pages 140–167*

FUNCTIONS	GRAMMAR	VOCABULARY	CULTURE	RE-ENTRY
• Discussing how often you do things • Talking about what you and your friends like to do together • Talking about what you do during a typical week • Giving today's date • Talking about the weather	• Negation • **¿quién?** and **¿quiénes?** • **les** and **a ustedes, a ellos, a ellas** • Regular **-er** and **-ir** verbs • Giving the date in Spanish	• Weekend activities • The seasons and the months • Weather expressions • Frequency terms	• Getting together with friends • **¿Cómo es una semana típica?** • Seasons in South America	• Gender • Subject pronouns with **-er** and **-ir** verbs • Days of the week

	FUNCTIONS	GRAMMAR	VOCABULARY	CULTURE	RE-ENTRY

Florida

CAPÍTULO 6 Entre familia, *Pages 168–177*

FUNCTIONS	GRAMMAR	VOCABULARY	CULTURE	RE-ENTRY
• Describing a family • Describing people • Discussing things a family does together • Discussing problems and giving advice	• Possessive adjectives • Present tense of **hacer** and **salir** • Present tense of **deber** • Present tense of **poner** • Understanding "personal **a**"	• Members of the family • Words that describe people • Household chores	• **el compadrazgo** • Privacy in Hispanic culture • **la familia** • Diminutives	• **hay** • Possessive adjectives • Colors • Descriptions of people • Pastimes/hobbies • **¿con qué frequencia?** • Forming questions

Ecuador

CAPÍTULO 7 ¿Qué te gustaría hacer?, *Pages 178–229*

FUNCTIONS	GRAMMAR	VOCABULARY	CULTURE	RE-ENTRY
• Talking on the telephone • Extending and accepting invitations • Making plans • Talking about getting ready • Turning down an invitation and explaining why	• **e** to **ie** stem-changing verbs • **pensar** + infinitive • **ir** + **a** + infinitive • Reflexive verbs • Expressions with **tener**	• Places and events • Words used to extend and accept invitations • Telephone vocabulary • Personal chores	• Common telephone expressions • Getting around without a car • **¿Qué haces para conocer a una persona?** • Party invitation	• **gustar** • Days of the week • **pensar** and **ir** • Future expressions

Ecuador

CAPÍTULO 8 ¡A comer!, *Pages 230–259*

FUNCTIONS	GRAMMAR	VOCABULARY	CULTURE	RE-ENTRY
• Talking about meals and food • Commenting on food • Making polite requests • Ordering dinner in a restaurant • Asking for and paying the bill in a restaurant	• Present tense of **encantar** and indirect object pronouns • Use of **estar** to talk about how things taste • **ser** and **estar** • **o** to **ue** stem-changing verbs • Expressions with **tener** • The forms of **otro**	• The table setting • Food and drink items for breakfast, lunch, and dinner • Words to describe food • Restaurant vocabulary	• **la comida de las Américas** • Breakfast in Spanish-speaking countries • Lunch in Spanish-speaking countries • Dinner in Spanish-speaking countries • **¿Cuál es un plato típico de tu país?** • *Calvin and Hobbes* comic strip • Table manners in Spanish-speaking countries • Common Andean dishes • Latin American and Spanish tortillas	• **e** to **ie** stem-changing verbs • Numbers 200–100,000 • Expressing likes and dislikes • Expressions with **tener** • **estar** and **ser**

FUNCTIONS	GRAMMAR	VOCABULARY	CULTURE	RE-ENTRY

CAPÍTULO 9 ¡Vamos de compras!, *Pages 264–291*

• Discussing gift suggestions • Asking for and giving directions downtown • Commenting on clothes • Making comparisons • Expressing preferences • Asking about prices and paying for something	• Indirect object pronouns: **le, les** • **es/son + de** + material or pattern • Comparisons: **más... que, menos... que, tan... como** • Demonstrative adjectives	• Gift suggestions • Stores downtown • Words describing clothes • Vocabulary for shopping	• Specialty stores in Spain • **¿Estás a la moda?** • Catalog page with clothing • *Tamalada* • Currency in some Spanish-speaking countries, the **euro**	• **ir + a** + infinitive • Talking about locations • Describing family • Numbers 0–100,000

CAPÍTULO 10 Celebraciones, *Pages 292–325*

• Talking about what you're doing right now • Asking for and giving an opinion • Asking for help and responding to requests • Telling a friend what to do • Talking about past events	• Present progressive • Informal commands • Preterite tense of regular **-ar** verbs • Direct object pronouns **lo** and **la**	• Festivals and holidays • Preparations for a party • Expressions for times in the past	• **día del santo** • **¿Qué hacen ustedes para celebrar?** • **la fiesta de quinceañera** • **¿Cómo se celebra una boda?** • **las piñatas**	• **estar** • **tú** versus **usted** • Dates, months, seasons • Extending, accepting, and turning down invitations • **¿quién?, ¿quiénes?**

CAPÍTULO 11 Para vivir bien, *Pages 326–355*

• Making suggestions and expressing feelings • Talking about moods and physical condition • Saying what you did • Talking about where you went and when	• The verb **sentirse** • The verb **doler** with **me, te,** and **le** • The verbs **ir** and **jugar** in the preterite	• Fitness activities • Words to describe moods and physical conditions • The human body • Locations for sports events	• Questionnaire about living well • Baseball in Spanish-speaking countries • **¿Qué deporte practicas?** • Magazine article on relieving stress • American football vs. soccer, **jai alai** • **remedios caseros**	• **estar** + condition • Stem-changing verbs • The preterite • Food vocabulary • Sports

CAPÍTULO 12 Las vacaciones ideales, *Pages 356–383*

REVIEW CHAPTER

• Talking about what you do and like to do every day • Making future plans • Discussing what you would like to do on vacation • Saying where you went and what you did on vacation	• **e** to **ie** and **o** to **ue** stem-changing verbs • Verbs followed by an infinitive • Uses of verbs **ser** and **estar** • Uses of the preterite	• Vacation activities and objects • Wilderness activities	• **¿Adónde vas y qué haces en las vacaciones?** • Spain's **paradores** • Spanish colloquialisms	• Chapter 12 is a global review of Chapters 1–11

¡Ven conmigo! Spanish Level 2
Scope and Sequence

	FUNCTIONS	GRAMMAR	VOCABULARY	CULTURE	RE-ENTRY
Andalucía	**CAPÍTULO 1 Mis amigos y yo,** *Pages 6–33*				
REVIEW CHAPTER	• Introducing yourself and others • Describing people • Talking about what you and others do • Saying what you like and don't like	• Present tense of **tener** • Adjective agreement • Present tense of regular verbs • Indirect object pronouns with verbs like **gustar**	• Nationalities • Numbers • Colors • Family members	• Description of appearance of Hispanics • **¿Qué es el euro?** • Planning evening activities in Spain • **¿Qué es un buen amigo?** • **cafeterías** • **¡Soy así!**	• Chapter 1 reviews Spanish taught in *¡Ven conmigo!* Level 1.
Andalucía	**CAPÍTULO 2 Un viaje al extranjero,** *Pages 34–61*				
REVIEW CHAPTER	• Talking about how you're feeling • Making suggestions and responding to them • Saying if something has already been done • Asking for and offering help • Describing your city or town	• The verb **estar** • Preterite of **-ar** verbs • Present tense of **querer** and **poder**	• Calendar expressions • Places around town • Weather expressions • Clothing	• Extended family living together • **¿En dónde te gustaría vivir?** • Celsius vs. Fahrenheit • Barcelona	• Chapter 2 reviews Spanish taught in *¡Ven conmigo!* Level 1.
Valle de México	**CAPÍTULO 3 La vida cotidiana,** *Pages 66–93*				
	• Talking about your daily routine • Talking about responsibilities • Complaining • Talking about hobbies and pastimes • Saying how long something has been going on	• Reflexive verbs and pronouns • **e** to **i** stem change in **vestirse** • Adverbs ending in **-mente** • Direct object pronouns: **lo, la, los, las** • **hace** + quantity of time + **que** + present tense	• Daily activities • Chores • Hobbies and pastimes	• **¿Cuál es tu profesión?** • Household chores • Expressions of agreement • Popular free-time activities among teenagers • **¿Estás aburrido/a de tu rutina?**	• Verbs of personal grooming • Adverbs of time and place • Vocabulary of household chores in Spain • Asking for help, responding to requests • Giving explanations • Vocabulary of hobbies and pastimes • Question formation

FUNCTIONS	GRAMMAR	VOCABULARY	CULTURE	RE-ENTRY

Valle de México

CAPÍTULO 4 ¡Adelante con los estudios! *Pages 94–123*

FUNCTIONS	GRAMMAR	VOCABULARY	CULTURE	RE-ENTRY
• Asking for and giving opinions • Giving advice • Talking about things and people you know • Making comparisons • Making plans	• **deberías** vs. **debes** • **ser** + adjective to describe people • **estar** + adjective to describe location • Present tense of the verb **conocer** • Direct object pronouns	• Classroom activities • School and computer terms • Describing people • Activities around town	• School levels in Mexico • Cost of university education in Latin America • **¿Qué haces después del colegio?** • **¿Quién es americano?**	• School subjects • **para** (in order to) + infinitive • **ser** vs. **estar** • Comparisons: **más... que, menos... que** • **ir** + **a** + infinitive

Texas

CAPÍTULO 5 ¡Ponte en forma!, *Pages 128–157*

FUNCTIONS	GRAMMAR	VOCABULARY	CULTURE	RE-ENTRY
• Talking about staying fit and healthy • Telling someone what to do and not to do • Giving explanations	• Preterite of the verb **dormir** • Preterite of regular **-er** and **-ir** verbs • Informal commands • Irregular informal commands • Preterite of **poder** • Reflexives with verbs of emotion	• Sports • Fitness activities • Health and fitness terms • Body parts • Injuries and explanations	• **¿Sanos o no?** • Student responses about health habits in Spanish-speaking countries • Snack foods in Spanish-speaking countries • **Garnachas, antojitos y bocadillos** • **¿Qué haces para mantenerte en forma?** • Flyers and radio ads	• Preterite of regular **-ar** verbs • Informal commands • Spelling changes in verbs that end in **-car, -gar, -zar** • Reflexive verbs

Texas

CAPÍTULO 6 De visita en la ciudad, *Pages 158–185*

FUNCTIONS	GRAMMAR	VOCABULARY	CULTURE	RE-ENTRY
• Asking for and giving information • Relating a series of events • Ordering in a restaurant	• Present tense of **saber** • **saber** vs. **conocer** • Preterite forms of **pedir, servir, traer**	• In the city • Places in the city • In the train station • In a restaurant	• San Antonio • **¿Cómo llegas al colegio?** • Birthday celebrations • **El festival de la música tejana**	• Direct object pronouns • **poder** • The preterite for listing events • Food vocabulary

El Caribe — CAPÍTULO 7 ¿Conoces bien tu pasado?, *Pages 190–219*

FUNCTIONS	GRAMMAR	VOCABULARY	CULTURE	RE-ENTRY
• Talking about what you used to do • Saying what you used to like and dislike • Describing what people and things were like • Using comparisons to describe people	• The imperfect tense of **-ar, -er, -ir** verbs • The imperfect tense of **ir** and **ver** • Spelling change of **o** to **u** and **y** to **e** to avoid vowel repetition • Imperfect of **ser** to describe people and things • The imperfect of **hay** • **tan** + adjective/adverb + **como**	• Childhood activities • Describing peole • Describing places • Conveniences	• **Lo mejor de lo antiguo** • Public services in Latin American cities • **dichos** • **¿De quién es esta estatua?** • **el merengue**	• The preterite • Talking about likes and dislikes using the preterite • Comparisons: **más/menos** + adjective + **que** • Complaining • Descriptive adjectives

El Caribe — CAPÍTULO 8 Diversiones, *Pages 220–247*

FUNCTIONS	GRAMMAR	VOCABULARY	CULTURE	RE-ENTRY
• Describing a past event • Saying why you couldn't do something • Reporting what someone said	• Adjectives with **-ísimo/a** • Superlatives • Verbs with prepositions • Using **mientras** in the past • Preterite of **decir**	• In the zoo, the amusement park, and movie theater • Running errands • At a festival	• **El Yunque** and **el coquí** • **¿Cuáles son las fiestas más importantes de tu ciudad o país?** • Holidays and festivals in Spanish-speaking countries • **Ponce es Ponce**	• Describing things • Describing what you did • The imperfect tense • Imperfect of **hay** • The preterite

Los Andes — CAPÍTULO 9 ¡Día de mercado!, *Pages 252–281*

FUNCTIONS	GRAMMAR	VOCABULARY	CULTURE	RE-ENTRY
• Asking for and giving directions • Asking for help in a store • Talking about how clothes look and fit • Bargaining in a market	• Formal commands with **usted, ustedes**	• Giving directions • In a clothing store • In a market	• **En la ventanilla tres, por favor** • Clothing/shoe sizes • **¿Dónde compras tu comida?** • Expressions for shopping • Mural art • **el mercado de Otavalo**	• Numbers • **ser** + **de** + material • Comparisons • Clothing material and pattern • Direct and indirect objects

FUNCTIONS	GRAMMAR	VOCABULARY	CULTURE	RE-ENTRY

Los Andes

CAPÍTULO 10   ¡Cuéntame!, *Pages 282–311*

FUNCTIONS	GRAMMAR	VOCABULARY	CULTURE	RE-ENTRY
• Setting the scene for a story • Continuing and ending a story • Talking about the latest news • Reacting to news	• The preterite vs. the imperfect • Preterite of **oír, creer, leer, caerse** • The preterite and the imperfect to tell a story • Preterite of **tener**	• Weather • Accidents, mishaps, and daily events • Science fiction and fairy tales • The latest news	• Weather map of Bolivia • **¿Te sabes algún cuento?** • A Chilean folk tale • An Ecuadorean legend • *Calvin and Hobbes* comic strip • **la Llorona**	• Reflexive verbs • Preterite of **ser** • Weather expressions

California

CAPÍTULO 11   Nuestro medio ambiente, *Pages 316–345*

FUNCTIONS	GRAMMAR	VOCABULARY	CULTURE	RE-ENTRY
• Describing a problem • Talking about consequences • Expressing agreement and disagreement • Talking about obligations and solutions	• Negative words • **si** clauses in present tense • **nosotros** commands	• Environmental problems • Animals • Protecting the environment • Materials and resources	• The rain forest • **El Yunque** • **¿Qué haces para el medio ambiente?** • Environmental programs • **el medio ambiente** • San Diego and Tijuana	• Affirmative and negative words • Giving an opinion • Cognates • Informal commands • Preterite of **decir**

California

CAPÍTULO 12   Veranos pasados, veranos por venir, *Pages 346–371*

	FUNCTIONS	GRAMMAR	VOCABULARY	CULTURE	RE-ENTRY
REVIEW CHAPTER	• Exchanging the latest news • Talking about where you went and what you did • Telling when something happened • Saying how you feel about people • Describing places • Saying when you're going to do something	• Review of regular and irregular verbs in the preterite tense • The subjunctive mood • Review of the imperfect tense	• Writing a letter • Vacation activities • Describing places	• Baja California • **¿Cómo celebran el fin de cursos?** • Interviews: **¡Nos llevamos muy bien!** • **viaje de curso** • *Calvin and Hobbes* comic strip	• Chapter 12 is a global review of Chapters 1–11, *Level 2*.

¡Ven conmigo! Spanish Level 3
Scope and Sequence

	FUNCTIONS	GRAMMAR	VOCABULARY	CULTURE	RE-ENTRY
La Coruña	**CAPÍTULO 1** ¡Qué bien lo pasé este verano!, *Pages 4–31*				
REVIEW CHAPTER	• Expressing interest, indifference, and displeasure • Asking for information • Describing yourself and others	• Stem-changing verbs in the present tense • The present tense • The preterite • **y** and **o** before vowels • Adjectives • **saber** vs. **conocer**	• Names of sports • Names of hobbies • Words and expressions to describe people	• Vacation activities of students from Costa Rica, Spain, and Miami • Seafood in Spain	• Chapters 1 and 2 are a global review of *¡Ven conmigo!* Levels 1 and 2
La Coruña	**CAPÍTULO 2** Por una vida sana, *Pages 32–61*				
REVIEW CHAPTER	• Asking for and giving advice • Talking about taking care of yourself	• Informal commands • Irregular informal commands • Reflexive verbs • The imperfect	• Expressions to tell how you are feeling today • Words and expressions to talk about stress • Expressions to talk about how to relieve stress	• Regional languages of Spain • Work schedules in Spain • Health habits of people in Spain and Latin America • Socializing with friends in Spain	• Chapters 1 and 2 are a global review of *¡Ven conmigo!* Levels 1 and 2
Caracas	**CAPÍTULO 3** El ayer y el mañana, *Pages 66–95*				
	• Talking about what has happened • Expressing and supporting a point of view • Using conversational fillers • Talking about future events • Talking about responsibilities	• The present perfect • **lo que** • The future tense	• Words and expressions related to technology • Words and expressions to talk about changes in the city • Things that may protect the environment	• Today's technology in the Spanish-speaking world • The role of oil in the Venezuelan economy • The benefits of technology for Venezuela	• Electrical appliances • Object pronouns • **todavía, ya, alguna vez** • Affirmatives and negatives • Comparisons of equality and inequality • **vamos a** + infinitive • Supporting opinions

Caracas

CAPÍTULO 4 Alrededor de la mesa, *Pages 96–123*

FUNCTIONS	GRAMMAR	VOCABULARY	CULTURE	RE-ENTRY
• Talking about how food tastes • Talking about unintentional events • Asking for help and requesting favors	• **se** with unintentional events • **por** and **para** • Double object pronouns	• Salads, meat, seafood, fruit, and desserts • Food stores • Repair shops	• The **sobremesa** • Ways of getting assistance from emergency service personnel • Foods and holiday dishes of Venezuela • Favorite foods of typical students from Miami, Quito, and Caracas • **causa picante**	• Ordering a meal • Giving explanations • Commands • Pronouns with commands • The suffix **-ísimo**

Guadalajara

CAPÍTULO 5 Nuestras leyendas, *Pages 128–155*

FUNCTIONS	GRAMMAR	VOCABULARY	CULTURE	RE-ENTRY
• Expressing qualified agreement and disagreement • Reporting what others say and think • Talking about hopes and wishes	• Impersonal **se** • The subjunctive to express hopes and wishes • Subjunctive of **ir, ser, dar, estar**	• Words and expressions to talk about war and peace	• **la "leyenda negra"** • Aztec pictographs • The legends **"La llorona"** and **"La carreta sin bueyes"** • The legend of **Quetzalcóatl** • The legend **"El Quetzal"**	• Verbs followed by an infinitive

Guadalajara

CAPÍTULO 6 El arte y la música, *Pages 156–185*

FUNCTIONS	GRAMMAR	VOCABULARY	CULTURE	RE-ENTRY
• Introducing and changing a topic of conversation • Expressing what needs to be done • Expressing an opinion • Making suggestions and recommendations • Turning down an invitation	• Gender of some words ending in **-a** and **-o** • The subjunctive after expressions of need • The subjunctive mood with recommendations • **nosotros** commands	• Words related to the arts • Words and expressions to describe works of art	• The murals of Orozco • The role of murals in Mexico • How some Hispanic students express themselves through art • Musical instruments • Mexican pop music star Luis Miguel • Life and works of Frida Kahlo	• The use of the infinitive vs. the subjunctive • Formation of the subjunctive • **dar, estar, ir,** and **ser** in the present subjunctive • Comparisons

FUNCTIONS	GRAMMAR	VOCABULARY	CULTURE	RE-ENTRY

Buenos Aires — **CAPÍTULO 7** **Dime con quién andas,** *Pages 190–219*

FUNCTIONS	GRAMMAR	VOCABULARY	CULTURE	RE-ENTRY
• Expressing happiness and unhappiness • Comforting someone • Making an apology • Describing an ideal relationship	• The subjunctive with expressions of feelings • Reflexive verbs for reciprocal actions • The present perfect subjunctive • The subjunctive with the unknown or nonexistent • The present subjunctive of **saber**	• Words and expressions to talk about friendship • Things that friends might do	• The use of **vos** • Cafés • The Organization of American States • The popularity of movies • The popularity of soccer • How Spanish-speaking teenagers solve interpersonal problems	• The use of the infinitive vs. the subjunctive • Irregular subjunctive • Past participle forms • Affirmative and negative words • Subjunctive forms

Buenos Aires — **CAPÍTULO 8** **Los medios de comunicación,** *Pages 220–247*

FUNCTIONS	GRAMMAR	VOCABULARY	CULTURE	RE-ENTRY
• Expressing doubt and disbelief • Expressing certainty • Talking about possibility and impossibility • Expressing surprise	• The subjunctive after expressions of doubt and disbelief • **por** in fixed expressions • The subjunctive after impersonal expressions	• Words to talk about television • Words and expressions to talk about information • Sections of a newspaper	• The use of the Internet in Argentina • How commercials affect our attitudes and behavior • Newsstands in Buenos Aires	• Uses of **se**

Nueva York — **CAPÍTULO 9** **Las apariencias engañan,** *Pages 252–279*

FUNCTIONS	GRAMMAR	VOCABULARY	CULTURE	RE-ENTRY
• Talking about your emotional reaction to something • Expressing disagreement • Expressing an assumption • Making hypothetical statements	• More on preterite versus imperfect • The preterite of **estar, ponerse, querer, saber,** and **sentirse** • The subjunctive with expressions of denial and disagreement • The conditional	• Words to describe people's behavior • Words and expressions to talk about prejudice and stereotypes	• Hispanics in the United States • Impressions Spanish-speaking people have of the United States • Spanish-language media in New York	• The subjunctive

Nueva York | **CAPÍTULO 10   La riqueza cultural,** *Pages 280–309*

FUNCTIONS	GRAMMAR	VOCABULARY	CULTURE	RE-ENTRY
• Talking about accomplishments • Talking about future plans • Expressing cause and effect • Expressing intention and purpose	• Verbs after prepositions • The subjunctive with **para que**	• Words and expressions to talk about achievements and future plans • Words and expressions to talk about your background and ambitions	• Hispanics in New York City • How Spanish-speaking students view themselves • **La Sociedad Hispánica de América** • **El Ballet Hispánico de Nueva York**	• The subjunctive with certain conjunctions • The present perfect • Reflexive pronouns • The conditional • The subjunctive

Costa Rica | **CAPÍTULO 11   El mundo en que vivimos,** *Pages 314–341*

FUNCTIONS	GRAMMAR	VOCABULARY	CULTURE	RE-ENTRY
• Pointing out problems and their consequences • Talking about how you would solve a problem • Talking about hypothetical situations	• The past subjunctive	• Today's problems	• Environmental issues facing North and Central America • Literacy in Costa Rica • Political stability in Costa Rica • Conservation in Costa Rica	• Impersonal **se** • Talking about consequences • The conditional • The preterite

Costa Rica | **CAPÍTULO 12   Mis planes para el futuro,** *Pages 342–371*

FUNCTIONS	GRAMMAR	VOCABULARY	CULTURE	RE-ENTRY
REVIEW CHAPTER • Talking about former jobs and goals • Talking about future career plans • Giving advice and making recommendations about work • Describing places • Saying when you're going to do something	• Preterite and imperfect • Future tense and **ir a** + infinitive • The subjunctive • Personal **a** before certain pronouns • The past subjunctive	• Names of professions • Words and expressions to talk about employment	• Universities in Costa Rica • Plans some Hispanic students have for the future • Employment in Costa Rica • Ecotourism in Costa Rica • Formality in the Spanish-speaking world	• Chapter 12 is a global review of Chapters 1–11, Level 3.

Pupil's Edition

¡Ven conmigo! offers an integrated approach to language learning. Presentation and practice of functional expressions, vocabulary, and grammar structures are interwoven with cultural information, language learning tips, and realia to facilitate both learning and teaching. The technology, audiovisual materials, and additional print resources are integrated throughout each chapter.

¡Ven conmigo! Level 1

¡Ven conmigo! Level 1 consists of a preliminary chapter that introduces students to Spanish and the Spanish-speaking world, followed by twelve instructional chapters. To facilitate articulation from one level to the next, Chapter 11 introduces minimal new material and Chapter 12 is a review chapter.

Following is a description of the various features in *¡Ven conmigo!* and suggestions on how to use them in the classroom.

Starting Out...

Location Opener In *¡Ven conmigo!*, chapters are arranged in groups of two, with each pair of chapters set in a different Spanish-speaking location. Each new location is introduced by four pages of colorful photos and information about the region.

Chapter Opener These two pages provide a visual introduction to the theme of the chapter and include a list of objectives students will be expected to achieve.

Setting The Scene...

De antemano Language instruction begins with this comprehensible input that models language in a culturally authentic setting. Presented also on video and audio CD, the highly visual presentation allows students to practice their receptive skills and to begin to recognize some of the new functions and vocabulary they will encounter in the chapter. Following **De antemano** is a series of activities to check comprehension.

Building Proficiency Step By Step...

Primer, Segundo, and **Tercer pasos** are the core instructional ·············▸
sections where most language acquisition will take place. The
communicative goals in each chapter center on the functional
expressions presented in **Así se dice** boxes. These expressions
are supported by material in the **Vocabulario, Gramática,**
and **Nota gramatical** sections. Activities following the
above features are designed to practice recognition or to
provide closed-ended practice. Activities then progress
from controlled to open-ended practice where students are
able to express themselves in meaningful communication.

Discovering the People and the Culture...

There are also two major cultural features to help students
develop an appreciation and understanding of the cultures
of Spanish-speaking countries.

Panorama cultural presents interviews conducted throughout
the Spanish-speaking world on a topic related to the chapter
theme. The interviews may be presented on video or done
as a reading supplemented by the compact disc recording.
Culminating activities on this page verify comprehension and
encourage students to think critically about the target culture
as well as their own.

◀·········· **Encuentro cultural** invites students to compare and contrast
other cultures with their own.

◀········· **También se puede decir...** helps students become familiar
with the linguistic richness of the Spanish-speaking world
by presenting regional alternatives for the vocabulary
introduced in the chapter.

También se puede decir...
In many Spanish-speaking countries, you'll also
hear **andar en bicicleta** or **pasear en bici** in
addition to **montar en bicicleta.**

◀······· **Nota cultural** helps students gain knowledge and understanding of other cultures.

Nota cultural

Many athletes from Spanish-speaking countries
broke new ground in the 2000 Olympic Games.
María Urrutia from Colombia and Soraya Jiménez
from Mexico gave their countries their first gold
in weightlifting. Cuba garnered six medals in
boxing, four of them gold, and a third con-
secutive gold by its women's volleyball team.
Costa Rica's swimmer Claudia Poll won two
bronze medals. In sailing, medals went to
Argentina's Carlos Espínola and Serena Amato.
Spain captured the gold in diverse competitions:
judo (Isabel Fernández), cycling (Juan Llaneras)
and gymnastics (Gervasio Deferr).

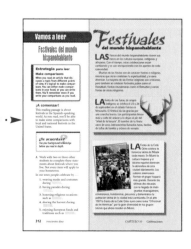

Understanding Authentic Documents...

Vamos a leer presents reading strategies that help students ·····▸
understand authentic Spanish documents and literature
presented in each chapter. The accompanying prereading,
reading, and postreading activities develop students' overall
reading skills and challenge their critical thinking abilities.

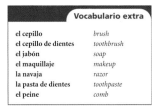

A lo nuestro

In Spanish, there are many ways to express how often you do things. Some of these expressions include: **una vez** (once), **de vez en cuando** (once in a while), **todo el tiempo** (all the time), **cada día** (each day), and **a menudo** (often).

Vocabulario extra

el cepillo	*brush*
el cepillo de dientes	*toothbrush*
el jabón	*soap*
el maquillaje	*makeup*
la navaja	*razor*
la pasta de dientes	*toothpaste*
el peine	*comb*

¿Se te ha olvidado?

gustar and encantar

Consulta la página 236

A lo nuestro

In Spanish, there are many ways to express how often you do things. Some of these expressions include: **una vez** (once), **de vez en cuando** (once in a while), **todo el tiempo** (all the time), **cada día** (each day), and **a menudo** (often).

LETRA Y SONIDO

A. 1. The letters ll and y are usually pronounced alike. Their pronunciation in many Spanish-speaking countries is similar to the y in the English word yes.

yo	yate	yema	yugo	yerno
llamo	lleva	llora	maquillaje	toalla

2. The single l in Spanish is pronounced like the l in the English word live. Keep the tip of the tongue behind the upper teeth when pronouncing l.

zoológico	lavarse	levantarse	¡Qué lástima!
lo siento	el lago	Aló	línea

B. Dictado
Lalo is trying to make plans with his friends. Write what he says.

C. Trabalenguas
La nublada neblina lava las lomas de un lugar lejano.

Targeting Students' Needs...

In each **Paso** several special features may be used to enhance language learning and cultural appreciation.

Sugerencia suggests effective ways for students to learn a foreign language.

A lo nuestro provides students with tips for speaking more natural-sounding Spanish.

Vocabulario extra presents optional vocabulary related to the chapter theme.

¿Te acuerdas? is a re-entry feature that lists and briefly explains previously learned vocabulary, functions, and grammar that students might need to review at the moment.

¿Se te ha olvidado? is a handy page reference to either an earlier chapter where material was presented or to a reference section in the back of the book.

At the end of each **Tercer paso** is **Letra y sonido,** which explains certain sounds and spelling rules. In a dictation exercise, students hear and write sentences using the targeted sounds and letters. Finally, a **trabalenguas** gives students an opportunity to practice the targeted sounds with challenging tongue-twisters.

Wrapping It All Up...

Más práctica gramatical provides additional practice on the grammar concepts presented in the chapter.

Repaso gives students the opportunity to review what they have learned and to apply their skills in new communicative contexts. Focusing on all four language skills as well as cultural awareness, the **Repaso** can help you determine whether students are ready for the Chapter Test.

Vamos a escribir helps students develop their writing skills by focusing on the writing process. Each **Vamos a escribir** gives students a topic related to the theme and functions of the chapter.

A ver si puedo... is a checklist that students can use on their own to see if they have achieved the goals stated on the Chapter Opener.

Vocabulario presents the chapter vocabulary grouped by **Paso** and arranged according to function or theme.

Technology Resources

Video Program-DVD Tutor

The *Video Program* and *DVD Tutor* provide the following video support:

- **Location Opener** documentaries

- **De antemano** and **A continuación** dramatic episodes

- **Panorama cultural** interviews on a variety of cultural topics

- **Videoclips** which present authentic footage from target cultures

The *Video Guide* contains background information, suggestions for presentation, and activities for all portions of the *Video Program.*

Interactive CD-ROM Tutor

The *Interactive CD-ROM Tutor* offers:

- a variety of supporting activities correlated to the core curriculum of *¡Ven conmigo!* and targeting all five skills

- a Teacher Management System (TMS) that allows teachers to view and assess students' work, manage passwords and records, track students' progress as they complete the activities, and activate English translations

- features such as a grammar reference section and a glossary to help students to complete the activities

Internet Connection

Keywords in the *Pupil's Edition* provide access to two types of online activities:

- **Juegos interactivos** are directly correlated to the instructional material in the textbook. They can be used as homework, extra practice, or assessment.

- **Actividades Internet** provide students with selected Web sites in Spanish-speaking countries and activities related to the chapter theme. A printable worksheet in PDF format includes pre-surfing, surfing, and post-surfing activities that guide students through their research.

For easy access, see the keywords provided in the *Pupil's* and *Teacher's Editions.* For chapter-specific information, see the F page of the chapter interleaf.

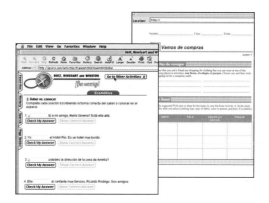

One-Stop Planner CD-ROM with Test Generator

The *One-Stop Planner CD-ROM* is a convenient tool to aid in lesson planning and pacing.

Easy navigation through menus or through lesson plans allows for a quick overview of available resources. For each chapter the *One-Stop Planner* includes:

- Editable lesson plans with direct links to teaching resources

- Printable worksheets from resource books

- Direct launches to the HRW Internet activities

- Video and audio segments

- Test Generator

- Clip Art for vocabulary items

Ancillaries

The *¡Ven conmigo!* Spanish program offers a comprehensive ancillary package that addresses the concerns of today's teachers and is relevant to students' lives.

Lesson Planning

One-Stop Planner
with Test Generator

- editable lesson plans
- printable worksheets from the resource books
- direct link to HRW internet activities
- entire video and audio programs
- Test Generator
- Clip Art for vocabulary items

Lesson Planner with Substitute Teacher Lesson Plans

- complete lesson plans for every chapter
- block scheduling suggestions
- correlations to Standards for Foreign Language Learning
- a homework calendar
- chapter-by-chapter lesson plans for substitute teachers
- lesson plan forms for customizing lesson plans

Student Make-Up Assignments

- diagnostic information for students who are behind in their work
- copying masters for make-up assignments

Listening and Speaking

TPR Storytelling Book

- step-by-step explanation of the TPR Storytelling method
- illustrated stories for each **Paso** with vocabulary lists and gestures
- teaching suggestions

Listening Activities

- print material associated with the *Audio Program*
- Student Response Forms for all *Pupil's Edition* listening activities
- Additonal Listening Activities
- scripts, answers
- lyrics to each chapter's song

Audio Compact Discs

Listening activities for the *Pupil's Edition*, the Additional Listening Activities, and the *Testing Program*

Activities for Communication

- Communicative activities for partner work based on an information gap
- Situation Cards to practice interviews and role-plays
- Realia: reproductions of authentic documents

Grammar

Cuaderno de gramática

- re-presentations of major grammar points
- additional focused practice
- *Teacher's Edition* with overprinted answers

Grammar Tutor for Students of Spanish

- presentations of grammar concepts in English
- re-presentations of Spanish grammar concepts
- discovery and application activities

Reading and Writing

Reading Strategies and Skills
- explanations of reading strategies
- copying masters for application of strategies

¡Lee conmigo!
- readings on familiar topics
- cultural information
- additional vocabulary
- interesting and engaging activities

Cuaderno de actividades
- activities for practice
- *Teacher's Edition* with overprinted answers

Teaching Transparencies
Colorful transparencies that help present and practice vocabulary, grammar, culture, and a variety of communicative functions

Exploratory Guide
- lessons with activity masters
- vocabulary lists
- review and assessment options

Native Speaker Activity Book
- a diagnostic test
- grammar and spelling exercises
- reading and listening comprehension exercises
- explanations of variances in vocabulary and pronunciation
- *Teacher's Edition* with an answer key

Assessment

Testing Program
- Grammar and Vocabulary quizzes
- **Paso** quizzes that test the four skills
- Chapter Tests
- Speaking Tests
- Midterm and Final Exams
- Score sheets, scripts, answers

Alternative Assessment Guide
- Suggestions for oral and written Portfolio Assessment
- Performance Assessment
- CD-ROM Assessment
- rubrics, portfolio checklists, and evaluation forms

Student Make-Up Assignments
Alternative Grammar and Vocabulary quizzes for students who missed class and have to make up the quiz

Standardized Assessment Tutor
Reading, writing, and math tests in a standardized, multiple-choice format

Annotated Teacher's Edition

Using the Chapter Interleaf

Each chapter of the *¡Ven conmigo!* *Annotated Teacher's Edition* includes the following interleaf pages to help you plan, teach, and expand your lessons.

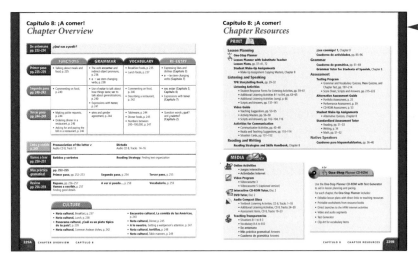

Chapter Overview

The Chapter Overview chart outlines at a glance the functions, grammar, vocabulary, re-entry, and culture featured in the chapter. You will also find a list of corresponding print and audiovisual resources organized by listening, speaking, reading, and writing skills, grammar, and assessment.

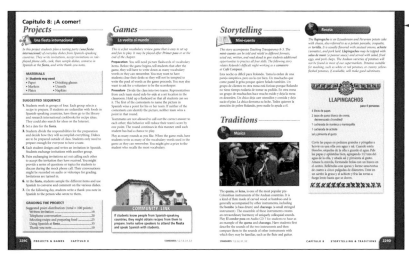

Projects/Games/ Storytelling/Traditions

Projects allow students to personalize and expand on the information from the chapter. Games reinforce the chapter content. In the Storytelling feature, you will find a story related to a *Teaching Transparency*. The Traditions feature concentrates on a unique aspect of the culture of the region. A recipe typical for the region accompanies this feature.

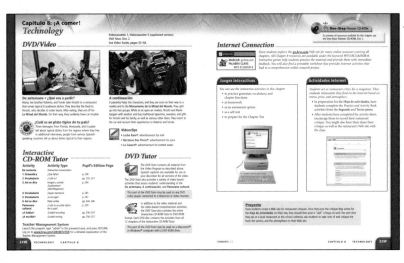

Technology

These pages assist you in integrating technology into your lesson plans. The Technology page provides a detailed list of video, DVD, CD-ROM, and Internet resources for your lesson. You will also find an Internet research project in each chapter.

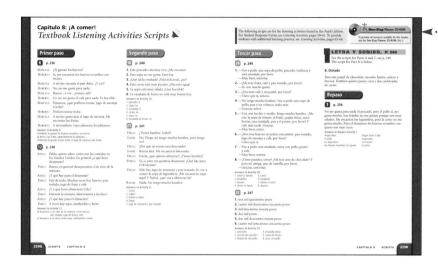

Textbook Listening Activities Scripts

Textbook Listening Activities Scripts provide the scripts of the chapter listening activities for reference or for use in class. The answers to each activity are provided below each script for easy reference.

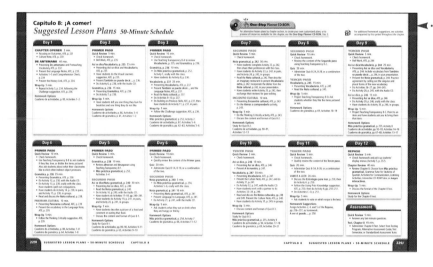

Suggested Lesson Plans— 50-Minute Schedule

This lesson plan is used for classes with 50-minute schedules. Each lesson plan provides a logical sequence of instruction along with homework suggestions.

Suggested Lesson Plans— 90-Minute Schedule

This lesson plan is used for classes with 90-minute schedules. Each lesson plan provides a logical sequence of instruction along with homework suggestions.

Using the Wrap-Around Teacher Text

Teaching Resources
pp. 21–26

PRINT
▸ Lesson Planner, p. 3
▸ TPR Storytelling Book, pp. 1, 4
▸ Listening Activities, pp. 3, 7
▸ Activities for Communication, pp. 1–2, 75, 78–79, 137–138
▸ Cuaderno de gramática, pp. 1–4
▸ Grammar Tutor for Students of Spanish, Chapter 1
▸ Cuaderno de actividades, pp. 4–6
▸ Cuaderno para hispanohablantes, pp. 1–5
▸ Testing Program, pp. 1–4
▸ Alternative Assessment Guide, p. 32
▸ Student Make-Up Assignments, Chapter 1

MEDIA
▸ One-Stop Planner
▸ Audio Compact Discs, CD 1, Trs. 11–13, 34–35, 29
▸ Teaching Transparencies, 1-1; **Más práctica gramatical** Answers; Cuaderno de gramática Answers
▸ Interactive CD-ROM Tutor, Disc 1

Resource boxes provide a quick list of all the resources you can use for each chapter section.

Presenting
Así se dice

Model these expressions, and have students repeat after you, imitating your gestures. (**regular** —thumb up; **horrible**—thumb down; **más o menos**—hand rocking side to side with palm down; **estupendo** and **excelente** —emphatic gestures) Then have pairs practice asking and answering how they are doing, using the appropriate gestures.

Presenting boxes offer useful suggestions for presenting new material.

Answers
14 *Possible answers:*
1. Bien, gracias.
2. Mucho gusto, Charín.
3. Regular.
4. Me llamo *(name)*.
5. Adiós.

24 VEINTICUATRO   PRIMER PASO

---

12 **Nuevos amigos** *New friends*

Hablemos Role-play the following conversation with a classmate using expressions from **Así se dice** on pages 21–22. If you'd like to use a Spanish name or nickname, choose one from the list on page 5. *Possible conversation:*

ESTUDIANTE 1 *Greet your classmate.* Hola; Buenos días; Buenas tardes.
ESTUDIANTE 2 *Respond and introduce yourself.* Buenos días, soy...; Hola, me llamo...
ESTUDIANTE 1 *Say "nice to meet you" and introduce yourself.* Mucho gusto, soy...; Encantado/a, me llamo...
ESTUDIANTE 2 *Respond to the introduction.* ¡Mucho gusto!; Igualmente.
ESTUDIANTE 1 *Say you have class now.* Bueno, tengo clase.
ESTUDIANTE 2 *Say that you also have class and say goodbye.* Tengo clase. Adiós.
ESTUDIANTE 1 *Say that you'll see your new friend tomorrow.* Hasta mañana.

Así se dice

Asking how someone is and saying how you are

To find out how a friend is, ask:

¿Cómo estás? *How are you?*   **¿Qué tal?** *How's it going?*
¿Y tú? *And you?*

Your friend might say:

Estoy (bastante) bien, gracias. *I'm (pretty) well, thanks.*   **Regular.** *Okay.*

Yo también. *Me too.*   **Más o menos.** *So-so.*

Estupendo/a. *Great.*   **(Muy) mal.** *(Very) bad.*

Excelente. *Great.*   **¡Horrible!** *Horrible!*

Más práctica gramatical, p. 38, Act. 2

Cuaderno de actividades, pp. 5–6, Acts. 5–7

Cuaderno de gramática, p. 3, Acts. 6–7

13 **¿Cómo estás?**

Escuchemos/Escribamos As each friend tells Sara how he or she is, write the person's name under the appropriate heading. *Scripts and answers on p.15G.*

CD 1
Tr. 13

MODELO   **Buenas tardes, Felipe. ¿Qué tal? Regular, gracias. ¿Y tú?**

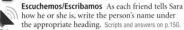
bien regular mal
Felipe

14 **¿Cómo contestas?** *How do you answer?*

Leamos/Escribamos How would you answer the following? Select your responses from the expressions you've learned. *See possible answers below.*
1. ¡Hola! ¿Qué tal?
2. Ésta es mi amiga Charín.
3. ¿Cómo estás?
4. Soy Eduardo Robledo. ¿Y tú?
5. ¡Hasta luego!

A lo nuestro

In Spanish, there are many ways to ask a person how he or she is doing. Throughout Spain and Latin America you will hear **¿Qué pasa?** *(What's happening?)* and **¿Qué hay?/¿Qué tal?** *(What's up?)* In Mexico, you'll also hear **¿Qué hubo?** or **¿Qué onda?**

Communication for All Students

Visual Learners
• Use gestures or sketch visual cues on index cards to represent each functional phrase. Have students call out the phrase as you perform the gesture or show the card.
• Students should make cards representing these phrases. They can use the cards to verify comprehension and also for pair and small-group practice.

Cooperative Learning
13 Divide the class into groups of three. Assign one student to be the scribe and two to be performers. After agreeing on the correct responses to the items in Activity 13, the group should then make up a conversation to present to the class. Group members should be assigned the same grade based on the group's written responses and performance.

STANDARDS: 1.1, 1.2

Communication for All Students
Under this head you will find helpful suggestions for students with different learning styles and abilities.

Correlations to the Standards for Foreign Language Learning are provided for your reference.

Gramática

Subject pronouns *tú* and *yo*

1. Use the pronoun **yo** to refer to yourself. In Spanish, **yo** *(I)* is not capitalized, except at the beginning of a sentence. Use **tú** *(you)* when you're talking to another student, a friend, or to someone who is about your own age. Notice that **tú** has an accent.

2. In Chapter 4 you'll learn a different pronoun to use when speaking to someone older than you or when you want to be polite to a stranger. You'll also discover that subject pronouns like these aren't used as often in Spanish as in English.

3. How many expressions can you find in **Así se dice** on pages 21–24 where the pronoun **yo** is implied but not stated? *

Cuaderno de gramática, p. 4, Acts. 8–10

Más práctica gramatical,
p. 38, Act. 3

---

15 **Gramática en contexto**

Leamos Which pronoun (**tú** or **yo**) is implied but not stated in each sentence?

1. ¿Cómo te llamas? tú
2. Me llamo Mercedes Margarita. yo
3. Soy Francisco. yo
4. ¿Cómo estás, Francisco? tú
5. Estoy bien, gracias. yo

16 **Charla** *Chitchat*

Escribamos Mercedes is talking to a new classmate. Using words or phrases you've learned, write their conversation.

MERCEDES	*greets her friend*
ELENA	*responds and introduces her friend Pedro*
MERCEDES	*says it is nice to meet Pedro*
PEDRO	*responds and asks Mercedes how she is*
MERCEDES	*responds and says she has class*
ELENA	*says she also has to go now*
ALL	*say goodbye*

Sample answer below.

17 **Mini-drama**

Hablemos The two teens in the photo have just been introduced to each other by a friend. Together with two partners, role-play the three students. You may use the conversation you created in Activity 16. Be creative and change the dialogue as needed to suit your group.

---

* **Yo** is implied in: **(Yo) tengo que...**, **(Yo) me llamo...**, **(Yo) soy...**, and in **(Yo) estoy...**

Connections and Comparisons

Native Speakers
Be aware that some native speakers from Latin America may use the second-person singular pronoun **vos** and its verb forms. Explain that while these are accepted regionally in colloquial contexts, **tú** is the internationally accepted pronoun and verb form.

Language Note
In Argentina, Uruguay, Paraguay, Central America, and the Mexican state of Chiapas, **vos** is typically used instead of **tú** as the informal subject pronoun. This practice is called **voseo**. There is regional variation in the conjugation of **vos** forms.

STANDARDS: 1.1, 1.3, 3.1, 4.1, 5.1

Presenting
Gramática

Subject pronouns tú and yo
Give several sentences with either **tú** or **yo**. Students point to themselves whenever you say **yo**, and to another student as you say **tú**. Point out the accent mark on **tú**.

Teaching Suggestion ▶
17 Allow time for students to prepare and practice the mini-drama. Circulate among the groups to check pronunciation and language.

Challenge
17 Ask groups to perform their mini-drama for the rest of the class.

Assess
▶ Testing Program, pp. 1–4
  Quiz 1-1A, Quiz 1-1B
  Audio CD 1, Tr. 29
▶ Student Make-Up Assignments, Chapter 1, Alternative Quiz
▶ Alternative Assessment Guide, p. 32

Answers
16 *Sample answer:*

MERCEDES:	¡Hola, Elena! ¿Qué tal?
ELENA:	Muy bien, Mercedes. Éste es mi amigo Pedro.
MERCEDES:	Mucho gusto, Pedro.
PEDRO:	Igualmente. ¿Cómo estás?
MERCEDES:	Muy bien, gracias, pero tengo clase.
ELENA:	Sí, yo tengo que irme.
TODOS:	¡Adiós! ¡Hasta luego!

The Annotated Teacher's Edition Wrap-Around Text offers helpful suggestions and information at point-of-use. You will also find annos, cultural information, correlations to the Standards for Foreign Language Learning, and references to other ancillaries.

Assessment
At the end of every **Paso** and again at the end of the chapter, you will find references to all the assessment material available for that section of the chapter.

Connections and Comparisons
Under this head you will find helpful information for connecting with other disciplines and developing insight into the nature of language and culture.

Bringing Standards into the Classroom

by Paul Sandrock, Foreign Language Consultant, Wisconsin Department of Public Education

The core question that guided the development of the National Standards and their accompanying goals was simply: what matters in instruction?

Each proposed standard was evaluated. Did the standard target material that will have application beyond the classroom? Was the standard too specific or not specific enough? Teachers should be able to teach the standard and assess it in multiple ways. A standard needs to provide a target for instruction and learning throughout a student's K–12 education.

In the development of standards, foreign languages faced other unique challenges. The writers could not assume a K–12 sequence available to all students. In fact, unlike other disciplines, they could not guarantee that all students would experience even any common sequence.

From this context, the National Standards in Foreign Language Education Project's task force generated the five C's, five goals for learning languages: communication, cultures, connections, comparisons, and communities. First presented in 1995, the standards quickly became familiar to foreign language educators across the US, representing our professional consensus and capturing a broad view of the purposes for learning another language.

To implement the standards, however, requires a shift from emphasizing the means to focusing on the ends. It isn't a matter of grammar versus communication, but rather how much grammar is needed to communicate. Instead of teaching to a grammatical sequence, teaching decisions become based on what students need to know to achieve the communicative goal.

The Focus on Communication

The first standard redefined communication, making its purpose **interpersonal, interpretive,** and **presentational** communication. Teaching to the purpose of interpersonal communication takes us away from memorized dialogues to spontaneous, interactive conversation, where the message is most important and where meaning needs to be negotiated between the speakers. Interpretive communication is not an exercise in translation, but asks beginners to tell the gist of an authentic selection that is heard, read, or viewed, while increasingly advanced learners tell deeper and deeper levels of detail and can interpret based on their knowledge of the target culture. In the presentational mode of communication, the emphasis is on the audience, requiring the speaker or writer to adapt language to fit the situation and to allow for comprehension without any interactive negotiation of the meaning.

Standards challenge us to refocus many of the things we've been doing all along. The requirements of speaking and our expectation of how well students need to speak change when speaking is for a different purpose. This focus on the purpose of the communication changes the way we teach and test the skills of listening, speaking, reading, and writing.

Standards help us think about how to help students put the pieces of language to work in meaningful ways. Our stan-

Standards for Foreign Language Learning

Communication Communicate in Languages Other than English	**Standard 1.1**	Students engage in conversations, provide and obtain information, express feelings and emotions, and exchange opinions.
	Standard 1.2	Students understand and interpret written and spoken language on a variety of topics.
	Standard 1.3	Students present information, concepts, and ideas to an audience of listeners or readers on a variety of topics.
Cultures Gain knowledge and understanding of Other Cultures	**Standard 2.1**	Students demonstrate an understanding of the relationship between the practices and perspectives of the culture studied.
	Standard 2.2	Students demonstrate an understanding of the relationship between the products and perspectives of the culture studied.
Connections Connect with other disciplines and Acquire Information	**Standard 3.1**	Students reinforce and further their knowledge of other disciplines through the foreign language.
	Standard 3.2	Students acquire information and recognize the distinctive viewpoints that are only available through the foreign language and its cultures.
Comparisons Develop Insight into the Nature of Language and Culture	**Standard 4.1**	Students demonstrate understanding of the nature of language through comparisons of the language studied and their own.
	Standard 4.2	Students demonstrate understanding of the concept of culture through comparisons of the cultures studied and their own.
Communities Participate in Multilingual Communities at Home and Around the World	**Standard 5.1**	Students use the language both within and beyond the school setting.
	Standard 5.2	Students show evidence of becoming life-long learners by using the language for personal enjoyment and enrichment.

dards answer *why* we are teaching various components of language, and we select *what* we teach in order to achieve those very standards.

The 5 C's

Originally the five C's were presented as five equal circles. During the years since the National Standards were printed, teachers implementing and using the standards to write curriculum, texts, and lesson plans have come to see that communication is at the core, surrounded by four C's that influence the context for teaching and assessing.

The four C's surrounding our core goal of **Communication** change our classrooms by bringing in real-life applications for the language learned:

- **Cultures:** Beyond art and literature, learning occurs in the context of the way of life, patterns of behavior, and contributions of the people speaking the language being taught.

- **Connections:** Beyond content limited to the culture of the people speaking the target language, teachers go out to other disciplines to find topics and ideas to form the context for language learning.

- **Comparisons:** Foreign language study is a great way for students to learn more about native language and universal principles of language and culture by comparing and contrasting their own to the target language and culture.

- **Communities:** This goal of the standards adds a broader motivation to the context for language learning. The teacher makes sure students use their new language beyond the class hour, seeking ways to experience the target culture.

Implementation at the Classroom Level: Assessment and Instruction

After the publication of the standards, states developed more specific performance standards that would provide evidence of the application of the national content standards. Standards provide the organizing principle for teaching and assessing. The standards-oriented teacher, when asked what she's teaching, cites the standard "students will sustain a conversation." With that clear goal in mind, she creates lessons to teach various strategies to ask for clarification and to practice asking follow-up questions that explore a topic in more depth.

Textbook writers and materials providers are responding to this shift. Standards provide our goals; the useful textbooks and materials give us an organization and a context. Standards provide the ends; textbooks and materials can help us practice the means. Textbooks can bring authentic materials into the classroom, real cultural examples that avoid stereotypes, and a broader exposure to the variety of people who speak the language being studied. Textbooks can model the kind of instruction that will lead students to successful demonstration of the knowledge and skill described in the standards.

To really know that standards are the focus, look at the assessment. If standards are the target, assessment won't consist only of evaluation of the means (grammatical structures and vocabulary) in isolation. If standards are the focus, teachers will assess students' use of the second language in context. The summative assessment of our target needs to go beyond the specific and include open-ended, personalized tasks. Regardless of how the students show what they can do, the teacher will be able to gauge each student's progress toward the goal.

Assessment is like a jigsaw puzzle. If we test students only on the means, we just keep collecting random puzzle pieces. We have to test, and students have to practice, putting the pieces together in meaningful and purposeful ways. In order to learn vocabulary that will help students "describe themselves," for example, students may have a quiz on Friday with an expectation of close to 100% accuracy. But if that is all we ever do with those ten words, they will quickly be gone from students' memory, and we will only have collected a puzzle piece from each student. It is absolutely essential to have students use those puzzle pieces to complete the puzzle to provide evidence of what they "can do" with the language.

During this period of implementing our standards, we've learned that the standards provide a global picture, the essence of our goals. But they are not curriculum, nor are they lesson plans. The standards influence how we teach, but do not dictate one content nor one methodology. How can we implement the standards in our classrooms? Think about the targets; think about how students will show achievement of those targets through our evaluation measures; then think about what we need to teach and how that will occur in our classrooms. Make it happen in your classroom to get the results we've always wanted: students who can communicate in a language other than English.

Reading Strategies and Skills

by Nancy Humbach, Miami University

Reading is the most enduring of the language skills. Long after a student ceases to study the language, the ability to read will continue to provide a springboard to the renewal of the other skills. We must consider all the ways in which our students will read and address the skills needed for those tasks.

How can we accomplish this goal? How can we, as teachers, present materials, encourage students to read, and at the same time foster understanding and build the student's confidence and interest in reading?

Selection of Materials

Reading material in the foreign language classroom should be relevant to students' backgrounds and at an accessible level of difficulty, i.e., at a level of difficulty only slightly above the reading ability of the student.

Authentic materials are generally a good choice. They provide cultural context and linguistic authenticity seldom found in materials created for students, and the authentic nature of the language provides a window on a new world. The problem inherent in the selection of authentic materials at early levels is obvious: the level of difficulty is frequently beyond the skill of the student. At the same time, however, readers are inspired by the fact that they can understand materials designed to be read by native speakers.

Presenting a Selection/ Reading Strategies

We assume that students of a second language already have a reading knowledge in their first language and that many of the skills they learned in their "reading readiness" days will serve them well. Too often, however, students have forgotten such skills as activating background knowledge, skimming, scanning, and guessing content based on context clues. Helping students to reactivate these skills is part of helping them become better readers.

Teachers should not assume their students' ability to transfer a knowledge set from one reading to another. Students use these skills on a regular basis, but often do not even realize they are doing so. To help students become aware of these processes, they need to be given strategies for reading. These strategies offer students a framework for the higher-level skills they need to apply when reading. Strategies also address learners of different learning styles and needs.

Advance Organizers

One way to activate the student's background knowledge is through advance organizers. They also serve to address the student's initial frustrations at encountering an unfamiliar text.

Advance organizers call up pertinent background knowledge, feelings, and experiences that can serve to focus the attention of the entire group on a given topic. In addition, they provide for a sharing of information among the students. Background information that includes cultural references and cultural information can reactivate in students skills that will help them with a text and provide for them clues to the meaning of the material.

A good advance organizer will provide some information and guide students to think about the scenarios being presented. An advance organizer might include photographs, drawings, quotations, maps, or information about the area where the story takes place. It might also be posed as a question, for example, "What would you do if you found yourself in….?" Having students brainstorm in advance, either as a whole class or in small groups, allows them to construct a scenario which they can verify as they read.

Prereading Activities

Prereading activities remind students of how much they really know and can prepare students in a number of ways to experience the language with less frustration. While we know that we must choose a reading selection that is not far beyond students' experience and skill level, we also know that no group of students reads at the same level. In the interest of assisting students to become better language learners, we can provide them with opportunities to work with unfamiliar structures and vocabulary ahead of time.

Preparing students for a reading selection can include a number of strategies that may anticipate but not dwell on potential problems to be encountered by students. Various aspects of grammar, such as differences in the past tenses and the meanings conveyed, can also cause problems. Alerting students to some of the aspects of the language allows them to struggle less, understand more quickly, and enjoy a reading selection to a greater degree.

Grouping vocabulary by category or simply choosing a short list of critical words for a section of reading is helpful. Providing an entire list of vocabulary items at one time can be overwhelming. With a bit of organization, the task becomes manageable to the point where students begin to master words they will find repeated throughout the selection.

Having students skim for a particular piece of information or scan for words, phrases, indicators of place or time, and names, and then asking them to write a sentence or two about the gist of a paragraph or story, gives them a sense of independence and success before they begin to read.

Getting into the Assignment

Teachers can recount the times they have assigned a piece of reading for homework, only to find that few students even attempted the work. Therefore, many teachers choose to complete the reading in class. Homework assignments should then be structured to have the student return to the selection and complete a assignment that requires critical thinking and imagination.

During class, several techniques assist students in maintaining interest and attention to the task. By varying these techniques, the teacher can provide for a lively class, during which students realize they *are* able to read. Partners can read passages to each other or students can take turns reading in small groups. The teacher might pose a question to be answered during that reading. Groups might also begin to act out short scenes, reading only the dialogue. Student might read a description of a setting and then draw what they imagine it to be. Of course, some selections might be silent reading with a specific amount of time announced for completion.

Reading aloud for comprehension and reading aloud for pronunciation practice are two entirely unrelated tasks. We can all recall classes where someone read aloud to us from weary lecture notes. Active engagement of the readers, on the other hand, forces them to work for comprehension, for the development of thought processes, and for improvement of language skills.

Postreading Activities

It is important to provide students with an opportunity to expand the knowledge

they have gained from the reading selection. Students should apply what they have learned to their own personal experiences. How we structure activities can provide students more opportunities to reflect on their reading and learn how much they have understood. We often consider a written test the best way to ensure comprehension; however, many other strategies allow students to keep oral skills active. These might include acting out impromptu scenes from the story and creating dialogues that do not exist in a story, but might be imagined, based on other information. Consider the possibility of debates, interviews, TV talk show formats, telephone dialogues, or a monologue in which the audience hears only one side of the conversation.

Written assignments are also valid assessment tools, allowing students to incorporate the vocabulary and structures they have learned in the reading. Students might be encouraged to write journal entries for a character, create a new ending, or retell the story from another point of view. Newspaper articles, advertisements, and other creations can also be a means of following up. Comparisons with other readings require students to keep active vocabulary and structures they have studied previously. Encourage students to read their creations aloud to a partner, to a group, or to the class.

Conclusion

Reading can be exciting. The combination of a good selection that is relevant and rates high on the interest scale, along with good preparation, guidance, and post reading activities that demonstrate to the students the level of success attained, can encourage them to continue to read. These assignments also allow for the incorporation of other aspects of language learning, and incorporate the Five C's of the National Standards. Communication and culture are obvious links, but so are connections (advance organizers, settings, and so on), comparisons (with other works in the

heritage or target language), and communities (learning why a type of writing is important in a culture).

¡Ven conmigo!

offers reading practice and develops reading skills and strategies in the following ways:

THE PUPIL'S EDITION

▶ Provides an extensive reading section in each chapter called **Vamos a leer.** Each **Vamos a leer** section offers a strategy students apply to an authentic text, as well as activities to guide understanding and exploration of the text.

THE ANNOTATED TEACHER'S EDITION

▶ Provides teachers with additional activities and information in every **Vamos a leer** section. Additional suggestions are provided for Prereading, Reading, and Postreading activities.

THE ANCILLARY PROGRAM

▶ *¡Lee conmigo!* This component offers reading selections of various formats and difficulty levels. Each chapter has a prereading feature, a reading selection with comprehension questions, and two pages of activities.

▶ The *Reading Strategies and Skills Handbook* offers useful strategies that can be applied to reading selections in the *Pupil's Edition,* *¡Lee conmigo!,* or a selection of your choosing.

▶ The Cuaderno de actividades contains a reading selection tied to the chapter theme, and reading activities for each chapter in ¡Ven conmigo!

▶ The Cuaderno para hispanohablantes offers reading selections and comprehension activities correlated to chapters in the Pupil's Edition.

Using Portfolios in the Language Classroom

by Jo Anne S. Wilson, J. Wilson Associates

Portfolios offer a more realistic and accurate way to assess the process of language teaching and learning.

The communicative, whole-language approach of today's language instruction requires assessment methods that parallel the teaching and learning strategies in the proficiency-oriented classroom. We know that language acquisition is a process. Portfolios are designed to assess the steps in that process.

What Is a Portfolio?

A portfolio is a purposeful, systematic collection of a student's work. A useful tool in developing a student profile, the portfolio shows the student's efforts, progress, and achievements for a given period of time. It may be used for periodic evaluation, as the basis for overall evaluation, or for placement. It may also be used to enhance or provide alternatives to traditional assessment measures, such as formal tests, quizzes, class participation, and homework.

Why Use Portfolios?

Portfolios benefit both students and teachers because they:

- **Are ongoing and systematic.** A portfolio reflects the real-world process of production, assessment, revision, and reassessment. It parallels the natural rhythm of learning.

- **Offer an incentive to learn.** Students have a vested interest in creating the portfolios, through which they can showcase their ongoing efforts and tangible achievements. Students select the works to be included and have a chance to revise, improve, evaluate, and explain the contents.

- **Are sensitive to individual needs.** Language learners bring varied abilities to the classroom and do not acquire skills in a uniformly neat and orderly fashion. The personalized, individualized assessment offered by portfolios responds to this diversity.

- **Provide documentation of language development.** The material in a portfolio is evidence of student progress in the language learning process. The contents of the portfolio make it easier to discuss their progress with the students as well as with parents and others.

- **Offer multiple sources of information.** A portfolio presents a way to collect and analyze information from multiple sources that reflects a student's efforts, progress, and achievements in the language.

Portfolio Components

The language portfolio should include both oral and written work, student self-evaluation, and teacher observation, usually in the form of brief, nonevaluative comments about various aspects of the student's performance.

The Oral Component

The oral component of a portfolio might be an audio- or videocassette. It may contain both rehearsed and extemporaneous monologues and conversations. For a rehearsed speaking activity, give a specific communicative task that students can personalize according to their individual interests (for example, ordering a favorite meal in a restaurant). If the speaking activity is extemporaneous, first acquaint students with possible topics for discussion or even the specific task they will be expected to perform. (For example, tell them they will be asked to discuss a picture showing a sports activity or a restaurant scene.)

The Written Component

Portfolios are excellent tools for incorporating process writing strategies into the language classroom. Documentation of various stages of the writing process—brainstorming, multiple drafts, and peer comments—may be included with the finished product.

Involve students in selecting writing tasks for the portfolio. At the beginning levels, the tasks might include some structured writing, such as labeling or listing. As students become more proficient, journals, letters, and other more complicated writing tasks are valuable ways for them to monitor their progress in using the written language.

Student Self-Evaluation

Students should be actively involved in critiquing and evaluating their portfolios and monitoring their own progress.

The process and procedure for student self-evaluation should be considered in planning the contents of the portfolio. Students should work with you and their peers to design the exact format. Self-evaluation encourages them to think about what they are learning (content), how they learn (process), why they are learning (purpose), and where they are going in their learning (goals).

Teacher Observation

Systematic, regular, and ongoing observations should be placed in the portfolio after they have been discussed with the student. These observations provide feedback on the student's progress in the language learning process.

Teacher observations should be based on an established set of criteria that has been developed earlier with input from the student. Observation techniques may include the following:

- Jotting notes in a journal to be discussed with the student and then placed in the portfolio

- Using a checklist of observable behaviors, such as the willingness to take risks when using the target language or staying on task during the lesson

- Making observations on adhesive notes that can be placed in folders

- Recording anecdotal comments, during or after class, using a cassette recorder.

Knowledge of the criteria you use in your observations gives students a framework for their performance.

Electronic Portfolios

Technology can provide help with managing student portfolios. Digital or computer-based portfolios offer a means of saving portfolios in an electronic format. Students can save text, drawings, photographs, graphics, audio or video recordings, or any combination of multimedia information. Teachers can create their own portfolio templates or consult one of the many commercial software programs available to create digital portfolios. Portfolios saved on videotapes or compact discs provide a convenient way to access and store students' work. By employing technology, this means of alternative assessment addresses the learning styles and abilities of individual students. Additionally, electronic portfolios can be shared among teachers, and parents have the ability to easily see the students' progress.

Logistically, the hypermedia equipment and software available for students' use determine what types of entries will be included in the portfolios. The teacher or a team of teachers and students may provide the computer support.

How Are Portfolios Evaluated?

The portfolio should reflect the process of student learning over a specific period of time. At the beginning of that time period, determine the criteria by which you will assess the final product and convey them to the students. Make this evaluation a collaborative effort by seeking students' input as you formulate these criteria and your instructional goals.

Students need to understand that evaluation based on a predetermined standard is but one phase of the assessment process; demonstrated effort and growth are just as important. As you consider correctness and accuracy in both oral and written work, also consider the organization, creativity, and improvement revealed by the student's portfolio over the time period. The portfolio provides a way to monitor the growth of a student's knowledge, skills, and attitudes and shows the student's efforts, progress, and achievements.

How to Implement Portfolios

Teacher-teacher collaboration is as important to the implementation of portfolios as teacher-student collaboration. Confer with your colleagues to determine, for example, what kinds of information you want to see in the student portfolio, how the information will be presented, the purpose of the portfolio, the intended purposes (grading, placement, or a combination of the two), and criteria for evaluating the portfolio. Conferring among colleagues helps foster a departmental cohesiveness and consistency that will ultimately benefit the students.

The Promise of Portfolios

The high degree of student involvement in developing portfolios and deciding how they will be used generally results in renewed student enthusiasm for learning and improved achievement. As students compare portfolio pieces done early in the year with work produced later, they can take pride in their progress as well as reassess their motivation and work habits.

¡Ven conmigo!

supports the use of portfolios in the following ways:

THE PUPIL'S EDITION

▸ Includes numerous oral and written activities that can be easily adapted for student portfolios, such as **En mi cuaderno, Vamos a escribir,** and **Situación.**

THE ANNOTATED TEACHER'S EDITION

▸ Suggests activities in the Portfolio Assessment feature that may serve as portfolio items.

THE ANCILLARY PROGRAM

▸ Includes criteria in the *Alternative Assessment Guide* for evaluating portfolios.

▸ Provides Speaking Tests in the *Testing Program* for each chapter that can be adapted for use as portfolio assessment items.

▸ Offers several oral and written scenarios on the *Interactive CD-ROM Tutor* that students can develop and include in their portfolios.

Teaching Culture

by Nancy A. Humbach, Miami University, and Dorothea Bruschke, Parkway School District

We must integrate culture and language in a way that encourages curiosity, stimulates analysis, and teaches students to hypothesize.

The teaching of culture has undergone some important and welcome changes in recent years. Instead of teaching the standard notions of cultures, language and regions, we now stress the teaching of analysis and the critical thinking skills required to evaluate a culture, not by comparing it to one's own, but within its own setting. The setting includes the geography, climate, history, and influences of peoples who have interacted within that cultural group.

The National Standards for the Teaching of Foreign Languages suggests organizing the teaching of culture into three categories: products, practices, and perspectives. Through the presentation of these aspects of culture, students should gain the skill to analyze the culture, evaluate it within its context, compare it to their culture and develop the ability to function comfortably in that culture.

Skill and practice in the analysis of cultural phenomena equip students to enter a cultural situation, assess it, create strategies for dealing with it, and accepting it as a natural part of the people. The ultimate goal of this philosophy is to reduce the "we vs. they" approach to culture. If students are encouraged to accept and appreciate the diversity of other cultures, they will be more willing and better able to develop the risk-taking strategies necessary to learn a language and to interact with people of different cultures.

There are many ways to help students become culturally knowledgeable and to assist them in developing an awareness of differences and similarities between the target culture and their own. Two of these approaches involve critical thinking, that is, trying to find reasons for a certain behavior through observation and analysis, and putting individual observations into larger cultural patterns. We must integrate culture and language in a way that encourages curiosity, stimulates analysis, and teaches students to hypothesize.

First Approach: Questioning

The first approach involves questioning as the key strategy. At the earliest stages of language learning, students begin to learn ways to greet peers, elders, and strangers, as well as the use of **tú** and **usted**. Students need to consider questions such as: "How do Spanish-speaking people greet each other? Are there different levels of formality? Who initiates a handshake? What's considered a good handshake?" Each of these questions leads students to think about the values that are expressed through word and gesture. They start to "feel" the other culture and, at the same time, understand how much of their own behavior is rooted in their cultural background.

Magazines, newspapers, advertisements, and television commercials are all excellent sources of cultural material. For example, browsing through a Spanish magazine, one finds an extraordinary number of advertisements for health-related products. Could this indicate a great interest in staying healthy? Reading advertisements can be followed up with viewing videos and films, or with interviewing native speakers or people who have lived in Spanish-speaking countries to learn about customs involving health. Students might want to find answers to questions such as: "How do Spanish speakers treat a cold? What is their attitude toward fresh air? toward exercise?" This type of questioning might lead students to discover that we view health matters and the curative properties of food and exercise differently. As in this country, many of the concepts have their roots in the traditions of the past.

An advertisement for a refrigerator or a picture of a Spanish or Latin American kitchen can provide an insight into practices of shopping for food. Students first need to think about the refrigerator at home, take an inventory of what is kept in it, and consider when and where their family shops. Next, students should look closely at a Spanish or Latin American refrigerator. Is it smaller? What could that mean? (Shopping takes place more often, stores are within walking distance, and people eat more fresh foods.)

Food wrappers and containers also provide good clues to cultural insight. For example, laundry detergent is packaged in small plastic bags in many Spanish-speaking countries. Further, instead of "blue-white" cleaning properties, a "red-white" is preferred and considered the epitome of clean. Because of the lack of paper board for boxes, the humidity in many areas, the use for hand laundry, and shopping habits, plastic bags are a more practical form of packaging.

Second Approach: Associating Words with Images

The second approach for developing cultural understanding involves forming associations of words with the cultural images they suggest. Language and culture are so closely related that one might actually say that language *is* culture. Most words, especially nouns, carry a cultural connotation. Knowing the literal equivalent of a word in another language is of little use to students in understanding this connotation. For example, **relación** cannot be translated simply as relationship, **comida** as food, or **paseo** as walk. The Spanish phrase **dar un paseo,** for instance, carries with it such social images as people out walking with friends or family, sitting in a sidewalk café, seeing people and being seen by others. In Spanish-speaking countries, "to go for a walk" often means something entirely different than it does for North Americans.

When students have acquired some sense of the cultural connotation of words—not only through teachers' explanations but, more importantly, through observation of visual images—they start to discover the larger underlying cultural themes, or what is often called "deep culture."

These larger cultural themes serve as organizing categories into which individual cultural phenomena fit to form a pattern. Students might discover, for example, that Spanish speakers, because they live in much more crowded conditions, have a great need for privacy (cultural theme), as reflected in such phenomena as closed doors, fences or walls around property, and sheers on windows. Students might also discover that love of nature and the outdoors is an important cultural theme, as indicated by such phenomena as flower boxes and planters in public places—even on small traffic islands—well-kept public parks in every town, and people going for a walk or going hiking.

As we teach culture, students learn to recognize elements not only of the target culture but also of their American cultural heritage. They see how elements of culture reflect larger themes or patterns. Learning what constitutes American culture and how that information relates to other people throughout the world can be an exciting journey for a young person.

As language teachers, we are able to facilitate that journey into another culture and into our own, to find our similarities as well as our differences from others. We do not encourage value judgments about others and their culture, nor do we recommend adopting other ways. We simply say to students, "Other ways exist. They exist for many reasons, just as our ways exist due to what our ancestors have bequeathed us through history, traditions, values, and geography."

¡Ven conmigo!

develops cultural understanding and awareness in the following ways:

THE PUPIL'S EDITION

▶ Informs students about Spanish-speaking countries through photo essays, maps, almanac boxes, and **Notas culturales** that invite comparison with the students' own cultural experiences.

▶ Engages students in analysis and comparison of live, personal interviews with native speakers in the **Panorama cultural** sections.

▶ Uses the **Encuentro cultural** section to expose students to cross-cultural situations that require observation, analysis, and problem-solving.

▶ Helps students integrate the language with its cultural connotations through a wealth of authentic art, documents, and literature.

THE ANNOTATED TEACHER'S EDITION

▶ Provides the teacher with additional culture, history, and language notes, background information on photos and almanac boxes, and multicultural links.

▶ Suggests problem-solving activities and critical thinking questions that allow students to hypothesize, analyze, and discover larger underlying cultural themes.

THE ANCILLARY PROGRAM

▶ Includes additional realia to develop cultural insight by serving as a catalyst for questioning and direct discovery.

▶ Offers activities that require students to compare and contrast cultures.

▶ Provides songs, short readings, and poems as well as many opportunities for students to experience regional variation and idioms in the video, audio, and CD-ROM programs.

Learning Styles and Multi-Modality Teaching

by Mary B. McGehee, Louisiana State University

Incorporating a greater variety of activities to accommodate the learning styles of all students can make the difference between struggle and pleasure in the foreign language classroom.

The larger and broader population of students who are enrolling in foreign language classes brings a new challenge to foreign language educators, calling forth an evolution in teaching methods to enhance learning for all our students. Educational experts now recognize that every student has a preferred sense for learning and retrieving information: visual, auditory, or kinesthetic. Incorporating a greater variety of activities to accommodate the learning styles of all students can make the difference between struggle and pleasure in the foreign language classroom.

Accommodating Different Learning Styles

A modified arrangement of the classroom is one way to provide more effective and enjoyable learning for all students. Rows of chairs and desks must give way at times to circles, semicircles, or small clusters. Students may be grouped in fours or in pairs for cooperative work or peer teaching. It is important to find a balance of arrangements, thereby providing the most comfort in varied situations.

Since visual, auditory, and kinesthetic learners will be in the class, and because every student's learning will be enhanced by a multi-sensory approach, lessons must be directed toward all three learning styles. Any language lesson content may be presented visually, aurally, or kinesthetically.

Visual presentations and practice may include the chalkboard, charts, posters, television, overhead projectors, books, magazines, picture diagrams, flash cards, bulletin boards, films, slides, or videos. Visual learners need to see what they are to learn. Lest the teacher think he or she will never have the time to prepare all those visuals, Dickel and Slak (1983) found that visual aids generated by students are more effective than ready-made ones.

Auditory presentations and practice may include stating aloud the requirements of the lesson, oral questions and answers, paired or group work on a progression of oral exercises from repetition to communication, tapes, CDs, dialogues, and role-playing. Jingles, catchy stories, and memory devices using songs and rhymes are good learning aids. Having students record themselves and then listen as they play back the cassette allows them to practice in the auditory mode.

Kinesthetic presentations entail the students' use of manipulatives, chart materials, gestures, signals, typing, songs, games, and role-playing. These lead the students to associate sentence constructions with meaningful movements.

A Sample Lesson Using Multi-Modality Teaching

A multi-sensory presentation on greetings might proceed as follows:

For Visual Learners

As the teacher begins oral presentation of greetings and introductions, he or she simultaneously shows the written forms on transparencies, with the formal expressions marked with an adult's hat, and the informal expressions marked with a baseball cap.

The teacher then distributes cards with the hat and cap symbols representing the formal and informal expressions. As the students hear taped mini-dialogues, they hold up the appropriate card to indicate whether the dialogues are formal or informal. On the next listening, the students repeat the sentences they hear.

For Auditory Learners

A longer taped dialogue follows, allowing the students to hear the new expressions a number of times. They write from dictation several sentences containing the new expressions. They may work in pairs, correcting each other's work as they "test" their own understanding of the lesson at hand. Finally, students respond to simple questions using the appropriate formal and informal responses cued by the cards they hold.

For Kinesthetic Learners

For additional kinesthetic input, members of the class come to the front of the room, each holding a hat or cap symbol. As the teacher calls out situations, the students play the roles, using gestures and props appropriate to the age group they are portraying. Non-cued, communicative role-playing with props further enables the students to "feel" the differences between formal and informal expressions.

Helping Students Learn How to Use Their Preferred Mode

Since we require all students to perform in all language skills, part of the assistance we must render is to help them develop strategies within their preferred learning modes to carry out an assignment in another mode. For example, visual students hear the teacher assign an oral exercise and visualize what they must do. They must see themselves carrying out the assignment, in effect watching themselves as if there were a movie going on in their heads. Only then can they also hear themselves saying the right things. Thus, this assignment will be much easier for the visual learners who have been taught this process, if they have not already figured it out for themselves. Likewise, true auditory students, confronted with a reading/writing assignment, must talk themselves through it, converting the entire process into sound as they plan and prepare their work. Kinesthetic students presented with a visual or auditory task must first break the assignment into tasks and then work their way through them.

Students who experience difficulty because of a strong preference for one mode of learning are often unaware of the degree of preference. In working with these students, I prefer the simple and direct assessment of learning styles offered by Richard Bandler and John Grinder in their book *Frogs into Princes,* which allows the teacher and student to quickly determine how the student learns. In an interview with the student, I follow the assessment with certain specific recommendations of techniques to make the student's study time more effective.

It is important to note here that teaching students to maximize their study does not require that the teacher give each student an individualized assignment. It does require that each student who needs it be taught how to prepare the assignment using his or her own talents and strengths. This communication between teacher and student, combined with teaching techniques that reinforce learning in all modes, can only maximize pleasure and success in learning a foreign language.

References

Dickel, M.J. and S. Slak. "Imaging Vividness and Memory for Verbal Material." *Journal of Mental Imagery* 7, i (1983):121–126.

Bandler, Richard, and John Grinder. *Frogs into Princes.* Real People Press, Moab, UT. 1978.

¡Ven conmigo!

accommodates different learning styles in the following ways:

THE PUPIL'S EDITION

▸ Presents basic material in audio, video, and print formats.

▸ Includes role-playing activities and a variety of multi-modal activities, including an extensive listening strand and many art-based activities.

THE ANNOTATED TEACHER'S EDITION

▸ Provides suggested activities for visual, auditory, and kinesthetic learners as well as suggestions for slower-paced learning and challenge activities.

▸ Includes Total Physical Response activities.

THE ANCILLARY PROGRAM

▸ Provides additional reinforcement activities for a variety of learning styles.

▸ Presents a rich blend of audiovisual input through the video program, audio program, CD-ROM tutor, transparencies, and blackline masters.

New Perspectives for Native Speakers

by Cecilia Rodríguez-Pino, New Mexico State University

Spanish teachers often simultaneously teach two groups of students whose learning needs are markedly different. The first group, the majority, for whom most curricula are developed, are English-proficient but at a beginner's level in Spanish. The second group consists of students whose proficiency in English varies but who already speak Spanish, often quite proficiently. From their own experience they already understand a great deal about the Spanish language and the cultures of Spanish speakers. Many schools have not yet set up Spanish for Native Speakers (SNS) sections with specialized curricula that would build on these students' linguistic and cultural strengths. As a result, in some schools native speakers who want to study Spanish are enrolled in courses where Spanish is taught as a foreign language. Addressing their learning needs thus becomes the particular challenge of the teacher, who must create and implement supplemental classroom materials.

Types of Native Spanish Speakers

The greatest number of native Spanish speakers in the classroom are Spanish-speaking immigrants and American students of Hispanic descent. Many immigrants have been uprooted from their native countries and find themselves in a new and foreign environment without the skills to communicate. Often they must struggle to adapt to mainstream sociocultural norms and values. Psychological adjustment, cultural integration, and the acquisition of new communicative skills are daily concerns for them. Building teacher-student and peer-peer learning relationships may be harder for such students.

American students of Hispanic descent are often bilingual. Some are highly proficient in both written and oral Spanish, but many are proficient to varying degrees, depending on the circumstances, topics, tasks, and informal situations. These students reflect the various socioeconomic classes of society and speak a wide range of Spanish dialects. Research indicates that the dialect they speak affects how they are viewed at school. When they speak a "standard" variety of Spanish and are from an educated class, as are many Cuban Americans in Florida, reactions to them are usually positive. But when Spanish speakers are from a rural background, speak a "nonstandard" dialect, or come from a nonliterate background, reactions in school are often negative. Attempting to modify their dialect can be detrimental to their linguistic and social development.

Linguistic Needs

Native Spanish speakers need to retrieve any Spanish they may have lost, maintain the competency they already have, and expand their knowledge and skills in Spanish.

The problem of native language loss is receiving much attention in the profession. Children appear to lose production skills more quickly than they lose comprehension ability. Thus retrieval efforts should focus on production. Rapid changes in society and in the patterns by which Spanish is transmitted from one generation to the next account for much of students' language loss. Word borrowing and code switching to English may also account for language loss. These practices are not unique to bilingual students in the United States; they are common linguistic phenomena, observed wherever languages are in contact. A native speaker may switch from Spanish to English when referring to activities generally associated with the dominant culture—even when the speaker is perfectly familiar with the relevant Spanish vocabulary. Efforts to eradicate code switching may harm students' linguistic and social development.

Affective Needs

Native Spanish-speaking students bring to class much valuable cultural and linguistic experience. Cultural opportunities need to be provided for them through which they can express their knowledge of their own particular Spanish-speaking culture and gain a greater overview of other Spanish-speaking communities and countries. They need to understand that their heritage, language, culture, dialect, and individual abilities are valuable to society. As teachers we must respect and value the different languages and dialects our students speak, and we must create an instructional context in which students will develop positive attitudes toward their own ethnic group and their own ethnic identity.

An SNS Program Approach

A task-based, whole-language approach is recommended. Receptive and productive skills can be developed through culturally meaningful activities whose contexts are community, school, home, and self. These activities can be carried out in conjunction with textbook thematic units. Such an approach creates a student-centered classroom in which the teacher acts as a facilitator connecting students to the bilingual community.

Expanding Receptive Skills

Students should perform activities in which they listen to their native language in a broad range of formal and informal contexts, from simple topics to complex ones. Audio- or videotaped versions of stories, songs, documentaries, speeches, or debates can be adapted for class assignments. Guest speakers from the community are extremely valuable resources for presentations or interviews on the chapter topic.

Students should have access to diverse, authentic reading materials from the popular culture as well as from more formal subject areas. Chicano, Cuban, Dominican, Colombian, Nicaraguan, Honduran, Panamanian, and Puerto Rican writings—which are underrepresented in the mainstream literary canon—can play an important role in instilling in students a sense of pride and awareness of their cultural heritage. Students relate well to literature written by contemporary Hispanic authors who have had experiences similar to the students' in the United States. For example, they might read the short story "Desde que se fue," from the collection *Madreselvas en flor* by literary prize-winning Chicano author Ricardo Aguilar-Melantzón, about growing up in a bilingual setting.

Developing Productive Skills

Oral history projects, ethnographic interviews, sociolinguistic surveys, dialogue journals, letter writing, and other purposeful authentic activities are effective techniques that focus on interactions among students, teacher, and community. These kinds of activities give students the opportunity to develop individual strengths and to explore their language and culture in a community context.

Classroom Environment

We can change the classroom space itself to create an environment that recognizes the prestige of the students' language and cultural heritage. Using a brief questionnaire, the teacher can find out the students' backgrounds and then display relevant posters, travel brochures, art, literature, or historical information. Students can contribute captioned photographs depicting cultural events and family traditions, so that the bulletin board reflects their personal view of the Spanish-speaking world rather than just the teacher's perspective.

Individual Assessment and Evaluation

Individual assessment at the beginning of the year should be based primarily on content so that students' errors are not the main focus. Use content, organization, and language as criteria for evaluating speaking and writing. In evaluating students' work for the year, take into account how students have broadened their functional range. This requires students to be responsible for the concepts that are essential to comprehension and production. A writing portfolio is a valuable component of the evaluation process. Oral presentations of ethnographic and sociolinguistic projects are contextualized activities for evaluating speaking.

¡Ven conmigo!

supports native speakers' continued development of Spanish in the following ways:

THE PUPIL'S EDITION

▸ Promotes pride and awareness of cultural heritage through Location Openers on U.S. Spanish-speaking areas, as well as cultural features, interviews with native speakers, and literary selections by U.S. and non-U.S. native speakers.

▸ Validates the use of regionally specific vocabulary and authentic expression in the **También se puede decir** and **A lo nuestro** features.

▸ Fosters the student's self-concept by encouraging individual expression in journal entries and other authentic tasks, such as letter writing.

THE ANNOTATED TEACHER'S EDITION

▸ Includes specific suggestions for activities to be performed by native speakers, both independently and with other students.

▸ Provides the teacher with additional vocabulary suggestions and language notes that validate regional variants.

▸ Suggests family and community links that strengthen students' ties to the wider bilingual community via family and community interviews and ethnographic reports.

THE ANCILLARY PROGRAM

▸ Offers a *Cuaderno para hispanohablantes* with a diagnostic instrument and, chapter by chapter, additional reading practice based on authentic literature on topics of interest to native speakers. In addition, this book addresses issues of formal usage and pronunciation and provides additional writing and speaking practice.

▸ Provides a **Para hispanohablantes** writing feature in each chapter of the *Interactive CD-ROM Tutor*.

Professional References

This section provides information about resources that can enrich your Spanish class. Included are addresses of Spanish and Latin American government offices, pen pal organizations, subscription agencies, and many others. Since addresses change frequently, you may want to verify them before you send your requests. You may also want to refer to the HRW Web site at http://www.hrw.com for current information.

PEN PAL ORGANIZATIONS

For the names of pen pal groups other than those listed below, contact your local chapter of AATSP. There are fees involved, so be sure to write for information.

**Student Letter Exchange
(League of Friendship)**
211 Broadway, Suite 201
Lynbrook, NY 11563
(516) 887-8628

World Pen Pals
1694 Como Avenue
St. Paul, MN 55108
(612) 647-0191

EMBASSIES AND CONSULATES

Addresses and phone numbers of embassies and consulates for Spanish-speaking countries are available in most U.S. city telephone directories. All are available in the directory for Washington, D.C.

PERIODICALS

Subscriptions to the following cultural materials are available through some larger bookstores or directly from the publishers. See also the section on Subscription Services.

- *El País,* a major Spanish newspaper
- *GeoMundo,* a cultural and environmental magazine
- *Hispanic,* an English-language magazine about Hispanics in the U.S.
- *El Nuevo Día,* a Puerto Rican newspaper
- *La Prensa,* a major daily paper in Argentina
- *Tú internacional,* a magazine for teens published in several Spanish-speaking countries
- *México desconocido,* a cultural and environmental magazine about Mexico

CULTURAL AGENCIES

For historical and tourist information about Spanish-speaking regions, contact:

Greater Miami Convention and Visitors Bureau
701 Brickell Ave., Suite 2700
Miami, FL 33131
(800) 283-2707

Mexican Government Tourism Office
10440 West Office Drive
Houston, TX 77042
(800) 446-3942

Tourist Office of Spain
666 Fifth Avenue
New York, NY 10022
(212) 265-8822

INTERCULTURAL EXCHANGE

CIEE Student Travel Services
205 East 42nd St.
New York, NY 10017
(888) 268-6245

American Field Service
198 Madison, 8th Floor
New York, NY 10016
(212) 299-9000

PROFESSIONAL ORGANIZATIONS

The American Council on the Teaching of Foreign Languages (ACTFL)
6 Executive Plaza
Yonkers, NY 10701
(914) 963-8830

American Association of Teachers of Spanish and Portuguese (AATSP)
Butler-Hancock Hall, Room 210
University of Northern Colorado
Greeley, CO 80639
(970) 351-1090

SUBSCRIPTION SERVICES

Spanish-language magazines can be obtained through subscription agencies in the United States. The following companies are among the many which can provide your school with subscriptions:

EBSCO Subscription Services
P.O. Box 1943
Birmingham, AL 35201-1943
(205) 991-6600

Continental Book Company
8000 Cooper Ave., Bldg. 29
Glendale, NY 11385
(718) 326-0560

MISCELLANEOUS

Educational Resources Information Center (ERIC)
2277 Research Blvd.
Rockville, MD 20852
(800) 538-3742

U.S. Department of Education
400 Maryland Ave., SW
Washington, D.C. 20202-0498
(800) USA-LEARN
- Information and resource center; publications and videos available

The International Film Bureau
332 South Michigan Ave.
Chicago, IL 60604-4382
(312) 427-4545
- Foreign language videos for sale and/or rent

Américas
Organization of American States
17th and Constitution Ave. NW
Room #307
Washington, D.C. 20006
(202) 458-3000
- Magazine available in English or Spanish text

A Bibliography for the Spanish Teacher

This bibliography is a compilation of resources available for professional enrichment.

SELECTED AND ANNOTATED LIST OF READINGS

I. Methods and Approaches

Cohen, Andrew D. *Assessing Language Ability in the Classroom,* **2/e.** Boston, MA: Heinle, 1994.
- Assessment processes, oral interviews, role-playing situations, dictation, portfolio assessment and computer-based testing.

Hadley, Alice Omaggio. *Teaching Language in Context,* **2/e.** Boston, MA: Heinle, 1993.
- Overview of the proficiency movement and a survey of past language teaching methods and approaches; application of the five skills in language education; includes sample activities, teaching summaries, and references.

Lafayette, R. (Ed.). *National Standards: A Catalyst for Reform.* Lincolnwood, IL: National Textbook Co., 1996.
- Outline and implications of the National Standards for the modern language classroom, addresses technology, teacher training, materials development, and the changing learning environment.

Lee, James F., and Bill VanPatten. *Making Communicative Language Teaching Happen.* New York: McGraw-Hill, 1995.
- Task-based approach to language education, includes activities and test sections to encourage communicative interaction in the classroom.

II. Second-Language Theory

Brown, H. Douglas. *Principles of Language Learning and Teaching* **(3rd. ed.).** Englewood Cliffs, NJ: Prentice Hall Regents, 1994.
- Addresses the cognitive, psychological, and sociocultural factors influencing the language learning process; also includes theories of learning, styles and strategies, motivation, and culture; as well as an introduction to assessment, error analysis, communicative competence and theories of acquisition.

Ellis, Rod. *The Study of Second Language Acquisition.* Oxford: Oxford University Press, 1994.
- Provides an overview of second language acquisition: error analysis, acquisition orders, social factors, affective variables, individual differences, and the advantages and disadvantages of classroom instruction.

Krashen, Stephen. *The Power of Reading.* New York: McGraw-Hill, 1994.
- Updates Optimal Input Theory by incorporating the reading of authentic texts.

Liskin-Gasparro, Judith. *A Guide to Testing and Teaching for Oral Proficiency.* Boston, MA: Heinle, 1990.
- Oral proficiency through interview techniques and speech samples.

III. Technology-Enhanced instruction

Bush, Michael D., and Robert M. Terry, (Eds.), in conjunction with ACTFL. *Technology Enhanced Language Learning.* Lincolnwood, IL: National Textbook Co., 1997.
- Articles deal with the application of technology in the modern language classroom, including: computer-mediated communication, electronic discussions, hypermedia, the Internet, multimedia, videos, and the WWW.

Muyskens, Judith Ann. (Ed.). *New Ways of Learning and Teaching: Focus on Technology and Foreign Language Education.* Boston: Heinle and Heinle, 1997.
- Compilation of articles on the use of technology in the classroom; techniques for applying technology tools to the four skills and culture; also discusses implementation, teacher training, and language laboratories.

Steen, Douglas R., Mark R. Roddy, Derek Sheffield, and Michael Bryan Stout. *Teaching With the Internet: Putting Teachers before Technology.* Bellevue, WA: Resolution Business Press, Inc., 1995.
- Designed for K–12 teachers and based on educational theory, provides tips and strategies for using the Internet in and out of the classroom, cites specific case studies; topics include the Internet, e-mail, mailing lists, newsgroups, the WWW, creating a Web page, and other research services.

IV. Teaching Native Speakers

Merino, Barbara J., Henry T. Trueba, and Fabián A. Samaniego. *Language and Culture in Learning: Teaching Spanish to Native Speakers of Spanish.* London, England: Falmer Press, 1993.

Rodríguez-Pino, Cecilia, and Daniel Villa. "A Student-Centered Spanish for Native Speakers Program: Theory, Curriculum Design and Outcome Assessment." In *Faces in a Crowd: The Individual Learner in Multisection Courses.* Edited by Carol A. Klee. American Association of University Supervisors Series. Boston, MA: Heinle, 1994.

Valdés, Guadalupe. "The Role of the Foreign Language Teaching Profession in Maintaining Non-English Languages in the United States." In *Northeast Conference Reports: Languages for a Multicultural World in Transition.* Edited by Heidi Byrnes. Lincolnwood, IL: National Textbook, 1992.

¡Ven conmigo!®

HOLT SPANISH

LEVEL 1

HOLT, RINEHART AND WINSTON

A Harcourt Classroom Education Company

Austin · New York · Orlando · Atlanta · San Francisco · Boston · Dallas · Toronto · London

ASSOCIATE DIRECTOR
Barbara Kristof

SENIOR EDITORS
Lynda Cortez
Janet Welsh Crossley
Jean Miller
Beatriz Malo Pojman
Paul Provence
Douglas Ward

MANAGING EDITOR
Chris Hiltenbrand

EDITORIAL STAFF
Hubert Bays
Nancy Bundy
Jeff Cole
Milagros Escamilla
Catherine Gavin
Martha Lashbrook
Zahydée Minnick
Carmen de la Morena
Jorge Muñoz
Todd Phillips
Brent Turnipseed
Todd Wolf
J. Elisabeth Wright

Mark Eells, *Editorial Coordinator*

EDITORIAL PERMISSIONS
Ann B. Farrar, *Senior Permissions Editor*
Yuri Muñoz, *Interpreter-Translator*

ART, DESIGN, & PHOTO

BOOK DESIGN
Richard Metzger, *Design Director*
Marta L. Kimball, *Design Manager*
Mary Wages, *Senior Designer*
Andrew Lankes
Alicia Sullivan
Ruth Limon

IMAGE SERVICES
Joe London, Director
Jeannie Taylor, *Photo Research Supervisor*
Diana Suthard

Michelle Rumpf, *Art Buyer Supervisor*
Coco Weir

DESIGN NEW MEDIA
Susan Michael, *Design Director*
Amy Shank, *Design Manager*
Kimberly Cammerata, *Design Manager*
Czeslaw Sornat, *Senior Designer*
Grant Davidson

MEDIA DESIGN
Curtis Riker, *Design Director*
Richard Chavez

GRAPHIC SERVICES
Kristen Darby, *Manager*
Linda Wilbourn
Jane Dixon
Dean Hsieh

COVER DESIGN
Richard Metzger, *Design Director*
Candace Moore, *Senior Designer*

PRODUCTION
Amber McCormick, *Production Supervisor*
Diana Rodriguez, *Production Coordinator*

MANUFACTURING
Shirley Cantrell, *Supervisor, Inventory & Manufacturing*
Deborah Wisdom, *Senior Inventory Analyst*

NEW MEDIA
Jessica Bega, *Senior Project Manager*
Elizabeth Kline, *Senior Project Manager*

VIDEO PRODUCTION
Video materials produced by Edge Productions, Inc., Aiken, S.C.

AUTHORS

Nancy A. Humbach
Miami University
Oxford, OH
Ms. Humbach collaborated in the development of the scope and sequence and video material, and created activities and culture features.

Dr. Oscar Ozete
University of Southern Indiana
Evansville, Indiana
Dr. Ozete collaborated in the development of the scope and sequence, reviewed all Pupil's Edition material, and wrote grammar explanations.

CONTRIBUTING WRITERS

Dr. Charles J. Bruno
Dr. Bruno wrote video materials.

Michael A. García
The University of Texas at Austin
Mr. García wrote the Location Openers.

Jean Rowe Miller
The University of Texas at Austin
Ms. Miller wrote the **Sugerencias.**

Susan Peterson
The Ohio State University
Columbus, OH
Mrs. Peterson selected realia for readings and developed reading activities.

The following people researched and wrote culture features:

Dolores Brown
Tucson, AZ

Mariana Colten
Frankfort, KY

Lisa Contreras
Lexington, KY

Melinda Gale
Portland, OR

Mary Maggi
Austin, TX

Jaime Ugaz
Austin, TX

CONSULTANTS

John DeMado
John DeMado Language Seminars, Inc.
Washington, CT

Dr. Ingeborg R. McCoy
Southwest Texas State University
San Marcos, TX

Jo Anne S. Wilson
J. Wilson Associates
Glen Arbor, MI

REVIEWERS

These educators reviewed one or more chapters of the Pupil's Edition.

Dr. Edward David Allen
The Ohio State University
Columbus, OH

Dr. Marjorie E. Artzer
Northern Kentucky University
Highland Heights, KY

Rocío Barajas
Native speaker reviewer
Mexico City, Mexico

Daniel J. Bender
Adlai Stevenson High School
Lincolnshire, IL

O. Lynn Bolton
Nathan Hale High School
West Allis, WI

Juanita Carfora
Central Regional High School
Bayville, NJ

Lolita Carfora
Central Regional High School
Bayville, NJ

Dr. June Carter
The University of Texas at Austin

Renato Cervantes
Pacific High School
San Bernardino, CA

Lucila Dorsett
Native speaker reviewer
Austin, TX

Myrtress G. Eddleman
Retired. Carver High School
Birmingham, AL

Rubén Garza
ESC XIII
Austin, TX

Dr. Gail Guntermann
Arizona State University
Tempe, AZ

Joseph N. Harris
Poudre School District
Fort Collins, CO

Dr. Audrey L. Heining-Boynton
The University of North Carolina
Chapel Hill, NC

Stephen L. Levy
Roslyn Public Schools
Roslyn, NY

Marcela Malo
Native speaker reviewer
Cuenca, Ecuador

Carmen Reyes
Jonesboro High School
Jonesboro, GA

Dr. Yolanda Russinovich Solé
The University of Texas at Austin

Elena Steele
Foreign Language Specialist
Clark County School District
Las Vegas, NV

Cristina Suárez
Native speaker reviewer
Madrid, Spain

Carol A. Villalobos
Hazelwood Central High School
St. Louis, MO

FIELD TEST PARTICIPANTS

We express our appreciation to the teachers and students who participated in the field test. Their comments were instrumental in the development of this program.

Bill Braden
South Junior High School
Boise, ID

Paula Critchlow
Indian Hills Middle School
Sandy, UT

Frances Cutter
Convent of the Visitation School
St. Paul, MN

Carlos Fernández
Sandy Creek High School
Tyrone, GA

Jan Holland
Lovejoy High School
Lovejoy, GA

Gloria Holmstrom
Emerson Junior High School
Yonkers, NY

K. A. Lagana
Ponus Ridge Middle School
Norwalk, CT

Michelle Mistric
Iowa High School
Iowa, LA

Rubén Moreno
Aycock Middle School
Greensboro, NC

Fred Pratt
San Marcos High School
San Marcos, TX

Regina Salvi
Museum Junior High School
Yonkers, NY

Lorraine Walsh
Lincoln Southeast High School
Lincoln, NE

FIELD TEST REVIEWERS

Maureen Fischer
Marian Catholic High School
Chicago Heights, IL

Nancy Holmes
Marian Catholic High School
Chicago Heights, IL

TO THE STUDENT

Some people have the opportunity to learn a new language by living in another country. Most of us, however, begin learning another language and getting acquainted with a foreign culture in a classroom with the help of a teacher, classmates, and a textbook. To use your book effectively, you need to know how it works.

¡Ven conmigo! *(Come along!)* is organized to help you learn Spanish and become familiar with the cultures of people who speak Spanish. The Preliminary Chapter presents basic concepts in Spanish and strategies for learning a new language. This chapter is followed by six Location Openers and twelve chapters.

Location Opener Six four-page photo essays called Location Openers introduce different Spanish-speaking places. You can also see these locations on video, the *CD-ROM Tutor*, and the *DVD Tutor*.

Chapter Opener The Chapter Opener pages tell you the chapter theme and goals.

De antemano *(Getting started)* This illustrated story, which is also on video, shows you Spanish-speaking people in real-life situations, using the language you'll learn in the chapter.

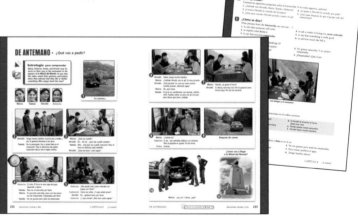

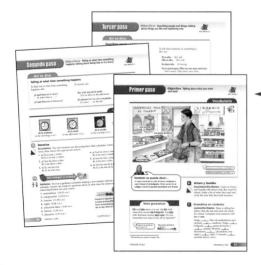

Primer, Segundo, and **Tercer paso** *(First, Second, and Third part)* After **De antemano,** the chapter is divided into three sections called **pasos.** Within the **paso** are **Así se dice** *(Here's how you say it)* boxes that contain the Spanish expressions you'll need to communicate and **Vocabulario** and **Gramática/Nota gramatical** boxes that give you the Spanish words and grammatical structures you'll need to know. Activities in each **paso** enable you to develop your skills in listening, reading, speaking, and writing.

Panorama cultural *(Cultural panorama)* On this page are interviews with Spanish-speaking people from around the world. You can watch these interviews on video or listen to them on audio CD. You can also watch them using the *CD-ROM Tutor* and the *DVD Tutor*, then check to see how well you understood by answering some questions about what the people say.

Encuentro cultural *(Cultural encounter)* This section, found in six of the chapters, gives you a firsthand encounter with some aspect of a Spanish-speaking culture.

Nota cultural *(Culture note)* In each chapter, there are notes with more information about the cultures of Spanish-speaking people.

Vamos a leer *(Let's read)* The reading section follows the three **pasos.** The selections are related to the chapter themes and will help you develop your reading skills in Spanish.

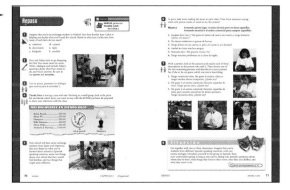

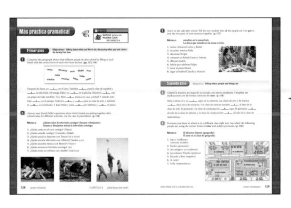

Más práctica gramatical *(Additional grammar practice)* This section begins the chapter review. You will find four pages of activities that provide additional practice with the grammar concepts you learned in the chapter.

Repaso *(Review)* The activities on these pages practice what you've learned in the chapter and help you improve your listening, reading, and communication skills. You'll also review what you've learned about culture. A section called **Vamos a escribir** *(Let's write)* in Chapters 3–12 will develop your writing skills.

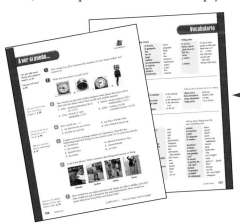

A ver si puedo... *(Let's see if I can . . .)* This page at the end of each chapter contains a series of questions and short activities to help you see if you've achieved the chapter goals.

Vocabulario *(Vocabulary)* In the Spanish-English vocabulary list on the last page of the chapter, the words are grouped by **paso.** These words and expressions will be on the quizzes and tests.

You'll also find special features in each chapter that provide extra tips and reminders.

Sugerencia *(Suggestion)* offers study hints to help you succeed in a foreign language class.

¿Te acuerdas? *(Do you remember?)* and **¿Se te ha olvidado?** *(Have you forgotten?)* remind you of expressions, grammar, and vocabulary you may have forgotten.

A lo nuestro *(Our way)* gives you additional expressions to add more color to your speech.

Vocabulario extra *(Extra vocabulary)* lists extra words you might find helpful. These words will not appear on the quizzes and tests unless your teacher chooses to include them.

You'll also find Spanish-English and English-Spanish vocabulary lists at the end of the book. The words you'll need to know for the quizzes and tests are in boldface type.

At the end of your book, you'll find more helpful material, such as:
- a summary of the expressions you'll learn in the **Así se dice** boxes
- a summary of the grammar you'll study
- additional vocabulary words you might want to use
- a grammar index to help you find where structures are presented.

¡Ven conmigo! Come along on an exciting trip to new cultures and a new language!

¡Buen viaje!

Explanation of icons in *¡Ven conmigo!*

Throughout ¡Ven conmigo!, you'll see these symbols, or icons, next to activities and presentations. The following key will help you understand them.

 Video/DVD Whenever this icon appears, you'll know there is a related segment in the *¡Ven conmigo! Video* and *DVD* Programs.

 Listening Activities

  Pair Work/Group Work Activities

 Writing Activities

 Interactive Games and Activities Whenever this icon appears, you'll know there is a related activity on the *¡Ven conmigo! Interactive CD-ROM Tutor* and on the *DVD Tutor*.

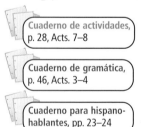

Cuaderno de actividades, p. 28, Acts. 7–8

Cuaderno de gramática, p. 46, Acts. 3–4

Cuaderno para hispano-hablantes, pp. 23–24

Practice Activities These icons tell you which activities from the *Cuaderno de actividades, Cuaderno de gramática*, and *Cuaderno para hispano-hablantes* practice the material presented.

Más práctica gramatical, p. 316, Act. 5 →

Más práctica gramatical This reference tells you where you can find additional grammar practice in the review section of the chapter.

 Internet Activities This icon provides the keyword you'll need to access related online activities at

¡Ven conmigo! Contents

Come along—to a world of new experiences!

¡Ven conmigo! offers you the opportunity to learn the language spoken by millions of people in the many Spanish-speaking countries around the world. Let's find out about the countries, the people, and the Spanish language.

¡VEN CONMIGO A
España!

¡Mucho gusto!.....16

Capítulo 2

¡Organízate! 46

CAPÍTULO 4

¿Qué haces esta tarde? 108

Florida!

El ritmo de la vida 140

CAPÍTULO 6

Entre familia 168

¡VEN CONMIGO A
Ecuador!

CAPÍTULO 7

¿Qué te gustaría hacer? 202

CAPÍTULO 8

¡A comer! 230

Texas!

LOCATION FOR CAPÍTULOS 9, 10 260

CAPÍTULO 9

¡Vamos de compras! 264

Capítulo 10

Celebraciones 292

¡VEN CONMIGO A
Puerto Rico!

Para vivir bien.....326

CAPÍTULO 12

Las vacaciones ideales 356

Cultural References

Page numbers referring to material in the Pupil's Edition *appear in regular type.*
For material located in the Annotated Teacher's Edition, *page numbers*
appear in boldface type.

La Península Ibérica

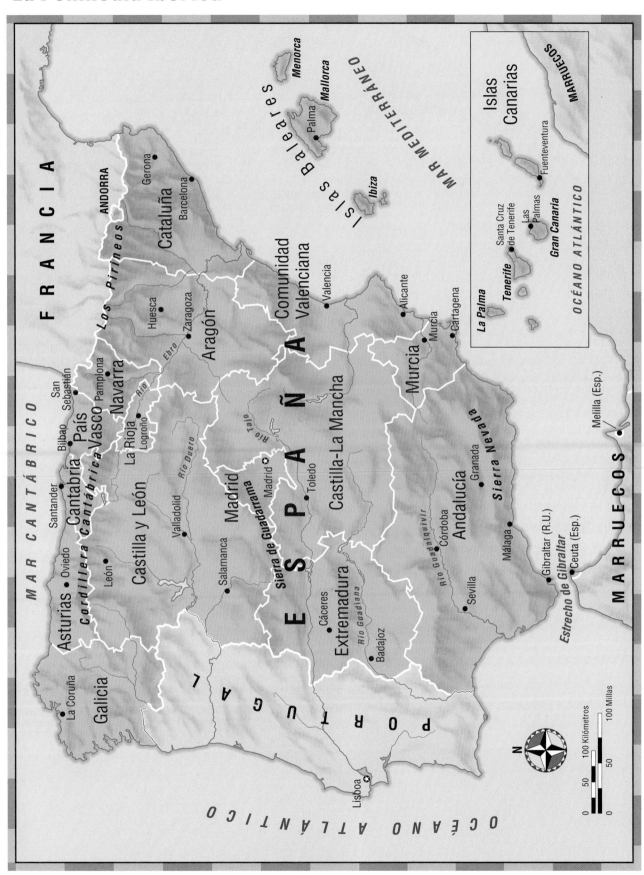

FRANCIA

MAR CANTÁBRICO

OCÉANO ATLÁNTICO

Menorca

Mallorca
Palma

Ibiza

MAR MEDITERRÁNEO

Islas Baleares

ANDORRA

Los Pirineos

Gerona

Cataluña

Barcelona

Comunidad
Valenciana

Valencia

Alicante

Murcia
Cartagena

Huesca

Zaragoza

Aragón

Río Ebro

Navarra

Pamplona

San
Sebastián

Bilbao

País Vasco

Cordillera Cantábrica

Cantabria

Santander

Asturias

Oviedo

La Rioja

Logroño

Río Duero

Río Tajo

Madrid

Madrid

Sierra de Guadarrama

Castilla-La Mancha

Toledo

Murcia

Granada

Sierra Nevada

Andalucía

Córdoba

Río Guadalquivir

E S P A Ñ A

Castilla y León

León

Valladolid

Salamanca

Cáceres

Extremadura

Badajoz

Río Guadiana

Sevilla

Málaga

Gibraltar (R.U.)

Ceuta (Esp.)

Estrecho de Gibraltar

Melilla (Esp.)

M A R R U E C O S

La Coruña

Galicia

P O R T U G A L

Lisboa

OCÉANO ATLÁNTICO

N

100 Kilómetros

100 Millas

50

50

50

50

0

0

Islas
Canarias

MARRUECOS

Fuenteventura

Santa Cruz
de Tenerife

Las
Palmas

Gran Canaria

Tenerife

La Palma

OCÉANO ATLÁNTICO

El mundo

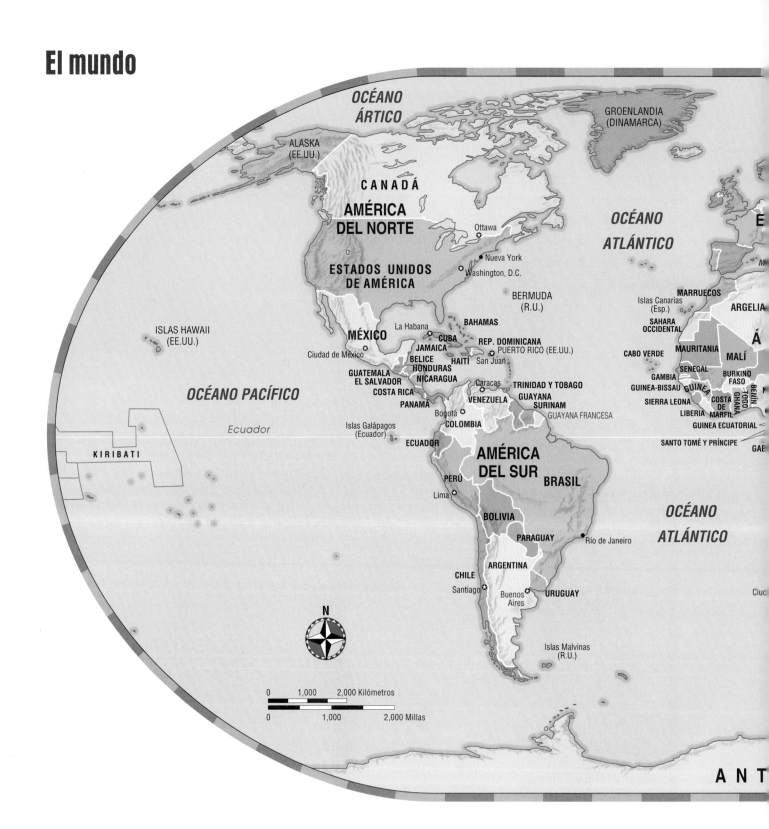

OCÉANO ÁRTICO

GROENLANDIA (DINAMARCA)

ALASKA (EE.UU.)

CANADÁ

AMÉRICA DEL NORTE

Ottawa

OCÉANO ATLÁNTICO

E

ESTADOS UNIDOS DE AMÉRICA

Nueva York
Washington, D.C.

BERMUDA (R.U.)

ISLAS HAWAII (EE.UU.)

Islas Canarias (Esp.)

MARRUECOS

ARGELIA

SAHARA OCCIDENTAL

La Habana

BAHAMAS

MÉXICO

CUBA
JAMAICA

REP. DOMINICANA

PUERTO RICO (EE.UU.)

Á

CABO VERDE

MAURITANIA

MALÍ

Ciudad de México

BELICE
HONDURAS

HAITÍ

San Juan

SENEGAL

BURKINO FASO

GUATEMALA
EL SALVADOR

NICARAGUA

GAMBIA

GUINEA-BISSAU

GUINEA

BENÍN

TOGO
GHANA

OCÉANO PACÍFICO

COSTA RICA

Caracas

TRINIDAD Y TOBAGO

SIERRA LEONA

COSTA DE MARFIL

PANAMÁ

VENEZUELA

GUAYANA
SURINAM

LIBERIA

Bogotá

GUAYANA FRANCESA

GUINEA ECUATORIAL

Islas Galápagos (Ecuador)

COLOMBIA

SANTO TOMÉ Y PRÍNCIPE

GAB

Ecuador

ECUADOR

KIRIBATI

AMÉRICA DEL SUR

PERÚ

BRASIL

OCÉANO ATLÁNTICO

Lima

BOLIVIA

PARAGUAY

Río de Janeiro

CHILE

ARGENTINA

Santiago

Buenos Aires

URUGUAY

Ciu

Islas Malvinas (R.U.)

N

0	1,000	2,000 Kilómetros
0	1,000	2,000 Millas

ANT

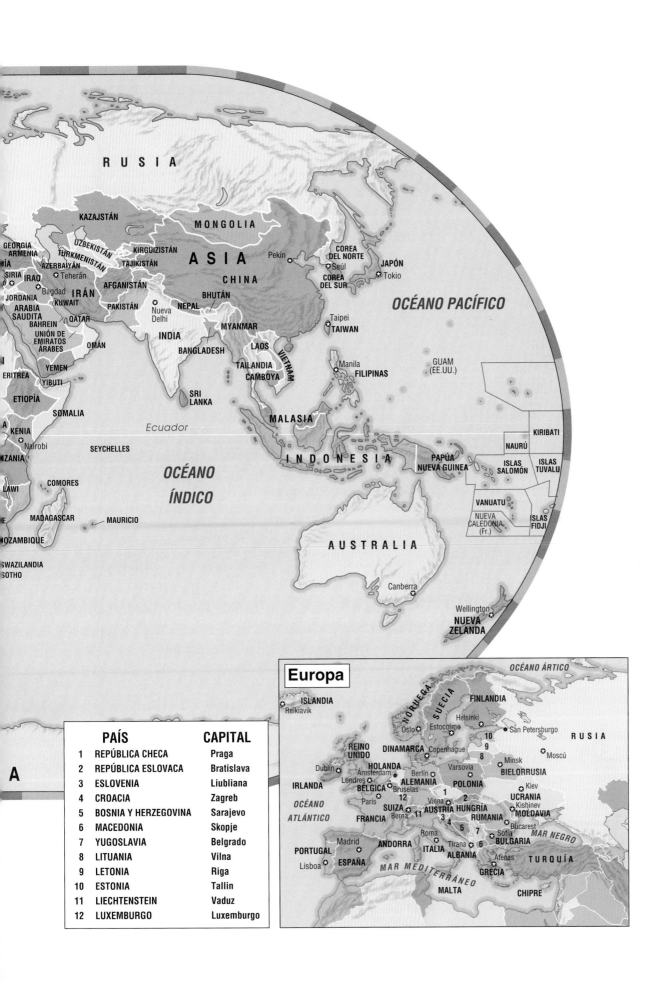

RUSIA

KAZAJSTÁN

MONGOLIA

GEORGIA
ARMENIA
UZBEKISTÁN
KIRGUIZISTÁN
TURKMENISTÁN
TAJIKISTÁN
AZERBAIYÁN
SIRIA
IRAQ
✪ Teherán
AFGANISTÁN
JORDANIA
✪ Bagdad
IRÁN
KUWAIT
ARABIA
SAUDITA
PAKISTÁN
✪ Nueva
Delhi
BAHREIN
QATAR
UNIÓN DE
EMIRATOS
ÁRABES
OMÁN
INDIA

ASIA

Pekín ✪

CHINA

BHUTÁN

NEPAL

MYANMAR

BANGLADESH

COREA
DEL NORTE
✪ Seúl
COREA
DEL SUR

JAPÓN
✪ Tokio

OCÉANO PACÍFICO

Taipei
TAIWAN

LAOS

YEMEN

ERITREA
YIBUTI

ETIOPÍA

SOMALIA

SRI
LANKA

TAILANDIA
CAMBOYA
VIETNAM

✪ Manila
FILIPINAS

GUAM
(EE.UU.)

Ecuador

MALASIA

KENIA
✪ Nairobi

ZANIA

SEYCHELLES

**OCÉANO
ÍNDICO**

KIRIBATI

NAURÚ

INDONESIA

PAPÚA
NUEVA GUINEA

ISLAS
SALOMÓN
ISLAS
TUVALU

LAWI

COMORES

MOZAMBIQUE

MADAGASCAR

MAURICIO

VANUATU

NUEVA
CALEDONIA
(Fr.)
ISLAS
FIDJI

SWAZILANDIA
SOTHO

AUSTRALIA

Canberra ✪

Wellington ✪
**NUEVA
ZELANDA**

A

PAÍS	CAPITAL
1 REPÚBLICA CHECA	Praga
2 REPÚBLICA ESLOVACA	Bratislava
3 ESLOVENIA	Liubliana
4 CROACIA	Zagreb
5 BOSNIA Y HERZEGOVINA	Sarajevo
6 MACEDONIA	Skopje
7 YUGOSLAVIA	Belgrado
8 LITUANIA	Vilna
9 LETONIA	Riga
10 ESTONIA	Tallin
11 LIECHTENSTEIN	Vaduz
12 LUXEMBURGO	Luxemburgo

Europa

OCÉANO ÁRTICO

ISLANDIA
Reikiavik

NORUEGA
SUECIA
FINLANDIA

Oslo
Estocolmo
Helsinki

✪ San Petersburgo
RUSIA

REINO
UNIDO
DINAMARCA
Copenhague
10
9
8
✪ Moscú

Dublín ✪
HOLANDA
Berlín
Varsovia
✪ Minsk
BIELORRUSIA

IRLANDA
Londres ✪
Amsterdam
ALEMANIA
POLONIA
✪ Kiev
UCRANIA

BÉLGICA
Bruselas
12
1
2
Kishinev ✪
MOLDAVIA

OCÉANO
ATLÁNTICO
París
SUIZA
Viena
AUSTRIA
HUNGRÍA
11
3
RUMANIA
FRANCIA
Berna
4
5
7
Sofía ✪
Bucarest
MAR NEGRO

Madrid
Roma
Tirana
6
BULGARIA

PORTUGAL
ANDORRA
ITALIA
ALBANIA
Atenas
TURQUÍA

Lisboa ✪
ESPAÑA
MAR MEDITERRÁNEO
GRECIA

MALTA
CHIPRE

América del Sur

MAR DE LAS ANTILLAS

OCÉANO

ATLÁNTICO

América Central

Cartagena
Maracaibo
Caracas
VENEZUELA
Orinoco
GUAYANA
SURINAM
Medellín
Ciudad Bolívar
Georgetown
Cayena
COLOMBIA
Paramaribo
GUAYANA FRANCESA
Bogotá

Islas Galápagos (Ecuador)
Quito
Río Putumayo
Ecuador
ECUADOR
Río
Manaus
Amazonas
Belén
Guayaquil
Cuenca

BRASIL

Cordillera de los

PERÚ
Recife

Lima
Cuzco
Salvador

Lago Titicaca
La Paz
Brasilia

BOLIVIA
Sucre

OCÉANO
Cordillera de los
PARAGUAY
Paraná
Río de Janeiro
Asunción
San Pablo

Trópico de Capricornio
CHILE
Tucumán
Río

ARGENTINA
PACÍFICO
Córdoba

Valparaíso
Mendoza
URUGUAY
Santiago
Montevideo
Buenos Aires
Río de la Plata

Andes

N

Bariloche
OCÉANO

ATLÁNTICO

Cordillera de los

0   500   1.000 Kilómetros
0   500   1.000 Millas

Andes
Estrecho de Magallanes
Islas Malvinas (R.U.)
Punta Arenas
Tierra del Fuego
Cabo de Hornos

América Central y las Antillas

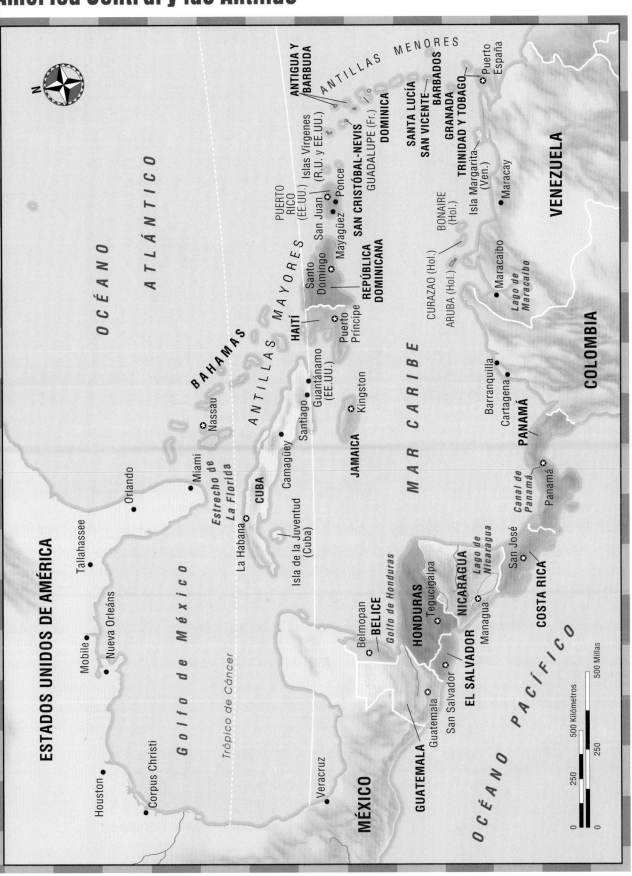

América Central y las Antillas

ESTADOS UNIDOS DE AMÉRICA

Houston ●
Corpus Christi ●
Mobile ●
Nueva Orleáns ●
Tallahassee ●
Orlando ●
Miami ●

Golfo de México

Trópico de Cáncer

MÉXICO

Veracruz ●

OCÉANO ATLÁNTICO

BAHAMAS
Nassau ✪

Estrecho de La Florida

La Habana
CUBA
Isla de la Juventud (Cuba)
Camagüey ●
Santiago ●
Guantánamo (EE.UU.)

ANTILLAS MAYORES

JAMAICA
Kingston ●

HAITÍ
Puerto Príncipe ✪

Santo Domingo ✪
REPÚBLICA DOMINICANA

PUERTO RICO (EE.UU.)
San Juan ✪
Ponce ●
Mayagüez ●

Islas Vírgenes (R.U. y EE.UU.)

ANTIGUA Y BARBUDA

ANTILLAS MENORES

SAN CRISTÓBAL-NEVIS
GUADALUPE (Fr.)
DOMINICA
SANTA LUCÍA
BARBADOS
SAN VICENTE
GRANADA
TRINIDAD Y TOBAGO

Isla Margarita (Ven.)

Puerto España ✪

VENEZUELA
Maracay ●

BONAIRE (Hol.)
CURAZAO (Hol.)
ARUBA (Hol.)

Maracaibo ●
Lago de Maracaibo

Barranquilla ●
Cartagena ●

COLOMBIA

MAR CARIBE

PANAMÁ
Panamá ✪
Canal de Panamá

San José ✪
COSTA RICA

NICARAGUA
Managua ✪
Lago de Nicaragua

HONDURAS
Tegucigalpa ✪

Belmopan ✪
BELICE
Golfo de Honduras

GUATEMALA
Guatemala ✪
San Salvador ✪
EL SALVADOR

OCÉANO PACÍFICO

N

500 Kilómetros
0   250   500 Millas
0   250

México

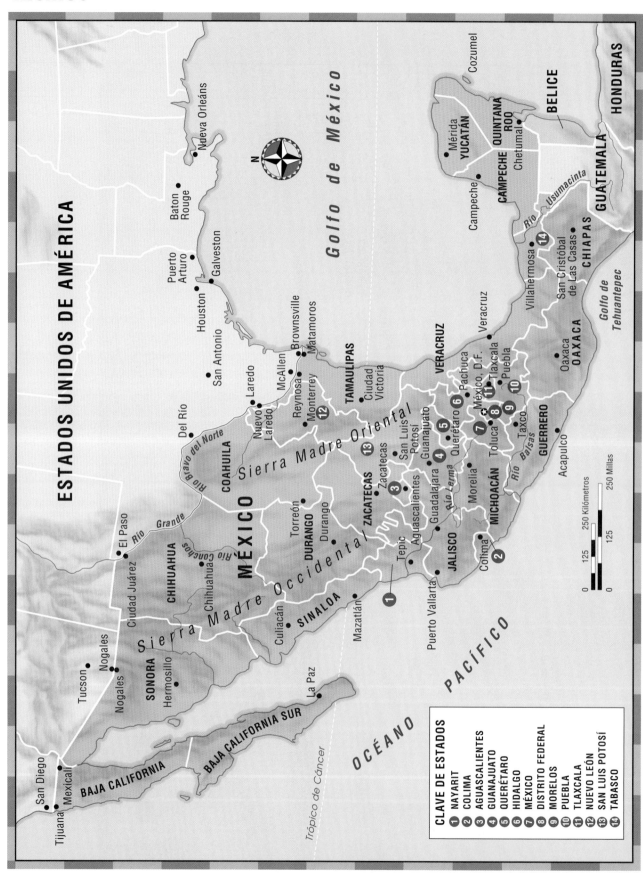

Estados Unidos de América

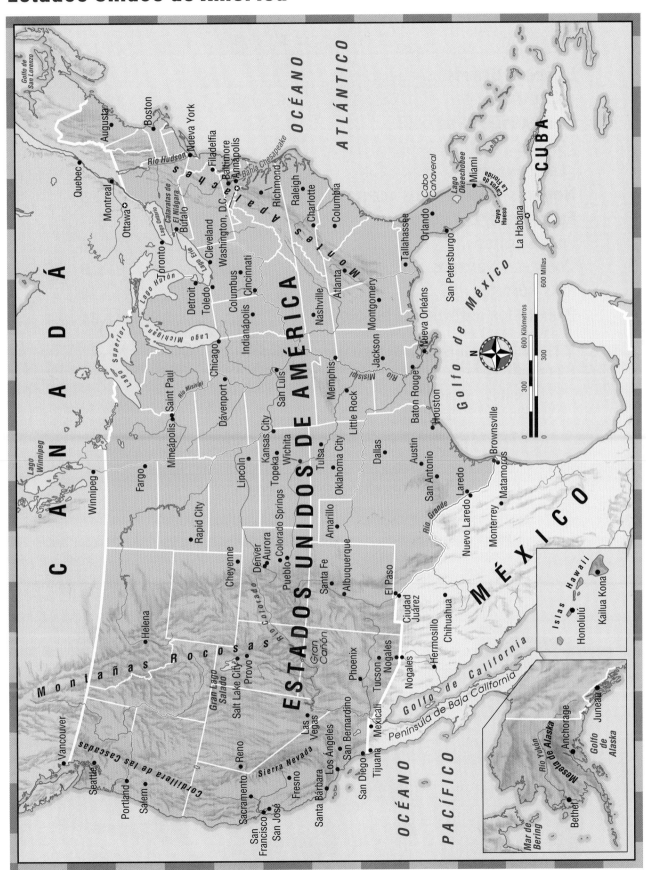

CONTENTS

The following material introduced in the **Capítulo preliminar** is presented again for testing in the chapters cited.

Acentos   Chapter 1, page 23

Colores   Chapter 6, page 178; Chapter 9, page 274

Números   Chapter 1, page 27

Teaching Resources
pp. T78–11

PRINT
- Lesson Planner, pp. X–1
- Listening Activities, pp. 2, 101
- Video Guide, pp. 1–2
- Cuaderno de actividades, pp. 1–2

MEDIA
- Video Program
  ¡Adelante!
  Videocassette 1, 1:15–4:30
- DVD Tutor, Disc 1
- Audio Compact Discs, CD 1, Trs. 1–8
- Map Transparency 4

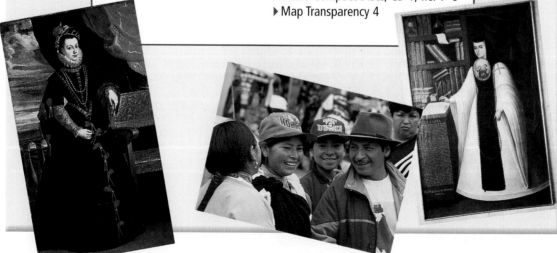

Capítulo preliminar: ¡Adelante!
Textbook Listening Activities Scripts

The following scripts are for the listening activities found in the *Pupil's Edition*. For Student Response Forms, see *Listening Activities*, page 2.

One-Stop Planner CD-ROM

To preview all resources available for this chapter, use the **One-Stop Planner CD-ROM**, Disc 1.

Nombres comunes, p. 5

The script is the same as the list of names in *Pupil's Edition*, page 5.

2   p. 5

Marta	Andrés	Isabel	Gregorio
Claudia	Miguel	Cristóbal	Antonio
Margarita	Luisa		

El alfabeto, pp. 6–7

A	**a** de águila	N	**ene** de naranja
B	**be** de bandera	Ñ	**eñe** de castañuelas
C	**ce** de ciclismo	O	**o** de oso
CH	**che** de chaleco	P	**pe** de piñata
D	**de** de dinero	Q	**cu** de quetzal
E	**e** de ensalada	R	**ere** de toro
F	**efe** de fruta	RR	**erre** de burro
G	**ge** de geografía	S	**ese** de salvavidas
H	**hache** de helicóptero	T	**te** de teléfono
I	**i** de iguana	U	**u** de uvas
J	**jota** de jabón	V	**ve** de violín
K	**ka** de karate	W	**doble ve** de Wálter
L	**ele** de lámpara	X	**equis** de examen
LL	**elle** de llanta	Y	**i griega** de yate
M	**eme** de máscara	Z	**zeta** de zapatos

6   p. 7

1. Pe, a, u, ele, a; Paula
2. I, ge, ene, a, ce, i, o; Ignacio
3. Jota, o, ere, ge, e; Jorge
4. Eme, a, ere, te, a; Marta
5. A, de, ere, i, a, ene, a; Adriana
6. Che, a, ere, o; Charo

Frases útiles para escuchar, p. 8

Abran el libro (en la página 20), por favor.
Levántense, por favor.
Siéntense, por favor.
Levanten la mano.
Bajen la mano.
Escuchen con atención.
Repitan después de mí.
Saquen una hoja de papel.
Silencio, por favor.
Miren la pizarra.

8   p. 8

1. Simón dice, "levántense, por favor".
2. Simón dice, "siéntense".
3. Simón dice, "saquen una hoja de papel".
4. Simón dice, "levanten la mano".
5. Bajen la mano.
6. Simón dice, "bajen la mano".
7. Miren la pizarra.
8. Simón dice, "repitan después de mí: ¡Gracias!"

Frases útiles para decir, p. 8

Buenos días.
Buenas tardes.
¿Cómo se dice... en español?
¿Cómo se escribe?
Más despacio, por favor.
¿Puedo ir por mi libro?
No entiendo.
No sé.
¿Puede repetir, por favor?
Perdón.
Tengo una pregunta.

13   p. 10

1. Me llamo Nicolás Guillén y mi número de teléfono es el 4-7-3-0-0-1-6.
2. Me llamo Juana Gómez Berea. Mi número de teléfono es el 3-9-1-2-3-4-6.
3. Soy Miguel Campos Romero. Mi número de teléfono es el 7-4-5-0-8-1-2.
4. Soy Cristina García. Mi número de teléfono es el 5-1-0-5-7-2-4.

¡ADELANTE!

CAPÍTULO PRELIMINAR

One-Stop Planner CD-ROM

For resource information, see the **One-Stop Planner**, Disc 1.

Teacher Note
The video for the Preliminary Chapter will introduce your students to some of the people they will view in the rest of *¡Ven conmigo!* Some are the actors in **fotonovelas** found in **De antemano**, and others are people interviewed on the street for the **Panorama cultural** and authentic Video Clips. You may wish to play the video as a preview to the program and to give your students an introduction to the Spanish language.

Photo Flash!
Photos on this page are of people that your students will view in the videos. Some are actors who play characters in the **fotonovelas**, and others are people interviewed on the street in numerous Spanish-speaking countries.

Culture Note
From the third century B.C. to the fifth century A.D., the Romans occupied the Iberian Peninsula. They brought not only their language—Latin—but also their civilization, culture, and customs.

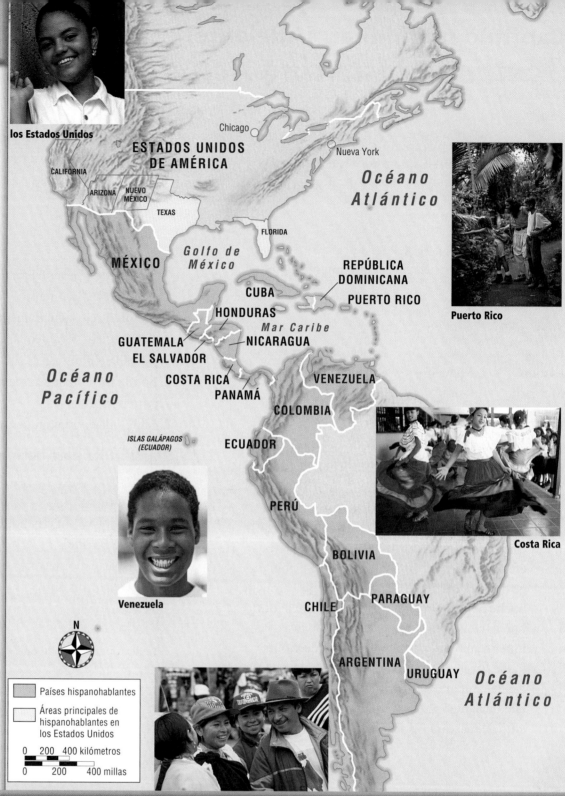

los Estados Unidos

Chicago

ESTADOS UNIDOS
DE AMÉRICA

CALIFORNIA

ARIZONA | NUEVO MÉXICO

TEXAS

FLORIDA

MÉXICO

Golfo de México

Nueva York

Océano Atlántico

REPÚBLICA DOMINICANA

CUBA

HONDURAS

PUERTO RICO

Puerto Rico

Mar Caribe

GUATEMALA
EL SALVADOR

NICARAGUA

Océano Pacífico

COSTA RICA

PANAMÁ

VENEZUELA

COLOMBIA

ISLAS GALÁPAGOS (ECUADOR)

ECUADOR

Venezuela

PERÚ

Costa Rica

BOLIVIA

PARAGUAY

CHILE

ARGENTINA

URUGUAY

Océano Atlántico

N

Países hispanohablantes

Áreas principales de hispanohablantes en los Estados Unidos

0   200   400 kilómetros

0   200   400 millas

Communication for All Students

Motivating Activity
Before students open their books, ask them to make a list of several Spanish-speaking countries. After they make their list, they should identify characteristics of the countries they have listed. The characteristics can include typical food, geography, products, economy, or climate. Have students work in small groups to compare their descriptions of the Spanish-speaking countries. The group should choose one country that most of the students have listed and reach a consensus about an accurate description of that country. Each group should present its description to the class.

T80   ¡ADELANTE!

STANDARDS: 3.1

México

España

Argentina

ESPAÑA

ISLAS BALEARES (ESPAÑA)

Mar Mediterráneo

ISLAS CANARIAS (ESPAÑA)

GUINEA ECUATORIAL

Océano Atlántico

CAPÍTULO PRELIMINAR

¡Adelante!

¡Bienvenido al mundo hispanohablante!

Spanish, one of the five official languages of the United Nations, is spoken by approximately 340 million people in the world today. Originally a dialect of Latin, Spanish was first recognized as a language in its own right about 700 years ago. Spanish is spoken in Spain (where it originated), in 19 Latin American countries, and in parts of Africa and the Philippines. It is also spoken in the United States, where about one out of ten residents speaks Spanish. Can you find the countries where these Spanish speakers live?

CAPÍTULO PRELIMINAR

History Link
The Spanish began colonizing the Philippines in 1565 and ruled the islands until 1898, when they were lost to the United States in the Spanish-American War. They named the islands after King Philip II (Felipe II). The Spanish legacy is still felt through religion. The Philippines has more Christians, most of whom are Roman Catholics, than any other Asian nation. Philippine food, a mixture of American, Chinese, Spanish, and indigenous Filipino cooking, is representative of the many cultures that have been a part of the nation. Although the two official languages of the Philippines are English and Filipino, a small number of Filipinos still speak Spanish.

Teaching Suggestion
Have students find the Philippines, Equatorial Guinea, and other Spanish-speaking countries on the map of the world on pages xxiv–xxv of the *Pupil's Edition* (pages T72–T73 of the *Teacher's Edition*).

Teacher Note
The **Capítulo preliminar** is a preparation for the study of Spanish. Students need not be expected to master the material—it will be presented again in subsequent chapters.

Connections and Comparisons

History Link
Equatorial Guinea is a country on the west coast of Africa. The territory that the country now occupies was ceded to Spain by Portugal in 1778, and today Spanish is the official language of Equatorial Guinea. Another language spoken is Bantu.

Pidgin English is spoken, and each ethnic group also speaks its own language. Hausa, an Afro-Asiatic language, has become a lingua franca that traverses ethnic and political boundaries throughout West Africa.

Motivating Activities

• Have students bring in help-wanted ads from national or local papers. Point out any bilingual jobs, and ask students in what ways they think learning Spanish might help them in work situations.

• Ask students who have traveled or lived in the Spanish-speaking world to share their experiences with the class.

Thinking Critically

A bilingual society is one in which most people speak two languages. What are the advantages or disadvantages of bilingualism for the society of the United States? Have students debate this question in small groups and then present their conclusions to the class.

Social Studies Link

Ask students to research the current status of trade between the United States and Mexico or another Spanish-speaking country. How do they think trade conditions affect job opportunities for bilingual workers in both countries?

Photo Flash!

Cristina María Saralegui was born on January 29, 1948, in Havana, Cuba. The Saraleguis owned and operated three successful magazines published in Cuba: *Bohemia, Carteles,* and *Vanidades*. In 1960, the Saralegui family moved to Miami, where Cristina studied communications at the University of Miami. She has received numerous awards, including an Emmy for her talk show, *Cristina*.

El español—¿Por qué? • *Why learn Spanish?*

There are many reasons for learning to speak Spanish. Which of these reasons is most important to you?

To Expand Your Horizons

You're living in one of the major Spanish-speaking countries right now—the United States! Learning Spanish can open up a whole new world of information, entertainment, and adventure. Spanish-language movies, books, videos, magazines, TV shows, and music are all around you.

For College

If you plan to go to college, you'll find that many university programs require some foreign-language study. Taking a language now can improve your chances of admission and give you a head start on meeting your degree requirements.

For Travel

Each language has its own personality. To really get to know someone, you have to speak that person's language. Chances are good that someday you'll travel to a Spanish-speaking country. Whatever your reason for going, whether it be vacation, study, or business, you'll get a lot more out of your stay if you can speak the language.

For Career Opportunities

Bilingual employees are always in demand in business, social work, health care, education, journalism, and many other fields. Learning Spanish will help you find a more interesting, better-paying job.

For Fun!

One of the best reasons for studying Spanish is for fun. Studying another language is a challenge to your mind, and you get a great feeling of accomplishment the first time you have a conversation in Spanish!

Communication for All Students

Native Speakers

• Write these questions on the board and have students turn in their answers:
  1. Where and how often do you use Spanish? at home? in certain situations?
  2. Do you use Spanish-language newspapers, television, or other media?
  3. Why do you want to learn Spanish?

• Native speakers might keep an interactive "language journal" during the school year. The journal should be written in Spanish, if the student prefers, and will contain written responses to Native Speaker suggestions. Students can begin the journal by elaborating on their answers to the questions about language background.

¿Sabías...? ▪ *Did you know . . .?*

Spanish language and culture are important parts of our national history. As you begin your study of Spanish, you should be aware that . . .

- the Spanish were among the first European explorers in what is today the U.S.
- the first European settlement in the United States was founded by the Spanish in 1565 at St. Augustine, Florida.
- parts of the U.S. once belonged to Mexico.
- many common words, such as *rodeo* and *patio*, came into English from Spanish.
- Spanish is the second most frequently spoken language in the U.S.
- many of the United States' most important trading partners in this hemisphere are Spanish-speaking nations.

Spanish Territory in North America in 1785

0 200 400 Kilómetros
0 200 400 Millas

① Herencia hispana *Hispanic heritage*   See possible answers below.

Leamos/Hablemos Working in small groups, choose and answer one of the following questions. Share your findings with the class.

1. Using your knowledge of geography, list several major U.S. cities with Spanish names. Also list states with names based on Spanish words.
2. Using the map on page xxx, name the major Spanish-speaking areas of the United States. What countries do many Spanish-speaking immigrants come from?
3. Under the headings *foods* and *cowboy lore*, list common English words you think may have been borrowed from Spanish.
4. Using the maps on pages xxiii–xxix, name 20 Spanish-speaking countries (one is a special part of the U.S.). Choose one country and list some things you know about it.
5. Name as many Spanish-language TV programs, radio stations, magazines, movies, and newspapers as you can.

Connections and Comparisons

History Link
In 1848 the Mexican Congress approved **el Tratado de Guadalupe Hidalgo**, ending the Mexican-American War. With this treaty Mexico ceded to the United States more than one-third of its total territory—the present-day states of Texas, California, Arizona, New Mexico, Nevada, and the Utah territory that included the present-day state of Utah and part of Colorado.

Language Note
The word **chocolate** came into Spanish from Nahuatl, an indigenous language spoken in central and western Mexico. **Xocolatl** *(show-ko-lat-ul)* is the Nahuatl word for chocolate, meaning *bitter water*. The Aztec nobility drank it without sugar. Today, there are over one million native Nahuatl speakers in Mexico.

CAPÍTULO PRELIMINAR

Background Information
St. Augustine, Florida, was founded in 1565 by the Spaniard Pedro Menéndez de Avilés. It is considered the first permanent European settlement in what is today the United States. St. Augustine is on the northeastern coast of Florida.

Social Studies Link
Have students research the Spanish explorers who traveled through North America. Among the most famous was Álvar Núñez Cabeza de Vaca. After being shipwrecked, Cabeza de Vaca spent nearly ten years in the Gulf region living among the indigenous peoples. His subsequent stories of the legendary El Dorado and the Seven Golden Cities of Cíbola inspired others, such as Francisco Vásquez de Coronado, to explore North America. Among these early explorers were Juan Ponce de León, who explored Florida searching for the mythical fountain of youth, and Hernando (or Fernando) de Soto, who explored the southern Gulf Coast area and the Mississippi River. As an extension, have students research the indigenous peoples of North or South America or the Spanish **conquistadores**.

Answers
① *Possible answers:*
1. Los Angeles, San Diego, San Antonio, Albuquerque, Santa Fe, Las Vegas; Colorado, New Mexico, Texas, Arizona, California, Montana, Florida, Nevada
2. Los Angeles, New York, Miami, Chicago, San Antonio, and the Southwest; Mexico, Puerto Rico, Cuba, and the countries of Central America
3. Foods: taco, enchilada, burrito, salsa, chocolate; Cowboy lore: lasso, lariat, ranch, chaps, chaparral, rodeo
4. *See maps on pages xxiii–xxix (T71–T77) for countries.* 5. *Answers will vary according to locale.*

¿Los conoces?

CAPÍTULO PRELIMINAR

Teaching Suggestion

Ask students to describe briefly other famous Spanish speakers or people of Hispanic heritage and have class-mates guess who it is they are describing. (Gloria Estefan, César Chávez, Kika de la Garza, Edward James Olmos, Rosie Pérez, Loretta Sánchez, Jennifer López, Andy García, Tish Hinojosa, Antonia Novello, Henry González, Jorge Ramos, María Amparo Escandón)

Background Information

• **Simón Bolívar** occupies a place in Latin American history analogous to that of George Washington in the history of the U.S. A soldier, general, political theorist, and pres-ident, Bolívar played a critical mili-tary and political role in the struggles for independence of Venezuela, Colombia, Ecuador, Peru, and Bolivia.

• **La reina Isabel I** *(Queen Isabella of Castile)* was named heir to the throne of Castile at the age of 17. She became queen in 1474 after a series of civil wars and palace intrigues. She and her husband, **Fernando de Aragón**, were able to consolidate the power of their two kingdoms and achieve political and religious unity within Spain with the expulsion of the last Moorish king of Granada in 1492. Legend has it that this "soldier queen" rode with her troops dur-ing the battles of the Reconquest. In addition to financing Columbus's voyages, Isabel was also an impor-tant patron of the arts. In 1492, she commissioned the Spanish humanist **Antonio de Nebrija** to write the *Gramática de la lengua castellana,* the first published Romance language grammar.

¿Los conoces? ▪ *Do you know them?*

Spanish speakers from all over the world have made valuable contributions in science, sports, politics, and the arts. These personality sketches may remind you of other famous Spanish speakers you know something about, like Gloria Estefan, Miguel Induráin, Edward James Olmos, or Celia Cruz.

◀**Frida Kahlo** (1907–1954), a Mexican artist born in Coyoacán, is best known for her powerful self-portraits. Like her husband, the famous muralist Diego Rivera, Frida Kahlo reflected the history and political life of her country in her work.

▲**Samuel (Sammy) Sosa** (b. 1968) was born in San Pedro de Macoris, Dominican Republic. He has broken several Major League, National League, and Chicago Cubs' records and became famous in 1998, along with Mark McGwire, for breaking Roger Maris's single-season home run record.

▶**Simón Bolívar** (1783–1830), born in Caracas, Venezuela, led a brilliant campaign against Spanish colonialism that eventu-ally resulted in independence for most of South America. He died in poverty and disgrace but is still honored as **el Libertador,** *the Liberator.*

▲**La reina Isabel** (Isabel I of Spain; 1451–1504) helped form the modern Spanish nation-state by marrying Fernando, king of Aragon. We know her best for financing Columbus's voyage to the New World.

▲**Miguel de Cervantes y Saavedra** (1547–1616) authored the book *Don Quijote de la Mancha.* His personal experiences of poverty, imprisonment, and warfare enabled him to paint a sharply realistic, yet sympa-thetic, picture of Spanish life at the turn of the 17th century.

◀**Sor Juana Inés de la Cruz** (1651–1695), was a favorite of the Spanish viceroys in Mexico before entering the convent and dedicating herself to intellectual pursuits. Her writings, literary and scientif-ic, have earned the respect of authors and historians.

Cultures and Communities

Culture Note

Cervantes, perhaps the greatest figure in Spain's Golden Age, had humble roots. He saw Renaissance culture as a soldier in Italy. Wounded in Lepanto, imprisoned in Algiers, he returned to work as a tax collector before writing poetry and drama. He earned great fame when the first part of his *Don Quijote* appeared in 1605. One of the most translated works of all time, it tells the adventures of a hero who fancies himself a knight errant and pursues, with his squire Sancho, the noble ideals of a lost era. These themes resonate among artists and audiences today. Students may know of don Quijote through modern Broadway plays or famous artwork by Pablo Picasso.

Nombres comunes ▪ *Common names*

1
1

Here are some common names from Spanish-speaking countries. Choose a name for yourself from the list if you wish.

Me llamo Ana Luisa.

Dolores (Lola)
Elena (Nena)
Graciela (Chela)
Inés
Isabel (Isa)
Juana
Luisa
Margarita
María
Marisol (Mari)

Adela
Alicia (Licha)
Ana, Anita
Ángela, Angélica
Beatriz
Carmen
Catalina (Cata)
Claudia
Cristina (Tina)
Daniela

Marta
Mercedes (Merche)
Natalia
Paloma
Pilar
Rosario (Charo)
Sara
Susana
Teresa
Verónica (Vero)

Alberto
Alejandro (Alejo)
Andrés
Antonio (Toño)
Carlos
Cristóbal
Diego
Eduardo (Lalo)
Francisco (Paco)
Gregorio
Guillermo
Ignacio (Nacho)
Jaime
Jesús (Chuy)
Jorge
José (Pepe)
Juan
Julio
Lorenzo
Luis

Me llamo Javier.

Manuel
Mario
Miguel
Pablo
Pedro
Rafael (Rafa)
Ricardo
Roberto (Beto)
Santiago
Tomás

2 **Nombres en español** *Names in Spanish*

Escuchemos/Hablemos Listen to a series of names in Spanish and repeat them aloud after the speaker. Try to guess the English equivalent of each one. Does your name have an equivalent in Spanish? Script on p. T79.

1
2

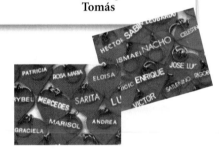

3 **Mis amigos** *My friends*

Escribamos Find and write Spanish names that match the names of at least six of your family members, friends, or classmates. Check to see that you've used accents in the correct places. Answers will vary. See names above.

4 **Me llamo...** *My name is . . .*

Hablemos Form a name chain in your row. The first person turns to a partner and asks his or her name. That person answers with a chosen name in Spanish, and then asks the next person's name. Keep going to the end of the row.

MODELO
—¿Cómo te llamas?
—Me llamo Carlos. ¿Cómo te llamas?

Los acentos

You may have noticed the accent mark (´) and the tilde (˜) on words in the name chart. They are used to help you pronounce the words correctly. You'll learn about these and other special marks, including the upside-down question mark and exclamation point, in Chapter 1.

Connections and Comparisons

Culture Note
It is quite popular in the Dominican Republic to give children Russian names. (Vladimir, Tatiana, Iván) It is also not uncommon there to name a child after a country or a city. (América, Venecia, Roma, Australia)

Language Note
An **apodo** is an affectionate nickname, such as **el gallo** or **la rubia**, which is frequently given to fellow students in high school. In Chapter 1, the **fotonovela** story line is based on two pen pals who don't realize they are acquaintances from school, since they had known each other only by their shortened names.

Motivating Activity

To help students build confidence, draw their attention to the words under the alphabet photos. Students should list words that are similar in English and Spanish (cognates and borrowed words, such as **ciclismo, ensalada, examen,** and **violín**). Have students identify spelling differences between words that are similar in the two languages. By examining these patterns, they can begin to develop tentative rules to explain the differences in the spelling of cognates. (**Ph** in *geography* is **f** in **geografía.**)

Teaching Suggestions

- Before students try to produce the sounds themselves, have them point to the corresponding letter and picture as they listen to *Audio CD 1.*
- Ask students if they can identify the Spanish vowel sounds. Point out that Spanish vowel sounds are different from English ones.
- Dictate the spelling of words as students find them in the illustrations.
- Dictate a list of items for students to remember on a trip to the grocery store. (**jabón, fruta, naranja, uvas, dinero**)

El alfabeto · *The alphabet*

CD 1
Tr. 3

The Spanish alphabet isn't quite the same as the English one. What differences do you notice? Listen to the names of the letters and repeat after the speaker.
Script on p. T79.

Although **ch** and **ll** have been officially dropped from the Spanish alphabet, dictionaries and glossaries published before 1994 will continue to show them as separate entries.

águila

bandera

ciclismo

chaleco

dinero

ensalada

fruta

geografía

helicóptero

iguana

jabón

karate

lámpara

llanta

 Los cognados *Cognates*

Leamos Cognates are words that look similar in both Spanish and English. Although they're pronounced differently, they often have the same meaning—but not always! For example, **embarazada** means *pregnant,* not *embarrassed.* How many cognates do you see in this ad? What happens to the spelling of English *-tion* in Spanish?

Communication for All Students

Kinesthetic Learners

Have students draw six blanks for a six-letter word. Dictate letters in Spanish one at a time in random order, giving the number of the blank in which each letter is to be written. (**ene** in the third blank, etc.: D I N E R O) The first student to guess the word chooses the next word for the teacher to dictate. Words should be within the students' experience, such as common names or cognates.

Auditory Learners

Students may like to chant rhymes or make up rap tunes to learn the correct sounds. (A–E–I–O–U. **Yo me llamo María. ¿Cómo te llamas tú?**)

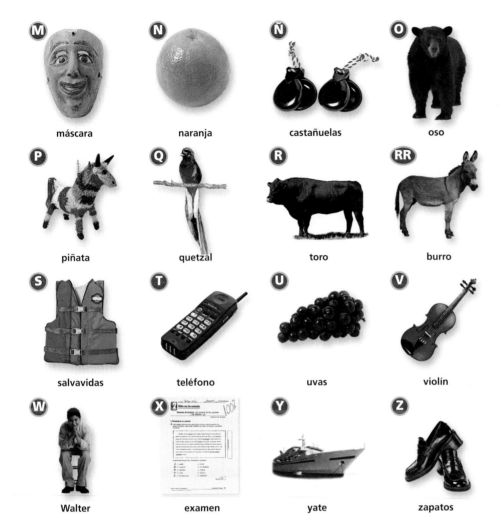

máscara naranja castañuelas oso

piñata quetzal toro burro

salvavidas teléfono uvas violín

Walter examen yate zapatos

6 **Por teléfono** *On the phone* Script on p. T79.

Escuchemos/Escribamos Imagine that you work as a receptionist answering the telephone. Listen as several Spanish speakers spell their names for you. Write each name as you hear it spelled.

7 **¿Cómo se escribe...?** *How is . . . written?* Answers will vary.

Hablemos/Escribamos Work with a partner. Choose from the following items and spell each one aloud, letter by letter, in Spanish. Your partner will write the words as you spell them, then guess the number of the item you chose. Then switch roles.

1. your first name
2. your last name
3. the name of your school
4. the name of your city or town
5. your best friend's first and last names
6. your favorite radio or TV station's call letters

CAPÍTULO PRELIMINAR

Challenge
6 Spell students' last names out loud in Spanish and ask them to raise their hand when they recognize their own name.

Teaching Suggestion
7 Teach students **con mayúscula**. Point out that names are capitalized in Spanish just as they are in English. Teach **con acento** or **lleva acento** as well. (eme con mayúscula, a, ere, i con acento, a: María)

Language Notes
• Although the **Real Academia Española** has deleted the letters **ch** and **ll** from the alphabet, many dictionaries still have separate entries for these letters. The end-of-book vocabulary (pp. R15–R40) follows the new rules, with **ch** and **ll** in sequence: "ce...ch...ci" and "li...ll...lo," with no separate entries for **ch** and **ll**.

• Although in the Americas **rr** is commonly recognized as a separate letter, the **Real Academia** does not officially recognize it.

Cultures and Communities

Community Link
Compile a class **abecedario** to be donated to a local children's center or library. Have students work in groups of three or four. Assign a portion of the alphabet to each group, and have students cooperate to design and illustrate their letters. Students may use a Spanish dictionary.

Language Note
Point out that an **abecedario** is a Spanish primer used to teach the alphabet.

Geography Link
Have students make up an alphabet book using the names of cities and countries in the maps on pages xxiv–xxv.

Frases útiles

Frases útiles

CAPÍTULO PRELIMINAR

 Games
- **Mímica** Have students play charades. One student acts out a phrase without speaking and the other students guess what the phrase is in Spanish.
- **Tiritas** Divide the class into groups of three to five. Have the groups write each word in the phrases on a separate scrap of paper (i.e., one word per piece of paper). Have students scramble the scraps. With books closed, dictate the phrases while students arrange the scraps to form the Spanish phrases. The first group to get the correct answer gets a point.

Additional Vocabulary
- **Para escuchar** If you use an overhead transparency instead of a chalkboard, you may wish to teach the phrase **Miren la transparencia**. Other commands you may find helpful are **¡Libros al suelo!** and **¡Cierren los libros!**
- **Para decir** Additional phrases you may wish to teach your students are **¿Qué significa...?**, **No oigo**, **¿Puedo ir al baño?**, **¿Puedo ir a la oficina?**, and **¿Puedo ir a mi *locker*?**

Answers
9 1. Buenas tardes.
2. ¿Puedo ir por mi libro?
3. No entiendo.
4. Más despacio, por favor./ ¿Puede repetir, por favor?
5. No sé.
6. Tengo una pregunta.
7. ¿Puede repetir, por favor?

Frases útiles · *Useful phrases*

CD 1 Tr. 5

Para escuchar Script on p. T79.
Here are some phrases you'll probably hear regularly in Spanish class. Learn to recognize them and respond appropriately.

Abran el libro (en la página 20), por favor.	*Open your books (to page 20), please.*
Levántense, por favor.	*Please stand up.*
Siéntense, por favor.	*Please sit down.*
Levanten la mano.	*Raise your hands.*
Bajen la mano.	*Put your hands down.*
Escuchen con atención.	*Listen closely.*
Repitan después de mí.	*Repeat after me.*
Saquen una hoja de papel.	*Take out a sheet of paper.*
Silencio, por favor.	*Silence, please.*
Miren la pizarra.	*Look at the chalkboard.*

8 **Simón dice** *Simon says* Script on p. T79.

CD 1 Tr. 6

Escuchemos Listen to some commands and perform the action called for, such as raising your hand or opening your book. Respond only if the speaker says **Simón dice.**

CD 1 Tr. 7

Para decir Script on p. T79.
Here are some phrases that you'll need to use often. Learn as many as you can and use them when they're appropriate.

Buenos días.	*Good morning.*
Buenas tardes.	*Good afternoon.*
¿Cómo se dice ... en español?	*How do you say . . . in Spanish?*
¿Cómo se escribe...?	*How do you spell . . . ?* (lit., *How do you write . . . ?*)
Más despacio, por favor.	*Slower, please.*
¿Puedo ir por mi libro?	*Can (May) I go get my book?*
No entiendo.	*I don't understand.*
No sé.	*I don't know.*
¿Puede repetir, por favor?	*Can you repeat, please?*
Perdón.	*Excuse me.*
Tengo una pregunta.	*I have a question.*

9 **Situaciones** See answers below.

Hablemos What would you say in the following situations? Choose your responses from above.

1. You see your teacher at the store one afternoon.
2. You left your book in your locker.
3. You don't understand the directions.
4. Your teacher is talking too fast.
5. You don't know the answer.
6. You'd like to ask a question.
7. You need to hear something again.

Communication for All Students

Kinesthetic Learners
Either play Audio CD 1 or pronounce the commands for students yourself. Use Total Physical Response and practice having students do the commands as you say them.

Additional Practice
8 Play SIMÓN DICE. Have students take turns being Simón. The following prepositions can be used for this activity's extension, as well as for TPR activities suggested in later chapters: **en, en medio de, a la derecha de, a la izquierda de, debajo de, detrás de, delante de, al lado de.**

Colores y números · *Colors and numbers*

10 Colores típicos

Hablemos What colors come to mind when you think of the following items? Say them in Spanish. See answers below.

1. the flag of the United States
2. a zebra
3. the sky
4. grass
5. a pumpkin
6. a cloudy day
7. coffee
8. a banana
9. snow
10. grape juice
11. a tire
12. a strawberry

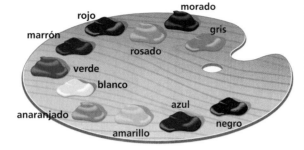

rojo · morado · gris · marrón · rosado · verde · blanco · azul · negro · anaranjado · amarillo

Vocabulario

cero · uno · dos · tres · cuatro · cinco
seis · siete · ocho · nueve · diez

11 ¿Cuántos dedos ves? *How many fingers do you see?*

Hablemos Using the photos above as a model, form a number with your hands and ask your partner to say the number. Switch roles after four or five tries.

12 Números cotidianos *Everyday numbers*

Hablemos/Escribamos What numbers come to mind when you think of the following items? Make up your own item for number 8.

1. a pair of shoes 2
2. your fingers 5,10
3. a tricycle 3
4. a pack of beverage cans 6
5. an octopus 8
6. a rectangle 4
7. a week 7
8. ¿? Answers will vary.

Connections and Comparisons

Multicultural Link

Europeans, Latin Americans, and North Africans write the numerals 1 and 7 a little differently than North Americans:

Culture Note

You may want to point out to students that the photos in **Vocabulario** show the typical method of finger counting used in Spanish-speaking countries. Hand gestures that represent numbers may be used in noisy markets or restaurants to clarify requests or instructions.

STANDARDS: 2.1, 5.2

Sidebar

CAPÍTULO PRELIMINAR

Teaching Suggestions

- For personalization, point to clothing items worn by students as you say the corresponding color.
- Ask students to name the colors of various classroom items. To evaluate comprehension, have students respond **cierto** or **falso** to your statements about colors in the room.
- Ask students what colors come to mind when they think of various holidays.
- Some of your students may be colorblind. (unable to distinguish between two or more of the colors red, green, and blue) With a color-blind student, you should stress color associations (fruits, plants, holidays) rather than color distinctions.

Game

Carreras Hang three sets of the nine colors (construction paper works well) vertically in three groups on the board. Divide the class into three teams. You call out a color in Spanish and a representative from each team goes to the board and writes a word in English associated with that color next to it on their section of the board. The first student to write a correct answer earns a point for his or her team. Continue until all students have played, tally the points, and declare a winning team.

Additional Vocabulary

violeta	*purple*
café, pardo	*brown*
azul claro	*light blue*
azul oscuro	*dark blue*
oro	*gold*
plata	*silver*

Answers

10
1. rojo, blanco, azul
2. blanco, negro
3. azul, gris
4. verde
5. anaranjado
6. gris, blanco, negro
7. marrón
8. amarillo
9. blanco
10. morado
11. negro
12. rojo

Más números

Group Work

14 Have students write the numbers on scraps of paper. Collect the scraps and have students divide into groups of four or five. Shuffle and give each student four or five numbers. Students take turns dictating the number they receive, and the members of the group write the number as it is read. After verifying answers, the next student dictates, and so on.

Background Information

15 Items **a.** and **b.** are registration stickers that change yearly. Item **c.** is a license plate from the State of Mexico, and item **d.** is from Tamaulipas. Cars keep the same plates for ten years. Registration stickers are placed on the inside of the windshield. Cars from Mexico City and surrounding areas must have a sticker to show that they have passed the six-month smog inspection. Cars must also have a sticker for pollution control, called **la calcomanía** or **el engomado**, which says **Hoy No Circula**. This sticker designates the day of the week when the car may not be driven. This includes holidays. There are no restrictions between 10 P.M. and 5 A.M. on weekdays and any time on weekends. When the level of air pollution is too high, newspapers publish changes in the laws reducing the number of cars that can be used. Cars from out of town, including those with foreign license plates, are also subject to pollution control laws that restrict use according to the license plate number.

13 **Números de teléfono**

CD 1
Tr. 8

Escuchemos Listen as four Spanish speakers tell you their telephone numbers. Based on what you hear, match each speaker's name with the right number. Script on p. T79.

1. Nicolás   3. Miguel
2. Juana   4. Cristina

745-08-12   473-00-16
510-57-24   391-23-46

Vocabulario

11	once	16	dieciséis	21	veintiuno	26	veintiséis
12	doce	17	diecisiete	22	veintidós	27	veintisiete
13	trece	18	dieciocho	23	veintitrés	28	veintiocho
14	catorce	19	diecinueve	24	veinticuatro	29	veintinueve
15	quince	20	veinte	25	veinticinco	30	treinta

14 **Datos importantes** *Important facts* Answers will vary.

Hablemos/Escribamos Use numbers in Spanish to give the following information.

1. your telephone number and area code
2. your zip code
3. the number of students in your row
4. your student I.D. number
5. the score of a recent game at your school or on TV

15 **Placas y permisos en México** Answers will vary.

Hablemos Your partner will read a number or name a color from these license plates and stickers. If you hear a number, name a color from the license plate that has that number, and vice versa. Switch roles after four or five tries.

MODELO   ¿QZB 7829?
—Verde.
—¡Sí!

a.

b.

c. QZB 7829 MEX MEX

d. KZY 8762 FRONT TAMPS

Cultures and Communities

Language Note

The numbers 16–19 and 21–29 can either be written as one word, **dieciséis**, or as three separate words, **diez y seis**. The form commonly listed in dictionaries is one word.

Culture Note

Increasingly, cities in Spanish-speaking countries use seven-digit, or even eight-digit (international) telephone numbers. Usually the first number is spoken alone, with the remaining ones expressed in pairs. They are usually hyphenated in pairs. (5-23-16-28: **el cinco, veintitrés, dieciséis, veintiocho**) In smaller towns, a phone number may be only five numbers.

Sugerencias para aprender el español
Tips for learning Spanish

Listen

It's important to listen carefully in class. Take notes and ask questions if you don't understand, even if you think your question seems a little silly. Other people are probably wondering the same thing you are. You won't be able to understand everything you hear at first, but don't feel frustrated. You're actually absorbing a lot even when you don't realize it.

Organize

Your memory is going to get a workout, so it's important to get organized. Throughout the textbook you'll see learning tips (**Sugerencias**) that can improve your study skills. For starters, here's a hint: see things with your mind. Associate each new word, sentence, or phrase with an exaggerated or unusual mental picture. For example, if you're learning the word **regla** *(ruler)*, visualize an enormous ruler on an enormous desk as you practice saying a sentence with the word.

Practice

Learning a foreign language is like learning to ride a bicycle or play an instrument. You can't spend one night cramming and then expect to be able to ride or play perfectly the next morning. You didn't learn English that way either! Short, daily practice sessions are more effective than long, once-a-week sessions. Also, try to practice with a friend or a classmate. After all, language is about communication, and it takes two to communicate.

Speak

Practice speaking Spanish aloud every day. Talking with your teachers and classmates is an easy and fun way to learn. Don't be afraid to experiment. Your mistakes will help identify problems, and they'll show you important differences in the way English and Spanish work as languages.

Expand

Increase your contact with Spanish outside of class in every way you can. You may be able to find someone living near you who speaks Spanish. It's easy to find Spanish-language programs on TV, on the radio, or at the video store. Many magazines and newspapers in Spanish are published or sold in the United States. Don't be afraid to read, watch, or listen. You won't understand every word, but that's okay. You can get a lot out of a story or an article by concentrating on the words you do recognize and doing a little intelligent guesswork.

Connect

Some English and Spanish words have common roots in Latin, and the two languages have influenced each other, so your knowledge of English can give you clues about the meaning of many Spanish words. Look for an English connection when you need to guess at unfamiliar words. You may also find that learning Spanish will help you in English class!

Have fun!

Above all, remember to have fun! The more you try, the more you'll learn. Besides, having fun will help you relax, and relaxed people learn better and faster. **¡Buena suerte!** *(Good luck!)*

Teaching Resources
pp. 12–15

PRINT
▸ Lesson Planner, p. 2
▸ Video Guide, pp. 3–4

MEDIA
▸ One-Stop Planner
▸ Video Program
  Videocassette 1, 4:31–7:06
▸ DVD Tutor, Disc 1
▸ Interactive CD-ROM Tutor, Disc 1
▸ Map Transparency 1

 go.hrw.com
WV3 SPAIN

Using the Almanac and Map

Terms in the Almanac

• **El gobierno:** The king serves as Spain's head of state. Although he does not have a direct role in running the government, he is an advisor. **El Primer Ministro** heads the **Consejo de Ministros** *(Cabinet),* which carries out the day-to-day operations of the government. The **Cortes** *(Parliament)* makes the country's laws.

• **Las industrias: productos alimenticios** *food products;* **calzado** *footwear;* **petroquímicos** *petrochemicals;* **acero** *steel;* **automóviles** *automobiles;* **buques** *ships*

• **Cosechas principales: granos** *grains;* **vegetales** *vegetables;* **frutas cítricas** *citrus fruits;* **aceitunas** *olives*

CAPÍTULOS 1 y 2

¡Ven conmigo a España!

Population: 40,000,000

Area: 194,898 sq. miles (504,788 sq. kms), consists of 85% of the Iberian Peninsula, the Balearic Islands, and the Canary Islands. Spain is larger than California but smaller than Texas.

Capital: Madrid; population: about 3 million

Government: constitutional monarchy (King Juan Carlos I since 1975), with an elected parliament

Industries: food products, textiles, footwear, petro-chemicals, steel, automobiles, ships, tourism

Chief crops: grains, vegetables, citrus fruits, olives

Monetary unit: euro

Main languages: Spanish, Catalan, Basque, Galician

go.hrw.com
WV3 SPAIN

La ciudad de Toledo a orillas del río Tajo ▸

Cultures and Communities

Background Information

• Toledo is the capital of the province of Toledo and is located 42 miles southwest of Madrid. The Tagus River (**el río Tajo**) flows in a deep ravine around the city, which is on a hill.

• From 712 to 1085, Toledo was ruled by the Moors, an Islamic people from North Africa. During the Moorish period, Toledo was a thriving center of culture and learning where Muslims, Jews, and Arabic-speaking Catholics (**mozárabes**) lived in relative peace and prosperity.

MAPQUEST.COM

HRW
go.hrw.com **Atlas Interactivo Mundial**

Have students use the interactive atlas at go.hrw.com to find out more about the geography of Spain and complete the Map Activities below.

Map Activities

- Have students identify the other country occupying the Iberian Peninsula. (Portugal) Have them identify Spain's neighbors to the north, west, and south. (France, Andorra, Portugal, Morocco)

- Have students locate Gibraltar. Ask if they have heard of the Rock of Gibraltar, a limestone mass that occupies most of Gibraltar's 2.3 square miles. Gibraltar has been a British possession since 1713.

- Point out the short distance between Spain and Morocco. It is a short ferry ride from the town of Algeciras to the coast of North Africa. Ceuta and Melilla, two towns on the coast of Morocco, are Spanish territory.

CNN enEspañol.com

Have students check the **CNN en español** Web site for news on Spain. The **CNN en español** site is also a good source of timely, high-interest readings for Spanish students.

Connections and Comparisons

Language Note
The Ladino language, based on 15th-century Castilian mixed with Hebrew, is spoken by some 200,000 people in areas of the Balkans, Israel, Turkey, North Africa, Argentina, and even the United States. It preserves Latin features now gone from modern Spanish, such as *fijo* for **hijo**, *fablar* for **hablar**, and *agora* for **ahora**.

Geography Link
Present the following list of geographical and climactic characteristics to the students: hot, cold, rain forest, tundra, desert, mountains, beaches, large cities, snow, forests, and glaciers. Have students work in small groups to decide if they think these features occur in Spain and then justify their answers after looking at the map and pictures on pp. 12–15.

Using the Photo Essay

②䷀ Catedral de la Sagrada Familia Antonio Gaudí y Cornet designed **El Templo de la Sagrada Familia** in Barcelona. He began the neo-Gothic cathedral around 1883. His plan included towers decorating the façade that resembled trees and vines. Due to his untimely death in 1926, Gaudí was unable to see his masterpiece completed. The **Sagrada Familia** is still under construction today and is one of the most remarkable features of Barcelona's skyline.

③ El traje andaluz Andalusia is the region that most closely fits many people's image of Spain. It is the home of **flamenco** (a dance involving guitar music, finger-snapping, castanets, and heel-stomping), **gazpacho** (a cold soup made with tomatoes, cucumbers, garlic, vinegar, and olive oil), and the **corrida de toros** (bull-fight). Much of Andalusian food, culture, and architecture is reminiscent of the ancient Moorish occupation.

⑤

Los Pirineos The Pyrenees, stretching over 270 miles with a maximum width of about 80 miles, form the boundary between France and Spain. Spain is Europe's second most mountainous country, surpassed only by Switzerland. The tallest peak of the Pyrenees is the Aneto Peak (**Pico de Aneto**) in Aragón, at 11,169 feet. The Pyrenees have many international ski resorts.

España

What comes to mind when you think of Spain? Spain is a country of varied landscapes. In the north you'll find lush, green hills, along with *los Pirineos* (the Pyrenees), a chain of rugged mountains separating Spain and France. Central Spain consists of a huge, dry plateau called the *Meseta,* home of the modern capital city of Madrid. Southern Spain has some of the most beautiful beaches in Europe. Spain's people are as diverse as its landscapes. They enjoy distinct customs and a strong sense of regional identity.

📶 internet

MARCAR: go.hrw.com
PALABRA CLAVE:
WV3 SPAIN

① Los rápidos
The swift rivers and rugged terrain in northern Spain are ideal for white-water rafting adventures.

② La catedral de la Sagrada Familia
Antonio Gaudí spent his career designing the Sagrada Familia cathedral, but he died without seeing his masterpiece finished.

③ El traje andaluz
This young woman is wearing a traditic costume of Andalusia. Costumes like th are often worn to dance flamenco, a music and dance tradition that originated with the gypsies in southern Spain.

④ La Costa Blanca en el Mediterráneo
Benidorm is a Mediterranean resort located on the Costa Blanca. The beautiful beaches make this one of Spain's most popular tourist destinations.

Connections and Comparisons

History Link
The Moors, from North Africa, conquered Spain in the early 700s and ruled for nearly 800 years. These Muslims (**musulmanes**) brought not only Islamic religion to Spain, but also their knowledge of mathematics and medicine. We owe much of the preservation of Greek, Latin, and Middle Eastern literature to their scholarly institutions.

Art Link
The decor of southern Spanish architecture is predominantly arabesque, with façades of patterned leaves, fruits, flowers, or geometric shapes. Have students research Spanish arabesque buildings. (the Alhambra, the Alcazaba, the Alcázar) Ask why their designs don't include people or animals. (Islam forbids their depiction.)

5 Los Pirineos
The Pyrenees Mountains form a natural border separating Spain and France. The highest peaks offer scenic views and excellent hiking.

Motivating Activity
Have students refer to the pictures on pp. 12–15. Are these types of places unique to Spain, or are there similar places in the United States? Ask students to compare and contrast places in these pictures to places they know of in the United States.

6 La Feria de Sevilla
The lively Feria de Sevilla is an annual celebration of Andalusian culture.

6 La Feria de Sevilla
Horsemanship plays an important role in Andalusian culture. Álvaro Domecq and the Royal Andalusian School of Equestrian Art (**Escuela Real Andaluza de Arte Ecuestre**) have won many awards in Spain and in America for their talented horses. Every Tuesday and Thursday at noon the Jerez riding school puts on an equestrian ballet called **Cómo bailan los caballos andaluces**, which features horses that strut, goose-step, leap, and dance. The rest of the working week, midday training sessions are open to the public. In May the whole city of Jerez de la Frontera celebrates these horses during the **Feria del Caballo**. Andalusian horses make up the stock of the Royal Lipizzaner Horses, which are trained at the Spanish Riding School of Vienna in Austria and regularly tour the United States.

7 Cultivo tradicional en la villa de Navacepeda
This farmer uses traditional farming methods in the village of Navacepeda in the Gredos Mountains. Fresh air and pine woods make this a popular weekend spot for residents of nearby Madrid.

7 Cultivo tradicional en la villa de Navecepeda Much of the land in Spain is used for farming, either as cropland or as pastureland. The country ranks among the world's leading producers of cork, lemons, olives, oranges, and grapes. Sheep are the chief livestock in Spain. Other important farm animals include beef and dairy cattle, chickens, goats, and pigs. About two-thirds of all Spanish farmers own their farms. Since about 1960, the government has introduced modern methods and equipment to Spanish farmers. Such advances have increased agricultural production, but some ancient Spanish agricultural practices are still in use today.

Cultures and Communities

Multicultural Link
Have students interview someone from another culture to find out what types of annual celebrations take place in their area. (patron saint festivals, folk art celebrations, memorials for local heroes)

Language Note
Many words in the Spanish language that begin with al- are Arabic in origin. Words like **alcalde** *mayor* or *judge*, **almacén** *store*, **almohada** *pillow*, **alquilar** *to rent*, and **albóndiga** *meatball* are examples of words from Arabic.

Capítulo 1: ¡Mucho gusto!
Chapter Overview

De antemano pp. 18–20	*¡Me llamo Francisco!*

	FUNCTIONS	GRAMMAR	VOCABULARY	RE-ENTRY
Primer paso pp. 21–26	• Saying hello and goodbye, p. 21 • Introducing people and responding to an introduction, p. 22 • Asking how someone is and saying how you are, p. 24	• Punctuation marks, p. 23 • Pronouns **tú** and **yo**, p. 25	• Greetings, p. 21 • Introductions, p. 22 • How you/others are, p. 24	• Accents (**Capítulo preliminar**)
Segundo paso pp. 27–31	• Asking and saying how old someone is, p. 27 • Asking where someone is from and saying where you're from, p. 28	• **Soy, eres,** and **es**, p. 28 • Forming questions with question words, p. 30	• Numbers 0–30, p. 27	• Numbers 0–30 (**Capítulo preliminar**)
Tercer paso pp. 32–35	• Talking about likes and dislikes, p. 32	• Nouns and definite articles, p. 33	• Sports, p. 32 • Food, p. 32 • Music, p. 32 • Classes, p. 32	

Letra y sonido p. 35	**The vowels:** Audio CD 1, Track 23	**Dictado** Audio CD 1, Tracks 24–27

Vamos a leer pp. 36–37	**Categorías**	**Reading Strategy:** Using cognates to determine meaning

Más práctica gramatical	**pp. 38–41**		
	Primer paso, p. 38	**Segundo paso,** pp. 39–41	**Tercer paso,** p. 41

Review pp. 42–45	**Repaso,** pp. 42–43	**A ver si puedo...,** p. 44	**Vocabulario,** p. 45

CULTURE

- **Nota cultural,** Greetings and goodbyes, p. 21
- **Nota cultural,** First names and Saints' Days, p. 23
- **Encuentro cultural, La distancia interpersonal,** p. 26
- **Panorama cultural, ¿De dónde eres?,** p. 31

Capítulo 1: ¡Mucho gusto!
Chapter Resources

PRINT

Lesson Planning
One-Stop Planner

Lesson Planner with Substitute Teacher Lesson Plans, pp. 3–7, 65

Student Make-Up Assignments
- Make-Up Assignment Copying Masters, Chapter 1

Listening and Speaking
TPR Storytelling Book, pp. 1–4

Listening Activities
- Student Response Forms for Listening Activities, pp. 3–5
- Additional Listening Activities 1-1 to 1-6, pp. 7–9
- Additional Listening Activities (song), p. 10
- Scripts and Answers, pp. 102–106

Video Guide
- Teaching Suggestions, pp. 5–7
- Activity Masters, pp. 8–10
- Scripts and Answers, pp. 88–89, 113

Activities for Communication
- Communicative Activities, pp. 1–6
- Realia and Teaching Suggestions, pp. 75–79
- Situation Cards, pp. 137–138

Reading and Writing
Reading Strategies and Skills Handbook, Chapter 1

¡Lee conmigo! 1, Chapter 1

Cuaderno de actividades, pp. 3–12

Grammar
Cuaderno de gramática, pp. 1–8

Grammar Tutor for Students of Spanish, Chapter 1

Assessment
Testing Program
- Grammar and Vocabulary Quizzes, **Paso** Quizzes, and Chapter Test, pp. 1–18
- Score Sheet, Scripts and Answers, pp. 19–26

Alternative Assessment Guide
- Portfolio Assessment, p. 18
- Performance Assessment, p. 32
- CD-ROM Assessment, p. 46

Student Make-Up Assignments
- Alternative Quizzes, Chapter 1

Standardized Assessment Tutor
- Reading, pp. 1–3
- Writing, p. 4

Native Speakers
Cuaderno para hispanohablantes, pp. 1–5

MEDIA

Online Activities
- Juegos interactivos
- Actividades Internet

Video Program
- Videocassette 1
- Videocassette 5 (captioned version)

Interactive CD-ROM Tutor, Disc 1

DVD Tutor, Disc 1

Audio Compact Discs
- Textbook Listening Activities, CD 1, Tracks 9–28
- Additional Listening Activities, CD 1, Tracks 34–40
- Assessment Items, CD 1, Tracks 29–33

Teaching Transparencies
- Situations 1-1 to 1-3
- Vocabulary 1-A to 1-C
- De antemano
- Más práctica gramatical Answers
- Cuaderno de gramática Answers

One-Stop Planner CD-ROM

Use the **One-Stop Planner CD-ROM with Test Generator** to aid in lesson planning and pacing.

For each chapter, the **One-Stop Planner** includes:
- Editable lesson plans with direct links to teaching resources
- Printable worksheets from resource books
- Direct launches to the HRW Internet activities
- Video and audio segments
- Test Generator
- Clip Art for vocabulary items

Capítulo 1: ¡Mucho gusto!

Projects ···

✂ ¿Por qué estudias español?

In this activity students consider reasons for studying Spanish and set personal objectives. They will present ideas to the class using posters, which may serve as motivation as well as class decoration. Students may make brochures for individual portfolios. This project should be done in English, unless Spanish speakers in class wish to use Spanish. It may be assigned as an individual or small-group project.

MATERIALS

✂ **Students may need**
- Poster board or construction paper
- Scissors
- Magazines
- Tape or glue
- Travel brochures

OUTLINE

Students should address three points:

- **Motivation** Why are you learning Spanish? Is it for personal, academic, or professional reasons?
- **Objectives** What would you like to achieve in Spanish this semester? (Be realistic.)
- **Long-Term Application** How will you apply Spanish over the course of your life?

SUGGESTED SEQUENCE

1. Discuss the importance of clarifying personal objectives and goals in language learning. Mention that perceptions often change during the learning process. Share your own experiences with students, explaining what inspired you to study Spanish. Tell how your goals and motivation changed over the years.

2. Describe the project and assign dates for oral presentations, providing a project assignment sheet. Set a firm time limit for presentations. Emphasize that students should be honest about their motivation, objectives, and goals.

3. Review project guidelines and elicit examples from the class.

4. Give students time in class to brainstorm and organize their thoughts.

5. Students create their posters based on their personal motivations, objectives, and goals. The posters may include information on culture, food, work opportunities, etc. Encourage creative use of words, photos, and drawings. Decide if the posters are to be done in class or at home, individually, or in groups.

6. Projects may be presented orally. The students may adopt some ideas presented as class goals.

TEACHER NOTE

Because of the subjective nature of the project, holistic grading should focus on completion, presentation, and effort.

GRADING THE PROJECT

Suggested point distribution: (total = 100 points)

Completion of assignment	30
Poster/Brochure	40
Effort	10
Presentation	20

Games ···

♞ Ponga

This game, played much like Bingo, lets students practice numbers in Spanish (p. 27) while enjoying a familiar game.

Materials   Index cards (or paper) and markers

Procedure   Students prepare their own PONGA card by drawing a card similar to a Bingo card with five horizontal and vertical spaces. Students write a number between zero and 30 in each space. Read a number between zero and 30 in Spanish and record it. Students cover or cross off numbers as they are called until a player has marked off an entire row or column. He or she then says PONGA. The student who then reads these numbers back correctly wins. You may laminate the cards for later use with water-based markers, or use paper scraps to cover the numbers.

PONGA

29	8	11	6	10
12	9	30	27	0
20	15	4	2	7
1	23	18	25	18
17	13	5	16	3

Storytelling

Mini-cuento

This story accompanies Teaching Transparency 1-C. The **mini-cuento** *can be told and retold in different formats, acted out, written, and read aloud, to give students additional opportunities to practice all four skills. The following story tells about Tina and José going to the cafeteria.*

Tina y José están en la cafetería. Tina le dice a una chica, "Hola. ¿De dónde eres?" La chica dice, "Soy de aquí. Me llamo Carolina". Tina le dice, "Mucho gusto. Me llamo Tina. Yo no soy de aquí. Éste es mi amigo José. Él no es de aquí". Carolina le dice a José, "Mucho gusto". José le dice, "Mucho gusto. Oye, ¿te gusta la comida china?" Carolina le dice, "No. Aquí la comida italiana es buena. Me gusta la pizza". Tina le dice, "¿Y te gusta la ensalada?" Carolina responde, "Sí. Es buena. Y a ti, José, ¿te gusta?" Tina dice, "¿A José? ¡No! A José sólo le gusta el chocolate!"

Traditions

Arte

Explain to students that at the beginning of the 20th century in Europe one of the most important and revolutionary art movements was born: cubism. Cubism is an abstract style in which paintings and sculpture are based on geometric forms (such as the intersection of cubes and cones). Pablo Picasso, a Spanish painter, and the French artist Georges Braque created this style. These artists influenced other European and Latin American painters such as Juan Gris and Diego Rivera. Divide the class into teams of six to research and create posters of the artists who used this technique and their famous works. The posters can be used to decorate the room. For examples of Picasso's work, log on to **go.hrw.com,** keyword WV3 SPAIN-PEOPLE, or consult library works. Discuss with students the consequences of changing the traditional forms of painting and perspective.

Receta

Horchata—a sweet, refreshing beverage—can be found in the Hispanic food sections of supermarkets and restaurants in the United States. Valencia, Spain, claims to make the original **horchata** *beverage from the* **chufa** *(sometimes called the tiger nut or earth almond) plant, which was imported from North Africa. In Spain and the Americas, the main ingredient of* **horchata** *is rice or almonds, or both. Sugar, cinnamon, and vanilla are usually added. The following recipe also includes lemon, which in addition to the almonds (and perhaps* **chufa***) is another Arabic influence in Spanish cuisine. Have students research* **horchata** *made with* **chufa** *in Valencia, Spain, or other variations of* **horchata** *(made with milk, coconut, served warm, etc.).*

HORCHATA DE ALMENDRA

para 8 personas

1 libra de almendras peladas

1/2–1 libra de azúcar o
   1–1 1/2 tazas de azúcar

1 limón, cortado en pedazos
   o trozos

1 palito de canela

2 1/2 litros de agua, al tiempo *(warm)*

2 cucharadas de vainilla

Machaque las almendras hasta formar una pasta. (Se puede hacer a mano o en una licuadora.) En la licuadora, combine el agua, el puré de almendras, la canela y el limón para hacer un puré. Cubra el puré y déjelo remojar por tres horas. Pase el puré por un colador y viértalo de nuevo en la licuadora. Repita hasta que se disuelva todo. Ponga azúcar al gusto y agregue la vainilla. Se puede dejar enfriar la horchata en el refrigerador, o ¡puede dejarla en el congelador para comerla helada!

Capítulo 1: ¡Mucho gusto!
Technology

DVD/Video

Videocassette 1, Videocassette 5 (captioned version)
DVD Tutor, Disc 1
See Video Guide, pages 5–10.

De antemano • ¡Me llamo Francisco!

Paco is hoping that Ramón, the mail carrier, is going to bring a letter from his new pen pal. Ramón pretends not to have a letter for Paco because the letter is addressed to "Francisco," Paco's full name. While Paco is reading the letter and daydreaming about his pen pal, his friend Felipe stops by for a visit.

A continuación

Paco and Felipe go to meet Mercedes, Paco's pen pal. She arrives at the pizzeria with her friend Juanita. Paco and Mercedes know each other from school as Paco and Merche. After some awkward moments, they realize that they are one another's pen pal, but under their full names, Francisco and Mercedes.

¿De dónde eres?

Students from Puerto Rico, Spain, Costa Rica, and Venezuela tell where they are from. In additional interviews, people from various parts of the Spanish-speaking world tell us where they are from.

Videoclips

Colombia: promotional piece directed by Édgar González

Interactive CD-ROM Tutor

Activity	Activity Type	Pupil's Edition Page
En contexto	*Interactive conversation*	
1. Así se dice	¿Qué falta?	pp. 21–22, 24
2. Así se dice	Patas arriba	pp. 21–22, 24
3. Vocabulario	¡Super memoria!	p. 27
4. Gramática	¡A escoger!	pp. 28, 30
5. Vocabulario	Imagen y sonido ¡Exploremos! ¡Identifiquemos!	pp. 27, 29
6. Vocabulario	¿Cuál es?	p. 32
Panorama cultural	¿De dónde eres? ¡A escoger!	p. 31
¡A hablar!	*Guided recording*	pp. 42–43
¡A escribir!	*Guided writing*	pp. 42–43

Teacher Management System

Launch the program, type "admin" in the password area, and press RETURN. Log on to **www.hrw.com/CDROMTUTOR** for a detailed explanation of the Teacher Management System.

DVD Tutor

The *DVD Tutor* contains all material from the *Video Program* as described above. Spanish captions are available for use at your discretion for all sections of the video. The *DVD Tutor* also provides a variety of video-based activities that assess students' understanding of the **De antemano, A continuación,** and **Panorama cultural.**

> This part of the *DVD Tutor* may be used on any DVD video player connected to a television or video monitor.

In addition to the video material and the video-based comprehension activities, the *DVD Tutor* also contains the entire *Interactive CD-ROM Tutor* in DVD-ROM format. Each DVD disc contains the activities from all 12 chapters of the *Interactive CD-ROM Tutor.*

> This part of the *DVD Tutor* may be used on a Macintosh® or Windows® computer with a DVD-ROM drive.

One-Stop Planner CD-ROM

To preview all resources available for this chapter, use the **One-Stop Planner CD-ROM**, Disc 1.

Internet Connection

MARCAR: go.hrw.com
PALABRA CLAVE:
WV3 SPAIN-1

*Have students explore the **go.hrw.com** Web site for many online resources covering all chapters. All Chapter 1 resources are available under the keyword **WV3 SPAIN-1**. Interactive games help students practice the material and provide them with immediate feedback. You will also find a printable worksheet that provides Internet activities that lead to a comprehensive online research project.*

Juegos interactivos

You can use the interactive games in this chapter

- to practice grammar, vocabulary, and chapter functions
- as homework
- as an assessment option
- as a self-test
- to prepare for the Chapter Test

Actividades Internet

Students look for information about famous Spanish-speakers online and record a little about each person, using the vocabulary and phrases from the chapter.

- In preparation for the **Hoja de actividades,** have students review the dramatic episode on Videocassette 1 or redo the activities in the **Panorama cultural** on page 31.

- After completing the activity sheet, have students work with a partner and share the information they gathered in activity B on that sheet. Then ask each pair of students to share what they learned with the class.

Proyecto

Have students list five things they enjoy doing and then exchange their list with another student. With their new lists, have the students search online for five Spanish-language Web sites that describe, show, or advertise those activities. Have each student record those URLs and return the list of sites to the list's creator.

Textbook Listening Activities Scripts

Primer paso

6 p. 21

1. —Hasta luego, Miguel Ángel. Tengo que irme.
—¡Chao, Alicia!

2. —Hola, Santiago.
—¿Qué tal, Miguel Ángel?

3. —Buenos días, don Alonso.
—Hola, Miguel Ángel.

4. —Adiós, Mariana.
—Sí, hasta mañana, Miguel Ángel.

5. —Buenas tardes, doña Luisa. ¿Cómo está?
—Buenas tardes. Estoy bien, gracias.

6. —Bueno, tengo clase.
—¡Hasta luego, David!

Answers to Activity 6
1. leaving 3. arriving 5. arriving
2. arriving 4. leaving 6. leaving

9 p. 23

1. Mucho gusto.

2. Me llamo Abel. ¿Y tú? ¿Cómo te llamas?

3. Éste es mi amigo. Se llama Felipe.

4. Ésta es Evita, la estudiante del programa internacional.

5. Encantada.

6. Soy la señora Rivas.

7. Mucho gusto.

Possible answers to Activity 9
1. ¡Mucho gusto! 3. ¡Mucho gusto!; 5. Igualmente.
2. Mucho gusto.   Encantado(a). 6. ¡Mucho gusto!
   Me llamo [name]. 4. Mucho gusto. 7. ¡Mucho gusto!;
                                          Igualmente.

13 p. 24

1. SARA ¿Cómo estás, Daniel?
DANIEL Ay, muy mal.

2. SARA ¿Qué tal, Marta?
MARTA Más o menos, Sara. ¿Y tú?

3. SARA Buenos días, Elena. ¿Cómo estás?
ELENA Estoy muy bien, gracias, Sara.

4. SARA Hola, José Luis. ¿Qué tal?
JOSÉ LUIS Pues, muy bien, Sara. ¿Y tú?

5. SARA Buenas tardes, Carlos. ¿Cómo estás?
CARLOS ¡Excelente!

6. SARA ¿Qué tal, Juan?
JUAN Pues, estoy muy mal, amiga, muy mal.

Answers to Activity 13
bien	regular	mal
Elena	Felipe (MODELO)	Daniel
José Luis	Marta	Juan
Carlos		

Segundo paso

18 p. 28

DANIEL Ésta es Marisa y tiene catorce años. Éste es José.

ARIANA ¿Cuántos años tiene?

DANIEL Tiene seis años.

ARIANA ¿Y éste? ¿Cómo se llama?

DANIEL Es David. Tiene once años.

ARIANA ¿Y ésta?

DANIEL Se llama Anita. Tiene veinticinco años.

ARIANA ¿Y éste?

DANIEL ¡Éste es Daniel! ¡Sí, soy yo! En esta foto tengo un año.

Answers to Activity 18
a. Marisa—14 c. Anita—25 e. José—6
b. Daniel—1 d. David—11

21 p. 29

1. —¿Cómo se llama?
—Se llama Gabriela y es de Buenos Aires, Argentina.

2. —¿Y ésta es Maricarmen?
—Sí, es Maricarmen y es de Santiago de Chile.

3. —¿De dónde es David?
—David es de Madrid, España.

4. —¿Cómo te llamas?
—Mi nombre es Antonio y soy de Quito, Ecuador.

5. —¿Y tú? Eres Laura, ¿verdad?
—Sí, Laura Alicia, encantada. Yo soy de San José, Costa Rica.

6. —¿De dónde es Pedro?
—Pedro es de Santa Fe de Bogotá, Colombia.

Answers to Activity 21
1. Gabriela es de Argentina. 4. Antonio es de Ecuador.
2. Maricarmen es de Chile. 5. Laura es de Costa Rica.
3. David es de España. 6. Pedro es de Colombia.

The following scripts are for the listening activities found in the *Pupil's Edition*. For Student Response Forms, see *Listening Activities*, pages 3–5. To provide students with additional listening practice, see *Listening Activities*, pages 7–10.

One-Stop Planner CD-ROM

To preview all resources available for this chapter, use the **One-Stop Planner CD-ROM**, Disc 1.

Tercer paso

29 p. 32

CARLOS ¿Te gusta el voleibol?

ELENA Bueno, no. No me gusta mucho.

CARLOS ¿Te gusta la pizza?

ELENA No, no me gusta.

CARLOS Oye, ¿te gusta la música pop?

ELENA Pues, no me gusta.

CARLOS Bueno, entonces, ¿qué te gusta?

ELENA A ver… ¿te gusta la comida mexicana?

CARLOS Sí, me gusta.

ELENA ¡Estupendo! A mí también me gusta. ¿Te gusta el restaurante Taco Paco?

CARLOS Mmm…, no, no me gusta mucho.

ELENA Ah, bueno…

Answers to Activity 29

Likes	Doesn't like
la comida mexicana	el voleibol
el restaurante	la pizza
Taco Paco	la música pop

Elena and Carlos should eat Mexican food together.

32 p. 33

AMIGO ¿Te gustan los deportes?

DIANA Sí, me gusta el béisbol. Y me gusta mucho el tenis. No me gusta mucho la natación.

AMIGO Bueno, y ¿qué comida te gusta?

DIANA Mmm, no me gusta la fruta. Me gusta la comida italiana. Y la ensalada. ¡Me gusta mucho la ensalada!

AMIGO Y a ti te gusta bastante la música, ¿verdad?

DIANA Sí, me gusta la música pero no me gusta el jazz. Me gusta más la música rock.

Answers to Activity 32

Likes	Dislikes
el béisbol	la natación
el tenis	la fruta
la ensalada	el jazz
la comida italiana	
la música rock	

LETRA Y SONIDO, P. 35

For the scripts for Parts A and C, see p. 35. The script for Part B is below.

B. Dictado

— Buenos días, Marta. ¿Qué tal?

— Muy bien, Ana. ¿Cómo estás?

— Bien. Bueno, tengo que irme.

— Hasta luego.

— Chao.

Repaso

1 p. 42

MODELO Me llamo Mariana Castillo. Soy de España. Tengo quince años y me gusta mucho la música pop. No me gusta el tenis.

— Hola. Me llamo <u>Liliana Rivera</u>. Soy de <u>Santiago de Chile</u> y tengo <u>dieciséis años</u>. Me gusta mucho <u>el tenis</u> pero no me gusta hacer <u>la tarea</u>.

— Hola, ¿qué tal? Soy <u>Pablo García</u>. Soy de <u>Monterrey</u>, <u>México</u>, y tengo <u>quince años</u>. Me gusta mucho <u>el inglés</u>. No me gusta <u>la música clásica</u>, pero <u>la música rock</u>, sí.

Capítulo 1: ¡Mucho gusto!
Suggested Lesson Plans 50-Minute Schedule

Day 1

CHAPTER OPENER, 5 min.
- Focusing on Outcomes, ATE, p. 17
- Culture Note, ATE, p. 17

DE ANTEMANO 40 min.
- Presenting **De antemano** and Preteaching Vocabulary, ATE, p. 18
- Culture Note and Language Note, ATE, p. 19
- Activities 1–5 and Comprehension Check, ATE, p. 20

Wrap-Up 5 min.
- Have students summarize the storyline of *¡Me llamo Francisco!*

Homework Options
Cuaderno de actividades, p. 3

Day 2

PRIMER PASO
Quick Review 5 min.
- Check homework.
- Bell Work, ATE, p. 21

Así se dice, p. 21 25 min.
- Presenting **Así se dice**, ATE, p. 21
- Do Activity 6, p. 21, with Audio CD.
- Have students read the **Nota cultural** and do the Kinesthetic Learners suggestion, ATE, p. 21
- Have students do Activities 7–8, p. 22, in pairs.

Así se dice, p. 22 10 min.
- Presenting **Así se dice**, ATE, p. 22
- Do Activity 9 with Audio CD, p. 23.

Wrap-Up 10 min.
- Pair work suggestion, ATE, p. 22

Homework Options
Cuaderno de actividades, p. 4, Activities 3–4
Cuaderno de gramática, p. 1, Activity 1

Day 3

PRIMER PASO
Quick Review 5 min.
- Check homework.

Nota gramatical, p. 23 20 min.
- Presenting **Nota gramatical**, ATE, p. 23
- Do Activities 10–11, p. 23.
- Have the students read **Nota cultural**, p. 23.
- Students do Activity 12, p. 24, in pairs.

Así se dice, p. 24 20 min.
- Presenting **Así se dice**, ATE, p. 24
- Do Activity 13, p. 24, with Audio CD, then Activity 14, p. 24.
- Have students read **A lo nuestro**, p. 24, and model pronunciation of the new phrases.
- Students practice alternative answers to Activity 14, p. 24, with a partner.

Wrap-Up 5 min.
- Ask individual students how they are. Have others show comprehension of their answer by pointing their thumb up for feeling fine, and down for not so good.

Homework Options
Más práctica gramatical, p. 38, Activities 1–2
Cuaderno de gramática, pp. 2–3, Activities 3–7
Cuaderno de actividades, p. 5, Activity 5

Day 4

PRIMER PASO
Quick Review 5 min.
- Check homework answers.

Gramática, p. 25 30 min.
- Have students read **Gramática**, checking their answers to number 3 in the footnote, then do Presenting **Gramática**, ATE, p. 25.
- Do Activity 15, p. 25, as a class.
- Students do Activity 16, p. 25, then exchange papers for peer evaluation.
- Have the groups of three do Activity 17, p. 25.

ENCUENTRO CULTURAL, p. 26 10 min.
- Presenting **Encuentro cultural**, ATE, p. 26
- Present the Multicultural Links, ATE, p. 26.

Wrap-Up 5 min.
- Review the Quiz format and ask students questions from the **Así se dice** sections of the **Paso**.

Homework Options
Study for Quiz 1-1, pp. 21–26.
Más práctica gramatical, p. 38, Activity 3
Cuaderno de gramática, p. 4, Activities 8–10
Cuaderno de actividades, p. 5, Activity 6; p. 6, Activities 7–8

Day 5

PRIMER PASO
Quick Review 5 min.
- Write the instructions for Bell Work, ATE, p. 27, on an overhead transparency.

Quiz 20 min.
- Administer Quiz 1-1A, 1-1B, or a combination of the two.

SEGUNDO PASO
Así se dice/Vocabulario, p. 27 20 min.
- Presenting **Así se dice** and **Vocabulario**, ATE, p. 27
- Do Activity 18, p. 28, with Audio CD.
- Have students do Activities 19–20, p. 28, in small groups.

Wrap-Up 5 min.
- Have several groups present their dialogues from Activity 20, p. 28, to the class.

Homework Options
Más práctica gramatical, p. 39, Activity 4
Cuaderno de gramática, p. 5, Activities 11–13
Cuaderno de actividades, p. 7, Activities 9–10

Day 6

SEGUNDO PASO
Quick Review 10 min.
- Check homework.
- Quickly review numbers from 0–30 and expressions for asking and saying how old someone is.

Así se dice/Nota gramatical, p. 28 35 min.
- Presenting **Así se dice** and **Nota gramatical**, ATE, p. 28
- Do Activity 21, p. 29, with Audio CD.
- Have students do Activities 22–23, p. 29, in small groups. See Additional Practice, ATE, p. 29.
- Students do Activity 24, p. 29, individually.

Wrap-Up 5 min.
- Play **¿De dónde eres?**, p. 31.

Homework Options
Cuaderno de gramática, p. 6, Activity 14
Cuaderno de actividades, p. 8, Activity 11
CD-ROM Disc 1, Chapter 1, **Segundo paso**, Activity 4

One-Stop Planner CD-ROM

For alternative lesson plans by chapter section, to create your own customized plans, or to preview all resources available for this chapter, use the **One-Stop Planner CD-ROM**, Disc 1.

 For additional homework suggestions, see activities accompanied by this symbol throughout the chapter.

Day 7

SEGUNDO PASO
Quick Review 5 min.
- Check homework.

Gramática p. 30 25 min.
- Presenting **Gramática**, ATE, p. 30
- Have students do Activities 25–26, p. 30, individually, checking answers as a class.
- Do Activity 27, p. 30, in small groups, and do Activity 28, p. 30, individually as a follow-up.
- Teacher-to-Teacher, ATE, p. 30

PANORAMA CULTURAL 15 min.
- Present **Panorama cultural**, p. 31, with the video or Audio CD.
- Ask students the **Preguntas**, p. 31, to check comprehension.
- Do **Para pensar y hablar…** activities, p. 31.

Wrap-Up 5 min.
- Review activity formats and provide sample questions for the Quiz.

Homework Options
Study for Quiz 1-2, pp. 27–30.
Más práctica gramatical, p. 41, Activity 7
Cuaderno de gramática, p. 6, Activity 15
Cuaderno de actividades, p. 8, Activities 12–13

Day 8

TERCER PASO
Quick Review 5 min.
- Bell Work, ATE, p. 32

Quiz 20 min.
- Have students complete Quiz 1-2A or Quiz 1-2B, or a combination of the two.

Así se dice, p. 32 10 min.
- Presenting **Así se dice**, ATE, p. 32
- Do Activity 29, with Audio CD.

Vocabulario, p. 32 10 min.
- Presenting **Vocabulario** and Additional Practice, ATE, p. 32
- Do Additional Listening Activities 1-5 and 1-6 with Audio CD, Listening Activities, p. 9.

Wrap-Up 5 min.
- Use flashcards made from magazine cut-outs to review the new vocabulary.

Homework Options
Más práctica gramatical, p. 41, Activity 8
Cuaderno de gramática, p. 7, Activities 16–17
Cuaderno de actividades, p. 9, Activity 14

Day 9

TERCER PASO
Quick Review 5 min.
- Check homework.

Gramática, p. 33 40 min.
- Ask for a volunteer to read the **Gramática**, p. 33, aloud, then do the Presenting suggestion.
- After going over the **modelo** as a class, have students do Activity 30, p. 33, individually.
- Model pronunciation of new words from the **También se puede decir…**, p. 33.
- Students do Activity 31, p. 33, in pairs.
- Do Activity 32, p. 33, with Audio CD, then have pairs continue with Activity 33, p. 33.
- Students do Activity 34, p. 34, individually, then exchange papers with a partner to peer-review. Pairs continue with Activity 35, p. 34.
- Go over words in **A lo nuestro**, p. 34.

Wrap-Up 5 min.
- Take the role of various famous people, and make likely and unlikely comments about what you like and dislike. Students show comprehension by responding with **sí** or **no**.

Homework Options
Have students work in pairs to do Activity 36, p. 35. Students also write Activity 37.

Day 10

TERCER PASO
Quick Review, pp. 34–35 5 min.
- Allow students to practice their interviews briefly (homework Activity 36, p. 35) with their partner.
- As you circulate, students show you their journal entry (homework Activity 37, p. 35). You may wish to mark a completion score in your gradebook.

Así se dice/Vocabulario/Gramática, pp. 32–35 30 min.
- Have pairs of students present their interviews from Activity 36, p. 35.

Letra y sonido, p. 35 10 min.
- Present using Audio CD.

Wrap-Up 5 min.
- Go over Quiz 1-3 format and provide sample questions.

Homework Options
Study for Quiz 1-3.
Más práctica gramatical, p. 41, Activity 9
Cuaderno de gramática, p. 8, Activities 18–20
Cuaderno de actividades, pp. 9–10, Activities 15–18

Day 11

TERCER PASO
Quick Review 5 min.
- Review **Paso** content quickly, using Teaching Transparency 1-3.

Quiz 20 min.
- Administer Quiz 1-3A or 1-3B.

VAMOS A LEER 20 min.
- Activities A–B, p. 36
- Activities C–E, p. 37

Wrap-Up 5 min.
- Have students state the reading strategy (using cognates to determine meaning) and give examples of true and false cognates from the reading.

Homework Options
Cuaderno de actividades, p. 11, Activity 19
A ver si puedo…, p. 44

Day 12

REPASO
Quick Review 5 min.
- Check homework.

Chapter Review 40 min.
- Review Chapter 1. Choose from **Más práctica gramatical,** Grammar Tutor for Students of Spanish, Activities for Communication, Listening Activities, Interactive CD-ROM Tutor, or **Juegos interactivos.**

Wrap-Up 5 min.
- Review Chapter 1 Test format.

Homework Options
Study for Chapter 1 Test.

Assessment

Test, Chapter 1 50 min.
- Administer Chapter 1 Test. Select from Testing Program, Alternative Assessment Guide, Test Generator, or Standardized Assessment Tutor.

Capítulo 1: ¡Mucho gusto!
Suggested Lesson Plans 90-Minute Block Schedule

Block 1

CHAPTER OPENER, 5 min.
- Focusing on Outcomes, ATE, p. 17
- Motivating Activity, ATE, p. 16

DE ANTEMANO, 40 min.
- Presenting **De antemano** and Preteaching Vocabulary, ATE, p. 18
- Culture Note and Language Note, ATE, p. 19
- Activities 1–5 and Comprehension Check, ATE, p. 20

Quick Review 5 min.
- Have students summarize the storyline of *¡Me llamo Francisco!*

PRIMER PASO
Así se dice, p. 21 25 min.
- Presenting **Así se dice**, ATE, p. 21
- Do Activity 6, p. 21, with Audio CD.
- Have students read the **Nota cultural** and do the Kinesthetic Learners suggestion, ATE, p. 21.
- Have students do Activities 7–8, p. 22, in pairs.

Así se dice, p. 22 10 min.
- Presenting **Así se dice**, ATE, p. 22
- Do Activity 9 with Audio CD, p. 23.

Wrap-Up 5 min.
- Teaching Suggestion for **Así se dice**, ATE, p. 22

Homework Options
Cuaderno de actividades, p. 4, Activities 3–4
Cuaderno de gramática, p. 1, Activities 1–2

Block 2

PRIMER PASO
Quick Review 5 min.
- Check homework.

Nota gramatical, p. 23 20 min.
- Presenting **Nota gramatical**, ATE, p. 23
- Do Activities 10–11, p. 23.
- Have the students read **Nota cultural**, p. 23.
- Students do Activity 12, p. 24, in pairs.

Así se dice, p. 24 20 min.
- Presenting **Así se dice**, ATE, p. 24
- Do Activity 13, p. 24, with Audio CD, then Activity 14.
- Have students read **A lo nuestro**, model pronunciation of the new phrases, and explain that using expressions from this feature will make their Spanish sound more natural.
- Students practice alternate answers to Activity 14 with a partner.
- Review phrases related to introductions, and ask individual students how they are. Have others show comprehension of their answer by pointing their thumb up for feeling fine, and down for not so good.

Gramática, p. 25 40 min.
- Have students read **Gramática**, checking their answers to number 3 in the footnote, then do Presenting **Gramática**, ATE, p. 25.
- Do Activity 15, p. 25, as a class.
- Students write their answers to Activity 16, then break into groups of three to exchange papers for peer evaluation.
- Have the groups of three do Activity 17. Challenge groups to perform the dialogues in front of the class.

Wrap-Up 5 min.
- Have students introduce their neighboring classmates to each other.

Homework Options
Más práctica gramatical, p. 38, Activities 1–3
Cuaderno de gramática, pp. 2–4, Activities 3–9
Cuaderno de actividades, p. 5–6 Activities 5–8
Study for Quiz 1-1, pp. 21–26.

Block 3

PRIMER PASO
Quick Review 5 min.
- Write p. 27, ATE, Bell Work instructions on a transparency.
- Check homework answers.

ENCUENTRO CULTURAL, 10 min.
- Presenting **Encuentro cultural**, ATE, p. 26
- Present the Multicultural Links, ATE, p. 26, and discuss cultural differences with the class.

Quick Review 5 min.
- Review the Quiz format and ask students questions from the **Así se dice** sections of the **Paso**.

Quiz 20 min.
Administer Quiz 1-1A, 1-1B, or a combination of the two.

SEGUNDO PASO
Así se dice and Vocabulario, p. 27 20 min.
- Presenting **Así se dice** and **Vocabulario**, ATE, p. 27
- Do Activity 18, p. 28, with Audio CD.
- Have students do Activities 19–20 in small groups.
- Have several groups present their dialogues from Activity 20 to the class.

Así se dice and Nota gramatical, p. 28 25 min.
- Quickly review numbers from 0–30, and expressions for asking and saying how old someone is.
- Presenting **Así se dice** and **Nota gramatical**, ATE, p. 28
- Do Activity 21, p. 29, with Audio CD.

Wrap-Up 5 min.
- Have different students pretend to be famous people. The rest of the class asks where the person is from and how old he or she is to guess the identity.

Homework Options
Más práctica gramatical, pp. 39–40, Activities 4–6
Cuaderno de gramática, pp. 4–5, Activities 8–13
Cuaderno de actividades, pp. 5–7, Activities 5–10
Study for Quiz 1-2, pp. 27–30.

One-Stop Planner CD-ROM

For alternative lesson plans by chapter section, to create your own customized plans, or to preview all resources available for this chapter, use the **One-Stop Planner CD-ROM**, Disc 1.

 For additional homework suggestions, see activities accompanied by this symbol throughout the chapter.

Block 4

SEGUNDO PASO

Quick Review 5 min.
- Bell Work, ATE, p. 27
- Check homework.

Así se dice, p. 28 20 min.
- Have students do Activities 22–23, p. 29, in small groups.
- Students do Activity 24 individually.
- Play **¿De dónde eres?**, ATE, p. 29.

Gramática, p. 30 25 min.
- Presenting **Gramática**, ATE, p. 30
- Have students do Activities 25–26, p. 30 individually, checking answers as a class.
- Do Activity 27 in small groups, and do Activity 28 individually as a follow-up.
- Teacher-to-Teacher, ATE, p. 30

PANORAMA CULTURAL, 10 min.
- Present **Panorama cultural** with the video or Audio CD.
- Ask students the **Preguntas**, ATE, p. 31, to check comprehension.

Quick Review 5 min.
- Ask review questions on **Segundo paso.**
- Review activity formats and provide sample questions for the Quiz.

Quiz 20 min.
- Have students complete Quiz 1-2A, Quiz 1-2B, or a combination of the two.

Wrap-Up 5 min.
You may wish to assign Additional Practice, p. 29, for homework.

Homework Options
Cuaderno de gramática, p. 6, Activities 14–15
Cuaderno de actividades, p. 8, Activities 11–13
CD-ROM Disc 1, Chapter 1, **Segundo paso,** Activity 4
Más práctica gramatical, p. 41, Activity 7

Block 5

TERCER PASO

Quick Review 5 min.
- Bell Work, ATE, p. 32

Así se dice, p. 32 10 min.
- Presenting **Así se dice**, ATE, p. 32
- Do Activity 29, p. 32, with Audio CD.

Vocabulario, p. 32 10 min.
- Presenting **Vocabulario** and Additional Practice, ATE, p. 32.
- Do Additional Listening Activities 1–5 and 1–6 with Audio CD, Listening Activities, p. 9.

Gramática, pp. 33–34 40 min.
- Ask for a volunteer to read the **Gramática** aloud, then do the Presenting suggestion, ATE, p. 33, as a whole-class activity.
- After going over the **modelo** as a class, have students do Activity 30 individually. Circulate to check comprehension.
- Model pronunciation of new words from the **También se puede decir...**
- Students do Activity 31 in pairs.
- Do Activity 32 with Audio CD, then have pairs continue with Activity 33.
- Have students write their answers to Activity 34 individually, then exchange papers with their partner to peer-review.
- Go over pronunciation of words in **A lo nuestro.**
- Pairs continue with Activity 35.

Letra y sonido, p. 35 10 min.
- Present using Audio CD.

Speaking Assessment, p. 35 10 min.
- Assign students to work with a partner to prepare Activity 36 for presentation.
- Allow students to practice their interviews briefly (Activity 36) with their partner.

Wrap-Up 5 min.
You may wish to do either Additional Practice suggestion, p. 35.

Homework Options
Writing assignment (Activity 37) p. 35
Más práctica gramatical, p. 41, Activities 8–9
Cuaderno de gramática, p. 7, Activities 16–17
Cuaderno de actividades, p. 9, Activity 14

Block 6

TERCER PASO

Quick Review 5 min.
- Bell Work, ATE, p.32
- Check homework.
- Students show you their journal entry (Activity 37) for a completion score or grade. See Writing Assessment, ATE, p. 43.

Speaking Assessment 20 min.
- Have students present their interviews from Activity 36. Use the Speaking Rubric, p. 35.

Quick Review 5–10 min.
- Review **Paso** with Teaching Transparency 1-3.
- Use magazine photos to review the vocabulary.
- Take the role of various famous people, and make comments about likes and dislikes. Students respond with **sí** or **no.**

Quiz 20 min.
- Administer Quiz 1-3A or 1-3B.

VAMOS A LEER 15–20 min.
- Activities A–B, p. 36
- Activities C–E, p. 37
- Cooperative Learning Activity, p. 37

REPASO, 10 min.
- Do Activity 1, p. 42, with Audio CD.
- Students do Activities 2, 3, and 4 individually.

Wrap-Up 5 min.
- Have students state the reading strategy and give examples of true and false cognates.
- Review Chapter 1 Test format.

Homework Options
Cuaderno de actividades, pp. 9–11, Activities 14–19
Write Activity 7 or Activity 9, p. 43
Más práctica gramatical, p. 41, Activity 8
Cuaderno de gramática, pp. 7–8, Activities 16–20

Block 7

REPASO

Homework Check 5 min.
- Pick up writing assignments for grade.

Chapter Review 10 min.
- Review Chapter 1. Choose from **Más práctica gramatical,** Grammar Tutor for Students of Spanish, Activities for Communication, Listening Activities, Interactive CD-ROM Tutor, or **Juegos interactivos.**

Test, Chapter 1 45 min.
- Administer Chapter 1 Test.

Motivating Activity 5–10 min.
Do a motivating activity to begin Chapter 2, p. 47.

CAPÍTULO 1

One-Stop Planner CD-ROM

For resource information, see the
One-Stop Planner, Disc 1.

Pacing Tips
As students have not yet
fallen into a rhythm this early in the
year, some exercises may take longer
than you have planned. Plan for cultural content, as this chapter presents
Panorama cultural, **Encuentro
cultural**, and more. See Suggested
Lesson Plans, pp. 15I–15L.

Meeting the Standards
Communication
• Saying hello and goodbye, p. 21
• Introducing people and responding
  to an introduction, p. 22
• Asking how someone is and saying
  how you are, p. 24
• Asking and saying how old some-
  one is, p. 27
• Asking where someone is from and
  saying where you're from, p. 28
• Talking about likes and dislikes,
  p. 32

Cultures
• Nota cultural, p. 20
• Nota cultural, p. 21
• Nota cultural, p. 23
• Culture Note, p. 23

Connections
• Multicultural Links, p. 26
• Culture Note, p. 29

Comparisons
• Culture Note, p. 19
• A lo nuestro, p. 24
• Encuentro cultural, p. 26
• También se puede decir, p. 33
• Language-to-Language, p. 37

Communities
• Thinking Critically, p. 31

Communication for All Students

Motivating Activity
Ask students to list greetings or introductions they
might say to a new student. Have students make
changes to the list as if they were meeting these
people: a five-year old girl, a new English teacher,
their mother's friend, their father's boss, their older
sister's boyfriend, or an elderly relative. Ask the
students to explain the changes they made in
their lists. Discuss with the class how the level
of formality changes when they address people
older or younger than themselves.

CAPÍTULO

1

¡Mucho gusto!

Objectives

In this chapter you will learn to

Primer paso

- say hello and goodbye
- introduce people and respond to an introduction
- ask how someone is and say how you are

Segundo paso

- ask and say how old someone is
- ask where someone is from and say where you're from

Tercer paso

- talk about likes and dislikes

 internet

 MARCAR: go.hrw.com
PALABRA CLAVE:
    WV3 SPAIN-1

◀ **Hola, me llamo Miguel. Y tú, ¿cómo te llamas?**

Photo Flash!
Interest in cultural heritage is important to young people of Hispanic heritage both in and outside the United States. San Antonio's array of cultural institutes and museums of history and art provide citizens a means of affirming this sense of heritage.

Focusing on Outcomes
Point out to students that an important use of a language is meeting and greeting people, having casual conversation, and getting to know one another better. By the end of the chapter, students will be able to appropriately greet people in Spanish, introduce themselves, ask and say how old someone is, ask where someone is from and tell where they are from, as well as talk about their likes and dislikes.

Connections and Comparisons

Culture Note
Social conventions regarding greeting old friends vary among cultures. Within Hispanic populations one can observe the conventional firm handshake, often accompanied with a squeeze of the upper arm with the left hand. Men sharing family ties or who are close friends often greet with an **abrazo** and vigorous pats on the back, and younger males are taught that not following this protocol is disrespectful. Women and men often greet with a token kiss on a cheek. Ask students to observe their own routines involving introductions or greetings and to define them. How do they differ from protocols seen in this chapter?

The **fotonovela** is an abridged version of the video episode.

CD 1 Trs. 9–10

Estrategia para comprender
Look at the characters in the **fotonovela**, or photo story. Where are they? What are their occupations? What do you think they're talking about? What do you suppose will happen in the story?

 Paco   **Felipe**   **Ramón**   **Abuela**

Teaching Resources
pp. 18–20

PRINT
▶ Lesson Planner, p. 2
▶ Video Guide, pp. 5–6, 8
▶ Cuaderno de actividades, p. 3

MEDIA
▶ One-Stop Planner
▶ Video Program
 De antemano
 Videocassette 1, 7:07–11:10
 Videocassette 5 (captioned version), 00:47–06:18
 A continuación
 Videocassette 1, 11:11–16:25
 Videocassette 5 (captioned version), 06:19–12:48
▶ DVD Tutor, Disc 1
▶ Audio Compact Discs, CD 1, Trs. 9–10
▶ **De antemano** Transparencies

Presenting
De antemano

Have students read and answer the questions in **Estrategia para comprender**. Then play the video once. Next, present the Preteaching Vocabulary. Discuss each picture and ask students what they understand. Follow up by modeling pronunciation of the **fotonovela** dialogue and having students repeat after you. Have students guess meanings from context.

 De antemano Transparencies

1
Mamá: ¡Ay, Paco!
Paco: ¡Lo siento, mamá!

2
Ramón: Hola, buenos días, Paco. ¿Cómo estás?
Paco: Muy bien, gracias. ¿Hay una carta para mí?

3
Ramón: No, ésta no es. Ésta es para... el señor Francisco Xavier López Medina. Tú no te llamas Francisco... tú te llamas Paco.
Paco: ¡Sí, soy yo! Yo soy Francisco, pero me llaman Paco. ¡Gracias! Hasta luego, ¿eh?
Ramón: Adiós, don Francisco Xavier López Medina.

4
Paco: Hola, Francisco. Me llamo Mercedes Margarita Álvarez García, y soy de Madrid...

Preteaching Vocabulary

Recognizing Cognates
De antemano contains several words that students will be able to recognize as cognates. Have students find these and have them guess what is happening in the story.

❷ hola
❷ mí
❺ pizza
❺ voleibol

❻ fantástica
❼ excelente
❾ secreto

STANDARDS: 1.2

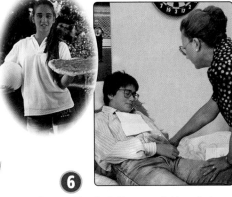

Madrid 3 de septiembre
¡Hola Francisco!
Me llamo Mercedes Margarita
Alvarez García y soy de Madrid.
Tengo 15 años. Me gusta la
pizza y me gusta mucho el
voleibol. ¿Cuántos años tienes?
¿Qué te gusta a ti?
Hasta luego,
Mercedes

5

Sr. Francisco Xavier López Medina
C/Echegaray 21, 1° D
28014 Madrid

6

Paco: ¡Sí, señor! ¡Una carta de Mercedes!
¡Una chica fantástica!
Abuela: ¡Paco! ¡Paco! Está aquí tu amigo Felipe.

Felipe: Hola, Paco. ¿Qué tal?
Paco: Excelente. ¿Y tú?

7

8

Felipe: Oye, ¿qué es eso?
Paco: Es una carta... de una chica.

9

Felipe: ¿Una chica? ¿Cómo se llama?
Paco: Felipe, es un secreto.
Felipe: Paco, soy tu amigo. Por favor... cuéntame.
Paco: Bueno... mira...

Cuaderno de actividades, p. 3, Acts. 1–2

Using the Captioned Video/DVD

As an alternative to reading the conversations in the book, you might want to show the captioned version of *¡Me llamo Francisco!* on Videocassette 5. As students hear the language and watch the story, anxiety about the new language will be reduced and comprehension facilitated. The reinforcement of seeing the written words with the gestures and actions in context will help students to do the comprehension activities on page 20. **NOTE:** The *DVD Tutor* contains captions for all sections of the *Video Program*.

DE ANTEMANO

CAPÍTULO 1

Culture Note
Mention that handwriting in Spanish-speaking countries is slightly different from handwriting in the U.S. Note the **m**, **s**, **p**, and **z** in Mercedes' letter. Also point out the number one (written with a tail) on the envelope. Ask students to mention any other differences they notice.

Language Notes
• Characters in the video episode for this chapter speak with a Peninsular Spanish accent. Point out to students that they will have an opportunity through the *Video Program* to hear a variety of authentic accents from at least nine locations around the Spanish-speaking world.

• Point out that **pizza** and **voleibol** are cognates (words that are similar in two languages, as in **voleibol** and *volleyball*). Tell students that looking and listening for cognates will help their comprehension.

A continuación
You may choose to continue with *¡Me llamo Francisco! (a continuación)* at this time or wait until later in the chapter. At this point, Paco and Felipe go to meet Mercedes. Francisco and Mercedes know each other from school as Paco and Merche, and they realize that they are pen pals under their full names. You may wish to have pairs of students predict what they think will happen in the second part of the video.

Teacher Notes

3 You may have asked students to write the expressions in Activity 3. In the early stages of language acquisition, copying is a valid writing activity. Assure students that it is normal for the productive skills of speaking and writing to develop more slowly than the receptive skills of listening and reading. Allow time for students to develop their passive skills before asking them to speak and write. Not all students will develop their productive skills at the same pace.

5 After students read the **Nota cultural**, ask for volunteers to say what their last name would be if they used this naming convention. To create a comfortable and nonthreatening atmosphere, it is especially important to ask only for volunteers to provide such personal examples.

Native Speakers

Ask native speakers if they know of any other **saludos** and **despedidas**. Have them share them with the class. Point out that **¡Hola!** as a greeting is spelled with **h,** and that the word for *wave* is spelled **ola,** without the **h.**

Answers

3 1. Hola.
2. Buenos días.
3. Me gusta mucho el voleibol.
4. Me llamo…
5. Gracias.
6. Hasta luego. Adiós.

4 1. carta
2. el señor Francisco Xavier López Medina
3. Soy
4. yo
5. me llamo
6. Hasta luego
7. Adiós

These activities check for comprehension only. Students should not yet be expected to produce language modeled in **De antemano.**

1 **¿Comprendes?** *Do you understand?*

How well do you understand what is happening in the **fotonovela**? Check by answering these questions. Don't be afraid to guess.

1. Who are the people in the **fotonovela**? Make a list of them. How are they related to Paco? Paco, his mother, his friend Felipe, and the mail carrier.
2. Why does Paco run out of the store? To see if the mail carrier has a letter for him.
3. What do you know about the family business? They operate a fruit stand.
4. What do you think will happen next? Paco will tell Felipe about his new pen pal.

2 **¿Cierto o falso?** *True or false?*

Con base en la fotonovela, indica **cierto** *(true)* si la oración es verdadera o **falso** *(false)* si no lo es. Si es falsa, cámbiala.

1. La carta es de *(from)* Felipe. Falso, la carta es de Mercedes.
2. El nombre completo de Paco es Francisco Xavier López Medina. Cierto
3. Felipe es el papá de *(of)* Paco. Falso, Felipe es el amigo de Paco.
4. Mercedes es de Toledo. Falso, Mercedes es de Madrid.
5. A Mercedes le gusta mucho el voleibol. Cierto

3 **Cortesías** *Courtesies* See answers below.

What Spanish phrases do the characters in the **fotonovela** use to say the following?

1. Hello.
2. Good morning!
3. I like volleyball.
4. My name is . . .
5. Thank you.
6. Goodbye.

4 **¡Soy yo!** *It's me!*

Completa el diálogo con palabras o expresiones de la **fotonovela**. See answers below.

PACO   ¿Hay una ___1___ para mí?

RAMÓN   No, ésta no es. Esta carta es para ___2___.

PACO   ¡___3___ yo! ¡Soy ___4___! ¡Yo Francisco! ¡Gracias! ___6___, ¿eh?

RAMÓN   ___7___, señor Francisco Xavier López Medina.

5 **¿Y tú?** *And you?*

What would your name be if you used both your father's and your mother's last name? Where would it be listed in the phone book? Answers will vary.

	LOPEZ - 89
LOPEZ MATEOS, N. - Galileo, 21	248 90 93
» **MATEOS, J.** - Alonso Cano, 33	730 18 83
» **MATUTE, R.** - Giralda, 204	775 89 64
» **MAYORAL, A.** - Palencia, 101	263 32 76
» **MAYORAL, C.** - Luis Buñuel, 12	437 18 06
» **MEDIAVILLA, P.** - Embajadores, 78	711 84 19
LOPEZ MEDINA, A. - Av. S. Eloy, 301	472 49 32
» **MEDINA, F.** - Amor Hermoso, 69	326 37 71
» **MEDINA, R.** - Echegaray, 21	775 89 64
» **MEDINA, T.** - Av. Valle, 35	464 76 91
» **MEDRANO, A.** - Cerro Blanco, 14	558 22 20
LOPEZ MEGIA, J. - Bolivia, 35	471 49 36
» **MEIRA, L.** - Libertad, 45	792 20 39

Nota cultural

You might think Francisco Xavier López Medina is an unusually long name. Actually, Spaniards and Latin Americans commonly use both their first and middle names. They also generally use two last names: first the father's (in Paco's case, López) and then the mother's maiden name (for Paco, it's Medina). In the phone book, Paco's name would be listed under "L" as **López Medina.**

Comprehension Check

Slower Pace

1 Have students work with a partner. Allow approximately five minutes for pairs to prepare answers to the questions. Review with the entire class.

Challenge

2 Have students work individually or in pairs to write three or four additional true-false statements based on *¡Me llamo Francisco!* Students might exchange papers and mark their answers, or you might call on individuals to read one of their statements and have other students respond.

Primer paso

Objectives Saying hello and goodbye; introducing people and responding to an introduction; asking how someone is and saying how you are

Así se dice
Here's how you say it

Saying hello and goodbye

To greet someone, say:

¡Hola! *Hello!*

Buenos días, señor.
Good morning, sir.

Buenas tardes, señorita.
Good afternoon, miss.

Buenas noches, señora.
Good evening, ma'am.
Good night, ma'am.

To say goodbye to someone, say:

Adiós.　　　　　*Goodbye.*

Bueno, tengo　　*Well, I have*
clase.　　　　　　*class.*

Chao.　　　　　　*'Bye.*

Hasta luego.　　*See you later.*

Hasta mañana.　*See you tomorrow.*

Tengo que irme.　*I have to go.*

> Cuaderno de actividades,
> p. 4, Act. 3

> Cuaderno de gramática,
> p. 1, Act. 1

6　Una recepción *A reception*

Escuchemos You're at an all-day open house celebration at Miguel Ángel's house. As you listen, decide whether the person is arriving or leaving. Scripts and answers on p.15G.

CD 1
Tr. 11

MODELO　　　—¡Hola, Miguel Ángel!
　　　　　　　　—Buenos días, señora de López. *(Mrs. López is arriving.)*

1. Alicia
2. Santiago
3. don Alonso
4. Mariana
5. doña Luisa
6. David

Nota cultural

Spanish speakers often greet each other with a handshake or a kiss. In Spain, friends may greet each other with a light kiss on both cheeks. Latin Americans kiss on only one cheek. When men greet each other, they often shake hands, pat each other on the back, or hug. Young people often shake hands when they meet or say goodbye. Family members usually greet each other with a kiss.

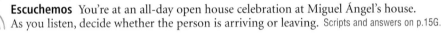

Communication for All Students

Kinesthetic Learners

Ask pairs of student volunteers to demonstrate in front of the class how they greet people. Have them do this in several situations as if they were greeting close friends of the same or opposite sex, parents, grandparents, the school principal, a small child, a new student in school.

Auditory Learners

6 Use the Student Response Form for this activity, in *Listening Activities*, p. 3, or have students number 1 to 6 on a separate sheet of paper. Play the recording again and have students repeat the Spanish. Encourage them to imitate the pronunciation they hear on the recording as closely as possible.

Teaching Resources
pp. 21–26

PRINT
- Lesson Planner, p. 3
- TPR Storytelling Book, pp. 1, 4
- Listening Activities, pp. 3, 7
- Activities for Communication, pp. 1–2, 75, 78–79, 137–138
- Cuaderno de gramática, pp. 1–4
- Grammar Tutor for Students of Spanish, Chapter 1
- Cuaderno de actividades, pp. 4–6
- Cuaderno para hispanohablantes, pp. 1–5
- Testing Program, pp. 1–4
- Alternative Assessment Guide, p. 32
- Student Make-Up Assignments, Chapter 1

MEDIA
- One-Stop Planner
- Audio Compact Discs, CD 1, Trs. 11–13, 34–35, 29
- Teaching Transparencies 1-1; **Más práctica gramatical** Answers; Cuaderno de gramática Answers
- Interactive CD-ROM Tutor, Disc 1

Bell Work
Have students refer to the **fotonovela** on pages 18–19 and write all of the expressions they can find to greet someone and to say goodbye.

Presenting
Así se dice

First model and then have the class repeat the expressions. Then hold up magazine photos of a man, a woman, a child, and a teenager. Students "greet" each photo with the appropriate phrase. Then model a phrase to say goodbye and have students respond accordingly, using a different phrase.

Teaching Resources
pp. 21–26

PRINT 📖

▸ Lesson Planner, p. 3
▸ TPR Storytelling Book, pp. 1, 4
▸ Listening Activities, pp. 3, 7
▸ Activities for Communication, pp. 1–2, 75, 78–79, 137–138
▸ Cuaderno de gramática, pp. 1–4
▸ Grammar Tutor for Students of Spanish, Chapter 1
▸ Cuaderno de actividades, pp. 4–6
▸ Cuaderno para hispanohablantes, pp. 1–5
▸ Testing Program, pp. 1–4
▸ Alternative Assessment Guide, p. 32
▸ Student Make-Up Assignments, Chapter 1

MEDIA 📀📹

▸ One-Stop Planner
▸ Audio Compact Discs, CD 1, Trs. 11–13, 34–35, 29
▸ Teaching Transparencies 1-1; **Más práctica gramatical** Answers; Cuaderno de gramática Answers
▸ Interactive CD-ROM Tutor, Disc 1

Presenting
Así se dice

Walk around the room greeting various students, using the suggested greetings. Encourage students to respond using the appropriate expression. Do a quick activity asking several students, **¿Cómo te llamas?** As they respond, shake each student's hand and reply **¡Mucho gusto!** or **Encantado/a.** Then introduce them to the class by saying **Éste es** or **Ésta es.**

---

7 Saludos y despedidas *Hellos and goodbyes* Answers will vary.

Escribamos How would you greet or say goodbye to the following people? How would they respond to your greetings? Choose your expressions from **Así se dice** on page 21.

a.

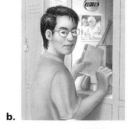
b.

c.

d.

e.

f.

8 Entre clases *Between classes* Answers will vary.

Hablemos Work with a partner. Imagine you just ran into each other in the hall between classes. Greet each other briefly. Then tell your partner you have to go, and say goodbye. Switch roles and replay the conversation, this time using different expressions.

Así se dice
Here's how you say it

Introducing people and responding to an introduction

To introduce yourself, say:

Me llamo... *My name is . . .*

Soy... *I am . . .*

¿Y tú? ¿Cómo te llamas?
And you? What's your name?

To introduce others, say:

Éste es mi amigo...
This is my (male) friend . . .

Ésta es mi amiga...
This is my (female) friend . . .

Se llama... *His/Her name is . . .*

> Cuaderno de gramática, p. 1, Act. 2

To respond to an introduction, say:

¡Mucho gusto! *Nice to meet you!*

Encantado/a.*
Delighted to meet you.

Igualmente. *Same here.*

> *If you're male, use **Encantado**. If you're female, use **Encantada**. You'll learn more about masculine and feminine endings in Chapter 2.

Communication for All Students

Pair Work

7 Ask students to work in pairs. Have them come up with as many **saludos** and **despedidas** as they can, referring to what they have learned so far.

Group Work

Así se dice Have students form groups of three and choose one person to be the "new student."

First, the other two students greet each other as friends, using expressions from **Así se dice** on page 21. Then one introduces the new student to the other, using the introductions presented in **Así se dice** on this page. You might then have students introduce themselves and their group members to other classmates.

9 **¿Cómo respondes?** *How do you respond?*

Escuchemos/Escribamos Look over the **Así se dice** section on page 22. Then, listen as some people at a party introduce themselves to you. Respond with one or two appropriate phrases. Scripts and answers on p.15G.

CD 1 Tr. 12

10 **Mini-situaciones**

Leamos/Hablemos What would you say in the following situations? First find the expressions you need in **Así se dice**. Then, with a partner, act out each mini-situation.

1. A friend introduces you to a new student.
   Possible answers: 1. ¡Mucho gusto!; Hola; Me llamo...
2. You want to ask the person sitting next to you what his or her name is. ¿Cómo te llamas?
3. You've just been introduced to your new Spanish teacher. Mucho gusto.
4. You want to tell the new classmate who you are. Me llamo...; Soy...
5. Your new counselor has just said **Mucho gusto.** ¡Mucho gusto!; Encantado/a.
6. You want to introduce your friend Ana to another classmate. Ésta es mi amiga Ana.

11 **Gramática en contexto**

Leamos/Escribamos A friend wants to introduce someone to you. Choose your responses from the expressions you've learned. Some blanks may have more than one possible answer.

TU AMIGO	Hola.
TÚ	___1___. ¡Hola!
TU AMIGO	Ésta es mi amiga Patricia.
TÚ	___2___, Patricia. Mucho gusto
PATRICIA	Igualmente. Eh, perdón. ¿Cómo te ___3___, por favor? llamas
TÚ	Me ___4___ ___5___. llamo [student's name]
TU AMIGO	Bueno, ___6___ clase. Tengo que irme. tengo
TÚ	Hasta ___7___. mañana/luego
PATRICIA	___8___. Chao

agosto

DOM	LUN	MAR	MIER	JUE	VIER	SAB
1 Sta. Esperanza	**2** N.S. de los Ang.	**3** Sta. Lydia	**4** Sto. Domingo de G.	**5** San Emigdio	**6** San Justo	**7** San Cayetano
8 San Emiliano	**9** San Román	**10** Sta. Paula	**11** Sta. Susana	**12** Sta. Clara	**13** Sta. Aurora	**14** Sta. Eusebia

---

Nota gramatical

Have you noticed that Spanish uses upside-down punctuation marks to begin a question (**¿**) and an exclamation (**¡**)? An accent mark is sometimes needed over a vowel (**á, é, í, ó, ú**), usually to show which syllable is stressed. The mark on the **ñ** (as in **mañana**) is called the *tilde*. It indicates the sound *ny* as in *canyon*. How many of these new punctuation marks can you find in the **Así se dice** sections on pages 21 and 22? All of them.

Cuaderno de gramática, p. 2, Acts. 3–5

Más práctica gramatical, p. 38, Act. 1

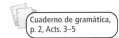

Nota cultural

Many people in Spain and Latin America are Roman Catholic. Children are often named after the Catholic saint celebrated on the day they are born, or after very important saints. Common first names are José and Juan Pablo for males, María José and Magdalena for females. Some common Jewish names include Miriam and Ester for girls, and Isaac and Jacobo for boys. Islamic names include Omar and Ismael for boys, and Jasmín and Zoraida for girls.

Cultures and Communities

Culture Note
Mesoamerican cultures, used to adopting the religion of conquering groups, assimilated the saints of the Spanish conquerors into their ritual life. The similarities in cultural themes (Christ as a sacrifice, saints viewed as minor deities) facilitated adaptation. Aztecs honored ancestors during autumn rites, just as the Spanish celebrated All Saints Day.

Game
Santo y Seña Stand at the door and show a picture flash card to students in a different row each day as they leave class. They must each tell you the appropriate word or phrase in Spanish before they can leave. Change the picture after every student, shuffling the cards periodically.

Teaching Resources
pp. 21–26

PRINT 📖

▸ Lesson Planner, p. 3
▸ TPR Storytelling Book, pp. 1, 4
▸ Listening Activities, pp. 3, 7
▸ Activities for Communication, pp. 1–2, 75, 78–79, 137–138
▸ Cuaderno de gramática, pp. 1–4
▸ Grammar Tutor for Students of Spanish, Chapter 1
▸ Cuaderno de actividades, pp. 4–6
▸ Cuaderno para hispanohablantes, pp. 1–5
▸ Testing Program, pp. 1–4
▸ Alternative Assessment Guide, p. 32
▸ Student Make-Up Assignments, Chapter 1

MEDIA

▸ One-Stop Planner
▸ Audio Compact Discs, CD 1, Trs. 11–13, 34–35, 29
▸ Teaching Transparencies, 1-1; **Más práctica gramatical** Answers; Cuaderno de gramática Answers
▸ Interactive CD-ROM Tutor, Disc 1

Presenting
Así se dice

Model these expressions, and have students repeat after you, imitating your gestures. (**regular** —thumb up; **horrible**—thumb down; **más o menos**—hand rocking side to side with palm down; **estupendo** and **excelente** —emphatic gestures) Then have pairs practice asking and answering how they are doing, using the appropriate gestures.

Answers
14 *Possible answers:*
1. Bien, gracias.
2. Mucho gusto, Charín.
3. Regular.
4. Me llamo *(name)*.
5. Adiós.

---

12 **Nuevos amigos** *New friends*

Hablemos Role-play the following conversation with a classmate using expressions from **Así se dice** on pages 21–22. If you'd like to use a Spanish name or nickname, choose one from the list on page 5. *Possible conversation:*

ESTUDIANTE 1	*Greet your classmate.*	Hola; Buenos días; Buenas tardes.
ESTUDIANTE 2	*Respond and introduce yourself.*	Buenos días, soy...; Hola, me llamo...
ESTUDIANTE 1	*Say "nice to meet you" and introduce yourself.*	Mucho gusto, soy...; Encantado/a, me llamo...
ESTUDIANTE 2	*Respond to the introduction.*	¡Mucho gusto!; Igualmente.
ESTUDIANTE 1	*Say you have class now.*	Bueno, tengo clase.
ESTUDIANTE 2	*Say that you also have class and say goodbye.*	Tengo clase. Adiós.
ESTUDIANTE 1	*Say that you'll see your new friend tomorrow.*	Hasta mañana.

Así se dice

Asking how someone is and saying how you are

To find out how a friend is, ask:

¿Cómo estás? *How are you?*   **¿Qué tal?** *How's it going?*

¿Y tú? *And you?*

Your friend might say:

Estoy (bastante) bien, gracias. *I'm (pretty) well, thanks.*   **Regular.** *Okay.*

Yo también. *Me too.*   **Más o menos.** *So-so.*

Estupendo/a. *Great.*   **(Muy) mal.** *(Very) bad.*

Excelente. *Great.*   **¡Horrible!** *Horrible!*

Más práctica gramatical, p. 38, Act. 2

Cuaderno de actividades, pp. 5–6, Acts. 5–7

Cuaderno de gramática, p. 3, Acts. 6–7

---

13 **¿Cómo estás?**

Escuchemos/Escribamos As each friend tells Sara how he or she is, write the person's name under the appropriate heading. *Scripts and answers on p.15G.*

CD 1 Tr. 13

MODELO   Buenas tardes, Felipe. ¿Qué tal?
Regular, gracias. ¿Y tú?

---

14 **¿Cómo contestas?** *How do you answer?*

Leamos/Escribamos How would you answer the following? Select your responses from the expressions you've learned. *See possible answers below.*

1. ¡Hola! ¿Qué tal?
2. Ésta es mi amiga Charín.
3. ¿Cómo estás?
4. Soy Eduardo Robledo. ¿Y tú?
5. ¡Hasta luego!

A lo nuestro

In Spanish, there are many ways to ask a person how he or she is doing. Throughout Spain and Latin America you will hear **¿Qué pasa?** *(What's happening?)* and **¿Qué hay?/¿Qué tal?** *(What's up?)* In Mexico, you'll also hear **¿Qué hubo?** or **¿Qué onda?**

Communication for All Students

Visual Learners

• Use gestures or sketch visual cues on index cards to represent each functional phrase. Have students call out the phrase as you perform the gesture or show the card.

• Students should make cards representing these phrases. They can use the cards to verify comprehension and also for pair and small-group practice.

Cooperative Learning

13 Divide the class into groups of three. Assign one student to be the scribe and two to be performers. After agreeing on the correct responses to the items in Activity 13, the group should then make up a conversation to present to the class. Group members should be assigned the same grade based on the group's written responses and performance.

Gramática

Subject pronouns *tú* and *yo*

1. Use the pronoun **yo** to refer to yourself. In Spanish, **yo** *(I)* is not capitalized, except at the beginning of a sentence. Use **tú** *(you)* when you're talking to another student, a friend, or to someone who is about your own age. Notice that **tú** has an accent.

2. In Chapter 4 you'll learn a different pronoun to use when speaking to someone older than you or when you want to be polite to a stranger. You'll also discover that subject pronouns like these aren't used as often in Spanish as in English.

3. How many expressions can you find in **Así se dice** on pages 21–24 where the pronoun **yo** is implied but not stated? *

Cuaderno de gramática, p. 4, Acts. 8–10

Más práctica gramatical, p. 38, Act. 3

15 Gramática en contexto

Leamos Which pronoun (**tú** or **yo**) is implied but not stated in each sentence?

1. ¿Cómo te llamas? tú
2. Me llamo Mercedes Margarita. yo
3. Soy Francisco. yo
4. ¿Cómo estás, Francisco? tú
5. Estoy bien, gracias. yo

16 Charla *Chitchat*

Escribamos Mercedes is talking to a new classmate. Using words or phrases you've learned, write their conversation.

MERCEDES	*greets her friend*
ELENA	*responds and introduces her friend Pedro*
MERCEDES	*says it is nice to meet Pedro*
PEDRO	*responds and asks Mercedes how she is*
MERCEDES	*responds and says she has class*
ELENA	*says she also has to go now*
ALL	*say goodbye*

Sample answer below.

17 Mini-drama

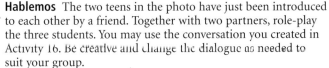

Hablemos The two teens in the photo have just been introduced to each other by a friend. Together with two partners, role-play the three students. You may use the conversation you created in Activity 16. Be creative and change the dialogue as needed to suit your group.

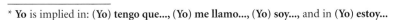

---

* **Yo** is implied in: **(Yo) tengo que...**, **(Yo) me llamo...**, **(Yo) soy...**, and in **(Yo) estoy...**

Connections and Comparisons

Native Speakers

Be aware that some native speakers from Latin America may use the second-person singular pronoun **vos** and its verb forms. Explain that while these are accepted regionally in colloquial contexts, **tú** is the internationally accepted pronoun and verb form.

Language Note

In Argentina, Uruguay, Paraguay, Central America, and the Mexican state of Chiapas, **vos** is typically used instead of **tú** as the informal subject pronoun. This practice is called **voseo**. There is regional variation in the conjugation of **vos** forms.

STANDARDS: 1.1, 1.3, 3.1, 4.1, 5.1

Presenting Gramática

Subject pronouns tú and yo
Give several sentences with either **tú** or **yo**. Students point to themselves whenever you say **yo**, and to another student as you say **tú**. Point out the accent mark on **tú**.

Teaching Suggestion

17 Allow time for students to prepare and practice the mini-drama. Circulate among the groups to check pronunciation and language.

Challenge

17 Ask groups to perform their mini-drama for the rest of the class.

Assess

▶ Testing Program, pp. 1–4
Quiz 1-1A, Quiz 1-1B
Audio CD 1, Tr. 29

▶ Student Make-Up Assignments, Chapter 1, Alternative Quiz

▶ Alternative Assessment Guide, p. 32

Answers

16 *Sample answer:*

MERCEDES:	¡Hola, Elena! ¿Qué tal?
ELENA:	Muy bien, Mercedes. Éste es mi amigo Pedro.
MERCEDES:	Mucho gusto, Pedro.
PEDRO:	Igualmente. ¿Cómo estás?
MERCEDES:	Muy bien, gracias, pero tengo clase.
ELENA:	Sí, yo tengo que irme.
TODOS:	¡Adiós! ¡Hasta luego!

La distancia interpersonal

In a Spanish-speaking country, you may encounter differences in "interpersonal distance," or the distance people keep from each other when they are together. Answer these questions to see if you can keep the right distance in various settings.

Para discutir...

1. You're sitting on a crowded bus. When one more passenger gets on, you should . . .
   a. move over and make room for the newcomer, even if it means rubbing shoulders with the person next to you.
   b. keep your place and avoid touching your neighbor.
2. You're standing on the street corner talking to a close friend. Your friend will probably expect you to stand . . .
   a. about an arm's length away.
   b. close enough to allow your friend to touch you without reaching.

Vamos a comprenderlo

1. a. Buses are often crowded, and people expect to squeeze together. This may take some getting used to!
2. b. Generally, Spanish speakers stand and sit closer to one another than most people in the United States do. Your Spanish-speaking friend might think you're a little bit unfriendly if you stand too far away.

Remember that there is seldom a single right answer in questions of etiquette. A good rule to follow in a new country is to watch what others do and let them take the lead in unfamiliar situations. As is said in Spanish, **Adónde fueres, haz lo que vieres**. *Wherever you go, do as you see. (When in Rome, do as the Romans do.)*

Connections and Comparisons

Multicultural Links

• Edwin Hall, an American anthropologist, has documented four distance zones in the United States: intimate (up to 18 inches apart), personal ($1^1/_2$ to 4 feet apart), social (4 to 12 feet apart), and public (12 to 25 feet apart).

• How people form lines can also indicate cultural differences. In Britain people usually form straight lines and stand quite far apart; in Latin America lines are tighter and meander more.

• Another cultural difference is how people walk together. For example, in the U.S., friends usually walk together side by side but do not touch; Arab, European, and Latin American women often walk with their arms linked.

Objectives Asking and saying how old someone is; asking where someone is from and saying where you are from

go.hrw.com
WV3 SPAIN-1

Así se dice

Asking and saying how old someone is

To ask how old someone is, say:

¿Cuántos años tienes?
How old are you?

¿Cuántos años tiene?
How old is (he/she)?

To answer, say:

Tengo ... años.
I'm . . . years old.

Tiene ... años.
(He/She) is . . . years old.

Vocabulario

Los números del 0 al 30

CD-ROM 1
DVD 1

cero

uno

dos

tres

cuatro

cinco

seis

siete

ocho

nueve

diez

Más práctica gramatical, p. 39, Act. 4 →

Cuaderno de actividades, p. 7, Acts. 9–10

Cuaderno de gramática, p. 5, Acts. 11–13

11 once	12 doce	13 trece	14 catorce	15 quince
16 dieciséis	17 diecisiete	18 dieciocho	19 diecinueve	20 veinte
21 veintiuno	22 veintidós	23 veintitrés	24 veinticuatro	25 veinticinco
26 veintiséis	27 veintisiete	28 veintiocho	29 veintinueve	30 treinta

Communication for All Students

Challenge/Math Link

Write number sequences on the board or overhead such as 1,3,5. . . (odd numbers) 1,2,4,8. . . (each number is added to itself to get the next number). Ask students to work in pairs to complete the number sequences up to 30. Have students read their solutions to the class. For further challenge, ask students to create their own number sequences and present them for the class to solve.

Auditory Learners

In some Spanish-speaking countries, telephone numbers are six digits. Dictate three, two-digit numbers to students. After dictating the numbers, show the correct number on a transparency so that students can check their accuracy. Alternatively, give students a list of imaginary names and phone numbers. Say a number and ask students to match that number with the correct name.

Teaching Resources
pp. 27–30

PRINT
▶ Lesson Planner, p. 4
▶ TPR Storytelling Book, pp. 2, 4
▶ Listening Activities, pp. 4, 8
▶ Activities for Communication, pp. 3–4, 76, 78–79, 137–138
▶ Cuaderno de gramática, pp. 5–6
▶ Grammar Tutor for Students of Spanish, Chapter 1
▶ Cuaderno de actividades, pp. 7–8
▶ Cuaderno para hispanohablantes, pp. 1–5
▶ Testing Program, pp. 5–8
▶ Alternative Assessment Guide, p. 32
▶ Student Make-Up Assignments, Chapter 1

MEDIA
▶ One-Stop Planner
▶ Audio Compact Discs, CD 1, Trs. 14–15, 36–37, 30
▶ Teaching Transparencies 1-2, 1-A; **Más práctica gramatical** Answers; Cuaderno de Gramática Answers
▶ Interactive CD-ROM Tutor, Disc 1

Bell Work
Have students use the questions **¿Cómo te llamas?** and **¿Cómo estás?** to write a dialogue between two people who have just met.

Presenting
Así se dice, Vocabulario
Make a set of cards numbered 1–30. Give a card to each student. Say the numbers and ask **¿Quién tiene... años?** The student with that card says **Tengo... años.** Write numbers in order on the board or use *Teaching Transparency 1-A.* Point to numbers and have students write or say them. To wrap up, do a dictation with numbers 0–30.

Teaching Resources
pp. 27–30

PRINT
▸ Lesson Planner, p. 4
▸ TPR Storytelling Book, pp. 2, 4
▸ Listening Activities, pp. 4, 8
▸ Activities for Communication, pp. 3–4, 76, 78–79, 137–138
▸ Cuaderno de gramática, pp. 5–6
▸ Grammar Tutor for Students of Spanish, Chapter 1
▸ Cuaderno de actividades, pp. 7–8
▸ Cuaderno para hispanohablantes, pp. 1–5
▸ Testing Program, pp. 5–8
▸ Alternative Assessment Guide, p. 32
▸ Student Make-Up Assignments, Chapter 1

MEDIA
▸ One-Stop Planner
▸ Audio Compact Discs, CD 1, Trs. 14–15, 36–37, 30
▸ Teaching Transparencies 1-2, 1-A; **Más práctica gramatical** Answers; Cuaderno de gramática Answers
▸ Interactive CD-ROM Tutor, Disc 1

Presenting
Así se dice, Nota gramatical

The verb ser: singular forms
Give students three-by-five index cards. On one side have students write a name from p. 5 and on the other side place names from maps on pp. xxiii–xxix. Model questions and responses by pointing to the cards and using **¿De dónde eres? Soy de...** and **¿De dónde es? Es de...**

Answers
20 *Possible conversation:*
—Hola, soy... Tengo ... años. ¿Cómo te llamas?; —Me llamo... ;
 —¿Cuántos años tienes?;
 —Tengo ... años.

18 **Edades** *Ages* Scripts and answers on p.15G.

Escuchemos Daniel is showing Adriana pictures in the family album. Listen as he tells how old each relative is. Then match the correct picture to the age he gives.

CD 1
Tr. 14

a.

b.

c.

d.

e.

19 **Número secreto** *Secret number*

Hablemos Try to guess the secret number your partner is thinking of (it must be between zero and 30). If you're wrong, your partner will point up or down to indicate a higher or lower number. Keep trying until you guess right. Then switch roles and play again.

20 **Presentaciones** *Introductions*

Hablemos Introduce yourself to the three classmates sitting closest to you. Greet them and ask each one's name and age. Then introduce your three new friends to the class.
See possible answers below.

MODELO —Hola, ¿cómo te llamas?
—Me llamo...

Nota gramatical

The words **soy**, **eres**, and **es** are all forms of the verb **ser**, which is one way to say *to be* in Spanish. When talking about where someone is from, forms of **ser** are always used.

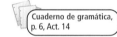
Cuaderno de gramática, p. 6, Act. 14

Más práctica gramatical, pp. 39–40, Acts. 5–6

Así se dice

Asking where someone is from and saying where you're from

To find out where someone is from, ask:

¿De dónde eres?
Where are you from?

¿De dónde es...?
Where is . . . from?

To answer, say:

Soy de los Estados Unidos.
I'm from the United States.

Es de...
(She/He) is from . . .

Cuaderno de actividades, p. 8, Acts. 11–13

Communication for All Students

Slower Pace
Students may ask how **soy, eres,** and **es** can all be forms of the same verb. Write in one column: *I'm the teacher. Are you the new student? This is my friend.* In a second column, write: **Soy la profesora. ¿Eres el estudiante nuevo? Éste es mi amigo.** Ask students to find the Spanish forms corresponding to the English verb. Then ask them what is similar about the forms of *to be* and **ser.**

Challenge
19 Teach students the phrase **Pienso en un número entre (uno y treinta)** and the words **más, menos, sí,** and **no.**

Re-Entry
Before having the students break into groups, briefly review expressions from **Así se dice,** pages 22, 24, and 27.

21 ¿De dónde es?

Escuchemos/Escribamos You'll overhear students talking at a party. As you listen, write the name of the country each person is from. Then choose three of the students and write a sentence telling where each one is from.

CD 1
Tr. 15

1. Gabriela
2. Maricarmen
3. David
4. Antonio
5. Laura Alicia
6. Pedro

Scripts and answers on p. 15G.

Vocabulario extra

Los países hispanohablantes

(la) Argentina	España	(el) Paraguay
Bolivia	los Estados	(el) Perú
Chile	Unidos	Puerto Rico
Colombia	Guatemala	(la) República
Costa Rica	Honduras	Dominicana
Cuba	México	(el) Uruguay
(el) Ecuador	Nicaragua	Venezuela
El Salvador	Panamá	

22 Gramática en contexto

Hablemos Ask five classmates where they are from and note each person's name and place of origin. Then introduce one of them to the class: **Ésta es Shawna; es de Allentown.** Anyone else from Allentown raises his or her hand and says **Yo también.**
Possible questions: ¿De dónde eres? ¿Cómo te llamas? *Possible answers:* Soy de.../Me llamo.../Soy....

23 Gramática en contexto

Hablemos You and your partner will each list five famous women and five famous men. Include as many Spanish speakers as you can. Then take turns asking and answering where each famous person is from.
See possible answers below.

MODELO —¿De dónde es Arantxa Sánchez Vicario?
—Es de España.

Arantxa Sánchez Vicario

24 Amigos hispanos *Hispanic friends*

Escribamos Write at least one sentence about each of these people. Tell each person's name and age, and what country he or she is from. What is the last name of each student's father and mother? Then, find the two countries on the map on pages xxiv–xxv and identify their capital cities. See possible answers below.

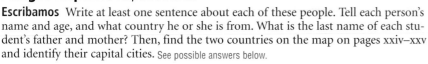

Cultures and Communities

Culture Notes

• Many high school students in Spain and Latin America have a photo I.D. card (**carné de identidad**). These cards double as library cards at school. National identification cards are issued to all citizens of Spain and of most Latin American countries.

• Tell students that **bachillerato** is equivalent to *high school degree* or *diploma*.

Game

¿De dónde eres? Holding a soft foam ball or beach ball, say **Soy de (Chile).** Tossing the ball to a student, ask **¿De dónde eres?** The student who catches answers **Soy de los Estados Unidos** and then tosses the ball to another student, asking **¿De dónde eres?** Students can answer with the town they are from or with Spanish-speaking cities or countries.

Additional Practice

22 As homework, have students interview at least five people. (school staff, faculty members, or other students) Have them write the names of the people they interview in large, colorful lettering and then write captions. For example, **Ésta es (la señora Carfora), es de (California)** or **Éste es (Nico), es de (El Salvador).**

Photo Flash!

At age 17, Spanish professional tennis player Arantxa Sánchez Vicario won the French Open, her first Grand Slam tournament. She has since won several international tournaments, including the Australian Open, the U.S. Open, and Wimbledon, and is considered one of the top tennis players in the world.

Language Note

24 Tell students that dates in Spanish-speaking countries are often abbreviated in a day-month-year format: 5-10-03. (5 de octubre de 2003)

Answers

23 *Possible answers:*
Roberto Alomar—Puerto Rico; don Francisco—Chile; Julio Iglesias—España; Alberto Fujimori—Perú; Rigoberta Menchú—Guatemala; Gloria Estefan—Cuba

24 *Possible answers:*
Jesús María García Jove es de España. En 2004 tiene diecisiete años. El apellido de su padre es García. El apellido de su madre es Jove. La capital de España es Madrid. María Elvira Ramírez Balboa es de Colombia. En 2004 tiene dieciséis años. El apellido de su padre es Ramírez y el apellido de su madre es Balboa. La capital de Colombia es Bogotá.

STANDARDS: 1.2, 1.3, 2.1, 5.2

Answers

25 1. Cómo
2. cómo
3. De dónde
4. Cuántos

26 1. ¿Cómo estás?
2. ¿De dónde eres?
3. ¿Cuántos años tienes?
4. ¿Cómo te llamas?

27 *Possible conversation:*
—¡Hola! ¿Cómo estás?
—Muy bien, gracias. ¿Y tú?
—Bastante bien. Me llamo... ¿Cómo te llamas tú?
—Me llamo... Y tú, ¿cómo te llamas?
—Me llamo... Mucho gusto. Y tú, ¿cómo te llamas?
—Me llamo... Tengo... años. ¿Cuántos años tienes tú?
—Tengo... años. ¿Y tú?
—Tengo... años, ¿y tú?
—Yo tengo... años. ¿De dónde eres?
—Soy de... ¿Y tú?
—Soy de... también.

Gramática

Forming questions with question words

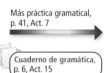

1. So far, you've asked questions using several different words.

¿Cómo estás? *How are you?*
¿Cómo te llamas? *What's your name?*
¿Cuántos años tienes? *How old are you?*
¿De dónde eres? *Where are you from?*

To ask questions like these, put the question word at the beginning of the sentence. These question words have accents.

2. Notice that **¿cómo?** can mean *how?* or *what?* depending on context. What does this tell you about translating?*

Más práctica gramatical, p. 41, Act. 7

Cuaderno de gramática, p. 6, Act. 15

25 **Gramática en contexto** See answers below.

Leamos/Escribamos It's the first day of school for Ana, a new student at a **colegio** *(secondary school)* in Madrid. Fill in each blank with the correct word.

ANA Buenos días. ¿____1____ (Cómo/Cuántos) estás?

FEDERICO Bien, ¿y tú?

ANA Regular. Oye, soy Ana. Y tú, ¿____2____ (de dónde/cómo) te llamas?

FEDERICO Me llamo Federico. Tú no eres de aquí, ¿verdad? ¿____3____ (Cuántos/De dónde) eres?

ANA Soy de Andalucía. ¿____4____ (Cuántos/Cómo) años tienes?

FEDERICO Tengo quince años. ¿Y tú?

ANA Yo tengo quince también.

26 **Gramática en contexto** See answers below.

Leamos You're listening to Javier as he is being interviewed over the phone for a survey. Below are the answers Javier gave. For each answer, choose the question from the box.

1. Bien, gracias.
2. De Madrid.
3. Catorce.
4. Javier Francisco González.

> ¿Cuántos años tienes?
> ¿Cómo te llamas?
> ¿Cómo estás?
> ¿De dónde eres?

27 **Tres amigos** *Three friends* See possible conversation below.

Hablemos Get to know the people in your class! Form a group with three students you don't know well and take turns interviewing each other. Ask each other's names, how you're feeling today, how old you are, and where you're from.

28 **Mi amigo/a se llama...** *My friend's name is . . .*

Escribamos Select one of your classmates from Activity 27 and write a brief paragraph telling what you've learned about him or her. *Possible answer:*
Mi amigo/a se llama... Tiene... años y es de...

*There's not always a one-to-one match between words in different languages.

Teacher to Teacher

For Patricia, the question is . . .

"Your students can practice forming questions playing a simple Jeopardy© game. Instead of subject categories, use small numbers (these will also help students review), and arrange them on the board. Place a bell on a small table between two students facing each other in their seats. One student picks the number category. Read a prepared answer such as **Ana tiene diez años**. The student who rings first gets to give the question **¿Cuántos años tiene Ana?**"

Patricia Ahrens
Central Junior High
West Lawn, Pennsylvania

CD 1
Trs. 16–20

¿De dónde eres?

Panorama cultural will introduce you to real Spanish speakers from around the globe, including Europe, Latin America, and the United States. In this chapter, we asked some people to tell us who they are and where they're from.

Miguel
Madrid, España

"Hola, buenas tardes. Me llamo Miguel Silva. Tengo dieciséis años y soy de Madrid".
CD 1
Tr. 18

Sandra
Venezuela

"Yo me llamo Sandra Terán y soy de Venezuela".
CD 1 Tr. 19

Ivette
Ponce, Puerto Rico

"Mi nombre es Ivette Marcano. Soy de Ponce, Puerto Rico".
CD 1
Tr. 17

Para pensar y hablar...
Things to think and talk about . . .

A. Can you find the places Mauricio, Ivette, Miguel, and Sandra are from on the maps in the front of your book? Using the legend on the maps, can you figure out how far apart all four countries are from each other?

B. What do you think these four countries are like? With a partner, describe each country in three or four sentences, using the maps in the front of the book and information you already know. Then, share your descriptions with another team.

Mauricio
San José, Costa Rica

"Me llamo Mauricio. Vivo aquí también en San José, Costa Rica y tengo quince años".
CD 1 Tr. 20

Teaching Resources
p. 31

PRINT
▸ Video Guide, pp. 5–7, 10
▸ Cuaderno de actividades, p. 12

MEDIA
▸ One-Stop Planner
▸ Video Program, Videocassette 1, 16:26–18:30
▸ DVD Tutor, Disc 1
▸ Audio Compact Discs, CD 1, Trs. 16–20
▸ Interactive CD-ROM Tutor, Disc 1

Presenting
Panorama cultural

Read the interviews as a class. Ask **¿De dónde es Miguel?** and **¿Cuántos años tiene él?** Repeat this process with the other interviewees. You may also want to play the video and then have students ask each other questions about the interviewees. Have students answer the **Preguntas**.

Preguntas

1. **¿Cómo se llama el chico de España?** (Miguel)
2. **¿De dónde es Ivette?** (Ponce, Puerto Rico)
3. **¿Cuántos años tiene la persona de Costa Rica?** (quince)
4. **¿De dónde es el chico que tiene dieciséis años?** (Madrid)
5. **¿Cómo se llama la chica de Venezuela?** (Sandra)

Connections and Comparisons

Thinking Critically

Analyzing Ask students whether they have visited someone from another country or state. When they introduced themselves, did they tell where they were from? Did their hosts make assumptions about them based on stereotypes?

Have students work in small groups to analyze how stereotypes about people from other states or countries influence their beliefs about those people. Have each group present its ideas to the class.

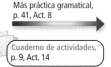
Teaching Resources
pp. 32–35

PRINT
▸ Lesson Planner, p. 5
▸ TPR Storytelling Book, pp. 3, 4
▸ Listening Activities, pp. 5, 9
▸ Activities for Communication, pp. 5–6, 77, 78–79, 137–138
▸ Cuaderno de gramática, pp. 7–8
▸ Grammar Tutor for Students of Spanish, Chapter 1
▸ Cuaderno de actividades, pp. 9–10
▸ Cuaderno para hispanohablantes, pp. 1–5
▸ Testing Program, pp. 9–12
▸ Alternative Assessment Guide, p. 32
▸ Student Make-Up Assignments, Chapter 1

MEDIA
▸ One-Stop Planner
▸ Audio Compact Discs, CD 1, Trs. 21–27, 31, 38–39
▸ Teaching Transparencies 1-3, 1-B, 1-C; **Más práctica gramatical** Answers; Cuaderno de gramática Answers
▸ Interactive CD-ROM Tutor, Disc 1

Bell Work
Have students answer the following questions in writing: ¿Cómo te llamas? ¿De dónde eres? ¿Cuántos años tienes?

Presenting
Así se dice
Using *Teaching Transparencies* 1-B and 1-C, point to a word and mime whether or not you like the item using **(No) me gusta…** and the Spanish equivalent.

Vocabulario
Model pronunciation by teaching a word's last syllable first and then building "backwards." (-ción, -tación, natación)

Así se dice

Talking about likes and dislikes

To find out what a friend likes, ask:

¿Qué te gusta?
What do you like?

¿Te gusta el fútbol?
Do you like soccer?

Your friend might answer:

Me gusta la comida mexicana.
I like Mexican food.

Me gusta mucho el tenis.
I like tennis a lot.

No me gusta la natación.
I don't like swimming.

Sí, pero me gusta más el béisbol.
Yes, but I like baseball more.

Más práctica gramatical, p. 41, Act. 8

Cuaderno de actividades, p. 9, Act. 14

29 Planes Scripts and answers on p.15H.

CD 1 Tr. 21

Escuchemos Elena and Carlos are trying to make plans. As you listen to them talk, note which items Elena likes and doesn't like. Is there anything she and Carlos both like? What would you suggest they do together?

1. el voleibol
2. la pizza
3. la música pop
4. la comida mexicana
5. el restaurante Taco Paco

Vocabulario

Los deportes *Sports*

el baloncesto
el béisbol
el fútbol
el fútbol norteamericano
la natación
el tenis
el voleibol

La comida *Food*

CD-ROM 1 / DVD 1

la cafetería
el chocolate
la comida mexicana (italiana, china…)
la ensalada
la fruta
la pizza

La música

el jazz
la música clásica
la música pop
la música rock
la música de…

Las clases

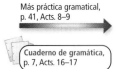

el español
la clase de inglés
la tarea *homework*

Más práctica gramatical, p. 41, Acts. 8–9

Cuaderno de gramática, p. 7, Acts. 16–17

Communication for All Students

Additional Practice
Write *Food*, *Sports*, and *School* as column heads across the top of a transparency. Ask students to name some things in English that they like and dislike in each category. Write their responses under the category heads. Leave room so that students can fill in the Spanish equivalents.

Visual Learners
Have students make review cards for new vocabulary. They can draw or paste pictures of sports, food, or school-related items on one side of each card and write the Spanish word on the back of the card. You might have students share their cards with their classmates by saying **Me gusta…** and **No me gusta…**

Gramática

Nouns and definite articles

All the words in the **Vocabulario** on page 32 are nouns—words used to name people, places, and things. As you can see, all the nouns in the list have **el** or **la** *(the)* before them. Generally **el** is used before masculine nouns and **la** before feminine nouns. When learning new nouns, always learn the definite article that goes with the noun at the same time.

Cuaderno de actividades, pp. 9–10, Acts. 15–16

Cuaderno de gramática, p. 8, Acts. 18–20

Más práctica gramatical, p. 41, Act. 9

---

30 **Gramática en contexto**

Escribamos For each category listed, write a sentence stating one thing in that category that you like and another that you don't like. Be sure to use the correct definite article (**el** or **la**) in your sentence.

MODELO   deportes
Me gusta el tenis.
No me gusta el fútbol.

1. deportes   3. música
2. comida   4. clases

31 **¿Te gusta...?** *Do you like . . .?*

Hablemos With a partner, take turns asking and answering whether you like the types of sports, music, food, and schoolwork listed in the **Vocabulario** on page 32. If your partner likes the same thing you do, you can say **¡A mí también!** *(Me too!)*

32 **Una fiesta**

Escuchemos/Escribamos You're in charge of planning a party for Diana. Listen as a friend asks Diana what she likes and doesn't like. Take notes. Then, based on your list, decide one sport, one food, and one kind of music you would include in a party to please her.
Scripts and answers on p. 15H.

CD 1
Tr. 22

33 **¡Juego de ingenio!** *Guessing game!*

Escribamos/Hablemos Work with a partner. First write three guesses about what your partner likes and doesn't like. Ask if your partner likes these items. Take turns asking and answering, to see if you guessed right.

MODELO   —¿Te gusta la natación?
—Sí, me gusta mucho la natación. *or* No, no me gusta.

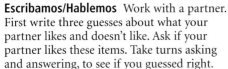

También se puede decir...

Just like English, Spanish has different words that express the same idea. The word you use often depends on where you're from.

In Spain, the common word for basketball is **el baloncesto**. In many parts of the Spanish-speaking world, you'll also hear **el basquetbol**, or **el básquet**.

Possible conversation:
¿A ti te gusta el béisbol?
Sí, me gusta.
A mí también. *or* Pues, a mí no.
¿Te gusta la música de Pearl Jam?
No, no me gusta.

SUGERENCIA

Although the best way to learn a new language is by spending time in a country where that language is spoken, you can still make the most out of your classroom opportunities to hear, speak, read, and write Spanish. From the moment you walk into the classroom, use as much Spanish as you can. Pay attention to everything your teacher says, even if you don't understand it all.

Connections and Comparisons

Challenge
31 Have students poll five people about their likes and dislikes. They should use sports, food, and school vocabulary. Have students report their findings to the class in an oral or written presentation. You might have them organize their collective results into graph or chart form.

Native Speakers
The **También se puede decir...** features offer an excellent chance to point out different dialects and vocabularies. Ask native speakers to share with the class regional vocabulary differences they may know.

Answers

35 *Sample answers:*
—¿Cómo te llamas?
—Me llamo Pilar. ¿Y tú?
—Me llamo Miguel. ¿Cuántos años tienes?
—Tengo catorce años. ¿Cuántos años tienes tú?
—Yo tengo dieciséis años. ¿Qué te gusta?
—Me gusta la música. También me gusta el béisbol.
—Me gusta el fútbol. Me gusta la ensalada. También me gusta la clase de historia.
—Pues, mucho gusto, Miguel.
—Igualmente, Pilar.

---

34 **La nueva estudiante** *The new student*

✏️ **Leamos/Escribamos** Felipe is interviewing the new exchange student from Managua for the school newspaper. Take the role of the new student and write the words for his or her part. Possible answers:

FELIPE	Hola. Soy Felipe. ¿Cómo te llamas?
ESTUDIANTE	**1.** ———. Me llamo...
FELIPE	¿Cómo estás?
ESTUDIANTE	**2.** ———. ¿———? *Regular. ¿Y tú?*
FELIPE	Bien. ¿De dónde eres?
ESTUDIANTE	**3.** ———. Soy de...
FELIPE	¿Y cuántos años tienes?
ESTUDIANTE	**4.** ———. Tengo ... años.

FELIPE	El béisbol es muy popular en Nicaragua. ¿Te gusta el béisbol?
ESTUDIANTE	**5.** ———. Sí, me gusta.
FELIPE	Personalmente, me gusta más el fútbol.
ESTUDIANTE	**6.** ¿———? ¿Te gusta el jazz?
FELIPE	No, no me gusta. Bueno, gracias y hasta luego.
ESTUDIANTE	**7.** ———. Chao.

35 **¡Mucho gusto!** See sample answers below.

👥 **Hablemos** Work with a partner and take turns playing the roles of Pilar and Miguel. Show each other the photos below from your scrapbooks to tell each other your name, how old you are, where you're from, and what you like.

A lo nuestro

There are many little words in Spanish that you can use to connect your ideas and to help you express yourself better. Some of these words are: **y** *(and)*, **también** *(too, also)*, and **más** *(more)*. Look back at the interviews in the **Panorama cultural** (p. 31) and see how one of these words is used.

Miguel Aguirre, 16 años
Barcelona, España

Pilar Morales, 14 años
Guatemala, Guatemala

VALENZUELA

Communication for All Students

Cooperative Learning

35 Write the following numbers and topics on the board: 1) Sports, 2) Food, 3) Music, 4) Classes. Divide students into groups of four and have each member select one topic. Each member will interview the other three, asking what each person likes and dislikes within the category chosen. Together they write what each person likes and report to the class.

Additional Practice

35 Have students draw or clip pictures from magazines that represent some sports, foods, music, and classes they like. They could then mount the pictures on larger sheets of paper and write short captions in Spanish for each photo. You might consider adding the scrapbook pages to student portfolios and having students develop them as the year progresses.

36 **Del colegio al trabajo** See possible questions below.

Hablemos You are a newspaper reporter interviewing a new student. Find out the student's name, age, and where he or she is from. Also, ask about at least three things he or she likes and dislikes. Be prepared to reenact your interview for the class.

37 **En mi cuaderno** *In my journal*

Escribamos Write a letter to a pen pal. Introduce yourself and give your age and where you're from. List three or four of your likes and dislikes. Then ask your pen pal some questions. Keep a copy of this letter in your journal.

> *Querido amigo / Querida amiga,*
>
> *Me llamo . . .   Tengo . . .*
> *Me gusta . . .   pero no . . .*
>
> *También me . . .   pero . . . más*
>
> *Con abrazos,*

LETRA Y SONIDO

CD 1
Trs. 23–27

A. The Spanish vowels (**a, e, i, o, u**) are pronounced clearly and distinctly. Learn to pronounce them by mimicking the recording or your teacher.

1. **a:** as in *father*, but with the tongue closer to the front of the mouth
   Ana   cámara   amiga   tarea   llama

2. **e:** as in *they*, but without the y sound
   este   eres   noche   excelente   café

3. **i:** as in *machine*, but much shorter
   íntimo   isla   legítimo   Misisipi   día

4. **o:** as in *low*, but without the w sound
   hola   moto   años   dónde   color

5. **u:** as in *rule*
   fruta   uno   fútbol   único   música

B. **Dictado** Script for Part B on p.15H.

Ana has just met several new friends in Madrid and is practicing the new phrases she has heard. Write what you hear.

C. **Trabalenguas**

¡A, e, i, o, u! Arbolito del Perú, ¿cómo te llamas tú?

Connections and Comparisons

Additional Practice

Write the following **trabalenguas** *(tongue twisters)* on a transparency and have students repeat them after you. **Ana practica el alemán para viajar a Alemania. Elena entiende el español en vez del francés. Lili invita a Ignacio y Martín a ir a Ibiza. El lobo se comió todos los conos de chocolate. Al duque le gusta mucho el zumo de uva.**

Music Link

You may want to play the song **La mar estaba serena** on Audio CD 1, Tr. 40. This song can be used to practice the Spanish vowels.

Tercer paso

CAPÍTULO 1

Additional Practice

36 In pairs, students role-play the following situation. One is a famous sports figure and the other a media interviewer. The interviewer asks the star questions related to his or her likes and dislikes (sports and food vocabulary). The star answers.

Teaching Suggestion

37 Refer to page T46 for names and addresses of pen pal organizations. Have students begin corresponding with a pen pal at the beginning of the school year. Maintain the correspondence through assignments throughout the year.

Assess

▶ Testing Program, pp. 9–12
Quiz 1-3A, Quiz 1-3B
Audio CD 1, Tr. 31

▶ Student Make-Up Assignments, Chapter 1, Alternative Quiz

▶ Alternative Assessment Guide, p. 32

Answers
36 *Possible questions:*
¡Mucho gusto! ¿Cómo te llamas?
¿De dónde eres? ¿Cuántos años tienes? ¿Te gusta el jazz?
Possible answers:
Me llamo...; Soy de...; Tengo... años.;
No, no me gusta el jazz.

LA ARQUEOLOGÍA

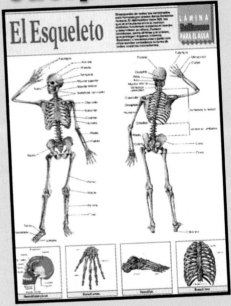

El misterio de las pirámides

La gran pirámide es una construcción magnífic...

Teaching Resources
pp. 36–37

PRINT
- Lesson Planner, p. 6
- Cuaderno de actividades, p. 11
- Cuaderno para hispanohablantes, pp. 1–5
- Reading Strategies and Skills Handbook, Chapter 1
- ¡Lee conmigo! 1, Chapter 1
- Standardized Assessment Tutor, Chapter 1

MEDIA
- One-Stop Planner

Prereading
Activities A and B
In each **Vamos a leer** section, the activities under **¡A comenzar!** focus on prereading skills.

Using Text Organizers
Have students look through English-language magazines, looking only at the headlines and captions. Ask the class to create a definition of a headline and a caption. Referring to their definitions, students should use as much Spanish as they can to rewrite a headline or a caption for one of the articles or pictures from one of the magazines.

Reading
Activities C and D

Using Context Clues
C. Have students work with a partner on Activity C, then go over the answers as a class.

Categorías

Estrategia para leer
Spanish shares many words with English. Words with similar meanings and spellings in both languages are called *cognates.** Recognizing cognates can help you understand more Spanish words.

¡A comenzar!
A. These illustrations are from different Spanish-language magazines. How many Spanish/English cognates can you find in one minute? Compare your list with a classmate's and try to guess what each word means. Look up any you're not sure of in a bilingual dictionary.

Al grano
B. Many cognates, like the ones in the reading, have similar beginnings in both languages: **extinción**, **vehículo**, **partes**, and **construcción**. Give the English equivalent of the following words. Check your work with a Spanish-English dictionary.

tecnología	restaurante	biología
república	etiqueta	bilingüe
ecología	historia	natural
technology	restaurant	biology
republic	etiquette	bilingual
ecology	history	natural

---

*So-called false cognates can be misleading. For example, **librería** means *bookstore*, not *library*.

El cuerpo humano

El Esqueleto

El esqueleto humano es maravilloso.
Las partes diferentes son increíbles.

Communication for All Students

Teacher Note
Be aware of your students' skill level in English. People seldom surpass their native-language abilities in a second language. If a student has difficulty reading in Spanish, he or she may lack English reading skills. Additionally, if you have students who have difficulty listening or spelling in Spanish, they may also be poor listeners or spellers in English. Talk to other teachers and to the students themselves to assess native-language abilities or deficiencies.

El transporte por el espacio

VEHÍCULO ORBITAL

DEPÓSITO EXTERNO DE COMBUSTIBLE

COHETES AUXILIARES

TRES... DOS... UNO... CEROOO...

Hay cinco motores: los tres principales del vehículo orbital y los dos cohetes auxiliares. Es una máquina fabulosa. Los astronautas son muy valientes.

Un animal en peligro de

extinción

El panda es nativo de las montañas Himalaya, pero hoy en día la población de los pandas no es grande. Su protección es esencial.

See answers below.

C. Refer to the magazine illustrations to answer the following:

Indicate the articles that . . .

1. might appear in a news-magazine
2. would be in a nature magazine
3. seem to deal with ancient history
4. provide terms for biology class
5. describe motors and machinery
6. deal with the future
7. tell about the past

See answers below.

D. Contesta las siguientes preguntas:

1. What part of the world is home to pandas?
2. Why do you think it's important to protect pandas?
3. Judging from the context of **El transporte por el espacio**, what do you think **cohetes auxiliares** are?
4. Which illustration is the easiest to understand? Why? Does the context help you guess the cognates?
5. Which magazine illustration first caught your attention? Why?

Cognados falsos

E. Some words look alike in Spanish and English but don't mean the same thing. These are called false cognates. For example, **vaso** means *drinking glass*, not *vase*. List a similar English equivalent for each Spanish word below. Then look up the Spanish words in a Spanish-English dictionary to see what they actually mean.

gripe	ropa	sopa
éxito	fábrica	nota
flu	clothing	soup
success	factory	grade

Cuaderno de actividades, p. 11, Act. 19

Vamos a leer

CAPÍTULO 1

Reading
Activities C and D

Cooperative Learning
D. Put students in groups of three. Ask them to choose a scribe, a proofreader, and an announcer. Give students a specific amount of time in which to complete Activity D. Monitor the groups' work as you walk around. Help students as necessary. At the end of the activity, call on each group announcer to read the group's results. Remind them that they will receive a common group grade. This will keep each person on task and engaged in the total process.

Postreading
Activity E

Using Prior Knowledge
After doing Activities A through D, have students brainstorm to think of as many English-Spanish cognates as they can in three minutes. Review their lists as a class. Clarify the meaning of any **cognados falsos** *(false cognates)* that may occur in the lists.

Answers

C 1. Endangered animals, Space shuttle
2. Endangered animals
3. Pyramids
4. Human skeleton
5. Space shuttle
6. Space shuttle
7. Pyramids

D 1. Himalayan mountains
2. Answers will vary. Possible answer: because their population is small
3. extra fuel tanks
4. Answers will vary.
5. Answers will vary.

Connections and Comparisons

Language-to-Language
Tell students that Spanish-English cognates are words derived from the same root word (usually by way of French or Latin). Point out that using cognates to decipher meaning is a useful strategy when reading other languages as well. Many of the cognates they find have cognates in other European languages, especially French.

Native Speakers
Some native speakers may use words that are considered anglicisms in standard Spanish. For example, they may use **carpeta** for *carpet* and **troca** for *truck*. You can ask students to think of other Spanish words for terms like these.

STANDARDS: 1.2, 3.1, 4.1, 5.2

For **Más práctica gramatical** Answer Transparencies, see the *Teaching Transparencies* binder.

Más práctica gramatical

CD-ROM 1
DVD 1

internet

MARCAR: go.hrw.com
PALABRA CLAVE:
WV3 SPAIN-1

Primer paso

Objectives Saying hello and goodbye; introducing people and responding to an introduction; asking how someone is and saying how you are

1 Help your friend by adding the correct punctuation and accent marks to her homework. (**p. 23**)

1. —Que tal, Paco
   —Yo, bien. Y como estas tu
2. —Adios, senor Montoya.
   —Adios, dona Carmen. Hasta manana.
3. —Maria, este es mi amigo, Jose Miguel.
   —Mucho gusto
4. —Como te llamas
   —Me llamo Rafael. Y tu

2 Can you match the different questions and answers that Guille overheard in the cafeteria? (**p. 24**)

1. Buenos días, profesora Guerrero.
2. Ésta es mi amiga Rebeca.
3. ¿Cómo se llama tu *(your)* amiga?
4. Bueno, tengo que irme.
5. ¿Qué tal, Fernanda?
6. Hola, ¿cómo te llamas?
7. Hasta luego, Adriana.

a. Mi amiga se llama Camila.
b. Yo también. Tengo clase.
c. Encantado, Rebeca. Soy Roberto.
d. ¡Horrible! ¿Y tú?
e. Chao, Tere. Hasta mañana.
f. Buenos días, señor Medina.
g. Soy Felipe. ¿Cómo te llamas tú?

3 Which subject pronoun, **tú** or **yo**, is implied but not stated in each sentence? (**p. 25**)

1. Buenos días, Paco. ¿Cómo estás?
2. ¿Te llamas Francisco?
3. Me llamo Mercedes Álvarez, y soy de Madrid.
4. Tengo quince años.
5. Me gusta la pizza y me gusta mucho el voleibol.
6. ¿Cuántos años tienes?
7. ¿Qué te gusta a ti?
8. Paco, soy tu amigo.

Answers

1
1. —¿Qué tal, Paco?
   —Yo, bien. ¿Y cómo estás tú?
2. —Adiós, Señor Montoya.
   —Adiós, doña Carmen. Hasta mañana.
3. —María, éste es mi amigo, José Miguel.
   —¡Mucho gusto!
4. —¿Cómo te llamas?
   —Me llamo Rafael. ¿Y tú?

2
1. f
2. c
3. a
4. b
5. d
6. g
7. e

3
1. tú
2. tú
3. yo
4. yo
5. yo
6. tú
7. tú
8. yo

Grammar Resources for Chapter 1

The **Más práctica gramatical** activities are designed as supplemental activities for the grammatical concepts presented in the chapter. You might use them as additional practice, for review, or for assessment.

For more grammar presentation, review, and practice, refer to the following:

• Cuaderno de gramática
• Grammar Tutor for Students of Spanish

• Grammar Summary on pp. R9–R13
• Cuaderno de actividades
• Grammar and Vocabulary quizzes (Testing Program)
• Test Generator
• Interactive CD-ROM Tutor
• **Juegos interactivos** at <u>go.hrw.com</u>.

Objectives Asking and saying how old someone is; asking where someone is from and saying where you are from

4 Write out these math problems for your little brother, following the **modelo**. (p. 27)

MODELO   2 + 8 = ——— **Dos y ocho son diez.**

1. 4 + 15 = ———

2. 12 + 3 = ———

3. 6 + 20 = ———

4. 11 + 13 = ———

5. 27 + 1 = ———

6. 14 + 16 = ———

5 Complete the conversation between Patricia, Ernesto, and Juan Luis with **soy, eres,** or **es.** (p. 28)

| soy | eres | es |

ERNESTO   Hola, buenos días.

PATRICIA   Hola, yo __1__ Patricia Méndez.

ERNESTO   Mucho gusto, Patricia. __2__ Ernesto Zaldívar.

PATRICIA   Encantada. Ernesto, éste __3__ mi amigo Juan Luis.

ERNESTO   Mucho gusto, Juan Luis. ¿Qué tal?

JUAN LUIS   Estupendo, gracias, Ernesto. ¿__4__ estudiante nuevo?

ERNESTO   Sí, yo __5__ de México.

PATRICIA   ¿Tú __6__ de México? ¡Qué bueno! Mi mamá __7__ de México también. Pero yo __8__ de los Estados Unidos.

ERNESTO   Y tú, Juan Luis, ¿de dónde __9__?

JUAN LUIS   Yo también __10__ de los Estados Unidos, pero mi papá __11__ de Guatemala.

Teacher to Teacher

Diana Goff
Chaparral High School
Scottsdale, Arizona

Diana's students really get into numbers

"I give each student a card with a different number on it. As I dictate math problems in Spanish, the student with the correct answer holds up the card and says the number. For more involvement, I have them become human math problems by standing as they hear their number in the dictated problem. Then the student with the correct answer to the problem stands and gives the answer aloud. "

Answers

4
1. Cuatro y quince son diecinueve.
2. Doce y tres son quince.
3. Seis y veinte son veintiséis.
4. Once y trece son veinticuatro.
5. Veintisiete y uno son veintiocho.
6. Catorce y dieciséis son treinta.

5
1. soy
2. Soy
3. es
4. Eres
5. soy
6. eres
7. es
8. soy
9. eres
10. soy
11. es

For **Más práctica gramatical** Answer Transparencies, see the *Teaching Transparencies* binder.

Más práctica gramatical

CD-ROM 1 · DVD 1 · go.hrw.com · WV3 SPAIN-1

6 What country is each of these students from? Look at the map of South America to find the answer. (**p. 28**)

MODELO   Marta/Buenos Aires
Marta es de Argentina.

1. Mario/Asunción
2. Orlando/Cuzco
3. Beatriz/Cuenca
4. Gabriel/Cartagena
5. Marcia/Caracas
6. Fernando/La Paz
7. Teresa/Montevideo
8. Cristina/Valparaíso

Communication for All Students

Additional Practice
Use the map on p. T74 (*Pupil's Edition*, p. xxvi) to help students develop mnemonic devices to remember the names and locations of Spanish-speaking countries in South America. For example, the eastern border of Colombia forms a letter *c* shape. Students can remember Uruguay by looking for the smallest Spanish-speaking country in South America.

Answers
6 1. Mario es de Paraguay.
2. Orlando es de Perú.
3. Beatriz es de Ecuador.
4. Gabriel es de Colombia.
5. Marcia es de Venezuela.
6. Fernando es de Bolivia.
7. Teresa es de Uruguay.
8. Cristina es de Chile.

STANDARDS: 3.1

7 Complete Vero and Lupe's conversation by filling in the blanks with the correct question words. (**p. 30**)

VERO   Hola. ¿___1___ tal?

LUPE   Bien, gracias. Y tú, ¿___2___ estás?

VERO   Bastante bien. ¿___3___ te llamas?

LUPE   Me llamo Lupe, ¿y tú?

VERO   Me llamo Verónica. Oye, Lupe, ¿___4___ años tienes?

LUPE   Tengo 15 años.

VERO   Yo también. ¿Y de ___5___ eres?

LUPE   Yo soy de San Juan, Puerto Rico. ¿Y tú?

VERO   Soy de Monterrey, México.

Tercer paso   Objective Talking about likes and dislikes

8 How would you ask the new student if . . . (**p. 32**)

1. she likes soccer?
2. she likes English class?
3. she likes Italian food?
4. she likes jazz?

How would you tell the new student that . . .

5. you like basketball a lot?
6. you don't like homework?
7. you like Italian food, but you like Chinese food more?
8. you like rock music?

9 Complete these statements with the correct article, **el** or **la**. (**p. 33**)

1. Me gusta ▭▭▭ comida mexicana.
2. No me gusta ▭▭▭ pizza.
3. ▭▭▭ natación es mi deporte favorito.
4. ▭▭▭ clase de inglés me gusta.
5. ▭▭▭ chocolate es delicioso.
6. ▭▭▭ español es excelente.
7. ▭▭▭ tarea no me gusta.
8. ¿Te gusta ▭▭▭ música rock?
9. Me gusta mucho ▭▭▭ tenis.
10. ▭▭▭ béisbol es un deporte popular.

Answers

7 1. Qué
2. cómo
3. Cómo
4. cuántos
5. dónde

8 1. ¿Te gusta el fútbol?
2. ¿Te gusta la clase de inglés?
3. ¿Te gusta la comida italiana?
4. ¿Te gusta el jazz?
5. Me gusta mucho el baloncesto.
6. No me gusta la tarea.
7. Me gusta la comida italiana, pero me gusta más la comida china.
8. Me gusta la música rock.

9 1. la
2. la
3. La
4. La
5. El
6. El
7. La
8. la
9. el
10. El

Review and Assess

You may wish to assign the **Más práctica gramatical** activities as additional practice or homework after presenting material throughout the chapter. Assign Activity 1 after **Nota gramatical** (p. 23), Activity 2 after **Así se dice** (p. 24), Activity 3 after **Gramática** (p. 25), Activity 4 after **Vocabulario** (p. 27), Activity 5 after **Así se dice** (p. 28), Activity 6 after **Vocabulario extra** (p. 29), Activity 7 after **Gramática** (p. 30), Activity 8 after **Así se dice** (p. 32), and Activity 9 after **Gramática** (p. 33). To prepare students for the **Paso** Quizzes and Chapter Test, have them do the **Más práctica gramatical** activities in the following order: complete Activities 1–3 before taking Quiz 1-1A or 1-1B; Activities 4–7 before taking Quiz 1-2A or 1-2B; and Activities 8–9 before taking Quiz 1-3A or 1-3B.

Repaso

The **Repaso** reviews all four skills and culture in preparation for the Chapter Test.

Teaching Resources
pp. 42–43

PRINT
▸ Lesson Planner, p. 6
▸ Video Guide, pp. 5–7, 10
▸ Grammar Tutor for Students of Spanish, Chapter 1
▸ Cuaderno para hispanohablantes, pp. 1–5
▸ Standardized Assessment Tutor, Chapter 1

MEDIA
▸ One-Stop Planner
▸ Video Program, Videocassette 1, 18:31–23:03
▸ DVD Tutor, Disc 1
▸ Audio Compact Discs, CD 1, Tr. 28
▸ Interactive CD-ROM Tutor, Disc 1

Teaching Suggestion
Before beginning the **Repaso**, have students turn to page 17 and review the learner outcomes. Ask them if they feel they have learned what was intended. Proceed through the **Repaso** activities. Encourage both group and individual work.

Answers

2 Mariana would be a good match. Both like rock music.

4 *Possible answer:*

PACO: ¡Hola! ¿Cómo estás?
MERCHE: Bien. ¿Y tú?
PACO: Excelente. ¿Te gusta el voleibol?
MERCHE: Sí, me gusta mucho. ¿Te gusta la pizza?
PACO: Sí, me gusta la pizza.

Repaso

MARCAR: go.hrw.com
PALABRA CLAVE:
WV3 SPAIN-1

1 Imagine that you work for a pen pal service. Your job is to complete a set of cards with information left by the clients on the answering machine. One card has been done for you as an example. Create two other cards and fill them in as you listen to the messages.

CD1
Tr. 28
Scripts and answers on p. 15H.

NOMBRE: Mariana Castillo
ORIGEN: Es de España
EDAD: Tiene 15 años
LE GUSTA: la música rock
NO LE GUSTA: el tenis

2 Read the following letter that a client has sent to the pen pal service. Then decide which of the three candidates in Activity 1 would be a good pen pal for him according to their likes and dislikes. See answer below.

Hola. Busco un amigo por correspondencia. Me llamo José Luis Bazán. Tengo quince años y soy de Guatemala. Me gustan mucho el fútbol y el béisbol. También me gusta la música rock, pero no me gusta la música clásica.

3 Look at the picture of Paco and his friends in front of the pizzeria. Keeping in mind what you've learned about gestures and interpersonal distance, explain how the picture would differ if it took place in your hometown. Possible answer: Paco and Mercedes would not kiss, and they would be standing farther apart.

4 Mira a los jóvenes en la fotografía. Escribe una conversación breve entre Paco y Mercedes. Possible answer below.

Apply and Assess

Additional Practice
1 Have students create a third card and fill it out for themselves. Then have students fill out a card for a partner, to practice asking in the **tú** form and reporting in the **él** or **ella** form.

Slower Pace
2 Have students make a list of José Luis's likes and dislikes. Then play the audio recording for Activity 1 again. Next, have students review in pairs their completed cards from Activity 1 and decide who is the best pen pal for José Luis.

5 Working with a partner, role-play each of your dialogues from the previous activity. Add a phrase or two to end the conversation politely. Be prepared to present one of your dialogues to the class.

6 Think of one item you like and one you dislike in each of the categories in the box. Interview your group members to find who shares at least two of your likes and two of your dislikes. See **Vocabulario**, page 32, for a list of vocabulary items students can use.

comida	música
deportes	clases

7 Write a short autobiographical paragraph. Be creative! Give yourself a new name, age, hometown, country, likes, and dislikes. Exchange papers with a partner and help each other correct mistakes. Possible answer below.

8 With your partner from Activity 7, introduce each other to the class. Give as much information as you can. You and your partner should be prepared to answer questions about your likes and dislikes. See possible answer below.

9 The editor of your school newspaper has asked you to come up with a standard questionnaire for interviewing new students. Create an interview form using the questions you've learned, and try it out on a classmate. See possible questionnaire below.

10 Juan's full name is Juan Luis Fernández Jiménez. Where would you find his name in the telephone book? Answer: Under "Fernández Jiménez."

11 **Situación**

ECUADOR TENIS Y SQUASH CLUB
Esta tarjeta da al socio derecho de ingresar al Club a sus instalaciones. La utilización de servicios. En caso de pérdida notificar al Ecuador Tenis y Squash Club.
Nombre MARIA LORENA DE MALO
Socio ESPECIAL N° 12-911
Fecha Nac. 13-08-1987
María Lorena De Malo

You've been asked to meet the new exchange student from Ecuador at the airport. Role-play the scene with a partner, using the information given. Be sure to exchange names, ages, where you're from, and several likes and dislikes in your conversation.

Possible conversation:
—Soy Pedro. ¿Cómo te llamas?
—Soy María Lorena de Malo.
—¿De dónde eres?
—Soy del Ecuador. Tú, ¿de dónde eres?
—Soy de California y tengo quince años. ¿Cuántos años tienes?
—Tengo dieciséis años. Me gusta mucho el tenis y el béisbol. ¿A ti qué te gusta?
—A mí me gusta el tenis también.

Apply and Assess

Thinking Critically
7 **Drawing Conclusions** Have students write an introductory letter to a new pen pal and post it on the board or wall. Ask students to read the letters to find one that describes interests similar to their own. As a modification, have students write a number on their letter instead of their names. Ask students to guess the name of the person with whom they have the most in common.

Additional Practice
9 Have students work in small groups using what they have learned about each other to write a dialogue. Include three or four participants who discuss where they are from, their ages, and their likes and dislikes.

Repaso

CAPÍTULO 1

Writing Assessment
7 Have pairs of students peer-evaluate their autobiographical paragraphs before handing them in for scoring. You may wish to evaluate their writing using the following rubric.

Writing Rubric	Points			
	4	3	2	1
Content (Complete–Incomplete)				
Comprehensibility (Comprehensible–Incomprehensible)				
Accuracy (Accurate–Seldom accurate)				
Organization (Well organized–Poorly organized)				
Effort (Excellent–Minimal)				

18–20: A   14–15: C   Under
16–17: B   12–13: D   12: F

Portfolio
7 **Written** Activity 7 may be used as a Portfolio entry. For Portfolio information, see *Alternative Assessment Guide*, pp. iv–17.

Answers
7 *Possible answer:*
Me llamo Pedro. Tengo 14 años. Soy de Cuba. Me gusta mucho la natación. No me gusta la tarea.

8 *Possible answer:*
Clase, éste es mi amigo Pedro. Es de Cuba.

9 *Possible questionnaire:*
¿Cómo te llamas? ¿De dónde eres? ¿Cuántos años tienes? ¿Qué te gusta? ¿Qué no te gusta?

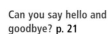

WV3 SPAIN-1

Teaching Resources
p. 44

PRINT
▸ Grammar Tutor for Students of Spanish, Chapter 1

MEDIA
▸ Interactive CD-ROM Tutor, Disc 1
▸ Online self-test

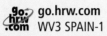
go.hrw.com
WV3 SPAIN-1

Teacher Note

This page is intended to help students prepare for the Chapter Test. The students should be reminded that this is only a checklist and does not necessarily include everything that will appear on the Chapter Test.

Answers

1 *Possible answers:*
1. ¡Hola!
2. Buenos días, señor(a).
3. Bueno, tengo clase.
4. Buenas noches; Adiós.
5. Hasta mañana.

2 *Possible answers:*
1. ¡Hola! ¿Cómo estás?
2. Me llamo...
3. Mucho gusto; Encantado/a.
4. Igualmente.

3 *Possible answers:*
1. ¿Qué tal?; ¿Cómo estás?
2. Bien; Regular.

4 *Possible answers:*
1. ¿Cuántos años tienes?
2. Tengo... años.
3. Juan tiene... años.

6 *Possible answers:*
1. ¿Te gusta la comida china?
2. ¿Te gusta la música rock?
3. ¿Te gusta el voleibol?
4. ¿Te gusta el béisbol?
5. ¿Te gusta la comida italiana?
6. ¿Te gusta la música pop?
7. ¿Te gusta la natación?
8. ¿Te gusta el baloncesto?
9. ¿Te gusta el jazz?... Me gusta...

Can you say hello and goodbye? p. 21

1 How would you greet or say goodbye to these people? Possible answers below.
1. your best friend
2. the principal before classes
3. a classmate as the bell rings
4. your neighbor as he or she leaves your house one evening
5. a friend at the end of the school day

Can you introduce people and respond to an introduction? p. 22

2 What would you say in the following situations? Possible answers below.
1. You want to introduce yourself to an interesting new classmate at a party.
2. The new Spanish teacher asks your name.
3. You have just been introduced to Juan, the new exchange student from Spain.
4. Juan has just said, "Mucho gusto."

Can you ask how someone is and say how you are? p. 24

3 Juan has just joined your class and you want to get to know him. How would you . . .? Possible answers below.
1. ask him how he is doing
2. tell him how you're doing

Can you ask and say how old someone is? p. 27

4 How would you . . .? See answers below.
1. ask Juan how old he is
2. tell him how old you are
3. tell your friend how old Juan is

Juan Luis Fernández Jiménez

Can you ask where someone is from, and say where you're from? p. 28

5 Can you . . .? Answers will vary.
1. tell Juan where you're from
2. ask him where he's from
3. tell your friend where Juan is from

Can you talk about likes and dislikes? p. 32

6 You'd like to ask Juan to do something with you on Saturday, but you don't know what he likes. Ask him if he likes these things, and tell him which ones you like. Possible answers below.
1. Chinese food
2. rock music
3. volleyball
4. baseball
5. Italian food
6. pop music
7. swimming
8. basketball
9. jazz

Review and Assess

Teacher Note

As this Chapter Test may be the first foreign-language test your students will have taken, you may wish to give them some tips on test preparation. Point out that this is a skills test, not a knowledge test. Cramming will not help them because memorization is not what they will be tested on. Communicating is what language is about, so it is a good idea for students to study together. For example, they could reread the **fotonovela** aloud, taking turns playing the characters' roles. Then they could identify vocabulary and phrases in the characters' lines from the presentations in the chapter. You may also want to refer them back to page 11 for language study tips.

Primer paso

Saying hello and goodbye

Adiós.	Goodbye.
Buenas noches.	Good night.
Buenas tardes.	Good afternoon.
Bueno, tengo clase.	Well, I have class (now).
Buenos días.	Good morning.
Chao.	'Bye.
Hasta luego.	See you later.
Hasta mañana.	See you tomorrow.
¡Hola!	Hello!
señor	sir, Mr.
señora	ma'am, Mrs.
señorita	miss
Tengo que irme.	I have to go.

Introducing people and responding to an introduction

¿Cómo te llamas?	What's your name?
Encantado/a.	Delighted to meet you.
Ésta es mi amiga.	This is my friend. (to introduce a female)
Éste es mi amigo.	This is my friend. (to introduce a male)
Igualmente.	Same here.
Me llamo...	My name is . . .
Mucho gusto.	Nice to meet you.
Se llama...	His/Her name is . . .
Soy...	I am . . .
¿Y tú?	And you? (familiar)

Asking how someone is and saying how you are

¿Cómo estás?	How are you? (to ask a friend)
Estoy (bastante) bien, gracias.	I'm (pretty) well, thanks.
Estupendo/a.	Great./Marvelous.
Excelente.	Great./Excellent.
Gracias.	Thanks.
Horrible.	Horrible.
Más o menos.	So-so.
(Muy) mal.	(Very) bad.
¿Qué tal?	How's it going?
Regular.	Okay.
tú	you (informal)
yo	I
Yo también.	Me too.

Segundo paso

Asking and saying how old someone is

¿Cuántos años tiene?	How old is (she/he)?
¿Cuántos años tienes?	How old are you?
el número	number
Tengo ... años.	I'm . . . years old.

Tiene ... años.	She/He is . . . years old.

Asking where someone is from and saying where you are from

¿De dónde eres?	Where are you from?

¿De dónde es?	Where is she/he from?
Es de...	He/She is from . . .
ser	to be
Soy de...	I'm from . . .

Numbers 0–30 See p. 27.

Tercer paso

Talking about likes and dislikes

el baloncesto	basketball
el béisbol	baseball
la cafetería	cafeteria
el chocolate	chocolate
la clase de inglés	English class
la comida mexicana/ italiana/china	Mexican/Italian/ Chinese food
el	the
la ensalada	salad
el español	Spanish
la fruta	fruit

el fútbol	soccer
el fútbol norteamericano	football
el jazz	jazz
la	the
más	more
Me gusta...	I like . . .
Me gusta más...	I like . . . more.
mucho	a lot
la música clásica/ pop/rock	classical/pop/rock music
la música de...	music by . . .

la natación	swimming
no	no
No me gusta...	I don't like . . .
pero	but
la pizza	pizza
¿Qué te gusta?	What do you like?
sí	yes
la tarea	homework
¿Te gusta...?	Do you like . . .?
el tenis	tennis
el voleibol	volleyball

Review and Assess

Game

¡A pescar! Each student makes a set of 31 playing cards, with the Spanish word and its corresponding numeral on one side. A pair of students shuffle their decks together and each draws five cards. Students play a variation of Go Fish—one student asks for the number in Spanish of a card that he or she has, (**¿cinco?**), and if the partner has it, he or she must hand it to the caller. Upon collecting a matching pair of cards, the player turns them face down on the desk. The turn continues until the caller asks for something the partner does not have, at which point the partner says **¡A pescar!** The caller must draw one card from the deck. The turn then goes to the partner. The winner is the first to make pairs of all the cards in his or her hand and therefore run out of cards.

CAPÍTULO 1

Kinesthetic Learners
Use actual objects as well as plastic replicas, drawings, and pictures to review the vocabulary. Put all items in a box. Have students take an item and use the name of the item in a Spanish phrase or sentence.

Teacher Note
As this chapter takes place in Spain, *¡Ven conmigo!* presents and tests the Spanish spelling of **voleibol**. If you prefer the spelling **volibol** used in the Americas, be aware that the spelling used in the Testing Program is **voleibol**.

Chapter 1 Assessment

▶ **Testing Program**
Chapter Test, pp. 13–18
Audio Compact Discs, CD 1, Trs. 32–33
Speaking Test, p. 343

▶ **Alternative Assessment Guide**
Performance Assessment, p. 32
Portfolio Assessment, p. 18
CD-ROM Assessment, p. 46

▶ **Interactive CD-ROM Tutor, Disc 1**

¡A hablar!
¡A escribir!

▶ **Standardized Assessment Tutor**
Chapter 1

▶ **One-Stop Planner, Disc 1**

Test Generator
Chapter 1

Capítulo 2: ¡Organízate!
Chapter Overview

De antemano pp. 48–50	¡Mañana es el primer día de clases!

	FUNCTIONS	GRAMMAR	VOCABULARY	RE-ENTRY
Primer paso pp. 51–54	• Talking about what you want and need, p. 52	• Indefinite articles **un** and **una**, p. 51 • Noun plurals, p. 52 • Indefinite articles (**un** and **unos**, **una**, and **unas**), p. 53 • Subject pronouns **él** and **ella**, p. 54	• School supplies, p. 51	• Subject pronouns: **yo**, **tú** (**Capítulo 1**)
Segundo paso pp. 56–59	• Describing the contents of your room, p. 57	• Agreement of **mucho** and **¿cuánto?** with nouns, p. 58	• Bedroom items, p. 56	• Talking about likes and dislikes (**Capítulo 1**)
Tercer paso pp. 60–63	• Talking about what you need and want to do, p. 60	• Identifying infinitives, p. 61	• Expressions with **necesitar** and **querer**, pp. 60–61 • After school activities, pp. 60–61 • Numbers 31–199, p. 62	• Numbers 0–30 (**Capítulo preliminar**) • Forming questions with **¿cuántos?** (**Capítulo 1**)

Letra y sonido p. 63	The letter **d** in Spanish: Audio CD 2, Track 11	**Dictado** Audio CD 2, Tracks 12–14
Vamos a leer pp. 64–65	**Portadas**	**Reading Strategy:** Reading titles: Looking at pictures, titles, and subtitles first
Más práctica gramatical	**pp. 66–69** **Primer paso,** pp. 66–67	**Segundo paso,** pp. 67–68 **Tercer paso,** pp. 68–69
Review pp. 70–73	**Repaso,** p. 70–71	**A ver si puedo...,** p. 72 **Vocabulario,** p. 73

CULTURE

• **También se puede decir...,** Regional terms for school vocabulary, p. 51
• **Nota cultural,** The school day in Spain and Latin America, p. 54
• **Panorama cultural, ¿Qué necesitas para el colegio?,** p. 55

• **También se puede decir...,** Regional terms for home vocabulary, p. 56
• **Nota cultural,** Apartments in Spain, p. 58
• **A lo nuestro,** Expressions for likes and dislikes, p. 59
• Realia, Spanish currency, p. 62

Capítulo 2: ¡Organízate!
Chapter Resources

PRINT

Lesson Planning

One-Stop Planner

Lesson Planner with Substitute Teacher Lesson Plans, pp. 8–12, 66

Student Make-Up Assignments
- Make-Up Assignment Copying Masters, Chapter 2

Listening and Speaking

TPR Storytelling Book, pp. 5–8

Listening Activities
- Student Response Forms for Listening Activities, pp. 11–13
- Additional Listening Activities 2-1 to 2-6, pp. 15–17
- Additional Listening Activities (song), p. 18
- Scripts and Answers, pp. 107–111

Video Guide
- Teaching Suggestions, pp. 11–13
- Activity Masters, pp. 14–16
- Scripts and Answers, pp. 90–91, 113–114

Activities for Communication
- Communicative Activities, pp. 7–12
- Realia and Teaching Suggestions, pp. 80–84
- Situation Cards, pp. 139–140

Reading and Writing

Reading Strategies and Skills Handbook, Chapter 2

¡Lee conmigo! 1, Chapter 2
Cuaderno de actividades, pp. 13–24

Grammar

Cuaderno de gramática, pp. 9–17
Grammar Tutor for Students of Spanish, Chapter 2

Assessment

Testing Program
- Grammar and Vocabulary Quizzes, **Paso** Quizzes, and Chapter Test, pp. 27–44
- Score Sheet, Scripts and Answers, pp. 45–52

Alternative Assessment Guide
- Portfolio Assessment, p. 19
- Performance Assessment, p. 33
- CD-ROM Assessment, p. 47

Student Make-Up Assignments
- Alternative Quizzes, Chapter 2

Standardized Assessment Tutor
- Reading, pp. 5–7
- Writing, p. 8
- Math, p. 51

Native Speakers

Cuaderno para hispanohablantes, pp. 6–10

 **MEDIA**

 Online Activities
- Juegos interactivos
- Actividades Internet

 Video Program
- Videocassette 1
- Videocassette 5 (captioned version)

Interactive CD-ROM Tutor, Disc 1

DVD Tutor, Disc 1

 Audio Compact Discs
- Textbook Listening Activities, CD 2, Tracks 1–16
- Additional Listening Activities, CD 2, Tracks 22–28
- Assessment Items, CD 2, Tracks 17–21

 Teaching Transparencies
- Situations 2-1 to 2-3
- Vocabulary 2-A to 2-C
- **De antemano**
- **Más práctica gramatical** Answers
- **Cuaderno de gramática** Answers

 One-Stop Planner CD-ROM

Use the **One-Stop Planner CD-ROM with Test Generator** to aid in lesson planning and pacing.

For each chapter, the **One-Stop Planner** includes:
- Editable lesson plans with direct links to teaching resources
- Printable worksheets from resource books
- Direct launches to the HRW Internet activities
- Video and audio segments
- Test Generator
- Clip Art for vocabulary items

Capítulo 2: ¡Organízate!

Projects

El regreso a clases

In this activity students will use all four skills as they create magazine advertisements, present them, and read and listen to those of others. Have students discuss seasonal advertising, how advertising influences them, and how it targets certain consumers. Have them say what kinds of ads they prefer. The theme of students' ads could be **El regreso a clases.**

MATERIALS

✂ **Students may need**

- Large sheets of white paper
- Old magazines
- A recent national newspaper
- Tape
- Scissors
- Markers
- Glue

SUGGESTED SEQUENCE

Have students work individually or in groups. They will need pictures of vocabulary items from page 73, found in magazines or drawn (encourage artistic students to create their own). Each item should include a price in **euros** reflecting the exchange rate, which they can find in the newspaper or on the Internet.

1. Remind students to use the chapter vocabulary in both a written and an oral context. Encourage them to be creative yet accurate in their ads.

2. Assign due dates for the rough draft, the completed ad, and the oral presentation. The rough draft may be a sketch with drawings labeled in Spanish.

3. After making sure the project is understood, allot class time for brainstorming and organizing in groups.

4. Allow for peer review after first draft completion.

5. Collect rough drafts from the students.

6. Have them do the final draft and give an oral presentation.

GRADING THE PROJECT

Suggested point distribution: (total = 100 points)

Newspaper Ad
Vocabulary use in ad 45
Creativity and appearance 25

Oral Presentation
Comprehensibility..10
Vocabulary use..10
Delivery (poise and confidence) 10

Games

Para la clase

This game promotes cooperation and gives students an opportunity to practice the vocabulary in Chapter 2. It can be played with the **Vocabulario** *in each* **Paso** *or as a chapter review using the vocabulary on page 73.*

Procedure With book closed, one student begins with **Para la clase necesito _____.** He or she adds any item from the **Vocabulario.** (**Para la clase necesito un cuaderno.**) The next student repeats, but adds an additional item. (**Para la clase necesito un cuaderno y un libro.**) The third student repeats what has been said and adds an item. The game goes on until a student cannot continue, in which case a student or the teacher points to an item in the classroom to help.

Plurals Review Ask each student to add two of the items. (**Para la clase necesito dos cuadernos.**) The next student repeats what the first student said and adds additional items. (**Para la clase necesito dos cuadernos y dos libros.**)

Numbers Review Ask each student to increase the number of the next item by one. (**Para la clase necesito un cuaderno.** Student 2 says, **Para la clase necesito un cuaderno y dos libros.**)

COMMUNITY LINK

Have students observe local billboard, magazine, and newspaper advertising. Discuss how these ads might be altered to target the Hispanic community. In areas with a large Hispanic presence, have students report on ads in Spanish or ads directed toward Latinos.

Storytelling

Mini-cuento

*This story accompanies Teaching Transparency 2-3. The **mini-cuento** can be told and retold in different formats, acted out, written, and read aloud, to give students additional opportunities to practice all four skills. The following story tells about four students, their desires, and their obligations.*

Andrés, Raquel, Guillermo y María son alumnos. Todos tienen obligaciones porque ya comienza un año nuevo de clases. Pero prefieren hacer otras cosas. Andrés quiere comprar discos compactos. Raquel quiere cenar con sus amigas. Guillermo prefiere mirar un programa cómico con su amigo Ernesto. A María le gusta ir de compras. Quiere comprar zapatos nuevos. Pero no pueden. Andrés necesita limpiar su cuarto sucio y organizar todo muy pronto. Raquel todavía tiene que comprar libros para sus clases. En el colegio de Guillermo, ya dan tarea y Guillermo necesita completarla. María necesita comprar útiles para su colegio. Para todos, ¡primero son las obligaciones!

Traditions

Música

Flamenco is one of the most intensely expressive kinds of music from Spain. There are three different elements of flamenco: the **baile** that is performed by **el bailaor** or **la bailaora**, the **cante** (song) and the **guitarra**. The music is created with a Spanish flamenco guitar while the **bailaoras** beat the rhythm with **castañuelas** (castanets) and a rhythmic **toque de palmas** (hand-clapping). Flamenco music is performed regularly in **cafés cantantes** (music cafes). Play a flamenco CD and have students describe the sound of the guitar, the voice, and the rhythm sections.

Receta

*Many cookbooks cite significant Moorish influence in Spanish desserts. **Alfajores** are candies made from **alajú**, a sweet paste that includes almonds, nuts, spices, and honey. **Alajú** is from the Arabic **al-hasu** (filling or stuffing). Have students find other Spanish desserts that use almonds; research foods brought by the Arabs to Spain between 711 and 1492; or compare the Spanish recipe for **alfajores** with those in Argentina.*

ALFAJORES

para 15 rosquillas

1 1/2 tazas de almendras peladas

2 tazas de almendras molidas

1 cucharadita de canela molida

1/2 cucharadita de anís

2/3 taza de miel

1/2 limón

Dore las almendras en el horno a 300°F. Hay que moverlas de vez en cuando para que no se quemen. Córtelas en trozos grandes. En un plato hondo combine las almendras molidas con la canela y el anís. Ralle la piel del limón sobre las almendras. Caliente la miel. Con una cuchara grande revuelva la miel con las almendras. Agregue los trozos de almendras y amase la mezcla. Luego separe la mezcla en 15 rosquillas para hacer caramelos. Puede envolverlas en papel festivo.

Capítulo 2: ¡Organízate!
Technology

Videocassette 1, Videocassette 5 (captioned version)
DVD Tutor, Disc 1
See Video Guide, pages 11–16.

DVD/Video ....

De antemano • ¡Mañana es el primer día de clases!
Paco explains to his grandmother that he needs to buy school supplies. His grandmother gives him money to buy what he needs but tells him he has to clean his room first. Paco tries to clean his room quickly by throwing everything in his desk drawer and under his bed. When he finishes, he realizes he has lost the money his grandmother gave him.

A continuación
Paco begins to tear apart his room looking for the lost money. His grandmother comes in and is shocked at the mess. While helping him look for the money, his grandmother realizes that Paco already has most of the school supplies he thought he needed. After finding the money, Paco and his friend Felipe go shopping for the things he still needs for school.

¿Qué necesitas para el colegio?
Students from Ecuador, Venezuela, and Argentina tell what they need to buy before the school year starts. In additional interviews, students from various Spanish-speaking countries tell us about what they need to buy for school.

Videoclips
• **Analfabetismo:** public service message about illiteracy

Interactive CD-ROM Tutor ....

Activity	Activity Type	Pupil's Edition Page
En contexto	*Interactive conversation*	
1. Vocabulario	Imagen y sonido	p. 51
	¡Exploremos!	
	¡Identifiquemos!	
2. Gramática	¿Qué falta?	pp. 52–53
3. Vocabulario	¿Cuál es?	p. 56
4. Gramática	¡A escoger!	p. 58
5. Así se dice	¡Super memoria!	p. 60
6. Vocabulario	Patas arriba	p. 62
Panorama cultural	¿Qué necesitas para el colegio? ¡A escoger!	p. 55
¡A hablar!	*Guided recording*	pp. 70–71
¡A escribir!	*Guided writing*	pp. 70–71

Teacher Management System
Launch the program, type "admin" in the password area, and press RETURN. Log on to **www.hrw.com/CDROMTUTOR** for a detailed explanation of the Teacher Management System.

DVD Tutor ....

The *DVD Tutor* contains all material from the *Video Program* as described above. Spanish captions are available for use at your discretion for all sections of the video. The *DVD Tutor* also provides a variety of video-based activities that assess students' understanding of the **De antemano, A continuación,** and **Panorama cultural.**

This part of the *DVD Tutor* may be used on any DVD video player connected to a television or video monitor.

In addition to the video material and the video-based comprehension activities, the *DVD Tutor* also contains the entire *Interactive CD-ROM Tutor* in DVD-ROM format. Each DVD disc contains the activities from all 12 chapters of the *Interactive CD-ROM Tutor.*

This part of the *DVD Tutor* may be used on a Macintosh® or Windows® computer with a DVD-ROM drive.

One-Stop Planner CD-ROM

To preview all resources available for this chapter, use the **One-Stop Planner CD-ROM**, Disc 1.

Internet Connection

MARCAR: go.hrw.com
PALABRA CLAVE:
WV3 SPAIN-2

*Have students explore the **go.hrw.com** Web site for many online resources covering all chapters. All Chapter 2 resources are available under the keyword WV3 SPAIN-2. Interactive games help students practice the material and provide them with immediate feedback. You will also find a printable worksheet that provides Internet activities that lead to a comprehensive online research project.*

Juegos interactivos

You can use the interactive activities in this chapter

- to practice grammar, vocabulary, and chapter functions
- as homework
- as an assessment option
- as a self-test
- to prepare for the Chapter Test

Actividades Internet

Students search online bookstores for books written about subjects they like. They then create a dialogue about going to the store for school supplies.

- To prepare students for the **Hoja de actividades**, have them complete the *Cuaderno de actividades* activities from the **Primer** and **Tercer pasos**.
- Once students complete the activity sheet, have them make an inventory of the school supplies they are carrying today. Then, ask them to estimate how many more of each item they are likely to need before the school year is out.

Proyecto

Have students search online stores for items they would like in an ideal bedroom. On a search engine, they can enter the chapter vocabulary or the word **hogar** *(home)*. You might have them start at a large site like www.elcorteingles.es (a large department store in Spain). Have them save images of lamps, beds, radios, and so on to their hard drive, and then attach the images to a brief description of each item.

CAPÍTULO 2   TECHNOLOGY   45F

Capítulo 2: ¡Organízate!
Textbook Listening Activities Scripts

Primer paso

6 p. 51

ARTURO Para las clases, necesito unas gomas de borrar, cuadernos y libros, claro. Tú, ¿qué necesitas?

SUMIKO Necesito lápices y cuadernos, y una regla nueva.

Answers to Activity 6
gomas de borrar, cuadernos, libros, lápices, regla

8 p. 52

Necesito papel, una calculadora, lápices y una carpeta. Ya tengo una mochila, varios cuadernos, los libros y los bolígrafos.

Answers to Activity 8
Necesito: papel, calculadora, lápices, carpeta.

Segundo paso

16 p. 56

En mi cuarto, hay dos camas y dos escritorios. También hay dos sillas, una mesa y un televisor. En mi cuarto tengo también una radio, una lámpara y tres carteles. Claro que también hay una puerta y una ventana, un armario y ropa en el armario.

Answers to Activity 16
camas, escritorios, sillas, mesa, televisor, radio, lámpara, carteles, puerta, ventana, armario, ropa; *comparisons will vary*

Tercer paso

27 p. 61

Primero les digo lo que necesito hacer yo. Necesito organizar mi cuarto, poner la ropa en el armario y encontrar mi mochila. Necesito hacer muchas cosas. Mi hermano Tomás también necesita hacer muchas cosas. Él necesita ir al centro comercial para comprar una mochila nueva, pero primero necesita hacer la tarea.

Answers to Activity 27
1. both
2. Tomás
3. Tomás
4. Victoria
5. Victoria/both
   (Students may point out that Tomás will need to find one in order to buy it.)
6. Victoria
7. Tomás

One-Stop Planner CD-ROM

To preview all resources available for this chapter, use the **One-Stop Planner CD-ROM**, Disc 1.

LETRA Y SONIDO, P. 63

For the scripts for Parts A and C, see p. 63.
The script for Part B is below.

B. Dictado

Quiero ir de compras. Necesito varias cosas—diez lápices, una calculadora, dos cuadernos y un diccionario. No necesito bolígrafos—ya tengo cinco. Y carpetas, ya tengo cuatro. ¿Qué más? Ah, sí, ¡necesito el dinero!

Repaso

1 p. 70

Para las clases necesitas muchas cosas. Necesitas una mochila, cuatro cuadernos, cinco carpetas, diez bolígrafos, seis lápices y un diccionario.

LIBRERIA "EL GRANDE"

librería

¡ TODO PARA EL COLEGIO !

una mochila   un cuaderno   un lápiz   un libro   un diccionario

un bolígrafo   una calculadora   una carpeta   una regla   papel   una goma de borrar

Capítulo 2: ¡Organízate!
Suggested Lesson Plans 50-Minute Schedule

Day 1

CHAPTER OPENER 5 min.
- Focusing on Outcomes, ATE, p. 47
- Culture Note, ATE, pp. 46–47

DE ANTEMANO 40 min.
- Presenting **De antemano** and Preteaching Vocabulary, ATE, p. 48
- Present the information in the Language Notes, ATE, p. 49.
- Activities 1–5 and Comprehension Check, ATE, p. 50

Wrap-Up 5 min.
- Do the Additional Practice activity, ATE, p. 50.

Homework Options
Cuaderno de actividades, p. 13, Activities 1–2

Day 2

PRIMER PASO
Quick Review 5 min.
- Check homework.

Vocabulario/Nota gramatical, p. 51 25 min.
- Presenting **Vocabulario** and **Nota gramatical**, ATE, p. 51
- Present and practice the vocabulary in **También se puede decir...**, p. 51.
- Do Activity 6 with the Audio CD, p. 51.
- Have students write Activity 7, p. 51. Check orally.

Así se dice, p. 52 15 min.
- Presenting **Así se dice**, ATE, p. 52
- Do Activity 8, p. 52, with the Audio CD.
- Present **Vocabulario extra**, p. 52, having students repeat. Have them do Activity 9, p. 52.

Wrap-Up 5 min.
- Ask students to list school supplies they need at the start of school. Call on students to read items from lists, spelling out the Spanish.

Homework Options
Más práctica gramatical, p. 66, Activity 1
Cuaderno de actividades, pp. 14–15, Activities 3–5
Cuaderno de gramática, pp. 9–10, Activities 1–4

Day 3

PRIMER PASO
Quick Review 5 min.
- Check homework.
- Review **Vocabulario** and **Así se dice** expressions using Transparency 2-A.

Gramática, p. 52 20 min.
- Presenting **Gramática**, ATE, p. 52
- Do **Más práctica gramatical**, p. 66, Activity 2.
- Have pairs do Activities 10 and 11, p. 53.
- Have students do Activity 12, p. 53, exchanging papers with partners for correction.

Gramática, p. 53 20 min.
- Presenting **Gramática**, ATE, p. 53
- Do the Thinking Critically activity, ATE, p. 53, and review the information in Language-to-Language.
- Do Activity 13, p. 54, orally with the class.
- Do **Más práctica gramatical**, p. 67, Activity 3.
- Present **Nota cultural**, p. 54.

Wrap-Up 5 min.
- Point to items on Transparency 2-1 and ask students if they need or want those items.

Homework Options
Cuaderno de actividades, p. 16, Activity 7
Cuaderno de gramática, pp. 11–12, Activities 5–8

Day 4

PRIMER PASO
Quick Review 5 min.
- Check homework.

Nota gramatical, p. 54 10 min.
- Present the **Nota gramatical**, p. 54.
- Have students do Activities 14–15, p. 54.

PANORAMA CULTURAL 10 min.
- Presenting **Panorama cultural**, ATE, p. 55

SEGUNDO PASO
Vocabulario, p. 56, 20 min.
- Presenting **Vocabulario**, ATE, p. 56
- Present **También se puede decir...**, p. 56.
- Do Activity 16, p. 56, with the Audio CD.
- Present **Vocabulario extra**. Explain cognates.
- Have students do Activity 17, p. 56.

Wrap-Up 5 min.
- Write the lists from Activity 17, p. 56, on the board as students read them to you.
- Discuss the content and format of Quiz 2-1.

Homework Options
Study for Quiz 2-1.
Más práctica gramatical, p. 67, Activities 4–5
Cuaderno de actividades, p. 16, Activity 8
Cuaderno de gramática, p. 13, Activities 9–10

Day 5

PRIMER PASO
Quick Review 10 min.
- Check homework.
- Quickly review the content of the **Primer paso**.

Quiz 20 min.
- Administer Quiz 2-1A, 2-1B, or a combination of the two.

SEGUNDO PASO
Así se dice, p. 57 15 min.
- Presenting **Así se dice**, ATE, p. 57
- Do Activity 18, p. 57, with the class.
- Have students do Activity 19, p. 57. Check orally, writing the students' sentences on the board as they read them.

Wrap-Up 5 min.
- Do the Challenge activity, ATE, p. 57.

Homework Options
Have students follow the **Sugerencia**, p. 57, to help them study the new vocabulary.
Más práctica gramatical, p. 68, Activity 6
Cuaderno de actividades, p. 17, Activities 9–10
Cuaderno de gramática, p. 14, Activities 11–12

Day 6

SEGUNDO PASO
Quick Review 5 min.
- Check homework.

Así se dice, p. 57 10 min.
- Review the vocabulary and **Así se dice** expressions from this **paso** using Transparency 2-B.
- Have students do Activity 20, p. 57, in pairs.

Gramática, p. 58 30 min.
- Presenting **Gramática**, ATE, p. 58
- Follow the Language Note activity, ATE, p. 58.
- Do Activity 21, p. 58.
- Read and discuss the **Nota cultural**, p. 58.
- Present the expressions in **A lo nuestro**, p. 59, giving examples of the appropriate use of each one. Have students do Activity 22, p. 59. Encourage them to incorporate the expressions from **A lo nuestro**.

Wrap-Up 5 min.
- Do the Additional Practice activity, ATE, p. 59, modeling it. Have students work in pairs.

Homework Options
Cuaderno de actividades, pp. 18–19, Activities 11–13
Cuaderno de gramática, p. 15, Activity 13

One-Stop Planner CD-ROM

For alternative lesson plans by chapter section, to create your own customized plans, or to preview all resources available for this chapter, use the **One-Stop Planner CD-ROM**, Disc 1.

 For additional homework suggestions, see activities accompanied by this symbol throughout the chapter.

Day 7

SEGUNDO PASO
Quick Review 5 min.
- Check homework.
- Bell Work, ATE, p. 60

Gramática, p. 58 20 min.
- Do **Más práctica gramatical,** p. 68, Activity 7.
- Use Transparency 2-2 to introduce and practice **Vocabulario extra,** p. 59.
- Have students do Activity 23, p. 59, in groups.

TERCER PASO
Así se dice, p. 60 20 min.
- Presenting **Así se dice,** ATE, p. 60
- Do Activity 25, p. 60.
- Have students do Activity 26, p. 60, in pairs. Call on a few volunteers to perform their dialogues for the class.

Wrap-Up 5 min.
- Ask students what they want or need to do right now.
- Discuss the content and format of Quiz 2-2.

Homework Options
Study for Quiz 2-2.
Assign Activity 24, p. 59, to be done as homework.
Cuaderno de actividades, p. 20, Activities 14–15

Day 8

TERCER PASO
Quick Review 10 min.
- Check homework.
- Collect the writing assignment (Activity 24, p. 59). You may wish to use the Writing Rubric, pp. 6–8 in the Alternative Assessment Guide to grade the assignment.
- Quickly review the content of the **Segundo paso,** using Transparencies 2-2 and 2-B.

Quiz 20 min.
- Administer Quiz 2-2A, 2-2B, or a combination of the two.

Vocabulario/Nota gramatical, p. 61 15 min.
- Presenting **Vocabulario,** ATE, p. 61
- Present **Nota gramatical,** p. 61. Also follow the Teaching Suggestion, ATE, p. 61.
- Do Activity 27, p. 61, with the Audio CD.

Wrap-Up 5 min.
- Do the Challenge activity, ATE, p. 60.

Homework Options
Más práctica gramatical, pp. 68–69, Activities 8–9
Cuaderno de actividades, pp. 20–22, Activities 16–18
Cuaderno de gramática, p. 16, Activities 14–15

Day 9

TERCER PASO
Quick Review 5 min.
- Check homework.

Vocabulario, pp. 61–62 20 min.
- Review the **Vocabulario,** p. 61, with Transparency 2-C.
- Have students do Activities 28–29, p. 61, then the suggestion for Auditory Learners, ATE, p. 60.
- Have students do Activity 30 p. 62, in pairs.

Vocabulario, p. 62 20 min.
- Presenting **Vocabulario,** ATE, p. 62
- Have students do Activity 31, p. 62 in pairs.
- Have students do Activity 32, p. 62 in pairs.
- Present the Culture Note, ATE, p. 62.

Wrap-Up 5 min.
- Call out a series of numbers. Have students write them down as a volunteer writes them on the board. Then have the class read the numbers aloud.

Homework Options
Assign Activity 33, p. 63, as homework.
Más práctica gramatical, p.69, Activity 10
Cuaderno de actividades, p. 22, Activity 19
Cuaderno de gramática, p. 17, Activities 16–17

Day 10

TERCER PASO
Quick Review 10 min.
- Check homework.
- Quickly review numbers by calling out a page number and having students turn to that page.

Vocabulario, p. 63 15 min.
- Have students do Activity 34, p. 63, in pairs.
- Follow the Thinking Critically suggestion, ATE, p. 62, then have students do Activity 35, p. 63. Have students exchange papers for peer editing.

VAMOS A LEER 20 min.
- Do Activities A and B, p. 64. Do the Thinking Critically activity, ATE, p. 64.
- Do Activities C–E, p. 65.

Wrap-Up 5 min.
- Ask students to list cognates from the reading and explain how the reading strategy helped them understand the text.
- Discuss the content and format of Quiz 2-3.

Homework Options
Study for Quiz 2-3.
Cuaderno de actividades, pp. 23–24, Activities 20–22

Day 11

TERCER PASO
Quick Review 5 min.
- Check homework.
- Quickly review the content of the **Tercer paso.**

Quiz 20 min.
- Administer Quiz 2-3A, 2-3B, or a combination of the two.

Letra y sonido, p. 63 10 min.
- Present **Letra y sonido,** p. 63, with the Audio CD.

REPASO 10 min.
- Do Activity 1, p. 70, with the Audio CD.
- Have students do Activity 4, p. 70, in groups.
- Do Activity 5, p. 70.

Wrap-Up 5 min.
- Discuss the key concepts and vocabulary learned in the chapter, listing them on the board.

Homework Options
Assign Activity 2, p. 70, as homework.
Have students prepare their role for the situation in Activity 8, p. 71.
A ver si puedo..., p. 72

Day 12

REPASO
Quick Review 5 min.
- Check **A ver si puedo...,** p. 72.
- Have students peer edit dialogues.

Chapter Review 40 min.
- Review Chapter 2. Choose from **Más práctica gramatical,** Grammar Tutor for Students of Spanish, Activities for Communication, Listening Activities, Interactive CD-ROM Tutor, or **Juegos interactivos.**

Wrap-Up 5 min.
- Discuss the format of the Chapter 2 test.

Homework Options
Study for the Chapter 2 Test.

Assessment

Quick Review 5 min.
- Answer last minute questions.

Test, Chapter 2 45 min.
- Administer Chapter 2 Test. Select from Testing Program, Alternative Assessment Guide, Test Generator, or Standardized Assessment Tutor.

Capítulo 2: ¡Organízate!

Suggested Lesson Plans 90-Minute Block Schedule

Block 1

CHAPTER OPENER 5 min.
- Focusing on Outcomes, ATE, p. 47

DE ANTEMANO 40 min.
- Presenting **De antemano** and Preteaching Vocabulary, ATE, p. 48
- Present the information in the Language Notes, ATE, p. 49.
- Activities 1–5 and Comprehension Check, ATE, p. 50

PRIMER PASO
Vocabulario/Nota gramatical, p. 51 25 min.
- Presenting **Vocabulario** and **Nota gramatical**, ATE, p. 51
- Present and practice the vocabulary in **También se puede decir...**, p. 51.
- Do Activity 6 with the Audio CD, p. 51.
- Have students write Activity 7, p. 51. Check orally.

Así se dice, p. 52 15 min.
- Presenting **Así se dice**, ATE, p. 52
- Do Activity 8, p. 52, with the Audio CD.
- Present **Vocabulario extra**, ATE, p. 52, by holding up the item and having students repeat after you. Have students do Activity 9, p. 52, then check.

Wrap-Up 5 min.
- Ask students to list the school supplies they need at the beginning of a school year. Call on students to read items from their lists, spelling out each item in Spanish.

Homework Options
Más práctica gramatical, p. 66, Activity 1
Cuaderno de actividades, pp. 13–15, Activities 1–5
Cuaderno de gramática, pp. 9–10, Activities 1–4

Block 2

PRIMER PASO
Quick Review 10 min.
- Check homework.
- Quickly review **Vocabulario** and **Así se dice** expressions from this **Paso** using Transparency 2-A.

Gramática, p. 52 25 min.
- Presenting **Gramática**, ATE, p. 52
- Do **Más práctica gramatical**, p. 66, Activity 2.
- Have students do Activities 10 and 11, p. 53, with a partner.
- Have students do Activity 12, p. 53, then exchange papers with their partner for correction.

Gramática, p. 53 20 min.
- Presenting **Gramática**, ATE, p. 53
- Do the Thinking Critically activity, ATE, p. 53, and review the information in Language-to-Language.
- Do Activity 13, p. 54, orally with the class.
- Do **Más práctica gramatical**, p. 67, Activity 3.
- Present **Nota cultural**, p. 54.

Nota gramatical, p. 54 15 min.
- Present the **Nota gramatical**, p. 54.
- Have students do Activity 14, p. 54, individually. Check orally with the class. Then do Activity 15, p. 54, with the class.

PANORAMA CULTURAL 10 min.
- Presenting **Panorama cultural**, ATE, p. 55
- Present the information in the Culture Note, ATE, p. 55.

Wrap-Up 10 min.
- Point to different items on Transparency 2-1 and ask students if they need or want one or some of those items. Then, based on those answers, ask the class who needs the items and have students answer with the subject pronouns **él** or **ella**.

Homework Options
Más práctica gramatical, p. 67, Activities 4–5
Cuaderno de actividades, p.15–16, Activities 6–8
Cuaderno de gramática, pp. 11–13 Activities 5–10

Block 3

PRIMER PASO
Quick Review 10 min.
- Check homework.
- Hold up one or two of the items from the vocabulary of this **Paso** and ask students what they are. Ask students who needs or wants the items.

Vocabulario/Así se dice/Gramática/Notas gramaticales, pp. 51–54 10 min.
- Additional Listening Activity 2-1, p. 15, Listening Activities
- Communicative Activity 2-1, pp. 7–8, Activities for Communication

SEGUNDO PASO
Vocabulario, p. 56, 20 min.
- Presenting **Vocabulario**, ATE, p. 56
- Present and practice the pronunciation of **También se puede decir...**, p. 56.
- Do Activity 16, p. 56, with the Audio CD.
- Present **Vocabulario extra** the same way as in Presenting **Vocabulario** using magazine photos. Explain that these words are also cognates.
- Have students do Activity 17, p. 56.

Así se dice, p. 57 20 min.
- Presenting **Así se dice**, ATE, p. 57
- Do Activity 18, p. 57, with the class.
- Have students do Activity 19, p. 57. Check orally, writing the students' sentences on the board as they read them. Then, have students do Activity 20, p. 57, in pairs.

Gramática, p. 58 20 min.
- Presenting **Gramática**, ATE, p. 58
- Follow the Language Note, ATE, p. 58.
- Have students do Activity 21, p. 58, individually, then check it with the class.
- Read and discuss the **Nota cultural**, p. 58.

Wrap-Up 10 min.
- Do the Additional Practice activity, p. 58, modeling it with the whole class, then have students work in pairs.
- Discuss the content and format of Quiz 2-1.

Homework Options
Study for Quiz 2-1.
Más práctica gramatical, p. 67, Activity 6
Cuaderno de actividades, pp. 17–18, Activities 9–11
Cuaderno de gramática, pp. 14–15, Activities 11–15

One-Stop Planner CD-ROM

For alternative lesson plans by chapter section, to create your own customized plans, or to preview all resources available for this chapter, use the **One-Stop Planner CD-ROM**, Disc 1.

 For additional homework suggestions, see activities accompanied by this symbol throughout the chapter.

Block 4

SEGUNDO PASO

Quick Review 10 min.
- Check homework.
- Quickly review the content of the **Primer paso.**

Quiz 20 min.
- Administer Quiz 2-1A, 2-1B, or a combination of the two.

Vocabulario/Así se dice, pp. 56-67 5 min.
- Review **Vocabulario** and **Así se dice,** pp. 56–57, using Transparency 2-B.

Gramática, p. 58 20 min.
- Quickly review **Gramática,** p. 58.
- Present the expressions in **A lo nuestro,** p. 59, giving examples of the appropriate use of each one. Have students do Activity 22, p. 59. Encourage them to incorporate the expressions from **A lo nuestro.**
- Use Transparency 2-2 to introduce and practice **Vocabulario extra,** p. 59.
- Have students do Activity 23, p. 59, in groups.

TERCER PASO

Así se dice, p. 60 15 min.
- Presenting **Así se dice,** ATE, p. 60
- Do Activity 25, p. 60.
- Have students do Activity 26, p. 60, in pairs.

Vocabulario and **Nota gramatical, p. 61** 15 min.
- Present **Vocabulario,** p. 61
- Present **Nota gramatical,** p. 61. Also follow the Teaching Suggestion, ATE, p. 61.
- Do Activity 27, p. 61, with the Audio CD.

Wrap-Up 5 min.
- Ask students what they want or need to do today.
- Discuss the content and format of Quiz 2-2.

Homework Options
Study for Quiz 2-2.
Assign Activity 24, p. 59, to be done as homework.
Más práctica gramatical, pp. 68–69, Activities 7–9
Cuaderno de actividades, p. 18–20, Activities 12–16
Cuaderno de gramática, p. 16, Activities 14–15

Block 5

TERCER PASO

Quick Review 10 min.
- Check homework.
- While students review for Quiz 2-2 with a partner, collect the writing assignment (Activity 24, p. 59). You may wish to use the Writing Rubric, pp. 3–9 in the Alternative Assessment Guide to grade the assignment.

Quiz 20 min.
- Administer Quiz 2-2A, 2-2B, or a combination of the two.

Vocabulario, pp. 61–62 15 min.
- Review the **Vocabulario,** p. 61, with Transparency 2-C.
- Do Activity 28, p. 61, with the class. Then have students do Activity 29, p. 61, and follow the suggestion for Auditory Learners, ATE, p. 60.
- Have students do Activity 30, p. 62, in pairs.

Vocabulario, p. 62 30 min.
- Presenting **Vocabulario,** ATE, p. 62
- Have students do Activity 31, p. 62, in pairs.
- Follow the Teaching Suggestion, ATE, p. 62. Then have students do Activity 32, p. 62, in pairs.
- Present the information in the Culture Note, ATE, p. 62.
- Have students do Activity 34, p. 63, in pairs.
- Follow the Thinking Critically suggestion, ATE, p. 62, then have students do Activity 35, p. 63. Have students exchange papers for peer editing.

Letra y sonido, p. 63 10 min.
- Present **Letra y sonido,** p. 63, with the Audio CD.

Wrap-Up 5 min.
- Call out a series of numbers and have students write them down as a volunteer writes them on the board. Then go back and have the class read the numbers aloud.
- Discuss the content and format of Quiz 2-3.

Homework Options
Study for Quiz 2-3.
Más práctica gramatical, p. 69, Activity 10
Cuaderno de actividades, pp. 21–22, Activities 17–19
Cuaderno de gramática, p. 17, Activities 16–17

Block 6

TERCER PASO

Quick Review 10 min.
- Check homework.

Así se dice/Vocabulario, pp. 60–62 10 min.
- Communicative Activity 2–3, pp. 11–12, Activities for Communication
- Practice numbers by calling out a page number and having students turn to that page.

Quiz 20 min.
- Administer Quiz 2-3A, 2-3B, or a combination.

VAMOS A LEER 20 min.
- Do Activities A and B, p. 64. Do the Thinking Critically activity, ATE, p. 64.
- Do Activities C–E, p. 65.

REPASO 25 min.
- Do Activity 1, p. 70, with the Audio CD, then Activity 5, p. 70, with the class.
- Have students do Activity 2, p. 70.
- Have students do Activities 3, 6, and 7, pp. 70–71, in pairs.
- Have students do Activity 4, p. 70, in groups.

Wrap-Up 5 min.
- Discuss concepts and vocabulary from the chapter, listing them on the board.
- Discuss test format, providing examples.

Homework Options
Have groups prepare Activity 8, p. 71.
A ver si puedo..., p. 72

Block 7

REPASO

Quick Review 10 min.
- Check homework.

Chapter Review 35 min.
- Review Chapter 2. Choose from **Más práctica gramatical,** Grammar Tutor for Students of Spanish, Activities for Communication, Listening Activities, Interactive CD-ROM Tutor, or **Juegos interactivos.**

Test, Chapter 2 45 min.
- Administer Chapter 2 Test. Select from Testing Program, Alternative Assessment Guide, Test Generator, or Standardized Assessment Tutor.

CAPÍTULO 2

One-Stop Planner CD-ROM

For resource information, see the
One-Stop Planner, Disc 1.

Pacing Tips

The **Primer paso** will
likely take longer to cover than the
Segundo or **Tercer pasos,** so you
might keep that in mind when planning your lessons. You may wish to
allow time for special projects, or
more directed oral practice. For more
tips on pacing, see Suggested Lesson
Plans, pages 45I–45L.

Meeting the Standards

Communication
• Talking about what you want and
  need, p. 52
• Describing the contents of your
  room, p. 57
• Talking about what you need and
  want to do, p. 60

Cultures
• Nota cultural, p. 54
• Culture Note, p. 55
• Nota cultural, p. 58

Connections
• Thinking Critically, p. 62
• Thinking Critically, p. 64
• Comparing and Contrasting, p. 64

Comparisons
• Culture Note, p. 46
• Language-to-Language, p. 53
• Thinking Critically, p. 55
• Language Note, p. 56
• A lo nuestro, p. 59
• Culture Note, p. 62

Communities
• Multicultural Link, p. 46
• Multicultural Link, p. 56
• Native Speakers, p. 65

Cultures and Communities

Multicultural Link
If possible, have students interview
exchange students or others from abroad regarding school schedules, school supplies, and the academic year in their countries. You might have
students choose a country they are interested in
and research these topics.

Culture Note
In Spanish-speaking countries many
items are sold in specialty shops like this
papelería. There are not as many supermarkets or
department stores that sell almost everything one
might need as there are in the United States.

CAPÍTULO

2

¡Organízate!

Objectives

In this chapter you will learn to

Primer paso

• talk about what you want and need

Segundo paso

• describe the contents of your room

Tercer paso

• talk about what you need and want to do

 internet

go.hrw.com MARCAR: go.hrw.com
.com PALABRA CLAVE:
WV3 SPAIN-2

◀ **Mañana es el primer día de clases.
¿Qué necesitas comprar?**

Photo Flash!

While the prevalence of specialty stores is declining in the United States, in many Spanish-speaking countries it is still common to see businesses specializing in a category of products. Here students in Spain shop at a **papelería** that sells paper products and office supplies.

Focusing on Outcomes

Explain to students that in this chapter they will be learning how to tell others what they need and want. Ask them to think of several items which they want at the beginning of a new school year and several additional items that they really need.

Chapter Sequence

Connections and Comparisons

Motivating Activity

Ask students to name items they purchase for school. Write the list on an overhead transparency or the board. Have the students make a list of things they use for school that are given to them by the school or teacher. When both lists are complete, ask the students to estimate how much they think they spend on school supplies and how much the school spends.

Building on Previous Skills

Remind students that they already know how to talk about likes and dislikes. How might the girl in the photo tell her friend that she likes her new notebook or ask him if he likes it? What might he answer?

Teaching Resources
pp. 48–50

PRINT
▶ Lesson Planner, p. 7
▶ Video Guide, pp. 11–12, 14
▶ Cuaderno de actividades, p. 13

MEDIA
▶ One-Stop Planner
▶ Video Program
  De antemano
  Videocassette 1, 23:18–28:16
  Videocassette 5 (captioned version), 10:12–15:09
  A continuación
  Videocassette 1, 28:17–35:07
  Videocassette 5 (captioned version), 15:10–22:04
▶ DVD Tutor, Disc 1
▶ Audio Compact Discs, CD 2, Trs. 1–2
▶ **De antemano** Transparencies

Presenting
De antemano

From the questions in **Estrategia para comprender** and from visual clues in the fotonovela, have students predict what will happen in the scene. Then play the Audio CD, as students read along in their books. Read the fotonovela frame by frame and have students repeat. Next, present the Preteaching Vocabulary to check for comprehension.

De antemano Transparencies

DE ANTEMANO ▪ *¡Mañana es el primer día de clases!*

The **fotonovela** is an abridged version of the video episode.

CD 2 Trs. 1–2

Paco   Abuela

Estrategia para comprender
Look at the pictures in the **fotonovela**. Who are the characters? Where are they? Is there a problem? What clues tell you this?

①
Abuela: Ta...ta...da...da...
Paco: Abuela... ¡Abuela! ... ¿Abuela?

②
Abuela: Ah, lo siento, Paco, ¿qué necesitas?
Paco: Pues, abuela... mañana es el primer día de clases y necesito muchas cosas. Necesito una mochila, ... unos cuadernos ... unos lápices ... libros ... papel ... bolígrafos ... una calculadora ... un diccionario ... y unas zapatillas de tenis.

③
Abuela: Sí, sí. Ven conmigo, Paco. ¡Ven conmigo!

④
Abuela: Paco, mira. ¡Tu cuarto es un desastre! Primero... organiza tu cuarto.

⑤
Abuela: Y ves, ya tienes lápices.

⑥
Abuela: Aquí tienes el dinero, pero para las cosas que necesitas.
Paco: Gracias, abuelita. Pero... ¿organizar mi cuarto?

Preteaching Vocabulary

Identifying Keywords

Help students use the Spanish they know and the images of school supplies to identify key words or phrases that tell them what is happening. Point out the phrase that gives them information about the time frame. **(title, ② primer día de clases)** They should then look for words that tell them what the focus of the conversation is (i.e., things that Paco needs for school). Here are some words in frame 2 that students might identify as keywords: **cuadernos, lápices, libros, papel, bolígrafos, calculadora, diccionario, zapatillas de tenis.**

7

¡Qué desastre!

8 **Paco:** Bueno, no necesito lápices... ni necesito bolígrafos. Y ya tengo una calculadora. Pero no tengo mucho papel... y necesito más cuadernos. Necesito también unas zapatillas de tenis. Y necesito una mochila.

9 **Abuela:** Bueno, Paco, ya tienes el dinero. Compra lo que necesitas. Pero, ¡sólo lo que necesitas!

10 **Paco:** ¡El dinero! El dinero...

11 **Paco:** ¿Dónde está el dinero?

Cuaderno de actividades, p. 13, Acts. 1–2

Using the Captioned Video/DVD

As an alternative to reading the conversations in the book, you might want to show the captioned version of *¡Mañana es el primer día de clases!* on Videocassette 5. As students hear the language and watch the story, anxiety about the new language will be reduced, and comprehension facilitated. The reinforcement of seeing the written words with the gestures and actions in context will help students to do the comprehension activities on page 50. **NOTE:** The *DVD Tutor* contains captions for all sections of the *Video Program*.

Language Notes
- The word **goma** means both *eraser* and *rubber*. Use **borrador** for a chalkboard eraser.
- While it may sound like Spaniards use a *th* sound, it's actually a valid phoneme of the language. Model how Spaniards would distinguish between pairs of words that are pronounced as homophones in Latin America. For example: **casa** *(ca sa)*, **caza** *(ca tha)*; **siento** *(syen to)*, **ciento** *(thyen to)*, **coser** *(ko ser)*, **cocer** *(ko ther)*.

Motivating Activities
- In the **fotonovela**, Paco persuades his grandmother that he needs money for school supplies. Have students discuss in small groups how they earn money or how they persuade family members to give them money for things they need or want.
- At the end of the **fotonovela**, Paco has misplaced the money that his grandmother gave him. Have students work in small groups to invent two or three endings for the **fotonovela**. Each group should explain which of their endings seems most likely.

A continuación
You may choose to continue with *¡Mañana es el primer día de clases! (a continuación)* at this time or wait until later in the chapter. After Paco's grandmother helps find the money, Paco and Felipe shop for school supplies and a gift for Paco's grandmother. You may wish to discuss with students where they buy school supplies and differences between stores in Spain and the U.S.

CAPÍTULO 2

Teaching Suggestions

1 Ask for volunteers to ask and answer questions. Have the class indicate whether or not answers are correct by thumbs up or thumbs down.

2 Write the words and phrases that make up these sentences on magnetic or felt board strips. Then ask students to manipulate the sentences to change what they say, changing negative sentences to positive ones and vice versa.

Answers

1 1. At the house where Paco and his grandmother (**abuela**) live.
2. Una mochila, unos cuadernos, unos lápices, libros, papel, bolígrafos, una calculadora, un diccionario y unas zapatillas de tenis.
3. She tells him to clean up his room before he goes shopping and to buy only the things he needs.
4. Paper, notebooks, tennis shoes, and a backpack.
5. Paco cannot find the money.

2 1. cierto
2. falso. Necesita más cuadernos.
3. cierto
4. falso. Paco organiza su cuarto.
5. falso. Paco tiene una calculadora y necesita unas zapatillas de tenis.

3 1. necesito
2. y necesito; necesito también
3. no necesito; ya tengo
4. necesito una mochila
5. ¿Dónde está el dinero?

These activities check for comprehension only. Students should not yet be expected to produce language modeled in **De antemano**.

1 **¿Comprendes?**

Do you understand what is happening in the **fotonovela**? Check your understanding by answering these questions. Don't be afraid to guess! See answers below.

1. Where does the story take place?
2. At the beginning of the **fotonovela**, what does Paco say he needs?
3. What does Paco's grandmother tell him to do? Why?
4. At the end of the **fotonovela**, what does Paco end up needing for school?
5. How does the scene end? What problem does Paco have?

2 **¿Cierto o falso?** See answers below.

Con base en la fotonovela, indica **cierto** *(true)* si la oración es verdadera o **falso** *(false)* si no lo es. Si es falsa, cámbiala.

1. Mañana es el primer día de clases.
2. Paco no necesita más cuadernos.
3. Paco no necesita más lápices ni *(nor)* bolígrafos.
4. La abuela organiza el cuarto de Paco.
5. Paco tiene unas zapatillas de tenis y necesita una calculadora.

3 **¿Cómo se dice...?**

Find the words and phrases Paco uses . . . See answers below.

1. to say he needs something
2. to say he also needs something else
3. to say that he already has something
4. to say that he needs a backpack
5. to ask where the money is

4 **¿Listos?** *Ready?*

Using the **fotonovela** as a guide, complete the following paragraph with the words from the box.

Ay, ¡mañana es el primer día de ___1___! Bueno, no ___2___ lápices ni necesito ___3___, y ya tengo una ___4___. Pero no tengo mucho ___5___ y necesito más ___6___. Y también necesito unas ___7___ de tenis. ¡Pero no tengo ___8___!

zapatillas	cuadernos
necesito	
dinero	clases
papel	
calculadora	bolígrafos

1. clases   3. bolígrafos   5. papel   7. zapatillas
2. necesito   4. calculadora   6. cuadernos   8. dinero

5 **¿Y tú?**

How about you? Have you run out of school supplies? Make a list of the supplies Paco mentions. Next to each, write (**No**) **necesito** or (**No**) **tengo** to say whether it is something you need or don't need, have or don't have.
Answers will vary. Example: cuadernos. No necesito cuadernos.

Comprehension Check

Cooperative Learning

1 Have students work in groups of three to answer the questions. One student reads each question to the group. Then all three group members look back at the **fotonovela** on pages 48–49 for the answer. The second student writes the answer to each question. The third student reads the answers aloud to the class when asked.

Additional Practice

2 Have partners make a shopping list for Paco. The list should include only the items he decides he needs after he has straightened his room. Ask students how much money Paco will have to spend on his school supplies. Ask pairs to compare their lists.

Objective Talking about what you want and need

Vocabulario

CD-ROM 1
DVD 1

MATERIALES PARA EL COLEGIO

LIBRERIA El Grande

- una mochila
- una goma de borrar
- un cuaderno
- un libro
- una regla
- papel
- una carpeta
- una calculadora
- un bolígrafo
- un lápiz
- un diccionario

Cuaderno de actividades, p. 14, Act. 3

Cuaderno de gramática, p. 9, Acts. 1–2

También se puede decir...

In many countries in Latin America, **la pluma** is used instead of **el bolígrafo**. Other words for **el colegio** include **la escuela secundaria** and **el liceo**.

Nota gramatical

Un and **una** mean *a* or *an*. Use **un** with masculine nouns: **un bolígrafo**. Use **una** with feminine nouns: **una regla**. Do you remember two ways to say *the* in Spanish?*

Cuaderno de gramática, p. 10, Acts. 3–4

Más práctica gramatical, p. 66, Act. 1

_____
* **El** and **la** are used to mean *the*.

6 Arturo y Sumiko

CD 2
Tr. 3

Escuchemos/Escribamos Listen as Arturo and Sumiko talk about what they need for school. Make a list of what they need and circle the item that they both mention. Scripts and answers on p. 45G.

7 Gramática en contexto

Leamos/Escribamos Elena is telling her father what she has and what she needs for school. Complete each sentence with **un** or **una**.

Tengo ___1 un___ libro de matemáticas pero necesito ___2 un___ cuaderno. Tengo ___3 un___ bolígrafo, ___4 una___ goma de borrar y ___5 una___ carpeta. Necesito ___6 un___ diccionario, ___7 una___ calculadora, una regla y ___8 un___ lápiz. Y necesito ___9 una___ mochila nueva *(new)*.

Teacher to Teacher

Norah L. Jones
Rustburg High School
Rustburg, Virginia

Norah's students name what's in the bag

"Into a personalized lunch bag students put a choice of eight school items. Students exchange bags, and then each student in turn identifies the bag. **Éste es el saco de Isabel.** The class then asks **¿Qué tiene Isabel?** and the student presents the contents, pulling out each item and noting **Isabel tiene un lápiz (una regla, etc.).** Variation: Class asks, **¿Necesita Isabel una calculadora?** Student answers **Sí, necesita una calculadora** or **No, ya tiene una calculadora.**"

Teaching Resources
pp. 51–54

PRINT
- Lesson Planner, p. 8
- TPR Storytelling Book, pp. 5, 8
- Listening Activities, pp. 11, 15
- Activities for Communication, pp. 7–8, 80, 83–84, 139–140
- Cuaderno de gramática, pp. 9–13
- Grammar Tutor for Students of Spanish, Chapter 2
- Cuaderno de actividades, pp. 14–16
- Cuaderno para hispanohablantes, pp. 6–10
- Testing Program, pp. 27–30
- Alternative Assessment Guide, p. 33
- Student Make-Up Assignments, Chapter 2

MEDIA
- One-Stop Planner
- Audio Compact Discs, CD 2, Trs. 3–4
- Teaching Transparencies 2-1, 2-A; **Más práctica gramatical** Answers; Cuaderno de Gramática Answers
- Interactive CD-ROM Tutor, Disc 1

Presenting
Vocabulario, Nota gramatical

Collect several school items and group into masculine (**un lápiz**) and feminine (**una carpeta**). Give the "masculine" items, one by one, to students, saying **un bolígrafo para Roberto,** etc. Then ask, **¿Quién tiene un _____** for each of the items. Hand out the "feminine" items, without naming them, to other students. Ask **¿Qué tiene Marta?** and so on. Draw a parallel between **un/una** and **el/la.** Use charts or flashcards to solidify the concept.

CAPÍTULO 2

Teaching Resources
pp. 51–54

PRINT 📖
- ▶ Lesson Planner, p. 8
- ▶ TPR Storytelling Book, pp. 5, 8
- ▶ Listening Activities, pp. 11, 15
- ▶ Activities for Communication, pp. 7–8, 80, 83–84, 139–140
- ▶ Cuaderno de gramática, pp. 9–13
- ▶ Grammar Tutor for Students of Spanish, Chapter 2
- ▶ Cuaderno de actividades, pp. 14–16
- ▶ Cuaderno para hispanohablantes, pp. 6–10
- ▶ Testing Program, pp. 27–30
- ▶ Alternative Assessment Guide, p. 33
- ▶ Student Make-Up Assignments, Chapter 2

MEDIA 💿📹💻
- ▶ One-Stop Planner
- ▶ Audio Compact Discs, CD 2, Trs. 3–4
- ▶ Teaching Transparencies 2-1, 2-A; **Más práctica gramatical** Answers; Cuaderno de gramática Answers
- ▶ Interactive CD-ROM Tutor, Disc 1

Presenting
Así se dice

Take an item from a student's desk and ask **¿Quieres (un libro)?** Prompt the student to say **Sí, quiero un libro.** Then ask the class **¿(Miguel) quiere un libro?** Repeat the process with **necesitar.**

Gramática

Making nouns plural Ask students to make plural the vocabulary items on page 47. Then hold up one or more of the items and ask **¿Cuántos hay?**

Así se dice

Talking about what you want and need

To find out what someone wants, ask:

¿Qué quieres?

¿Paco quiere una mochila?

To answer, say:

Quiero una mochila.

Sí, él **quiere** una mochila.

To find out what someone needs, ask:

¿Qué necesitas?

¿Necesitas papel?

¿Qué necesita Merche?

Necesito un cuaderno.

No, **ya tengo** papel.
. . . I already have . . .

¡Ella necesita muchas cosas!
She needs a lot of things!

---

8 **¿Qué necesito?**

CD 2 Tr. 4

Escuchemos/Escribamos Blanca is stocking up on school supplies before school starts. Listen as she makes up her shopping list. Ignoring the things she already has, write only the things she needs. Start your answer with **Necesito...** Scripts and answers on p. 45G.

9 **¿Qué necesitas para...?** *What do you need for . . .?*

Escribamos Using the drawing of the items in the bookstore and **Vocabulario extra,** identify the Spanish words for the things you might need. . .

1. to write a report papel y un bolígrafo
2. to carry loose papers una carpeta
3. to make a poster for art class un marcador
4. to add up your bill una calculadora
5. to do your geometry homework una regla
6. to take notes in class un bolígrafo, papel
7. to carry your supplies una mochila
8. to look up unknown words un diccionario

Vocabulario extra	
un lápiz de color	*colored pencil*
un marcador	*marker*
un pincel	*paintbrush*
(la) pintura	*paint*

Gramática

Making nouns plural

1. So far, you've been talking about single things. To make a noun plural, add **-s** if it ends in a vowel: **diccionario** → **diccionarios**. If the noun ends in a consonant, add **-es: papel** → **papeles.**

2. If a noun ends in **-z**, change **-z** to **-c** and add **-es: lápiz** → **lápices.**

3. How would you make these nouns plural?
   a. cruz b. luz c. vez*

 Cuaderno de gramática, p. 11, Acts. 5–6

Más práctica gramatical, p. 66, Act. 2 →

---

* The plurals are **cruces, luces, veces.**

Communication for All Students

Additional Practice
You might set up a classroom store with play money and a list of school supplies for each student. Ask a few students to serve as clerks. The rest will be shoppers. Give shoppers a list of school supplies and ask them to check their own supplies against the items on the list. If students do not have something, they will need to buy it at the classroom store.

Slower Pace
10 Have students write the words for the numerals of how many items Paco has before joining their partner. Allow them to use the written responses as they role-play Paco and his friend.

10 Gramática en contexto

Hablemos With a partner, play the roles of Paco and a friend. Each time Paco says he wants an item, his friend tells him he already has several. Use the numbers in parentheses.

MODELO **(6) libro de béisbol** See answers below.
—**Quiero un libro de béisbol.**
—**Pero Paco, ¡ya tienes seis libros de béisbol!**

1. (3) calculadora
3. (9) cuaderno
5. (15) bolígrafo
7. (20) goma de borrar

2. (11) lápiz
4. (2) mochila
6. (5) carpeta
8. (4) regla

11 Una lista

Hablemos/Escribamos Work in pairs. Find out if your partner needs or already has these ¿Necesitas...? school supplies. Then tell your partner which ones you need. Make a list for each partner. Yo necesito...

una carpeta · una calculadora · papel · una regla

un cuaderno · un libro · un bolígrafo · un lápiz

12 La lista de mi compañero/a *My partner's list*

Escribamos Based on Activity 11, write a brief paragraph telling what school supplies your partner already has and what she or he needs. Use **Ya tiene…** and **Necesita…**

Possible answers: (Name) ya tiene...; (Name) necesita...

Gramática

Indefinite articles (*un, una, unos, unas*)

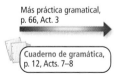
CD-ROM 1
DVD 1

1. You've already learned that **un** and **una** mean *a* or *an*. **Unos** and **unas** mean *some* or *a few*. This chart shows how the four forms of the indefinite article are used.

	SINGULAR	PLURAL
MASCULINE	**un** bolígrafo	**unos** bolígrafos
FEMININE	**una** mochila	**unas** mochilas

2. Use **unos** with a masculine plural noun. When referring to a group of people that includes both males and females, the masculine plural is used (**unos estudiantes**).

Más práctica gramatical, p. 66, Act. 3

3. In a negative sentence, **un, una, unos,** and **unas** are often dropped.

¿Necesitas **unos** bolígrafos? No, no necesito bolígrafos.

Cuaderno de gramática, p. 12, Acts. 7–8

Connections and Comparisons

Thinking Critically
Drawing Inferences Ask students why **el, la, los,** and **las** are called definite articles and why **un, una, unos,** and **unas** are called indefinite articles. (The indefinite articles don't refer to a specific person, place, or thing.)

Language-to-Language
In English we say *the folder* and *the books* when speaking about specific items, and *a folder* and *some books* when referring to things in a general way. Arrange school supplies on your desk. Say **Necesito la carpeta**, and pick up the folder. Then say **Necesito una carpeta** and look around, as if any folder will do. Ask students which word corresponds to the specific folder, **la** or **una**.

Presenting
Nota gramatical

Subject pronouns *él* and *ella*

After presenting an explanation of pronouns for first, second, and third persons using a triangular diagram on the board, have two student volunteers model greetings and simple questions (see Chapter 1), then ask what each needs for school. Next, choose another student from the class, and have the first two students form the same questions and answers about him or her in the third person with pronouns. Choose still other students until you feel the concept is well-covered and practiced.

Assess

▸ Testing Program
Quiz 2-1A, Quiz 2-1B, pp. 27–30
Audio CD 2, Tr. 17

▸ Student Make-Up Assignments, Chapter 2, Alternative Quiz

▸ Alternative Assessment Guide, p. 33

Answers

14 1. Él tiene unos bolígrafos.
2. Ella quiere una mochila.
3. Él necesita un cuaderno.
4. Ella tiene unos libros.
5. Él necesita unas carpetas.
6. Ella quiere papel.
7. Ella necesita una calculadora.
8. Él tiene una regla.

15 1. Cierto
2. Falso; Tú no necesitas ir.
3. Cierto
4. Cierto
5. Cierto

---

13 ## Gramática en contexto

A. Leamos/Hablemos Read the conversation between Leo and Marta, choosing the correct indefinite article. Then answer Part B to tell what the two students will probably shop for.

LEO   Ya tengo (un, una) cuaderno rojo pero necesito (un, una) goma de borrar.

MARTA Pues, yo tengo (un, unos) cuadernos pero no tengo (una, un) calculadora para la clase de matemáticas. ¿Qué quieres?

LEO   Quiero (unos, un) lápices, (una, un) regla azul y (una, un) mochila grande.

MARTA Yo también quiero (una, unas) mochila. ¡Necesitamos dinero!

B. Hablemos What do Leo and Marta each need, want, and already have?

Nota gramatical

In Chapter 1 you learned to use the subject pronoun **yo** when talking about yourself and **tú** when talking to another student or someone your own age. When you want to talk about someone else, use **él** to mean *he* and **ella** to mean *she*.

Paco y **Merche** quieren ir a la tienda. **Él** necesita una mochila y **ella** necesita muchas cosas.

Cuaderno de gramática, p. 13, Acts. 9–10

Más práctica gramatical, p. 67, Acts. 4–5

Nota cultural

In many high schools in Spain and Latin America, students stay in the same room for their classes all day and the teachers change classrooms. Because of this, it's rare to find a school that has lockers. Students carry their supplies to and from school each day in book bags or backpacks.

14 ## Gramática en contexto

Hablemos/Escribamos Answer the questions using the correct pronoun (**él** or **ella**). See answers below.

MODELO   ¿Qué tiene Marta? (lápiz)
          Ella tiene un lápiz.

1. ¿Qué tiene Paco? (bolígrafos)
2. ¿Qué quiere Merche? (mochila)
3. ¿Qué necesita Carlos? (cuaderno)
4. ¿Qué tiene la abuela? (libros)

5. ¿Qué necesita tu amigo? (carpetas)
6. ¿Qué quiere Beatriz? (papel)
7. ¿Qué necesita Ana? (calculadora)
8. ¿Qué tiene Raúl? (regla)

15 ## ¿Cierto o falso? See answers below.

Leamos/Escribamos Imagine you are the older brother in the drawing. Are these statements true (**cierto**) or false (**falso**)? If they're false, change them to make them true.

1. Yo necesito ir al colegio.
2. Tú necesitas ir también.
3. Tú quieres ir a la escuela.
4. Yo tengo una mochila.
5. Yo tengo un libro y tú tienes un libro también.

Yo necesito ir al colegio. Tú sólo tienes cuatro años. No puedes ir.

Yo quiero ir también. ¡Soy muy inteligente!

Cultures and Communities

Game

Dibujos To review material from this **Paso**, divide the class into two teams and play this game. Ask the first player to go to the board. Show the student a vocabulary word. He or she draws a picture of the word and his or her team says the word in Spanish, including the correct definite arti-cle (**el** or **la**). The team has thirty seconds to draw and guess the word before the opposing team may try. The successful team gets the point. The other team sends a student to the board next. Continue, this time with the indefinite articles.

CD 2
Trs. 5–8

¿Qué necesitas para el colegio?

In this chapter, we asked some people what they need to buy before the school year starts.

Jimena CD 2 Tr. 8
Buenos Aires, Argentina
"Tuve que comprar lápices, lapiceras, gomas, reglas, cartuchera, mochila, cuadernos y carpetas".

Fabiola CD 2 Tr. 7
Caracas, Venezuela
"Bueno, cuadernos, lápices, libros, borradores, calculadora".

Paulina CD 2 Tr. 6
Quito, Ecuador
"Tengo que comprar todos los cuadernos, los libros y mi uniforme".

Para pensar y hablar...

A. What do you need to buy before the school year starts? In some countries of the Spanish-speaking world, there's a basic list of school supplies. Do you find differences and similarities between the supplies you buy and the items mentioned by these Latin American students?

B. Paulina mentions having to buy a uniform. How do you feel about wearing uniforms to school? What would be the advantages and disadvantages?

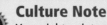
Cuaderno para hispanohablantes, p. 10

Connections and Comparisons

Thinking Critically

Comparing and Contrasting Some students in both the U.S. and Latin America have to wear school uniforms. Have students work in small groups to list the advantages and disadvantages of school uniforms. Each group should attempt to arrive at a consensus about whether schools should require uniforms. Have students explain their conclusion to the class.

Culture Note

You might point out that many schools in Spain and Latin America require their students to wear uniforms and that usually, the students must purchase them. It is also normal for students to have to buy their own textbooks, since these are not provided by the schools.

Teaching Resources
p. 55

PRINT 📖
▶ Video Guide, p. 11–13, 16
▶ Cuaderno de actividades, p. 24
▶ Cuaderno para hispanohablantes, p. 10

MEDIA
▶ One-Stop Planner
▶ Video Program
  Videocassette 1, 35:38–39:37
▶ DVD Tutor, Disc 1
▶ Audio Compact Discs, CD 2, Trs. 5–8
▶ Interactive CD-ROM Tutor, Disc 1

Presenting
Panorama cultural

Read the interviews aloud or have students watch the video without looking at the written interview. Have the students recall the supplies that they heard. Then have students read the interviews while listening to the tape and check the answers that were given. Then play the video again and have students answer the **Preguntas**.

Preguntas

1. **¿Qué persona necesita un uniforme?** (Paulina)

2. **¿El estudiante de qué país tiene que comprar una calculadora?** (Venezuela)

3. **En la Argentina, ¿necesitan los chicos comprar los libros?** (No.)

Segundo paso

Objective Describing the contents of your room

go.
hrw
.com

WV3 SPAIN-2

Teaching Resources
pp. 56–59

PRINT
▸ Lesson Planner, p. 9
▸ TPR Storytelling Book, pp. 6, 8
▸ Listening Activities, pp. 12, 16
▸ Activities for Communication, pp. 9–10, 81, 83–84, 139–140
▸ Cuaderno de gramática, pp. 14–15
▸ Grammar Tutor for Students of Spanish, Chapter 2
▸ Cuaderno de actividades, pp. 17–19
▸ Cuaderno para hispanohablantes, pp. 6–10
▸ Testing Program, pp. 31–34
▸ Alternative Assessment Guide, p. 33
▸ Student Make-Up Assignments, Chapter 2

MEDIA
▸ One-Stop Planner
▸ Audio Compact Discs, CD 2, Tr. 9
▸ Teaching Transparencies 2-2, 2-B; **Más práctica gramatical** Answers; Cuaderno de gramática Answers
▸ Interactive CD-ROM Tutor, Disc 1

Bell Work

Display Teaching Transparency 2-A. Have students write down any items they have in class today. They must use an article. They can check their work with the overlay.

Presenting
Vocabulario
Have students pick out cognates in **Vocabulario**, then model pronunciation and have students repeat the new words. Use Chapter Opener photo three to present vocabulary. For additional practice, use *Teaching Transparency 2-B.*

Vocabulario

El cuarto de Débora

CD-ROM 1
DVD 1

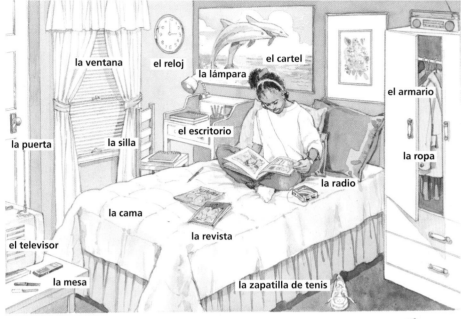

la ventana — el reloj — el cartel — la lámpara — el armario — el escritorio — la ropa — la puerta — la silla — la radio — la cama — la revista — el televisor — la zapatilla de tenis — la mesa

Cuaderno de gramática, p. 14, Acts. 11–12

16 ¿Qué hay?
Escuchemos/Escribamos Listen as Julio describes what's in his room. Write the items he mentions. How is the room he describes different from Débora's room in the picture? Scripts and answers on p. 45G.

CD 2
Tr. 9

17 En la sala de clase *In the classroom*
Escribamos Which of the things in Débora's room are also found in your classroom? Make two lists, one showing how many there are (**hay**) of each item, and another one showing what isn't in the classroom (**no hay**). Answers will vary.

También se puede decir...
In many Spanish-speaking countries, you will also hear **el pupitre** for **el escritorio** and **el afiche** or **el póster** for **el cartel**.

Vocabulario extra

la computadora	*computer*
el DVD	*DVD*
el estéreo	*stereo*
el teléfono (celular)	*(cellular) telephone*
la videocasetera	*VCR*

Cultures and Language

Language Note
Las zapatillas de tenis is the common term for *tennis shoes* in Spain. In other Spanish-speaking countries, however, one much more commonly hears **los zapatos de tenis**, or simply **los tenis**.

Multicultural Link
Have students interview exchange students or immigrants. Do students in their country of origin follow the same kind of schedule as students in your school? Do they wear uniforms? You may wish to set up a pen pal or e-pal exchange with a school in a Spanish-speaking country. See page T46 for suggestions.

STANDARDS: 1.2, 4.2

Así se dice

Describing the contents of your room

Más práctica gramatical,
p. 67, Act. 6 →

To find out what there is in someone's room, ask:

¿Qué hay en tu cuarto?

¿Qué hay **en el cuarto de Paco?**
. . . in Paco's room?

¿Tienes un televisor?
Do you have a TV set?

¿Qué tiene Merche **en su cuarto?**
. . . in her room?

To answer, say:

Tengo una mesa y dos sillas **en mi cuarto.** *I have . . . in my room.*

Hay libros y cuadernos **en su cuarto.** *There are . . . in his room.*

No, **no tengo** televisor.

Merche **tiene** unos carteles y una radio **en su cuarto.**

18 **Describir el cuarto**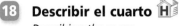

Describing the room

Escribamos Look at the **Vocabulario** on page 56. How many of each item does Débora have in her room? Start your descriptions with **En el cuarto de Débora hay...** or **Ella tiene...**

1. bolígrafo dos
2. ventana una
3. revista tres
4. cuaderno tres
5. lápiz cuatro
6. lámpara una
7. cama una
8. cartel un
9. armario un
10. zapatilla de tenis una
11. silla una
12. radio una
13. televisor un
14. reloj un
15. puerta dos (o tres)

Try making Spanish labels for things you use every day at school and at home (your school supplies, things in your room, etc.). This way, every time you look at an item you'll be reminded of how to say it in Spanish. And don't forget to include **el** and **la** to remind you which words are masculine and which ones are feminine.

19 **Un cuarto perfecto**

Escribamos Look at the picture of this bedroom and write five sentences about it. Begin your description with **En el cuarto hay...** Be as detailed as you can.
See sample answer below.

20 **¿Qué hay en tu cuarto?**

Hablemos With a partner, take turns asking each other about what's in your rooms. Use both **¿Hay...?** and **¿Tienes...?** and refer to the art on page 56 for ideas. Feel free to describe an imaginary room.
See possible questions below.

Communication for All Students

Visual Learners

18 To help students remember vocabulary, have them make labels for vocabulary items found in your classroom.

Challenge

18 Teach the prepositions **al lado de**, **encima de**, and **debajo de**. Ask students to tell you where an item is in relation to another. Use the picture of **el cuarto de Débora** and ask questions like **¿Qué hay en el cuarto de Débora?**

Answers

19 *Sample answer:*
En el cuarto hay una cama, una ventana y una lámpara blanca. Hay unas carpetas, unos libros y unos cuadernos. Hay una mesa y una silla. No hay televisor. No hay reloj.

20 *Possible questions:*
¿Hay un reloj?
¿Tienes una silla?

Teaching Resources
pp. 56–59

PRINT
▶ Lesson Planner, p. 9
▶ TPR Storytelling Book, pp. 6, 8
▶ Listening Activities, pp. 12, 16
▶ Activities for Communication, pp. 9–10, 81, 83–84, 139–140
▶ Cuaderno de gramática, pp. 14–15
▶ Grammar Tutor for Students of Spanish, Chapter 2
▶ Cuaderno de actividades, pp. 17–19
▶ Cuaderno para hispanohablantes, pp. 6–10
▶ Testing Program, pp. 31–34
▶ Alternative Assessment Guide, p. 33
▶ Student Make-Up Assignments, Chapter 2

MEDIA
▶ One-Stop Planner
▶ Audio Compact Discs, CD 2, Tr. 9
▶ Teaching Transparencies 2-2, 2-B; **Más práctica gramatical** Answers; Cuaderno de gramática Answers
▶ Interactive CD-ROM Tutor, Disc 1

Presenting
Gramática

Agreement of *mucho* and *¿cuánto?* with nouns

Tell students that **cuánto/a** and **mucho/a** are used with things we don't usually count. (**¿Cuánto papel tienes? Tengo mucho. ¿Cuánta ropa hay? Hay mucha.**) **Cuántos/as** and **muchos/as** are used when we can count the things to which we refer.

Answers

21 1. Cuántas   6. Cuántos
     2. Cuánta   7. cuántos
     3. mucha   8. muchos
     4. muchas   9. muchos
     5. muchas   10. muchos

Gramática

Agreement of *mucho* and *¿cuánto?* with nouns

1. Many nouns and adjectives have the following endings:

	SINGULAR	PLURAL
MASCULINE	–o	–os
FEMININE	–a	–as

Making the endings of adjectives and nouns match is called *agreement in gender* (masculine/feminine) *and number* (singular/plural).*

2. The forms of **¿cuánto?** are used to ask *how much?* or *how many?* Like other adjectives, **¿cuánto?** matches the noun it describes.

(el papel) **¿Cuánto** papel tienes?
(la tarea) **¿Cuánta** tarea?
(los bolígrafos) **¿Cuántos** bolígrafos?
(las carpetas) **¿Cuántas** carpetas?

3. The forms of **mucho** mean *a lot, much,* or *many*. Like **¿cuánto?**, **mucho** changes to match the noun it modifies.

No necesito **muchas** carpetas, pero necesito **muchos** bolígrafos y **mucho** papel.

Tengo **mucha** tarea.

Más práctica gramatical, p. 68, Act. 7

Cuaderno de actividades, pp. 18–19, Acts. 11–13

Cuaderno de gramática, p. 15, Act.13

---

21   **Gramática en contexto** See answers below.

Leamos/Escribamos Patricia has just moved here, and her new friend David wants to know more about her. Fill in the blanks of their conversation using forms of **¿cuánto?** and **mucho.**

DAVID   ¿Te gusta el colegio? ¿___1___ clases tienes? ¿___2___ tarea hay?

PATRICIA   Me gusta el colegio. Tengo siete clases y hay ___3___ tarea.

DAVID   ¿Te gusta tu cuarto? ¿Hay ___4___ ventanas?

PATRICIA   No hay ___5___ ventanas. Sólo (*only*) hay una.

DAVID   ¿___6___ carteles hay? ¿Y ___7___ libros tienes?

PATRICIA   Tengo ___8___ carteles y ___9___ libros. Pero David… no tengo ___10___ amigos.

DAVID   Ay, Patricia… ¡yo soy tu amigo!

---
* You will learn more about *agreement* in Chapter 3.

Nota cultural

In Spain, most people live in **pisos** (*apartments*) in cities or towns. Bedrooms are often smaller, and sisters or brothers will sometimes have to share a room. Generally, the family shares a single TV set and a single phone. It's not as common for teenagers to have a TV or a phone of their own in their bedroom.

Communication for All Students

Language Note
Point out to students that **mucho** does not change form when used as an adverb: **Me gusta mucho la natación. Mucho** changes form only when used as an adjective, to say *how much* or *how many* of something there is. **Necesito mucho dinero. ¿Tienes muchas clases?**

Additional Practice
Have partners ask and answer questions about classroom objects using **cuántos** and **muchos.** (**¿Cuántos diccionarios hay en la clase? Hay muchos diccionarios en la clase.**) Each student should ask a minimum of five questions.

22 Comparación de cuartos
Comparing rooms

Hablemos Work with a partner. One of you is staying in the **Hotel Dineral,** and the other is staying in the **Hotel Pocovale.** Imagine that you're on the telephone with each other comparing your rooms. Tell your partner what's in your room, or tell about what's not there.

MODELO —En mi cuarto hay dos camas. No tengo televisor pero hay dos lámparas.

See sample answer below.

Hotel Pocovale

Hotel Dineral

23 La sala de clase

Hablemos Work with three to five class-mates to find out what's in the ideal classroom. Be prepared to tell the class what kind of classroom your group would design.

MODELO —En la sala de clase ideal hay…

Vocabulario extra	
una alfombra	*rug*
un balcón	*balcony*
unos discos compactos	*CDs*
un estante	*bookcase*
una pecera	*fishbowl*
unas plantas	*plants*
un tocador de discos compactos	*CD player*

24 En mi cuaderno
Answers will vary. Example: En mi cuarto ideal hay dos camas,...

Escribamos Choose a picture of your ideal room from a magazine, or draw a room yourself. Imagine that it is your room, and write how many there are of each item in it.

A lo nuestro

You have already learned to say if you like something using **(no) me gusta.** Here are some new phrases to express stronger reactions. If you like something a lot you can say **¡Genial!, ¡Increíble!,** or **¡Qué padre!** If you think something is just all right, you can say **Está bien** or **No está mal.** If you think it's terrible, you can say **¡Qué horrible!, ¡Qué pesado!,** or **¡Pésimo!**

Writing Assessment
24 You may wish to evaluate this assignment using the following rubric.

Writing Rubric	Points			
	4	3	2	1
Content (Complete– Incomplete)				
Comprehensibility (Comprehensible– Incomprehensible)				
Accuracy (Accurate– Seldom accurate)				
Organization (Well organized– Poorly organized)				
Effort (Excellent–Minimal)				

18–20: A   14–15: C   Under
16–17: B   12–13: D   12: F

Assess
▶ Testing Program
Quiz 2-2A, Quiz 2-2B, pp. 31–34
Audio CD 2, Tr. 18

▶ Student Make-Up Assignments, Chapter 2, Alternative Quiz

▶ Alternative Assessment Guide, p. 33

Answers
22 *Sample answer:*
Tengo un cuarto grande. Hay una cama y tres ventanas. También hay un armario y un televisor.

Teaching Resources
pp. 60–63

PRINT 📖
▸ Lesson Planner, p. 10
▸ TPR Storytelling Book, pp. 7, 8
▸ Listening Activities, pp. 12, 17
▸ Activities for Communication, pp. 11–12, 82, 83–84, 139–140
▸ Cuaderno de gramática, pp. 16–17
▸ Grammar Tutor for Students of Spanish, Chapter 2
▸ Cuaderno de actividades, pp. 20–22
▸ Cuaderno para hispanohablantes, pp. 6–10
▸ Testing Program, pp. 35–38
▸ Alternative Assessment Guide, p. 33
▸ Student Make-Up Assignments, Chapter 2

MEDIA 💿📹
▸ One-Stop Planner
▸ Audio Compact Discs, CD 2, Trs. 10–15
▸ Teaching Transparencies 2-3, 2-C; **Más práctica gramatical** Answers; Cuaderno de gramática Answers
▸ Interactive CD-ROM Tutor, Disc 1

Bell Work
Tape a magazine picture or newspaper ad for furniture on the board. Ask students to imagine they are decorating a college dorm room. Ask them to write what they would put in their room. (**dos lámparas, un escritorio, una cama**)

Presenting
Así se dice

Model the expressions in **Así se dice.** Have students repeat after you. Put a list of activities on the board in Spanish and have students tell you whether they want or need to do these things.

Tercer paso

Objective Talking about what you need and want to do

WV3 SPAIN-2

Así se dice

Talking about what you need and want to do

To find out what someone needs to do, ask:

¿Qué necesitas hacer?
What do you need to do?

¿Y qué **necesita** hacer Paco?

To answer, say:

Necesito organizar mi cuarto.
. . . to organize my room.

Necesita ir a la librería.
. . . to go to the bookstore.

To find out what someone wants to do, ask:

¿Qué quieres hacer?

¿Y qué **quiere hacer** Merche?

No sé, pero no quiero hacer la tarea.
I don't know, but I don't want . . .

Quiere ir a la **pizzería.**

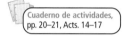

Cuaderno de actividades, pp. 20–21, Acts. 14–17

Más práctica gramatical, p. 68, Act. 8

---

25 ¿Qué necesita comprar?

Leamos/Escribamos Complete Paco and Abuela's conversation with the phrases in the box. First, read the sentences that come after the missing phrases so that the conversation makes sense.

ABUELA Oye, Paco. Mañana es el primer día de clases, ¿verdad? **1.** ¿════?

PACO Sí, es el primer día de clases. **2.** Necesito ════.

ABUELA ¿Qué cosas necesitas hacer?

PACO **3.** ════.

ABUELA Sí, es cierto. No tienes mucho papel.

PACO **4.** Y también quiero comprar ════.

- 3 • necesito comprar papel
- 4 • zapatillas de tenis
- 7 • no necesitas una calculadora
- 2 • hacer muchas cosas
- 8 • necesitas organizar
- 5 • necesito comprar cuadernos
- 1 • qué necesitas hacer
- 6 • pero necesito una calculadora

ABUELA Sí, también necesitas zapatillas de tenis. ¿Y cuadernos?

PACO **5.** No, no ════.

ABUELA Bueno, no necesitas cuadernos.

PACO **6.** ¡════ para la clase de álgebra!

ABUELA ¡Paco! **7.** ¡════! Y tu cuarto es un desastre. **8.** ════ tu cuarto.

26 Paco y su abuela

Hablemos Now, with a partner, act out the roles of Paco and his grandmother, using the dialogue from the previous activity. Then switch roles and try to vary what the two characters say. Be creative! Answers modeled in Activity 25.

Communication for All Students

Challenge
25 Ask students to complete the following sentences in as many original ways as possible.
1. Necesito poner...
2. Necesito encontrar...
3. Necesito ir a...
4. Necesito conocer a...
5. Necesito comprar...

Auditory Learners
29 After students write the answers, have them orally check answers in pairs, asking each other what the various people need. (**¿Qué necesita hacer Juanita? Necesita comprar un reloj.**)

STANDARDS: 1.1

Vocabulario

Necesito...

poner la ropa en
el armario

encontrar el dinero primero

Nota gramatical

Comprar, poner, conocer, and **ir** are
infinitives. The infinitive is a form of the
verb found in the dictionary. There are
three kinds of infinitive endings in Spanish:
-ar, -er, and **-ir.**

Cuaderno de gramática, p. 16, Act. 15

Quiero...

ir al centro comercial

conocer a muchos nuevos amigos

comprar muchas cosas

Cuaderno de actividades,
pp. 20–21, Acts. 16–17

Cuaderno de gramática, p. 16, Act. 14

Más práctica gramatical,
p. 69, Act. 9

Cuaderno de gramática, p. 16, Act. 15
Cuaderno de actividades, pp. 20–21, Acts. 16–17
Cuaderno de gramática, p. 16, Act. 14
Más práctica gramatical, p. 69, Act. 9

27 **Victoria y Tomás** Scripts and answers on p. 45G.

CD 2
Tr. 10

Escuchemos/Escribamos Listen as Victoria lists what she and Tomás need to do before Monday.
Write the name of the person who needs to do each thing. What do both of them need to do?

1. hacer muchas cosas
2. ir al centro comercial
3. comprar una mochila
4. organizar el cuarto
5. encontrar la mochila
6. poner la ropa en el armario
7. hacer la tarea

28 **Gramática en contexto**

Leamos/Hablemos Use verbs from the first column with phrases from the second to talk about
some things you plan to do this week. Start each
sentence with (**No**) **Necesito...** or (**No**) **Quiero...**
Possible answers: No quiero organizar la sala
de clase.Necesito poner los lápices en la mesa.

poner	mi cuarto
hacer	a clase
comprar	los lápices en la mesa
organizar	la sala de clase
ir	la tarea para mañana
encontrar	el dinero
	un diccionario de español
	mi libro de español en la mochila
	a la librería

29 **Problemas**

Escribamos The following people need your help. Write what each person needs to do,
wants to buy, or where each one needs to go, using as many new expressions as you can.

1. Juanita never knows what time it is.
2. Jorge's room is too dark.
3. María doesn't have enough clothes.
4. Isabel can't find tomorrow's homework in her cluttered room.
5. Rafael is trying to build his vocabulary.
6. Diego is totally out of pens, pencils, and paper.
7. Inés is new in town and is feeling lonely.
See possible answers below.

Cultures and Communities

Culture Note

The **centro comercial** in Latin America
has become a new focal point for some
Latin teenagers. Just as teens in the USA enjoy
visiting malls to shop, to eat, or just to see and be
seen, many youths in large cities spend time in malls
doing similar things. Latin teenagers tend to meet in
larger groups, often gathering in cafés to chat.

Native Speakers

Native speakers might make an entry in their journal (see Native Speakers, p. 2) using the pictures in
Vocabulario to tell a story. Tell them they may use
other verb forms in addition to the infinitives if
they feel comfortable doing so.

(see Native Speakers, p. 2)

Presenting
Vocabulario, Nota gramatical

Infinitives Model the pronunciation of the phrases on
Teaching Transparency 2–C,
having students repeat after you.
Then ask the class ¿**Necesitas
poner la ropa en el armario
en tu cuarto?** Have the class
answer chorally first, then call on
some individual students. Next
practice ¿**Quieres ir al centro
comercial esta tarde?** and
¿**Quieres comprar muchas
cosas?** ¿**Necesitas muchas
cosas o solamente quieres
muchas cosas?** Then have
students practice using the new
phrases in pairs.

Teaching Suggestion
Tell students to imagine that they are
getting ready to go back to school.
Ask, ¿**Necesitas comprar muchas
cosas?**, and ¿**Qué necesitas
comprar?** Then have them imagine
that they are packing their backpacks
the night before their first day back
at school. Ask, ¿**Qué necesitas
poner en la mochila?** and ¿**Qué
más necesitas hacer?**

Answers
29 *Possible answers:*
1. Juanita necesita comprar un reloj.
2. Jorge necesita una ventana.
3. María necesita comprar ropa.
4. Ella necesita organizar el cuarto
y hacer la tarea.
5. Rafael necesita un diccionario.
6. Diego necesita ir al centro comercial. Él necesita comprar muchas
cosas.
7. Inés necesita conocer a nuevos
amigos.

Teaching Resources
pp. 60–63

PRINT
- Lesson Planner, p. 10
- TPR Storytelling Book, pp. 7, 8
- Listening Activities, pp. 12, 17
- Activities for Communication, pp. 11–12, 82, 83–84, 139–140
- Cuaderno de gramática, pp. 16–17
- Grammar Tutor for Students of Spanish, Chapter 2
- Cuaderno de actividades, pp. 20–22
- Cuaderno para hispanohablantes, pp. 6–10
- Testing Program, pp. 35–38
- Alternative Assessment Guide, p. 33
- Student Make-Up Assignments, Chapter 2

MEDIA
- One-Stop Planner
- Audio Compact Discs, CD 2, Trs. 10–15
- Teaching Transparencies 2-3, 2-C; **Más práctica gramatical** Answers; Cuaderno de gramática Answers
- Interactive CD-ROM Tutor, Disc 1

Presenting
Vocabulario

Count by two's from 20 to 30. From 30 on, model the first number in each series (30, 40, 50, etc.) and have students continue until the next series is reached. Then play PONGA (see page 15C) to further practice the numbers. Students should prepare their PONGA card with numbers from 31 through 100.

Answers
32 1. 70, 30   4. 55, 45
2. 48, 52   5. 23, 77
3. 34, 66   6. 12, 88

---

30 **¿Qué necesitas hacer?**

 Hablemos Work in pairs. Tell your partner what each person in Activity 29 needs to do. Then find out if your partner wants or needs to do the same things. Switch roles after number four.

MODELO —Diego necesita ir a la librería. ¿Y tú? ¿Quieres ir a la librería?
—No, no quiero ir a la librería, pero necesito...

31 **De vuelta al colegio** *Back to school*

Hablemos With a partner, take turns asking and telling each other how many of each item you need to buy and how much money you need.

regla   diccionario
cuaderno   lápiz
mochila   goma de borrar
libro   bolígrafo

MODELO —¿Cuántas carpetas necesitas comprar?
—Necesito comprar siete carpetas.
—Necesitas ... dólares y ... centavos.

Vocabulario

¿Cuánto es en dólares?

31	treinta y uno	40	cuarenta	101	ciento uno
32	treinta y dos	50	cincuenta	102	ciento dos
33	treinta y tres	60	sesenta	103	ciento tres
34	treinta y cuatro	70	setenta		...
35	treinta y cinco	80	ochenta		...
36	treinta y seis	90	noventa		...
...		100	cien	199	ciento noventa y nueve

Uno at the end of a number changes to **un** before a masculine noun and **una** before a feminine noun: **veintiún dólares** *(dollars)*, **veintiuna reglas.**

CD-ROM 1
DVD 1

Más práctica gramatical, p. 69, Act. 10 →

Cuaderno de gramática, p. 17, Acts. 16–17

Cuaderno de actividades, p. 22, Act. 19

32 **Del colegio al trabajo** See answers below.

Hablemos Play the roles of clerks in a **papelería**. The store needs to have 100 of each of the following items for the upcoming semester. Working with a partner, tell how many of each are needed, given the quantity on hand.

MODELO —Hay cuarenta carpetas.
—Necesitamos sesenta más.

1. gomas de borrar (70)
2. bolígrafos (48)
3. cuadernos (34)
4. lápices (55)
5. reglas (23)
6. mochilas (12)

Connections and Comparisons

Culture Note

People in Spanish-speaking countries do not use personal checks for purchases as often as people in the United States do. In Mexico many people pay their utility bills with personal checks, but in Spain bills are usually paid by direct withdrawal. Cash is universally accepted, and most stores also accept credit cards, especially in larger cities.

Thinking Critically

Drawing Inferences Remind students that a store that sells paper (**papel**) is called a **papelería**, and that a store that sells books (**libros**) is called a **librería**. Have students guess what a store is called that sells shoes (**zapatos**), flowers (**flores**), or watches (**relojes**). (**zapatería, florería, relojería**)

33 **¿Cuántos años tiene?**

Hablemos/Escribamos In Chapter 1 you learned how to say how old someone is. Give the ages of the following people, using the person's name and **tiene _____ años.** If you don't know, you'll ask! If you can't ask, just guess. *Answers will vary. Example:* Mi padre tiene cincuenta años.

1. your parent or guardian
2. your principal
3. the person sitting next to you
4. a TV star
5. the President

6. a grandparent or elderly person
7. your best friend
8. the person in your family nearest your age
9. your favorite movie star
10. a recording artist

34 **Números de teléfono**

 Hablemos/Escribamos Your partner will say a name and a telephone number. Write the number, then repeat it to your partner to verify that you copied it correctly. Write three names and numbers, then switch roles and start over.

> **MODELO** El teléfono de Mark es el cinco, cincuenta y cinco, ochenta y siete, treinta y seis.

35 **En mi cuaderno**

Escribamos Most of us could use a little more organization in our lives. In your journal, write a paragraph about what you need to do this week. Include some things you need to do, where you need to go, and what you need to buy. Write how much money you need. See sample answer below.

LETRA Y SONIDO

CD 2
Trs. 11–15

A. The letter **d** in Spanish represents two possible pronunciations.

  1. At the very beginning of a phrase, or after an **l** or **n**, it sounds like the *d* in the English word *did* except with the tip of the tongue closer to the back of the teeth.

    dinero   diez   diccionario   dar   andar   dónde   el día   falda

  2. Anywhere else in the word or phrase (especially between vowels) its pronunciation is softened and is similar to the *th* in the English word *they*.

    qué día   cerdo   modo   cada   verdad   estudiar   calculadora

B. Dictado Script for Part B on p. 45H.

  Adriana is making a shopping list. Complete her list based on what she says.

    Tengo...   Necesito...

C. Trabalenguas

  Pronounce this tongue twister after your teacher or after the recording.
    Cada dado da dos dedos,
    dice el hado, y cada lado
    de dos dados, o dos dedos,
    da un dos en cada uno de los lados.

Communication for All Students

Kinesthetic Learners

34 Write two sets of identical phone numbers on slips of paper and put them in two jars. Have each student pick one number from each jar. The number from the first jar is hers and the number from the second is the number she calls. Students call classmates by saying the second number. The person who hears his number moves next to the one who called.

Slower Pace

35 Ask students to work in pairs to make a chart with days of the week listed at the top. Under each day, list activities they need to do that day. Use the chart as a graphic organizer to write a journal entry for Activity 35. Have students read the journal entries to each other and compare them with the graphic organizers to check for completeness.

Challenge
To reinforce writing skills, have students write the tongue twister in the **Letra y sonido** as you dictate it. After they have finished, ask them to look at the text to correct their work.

Additional Practice
To review material from this **Paso**, set up a **papelería** in the classroom with a variety of classroom objects "for sale" at various prices. Ask students to take the roles of salesclerk and customer and to practice buying things in the store.

Assess
▸ Testing Program
  Quiz 2-3A, Quiz 2-3B, pp. 35–38
  Audio CD 2, Tr. 19

▸ Student Make-Up Assignments, Chapter 2, Alternative Quiz

▸ Alternative Assessment Guide, p. 33

Answers
35 *Sample answer:*
  Necesito organizar mi cuarto. También necesito hacer la tarea. Necesito ir de compras. Necesito comprar una calculadora. Necesito 50 dólares.

Vamos a leer

CAPÍTULO 2

Teaching Resources
pp. 64–65

PRINT
▶ Lesson Planner, p. 11
▶ Cuaderno de actividades, p. 23
▶ Cuaderno para hispanohablantes, pp. 6–10
▶ Reading Strategies and Skills Handbook, Chapter 2
▶ ¡Lee conmigo! 1, Chapter 2
▶ Standardized Assessment Tutor, Chapter 2

MEDIA
▶ One-Stop Planner

Prereading
Activities A and B

Comparing and Contrasting
Ask students to name some books and movies whose storyline or setting is from another country or culture. *(Evita, Zorro, Romeo and Juliet, The Diary of Anne Frank)* How are these books or movies similar to or different from those set in the United States? Is setting the only difference? Have students discuss these questions in small groups or discuss them with the whole class.

Reading
Activities C and D

Drawing Inferences
C. Ask students to choose three of the items. What kinds of people would like these as gifts? (e.g., ***50 cosas que los niños pueden hacer para salvar la Tierra:** people who like nature, animals, the sea)*

Answers

B 1. *50 cosas que los niños pueden hacer para salvar la tierra*
2. *Nutrición y salud*
3. *Guía completa para el adiestramiento del perro*
4. *Mundo marino*

Portadas

A trip to the bookstore to buy school supplies is also a good opportunity to browse through some other interesting and fun items.

Estrategia para leer
Look at pictures, titles, and subtitles before you begin to read. Also look for other words that stand out (bold or large print). By looking at these first, you can often tell what a passage is about without reading every word.

¡A comenzar!

A. Look at the pictures and titles on these two pages. Are these items…
1. advertisements? no
2. movie reviews? no
3. book covers, CD-ROMs, magazines, and videotapes? yes
4. posters? no

B. By looking at just the <u>pictures</u> on the covers, can you tell which item is about… See answers below.
1. the environment?
2. food?
3. dogs?
4. marine life?

¿Te acuerdas?
Do you remember?
Remember the strategy you learned in Chapter 1. Use cognates to figure out meaning.

NUTRICIÓN Y SALUD
Mitos, peligros y errores de las dietas de adelgazamiento *Información sobre comidas y hábitos sanos.*

YA SOY COMPOSITOR
Nuevo CD-ROM con el que se convierte música en señales digitales. Crea tus propias melodías en la computadora.

Educar para el futuro. **50 COSAS QUE LOS NIÑOS PUEDEN HACER PARA SALVAR LA TIERRA** *The earth works group.* Ed. Emecé.

Buscando la utilidad
GUÍA COMPLETA PARA EL ADIESTRAMIENTO DEL PERRO
V. Rossi. De Vecchi.

Connections and Comparisons

Thinking Critically
Drawing Inferences Ask students what they think they could learn from each of the items. Other than what the titles say, what information might be included? (e.g., ***Guía completa para el adiestramiento del perro:** dog breeds, dog health, safety tips)*

Comparing and Contrasting
On the board write the following **refrán: Cara vemos, corazón no sabemos.** Then give the students a literal translation *(We can see the face, but we do not know the heart.)* Ask if anyone can think of an analogous saying in English. (You can't judge a book by its cover.)

LAROUSSE ILUSTRADO
Diccionario
Enciclopédico

LENGUA
Definiciones de la
palabra
Sinónimos y antónimos
Dificultades del idioma
Reglas gramaticales
CULTURA
Historia y geografía
Tecnología y biología
Ciencias naturales
Arte y literatura

GEOMUNDO
Revista de la naturaleza
mundial: animales,
lugares y situaciones
interesantes.

**BILLIKEN PRESENTA:
MUNDO MARINO**
Video documental filmado
en el oceanario de San
Clemente del Tuyú.
ATLÁNTIDA

Al grano For answers to C, D, and E, see below.

Now take a little more time and
look at the words in bold print.

C. Which item would you buy as a
gift for each of these people?
For someone who. . .

1. loves music
2. likes animals
3. wants to be a marine
biologist
4. wants to learn about ecology

D. Now read the information
accompanying each picture and
answer the questions.

1. Look at the *Pequeño
Larousse Ilustrado*. Does it
have cultural information?
Which cognates tell you this?

2. Look at the *Guía completa
para el adiestramiento del
perro*. **Guía** means *guide*.
What kind of a guide is this?

3. Look at *50 cosas que los niños
pueden hacer para salvar la
Tierra*. What's this book
about? How do you know?

4. Look at the *GeoMundo*.
What kind of magazine is it?
What do you think you'd
learn about if you read it?

E. Quieres comprar un video y
un libro. Completa el párrafo
(paragraph) para explicar *(to
explain)* adónde necesitas ir y
qué te gusta.

tienda   *store*
interesante   *interesting*
bueno   *good*

Quiero comprar unos...
Primero, necesito ir... donde está
mi... favorita. De los videos que
hay, me gusta... porque es... El
libro que quiero comprar es...
porque es...

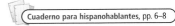

Cuaderno para hispanohablantes, pp. 6–8

Cuaderno de actividades, p. 23, Act. 20

Cuaderno para hispanohablantes, pp. 6–8

Cuaderno de actividades, p. 23, Act. 20

Vamos a leer

CAPÍTULO 2

Postreading
Activity E

Drawing on Your Experience
Ask students to think about their
favorite book. What is the title? What
do they like about the book? In their
opinion, can they tell from the title
everything the book is about?

Teaching Suggestion
All students may enjoy the challenge
of doing the last activity in the
Vamos a leer section in Spanish.
It is also particularly suitable for
native speakers of Spanish.

Native Speakers
Ask native speakers to bring in
their favorite book or video or a
photocopy of the cover. You may
want to preview the materials that
students bring in for age-appropriate
content. See if non-native speakers
can tell what a book or video is
about by reading the title. Then ask
the person who brought the book
or video in to describe its contents
and say why they like it.

C Answers
1. *Ya soy compositor*
2. *GeoMundo, Mundo Marino, Guía
completa para el diestramiento
del perro*
3. *Mundo marino*
4. *50 cosas que los niños pueden
hacer para salvar la tierra*

D 1. Yes; cultura, historia, arte,
literatura
2. The guide is about dog training.
3. The book is about 50 things that
children can do to save the Earth.
The number 50, the picture of
the planet Earth, and the English
phrase *The Earth-Works Group*
provide the clues.
4. It's a nature magazine. *Possible
answers:* animals, penguins,
cheetahs, Hong Kong

E *Answers will vary.*

Communication for All Students

Challenge
Students write **"Me gusta..."** lists on strips of
paper, trying to relate two or three of their likes
to one of the books pictured, signing their names
to their list. Have each student draw one. Each
student then decides which book is appropriate,
faces the person whose list he or she has drawn,
and says **"Necesitas comprar _____ porque
te gusta _____."**

Visual Learners
Have each student use these titles as a springboard
to come up with an original title for a book. Have
students exchange titles with a partner. Each then
considers the contents of his or her partner's book
and creates an appropriate book cover with pencil,
pen, and marker on paper or poster board. Display
the book covers around the room.

For **Más práctica gramatical** Answer Transparencies, see the *Teaching Transparencies* binder.

Más práctica gramatical

MARCAR: go.hrw.com
PALABRA CLAVE: WV3 SPAIN-2

Primer paso

Objective Talking about what you want and need

1 Complete Susana's school shopping list by filling in each blank with the correct indefinite article, **un** or **una**. (p. 51)

La lista de Susana

1. _____ bolígrafo
2. _____ regla
3. _____ goma de borrar
4. _____ carpeta
5. _____ diccionario
6. _____ mochila
7. _____ libro
8. _____ lápiz

2 You've offered to help Susana shop for school supplies. Make a joint list to take to the bookstore by combining her list from Activity 1 with yours. (p. 52)

1. _____
2. _____
3. _____
4. _____
5. _____
6. _____
7. _____
8. _____
9. _____
10. _____

Mi lista
1 regla
1 goma de borrar
1 libro
1 lápiz
1 diccionario
1 cuaderno
1 calculadora

3 Rosa and Luis are talking in a bookstore. Complete their conversation by filling in each blank with the correct indefinite article: **un, una, unos,** or **unas**. (p. 53)

ROSA Luis, ¿qué necesitas para las clases?

LUIS A ver... necesito __1__ mochila y __2__ calculadora. ¿Y tú, Rosa?

ROSA Pues, para mi clase de arte necesito __3__ lápices y __4__ cuadernos. Y quiero __5__ regla y __6__ gomas de borrar para la clase de matemáticas.

LUIS ¿Y qué necesitas para las clases de inglés y español?

ROSA Necesito __7__ diccionarios y __8__ carpetas.

Answers

1
1. un
2. una
3. una
4. una
5. un
6. una
7. un
8. un

2
1. un bolígrafo
2. dos reglas
3. dos gomas de borrar
4. una carpeta
5. dos diccionarios
6. una mochila
7. dos libros
8. dos lápices
9. un cuaderno
10. una calculadora

3
1. una   5. una
2. una   6. unas
3. unos   7. unos
4. unos   8. unas

Grammar Resources for Chapter 2

The **Más práctica gramatical** activities are designed as supplemental activities for the grammatical concepts presented in the chapter. You might use them as additional practice, for review, or for assessment.

For more grammar presentation, review, and practice, see the:
• Cuaderno de gramática
• Grammar Tutor for Students of Spanish

• Grammar Summary on pp. R9–R13.
• Cuaderno de actividades
• Grammar and Vocabulary quizzes (Testing Program)
• Test Generator on the One-Stop Planner CD-ROM
• Interactive CD-ROM Tutor
• **Juegos interactivos** at <u>go.hrw.com</u>.

4 Which subject pronoun, **yo, tú, él,** or **ella,** would you use to . . .? (**p. 54**)

1. ask your friend Alicia a question
2. tell what Alicia needs to buy
3. talk to your friend Marcos
4. explain what Marcos wants
5. talk about your art teacher, Mr. Vargas
6. describe your math teacher, Mrs. Cisneros
7. say what you need

5 Answer these questions about what school supplies different people need. Use the subject pronouns **yo, él,** or **ella** in your answers. (**p. 54**)

MODELO   **¿Qué necesita Miguel Ángel? (cuadernos)**
Él necesita unos cuadernos.

1. ¿Qué necesita el profesor Delgado? (carpetas)
2. ¿Qué necesita Carmen? (reglas)
3. ¿Qué necesitas tú? (bolígrafos)
4. ¿Qué necesita tu amigo? (lápices)
5. ¿Qué necesita la profesora Rivera? (gomas de borrar)
6. ¿Qué necesita José Alberto? (papel)

Segundo paso

Objective Describing the contents of your room.

6 Paco is describing his room to Merche. Complete his description by filling in each blank with the correct word. (**p. 57**)

¿Qué hay en ___1___ (mi/su) cuarto? Pues, yo ___2___ (tengo/tienes) un escritorio, una cama, una lámpara y ___3___ (un/una) reloj. También hay ___4___ (un/una) radio. Quiero una computadora, ___5___ (un/una) televisor y un estéreo. Ya hay ___6___ (unos/unas) carteles en mi cuarto, pero quiero más. Mi amigo Felipe ___7___ (tienes/tiene) muchos libros en ___8___ (mi/su) cuarto. ¿Y tú, Merche? ¿Qué ___9___ (tienes/tiene) en ___10___ (su/tu) cuarto?

Answers

4
1. tú   5. él
2. ella   6. ella
3. tú   7. yo
4. él

5
1. Él necesita unas carpetas.
2. Ella necesita unas reglas.
3. Yo necesito unos bolígrafos.
4. Él necesita unos lápices.
5. Ella necesita unas gomas de borrar.
6. Él necesita papel.

6
1. mi
2. tengo
3. un
4. una
5. un
6. unos
7. tiene
8. su
9. tienes
10. tu

Teacher to Teacher

Mani Hernández
Presentation High School
San José, California

Mani's students get the last word
❝I give each student a word or phrase from the vocabulary listed at the end of the unit, then ask them to stand up. Two designated students take turns calling out these words from a list I have prepared, in any order. The student with the word or phrase called out sits down. Since I repeat some words, more than one student may have to take a seat, and more than one may be left standing. The student or students with the last word or phrase may be given a winner's prize—either extra points or token trinkets.❞

Más práctica gramatical

WV3 SPAIN-2

CAPÍTULO 2

 For **Más práctica gramatical** Answer Transparencies, see the *Teaching Transparencies* binder.

7 Your sister has a lot of questions about school. Write her questions and your answers, using the correct forms of **cuánto** and **mucho**. (p. 58)

MODELO   estudiantes en la clase de español
　　　　　　—¿Cuántos estudiantes hay en la clase de español?
　　　　　　—Hay muchos estudiantes.

1. carteles en la clase de español
2. tarea en tu clase de inglés
3. sillas en la cafetería
4. televisores en el colegio
5. libros en la librería
6. mesas en la cafetería
7. ventanas en la clase de arte
8. dinero en tu mochila

Tercer paso

Objective Talking about what you want and need to do

8 You've written a letter to your cousin Teresa about this coming weekend. Fill in each blank with the correct form of the verb in parentheses. (p. 60)

Este fin de semana yo ___1___ (necesitar) comprar cosas para la escuela. Luis ___2___ (querer) ir al centro comercial pero ___3___ (necesitar) encontrar su dinero. Yo ___4___ (querer) ir al centro comercial porque ___5___ (necesitar) comprar una goma de borrar y unos cuadernos. Yo ___6___ (tener) calculadoras y lápices pero ___7___ (necesitar) comprar los libros.

Answers

7 1. ¿Cuántos carteles hay en la clase de español? Hay muchos carteles.
2. ¿Cuánta tarea hay en tu clase de inglés? Hay mucha tarea.
3. ¿Cuántas sillas hay en la cafetería? Hay muchas sillas.
4. ¿Cuántos televisores hay en el colegio? Hay muchos televisores.
5. ¿Cuántos libros hay en la librería? Hay muchos libros.
6. ¿Cuántas mesas hay en la cafetería? Hay muchas mesas.
7. ¿Cuántas ventanas hay en la clase de arte? Hay muchas ventanas.
8. ¿Cuánto dinero hay en tu mochila? Hay mucho dinero.

8 1. necesito
2. quiere
3. necesita
4. quiero
5. necesito
6. tengo
7. necesito

Communication for All Students

Additional Practice

Fill a shopping bag or basket with school items already presented. Put in two or three of some items. One by one, have students come up to the front. Tell each person what he or she is to take using either **tienes**, **necesitas**, or **quieres** and an item or items in the container. If you say **Miguel, necesitas cuadernos**, the student is to pick the item or items from the container and say a sentence using the **yo** form of the verb you have used and the items taken. (**Necesito unos cuadernos**). Students should refer to the items they find in the container using **un** or **unos** and **una** or **unas**.

9 Explain what you and your friends need to do after school today, using the chart and the verb **necesitar**. (**p. 61**)

MODELO   **Sarita**
          Sarita necesita comprar cosas para las clases. También...

	YO	TÚ	RAFAEL	SARITA
comprar cosas para las clases	✔			✔
ir a la librería	✔	✔		
hacer la tarea			✔	
ir al centro comercial		✔		✔
organizar el cuarto			✔	✔

1. Yo...   **3.** Rafael...
2. Tú...   **4.** Sarita...

10 Tell your friend Jaime how much money he needs to buy the following things. Write out the numbers. (**p. 62**)

MODELO   **2 carteles a $15.00 c/u (cada uno - *each*)**
          —Necesitas treinta dólares para comprar dos carteles.

1. 3 lámparas a $21.00 c/u
2. 4 pizzas a $11.00 c/u
3. 1 radio a $17.00
4. 10 revistas a $3.50 c/u
5. 2 pares de zapatillas de tenis a $89.00 c/u
6. 1 silla a $57.00
7. 2 mochilas a $26.00 c/u

Answers

9 **1.** Yo necesito comprar cosas para las clases. También necesito ir a la librería.
2. Tú necesitas ir a la librería. También necesitas ir al centro comercial.
3. Rafael necesita hacer la tarea. Él necesita organizar su cuarto también.
4. Sarita necesita comprar cosas para las clases. También necesita ir al centro comercial y organizar su cuarto.

10 **1.** Necesitas sesenta y tres dólares para comprar tres lámparas.
2. Necesitas cuarenta y cuatro dólares para comprar cuatro pizzas.
3. Necesitas diecisiete dólares para comprar una radio.
4. Necesitas treinta y cinco dólares para comprar diez revistas.
5. Necesitas ciento setenta y ocho dólares para comprar dos pares de zapatillas de tenis.
6. Necesitas cincuenta y siete dólares para comprar una silla.
7. Necesitas cincuenta y dos dólares para comprar dos mochilas.

Review and Assess

You may wish to assign the **Más práctica gramatical** activities as additional practice or homework after presenting material throughout the chapter. Assign Activity 1 after **Nota gramatical** (p. 51), Activity 2 after **Gramática** (p. 52), Activity 3 after **Gramática** (p. 53), Activities 4–5 after **Nota gramatical** (p. 54), Activity 6 after **Así se dice** (p. 57), Activity 7 after **Gramática** (p. 58), Activity 8 after **Así se dice** (p. 60), Activity 9 after **Nota gramatical** (p. 61), and Activity 10 after **Vocabulario** (p. 62). To prepare students for the **Paso** Quizzes and Chapter Test, have them do the **Más práctica gramatical** activities in the following order: complete Activities 1–5 before taking Quiz 2-1A or 2-1B; Activities 6–7 before taking Quiz 2-2A or 2-2B; and Activities 8–10 before taking Quiz 2-3A or 2-3B.

CAPÍTULO 2

The **Repaso** reviews and integrates all four skills and culture in preparation for the Chapter Test.

MARCAR: go.hrw.com
PALABRA CLAVE:
WV3 SPAIN-2

internet

Teaching Resources
pp. 70–71

PRINT

▶ Lesson Planner, p. 11
▶ Video Guide, p. 16
▶ Grammar Tutor for Students of Spanish, Chapter 2
▶ Cuaderno para hispanohablantes, pp. 6–10
▶ Standardized Assessment Tutor, Chapter 2

MEDIA

▶ One-Stop Planner
▶ Video Program
  Videocassette 1, 39:38–40:18
▶ DVD Tutor, Disc 1
▶ Audio Compact Discs, CD 2, Tr. 16
▶ Interactive CD-ROM Tutor, Disc 1

Portfolio

2 **Written** Suggest that each student write a dialogue between him- or herself and a classmate using vocabulary and functions from this chapter. Students may wish to include their dialogues in their portfolios. For Portfolio information, see *Alternative Assessment Guide*, pp. iv–17.

Answers

2 **3** *Possible dialogue for Activities 2 and 3:*
—Paco, necesitas organizar tu cuarto.
—Pero Abuela, necesito ir de compras.
—¡Primero, a organizar tu cuarto!
—Bien, pero necesito muchas cosas. Necesito una mochila.
—Aquí tienes una mochila.
—Bien. Voy a organizar mi cuarto.

---

1 CD 2 Tr. 16 — Imagine that you're an exchange student in Madrid. Your host brother Juan Carlos is helping you decide what you'll need for school. Based on what Juan Carlos says, how many of each item do you need? Script on p. 45H.

a. cuaderno 4   **d.** carpeta 5
b. diccionario 1 **e.** lápiz 6
c. bolígrafo 10   **f.** mochila 1

2 Paco and Felipe want to go shopping, but first Paco must clean his room. Write a dialogue and include Felipe's questions about what Paco needs to do, and Paco's answers. Be sure to use **querer** and **necesitar.**
See sample answer below.

3 Con un/a compañero/a, presenten los diálogos que crearon para la actividad 2.
See sample answer below.

4 **Tienda Deco** is having a year-end sale. Working in a small group, look at the price list and decide which items you want to buy with the $199.00 you have. Be prepared to share your selections with the class.

MES DEL MUEBLE EN TIENDA DECO

Reloj Pared	$39.00
Mesa TV	$79.00
Lámpara	$26.00
Silla Danesa	$50.00
Mesa Nido	$35.00
Armario 2 Puertas	$150.00

reloj pared   lámpara

5 Your school will have some exchange students from Spain and Argentina this year. Based on what you've learned about schools in Spanish-speaking countries, name two things about your school that they would find familiar, and two things that might seem different.
Familiar: desks, books;
Different: lockers, changing rooms

Apply and Assess

Slower Pace

1 Have students list the items before beginning this activity. If possible, have actual labeled items available.

Additional Practice

2 Suggest that each student write a paragraph about him- or herself, a classmate, or Paco using vocabulary and functions learned in this chapter. A complete paragraph should include the following: what the person needs or wants to do, what he or she needs or wants to buy, and places he or she needs or wants to go.

6 In pairs, take turns reading the items to each other. Then form sentences saying what each person wants or needs to do. Be creative!

MODELO Armando quiere jugar *(to play)* al tenis pero no tiene zapatillas.
Armando necesita ir al centro comercial para comprar zapatillas.

1. Joaquín dice *(says)*, "Me gusta la música de Juan Luis Guerra y tengo bastante *(plenty of)* dinero."

2. No tienes cuadernos ni gomas de borrar.

3. Tengo dinero en mi cuarto, sí, pero ¡el cuarto es un desastre!

4. Anabel no tiene muchos amigos.

5. Manuela dice, "Me gusta la revista *Tú*."

6. Tengo muchos problemas en la clase de inglés.
Answers will vary. See example below.

7 With a partner, look at the pictures and match each of these descriptions to the person who said it. Then choose one of the two remaining pictures and describe it to your partner. See if she or he can guess which one you're describing.

1. Tengo veintiocho años. Me gusta la música clásica y tengo muchos discos compactos. ¿Quién soy?

2. Me gusta ir al centro comercial. Necesito zapatillas de tenis. Tengo quince años. ¿Quién soy?

3. Me gusta ir al centro comercial. Necesito zapatillas de tenis, pero necesito encontrar mi dinero primero. Tengo cincuenta años. ¿Quién soy?

3.

2.

1.

8 **Situación**

Get together with two or three classmates. Imagine that you're students from different Spanish-speaking countries, with new names and ages. Introduce yourself to the group in Spanish. Keep your conversation going as long as you can by asking your partners questions about where they're from, what things they have in their room, their likes and dislikes, and what they want to do.

Cuaderno para hispanohablantes, p. 10

Additional Practice
Students work in pairs. One student says a sentence or two that set forth a problem to his or her partner. **(No tengo dinero. Necesito un cuaderno.)** The partner should then offer a solution, using the phrases and vocabulary in the chapter. **(Necesitas ir al banco. Tienes que comprar un cuaderno.)**

Speaking Assessment
8 Allow students to practice their conversation in small groups for ten minutes. You may wish to have each group present their conversation to the class, during which time you can use the following rubric to evaluate their speaking progress.

Speaking Rubric	Points			
	4	3	2	1
Content (Complete– Incomplete)				
Comprehension (Total–Little)				
Comprehensibility (Comprehensible– Incomprehensible)				
Accuracy (Accurate– Seldom accurate)				
Fluency (Fluent–Not fluent)				

18–20: A   14–15: C   Under
16–17: B   12–13: D   12: F

Apply and Assess

Group Work

Have students work in pairs or small groups to develop a conversation between an older and a younger sibling. The older sibling must buy his or her younger sibling what he or she needs for school. As the younger sibling says **Necesito tres bolígrafos**, the older sibling is to question whether the younger child needs or wants the item by saying **¿Tienes bolígrafos?**, **¿Qué hay en tu mochila?**, or another appropriate question. The younger sibling should respond, and then the two siblings will decide to buy only what is needed. Encourage students to be creative.

Answers
Sample answer:
6 1. Joaquín necesita ir a la tienda de música para comprar unos discos compactos de Juan Luis Guerra.

A ver si puedo

Teaching Resources
p. 72

PRINT
▶ Grammar Tutor for Students of Spanish, Chapter 2

MEDIA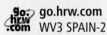
▶ Interactive CD-ROM Tutor, Disc 1
▶ Online self-test

go.hrw.com
WV3 SPAIN-2

Answers

1 *Possible answers:*
1. —Juanita, ¿tienes unos bolígrafos y papel?
   —Sí, tengo unos bolígrafos y papel.
2. —Paco, ¿necesitas una calculadora?
   —No, no necesito una calculadora.
3. —Felipe, ¿necesitas unos cuadernos?
   —Sí, necesito unos cuadernos.
4. —Mercedes, ¿necesitas una mochila?
   —No, no necesito una mochila.
5. —(Mari), ¿necesitas un lápiz?
   —Sí, necesito un lápiz.

2 Hay _____ en mi cuarto. No tengo _____, pero quiero _____. ¿Tienes un armario en tu cuarto? ¿una cama? ¿una radio? ¿un televisor?

3 1. ¿Cuánto papel necesitas?
2. ¿Cuántos libros necesitas?
3. ¿Cuántas reglas necesitas?
4. ¿Cuántos cuadernos necesitas?
5. ¿Cuántas carpetas necesitas?
6. ¿Cuántos lápices necesitas?

4 1. Necesito organizar mi cuarto. Quiero organizar mi cuarto.
2. Necesito poner mis zapatillas de tenis en el armario. Quiero poner...
3. Necesito encontrar mi dinero. Quiero encontrar mi dinero.
4. Necesito ir a la librería. Quiero ir...
5. Necesito comprar muchas cosas. Quiero comprar...
6. Necesito conocer a unos amigos nuevos. Quiero conocer...

A ver si puedo...

WV3 SPAIN-2

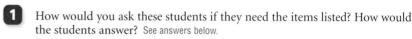

Can you talk about what you want and need? p. 52

1 How would you ask these students if they need the items listed? How would the students answer? See answers below.
1. Juanita   some pens and paper
2. Paco   a calculator
3. Felipe   some notebooks
4. Mercedes   a backpack
5. Tú   ¿?

Can you describe the contents of your room? p. 57

2 How would you tell a friend how many, if any, of each item is in your room? How would you say you don't have a certain item but want one? Now write out the questions you would use to ask your friend if she or he has these items in his or her room. See answers below.

3 Tomorrow is the first day of class. Ask a friend how much or how many he or she needs of these things. How would your friend answer? See answers below.
1. paper   4. notebooks
2. books   5. folders
3. rulers   6. pencils

Can you talk about what you need and want to do? p. 60

4 How would you say you need to do the following things? How would you say you want to do the same things? See answers below.
1. to organize your room
2. to put your tennis shoes in the closet
3. to find your money
4. to go to the bookstore
5. to buy a lot of things
6. to meet some new friends

Communication for All Students

Challenge
2 Ask students to interview classmates to find out what is in their rooms and what they need or want in their rooms. Based on the answers to the interview questions, have each student write a paragraph describing his or her partner's ideal room. The paragraph should include items their partners need or want for the room. Students should check with each other for accuracy.

Building on Previous Skills
4 Juan, Susana, and Diego want to spend the afternoon together. Juan is hungry and wants to go out to eat. Susana needs to buy school supplies. Diego wants to go with Juan and Susana, but he has to clean his room first. Divide students into groups of three and assign a role to each student. Ask students to write and role-play a conversation among the three friends.

Primer paso

Talking about what you want and need

el bolígrafo	ballpoint pen	la librería	bookstore	quieres	you want
Bueno	Well . . .	el libro	book	quiero	I want
la calculadora	calculator	la mochila	book bag,	la regla	ruler
la carpeta	folder		backpack	tengo	I have
el colegio	high school	necesita	she/he needs	un	a, an (masc. sing.)
el cuaderno	notebook	necesitar	to need	una	a, an (fem. sing.)
el diccionario	dictionary	necesitas	you need	unas	some, a few
él	he	necesito	I need		(fem. pl.)
ella	she	el papel	paper	unos	some, a few
la goma de borrar	eraser	querer (ie)	to want		(masc. pl.)
el lápiz	pencil	quiere	he/she wants	ya	already

Segundo paso

Describing the contents of your room

el armario	closet	mi	my	su	his; her
la cama	bed	mucho/a	a lot (of)	el televisor	TV set
el cartel	poster	muchos/as	many, a lot (of)	tener (ie)	to have
¿Cuánto/a?	How much?	la puerta	door	tiene	he/she has
¿Cuántos/as?	How many?	¿Qué hay en...?	What's in . . .?	tienes	you have
el cuarto	room	la radio	radio		(familiar)
el escritorio	desk	el reloj	clock; watch	tu	your (familiar)
hay	there is, there are	la revista	magazine	la ventana	window
la lámpara	lamp	la ropa	clothes, clothing	las zapatillas de	tennis shoes
la mesa	table	la silla	chair	tenis	(Spain)

Tercer paso

Talking about what you need and want to do

el centro comercial	shopping mall	el dinero	money	nuevos amigos	new friends
comprar	to buy	el dólar	dollar	organizar	to organize
conocer	to get to know (someone)	encontrar (ue)	to find	la pizzería	pizzeria
		hacer	to do, to make	poner	to put
		ir	to go	primero	first
la cosa	thing	No sé.	I don't know.		

Numbers 31–199 See p. 62.

Review and Assess

Game

¿Qué ves? Any number of students may play, but this game works well with small groups. One player tells the group that he or she sees something in the room (vocabulary restricted to this chapter). The others, each in turn, quickly try to guess what he or she sees. Whoever guesses correctly is the next student to describe. You will

need to teach them **veo, ves,** and **cosa** as words to facilitate the game.

Player 1: Veo algo.
Player 2: ¿Es una persona o una cosa?
Player 1: Una cosa.
Player 3: ¿Con qué letra?
Player 1: Con la letra "c".
Player 4: ¿Es un cartel?
Player 1: Sí, por supuesto.

Teaching Suggestions

- In the Chapter Opener Presentation (p. 42), the students made a list of items in the window of the **papelería**. Ask them to check their list to see which things they now know how to say in Spanish.

- Have students work in groups of three or four. Each group should make removable labels using the vocabulary for 15 things they see in the classroom. Groups should exchange labels and see which group can attach their labels to the items the fastest.

Chapter 2 Assessment

▸ **Testing Program**
Chapter Test, pp. 39–44
Audio Compact Discs, CD 2, Trs. 20–21
Speaking Test, p. 343

▸ **Alternative Assessment Guide**
Performance Assessment, p. 33
Portfolio Assessment, p.19
CD-ROM Assessment, p. 47

▸ **Interactive CD-ROM Tutor, Disc 1**
¡A hablar!
¡A escribir!

▸ **Standardized Assessment Tutor**
Chapter 2

▸ **One-Stop Planner, Disc 1**

Test Generator
Chapter 2

Teaching Resources
pp. 74–77

PRINT
▶ Lesson Planner, pp. 12, 67
▶ Video Guide, pp. 17–18

MEDIA
▶ One-Stop Planner
▶ Video Program
  Videocassette 1, 40:32–43:02
▶ DVD Tutor, Disc 1
▶ Interactive CD-ROM Tutor, Disc 1
▶ Map Transparency 5

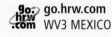 **go.hrw.com**
WV3 MEXICO

Using the Almanac and Map

Terms in the Almanac

- **La bandera:** The emblem on the flag depicts the legend of the founding of **Tenochtitlán,** the Aztec capital and the site of present-day Mexico City.

- **Capital:** Mexico City may be referred to simply as **México,** as **México, Distrito Federal,** or as **México, D.F.**

- **República federal:** Mexico is composed of 31 states and a federal district.

- **Industrias: acero** *steel;* **plata** *silver;* **químicos** *chemicals;* **electrodomésticos** *electrical household appliances;* **caucho** *rubber*

- **Cosechas principales: algodón** *cotton;* **café** *coffee;* **trigo** *wheat;* **arroz** *rice;* **caña de azúcar** *sugar cane*

- **Idiomas:** Spanish is the official language of Mexico, but many people speak indigenous languages, especially in the rural areas of Oaxaca, Chiapas, Michoacán, and Yucatán. The main indigenous languages are **maya, mixteco, náhuatl, otomí, purépecha,** and **zapoteco.**

¡Ven conmigo a México!

Población: 98.000.000

Área: 1.949.706 km² (761.604 millas cuadradas); tres veces más grande que el estado de Texas

Capital: Ciudad de México (Distrito Federal), población más de 20.000.000 (área metropolitana)

Gobierno: república federal

Industrias: acero, plata, químicos, electrodomésticos, textiles, caucho, petróleo, turismo

Cosechas principales: algodón, café, trigo, arroz, caña de azúcar, tomates, maíz, frutas

Unidad monetaria: el nuevo peso

Idiomas: español, más de cincuenta lenguas indígenas

 go.hrw.com
WV3 MEXICO

Ruinas de una civilización pre-azteca en Teotihuacán ▶

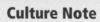 Culture Note

Teotihuacán means *city of the gods* in Náhuatl. According to legend, a huge pyre was built and the brave god Nanahuatzin leaped into the fire and was transformed into the sun. The richly-clad Tecciztécatl, who had claimed to be brave, hesitated before diving into the fire, and thus became the pale moon.

 Multicultural Link

Ask students if they know how Egyptian pyramids differ from those in the Americas. (Americas: steps, flat tops, primarily used as temples; Egypt: smooth sides, pointed tops, used as tombs and monuments)

≥MAPQUEST.COM™

HRW
go. Atlas Interactivo
hrw. Mundial
.com

Have students use the interactive atlas at go.hrw.com to find out more about the geography of Mexico and to complete the Map Activities below.

Map Activities

Refer students to the map of Mexico on page xxviii to answer the following questions.

1. Ask students to point out countries that border Mexico. (United States, Guatemala, Belize)

2. Have students point out D.F. (Teotihuacán is about 30 miles from D.F.)

3. Point out to students that Mexico is divided into states. Ask if anyone can figure out which states have names from Spanish (Hidalgo, Guerrero, Veracruz, and so on) and which have names from indigenous languages. (Oaxaca, Coahuila, Tlaxcala, and so on)

4. Have students locate Monterrey, an important industrial center.

5. Ask students to locate Guadalajara, an important agricultural and industrial center.

6. Have students locate Acapulco, Cozumel, Mazatlán, and Puerto Vallarta. Have they visited these popular places?

CNNenEspañol.com

Have students check the **CNN en español** Web site for news on Mexico. The **CNN en español** site is also a good source of timely, high-interest readings for Spanish students.

Connections and Comparisons

History Link

According to legend, the god Huitzilopochtli told the Aztecs to establish their capital, Tenochtitlán, where they saw an eagle perched on a cactus with a serpent in its mouth. They saw the eagle on an island in the middle of Lake Texcoco, a large saline lake surrounded by volcanic peaks. Some parts of Tenochtitlán, now Mexico City, were built on artificial garden-islands known as **chinampas**, which also provided much of the city's food supply. The Spanish conquerors were astounded at how developed Tenochtitlán was and took over the city for their own capital.

Using the Photo Essay

1 **Alfarero de Oaxaca** In Oaxaca you can find indigenous black pottery as well as Spanish-style green-glazed pottery. Also for sale in the **mercados** are weavings, textiles, filigree jewelry, ceramics, sculptures, baskets, and colorful native dresses called **huipiles**. The name **Oaxaca** comes from the indigenous Nahuatl language. The **x** is pronounced like the **x** in **México**.

2 "El Popo," as **Popocatépetl** is often called, is located 45 miles southeast of Mexico City. At 17,887 feet, it is the second-highest peak in Mexico and the world's highest active volcano. **Popocatépetl** means *smoking mountain* in Náhuatl.

3 **El Palacio de Bellas Artes**, built between 1904 and 1934, is constructed almost entirely of marble. Its great weight has caused it to sink several inches per year. It has been tied and lifted with cranes on several occasions. This major cultural center houses the National Theater, where concerts, dance programs, operas, and plays are performed, and art galleries feature 19th- and 20th-century Mexican paintings.

México

Mexico, a rich and diverse nation with a wealth of resources, culture, and history, has been a cradle of advanced civilizations for more than two thousand years. Many Mexicans are of mixed indigenous and European descent. The country is a leading producer of petroleum, silver, corn, coffee, oranges, and cotton. Mexico City, the national capital, is the world's largest city.

internet

MARCAR: go.hrw.com
PALABRA CLAVE:
WV3 MEXICO

1 **Alfarero de Oaxaca**
The markets of Oaxaca are a great place to find colorful pottery, weavings, jewelry, ceramics, and baskets.

2 "El Popo"
Popocatépetl, one of two volcanoes near Mexico City, means "smoking mountain" in Náhuatl, the language of the ancient Aztecs and the native language of over one million Mexicans today

3 **Bellas Artes**
El Palacio de Bellas Artes, home of the *Ballet Folklórico*, is Mexico's most important theater.

Cultures and Communities

Geography Link

Ask students to think about why buildings in Mexico City are sinking. When the Spaniards took over Tenochtitlán, frequent floods forced them to undertake ambitious drainage projects. The drained lakebed formed the plains upon which Mexico City expanded. The city's growing population required more and more drinking water, formerly obtained from wells and springs south of the valley, but taken increasingly from the lake. The ground beneath parts of the city has compacted due to years of water removal, and thus many buildings have been sinking over the years. The silty soils of the former lakebed are unstable during earthquakes, which can cause dramatic destruction, as happened in 1985.

5 Cabeza olmeca
The Olmecs, Mexico's earliest recorded civilization, left behind huge carved stone heads, the earliest portraits of Native Americans.

4 La UNAM The mural at the library of the National Autonomous University of Mexico was created by Juan O'Gorman in 1950. It depicts a symbolic history of Mexican culture.

5 Cabeza olmeca The statues probably came from San Lorenzo, one of the three major Olmec centers in the Tabasco region of the southern Gulf Coast. The heads were carved out of basalt, a volcanic rock, some time between 1200 and 900 B.C. They are believed to represent ancient tribal chiefs whose likenesses were merged with images of serpents and tigers. Besides being highly-skilled sculptors, the Olmecs were possibly the Mesoamerican inventors of numbers, writing, and the calendar. They strongly influenced the development of later peoples such as the Mayans and Aztecs.

4 La UNAM
Spectacular murals are found throughout Mexico, like this mosaic mural at the *Universidad Nacional Autónoma de México.*

6 El Parque de Chapultepec is a favorite spot for residents of Mexico City. It covers 40 square miles. Chapultepec has an amusement park, three lakes, and eight museums, including the famous Chapultepec Castle (**Castillo de Chapultepec**), which was the residence of the president until 1940. In Náhuatl, **Chapultepec** means *grasshopper hill.*

In Chapters 3 and 4
you will meet several students who live in Cuernavaca, a historic city of about 400,000 people that is the capital of the Mexican state of Morelos. Cuernavaca is a popular place where people from all over the world come to study Spanish. Young people from Mexico City come to Morelos for a fun-filled weekend of skiing on natural lakes, swimming in spring-fed pools, sailboat racing, and visiting historical sites like the *Palacio de Cortés* or the ruins at Xochicalco.

6 El parque de Chapultepec
Chapultepec Park, the largest wooded area in Mexico City, is one of the best places for outdoor relaxation in the capital.

7 Charreadas are rodeo-like competitions popular in western Mexico. The male horsemen, called **charros,** wear suits made of doeskin or velvet with a short jacket known as a **bolero** and riding pants with gold or silver buttons down the sides. The **charras** wear a feminine version of the charro suit, and the **amazonas** wear long, colorful dresses.

7 Las charreadas
The biggest rodeo rings in Mexico are in Mexico City and Guadalajara. These women are dressed in typical *amazona* costume.

Connections and Comparisons

Art Link
Ask students if they know what a mural is. (a large picture painted on a wall or a ceiling) Can they describe a mosaic? (pictures or designs made by inlaying small bits of colored stone, glass, or tile in mortar) Who are some famous Mexican muralists? (Diego Rivera, José Clemente Orozco, David Siqueiros)

Multicultural Link
The Olmecs are noted for their contribution to the development of the calendar. Ask students what other ancient cultures developed calendars. (Egyptian, Babylonian, Roman, Arabic, Chinese, Mayan)

Capítulo 3: Nuevas clases, nuevos amigos
Chapter Overview

Capítulo 3: Nuevas clases, nuevos amigos
Chapter Resources

PRINT

Lesson Planning
One-Stop Planner
Lesson Planner with Substitute Teacher Lesson Plans, pp. 13–17, 67
Student Make-Up Assignments
- Make-Up Assignment Copying Masters, Chapter 3

Listening and Speaking
TPR Storytelling Book, pp. 9–12
Listening Activities
- Student Response Forms for Listening Activities, pp. 19–21
- Additional Listening Activities 3-1 to 3-6, pp. 23–25
- Additional Listening Activities (song), p. 26
- Scripts and Answers, pp. 112–116

Video Guide
- Teaching Suggestions, pp. 19–21
- Activity Masters, pp. 22–24
- Scripts and Answers, pp. 91–93, 114

Activities for Communication
- Communicative Activities, pp. 13–18
- Realia and Teaching Suggestions, pp. 85–89
- Situation Cards, pp. 141–142

Reading and Writing
Reading Strategies and Skills Handbook, Chapter 3

¡Lee conmigo! 1, Chapter 3
Cuaderno de actividades, pp. 25–36

Grammar
Cuaderno de gramática, pp. 18–26
Grammar Tutor for Students of Spanish, Chapter 3

Assessment
Testing Program
- Grammar and Vocabulary Quizzes, **Paso** Quizzes, and Chapter Test, pp. 53–70
- Score Sheet, Scripts and Answers, pp. 71–78

Alternative Assessment Guide
- Portfolio Assessment, p. 20
- Performance Assessment, p. 34
- CD-ROM Assessment, p. 48

Student Make-Up Assignments
- Alternative Quizzes, Chapter 3

Standardized Assessment Tutor
- Reading, pp. 9–11
- Writing, p. 12
- Math, pp. 25–26

Native Speakers
Cuaderno para hispanohablantes, pp. 11–15

MEDIA

 Online Activities
- Juegos interactivos
- Actividades Internet

 Video Program
- Videocassette 1
- Videocassette 5 (captioned version)

Interactive CD-ROM Tutor, Disc 1

DVD Tutor, Disc 1

 Audio Compact Discs
- Textbook Listening Activities, CD 3, Tracks 1–17
- Additional Listening Activities, CD 3, Tracks 23–29
- Assessment Items, CD 3, Tracks 18–22

 Teaching Transparencies
- Situations 3-1 to 3-3
- Vocabulary 3-A to 3-C
- **De antemano**
- **Más práctica gramatical** Answers
- **Cuaderno de gramática** Answers

  One-Stop Planner CD-ROM

Use the **One-Stop Planner CD-ROM with Test Generator** to aid in lesson planning and pacing.

For each chapter, the **One-Stop Planner** includes:

- Editable lesson plans with direct links to teaching resources
- Printable worksheets from resource books
- Direct launches to the HRW Internet activities
- Video and audio segments
- Test Generator
- Clip Art for vocabulary items

Capítulo 3: Nuevas clases, nuevos amigos

Projects ·········

Folletos informativos

In this activity students create brochures of their school or town. The activity may be done in class or as an outside assignment. Students create brochures for a foreign exchange program, keeping in mind that exchange students from Spanish-speaking countries will use them to decide where they want to attend classes.

MATERIALS
✄ **Students may need**
- Old magazines
- Old newspapers
- Construction paper
- Scissors
- Glue or tape
- Markers

SUGGESTED SEQUENCE

1. Divide the class into groups and set due dates for the brochure and oral presentation.
2. Review chapter vocabulary.
3. Students find illustrations in magazines and newspapers, draw, or take photos. Groups decide which images to use.
4. Students prepare short written descriptions in Spanish of each picture. Each student describes at least one.
5. Groups first make a two-page layout showing where pictures and descriptions will go.
6. Peer groups review, proofread, and critique the brochures.
7. Groups affix pictures on clean paper and write descriptions for each.
8. Groups decide on a cover and a title for their brochures.
9. Each student reads his or her descriptions to the class.

GRADING THE PROJECT
Suggested point distribution: (total = 100 points)

Brochure content	40
Correct vocabulary and grammar	20
Originality	10
Appearance	10
Oral presentation	20

TEACHER NOTE

If your class has a pen pal program, your students might send the brochure to their pen pal's school and ask for one in return.

Games ·········

Las escaleras

In this game, current and previous vocabulary is practiced.

Preparation On the board draw two sets of stairs with eight to ten steps for students to write words on.

Procedure Divide the class into two teams. One member from each team goes to the board. A word category is announced. (school subjects, class schedules, time expressions, and so on) A student writes a word from that category on the lowest step. When the student is finished, he or she is replaced by a teammate. The team filling all the spaces on the ladder correctly in the shortest time is the winner.

Palabras revueltas

This game is good for tactile learners. The goal is for students to construct five Spanish words from scrambled letters.

Materials Ten small squares of paper for each student.

Procedure Divide the class into two teams. Each person finds a Spanish word from p. 107 and writes each letter of that word on one of the pieces of paper. After everyone is finished, team members exchange their letters with a person on the other team. Students quickly try to arrange the letters to form the word. The student who unscrambles a word before his or her counterpart wins a point for his or her team.

COMMUNITY LINK

Businesses and government agencies often use bilingual brochures. Can students find examples and bring them to class? You may look at brochures from telephone and utility companies, real estate groups, public safety, tax, and voting offices. How is the message presented?

Storytelling

Mini-cuento

This story accompanies Teaching Transparency 3-1. *The* **mini-cuento** *can be told and retold in different formats, acted out, written, and read aloud, to give students additional opportunities to practice all four skills. The following story relates Sergio's difficulty studying in* **la biblioteca.**

Para Paco y Carmen, estudiar en la biblioteca es divertido. Son morenos, inteligentes y simpáticos. A Sergio no le gustan porque hacen mucho ruido. Sergio es rubio y serio. Sergio está de mal humor porque necesita terminar un trabajo difícil para su clase de filosofía. Pero no puede estudiar porque Paco y Carmen practican francés en voz alta. El señor Ureña, el bibliotecario, lee el periódico y no presta atención. La señora Muñoz, la otra bibliotecaria, trabaja con los libros y no presta atención. Los bibliotecarios necesitan ser más serios. Pero Carmen y Paco no son un problema para todos. Rafael es muy inteligente y trabaja sin distracciones. No tiene prisa. Estudia para su clase de computación. Eugenia es guapa, morena, e inteligente, pero está aburrida. Por eso duerme en el sofá. Todos están contentos, excepto pobre Sergio.

Traditions

Las pirámides

Pyramids were built in Mexico as ceremonial centers to worship the gods or as astronomical observatories. The first pyramid was built by the Olmecs around 1500 B.C. There are hundreds of archeological sites with pyramids in Mesoamerica. In **Teotihuacán** there are two incredible pyramids: the Pyramid of the Sun and the Pyramid of the Moon. In southern Mexico, **Monte Albán** and **Tajín** are two beautiful cities with pyramids and platforms. Other important centers are the Mayan cities **Palenque, Uxmal,** and **Chichén Itzá** with distinctive pyramids and palaces. Have students check our Web site by entering the keyword WV3 VALLE DE MEXICO to see examples of pyramids and other early structures. Assign groups to research the architecture and history of the Aztec, Toltec, Zapotec, and Maya ceremonial centers. You might have groups create plaster-of-paris molds or clay replicas of specific sites.

Receta

The practice of grinding corn into **tortillas de maíz** *dates back to pre-Columbian civilizations in what is now Mexico and Central America. The corn is boiled with lime before it is ground on a* **metate,** *or flat stone. The resulting lime-whitened corn dough is then pressed into thin round pieces and cooked on a dry surface. Nowadays, factories produce most tortillas, and flour is a popular alternative to corn. Homemade tortillas no longer involve boiling and grinding corn; the dough is sold at stores as* **masa para tortillas** *or* **masa harina.**

TORTILLAS DE MAÍZ

12 tortillas

1 libra de masa harina
4 cucharaditas de sal
agua fría

Añada suficiente agua a la masa harina y sal para que la masa no se deshaga en la prensa (*tortilla press*). Abra la prensa y cubra la parte superior e inferior con plástico transparente. Ponga una bolita de masa entre el plástico y aplástela con la prensa. Coloque la tortilla en un comal (*griddle*) caliente. Voltee la tortilla varias veces hasta que se dore. ¡Las tortillas recién hechas son riquísimas!

Technology

Videocassette 1, Videocassette 5 (captioned version)
DVD Tutor, Disc 1
See Video Guide, pages 19–21.

DVD/Video

De antemano • ¡Bienvenida al colegio!

Claudia is starting the year at a new school. She meets the school principal, who introduces her to the students in her first class. While waiting for her teacher to arrive, Claudia talks with her new classmates, Fernando and María Inés. María Inés stands at the front of the class and jokingly begins to imitate the teacher, not realizing that he is standing in the doorway of the classroom.

A continuación

María Inés receives an extra assignment from her teacher. After school, Fernando and María Inés introduce Claudia to some of their friends, including Luis. Claudia, Luis, and María Inés decide to go to the park to buy popsicles.

¿Cómo es un día escolar típico?

Students from Costa Rica, Argentina, and Venezuela tell what a typical school day is like for them. In additional interviews, students from various Spanish-speaking countries tell us about their school day.

Videoclips

• **I.C.E.:** advertisement for lower telephone rates during the holidays

Interactive CD-ROM Tutor

Activity	Activity Type	Pupil's Edition Page
En contexto	*Interactive conversation*	
1. Así se dice	Patas arriba	pp. 84–85
2. Gramática	¡Super memoria!	p. 86
3. Vocabulario	¡A escoger!	p. 83
4. Así se dice	¿Qué falta?	pp. 88, 90
5. Así se dice	¿Cuál es?	pp. 92, 95
6. Vocabulario	Imagen y sonido ¡Exploremos! ¡Identifiquemos!	p. 92
Panorama cultural	¿Cómo es un día escolar típico?	p. 87
¡A hablar!	*Guided recording*	pp. 104–105
¡A escribir!	*Guided writing*	pp. 104–105

Teacher Management System

Launch the program, type "admin" in the password area, and press RETURN. Log on to **www.hrw.com/CDROMTUTOR** for a detailed explanation of the Teacher Management System.

DVD Tutor

The *DVD Tutor* contains all material from the *Video Program* as described above. Spanish captions are available for use at your discretion for all sections of the video. The *DVD Tutor* also provides a variety of video-based activities that assess students' understanding of the **De antemano, A continuación,** and **Panorama cultural.**

This part of the *DVD Tutor* may be used on any DVD video player connected to a television or video monitor.

In addition to the video material and the video-based comprehension activities, the *DVD Tutor* also contains the entire *Interactive CD-ROM Tutor* in DVD-ROM format. Each DVD disc contains the activities from all 12 chapters of the *Interactive CD-ROM Tutor.*

This part of the *DVD Tutor* may be used on a Macintosh® or Windows® computer with a DVD-ROM drive.

One-Stop Planner CD-ROM

To preview all resources available for this chapter, use the **One-Stop Planner CD-ROM**, Disc 1.

Internet Connection

*Have students explore the **go.hrw.com** Web site for many online resources covering all chapters. All Chapter 3 resources are available under the keyword **WV3 MEXICO-3**. Interactive games help students practice the material and provide them with immediate feedback. You will also find a printable worksheet that provides Internet activities that lead to a comprehensive online research project.*

Juegos interactivos

You can use the interactive activities in this chapter

- to practice grammar, vocabulary, and chapter functions
- as homework
- as an assessment option
- as a self-test
- to prepare for the Chapter Test

Actividades Internet

Students find out what kinds of classes schools in other countries offer and create a schedule of classes they would take if they were exchange students.

- As preparation for the **Hoja de actividades,** have students review the **Primer paso** or watch the **Panorama cultural** on Videocassette 1 or CD-ROM, Disc 1.
- After completing the activity sheet, ask students to create a schedule for an exchange student coming to their school for a year. Have them include classes and activities offered at their school that they think a foreign student would like.

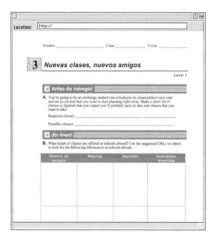

Proyecto

Have students post the schedule they create for the **Hoja de actividades** on a personal Web site. Ask them to create a link from each class to the page on the Web where they learned about that class. If this is not possible, have students include with each class a list of two things covered in that course. (From the site of a school in Spain, they might find an art class that covers Goya and Velázquez.)

Primer paso

6   p. 83

— Hola, Lupita. ¿Qué tal?

— Hola, Álvaro. ¿Cómo estás?

— Bien, ¿y tú?

— Bueno, más o menos. Es el primer día de clase y ya tengo mucha tarea.

— ¿Qué clases tienes?

— Tengo ciencias, francés, arte, matemáticas, computación, educación física e historia con el profesor Maldonado. ¿Qué clases tienes tú?

— Yo tengo historia con la profesora Vázquez, álgebra, biología, computación y geografía.

— ¿A qué hora tienes clase de computación?

— A la una menos cinco.

— ¡Qué bien! Estamos en la misma clase, entonces.

— ¡Ay, no, llegamos tarde!

— ¡Vamos!

Answer to Activity 6
Lupita and Álvaro have the class of **computación** together.

10   p. 85

1. — Oye, Bernardo, ¿qué hora es?
— Son las dos y media.

2. — Bernardo, dime, ¿qué hora es?
— Son las tres y cuarto.

3. — No tengo reloj, Bernardo. ¿Qué hora es?
— Son las seis.

4. — ¿Qué hora es, por favor?
— Es la una y cuarto, mi hijo.

5. — Ahora, ¿qué hora es?
— Son las diez. Vete a jugar.

6. — Bueno, Geraldo. ¡Despiértate!
— ¿Qué hora es?
— Son las ocho.

7. — Ya es tarde.
— Pero, Bernardo, ¿qué hora es?
— Son las ocho y media.

8. — Bernardo, ¿qué hora es?
— Son las cuatro. ¡Vamos al parque!

Answers to Activity 10

1. h	5. c
2. f	6. e
3. g	7. b
4. a	8. d

13   p. 86

MODELO   Son las doce y diez. Tengo la clase de computación. *12:10, la clase de computación*

1. Ya son las nueve y cuarto. Tengo la clase de arte.

2. Ahora tengo ciencias sociales. Son las ocho y veinticinco.

3. Son las once y cuarenta. Por fin tengo almuerzo.

4. ¡Ya es la una! Tengo clase de matemáticas.

5. Ya son las dos menos cinco. Tengo educación física.

6. Son las tres menos cuarto. Tengo la clase de francés.

7. ¿Son las diez y cinco? ¡Tengo geografía!

Answers to Activity 13
1. 9:15, arte
2. 8:25, ciencias sociales
3. 11:40, almuerzo
4. 1:00, matemáticas
5. 1:55, educación física
6. 2:45, francés
7. 10:05, geografía

Segundo paso

15   p. 88

1. Necesito ir a clase. ¿Qué hora es?

2. ¿A qué hora es el descanso?

3. Necesito organizar mi cuarto. ¿Ya son las tres?

4. ¿A qué hora es el almuerzo?

5. ¿A qué hora necesitas ir a la clase de inglés?

6. Quiero ir al centro comercial. ¿Qué hora es?

Answers to Activity 15

1. a	4. b
2. b	5. b
3. a	6. a

The following scripts are for the listening activities found in the *Pupil's Edition.* For Student Response Forms, see *Listening Activites,* pages 19–21. To provide students with additional listening practice, see *Listening Activities,* pages 23–26.

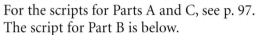

One-Stop Planner CD-ROM

To preview all resources available for this chapter, use the **One-Stop Planner CD-ROM**, Disc 1.

Tercer paso

29 p. 95

— Hola, Patricia, soy Gregorio. ¿Cómo estás?

— Muy bien. ¿Y tú?

— Bien. Oye, ¿qué haces esta tarde? Hay una fiesta a las ocho.

— ¡Ay, no, una fiesta no, por favor! No me gustan las fiestas. Pero me gustan los partidos de fútbol.

— Este, pues... No me gustan los partidos de fútbol. No son interesantes. Pero, a ver... me gustan los videojuegos. ¿A ti te gustan?

— Los videojuegos no me gustan. Bueno, Gregorio, ¿te gustan los partidos de tenis?

— Es que no me gustan los deportes. Pero me gustan los conciertos.

— ¡Ay, sí! Me encantan los conciertos. ¿Qué música te gusta? ¿Te gusta la música rock?

— Sí, me gusta la música rock. ¡Vamos a un concierto!

— ¡Fantástico! Oye, Gregorio, ¿tienes un coche?

— Pues, no...

Answers to Activity 29
1. cierto
2. falso
3. falso
4. cierto

LETRA Y SONIDO, P. 97

For the scripts for Parts A and C, see p. 97.
The script for Part B is below.

B. Dictado

Necesito una goma de borrar y una regla en matemáticas. En geografía, necesito un bolígrafo y un cuaderno.

Repaso

1 p. 104

1. Son las tres de la mañana en la ciudad de Panamá.

2. En la ciudad de Los Ángeles son las doce del mediodía.

3. Aquí en Nueva York es la una y veinticinco de la tarde.

4. Son las tres y media de la tarde de un día fresco y nublado aquí en la bella ciudad de Miami.

5. Aquí en Caracas son las nueve menos cinco de la noche.

Answers to Repaso Activity 1
Answers will vary according to locale.

Capítulo 3: Nuevas clases, nuevos amigos
Suggested Lesson Plans 50-Minute Schedule

Day 1

CHAPTER OPENER 5 min.
- Focusing on Outcomes, ATE, p. 79
- Native Speakers, ATE, p. 79

DE ANTEMANO 40 min.
- Presenting **De antemano** and Preteaching Vocabulary, ATE, p. 80
- View video of **De antemano**, Video Guide, p. 22.
- Activities 1–5, p. 82, and Comprehension Check, ATE, p. 82

Wrap-Up 5 min.
- Have students state the main ideas of *¡Bienvenida al colegio!*

Homework Options
Cuaderno de actividades, p. 25, Activities 1–2

Day 2

PRIMER PASO
Quick Review 5 min.
- Check homework.
- Bell Work, ATE, p. 83

Vocabulario/Nota gramatical, p. 83 20 min.
- Presenting **Vocabulario** and **Nota gramatical**, ATE, p. 83
- Present **Vocabulario extra**, p. 83.
- Do Activity 6, p. 83, with Audio CD.
- **Más práctica gramatical**, p. 100, Act. 1
- Read and discuss the **Nota cultural** with the class, p. 83.

Así se dice, p. 84 20 min.
- Presenting **Así se dice**, ATE, p. 84
- Do Activities 7–8, p. 84. See Auditory Learners, ATE, p. 84.
- Have students do Activity 9 in pairs, p. 85.

Wrap-Up 5 min.
- Do Additional Practice suggestion, ATE, p. 84.

Homework Options
Cuaderno de actividades, pp. 26–27, Activities 3–6
Cuaderno de gramática, p. 18–19, Activities 1–5

Day 3

PRIMER PASO
Quick Review 5 min.
- Check homework.
- Ask students about what classes they have to review the **Vocabulario** and **Así se dice**.

Así se dice, p. 85 15 min.
- Presenting **Así se dice**, ATE, p. 85
- Present Language Notes, ATE, p. 85.
- Do Activity 10, p. 85, with Audio CD. See Slower Pace suggestion, ATE, p. 85.
- Do Activity 11. See Kinesthetic Learners suggestion, ATE, p. 85.

Gramática, p. 86 25 min.
- Presenting **Gramática**, ATE, p. 86
- Have students do Activity 12, p. 86, in pairs.
- Do Activity 13 with Audio CD, p. 86.
- Have students do Activity 14, p. 86, individually, then exchange papers for peer-editing.

Wrap-Up 5 min.
- Do the TPR suggestion, ATE, p. 86.

Homework Options
Study for Quiz 3-1.
Cuaderno de actividades, p. 28, Activities 7–8
Cuaderno de gramática, p. 20, Activities 6–7

Day 4

PRIMER PASO
Review 15 min.
- **Más práctica gramatical**, p. 100, Activity 2
- Check homework.
- Use Transparencies 3-1 and 3-A to review **Primer paso** content.

Quiz 20 min.
- Administer Quiz 3-1A, 3-1B, or a combination of the two.

PANORAMA CULTURAL, p. 87 10 min.
- Present **Panorama cultural**, p. 87.
- Present Language-to-Language, ATE, p. 87.

Wrap-Up 5 min.
- Ask students what their ideal class schedule would be if they could choose all their courses, and why.

Homework Options
Preview the **Segundo paso**.

Day 5

SEGUNDO PASO
Quick Review 5 min.
- Bell Work, ATE, p. 88

Así se dice/Vocabulario, p. 88 25 min.
- Presenting **Así se dice** and **Vocabulario**, ATE, p. 88
- Do Activity 15 with Audio CD, p. 88.
- Have students read the **Nota cultural**, p. 88.
- Have students do Activities 16–17 in pairs, pp. 88–89.
- Have students do Activity 18 in groups, p. 89. Then call on a few students to present their group members' schedules to the class.

Nota gramatical, p. 89 15 min.
- Presenting **Nota gramatical**, ATE, p. 89. See Language-to-Language suggestion, ATE, p. 89.
- **Más práctica gramatical**, p. 102, Activity 5
- Have students do Activity 19 in groups, p. 89.

Wrap-Up 5 min.
- Using the items in Activity 19, ask students about their favorite people and things.

Homework Options
Más práctica gramatical, p. 101, Activities 3–4
Cuaderno de gramática, pp. 21–22, Activities 8–11
Cuaderno de actividades, p. 29–30, Activity 10

Day 6

SEGUNDO PASO
Quick Review 10 min.
- Check homework.
- Ask students what time they have different classes. Then ask yes/no questions about which classroom objects belong to whom.

Así se dice, p. 90 15 min.
- Presenting **Así se dice**, ATE, p. 90
- Present **También se puede decir** and do Activity 20 with the class, p. 90.
- Have students do Activity 21 individually, then do Activity 22 in pairs, p. 90.

ENCUENTRO CULTURAL, p. 91 10 min.
- Present **Encuentro cultural**, p. 91.
- Have the suggested Thinking Critically discussions, ATE, p. 91.

Wrap-Up 15 min.
- Project Transparency 3-2. Review the content from the **Segundo paso** by asking students questions about the transparency.
- Do Activities 9 and 11 on pp. 29–30 of the Cuaderno de actividades.

Homework Options
Study for Quiz 3-2.
Cuaderno de actividades, p. 31, Activities 12–13

One-Stop Planner CD-ROM

For alternative lesson plans by chapter section, to create your own customized plans, or to preview all resources available for this chapter, use the **One-Stop Planner CD-ROM**, Disc 1.

 For additional homework suggestions, see activities accompanied by this symbol throughout the chapter.

Day 7

SEGUNDO PASO

Quick Review 5 min.
- Check homework.
- Answer any questions students may have about the upcoming quiz.

Quiz 20 min.
- Administer Quiz 3-2A, 3-2B, or a combination of the two.

TERCER PASO

Así se dice/Vocabulario/Nota gramatical 20 min.
- Presenting **Así se dice/Vocabulario**, ATE, p. 92
- Present the **Nota gramatical** by describing yourself and the students in the classroom.
- Do Activity 23, p. 92, with the class.

Wrap-Up 5 min.
- Describe different students in the room and have students guess who you are describing.

Homework Options
Cuaderno de actividades, p. 33, Activity 15
Cuaderno de gramática, p. 23, Activity 12
Más práctica gramatical, p. 102, Activity 6

Day 8

TERCER PASO

Quick Review 15 min.
- Check homework.
- Use Transparency 3-3 to review **ser, Así se dice** expressions, and **Vocabulario**, p. 92.

Gramática, p. 93 30 min.
- Presenting **Gramática**, ATE, p. 93
- Do Teaching Suggestions, ATE, p. 93.
- Have students write Activities 24–25, pp. 93–94. Check.
- Present the information in the Teacher Notes and for **A lo nuestro**, ATE, p. 94, then have students do Activities 26–27 in pairs, p. 94.

Wrap-Up 5 min.
- Write the names of two male and two female celebrities on the board. Have students describe the celebrities individually, then describe what they have in common.

Homework Options
Más práctica gramatical, p. 103, Activity 7
Cuaderno de gramática, pp. 24–25, Activities 14–17
Cuaderno de actividades, pp. 33–34, Activities 16–17

Day 9

TERCER PASO

Quick Review 10 min.
- Have students do Activity 28, p. 94.
- Check homework.

Así se dice/Vocabulario, p. 95 25 min.
- Presenting **Así se dice/Vocabulario**, ATE, p. 95.
- Follow the Additional Practice and Language-to-Language suggestions, ATE, p. 95.
- Do Activity 29 with Audio CD, p. 95.
- Point out the tag questions in the models for Activities 30–31, p. 96, then present the **Nota gramatical.** Have students do Activities 30–31, p. 96.

Letra y sonido, p. 97 10 min.
- Present using Audio CD. See Visual Learners, ATE, p. 97.

Wrap-Up 5 min.
- Ask students questions about the classes they are taking and which ones they like and do not like.

Homework Options
Have students write the journal entry in Activity 35, p. 97.
Cuaderno de gramática, p. 26, Activities 18–19

Day 10

TERCER PASO

Quick Review 10 min.
- Check homework.
- Quickly review the grammar, vocabulary, and expressions from the **paso.**

Así se dice/Vocabulario, p. 95 15 min.
- Cuaderno de actividades, p. 34, Activities 18–19
- Have students do Activities 32 and 34, pp. 96–97, in groups.
- Assign partners, then have students do Activity 33, p. 97, in pairs.

VAMOS A LEER 20 min.
- Activities A–B, p. 98
- Activities C–E, p. 99

Wrap-Up 5 min.
- Have students briefly explain how their background knowledge helped them understand the reading.
- Go over Quiz 3-3 format and content.

Homework Options
Study for Quiz 3-3.

Day 11

TERCER PASO

Quick Review 5 min.
- Review **Tercer paso** content quickly.

Quiz 20 min.
- Administer Quiz 3-3A, 3-3B, or a combination of the two.

REPASO 20 min.
- Do Activity 1, p. 104, with Audio CD.
- Have students do Activities 2 and 4, p. 104, individually.
- Have students do Activity 3, p. 104, in pairs and Activity 5, p. 105, in groups.

Wrap-Up 5 min.
- See Additional Practice, ATE, p. 104.
- Explain Process Writing as described on ATE p. 105 and discuss Activity 6, p. 105.

Homework Options
Assign Activity 6, p. 105.
Assign students to work with a partner to prepare the situation in Activity 7, p. 105.
A ver si puedo..., p. 106

Day 12

REPASO

Quick Review 10 min.
- Allow students to practice their situations (Activity 7, p. 105) with their partner while you check Activity 6, p. 105.

Chapter Review 40 min.
- Review Chapter 3. Choose from **Más práctica gramatical,** Grammar Tutor for Students of Spanish, Activities for Communication, Listening Activities, Interactive CD-ROM Tutor, or **Juegos interactivos.**

Homework Options
Study for the Chapter 3 Test.

Assessment

Quick Review 5 min.
- Answer any last-minute questions.

Test, Chapter 3 45 min.
- Administer Chapter 3 Test. Select from Testing Program, Alternative Assessment Guide, Test Generator, or Standardized Assessment Tutor.

Capítulo 3: Nuevas clases, nuevos amigos
Suggested Lesson Plans 90-Minute Block Schedule

Block 1

CHAPTER OPENER 5 min.
- Focusing on Outcomes, ATE, p. 79

DE ANTEMANO 40 min.
- Presenting **De antemano** and Preteaching Vocabulary, ATE, p. 80
- View video of **De antemano,** Video Guide, p. 22.
- Activities 1–5 and Comprehension Check, p. 82

PRIMER PASO
Vocabulario/ Nota gramatical, p. 83 25 min.
- Presenting **Vocabulario/Nota gramatical,** ATE, p. 83
- Present **Vocabulario extra,** p. 83.
- Do Activity 6, p. 83, with Audio CD.
- **Más práctica gramatical,** p. 100, Activity 1
- Read and discuss the **Nota cultural** with the class, p. 83.

Así se dice, p. 84 15 min.
- Presenting **Así se dice,** ATE, p. 84
- Do Activities 7–8, p. 84.
- See Auditory Learners suggestion for Activity 7, ATE, p. 84

Wrap-Up 5 min.
- Do Additional Practice suggestion, ATE, p. 84.

Homework Options
Cuaderno de actividades, pp. 25–27, Activites 1–6
Cuaderno de gramática, pp. 18–19, Activities 1–5

Block 2

PRIMER PASO
Así se dice, p. 85 20 min.
- Check homework.
- Have students do Activity 9 in pairs, p. 85.
- Presenting **Así se dice,** ATE, p. 85
- Present Language Notes, ATE, p. 85.
- Do Activity 10, p. 85, with Audio CD. See Slower Pace suggestion, ATE, p. 85.
- Do Activity 11. See Kinesthetic Learners suggestion, ATE, p. 85.

Gramática, p. 86 30 min.
- Presenting **Gramática,** ATE, p. 86
- Have students do Activity 12, p. 86, in pairs.
- Do Activity 13 with Audio CD, p. 86.
- Have students do Activity 14, p. 86, individually, then exchange papers for peer-editing.
- **Más práctica gramatical,** p. 100, Activity 2

PANORAMA CULTURAL, p. 87 10 min.
- Present **Panorama cultural,** p. 87.
- Present Language-to-Language, ATE, p. 87.

SEGUNDO PASO
Así se dice/Vocabulario, p. 88 20 min.
- Presenting **Así se dice/Vocabulario,** ATE, p. 88
- Do Activity 15 with Audio CD, p. 88.
- Have students read the **Nota cultural,** p. 88.
- Have students do Activity 16, p. 88, in pairs.

Wrap-Up 10 min.
- Use Transparencies 3-1 and 3-A to review the content of the **Primer paso.**

Homework Options
Study for Quiz 3-1.
Cuaderno de actividades, p. 28, Activities 7–8
Cuaderno de gramática, p. 20, Activities 6–7

Block 3

PRIMER PASO
Quick Review 5 min.
- Check homework.
- Review **Primer paso** content.

Quiz 20 min.
- Administer Quiz 3-1A, 3-1B, or a combination of the two.

SEGUNDO PASO 20 min.
- Review expressions in **Así se dice** and **Vocabulario,** p. 88.
- Cuaderno de gramática, p. 21, Activity 8
- Have students do Activity 17 in pairs, p. 89.
- Have students do Activity 18 in groups, p. 89. Then call on students to present their group members' schedules to the class.

Nota gramatical, p. 89 15 min.
- Presenting **Nota gramatical,** ATE, p. 89 See Language-to-Language suggestion, ATE, p. 89.
- **Más práctica gramatical,** p. 102, Activity 5
- Have students do Activity 19 in groups, p. 89.

Así se dice, p. 90 15 min.
- Presenting **Así se dice,** ATE, p. 90
- Present **También se puede decir** and do Activity 20 with the class, p. 90.
- Have students do Activity 21 individually, then Activity 22 in pairs, p. 90.

ENCUENTRO CULTURAL, p. 91 10 min.
- Have the first suggested Thinking Critically discussion, ATE, p. 91.
- Present the **Encuentro cultural,** p. 91.

Wrap-Up 5 min.
- Have the second suggested Thinking Critically discussion, ATE, p. 91.
- Discuss the content and format of Quiz 3-2.

Homework Options
Study for Quiz 3-2.
Más práctica gramatical, pp. 101–102, Activities 3–5
Cuaderno de gramática, pp. 21–22, Activities 9–11
Cuaderno de actividades, p. 29–30, Activities 9–11

One-Stop Planner CD-ROM

For alternative lesson plans by chapter section, to create your own customized plans, or to preview all resources available for this chapter, use the **One-Stop Planner CD-ROM**, Disc 1.

For additional homework suggestions, see activities accompanied by this symbol throughout the chapter.

Block 4

SEGUNDO PASO

Quick Review 15 min.
- Check homework.
- **Cuaderno de actividades,** p. 31, Activities 12–13
- Quickly review content from **Segundo paso.**

Quiz 20 min.
- Administer Quiz 3-2A, 3-2B, or a combination of the two.

TERCER PASO

Así se dice/ Vocabulario/Nota gramatical 20 min.
- Presenting **Así se dice, Vocabulario,** ATE, p. 92
- Present the **Nota gramatical** by describing yourself and the students in the classroom.
- Do Activity 23, p. 92, with the class.

Gramática, p. 93 30 min.
- Presenting **Gramática,** ATE, p. 93
- Do Teaching Suggestions, ATE, p. 93.
- Have students write Activities 24–25, pp. 93–94. Check.
- Present the information in the Teacher Notes and in **A lo nuestro,** p. 94. Then have students do Activities 26–27 in pairs, p. 94.

Wrap-Up 5 min.
- Describe different students in the room and have others guess whom you are describing.

Homework Options
Activity 28, p. 94
Cuaderno de actividades, p. 33, Activities 15–16
Cuaderno de gramática, pp. 23–24, Activities 12–16
Más práctica gramatical, pp. 102–103, Activities 6–8

Block 5

TERCER PASO

Quick Review 20 min.
- Check homework.
- Using Transparency 3-3, review the content presented thus far in the **Tercer Paso.**
- Write the names of two male and two female celebrities on the board. Have students describe the celebrities individually, then describe what they have in common.
- Cuaderno de gramática, p. 25, Activity 17

Así se dice/Vocabulario, p. 95 30 min.
- Presenting **Así se dice/Vocabulario,** ATE, p. 95
- Follow the Additional Practice and Language-to-Language suggestions, ATE, p. 95.
- Do Activity 29 with Audio CD, p. 95.
- Point out the tag questions in the models for Activities 30–31, p. 96, then present the **Nota gramatical.** Have students do Activities 30–31, p. 96.
- Have students do Activity 32 in groups, p. 96, and Activity 33, p. 97, in pairs.

Letra y sonido, p. 97 10 min.
- Present using Audio CD. See Visual Learners, ATE, p. 97.

VAMOS A LEER 20 min.
- Activities A–B, p. 98
- Activities C–E, p. 99

Wrap-Up 10 min.
- Have students briefly explain how their background knowledge helped them understand the reading.
- Activity 34, p. 97

Homework Options
Study for Quiz 3-3.
Have students write the journal entry in Activity 35, p. 97.
Cuaderno de gramática, p. 26, Activities 18–19
Cuaderno de actividades, p. 34, Activities 17–19

Block 6

TERCER PASO

Quick Review 10 min.
- Check homework.
- Use Transparencies 3-3 and 3-C to review for the quiz.

Quiz 20 min.
- Administer Quiz 3-3A, 3-3B, or a combination of the two.

REPASO 50 min.
- Do Activity 1, p. 104, with Audio CD.
- Have students do Activities 2 and 4, p. 104, individually.
- Have students do Activity 3, p. 104, in pairs and Activity 5, p. 105, in groups.
- Assign Activity 6, **Vamos a escribir,** p. 105. See Process Writing suggestion and Teacher Notes, ATE, p. 105.
- Assign partners to prepare and practice the situation in Activity 7, p. 105.

Wrap-Up 10 min.
- See Reteaching Suggestion (reviewing learner outcomes), ATE, p. 105.
- Review the format of the **Chapter** 3 Test and provide some sample questions.

Homework Options
Have students write a final draft of the Activity 6 assignment, p. 105.
Study for the Chapter 3 Test.
A ver si puedo, p. 106

Block 7

REPASO

Quick Review 10 min.
- Allow students to practice their situations (Activity 7, p. 105) while you check homework.

Chapter Review 35 min.
- Review Chapter 3. Choose from **Más práctica gramatical,** Grammar Tutor for Students of Spanish, Activities for Communication, Listening Activities, Interactive CD-ROM Tutor, or **Juegos interactivos.**

Test, Chapter 3 45 min.
- Administer Chapter 3 Test. Select from Testing Program, Alternative Assessment Guide, Test Generator, or Standardized Assessment Tutor.

CAPÍTULO 3

One-Stop Planner CD-ROM

For resource information, see the **One-Stop Planner,** Disc 1.

Pacing Tips
New vocabulary and grammar are presented, especially in the first and third **Pasos,** accompanying some involved cultural content. Make sure ample time is allotted for review and practice. See Suggested Lesson Plans, pp. 77I–77L.

Meeting the Standards
Communication
- Talking about classes and sequencing events, p. 84
- Telling time, p. 85
- Telling at what time something happens, p. 88
- Talking about being late or in a hurry, p. 90
- Describing people and things, p. 92
- Talking about things you like and explaining why, p. 95

Cultures
- Culture Note, p. 78
- Language Notes, p. 85
- Nota cultural, p. 88
- Encuentro cultural, p. 91

Connections
- Map Activities, p. 75
- Geography Link, p. 76
- Art Link, p. 77
- Multicultural Link, p. 98

Comparisons
- Nota cultural, p. 83
- Language-to-Language, p. 87
- Language-to-Language, p. 89
- Thinking Critically, p. 91
- Language-to-Language, p. 95

Communities
- Family Link, p. 89
- Community Link, p. 105

Cultures and Communities

Culture Note
Mexican high-school students planning to go on to a university attend three years of **preparatoria,** known as **prepa,** after the **secundaria.** There are public and private **preparatorias,** and students must pass rigorous exams to enter, to graduate, and to be accepted for university studies. A degree from a **preparatoria** is called a **bachillerato.** Students refer to themselves as being in the **primer, segundo,** or **tercer año.** In the third year, **preparatoria** students are required to choose their subject area for university study. Students not planning to enter a university may do vocational or technical training during their high school years at an **escuela vocacional.**

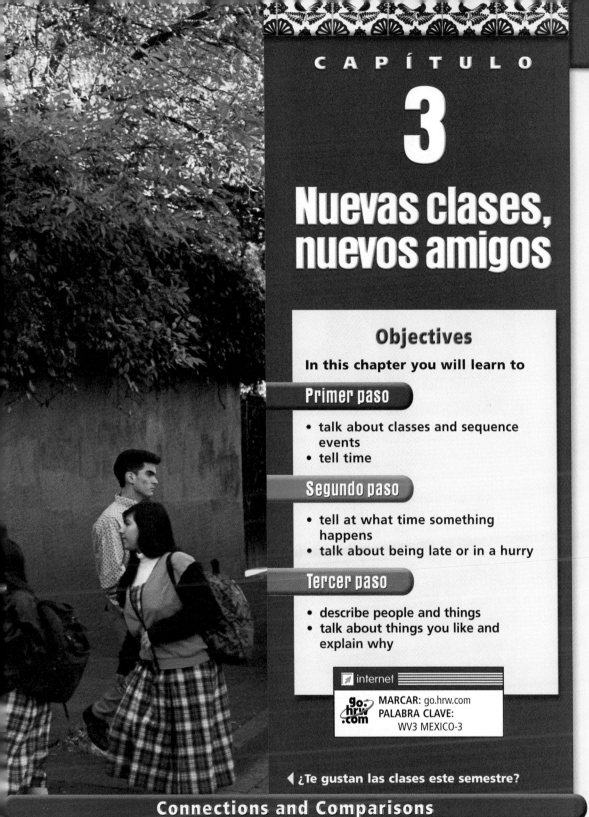

CAPÍTULO

3

Nuevas clases, nuevos amigos

Objectives

In this chapter you will learn to

Primer paso

- talk about classes and sequence events
- tell time

Segundo paso

- tell at what time something happens
- talk about being late or in a hurry

Tercer paso

- describe people and things
- talk about things you like and explain why

internet

MARCAR: go.hrw.com
PALABRA CLAVE:
WV3 MEXICO-3

◄ ¿Te gustan las clases este semestre?

Connections and Comparisons

Native Speakers

If any of your students have lived in or visited Mexico, ask them if they would be willing to share some of their knowledge. Ask them how Mexico is similar to the United States. In what ways are the two countries different? What are Mexican schools like compared with those in the U.S.? Your advanced students may enjoy reading the interview with a Mexican exchange student that may be found on pp. 114–115 of *¡Ven conmigo! Holt Spanish Level 2.*

CAPÍTULO 3

Photo Flash!

In some private schools in Mexico, middle school (**secundaria**) and high school (**preparatoria**) students may attend the same institution. Students have a little time to socialize between classes because the passing periods may be up to 15 minutes.

Focusing on Outcomes

An important use of language is talking about classes, class schedules, and classmates. Point out to students that these language skills are valuable because most of the people they meet are classmates and much of their time is spent in school. Talking about school includes being able to tell time, sequence events, describe people and things, and express likes and dislikes. By the end of this chapter, students will be able to describe teachers and other students, read a class schedule, and write to a friend about their experiences at school.

Teaching Resources
pp. 80–82

PRINT
▶ Lesson Planner, p. 12
▶ Video Guide, pp. 19–20, 22
▶ Cuaderno de actividades, p. 25

MEDIA
▶ One-Stop Planner
▶ Video Program
  De antemano
  Videocassette 1, 43:03–48:33
  Videocassette 5 (captioned version), 22:05–27:35
  A continuación
  Videocassette 1, 48:34–53:50
  Videocassette 5 (captioned version), 27:36–32:57
▶ DVD Tutor, Disc 1
▶ Audio Compact Discs, CD 3, Trs. 1–2
▶ **De antemano** Transparencies

Presenting
De antemano

While students read or view the **fotonovela**, periodically stop to ask questions, such as those in the **Estrategia para comprender**. Then present the Preteaching Vocabulary. Follow up by modeling pronunciation of the **fotonovela** dialogue and having students repeat after you. Have students guess meanings from context.

De antemano
Transparencies

DE ANTEMANO · *¡Bienvenida al colegio!*

The **fotonovela** is an abridged version of the video episode.

CD 3 Trs. 1–2

Estrategia
para comprender
Look at the photos that accompany the story. Where and when do you think these scenes are taking place? What clues tell you this? What do you think will happen in the story?

María Inés

Fernando

Claudia

Director Altamirano

Profesor Romanca

1 **Director:** Bueno, ya son las ocho menos cinco. Aquí tienes el horario. Ahorita tienes clase de ciencias sociales... y a las ocho y cincuenta tienes clase de francés. El descanso es a las nueve y cuarenta...

2 **Director:** Muchachos, buenos días. Ella es una compañera nueva. Se llama Claudia Obregón Sánchez. Es de la Ciudad de México.

3 **María Inés:** Me llamo María Inés.
Fernando: Y yo soy Fernando. Encantado. Y ¡bienvenida a Cuernavaca!
María Inés: Eres de la Ciudad de México, ¡ay, qué padre! Hay muchas cosas interesantes allá, ¿no?

4 **Claudia:** Sí, la capital es muy divertida. Mira, me gusta ir al parque... visitar los museos... y también me gusta mucho jugar al basquetbol.
Fernando: Miren, ya son las ocho. ¿Dónde está el profesor? Está atrasado.

Preteaching Vocabulary

Activating Prior Knowledge
Point out that the setting for this **fotonovela** is a school and that the young people are meeting a new student. What kinds of statements might they be making or what kinds of questions might they be asking?

What information do they give to the new students about the school? Have students guess the meanings of the following school-related expressions: **1** horario, **1** ciencias sociales, **1** francés, **1** descanso, **4** profesor, **5** exámenes, **6** estudiar.

Claudia: Fernando, ¿cómo es esta clase?

Fernando: Ay, es horrible. El profesor es muy aburrido... ¡y no le gustan los exámenes fáciles!

María Inés: No te preocupes, Claudia, no es verdad. Esta clase es mi favorita. Es muy interesante, y el profesor, pues, es... así.

María Inés: Señor Rodríguez, una pregunta, ¿le gustan las ciencias sociales?

Fernando: Sí, "profesora"... me gustan.

María Inés: ¿Y le gusta estudiar?

Fernando: Sí, me gusta estudiar.

María Inés: Entonces, ¿por qué no le gusta estudiar las ciencias sociales?

¡Ay, no!

Cuaderno de actividades, p. 25, Acts. 1–2

Using the Captioned Video/DVD

As an alternative to reading the conversations in the text, you might want to show the captioned version of **¡Bienvenida al colegio!** on Videocassette 5. As students hear the language and watch the story, anxiety about the new language will be reduced, and comprehension facilitated. The reinforcement of seeing the written words with the gestures and actions in context will help students do the comprehension activities on p. 82. **NOTE:** The *DVD Tutor* contains captions for all sections of the *Video Program*.

Teaching Suggestions

- Point out that **bienvenida** in the title refers to Claudia, and that **bienvenido** changes in gender and number depending on who is being addressed.

- After students read the **fotonovela**, ask them if they have ever been in a similar situation (a new student in another country or simply in a new school). If so, how did they handle it? Were there differences in language or culture?

- Explain some colloquial Mexican expressions that appear in the **fotonovela**:
  ¡Qué padre! *Cool!*
  ¡Miren! *Look!, Hey!*

- Have students find examples of exclamations in other dialects of Spanish by consulting dictionaries or native speakers. Example: **¡Qué chévere!** *How cool!* (Venezuela and the Caribbean)

A continuación

You may choose to continue with **¡Bienvenida al colegio! (a continuación)** at this time or wait until later in the chapter. At this point, María Inés receives an extra assignment from the teacher. After school María Inés meets more of Claudia's friends. You may wish to discuss with students differences between schools in Mexico and the U.S.

Teaching Suggestion

1 Have students review questions with a partner. Ask pairs to scan the **fotonovela** and find words and phrases to justify their answers. Then ask for volunteers to answer the questions. Ask the class to use thumbs up or thumbs down to indicate whether the answers are correct.

Answers

1 1. 7:55
2. the school schedule
3. places in Mexico City
4. Fernando: doesn't like, horrible, professor boring, exams hard; Claudia: favorite class, interesting
5. María Inés; she mimics the teacher
6. The teacher discovers María Inés imitating him; embarrassed

2 *Possible answers:*
1. La primera clase de Claudia no es la clase de francés.
2. Claudia es (una/la) nueva estudiante en la clase.
3. Claudia es de la Ciudad de México.
4. La capital es muy divertida.
5. Para Fernando, la clase no es fácil.

3 1. también me gusta
2. ¿cómo es esta clase?
3. No te preocupes, Claudia.
4. no es verdad
5. es... así
6. son las
7. a las ocho y cincuenta tienes clase de francés
8. me gustan
9. no le gustan

These activities check for comprehension only. Students should not yet be expected to produce language modeled in **De antemano**.

1 **¿Comprendes?** See answers below.

Check your understanding of the **fotonovela** by answering these questions. Remember that intelligent guessing is a useful way to increase your understanding in a foreign language.

1. What time is it when this story begins?
2. What do you think the principal is discussing with Claudia?
3. What's in the photographs that Claudia is showing Fernando and María Inés?
4. How do María Inés and Fernando's opinions of this class differ?
5. Which of the students seems to be mischievous? How?
6. How does the **fotonovela** end? How do you think María Inés feels?

2 **Errores** See answers below.

Con base en la fotonovela, cambia las oraciones para hacerlas verdaderas.

1. La primera clase de Claudia es la clase de francés.
2. Claudia es una profesora nueva en la clase.
3. Claudia es de España.
4. La capital de México es muy aburrida.
5. Para Fernando, la clase es fácil.

3 **¿Cómo se dice...?** See answers below.

What phrases do these characters use in each situation?

Claudia
1. to say she also likes to do something
2. to ask Fernando what this class is like

the principal
6. to say what time it is
7. to tell Claudia at what time she has French

María Inés
3. to tell Claudia not to worry
4. to say "it's not true"
5. to say the professor is "like this"

Fernando
8. to say he likes social sciences
9. to say what the teacher doesn't like

4 **¡Opiniones!**

Using the **fotonovela** as a guide, fill in the blanks with words from the box.

Tengo la clase de ___1___ a las ocho. No ___2___ la clase. Es ___3___ y los exámenes son ___4___. Necesito más clases ___5___. Mi clase de español es mi ___6___ porque es ___7___.

ciencias sociales 1   me gusta 2
horrible 3   interesantes 5
divertida 7   favorita 6
difíciles 4

5 **¿Y tú?** Answers will vary.

Complete the following with your own ideas about what's fun, boring, easy, or difficult.

1. La capital de mi estado es (divertida/aburrida).
2. Mis clases son (fáciles/difíciles).
3. La clase de español es (fácil/difícil).
4. La música clásica es (divertida/aburrida).
5. El tenis es (divertido/aburrido).

Comprehension Check

Additional Practice

2 Give the students these additional items: **Fernando es de la Ciudad de México. La compañera nueva se llama María Inés. La clase es de matemáticas. María Inés es la profesora de la clase.** Put words and phrases that make up these sentences on sentence strips or a felt board, and have students move the words to make the false sentences true.

Captioned Video

3 Play Videocassette 5 and have students find three of these answers. You may want to stop the tape every 30 seconds to give students a chance to say what they found.

Objectives Talking about classes and sequencing events; telling time

WV3 MEXICO-3

Vocabulario

¿Qué materias estudias? *What subjects are you studying?*

CD-ROM 1
DVD 1

el arte

las ciencias

las ciencias sociales

la computación

el almuerzo

la educación física

el francés

la geografía

las matemáticas

el descanso

> Cuaderno de actividades, p. 26, Act. 3
>
> Cuaderno de gramática, p. 18, Acts. 1–2

6 **¡Tenemos la misma clase!**

Escuchemos Listen to Álvaro and Lupita discuss their new class schedules. What class do they have together?

CD 3
Tr. 3   Scripts and answers on p. 77G.

Vocabulario extra

el alemán	*German*
el coro	*choir*
la informática	*computer science*
Internet	*Internet*
la química	*chemistry*
el Web, la Telaraña Mundial	*World Wide Web*

Nota cultural

How would you feel if you got a score of 18 on a test? In Peru, this would actually be a high grade, equivalent to a 90.

• Peruvian schools use a scale of 1 to 20, with 11 the lowest passing score.

• Mexican schools use a scale of 1 to 10; 6 is passing.

What would your grades be if you went to school in Peru? in Mexico?

Nota gramatical

With nouns referring to more than one thing, like **libros** or **clases**, use **los** or **las**. Both words mean *the*.

> Tengo **los** libros.
> ¿Tienes **las** gomas de borrar?

Also use **los** when referring to a group of people that includes both males and females.

> **Los** profesores son buenos.

Más práctica gramatical, p. 100, Act. 1

> Cuaderno de actividades, p. 27, Act. 5
>
> Cuaderno de gramática, p. 19, Acts. 3–5

Teacher to Teacher

Diane Kalata
Pioneer High School
Ann Arbor, Michigan

Diane's students know a visual image is worth a thousand words
"I use Clip Art from the **One-Stop Planner** for teaching chapter vocabulary. After I introduce the vocabulary, I group students into pairs and have them practice using the vocabulary in short sentences. I often create a crossword puzzle using the pictures as hints. The same pictures can later become the basis of a vocabulary quiz. Students tell me that working with the pictures helps them remember the vocabulary throughout the year."

Presenting
Así se dice

Ask students to imagine that the class schedule on this page is their own. Model the questions in **Así se dice**. Ask: **Gloria, ¿qué clases tienes este semestre? Ustedes, ¿qué clases tienen los martes?** Encourage students to respond using the correct pronoun and form of **tener**. (**Ella tiene ciencias sociales y francés. Nosotros tenemos...**)

Así se dice

Talking about classes and sequencing events

To find out what classes a friend has, ask:

¿Qué clases tienes este semestre?
. . . this semester?

¿Qué clases tienes hoy?
. . . today?

¿Y cuándo tienes un día libre?
And when do you have a free day?

Your friend might answer:

Bueno, **tengo** matemáticas, inglés, español y ciencias sociales.

Primero tengo geografía, **después** computación y **luego** francés.
First I have . . . afterward . . . then . . .

¡Mañana por fin tengo un día libre!
Tomorrow at last I have a free day!

7 Gramática en contexto

Leamos/Escribamos Today is the first day of the new school year. The students have just received their class schedule. Explain what school supplies they need for the classes they are taking. Use **los** and **las** in your answers. Answers will vary.

MODELO Los estudiantes necesitan las reglas para la clase de geometría.

reglas	geometría
mapas (m.)	francés y español
lápices, gomas de borrar	arte
zapatillas de tenis	educación física
calculadoras	informática
diccionarios	geografía
computadoras	matemáticas

8 Primero tiene...

Leamos/Escribamos Complete this description of Claudia's Monday morning schedule, using the words provided.

luego 3, 4	**después** 3, 4	**mañana** 5
primero 2		**hoy** 1

___1___ Claudia tiene siete clases. ___2___ tiene la clase de ciencias sociales con el profesor Romanca. ___3___ tiene francés y un descanso. ___4___ tiene química, computación y un descanso. ___5___ tiene física a las 10:00 y música a las 10:50.

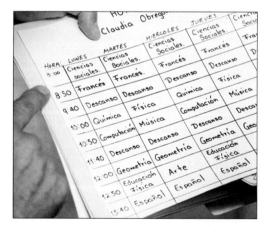

Communication for All Students

Additional Practice

8 Have students write a description of their class schedule in their journal. Ask them to use the adverbs **primero, después, luego,** and **por fin** for sequencing the classes. For an additional journal entry suggestion for Chapter 3, see *Cuaderno de actividades,* p. 147.

Auditory Learners

Practice the adverbs **primero, después, luego,** and **por fin** in a conversation with students. (**Carlos, ¿qué clase tienes primero? ¿Y qué tienes después? ¿Luego qué clase tienes?**) Then have students practice with a partner for three to four minutes.

9 Pues, tengo...

Hablemos Get together with a partner. Greet one another and ask how your partner is. Find out what classes you each have and in what order. Use the expressions you've learned for talking about your schedule.

Así se dice

Telling time

To find out what time it is, ask:

¿Qué hora es?

¡Ay! **¿Ya son** las tres?

To answer, say:

Son las ocho. *It's eight o'clock.*
Son las once y media. *It's 11:30.*
Es la una y cuarto. *It's 1:15.*
(It's a quarter after one.)

Sí, hombre, es tarde. ¡Vamos!
Yes, man, it's late. Let's go!

CD-ROM 1
DVD 1

10 El reloj

CD 3
Tr. 4

Escuchemos Bernardo is babysitting today. You'll hear his brother at different times throughout the day ask him what time it is. Match each time mentioned with the correct clock below. Scripts and answers on p. 77G.

a.

b.

c.

d.

f.

g.

h.

e.

11 Hora local

Escribamos Generally, what time is it when . . .?

1. the sun comes up
2. you wake up
3. you get out of bed
4. the school day begins
5. you eat lunch
6. you leave school
7. you eat dinner
8. you get in bed
9. you go to sleep

Presenting
Así se dice

Use a large clock (or draw one on the board or a transparency) to model pronunciation and the use of the singular and plural forms of **ser** to express time. Have students in small groups construct paper-plate clocks, using pens or pencils for the hands. Students take turns calling out a time. The others move the hands on their clock to the right time. You might do this as a whole class activity as you check comprehension.

Visual Learners
9 You might want to write times on the board and have students structure their conversation around them. (10:30: **¿Qué clase tienes a las diez y media?**)

Slower Pace
10 To prepare students for the listening task, ask them what time it is in each picture before playing the audio recording.

Kinesthetic Learners
11 Have one or two volunteers pantomime several of the actions mentioned in this activity while the rest of the class guesses the associated time.

Cultures and Communities

Language Notes
- Point out the difference between **cuatro** and **cuarto**. When telling time, in many countries **y quince** is used instead of **y cuarto**. A variation of **...menos quince** is **Faltan quince para la(s)...** Because of digital watches, it is becoming more common to hear **Son las ocho y cuarenta y cinco.**

- Some native speakers may also say **¿Qué horas son?** Ask native speakers for other expressions they may use to tell time. Make sure to review the spelling of these additional phrases.

Presenting
Gramática

Telling Time Before beginning this section, prepare large flash-cards. On each card write a time, such as 3:25. As you begin the presentation, point to the clock on the wall and tell the time: **Clase, son las diez y doce.** Then ask **Clase, ¿qué hora es?** Elicit a choral response and say with them **Son las diez y doce, profesor/a.** Next, show the cards one at a time and have the class chorally tell you the time in Spanish.

Assess

▸ Testing Program, pp. 53–56
Quiz 3-1A, Quiz 3-1B
Audio CD 3, Tr. 18

▸ Student Make-Up Assignments, Chapter 3, Alternative Quiz

▸ Alternative Assessment Guide, p. 34

Gramática

Telling Time

1. To tell the hour (except for times around one o'clock), use **Son las…** plus the hour. **Son las ocho.** *It's 8 o'clock.*

2. For times after the hour, follow this pattern:
   Son las siete **y cuarto.** *It's a quarter after 7.*
   Son las ocho **y veinticinco.** *It's 8:25.*
   Son las once **y media.** *It's 11:30.*

3. For times before the hour, say:
   Es la una **menos veinte.** *It's 20 minutes to 1.*
   Son las doce **menos cuarto.** *It's a quarter to 12.*
   Son las ocho **menos diez.** *It's 10 minutes to 8.*

4. For times including 1:00, use **Es la una…**
   Es la una y veinte. *It's 1:20.*

Cuaderno de actividades, p. 28, Acts. 7–8

Cuaderno de gramática, p. 20, Acts. 6–7

Más práctica gramatical, p. 100, Act. 2

12 **Gramática en contexto** See answers below.

Hablemos Intercambia papeles con tu compañero/a. Indiquen qué hora es en cada reloj.

1. 2. 3.

4. 5. 6.

13 **¿Qué clase tengo ahora?**

CD 3
Tr. 5

Escuchemos/Escribamos Imagine that you're keeping your new friend Alberto company during a typical school day. Listen as he tells you about his schedule. First write the times of day he mentions. Then listen again and write the class he has at each time.

MODELO   —Son las doce y diez. Tengo la clase de computación.
            12:10—computación Scripts and answers on p. 77G.

14 **Gramática en contexto**

Escribamos Para cada una de las siguientes oraciones, escribe qué hora es. Tus respuestas pueden variar.

1. Ya no tengo clases.
2. Necesito hacer la tarea.
3. Necesito ir al colegio.
4. Hay un descanso.

5. Tengo clase de español.
6. Es la hora del almuerzo.
7. Quiero ir a la pizzería con amigos.
8. Quiero ir al centro comercial.

Communication for All Students

TPR Ask a volunteer to come to the front of the class. Show the student a flashcard, but do not let the rest of the class see it. The student moves his or her body to visually represent the time. (3:00—Facing the class, the student may hold the right arm straight up and the left one perpendicular to the shoulder.) The rest of the class guesses the time in Spanish. Continue with other volunteers.

Tactile Learners

Gramática Have students work in pairs. Each pair should make six sets of cards showing times of day. Each set should include one card with the time written in words and the other showing the time as it would appear on a clock face. Then students turn all the cards face down, mix them up, and play Concentration®.

Answers

12 1. Son las tres y media.
2. Son las doce menos veinte.
3. Son las cinco.
4. Son las diez y cuarto.
5. Son las seis y cinco.
6. Son las nueve menos cinco.

CD 3
Trs. 6–9

¿Cómo es un día escolar típico?

In this chapter, we asked some students at what time they usually go to school, what they do after class, and which classes they like.

Teaching Resources
p. 87

PRINT
▸ Video Guide, pp. 19–21, 24
▸ Cuaderno de actividades, p. 36
▸ Cuaderno para hispanohablantes, p. 14

MEDIA
▸ One-Stop Planner
▸ Video Program, Videocassette 1, 53:51–56:52
▸ DVD Tutor, Disc 1
▸ Audio Compact Discs, CD 3, Trs. 6–9
▸ Interactive CD-ROM Tutor, Disc 1

Mario CD 3 Tr. 7
Lagunilla de Heredia, Costa Rica

"Bueno... son varios horarios. En el horario de la mañana voy a las siete de la mañana, y en el horario de la tarde a las doce y media, más o menos".

Lucía CD 3 Tr. 8
Buenos Aires, Argentina

"Bueno... el día es tranquilo. En general es lindo. Me la paso bien acá dentro del colegio y tengo alrededor de doce materias. Mi materia preferida es literatura y todas las que tengan que ver con lo humanístico".

Natalie CD 3 Tr. 9
Maracaibo, Venezuela

"Bueno... voy a la escuela de [las] 7 de la mañana a [la] 1:30 de la tarde; de ahí voy a mi casa, almuerzo; normalmente después me acuesto como hasta las 3 de la tarde y después me pongo a estudiar si tengo algo que estudiar".

Para pensar y hablar...

A. At what time do you usually go to school? How many hours are you in school? What do you do after school? In Costa Rica, Mario has classes almost all day with a lunch break. Why do you think he has such a schedule? What are the advantages and disadvantages of going to school for a longer period during the day?

B. In groups, ask your classmates what their favorite classes are and why. Discuss why some people like sciences and others humanities or social sciences.

Cuaderno para hispanohablantes, p. 14

Presenting
Panorama cultural

After reading or watching each interview, ask students to summarize what the person said. When all three interviews have been viewed or read, have students answer the questions in the text. Then have them answer the **Preguntas**.

Preguntas

1. **¿De dónde es Natalie? ¿Lucía? ¿Mario?** (Venezuela, Argentina, Costa Rica)
2. **¿Quién tiene dos horarios?** (Mario)
3. **¿A qué hora va Mario al colegio por la tarde?** (a las doce y media)
4. **¿Quiénes tienen clase a las siete de la mañana?** (Mario y Natalie)
5. **¿A Lucía le gusta el colegio?** (Sí)

Connections and Comparisons

Language-to-Language

• Lucía uses the expression **la paso bien** to say *I have a good time.* You might point out to students that **lo paso bien** is also used in Spanish-speaking countries. In these phrases, the pronouns **lo** or **la** have no antecedent. Ask them to think of English expressions in which the word *it* has no antecedent. (*It's raining, It's late, It's now or never.*)

• Natalie says **...almuerzo...** which may be translated as *I eat lunch.* However, *lunch,* or **el almuerzo** in Spanish-speaking countries, may mean anything from a late breakfast to a lengthy lunch beginning at home around 1–2 p.m. and lasting up to two hours. Have students discuss how their routines would change if they spent one to two hours at home for lunch.

Segundo paso

Objectives Telling at what time something happens; talking about being late or in a hurry

WV3 MEXICO-3

Teaching Resources
pp. 88–90

PRINT
- Lesson Planner, p. 14
- TPR Storytelling Book, pp. 10, 12
- Listening Activities, pp. 21, 24
- Activities for Communication, pp. 15–16, 86, 88–89, 141–142
- Cuaderno de gramática, pp. 21–22
- Grammar Tutor for Students of Spanish, Chapter 3
- Cuaderno de actividades, pp. 29–31
- Cuaderno para hispanohablantes, pp. 11–15
- Testing Program, pp. 57–60
- Alternative Assessment Guide, p. 34
- Student Make-Up Assignments, Chapter 3

MEDIA
- One-Stop Planner
- Audio Compact Discs, CD 3, Trs. 10, 25–26, 19
- Teaching Transparencies 3-2; **Más práctica gramatical** Answers; Cuaderno de gramática Answers
- Interactive CD-ROM Tutor, Disc 1

Bell Work Have students write answers to these questions: **¿Qué materias tienes este semestre? ¿Qué clases tienes hoy? ¿Qué clase tienes ahora?**

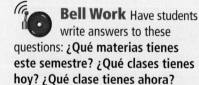

Presenting
Así se dice, Vocabulario

List upcoming school activities. Ask **¿A qué hora es?** and model the response: **Es a las ___**. Have pairs ask each other when they have certain classes. Circulate, asking, **¿...de la tarde? ¿...de la mañana?**

Así se dice

Telling at what time something happens

Más práctica gramatical, p. 101, Act. 3

To find out at what time something happens, ask:

¿A qué hora es la clase?
At what time is . . .?

¿A qué hora es el almuerzo?

To answer, say:

(Es) a las tres de la tarde.
(It's) at three in the afternoon.

¡Es ahora! Son las doce **en punto.**
It's now! . . . on the dot.

Vocabulario

Más práctica gramatical, p. 101, Act. 4

de la mañana
in the morning (A.M.)

de la tarde
in the afternoon (P.M.)

de la noche
in the evening (P.M.)

Cuaderno de actividades, p. 29, Act. 10

Cuaderno de gramática, p. 21, Acts. 8–9

---

15 **Horarios**

CD 3
Tr. 10

Escuchemos Two new students are discussing their daily schedules. Listen to the questions, then choose the appropriate answer. Scripts and answers on p. 77G.

1. **a)** Es la una y veinte.
   b) Es a la una y veinte.

2. **a)** Son las doce y diez.
   b) A las doce y diez.

3. **a)** Sí, son las tres.
   b) Sí, es a las tres.

4. **a)** Son las once y media.
   b) A las once y media.

5. **a)** Son las tres y ocho.
   b) A las tres y ocho.

6. **a)** Son las seis de la tarde.
   b) Es a las seis de la tarde.

---

16  **Del colegio al trabajo**

Hablemos You are a guidance counselor helping a new student with his or her class schedule. Answer the student's questions about at what time the classes meet. Use the times listed below for each course.

1. matemáticas (10:35 A.M.)
2. computación (2:10 P.M.)
3. ciencias (11:40 A.M.)
4. inglés (9:40 A.M.)
5. educación física (3:40 P.M.)
6. francés (1:20 P.M.)
7. almuerzo (1:55 P.M.)

Nota cultural

Students in Spanish-speaking countries may take as many as nine different courses. They can take more courses because their schedules vary from day to day. Most of these are required courses.

Communication for All Students

Motivating Activity

Ask students why it is important to know when something starts. (so they can get someplace on time) Are they ever late? When do they have to hurry to get somewhere? In this **Paso** they will learn to talk about these things in Spanish.

Ask students to demonstrate through gestures what they might be doing at the times you call out. (**Son las seis de la mañana.** Students might raise their arms and stretch, as though waking up.)

STANDARDS: 1.1, 1.2, 3.2, 4.2

17 Los programas de televisión

Hablemos/Leamos Choose two programs from this television listing from Mexico City and tell your partner what time they begin. Your partner will guess which programs you chose. Then think of two television programs you like to watch at home. Tell your partner at what time they begin, and your partner will guess the programs.

18 Entrevista

Hablemos/Escribamos Get together with two classmates. Imagine that you have just met. Exchange greetings with them and ask where they are from and how they're doing. Find out what classes they have today and at what times the classes meet. Then write their schedules, including classes and times. Be sure to use words like **primero**, **después**, and **luego** to help you sequence their schedules.

JUEVES

7:00 ⑤ BEETLEJUICE. Dibujos animados.
NOCHE ⑦ ALF. Comedia.
⑨ ESPECIAL MUSICAL. Variedades. "Timbiriche".
⑪ HOY EN LA CULTURA Entrevista especial a Octavio Paz. Premio Nobel de Literatura y Orgullo de México. Conducción: Sari Bermúdez.
7:30 ② ¡LLEVATELO! Concursos para toda la familia, con Paco Stanley y Gabriela Ruffo.
⑤ BATMAN. Dibujos animados.
⑦ SALVADO POR LA CAMPANA. Aventuras.
⑪ EL HOMBRE Y LA INDUSTRIA. Reportajes. Juventud.
⑬ SEÑORA. Telenovela.
22 POR AQUI PUEDEN PASAR. Animación infantil. Cuentos alrededor del mundo: Rumpelstiltskin.
7:50 22 ENCUADRE. Cartelera cinematográfica. Con Leonardo García Tsao y Nelson Carro.
8:00 ④ LOS INTOCABLES. Aventuras policíacas.
⑤ INTRIGA TROPICAL. Aventuras de un ex-agente antinarcóticos y su socia detective. Rob Stewart "Nick Slaughter", Carolyn Dunn "Sylvie Girard", Pedro Armendáriz "Lt. Carrillo".

Nota gramatical

In Spanish, to show that something belongs to someone, use **de.** This is the equivalent of *'s* (apostrophe s) in English.

los zapatos de David   *David's shoes*
las clases de Eva   *Eva's classes*

De combines with **el** to form the contraction **del.**

el perro del profesor   *the teacher's dog*
la directora del colegio   *the school's director*

Cuaderno de gramática, p. 22, Acts. 10–11

Más práctica gramatical, p. 102, Act. 5

SUGERENCIA

Sometimes students often don't know *how* to study a foreign language. Learning a language is like learning a new sport—you have to do a little bit every day. You also have to practice. Set aside time each day for Spanish. Study in a quiet place, where you can say words out loud. Review what you did in Spanish class that day, then go on to your homework. Keep at it and plan to study regularly with a classmate. All your hard work will pay off!

19 Gramática en contexto

Hablemos/Escribamos Work in a group of three. Each student completes the sentences below. Then exchange answers with your partners. Take turns reporting to the group.

MODELO   —Mi actor favorito es Andy García.
—El actor favorito de Luis es Andy García.

1. Mi actor favorito es...
2. Mi actriz favorita es...
3. Mi libro favorito es...
4. Mi deporte favorito es...
5. Mi clase favorita es...
6. Mi color favorito es...
7. Mi programa de televisión favorito es...
8. Mi grupo musical favorito es...
9. Mi comida favorita es...

Group Work

17 This activity requires index cards and several TV guides. In groups of five, have students write the name and time of five of their favorite TV programs, one on each card. Give each group a TV schedule so that they may verify the program times. Then have groups exchange their index cards with other groups. On the back of each card, students write the time of the program in Spanish. Students return the completed cards to the group. Have groups write up their ideal night of television in Spanish.

Presenting
Nota gramatical

Possession using *de* First, have the students read the grammar explanation. Then, walk around the class and pick up various objects. Ask for volunteers to answer questions such as **¿De qué color es la mochila de Beth?** Elicit answers such as **La mochila de Beth es roja.**

Teaching Suggestion

19 Do students share common preferences or do their preferences vary greatly? Based on the information that students have gathered in their **encuesta**, ask them to predict whether their classmates are similar or diverse in their preferences for music, sports, classes, or other categories. In order to verify (or disprove) the students' predictions, ask each group to share their findings on several items in the interview. When students report data, they can use the same sentence structure they used in the original activity. (**El grupo musical favorito de Luis es Maná.**) Tabulate the data on the board or on an overhead. For further discussion, ask students to explain why the similarities or differences exist in the preferences of the class.

Connections and Comparisons

Language-to-Language
Stress the differences in English and Spanish possessive constructions. Have students practice Spanish possession: **la mochila de Stephen, la clase de Rebecca.** Ask the class to think of examples of a similar construction in English: *David is a friend of mine. Tom is a friend of Dianne's.*

Family Link
Ask students to get together with someone at home and write out his or her daily schedule. Does the person do the same things at the same time every day, or does his or her schedule vary? Have students report their findings to the class, describing in Spanish a typical day in a family member's life.

Presenting
Así se dice

Prepare a transparency with a list of names, events and times. **(José, concierto—8:00 P.M.; Samuel, clase de inglés—1:15 P.M.)** Revealing one at a time, first tell students what time it is, giving a time that is later than the time of the event on the transparency. **(Son las ocho y media. ¡José, date prisa, estás atrasado!)** After you have modeled several expressions in this way, show the entire list and call out a time to the class, to which they respond appropriately. **(—Es la una y veinticinco. —Samuel, estás atrasado, ¡córrele!)**

Assess

▶ Testing Program, pp. 57–60
Quiz 3-2A, Quiz 3-2B
Audio CD 3, Tr. 19

▶ Student Make-Up Assignments, Chapter 3, Alternative Quiz

▶ Alternative Assessment Guide, p. 34

Así se dice

Talking about being late or in a hurry

To tell someone you are late, say:

Estoy atrasada.	*(if you're female)*
Estoy atrasado.	*(if you're male)*

To say that someone else is late, say:

Está atrasada.	*(if the person is female)*
Está atrasado.	*(if the person is male)*

To tell someone you are in a hurry, say:
Tengo prisa.

To tell a friend to hurry up, say:
¡Date prisa!

Cuaderno de actividades, pp. 30–31, Acts. 11–12

También se puede decir...
To tell a friend to hurry up, Mexicans also may say ¡Ándale!, ¡Apúrate!, or ¡Córrele!

20 **¡Ya es tarde!**

Leamos/Escribamos Everyone's running late today! Match the correct photos to the sentences below. Then, using phrases from **Así se dice,** create a caption for the remaining photo.

a.
b.
c.
d.

1. ¡Date prisa! Ya tengo todo en mi mochila. a
2. Buenos días, señor Rodríguez. Usted está atrasado, ¿no? c
3. ¡Ay, ya son las nueve y media! ¡Tengo prisa! b
4. ¿ ? Answers will vary.

21 **¿Quién está atrasado?**

Escribamos Of the people you know, who is always late and who is never late? Write sentences about five people you know, using **siempre** for always, and **nunca** for never.

MODELO   Mi amigo Juan siempre está atrasado.

22 **Lo siento, no tengo tiempo.** *I'm sorry, I don't have time.*

Escribamos Imagine that you and your friend have just run into each other. Write a dialogue in which one of you keeps on chatting while the other tries to end the conversation.

Communication for All Students

Auditory Learners

21 Model sentence structure by reading aloud sentences about known or famous people, using **siempre** and **nunca**. **(La directora del colegio siempre tiene prisa. Super-hombre nunca está atrasado.)** As a follow-up activity, ask for volunteers to read their sentences aloud to the class.

Building on Previous Skills

22 Before students begin to write their dialogue, review the functional expressions in the **Así se dice** sections of pages 22, 27, 28, 32, 52, 60, 84, 85, and 88. This will refresh in students' minds several possible real-life contexts for the imaginary dialogues they are about to write.

Encuentro cultural

Hora latina

Eric recently moved to Taxco, Mexico, from Minnesota. Last weekend, he was invited to a party by his new friends Paloma and Consuelo. He arrived at 8:00 P.M., as Paloma and Consuelo had told him. When he got there, however, none of the other guests had arrived and the two girls weren't even ready. Eric felt really awkward.

Tomorrow, Eric has an interview with the principal at the school he'll be attending. His appointment is for 9:00 A.M. Eric isn't sure when to show up. Working with a partner, decide how to answer the questions under **Para discutir…** below. Then check your answers in the **Vamos a comprenderlo** section to see if they are reasonable.

COLEGIO SAN ROQUE

Para discutir…

1. Should Eric show up for his interview at 9:00 on the dot?
2. What would have been a good time for Eric to arrive at Paloma and Consuelo's party?
3. What would you do if you arrived at a party before the hosts were ready?

Vamos a comprenderlo

In Mexico, as in other Spanish-speaking countries, people are expected to arrive a little late for a party—a half-hour to an hour later than they are told to come. This custom is called **hora latina** *(Latin time)*. But at school or on the job, people are expected to be on time. There's no set rule for what to do if you arrive too early to a social event. Eric could have made a polite excuse to leave and come back later, but it's likely that his hosts would have invited him in for a soft drink while he waited for the other guests.

Motivating Activity
Ask students to imagine they are friends with a visiting student from a Latin American country. They get along well and have common interests, but their friend often arrives late to various activities. Ask students to work in pairs to think of a way to explain the North American understanding of punctuality. Students should be sure the explanation is clear but not offensive to their foreign friend.

Presenting
Encuentro cultural
Many university schedules from Latin American countries show lengthy "passing time" between classes, often 15 minutes, sometimes more. You might create your own schedule, simulating a known university, or find one on the Internet, and use this as a springboard for conversation before reading **Encuentro cultural**. Ask students why they think the time between classes is so lengthy, and if they feel it is necessary. Ask if they think this long passing time would help make their school run more efficiently.

Additional Practice
After students have read the **Encuentro cultural,** ask them to compare their conclusions about punctuality in the U.S. with what they have learned about Hispanic attitudes towards time. What are the similarities and differences? Can students account for these differences?

Native Speakers
Ask native speakers to share expressions telling a friend to hurry up. Some examples may include ¡Avanza!, ¡Date prisa!, ¡Corre!, ¡Órale!, ¡Termina!, ¡Venga!

Connections and Comparisons

Thinking Critically
Comparing and Contrasting Discuss punctuality in the United States. Ask students when and under what circumstances it is important to be on time and when it is acceptable to be late. Is it all right to be late to a dentist appointment? an after-school practice? a babysitting job? when meeting friends at the mall? How late is late? Try to show students that in the U.S. there are also circumstances when it is all right to be late. You might ask a volunteer to list these circumstances on the board.

Tercer paso

Objectives Describing people and things; talking about things you like and explaining why

WV3 MEXICO-3

Teaching Resources
pp. 92–97

PRINT
▸ Lesson Planner, p. 15
▸ TPR Storytelling Book, pp. 11, 12
▸ Listening Activities, pp. 21, 25
▸ Activities for Communication, pp. 17–18, 87, 88–89, 141–142
▸ Cuaderno de gramática, pp. 23–26
▸ Grammar Tutor for Students of Spanish, Chapter 3
▸ Cuaderno de actividades, pp. 32–34
▸ Cuaderno para hispanohablantes, pp. 11–15
▸ Testing Program, pp. 61–64
▸ Alternative Assessment Guide, p. 34
▸ Student Make-Up Assignments, Chapter 3

MEDIA
▸ One-Stop Planner
▸ Audio Compact Discs, CD 3, Trs. 11–16, 20, 27–28
▸ Teaching Transparencies 3-3, 3-B, 3-C; **Más práctica gramatical** Answers; Cuaderno de gramática Answers
▸ Interactive CD-ROM Tutor, Disc 1

Bell Work
Write these questions on the board or a transparency and have students write their answers. **¿Qué hora es? ¿A qué hora tienes el almuerzo? ¿Te gusta el español?**

Presenting
Así se dice, Vocabulario, Gramática

Using *Teaching Transparency 3-3*, describe several characters. Then tape magazine cutouts of different figures to the board and ask students to guess which one you are thinking of by asking questions. (**¿Es rubio? ¿Es baja?**)

Así se dice

Describing people and things

To find out what people and things are like, ask:

¿Cómo es tu compañero/a nuevo/a?
What's your new friend like?

¿Cómo es la clase?

¿Cómo son los profesores?
What are the teachers like?

To tell what someone or something is like, say:

Él es alto. *He's tall.*
Ella es alta. *She's tall.*

Es aburrida. *It's boring.*

No te preocupes. Ellos no son muy estrictos.
Don't worry. They aren't very strict.

Nota gramatical

You're familiar with the singular forms of **ser** *(to be)*. Here are all forms of the verb.

Soy alto/a.	Nosotros/as **somos** altos/as.
Eres bajo/a.	Vosotros/as **sois** bajos/as.
Es cómico/a.	**Son** cómicos/as.

Cuaderno de gramática, p. 23, Acts. 12–13

Más práctica gramatical, p. 102, Act. 6

Vocabulario

CD-ROM 1
DVD 1

antipático/a *disagreeable*	**inteligente** *intelligent*
bajo/a *short*	**interesante** *interesting*
bonito/a *pretty*	
bueno/a *good*	**malo/a** *bad*
cómico/a *funny*	**moreno/a** *dark-haired, dark-skinned*
difícil *difficult*	
divertido/a *fun, amusing*	**nuevo/a** *new*
fácil *easy*	**pequeño/a** *small*
feo/a *ugly*	**rubio/a** *blond*
grande *big*	**simpático/a** *nice*
guapo/a *good-looking*	

Cuaderno de gramática, p. 24, Acts. 14–16

Más práctica gramatical, p. 103, Act. 7

23 **Gramática en contexto**

Leamos Empareja cada uno de los dibujos con la descripción correcta.

a.

b.

c.

d.

1. Es nuevo pero es aburrido. c.
2. Son bajos y muy cómicos. d.
3. Son pequeños pero son muy malos. a.
4. Es alta y fea. b.

Communication for All Students

Motivating Activity
Así se dice Ask volunteers to ad-lib a conversation in English at the lost-and-found counter of a shopping mall. One student has lost a small child. The attendant at the counter must ask numerous questions to get an accurate description of the child. Have the class count the number of descriptors necessary to describe the child really well.

Slower Pace
23 Model the word **empareja** by matching familiar items. For example, you may choose to match numerals with Spanish number words. Preteach other vocabulary in the instructions so that students know what to do. To complete the activity, have students refer to the **Vocabulario**.

Gramática

Adjective Agreement

Have you noticed that adjectives such as **divertido** change to match the nouns they modify?

	MASCULINE	FEMININE
SINGULAR	un libro **divertido**	una clase **divertida**
PLURAL	unos libros **divertidos**	unas clases **divertidas**

1. To describe one person or thing, use **es** + a singular adjective.

   El libro **es divertido**.   La clase **es divertida**.

2. To describe more than one person or thing, use **son** + a plural adjective.

   Los libros **son buenos**.   Las clases **son buenas**.

3. If you're describing a group of males and females, use a masculine plural adjective.

   Mis compañeros **son simpáticos**.

   Más práctica gramatical, p. 103, Act. 7

4. Adjectives ending in **-e** or a consonant such as **l, r,** or **n** have only two forms: singular and plural. To make these adjectives plural, add **-s** or **-es**.

   El libro es **interesante**. → Los libros son **interesantes**.
   La clase es **difícil**. → Las clases son **difíciles**.

   Cuaderno de actividades, pp. 33–34, Acts. 16–17

   Cuaderno de gramática, p. 25, Act. 17

24 **Gramática en contexto**

Leamos/Escribamos Claudia is writing to her cousin Marisa, telling her about her new school and her friends there. Complete her letter with the correct forms of the adjectives in the word box. Use each adjective only once.

See possible answers below.

> bonito   simpático   inteligente
>
> interesante   divertido
>
> difícil
>
> guapo   cómico

> Querida Marisa,
> ¡Hola! ¿Cómo estás? Bueno, aquí estoy en el Instituto Centro Unión. Me gusta mucho. Las clases son ___1___ y ___2___, pero no son ___3___. Los profesores son muy ___4___. Los estudiantes en este colegio son ___5___. Mi amiga María Inés es ___6___ y ___7___. Fernando es el amigo de Sandra. Él es muy ___8___. Bueno, ahora tengo clase. ¡Ya estoy atrasada!
> ¡Hasta luego!
> Claudia

Cultures and Communities

Language Notes

- **Así se dice** Dominicans and other native speakers from Caribbean countries often use **bien** to replace **muy**.

- **Vocabulario** You might point out to students that **rubio/a** may also be used to describe someone who is fair-skinned. **Moreno/a** is often used to describe someone with dark coloring.

Presenting
Gramática

Adjective agreement Point out and model the four combinations of adjective agreement (feminine singular, masculine singular, feminine plural, and masculine plural) using **carpeta(s)** and **video(s)**. Then, ask students questions about objects in the room and have them answer using adjectives. (—¿Qué son? —Son plantas verdes.)

Teaching Suggestions

- Put magazine pictures of people in an envelope. Ask students to choose a picture and describe him or her to a partner.

- Place pictures of famous people in a bag. Have one student go to the front of the room. Select a picture from the bag and place it on the student's back. Other students take turns making up a descriptive sentence as a hint for who the famous person is. After each sentence, the student who is "it" must guess the name of the celebrity.

Additional Practice

24 Using Claudia's letter as a model, have students write a brief description of school, their friends, classes, and teachers.

Answers
24 *Possible answers:*
1. interesantes
2. divertidas
3. difíciles
4. inteligentes
5. simpáticos
6. bonita
7. cómica
8. guapo

Teaching Resources
pp. 92–97

PRINT

▸ Lesson Planner, p. 15
▸ TPR Storytelling Book, pp. 11, 12
▸ Listening Activities, pp. 21, 25
▸ Activities for Communication, pp. 17–18, 87, 88–89, 141–142
▸ Cuaderno de gramática, pp. 23–26
▸ Grammar Tutor for Students of Spanish, Chapter 3
▸ Cuaderno de actividades, pp. 32–34
▸ Cuaderno para hispanohablantes, pp. 11–15
▸ Testing Program, pp. 61–64
▸ Alternative Assessment Guide, p. 34
▸ Student Make-Up Assignments, Chapter 3

MEDIA

▸ One-Stop Planner
▸ Audio Compact Discs, CD 3, Trs. 11–16, 27–28, 20
▸ Teaching Transparencies 3-3, 3-B, 3-C; **Más práctica gramatical** Answers; Cuaderno de gramática Answers
▸ Interactive CD-ROM Tutor, Disc 1

Teacher Notes

25 Point out to students that in item three, the adjective for *Texas* agrees with **el estado,** a masculine noun. You may also wish to explain gender agreement with **el país, la ciudad,** and **la provincia.**

Answers

25 *Possible answers:*

1. Tus clases no son fáciles. Son difíciles.
2. La clase de español no es aburrida. Es interesante.
3. Texas no es pequeño. Es grande.
4. Los profesores no son antipáticos. Son simpáticos.
5. Alberto no es alto. Es bajo.
6. Tus compañeros no son malos. Son buenos.

---

25 **Gramática en contexto**

Leamos/Escribamos Your friend is always talking, but everything he says is wrong. Change each statement to say the opposite of what your friend says. See answers below.

> **MODELO**   Fernando es moreno.
> —No, no es moreno. Es rubio.

1. Mis clases son fáciles.
2. La clase de español es aburrida.
3. Texas es pequeño.
4. Los profesores son antipáticos.
5. Alberto es alto.
6. Mis compañeros son malos.

26 **Descripciones**

 Hablemos Work with a partner and form as many sentences as you can describing the picture. Use the words from the **Vocabulario** on page 92.

 A lo nuestro

What words do you use to get someone's attention? In Spanish, two common expressions are **¡Mira!** *(Look!)* and **¡Oye!** *(Listen!).* When speaking to more than one person, use **miren** or **oigan.**

Oye, ¿cómo es la clase?
Hey, what's the class like?

Mira, es fácil, pero hay mucha tarea.
Look, it's easy, but there's a lot of homework.

Although **oye** and **oigan** mean *listen,* they are used like the English expression *"hey."*

Mario

El carro

Ana

27 **Mis amigos son...**

Hablemos Con un/a compañero/a describe las cosas y a las personas siguientes.

> **MODELO**   —Oye, ¿cómo es tu cuarto?
> —Mira, es pequeño, pero bonito.

1. el libro de...
2. los profesores de...
3. la cafetería
4. los centros comerciales
5. la clase de...
6. la tarea de...
7. tus amigos
8. la música de...

28 **¿Cómo son tus clases?**

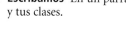 **Escribamos** En un párrafo de seis o siete oraciones describe a tus maestros, amigos y tus clases.

Communication for All Students

Slower Pace

25 Have students brainstorm and list as many descriptors and adjectives from this chapter as they can before beginning this activity.

Tactile Learners

27 Have students collect several things from around the room (books, notebooks, pens, etc.) and pass them to each other as they describe them in Spanish. For added interest, have students close their eyes and guess what is passed to them. You may wish to introduce *heavy* **(pesado)**, *light* **(ligero)**, *hard* **(duro)**, and *soft* **(suave)**. As a follow-up, have students label objects in the room.

STANDARDS: 1.1, 1.3, 5.1

Así se dice

Talking about things you like and explaining why

CD-ROM 1
DVD 1

To find out if a friend likes more than one thing, ask:

Your friend might answer:

¿Te gustan las clases?

Sí, **me gustan**. Son fáciles.

¿Cuál es tu clase favorita?
Which is . . .?

Mi clase **favorita** es inglés.

¿A Claudia le gustan las ciencias?
Does Claudia like . . .?

Sí. **Le gustan** mucho y también **le gusta** la geografía.

¿Por qué?
Why?

Porque son muy interesantes.
Because . . .

Más práctica gramatical, p. 103, Act. 8

Vocabulario

el baile

el concierto

los deportes

el examen
(pl. los exámenes)

la fiesta

la novela

el partido de...

el videojuego

Cuaderno de gramática, p. 26, Acts. 18–19

Más práctica gramatical, p. 103, Act. 8

29 **Patricia y Gregorio**

CD 3
Tr. 11

Escuchemos/Leamos Patricia and Gregorio have just met at school. Listen to their conversation as they try to decide what to do. Based on their conversation, respond to these statements with **cierto** or **falso**. Scripts and answers on p. 77H.

1. A Patricia no le gustan las fiestas.
2. A Gregorio le gustan los partidos de fútbol porque son interesantes.
3. A Patricia no le gustan los conciertos.
4. A Gregorio le gusta la música rock.

Connections and Comparisons

Language-to-Language

Students often have trouble with the **gustar** construction and complain that it seems backwards or upside-down to them. It may be helpful to make comparisons with similar constructions in English: *Music interests me. Football bores my mom.* Ask students to think of more examples, with different verbs: *Do exams scare you? My little brother really bugs me.* Ask students to explain the parallels between these examples and the expressions in **Así se dice**.

Teaching Resources
pp. 92–97

PRINT

▶ Lesson Planner, p. 15
▶ TPR Storytelling Book, pp. 11, 12
▶ Listening Activities, pp. 21, 25
▶ Activities for Communication, pp. 17–18, 87, 88–89, 141–142
▶ Cuaderno de gramática, pp. 23–26
▶ Grammar Tutor for Students of Spanish, Chapter 3
▶ Cuaderno de actividades, pp. 32–34
▶ Cuaderno para hispanohablantes, pp. 11–15
▶ Testing Program, pp. 61–64
▶ Alternative Assessment Guide, p. 34
▶ Student Make-Up Assignments, Chapter 3

MEDIA

▶ One-Stop Planner
▶ Audio Compact Discs, CD 3, Trs. 11–16, 27–28, 20
▶ Teaching Transparencies 3-3, 3-B, 3-C; **Más práctica gramatical** Answers; Cuaderno de gramática Answers
▶ Interactive CD-ROM Tutor, Disc 1

Additional Practice

30 After students have completed the pairwork, create a graph of class **gustos** by having students report their partner's preferences.

Presenting
Nota gramatical

Present tag questions to students. Model incorrect descriptions such as **Juan es bajo, ¿verdad?,** then correct them with sentences like **No, Juan no es bajo. Es alto.** Have students write tag questions with incorrect descriptions of classmates, then read them aloud for classmates to correct.

---

30 ¿Por qué te gusta?

  Leamos/Hablemos Working with a partner, take turns asking whether or not you like the things in the list below. Explain why or why not, using the adjectives you've learned so far. Be prepared to report five of your partner's answers to the class. Answers will vary.

MODELO —Te gustan las clases, ¿no?
—Sí, me gustan mucho.
—¿Por qué?
—Porque son divertidas.

1. la música pop
2. los exámenes
3. el basquetbol
4. las fiestas
5. el fútbol
6. los bailes
7. la música clásica
8. las novelas
9. la natación
10. los conciertos
11. el programa de...
12. los deportes
13. los videojuegos
14. el tenis
15. los videos de...

CALENDARIO DE EVENTOS

12h00:
FESTIVAL DE CINE FRANCES
LOCAL: AUDITORIO DEL MUSEO

15h00:
EXPOSICION DE ARTE
LOCAL: NUEVO MUSEO

17h00:
CONCIERTO DE PIANO
LOCAL: AUDITORIO DEL MUSEO

18h30:
PRESENTACION DE DANZA
LOCAL: TEATRO CARLOS TAMARIZ

20h00:
FESTIVAL VIDEO-ROCK
LOCAL: AUDITORIO DEL MUSEO

22h00:
GRAN BAILE: "LOS PRISIONEROS"
LOCAL: PARQUE DE SAN SEBASTIAN

Nota gramatical

One way of asking a question is by adding **¿no?** or **¿verdad?** to the end of a sentence. These are called *tag questions*. The tag question can be translated several different ways, depending on the English context.

La clase es difícil, **¿no?**
isn't it? right?
Te gustan los bailes, **¿verdad?**
don't you? right?

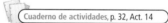
Cuaderno de actividades, p. 32, Act. 14

---

31 Gramática en contexto

  Hablemos With a partner, take a look at this entertainment guide and try to figure out what to do. Take turns asking each other whether or not you like the events listed in the entertainment guide and at what time they take place. When possible, try to use tag questions like those explained in the **Nota gramatical**.

MODELO —Te gustan los festivales de cine, ¿verdad?
—Sí, me gustan mucho. ¿A qué hora es el festival?
—A las doce de la tarde.

---

32 De visita Answers will vary.

  Escribamos/Hablemos Work in groups of three. Imagine that you are students at the Instituto Centro Unión in Cuernavaca. Prepare a list of questions you can use to interview a student from the U.S. Include questions about age, classes, friends, and teachers. Also, ask about likes and dislikes.

Connections and Comparisons

Thinking Critically

32 **Comparing and Contrasting** Ask students to write to the Mexican Embassy or the Mexican Government Tourism Office (see p. T46) to obtain information on specific cities such as Cuernavaca. Students may also supplement their knowledge by searching the Internet or with travel books on Mexico from bookstores or public libraries.

Visit the HRW Web site at **http://go.hrw.com** for online resources and additional information about Mexico. After they have finished their research, students should write a report in which they compare their hometown to the Mexican city they researched.

33 Ahora, dime...

Hablemos Choose a classmate to take the role of the visiting student in Activity 32. Interview your partner using the questions you've prepared. Then switch roles, allowing your partner to ask you his or her questions.

 34 Soy...

Hablemos/Escribamos Form a group of five and write a detailed description of one person in your group. Include the person's age, personality traits, and physical characteristics, and things she or he likes or dislikes. Then read your group's description to the class and have them guess who it is.

35 En mi cuaderno

Escribamos In your journal, write seven or eight sentences about what you need and want to do at different times tomorrow. Include going to class, doing homework, and going shopping. Use **me gusta(n)** to tell how you feel about the classes and places you mention, and explain why. Answers will vary.

LETRA Y SONIDO

CD 3
Trs. 12–16

A. 1. h: The letter **h** in Spanish is always silent.

hora	ahora	héroe	Hugo	hijo	hospital

2. j: The letter **j** in Spanish represents a sound that has no equivalent in English. It's pronounced like the *h* in the English word *house*, but much stronger and with the back of the tongue near the soft palate.

jugar	jefe	ají	joven	pasaje	caja	juego

3. g: The letter **g** before the vowels **e** and **i** has the same sound as the letter **j** in the examples above.

gente	general	geografía	gimnasio	corregir	agitar

4. Before the vowels *a, o,* and *u,* the letter *g* is pronounced like the *g* in the English word *go.*

ángulo	tengo	gusto	mango

Between vowels this sound is much softer.

haga	agua	agotar	mucho gusto

5. The **g** is pronounced "hard," like the *g* in *get,* when it's followed by **ue** or **ui.**

guerra	llegué	guitarra	guía

B. Dictado Script for Part B on p. 77H.

Jimena describes for us what she needs in two of her classes. Write what Jimena is saying.

C. Trabalenguas

La gente de San José generalmente juega a las barajas con ganas de ganar.

Communication for All Students

Slower Pace

30 Put pictures of famous people on the board and number each one. Ask students if they can remember what adjectives were used to describe each person and have them write a list of adjectives that go with each picture. It may be helpful for them to associate an image with adjectives. (a frog with **feo**) Then, have them check their adjective endings to be sure the form is correct.

Visual Learners

Letra y sonido Make flashcards with the words in **Letra y sonido**. Hold up a card and have all students say the word until you have heard the correct pronunciation. As a follow-up, recite the list of words on the flashcards and have students write them.

Tercer paso

CAPÍTULO 3

 TPR Hold up photos of famous people clipped from magazines. Ask students to describe each one with at least three phrases. For a photo of an athlete, you could ask: **Clase, ¿quién es? ¿Cómo es él/ella? ¿Qué le gusta a él/ella?**

Additional Practice

Have students form groups of three and create a dialogue using **ser** and singular and plural adjectives. One student makes an observation in the singular, which the other two students convert to the plural. (—**Yo soy simpática.** —**Ah, sí. Y nosotros somos simpáticos también.**)

Speaking Assessment

33 Have pairs of partners peer-evaluate each other's dialogues.

Speaking Rubric	Points			
	4	3	2	1
Content (Complete–Incomplete)				
Comprehension (Total–Little)				
Comprehensibility (Comprehensible–Incomprehensible)				
Accuracy (Accurate–Seldom accurate)				
Fluency (Fluent–Not fluent)				

18–20: A   14–15: C   Under
16–17: B   12–13: D   12: F

Assess

▸ Testing Program, pp. 61–64
  Quiz 3-3A, Quiz 3-3B
  Audio CD 3, Tr. 20

▸ Student Make-Up Assignments, Chapter 3, Alternative Quiz

▸ Alternative Assessment Guide, p. 34

Vamos a leer

MATRÍCULA	ÓSCAR GONZÁLEZ LÓPEZ				(MÉXICO)	
B0847842	SEPT.	OCT.	NOV.	ENE.	FEB.	MAR.
ESPAÑOL	7.7	9.8	9.5	9.5	9.2	8.4
MATEMÁTICAS	8.8	8.2	9.0	6.4	7.1	8.0
LENG.A.A/ESPAÑOLA	8.5	6.5	7.5	9.0	10.0	10.0
C. NATURALES	7.2	7.4	7.6	8.1	8.8	7.7
C. SOCIALES	9.0	7.7	9.6	10.0	9.7	9.4
EDUC. FÍSICA	10.0	7.5	10.0	9.5	9.6	9.5
EDUC. ARTÍSTICA	10.0	10.0	10.0	10.0	9.5	9.5
EDUC. TECNOLÓGICA	10.0	10.0	10.0	10.0	10.0	10.0

ALUMNA: JUANA ACOSTA RUIZ					(ESPAÑA)	
	PRIMERA EVALUACIÓN			TERCERA EVALUACIÓN		
Segundo De B.U.P.	Faltas de asistencia	conoci- mientos	Actitud	Faltas de asistencia	conoci- mientos	Actitud
L. y L. Españolas		7	C		7'5	C
Latín		8	B	1	5'5	C
Lengua Extranjera (___)		6'5	C		5	C
Geografía Humana		8	C		7	C
F. Polít. Soc. y Econ.						
Matemáticas		4'5	C		4'5	C
Física-Química		9	C		5'5	C
Religión		7	C		7	B
Educ. Física y Deport.					6	C
EATP. Ens. Ac. Tec-Prof.		4'5	C		5	C

Teaching Resources
pp. 98–99

PRINT
- Lesson Planner, p. 16
- Cuaderno de actividades, p. 35
- Cuaderno para hispanohablantes, pp. 11–13
- Reading Strategies and Skills Handbook, Chapter 3
- ¡Lee conmigo! 1, Chapter 3
- Standardized Assessment Tutor, Chapter 3

MEDIA
- One-Stop Planner

Prereading
Activities A and B

Motivating Activity
Have the class consider how schedules and report cards help students and teachers. Ask students to work in small groups to develop alternatives to traditional schedules and report cards. You may want to ask students to explain to the class how their ideas would improve the existing system.

Using Prior Knowledge
Discuss the 24-hour clock with the class prior to beginning the reading. To do this, use a clock with movable arms and review telling time in Spanish.
—¿Qué hora es, clase? (11:00)
—Son las once.
—¿Y ahora? (12:00)
—Son las doce.

Then move the clock hands to 1:00 and ask:
—¿Son las trece?
—No, es la una.
—Sí, es la una. Pero también son las trece.

Check comprehension briefly in English, clarifying that 12:00 is midnight (**medianoche**).

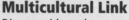

Calificaciones y horarios

Estrategia para leer

As soon as you know the topic of a reading, spend a couple of minutes just thinking about the topic. What do you already know about it? The reading should then be easier to understand, and you'll be better able to guess unknown words and make sense of difficult passages.

¡A comenzar!

A. You're probably already familiar with the items above. Skim them briefly and then complete the following statement.

These items are . . .
1. TV schedules and sports scores
2. report cards and TV schedules
3. sports scores and class schedules
4. class schedules and report cards

B. Now, before you read them again more carefully, think about what you already know about these two topics. Would the following probably be found in a school schedule, in a report card, in both, or in neither?

1. letter grades report card
2. name(s) of parent(s) report card (or neither)
3. class names both
4. days of the week schedule
5. student's name both
6. textbook names neither
7. numerical grades report card
8. best friend's name neither
9. class times schedule

Connections and Comparisons

Multicultural Link
Discuss with students ways of obtaining schedules and report cards from other countries. If students have pen pals, their correspondents might supply them. See p. T46 for addresses of pen pal organizations. Also, visit the HRW Web site at **http://go.hrw.com** for online resources and additional information.

Culture Note
Students in Spain often receive comments instead of grades: **sobresaliente, bien, suficiente,** or **deficiente.** Students in many Spanish-speaking countries may be exempt from exams in a course if they have a good grade. Ask students to discuss the benefits and deficits of different grading systems.

El horario de Gloria (México)

Hora	lunes	martes	miércoles	jueves	viernes
7:30-8:20	música	civismo	geografía	biología	historia
8:30-9:20	español	inglés	inglés	matemáticas	matemáticas
9:30-10:20	matemáticas	español	historia	educación física	civismo
10:30-11:20	historia	música	matemáticas	geografía	educación física
11:30-12:20	inglés	descanso	descanso	descanso	español
12:30-13:20	biología	matemáticas	español	español	biología
13:30-14:20					

El horario de María (España)

	lunes	martes	miércoles	jueves	viernes
9:20-10:10	historia	e. física	lit. gallega	latín	filosofía
10:10-11:00	latín	inglés	historia	l. gallega	matemáticas
11:00-11:50	inglés	filosofía	lit. española	l. española	latín
	descanso	descanso	descanso	descanso	descanso
12:10-13:00	matemáticas	inglés	diseño	diseño	inglés
13:00-13:50	e. física	latín	filosofía	filosofía	historia
13:50-14:40			matemáticas		lit. española
15:30-16:20	lit. española	religión			
16:20-17:10	religión	matemáticas			
17:10-18:00		lit. gallega			

Reading
Activities C and D

Using Context Clues
Have students work in groups of three. Ask them to scan the reading to find as many cognates as they can. Set a time limit of three minutes.

Postreading
Activity E

Making Inferences
Have students choose either Spain or Mexico and make up their own "ideal" school schedule and report card as if they were a student in one of those countries.

Al grano
C. Comparaciones. Look at the last columns of the documents for Óscar and Juana. See answers below.

1. The numerical grades are the achievement grades for the class. There are also letter grades. What do the letter grades on Juana's report card represent?
2. What is the highest grade each student got in science?
3. Who did better in physical education?
4. Who did better in Spanish?

D. ¿Qué horario prefieres? Read the class schedules carefully. Do you prefer Gloria's schedule, María's schedule, or your schedule? These questions may help you decide. See answers below.

1. Which classes do all three of you have?
2. How many days a week does each of you have English?

3. What kinds of language classes does each of you take?
4. How many days a week do you each take physical education?

E. ¿Dónde te gustaría estudiar? Contesta las siguientes preguntas. See answers below.

1. ¿Cuántas clases tiene Gloria? ¿María? ¿Óscar? ¿Juana?
2. ¿Te gustan las clases de Gloria? ¿de María? ¿Por qué?
3. ¿A qué hora empiezan *(begin)* las clases de Gloria? ¿de María?

Cuaderno para hispanohablantes, pp. 11–13
Cuaderno de actividades, p. 35, Act. 20

Answers

C 1. her attitude/behavior
2. Óscar: 8.8; Juana: 9
3. Óscar
4. Óscar

D *Answers will vary.*
1. Gloria and María both have *inglés, matemáticas, historia,* and *educación física.*
2. Gloria has English three times a week. María has it twice a week.
3. Gloria: inglés, español; María: inglés, latín
4. Gloria: twice; María: twice

E 1. Gloria: 10; María: 10; Óscar: 8; Juana: 10
2. *Answers will vary.*
3. Gloria, 7:30; María, 9:20

Communication for All Students

Slower Pace
C. Have students work with just one schedule until they understand its components.

Group Work
D. Have groups of three review the schedules. Each student takes a schedule and presents its advantages. Have the class vote on the most appealing schedule.

Pair Work
E. Have students work with a partner to answer these questions. Watch for students having difficulty. When finished, go over the answers as a class.

Más práctica gramatical

CAPÍTULO 3

For **Más práctica gramatical** Answer Transparencies, see the *Teaching Transparencies* binder.

Más práctica gramatical

MARCAR: go.hrw.com
PALABRA CLAVE:
WV3 MEXICO-3

Primer paso **Objectives** Talking about class schedules and sequencing events; telling time

1 Víctor is checking to make sure he has everything in his backpack. Complete what he says by filling in each blank with the correct definite article: **el, la, los,** or **las**. (p. 83)

A ver... ¿tengo ___1___ cuadernos? Sí, aquí están, con ___2___ lápices y bolígrafos. Y necesito ___3___ libros de historia y español. También necesito ___4___ carpetas para ___5___ clases de inglés y geografía. Y para ___6___ clase de educación física... ___7___ zapatillas de tenis. ¿Qué más? Necesito encontrar ___8___ calculadora y ___9___ regla. ¿Dónde están? Y, ¡ay! necesito encontrar ___10___ dinero ahora mismo.

2 Mira el horario de clases de Gloria y di a qué hora tiene sus clases. (p. 86)

MODELO Tiene la clase de arte.
Son las diez y diez.

HORA	MIÉRCOLES	JUEVES
7:20	geografía	biología
8:25	inglés	matemáticas
9:15	historia	educación física
10:10	matemáticas	arte
11:05	almuerzo	almuerzo
11:45	español	español
12:35	francés	computación
1:40	ciencias sociales	ciencias sociales

1. Tiene la clase de educación física.
2. Quiere comprar una ensalada en la cafetería.
3. Su clase de biología es ahora.
4. Ahora tiene la clase de español.
5. Necesita ir a la clase que tiene después de historia.
6. Tiene inglés ahora.
7. Necesita ir a la clase de computación.
8. Su clase de ciencias sociales es ahora.

Answers

1
1. los
2. los
3. los
4. las
5. las
6. la
7. las
8. la
9. la
10. el

2
1. Son las nueve y cuarto.
2. Son las once y cinco.
3. Son las siete y veinte.
4. Son las doce menos cuarto.
5. Son las diez y diez.
6. Son las ocho y veinticinco.
7. Es la una menos veinticinco.
8. Son las dos menos veinte.

Grammar Resources for Chapter 3

The **Más práctica gramatical** activities are designed as supplemental activities for the grammatical concepts presented in the chapter. You might use them as additional practice, for review, or for assessment.

For more grammar presentations, review, and practice refer to the following:
• Cuaderno de gramática
• Grammar Tutor for Students of Spanish

• Grammar Summary on pp. R9–R13
• Cuaderno de actividades
• Grammar and Vocabulary quizzes (Testing Program)
• Test Generator on the One-Stop Planner CD-ROM
• Interactive CD-ROM Tutor
• **Juegos interactivos** at **go.hrw.com**

Segundo paso

Objectives Telling at what time something happens; talking about being late or in a hurry

3 Tell what Javier plans to do after school today. Be sure to write out the time he will do things. (**p. 88**)

MODELO
Primero/quiere/ir a la pizzería/3:45 P.M.
Primero, Javier quiere ir a la pizzería a las cuatro menos cuarto de la tarde.

1. Después/quiere/ir al centro comercial/4:30 P.M.
2. Luego/necesita/comprar zapatillas de tenis/4:45 P.M.
3. Luego/necesita/ir a la librería/5:00 P.M.
4. Después/quiere/comprar una mochila/5:15 P.M.
5. Luego/necesita/organizar su cuarto/7:30 P.M.
6. Por fin/necesita/hacer la tarea/8:00 P.M.

4 Look at these courses offered at Colegio Benito Juárez. Then, write when the students below have their favorite classes. (**p. 88**)

MODELO
La clase favorita de Virginia es biología.
Su clase favorita es a las once y cuarto de la mañana.

MATERIA	HORA	MATERIA	HORA
arte	8:50	geografía	7:55
biología	11:15	historia	14:20
computación	9:20	literatura	10:30
educación física	10:05	inglés	9:50
español	13:45	música	15:25

1. La clase favorita de Yolanda es inglés.
2. La clase favorita de Simón es historia.
3. La clase favorita de Teresa es computación.
4. La clase favorita de Paloma es música.
5. La clase favorita de Fabián es geografía.
6. La clase favorita de Leonor es educación física.
7. La clase favorita de Jaime es arte.
8. La clase favorita de Fernanda es literatura.

Answers

3
1. Después, Javier quiere ir al centro comercial a las cuatro y media de la tarde.
2. Luego, necesita comprar zapatillas de tenis a las cinco menos cuarto de la tarde.
3. Luego, necesita ir a la librería a las cinco de la tarde.
4. Después, quiere comprar una mochila a las cinco y cuarto de la tarde.
5. Luego, necesita organizar su cuarto a las siete y media de la tarde/noche.
6. Por fin, necesita hacer la tarea a las ocho de la tarde/noche.

4
1. Su clase favorita es a las diez menos diez de la mañana.
2. Su clase favorita es a las dos y veinte de la tarde.
3. Su clase favorita es a las nueve y veinte de la mañana.
4. Su clase favorita es a las tres y veinticinco de la tarde.
5. Su clase favorita es a las ocho menos cinco de la mañana.
6. Su clase favorita es a las diez y cinco de la mañana.
7. Su clase favorita es a las nueve menos diez de la mañana.
8. Su clase favorita es a las diez y media de la mañana.

Teacher to Teacher

Latanza Garvin
Lexington Catholic
High School
Lexington, Kentucky

Latanza's students race to match articles
"I give each student four note cards and have them write the singular and plural definite articles on them. I call out different class subjects and students hold up the corresponding article as quickly as possible. This can be done as a race to see who can identify the article the fastest."

Más práctica gramatical

CAPÍTULO 3

For **Más práctica gramatical** Answer Transparencies, see the *Teaching Transparencies* binder.

Más práctica gramatical

WV3 MEXICO-3

5 Tell which items in the teachers' lounge belong to each teacher, so they don't get misplaced. (**p. 89**)

> **MODELO**   exámenes/el profesor Vargas
> **Son los exámenes del profesor Vargas.**

1. cuadernos/la profesora Jiménez
2. radio/el profesor Vega
3. papeles/el director Iriarte
4. carpetas/el profesor Rico
5. revistas/la profesora Guillén
6. calculadora/la profesora Elizondo
7. diccionario/el profesor Román

Tercer paso

Objectives Describing people and things; talking about things you like and explaining why

6 Completa la descripción de Claudia de su nueva escuela con las formas correctas del verbo **ser**. (**p. 92**)

> ¡Me gusta mucho mi colegio! ___1___ grande y nuevo. Tengo ocho clases. La clase de ciencias sociales ___2___ a las ocho menos cinco. El profesor de ciencias sociales ___3___ el profesor Romanca. Él ___4___ estricto pero interesante. Yo ___5___ la estudiante nueva de la clase. Mis compañeros de clase ___6___ simpáticos y divertidos. Mi compañera María Inés ___7___ muy cómica. Nosotras ya ___8___ buenas amigas. Bueno, ya ___9___ las cuatro de la tarde y necesito hacer la tarea.

Answers

5
1. Son los cuadernos de la profesora Jiménez.
2. Es la radio del profesor Vega.
3. Son los papeles del director Iriarte.
4. Son las carpetas del profesor Rico.
5. Son las revistas de la profesora Guillén.
6. Es la calculadora de la profesora Elizondo.
7. Es el diccionario del profesor Román.

6
1. Es
2. es
3. es
4. es
5. soy
6. son
7. es
8. somos
9. son

Communication for All Students

Challenge

5 After completing Activity 5, have students close the book and try to identify the item(s) their partner has in mind by asking four questions: **¿Cómo es/son?** to elicit a possible description, **¿Dónde está/n?** to suggest a possible location of the item or items, **¿De quién es/son?** to identify the owner, and finally, **¿Qué es/son?** for the definitive identification. Students then switch roles.

Slower Pace

6 Provide a two-column chart listing the grammatical subjects from Activity 6 on the left and a space to the right. Have students complete the chart with **ser** and the complement. The chart should list the nine subjects in mixed order.

Mi colegio	*es grande y nuevo*
Yo	*soy la estudiante nueva*
Nosotras	*somos buenas amigas*

7 Write a sentence describing each thing or person below, using the verb **ser** and the correct Spanish form of the adjective in parentheses. (**pp. 92, 93**)

MODELO   profesores *(intelligent)*
          Los profesores son inteligentes.

1. cafetería *(ugly)*
2. matemáticas *(interesting)*
3. compañeros *(nice)*
4. clases por la mañana *(boring)*
5. director *(strict)*
6. colegio *(big)*
7. María Inés *(funny)*
8. tarea *(hard)*

8 You and your friend Isabel have different opinions. Tell what you each like and dislike, using the information in the chart. (**p. 95**)

MODELO   **Me gustan las fiestas. A Isabel no le gustan.**

	YO	ISABEL
las fiestas	sí	no
las matemáticas	no	sí
los deportes	sí	no
los videojuegos	sí	no
los bailes	no	sí
los partidos	no	sí
los conciertos	sí	no

1. las matemáticas
2. los deportes
3. los videojuegos
4. los bailes
5. los partidos
6. los conciertos

Answers

7
1. La cafetería es fea.
2. Las matemáticas son interesantes.
3. Los compañeros son simpáticos.
4. Las clases por la mañana son aburridas.
5. El director es estricto.
6. El colegio es grande.
7. María Inés es cómica.
8. La tarea es difícil.

8
1. No me gustan las matemáticas. A Isabel le gustan.
2. Me gustan los deportes. A Isabel no le gustan.
3. Me gustan los videojuegos. A Isabel no le gustan.
4. No me gustan los bailes. A Isabel le gustan.
5. No me gustan los partidos. A Isabel le gustan.
6. Me gustan los conciertos. A Isabel no le gustan.

Review and Assess

You may wish to assign the **Más práctica gramatical** activities as additional practice or homework after presenting material throughout the chapter. Assign Activity 1 after **Nota gramatical** (p. 83), Activity 2 after **Gramática** (p. 86), Activities 3–4 after **Así se dice** (p. 88), Activity 5 after **Nota gramatical** (p. 89), Activity 6 after **Nota gramatical** (p. 92), Activity 7 after **Vocabulario** (p. 92) and **Gramática** (p. 93), and Activity 8 after **Así se dice** (p. 95). To prepare students for the **Paso** quizzes and Chapter Test, have them do the **Más práctica gramatical** activities in the following order: complete Activities 1–2 before taking Quiz 3-1A or 3-1B; Activities 3–5 before taking Quiz 3-2A or 3-2B; and Activities 6–8 before taking Quiz 3-3A or 3-3B.

Repaso

CAPÍTULO 3

The **Repaso** reviews and integrates all four skills and culture in preparation for the Chapter Test.

Teaching Resources
pp. 104–105

PRINT
▶ Lesson Planner, p. 16
▶ Listening Activities, p. 21
▶ Video Guide, pp. 19–24
▶ Grammar Tutor for Students of Spanish, Chapter 3
▶ Cuaderno para hispanohablantes, pp. 14–15
▶ Standardized Assessment Tutor, Chapter 3

MEDIA
▶ One-Stop Planner
▶ Video Program, Videocassette 1, 56:53–57:42
▶ DVD Tutor, Disc 1
▶ Audio Compact Discs, CD 3, Tr. 17
▶ Interactive CD-ROM Tutor, Disc 1

📁 **Portfolio**

2 **Written** Mention to your students that this assignment would be an appropriate entry in their Portfolio.

3 **Oral** You may suggest that students include the conversation in their Portfolio. For Portfolio suggestions, see *Alternative Assessment Guide*, p. 20.

Repaso

MARCAR: go.hrw.com
PALABRA CLAVE:
WV3 MEXICO-3

1 Look at the time zone map. Listen as times around Latin America and the U.S. are announced. For each time you hear, figure out what time it is where you are.
Script on p. 77H.

CD 3, Tr. 17

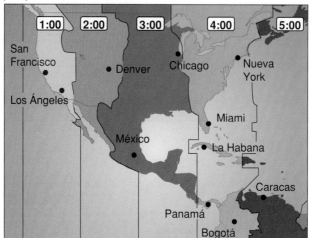

2 These are the classes that Martín and Gabriela have on Monday. Answer the following questions in Spanish.
See answers below.

1. ¿A qué hora tiene Gabriela la clase de español? ¿y Martín?

2. ¿Qué clase tiene Gabriela primero? ¿y Martín?

3. A las diez y media, ¿qué clase tiene Gabriela? ¿y Martín?

4. Son las 8:40. ¿Qué clase tiene Gabriela? ¿y Martín?

Hora	Martín	Gabriela
7:50 - 8:40	Francés	Ciencias sociales
8:40 - 9:30	Geografía	Computación
9:30 - 9:40	DESCANSO	DESCANSO
9:40 - 10:30	Arte	Inglés
10:30 - 11:20	Computación	Geografía
11:20 - 11:40	Inglés	Arte
11:40 - 12:30	ALMUERZO	ALMUERZO
12:30 - 13:20	Ciencias sociales	Español
13:20 - 13:30	DESCANSO	DESCANSO
13:30 - 14:20	Español	Educación física

3 Working with a partner, create two blank class schedules like the one in Activity 2. As you name your classes and the times they meet, your partner will fill in your schedule. Then switch roles. Discuss what your classes are like. Are they big? fun? interesting?

4 Answer the following questions according to the culture sections of this chapter.

1. Would you be pleased if you got a 9 on your report card in Peru? in Mexico? no, yes

2. Do students in Spanish-speaking countries have the same classes every day? How many classes can they take? no, nine

3. **Hora latina** means . . . Latin time, custom of arriving late at parties

Apply and Assess

Additional Practice

3 Ask students to write and present a dialogue about classes and teachers they like. Students should explain why they like that class. Teach the phrase ¿**Por qué no tomas...?** so that students can make recommendations to each other about classes they should take. In the recommendations, students should explain why they think that class is a good one.

Cooperative Learning

4 Have students work in groups of three to answer these questions. Each student is responsible for finding the answer to one question. As a group, have them add one question that they create from one of the culture sections of the chapter. They should then elect one group member to present this question to the class.

Answers
2 1. 12:30; 1:30
2. ciencias sociales; francés
3. geografía; computación
4. computación; geografía

5 Form a group of four. Role-play a dialogue in which your partners ask you what you and a few of your friends are like, where each one is from, what they like or dislike, where they go to school, and what courses they take. Keep the conversation going as long as you can.

6 # Vamos a escribir

You're creating a Spanish page for your school's Web site. Include information about your Spanish class: when it meets, what your teacher and some classmates are like, and what you like about the class. Before you start, organize your ideas in a cluster diagram.

> ### Estrategia para escribir
> Cluster diagrams are a useful way to organize ideas and to see how different ideas and information about a topic are related. The steps below give an example of how to create this kind of diagram.

1. Draw a central circle and label it **la clase de español.**

2. Draw four more circles and connect them to the original one. Label each circle with a category: **la hora y una descripción de la clase, el profesor/la profesora, mis compañeros,** and **yo.** Continue adding circles with more specific information.

3. Use your cluster diagram to write the entries for the Web page.

7 ## Situación

A reporter for the school newspaper is interviewing Alejandro Morales, an exchange student from Cuernavaca. The reporter asks Alejandro questions about his classes, his schedule, and the things he likes and doesn't like. Working with a partner, take the roles of the reporter and Alejandro. One of you ends the interview by saying you're late and in a hurry.

> Cuaderno para hispanohablantes, p. 15

Teacher Note
At the end of each chapter, students will learn and practice different strategies to help them improve their Spanish writing skills. You might incorporate the following suggestions:

- Explain process writing stages. Use class time to get students started on their first drafts. Assign the first draft for homework. Use part of the next day for revising, and then assign the final draft for homework.

- Incorporate a variety of methods: model a prewriting sample or have class brainstorming sessions.

- Set clear guidelines for evaluation: grade only on use of target vocabulary or on a targeted grammar point.

Community Link

7 Have students write a proposal for their city council or the school board explaining why their school would benefit from having more exchange students. Have them expand on their essays about their school. Why is their school excellent for exchange students? What is good about their town for exchange students? Why is it important to have such programs?

Apply and Assess

Reteaching
***Ser,* Adjective agreement** Prepare a board with sentences made from different color-coded cards. (verb = red, noun = blue, adjective = green) Have students replace existing cards with already-prepared plural verb/noun/adjective cards. Use various examples, changing feminine to masculine and vice-versa. Build up sentence structure slowly.

Process Writing
6 Explain that clustering is another way of making an outline. Do a class cluster diagram to get students started. Begin the **clase de español** cluster on the board, and have students fill in words to write about the subtopics. As you fill in the circles, emphasize how the topics are related by pointing out the branches in the diagram.

A ver si puedo

Teaching Resources
p. 106

PRINT
▸ Grammar Tutor for Students of Spanish, Chapter 3

MEDIA
▸ Interactive CD-ROM Tutor, Disc 1
▸ Online self-test

go.hrw.com
WV3 MEXICO-3

Teacher Note
This page is intended to help students prepare independently for the Chapter Test. It is a brief checklist of the major points covered in the chapter. The students should be reminded that it is only a checklist and does not necessarily include everything that will appear on the Chapter Test.

Answers

2
a. seis menos catorce
b. ocho y media
c. ocho menos diez
d. diez y diez

3 *Sample answer:*
— Sofía, ¿tienes clase de educación física? ¿y de arte?
— Sí, tengo educación física a las ocho y trece de la mañana y arte a las dos y diez de la tarde.

4
1. Tengo prisa.
2. Estoy atrasado/a.
3. Está atrasado/a.
4. ¡Date prisa!

6 *Sample answer:*
Yolanda es inteligente y estudia mucho.

A ver si puedo...

WV3 MEXICO-3

Can you talk about classes and sequence events? p. 84

1 How would you tell a classmate the sequence of your classes today? and tomorrow? Primero... luego... después... Mañana...

Can you tell time? p. 85

2 Write the time shown on each clock. See answers below.

a.   b.   c.   d.

Can you tell at what time something happens? p. 88

3 How would you ask each of these students what classes they have and at what time the classes meet? How would each student answer?
1. Sofía –physical education (8:13) –art (2:10)
2. César –French (11:40) –geography (2:25)
3. Simón –social sciences (9:07) –mathematics (3:15)
4. Adela –science (10:38) –computer science (12:54)

See sample answer below.

Can you talk about being late or in a hurry? p. 90

4 How would you . . .? See answers below.
1. say that you are in a hurry
2. say that you are late
3. say that a friend is late
4. tell a friend to hurry up

Can you describe people and things? p. 92

5 Imagine you're an exchange student in Cuernavaca. Describe the following people and things in your school in the U.S. to your new friends in Cuernavaca.
1. the teachers
2. Spanish class
3. the exams
4. physical education class
5. school friends
6. art class

6 Look at the photos. Write a sentence describing each person or thing.

   Yolanda   **Andrés**   **Simón**   **Bruto**

See sample answer below.

Can you talk about things you like and explain why? p. 95

7 How would you say which activities and classes you like or dislike, and why? How would you ask a friend for the same information? How would you report what your friend likes and doesn't like?

Review and Assess

Group Work
Divide the class into pairs. Tell them that they will create a conversation for a classroom competition. One of each pair plays a student who has recently arrived from Mexico to study at your school. He or she is unfamiliar with U.S. school schedules, classes, and what should be done at what time. The partner answers his or her questions. Partners are given fifteen to twenty minutes to plan the dialogues, which they then present to the class. At the end of the competition, the class votes on which pair has the most spontaneous, interesting, or humorous conversation. You may want to consider offering a prize, such as extra-credit points, to the winning pair.

Primer paso

Talking about classes and sequencing events

el almuerzo	lunch	el francés	French
el arte	art	la geografía	geography
las ciencias	science	hoy	today
las ciencias sociales	social studies	las, los	the
		luego	then
la computación	computer science	mañana	tomorrow
¿Cuándo?	When?	las matemáticas	mathematics
el descanso	recess, break	la materia	subject
después	after, afterward	por fin	at last
el día libre	a free day	primero	first
la educación física	physical education	el semestre	semester

Telling time

Es la una.	It's one o'clock.
menos cuarto	quarter to (the hour)
¿Qué hora es?	What time is it?
Son las...	It's . . . o'clock.
tarde	late, afternoon
y cuarto	quarter past (the hour)
y media	half past (the hour)

Segundo paso

Telling at what time something happens

ahora	now	de la mañana	in the morning (A.M.)
¿A qué hora...?	At what time . . . ?	de la noche	in the evening (P.M.)
de	of, from	de la tarde	in the afternoon, (P.M.)
del	of the, from the	en punto	on the dot

Talking about being late or in a hurry

¡Date prisa!	Hurry up!
Está atrasado/a.	He/She is late.
Estoy atrasado/a.	I'm late.
Tengo prisa.	I'm in a hurry.

Tercer paso

Describing people and things

aburrido/a	boring	estricto/a	strict
alto/a	tall	fácil	easy
antipático/a	disagreeable	feo/a	ugly
bajo/a	short (to describe people)	grande	big
		guapo/a	good-looking
bonito/a	pretty	inteligente	intelligent
bueno/a	good	interesante	interesting
cómico/a	funny	malo/a	bad
¿Cómo es...?	What's . . . like?	moreno/a	dark-haired, dark-skinned
¿Cómo son...?	What are . . . like?		
el (la) compañero/a	friend, pal	No te preocupes.	Don't worry.
		nuevo/a	new
difícil	difficult	pequeño/a	small
divertido/a	fun, amusing	el (la) profesor/a	teacher
ellas, ellos	they	rubio/a	blond
eres	you are	simpático/a	nice
es	he/she/it is	somos	we are

Talking about things you like and explaining why

el baile	dance
el concierto	concert
¿Cuál?	Which?
los deportes	sports
el examen	exam (pl. los exámenes)
favorito/a	favorite
la fiesta	party
le gusta(n)	he/she likes
me gusta(n)	I like
¿no?	isn't it?/right?
la novela	novel
el partido de...	game of . . . (sport)
¿Por qué?	Why?
porque	because
te gusta(n)	you like
¿verdad?	don't you?/right?
el videojuego	videogame

Game

¿A qué hora es...? Put a mock class schedule on a transparency or on the board. Divide the class into two teams. A member of Team A asks what time a class is. A member of Team B must answer in Spanish. Continue, alternating teams. Teams get one point for each correct response, and the winner is the team with the highest score.

Chapter 3 Assessment

▸ **Testing Program**
Chapter Test, pp. 65–70
Audio Compact Discs, CD 3, Trs. 21–22
Speaking Test, p. 344

▸ **Alternative Assessment Guide**
Performance Assessment, p. 34
Portfolio Assessment, p. 20
CD-ROM Assessment, p. 48

▸ **Interactive CD-ROM Tutor, Disc 1**
¡A hablar!
¡A escribir!

▸ **Standardized Assessment Tutor**
Chapter 3

▸ **One-Stop Planner, Disc 1**
Test Generator,
Chapter 3

Review and Assess

Game

Arreglar palabras Cut heavy paper or cardboard into one-inch squares. Leave a third of them blank and write the Spanish alphabet on the rest. (You may want to make extra squares with the most common letters: vowels, **s**, **t**, etc.) A blank may serve as any letter. Place the letters face down in one pile and the blanks in another pile.

Each student picks ten letters and five blanks. Using learned vocabulary, students arrange letters and blanks to form as many words as possible. The students with the most words and the longest words are the winners. This game may also be played in small teams.

Capítulo 4: ¿Qué haces esta tarde?
Chapter Overview

De antemano pp. 110–112	¿Dónde está María Inés?			

	FUNCTIONS	**GRAMMAR**	**VOCABULARY**	**RE-ENTRY**
Primer paso pp. 113–117	• Talking about what you like to do, p. 113 • Discussing what you and others do during free time, p. 114	• Present tense of regular -ar verbs, p. 114 • The verb **jugar** and the contraction **al**, p. 114 • **con, conmigo, contigo**, p. 116 • The relative pronoun **que**, p. 117	• Everyday activities around the house, p. 113 • More everyday activities, p. 115	• Present tense of **tener** (**Capítulo 2**) • Present tense of **gustar** (**Capítulo 3**)
Segundo paso pp. 118–122	• Telling where people and things are, p. 118	• The verb **estar**, p. 118 • Subject pronouns, p. 121	• Places, p. 119 • Prepositions of location, p. 119 • Subject Pronouns, p. 121	• Subject pronouns **yo, tú, él, ella** (**Capítulo 1, Capítulo 2**) • Describing with **ser** (**Capítulo 3**)
Tercer paso pp. 123–125	• Talking about where you and others go during free time, p. 123	• The verb **ir**, p. 123 • Days of the week, p. 124	• Days of the week, p. 124	• Telling time (**Capítulo 3**)

Letra y sonido p. 125	**The letters *b* and *v*** Audio CD 4, Track 13	**Dictado** Audio CD 4, Tracks 14–17
Vamos a leer pp. 126–127	**Anuncios personales**	**Reading Strategy:** Scanning for specific information
Más práctica gramatical	**pp. 128–131** **Primer paso,** pp. 128–129	**Segundo paso,** pp. 129–130 **Tercer paso,** pp. 130–131
Review pp. 132–135	**Repaso,** pp. 132–133 **Vamos a escribir,** p. 133 Using drawings to help you write	**A ver si puedo...,** p. 134 **Vocabulario,** p. 135

CULTURE

- **Nota cultural,** Popular sports in Spanish-speaking countries, p. 115
- **A lo nuestro,** Greetings in Spanish-speaking countries, p. 117
- **Nota cultural, tú** and **usted,** p. 121
- **Panorama cultural, ¿Te gusta pasear con tus amigos?,** p. 122
- **Nota cultural,** Extracurricular activities in Spanish-speaking countries, p. 124

Capítulo 4: ¿Qué haces esta tarde?
Chapter Resources

PRINT

Lesson Planning
One-Stop Planner

Lesson Planner with Substitute Teacher Lesson Plans, pp. 18–22, 68

Student Make-Up Assignments
- Make-Up Assignment Copying Masters, Chapter 4

Listening and Speaking
TPR Storytelling Book, pp. 13–16

Listening Activities
- Student Response Forms for Listening Activities, pp. 27–29
- Additional Listening Activities 4-1 to 4-6, pp. 31–33
- Additional Listening Activities (song), p. 34
- Scripts and Answers, pp. 117–121

Video Guide
- Teaching Suggestions, pp. 25–27
- Activity Masters, pp. 28–30
- Scripts and Answers, pp. 93–95, 114

Activities for Communication
- Communicative Activities, pp. 19–24
- Realia and Teaching Suggestions, pp. 90–94
- Situation Cards, pp. 143–144

Reading and Writing
Reading Strategies and Skills Handbook, Chapter 4

¡Lee conmigo! 1, Chapter 4
Cuaderno de actividades, pp. 37–48

Grammar
Cuaderno de gramática, pp. 27–36
Grammar Tutor for Students of Spanish, Chapter 4

Assessment
Testing Program
- Grammar and Vocabulary Quizzes, **Paso** Quizzes, and Chapter Test, pp. 79–96
- Score Sheet, Scripts and Answers, pp. 97–104

Alternative Assessment Guide
- Portfolio Assessment, p. 21
- Performance Assessment, p. 35
- CD-ROM Assessment, p. 49

Student Make-Up Assignments
- Alternative Quizzes, Chapter 4

Standardized Assessment Tutor
- Reading, pp. 13–15
- Writing, p. 16
- Math, pp. 25–26

Native Speakers
Cuaderno para hispanohablantes, pp. 16–20

MEDIA

 Online Activities
- Juegos interactivos
- Actividades Internet

 Video Program
- Videocassette 2
- Videocassette 5 (captioned version)

 Interactive CD-ROM Tutor, Disc 1

DVD Tutor, Disc 1

 Audio Compact Discs
- Textbook Listening Activities, CD 4, Tracks 1–18
- Additional Listening Activities, CD 4, Tracks 24–30
- Assessment Items, CD 4, Tracks 19–23

 Teaching Transparencies
- Situations 4-1 to 4-3
- Vocabulary 4-A to 4-C
- **De antemano**
- **Más práctica gramatical** Answers
- **Cuaderno de gramática** Answers

One-Stop Planner CD-ROM

Use the **One-Stop Planner CD-ROM with Test Generator** to aid in lesson planning and pacing.

For each chapter, the **One-Stop Planner** includes:
- Editable lesson plans with direct links to teaching resources
- Printable worksheets from resource books
- Direct launches to the HRW Internet activities
- Video and audio segments
- Test Generator
- Clip Art for vocabulary items

Capítulo 4: ¿Qué haces esta tarde?

Projects

Recorrido turístico

*This activity uses **cooperative learning**, as students help visitors get around town by giving directions. They create a map and use it to orally present a guided tour.*

INTRODUCTION

Discuss the importance of using Spanish when traveling, meeting people, and helping others get around. The class imagines that a tourist group from Mexico is coming to visit your city. Ask students who have been on a tour to imagine what a guided tour of your city would be like. The project is divided into two parts: the map and the guided tour.

MATERIALS
Students may need
- Poster board
- Rulers
- Markers
- Blank overhead transparencies
- Toy vehicle (optional)
- Pens/pencils

SUGGESTED SEQUENCE

1. Groups of four are assigned a script writer, proofreader, tour guide, and tour demonstrator.
2. Groups draw maps of their town or area on posters or transparencies. They must include terms from page 135.
3. Students create a script for the tour including what is said upon arrival at each site and a description (what it's near; what it looks like; what is done there). The script writer puts the tour in writing.
4. The proofreader peer-edits the written copy.
5. The tour guide narrates the tour shown on the group's map, aided by the demonstrator, who indicates the sequence on the map, pointing or moving an object to each site as it is mentioned.

GRADING THE PROJECT

Suggested point distribution: (total = 100 points)
Map
Creativity and appearance..................................20
Legibility 10
Script
Appropriate vocabulary and detail....................30
Spelling and grammar usage.............................10
Tour
Coordination – script / demonstration 10
Comprehensibility 20

Games

¿Dónde está?

*This game reviews the classroom vocabulary and provides the opportunity to work with the verb **estar**.*

Procedure   One student writes the Spanish word for an object in the classroom on a sheet of paper and gives it to you. The other students ask questions of the first to locate the object. (**¿Está debajo de la mesa?** or **¿Está cerca del escritorio?**) The one who guesses the object writes a new word and answers questions.

Cerebro

This game, played like Concentration®, helps students learn and review through concentration and recall.

Preparation   Have students make three pairs of cards.

1. On one card write a question from **Así se dice,** and on its mate, an appropriate response.
2. On one card write a verb from the chapter, and on its mate, draw a figure depicting the action.
3. Turn to page 116. On one card write a verb from the second box of Activity 11, and on its mate, write an appropriate phrase from the third box.

Procedure   Divide the class into pairs or small groups. Have students place a set of cards in a pattern on the desk, blank side up. Players take turns turning over two cards each. If they match, the player removes them. If they don't, they are returned to their original place. Play continues until all the cards are paired. The player with the most matches wins.

FAMILY LINK

Teach a relative or friend five Spanish words. Have students take home their own set of *Cerebro* cards. The assignment is to teach someone the three phrases by playing the game. Have students report orally how their student is doing.

Storytelling

Mini-cuento

This story accompanies Teaching Transparency 4-1. *The **mini-cuento** can be told and retold in different formats, acted out, written, and read aloud, to give students opportunities to practice all four skills. The following story relates Saturday's activities at **Condominios Miramar**.*

Para muchos inquilinos, el sábado es un día activo. El señor Suárez tiene que lavar la ropa. Encima de la lavandería vive la familia Rendón. Nicolás Rendón no está contento, porque tiene que sacar la basura. ¡No le gusta oler la basura! Después de pasar la aspiradora, la señora Rendón descansa y mira la televisión. A Leticia le gusta la pintura, y pinta un cuadro mientras su mamá mira la tele. Patricia, la vecina de los Rendón, odia trabajar, pero tiene que lavar el carro. Escucha su música favorita para no pensar en su quehacer. Pero eso no ayuda. No está contenta.

Traditions

Las piñatas

It is said that **piñatas** originated in China, where they were made of colored paper and adorned with ribbons. After breaking them, people picked up the pieces for good luck. This tradition then took root in Italy and later on in Spain, where a clay container was used instead. Later, Spanish missionaries in the New World used the **piñata** for religious instruction. For them, the pot (**olla**) symbolized the Devil and his attempts to lure human souls, and the fruits and candies represented temptation. Nowadays **piñatas** filled with good things to eat and with toys have lost much of their religious symbolism, and are intended only for fun. Have students make their own **piñatas** as individual or group projects. They will need balloons, newspaper, colored

tissue paper, scissors, and glue. Instruct them to inflate the balloons and cover them with papier-mâché. Then they will make a design with the tissue paper. The final step is to fill the **piñata** with candy!

Receta

*Champurrado is a form of **atole**, or a hot thick beverage similar to that prepared by the Aztecs for ceremonial purposes centuries ago. The **xocoatl**, or "bitter water," of a fermented cocoa bean paste—to which ground corn and **chiles**, vanilla and other herbs were added—was subsequently altered by the Spaniards, who introduced ingredients such as milk, sugar, cinnamon, and even ground almonds. These are now common in Mexican cooking and have replaced the ground chili peppers and ground corn in **champurrado**, depending on the recipe. **Champurrado** is traditionally served during Mexican holiday festivities, such as the **posadas** and **Día de los Reyes Magos**.*

CHAMPURRADO

para 8 personas

8 tazas de agua

1 taza de azúcar moreno

8 onzas de chocolate sin azúcar

1 taza de masa harina

2 rajitas de canela

2 cucharaditas de vainilla

Vierta dos tazas de agua con la canela, la vainilla y el chocolate en una olla. Caliente y remueva la mezcla constantemente hasta que se derrita el chocolate. En otra olla, disuelva la masa harina con seis tazas de agua a fuego lento. Bata constantemente con un molinillo *(whisk)*. Después de media hora, agregue el chocolate y el azúcar, moviéndolo constantemente para disolver el azúcar. Puede espumarlo con el molinillo.

Capítulo 4: ¿Qué haces esta tarde?
Technology

Videocassette 2, Videocassette 5 (captioned version)
DVD Tutor, Disc 1
See Video Guide, pages 25–27.

DVD/Video ....

De antemano • ¿Dónde está María Inés?
Claudia and Luis plan to go to Taxco with Claudia's sister Rosa. Knowing that María Inés enjoys Taxco, Claudia and Luis decide to invite her to go with them. They look for María Inés at all the places she usually goes on Saturdays. Unfortunately they miss her by just a few minutes at each place.

A continuación
After failing to find María Inés, Claudia and Luis return to Claudia's house, where María Inés meets up with them. They go sightseeing in Taxco and visit Claudia's uncle, a local silversmith. He makes a special gift for Claudia to take back for her mother's birthday.

¿Te gusta pasear con tus amigos?
Teenagers from California, Argentina, Mexico, and Spain talk about enjoying the **paseo**. In additional interviews, people from various Spanish-speaking countries tell their opinions about the **paseo**.

Videoclips
- **Banco Popular:** advertisement by a bank promoting respect for people with disabilities

Interactive CD-ROM Tutor ....

Activity	Activity Type	Pupil's Edition Page
En contexto	*Interactive conversation*	
1. Vocabulario	¿Cuál es?	p. 113
2. Gramática	¿Qué falta?	p. 114
3. Así se dice	Patas arriba	p. 118
4. Gramática	¿Qué falta?	p. 118
5. Gramática	¡A escoger!	p. 123
6. Vocabulario	¡Super memoria!	p. 124
	¿Te gusta pasear con tus amigos?	
Panorama cultural	¡A escoger!	p. 122
¡A hablar!	*Guided recording*	pp. 132–133
¡A escribir!	*Guided writing*	pp. 132–133

Teacher Management System
Launch the program, type "admin" in the password area and press RETURN. Log on to **www.hrw.com/CDROMTUTOR** for a detailed explanation of the Teacher Management System.

DVD Tutor ....

The *DVD Tutor* contains all material from the *Video Program* as described above. Spanish captions are available for use at your discretion for all sections of the video. The *DVD Tutor* also provides a variety of video-based activities that assess students' understanding of the **De antemano, A continuación,** and **Panorama cultural.**

This part of the *DVD Tutor* may be used on any DVD video player connected to a television or video monitor.

In addition to the video material and the video-based comprehension activities, the *DVD Tutor* also contains the entire *Interactive CD-ROM Tutor* in DVD-ROM format. Each DVD disc contains the activities from all 12 chapters of the *Interactive CD-ROM Tutor.*

This part of the *DVD Tutor* may be used on a Macintosh® or Windows® computer with a DVD-ROM drive.

One-Stop Planner CD-ROM

To preview all resources available for this chapter, use the **One-Stop Planner CD-ROM**, Disc 1.

Internet Connection ....

🔗 internet ≡≡≡≡

MARCAR: go.hrw.com
PALABRA CLAVE:
WV3 MEXICO-4

*Have students explore the **go.hrw.com** Web site for many online resources covering all chapters. All Chapter 4 resources are available under the keyword **WV3 MEXICO-4**. Interactive games help students practice the material and provide them with immediate feedback. You will also find a printable worksheet that provides Internet activities that lead to a comprehensive online research project.*

Juegos interactivos

You can use the interactive activities in this chapter

- to practice grammar, vocabulary, and chapter functions
- as homework
- as an assessment option
- as a self-test
- to prepare for the Chapter Test

Actividades Internet

Students write about the activities they would do on a weekend if they were an exchange student in Mexico.

- In preparation for the **Hoja de actividades,** have students review the chapter vocabulary on page 135. You might have them complete the vocabulary activities in the **Cuaderno de gramática.**
- After they have completed the activity sheet, have students create a similar schedule of activities appropriate for a grandparent or older person visiting Mexico City.

Proyecto

Have students work with a partner to find a tourism Web site for a Mexican city. Ask them to find activities that the city promotes. Then ask the pairs to create a brief brochure that highlights city activities they think appeal to people their age. You might have them create an online brochure: have them post descriptions and images on a personal Web site.

Primer paso

6   p. 113

1. Hola. Me llamo Tomás. Me gusta comprar muchas cosas. Por eso me gusta ir de compras.

2. ¿Qué tal? Me llamo Arturo. No me gustan las fiestas porque son muy aburridas.

3. Yo soy Bárbara. A mí me gusta hablar por teléfono... ¡día y noche!

4. Hola. Soy Patricia. No me gusta estudiar mucho, pero me gusta mirar la televisión.

Answers to Activity 6
1. c
2. b
3. a
4. d

8   p. 114

1. Hola, soy Carmen. Escucho música y miro la televisión en mi cuarto.

2. Me llamo Javier. Hablo por teléfono con Sofía, Manuel, Rebeca, y Raúl...

3. Soy Armando. Ana y yo estudiamos en la biblioteca día y noche.

4. Me llamo Susana. Después de clases, practico el béisbol y el tenis.

5. Soy Pablo. En el tiempo libre, bailo y canto con mis amigos. Toco la guitarra también.

Answers to Activity 8
1. d
2. b
3. e
4. c
5. a

Segundo paso

18   p. 118

1. ¿El correo? Está en la Plaza de la Constitución.

2. Necesito encontrar mi mochila. No está en mi cuarto.

3. Hola. ¿Qué tal? Estoy atrasado. Todavía estoy en el trabajo.

4. ¡Estoy aquí, José! Mira, José, ¡estoy aquí!

Answers to Activity 18
1. c
2. d
3. b
4. a

21   p. 120

MODELO   Paco es bajo y moreno. Le gusta jugar con su perro. Está en el parque.

1. Marisa y Ana Luisa son guapas y morenas. Tienen catorce años. Están en el restaurante.

2. El señor Contreras es bajo y le gusta comprar ropa. Está en la tienda.

3. Eva es muy inteligente y le gusta estudiar matemáticas. Está en la biblioteca.

4. Isabel tiene seis años y le gustan los videos cómicos. Está en la casa.

5. Mario y José son antipáticos. Siempre necesitan hablar con el director del colegio. Están al lado de la oficina del director.

6. Anabel nada muy bien. Tiene treinta y cinco años y es muy bonita. Está en la piscina.

7. Guillermo es alto y rubio. Juega mucho al basquetbol con sus amigos. Está en el gimnasio.

Answers to Activity 21
1. f
2. g
3. e
4. c
5. h
6. b
7. d

One-Stop Planner CD-ROM

To preview all resources available for this chapter, use the **One-Stop Planner CD-ROM**, Disc 1.

Tercer paso

26 p. 123

1. —Y Pedro, ¿adónde va él?
—Él va a la casa de Graciela.

2. —David y Luisa, entonces. ¿Adónde van ellos?
—Ellos van al gimnasio.

3. —Y tú, Alicia, ¿adónde vas?
—Voy a la piscina. Trabajo allí hoy.

4. —Y Carlos, ¿va al cine?
—Sí, Carlos va al cine.

5. —Hola Carlos.
—Hola Filiberto. ¿Adónde vas?
—Voy al cine. ¡Contigo!

Answers to Activity 26
1. Pedro va a la casa de Graciela.
2. David y Luisa van al gimnasio.
3. Alicia va a la piscina.
4. Carlos va al cine.
5. Filiberto va al cine. Carlos can give Filiberto a ride to the movies.

LETRA Y SONIDO, P. 125

For the scripts for Parts A and C, see p. 125. The script for Part B is below.

B. Dictado

veinte, bolígrafo, librería, basura, el tiempo libre, jueves

Repaso

1 p. 132

MODELO Hola, soy Carlos. El sábado vamos al parque para jugar al tenis. Vamos a las 10:00. ¿Quieres ir también?

1. Buenos días. Soy Carmen. Enrique y yo vamos a estudiar en la biblioteca hoy a las tres y media. ¿Quieres ir con nosotros?

2. Hola. Soy Gaby. ¿Cómo estás? Voy a la piscina mañana a las cuatro y media. ¿Quieres ir conmigo?

3. Buenos días. Soy Victoria. ¿Cómo estás? Sara y yo vamos al cine el domingo a las tres. A ti te gustan las películas, ¿no? Pues, ¡vamos!

Answers to Repaso Activity 1
Notes:
1. Carmen y Enrique van a la biblioteca hoy, a las 3:30.
2. Gaby va a la piscina mañana, a las 4:30.
3. Victoria y Sara van al cine el domingo, a las 3:00.

Capítulo 4: ¿Qué haces esta tarde?
Suggested Lesson Plans 50-Minute Schedule

Day 1

CHAPTER OPENER 5 min.
- Focusing on Outcomes, ATE, p. 109
- Culture Notes, ATE, pp. 108–109
- Photo Flash!, ATE, p. 109

DE ANTEMANO 40 min.
- Presenting **De antemano** and Preteaching Vocabulary, ATE, p. 110.
- **De antemano** Transparencies
- Present the information in Background Information, ATE, p. 111.
- Activities 1–5 and Comprehension Check, ATE, p. 112

Wrap-Up 5 min.
- Have students present their ideas from Activity 5, p. 112, to the class.

Homework Options
Cuaderno de actividades, p. 37, Activities. 1–2

Day 2

PRIMER PASO
Quick Review 5 min.
- Check homework.
- Bell Work, ATE, p. 113

Así se dice/Vocabulario, p. 113 20 min.
- Presenting **Así se dice/Vocabulario**, ATE, p. 113
- Do Activity 6 with Audio CD.
- Have students do Activity 7 in pairs, then present their partner's list to the class.

Gramática, p. 114 20 minutes
- Presenting **Gramática**, ATE, p. 114
- **Más práctica gramatical**, p. 128, Activity 1

Wrap-Up 5 min.
- Display Transparency 4-1. Ask students if they do the activities pictured. Then ask them if they like to do those activities.

Homework Options
Cuaderno de actividades, pp. 38–39, Activities 3–4
Cuaderno de gramática, pp. 27–28, Activities 1–4

Day 3

PRIMER PASO
Quick Review 5 min.
- Check homework.
- Quickly review **-ar** verb conjugations, using the vocabulary on p. 113.

Así se dice/Nota gramatical, p. 114 15 min.
- Presenting **Así se dice/Nota gramatical**, ATE, p. 114
- Do Activity 8, p. 114, with the Audio CD.
- **Más práctica gramatical**, p.131, Activity 8

Vocabulario, p. 115 25 min.
- Presenting **Vocabulario**, ATE, p. 115
- Present **También se puede decir...**, p. 115, then have students write Activity 9. Check orally.
- Read and discuss the **Nota cultural**, p. 115.
- Do Activities 10 and 11, p. 116.
- Have students do Activity 12, p. 116, in pairs, then report their findings to the class.

Wrap-Up 5 min.
- Ask students questions about what they and their classmates do in their free time.

Homework Options
Cuaderno de actividades, pp. 39–40, Activities 5–6
Cuaderno de gramática, p. 29, Activities 5–7

Day 4

PRIMER PASO
Quick Review 5 min.
- Check homework.

Nota gramatical, p. 116 20 min.
- Presenting **Nota gramatical**, ATE, p. 116
- Have students do Activity 13 in pairs, p. 116, and Activity 14 in groups, p. 117. See Cooperative Learning for Activity 14, ATE, p. 116.
- Have students do Activity 15, p. 117, individually, then exchange papers.

Nota gramatical, p. 117 15 min.
- Presenting **Nota gramatical**, ATE, p. 117
- Present **A lo nuestro**, p. 117.
- Have students circulate to do Activity 16, p. 117. Encourage them to use **A lo nuestro** terms.
- Have students do Activity 17, p. 117, in pairs.

Wrap-Up 10 min.
- Review **Primer paso** using Transparencies 4-1 and 4-A.
- Go over the Quiz 4-1 content.

Homework Options
Study for Quiz 4-1.
Cuaderno de gramática, p. 30, Activities 8–9
Cuaderno de actividades, p. 40, Activity 7

Day 5

PRIMER PASO
Quick Review 10 min.
- Check homework.
- Review **Primer paso** content.

Quiz 20 min.
- Administer Quiz 4-1A, 4-1B, or a combination of the two.

SEGUNDO PASO
Así se dice/Nota gramatical, p. 118 15 min.
- Presenting **Así se dice** and **Nota gramatical**, ATE, p. 118
- Do Activity 18, p. 118, with Audio CD.
- Do Activities 19 and 20, pp. 118–119.

Wrap-Up 5 min.
- Ask the class where different students are in the class. Have them respond by pointing to the students and using the correct conjugation of **estar** and **allí** or **aquí**.

Homework Options
Cuaderno de gramática, p. 31, Activity 10
Cuaderno de actividades, p. 41, Activity 8
Más práctica gramatical, p. 129, Activity 4

Day 6

SEGUNDO PASO
Quick Review 5 min.
- Check homework.
- Review conjugations of **estar** by asking questions with **Así se dice** terms, p. 118.

Vocabulario, p. 119 40 min.
- Presenting **Vocabulario**, ATE, p. 119
- Present **También se puede decir...**, p. 119.
- Additional Practice, TPR suggestions, ATE, p. 118
- **Sugerencia**, p. 120
- Activity 21, p. 120, with Audio CD.
- Have students do Activities 22–24, pp. 120–121, in pairs.

Wrap-Up 5 min.
- Have students answer yes/no questions about where people are in the room.

Homework Options
Cuaderno de gramática, pp. 31–32, Activities 11–13
Cuaderno de actividades, pp. 41–42, Activity 9
Más práctica gramatical, p. 129, Activity 5

One-Stop Planner CD-ROM

For alternative lesson plans by chapter section, to create your own customized plans, or to preview all resources available for this chapter, use the **One-Stop Planner CD-ROM**, Disc 1.

 For additional homework suggestions, see activities accompanied by this symbol throughout the chapter.

Day 7

SEGUNDO PASO

Quick Review 15 min.
- Check homework.
- Use Transparency 4-2 to review vocabulary from the **paso** and **estar.**
- Activities for Communication, pp. 21–22, Activity 4-2

Gramática, p. 121 20 min.
- Presenting **Gramática,** ATE, p. 121. Also follow Kinesthetic Learners suggestion, ATE, p. 121.
- Read **Nota cultural,** p. 121.
- Do Activity 25, p. 121
- **Cuaderno de gramática,** p. 33, Activities 14–16

PANORAMA CULTURAL, p. 122 10 min.
- Present Background Information, ATE, p. 122.
- Present the Culture Note, ATE, p. 122.

Wrap-Up 5 min.
- Ask students to explain what a **paseo** is.
- Discuss the format and content of Quiz 4-2.

Homework Options
Study for Quiz 4-2.
Cuaderno de actividades, p. 43, Activity 10

Day 8

SEGUNDO PASO

Quick Review 5 min.
- Quickly review the content of the **Segundo paso.**

Quiz 20 min.
- Administer Quiz 4-2A, 4-2B, or a combination of the two.

TERCER PASO

Así se dice/Nota gramatical, p. 123 20 min.
- Presenting **Así se dice/Nota gramatical,** ATE, p. 123
- Do Activity 26, p. 123, with Audio CD.
- Do Activities 27, p. 123, and 28, p. 124.
- Have students write Activity 29, p. 124. Ask students to share their sentences with the class.

Wrap-Up 5 min.
- Do Building on Previous Skills suggestion for Activity 29, ATE, p. 124.

Homework Options
Más práctica gramatical, p. 130, Activity 7.
Cuaderno de actividades, p. 44, Activities 11–12
Cuaderno de gramática, p. 34, Activities 17–18

Day 9

TERCER PASO

Quick Review 10 min.
- Review the conjugations of **ir** and the **Así se dice** expressions, p. 123.
- Check homework.

Vocabulario/Nota gramatical, p. 124 25 min
- Presenting **Vocabulario** and **Nota gramatical,** ATE, p. 124. Follow Language-to-Language suggestion, ATE, p. 125.
- Read and discuss the **Nota cultural,** p. 124
- Present the Culture Note, ATE, p. 125
- Have students do Activity 30, p. 125, in pairs.
- **Cuaderno de gramática,** pp. 35–36, Activities 19, 21, and 22
- Have students do Activity 31, p. 125, in groups, and present their results.

Letra y sonido, p. 125 10 min.
- Present using Audio CD.

Wrap-Up 5 min.
- Ask students where they go on different days of the week.

Homework Options
Assign Activity 32, p. 125.
Más práctica gramatical, p. 130, Activity 8
Cuaderno de actividades, pp. 45–46, Activities 13–15

Day 10

TERCER PASO

Quick Review 15 min.
- Check homework.
- Use Transparencies 4-3 and 4-C to review **Tercer paso.**
- Have students do Activity 4-3 on pp. 23–24 of Activities for Communication as you circulate to check writing assignment.

VAMOS A LEER 20 min.
- Activities A–B, p. 126
- Activities C–E, p. 127
- Follow the Teaching Suggestion, ATE, p. 126 for Activities C and D, and do the Thinking Critically activity, ATE, p. 127.

REPASO 10 min.
- Have students begin the writing assignment in **Vamos a escribir,** Activity 6, p. 133. See suggestion for Process Writing, ATE, p. 133.

Wrap-Up 5 min.
- Discuss the format and content of Quiz 4-3. Answer questions about writing assignment.

Homework Options
Have students complete the writing assignment from Activity 6, p. 133.
Study for Quiz 4-3.

Day 11

TERCER PASO

Quick Review 5 min.
- Review **Tercer paso** content quickly and collect writing assignment. You may wish to assess the students' writing skills using the Writing Rubric, ATE, p.125.

Quiz 20 min.
- Administer Quiz 4-3A, 4-3B, or a combination of the two.

REPASO 20 min.
- Do Activity 1, p. 132 with the Audio CD.
- Have students do Activities 2, 4, and 5 individually, pp. 132–133. Go over answers as a class.
- Students do Activity 3, p. 132, in pairs.

Wrap-Up 5 min.
- Have students list what they need to study for the chapter test based on the **Repaso.**

Homework Options
A ver si puedo..., p. 134.
Assign small groups to prepare and perform the situation in Activity 7, p. 133.

Day 12

REPASO

Quick Review 10 min.
- Check homework and discuss any questions students may have about the chapter.

Chapter Review 40 min.
- Review Chapter 4. Choose from **Más práctica gramatical,** Grammar Tutor for Students of Spanish, Activities for Communication, Listening Activities, Interactive CD-ROM Tutor, or **Juegos Interactivos.**

Homework Options
Study for the Chapter 4 Test.

Assessment

Quick Review 5 min.
- Answer any last-minute questions.

Test, Chapter 4 45 min.
- Administer Chapter 4 Test. Select from Testing Program, Alternative Assessment Guide, Test Generator, or Standardized Assessment Tutor.

Capítulo 4: Qué haces esta tarde?
Suggested Lesson Plans 90-Minute Block Schedule

CHAPTER OPENER 5 min.
- Focusing on Outcomes, ATE, p. 109
- Photo Flash, ATE, p. 109

DE ANTEMANO 40 min.
- Presenting **De antemano** and Preteaching Vocabulary, ATE, p. 110.
- Present the Background Information, ATE, p. 111.
- Activities 1–5, p. 112, and Comprehension Check, ATE, p. 112

PRIMER PASO
Así se dice/Vocabulario, p. 113 20 min.
- Presenting **Así se dice/Vocabulario**, ATE, p. 113
- Do Activity 6 with Audio CD.
- Have students do Activity 7 in pairs, then present their partners' lists to the class.

Gramática, p. 114 20 min.
- Presenting **Gramática**, ATE, p. 114
- **Más práctica gramatical**, p. 128, Activity 1

Wrap-Up 5 min.
- Project Transparency 4-1. Ask students if they do the activities pictured. Then ask them if they like to do those activities.

Homework Options
Cuaderno de actividades, pp. 37–39, Activities 1–4
Cuaderno de gramática, pp. 27–28, Activities 1–4

PRIMER PASO
Quick Review 10 min.
- Check homework.
- Use Transparency 4-1 to review **-ar** verbs and how to conjugate them.

Así se dice/Nota gramatical, p. 114 15 min.
- Presenting **Así se dice/Nota gramatical**, ATE, p. 114
- Do Activity 8, p. 114, with the Audio CD.
- **Más práctica gramatical**, p. 131, Activity 8

Vocabulario, p. 115 25 min.
- Presenting **Vocabulario**, ATE, p. 115
- Present **También se puede decir...**, p. 115, then have students write Activity 9. Check orally.
- Read and discuss the **Nota cultural**, p. 115.
- Do Activities 10 and 11, p. 116.
- Have students do Activity 12, p. 116, in pairs, then report their findings to the class.

Nota gramatical, p. 116 20 min.
- Presenting **Nota gramatical**, ATE, p. 116
- Have students do Activity 13, p. 116, in pairs and Activity 14, p. 117 in groups. See Cooperative Learning suggestion for Activity 14, ATE, p. 116.
- Have students do Activity 15, p. 117, individually, then exchange papers for peer editing.

Nota gramatical, p. 117 15 min.
- Presenting **Nota gramatical**, ATE, p. 117
- Present **A lo nuestro**, p. 117.
- Have students circulate around the room to do Activity 16, p. 117. Encourage students to use expressions from **A lo nuestro** in their conversations.
- Have students do Activity 17, p. 117, in pairs.

Wrap-Up 5 min.
- Ask students questions about what they and their classmates do in their free time.

Homework Options
Cuaderno de actividades, pp. 39–40, Activities 5–7
Cuaderno de gramática, pp. 29–30, Activities 5–9
Más práctica gramatical, p. 128, Activity 1

PRIMER PASO
Review 25 min.
- Check homework.
- Use Transparencies 4-1 and 4-A to review **Primer paso** vocabulary, **Así se dice** expressions, and grammar.
- Have students do **Más práctica gramatical**, p. 128, Activities 2–3, individually. Check answers orally with the class.
- Have students work in pairs to do Communicative Activity 4-1, p. 19, in Activities for Communication.

SEGUNDO PASO
Así se dice/Nota gramatical, p. 118 15 min.
- Presenting **Así se dice/Nota gramatical**, ATE, p. 118
- Do Activity 18, p. 118, with Audio CD.
- Do Activities 19 and 20, pp. 118–119.

Vocabulario, p. 119 40 min.
- Presenting **Vocabulario**, ATE, p. 119
- Present **También se puede decir...**, p. 119.
- Do Additional Practice, p. 119, and TPR suggestions, ATE, p. 118.
- Have students read the **Sugerencia**, p. 120, then do Activity 21, p. 120, with Audio CD.
- Have students do Activities 22–24, p. 120–121, in pairs.

Wrap-Up 10 min.
- Have students answer yes/no questions about where people are located in relationship to one another in the room.
- Go over the Quiz 4-1 content and discuss sample questions.

Homework Options
Study for Quiz 4-1.
Cuaderno de gramática, p. 31–32, Activities. 10–13
Cuaderno de actividades, pp. 41–42, Activities 8–9

One-Stop Planner CD-ROM

For alternative lesson plans by chapter section, to create your own customized plans, or to preview all resources available for this chapter, use the **One-Stop Planner CD-ROM**, Disc 1.

 For additional homework suggestions, see activities accompanied by this symbol throughout the chapter.

Block 4

PRIMER PASO

Quick Review 5 min.
- Review **Primer paso** content.

Quiz 20 min.
- Administer Quiz 4-1A, 4-1B, or a combination of the two.

SEGUNDO PASO

Quick Review 15 min.
- Check homework.
- Review the conjugations of **estar** and the vocabulary and expressions from the **Segundo paso** using Transparency 4-2.

Gramática, p. 121 15 min.
- Presenting **Gramática**, ATE, p. 121. Also follow Kinesthetic Learners suggestion, ATE, p. 121.
- Read **Nota cultural**, p. 121.
- Do Activity 25, p. 121.
- Cuaderno de gramática, p. 33, Activities 14–15

PANORAMA CULTURAL, p. 122 10 min.
- Present **Nota cultural**, p. 122.
- Present the Culture Note, ATE, p. 122.

Así se dice/Nota gramatical, p. 123 20 min.
- Presenting **Así se dice/Nota gramatical**, ATE, p. 123
- Do Activity 26, p. 123, with Audio CD.
- Do Activities 27, p. 123, and 28, p. 124.
- Have students write Activity 29, p. 124. Ask students to share their sentences with the class.

Wrap-Up 5 min.
- Do Building on Previous Skills suggestion for Activity 29, ATE, p. 124.
- Discuss the format and content of Quiz 4-2.

Homework Options
Study for Quiz 4-2
Más práctica gramatical, pp. 129–130, Activities 4–6
Cuaderno de actividades, pp. 43–44, Activities 10–12
Cuaderno de gramática, p. 34, Activities 17–18

Block 5

SEGUNDO PASO

Quick Review 5 min.
- Review content of the **Segundo paso**.

Quiz 20 min.
- Administer Quiz 4-2A, 4-2B, or a combination of the two.

TERCER PASO

Quick Review 10 min.
- Check homework.
- Review **ir** conjugations and **Así se dice** expressions, p. 123, by asking students where different people are going based on what they want or need to do.

Vocabulario/Nota gramatical, p. 124 25 min
- Presenting **Vocabulario/Nota gramatical**, ATE, p. 124. Follow Language-to-Language suggestion, ATE, p. 125.
- Read and discuss the **Nota cultural**, p. 124
- Present the Culture Note, ATE, p. 125
- Have students do Activity 30, p. 125, in pairs.
- Cuaderno de gramática, pp. 35–36, Activities 19, 21, and 22
- Have students do Activity 31, p. 125, in groups, and present their results.

VAMOS A LEER 20 min.
- Activities A–B, p. 126
- Activities C–E, p. 127.
- Follow the Teaching Suggestion, ATE, p. 126 for Activities C and D, and do the Thinking Critically activity, ATE, p. 127.

Wrap-Up 10 min.
- Ask students which pen pal they would choose from the reading and why.
- Review **Tercer paso** content by asking students where they go on different days of the week.
- Discuss the format and content of Quiz 4-3.

Homework Options
Study for Quiz 4-3.
Assign Activity 32, p. 125, as homework.
Más práctica gramatical, pp. 130–131, Activities 7–8
Cuaderno de actividades, pp. 45–46, Activities 13–15

Block 6

TERCER PASO

Quick Review 10 min.
- Check homework.
- Use Transparencies 4-3 and 4-C to review the content of the **Tercer paso**.

Quiz 20 min.
- Administer Quiz 4-3A, 4-3B, or a combination of the two.

Letra y sonido, p. 125 10 min.
- Present using Audio CD.

REPASO 45 min.
- Do Activity 1, p. 132 with the Audio CD.
- Students do Activity 3, p. 132, in pairs.
- Have students do Activities 2, 4, and 5 individually, pp. 132–133. Go over answers as a class.
- Students write rough draft of **Vamos a escribir** assignment, Activity 6, p. 133. See suggestion for Process Writing, ATE, p. 133. Students then exchange papers for peer-editing.
- Divide the class into small groups to prepare the situation described in Activity 7, p. 133.

Wrap-Up 5 min.
- Have students list what they need to study for the chapter test based on their work from the **Repaso**.
- Review the test format and sample questions for students.

Homework Options
Students practice situation from Activity 7, p. 133.
Students write final draft of **Vamos a escribir** assignment, p. 133.
Study for the Chapter 4 Test.
A ver si puedo..., p. 134.

Block 7

REPASO

Quick Review 10 min.
- Check homework and writing assignment. You may wish to use the Writing Rubric, ATE, p. 125.

Chapter Review 25 min.
- Review Chapter 4. Choose from **Más práctica gramatical**, Grammar Tutor for Students of Spanish, Activities for Communication, Listening Activities, Interactive CD-ROM Tutor, or **Juegos interactivos**.

Test, Chapter 4 45 min.
- Administer Chapter 4 Test. Select from Testing Program, Alternative Assessment Guide, Test Generator, or Standardized Assessment Tutor.

CAPÍTULO 4

One-Stop Planner CD-ROM

For resource information, see the **One-Stop Planner**, Disc 1.

Pacing Tips
Several new verbs are presented, along with interrogatives and prepositional phrases. Be sure to balance needed speaking practice and cultural notes with grammar objectives in this chapter. See Suggested Lesson Plans, pp. 107I–107L.

Meeting the Standards
Communication
- Talking about what you like to do, p. 113
- Discussing what you and others do during free time, p. 114
- Telling where people and things are, p. 118
- Talking about where you and others go during free time, p. 123

Cultures
- Culture Note, p. 108
- Nota cultural, p. 121
- Panorama cultural, p. 122
- Nota cultural, p. 124

Connections
- Background Information, p. 111
- Culture Notes, p. 109
- Thinking Critically, p. 127

Comparisons
- Culture Notes, p. 109
- Language-to-Language, p. 113
- Culture Note, p. 122
- Culture Note, p. 126

Communities
- Background Information, p. 122

Cultures and Communities

Culture Note
Along streets in Mexico, one finds many fruit, ice cream, **paleta**, and **jugo** stands. The freshness and variety of fruits (mangos, papayas, **guanábanas**, **guayabas**, **tamarindos**, and **mameyes**, as well as oranges, strawberries, and bananas) can be a surprise to foreigners. The iced **paletas** may be any flavor—even corn or avocado! While "smoothies" shops in the United States are a newer phenomenon serving what is considered "health food," they have long been popular in Mexico. **Licuados** of fruit and egg, in a base of orange or carrot juice, **alfalfa y limón**, **betabel**, or milk (called an **eskimo**), are enjoyed throughout Mexico. Ask students how mass production of food and the proliferation of "chains" in the United States have affected our consumption habits.

STANDARDS: 2.2, 4.2

CAPÍTULO

4

¿Qué haces esta tarde?

Objectives

In this chapter you will learn to

Primer paso

- talk about what you like to do
- discuss what you and others do during free time

Segundo paso

- tell where people and things are

Tercer paso

- talk about where you and others go during free time

internet

go.hrw.com
MARCAR: go.hrw.com
PALABRA CLAVE:
WV3 MEXICO-4

◀ **Después de clases, nos gusta tomar helado.**

CAPÍTULO 4

Photo Flash!
Small shops or stands selling refreshments such as **paletas** or **jugos** are popular among Mexican high school students. These refreshments come in both fruit (**de frutas**) and vegetable (**de verduras**) flavors. Like many high school students, the young people pictured here wear a school uniform.

Focusing on Outcomes
Point out to students that an important use of language is talking about what you like to do in your free time and telling where you go for leisure activities. This includes being able to find out if another person shares your interests. By the end of this chapter, students will be able to discuss and plan with their classmates how they want to spend their free time and where they like to go.

Chapter Sequence

Connections and Comparisons

Culture Notes
• For economic and other reasons, it is not uncommon for Latin Americans to live, work, or study abroad, often in the United States. Many people have friends or relatives in other countries. Ask students if they have been to another country or know someone abroad.

• Point out that families in Spanish-speaking countries often do not own more than one car. Teenagers may walk, take the bus, or ride a moped to get where they need to go. Have students plan their after-school or weekend activities as if they had no family car. How would they have to change their plans if they had to use other means of transportation?

DE ANTEMANO ▪ *¿Dónde está María Inés?*

The **fotonovela** is an abridged version of the video episode.

CD 4 Trs. 1–2

Estrategia
para comprender
You met Claudia and her new friends in Chapter 3. Look at the **fotonovela**. What do you think happens in this story? Where do you think Claudia and her new friends are going? Read the story and find out!

 Rosa   Claudia   Luis   María Inés

1
Claudia: Papi, él es mi amigo Luis. Después de clases, yo canto en el coro con Luis.
Papi: Sí, los miércoles y los viernes, ¿verdad?
Claudia: No, papi, los martes y los jueves.
Papi: Ah... Entonces, Luis... ¿vas a Taxco con Claudia y Rosa?
Luis: Sí, señor... voy con ellas.

2
Rosa: Hola, Luis. Claudia habla mucho de ti. Tú juegas al basquetbol muy bien, ¿no?
Luis: Pues... no sé.
Rosa: Bueno, Luis, vamos a Taxco porque mi tío Ernesto tiene un regalo especial para mamá.

3
Claudia: ¡Tengo una muy buena idea! A María Inés le gusta mucho Taxco. ¿Llamo a María Inés?
Rosa: Sí, cómo no. Buena idea.

4
Claudia: Ah, pero los sábados por la mañana practica con su grupo de baile folklórico.
Luis: Pues, vamos allá. La escuela de baile donde tiene clase está en la Avenida Juárez.

Preteaching Vocabulary

Guessing Words from Context

Ask students what types of extracurricular activities they participate in. Have students identify expressions in **De antemano** that they think would be categorized as extracurricular activities. (❶ Canto en el coro. ❷ Juegas al basquetbol. ❹ Practica baile folklórico. ❺ Voy al centro. ❻ Necesito ir al correo. ❼ Estudia en la biblioteca.) For each activity mentioned, have students list the days on which the character participates in the activity.

5

Juan: Oye, María Inés... voy al centro. ¿Me acompañas?

María Inés: Gracias, Juan, pero no. Necesito ir al correo. ¡Adiós!

6

Claudia: ¿Está aquí María Inés Hernández?

Juan: No, va ahorita hacia el correo.

Claudia: ¿Dónde está?

Luis: En la Plaza de la Constitución.

7

Claudia: Bueno, ¿qué hacemos? ¿Regresamos a casa?

Luis: Sí. Aquí no está.

Claudia: Momento... Por lo general, estudia en la biblioteca después de bailar. ¿Por qué no vamos allá?

8

Claudia: María Inés no está en la escuela de baile, no está en el correo, y no está aquí en la biblioteca. ¿Qué hacemos?

Cuaderno de actividades, p. 37, Acts. 1–2

Using the Captioned Video/DVD

As an alternative to reading the conversations in the book, you might want to show the captioned version of *¿Dónde está María Inés?* on Videocassette 5. As students hear the language and watch the story, anxiety about the new language will be reduced, and comprehension

facilitated. The reinforcement of seeing the written words with the gestures and actions in context will help students do the comprehension activities on p. 112. **NOTE:** The *DVD Tutor* contains captions for all sections of the *Video Program*.

Background Information

• Taxco is a beautiful city in the state of Guerrero. The government has declared it to be a national monument. There are flowers and bougainvillea throughout the city. Its buildings are mostly white with red tile roofs, and winding, cobblestone streets climb its steep hills. The church of Santa Prisca was ordered built in 1751 by José (Joseph) de la Borda, a Frenchman made wealthy by developing the local silver mines.

• Folk dancing is a tradition carried on by many contemporary Mexicans. There are numerous regional dances performed by men, women, and children who wear traditional costumes at festivals and celebrations throughout the year. The **Ballet Folklórico de México** has contributed to the popularity of folk dancing. The dancers perform in the **Palacio de Bellas Artes** in Mexico City and in theaters throughout the world.

A continuación

You may choose to continue with *¿Dónde está María Inés? (a continuación)* at this time or wait until later in the chapter. At this point in the story, Claudia and Luis return home, where María Inés meets up with them. The three friends go to Taxco for the afternoon with Rosa, where they visit relatives and go sightseeing. You may wish to discuss with students the types of places they might visit or activities they might pursue in their free time.

Native Speakers

- You could assign native speakers the various roles in the **fotonovela** and ask them to act it out. Then, you might have these students act out the roles again, this time using their own words. This demonstration will also help those students who are auditory learners.

- Have native speakers supply a dialogue for the panels of the **fotonovela** that tells a different story from the one presented there. You might suggest a topic: for instance, students can write dialogues that talk about the relationships among the friends. You can restrict them to material they have learned in Chapters 1 through 3, or you can allow them to use whatever Spanish they know.

These activities check for comprehension only. Students should not yet be expected to produce language modeled in **De antemano**.

1 **¿Comprendes? ¡Contesta las preguntas!**

Do you understand who the characters are and what they're doing in the **fotonovela**? Check your comprehension by answering these questions. Don't be afraid to guess!

1. Where does the story begin? Claudia's house
2. Where do Luis, Claudia, and Rosa plan to go? Taxco
3. Who are Luis and Claudia looking for? María Inés
4. Where do they look? dance school, plaza, post office, library

2 **¿Cierto o falso?**

Con base en la fotonovela, indica **cierto** si la oración es verdadera o **falso** si no lo es. Si es falsa, cámbiala. See answers below.

1. Luis y Claudia cantan en el coro los miércoles y los viernes.
2. Tío Ernesto tiene un regalo para la madre de Claudia y Rosa.
3. María Inés practica el béisbol los sábados por la mañana.
4. Claudia y Luis van al correo.
5. Por lo general, María Inés estudia en casa después de la clase de baile.

3 **¿Dónde está ella?** *Where is she?*

In the **fotonovela**, Luis and Claudia go all over downtown Cuernavaca. Retrace their steps by putting the following events in order.

a. Claudia y Luis van a la clase de baile. 2
b. Ellos van al correo. 4
c. Luis va a la casa de Claudia. 1
d. Van a la biblioteca. 5
e. María Inés va al correo. 3

4 **¿Qué hacemos?**

Complete these three conversations with words from the box. Use the **fotonovela** as a guide. One word will be used more than once.

CLAUDIA Ah, pero los ——**1**—— por la mañana María Inés ——**2**—— con su grupo de baile folklórico.

LUIS Pues, ——**3**—— allá. La escuela de baile donde tiene clase ——**4**—— en la Avenida Juárez.

CLAUDIA Vamos al ——**5**——. ¿Dónde está?

LUIS ——**6**—— en la Plaza de la Constitución.

CLAUDIA Momento... Por lo general ——**7**—— en la ——**8**—— después de bailar. ¿Vamos allá?

LUIS Sí, ¿por qué no?

correo 5	**vamos** 3
practica 2	**sábados** 1 **está** 6, 4
estudia 7	**biblioteca** 8

5 **¿Y tú?**

 Claudia and Luis have looked all over for María Inés without finding her. What do you think will happen next in the story? Discuss your ideas with a partner. Answers will vary.

Comprehension Check

Auditory Learners

2 This activity can be used as a listening comprehension activity. Read the sentences aloud and have students write **cierto** or **falso** on their papers. As a class, go over the corrected statements for the false items, based on **De antemano**.

Slower Pace

3 Have students look back at the **fotonovela** and scan for key words (**coro, correo, practica, estudia**) to help them find the information they need to answer the questions.

Answers

2 1. Falso: Cantan en el coro los martes y los jueves.
2. Cierto
3. Falso: María Inés baila con un grupo de baile folklórico.
4. Cierto
5. Falso: María Inés estudia en la biblioteca después de la clase de baile.

Objectives Talking about what you like to do; discussing what you and others do during free time

WV3 MEXICO-4

Así se dice

Talking about what you like to do

To find out what a friend likes to do, ask:

A ti, ¿qué te gusta hacer?
What do you like to do?

¿A Manuel le gusta estudiar?
Does Manuel like to study?

¿A quién le gusta bailar y cantar?
Who likes to dance and sing?

Your friend might respond:

Me gusta pintar.
I like to paint.

No, **no le gusta** estudiar.
Pero le gusta **hablar por teléfono.**
. . . he doesn't like . . .
. . . to talk on the phone.

A mí me gusta bailar y cantar.
Por eso me gustan las fiestas.
I like . . .
That's why I like . . .

Vocabulario

cuidar a tu hermano/a	*to take care of your brother/sister*	lavar la ropa	*to wash the clothes*
descansar en el parque	*to rest in the park*	mirar la televisión	*to watch TV*
dibujar	*to draw*	nadar en la piscina	*to swim in the pool*
escuchar música	*to listen to music*	sacar la basura	*to take out the trash*
jugar a	*to play (a sport or game)*	tocar	*to play (an instrument)*
lavar el carro	*to wash the car*		

CD-ROM 1
DVD 1

Cuaderno de gramática,
p. 27, Acts. 1–2

Más práctica gramatical,
p. 128, Act. 1

Cuaderno de actividades,
p. 38, Act. 3

6 **Actividades**

Escuchemos Listen to what the following people like to do. Match the name of each person with the appropriate picture.

CD 4 Tr. 3
1. Tomás
3. Bárbara
2. Arturo
4. Patricia

Scripts and answers on p. 107G.

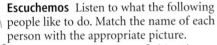

c.

d.

7 **¿Qué te gusta hacer?**

Escribamos/Hablemos Look at the activities in **Así se dice** and the **Vocabulario** on this page. List three activities you like to do and three that you don't like to do. Get together with a partner and compare lists. Be prepared to tell the class what your partner likes and doesn't like to do. Answers will vary.

Connections and Comparisons

Language-to-Language

Point out that English often uses the *-ing* form of the verb where Spanish uses the infinitive (the form that ends in **-ar**, **-er**, or **-ir**). Write **Me gusta ir al centro comercial** and *I like going to the mall* on the board. Then ask students how they would say the following in Spanish: *I like going to lunch. I don't like cleaning my room.*

Teaching Resources
pp. 113–117

PRINT
▸ Lesson Planner, p. 18
▸ TPR Storytelling Book, pp. 13, 16
▸ Listening Activities, pp. 27, 31
▸ Activities for Communication, pp. 19–20, 90, 93–94, 143–144
▸ Cuaderno de gramática, pp. 27–30
▸ Grammar Tutor for Students of Spanish, Chapter 4
▸ Cuaderno de actividades, pp. 38–40
▸ Cuaderno para hispanohablantes, pp. 16–20
▸ Testing Program, pp. 79–82
▸ Alternative Assessment Guide, p. 35
▸ Student Make-Up Assignments, Chapter 4

MEDIA
▸ One-Stop Planner
▸ Audio Compact Discs, CD 4, Trs. 3–4, 24–25, 19
▸ Teaching Transparencies 4-1, 4-A, 4-B; **Más práctica gramatical** Answers; Cuaderno de gramática Answers
▸ Interactive CD-ROM Tutor, Disc 1

Bell Work Have students write responses to: ¿Te gusta la historia? ¿Te gustan las matemáticas? ¿A qué hora es tu clase favorita?

Presenting

Así se dice, Vocabulario

Use *Teaching Transparency 4-1* or *4-A* to model **Así se dice** and **Vocabulario.** As students master **¿Qué te gusta hacer?**, introduce **¿A _____ le gusta estudiar? ¿A quién le gusta _____?** Have students ask others what they like to do, then tell what they found out.

Gramática

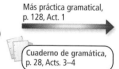

Present tense of regular -ar verbs

1. In Spanish and English, verbs change depending on the *subject* (the person doing the action). This is called *conjugating the verb*.

2. In Spanish, there are three main groups of verbs; their infinitive (the unchanged form of a verb) ends in **-ar**, **-er**, or **-ir**. The first group you'll learn to conjugate is the **-ar** verbs.

3. To conjugate **hablar** or any other regular **-ar** verb, take the part of the verb called the *stem* (**habl-**) and add these endings:

(yo)	habl**o**	(nosotros/as)	habl**amos**	*we speak*
(tú)	habl**as**	(vosotros/as)	habl**áis**	*you speak (plural, Spain)*
(usted) (él) (ella)	habl**a**	(ustedes) (ellos) (ellas)	habl**an**	*you or they speak*

> Más práctica gramatical, p. 128, Act. 1

> Cuaderno de gramática, p. 28, Acts. 3–4

Así se dice

Discussing what you and others do during free time

> Cuaderno de gramática, p. 29, Acts. 5–6

To ask what a friend does after school, say:

¿Qué haces después de clases?
What do you do after school?

¿Tocas el piano?
Do you play the piano?

¿Bailan ustedes antes de regresar a casa?
Do you (plural) dance before returning home?

¿Practican deportes Luis y Carmen en el tiempo libre?
Do Luis and Carmen practice sports during free time?

Your friend might answer:

Descanso. Después **juego al** fútbol.
I rest . . . I play . . .

No, pero **toco la guitarra.**
. . . I play the guitar.

Sí, **nosotros bailamos con** un grupo de baile. Y también **jugamos al** tenis.
Yes, we dance with a dance troupe . . . we play . . .

No, ellos **no practican** deportes. **Juegan** a los videojuegos.
. . . they don't practice . . . They play

---

8 **El tiempo libre** Scripts and answers on p. 107G.

CD 4
Tr. 4

Escuchemos/Leamos Listen as each person tells you what he or she does during his or her free time. Match the person with the correct activity.

1. Carmen
2. Javier
3. Armando y Ana
4. Susana
5. Pablo

a. bailar y cantar
b. hablar con amigos
c. practicar deportes
d. escuchar música
e. estudiar

Nota gramatical

The verb **jugar** has the following conjugation:

j**ue**go	jugamos
j**ue**gas	jugáis
j**ue**ga	j**ue**gan

The preposition **a** combines with **el** to form the contraction **al.**

¿Juegas al tenis?

Communication for All Students

Additional Practice

For more practice with **Gramática**, use **Más práctica gramatical**, Acts. 2–3, pp. 128–129; *Cuaderno de gramática*, Acts. 3–6, pp. 28–29; *Cuaderno de actividades*, Acts. 6–7, p. 40; and *Interactive CD-ROM*. For **Así se dice**, use **Más práctica gramatical**, Act. 1, p. 128; *Cuaderno de gramática*, Act. 1, p. 27 and Act. 7, p. 29; *Cuaderno de actividades*, Acts. 3–5, pp. 38–39.

Auditory Learners

Vocabulario Cut pictures from magazines or draw new vocabulary items. Then randomly number them, and, as you say the Spanish for a picture, students say the number in Spanish. Once they are familiar with the words, the students can say the Spanish words for each picture as you cue them with the number.

Vocabulario

pasar el rato con amigos

caminar con el perro

montar en bicicleta

trabajar en un restaurante

tomar un refresco

tomar un helado

preparar la cena

Cuaderno de gramática,
p. 29, Act. 7

También se puede decir...

In many Spanish-speaking countries, you'll also hear **andar en bicicleta** or **pasear en bici** in addition to **montar en bicicleta**.

9 **Gramática en contexto** [H]

Escribamos Tell Mariana, your new class-mate, what these people do in their free time. Write complete sentences using the information provided. See answers below.

1. Yo/tocar/la guitarra en el tiempo libre
2. Mi hermana/trabajar/después de clases
3. Mi padre/caminar con el perro/en el parque a las cinco
4. Beto y Shoji/hablar por teléfono/después de clases
5. Maya y yo/nadar en la piscina/antes de regresar a casa
6. Ellas/escuchar la radio/antes de clases

Nota cultural

Many athletes from Spanish-speaking countries broke new ground in the 2000 Olympic Games. María Urrutia from Colombia and Soraya Jiménez from Mexico gave their countries their first gold in weightlifting. Cuba garnered six medals in boxing, four of them gold, and a third con-secutive gold by its women's volleyball team. Costa Rica's swimmer Claudia Poll won two bronze medals. In sailing, medals went to Argentina's Carlos Espínola and Serena Amato. Spain captured the gold in diverse competitions: judo (Isabel Fernández), cycling (Juan Llaneras) and gymnastics (Gervasio Deferr).

Presenting
Vocabulario

Display *Teaching Transparency 4-B.* After looking at the pictures, ask students to raise their hands to answer the following questions about their own activities.
(**¿A quién le gusta montar en bicicleta? ¿A quién no le gusta preparar la cena? ¿A quién le gusta caminar con el perro? ¿Quiénes de ustedes no toman el refresco _____ ? ¿Quiénes trabajan en un restaurante? ¿Cuántos de ustedes pasan el rato con amigos?**)

Challenge

9 Once students have formed the sentences, have them work indi-vidually or in pairs to create new sen-tences by adding original endings:
Toco la guitarra con mi hermano.
Mi hermana trabaja los sábados.

Teaching Suggestion

9 You may want to have students do this activity orally.

Answers

9 1. Yo toco la guitarra en mi tiempo libre.
2. Mi hermana trabaja después de clases.
3. Mi padre camina con el perro en el parque a las cinco.
4. Beto y Shoji hablan por teléfono después de clases.
5. Maya y yo nadamos en la piscina antes de regresar a casa.
6. Ellas escuchan la radio antes de clases.

Teacher to Teacher

Shelli Albertson
Shorewood High School
Shorewood, Wisconsin

Shelli's activity cuts through conjugation problems
"I do this hands-on activity to practice verb conjugations. On a sheet I pass out to pairs of students there are six subject pronouns (**yo, Paco, ellos,** etc.), six verb stems (**escuch-, lav-, sac-,** etc.), and six verb endings (**-o, -a, -an,** etc.), all in random order. Students have to cut out elements separately, place them in the correct order, and glue them onto a colored piece of paper. At the end of each phrase, they write three to seven words in Spanish to form six complete sentences. Finally, underneath they write the translation in English."

Teaching Resources
pp. 113–117

PRINT 📖
- ▶ Lesson Planner, p. 18
- ▶ TPR Storytelling Book, pp. 13, 16
- ▶ Listening Activities, pp. 27, 31
- ▶ Activities for Communication, pp. 19–20, 90, 93–94, 143–144
- ▶ Cuaderno de gramática, pp. 27–30
- ▶ Grammar Tutor for Students of Spanish, Chapter 4
- ▶ Cuaderno de actividades, pp. 38–40
- ▶ Cuaderno para hispanohablantes, pp. 16–20
- ▶ Testing Program, pp. 79–82
- ▶ Alternative Assessment Guide, p. 35
- ▶ Student Make-Up Assignments, Chapter 4

MEDIA 💿📼📚
- ▶ One-Stop Planner
- ▶ Audio Compact Discs, CD 4, Trs. 3–4, 24–25, 19
- ▶ Teaching Transparencies 4-1, 4-A, 4-B; **Más práctica gramatical** Answers; Cuaderno de gramática Answers
- ▶ Interactive CD-ROM Tutor, Disc 1

Presenting
Nota gramatical

Prepare questions and responses using **con, conmigo** and **contigo**. For example, **¿Quién nada contigo? Arturo nada conmigo.** Practice this type of question and response with students several times. Have students work together asking each other about activities they do with others. Students should be ready to tell the class what they have found out from their classmates.

---

10 **Después de clases**

Leamos/Escribamos Read what each person or group likes, then write a sentence telling what these people probably do after school. Answers may vary.

> **MODELO**   **A Reynaldo le gustan los animales.**
> **Reynaldo camina con el perro.**

1. A Emilia le gusta hablar con sus amigos.
2. A Luisa le gusta la clase de arte. A mí me gusta también.
3. A Tyrone le gusta la comida.
4. A Pablo le gustan los deportes. A Marcela le gustan los deportes también.
5. A Joaquín le gusta mucho trabajar en casa.
6. A mí me gusta la música.
7. A Paola le gustan los bailes del colegio.

11 **Combina las frases** Answers will vary.

Leamos/Escribamos Combina las palabras de los tres cuadros y escribe todas las oraciones que puedas.

yo	practicar	tomar		el piano	un helado	en la piscina
tú	nadar	escuchar		un refresco	por teléfono	en bicicleta
ella	hablar	tocar		música	el voleibol	en una fiesta
él	montar	jugar a		el béisbol	en el parque	en un baile

12 **¿Qué haces después de clases?** Answers will vary.

Hablemos/Escribamos Work in pairs. Find out what your partner does in his or her free time with friends. Use the expressions **después de clases, antes de regresar a casa,** and **en el tiempo libre.** Take notes on your partner's responses and be prepared to report your findings to the class.

Nota gramatical

To talk about doing things with someone else, **con** is used with a pronoun like **él** or **ella.**

> ¿Quién trabaja **con** Luisa?
> Yo trabajo **con ella.**
> ¿Quién toma un refresco **con** David?
> Alegría toma limonada **con él.**

The expressions *with me* and *with you* (familiar) have special forms.

> ¿Quién estudia **contigo?**
> *Who … with you?*
> Mi amigo Miguel estudia **conmigo.** *… with me.*

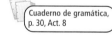

Cuaderno de gramática, p. 30, Act. 8

Más práctica gramatical, p. 128, Act. 2 ➡

---

13 **Gramática en contexto** Answers will vary.

Hablemos Think about all the people you see every day. Ask your partner who does the following activities with him or her each day. Then tell who does the activities with you. Take turns asking and answering the questions.

> **MODELO**   **tocar un instrumento**
> **—¿Quién toca un instrumento contigo?**
> **—Mi papá toca el piano conmigo.**

1. tomar un refresco
2. jugar a un deporte
3. dibujar
4. estudiar
5. mirar la televisión
6. escuchar música
7. caminar con el perro
8. montar en bicicleta
9. tomar un helado

Communication for All Students

Kinesthetic Learners

11 Put these verbs and expressions on cards and give one to each student. Ask a student to stand and read his or her card aloud. Students who have a card with a meaningful completion should stand and say the full phrase. (A student with **practicar** stands and says **practico,** showing the card. A student with the card **deportes** stands and says **Practico deportes.**)

Cooperative Learning

14 Have students do this activity in an interview format. One student asks a question, and the second answers. The third either writes the response or monitors his or her partners. After a few questions, have students switch roles. The interviewer might ask: **¿Qué haces en el tiempo libre? ¿Qué te gusta hacer después de clases?**

---

14 Con mis amigos

Hablemos Form a small group with two other class-mates. Ask your partners what they do in their free time and with whom they do each activity. Switch roles after four questions. Use **siempre** *(always)* or **nunca** *(never)* before the verb when appropriate. Be prepared to share your findings with the class.

15 ¿Con quién?

Leamos/Escribamos For each person or group listed, write two sentences telling what the person is like and what you or others do with that person. Use some of the activities in the box. Answers will vary.

MODELO
Carlos
Carlos es muy simpático. Lava la ropa y prepara la cena con su mamá.

1. yo
2. tu mejor amigo/a *(best friend)*
3. tus compañeros de clase
4. el profesor/la profesora de español
5. mamá
6. tu novio/a
   (boyfriend/girlfriend)
7. nosotros

> trabajar
> montar en bicicleta
> estudiar
> hablar por teléfono
> preparar la cena
> lavar la ropa
> mirar la televisión

Nota gramatical

Que is a very common word in Spanish. It can refer to either people or things and can mean *that*, *which*, or *who*.

Tengo **una amiga que canta** bien.

La música que me gusta escuchar es rock en español.

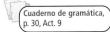

Cuaderno de gramática, p. 30, Act. 9

Más práctica gramatical, p. 129, Act. 3

16 Gramática en contexto

Hablemos Take turns asking and answering questions with two or three of your classmates. Be sure to use **que** in your answer.
Answers will vary.

MODELO
la clase/te gusta más
—¿Qué clase te gusta más?
—La clase que me gusta más es el español.

1. la música/te gusta escuchar
2. el estado/quieres visitar
3. el programa de televisión/te gusta mirar
4. el refresco/quieres tomar
5. el deporte/te gusta practicar
6. la cena/te gusta preparar
7. el restaurante/te gusta más

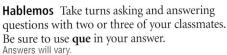

A lo nuestro

In Spanish there are many different ways to refer to your classmates and friends. To greet a friend in Peru, say **¡Hola, pata!** Throughout Latin America and Mexico, men call each other **compadre**. You'll hear friends call each other **'mano/a** (short for **hermano/a**) or **compañero/a** in Mexico and Central America. Another Mexican expression for a friend is **cuate**.

17 Pienso en... *I'm thinking about*

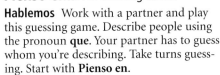

Hablemos Work with a partner and play this guessing game. Describe people using the pronoun **que**. Your partner has to guess whom you're describing. Take turns guessing. Start with **Pienso en**.

MODELO
—Pienso en una persona famosa que es de México, y canta y toca en *Supernatural.*
—¿Es Carlos Santana?
—¡Sí, es él!

Building on Previous Skills

15 Remind students to use times of day, days of the week, and places in their answers.

Presenting
Nota gramatical

The relative pronoun *que*
Present magazine photos of people displaying action –ar verbs. For example, hold up an image of a person singing and ask **¿Qué hace la persona?** Write the question on the board. After you have elicited **canta**, write it on the board. Then model the construction with **que** by saying **Es una persona que canta.** Ask the original question with the other magazine photos, eliciting first the correct verb form, then the construction **Es una persona que...** You might want to point out the difference between **qué** *(what)* and **que** *(that, which, who).*

Assess

▶ Testing Program, pp. 79–82
  Quiz 4-1A, Quiz 4-1B
  Audio CD 4, Tr. 19

▶ Student Make-Up Assignments, Chapter 4, Alternative Quiz

▶ Alternative Assessment Guide, p. 35

Cultures and Communities

Native Speakers

A lo nuestro Ask native speakers to contribute expressions they know for referring to friends or acquaintances. Start by suggesting terms such as **chavo/a, vato,** or **ése,** and see if they can come up with more, including local ones. **Argentinos** may use **che,** while those from western Mexico may have heard or used **vale.** Ask if they know of other terms their parents or grandparents may have used that are now out of date. Have them generate more expressions in groups, listing those used in their particular homes and those considered out of date, then contrasting these with the current terms written on another list. Ask students to speculate about how they may change in the future, or about why certain expressions are in use.

Segundo paso

Objective Telling where people and things are

go.hrw.com

WV3 MEXICO-4

Así se dice

Telling where people and things are

To find out where someone or something is, ask:

¿Dónde estás?
Where are you?

¿No está en la escuela de baile?
Isn't she . . .?

Your friend might answer:

Estoy en el centro. Necesito encontrar a María Inés.   *I'm downtown.*

No, no está aquí.
No, she's not here.

Está en el trabajo.
She's at work.

CD-ROM 1 / DVD 1

---

18 **¿Dónde está?**

Escuchemos Listen to these people talking about where things are. Match each statement you hear with the correct picture. Scripts and answers on p. 107G.

CD 4 Tr. 5

a.

b.

c.

d.

Nota gramatical

The verb **estar** *(to be)* is used to talk about location. Here are the present tense forms of the verb.

Estoy en la librería.
Estás con tu familia.
Está en el centro.

Estamos en casa.
Estáis en la clase.
Están en el cuarto.

CD-ROM 1 / DVD 1

 Cuaderno de gramática, p. 31, Acts. 10–11

Más práctica gramatical, p. 129, Acts. 4–5

---

19 **Gramática en contexto**

Leamos/Escribamos This is the first time Luis has been to Taxco, so María Inés is acting as his guide. Read her description of the city and fill in each blank with the correct form of **estar**. See answers on p. 119.

Estamos en un lugar magnífico. Luis, es la primera vez que tú ___1___ en Taxco, ¿no? Bueno, allá ___2___ el parque, y allá ___3___ Los Arcos. El Museo ___4___ en la Plaza Borda. Muchos hoteles buenos ___5___ en la calle Hidalgo. El cine y una tienda ___6___ en la Plazuela de San Juan.

Communication for All Students

Kinesthetic Learners

20 Have students look at the vocabulary list. Then allow them to move around the room and review prepositions. Place items (pencil, book, magazine, watch, etc.) at different locations in the room. Ask: **¿Dónde está el lápiz?** Select a student to go get the pencil and reply: **El lápiz está encima de la mesa.** Continue the activity until you have reviewed all of the vocabulary.

Auditory/Visual Learners

Vocabulario Model descriptions of the town in *Teaching Transparency 4-2.* (**El cine está al lado del supermercado.**) Tell students you will use both correct and incorrect descriptions of the town and ask them to distinguish between the two. To wrap up, have students point to and describe the places on the transparency using **estar** and the prepositions on p. 119.

20 ¿Quiénes y qué?

Hablemos/Escribamos Name some people or things that are in the following places right now. Give as many answers as you can think of for each item. Answers will vary.

MODELO Mis padres están en el trabajo.

1. en la clase de español
2. en tu cuarto
3. en el centro
4. en tu armario
5. en tu casa
6. en México

Vocabulario

al lado de	next to; to one side of
allá	there
aquí	here
cerca de	near
debajo de	under; beneath
encima de	on top of
lejos de	far from

Cuaderno de actividades, pp. 41–42, Acts. 8–9

Cuaderno de gramática, p. 32, Acts. 12–13

También se puede decir...

In Mexico, people say **la alberca** instead of **la piscina**; in Argentina and Uruguay, you'll hear **la pileta**.

Connections and Comparisons

History/Geography Link

While middle- and upper-class suburbs tend to surround most North American cities, in Latin America it is mostly the poor who live on the outskirts and commute to work in the city. Another traditional difference is the tendency for many Latin American business districts to be organized into separate sections. (Jewelry stores might be clustered together, while baby clothes are in another section, and shoes in yet another.) Such differences stem from the way places were settled by Europeans, as well as when. Indeed, cities such as Bogotá, Lima, Mexico City, Havana, and Guatemala City were built long before cars were invented, and have therefore kept many of their pre-automobile features, whereas most North American cities began to grow rapidly after cars became available.

Presenting
Vocabulario

Use local places to present the new vocabulary. **(El cine "Expo" está en la calle Guadalupe. El supermercado "Mack's" está en la avenida Lincoln. Clase, ¿qué otros supermercados hay?)** Check comprehension by making some false statements and having the students correct them. **(—El cine "Expo" está en la avenida Lincoln. —No, profesora, está en la calle Guadalupe.)** Have students practice with a partner: one gives a new vocabulary word and the other responds with a proper name. They should create their own false statements to check comprehension.

Additional Practice

Teach the class the words for floor, wall, and ceiling. **(piso, pared, techo)** Then walk around the class asking students if statements you make are true **(cierto)** or false **(falso)**. Have students correct false statements.

1. **La pizarra está en la pared.**
2. **El/la profesor(a) está detrás de** (student's name).
3. **El techo está al lado del piso.**
4. **El escritorio está encima de la pizarra.**
5. **La mesa está cerca de** (student's name).
6. **El borrador está lejos de la pizarra.**
7. **El reloj está debajo del piso.**
8. **El pupitre está encima del techo.**

Answers
19
1. estás
2. está
3. están
4. está
5. están
6. están

Answers

 Possible answers:

1. Reynaldo necesita ir a la tienda. Está cerca del restaurante y al lado del gimnasio.
2. Berta necesita ir al parque. Está cerca del cine.
3. Alejandro necesita ir al correo. Está cerca del restaurante y al lado de la biblioteca.
4. Paula y Sergio necesitan ir a la piscina. Está cerca del restaurante.
5. Álvaro necesita ir al cine. Está cerca de la casa.
6. Bárbara necesita ir al parque. Está cerca del supermercado.

---

21 **¿Quiénes son y dónde están?**

Escuchemos Listen as Luis Miguel describes his friends and family. Match each picture with the description you hear. Scripts and answers on p. 107G.

 CD 4 Tr. 6

MODELO Paco es bajo y moreno. Le gusta jugar con su perro. Está en el parque.

a.   b.   c.   d.

e.   f.   g.   h.

22 **Del colegio al trabajo**

 Hablemos You work as a waitperson at a restaurant and a busload of tourists has just arrived. You know the city well and offer them directions. With a partner, refer to the downtown scene on page 119 to explain where everyone needs to go. Take turns being the waitperson and tourists. Use the prepositions **en, cerca de, al lado de,** and **lejos de** to explain your directions from the restaurant (**el restaurante**). See answers below.

MODELO Juan Luis quiere comprar fruta y chocolate.
—Él necesita ir al super-mercado. Está cerca del restaurante y al lado del cine.

1. Reynaldo necesita comprar ropa.
2. Berta quiere caminar con el perro.
3. Alejandro necesita comprar estampillas *(stamps).*
4. Paula y Sergio quieren nadar.
5. Álvaro quiere ver una película *(to see a film).*
6. Bárbara quiere jugar al voleibol.

SUGERENCIA

Do you sometimes feel that all the Spanish you hear is too fast? It's frustrating to feel lost, but are you really missing *everything?* Try not to let anxiety get in the way of listening carefully and picking out the words you do understand. When you listen to your teacher or an audio CD, or when you watch a video in Spanish, focus on the words you recognize. Then do some intelligent guesswork to fill in the gaps. Don't give up!

23 **¿Dónde están las cosas en tu escritorio?**

 Hablemos Get together with a classmate. With your backs to each other, take turns arranging four things on your desks and describing their location to each other. As your partner describes, draw what you hear. Then compare the drawings to the arrangements and make corrections: **No, el lápiz no está encima del libro. Está al lado del libro.**

Communication for All Students

Cooperative Learning

21 In this activity, students will make verb phrase flash cards. Divide the class into groups of three. Give each person a blank index card. Each group will choose two verb phrases using verbs they have learned. (**hablar español, ir al parque**) Each of the three students is responsible for writing two pronouns and two verb forms so that all six forms are covered by the group.

Cards should have one verb phrase and the two pronouns on the front (**hablar español— yo/usted**), and the two completed sentences on the back. (**Yo hablo español./Usted habla español.**) Every group will end up with two complete sets of cards. Students then turn in their sets of cards. Keep the cards in sets for later use.

24 En mi ciudad... *In my city*

Hablemos/Escribamos Completa las oraciones sobre los lugares que conoces. Puedes cambiar las oraciones a la forma negativa. See sample answers below.

1. El supermercado está lejos de...
2. El cine está al lado de...
3. El centro comercial está cerca de...
4. El restaurante está al lado de...
5. Hay ... debajo de mi cama.
6. En mi armario, hay...
7. Mi ventana está...
8. Normalmente mis libros están...

Gramática

Subject pronouns

Spanish speakers don't use subject pronouns as often as English speakers do. That's because the verb ending usually indicates the subject of the verb. But the pronoun may be used to clarify or to emphasize the subject.

yo	compr**o**	**nosotros, nosotras**	compr**amos**
tú	compr**as**	**vosotros, vosotras**	compr**áis**
usted **él, ella** } compr**a**		**ustedes** **ellos, ellas** } compr**an**	

1. In general, **tú** is used to speak to people with whom you are on a first-name basis. Use **usted** with adults and people in authority.

2. In Spain, **vosotros** is the plural of **tú**, while **ustedes** is the plural of **usted**. In the Americas, **ustedes** is the plural of both **tú** and **usted**.

3. The masculine forms (**nosotros** and **vosotros**) are used to refer to groups of males or groups including both males and females. The feminine forms **nosotras** and **vosotras** refer to groups including only females.

Más práctica gramatical,
p. 130, Act. 6

Cuaderno de actividades,
p. 43, Act. 10

Cuaderno de gramática,
p. 33, Acts. 14–16

25 Gramática en contexto

Escribamos Write sentences to tell where the following people are. Use the correct subject pronoun. See possible answers below.

MODELO los estudiantes
Ellos están en la biblioteca.

1. tú y tus amigos
2. tu abuela
3. tú
4. nosotros

Hablemos Now, ask the following people what they do during the week. Be sure to use the correct form of address, **tú** or **usted**.

MODELO el señor Pérez
¿Trabaja usted en el supermercado?

5. el director del colegio
6. tu mejor amigo
7. una profesora
8. el señor y la señora Navarro

Nota cultural

The use of **tú** and **usted** varies from country to country. Children in some areas are likely to address a parent as **usted**, while children in other areas use **tú**. If you're in a Spanish-speaking area, listen to others and try to use **tú** and **usted** as they do. When in doubt, use **usted** and wait for the other person to invite you to be less formal.

Communication for All Students

Group Work

24 Divide the class into groups. Each group creates sentences telling the location of a thing in the classroom or a place on the school campus without naming the thing or place. Have groups trade sentences to guess what thing or place the other group has in mind. Reward correct answers.

Challenge

25 Have students sit in a circle and build on a "chain" of statements about where people work and where they are. List places on the board. Have students use each other's names to elicit **yo**-form responses, calling on each other: **Paco trabaja en la biblioteca pero está en el garaje donde trabaja** *Juan.* *Yo* **trabajo en el garaje pero estoy en la tienda donde trabaja** *Claudia.*

Presenting
Gramática

Subject pronouns Point out that there are six different endings for regular -**ar** verbs, and that each ending corresponds to a subject pronoun (or group of pronouns). Because of this, the verb alone can often show who the subject is. Give students several sentences without subject pronouns and have them identify the subject. **Habla francés. (usted, él, ella)**

Kinesthetic Learners

Gramática Using gestures, demonstrate each pronoun. After you have modeled this, ask students to break into groups of three or four and demonstrate each pronoun as you say it.

Assess

▸ Testing Program, pp. 83–86
Quiz 4-2A, Quiz 4-2B
Audio CD 4, Tr. 20

▸ Student Make-Up Assignments, Chapter 4, Alternative Quiz

▸ Alternative Assessment Guide, p. 35

Answers

24 *Sample answers:*
1. El supermercado está lejos de la escuela.
2. El cine está al lado de las tiendas.

25 *Possible answers:*
1. Ustedes están en la clase de español.
2. Ella está en la oficina.
3. Tú estás en la escuela.
4. Nosotros estamos en los Estados Unidos.
5. ¿Qué hace usted los sábados?
6. ¿Necesitas organizar el cuarto?
7. ¿Camina usted con el perro en la tarde?
8. ¿Comen ustedes en la cafetería?

Teaching Resources
p. 122

PRINT
▸ Video Guide, pp. 25–27, 30
▸ Cuaderno de actividades, p. 48
▸ Cuaderno para hispanohablantes, p. 20

MEDIA
▸ One-Stop Planner
▸ Video Program, Videocassette 2, 15:53–17:43
▸ DVD Tutor, Disc 1
▸ Audio Compact Discs, CD 4, Trs. 7–11
▸ Interactive CD-ROM Tutor, Disc 1

Presenting
Panorama cultural

After doing the Motivating Activity, have students read, listen to, or watch the interviews. Ask them who mentions a way of spending time with friends that they also do and have them explain. Then have students answer the **Preguntas**.

Preguntas

1. ¿Qué hacen David y sus amigos cuando pasean? (Van a las casas de amigos.)

2. ¿A quién le gusta ir de compras? (a Patricia)

3. ¿A Jimena le gusta salir en grupo? (Sí.)

4. ¿Adónde van Juan Pablo y sus amigos? (al parque)

CD 4
Trs. 7–11

¿Te gusta pasear con tus amigos?

The **paseo** is a tradition in Spanish-speaking countries; people stroll around the **plaza** or along the streets of a town in the evening to socialize, and to see and be seen by others. In this chapter we asked some teens about the **paseo**.

CD 4 Tr. 10
David
Ciudad de México, México

"Sí, con mis amigos sí me gusta pasear... Podemos ir de la casa de uno a la casa de otro".

CD 4 Tr. 8
Patricia
San Diego, California

"Me gusta ir con mis amigos a las tiendas, de compras... me gusta ir mucho... al parque, para ir a ver a los muchachos, y también a la playa".

CD 4 Tr. 9
Jimena
Buenos Aires, Argentina

"Vamos a pasear, vamos a muchísimos lugares... Me parece divertido estar todos juntos, es una manera de hacerse más amigos de todos".

CD 4 Tr. 11
Juan Pablo
Sevilla, España

"Sí, me gusta pasear. Vamos a la Cartuja, [al parque de] María Luisa, y hablamos de todo un poco... Que aquí en Sevilla es muy común, si no se sale de vacaciones, dar una vuelta ya que con el calor la casa es un infierno... y vamos, se pasa bien aquí con los amigos".

Para pensar y hablar...

A. Which interviewee has the best reason for going out on a **paseo**? Why?

B. Why do you think people enjoy the **paseo**? What activity do you participate in that serves the same purpose as the **paseo**?

 Cuaderno para hispanohablantes, p. 20

Cultures and Communities

Culture Note
Although the **paseo** is no longer a tradition in very large Latin American cities, urban families may still take strolls in their **barrio**. Urban neighborhoods in Latin American countries often have the feel of small towns, with family-owned shops and small cafés and restaurants. This is also true in urban **barrios** of the United States.

Background Information
• **María Luisa** is a park in downtown Seville, with fountains, trees, walkways, and a conservatory.
• **La Cartuja**, also known as **Isla de la Cartuja**, is a neighborhood in Seville, and was the site of Expo '92, the 1992 World's Fair.

Objective Talking about where you and others go during free time

go.
hrw
.com

WV3 MEXICO-4

Tercer paso

CAPÍTULO 4

Así se dice

Talking about where you and others go during free time

To ask where someone is going, say:

¿Adónde vas?
Where are you going?

¿Adónde va María Inés?
Where is María Inés going?

Your friend might answer:

Voy a la biblioteca **para estudiar.**
I'm going . . . in order to study.

María Inés va al correo. Luego va al cine
para ver una película.
. . . in order to see a movie.

Nota gramatical

Ir *(to go)* is an irregular verb, since its conjugation doesn't follow any pattern. To ask where someone is going, use the question word **¿adónde?** *([to] where?).*

CD-ROM 1
DVD 1

Voy al cine.
¿Adónde vas ahora?
Va al gimnasio.

Vamos a la piscina.
Vais a casa.
Van al baile.

Más práctica gramatical,
p. 130, Act. 7

Cuaderno de actividades,
p. 44, Acts. 11–12

Cuaderno de gramática,
p. 34, Acts. 17–18

---

26 **¿Adónde vas?**

CD 4
Tr. 12

Escuchemos/Escribamos Listen as Filiberto asks his friend Alicia where everyone is going this afternoon after school. Write each person's name and where he or she is going. Then decide who can give Filiberto a ride to the movies. Scripts and answers on p. 107H.

---

27 **Gramática en contexto**

Leamos/Escribamos Claudia and her friends are visiting Taxco and everyone is going to a different place. Fill in the blanks with the correct forms of the verb **ir**. See answers below.

ROSA   Claudia ___1___ a la casa de mi tío y yo ___2___ con ella. Luis, ¿adónde ___3___ tú?

LUIS   Yo ___4___ al parque. Oye, María Inés, ¿adónde ___5___ tú?

MARÍA INÉS   Yo ___6___ al centro.

LUIS   ¿A qué hora ___7___ ustedes a la casa de su tío?

CLAUDIA   ¡Nosotros ___8___ a Cuernavaca a las nueve!

Teaching Resources
pp. 123–125

PRINT
▶ Lesson Planner, p. 20
▶ TPR Storytelling Book, pp. 15, 16
▶ Listening Activities, pp. 29, 33
▶ Activities for Communication, pp. 23–24, 92, 93–94, 143–144
▶ Cuaderno de gramática, pp. 34–36
▶ Grammar Tutor for Students of Spanish, Chapter 4
▶ Cuaderno de actividades, pp. 44–46
▶ Cuaderno para hispanohablantes, pp. 16–20
▶ Testing Program, pp. 87–90
▶ Alternative Assessment Guide, p. 35
▶ Student Make-Up Assignments, Chapter 4

MEDIA
▶ One-Stop Planner
▶ Audio Compact Discs, CD 4, Trs. 12–17, 28–29, 21
▶ Teaching Transparencies 4-3, 4-C; **Más práctica gramatical** Answers; Cuaderno de gramática Answers
▶ Interactive CD-ROM Tutor, Disc 1

Bell Work
Write two columns of phrases. Students match them to form sentences. (Column 1: **El libro está, Uds. están,** etc.; Column 2: **en el cine, debajo de la mesa,** etc.)

Presenting
Así se dice,
Nota gramatical

Ask students **¿Adónde vas a las nueve? (diez,** etc.). Use all forms of **ir,** asking who is going somewhere at a specific time.

Answers
27 1. va   4. voy   7. van
2. voy   5. vas   8. vamos
3. vas   6. voy

Communication for All Students

Auditory/Visual Learners
26 Copy and enlarge the map from Additional Listening Activity 9-2, *Listening Activities,* p. 146, or invent one, displaying it. For each map site, make a card. Eight students draw two each, one a starting point, the other a destination. Students say, **Estoy en... y voy a...** Others take turns drawing the route on the map. Note which routes intersect. Ask who could go with whom to a destination.

Kinesthetic Learners
27 Label sections of your class after places in town seen in **De antemano** or Activity 27. Put students' names in one hat and the places in another. One student draws the names, asking, **¿Adónde va Luis?** Another draws a place, answering, **Va al centro**. The student called must go to the proper area. Return places to the hat so that they may be used again.

Teaching Resources
pp. 123–125

PRINT 📖

▸ Lesson Planner, p. 20
▸ TPR Storytelling Book, pp. 15–16
▸ Listening Activities, pp. 29, 33
▸ Activities for Communication, pp. 23–24, 92, 93–94, 143–144
▸ Cuaderno de gramática, pp. 34–36
▸ Grammar Tutor for Students of Spanish, Chapter 4
▸ Cuaderno de actividades, pp. 44–46
▸ Cuaderno para hispanohablantes, pp. 16–20
▸ Testing Program, pp. 87–90
▸ Alternative Assessment Guide, p. 35
▸ Student Make-Up Assignments, Chapter 4

MEDIA 🎥💿

▸ One-Stop Planner
▸ Audio Compact Discs, CD 4, Trs. 12–17, 28–29, 21
▸ Teaching Transparencies 4-3, 4-C; **Más práctica gramatical** Answers; Cuaderno de gramática Answers
▸ Interactive CD-ROM Tutor, Disc 1

Presenting
Vocabulario, Nota gramatical

Show a transparency of a calendar. After modeling **¿Qué día es hoy?** and its answer, ask **¿Y mañana?** Use dates to elicit other days: **¿Qué día es el doce? ¿el trece?** Ask **¿Qué haces los lunes? ¿los jueves?** to contrast use and omission of articles. Correct omitted articles or unneeded prepositions. Have students find out the day on which their birthday falls this year, then have them write it out.

---

28 **Cosas que hacer** *Things to do*

Leamos/Hablemos You and a friend are trying to think of something to do this weekend. Look at the entertainment guide and say where you're going. Base your answers on the following. *Answers may vary.*

1. Te gusta jugar al tenis.
2. A tu compañero le gusta nadar.
3. Quieres hacer ejercicios aeróbicos *(to do aerobics)*.
4. Quieres ver una película.

CINES

CINES LUMIERE. Pasaje Martín de los Heros o Princesa, 5. Tel. 542 11 72. Acceso directo desde el parking. Precio por sesión, 3€ y otra película sin determinar. Confirmar cambios de horarios y película en taquilla.

GIMNASIOS

GIMNASIO GARCÍA. Andrés Bello, 21-23. Teléfono. 312 86 01. Karate (club campeón de España), clases de aeróbicos, gimnasia, jazz, voleibol, basquetbol y baile. Máquinas Polaris.

PISCINAS

MUNICIPALES ALUCHE (Latina). A. General Fanjul, 14 (metro Aluche, autobuses 17, 34 y 39). Tel. 706 28 68.

TENIS

CLUB DE TENIS LAS LOMAS. Avenida de Las Lomas. Tel. 633 04 63. Escuela de tenis. Todos los niveles. Todos los días de la semana.

29 **Destinos**

 Escribamos Escribe seis oraciones con el vocabulario de la página 119. Nombra los lugares adónde van tú, tus amigos/as y tus padres en su tiempo libre. *Answers will vary.*

MODELO **Voy al parque para montar en bicicleta.**

Vocabulario

Los días de la semana *The days of the week*

💿 CD-ROM 1
📀 DVD 1

Monday					el fin de semana	
lunes	martes	miércoles	jueves	viernes	sábado	domingo
1	2	3	4	5	6
7	8	9	10	11	12	13

OCTUBRE

Cuaderno de gramática, p. 35, Acts. 19–20

Nota gramatical

1. Always use **el** before a day of the week except when stating what day it is. **Hoy es martes.**
2. To make **sábado** and **domingo** plural, add **-s.**
3. To say *on Monday, on Tuesday,* etc., use **el lunes, el martes.**
   Voy al gimnasio **el jueves.**
4. To say *on Mondays, on Tuesdays,* etc., use **los lunes, los martes.**
   Los lunes, vamos al colegio.
5. Days of the week are not capitalized in Spanish.

Cuaderno de gramática, p. 36, Acts. 21–23

Más práctica gramatical, p. 131, Acts. 8–9 →

Nota cultural

In Spain and Latin America, there are fewer school-sponsored extracurricular activities for high school students than in the United States. Teenagers who play sports will often join independent teams, since many schools don't have their own teams.

Communication for All Students

Building on Previous Skills

29 Have pairs of students recycle question formation as well as previously-learned vocabulary in an oral variation. (—**¿Vas a la piscina? —Sí, voy a la piscina. —A qué hora vas? —Voy a las cuatro.**)

Visual Learners

Vocabulario Ask students to develop a Spanish calendar for the current month, putting the days of the week and the dates in their proper places. Remind them that the days of the week are not capitalized. You might then have them fill in one week of the calendar with one sentence for each day, telling what they or someone they know normally does or is going to do on that day.

30 **Gramática en contexto**

Leamos/Hablemos Compare schedules with a partner. Ask each other where you are at the following times during the week. Answers will vary.

MODELO   —¿Dónde estás los lunes a las ocho de la mañana?
               —Estoy en la clase de inglés.

1. los viernes a las cuatro de la tarde
2. los sábados a las diez y media de la mañana
3. los sábados por la noche
4. los martes a la una de la tarde
5. los jueves a las once de la mañana
6. los lunes por la noche
7. los domingos por la mañana
8. los miércoles por la tarde

31 **¡Una encuesta!**

Hablemos/Escribamos Take a survey of three classmates to find out where they go on the weekend. Write the name of each person and at least two places where he or she goes. Be prepared to present the class with the results of your survey.

32 **En mi cuaderno** Possible answers below.

Escribamos Write a short description of a typical week in your life. Make a calendar for the week and include at least two activities for each day. Start some of your sentences with the phrases in the word box.

> Después de clases, voy a...
>
> En mi tiempo libre...
>
> Los sábados estoy en...

LETRA Y SONIDO

CD 4
Trs. 13–17

A. The letters **b** and **v** in Spanish represent the same sound. That single sound has two possible variations.

   1. At the beginning of a phrase, or after an **m** or an **n**, these letters sound like the *b* in the English word *bean*.

      biblioteca   **basquetbol**   **bailar**   **invierno**   **viernes**

   2. Between vowels and after other consonants, their pronunciation is softened, with the lower lip slightly forward and not resting against the upper teeth.

      lobo   **lo bueno**   **uva**   **Cuba**

   3. Note that the **b** and **v** in the following pairs of words and phrases have exactly the same pronunciation.

      tubo/tuvo   **a ver/haber**
      vienes/bienes   **botar/votar**

B. Dictado Script for Part B on p. 107H.

   Pablo hasn't learned to spell words that use **b** and **v** yet. As he says the words he's not sure of, write what you hear.

C. Trabalenguas

   El lobo sabe bailar bien el vals bajo el árbol.

Connections and Comparisons

Culture Note

Spanish calendars look slightly different than calendars in English; **el lunes** (Monday), not **el domingo** (Sunday), is the first day of the week. Point out to your students that this makes more sense of the term "weekend," as Saturday and Sunday are together at the end of the week.

Language-to-Language

Review the **Nota gramatical**, then write the following on the board:
1. *On Wednesdays* I have soccer practice.
2. *Today is* *Wednesday*.
3. *On Wednesday* there is an exam.
   Then write **a. miércoles, b. el miércoles, c. los miércoles**, and ask students to match the correct phrase to the underlined English expressions.

Writing Assessment

32 You may wish to use the following rubric to assess students' writing progress at this time. Having pairs peer-edit each other's first draft of the calendar, then turning in a revised version will often improve the quality of submissions.

Writing Rubric	Points			
	4	3	2	1
Content (Complete– Incomplete)				
Comprehensibility (Comprehensible– Incomprehensible)				
Accuracy (Accurate– Seldom accurate)				
Organization (Well organized– Poorly organized)				
Effort (Excellent–Minimal)				

18–20: A   14–15: C   Under
16–17: B   12–13: D   12: F

Assess

▶ Testing Program, pp. 87–90
   Quiz 4-3A, Quiz 4-3B
   Audio CD 4, Tr. 21

▶ Student Make-Up Assignments, Chapter 4, Alternative Quiz

▶ Alternative Assessment Guide, p. 35

Answers

32 *Possible answers:*
Los lunes voy a la escuela. Después de clase toco el piano. Los martes voy a la clase de piano. En mi tiempo libre estudio. Los sábados estoy en el centro comercial todo el día.

STANDARDS: 1.1, 1.3, 3.1, 4.1, 5.1, 5.2

Teaching Resources
pp. 126–127

PRINT

▸ Lesson Planner, p. 21
▸ Cuaderno de actividades, p. 47
▸ Cuaderno para hispanohablantes, pp. 16–19
▸ Reading Strategies and Skills Handbook, Chapter 4
▸ ¡Lee conmigo! 1, Chapter 4
▸ Standardized Assessment Tutor, Chapter 4

MEDIA

▸ One-Stop Planner

Prereading
Activities A and B

Connecting through Your Experience
Ask students to think about their closest friends or pen pals. What makes these friendships close? Do they have similar or divergent interests? Are their personalities alike or different? Ask students to use these questions to create a profile of an ideal friend or pen pal. Ask students to think of times, such as looking up a name in the phone directory, when they must scan for information.

Reading
Activities C and D

Monitoring Comprehension
Have students scan the pen pal ads for obvious cognates (**música rock, teléfono**) and make a list of the ones they find. Then ask them to scan again for words or cognates that are not so easy to spot. (**turista, estudiar**) See if they can guess or derive their meanings.

Vamos a leer

Anuncios personales

Estrategia para leer
Scanning for specific information means looking for one thing at a time, without concerning yourself with the rest of the information there. Some examples of scanning are looking up the spelling of a word in a dictionary or hunting through the TV listing to see what time a certain show comes on.

¡A comenzar!
The ads on these pages are for pen pals. They come from *Tú*, a magazine for Spanish-speaking teens. Before doing any scanning, gather more general information.

¿Te acuerdas?
Use your background knowledge before you read in depth.

A. If you were writing an ad for a pen pal, what kind of information would you include? Choose the items you would want to include. *Answers will vary.*
- your name
- your best friend's name
- your address
- the name of your school
- your age
- what you look like
- what your parents do
- your hobbies

B. Now look briefly at the ads. Of the eight possibilities listed above, which four are included in the ads? *person's name, address, age, and hobbies*

LÍNEA DIRECTA

Nombre: Sandra Duque
Edad: 17 años
Dirección: P.O. Box # 1752, Colón, REPÚBLICA DE PANAMÁ.
Pasatiempos: Escuchar música, coleccionar unicornios, ver televisión, ir al cine, escribir cartas.

▲▲▲▲▲▲▲▲▲▲▲▲▲▲▲▲▲▲

Nombre: Susana Tam
Edad: 13 años
Dirección: 4ta. Ave., N #41-07, La Flora, Cali, REPÚBLICA DE COLOMBIA.
Pasatiempos: Ir al cine, a fiestas, a bailar y hablar por teléfono. Pueden escribirme en inglés.

▲▲▲▲▲▲▲▲▲▲▲▲▲▲▲▲▲▲

Nombre: Juan Dos Santos
Edad: 15 años
Dirección: 55mts sur, Bomba Gasotica, Pérez Zeledón, COSTA RICA.
Pasatiempos: Oír música rock, hablar con los turistas y tener amigos.

▲▲▲▲▲▲▲▲▲▲▲▲▲▲▲▲▲▲

Nombre: Juana Saldívar
Edad: 16 años
Dirección: P.O. Box 678, Hato Rey 00919, PUERTO RICO.
Pasatiempos: Conocer a chicos de otros países, oír música y pasear.

▲▲▲▲▲▲▲▲▲▲▲▲▲▲▲▲▲▲

Nombre: Wilmer Ramírez
Edad: 16 años
Dirección: Urb. Las Batallas, Calle La Puerta #2, San Félix, Edo. Bolívar, VENEZUELA.

Pasatiempos: Leer, escuchar música e intercambiar correspondencia y estudiar.

Connections and Comparisons

Culture Note
After reading, have students scan the entries again, paying attention to the addresses. Point out that in most Spanish-speaking countries, addresses give the street name first, then the number. **Yapeyú 9550** means *9550 Yapeyú Street.* Have students figure out the address of the entry from Costa Rica on this page. Explain that in Central America, directions and distances from landmarks, rather than names and numbers, often indicate addresses. Ask students how far the Costa Rican pen pal lives from the **Bomba Gasotica** (55 meters to the south). Model the Spanish address style using your school's address, and give students the vocabulary for cardinal points: **norte, sur, este, oeste**. Have students practice writing other addresses using both formats.

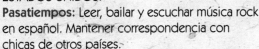

Nombre: Gerardo Vargas
Edad: 14 años
Dirección: P.O. Box 2002,
Borrego Springs,
California 92004,
ESTADOS UNIDOS.
Pasatiempos: Leer, bailar y escuchar música rock
en español. Mantener correspondencia con
chicas de otros países.

▲▲▲▲▲▲▲▲▲▲▲▲▲▲▲▲▲▲▲▲▲▲▲▲▲▲

Nombre: Julia Ileana Oliveras
Edad: 15 años
Dirección: Yapeyú 9550 (1210) Cap. Fed. Buenos
Aires, ARGENTINA.
Pasatiempos: Escuchar la radio, leer, nadar y
jugar al tenis. Pueden escribirme también
en inglés y en alemán.

▲▲▲▲▲▲▲▲▲▲▲▲▲▲▲▲▲▲▲▲▲▲▲▲▲▲

Nombre: Pedro Manuel Yue
Edad: 17 años
Dirección: Apartado Postal 9054, La Habana 9,
Ciudad Habana C.P.10900, CUBA.
Pasatiempos: Leer, bailar y escuchar
música romántica.

▲▲▲▲▲▲▲▲▲▲▲▲▲▲▲▲▲▲▲▲▲▲▲▲▲▲

Nombre: Esteban Hernández
Edad: 15 años
Dirección: Apartado 8-3009, El Dorado,
PANAMÁ
Pasatiempos: Ir al cine, practicar deportes, jugar
a los videojuegos.

▲▲▲▲▲▲▲▲▲▲▲▲▲▲▲▲▲▲▲▲▲▲▲▲▲▲

Nombre: Bessy Ortiz
Edad: 15 años
Dirección: Res. Carro Grande, Zona 4,
B-12 C. 2111, Tegucigalpa,
D.C. HONDURAS.
Pasatiempos:
Ver televisión, tocar la
flauta, pasear en bicicleta.

Al grano

Now that you have a general
overview of the pen pal ads, you can
scan for more details. See answers below.

C. Imagine that you're organizing a
letter exchange for your Spanish
class. Your classmates have listed
their preferences regarding age
and country where the pen pal
lives. Which pen pal would be
best for each classmate?

1. someone from Venezuela
2. someone who's 14 years old
3. a boy from Panama
4. a 16-year-old girl
5. someone from the United
States
6. someone who lives in the city
of Buenos Aires
7. a 17-year-old boy

D. Now it's time to choose a pen
pal for yourself. You're hoping to
develop a long-term friendship
with someone who shares your
own interests and hobbies.
Whom will you choose if you . . .? See answers below.

1. like to dance
2. like to ride a bike
3. prefer to write letters in
English
4. love listening to music

Whom *won't* you choose if
you . . .?

5. don't like to study
6. don't like video games
7. don't like to swim

E. Escribe un anuncio *(ad)* personal
en español. Usa vocabulario
conocido. Después, lee el
anuncio de un/a compañero/a y
trata de encontrarle un/a amigo/a
por correspondencia *(pen pal)*.
Explícale a tu compañero/a por
qué esta persona es su amigo/a
por correspondencia ideal.
Individual ads will vary.

> Cuaderno para hispanohablantes, pp. 16–19

> Cuaderno de actividades, p. 47, Act. 17

Postreading
Activity E

Connecting through Your Experience
Have students copy their pen pal
ad without putting their name or
street address on it, and then have
them turn it in. Randomly number
the anonymous ads. Tape the ads
around the room. Have students walk
around the room and find the ad of
someone they would like to get to
know. They should copy the number
of the ad they like and that of their
own ad and sit down. Then ask individual students why the pen pal ad
they chose was interesting to them.
You might ask volunteers to say
which ad was theirs.

Native Speakers
Activity E might be a good
homework assignment for your
native speakers or advanced learners.

Answers

C 1. Wilmer Ramírez
2. Gerardo Vargas
3. Esteban Hernández
4. Juana Saldívar
5. Gerardo Vargas
6. Julia Ileana Oliveras
7. Pedro Manuel Yue

D *Answers may vary.*
1. Pedro, Gerardo, or Susana
2. Bessy
3. Julia or Susana
4. Pedro, Julia, Gerardo, Wilmer,
Juana, Juan, or Sandra
5. Wilmer
6. Esteban
7. Julia

Communication for All Students

Thinking Critically
Analyzing Ask students why they think they
see so many cognates in Spanish. Tell them that
English, although a Germanic language, has a
great many loanwords of French origin, and that
both Spanish and French come from Latin; also,

modern Spanish has borrowed many English
words, given the universality of English in the
fashion, travel, and business worlds. Encourage
students with this fact: Spanish may be easier
to learn than they think!

For **Más práctica gramatical** Answer Transparencies, see the *Teaching Transparencies* binder.

Más práctica gramatical

internet

MARCAR: go.hrw.com
PALABRA CLAVE:
WV3 MEXICO-4

Primer paso   **Objectives** Talking about what you like to do; discussing what you and others do during free time

1 Complete the paragraph about what different people do after school by filling in each blank with the correct form of each verb from the box. (**pp. 113, 114**)

cantar	descansar	mirar	dibujar	tocar
pintar	nadar		bailar	
estudiar	escuchar	hablar		cuidar

Después de clases, yo ___1___ en el coro. También ___2___ para la clase de español y ___3___ la televisión. Mi amiga Talía y yo ___4___ en la piscina. Nosotros ___5___ con un grupo de baile también. Tú y Beni ___6___ música en casa, ¿verdad? Y ustedes también ___7___ en el parque. Federico ___8___ y ___9___ para su clase de arte, y también él ___10___ a su hermano. Y Juan Pablo y Luisa ___11___ por teléfono y ___12___ el piano.

2 Answer your friend Pablo's questions about which friends are getting together after school today for different activities. Use the cues in parentheses. (**p. 116**)

MODELO   **¿Quién mira la televisión contigo? (Susana y Benjamín)**
Susana y Benjamín miran la televisión conmigo.

1. ¿Quién canta en el coro contigo? (Diana)
2. ¿Quién estudia contigo? (Carmela y Rafael)
3. ¿Quién practica deportes con Teresa? (tú y Javier)
4. ¿Quién mira la televisión con Gilberto? (Sandra y yo)
5. ¿Quién escucha música con Beatriz? (Víctor)
6. ¿Quién monta en bicicleta conmigo? (yo)
7. ¿Quién toma un refresco con Adolfo? (José Luis)

Answers

1
1. canto
2. estudio
3. miro
4. nadamos
5. bailamos
6. escuchan
7. descansan
8. pinta/dibuja
9. dibuja/pinta
10. cuida
11. hablan
12. tocan

2
1. Diana canta en el coro conmigo.
2. Carmela y Rafael estudian conmigo.
3. Tú y Javier practican deportes con ella.
4. Sandra y yo miramos la televisión con él.
5. Víctor escucha música con ella.
6. Yo monto en bicicleta contigo.
7. José Luis toma un refresco con él.

Grammar Resources for Chapter 4

The **Más práctica gramatical** activities are designed as supplemental activities for the grammatical concepts presented in the chapter. You might use them as additional practice, for review, or for assessment.

For more grammar presentations, review, and practice, refer to the following:
• Cuaderno de gramática
• Grammar Tutor for Students of Spanish

• Grammar Summary on pp. R7–R11.
• Cuaderno de actividades
• Grammar and Vocabulary quizzes (Testing Program)
• Test Generator on the One-Stop Planner CD-ROM
• Interactive CD-ROM Tutor
• **Juegos interactivos** at <u>go.hrw.com</u>.

3 You're in the café after school. Tell the new student who all the people are. Use **que** to join the two parts of your sentence together. (**p. 117**)

MODELO estudiar en la mesa/Inés
La chica que estudia en la mesa es Inés.

1. tomar refrescos/Carlos y Rafael
2. escuchar música/Alida
3. descansar/Sergio
4. comprar un helado/Laura y Jimena
5. dibujar/Andrés
6. hablar por teléfono/Felipe
7. tocar el piano/María
8. jugar al béisbol/Claudia y Marisol

Segundo paso   **Objective** Telling where people and things are

4 Gabriel le muestra un mapa de su escuela a un nuevo estudiante. Completa sus explicaciones con las formas correctas de **estar**. (**p. 118**)

Mira, Leticia, tú y yo ___1___ aquí, en la cafetería. Las clases de arte y de música ___2___ muy cerca de nosotros. Y la clase de ciencias sociales ___3___ al lado de la clase de arte. El gimnasio y la clase de computación ___4___ aquí. El gimnasio ___5___ al lado de la clase de alemán, y la clase de computación ___6___ al lado de la clase de matemáticas.

5 Everyone you know at school is in a different class right now. Say where the following people are, using the correct forms of **estar** and subject pronouns. (**p. 118**)

MODELO El director Ramos (geografía)
Él está en la clase de geografía.

1. Sara y Guillermo (ciencias sociales)
2. Nacho (gimnasio)
3. mis amigos y yo (cafetería)
4. la profesora Pineda (química)
5. Ricardo y Beto (español)
6. tú (arte)
7. Sofía (matemáticas)

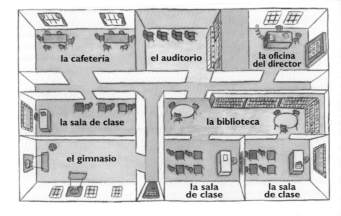

la cafetería   el auditorio   la oficina del director

la sala de clase   la biblioteca

el gimnasio   la sala de clase   la sala de clase

Answers

3 1. Los chicos que toman refrescos son Carlos y Rafael.
2. La chica que escucha música es Alida.
3. El chico que descansa es Sergio.
4. Las chicas que compran un helado son Laura y Jimena.
5. El chico que dibuja es Andrés.
6. El chico que habla por teléfono es Felipe.
7. La chica que toca el piano es María.
8. Las chicas que juegan al béisbol son Claudia y Marisol.

4 1. estamos
2. están
3. está
4. están
5. está
6. está

5 1. Ellos están en la clase de ciencias sociales.
2. Él está en el gimnasio.
3. Nosotros estamos en la cafetería.
4. Ella está en la clase de química.
5. Ellos están en la clase de español.
6. Tú estás en la clase de arte.
7. Ella está en la clase de matemáticas.

Communication for All Students

Group Work

3 Create three sets of 24 strips of paper, each with a portion of a sentence from Activity 3: a subject (**Los chicos, La chica**), a clause (**que toman refrescos, que escucha música**), and a verb phrase (**son Carlos y Rafael, es Alicia**). Divide the class into three groups and distribute the jumbled fragments. See which group is able to arrange eight correct sentences first.

Kinesthetic Learners

4 Divide the class into groups. On cards, depict school buildings and people. Have students label them: **tú y yo, el gimnasio, la cafetería, la clase de inglés**. Tape them to the board. Have each group create sentences using **estar** with prepositions (p. 119) to indicate a location for each. Have a volunteer arrange cards to match the sentences.

For **Más práctica gramatical**
Answer Transparencies, see the
Teaching Transparencies binder.

WV3 MEXICO-4

6 ¿**Tú** o **usted**? Completa las oraciones con la forma correcta del verbo. (**p. 121**)

1. Buenos días, señora Silva. ¿Cómo (está usted/estás) hoy?
2. Oye, Maripili, ¿qué (necesita usted/necesitas) comprar para las clases?
3. Profesora Benavente, ¿(mira usted/miras) la televisión mucho?
4. Suso, ¿a qué hora (trabaja usted/trabajas) hoy? ¿Quieres ir al centro comercial?
5. Señor Durán, ¿(habla usted/hablas) inglés?
6. Margarita, ¿(quiere usted/quieres) montar en bicicleta conmigo después de clases?
7. Sergio, te gustan los deportes, ¿no? ¿Cuántos deportes (practica usted/practicas)?

Tercer paso

Objective Talking about where you and others go during free time

7 Tell where the following people are going after school, using a different location from the box in each sentence. (**p. 123**)

MODELO   **Santiago necesita preparar la cena.**
              Él va a casa.

casa	parque	cine	supermercado
pizzería	gimnasio	piscina	biblioteca

1. A Marcos le gusta mucho la pizza.
2. Virginia necesita comprar unos refrescos para una fiesta.
3. Esteban y Lupe necesitan estudiar.
4. Quiero ver la nueva película.
5. Necesitas caminar con el perro.
6. Mi amigo y yo tomamos una clase de natación.
7. Fernanda y Luisa toman una clase de karate.
8. El profesor Arce necesita descansar.

Answers

6 1. está usted
2. necesitas
3. mira usted
4. trabajas
5. habla usted
6. quieres
7. practicas

7 1. Él va a la pizzería.
2. Ella va al supermercado.
3. Ellos van a la biblioteca.
4. Yo voy al cine.
5. Vas al parque.
6. Nosotros vamos a la piscina.
7. Ellas van al gimnasio.
8. Él va a la casa.

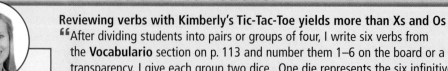

Teacher to Teacher

Kimberly Bromley
Warren Township
High Schools
Gurnee, Illinois

Reviewing verbs with Kimberly's Tic-Tac-Toe yields more than Xs and Os
"After dividing students into pairs or groups of four, I write six verbs from the **Vocabulario** section on p. 113 and number them 1–6 on the board or a transparency. I give each group two dice. One die represents the six infinitive verbs, while the other die represents the six forms of a conjugated verb (1 for first person singular, 2 for second person singular, and so on). Students roll the dice and the first person or group to conjugate the correct verb in the correct form puts an X or O on his or her Tic-Tac-Toe board. The students peer-correct their answers."

STANDARDS: 1.2

8 Use the after-school schedules for Miguel, Merche, and Ana to state on what days they do the activities listed. If an activity is used twice, give both days. (**p. 124**)

MODELO   tomar un refresco en el café
          Merche toma un refresco en el café los miércoles.

	LUNES	MARTES	MIÉRCOLES	JUEVES	VIERNES
Miguel	biblioteca	parque	biblioteca	parque	plaza
Merche	plaza	gimnasio	café	gimnasio	cine
Ana	piscina	clase de baile	piscina	clase de baile	restaurante

1. estudiar en la biblioteca
2. nadar en la piscina
3. ir al parque
4. practicar deportes en el gimnasio
5. trabajar en un restaurante
6. tener clase de baile
7. ver una película con amigos

9 Look back at the after-school schedules for Miguel, Merche, and Ana in the previous activity. Based on that information and the information in the following sentences, tell what day of the week it is. More than one answer is possible in some cases. Guess what day it could be in number 7, based on your own experiences. (**p. 124**)

MODELO   **Miguel está en la biblioteca porque...**
          ...hoy es lunes.

1. Ana está en la piscina porque...
2. Merche va al cine porque...
3. Ana tiene clase de baile porque...
4. Miguel va a la plaza porque...
5. Merche va a la plaza porque...
6. Miguel está en la biblioteca porque...
7. Miguel, Merche y Ana no van a la escuela porque...

Review and Assess

You may wish to assign the **Más práctica gramatical** activities as additional practice or homework after presenting material throughout the chapter. Assign Activity 1 after **Vocabulario** (p. 113) and **Gramática** (p. 114), Activity 2 after **Nota gramatical** (p. 116), Activity 3 after **Nota gramatical** (p. 117), Activities 4–6 after **Nota gramatical** (p. 118) and **Gramática** (p. 121), Activity 7 after

Nota gramatical (p. 123), and Activities 8–9 after **Vocabulario** and **Nota gramatical** (p. 124). To prepare students for the **Paso** Quizzes and Chapter Test, have them do the **Más práctica gramatical** activities in the following order: complete Activities 1–3 before taking Quiz 4-1A or 4-1B; Activities 4–6 before taking Quiz 4-2A or 4-2B; and Activities 7–9 before taking Quiz 4-3A or 4-3B.

Answers

8 1. Miguel estudia en la biblioteca los lunes y los miércoles.
2. Ana nada en la piscina los lunes y los miércoles.
3. Miguel va al parque los martes y los jueves.
4. Merche practica deportes en el gimnasio los martes y los jueves.
5. Ana trabaja en un restaurante los viernes.
6. Ana tiene clase de baile los martes y los jueves.
7. Merche ve una película con amigos los viernes.

9 1. ...hoy es lunes o miércoles.
2. ...hoy es viernes.
3. ...hoy es martes o jueves.
4. ...hoy es viernes.
5. ...hoy es lunes.
6. ...hoy es lunes o miércoles.
7. ...hoy es sábado o domingo.

CAPÍTULO 4

The **Repaso** reviews and integrates all four skills and culture in preparation for the Chapter Test.

Teaching Resources
pp. 132–133

PRINT
▶ Lesson Planner, p. 21
▶ Listening Activities, p. 29
▶ Video Guide, pp. 25–27, 30
▶ Grammar Tutor for Students of Spanish, Chapter 4
▶ Cuaderno para hispanohablantes, pp. 16–20
▶ Standardized Assessment Tutor, Chapter 4

MEDIA
▶ One-Stop Planner
▶ Video Program, Videocassette 2, 17:44–18:40
▶ DVD Tutor, Disc 1
▶ Audio Compact Discs, CD 4, Tr. 18
▶ Interactive CD-ROM Tutor, Disc 1

Answers

2 1. estoy
2. gusta
3. vamos
4. voy
5. hablo
6. habla
7. estudiamos
8. trabajan
9. practican
10. voy
11. camino
12. se llama

4 1. Los lunes a las ocho menos quince va al colegio.
2. Los martes a las cinco habla por teléfono con Claudia.
3. Los lunes a las seis y media practica el basquetbol.
4. Los jueves estudia con Luis por tres horas.
5. Los viernes después de clases toma refrescos con amigos.
6. Los sábados y domingos monta en bicicleta en el parque.

go.
hrw
.com

▮ internet ▮

MARCAR: go.hrw.com
PALABRA CLAVE: WV3 MEXICO-4

CD-ROM **1**
DVD **1**

1 A friend has asked you to listen to some messages left on the answering machine. Take notes about who calls, what they want, and times or days they mention. Script and answers on p. 107H.

CD 4 Tr. 18

Recado Telefónico

Nombre: *Carlos*
Asunto: *10:00, el sábado jugar al tenis en el parque*

2 Complete María Elena's letter to her family using forms of the verbs you've learned. See answers below.

> Queridos papás,
>
> Aquí ___1___ yo en St. Louis. Me ___2___ mucho mi colegio. Es muy grande y está cerca de mi casa. Mis amigos son muy simpáticos. Nosotros ___3___ al partido de fútbol los viernes, y yo ___4___ con Gloria y Linda al centro comercial los sábados. Yo ___5___ inglés, pero Miguel Ángel, un chico de Colombia, ___6___ mejor *(better)*. Todos nosotros ___7___ juntos en la biblioteca y hacemos la tarea. Mis amigos Ricardo y Andrés ___8___ los sábados y domingos en el cine porque necesitan dinero, pero ___9___ al fútbol todas las tardes a las cuatro. Yo ___10___ a casa después de clases y ___11___ con el perro. El perro ___12___ "Spot". Es blanco y negro. Bueno, tengo que estudiar para un examen mañana. ¡Hasta luego!
>
> Un abrazo para todos,
> María Elena

3 With a partner, create a conversation in which Claudia, Rosa, Luis, and María Inés talk about what they do in their free time. Be sure to include times of day and days of the week. Answers will vary.

4 Use these notes to report María Inés' activities during the week. See answers below.

1. lunes (7:45) - ir al colegio
2. martes (5:00) - hablar por teléfono con Claudia
3. lunes (6:30) - practicar el basquetbol
4. jueves - estudiar con Luis por tres horas
5. viernes (después de clases) - tomar refrescos con amigos
6. sábado y domingo - montar en bicicleta en el parque

Apply and Assess

Challenge

2 Have students write questions about the contents of the letter. With a partner, have them write five questions that María Elena's father could have asked her mother about the letter. Each pair might then role-play the conversation between the mother and father. They may wish to include the expression **María Elena dice _____** or simply **Dice _____**.

Slower Pace

3 Allow students to prepare by outlining the conversation or by writing some key words in Spanish before joining their partner.

5 En las siguientes oraciones, corrige *(correct)* las oraciones falsas. Basa tus respuestas en las **Notas culturales** y el **Panorama cultural** de este capítulo. See answers below.

1. El paseo ya no existe en Latinoamérica.

2. En los países hispanohablantes *(Spanish-speaking countries)* los colegios tienen muchas actividades después de clases.

3. Muchos atletas hispanos participaron *(participated)* en los Juegos Olímpicos *(Olympic Games)* en el 2000.

4. El paseo no es muy común en España.

5. Por lo general, los jóvenes *(young people)* usan el **tú** para hablar con su padre o su madre.

---

6 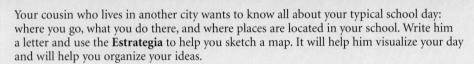 **Vamos a escribir**

Your cousin who lives in another city wants to know all about your typical school day: where you go, what you do there, and where places are located in your school. Write him a letter and use the **Estrategia** to help you sketch a map. It will help him visualize your day and will help you organize your ideas.

Estrategia para escribir
Use drawings to help you write and to organize your thoughts and ideas. If you can see your ideas on paper, you'll be able to write more effectively.

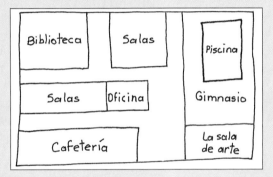

1. Draw a simple map of your school and label five places you go during a typical day.

2. Under each place write two activities you do there.

3. Tell what you do in each place and where it's located. Use phrases like **al lado de, cerca de,** and **lejos de.**

---

7 **Situación**

Work with two or three classmates to create a conversation. You want to get together to do something for fun, but you're all really busy. Discuss your schedules and responsibilities, and decide on the activity, the time, and the place where you'll meet.

Cuaderno para hispanohablantes, p. 20

Apply and Assess

Process Writing

6 Remind students to take each writing task through stages: prewriting, rough draft, revision, and final draft. In the prewriting stage, they can use lists, maps, charts, outlines, story webs, or other graphic organizers to help structure their thoughts before writing. As they prepare their rough draft, they can organize their writing chronologically, thematically, or in order of importance. In the prewriting and rough draft stages, it is important to classify information so that it will be useful later. When students revise their rough draft, they should use tools such as dictionaries, thesauruses, grammar references, online databases, or encyclopedias to improve their writing. Final drafts should incorporate changes made during revisions and last-minute corrections.

Pair Work

5 You may wish to let students work with a partner to answer the questions on cultural content. In addition to correcting the false statements, they should discuss how the answers are similar to and different from their own culture.

Teacher Note

6 It is helpful in the development of writing skills for students to edit one another's work. You may wish to provide copies of the Peer Editing Rubric on page 9 of the *Alternative Assessment Guide* for the **Vamos a escribir** writing assignments. Students complete the rubric by checking content and proofreading their classmate's work.

📁 Portfolio

6 **Written** Your students might want to include this activity in their Portfolio. For Portfolio information, see *Alternative Assessment Guide,* pp. iv–17.

Native Speakers

7 After completing this activity, have native speakers choose one of the corrected five sentences and write a paragraph on the topic to include in their journals. Remind them that they can use cluster diagrams (p. 93) or other visual aids to help structure their essay.

Answers
5 1. El paseo todavía existe en Latinoamérica.
2. En los países hispanohablantes los colegios no tienen muchas actividades después de clases.
3. Cierta
4. El paseo es muy común en España.
5. A veces, los jóvenes usan el **tú** para hablar con su padre o su madre.

Teacher Note

This page is intended to prepare students for the Chapter Test. It is a brief checklist of the major points covered in the chapter. The students should be reminded that it is a checklist only and does not necessarily reflect everything that will appear on the Chapter Test.

Answers

3 *Answers may vary.*
1. Rosa está en la biblioteca.
2. Claudia está en el centro comercial.
3. Geraldo está en el parque.
4. Sofía está en el gimnasio.
5. Nosotros estamos en el cine.
6. Estoy en casa.

4
1. El supermercado está al lado del parque.
2. La librería está lejos de la tienda.
3. El gimnasio está cerca de la biblioteca.

5
1. Mariana va a la librería para comprar libros, cuadernos y lápices.
2. Pedro va a la escuela para hablar con su profesor de inglés.
3. Lupe va a la casa para hablar con su amiga.
4. La señora Suárez y su hermana van a la piscina para nadar.
5. Carlos y Adriana van al correo para comprar estampillas.
6. Un amigo y yo vamos al parque para jugar al tenis.

A ver si puedo...

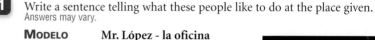

Can you talk about what you like to do?
p. 113

1 Write a sentence telling what these people like to do at the place given. Answers may vary.

MODELO   Mr. López - la oficina
              Le gusta trabajar.

1. Cecilia - la piscina
2. Gustavo - el centro comercial
3. Diego y Berta - una fiesta
4. Carlos y yo - el parque
5. Linda y Eva - la biblioteca
6. yo - el colegio

Can you discuss what you and others do during free time?
p. 114

2 How would you tell someone that you . . .? Answers will vary.
1. play the guitar   4. paint and draw
2. wash the car   5. watch television
3. prepare dinner   6. swim in the pool

Can you tell where people and things are? p. 118

3 Write sentences in Spanish telling where the following people are. See answers below.
1. Rosa is reading books and must be very quiet.
2. Claudia is shopping for gifts for her parents.
3. Geraldo is walking the dogs.
4. Sofía is exercising and lifting weights.
5. You and your friends are watching a movie.
6. You're talking on the phone.

4 How would you tell a visitor who needs directions that . . .? See answers below.
1. the supermarket is next to the park
2. the bookstore is far from the store
3. the gym is near the library

Can you talk about where you and others go during free time?
p. 123

5 Create a sentence telling where each person is going and why. See answers below.

MODELO   Mr. Suárez is really thirsty.
              Él va al restaurante para tomar un refresco.

1. Mariana wants to buy some books, notebooks, and pencils.
2. Pedro needs to talk to his English teacher.
3. Lupe wants to spend time with her friend.
4. Mrs. Suárez and her sister want to go swimming.
5. Carlos and Adriana need to buy stamps.
6. You and a friend want to play tennis.

6 Think of a typical week in your life. Write a sentence telling at what time and on which day you're at the following places. Answers will vary.
1. el centro comercial   3. la casa de un amigo o una amiga
2. el cine   4. el parque

Review and Assess

Cooperative Learning

To assess knowledge of material presented in **De antemano**, have students form groups of three to create directed dialogues. One student plays the role of a parent, another the son or daughter, and a third a friend of the opposite sex to be introduced. The friend answers a few questions about what he or she likes to do. The son or daughter must ask permission to do a variety of things with the friend. The questions that ensue elicit responses as to where they will be at certain hours. Use one of the oral assessment rubrics (pages 3–4, *Alternative Assessment Guide*) to grade for correct use of grammar in Chapter 4, especially expressing time, the conventions of introduction, place vocabulary, fluidity, and creativity.

Primer paso

Talking about what you like to do

A mí me gusta + inf.	I (emphatic) like to . . .	pintar	to paint	jugar (ue) a	to play (a sport or game)
¿A quién le gusta + inf.?	Who likes to . . . ?	la piscina	swimming pool	montar en bicicleta	to ride a bicycle
A ti, ¿qué te gusta hacer?	What do you (emphatic) like to do?	por eso	that's why	pasar el rato con amigos	to spend time with friends
		¿Quién?	Who?	el piano	piano
		sacar la basura	to take out the trash	practicar	to practice
bailar	to dance			preparar	to prepare
cantar	to sing	**Discussing what you and others do during free time**		que	that, which, who
cuidar a tu hermano/a	to take care of your brother/sister	al	to the	¿Qué haces después de clases?	What do you do after school?
descansar en el parque	to rest in the park	antes de	before		
		caminar con el perro	to walk the dog	el refresco	soft drink
dibujar	to draw	la cena	dinner	regresar	to return
escuchar música	to listen to music	con	with	el restaurante	restaurant
estudiar	to study	conmigo	with me	tocar	to play (an instrument)
hablar por teléfono	to talk on the phone	contigo	with you		
lavar el carro	to wash the car	después de	after	tomar	to drink, to take
lavar la ropa	to wash the clothes	(en) el tiempo libre	(during) free time	trabajar	to work
mirar la televisión	to watch TV	la guitarra	guitar		
nadar	to swim	el helado	ice cream		

Segundo paso

Telling where people and things are

al lado de	next to	debajo de	under, beneath	el supermercado	supermarket
allá	there	¿Dónde?	Where?	la tienda	store
aquí	here	encima de	on top of	el trabajo	work, job
la biblioteca	library	estar	to be	usted	you (formal)
la casa	house, home	el gimnasio	gym	ustedes	you (plural, formal)
el centro	downtown	lejos de	far from		
cerca de	near	nosotros/nosotras	we	vosotros/vosotras	you (plural, informal)
el cine	movie theater	el parque	park		
el correo	post office	el paseo	walk, stroll (social)		

Tercer paso

Talking about where you and others go during free time

¿Adónde?	Where (to)?	el jueves	Thursday	el sábado	Saturday
¿Adónde vas?	Where are you going?	el lunes	Monday	la semana	week
		el martes	Tuesday	ver	to see
el día	day	el miércoles	Wednesday	el viernes	Friday
el domingo	Sunday	para + inf.	in order to . . .		
el fin de semana	weekend	la película	movie		

Game

Clave Divide the class into two teams. On a dry-erase board, chalkboard, or flipchart paper, write various Spanish phrases, verbs, and nouns. Give a verbal clue describing one of the items listed. **(el sábado y el domingo)** A representative from each team points to the words described. **(el fin de semana)** The first to correctly identify it circles the item with that team's colored marker. The team with the most words circled at the end wins.

Chapter 4 Assessment

▸ **Testing Program**
Chapter Test, pp. 91–96
Audio Compact Discs, CD 4, Trs. 22–23
Speaking Test, p. 344

▸ **Alternative Assessment Guide**
Performance Assessment, p. 35
Portfolio Assessment, p. 21
CD-ROM Assessment, p. 49

▸ **Interactive CD-ROM Tutor, Disc 1**

¡A hablar!
¡A escribir!

▸ **Standardized Assessment Tutor**
Chapter 4

▸ **One-Stop Planner, Disc 1**
Test Generator
Chapter 4

Review and Assess

Game

Play **Mímica** to review verbs and prepositions. Write action verbs and prepositional phrases on cards. **(nadar, debajo de la mesa).** Divide the class into teams and give one card to each student. Taking turns, students act out their word or words while the other team guesses in Spanish. You may consider limiting the time that each team has to guess. As a challenge, have the teams combine a number of students' cards to create sentences, assigning nouns and other necessary parts of speech to individuals. The team acts out its string of words while the other team tries to figure out the sentence that is being presented.

Teaching Resources
pp. 136–139

PRINT
▶ Lesson Planner, p. 22
▶ Video Guide, pp. 31–32

MEDIA
▶ One-Stop Planner
▶ Video Program, Videocassette 2, 18:54–20:56
▶ DVD Tutor, Disc 1
▶ Interactive CD-ROM Tutor, Disc 2
▶ Map Transparency 6

 go.hrw.com
WV3 FLORIDA

 Using the Almanac and Map

Terms in the Almanac

• **La bandera:** The Florida state flag features crossed diagonal red bars on a white field. Its centerpiece is the state seal with a Native American woman strewing flowers, a sabal palm (the state tree), a steamboat, and the rising sun in the background.

• **Miami:** The name comes from the Native American word **Mayaimi,** which means *big water,* and perhaps referred to Lake Okeechobee.

• **Los Seminole:** The Seminole fled from the British in Georgia and Alabama and settled in south Florida in the 18th century. In 1830, the U.S. government ordered them deported to the Oklahoma Indian Territory. The Seminole preferred to fight rather than leave their homes. Most ultimately surrendered and were forcibly resettled, or were driven deep into the Everglades. A few descendants of those who escaped still live in the Everglades today.

CAPÍTULOS 5 y 6

¡Ven conmigo a la Florida!

Población: Más de 16.000.000 de habitantes, de los cuales más de 16% son de origen hispano

Área: 58.664 millas cuadradas (151.940 km²)

Capital: Tallahassee

Ciudad principal: Miami y área metropolitana, 3.711.000 habitantes

Clima: subtropical

Economía: manufactura, turismo, productos de frutas cítricas, caña de azúcar, pesca comercial, electrónica, comercio con Latinoamérica

Historia: Poblada por indígenas norteamericanos antes de la llegada del explorador español Ponce de León en 1513. Colonia francesa establecida en 1564. Colonia española establecida en 1565. Poblada, en parte, por los Seminole en el siglo XVIII. España cedió el territorio a los Estados Unidos en 1819.

 WV3 FLORIDA   VIDEO   CD-ROM 2 DVD 1

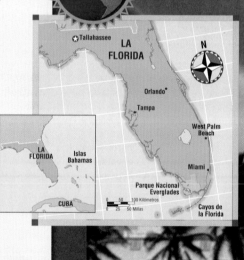

La zona "art deco" de la ciudad de Miami Beach ▶

Connections and Comparisons

Art Link

The Art Deco District of Miami Beach, a recognized national treasure, became the youngest historic district in the nation when placed on the *National Register of Historic Places* in 1979. Art Deco was a decorative style used mostly in architecture, furniture, pottery, and textiles from 1925–1940. It is characterized by geometric designs, bold colors, and use of plastic, chrome, and other industrial materials. Ask students to research Art Deco to find how it reflected the values of the times. (Artists sought to characterize the new modernity, while designers had mass-production in mind.) Ask them to think of famous examples of Art Deco in architecture. (the Chrysler Building, Radio City Music Hall, New York) Do students associate Art Deco with architectural styles considered typically Hispanic?

MAPQUEST.COM™

HRW
Atlas Interactivo Mundial

go.hrw.com

Have students use the interactive atlas at <u>go.hrw.com</u> to find out more about the geography of Florida and complete the Map Activities below.

Map Activities

You may want to have students refer to the map on *Pupil's Edition* page xxix.

- Ask students to identify the two states that border Florida. (Alabama and Georgia)

- Have students measure the distance between Miami and Havana. (approximately 237 miles) What significance might this short distance have? (Miami boasts a large Cuban-American population and heavy Cuban influence in its food, music, business, and media.)

- Tourism is crucial to Florida's economy. Ask students to locate some of the tourist spots on the map and to discuss the attractions.

CNN enEspañol.com

Have students check the **CNN en español** Web site for news on Florida. The **CNN en español** site is also a good source of timely, high-interest readings for Spanish students.

Cultures and Communities

Culture Note

Southern Florida has a diverse population with a Hispanic flavor. Many of the state's Hispanic residents are of Cuban heritage and came to the United States after 1959, dissatisfied with the results of Fidel Castro's revolution. Cubans who came to the United States in the early 1960s had successful academic, business, or professional careers in Cuba. Some immigrants overcame difficult circumstances to continue careers and excel in many fields including politics, business, sports, art, and entertainment. (political leaders U.S. Rep. Lincoln Díaz-Balart, former Governor Bob Martínez; baseball player Luis González; musicians Willy Chirino, Celia Cruz, and Gloria Estefan; actor Andy García; and financier and patron of the arts Alberto Vilar.)

Using the Photo Essay

1 Los arrecifes de coral Tell students that Florida is the site of the first undersea park in the continental U.S., the John Pennekamp Coral Reef State Park near Key Largo. Florida is warm year-round and has more coastline than any other state except Alaska.

2 Las tierras pantanosas At the turn of the century, Miami began to boom, and the Everglades were in danger of being destroyed. In 1916, the Florida Federation of Women's Clubs purchased the first 4,000 acres of what would become Everglades National Park and set them aside for preservation. Southern Florida's metropolitan areas kept growing, but efforts continued to be made to protect the Everglades. In 1994, the Everglades Forever Act was signed, protecting the quality of water entering the park. Other conservation efforts have included expansion of the park and restoration of a more natural water flow to the wetlands.

Additional Vocabulary

You may want to present the following words with the Location Opener:

bucear   *to scuba dive*
la sombrilla   *parasol*
jugar al ajedrez   *to play chess*
jugar al dominó   *to play dominoes*
el arrecife
   de coral   *coral reef*
el pantano   *wetland*
la garza   *heron*

Language Note

The English word *alligator* comes from the Spanish **el lagarto** (*lizard*).

La Florida

Florida has many attractions, such as the Kennedy Space Center, the wetlands of the Everglades, and hundreds of miles of fantastic beaches. The Spanish came in the early 1500s, followed by other European settlers. A wide variety of ethnic heritages from other countries and other parts of the U.S. have greatly enriched the peninsula's population.

internet

MARCAR: go.hrw.com
PALABRA CLAVE:
   WV3 FLORIDA

1 Los arrecifes de coral
The warm waters of Biscayne Bay and the nearby Gulf Stream provide a fine setting for year-round water sports. Coral reefs and keys (small islands) provide a magical world for scuba divers to explore.

2 Las tierras pantanosas
Home to alligators, manatees, and a riot of colorful aquatic birds, Everglades wetlands are one of the United States' great natural treasures.

Cultures and Communities

Culture Note
Thanks to its Latin influence, southern Florida is virtually bilingual. Spanish is heard everywhere: in schools and shops, on the streets, and over the airwaves. Spanish-language radio, television, and newspapers are popular and profitable. Florida's bilingualism is doubtless a strong attraction for Spanish-speaking tourists and business people from around the world.

Background Information
The Florida East Coast Railroad was extended to Miami and completed in 1896. The railway boosted tourism and business in the region and enabled Miami to reach a population of 250,000 over the next fifty years.

Chapters 5 and 6

will introduce you to Patricia, José Luis, and Raquel, some students who live in Miami. Spanish speakers make up about two-thirds of the city's population. The great majority of Spanish speakers here are of Cuban heritage. You'll have a chance to find out a little about what ordinary life is like in this extraordinary North American city!

❸ El Festival de la Calle Ocho
People of many backgrounds converge in Miami to play and hear Caribbean music.

❹ La Piscina de Coral
The Venetian Municipal Pool, carved out of solid coral, attracts visitors from around the world.

❺ Un partido de ajedrez
Little Havana is the symbolic center of South Florida's thriving Cuban community, a place to enjoy a delicious meal or a game of chess or dominoes with good friends.

❸ El Festival de la Calle Ocho
People who visit Miami during Carnival celebrations may be struck by the bright colors and wide variety of costumes worn by different ethnic groups. Musicians enjoy a great deal of exposure as well each year during the **Festival de la Calle Ocho,** which culminates in Carnival Miami. Crowds of people walk along the 23 city blocks that are roped off for the festival. They can sample snacks from food stands and hear musicians on several stages.

❹ La Piscina de Coral Built in 1924 by George Merrick, the Venetian Pool is part of Coral Gables, one of the first fully planned communities in the nation.

❺ Un partido de ajedrez
El parque Máximo Gómez, better known as Domino Park, is located on **la Calle Ocho,** in the heart of Miami's Little Havana **(la Pequeña Habana)**. The park is popular with members of the Cuban American community who come to play dominoes and chess. Ask students which article of the men's clothing would suggest that they might be Cuban. (their **guayabera** shirts)

Connections and Comparisons

History/Geography Link

- Florida and the states bordering Mexico bear the unmistakable stamp of Spanish and Latin American influence. Ask students which states in the United States reveal a strong French heritage. (Louisiana, northern New England)

- Ask students if they can think of a Caribbean island that was colonized by both the French and the Spanish. (Hispaniola, divided between Haiti, a former French colony, and the Dominican Republic, a former Spanish colony) Have them locate it on the map on page xxvii.

Capítulo 5: El ritmo de la vida
Chapter Overview

De antemano pp. 142–144	¿Cómo es el ritmo de tu vida?

	FUNCTIONS	**GRAMMAR**	**VOCABULARY**	**RE-ENTRY**
Primer paso pp. 145–147	• Discussing how often you do things, p. 145	• Negation, p. 145 • The question words **¿quién?** and **¿quiénes?**, p. 146	• Describing how often things are done, p. 145	• Present tense of regular **-ar** verbs (**Capítulo 4**) • **¿quién?** (**Capítulo 4**)
Segundo paso pp. 148–153	• Talking about what you and your friends like to do together, p. 148 • Talking about what you do during a typical week, p. 151	• Indirect object pronoun **les**, and **a ustedes, a ellos**, p. 149 • **-er** and **-ir** verbs, p. 150	• Typical activities, p. 149 • Food, pastimes, p. 149	• **gustar** (**Capítulo 3**) • Subject pronouns (**Capítulo 4**) • Gender (**Capítulo 1**)
Tercer paso pp. 154–157	• Giving today's date, p. 154 • Talking about the weather, p. 156	• Giving today's date, p. 154	• Months of the year, seasons, p. 154 • Describing the weather, p. 156	• Days of the week (**Capítulo 4**)

Letra y sonido p. 157	**Accent marks** Audio CD 5, Track 11	**Dictado** Audio CD 5, Tracks 12–15	
Vamos a leer pp. 158–159	**Deportes en el agua**	**Reading Strategy:** Using context to guess meaning	
Más práctica gramatical	**pp. 160–163** **Primer paso,** pp. 160–161	**Segundo paso,** pp. 161–162	**Tercer paso,** pp. 162–163
Review pp. 164–167	**Repaso,** pp. 164–165 **Vamos a escribir,** p. 165 Making a writing plan	**A ver si puedo...,** p. 166	**Vocabulario,** p. 167

CULTURE

- **Realia, Tira cómica,** p. 147
- **Nota cultural,** Getting together with friends, p. 150
- **A lo nuestro,** Expressions of frequency, p. 151
- **Panorama cultural, ¿Cómo es una semana típica?,** p. 153

- **Nota cultural,** The seasons of the year in South America, p. 155
- **A lo nuestro,** Weather expressions, p. 157

Capítulo 5: El ritmo de la vida
Chapter Resources

PRINT

Lesson Planning

One-Stop Planner

Lesson Planner with Substitute Teacher Lesson Plans, pp. 23–27, 69

Student Make-Up Assignments
- Make-Up Assignment Copying Masters, Chapter 5

Listening and Speaking

TPR Storytelling Book, pp. 17–20

Listening Activities
- Student Response Forms for Listening Activities, pp. 35–37
- Additional Listening Activities 5-1 to 5-6, pp. 39–41
- Additional Listening Activities (song), p. 42
- Scripts and Answers, pp. 122–126

Video Guide
- Teaching Suggestions, pp. 33–35
- Activity Masters, pp. 36–38
- Scripts and Answers, pp. 96–97, 115

Activities for Communication
- Communicative Activities, pp. 25–30
- Realia and Teaching Suggestions, pp. 95–99
- Situation Cards, pp. 145–146

Reading and Writing

Reading Strategies and Skills Handbook, Chapter 5

¡Lee conmigo! 1, Chapter 5

Cuaderno de actividades, pp. 49–60

Grammar

Cuaderno de gramática, pp. 37–44

Grammar Tutor for Students of Spanish, Chapter 5

Assessment

Testing Program
- Grammar and Vocabulary Quizzes, **Paso** Quizzes, and Chapter Test, pp. 105–122
- Score Sheet, Scripts and Answers, pp. 123–130

Alternative Assessment Guide
- Portfolio Assessment, p. 22
- Performance Assessment, p. 36
- CD-ROM Assessment, p. 50

Student Make-Up Assignments
- Alternative Quizzes, Chapter 5

Standardized Assessment Tutor
- Reading, pp. 17–19
- Writing, p. 20
- Math, pp. 25–26

Native Speakers

Cuaderno para hispanohablantes, pp. 21–25

MEDIA

 Online Activities
- Juegos interactivos
- Actividades Internet

 Video Program
- Videocassette 2
- Videocassette 5 (captioned version)

 Interactive CD-ROM Tutor, Disc 2

 **DVD Tutor,** Disc 1

 Audio Compact Discs
- Textbook Listening Activities, CD 5, Tracks 1–16
- Additional Listening Activities, CD 5, Tracks 22–28
- Assessment Items, CD 5, Tracks 17–21

 Teaching Transparencies
- Situations 5-1 to 5-3
- Vocabulary 5-A to 5-C
- **De antemano**
- **Más práctica gramatical** Answers
- **Cuaderno de gramática** Answers

One-Stop Planner CD-ROM

Use the **One-Stop Planner CD-ROM with Test Generator** to aid in lesson planning and pacing.

For each chapter, the **One-Stop Planner** includes:

- Editable lesson plans with direct links to teaching resources
- Printable worksheets from resource books
- Direct launches to the HRW Internet activities
- Video and audio segments
- Test Generator
- Clip Art for vocabulary items

Capítulo 5: El ritmo de la vida
Projects ···········

Calendarios

In this class project students create a day calendar. They will prepare a matte board for the class with the day of the week, the date, the month, and the current weather and temperature. The class may designate a different student each day to update the information.

MATERIALS

✄ **Students may need**
- Large matte board
- Velcro®
- Large-tip colored markers
- 4×6 colored index cards
- 4×6 index card box

SUGGESTED SEQUENCE

1. Divide students into four groups.

2. Have Group 1 write and letter the following questions and answers on the matte board, and place a strip of Velcro® in the appropriate spaces as indicated below.

   A. ¿Qué día de la semana es hoy? *(Velcro®)*

   B. ¿Cuál es la fecha?
   Hoy es el *(Velcro®)* de *(Velcro®)*.

   C. ¿Qué tiempo hace? *(Velcro®)*

   D. ¿Cuál es la temperatura?
   Estamos a *(Velcro®)* grados.

3. Have Group 2 prepare index cards with the appropriate answers for questions A and C, and place a strip of Velcro® on the back of each index card.

   Day cards: **lunes, martes, miércoles, jueves, viernes**

   Weather phrases: **Hace frío, Hace calor, Hace mal tiempo, Hace buen tiempo, Llueve, Nieva, Hace viento, Hace sol, Está nublado**

4. Group 3 prepares index cards with the appropriate answers for question B and places Velcro© on the back of each index card.

   Number cards: **1–31**

   Month cards: **enero, febrero, marzo, abril, mayo, junio, julio, agosto, septiembre, octubre, noviembre, diciembre**

5. Group 4 prepares number cards for temperatures and places Velcro® on the back of each index card.

6. Have the class designate the first student to place the appropriate information for that day. The rest of the cards may be kept in a box near the matte board.

7. Suggest that the class create a schedule for when each student updates the information on the matte board.

GRADING THE PROJECT

Suggested point distribution: (total = 100 points)
Completeness..25
Content 25
Grammar and vocabulary 25
Creativity..25

Games ·······························

La fecha en diez preguntas

In this game students practice asking questions and use critical thinking to determine a date.

Procedure Write a date (day and month) on a piece of paper. Students take turns asking questions answerable by **sí** or **no** to determine the date. Those who guess the date with ten questions or fewer win.

Give examples of sharply focused questions. They should include **antes** or **después**: (¿Es antes de junio? ¿Es después de marzo? ¿Es antes del 15?)

Individual Needs Encourage students to determine the date with just five questions.

Tic-Tac-Toe

In this game students practice vocabulary terms and sentence construction with input from classmates.

Procedure Draw a Tic-Tac-Toe grid on the board. On pieces of paper, write new words. Tape papers face down on each square. Members of two teams take turns picking a word from a square and using it in a sentence. If the sentence is logical, the student marks an **X** or an **O** in the square chosen. If not, the other team attempts to do so. If the second team fails, replace the word with a new one. The team first connecting three squares in a line wins. (You can make the game more challenging by using a grid of four by four squares.)

Storytelling

Mini-cuento

This story may be used with Teaching Transparency 5-2. The **mini-cuento** *can be told and retold in different formats, acted out, written, and read aloud, to give students additional opportunities to practice all four skills. The following story relates two* **novios'** *day at the* **Lago Encantado.**

Los novios Rogelio y Beatriz pasan un fin de semana en el Lago Encantado, y allí ven a muchas personas que conocen. Es el 5 de junio, y es un día fantástico. Por eso disfrutan la belleza en el muelle. Ven a María y a Juanita, que pasan en barco. Pescan, pero no sacan nada. La familia Gómez está también en el agua caminando cerca de la orilla. En la distancia, hay un barco amarrado a un árbol, pero no hay nadie adentro. A Ricardo y a Julia les gusta hacer ejercicio. Están contentos al correr por la playa. Adriana y su hija Sandra acampan con frecuencia, y este fin de semana van también al Lago Encantado. En este momento charlan y comen unos sándwiches. Beatriz y Rogelio deciden tomar el barquito desocupado para dar un paseo. Pero no pueden. El perro Duque está furioso, y ladra porque están en el muelle con él. ¡Él cree que es su territorio! Todos están contentos excepto el perro Duque.

and merengue are especially highlighted during this festive event, and some of the most popular Latin musicians, including Celia Cruz and Gloria Estefan, have performed for crowds of up to a million people. To give your students a sample of the music one might hear in the streets of Little Havana, play "Guantanamera" on Audio CD 6 and ask the class to identify different instruments in the song. You might give them a copy of the lyrics found on p. 50 of the *Listening Activities* book, blanking out selected words to be filled in as they listen. Then have small groups of students make plans for a block party that would celebrate their own city or region. What representative songs, artists, and food would they choose and why? To practice Chapter 5 vocabulary, have the groups specify what time of year the event should take place and why.

Receta

Cuban cuisine is popular in South Florida, where many Cubans have settled. Dishes with plantains are common in Cuba, which shares a Spanish and African cultural heritage with much of the rest of the Caribbean. Fried, baked, and puréed plantains are typical in Cuban and African cuisine. The following recipe is for fried sweet plantains, which make a delicious snack or dessert.

Traditions

Festivales

The annual Calle Ocho Festival in Miami's Little Havana has become a major tourist attraction since its inception in 1977. This enormous block party, which takes place in March, celebrates Hispanic culture, food, and music. Salsa

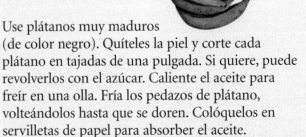

PLÁTANOS FRITOS

para 5 personas

2 plátanos *(plantains)* muy maduros

aceite para freír

azúcar (opcional)

Use plátanos muy maduros (de color negro). Quíteles la piel y corte cada plátano en tajadas de una pulgada. Si quiere, puede revolverlos con el azúcar. Caliente el aceite para freír en una olla. Fría los pedazos de plátano, volteándolos hasta que se doren. Colóquelos en servilletas de papel para absorber el aceite.

Capítulo 5: El ritmo de la vida
Technology

Videocassette 2, Videocassette 5 (captioned version)
DVD Tutor, Disc 1
See Video Guide, pages 33–38.

DVD/Video ....

De antemano • ¿Cómo es el ritmo de tu vida?

Students in Miami prepare a news broadcast program for their high school. José Luis gives the national weather forecast, and Raquel interviews students about what they do during their free time. After Raquel's last interview, there is a problem with the camera in the studio and the broadcast is interrupted.

A continuación

The students resolve the camera problem and finish their news broadcast. The next day they show Armando, the new student from Panama, around the gardens of Vizcaya.

¿Cómo es una semana típica?

Teenagers from Ecuador, Venezuela, and Argentina tell us what they usually do during the week and on weekends. In additional interviews, people from various Spanish-speaking countries tell us what a typical week is like for them.

Videoclips

• **Pronóstico del tiempo:** weather report from Costa Rica

Interactive CD-ROM Tutor ....

Activity	Activity Type	Pupil's Edition Page
En contexto	*Interactive Conversation*	
1. Así se dice	Imagen y sonido	p. 145
	¡Exploremos!	
	¡Identifiquemos!	
2. Gramática	¡A escoger!	p. 145
3. Vocabulario	¡Super memoria!	p. 149
4. Gramática	¿Qué falta?	p. 150
5. Vocabulario	¡Super memoria!	pp. 154–156
6. Vocabulario	¡A escoger!	p. 154
Panorama cultural	¿Cómo es una semana típica?	p. 153
¡A hablar!	*Guided recording*	pp. 164–165
¡A escribir!	*Guided writing*	pp. 164–165

Teacher Management System

Launch the program, type "admin" in the password area, and press RETURN. Log on to **www.hrw.com/CDROMTUTOR** for a detailed explanation of the Teacher Management System.

DVD Tutor ....

The *DVD Tutor* contains all material from the *Video Program* as described above. Spanish captions are available for use at your discretion for all sections of the video. The *DVD Tutor* also provides a variety of video-based activities that assess students' understanding of the **De antemano, A continuación,** and **Panorama cultural.**

This part of the *DVD Tutor* may be used on any DVD video player connected to a television or video monitor.

In addition to the video material and the video-based comprehension activities, the *DVD Tutor* also contains the entire *Interactive CD-ROM Tutor* in DVD-ROM format. Each DVD disc contains the activities from all 12 chapters of the *Interactive CD-ROM Tutor.*

This part of the *DVD Tutor* may be used on a Macintosh® or Windows® computer with a DVD-ROM drive.

One-Stop Planner CD-ROM

To preview all resources available for this chapter, use the **One-Stop Planner CD-ROM**, Disc 2.

Internet Connection ....

MARCAR: go.hrw.com
PALABRA CLAVE:
WV3 FLORIDA-5

*Have students explore the __go.hrw.com__ Web site for many online resources covering all chapters. All Chapter 5 resources are available under the keyword **WV3 FLORIDA-5**. Interactive games help students practice the material and provide them with immediate feedback. You will also find a printable worksheet that provides Internet activities that lead to a comprehensive online research project.*

Juegos interactivos

You can use the interactive activities in this chapter

- to practice grammar, vocabulary, and chapter functions
- as homework
- as an assessment option
- as a self-test
- to prepare for the Chapter Test

Actividades Internet

Students find out what the weather is like today in Miami. Based on their findings, they write activities they would like to do there.

- To prepare for the **Hoja de actividades,** have students watch the dramatic episode on Videocassette 2.
- After completing the activity sheet, ask students to choose a Spanish-speaking city with a very different climate than Miami's and do the same activity. Encourage students to learn more about that city than just the weather: what can they do there? what are typical leisure activities? what do people do at other times of year?

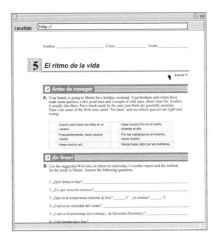

Proyecto

Students work in pairs: one student is a travel agent, and the other is a client. The agent asks the client what activities he or she enjoys. Based on that information, the pair searches online together for a Spanish-speaking city that offers those activities this time of year. They plan a three-day vacation for the client. You might have them post the itinerary on a personal Web site.

Capítulo 5: El ritmo de la vida
Textbook Listening Activities Scripts

Primer paso

6 p. 145

— Hola, Teresa, ¿qué tal?

— Bien, Carlos, ¿y tú?

— ¡Fantástico! Oye, ¿cómo va todo en el trabajo?

— Bien...

— ¿Está todavía Alejandro?

— Sí... Alejandro está allí todos los días. Trabaja mucho.

— ¿Y los otros?

— Bueno... Maite trabaja los fines de semana. Ramón no está aquí mucho; trabaja sólo cuando tiene tiempo los jueves.

— ¿Y Flora? ¿Todavía trabaja con ustedes?

— Sí... Flora siempre trabaja los lunes, y a veces los jueves.

— ¿Y qué pasa con Juan Luis?

— Ay, no sé. Juan Luis nunca está aquí. Qué lástima, ¿verdad?

Answers to Activity 6
1. D, Juan Luis, nunca
2. B, Maite, los fines de semana
3. A, Alejandro, todos los días
4. E, Flora, siempre los lunes, a veces los jueves
5. C, Ramón, sólo cuando tiene tiempo los jueves

Segundo paso

13 p. 148

GLORIA   Oye, Carlos, ¿qué les gusta a ti y a Eddie? ¿Les gusta practicar un deporte?

CARLOS   Bueno, a mí me gusta esquiar, pero a Eddie no.

GLORIA   ¿Les gusta bucear juntos?

CARLOS   Pues sí, nos gusta bucear juntos. Especialmente los fines de semana.

GLORIA   Eddie, ¿te gusta acampar con frecuencia?

EDDIE   A mí me gusta mucho. Pero a Carlos no le gusta.

GLORIA   Pero a ustedes les gusta pescar, ¿no?

CARLOS   ¿Pescar? No, no pescamos nunca.

Answers to Activity 13
1. a
2. c
3. b
4. d

18 p. 152

Ese Miguel es inteligente y es un chico bueno. ¡Pero no le gusta hacer cosas difíciles! Por la mañana toma el autobús al colegio porque montar en bicicleta es muy difícil. A las doce sólo bebe jugo porque preparar un sándwich es muy difícil. Por la tarde, después de clases, sólo quiere descansar. No quiere ni asistir a clases ni practicar deportes. No, señor, ¡jugar al fútbol es muy difícil! Y no le gusta leer. Sólo lee las tiras cómicas, porque son fáciles. Y eso sí, a veces escribe a su amigo Pepe en Nueva York. Pero sólo tarjetas postales, ¡porque escribir cartas es muy difícil!

Answers to Activity 18
a. Incorrecto; A Miguel no le gusta escribir cartas porque es difícil.
b. Correcto
c. Correcto

Tercer paso

23 p. 155

1. Hoy es el veinticinco de diciembre.

2. Hoy es el veintiséis de abril.

3. Hoy es el treinta y uno de octubre.

4. Hoy es el veintiséis de noviembre.

5. Hoy es el catorce de febrero.

6. Hoy es el cuatro de julio.

Answers to Activity 23

1. b
2. d
3. a
4. f
5. e
6. c

LETRA Y SONIDO, P. 157

For the scripts for Parts A, B, and D, see p. 157. The script for Part C is below.

C. Dictado

Voy al almacén hoy porque necesito una cámara nueva. Pero, ¿dónde está mi suéter? ¿Y el cinturón para mi falda? Ah, aquí están. ¿Tú quieres ir conmigo?

Repaso

1 p. 164

1. Hoy en Nueva York, hace mal tiempo. No hace mucho frío, pero está lloviendo muchísimo.

2. En Chicago hace mucho viento otra vez. No va a llover hoy, y la temperatura va a llegar a los setenta grados.

3. En Miami va a ser un día maravilloso. Hace buen tiempo. Hace sol y la temperatura es de ochenta grados. Un buen día para la playa.

4. Hace frío en las montañas de Colorado. La temperatura es de treinta y dos grados. Un día perfecto para esquiar.

Answers to Repaso Activity 1

1. c   3. a
2. d   4. b

Capítulo 5: El ritmo de la vida
Suggested Lesson Plans 50-Minute Schedule

Day 1

CHAPTER OPENER 5 min.
- Focusing on Outcomes, ATE, p. 141

DE ANTEMANO 40 min.
- Presenting **De antemano** and Preteaching Vocabulary, ATE, p. 142
- Do the Thinking Critically activity, ATE, p. 143
- Activities 1–5 and Comprehension Check, ATE, p. 144

Wrap-Up 5 min.
- Do the Building on Previous Skills activity, ATE, p. 144

Homework Options
Cuaderno de actividades, p. 49, Activity 1

Day 2

PRIMER PASO
Quick Review 5 min.
- Check homework.
- Bell Work, ATE, p. 145

Así se dice/Gramática, p. 145 35 min.
- Presenting **Así se dice/Gramática**, p. 145
- Do Activity 6 with the Audio CD, p, 145.
- Have students do Activity 7 in pairs, then Activity 8 individually, p. 146. Call on volunteers to write their sentences from Activity 8 on the board.
- Have students circulate to do Activity 9, p. 146. Then have them do the suggested Thinking Critically activity, ATE, p. 146.

Wrap-Up 10 min.
- Have students read Activity 7, p. 52, in the Cuaderno de actividades, then discuss.

Homework Options
Más práctica gramatical, p. 160, Activities 1–2
Cuaderno de gramática, pp. 37–38, Activities 1–3
Cuaderno de actividades, pp. 50–51, Activities 2–5

Day 3

PRIMER PASO
Quick Review 10 min.
- Check homework.
- Review **Así de dice** and **Gramática**, p. 145, asking students how often they do things.

Nota gramatical, p. 146 20 min.
- Presenting **Nota gramatical**, ATE, p. 146
- Do Activity 10, p. 146, with the class.
- Have students do Activity 11 in pairs and Activity 12 in groups, p. 147.
- **Tira Cómica** after Teaching Suggestion, ATE, p. 147.

SEGUNDO PASO
Así se dice, p. 148 15 min.
- Presenting **Así se dice**, ATE, p. 148
- Do Activity 13 with the Audio CD, p. 148.
- Cuaderno de gramática, p. 39, Activity 5

Wrap-Up 5 min.
- Do the Thinking Critically activity, ATE, p. 148.
- Review the content and format for Quiz 5-1.

Homework Options
Study for Quiz 5-1.
Más práctica gramatical, pp. 160–161, Activities 3–4
Cuaderno de actividades, p. 52, Activity 6
Cuaderno de gramática, p. 38, Activity 4

Day 4

PRIMER PASO
Quick Review 10 min.
- Check homework.
- Quickly review the content of the **Primer paso.**

Quiz 20 min.
- Administer Quiz 5-1A, 5-1B, or a combination of the two.

SEGUNDO PASO
Vocabulario, p. 149 15 min.
- Presenting **Vocabulario**, ATE, p. 149. You might also want to present the Additional Vocabulary, ATE, p. 149
- Do Additional Listening Activity 5-3, p. 40, in Listening Activities.
- Do Activity 14, p. 149.

Wrap-Up 5 min.
- Use Transparency 5-2 to ask students yes/no questions about whether the people in the transparency like doing different activities.

Homework Options
Cuaderno de actividades, p. 53, Activity 9
Cuaderno de gramática, p. 39, Activity 6

Day 5

SEGUNDO PASO
Quick Review 5 min.
- Check homework.
- **Así se dice**, p. 148, **Vocabulario**, p. 149.

Nota gramatical, p. 149 15 min.
- Presenting **Nota gramatical**, ATE, p. 149
- Do **Más práctica gramatical**, p. 161, Activity 4.
- Have students do Activity 15, p. 149, in pairs.

Gramática, p. 150 25 min.
- Presenting **Gramática**, ATE, p. 150
- Activities 16–17, pp. 150–151. Review ¿Te acuerdas? Do Activity 17. Group Work, ATE, p. 151.
- Discuss **Nota cultural**, p. 150. Include Architectural Link, ATE, p. 150.

Wrap-Up 5 min.
- Ask students who does the activities in **Vocabulario.** Then ask how often they do each.

Homework Options
Más práctica gramatical, pp. 161–162, Activities 5–6
Cuaderno de gramática, p. 40, Activities 7–8
Cuaderno de actividades, p. 54, Activities 10–11

Day 6

SEGUNDO PASO
Quick Review 10 min.
- Check homework.
- Use Transparency 5-A to review –er and –ir verb conjugations.

Así se dice, p. 151 25 min.
- Presenting **Así se dice**, ATE, p. 151
- Present and practice the expressions in **A lo nuestro**, p. 151.
- Do Activity 18, p. 152, with the Audio CD. Follow the Teaching Suggestion, ATE, p. 152.
- Activities 19–20, p. 152, in pairs. Suggestions for activities, ATE, p. 152.
- Assign Activity 21, p. 152, having students create an outline for their essays in class.

PANORAMA CULTURAL 10 min.
- Presenting **Panorama cultural**, ATE, p. 153

Wrap-Up 5 min.
- Review the content and format for Quiz 5-2.

Homework Options
Have students finish the Activity 21 essay, p. 152, for homework.
Study for Quiz 5-2.
Cuaderno de actividades, p. 55, Activity 12
Cuaderno de gramática, p. 41, Activities 9–10

One-Stop Planner CD-ROM

For alternative lesson plans by chapter section, to create your own customized plans, or to preview all resources available for this chapter, use the **One-Stop Planner CD-ROM,** Disc 2.

 For additional homework suggestions, see activities accompanied by this symbol throughout the chapter.

Day 7

SEGUNDO PASO

Quick Review 10 min.
- Have students review the content of the **Segundo paso** with a partner as you check or pick up their writing assignment. You may wish to use the Writing Rubric, ATE, p. 125, to grade the assignment.

Quiz 20 min.
- Administer Quiz 5-2A, 5-2B, or a combination of the two.

TERCER PASO

Vocabulario, p. 154 15 min.
- Present **Vocabulario,** p. 154
- Read and discuss the **Nota cultural,** p. 155. Do the Science Link, ATE, p. 155.

Wrap-Up 5 min.
- Ask students what their favorite season is. Then ask them what they like to do during that season.

Homework Options
Cuaderno de actividades, p. 57, Activity 15
Cuaderno de gramática, p. 42, Activity 11

Day 8

TERCER PASO

Quick Review 10 min.
- Check homework.
- Bell Work, ATE, p. 154

Así se dice/Nota gramatical/Vocabulario, p. 154 30 min.
- Review **Vocabulario,** using Transparency 5-3.
- Presenting **Así se dice,** ATE, p. 154
- Present the **Nota gramatical,** p. 154.
- Do Activity 23, p. 155, with the Audio CD.
- Have students do Activity 24, p. 155, individually, then Activity 25, p. 155, in pairs.
- Have students do Activity 26 in pairs, p. 155.

Wrap-Up 10 min.
- Have students do Activity 22, p. 154. Have students share what they found out about their partner with the class.

Homework Options
Más práctica gramatical, p. 163, Activity 8
Cuaderno de gramática, pp. 42–43, Activities 12–14
Cuaderno de actividades, p. 56, Activities 13–14

Day 9

TERCER PASO

Quick Review 5 min.
- Check homework.

Así se dice/Vocabulario, p. 156 40 min.
- Presenting **Así se dice/Vocabulario,** p. 156
- Do Activity 27, p. 156, orally with the class.
- Present and practice the expressions in **A lo nuestro,** p. 157.
- Have students do Activities 28 and 29, p. 157, in pairs.
- Ask students to write Activity 30, then peer-edit another student's work. Call on volunteers to read their paragraphs.

Wrap-Up 5 min.
- Use Transparency 5-B to ask students questions about the weather.

Homework Options
Ask students to bring in a weather map from a recent copy of a local newspaper.
Más práctica gramatical, p. 162, Activity 7
Cuaderno de gramática, p. 44, Activities 15–16
Cuaderno de actividades, pp. 57–58, Activities 16–18

Day 10

TERCER PASO

Quick Review 5 min.
- Check homework.

Así se dice/Vocabulario, p. 156 10 min.
- Quickly review weather terms and expressions by asking students questions about the weather during different months and/or seasons of the year.

Letra y sonido, p. 157 10 min.
- Present using Audio CD.

VAMOS A LEER 20 min.
- Activities A–B, p. 158
- Do Activities C–E, p.159. Follow the Teaching Suggestion for C, ATE, p. 159.

Wrap-Up 5 min.
- Have students share their answers for Activity E, p. 159, with the class.
- Discuss the content and format of Quiz 5-3.

Homework Options
Study for Quiz 5-3.
Cuaderno de actividades, pp. 59–60, Activities 19–22

Day 11

TERCER PASO

Quick Review 10 min.
- Check homework.
- Review the content of the **Tercer paso** using Transparencies 5-B and 5-C.

Quiz 20 min.
- Administer Quiz 5-3A, 5-3B, or a combination of the two.

REPASO 15 min.
- Do Activity 1, p. 164, with Audio CD.
- Have students write Activities 2 and 4, p. 164. Go over the answers on the board.
- Do Activity 6, p. 165 with the class.

Wrap-Up 5 min.
- Ask students to summarize the concepts learned in Chapter 5.

Homework Options
Have students do Activity 7, p. 165, as homework.
A ver si puedo..., p. 166

Day 12

REPASO

Quick Review 10 min.
- Check homework while students do Activity 5, p. 164.

Chapter Review 35 min.
- Review Chapter 5. Choose from **Más práctica gramatical,** Grammar Tutor for Students of Spanish, Activities for Communication, Listening Activities, Interactive CD-ROM Tutor, or **Juegos interactivos.**

Wrap-Up 5 min.
- Discuss the format of the Chapter 5 Test.

Homework Options
Study for the Chapter 5 Test.

Assessment

Quick Review 5 min.
- Answer any last-minute questions.

Test, Chapter 5 45 min.
- Administer Chapter 5 Test. Select from Testing Program, Alternative Assessment Guide, Test Generator, or Standardized Assessment Tutor.

Capítulo 5: El ritmo de la vida
Suggested Lesson Plans 90-Minute Block Schedule

Block 1

CHAPTER OPENER 5 min.
- Focusing on Outcomes, p. 141
- Teacher Notes, pp. 140–141

DE ANTEMANO 40 min.
- Presenting **De antemano** and Preteaching Vocabulary, p. 142
- Do the Thinking Critically activity, ATE, p. 143.
- Do Activities 1–5, p.144, and Comprehension Check, ATE, p. 144.

Así se dice/Gramática, p. 145 35 min.
- Presenting **Así se dice/Gramática**, p. 145
- Do Activity 6 with the Audio CD, p, 145.
- Have students do Activity 7 in pairs, then Activity 8 individually, p. 146. Call on volunteers to write their sentences from Activity 8 on the board.
- Have students do Activity 9, p. 146. Then have them do the suggested Thinking Critically activity, ATE, p. 146.

Wrap-Up 10 min.
- Have students read Activity 7, p. 52, in the Cuaderno de actividades, then discuss.

Homework Options
Más práctica gramatical, p. 160, Activities 1–2
Cuaderno de gramática, pp. 37–38, Activities 1–3
Cuaderno de actividades, pp. 49–50, Activities 1–3

Block 2

PRIMER PASO
Quick Review 10 min.
- Check homework.
- Quickly review the content of **Así de dice** and **Gramática**, p. 145, by asking students how often they do various activities.

Así se dice/Gramática, pp. 145–146 15 min.
- Have students do Cuaderno de actividades, p. 51, Activities 4 and 5, individually. Check Activity 4 orally with the class, then ask volunteers to write their sentences from Activity 5 on the board for the class to check.
- Activities for Communication, pp. 25–26, Activity 5-1

Nota gramatical, p. 146 20 min.
- Presenting **Nota gramatical**, ATE, p. 146
- Do Activity 10, p. 146, orally with the class.
- Have students do Activity 11 in pairs and Activity 12 in groups, p. 147.
- Read the **Tira Cómica**, following the Slower Pace suggestion, ATE, p. 147.

SEGUNDO PASO
Así se dice, p. 148 15 min.
- Presenting **Así se dice**, ATE, p. 148
- Do Activity 13 with the Audio CD, p. 148.
- **Cuaderno de gramática**, p. 39, Act. 5

Vocabulario, p. 149 20 min.
- Presenting **Vocabulario**, ATE, p. 149. You might also want to present the Additional Vocabulary, ATE, p. 149
- Do Additional Listening Activity 5-3, p. 40, in Listening Activities.
- Do Activity 14, p. 149.

Wrap-Up 10 min.
- Do the Thinking Critically activity, ATE, p. 148.
- Review the content and format for Quiz 5-1.

Homework Options
Study for Quiz 5-1.
Más práctica gramatical, p. 160, Activity 3
Cuaderno de actividades, pp. 52–53, Activities 6, 8
Cuaderno de gramática, pp. 38–39, Activities 4–6

Block 3

PRIMER PASO
Quick Review 10 min.
- Check homework.
- Quickly review the content of the **Primer paso.**

Quiz 20 min.
- Administer Quiz 5-1A, 5-1B, or a combination of the two.

SEGUNDO PASO
Así se dice/Vocabulario, pp. 148–149 15 min.
- Review the content of **Así se dice** and **Vocabulario**, pp. 148–149, using Transparency 5-2. Then ask students yes/no questions about whether they or other students in the class like doing the activities in the transparency.

Nota gramatical, p. 149 15 min.
- Presenting **Nota gramatical**, ATE, p. 149
- Do **Más práctica gramatical**, p. 161, Activity 4.
- Have students do Activity 15, p. 149, in pairs.

Gramática, p. 150 25 min.
- Presenting **Gramática**, ATE, p. 150
- Do Activities 16 and 17, pp. 150–151. Review the information in **¿Te acuerdas?** before students complete Activity 17. As a follow-up, have students do the Group Work activity, p. 151.
- Read and discuss the **Nota cultural**, p. 150. Include the information in the Architectural Link, ATE, p. 150.

Wrap-Up 5 min.
- Ask students who in the class does the activities listed in the **Vocabulario** of this **Paso.** Then ask students how often they do each activity.

Homework Options
Más práctica gramatical, pp. 161–162, Activities 5–6
Cuaderno de actividades, pp. 53–54, Activities 9–11
Cuaderno de gramática, p. 40, Activities 7–8

One-Stop Planner CD-ROM

For alternative lesson plans by chapter section, to create your own customized plans, or to preview all resources available for this chapter, use the **One-Stop Planner CD-ROM,** Disc 2.

 For additional homework suggestions, see activities accompanied by this symbol throughout the chapter.

Block 4

SEGUNDO PASO
Quick Review 10 min.
- Check homework.
- Use Transparency 5-A to review –**er** and –**ir** verb conjugations. Then, ask students who likes doing the various activities pictured.

Así se dice, p. 151 25 min.
- Presenting **Así se dice,** ATE, p. 151
- Present and practice the expressions in **A lo nuestro.**
- Do Activity 18, p. 152, with the Audio CD. Follow the Teaching Suggestion, ATE, p. 152.
- Have students do Activities 19–20, p. 152, in pairs. Follow the Teaching Suggestions for both activities, ATE, p. 152.
- Assign Activity 21, p. 152, having students create an outline for their essays in class.

PANORAMA CULTURAL 10 min.
- Presenting **Panorama cultural,** ATE, p. 153

TERCER PASO
Vocabulario, p. 154 15 min.
- Present **Vocabulario,** p. 154
- Read and discuss the **Nota cultural,** p. 155. Do the Science Link, ATE, p. 155.

Así se dice/Nota gramatical, p. 154 20 min.
- Presenting **Así se dice,** ATE, p. 154
- Present the **Nota gramatical,** p. 154.
- Do Activity 23, p. 155, with the Audio CD.
- Have students do Activity 24, p. 155, individually, then Activity 25, p. 155, in pairs.
- Have students do Activity 26 in pairs, p. 155.

Wrap-Up 10 min.
- Have students do Activity 22, p. 154, then share what they found out about their partner with the class.
- Review the content and format for Quiz 5-2.

Homework Options
Have students write the Activity 21 essay, p. 152.
Study for Quiz 5-2.
Cuaderno de actividades, pp. 55–57, Activities 12–15
Cuaderno de gramática, pp. 41–42, Activities 9–12

Block 5

SEGUNDO PASO
Quick Review 10 min.
- Check homework.
- Have students review the content of the **Segundo paso** with a partner as you check or pick up their writing assignment. You may wish to use the Writing Rubric, pp. 3–9 in the Alternative Assessment Guide to grade the assignment.

Quiz 20 min.
- Administer Quiz 5-2A, 5-2B, or a combination of the two.

TERCER PASO
Así se dice/Vocabulario/Nota gramatical, pp. 154–155 10 min.
- Use Transparency 5-3 to review the seasons, months, and the date.
- Do Activities 13–14, p. 43, in the **Cuaderno de gramática.**

Así se dice/Vocabulario, p. 156 40 min.
- Presenting **Así se dice** and **Vocabulario,** ATE, p. 156
- Do Activity 27, p. 156, orally with the class.
- Present and practice the expressions in **A lo nuestro,** p. 157.
- Have students do Activities 28–29, p. 157, in pairs.
- Ask students to write Activity 30, then peer-edit another student's work. Call on volunteers to read their paragraphs.

Wrap-Up 10 min.
- Ask students what their favorite season is. Then ask them what the weather is like during that season. Finally, ask them what the weather is like on a particular date in different locations around the world.
- Review the content and format of Quiz 5-3.

Homework Options
Study for Quiz 5-3.
Más práctica gramatical, pp. 162–163, Activities 7–8
Cuaderno de gramática, p. 44, Activities 15–16
Cuaderno de actividades, pp. 57–58, Activities 16–18

Block 6

TERCER PASO
Quick Review 10 min.
- Check homework.
- Review the content of the **Tercer paso** using Transparencies 5-B and 5-C.

Quiz 20 min.
- Administer Quiz 5-3A, 5-3B, or a combination of the two.

Letra y sonido, p. 157 10 min.
- Present using Audio CD.

VAMOS A LEER 20 min.
- Activities A–B, p. 158
- Do Activities C–E, p.159. Follow the Teaching Suggestion for Activity C, ATE, p. 159.

REPASO 25 min.
- Do Activity 1, p. 164, with Audio CD.
- Have students write Activities 2, 4, and 5, p. 164. Go over the answers on the board.
- Have students do Activity 3, p. 164, in pairs.
- Do Activity 6, p. 165 with the class.
- Have students make their writing plan for Activity 7, p. 165.

Wrap-Up 5 min.
- Ask students to summarize the concepts learned in Chapter 5.
- Review the format and provide sample questions from the Chapter 5 Test.

Homework Options
Study for the Chapter 5 Test.
Have students complete Activity 7, p. 165, for homework.
A ver si puedo..., p. 166

Block 7

REPASO
Quick Review 10 min.
- Do Activity 8 in pairs, p. 165; Check homework.

Chapter Review 35 min.
- Review Chapter 5. Choose from **Más práctica gramatical,** Grammar Tutor for Students of Spanish, Activities for Communication, Listening Activities, Interactive CD-ROM Tutor, or **Juegos interactivos.**

Test, Capítulo 5 45 min.
- Administer Chapter 5 Test. Select from Testing Program, Alternative Assessment Guide, Test Generator, or Standardized Assessment Tutor.

CAPÍTULO 5

One-Stop Planner CD-ROM

For resource information, see the **One-Stop Planner**, Disc 2.

Pacing Tips

Increased reading content **(Vamos a leer)** will challenge many students. Terms learned in the readings will add to an already difficult vocabulary list. Allot sufficient time for assessment of reading comprehension and retention of vocabulary. For lesson plan and timing suggestions, see pp. 139I–139L.

Meeting the Standards

Communication

- Discussing how often you do things, p. 145
- Talking about what you and your friends like to do together, p. 148
- Talking about what you do during a typical week, p. 151
- Giving today's date, p. 154
- Talking about the weather, p. 156

Cultures

- Nota cultural, p. 150
- Panorama cultural, p. 153

Connections

- Architectural Link, p. 150
- Science Link, p. 155
- Nota cultural, p. 155
- Career Path, p. 157
- Geography Link, p. 165

Comparisons

- Culture Note, p. 141
- Thinking Critically, p. 148
- Native Speakers, p. 153

Communities

- Career Path, p. 157
- Del colegio al trabajo, p. 157

Cultures and Communities

Background Information

Although there were already many Cuban-Americans when Castro came to power in 1959, most have arrived since the Revolution. The immigrants of the early 1960s were often wealthy, and left either because they wanted to preserve assets or because they were forced to leave. A second wave occurred in 1980 when restrictions on departure from Cuba were relaxed. Thousands left for political and economic reasons. The collapse of the Soviet Union in 1990 caused economic decline and shortages of commodities in Cuba, producing a third wave of immigration. Have students research how political and economic events have affected immigration from other countries in Latin America. Discuss the motives for emigration of different groups.

CAPÍTULO

5
El ritmo de la vida

Objectives

In this chapter you will learn to

Primer paso

- discuss how often you do things

Segundo paso

- talk about what you and your friends like to do together
- talk about what you do during a typical week

Tercer paso

- give today's date
- talk about the weather

 internet

MARCAR: go.hrw.com
PALABRA CLAVE:
WV3 FLORIDA-5

◀ **Nos gusta ir al parque cuando hace buen tiempo.**

Photo Flash!
Cyclists take a break in **Plaza Alvear**, a city park located in a fashionable area of Buenos Aires, Argentina, known as **La Recoleta**.

Focusing on Outcomes
Two important language skills are talking about the weather and expressing likes and dislikes. Point out to students that these skills are valuable because making plans for activities may depend on the weather. Talking about these activities includes describing frequency and telling the date. By the end of the chapter, students will be able to ask what friends like to do and plan events for a certain date.

Chapter Sequence

Connections and Comparisons

Culture Note
City parks in Spanish-speaking countries are a focal point of leisure for many. The custom of strolling, relaxing with family, playing informal soccer, picnicking, or even napping in the sun, contrasts with the scheduled routines that mark life in the United States. Here city parks are often empty, or the scene of sponsored activities. Have students discuss reasons for these contrasts.

Language Note
pasar un rato - *to spend time*
a poco rato - *soon; shortly*
luego - *a while later; later on*
a menudo - *frequently, repeatedly*
matar el tiempo - *to kill time*
gastar tiempo - *to waste time*

Teaching Resources
pp. 142–144

PRINT
▸ Lesson Planner, p. 22
▸ Video Guide, pp. 33–34, 36
▸ Cuaderno de actividades, p. 49

MEDIA
▸ One-Stop Planner
▸ Video Program
  De antemano
  Videocassette 2, 20:57–25:03
  Videocassette 5 (captioned version), 47:21–51:28
  A continuación
  Videocassette 2, 25:04–29:36
  Videocassette 5 (captioned version), 51:29–56:05
▸ DVD Tutor, Disc 1
▸ Audio Compact Discs, CD 5, Trs. 1–2
▸ **De antemano** Transparencies

Presenting
De antemano

Have students scan the **foto-novela** to predict what will happen. Then have students answer the questions in **Estrategia para comprender**. Play the audio CD once, having students repeat each character's lines while reading along. Next, present the Preteaching Vocabulary and follow-up by having students read aloud in pairs. Finally, play the video and have students see how accurate their predictions were.

De antemano Transparencies

DE ANTEMANO · ¿Cómo es el ritmo de tu vida?

The **fotonovela** is an abridged version of the video episode.

CD 5 Trs. 1–2

Estrategia
para comprender
Look at the pictures in the **foto-novela**. Can you tell what Patricia, José Luis, and Raquel are doing? Where are they? Does something go wrong? How can you tell?

Patricia **José Luis** **Raquel** **Armando**

1

Patricia: ¡Bienvenidos! Hoy es el seis de noviembre y ésta es la nueva edición de "Noticias Colegio Seminole". Soy Patricia Carter...

José Luis: Y yo soy José Luis Jiménez. Como siempre, tenemos un programa muy interesante para ustedes esta semana.

2

José Luis: Pero primero, ¿qué tiempo hace? Aquí en Miami, hace buen tiempo. Hace mucho sol. En Nueva York, hace un poco de frío... Y en Texas, está lloviendo... ¡a cántaros!

3

Patricia: Gracias, José Luis. Ahora, vamos al reportaje especial de Raquel. Esta semana, ella habla con la gente del colegio sobre el ritmo de sus actividades en una semana típica.

4

Raquel: ¡Hola! Raquel Villanueva a sus órdenes. Todos estamos aquí, en el colegio, durante las horas de clase. ¿Pero qué hacemos cuando no estamos aquí? Ramón... ¿qué haces por la tarde?

Ramón: Bueno... los martes y los jueves, trabajo en el restaurante de mis padres. Y cuando no trabajo, hago la tarea o paso el rato con mis amigos.

Preteaching Vocabulary

Recognizing cognates

De antemano contains several words that students will be able to recognize as cognates. Have students find these and have them guess what is happening in the story.

❶ edición
❷ programa
❸ reportaje
❸ ritmo

❹ restaurante
❺ periódico
❻ música
❾ problema

⑤

Raquel: ¿Qué tal, Anita y Josué? Dime, Anita... ¿qué haces típicamente los domingos?

Anita: Eh... todos los domingos, descanso y leo el periódico. Y Josué y yo siempre corremos juntos por la tarde.

Raquel: Ah, ¿sí? ¿Y corren mucho?

Josué: Sí, mucho. Nos gusta correr. ¡Pero en el verano no, porque hace demasiado calor!

⑥

Raquel: Buenos días, profesor Williams. ¿Qué hace usted por la noche cuando está en casa?

Prof. Williams: Bueno, Raquel... primero la señora Williams y yo preparamos la cena. Después, a veces escucho música o escribo cartas.

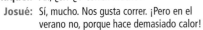

⑦

Raquel: ¡Tenemos un nuevo estudiante en el Colegio Seminole! ¿Quién es? Es Armando Tamayo, y es de Panamá. Armando, ¿qué haces en tu tiempo libre?

Armando: En mi tiempo libre, yo pinto y dibujo.

Raquel: ¿En serio? A mí también me gusta mucho pintar y dibujar. Qué casualidad, ¿no?

⑧

Raquel: Bueno, amigos... aquí termina mi reportaje. Quiero recibir tarjetas postales de ustedes. ¿Les gusta el programa? ¡Escríbanme! ¡Y hasta la próxima!

⑨

Patricia: Gracias, Raquel, y ahora... ¿qué pasa?

José Luis: ¿Hay un problema con la cámara?

Cuaderno de actividades, p. 49, Act. 1

⑩

Using the Captioned Video/DVD

Use Videocassette 5 to allow students to see the Spanish captions for *¿Cómo es el ritmo de tu vida?* Hearing the language and watching the story will reduce anxiety about the new language and facilitate comprehension. The reinforcement of seeing the written words with the gestures and actions in context will help prepare students to do the comprehension activities on p. 144. **NOTE:** The *DVD Tutor* contains captions for all sections of the *Video Program*.

CAPÍTULO 5

Thinking Critically
Comparing and Contrasting On a current weather map, ask students to locate Miami. Is the weather in Miami today the same as it is in the **fotonovela**? Students might then compare the weather in the other locations mentioned in the **fotonovela** with the current weather.

A continuación

You may choose to continue with *¿Cómo es el ritmo de tu vida? (a continuación)* at this time or wait until later in the chapter. At this point, the students resolve the camera problems and clean up the spilled papers. Later they take Armando to the Vizcaya Gardens. You may wish to discuss with students attractions in their hometown that they would show to a visitor from another country.

CAPÍTULO 5

Building on Previous Skills
Ask students to introduce the characters in the **fotonovela** using skills they have learned in Chapters 1 through 4. Have them give each character's name, age, country of origin, and likes or dislikes.

Teaching Suggestion
5 You may wish to have students compare their list with a partner's to see which activities they have in common and if their times for doing them are the same.

These activities check for comprehension only. Students should not yet be expected to produce language modeled in **De antemano**.

1 **¿Comprendes?**

Contesta las preguntas *(Answer the questions).* Si no estás seguro/a sobre lo que pasa en la fotonovela, ¡adivina! See answers below.

1. What are the teenagers in the story doing?
2. What kind of report does José Luis give?
3. What does Raquel do in her special report?
4. Who is Armando, and what does he have in common with Raquel?
5. How will the crew deal with the accident at the end of the broadcast?

2 **¿Cómo se dice?**

Using the **fotonovela** as a guide, find the words and phrases you could use to . . . See answers below.

1. say that the weather is nice
2. ask what a friend does on Sundays
3. say that you and a friend run a lot
4. say that you write letters
5. say that you paint and draw in your free time

3 **Equivocaciones** *Errors*

There are five errors in this paragraph describing Raquel and her friends. Find and correct the errors, and then read the corrected paragraph aloud. See answers below.

Patricia y José Luis están en <u>Nueva York,</u> donde hace mucho sol. <u>Anita</u> trabaja en un restaurante los martes y los jueves. Josué y Anita corren <u>todos los días.</u> Raquel y Armando <u>miran la televisión</u> en su tiempo libre. ¿Y el profesor Williams? Él <u>lee el periódico</u> después de clases y prepara la cena con su esposa.

4 **Cuando hace mal tiempo...** *When the weather's bad . . .*

Read what Raquel says she and her friends do when the weather is bad. Then match the correct character's name with each activity.

Cuando hace frío, yo escucho música. Mi amiga Anita lee el periódico y el profesor Williams trabaja en casa. Cuando está lloviendo, Armando y yo dibujamos, Anita descansa y el profesor Williams y su señora escriben cartas.

1. Anita a, c
2. el profesor Williams b, e
3. Raquel d, f
4. Armando f
5. la señora del profesor b

a. leer el periódico
b. escribir cartas
c. descansar
d. escuchar música
e. trabajar en casa
f. dibujar

5 **¿Y tú?**

Usa la fotonovela como modelo. Describe lo que *(what)* haces, y cuándo, en un típico fin de semana. Answers will vary.

Answers
1
1. filming a TV show
2. weather report
3. interviews people about free-time activities
4. a new student; drawing and painting
5. *Answers will vary.*

2
1. Hace buen tiempo.
2. ¿Qué haces los domingos?
3. Corremos mucho.
4. Escribo cartas.
5. Pinto y dibujo en el tiempo libre.

3
1. Miami
2. Ramón
3. los domingos
4. pintan y dibujan
5. escucha música o escribe cartas

Comprehension Check

Slower Pace
1 Distribute a chart showing the various activities each character in **De antemano** likes to do. Have students review Raquel's interviews and mark the activities under the appropriate name. In groups, allow peer review and have them ask each other when each character engages in the activity.

Challenge
5 Motivated students may create their own charts as "information gap" activities, varying the activities and using fictitious people, classmates, or themselves as characters.

Así se dice

Discussing how often you do things

CD-ROM 2 / DVD 1

To find out how often a friend does things, ask:

¿Con qué frecuencia desayunas?
How often do you eat breakfast?

¿Siempre organizas tu cuarto?
(Do you) always . . .?

¿Y qué haces **durante** la semana?
. . . during the week?

¿Todavía tocas la guitarra?
(Do you) still . . .?

Your friend might respond:

Desayuno todos los días.
I eat breakfast every day.

Nunca organizo mi cuarto.
(I) never . . .

A veces cuido a mi hermano.
Sometimes . . .

Muchas veces ayudo en casa.
Often I help at home.

Sí, pero **sólo cuando** no tengo tarea.
. . . only when . . .

6 **Viejos amigos** *Old friends*

CD 5
Tr. 3

Escuchemos Listen as Teresa tells Carlos what some of his old friends are doing. Match the name of each friend with when he or she works with Teresa. Scripts and answers on p. 139G.

1. Juan Luis
2. Maite
3. Alejandro
4. Flora
5. Ramón

a. todos los días
b. los fines de semana
c. sólo cuando tiene tiempo los jueves
d. nunca
e. siempre los lunes, a veces los jueves

Gramática

Negation

CD-ROM 2 / DVD 1

In Chapter 2 you learned to make sentences negative by putting **no** before the verb. To say *never* or *not ever*, put **nunca** before the verb.

Nunca tomo el autobús.　　*I never take the bus.*

In Spanish, you'll often use **no** and **nunca** or **no** and **nada** (nothing) together in the same sentence. In that case, be sure to put **no** in front of the verb, and **nunca** or **nada** after the verb.

No tomo el autobús **nunca**.　　*I never take the bus.*
Los sábados **no** hago **nada**.　　*On Saturdays I don't do anything.*

Another negative word is **nadie**. It is always used with a singular verb form.

No toca la guitarra **nadie**.　　} *Nobody plays the guitar.*
Nadie toca la guitarra.

Más práctica gramatical, p. 160. Acts. 1–2

Cuaderno de gramática, pp. 37–38, Acts. 1–3

Cuaderno de actividades, pp. 50–51, Acts. 2–5

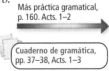

Communication for All Students

Building on Previous Skills

Review phrases to describe time and sequence of events. (antes de, después de, ¿A qué hora?) Model questions and answers using known phrases and new ones from **Así se dice** and **Gramática**. (¿Desayunas antes de ir a la escuela? Sí, siempre desayuno antes de ir a la escuela.) Have students write questions with these phrases. Students may practice questions in small groups to create dialogues.

Tactile Learners

Using phrases in **Así se dice** and **Gramática**, write sentences on the board for students to copy on strips of paper. Ask students to cut the sentences they have written into individual words and work in small groups to make new sentences. You may want to challenge students to create as many new sentences as they can.

Teaching Resources
pp. 145–147

PRINT
- Lesson Planner, p. 24
- TPR Storytelling Book, pp. 17, 20
- Listening Activities, pp. 35, 39
- Activities for Communication, pp. 25–26, 95, 98–99, 145–146
- Cuaderno de gramática, pp. 37–38
- Grammar Tutor for Students of Spanish, Chapter 5
- Cuaderno de actividades, pp. 50–52
- Cuaderno para hispanohablantes, pp. 21–25
- Testing Program, pp. 105–108
- Alternative Assessment Guide, p. 36
- Student Make-Up Assignments, Chapter 5

MEDIA
- One-Stop Planner
- Audio Compact Discs, CD 5, Trs. 3, 22–23, 17
- Teaching Transparencies 5-1; **Más práctica gramatical** Answers; Cuaderno de gramática Answers
- Interactive CD-ROM Tutor, Disc 2

 go.hrw.com
WV3 FLORIDA

 Bell Work
List classroom objects. Have students write where each thing is: **El reloj está al lado de la mesa.**

Presenting
Así se dice / Gramática

Write the days of the week, listing under each things you do that day. Say how often using **Así se dice** phrases. Then ask students what they do and how often. Record responses.

Teaching Resources
pp. 145–147

PRINT
- Lesson Planner, p. 23
- TPR Storytelling Book, pp. 17, 20
- Listening Activities, pp. 35, 39
- Activities for Communication, pp. 25–26, 95, 98–99, 145–146
- Cuaderno de gramática, pp. 37–38
- Grammar Tutor for Students of Spanish, Chapter 5
- Cuaderno de actividades, pp. 50–52
- Cuaderno para hispanohablantes, pp. 21–25
- Testing Program, pp. 105–108
- Alternative Assessment Guide, p. 36
- Student Make-Up Assignments, Chapter 5

MEDIA
- One-Stop Planner
- Audio Compact Discs, CD 5, Trs. 3, 22–23, 17
- Teaching Transparencies 5-1; **Más práctica gramatical** Answers; Cuaderno de gramática Answers
- Interactive CD-ROM Tutor, Disc 2

Presenting
Nota gramatical

Choose sentences from Activity 3, **Equivocaciones**, for display on an overhead. Have volunteers underline the subjects, then challenge students to form and ask **quién/quiénes** questions that elicit the subjects. Stress the singular/plural distinction through emphatic modeling and correcting.

Answers
10 1. Quién
2. quiénes
3. Quién
4. quiénes

---

7 Gramática en contexto

Leamos Think of the following people you know and complete the sentences with one of the activities below. Answers will vary.

1. Yo nunca...
2. Mi mejor amigo/a siempre...
3. A veces mi hermano/a...
4. Mis abuelos siempre...
5. Todos los días la profesora...
6. Mi perro/a nunca...
7. A veces tú...
8. Los fines de semana yo...

> practicar un deporte   desayunar   cuidar a tu hermano/a   trabajar
>
> caminar con el perro   pintar
>
> estudiar en la biblioteca   tocar un instrumento   preparar la cena   ir al colegio

8 Mi semana

Escribamos What do you do during a typical week? Write six sentences using activities from the box above. Be sure to explain how often you do each activity. Include two activities you never do. Answers will vary.

9 Una encuesta

Hablemos Interview five classmates to find out how often they do the things mentioned in the first column. Your classmates will respond by using words from both columns.

lavar la ropa	nunca
organizar tu cuarto	a veces
hablar por teléfono	sólo cuando tengo tiempo
ayudar en casa	los lunes, los martes, etc.
tomar el autobús	los fines de semana
sacar la basura	todos los días
mirar la televisión	

MODELO —¿Con qué frecuencia lavas la ropa?
—Nunca lavo la ropa.

Nota gramatical

You've already learned the question word **¿quién?** *(who?)*. **¿Quién?** is used to ask about one person. When asking about more than one person, use **¿quiénes?** *(who?)*. Compare the two sentences below.

¿Quién es el chico rubio?
Who is the blond boy?

¿Quiénes son las chicas altas?
Who are the tall girls?

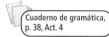

Cuaderno de gramática, p. 38, Act. 4   Más práctica gramatical, pp. 160–161, Act. 3

See answers below.

10 Gramática en contexto

Escribamos Fill in the blanks with **quién** or **quiénes** to complete David and Ana's conversation about guests at Ana's party.

DAVID Ana, hay muchas personas aquí, ¿no? ¿___1___ es el chico alto?

ANA Se llama Andrés.

DAVID ¿Y ___2___ son las chicas al lado de Andrés?

ANA Se llaman Veronique y Marie Agnès. Son de París.

DAVID Ah, ¿sí? Yo tengo familia de Francia también.

ANA ¿___3___ es de Francia en tu familia?

DAVID Mi abuela. ¿Y ___4___ son los chicos cerca de la puerta?

ANA Se llaman Mario, Roberto y Julia.

Communication for All Students

Thinking Critically

9 Drawing Conclusions After students complete their interviews, have them assign a number from 1 to 5 to the classmates they interviewed, in order of who is the most and least busy. Follow up by asking students to explain their rankings, using information from their interviews.

Slower Pace

10 Point out the clues in the text that signal the proper choice. (In item 1, students may choose **¿Quiénes?** based on **muchas personas** rather than **¿Quién?** based on **chico**.) Review forms of **ser** with the interrogatives by pointing to individual students and having the class respond **¿Quién es?** or **¿Quiénes son?**

11 ¿Quién hace eso? *Who does that?*

Hablemos Who is doing what in the drawings? Get together with a partner and take turns asking and answering questions about the people and activities pictured. See answers below.

MODELO   ¿Quiénes nadan en la Piscina Alberti?
            Julia y Silvia nadan en la Piscina Alberti.

1. estar/gimnasio
2. mirar/televisión
3. ir/parque
4. cuidar a/su hermano
5. pintar/la clase de arte
6. tomar/helado

Julia y Silvia

Rita

Li

Micki y Pablo

Roberto y Laura

Keesha

Ricardo y Daniel

Possible answers below.

12 ¿Tienes buena memoria?

Escribamos/Hablemos Work in groups of five. On three slips of paper each person writes the categories **siempre, a veces,** and **nunca.** Under each category write one activity that you always, sometimes, and never do. Then shuffle the papers. Each person draws three slips and asks **¿Quién...?** or **¿Quiénes...?,** the activity, and the category to try to guess who wrote the activity on each slip.

SUGERENCIA

At first, it's often hard to write in a foreign language. Remember that learning to write is like learning other skills in Spanish. Take it slowly, and go in small steps. Begin by writing short messages. For example, you can write brief reminders to yourself about what you need to do, or try writing out your weekly schedule in Spanish. Start now by making a list of activities you usually do during a particular day—for example, on Mondays.

CALVIN AND HOBBES © Watterson. Dist. by Universal Press Syndicate. Reprinted with permission. All rights reserved.

Connections and Comparisons

Additional Vocabulary

echarse un clavado *to dive*
el trampolín *diving board*
el cochecito *stroller*
la banca *bench*
los árboles *trees*
el pincel *paintbrush*
la paleta *palette*
el lienzo *canvas*

el caballete *easel*
pintar al óleo *to paint in oils*
pintar a la acuarela *to paint in watercolors*
la silla de ruedas *wheelchair*
levantar pesas *to lift weights*
pasear *to take a walk*
la bolsa *purse*

Slower Pace
Tira cómica First, ask your students to scan the comic for cognates and familiar words. What do they think is happening?

Assess
▶ Testing Program, pp. 105–108
   Quiz 5-1A, Quiz 5-1B
   Audio CD 5, Tr. 17

▶ Student Make-Up Assignments, Chapter 5, Alternative Quiz

▶ Alternative Assessment Guide, p. 36

Answers
11 1. ¿Quién está en el gimnasio? Keesha está en el gimnasio.
2. ¿Quiénes miran la televisión? Roberto y Laura miran la tele.
3. ¿Quiénes van al parque? Ricardo y Daniel van al parque.
4. ¿Quién cuida a su hermano? Rita cuida a su hermano.
5. ¿Quiénes pintan en la clase de arte? Micki y Pablo pintan en la clase de arte.
6. ¿Quién toma helado? Li toma helado.

12 *Possible questions and answers:*
(A veces preparo la cena.) —¿Quién prepara la cena a veces? ¿Tú, Roberto? —Sí, a veces yo preparo la cena. (Nunca organizo el cuarto.) —¿Quién no organiza el cuarto nunca? ¿Tú, Juana? —No, yo no. Yo siempre organizo el cuarto.

Teaching Resources
pp. 148–152

PRINT 📖
▸ Lesson Planner, p. 24
▸ TPR Storytelling Book, pp. 18, 20
▸ Listening Activities, pp. 35–36, 40
▸ Activities for Communication, pp. 27–28, 96, 98–99, 145–146
▸ Cuaderno de gramática, pp. 39–41
▸ Grammar Tutor for Students of Spanish, Chapter 5
▸ Cuaderno de actividades, pp. 53–55
▸ Cuaderno para hispanohablantes, pp. 21–25
▸ Testing Program, pp. 109–112
▸ Alternative Assessment Guide, p. 36
▸ Student Make-Up Assignments, Chapter 5

MEDIA 💿📼
▸ One-Stop Planner
▸ Audio Compact Discs, CD 5, Trs. 4–5, 24–25, 18
▸ Teaching Transparencies 5-2, 5-A; **Más práctica gramatical** Answers; Cuaderno de gramática Answers
▸ Interactive CD-ROM Tutor, Disc 2

Bell Work
Write infinitives from Activities 9 and 11 in a column on the board, and phrases relating to the verbs in a column to the right. Have students link the verb to the phrase by drawing lines.
montar   a bicicleta
sacar   la basura

Presenting
Así se dice
Ask groups of students or the whole class ¿**Qué les gusta hacer?** Elicit responses by acting out swimming, dancing, etc.

Segundo paso

Objectives Talking about what you and your friends like to do together; talking about what you do during a typical week

Así se dice

Talking about what you and your friends like to do together

So far, you've been using **gusta** with the pronouns **me, te,** and **le** to talk about what just one person likes and dislikes.

To find out what some of your friends like to do, ask them:

¿Qué **les gusta** hacer?
    . . . do you like . . .?

Y a Celia y Roberto, **¿les gusta esquiar?**
    . . . do they like to ski?

¿Les gusta **acampar** y **pescar?**
    . . . to camp . . . to fish?

Your friends might answer:

Nos gusta hacer ejercicio o correr por la playa.
    We like to exercise or run on the beach.

No sé, pero les gusta **bucear juntos.**
    . . . to scuba dive together.

Sí, **especialmente** durante **las vacaciones.**
    . . . especially . . . vacation.

> Cuaderno de gramática, p. 39, Act. 5

Scripts and answers on p. 139G.

13 Mejores amigos

Escuchemos Gloria is writing an article about best friends for the school newspaper. Listen as she interviews Carlos and Eddie. Then, for each activity shown, choose the best answer.

CD 5
Tr. 4

1. Les gusta.
2. No les gusta.
3. Sólo le gusta a Carlos.
4. Sólo le gusta a Eddie.

a.

b.

c.

d.

Connections and Comparisons

Thinking Critically
Write these Spanish sayings on the board before class: **de gustos no hay nada escrito, eso va en gustos, de mal gusto, le toma el gusto.** Ask if students can guess the English equivalents *(to each his own, that's a matter of taste, in poor taste, he takes a liking to).* Ask them to think about why people develop certain likes and preferences rather than others. Are there things everyone likes? How does a specific culture shape the tastes of a community? Have students think of **gustos** they would consider typically Hispanic to compare with their own. Ask if they can explain why preferences in activities, food, or music reflect or define a culture. Some tastes may have developed over time. Others may have been adopted from another culture. Have them contribute thoughts and ideas.

Vocabulario

asistir a una clase de ejercicios aeróbicos

comer un sándwich o una hamburguesa con papas fritas

beber agua o jugo

leer las tiras cómicas en el periódico

escribir tarjetas postales

recibir cartas

CD-ROM 2 DVD 1

Cuaderno de gramática, p. 39, Act. 6

Cuaderno de actividades, p. 54, Act. 11

14 **¿Qué les gusta hacer?**

Hablemos Tell what you and your friends like to do at each of these times and places. For each answer, choose at least one item from the **Vocabulario** and at least one from vocabulary you already know. *Answers will vary.*

MODELO después de correr
Nos gusta descansar y beber jugo. A veces nos gusta nadar después de correr.

1. en casa los domingos
2. después de jugar a un deporte
3. los sábados (en el gimnasio, por ejemplo)
4. en la biblioteca
5. en la playa los fines de semana
6. durante las vacaciones

Nota gramatical

Look at the examples in the **Así se dice** box on page 148. When **les gusta** is translated literally, it means *is pleasing to them* or *is pleasing to you* (plural). Sometimes the phrases **a ustedes** and **a ellos** or **a ellas** are added for clarification.

Look at the literal translations of these questions.

¿A ustedes les gusta nadar?
Is swimming pleasing to you?

¿A ellos les gusta preparar la cena juntos?
Is preparing dinner together pleasing to them?

What would the non-literal English translations be?*

Más práctica gramatical, p. 161, Act. 4

Cuaderno de gramática, p. 40, Act. 7

Do you like to swim? Do they like to fix dinner together?

15 **Gramática en contexto**

Leamos/Hablemos Work in pairs. Using the cues, ask a series of questions to find out which activities your partner likes to do and how often. Be prepared to tell the class what you learn. For an activity you both like to do, use **nos gusta**.
Possible answer below.

MODELO correr: playa/parque
—¿Te gusta correr por la playa o en el parque?
—Me gusta correr en el parque.
—¿Y con qué frecuencia?

1. escribir: cartas/tarjetas postales
2. recibir: notas de amigos/cartas de amor *(love letters)*
3. comer: ensalada/un sándwich
4. leer: revistas/el periódico
5. asistir: a clases/a un concierto de...
6. beber: jugo/agua

Presenting
Vocabulario, Nota gramatical

The plural pronouns *les* and *nos* Have students close their books as you show *Teaching Transparency 5-A* without its overlay. Model pronunciation of the terms, then have pairs of students discuss the activities they enjoy. They then must say which activities one partner likes but the other doesn't, which they both like, and which neither likes. (**Nos gusta leer tiras cómicas. A mí me gusta escribir tarjetas postales, pero a Ana no le gusta escribirlas.**) As partners report, display the overlay to provide a reference. After briefly reviewing **me gusta** and **le gusta,** show magazine photos of people doing different things, labeling each with an infinitive phrase (**escribir cartas**). Select one or two photos and model a **les gusta** sentence, emphasizing the pronoun. Then ask **¿Qué les gusta a ellos?** pointing to each photo one by one. Then you may use people known around school, well-known figures, or more photos to continue practicing **les**, as well as reviewing **me gusta, te gusta,** and **le gusta.**

Communication for All Students

Additional Practice
For more practice with **Vocabulario,** use **Más práctica gramatical,** Act. 5, p. 162; *Cuaderno de gramática,* Act. 6, p. 39; and *Interactive CD-ROM,* **¡Super memoria!** For more practice with **Nota gramatical,** use *Cuaderno de gramática,* Act. 7, p. 40; and *Cuaderno de actividades,* Acts. 8–9, p. 53.

Additional Vocabulary
coleccionar sellos o monedas *to collect stamps or coins*
practicar artes marciales *to practice martial arts*
actuar en obras de teatro *to act in a play*
jugar a las cartas *to play cards*
jugar al ajedrez *to play chess*

Answers
15 *Possible answer:*
1. —¿Te gusta escribir cartas o tarjetas postales?
—Me gusta escribir tarjetas postales.
—¿Y con qué frecuencia te gusta escribir?
—Me gusta escribir tarjetas todos los viernes.

Teaching Resources
pp. 148–152

PRINT

▶ Lesson Planner, p. 24
▶ TPR Storytelling Book, pp. 18, 20
▶ Listening Activities, pp. 35–36, 40
▶ Activities for Communication, pp. 27–28, 96, 98–99, 145–146
▶ Cuaderno de gramática, pp. 39–41
▶ Grammar Tutor for Students of Spanish, Chapter 5
▶ Cuaderno de actividades, pp. 53–55
▶ Cuaderno para hispanohablantes, pp. 21–25
▶ Testing Program, pp. 109–112
▶ Alternative Assessment Guide, p. 36
▶ Student Make-Up Assignments, Chapter 5

MEDIA

▶ One-Stop Planner
▶ Audio Compact Discs, CD 5, Trs. 4–5, 24–25, 18
▶ Teaching Transparencies 5-2, 5-A; **Más práctica gramatical** Answers; Cuaderno de gramática Answers
▶ Interactive CD-ROM Tutor, Disc 2

Presenting
Gramática

-er and -ir verbs
Have volunteers write out **escuchar** on the board. Then write out the **-er** and **-ir** paradigms, showing similarities and differences. To practice **-er** forms, pass out pictures of foods and ask questions with **comer.** For **-ir** forms, ask students about events or classes with **asistir a.**

Answers
16. 1. corremos   5. ven
    2. leo   6. escribes
    3. asisten   7. recibimos
    4. come

Gramática

-er and -ir verbs

In Chapter 4 you learned to work with **-ar** verbs, such as **hablar.** Look at the conjugations of **comer** and **escribir** to see how **-er** and **-ir** verbs work. Which two endings aren't identical for both types of verbs?*

(yo)	como	(nosotros, nosotras)	comemos
(tú)	comes	(vosotros, vosotras)	coméis
(él, ella, usted)	come	(ellos, ellas, ustedes)	comen

(yo)	escribo	(nosotros, nosotras)	escribimos
(tú)	escribes	(vosotros, vosotras)	escribís
(él, ella, usted)	escribe	(ellos, ellas, ustedes)	escriben

You also know the verb **ver.** It is regular except in the **yo** form.

(yo)	veo	(nosotros, nosotras)	vemos
(tú)	ves	(vosotros, vosotras)	veis
(él, ella, usted)	ve	(ellos, ellas, ustedes)	ven

Más práctica gramatical, p. 161, Act. 5

Cuaderno de gramática, pp. 40–41, Acts. 8–10

Cuaderno de actividades, p. 54, Act. 11

16 **Gramática en contexto**

Leamos/Escribamos Completa las oraciones sobre las vacaciones de Antonio y su familia. Usa la forma correcta del verbo entre paréntesis. See answers below.

1. Ana y yo (correr) por la playa.
2. Luego descansamos y yo (leer) las tiras cómicas en inglés.
3. Los lunes y los miércoles mis padres (asistir) a una clase de ejercicios.
4. A Miguel le gustan las hamburguesas y las papas fritas. ¡Siempre (comer) mucho!
5. Mis padres no (ver) muchas películas. Les gustan las novelas.
6. Y tú, Diana, ¿por qué no me (escribir) una tarjeta postal?
7. Todos los días nosotros (recibir) cartas, pero ¡no de ti! *Not from you!*

Nota cultural

Spending time with a group of friends is an important part of life for young adults in the Spanish-speaking world. Fewer young people own cars in Spain or Latin America than in the United States, so they often share rides with friends. Meeting friends in public is a big part of life for both young and old. Public gathering places like parks and cafés are common meeting places. The streets of a Spanish-speaking town are usually alive both day and night.

---

*The **nosotros** forms are different: **comemos, escribimos.** And the **vosotros** forms are different: **coméis, escribís.**

Connections and Comparisons

Architectural Link

The *cloister,* a medieval architectural feature adapted by Renaissance builders, has Byzantine, Roman, and Islamic origins. It has remained popular throughout the Spanish-speaking world. A courtyard, often adorned with plants, a fountain, or a sculpture, is surrounded on four sides by arches supporting a covered walkway shading the building of one or many stories. Many government buildings, museums, **haciendas**, and even hotels and restaurants throughout Spain and the Americas are examples of this architecture; in the Americas they are left over from colonial times. Have students think of other places where this architectural style is popular.

17 Gramática en contexto

Hablemos What do the people in these pictures do during the week? *See answers below.*

MODELO   Alejandra y sus amigos hacen la tarea juntos.

Alejandra y sus amigos

ustedes

la señora Pérez

tú

yo

nosotros

¿Te acuerdas?

Do you remember that masculine plural adjectives and nouns can refer to mixed groups of males and females as well as all-male groups? If you're talking about two males or a male and a female together, use **juntos**. If you're talking about two females, use **juntas**.

A lo nuestro

In Spanish, there are many ways to express how often you do things. Some of these expressions include: **una vez** *(once)*, **de vez en cuando** *(once in a while)*, **todo el tiempo** *(all the time)*, **cada día** *(each day)*, and **a menudo** *(often)*.

Así se dice

Talking about what you do during a typical week

To find out what your friends typically do during the week, ask:

¿Qué haces **típicamente** durante el día?

¿Qué hace Josué **por la mañana?**
    . . . *in the morning?*

¿Hacen ustedes ejercicio juntos?

¿Y qué hacen Raquel y Anita **por la noche?**
    . . . *at night?*

Some responses might be:

Asisto a clases, trabajo y paso el rato con amigos.

Corre **dos millas** por la playa.
    . . . *two miles* . . .

Sí, pero sólo **por la tarde.**
    . . . *in the afternoon.*

A veces van a un restaurante.

> Cuaderno de actividades, p. 55, Act. 12

Group Work

17 Have students look at the photos in Activity 17. Divide the class into groups of three and challenge them to come up with two activities the people pictured like and do not like to do. Ask them to report their ideas to the class.

Presenting
Así se dice

Tell the class a story about yourself, using the vocabulary in **Así se dice**. Draw a schedule on the board, then describe what you do in a day. **Típicamente, trabajo aquí en el colegio de siete a cuatro. Por la mañana y por la tarde enseño. Después de las cuatro, regreso a casa. Por la tarde a veces corro, o voy al gimnasio. Por la noche, típicamente preparo la cena para mi familia. A veces salimos a un restaurante, pero no con mucha frecuencia.** Then ask the students to respond to comprehension questions. **(Clase, ¿qué hago típicamente por la mañana?)** Extend the pattern to students, asking questions based on **Así se dice**. Once comprehension is high, have students practice in pairs, using vocabulary from **A lo nuestro**.

Answers
17 *Possible answers:*
Ustedes corren en la mañana.
La señora Pérez escribe tarjetas postales.
Comes hamburguesas con amigos en un restaurante.
Yo asisto a la clase de ejercicios aeróbicos.
Leemos las tiras cómicas en el periódico.

18 **Un día típico en la vida de...** Scripts and answers on p. 139G.

Escuchemos/Hablemos Listen as Miguel's mother describes a typical day in his life, and decide which of these illustrations shows the real Miguel. Explain what is wrong with the incorrect illustrations.

CD 5 Tr. 5

a.   b.   c.

19 **¿Quién lo hace?** Answers will vary.

 Hablemos/Escribamos Try to identify at least one person in your partner's family or circle of friends who does each of the activities listed. Also find out how often each person does the activity. Take notes, and try to find activities that your friends or family members have in common. If nobody does the activity, use **Nadie...** in your answer.

MODELO
—Juana, ¿quién en tu familia lee revistas?
—Nadie, pero mi padre lee el periódico todos los días por la mañana.

> leer: revistas, las tiras cómicas, el periódico, novelas
> asistir a: una clase de ejercicios, bailes, conciertos
> escribir: poemas, cartas, tarjetas postales
> comer: ensaladas, fruta, hamburguesas
> correr: en el parque, después de clases, cinco millas

20 **¿Cómo pasas tú los días?** *How do you spend your days?*

 Hablemos Interview a partner to find out how she or he spends a typical weekday. Ask about morning, afternoon, and evening activities. Switch roles and answer your partner's questions about a typical weekend morning, afternoon, or evening.

MODELO
—¿Qué haces los lunes por la mañana?
—Los lunes asisto al colegio y hablo con mis amigos.

21 **Los sábados**

 Escribamos With whom do you usually spend Saturdays? Write three paragraphs, one for the morning, one for the afternoon, and one for the evening. In each paragraph, tell whom you're with, where you go, and what you typically do together. Use some of the expressions listed in the word box to make your paragraphs flow naturally. See sample answer below.

> siempre   especialmente
>   primero
> vamos a   a veces
>   nunca
>   por fin
> típicamente nos gusta   luego

Communication for All Students

Additional Practice

To review the functions and grammar of this **paso**, have your students do the following activity. Have students form groups, then give each group a list of several activities. Have students divide the activities into three categories—**por la mañana, por la tarde,** and **por la noche**—according to the time of day that they do each. Ask each group member to report to the class when one activity is done, using the correct form of the verb for each. You might record their answers on the board as they go along.

¿Cómo es una semana típica?

In this chapter, we asked some students what they usually do during the week and on weekends.

Matías
Buenos Aires, Argentina CD 5 Tr. 9

"Vengo al colegio a las ocho y cuarto; salgo [a las] doce y cuarto para irme a comer, vuelvo a la una y media y salgo de nuevo a las cuatro y cuarto, llego a mi casa, veo tele y como, y voy a dormir."

¿Y los fines de semana?
"Voy a andar en velero al club náutico, y después vuelvo tarde a eso de las ocho y vuelvo a mi casa directo a dormir".

Maikel CD 5 Tr. 8
Caracas, Venezuela

"Ir al liceo, llegar a casa en la tarde, hacer mis tareas y descansar".

¿Y los fines de semana?
"Bueno, quedarme en mi casa o si no, salgo con mis padres".

María Luisa
Quito, Ecuador CD 5 Tr. 7

"Vengo al colegio y del colegio a la casa, y de ahí no hago nada más".

¿Y los fines de semana?
"Salgo a comer con mis amigas, me voy a casa de ellas o ellas vienen a mi casa".

Para pensar y hablar...

A. Read the interviews carefully. Whose weekday routine is most like yours? Whose weekend routine is similar to yours?

B. What you do says a lot about you. What do you think María Luisa, Matías, and Maikel are like?

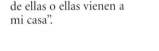
Cuaderno para hispanohablantes, pp. 24–25

Connections and Comparisons

Motivating Activity
Ask students to imagine what routines are like for teenagers in Spain and Latin America. Discuss how much time they believe these students spend going to school, doing homework or chores, watching TV, or doing other leisure activities. (Students in Spanish-speaking countries may start school later, have a longer lunch, and watch less TV.) Why do they think similarities or differences exist?

Native Speakers
If you have students from a Spanish-speaking country, ask if they are willing to share with the class how their daily routine is the same or different from the one they had in their country of origin. Students from other, non-Spanish-speaking cultures may also share what their daily routines were like before they came to the United States.

Teaching Resources
p. 153

PRINT
▸ Video Guide, pp. 33–35, 38
▸ Cuaderno de actividades, p. 60
▸ Cuaderno para hispanohablantes, p. 24

MEDIA
▸ One-Stop Planner
▸ Video Program, Videocassette 2, 29:37–32:37
▸ DVD Tutor, Disc 1
▸ Audio Compact Discs, CD 5, Trs. 6–9
▸ Interactive CD-ROM Tutor, Disc 2

Presenting
Panorama cultural

Read each interview as a class, or stop the video after each interview and ask students to summarize in English what the person on the video said. When all interviews have been viewed, have students answer the questions in the text. Then show the video again and have students answer the **Preguntas**.

Preguntas

1. **¿Cuál de los chicos no hace nada después del colegio?** (María Luisa)
2. **¿Qué significa** *liceo*? (high school)
3. **¿Quiénes salen con gente los fines de semana?** (María Luisa, Maikel)
4. **¿Con quiénes salen?** (sus amigas, sus padres)
5. **¿Qué quiere decir** *andar en velero* y *a eso de*? (to go sailing; "around," in terms of time)

Tercer paso

Objectives Giving today's date; talking about the weather

go.
hrw
.com
WV3 FLORIDA-5

Teaching Resources
pp. 154–157

PRINT
▶ Lesson Planner, p. 26
▶ TPR Storytelling Book, pp. 19–20
▶ Listening Activities, pp. 36, 41
▶ Activities for Communication, pp. 29–30, 97, 98–99, 145–146
▶ Cuaderno de gramática, pp. 42–44
▶ Grammar Tutor for Students of Spanish, Chapter 5
▶ Cuaderno de actividades, pp. 56–58
▶ Cuaderno para hispanohablantes, pp. 21–25
▶ Testing Program, pp. 113–116
▶ Alternative Assessment Guide, p. 36
▶ Student Make-Up Assignments, Chapter 5

MEDIA
▶ One-Stop Planner
▶ Audio Compact Discs, CD 5, Trs. 10–15, 26–27, 19
▶ Teaching Transparencies 5-3, 5-B, 5-C; **Más práctica gramatical** Answers; Cuaderno de gramática Answers
▶ Interactive CD-ROM Tutor, Disc 2

Bell Work
Write simple addition or subtraction problems with numbers from 1 to 31. Students write out the problems and their answers in Spanish.

Presenting
Así se dice, Nota gramatical Vocabulario

Write the date on the board using **Hoy es el... de....** Elicit this phrase as a response to **¿Cuál es la fecha?** Then write the months on the board. Model the Spanish for the seasons, and ask students which months correspond to each.

Así se dice

Giving today's date

To find out today's date, ask:

¿Cuál es la fecha?
¿Qué fecha es hoy?

To give today's date, say:

Hoy **es el primero de diciembre.**
   . . . is the first of December.

Es el quince de enero.
   It's the fifteenth of January.

To tell on what date something happens, say:

El cuatro de este mes hay un examen.
   On the fourth of this month . . .

Nota gramatical

The formula for giving today's date is **el** + *number* + **de** + *month*: **el quince de junio**. The first day of the month is called **el primero.** Note that in Spanish you omit the "on" in expressions like *on the fifth*.

La fiesta es el cinco de mayo.
   The party is on the fifth of May.

Cuaderno de gramática, pp. 42–43, Acts.12–14

Más práctica gramatical, p. 162, Act. 7

---

22 **Gramática en contexto** Answers will vary.

Escribamos/Hablemos Working individually first, write a special date for each month of the year. You might include holidays and more personal dates like birthdays or upcoming special events. Then compare lists with your partner. For each date that you don't recognize, ask why that date is special to your partner. For holidays or other special occasions, see page R5.

Vocabulario

la primavera
• marzo
• abril
• mayo

el verano
• junio
• julio
• agosto

CD-ROM 2
DVD 1

el invierno
• diciembre
• enero
• febrero

el otoño
• septiembre
• octubre
• noviembre

Cuaderno de actividades, p. 56, Acts. 13–15

El otoño es una estación.
Hay cuatro estaciones en un año.

Octubre es un mes.
Hay doce meses en un año.

Cuaderno de gramática, p. 42, Act. 11

Communication for All Students

Auditory Learners
24 Have students work in groups of four to form sentences. The first students says something from the first column. (**En el invierno...**) The second student says something from the second column. (**...hago ejercicio...**) The third student says something from the third column. (**...en el gimnasio.**) The fourth student records what the others say. Ask students to switch roles throughout the activity.

Challenge
26 After discussing the **Nota cultural,** give dates and places (**el quince de julio en Santiago de Chile**) and ask students to name activities they might do based on what the weather might be. (**El quince de julio en Santiago de Chile, leo revistas en casa. El veinte de abril en Miami, juego al béisbol.**) You may wish to use *Teaching Transparency 2A.*

23 Meses y estaciones — Scripts and answers on p. 139H.

Escuchemos Listen and match the date you hear with the correct picture.

CD 5 Tr. 10

a.

b.

c.

d.

e.

f.

24 Actividades — Possible answer below.

Leamos/Escribamos What do you usually do during different seasons of the year? Combine elements from all three columns to form answers. Then, create a sentence telling what you like to do in the places mentioned.

MODELO En el verano voy a la playa. Me gusta bucear, jugar al voleibol y descansar.

En el invierno	ir a...	el colegio
En la primavera	trabajar en...	el gimnasio
En el verano	hacer ejercicio...	el parque
En el otoño	comer...	la piscina
	beber...	la playa
	asistir a...	en casa
	leer...	el centro
	escribir...	comercial
	jugar al...	

Nota cultural

The seasons in the southern cone of South America occur at opposite times of year from seasons north of the equator. Summer begins in December, and winter begins in June. The equator runs through northern South America, where the weather is warm all year round. Here there are only two seasons, wet and dry. In the tropics, altitude plays a major role in climate. The Andes region is quite cold even though it's near the equator.

25 Y tú, ¿adónde vas?

Hablemos Get together with a partner. Try to guess at least five sentences your partner wrote in Activity 24. Check how many of your guesses were right. What activities do you and your partner have in common?

26 ¿Cuál es la fecha?

Escribamos/Hablemos Make a list of six dates, including at least one from each season. Then read them to your partner one at a time. Your partner will tell you what season it is, and at least one activity she or he associates with that time of year. Possible answer below.

MODELO —Es el treinta de abril.
—Es la primavera, y juego al béisbol.

Tercer paso

CAPÍTULO 5

Additional Practice
Before class begins write on a transparency: ¿Quién cumple años el... de...? Yo, yo cumplo años el... de..., and ____, ¿no cumples años el... de...?

In Spanish, have students write their birthday and their name on an index card. Collect the cards and have a volunteer shuffle and pass them out. Tell students not to let anyone know whose card they receive.

Display the transparency and call on a student to ask the first question using the date on their card: ¿Quién cumple años el... de...? The student recognizing his or her birthday answers **Yo, yo cumplo años el... de...** If no one answers, the student who holds the card with that birthday should ask the student named on the card: **Juan, ¿no cumples años el cuatro de enero?**

Continue until all students have participated. You may wish to save the cards for a quick review activity later in the chapter.

Teaching Suggestion
24 Have several students write sentences on the board or on a transparency to share with the class. You may wish to have the class peer-correct.

Answers
24 *Possible answer:*
En el invierno estoy mucho en casa. Me gusta leer novelas y mirar la televisión.

26 *Possible answer:*
—Es el catorce de agosto.
—Es el verano. Nadamos mucho en el verano.

Connections and Comparisons

Science Link

After students read **Nota cultural**, have them explain why seasons occur at opposite times of the year in the Southern and Northern Hemispheres. (Due to the tilt of the Earth's axis, sunlight is more direct in the Southern Hemisphere in December than in June and vice-versa in the Northern Hemisphere.) You may have students research weather patterns throughout the Spanish-speaking world, and then report on where they would go to follow what they consider an ideal climate as the seasons change. As a larger project, have them do this month by month, researching and reporting on twelve different places. Once they report on the places selected, have the class defend them as having more desirable climates in given months than the places classmates chose.

Teaching Resources
pp. 154–157

PRINT
- Lesson Planner, p. 25
- TPR Storytelling Book, pp. 19–20
- Listening Activities, pp. 36, 41
- Activities for Communication, pp. 29–30, 97, 98–99, 145–146
- Cuaderno de gramática, pp. 42–44
- Grammar Tutor for Students of Spanish, Chapter 5
- Cuaderno de actividades, pp. 56–58
- Cuaderno para hispanohablantes, pp. 21–25
- Testing Program, pp. 113–116
- Alternative Assessment Guide, p. 36
- Student Make-Up Assignments, Chapter 5

MEDIA
- One-Stop Planner
- Audio Compact Discs, CD 5, Trs. 10–15, 26–27, 19
- Teaching Transparencies 5-3, 5-B, 5-C; **Más práctica gramatical** Answers; Cuaderno de gramática Answers
- Interactive CD-ROM Tutor, Disc 2

Presenting
Así se dice, Vocabulario

Have students follow along in their books as you talk about the weather map. **¿Qué tiempo hace hoy? En Portland está lloviendo. Llueve mucho. En Fargo, está nevando. En Chicago hace viento. En Los Ángeles hace buen tiempo, pero en Milwaukee...,** and so on. Next, ask true/false questions using **¿verdad?** Finally, have the class answer questions. **(Clase, ¿qué tiempo hace hoy en Nueva York?)**

Así se dice

Talking about the weather

To find out what the weather is like, ask:

¿Qué tiempo hace?

To answer, say:

Hace buen tiempo.
Hace muy mal tiempo hoy.

Más práctica gramatical, p. 163, Acts. 8–9

Vocabulario

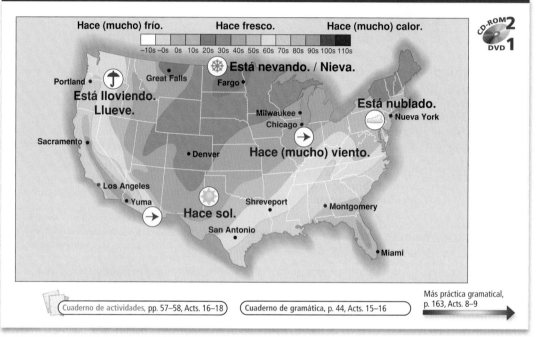

Hace (mucho) frío.   Hace fresco.   Hace (mucho) calor.

–10s –0s 0s 10s 20s 30s 40s 50s 60s 70s 80s 90s 100s 110s

Está nevando. / Nieva.

Portland • Great Falls Fargo •

Está lloviendo.
Llueve.

Milwaukee •   Está nublado.
Chicago •   • Nueva York

Sacramento •

• Denver   Hace (mucho) viento.

• Los Angeles

• Yuma   Hace sol.   Shreveport • Montgomery

San Antonio •   • Miami

Cuaderno de actividades, pp. 57–58, Acts. 16–18   Cuaderno de gramática, p. 44, Acts. 15–16

Más práctica gramatical, p. 163, Acts. 8–9

27 **El pronóstico del tiempo** *The weather report*

Leamos Mira el mapa e indica qué tiempo hace en cada ciudad. Answers may vary. Possible answers:

1. Miami a, c, d, h   **a.** hace sol y hace buen tiempo
2. Nueva York i   **b.** está lloviendo
3. Portland c   **c.** hace buen tiempo
4. Sacramento a, c, d, h **d.** hace calor y hace sol
5. San Antonio a, c   **e.** hace viento
6. Milwaukee e   **f.** hace mucho frío
7. Shreveport a, c   **g.** hace frío y está nevando
8. Chicago e   **h.** hace calor
                          i. hace fresco

Teacher to Teacher

Linda Hale
Sonoma Valley High School
Sonoma, California

For Linda's class, a *noticiero* tells it all

"For this unit I have students write and practice a TV broadcast like the one in the **fotonovela**. In pairs, students make maps and practice a weather report or they write interview questions for a famous person or another student and practice them out loud. Another pair of students in the group tells about upcoming events or sports. Then we videotape their shows. Students love to see themselves on television and really practice to sound authentic."

Note: You may wish to use the rubric on p. 182 for evaluation.

28 Del colegio al trabajo

Escribamos A travel agency has contracted you to help develop an informational Web page for Spanish-speaking visitors to your area. Describe the weather in your city during different months for tourists planning to visit. *Answers will vary.*

MODELO en diciembre y enero
En diciembre y enero, hace mucho frío y nieva.

1. en julio y agosto
2. en septiembre y octubre
3. en febrero y marzo
4. en marzo y abril

A lo nuestro

When it's really cold or hot, you can say **¡Hace un frío/calor tremendo!** If it's raining especially hard, you can say **Está lloviendo a cántaros** (*It's raining cats and dogs*). If it's a beautiful day and you really can't complain, you can tell your friends **Hace un tiempo precioso.**

29 ¿Qué haces cuando...? *Possible answers below.*

Hablemos Find out what activities your partner does in the following kinds of weather. Use the **-ar**, **-er**, and **-ir** verbs you know. Be prepared to report your findings to the class.

1. cuando hace frío
2. cuando llueve
3. cuando nieva
4. cuando hace mal tiempo
5. cuando hace sol
6. cuando hace calor

30 En mi cuaderno *Answers will vary.*

Escribamos Write two paragraphs describing your favorite season and explaining why you like it. First, tell which months are in that season and describe the weather. Then, write about the activities that you and your friends like to do, and any special places where you go at that time.

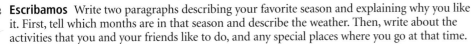

LETRA Y SONIDO

CD 5
Trs. 11–15

A. One of the purposes of accent marks is to tell you which syllable to stress.

1. Words ending in a vowel, **n**, or **s** are stressed on the next to the last syllable.

   examen   hablan   discos   toma   quiero

2. Words ending in any consonant besides **n** or **s** are stressed on the last syllable.

   animal   feliz   Madrid   hablar

3. Exceptions to rules 1 and 2 get an accent mark over the syllable to be stressed.

   semáforo   lápices   rápido   lámpara   música   Víctor   suéter

4. All question words have an accent mark.

   ¿qué?   ¿cuándo?   ¿quién?   ¿cómo?   ¿cuánto?   ¿dónde?

B. Some words have an accent mark to tell them apart from a similar word.

   mi *my*   **tu** *your*   **si** *if*
   mí *me*   **tú** *you*   **sí** *yes*

C. Dictado *Script for Part C on p. 139H.*

Listen and read the phone conversation and rewrite the words that need accent marks.

Voy al almacen hoy porque necesito una camara nueva. Pero, ¿donde esta mi sueter? ¿Y el cinturon para mi falda? Ah, aqui estan. ¿Tu quieres ir conmigo?

D. Trabalenguas

Tin marín dedós pingüé, cúcara, mácara, títere fue

Connections and Comparisons

TPR Divide students into groups of three or four. Give each group a piece of paper with a month or a season on it. They are to develop a pantomime based on their month or season, and the class is to guess which one it is. Each student in the group should play a part in the pantomime.

Career Path

Ask students to form small groups and write as many careers as they can think of that incorporate or are affected by weather. Give them five minutes to brainstorm and then call the class together. Now ask the class to consider which of these careers would also use Spanish. You might get them started with some hints: meteorologist, international tour guide, scientist, pilot, travel agent.

Writing Assessment

30 Refer to **Cuaderno de actividades,** p. 149, or the *Alternative Assessment Guide,* p. 22, for more writing ideas. You may wish to use the following rubric to assess the assignment.

Writing Rubric	Points			
	4	3	2	1
Content (Complete– Incomplete)				
Comprehensibility (Comprehensible– Incomprehensible)				
Accuracy (Accurate– Seldom accurate)				
Organization (Well organized– Poorly organized)				
Effort (Excellent–Minimal)				

18–20: A   14–15: C   Under
16–17: B   12–13: D   12: F

Assess

▶ Testing Program, pp. 113–116
  Quiz 5-3A, Quiz 5-3B
  Audio CD 5, Tr. 19

▶ Student Make-Up Assignments, Chapter 5, Alternative Quiz

▶ Alternative Assessment Guide, p. 36

Answers

29 *Possible answers:*
1. —¿Qué haces cuando hace frío?
   —Cuando hace frío, me gusta leer en casa.
2. —¿Qué te gusta hacer cuando llueve?
   —Cuando llueve voy al cine.

 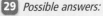

Vamos a leer

Teaching Resources
pp. 158–159

PRINT
▸ Lesson Planner, p. 27
▸ Cuaderno de actividades, p. 59
▸ Cuaderno para hispanohablantes, pp. 21–23
▸ Reading Strategies and Skills Handbook, Chapter 5
▸ ¡Lee conmigo! 1, Chapter 5
▸ Standardized Assessment Tutor, Chapter 5

MEDIA
▸ One-Stop Planner

Prereading
Activity A

Using Text Structures
You may wish to ask students to look at the pictures and to guess what the reading will be about. You might then ask them what their favorite water sport is and if it is pictured here. Also, ask them which words they already know as a result of their knowledge of English.

Deportes en el agua

Estrategia para leer
As you know, it's easy to understand pictures, cognates, and words you have already studied. Many other words can be understood, too, based on how they're used in the sentence or paragraph. When you come to an unknown word, try to guess its meaning based on context (the other words around it).

¡A comenzar!

A. Before you do any in-depth reading, first remember to get the general idea and to recall your background knowledge of the topic. It should be easy to tell what these readings are about because of the pictures.

¿Te acuerdas?

Look at pictures and titles first. What is the reading about?
a. a sporting goods store
b. racing
c. water sports
d. the environment

Al grano

B. Imagine that your family will be vacationing in Miami this summer. Each of you wants to try out a different sport. Read the passages and decide which sport would be best for each member of your family. Then, find an appropriate activity for each family member on page 159. Be sure to tell what words or phrases support your choice.
See answers below.

El motoesquí es para los fanáticos de la velocidad. El piloto necesita moverse con el ritmo de las <u>olas</u> del océano. Es fácil usar estas máquinas y no es muy caro. Es posible <u>alquilar</u> una por $25 la hora.

¿Te gusta mirar deportes en la televisión? Las <u>lanchas</u> del offshore son un deporte similar a la Fórmula 1. Estas lanchas corren a aproximadamente 110 millas por hora. Pero no son baratas — ¡estas lanchas <u>cuestan</u> más de 200.000 dólares! Naturalmente, no hay muchas personas que participen en este deporte.

Cultures and Communities

Native Speakers
• Have native speakers write an entry in their journals about their favorite sport or pastime. Encourage them to review a magazine or newspaper article or an Internet document about their favorite activity, telling how well they think it is depicted. Have them wrap up the entry by saying why they like this pastime most.

• Encourage native speakers to find synonyms for the words underlined in **Vamos a leer**. Have them use six of the underlined words in a mock article for the sports page of a newspaper. Encourage students to be creative and humorous!

La natación es siempre el favorito de la estación. Es posible nadar en el océano o en una piscina. Hay muchas piscinas de <u>tamaño</u> olímpico que son muy grandes. Es bueno practicar aquí. La piscina está dividida en muchas <u>calles</u>, y todas las personas nadan en una <u>calle</u> diferente.

El windsurf es buen deporte para el verano. Si no tienes experiencia, es muy importante tomar <u>lecciones</u> de un instructor. También necesitas tener un buen <u>sentido</u> de equilibrio. Tu primera experiencia debe ser en el verano porque el viento es ideal. En la primavera, hace demasiado viento para las personas que no tienen experiencia en el deporte.

En el verano, hay muchos kayaks en el agua. Son barcos pequeños para una o dos personas. Las personas controlan el kayak con <u>remos</u> largos. Es normal operar un kayak en el <u>río</u>, no en el océano.

1. your father, who loves high speeds (What phrase in the text supports that decision?)
2. your mother, who likes the most popular of all water sports (What sentence says this sport is the most popular?)
3. your sister, who likes small, one- or two-person boats (What words in the text tell you this?)
4. your brother, who would rather watch sports than participate (What phrase says this is primarily a sport to watch?) See answers below.

C. Your parents are trying to read the descriptions of these sports, but they don't know Spanish as well as you do. They underlined the words they didn't know so that you could help them. Use your knowledge of context to help them guess the meanings of these words. See answers below.

D. Choose one easy-to-recognize noun from each of the sports in the reading, but don't choose the name of the sport itself. Then tell your partner the noun you chose. Your partner will say which sport the noun is associated with. Switch roles after four nouns.

MODELO —Piscina.
—¡La natación!

E. Tus padres dicen que tienes todo el día libre para participar en tu deporte acuático favorito. ¿Cuál de estos cinco deportes prefieres? Busca dos o tres frases en la lectura *(reading)* que explican por qué prefieres este deporte.

Cuaderno para hispanohablantes, pp. 21–23

Cuaderno de actividades, p. 59, Act. 19

Vamos a leer

CAPÍTULO 5

Reading
Activities B and C

Using Context Clues
C. There may be translations of the words other than those listed. Praise students for making a logical guess, even if it is not the exact word. For instance, **alquilar** could be translated as *use* or *get* in this context. After they've done one or two, check to see if they are guessing correctly. Talk them through the process in English if they are having difficulty. ("It's very important to take _____ from an expert.") Then ask the class to give you logical guesses.

Postreading
Activities D and E

Monitoring Comprehension
D. As a follow-up activity, put students in groups of two or three, give them a picture of a different sport from those listed here, and have them compose a brief caption.

Answers

B 1. jet ski; "los fanáticos de la velocidad"
2. natación; "La natación es siempre el favorito de la estación".
3. kayaks; "barcos pequeños para una o dos personas"
4. offshore boating; "¿Te gusta mirar deportes en la televisión?" or "no hay muchas personas que participen"

C 1. waves; to rent
2. boats; cost / they cost
3. size; lanes; lane
4. lessons; sense
5. oars; river

Communication for All Students

Auditory Learners
Write the names of the sports in the photos on a transparency or on the board. Have students close their books. Then read a portion of the description of each photo from the text and ask students to identify the sport you are describing.

Additional Practice
Ask each student to select the text from one of the photos and to record it on an audiocassette tape. Replay the tape and ask the student to assess how he or she sounds. You may wish to provide feedback to each student.

CAPÍTULO 5

For **Más práctica gramatical**
Answer Transparencies, see the
Teaching Transparencies binder.

Más práctica gramatical

internet

MARCAR: go.hrw.com
PALABRA CLAVE:
WV3 FLORIDA-5

Primer paso **Objective** Discussing how often you do things

1 Daniel is complaining about all the responsibilities he has and all the fun things he never gets a chance to do. Create a sentence for each of his complaints. (**p. 145**)

> **MODELO**   cuidar a mi hermano/mirar la televisión
> ¡Siempre cuido a mi hermano! Nunca miro la televisión.

1. practicar el piano/montar en bicicleta
2. preparar la cena/tomar un refresco con amigos
3. estudiar/nadar en la piscina
4. lavar la ropa/ir al gimnasio
5. sacar la basura/descansar
6. organizar mi cuarto/escuchar música
7. lavar el carro/ir al parque

2 Pilar has just transferred to a new school and is feeling lonely. Complete her letter to an advice columnist by filling in each blank with **nunca, nada,** or **nadie.** (**p. 145**)

Quiero conocer a los estudiantes pero es difícil.
En la cafetería, ___1___ pasa el rato conmigo.
Después de clases, mis compañeros van al café a
tomar un refresco, pero ___2___ voy con ellos.
Después de clases, ___3___ habla por teléfono
conmigo. Los fines de semana, no hago ___4___.
Por ejemplo, ___5___ voy a la pizzería con los
compañeros. Cuando voy al parque,
no hablo con ___6___. ¡Qué horrible! ¿Qué
necesito hacer para tener amigos?

Answers

1 1. ¡Siempre practico el piano! Nunca monto en bicicleta.
2. ¡Siempre preparo la cena! Nunca tomo un refresco con amigos.
3. ¡Siempre estudio! Nunca nado en la piscina.
4. ¡Siempre lavo la ropa! Nunca voy al gimnasio.
5. ¡Siempre saco la basura! Nunca descanso.
6. ¡Siempre organizo mi cuarto! Nunca escucho música.
7. ¡Siempre lavo el carro! Nunca voy al parque.

2 1. nadie
2. nunca
3. nadie
4. nada
5. nunca
6. nadie

3 Completa la conversación sobre los estudiantes en una fiesta. Usa **quién** o **quiénes**. (**p. 146**)

MATEO Sonia, ¿___1___ es la chica alta?

SONIA Es Soledad, la amiga de Felipe. ¿Y sabes ___2___ son los jóvenes bajos y rubios allí?

MATEO Sí, sí. Son Pablo y Tomás. ¿___3___ es la chica baja? Es Estela, ¿verdad?

Grammar Resources for Chapter 5

The **Más práctica gramatical** activities are designed as supplemental activities for the grammatical concepts presented in the chapter. You might use them as additional practice, for review, or for assessment.

For more grammar presentation, review, and practice refer to the following:

• Cuaderno de gramática
• Grammar Tutor for Students of Spanish

• Grammar Summary on pp. R9–R13
• Cuaderno de actividades
• Grammar and Vocabulary quizzes (Testing Program)
• Test Generator on the One-Stop Planner CD-ROM
• Interactive CD-ROM Tutor
• **Juegos interactivos** at go.hrw.com

STANDARDS: 1.2

SONIA   No, es Lola, la hermana de Estela. ¿__4__ es el chico guapo con ella?

MATEO   Es mi amigo Simón. Oye, ¿__5__ tocan la guitarra y el piano?

SONIA   La chica que toca la guitarra es Laura. ¿__6__ toca el piano, sabes?

Segundo paso   Objectives Talking about what you and your friends like to do together; talking about what you do during a typical week

4 What do the following people like to do? Use a verb from the box in each sentence you create to say what they like. Be sure to include **a ustedes, a ellos,** or **a ellas** for clarification. (p. 149)

MODELO   **Héctor y Olivia van a la piscina.**
           A ellos les gusta nadar.

1. Martín y Enrique compran una pizza grande.
2. Raimundo y Laura van al gimnasio.
3. Daniela y Linda compran jugo de frutas.
4. Tú y Rita van al parque.
5. Guillermo y Ana van al correo.
6. Tú y Yolanda compran el periódico.

> leer las tiras cómicas
> beber jugo
> correr
> hacer ejercicio
> comer
> escribir tarjetas postales

5 Complete the description of the cafeteria at lunch break by filling in each blank with the correct form of the verbs from the box. Some verbs may be used more than once. (p. 150)

> comer   beber   escribir
> hacer   leer   correr

Hay muchos estudiantes en la cafetería. En una mesa, Fernanda __1__ el periódico. Cerca de ella, Diego y Esteban __2__ pizza. Al lado de Fernanda, José Patricio __3__ una carta y __4__ una ensalada. Yo __5__ jugo con Martín. Nosotros también __6__ la tarea para la clase de inglés. ¿Y qué __7__ Sara? Ella __8__ un sándwich muy rápido porque tiene clase en tres minutos. Y Luis __9__ para comprar otra hamburguesa, porque la cafetería se cierra *(closes)* ahora.

Communication for All Students

Additional Practice

1 3 4 Have students work in small groups. Each group should conduct a poll among themselves using questions with **¿A quién le gusta...?** and **¿A quiénes les gusta...?** The groups should try to identify two or more activities that everyone in the group likes and two or more activities that everyone dislikes. Then one member from each group moves to another group to explain his or her group's likes and dislikes and to find out about the preferences of the other group. Finally, all students return to their original group to explain what they found out about the likes and dislikes of the other students. (**A ellos les gusta..., A ellos no les gusta...**)

Answers

3 1. quién
2. quiénes
3. Quién
4. Quién
5. quiénes
6. quién

4 1. A ellos les gusta comer.
2. A ellos les gusta hacer ejercicio.
3. A ellas les gusta beber jugo.
4. A ustedes les gusta correr.
5. A ellos les gusta escribir tarjetas postales.
6. A ustedes les gusta leer las tiras cómicas.

5 1. lee
2. comen
3. escribe/lee
4. come
5. bebo
6. hacemos/escribimos
7. hace
8. come
9. corre

Más práctica gramatical

WV3 FLORIDA

CAPÍTULO 5

For **Más práctica gramatical**
Answer Transparencies, see the
Teaching Transparencies binder.

6 Indica lo que a la gente le gusta y lo que no le gusta hacer. Completa cada oración con el pronombre correcto: **me, te, le** o **les**. (p. 149)

1. A María ___1___ gusta asistir a su clase de aeróbicos, pero a Patricia y a Lourdes no ___2___ gusta hacer ejercicio.
2. A mí ___3___ gusta beber jugo todos los días, pero a Daniel no ___4___ gusta.
3. A Elena y a Pedro ___5___ gusta leer las tiras cómicas en el periódico, pero a mí ___6___ gusta más leer un libro interesante.
4. ¿A ti ___7___ gusta recibir cartas? No, a mí no ___8___ gusta.

Tercer paso

Objectives Giving today's date; talking about the weather

7 Indica la fecha de las siguientes actividades con base en el calendario de Paloma. Deletrea *(Spell out)* los números. (p. 154)

MODELO   el partido de voleibol
El partido de voleibol es el dieciséis de noviembre.

NOVIEMBRE

lunes	martes	miércoles	jueves	viernes	sábado	domingo
		1 examen de historia	2	3 partido de fútbol	4	5
6 examen de español	7 clase de natación	8	9 clase de natación	10	11 ¡¡Día Libre!!	12 baile
13	14 concierto	15	16 partido de voleibol	17	18 fiesta para Julia	19

1. las clases de natación
2. el concierto
3. el examen de español
4. el examen de historia
5. la fiesta para Julia
6. el baile
7. el día libre
8. el partido de fútbol

Answers

6 1. le
2. les
3. me
4. le
5. les
6. me
7. te
8. me

7 1. Las clases de natación son el siete y el nueve de noviembre.
2. El concierto es el catorce de noviembre.
3. El examen de español es el seis de noviembre.
4. El examen de historia es el primero de noviembre.
5. La fiesta para Julia es el dieciocho de noviembre.
6. El baile es el doce de noviembre.
7. El día libre es el once de noviembre.
8. El partido de fútbol es el tres de noviembre.

Teacher to Teacher

Patricia Wells
C.C. Sweeting
Junior High School
Nassau, Bahamas

Patricia's students make global forecasts
"I reinforce weather terms by having students play the role of weather forecasters from abroad. I assign students countries from different hemispheres or climatic zones and encourage them to watch the weather channel to learn about conditions and to facilitate role-playing. I have them give a brief weather report in Spanish in class. Since there are so many students, I select a few students every class to give a weather report from their corner of the globe."

8 Ana keeps a diary throughout the year. Read these excerpts, and then match each one with the weather and the season. (**pp. 154, 156**)

> **a.** nieva; invierno
> **b.** hace fresco; otoño
> **c.** llueve; primavera
> **d.** hace sol; primavera
> **e.** hace calor; verano
> **f.** está nublado; otoño

1. Hoy es un día estupendo. Es el quince de abril y voy al parque con el perro.
2. ¡Qué mal tiempo hace! Hoy es el primero de mayo y voy al cine con unos amigos.
3. El tres de diciembre—¡me encanta el frío! Beto y yo vamos esta tarde a esquiar.
4. No me gusta el tiempo así, ¡está tan gris! Es el diecisiete de octubre y Mamá escribe cartas en la sala.
5. Hoy es el nueve de agosto y hace mucho sol. Laura y Rafa van a nadar en la piscina.
6. Me gusta el tiempo así. Es el doce de septiembre y mi familia acampa este fin de semana.

9 As you read each description below, decide which picture best illustrates it. Answer **ninguna foto** if no picture illustrates it. (**p. 156**)

a.

b.

c.

1. Hace muy buen tiempo hoy.
2. Hoy no hace buen tiempo. Está lloviendo.
3. Aquí nieva mucho y qué bien porque me gusta esquiar.
4. Hace fresco por la tarde y no está lloviendo.
5. Está nevando y está nublado también.
6. Nos gusta bucear cuando hace fresco.
7. A Julián le gusta acampar cuando hace fresco.

Review and Assess

You may wish to assign **Más práctica gramatical** as additional practice or homework. Assign Activities 1–2 after **Gramática** (p. 145), Activity 3 after **Nota gramatical** (p. 146), Activity 4 after **Nota gramatical** (p. 149), Activity 5 after **Gramática** (p. 150), Activity 6 after **Nota gramatical** (p. 149), Activity 7 after **Nota gramatical** (p. 154), Activity 8 after **Nota gramatical** (p. 154), and **Vocabulario** (p. 156), and Activity 9 after **Vocabulario** (p. 156).

To prepare students for the **Paso** quizzes and Chapter Test, have them do the **Más práctica gramatical** activities in the following order: complete Activities 1–3 before taking quiz 5-1A or 5-1B; Activities 4–6 before taking quiz 5-2A or 5-2B; and Activities 7–9 before taking quiz 5-3A or 5-3B.

Answers

8 1. d
2. c
3. a
4. f
5. e
6. b

9 1. b *or* c
2. a
3. b
4. c
5. ninguna foto
6. ninguna foto
7. c

Repaso

🖥 internet

go.hrw.com
MARCAR: go.hrw.com
PALABRA CLAVE:
WV3 FLORIDA-5

CAPÍTULO 5

The **Repaso** reviews and integrates all four skills and culture in preparation for the Chapter Test.

Teaching Resources
pp. 164–165

PRINT
▶ Lesson Planner, p. 26
▶ Listening Activities, p. 37
▶ Video Guide, pp. 33–35, 38
▶ Grammar Tutor for Students of Spanish, Chapter 5
▶ Cuaderno para hispanohablantes, pp. 21–25
▶ Standardized Assessment Tutor, Chapter 5

MEDIA
▶ One-Stop Planner
▶ Video Program, Videocassette 2, 32:28–33:19
▶ DVD Tutor, Disc 1
▶ Audio Compact Discs, CD 5, Tr. 16
▶ Interactive CD-ROM Tutor, Disc 2

Teaching Suggestion

2 You might like to videotape the interview, asking one of the students to assume the role of Raquel. They can then reverse their roles.

---

1 For each weather report you hear, determine which of the photos is being described.
Scripts and answers on p. 139H.

CD 5
Tr. 16

a.

b.

c.

d.

2 Raquel necesita entrevistarte para poder terminar su segmento en *Noticias Colegio Seminole.* Contesta sus preguntas.   Answers will vary.

1. Típicamente, ¿qué haces con tus amigos?
2. ¿Qué haces con tu familia durante la semana?
3. A tus amigos, ¿les gusta mirar la televisión? ¿Con qué frecuencia?
4. Cuando hace buen tiempo, ¿qué te gusta hacer?
5. ¿Qué haces con tus amigos cuando hace mal tiempo?

3 See if your partner knows who in your class likes to do the following activities and how often. Answers will vary.

1. escribir poemas
2. bailar
3. pescar
4. tocar el piano
5. dibujar
6. correr
7. comer ensaladas
8. organizar el cuarto
9. acampar
10. leer el periódico
11. asistir a conciertos
12. hacer ejercicio

4 Write the following dates in correct Spanish form. See if you can locate a Spanish-language almanac or calendar to find out what special day each one represents. See answers below.

1. May 5   2. December 28   3. June 24   4. October 12   5. January 6

5 Pick four different cities from the weather map on page 165. Describe the weather there and list two different activities you might do in each place. Answers will vary.

Apply and Assess

Native Speakers

4 Ask students to share with the class details about the celebration of these holidays and others. You might try to determine if the festivities for each holiday vary from country to country.

Additional Practice

5 Ask students to read or listen to the local weather forecast and to prepare their own brief **pronóstico del tiempo** for your city or town for the following day. It could be done as an audio or video recording or as a newspaper article. (You may wish to bring in a newspaper in case some students do not have access to a forecast.)

Answers
4 1. el Cinco de Mayo; la Batalla de Puebla de 1862
2. el veintiocho de diciembre; el Día de los Inocentes *(April Fools' Day)*
3. el veinticuatro de junio; el Día de San Juan Bautista
4. el doce de octubre; el Día de la Raza *(Columbus Day)*
5. el seis de enero; el Día de los Reyes Magos

6 Decide if the following statements would most likely be made by someone from the United States (**un/a estadounidense**) or someone from a Spanish-speaking country (**una persona de un país hispanohablante**). Some statements might be made by both! See answers below.

1. Bueno, durante la semana juego al fútbol con el equipo de mi colegio.
2. ¿En una semana típica? Pues, de lunes a sábado asisto a clases en mi colegio. Los domingos, mi familia y yo hacemos cosas juntos.
3. Trabajo todos los días después de clases en un restaurante.
4. Por la tarde, mis amigos y yo paseamos por el centro y tomamos algo en un café.

Vamos a escribir

7

You're exchanging e-mail with a student from Argentina who wants to know what you normally do during the day. Start by making a writing plan. Then, based on your plan, write a detailed description of what you and your friends like to do and how often. Describe different activities you do depending on the weather. End your e-mail by asking about your Argentine friend's favorite activities.

Caracas	30°C/86°F
Bogotá	19°C/66°F
Quito	23°C/74°F
Lima	19°C/66°F
La Paz	2°C/35°F
Asunción	17°C/63°F
Santiago	12°C/53°F
Buenos Aires	16°C/61°F
Montevideo	10°C/50°F

Estrategia para escribir
Making a writing plan before you begin is important. Think about your topic carefully. Do you know all the vocabulary you'll need? Will your topic require you to use certain verbs or grammatical structures frequently? If you're not sure, consult your textbook or your teacher.

1. First brainstorm to come up with the vocabulary you'll need. Think of indoor and outdoor activities you've talked about in this chapter. Include the people you're with and where you like to go.

2. Now think about what verbs and grammar structures you'll need. Can you talk about what you like to do and what the weather is like? Use the weather vocabulary on page 156 to get started.

Situación

8

You are the host of your own late night talk show. With a partner, choose a famous person and role-play the interview. Be sure to ask what your guest does during certain times of the year, what he or she likes to do, where he or she likes to go, and why.

Cuaderno para hispanohablantes, p. 25

Apply and Assess

Process Writing

7 Remind students that much of the grammar they have learned in earlier chapters will be useful when they develop their writing plan. Suggest that they review the grammar points and functions on pp. 32, 113, 114, 145, 148, and 151 to get them started. Encourage students to begin by listing ways of saying things that could be used in writing their e-mail.

Geography Link
Challenge students to evaluate some common stereotypes about geography and climate in the Spanish-speaking world by writing the following statement on the board: **Siempre hace calor y sol en Ecuador, México y España.** Ask students what is incorrect about that statement, and assign individuals or teams to gather information to refute this stereotype. Have students look in atlases, almanacs, encyclopedias, newspapers, and on the Internet to find the following information: the average seasonal temperatures in these countries; average snowfall amounts; the different geographical regions and mountain ranges; the height above sea level; and the latitude. Have students compile their findings about each country into one report to share with the class.

📁 Portfolio
8 **Oral** You might suggest that students include the **Situación** interview in their Portfolio. For Portfolio information, see *Alternative Assessment Guide,* pp. iv–17.

Answers
6 1. un estadounidense
2. un hispano
3. un estadounidense
4. un hispano/los dos

STANDARDS: 1.1, 1.3, 3.1, 4.2, 5.1, 5.2

Teaching Resources
p. 166

PRINT 📖
▸ Grammar Tutor for Students of Spanish, Chapter 5

MEDIA
▸ Interactive CD-ROM Tutor, Disc 2
▸ Online self-test

go.hrw.com
WV3 FLORIDA-5

Answers

1 1. Nunca nado.
2. Siempre desayuno. *or* Todos los días desayuno.
3. A veces hablo con Luisa.
4. Siempre trabajo los fines de semana.
5. A veces voy al cine los viernes.
6. Nunca estudio en la biblioteca.
7. Siempre ayudo en casa.

2 1. Franco, ¿te gusta organizar tu cuarto?
2. Cristina y Marta, ¿a ustedes les gusta correr en el parque?
3. Geraldo y Esteban, ¿a ustedes les gusta bucear?
4. Pablo, ¿te gusta leer novelas?
5. Linda y Laura, ¿les gusta esquiar?
6. Daniel, ¿te gusta hacer ejercicio en el gimnasio?
7. Isabel, ¿te gusta escribir cartas?

4 1. El examen de español es el cinco de marzo.
2. El partido de fútbol americano es el catorce de septiembre.
3. La fiesta de Juan es el primero de mayo.
4. El baile del colegio es el veintinueve de julio.
5. El concierto de jazz es el dieciocho de enero.

5 1. Hace frío y está lloviendo.
2. Hace buen tiempo y hace sol.
3. Hace frío y mucho viento.
4. Nieva mucho hoy.
5. Hace calor y mucho sol.
6. Está nublado.
7. Hace fresco.
8. Hace mal tiempo y está lloviendo.

Can you discuss how often you do things?
p. 145

1 How would José Luis say that . . .? See answers below.
1. he never swims
2. he always eats breakfast
3. he sometimes talks to Luisa
4. he always works on the weekends
5. he sometimes goes to the movies on Fridays
6. he never studies in the library
7. he always helps at home

Can you talk about what you and your friends like to do together? p. 148

2 How would you ask the following people or groups of people if they like to do each of the following activities? How would each person or group answer you? See answers below.
1. Franco/to organize his room
2. Cristina y Marta/to run in the park together
3. Geraldo y Esteban/to scuba dive together
4. Pablo/to read novels
5. Linda y Laura/to ski together
6. Daniel/to exercise in the gym
7. Isabel/to write letters

Can you talk about what you do during a typical week? p. 151

3 How would you tell a classmate about five activities you typically do each week? Answers will vary.

Can you give today's date? p. 154

4 How would you tell a classmate the date of the following things?
See answers below.
1. the Spanish test - March 5
2. the football game - September 14
3. John's party - May 1
4. the school dance - July 29
5. the jazz concert - January 18

Can you talk about the weather? p. 156

5 How would you describe the weather if it were . . .? See answers below.
1. rainy and cold
2. a nice, sunny day
3. cold and windy
4. snowy
5. hot and sunny
6. a cloudy day
7. cool
8. a terrible, rainy day

6 What would be a typical weather description of your hometown during the following times of the year? Answers will vary.
1. el otoño
2. el invierno
3. la primavera
4. el verano

Review and Assess

Reteaching Suggestions

1 Give students additional verb conjugation practice by having them describe what José Luis would say about what he, his brother Jorge, and his sister Claudia do.

3 Ask students to list five activities they do only under special circumstances in sentences using **sólo cuando. (Buceo sólo cuando voy a Miami. Miro la tele sólo cuando no tengo tarea.)**

4 5 6 Have students work in small groups. Each student writes four sentences describing the weather in a certain place, during a particular month, and what they like to do there. Two sentences should be probable and two should be improbable. Ask students to read their sentences to each other to determine reasonableness.

Vocabulario

Primer paso

Discussing how often you do things

a veces	sometimes	durante	during	siempre	always
ayudar en casa	to help at home	muchas veces	often	sólo cuando	only when
la chica	girl	nada	nothing	todavía	still, yet
el chico	boy	nadie	nobody	todos los días	every day
¿Con qué frecuencia?	How often?	nunca	never	tomar el autobús	to take the bus
desayunar	to eat breakfast	¿quiénes?	who? (plural)		

Segundo paso

Talking about what you and your friends like to do together

a ellos/as	to them	especialmente	especially	el sándwich	sandwich
a Uds.	to you (plural)	esquiar	to ski	las tarjetas postales	postcards
acampar	to camp	hacer ejercicio	to exercise	las tiras cómicas	comics
el agua	water (f.)	la hamburguesa	hamburger	las vacaciones	vacation
asistir a	to attend	el jugo	juice		
beber	to drink	juntos/as	together		
bucear	to scuba dive	leer	to read	**Talking about what you**	
la carta	letter	les gusta	they/you (pl.) like	**do during a typical week**	
la clase de ejercicios aeróbicos	aerobics class	nos gusta	we like	la milla	mile
		las papas fritas	french fries	por la mañana	in the morning
		el periódico	newspaper	por la noche	at night (in the evening)
comer	to eat	pescar	to fish		
correr	to run	por la playa	along the beach	por la tarde	in the afternoon
escribir	to write	recibir	to receive	típicamente	typically

Tercer paso

Giving today's date

				Talking about the weather	
abril	April	el invierno	winter	Está lloviendo.	It's raining.
agosto	August	julio	July	Está nevando.	It's snowing.
el año	year	junio	June	Está nublado.	It's cloudy.
¿Cuál es la fecha?	What is the date?	marzo	March	Hace buen/mal tiempo.	The weather is nice/bad.
		mayo	May	Hace calor.	It's hot.
diciembre	December	el mes	month	Hace fresco.	It's cool.
El... de este mes...	On the (date) of this month . . .	noviembre	November	Hace (mucho) frío.	It's (very) cold.
enero	January	octubre	October		
Es el... de...	It's the (date) of (month).	el otoño	fall	Hace (mucho) viento.	It's (very) windy.
		la primavera	spring		
		el primero	the first (of the month)	Hace sol.	It's sunny.
la estación	season			Llueve.	It's raining.
febrero	February	¿Qué fecha es hoy?	What's today's date?	Nieva.	It's snowing.
Es el... de...	It's the (date) of (month).	septiembre	September	¿Qué tiempo hace?	What's the weather like?
		el verano	summer		

Review and Assess

Game

Ponga Ask students to prepare a card as in a game of Bingo, but not to write anything in the spaces. You will need to designate the number of spaces across and down. Then ask the students to fill in the spaces at random with words or expressions in Spanish from the vocabulary list. Call out each word or expression in English, and if students have the Spanish equivalent on their card, they place a mark on the space. The first student to mark a straight or a diagonal line of spaces is the winner. A variation is to ask students to prepare a card and then exchange the card with another student before play begins.

Vocabulario

CAPÍTULO 5

Teaching Suggestion
To review vocabulary quickly, you may want to play Tic-Tac-Toe (see p. 139C), Ponga (see p. 15C), or Cerebro (see p. 107C).

Chapter 5 Assessment

▶ **Testing Program**
Chapter Test, pp. 117–122
 Audio Compact Discs, CD 5, Trs. 20–21
Speaking Test, p. 345

▶ **Alternative Assessment Guide**
Performance Assessment, p. 36
Portfolio Assessment, p. 22
CD-ROM Assessment, p. 50

▶ **Interactive CD-ROM Tutor, Disc 2**
 ¡A hablar!
¡A escribir!

▶ **Standardized Assessment Tutor**
Chapter 5

▶ **One-Stop Planner, Disc 2**
 Test Generator
Chapter 5

Capítulo 6: Entre familia
Chapter Overview

De antemano pp. 170–172	¿Cómo es tu familia?

	FUNCTIONS	GRAMMAR	VOCABULARY	RE-ENTRY
Primer paso pp. 173–177	• Describing a family, p. 174	• Possessive adjectives, p. 174	• Family members, p. 173 • Domestic animals, p. 176	• hay (Capítulo 2) • Possessive adjectives (Capítulo 2) • Use of de (Capítulo 3)
Segundo paso pp. 178–183	• Describing people, p. 178 • Discussing things a family does together, p. 180	• The verbs hacer and salir, p. 180 • The personal a, p. 181	• Descriptions of people, p. 178 • Descriptive adjectives, p. 179	• Colors (Capítulo preliminar) • Descriptions of people (Capítulo 3) • Pastimes/hobbies (Capítulo 5) • ¿con qué frecuencia? (Capítulo 5) • Adjective agreement (Capítulo 3)
Tercer paso pp. 184–187	• Discussing problems and giving advice, p. 184	• The verb deber, p. 184 • The verb poner, p. 185	• Household chores, p. 185	• Forming questions (Capítulo 3)

Letra y sonido p. 187	**The Spanish r** Audio CD 6, Track 12	**Dictado** Audio CD 6, Tracks 13–16
Vamos a leer pp. 188–189	**Cinco cosas curiosas para hacer en la Pequeña Habana**	**Reading Strategy:** Using pictures, titles, and subtitles to determine text organization
Más práctica gramatical	**pp. 190–193** **Primer paso,** p. 190	**Segundo paso,** pp. 190–192 **Tercer paso,** pp. 192–193
Review pp. 194–197	**Repaso,** pp. 194–195 **Vamos a escribir,** p. 195 Outlining to help organize your topic	**A ver si puedo...,** p. 196 **Vocabulario,** p. 197

CULTURE

- **Nota cultural, El compadrazgo,** p. 175
- **Encuentro cultural, ¿Estás bien, hija?,** p. 177
- **Panorama cultural, ¿Cuántas personas hay en tu familia?,** p. 183
- **A lo nuestro,** Diminutives, p. 187

Capítulo 6: Entre familia
Chapter Resources

PRINT

Lesson Planning

One-Stop Planner

Lesson Planner with Substitute Teacher Lesson Plans, pp. 28–32, 70

Student Make-Up Assignments
- Make-Up Assignment Copying Masters, Chapter 6

Listening and Speaking

TPR Storytelling Book, pp. 21–24

Listening Activities
- Student Response Forms for Listening Activities, pp. 43–45
- Additional Listening Activities 6-1 to 6-6, pp. 47–49
- Additional Listening Activities (song), p. 50
- Scripts and Answers, pp. 127–131

Video Guide
- Teaching Suggestions, pp. 39–41
- Activity Masters, pp. 42–44
- Scripts and Answers, pp. 97–99, 115–116

Activities for Communication
- Communicative Activities, pp. 31–36
- Realia and Teaching Suggestions, pp. 100–104
- Situation Cards, pp. 147–148

Reading and Writing

Reading Strategies and Skills Handbook, Chapter 6

¡Lee conmigo! 1, Chapter 6

Cuaderno de actividades, pp. 61–72

Grammar

Cuaderno de gramática, pp. 45–52

Grammar Tutor for Students of Spanish, Chapter 6

Assessment

Testing Program
- Grammar and Vocabulary Quizzes, **Paso** Quizzes, and Chapter Test, pp. 131–148
- Score Sheet, Scripts and Answers, pp. 149–156
- Midterm Exam, pp. 157–164
- Score Sheet, Scripts and Answers, pp. 165–170

Alternative Assessment Guide
- Portfolio Assessment, p. 23
- Performance Assessment, p. 37
- CD-ROM Assessment, p. 51

Student Make-Up Assignments
- Alternative Quizzes, Chapter 6

Standardized Assessment Tutor
- Reading, pp. 21–23 • Writing, p. 24 • Math, pp. 25–26

Native Speakers

Cuaderno para hispanohablantes, pp. 26–30

MEDIA

 Online Activities
- Juegos interactivos
- Actividades Internet

 Video Program
- Videocassette 2
- Videocassette 5 (captioned version)

 Interactive CD-ROM Tutor, Disc 2

 DVD Tutor, Disc 1

 Audio Compact Discs
- Textbook Listening Activities, CD 6, Tracks 1–17
- Additional Listening Activities, CD 6, Tracks 27–33
- Assessment Items, CD 6, Tracks 18–26

 Teaching Transparencies
- Situations 6-1 to 6-3
- Vocabulary 6-A to 6-C
- **De antemano**
- **Más práctica gramatical** Answers
- **Cuaderno de gramática** Answers

  One-Stop Planner CD-ROM

Use the **One-Stop Planner CD-ROM with Test Generator** to aid in lesson planning and pacing.

For each chapter, the **One-Stop Planner** includes:
- Editable lesson plans with direct links to teaching resources
- Printable worksheets from resource books
- Direct launches to the HRW Internet activities
- Video and audio segments
- Test Generator
- Clip Art for vocabulary items

Capítulo 6: Entre familia

Projects ···

Árbol genealógico

In this activity, students create family trees. Students may diagram their own family, a fictitious family, or a famous one. Have them write an essay or give an oral presentation explaining the relationships on the tree.

MATERIALS
Students may need
- Poster board
- Markers
- Photos

SUGGESTED SEQUENCE

1. Explain the assignment. Draw a simple family tree on the board or a transparency to teach the diagramming format, or use *Teaching Transparency 6-1.*

2. Have students sketch a rough draft of their tree. Have them begin with one set of grandparents, adding all their children. Then have them add the marriages and children of the second generation, and so on. Have them do the same for the next set of grandparents.

3. When a rough draft of the entire family is done, have them outline the tree on poster board, then transfer the information from the rough draft onto the final draft.

4. Have students embellish their trees with drawings, photos, or magazine images.

5. Have them either write a description in Spanish or present their tree to the class, explaining the relationships.

TEACHING SUGGESTION

Since some students feel uncomfortable discussing their family, offer the option of using an imaginary family, a TV family, or simply creating a poster of someone important to them.

GRADING THE PROJECT

Suggested point distribution: (total = 100 points)
Completeness..30
Presentation / appearance................................30
Use / spelling of vocabulary 20
Oral or written presentation 20

Games ···

¿Cómo te diré?

This game helps your students develop circumlocution skills. Explain that when they find themselves at a loss to express something, they can paraphrase, use synonyms, or describe to communicate effectively.

Preparation Set desks in front so that two sets of partners face each other. From a list of related vocabulary words, write one each on index cards, and place them face down. On the board, write words and several key phrases:

Se usa para... Es lo contrario de...

Es un lugar donde... Tiene...

Es un(a) cosa, persona, animal que...

Está hecho de (plástico, metal, madera, vidrio).

Es viejo(a)/nuevo(a). Es similar a...

Procedure Have two players from each team sit at the desks. A Team A player selects a card and shows it to just one Team B player. The Team A player expresses the word's sense without saying it. (For **elefante** one could say **Es un animal gris.**) If the partner guesses the word, Team A earns five points. (30 seconds per guess!) If not, the Team B player gives a clue to his or her partner. If he or she guesses, Team B receives four points. Play alternates between teams, with point value dropping by one after each incorrect guess. Give the answer if no one guesses correctly. After four words, select four new players for the next round.

Una palabra más

This game helps students build on words and ideas to make complete sentences. The sentences can be odd or funny, but they should be grammatically correct.

Procedure Create any number of teams. Begin a sentence on the board with a word. (**Mi**) Have one player write a word to continue the sentence. (**papá**) The next team's player writes another word. (**tiene**) Once the sentence becomes complicated, students may add words before or after others. For example, **inteligente** could go between **papá** and **tiene.** Players score a point for a logical contribution.

Storytelling

Mini-cuento

This story accompanies Teaching Transparency 6-3. The **mini-cuento** *can be told and retold in different formats, acted out, written, and read aloud, to give students additional opportunities to practice all four skills. The following story relates the problems at the Peralta house, where no one tends to daily* **quehaceres.**

Los miembros de la familia Peralta son desordenados. Nadie hace lo que debe. Un día la señora Peralta prepara la comida en una cocina sucia. Debe lavar los platos primero, pero siempre se olvida. Jaime debe dar de comer al gato, pero está afuera jugando. Ahora el gato tiene hambre. Cristina debe sacar la basura todos los días. Pero a Cristina le gusta más charlar por teléfono y mirar la televisión. Rebeca debe pasar la aspiradora por la sala pero no puede. Su excusa es que necesita terminar un informe. Comienza tarde porque nunca encuentra lo que busca en su cuarto. ¡Está desesperada! Gregorio Peralta, el padre, no ayuda. Debe cortar el césped, pero está jugando al golf. ¿Quién va a salvar a la familia Peralta?

Traditions

Historia

The state of Florida has had cultural ties with Spanish speakers for almost 500 years. Juan Ponce de León is credited with being the first European to see the territory shortly after Easter Sunday, 1513, and perhaps named it after **la Pascua Florida.** Florida also boasts the oldest perma-

nently occupied European settlement in the United States, St. Augustine. Spanish explorer Pedro Menéndez established a small settlement there in 1565 in an attempt to block French colonization of the peninsula. Other famous conquistadors, including Hernando de Soto, explored Florida in the sixteenth century. Have students log on to **go.hrw.com** and enter the keyword **WV3 FLORIDA** to learn more about Spaniards who had an impact on the history of the state. Ask students to find out about the motivations of the conquistadors.

Receta

Cuban sandwiches are very common in restaurants in Florida. These sandwiches are delicious and simple to prepare. Cubans in Florida usually call this dish **tortas** *or* **sándwiches a la plancha.**

SÁNDWICHES CUBANOS

para 2 personas

Un trozo mediano de pan *(French or Italian bread or hard crust loaf)*

mantequilla, o mostaza y mayonesa (opcional)

1 rebanada de carne de puerco horneado

1 o 2 rebanadas de jamón

2 rebanadas pequeñas de queso suizo

1 pepino en escabeche

Caliente una sartén o si tiene una waflera *(waffle iron)* es mejor. Corte en dos partes el pan. Embarre la mantequilla o la mostaza y la mayonesa en cada una de las mitades. Coloque en una de las mitades las rebanadas de puerco y de jamón junto con el queso y el pepino en escabeche. Después junte las dos partes y colóquelas en la sartén caliente o en la waflera y presione *(press)* de tres a cuatro minutos hasta que quede dorado el pan.

Capítulo 6: Entre familia
Technology

Videocassette 2, Videocassette 5 (captioned version)
DVD Tutor, Disc 1
See Video Guide, pages 39–44.

DVD/Video ....

De antemano • ¿Cómo es tu familia?
Armando goes to Raquel's house, and she shows him photos of her family. She describes what her family is like and what they like to do together. While she is showing Armando the photos, they are interrupted by a loud crash.

A continuación
Raquel discovers that her dog, Pepe, has come into the house and knocked something over in the other room. She scolds him and sends him outside. Later, she cannot find him and is afraid that he has run away. After Raquel and her friends scour the neighborhood, they finally find Pepe hiding under a table in Raquel's living room.

¿Cuántas personas hay en tu familia?
Teenagers from Ecuador, Spain, and Texas tell how many people are in their family and what they do to help around the house. In additional interviews, people from various Spanish-speaking countries describe their families and what they do to help around the house.

Videoclips
- **Estar en familia:** public service message supporting spending time with family

Interactive CD-ROM Tutor ....

Activity	Activity Type	Pupil's Edition Page
En contexto	*Interactive Conversation*	
1. Vocabulario	¡Super memoria!	p. 173
2. Gramática	¡A escoger!	p. 174
3. Gramática	¿Qué falta?	p. 180
4. Así se dice	Imagen y sonido ¡Exploremos! ¡Identifiquemos!	p. 178
5. Vocabulario	¡Super memoria!	p. 185
6. Gramática	¿Qué falta?	pp. 184–185
Panorama cultural	¿Cuántas personas hay en tu familia?	p. 183
¡A hablar!	*Guided recording*	pp. 194–195
¡A escribir!	*Guided writing*	pp. 194–195

Teacher Management System
Launch the program, type "admin" in the password area, and press RETURN. Log on to **www.hrw.com/CDROMTUTOR** for a detailed explanation of the Teacher Management System.

DVD Tutor ....

The *DVD Tutor* contains all material from the *Video Program* as described above. Spanish captions are available for use at your discretion for all sections of the video. The *DVD Tutor* also provides a variety of video-based activities that assess students' understanding of the **De antemano, A continuación,** and **Panorama cultural.**

This part of the *DVD Tutor* may be used on any DVD video player connected to a television or video monitor.

In addition to the video material and the video-based comprehension activities, the *DVD Tutor* also contains the entire *Interactive CD-ROM Tutor* in DVD-ROM format. Each DVD disc contains the activities from all 12 chapters of the *Interactive CD-ROM Tutor.*

This part of the *DVD Tutor* may be used on a Macintosh® or Windows® computer with a DVD-ROM drive.

One-Stop Planner CD-ROM

To preview all resources available for this chapter, use the **One-Stop Planner CD-ROM**, Disc 2.

Internet Connection

MARCAR: go.hrw.com
PALABRA CLAVE:
WV3 FLORIDA-6

*Have students explore the **go.hrw.com** Web site for many online resources covering all chapters. All Chapter 6 resources are available under the keyword WV3 FLORIDA-6. Interactive games help students practice the material and provide them with immediate feedback. You will also find a printable worksheet that provides Internet activities that lead to a comprehensive online research project.*

Juegos interactivos

You can use the interactive activities in this chapter

- to practice grammar, vocabulary, and chapter functions
- as homework
- as an assessment option
- as a self-test
- to prepare for the Chapter Test

Actividades Internet

Students will create the script for a television show that is about two families coming together.

- Have students prepare for the **Hoja de actividades** by reviewing the vocabulary from the **Primer paso.** You might also have them complete the Listening Activities for that **Paso.**
- When students have finished the activity sheet, have them describe their show's cast and plot (the family activities they chose in Activity A).

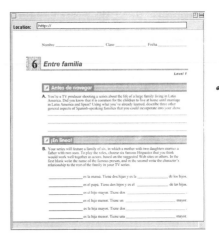

Proyecto

Have students search Spanish-language Web sites such as television networks or online magazines for images and descriptions of actors. They should choose possible cast members for their show about families from the **Hoja de actividades.** For each person they cast, have students describe his or her physical appearance and say which role each would play.

Capítulo 6: Entre familia
Textbook Listening Activities Scripts

6 **p. 173**

1. Es una familia bastante grande. Hay nueve personas en total.
2. La familia es muy simpática. Tiene un perro muy travieso.
3. Los abuelos son de España. ¡Imagínate!
4. Es una familia muy unida. El padrastro es muy cariñoso con los hijos.
5. Los muchachos se ven muy guapos. El gato también.

Answers to Activity 6
1. b   2. d   3. ninguna foto   4. c   5. a

Segundo paso

15 **p. 178**

1. Alma tiene veintidós años y tiene el pelo blanco.
2. Guillermo es pelirrojo. Tiene los ojos negros.
3. Olivia tiene el pelo rubio y tiene ojos azules.
4. Adolfo tiene ochenta y cinco años. Tiene el pelo negro.
5. Liliana tiene los ojos blancos y el pelo verde.
6. Anselmo tiene pelo rubio y ojos de color café.

Answers to Activity 15
1. improbable	4. improbable
2. improbable	5. improbable
3. probable	6. probable

16 **p. 179**

1. Es pelirrojo, tiene ojos azules y es muy alto.
2. Es muy simpática y guapa. Tiene pelo negro y ojos de color café.
3. Ella es baja, tiene pelo rubio y ojos verdes. Él es alto y tiene ojos verdes, también.
4. Es una persona muy especial. Es muy cariñosa conmigo. Tiene cincuenta años, pero se ve joven.
5. Son muy cómicos cuando están juntos. Uno de ellos es delgado y el otro es un poco gordo. Son muy traviesos.

Answers to Activity 16
1. David	4. Maki
2. Rebeca	5. Simón y Quique
3. Gabriel y Conchita	

21 **p. 180**

1. Durante el verano mi familia y yo hacemos un viaje. Casi siempre visitamos a nuestros primos. Ellos viven en Colorado.
2. Salgo con frecuencia con mis amigos. A veces vamos a la playa.
3. Soy muy atlética. Hago ejercicio por la mañana con mis amigos. A veces los sábados corro con ellos en el parque.
4. Mi familia y yo salimos a comer juntos todos los viernes. Nos gusta hablar sobre nuestras actividades, las clases y el trabajo.

Answers to Activity 21
1. b   2. d   3. c   4. a

The following scripts are for the listening activities found in the *Pupil's Edition*. For Student Response Forms, see *Listening Activities*, pages 43–45. To provide students with additional listening practice, see *Listening Activities*, pages 47–50.

One-Stop Planner CD-ROM

To preview all resources available for this chapter, use the **One-Stop Planner CD-ROM**, Disc 2.

Tercer paso

28   p. 184

Mi tía es divorciada y vive con nosotros. Ella dice que mi mamá trabaja demasiado. Mi mamá sale de la casa a las siete de la mañana y regresa a las nueve de la noche. Debe descansar más, ¿verdad? Mi hermana es muy inteligente. Estudia ciencias y siempre está en la biblioteca con sus libros. Debe salir con amigos a veces. ¿Y yo? Pues, soy bastante perezosa. Toco la guitarra pero toco muy mal. Claro, debo practicar más.

Answers to Activity 28
1. c
2. a
3. b
4. not pictured

LETRA Y SONIDO, P. 187

For the scripts for Parts A and C, see p. 187. The script for Part B is below.

B. Dictado

Rafael Ramírez es rubio y tiene ojos verdes. Él corre muy rápido en sus zapatos rojos de rayas.

Repaso

1   p. 194

Roberto, ésta es mi familia. Ésta es mi madre. Ella es inteligente y muy cariñosa. Lee muchas novelas. Y éste es mi padre. Él es muy alto, ¿verdad? También es muy cómico. Es artista y trabaja en un museo. Debe trabajar menos. Ésta es mi hermana. Ella es muy lista, pero debe estudiar más. Trabaja mucho en el jardín. Éste es mi tío Miguel. Es joven, tiene veinte años. A él le gusta tocar la guitarra día y noche. Éste es nuestro perro. Es muy travieso. También es un poco gordo porque come demasiado. Y finalmente éste soy yo. Yo soy muy simpático, y siempre limpio mi cuarto.

Answers to Repaso Activity 1
1. el perro
2. el padre
3. la madre
4. Marcos
5. el tío Miguel
6. la hermana

Capítulo 6: Entre familia
Suggested Lesson Plans *50-Minute Schedule*

Day 1

CHAPTER OPENER 5 min.
- Focusing on Outcomes, ATE, p. 169
- Culture Notes, ATE, pp. 168–169

DE ANTEMANO 40 min.
- Presenting **De antemano** and Preteaching Vocabulary, ATE, p. 170
- Follow the Additional Practice suggestion, ATE, p. 171.
- Activities 1–5, p. 172, and Comprehension Check, ATE p. 172

Wrap-Up 5 min.
- Ask students to explain what *¿Cómo es tu familia?* is about. Then have them share their answers to Activity 5, p. 172.

Homework Options
Cuaderno de actividades, p. 61, Activities 1–2

Day 2

PRIMER PASO
Quick Review 5 min.
- Check homework.
- Bell Work, ATE, p. 173

Vocabulario, p. 173 25 min.
- Presenting **Vocabulario**, ATE, p. 173
- Do Activity 6, p. 173, with the Audio CD.

Así se dice, p. 174 15 min.
- Presenting **Así se dice**, ATE, p. 174
- Have students do Activity 7, p. 174, in pairs.

Wrap-Up 5 min.
- Show students a picture of a family. Ask students yes/no questions about the family and its members.

Homework Options
Cuaderno de actividades, p. 62, Activity 3
Cuaderno de gramática, p. 45, Activities 1–2

Day 3

PRIMER PASO
Quick Review 10 min.
- Check homework.
- Use Transparency 6-1 to review the **Vocabulario** and expressions from **Así se dice**, pp. 173–174.

Nota gramatical, p. 174 35 min.
- Presenting **Nota gramatical**, ATE, p. 174
- Do Activity 8, p. 174, orally with the class.
- Have students do Activity 9, p. 175, in pairs, then share their paragraphs with the class.
- Present and discuss the **Nota cultural**, p. 175, and the Culture Notes, ATE, p. 174.
- Have students do Activity 10, p. 175, in pairs.

Wrap-Up 5 min.
- Do the Visual Learners suggestions, ATE, p. 175, incorporating possessive adjectives into your questions.

Homework Options
Más práctica gramatical, p. 190, Activities 1–2
Cuaderno de gramática, p. 46, Activities 3–4
Cuaderno de actividades, p. 63, Activities 5–6

Day 4

PRIMER PASO
Quick Review 10 min.
- Check homework.
- Cuaderno de actividades, p. 64, Activity 7

Vocabulario/Así se dice/Nota gramatical, pp. 173–174 25 min.
- Have students do Activity 11, p. 175, in pairs.
- Ask students to do Activity 12, p. 176, individually. Check orally with the class.
- Present **Vocabulario extra** using pictures or drawings, p. 176.
- Have students do Activity 13, p. 176, individually, then Activity 14, p. 176, in pairs.

ENCUENTRO CULTURAL 10 min.
- Presenting **Encuentro cultural**, ATE, p. 177

Wrap-Up 5 min.
- Ask students how privacy is regarded among people they know.
- Explain the content and format of Quiz 6-1.

Homework Options
Study for Quiz 6-1.
Cuaderno de actividades, p. 64, Activity 8

Day 5

PRIMER PASO
Quick Review 5 min.
- Check homework.
- Quickly review the content of the **Primer paso** using Transparency 6-A.

Quiz 20 min.
- Administer Quiz 6-1A, 6-1B, or a combination of the two.

SEGUNDO PASO
Así se dice, p. 178 10 min.
- Presenting **Así se dice**, ATE, p. 178
- Do Activity 15, p. 178, with Audio CD.

Vocabulario, p. 178 10 min.
- Do Presenting **Vocabulario**, ATE, p. 178. Include the words from **También se puede decir...** p. 178 in your presentation.
- Present the information in Native Speakers, ATE, p. 178.

Wrap-Up 5 min.
- Make incorrect statements describing people in the school community. Have students correct your statements.

Homework Options
Cuaderno de actividades, p. 65, Activity 9
Cuaderno de gramática, pp. 47–48, Activities 5–7

Day 6

SEGUNDO PASO
Quick Review 5 min.
- Check homework.
- Review **Vocabulario** and **Así se dice**, p. 178, using Transparency 6-B.

Vocabulario/Así se dice/Vocabulario extra, pp. 178–179 25 min.
- Do Activity 16, p. 179, with the Audio CD.
- Present **Vocabulario extra** using TPR. Do the Additional Practice, ATE, p. 179.
- Have students do Activity 17, p. 179. Next, ask partners to do Actvity 18, p. 179.
- Do the Visual Learners suggestion, ATE, p. 179. Then have students do Activity 19.

Así se dice/Nota gramatical, p. 180 15 min.
- Presenting **Así se dice** and **Nota gramatical**, ATE, p. 180
- Do Activity 21, p. 180, with the Audio CD.

Wrap-Up 5 min.
- Discuss Language-to-Language, ATE, p. 180.

Homework Options
Have students do Activity 20, p. 179, for homework.
Más práctica gramatical, p. 191, Activities 3–4
Cuaderno de gramática, pp. 48–49, Activities 8–9

One-Stop Planner CD-ROM

For alternative lesson plans by chapter section, to create your own customized plans, or to preview all resources available for this chapter, use the **One-Stop Planner CD-ROM**, Disc 2.

 For additional homework suggestions, see activities accompanied by this symbol throughout the chapter.

Day 7

SEGUNDO PASO
Quick Review 10 min.
- Check homework.
- Have students do Activity 22, p. 181, following the Auditory Learners suggestion, ATE, p. 181, while you check the writing assignment (Activity 20, p. 179) for completion.

Nota gramatical, p. 181 25 min.
- Presenting **Nota gramatical**, ATE, p. 181
- Present the Culture Note, ATE, p. 181.
- Do Activities 23–24, p. 181.
- Have students do Activities 25–27 in pairs, p. 182, switching partners after each activity. Call on some students to report their findings from Activity 25. Call on others to read their dialogues from Activity 27.

PANORAMA CULTURAL 10 min.
- Presenting **Panorama cultural**, ATE, p. 183

Wrap-Up 5 min.
- Discuss the content and format of Quiz 6-2.

Homework Options
Study for Quiz 6-2.
Más práctica gramatical, p. 192, Activity 6
Cuaderno de actividades, pp. 66–67, Activities 11–13
Cuaderno de gramática, p. 49, Activity 10

Day 8

SEGUNDO PASO
Quick Review 10 min.
- Check homework.
- Quickly review the content of the **Segundo paso** using Transparencies 6-2 and 6B.

Quiz 20 min.
- Administer Quiz 6-2A, 6-2B, or a combination of the two.

TERCER PASO
Así se dice/Nota gramatical, p. 184 15 min.
- Presenting **Así se dice** and **Nota gramatical**, ATE, p. 184
- Point out the information in the Language Note, ATE, p. 184.
- Do Activity 28, p. 184, with the Audio CD.
- Have students do Activity 29, p. 184, in pairs. Call on volunteers to present some of their ideas to the class.

Wrap-Up 5 min.
- Ask students questions about what they and their classmates should do every day to elicit different conjugations of **deber**.

Homework Options
Cuaderno de gramática, p. 50, Activities 11–12
Cuaderno de actividades, pp. 68–69, Activities 14–15

Day 9

TERCER PASO
Quick Review 5 min.
- Check homework.

Vocabulario/Nota gramatical, p. 185 25 min.
- Presenting **Vocabulario** and **Nota gramatical**, ATE, p. 185
- Do Activities 30–31, pp. 185–186, and follow the Additional Practice suggestion, ATE, p. 185.
- Have students do Activities 32–33, p. 186.
- Have students do Activity 35, p. 187, in pairs.
- Have students circulate around the classroom to do Activity 34, p. 186.
- Present **A lo nuestro**, p. 187.

Letra y sonido, p. 187 10 min.
- Present **Letra y sonido**, p. 187.
- Present and practice the **trabalenguas** in **Letra y sonido**, p. 187.

Wrap-Up 10 min.
- Do the Additional Practice suggestion for Activity 33, ATE, p. 186.

Homework Options
Más práctica gramatical, pp. 192–193, Activities 7–9
Cuaderno de gramática, p. 51, Activities 13–15

Day 10

TERCER PASO
Quick Review 10 min.
- Check homework.
- Review vocabulary and grammar from this **Paso** using Transparency 6-C.

Vocabulario/Gramática, p. 185 15 min.
- Do Activities 16–17, p. 52, in Cuaderno de gramática. Ask volunteers to write their sentences on the board.
- Have small groups do Activity 36, p. 187.

VAMOS A LEER 20 min.
- Do Activity A, p. 188. Do the Building on Previous Skills suggestion, ATE, p. 188.
- Do Activities B–D, pp. 188–189
- Present the Culture Note, ATE, p. 188.

Wrap-Up 5 min.
- Ask students to explain how **Vamos a leer** was organized and how the organization helped them understand the reading.
- Quickly review the content and format of Quiz 6-3.

Homework Options
Assign Activity 37, p. 187, as homework.
Study for Quiz 6-3.

Day 11

TERCER PASO
Quick Review 5 min.
- Have students review **Tercer paso** while you pick up the homework.

Quiz 20 min.
- Administer Quiz 6-3A, 6-3B, or a combination of the two.

REPASO 20 min.
- Do Activity 1, p. 194, with Audio CD.
- Do Activities 2, 5, pp. 194–195, orally with the class.
- Have students do Activities 3–4, p. 194. Then, have students exchange papers for peer-editing.
- Have students work with a partner to do Activity 7, p. 195.

Wrap-Up 5 min.
- Ask students to list items they need to study for the Chapter Test. Review the most difficult item.

Homework Options
Practice the situations for Activity 7, p. 195.
A ver si puedo..., p. 196

Day 12

REPASO
Quick Review 5 min.
- Check homework.

Chapter Review 40 min.
- Review Chapter 6. Choose from **Más práctica gramatical**, Grammar Tutor for Students of Spanish, Activities for Communication, Listening Activities, Interactive CD-ROM Tutor, or **Juegos interactivos**.

Wrap-Up 5 min.
- Discuss the content of the Chapter 6 Test and provide sample questions.

Homework Options
Study for the Chapter 6 Test.

Assessment

Quick Review 5 min.
- Answer any last-minute questions.

Test, Chapter 6 45 min.
- Administer Chapter 6 Test. Select from Testing Program, Alternative Assessment Guide, Test Generator, or Standardized Assessment Tutor.

Capítulo 6: Entre familia
Suggested Lesson Plans *90-Minute Block Schedule*

CHAPTER OPENER 5 min.
- Focusing on Outcomes, ATE, p. 169
- Teacher Notes, ATE, pp. 168–169

DE ANTEMANO 40 min.
- Presenting **De antemano** and Preteaching Vocabulary, ATE, p. 170
- Follow the Additional Practice suggestion, ATE, p. 171.
- Do Activities 1–5, p. 172, and Comprehension Check, ATE, p. 172.

PRIMER PASO
Vocabulario, p. 173 25 min.
- Presenting **Vocabulario,** ATE, p. 173
- Do Activity 6, p. 173, with the Audio CD.

Así se dice, p. 174 15 min.
- Presenting **Así se dice,** ATE, p. 174
- Have students do Activity 7, p. 174, in pairs.

Wrap-Up 5 min.
- Show students a picture of a family. Ask students yes/no questions about the family and its members.

Homework Options
Cuaderno de actividades, pp. 61–62, Activities 1–3
Cuaderno de gramática, p. 45, Activities 1–2

PRIMER PASO
Quick Review 10 min.
- Check homework.
- Use Transparency 6-1 to review the **Vocabulario** and expressions from **Así se dice,** pp. 173–174.

Nota gramatical, p. 174 60 min.
- Presenting **Nota gramatical,** ATE, p. 174
- Do Activity 8, p. 174, orally with the class.
- Have students do Activity 9, p. 175, in pairs, then share their paragraphs with the class.
- Present and discuss the **Nota cultural,** p. 175, and the Culture Notes, ATE, p. 174.
- Have students do Activities 10–11, p. 175, in pairs.
- Ask students to do Activity 12, p. 176, individually. Check orally with the class.
- Present **Vocabulario extra** using pictures or drawings, p. 176.
- Have students do Activity 13, p. 176, individually, then Activity 14, p. 176, in pairs.

ENCUENTRO CULTURAL 10 min.
- Presenting **Encuentro cultural,** ATE, p. 177

Wrap-Up 10 min.
- Ask students how privacy is regarded among people they know.
- Do the Visual Learners suggestions, ATE, p. 175, incorporating possessive adjectives into your questions.
- Explain the content and format of Quiz 6-1.

Homework Options
Más práctica gramatical, p. 190, Activities 1–2
Cuaderno de gramática, p. 46, Activities 3–4
Cuaderno de actividades, p. 63, Activities 5–6

PRIMER PASO
Quick Review 10 min.
- Check homework.
- Bell Work, ATE, p. 178

Vocabulario/Así se dice/Nota gramatical, pp. 173–174 10 min.
- Quickly review the content of the **Primer paso** using Transparencies 6-1 and 6-A.
- Do Activity 7 in Cuaderno de actividades, p. 64, with the class.

Quiz 20 min.
- Administer Quiz 6-1A, 6-1B, or a combination of the two.

SEGUNDO PASO
Así se dice, p. 178 10 min.
- Presenting **Así se dice,** ATE, p. 178
- Do Activity 15, p. 178, with Audio CD.

Vocabulario, p. 178 35 min.
- Do Presenting **Vocabulario,** ATE, p. 178. Include the words from **También se puede decir...** in your presentation.
- Present the information in the Native Speakers suggestion, ATE, p. 178.
- Do Activity 16, p. 179, with the Audio CD.
- Present **Vocabulario extra,** p. 179, using TPR and by describing characters from television programs. Do the Additional Practice suggestion, ATE, p. 179.
- Have students do Activity 17, p. 179, individually, then exchange papers with a partner for peer-editing. Next, ask partners to do Actvity 18, p. 179.
- Have students do Activity 19, p. 179, in small groups.

Wrap-Up 5 min.
- Do the Visual Learners suggestion, ATE, p. 179.

Homework Options
Assign Activity 20, p. 179, for homework.
Cuaderno de actividades, p. 65, Activities 9–10
Cuaderno de gramática, pp. 47–48, Activities 5–7

One-Stop Planner CD-ROM

For alternative lesson plans by chapter section, to create your own customized plans, or to preview all resources available for this chapter, use the **One-Stop Planner CD-ROM**, Disc 2.

 For additional homework suggestions, see activities accompanied by this symbol throughout the chapter.

Block 4

SEGUNDO PASO

Quick Review 10 min.
- Check homework.
- Pick up Activity 20, p. 179, then follow the Auditory Learners suggestion, ATE, p. 179.

Así se dice/Nota gramatical, p. 180 20 min.
- Presenting **Así se dice** and **Nota gramatical**, ATE, p. 180
- Present the information in Language-to-Language, ATE, p. 180.
- Do Activity 21, p. 180, with the Audio CD.
- Do **Más práctica gramatical**, pp. 190–191, Activities 3–4 with the class.
- Follow the Auditory Learners suggestion for Activity 22, ATE, p. 181.

Nota gramatical, p. 181 25 min.
- Presenting **Nota gramatical**, ATE, p. 181
- Present the Culture Note, ATE, p. 181.
- Do Activities 23–24, p. 181.
- Have students do Activities 25–27 in pairs, p. 182, switching partners after each activity. Call on some students to report their findings from Activity 25. Call on others to read their dialogues from Activity 27.

PANORAMA CULTURAL 10 min.
- Presenting **Panorama cultural**, ATE, p. 183

TERCER PASO

Así se dice/Nota gramatical, p. 184 15 min.
- Presenting **Así se dice/Nota gramatical**, ATE, p. 184
- Point out the information in Language Note, ATE, p. 184.
- Do Activity 28, p. 184, with the Audio CD.
- Have students do Activity 29, p. 184, in pairs. Call on volunteers to present some of their ideas to the class.

Wrap-Up 10 min.
- Ask students questions about what they and their classmates should do every day to elicit different conjugations of **deber**.
- Discuss the content and format of Quiz 6-2.

Homework Options
Study for Quiz 6-2.
Más práctica gramatical, pp. 191–192, Activities 5–6
Cuaderno de actividades, pp. 66–69, Activities 11–15
Cuaderno de gramática, pp. 48–50, Activities 8–12

Block 5

SEGUNDO PASO

Quick Review 10 min.
- Check homework.
- Quickly review content of the **Segundo paso** using Transparencies 6-2 and 6-B.

Quiz 20 min.
- Administer Quiz 6-2A, 6-2B, or a combination of the two.

TERCER PASO

Vocabulario/Nota gramatical, p. 185 30 min.
- Presenting **Vocabulario** and **Nota gramatical**, ATE, p. 185
- Do Activities 30–31, pp. 185–186, with the class. Follow the Additional Practice suggestion, ATE, p. 185.
- Have students do Activities 32–33, p. 186, individually. Check the answers orally. Then, have students do Activity 35, p. 187, in pairs.
- Have students circulate around the classroom to do Activity 34, p. 186. Call on students at random to share their findings.
- Present **A lo nuestro**, p. 187.
- Have students do Activity 36, p. 187, in pairs.

VAMOS A LEER 20 min.
- Do Activity A, p. 188. Do the Building on Previous Skills suggestion, ATE, p. 188.
- Do Activities B–D, pp. 188–189
- Present the information in the Culture Note, ATE, p. 188.

Wrap-Up 10 min.
- Ask students to explain how the reading in **Vamos a leer** was organized and how the organization helped them understand the reading.
- Quickly review the content and format of Quiz 6-3.

Homework Options
Study for Quiz 6-3.
Assign Activity 37, p. 187, for homework.
Cuaderno de gramática, p. 52, Activities 16–17
Cuaderno de actividades, pp. 69–70, Activities 16–18

Block 6

TERCER PASO

Quick Review 10 min.
- Check homework.
- Have students review **Tercer paso** while you pick up the homework.

Así se dice/Notas gramaticales/Vocabulario, pp. 184–185 20 min.
- Review the content of the **Tercer paso** with Transparencies 6-3 and 6-C.
- Do Additional Listening Activity 6-6, p. 49.
- Do **Más práctica gramatical**, pp. 192–193, Activities 7–9.

Quiz 20 min.
- Administer Quiz 6-3A, 6-3B, or a combination of the two.

Letra y sonido, p. 187 10 min.
- Present **Letra y sonido**, p. 187.
- Present and practice the **trabalenguas** in **Letra y sonido**, p. 187.

REPASO 20 min.
- Do Activity 1, p. 194, with Audio CD.
- Do Activities 2 and 5, pp. 194–195.
- Have students do Activities 3–4, p. 194.
- Have students work in pairs to do Activity 7, p. 95.

Wrap-Up 10 min.
- Ask students to list items they need to study for the Chapter Test.
- Provide sample questions for the Chapter 6 Test.

Homework Options
Study for the Chapter 6 Test.
Practice the situations for Activity 7, p. 195.
A ver si puedo..., p. 196

Block 7

REPASO

Quick Review 5 min.
- Check homework.

Chapter Review 40 min.
- Review Chapter 6. Choose from **Más práctica gramatical**, Grammar Tutor for Students of Spanish, Activities for Communication, Listening Activities, Interactive CD-ROM Tutor, or **Juegos interactivos**.

Test, Chapter 6 45 min.
- Administer Chapter 6 Test. Select from Testing Program, Alternative Assessment Guide, Test Generator, or Standardized Assessment Tutor.

Chapter Opener

CAPÍTULO 6

 One-Stop Planner CD-ROM

For resource information, see the **One-Stop Planner**, Disc 2.

Pacing Tips
This chapter presents a great deal of interesting and useful vocabulary that many students will enjoy personalizing in conversational activities. Plan for ample time for students to describe friends and family and what they do. See Suggested Lesson Plans, pp. 167I–167L.

Meeting the Standards

Communication
- Describing a family, p. 174
- Describing people, p. 178
- Discussing things a family does together, p. 180
- Discussing problems and giving advice, p. 184

Cultures
- Culture Notes, p. 168
- Culture Notes, p. 174
- Native Speakers, p. 178

Connections
- A lo nuestro, p. 187
- Culture Note, p. 188
- Vamos a leer, pp. 188–189

Comparisons
- Culture Notes, p. 168
- Encuentro cultural, p. 177
- Language-to-Language, p. 180
- Comparing and Contrasting, p. 183
- Language Note, p. 184

Communities
- Family Link, p. 183
- Career Path, p. 189

Cultures and Communities

 Culture Notes
- Many Spanish speakers in Miami identify themselves as Cuban Americans, **cubanos,** or Cubans. Others, however, use the broader terms *Hispanic* and *Latino*. These are more general terms used to describe people who speak Spanish as their first language or whose ancestors did.

- A family in which relatives beyond the nuclear family live together is an *extended family*. In Spanish-speaking countries, **la familia** often includes aunts, uncles, cousins, and grandparents. An extended family may include members who are not biological relatives: stepparents, stepsiblings, and so on. In the United States, extended families are not as common as in Spanish-speaking countries.

STANDARDS: 3.2

C A P Í T U L O

6
Entre familia

Objectives

In this chapter you will learn to

Primer paso

- describe a family

Segundo paso

- describe people
- discuss things a family does together

Tercer paso

- discuss problems and give advice

internet

MARCAR: go.hrw.com
PALABRA CLAVE:
WV3 FLORIDA-6

◀ **Mi abuelo y yo somos muy unidos.**

Photo Flash!
This family is from Ciudad Real, although the photo was taken in Madrid. The grandfather is wearing a **boina,** the woolen beret typical of northern Spain. His grandsons and wife are sitting by him on the benches.

Focusing on Outcomes
An important use of language is describing people. Point out to students that these skills are valuable for describing members of their families. Talking about families includes describing the activities that families do together as well as discussing problems and giving advice. By the end of the chapter, students will be able to describe the members of their family and ask friends questions to learn about their families.

Connections and Comparisons

Culture Note
It is common to see men, particularly older men, wearing berets in some Spanish-speaking countries, especially Spain. Indeed, it is as much a Spanish tradition as a French one. The beret was originally worn by men in the Basque country in northern Spain and southern France.

Thinking Critically
Comparing and Contrasting Have students write a short essay telling what it would be like to change places with a parent or sibling. In making comparisons, students should consider both the privileges and the responsibilities that the other family member has. Ask them to be honest and fair in their evaluation.

The **fotonovela** is an abridged version of the video episode.

Teaching Resources
pp. 170–172

PRINT 📖
▸ Lesson Planner, p. 27
▸ Video Guide, pp. 39–40, 42
▸ Cuaderno de actividades, p. 61

MEDIA 💿📼
▸ One-Stop Planner
▸ Video Program
  De antemano
  Videocassette 2, 33:41–37:51
  Videocassette 5 (captioned version), 56:06–1:00:16
  A continuación
  Videocassette 2, 37:52–44:14
  Videocassette 5 (captioned version), 1:00:17–1:06:39
▸ DVD Tutor, Disc 1
▸ Audio Compact Discs, CD 6, Trs. 1–2
▸ **De antemano** Transparencies

CD 6 Trs. 1–2

Estrategia para comprender
Look at the pictures below. What is going on? Who is Raquel talking about with Armando? Does something surprising happen at the end? What could have happened?

 Raquel   Armando   Pepe

Presenting
De antemano

From the questions in **Estrategia para comprender** and from visual clues in the **fotonovela,** have students predict what will happen in the scene. Then play the video as students read along in their books. Have students read the **fotonovela** with a partner to see if they agree about what is happening. Next present the Preteaching Vocabulary to check for comprehension.

 De antemano Transparencies

1
Armando: A ver, Raquel, ¿cómo es tu familia?
Raquel: Bueno, es bastante grande... tengo tres hermanos, una hermana... y muchísimos primos...
Armando: ¿Y cuántos viven aquí?
Raquel: Somos ocho en casa: mis padres, todos mis hermanos menos uno, una abuela y una tía.

2
Armando: ¿Y cómo son tus padres? ¿Son simpáticos?
Raquel: Sí, son muy simpáticos. ¿Por qué no miramos mi álbum de fotos? Así puedes conocer a toda la familia.

3
Raquel: Éstos son mis padres. Ellos son de Cuba. Les gusta mucho trabajar en el jardín. Mi mamá es muy buena cocinera. Alguna vez debes probar la barbacoa que ella prepara. ¡Es fenomenal!

4
Raquel: Éstos son mis hermanos mayores. Y ella es mi hermana menor.

Preteaching Vocabulary

Identifying Keywords
First ask students to guess the context of the **De antemano** (descriptions of families). Then have them identify words or phrases that tell them what is happening. They should first find words that give them information about the people being described. (❶ hermanos, ❶ hermana, ❶ primos, ❶ padres, ❶ abuela, ❶ tía, ❽ perro) They should then look for words that tell them what the focus of the

conversation is. (family members, things families do together) Here are some key expressions they might identify:
❸ trabajar en el jardín, ❺ vamos a la iglesia,
❺ comemos juntos, ❺ salimos al parque,
❻ jugar al fútbol americano.

STANDARDS: 1.2

5 Raquel: Nosotros hacemos muchas cosas juntos, especialmente los domingos. Primero, vamos a la iglesia. Después, comemos juntos y salimos a alguna parte. En esta foto, salimos al parque.

6 Raquel: Aquí estamos en el parque. A mis hermanos les gusta mucho jugar al fútbol americano... y a mí también. Juego con ellos un poco todos los fines de semana.

7 Raquel: Comemos de todo: arroz con frijoles negros, maduros, tostones, pollo asado... Ummm, el pollo asado de mi tía Gloria es fenomenal.

8 Raquel: Aquí hay una foto de nuestro perro Pepe y de mí.

¡CRAC!

9 Raquel: ¡Ay, no! ¿Dónde está Pepe?

Cuaderno de actividades, p. 61, Acts. 1-2

Using the Captioned Video/DVD

As an alternative to reading the conversations in the book, you might want to show the captioned version of *¿Cómo es tu familia?* on Videocassette 5. As students hear the language and watch the story, anxiety about the new language will be reduced, and comprehension

facilitated. The reinforcement of seeing the written words with the gestures and actions in context will help students do the comprehension activities on page 172. **NOTE:** The *DVD Tutor* contains captions for all sections of the *Video Program*.

Teaching Suggestion
The reading for this **fotonovela** is relatively easy and students will probably be able to answer the questions on the next page without difficulty. Point out how much they are able to understand after having studied Spanish for only a short time.

Additional Practice
After you have presented the **fotonovela,** have students review the learner outcomes listed on page 169. Ask them to identify the phrases in the **fotonovela** that correspond to describing family and to describing people. Discussing problems and giving advice are functions modeled in the continuation of the **fotonovela** on the *Video Program.*

A continuación
You may choose to continue with *¿Cómo es tu familia? (a continuación)* at this time or wait until later in the chapter. At this point, Raquel discovers that her dog, Pepe, has made a mess. Later Raquel cannot find Pepe. She and her friends search the neighborhood for the dog. You may wish to have pairs of students predict where they think Raquel will find Pepe.

CAPÍTULO 6

Teaching Suggestions

2 Have students identify the scene that proves or disproves each statement.

3 As an option, orally give the answers to the activity out of order and ask students to tell you the number of the item you have just modeled.

4 Turn one or two of the statements into questions and have students answer as they look at the **fotonovela.** Then have pairs of students make and answer questions for the other items in the activity.

These activities check for comprehension only. Students should not yet be expected to produce language modeled in De antemano.

1 **¡Contesta las preguntas!** See answers below.

Contesta las preguntas sobre la fotonovela. Si no estás seguro/a, ¡adivina!

1. ¿Dónde están Raquel y Armando?
2. ¿De qué hablan Raquel y Armando?
3. ¿Cómo es la familia de Raquel?
4. ¿Qué hacen juntos Raquel y su familia?
5. ¿Quién es Pepe y cómo es él?

2 **¿Son ciertas o falsas las oraciones?** See answers below.

Con base en la fotonovela, indica **cierto** si la oración es verdadera y **falso** si no lo es. Si es falsa, cámbiala.

1. Armando y Raquel son hermanos.
2. Una tía de Raquel vive en casa con ella.
3. Raquel y sus hermanos tocan el piano.
4. Toda la familia hace algo los sábados.
5. Pepe es un primo de Raquel.

3 **¿Cómo se dice?** See possible answers below.

Look through the **fotonovela** and find the words and phrases you would use . . .

1. to ask what someone's family is like
2. to point out your parents in a photo
3. to ask a friend how many people live in his or her house
4. to say that you and a family member go out together on Sundays
5. to say that a friend should try your mom's barbecue

4 **La familia de Raquel**

Mira las fotos de la familia de Raquel en las páginas 170–171 y decide a qué foto corresponde cada descripción.

a. Sus padres trabajan en el jardín. 3
b. La comida es deliciosa. 7
c. Sus hermanos tocan la guitarra. 4

d. Raquel juega al fútbol americano en el parque. 6
e. La familia va al parque en su carro. 5
f. Raquel tiene un perro muy bonito. 8

Answers

1 1. Raquel and Armando are in the kitchen of Raquel's house.
2. They are talking about her family.
3. Raquel's family is fairly large.
4. Raquel and her family go to church and on picnics, play football, work in the garden, play music, and sing.
5. Pepe is Raquel's dog. He is large, brown, and mischievous.

2 1. Falso; Son amigos.
2. Cierto
3. Falso; Tocan la guitarra y la flauta.
4. Falso; los domingos.
5. Falso; Es el perro de Raquel.

3 1. ¿Cómo es tu familia?
2. Éstos son mis padres.
3. ¿Cuántas personas viven en tu casa?
4. Salimos a alguna parte juntos los domingos.
5. Debes probar la barbacoa que prepara mi mamá.

5 **Y tú, ¿qué piensas?** *What do you think?* Answers will vary.

Completa las oraciones con tus opiniones personales.

1. La familia ideal es...
   a. grande b. pequeña c. ni *(neither)* grande ni *(nor)* pequeña
2. Las personas en una familia ideal hacen cosas juntas...
   a. a veces b. muchas veces c. todos los fines de semana
3. La familia ideal es...
   a. unida b. independiente c. independiente y unida también

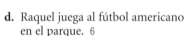

Comprehension Check

Slower Pace

2 Make sure that students understand key vocabulary in the instructions (**cierto, falso, cámbiala**). Help students locate the information they need by guiding them to the relevant videoframes in **De antemano** (for number one, videoframe one; number two, videoframe one; number three, videoframe four; number four, videoframe five; number five, videoframe eight). Ask students to read the sentences they correct to a partner to check for accuracy.

Vocabulario

a. Ésta es **la familia** de Miguel: su **madre**, su **media hermana** *(half sister)* y su **gato**.

b. La familia Pérez es grande. Están aquí **el padre** y su **esposa** *(wife)*, los dos **hijos** y una **hija**, **la abuela** y **el tío** *(uncle)* de los chicos. **La tía** *(aunt)* Catalina y **el abuelo** *(grandfather)* no están en la foto.

c. **Éstas** son las personas en mi familia: mi **medio hermano**, mi **madre** y yo, y **el esposo** *(husband)* de **mamá**, Rolando. Es mi **padrastro** *(stepfather)*.

los hermanos	brothers and sisters
los hijos	children
los abuelos	grandparents
la madrastra	stepmother
el hermanastro	stepbrother
la hermanastra	stepsister

d. Soy María. **Éstos** son aquí mis **padres** (mi **padre** y mi **madre**) y mi **perro** Chuleta.

Cuaderno de actividades, p. 62, Act. 3   Cuaderno de gramática, p. 45, Acts. 1–2

6 **¿Quién es quién?** Scripts and answers on p. 167G.

Escuchemos Imagine that you're on the phone with the photographer who took the family portraits above. As she describes members of each family, find the picture that matches. If no picture matches, answer **ninguna foto.** Have students read the captions and familiarize themselves with the photos before attempting this activity.

CD 6 Tr. 3

Connections and Comparisons

Language Note
Tell students that cognates in Spanish often have an **e** preceding the consonant clusters **sp, st,** or **sc,** and others. Then ask them what they think a cognate for **esposo** or **esposa** might be *(spouse)*. You may wish to provide them with more examples (**escuela, escala, estable, espacio**), and follow up by giving various words in English, to see if they can guess the Spanish.

Additional Vocabulary
bisabuelo/a *great-grandfather/great-grandmother*
tío abuelo/tía abuela *great-uncle/great-aunt*
cuñado/a *brother/sister-in-law*
suegro/a *father/mother-in-law*
yerno *son-in-law*
nuera *daughter-in-law*
marido *husband*

Teaching Resources
pp. 173–176

PRINT
▸ Lesson Planner, p. 29
▸ TPR Storytelling Book, pp. 21, 24
▸ Listening Activities, pp. 43, 47
▸ Activities for Communication, pp. 31–32, 100, 103–104, 147–148
▸ Cuaderno de gramática, pp. 45–46
▸ Grammar Tutor for Students of Spanish, Chapter 6
▸ Cuaderno de actividades, pp. 62–64
▸ Cuaderno para hispanohablantes, pp. 26–30
▸ Testing Program, pp. 131–134
▸ Alternative Assessment Guide, p. 37
▸ Student Make-Up Assignments, Chapter 6

MEDIA
▸ One-Stop Planner
▸ Audio Compact Discs, CD 6, Trs. 3, 27–28, 18
▸ Teaching Transparencies 6-1, 6-A; **Más práctica gramatical** Answers; Cuaderno de gramática Answers
▸ Interactive CD-ROM Tutor, Disc 2

Bell Work
Have students write five sentences listing what their families like or do not like to do together, using (no) nos gusta... juntos.

Presenting Vocabulario
Present family vocabulary and relationships using Teaching Transparency 6-1, then ask ¿quién es...?, ¿quiénes son...? questions. Display Teaching Transparency 6-A and have students speculate about relationships depicted.

Teaching Resources
pp. 173–176

PRINT
- Lesson Planner, p. 28
- TPR Storytelling Book, pp. 21, 24
- Listening Activities, pp. 43, 47
- Activities for Communication, pp. 31–32, 100, 103–104, 147–148
- Cuaderno de gramática, pp. 45–46
- Grammar Tutor for Students of Spanish, Chapter 6
- Cuaderno de actividades, pp. 62–64
- Cuaderno para hispanohablantes, pp. 26–30
- Testing Program, pp. 131–134
- Alternative Assessment Guide, p. 37
- Student Make-Up Assignments, Chapter 6

MEDIA
- One-Stop Planner
- Audio Compact Discs, CD 6, Trs. 3, 27–28, 18
- Teaching Transparencies 6-1, 6-A; **Más práctica gramatical** Answers; Cuaderno de gramática Answers
- Interactive CD-ROM Tutor, Disc 2

Presenting

Así se dice

Ask students questions from **Así se dice.** Assure them that they may give fictitious answers.

Nota gramatical

Review the singular possessive adjectives. Then model plural possessive adjectives.

Answers
 1. nuestra
2. mis
3. su
4. tus
5. su
6. mi
7. nuestra
8. nuestros

Así se dice

Describing a family

To find out about a friend's family, ask:

¿Cuántas personas hay en tu familia?

¿Cómo es tu familia?

Your friend might answer:

Hay cinco personas **en mi familia.**
Mi abuela **vive** con nosotros.
. . . lives . . .

Somos cinco.
There are . . . of us.

También **tenemos** un perro.
. . . we have . . .

Nuestra familia es muy grande. Tenemos muchos **primos.**
. . . cousins.

Somos muy **unidos.**
We're . . . close-knit.

Nota gramatical

You've been using **mi(s)**, **tu(s)**, and **su(s)**, which are *possessive adjectives.* Here are the others:

nuestro/a(s)   our
vuestro/a(s)   your (when "you" is plural)
su(s)   your (when "you" is plural)
su(s)   their

1. Note that **nuestro** and **vuestro** also have a feminine form:

   Nuestra famil**ia** es pequeña.

2. Like **mi, tu,** and **su,** these forms add an **-s** when they modify a plural noun:
   sus primos, nuestros gatos.

Cuaderno de gramática, p. 46, Acts. 3–4

Más práctica gramatical, p. 190, Acts. 1–2

7 **Retrato de familia** *Family portrait*

Hablemos Work in pairs. Take the role of one of the people in the family pictures in the **Vocabulario** on page 173. Introduce yourself and the other members of your family to your partner.

MODELO   **Ésta es mi madre y aquí están mi padrastro y mi hermano.**

hijo	padrastro
media hermana	perro
tía	abuelo

8 **Gramática en contexto** See answers below.

Leamos/Escribamos Pati y Luis están mirando las fotos de la familia de Pati. Completa su conversación con el adjetivo posesivo correcto.

PATI   Aquí está ___1___ *(our)* abuela conmigo y con ___2___ *(my)* primos.

LUIS   ¿Y quién es este señor?

PATI   ¿Con mi tía? Es ___3___ *(her)* esposo, Adolfo. Es el padrastro de mis primos.

LUIS   Es bastante grande la familia de ___4___ *(your)* primos, ¿verdad?

PATI   Sí, hay siete personas en ___5___ *(their)* familia. En ___6___ *(my)* familia somos cuatro.

LUIS   En ___7___ *(our)* familia somos cuatro también. Pero si *(if)* contamos *(count)* a ___8___ *(our)* perros también, ¡somos siete!

Cultures and Communities

Culture Notes

- Emphasize to students that **los parientes** means *relatives.* Ask students to recall that the Spanish words for *parents* are **padres** and **papás.** Many Spanish speakers refer to their parents individually as **mami** and **papi** and address them using the informal **tú** form, although some speakers use **usted** with their parents.

- Many Spanish-speaking parents select close friends or relatives to be godparents for their children. The godfather (**el padrino** or **el compadre**) is often an uncle or brother, while the godmother (**la madrina** or **la comadre**) may be an aunt or sister. Godparents are often traditional in the United States and in Spanish-speaking countries.

9 **La familia extendida** See sample answer below.

Hablemos/Escribamos Work with a partner to write a paragraph about an extended family. Use the family picture below to help you. Answer the following questions and be prepared to share your paragraph with the class.

1. ¿Cuántas personas hay en la familia?
2. ¿Qué les gusta hacer a tres de las personas?
3. ¿Es grande la familia? ¿pequeña?

4. ¿Cómo son? Describe a tres de las personas. (Usa los adjetivos posesivos.)
5. ¿Qué actividades les gusta hacer juntos?

 10 **¿Quién en tu familia es...?**

Hablemos Work in pairs. Ask your partner, **¿Quién en tu familia es...?** using adjectives like those in the box.

guapo moreno bonito alto
simpático cómico
bajo inteligente rubio

 11 **Una entrevista**

Hablemos/Escribamos Work with a partner. Create six to eight questions about someone's family and take turns interviewing each other. Then, using forms of **nuestro** as needed, work together to write a paragraph telling two or three things you have in common.

Nota cultural

When a man and a woman serve as **padrino** *(godfather)* and **madrina** *(godmother)* at a baby's baptism, it's understood that they'll have a special lifelong relationship with their godchild. The godparents give their **ahijados** love, advice, and help with education and careers. El **compadrazgo** is the relationship between the parents and godparents of a child. **Compadres** and **comadres** often consider each other family. Should a parent die, **compadres** and **comadres** are expected to care for each other's children.

 Cuaderno de actividades, p. 72, Act. 20

Visual Learners

Use the pictures on *Teaching Transparency 6-A* or bring in magazine photos. With the photos visible to everyone in the class, ask several students **¿Quién es alto? ¿Quién es cómico?** Students should answer appropriately according to the pictures displayed.

Teaching Suggestion

11 Have students write their paragraphs separately, then consult with a partner on a final version to be turned in.

Native Speakers

Have native speakers write an entry in their journals describing a favorite family member: a grandparent, an aunt or uncle, a godparent, or a cousin. Content should include the person's appearance, personality, likes, and dislikes. Encourage students to share an anecdote that shows why that family member is special.

Additional Practice

Ask students to create a three-tiered family tree, using the names of their favorite celebrities. Encourage them to come up with unusual combinations of relatives, and to incorporate new family vocabulary. Have students write sentences explaining the relationships of the different family members to one another. (**Los abuelos son Arnold Schwarzenegger y Wynona Judd. Ethan Hawke, Michael Chang y Bart Simpson son hermanastros.**)

Communication for All Students

Cooperative Learning

10 Find four pictures of people of varying ages and sexes, then copy two pictures each onto four sheets of paper, making sure no two papers are alike. Each student in a group of four will see only one sheet, and will listen to descriptions to determine which group member is searching for the person on the top of his or her paper, and in turn he or she describes the person on the bottom.

Auditory Learners

11 Have students ask each other questions to see what has been learned about the partner's family. The questions must begin with **¿Cómo es...** or **¿Cómo son...** and *not* contain the family relation, but use circumlocution (**el esposo de mi madre**) following the interrogative phrase. The answer must contain the description and the relationship. (**Tu tío es alto y moreno.**)

Answers

9 *Sample answer:*
En la familia hay cinco personas. A ellos les gusta estar en casa juntos. La familia es grande y es muy unida. La madre es morena y guapa. Sus hijos son rubios y divertidos.

Cooperative Learning

Have students work in groups of four to create a questionnaire. Each group member prepares two questions about a different family in the photos on page 173. (**¿Cuántos hermanos tiene Miguel? ¿Hay una hija en la familia Pérez?**) One person proofreads the questions and another puts them together as a questionnaire. Groups exchange questionnaires and answer their classmates' questions. Each questionnaire is then returned to the group that created it. The two remaining group members in each group check the answers to see if they are correct.

Assess

▶ Testing Program, pp. 131–134
Quiz 6-1A, Quiz 6-1B
Audio CD 6, Tr. 18

▶ Student Make-Up Assignments, Chapter 6, Alternative Quiz

▶ Alternative Assessment Guide, p. 37

12 Cuestionario sobre la familia

Leamos/Escribamos Based on what you see in the questionnaire below, how would you describe this family? The verb **vivir** means *to live.* See possible answers below.

1. Ésta es una familia...
2. En la familia, hay...
3. Viven en...
4. Probablemente tienen...
5. Les gusta...
6. Cuando tienen problemas...

INFORMACIÓN PERSONAL

❶ Datos personales
  a. Nombre completo: Apellido *Young*
                  Nombre(s) *Kelly*
  b. Edad: *14* años
  c. Domicilio una casa ☐ un apartamento ☒

❷ Vivo con unos parientes ☐ con una familia extensa ☐
         en una familia nuclear ☒

❸ Datos familiares
  a. ¿Tienes hermanos? *Sí* ¿Cuántos? *2*
  b. ¿Cuántos años tiene cada uno?
    Mi hermano mayor Mike tiene 16 años
    Mi hermana menor Lynn tiene 12 años

❹ Actividades
  ¿Qué haces con tu familia? ¿Con qué frecuencia?
  a. pescar
  b. visitar a los parientes
  c. ir al cine *todos los viernes*
  d. limpiar la casa
  e. acampar *a veces/durante el verano*
  f. ir de vacaciones

13 ¿Cómo es tu familia?

Escribamos Create your own questionnaire to find out about another family. Include questions about how people look, what they are like, what their house is like, and whether or not they have any pets.

14 Mi familia imaginaria

Hablemos/Escribamos First create an imaginary family or think of a TV family you and your partner are familiar with. Using the questionnaire you created in Activity 13, interview your partner about his or her "family," filling in the blanks as you go. Then switch roles. What characteristics do the families have in common?

Vocabulario extra	
el animal doméstico, la mascota	*pet*
el caballo	*horse*
el conejo	*rabbit*
la culebra	*snake*
el pájaro	*bird*
el pez dorado	*goldfish*
el ratón	*mouse*
la tortuga	*turtle*

Communication for All Students

Visual Learners

13 Pass out magazine pictures of individuals or families. Ask students to imagine that the people in the picture are long-lost relatives. Have students describe their new-found family members and share their descriptions with a partner.

Building on Previous Skills

14 Have students switch questionnaires with a partner and read the description of the imaginary family to him or her. In addition to describing the people, their house, and their pets, include the activities they like and dislike. The partner responds to the description by describing another family that is exactly opposite. Students may refer to **Vocabulario** on pp. 92, 107, 113, and 135.

Answers
12 *Possible answers:*
1. ...pequeña.
2. ...tres hijos.
3. ...un apartamento.
4. ...cinco personas en la familia.
5. ...ir al cine.
6. *Answers will vary.*

STANDARDS: 1.1, 1.3, 3.1, 5.1

¿Estás bien, hija?

Alison's spending her summer with Mrs. Saralegui and her children Marcela and Cristián in Concepción, Chile. After a busy day, Alison goes to her room to read and relax. Read the dialogues and try to answer the questions that follow.

MARCELA Oye, Alison, ¿no quieres tomar un té con nosotros? Estamos en la sala.

ALISON No, gracias, Marcela. Quiero leer esta novela.

Diez minutos después...

SRA. CECILIA ¿Te sientes mal, hijita? ¿Te hace falta* tu familia?

ALISON No. Estoy leyendo, nada más.

Quince minutos después...

CRISTIÁN Alison, ¿qué haces aquí solita? ¿Estás bien?

ALISON Sí, estoy bien. Sólo quiero leer ahora, gracias.

Para discutir...

A. Why do you think everyone assumes that Alison is upset or sick?

B. What do you do when you want to be alone?

C. In small groups, discuss what you think Alison is learning about privacy in Hispanic culture.

Vamos a comprenderlo

The concept of privacy is different in Spanish-speaking countries. People spend less time alone and more time among friends and family. Even though Alison just wants a few moments alone, the Saralegui family is worried that something must be wrong. Checking on her is their way of expressing concern.

_____

* ¿Te hace falta...? Do you miss …?

Connections and Comparisons

Multicultural Link

If your students have access to the Internet, have them ask a keypal in a Spanish-speaking country how privacy is regarded. Ask students to compare their concept of privacy with that of their keypal. If the Internet is unavailable, suggest that students write to Spanish-speaking pen pals and ask the same question. A list of pen pal organizations is provided on page T46. Visit the HRW Web site at **go.hrw.com** for online resources and additional information about pen pal organizations.

Teaching Resources
pp. 178–182

PRINT 📖

▸ Lesson Planner, p. 29
▸ TPR Storytelling Book, pp. 22, 24
▸ Listening Activities, pp. 43–44, 48
▸ Activities for Communication, pp. 33–34, 101, 103–104, 147–148
▸ Cuaderno de gramática, pp. 47–49
▸ Grammar Tutor for Students of Spanish, Chapter 6
▸ Cuaderno de actividades, pp. 65–67
▸ Cuaderno para hispanohablantes, pp. 26–30
▸ Testing Program, pp. 135–138
▸ Alternative Assessment Guide, p. 37
▸ Student Make-Up Assignments, Chapter 6

MEDIA 💿

▸ One-Stop Planner
▸ Audio Compact Discs, CD 6, Trs. 4–6, 29–30, 19
▸ Teaching Transparencies 6-2, 6-B; **Más práctica gramatical** Answers; Cuaderno de gramática Answers
▸ Interactive CD-ROM Tutor, Disc 2

Bell Work
Have students imagine they attended a family reunion where every relative imaginable was present. Have them write descriptions of as many guests as possible.

Presenting
Así se dice
Pointing out the definite articles with parts of the body, ask who has **los ojos azules** or **el pelo negro**.

Vocabulario
Model pronunciation, and ask questions based on the captions.

Segundo paso

Objectives Describing people; discussing things a family does together

WV3 FLORIDA-6

Así se dice

Describing people

To ask for a description of someone, say:

¿**Cómo es** tu abuelo?

¿**De qué color son los ojos** de Pedro?
What color are . . . eyes?

¿**De qué color es el pelo** de tu padre?
What color is . . . hair?

Some responses might be:

Él es alto y cariñoso.

Tiene (los) ojos verdes.
He has green eyes.

Tiene canas.
He has gray hair.

Cuaderno de actividades, p. 65, Act. 9

También se puede decir…
Other words for *brown* are **marrón, castaño,** and **pardo.**

15 **¿Ciencia ficción?**

Escuchemos Listen to the following descriptions of some fictional characters and use **probable** or **improbable** to tell what you think of their appearance.
Scripts and answers on p. 167G.

CD 6
Tr. 4

Vocabulario

La profesora Fajardo es muy lista. Es pelirroja, delgada y tiene (los) ojos azules.

Los hijos de Julio son traviesos. Pepe es mayor y Pedro es menor. Julio y sus hijos tienen pelo negro y (los) ojos de color café.

Los abuelos son muy cariñosos. La abuela es atractiva y un poco gorda. El abuelo es viejo. Tiene canas pero se ve joven.

Cuaderno de actividades, p. 65, Act. 10   Cuaderno de gramática, pp. 47–48, Acts. 5–7

Cultures and Communities

Native Speakers
Explain to students that **gordo** and **gorda** (or **gordito** and **gordita**) are often used as terms of affection or nicknames. Other nicknames based on physical characteristics include **prieto/a** *(dark-skinned)*, **güero/a** *(blond or light-skinned)*, or **chaparro/a** *(short)*. Ask native speakers to contribute nicknames or terms of affection that they have heard in their families or among their friends.

Additional Vocabulary
Some color words are actually nouns that are used as adjectives. As such, they do not change either number or gender to agree with the noun that they modify. Sometimes the phrases **color de...** or **de color...** precede these nouns.

violeta *violet*	**lila** *lilac*
rosa *pink*	**turquesa** *turquoise*
añil *indigo*	**escarlata** *scarlet*

16 ¿Cómo son tus amigos? Scripts and answers on p. 167G.

 Escuchemos Listen as Rogelio describes some people and his cat to his aunt Maki. Identify each character by name. Does Maki know one of them especially well?

CD 6
Tr. 5

Simón y Quique

David

Rebeca

Gabriel y Conchita

Maki

 17 Los amigos de Rogelio Answers will vary.

Escribamos Escribe una descripción de cada personaje de la Actividad 16. Incluye la edad y el color del pelo y de los ojos en tu descripción. Usa algunas de las palabras nuevas del **Vocabulario** en la página 178.

 18 Una entrevista

Hablemos Work with a partner and interview each other about three of your relatives or characters in a TV series. Include at least one adult and at least one teenager. Describe each person as fully as possible, telling where he or she lives and works and some things that person does. Be prepared to tell the class about one of the people you learned about.

 19 Adivina... ¿quién es?

Hablemos Work in groups of three. Each should pick a famous person and describe him or her in two to five sentences to the group. Your partners must guess whom you're describing.

Vocabulario extra	
egoísta	*selfish* (masc., fem.)
leal	*loyal*
perezoso/a	*lazy*
trabajador/a	*hard-working*

What do you think these words mean?

agresivo/a	**generoso/a**
artístico/a	**responsable**
atlético/a	**independiente**
creativo/a	**romántico/a**
desorganizado/a	**tímido/a**

 20 Así soy yo. See sample answer below.

Escribamos Imagine that you're going to spend the next school year in Spain. Write a description of yourself for the agency that places students with host families. What do you look like? What things do you especially like or dislike? Make your description as detailed as you can. Be prepared to share your description with the class.

Communication for All Students

Slower Pace

16 Have students describe the pictures before listening to the recording.

Visual Learners

19 Display photos of several well-known personalities cut from magazines. Have a student describe one of the people in the photos. The other students guess which person is being described.

Auditory Learners

20 Read several of the students' descriptions of themselves aloud and see if the class can guess who is being described. You may want to ask students in advance for permission to read their description to the class.

Segundo paso

CAPÍTULO 6

TPR To review colors and body parts, each student will need a set of items in various colors to move (small pieces of colored paper or crayons). Have students respond to simple commands in Spanish, such as: **Pon el azul en el pelo.** Move into more complicated directions, such as **Si tienes el pelo castaño, pon el color verde en la silla,** or **Si tienes los ojos azules, pon el color negro en el suelo.** You may wish to have students peer-correct.

Additional Practice

Have students work in groups of four or five. Using the **Vocabulario** and the words from **Vocabulario extra,** ask each group to select at least five of the adjectives and think how they might mime them for the class. Ask each student to mime one of the words and ask the rest of the class to guess what the word is.

Teaching Suggestion

Students work in small groups to create a short skit based on the following situation: A hit-and-run driver has just left the scene of an accident. Fortunately, several witnesses got a good look at the driver. A police officer has just arrived and is taking the witnesses' descriptions of the suspects.

Answers

20 *Sample answer:*
Soy morena y baja. Tengo pelo y ojos de color café. Tengo 15 años y soy delgada. Soy tímida. También soy inteligente, trabajadora y responsable. Me gusta leer y viajar.

Presenting
Así se dice

Write several familiar verbs on the board and ask **¿Qué haces los fines de semana?** Elicit first-person plural responses by addressing groups. Then have students ask others about weekend activities in the **ustedes** form.

Nota gramatical

Use **salir** and **hacer** to describe photos in Activity 21. (**Salen a cenar. Hacen ejercicio.**) Ask questions about the photos, using the same verbs.

Así se dice

Discussing things a family does together

To find out what a family does together, ask:

¿Qué hacen ustedes los fines de semana?
What do you do . . .?

¿Hacen ustedes **algo** durante el verano?
. . . something . . .

Some responses might be:

Salimos juntos y **visitamos a** nuestros abuelos. **Casi siempre cenamos** con ellos los domingos.
We go out . . . we visit . . .
We almost always eat dinner . . .

Sí. Siempre **hacemos un viaje.**
. . . we take a trip.

Caracas, Venezuela

Nota gramatical

Hacer *(to do, make)* and **salir** *(to go out)* are regular verbs in the present tense except in the **yo** form, which has an irregular **-go** ending.

hago	hacemos	**salgo**	salimos
haces	hacéis	sales	salís
hace	hacen	sale	salen

Cuaderno de actividades, p. 67, Act. 13

Cuaderno de gramática, pp. 48–49, Acts. 8–9

Más práctica gramatical, p. 191, Acts. 3–5 →

21 **Con la familia**

Escuchemos Listen as four friends discuss what they do with their families and friends. Match the description you hear with the correct photo. Scripts and answers on p. 167G.

CD 6 Tr. 6

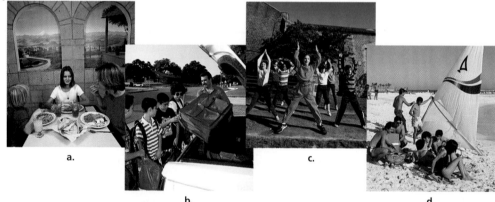

a.

b.

c.

d.

Connections and Comparisons

Language-to-Language
Point out a similarity between the Spanish verb **hacer** and the English verb *to do:* when you use them in a question, you often don't need them in the answer. If your students are repeating **hacer** in their responses, write **¿Qué** <u>haces</u> **los sábados?** on the board. Answer for yourself, writing some of your answers: **Descanso con mi familia. Lavo la** ropa. **Voy al cine.** Then write *What* <u>do you do</u> *on Saturdays?* on the board. Call on several students to answer and write their responses: *I go to the mall. I play soccer. I sleep.* Help students notice that neither language repeats the verb **hacer***/to do.* Then repeat the Spanish question, writing student responses on the board.

STANDARDS: 1.2, 4.1

22 Gramática en contexto

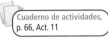

Leamos/Escribamos Escribe un párrafo sobre lo que haces cuando sales. Utiliza las siguientes preguntas como guía.

1. ¿Sales los fines de semana?
2. ¿Qué te gusta hacer cuando sales?
3. ¿Con quién o con quiénes sales?
4. ¿Qué haces cuando sales con tus amigos?
5. ¿Qué te gusta hacer cuando sales con tu familia?
6. Si no sales mucho, ¿qué haces?

Nota gramatical

When a direct object refers to a person who receives the action of a verb, use the "personal **a**" before the noun. If the direct object is a place or thing, no **a** is used.

Visito a mis tíos en Guatemala todos los veranos. Cuando estoy con ellos, siempre **visitamos las ruinas** mayas.

Cuaderno de actividades, p. 66, Act. 11

Más práctica gramatical, p. 192, Act. 6

Cuaderno de gramática, p. 49, Act. 10

24 Una excursión *Answers will vary.*

Leamos/Hablemos You and your family are planning a trip to Miami. Combine phrases from each box to make a list of people and places you each need to visit. Use the personal **a** as needed.

yo
mis padres
mi hermano/a
todos nosotros
mis abuelos

la piscina de Venecia
mis tíos en Coral Gables
los museos históricos
nuestros primos
una amiga de la familia

MODELO   Yo necesito visitar a un primo en Hialeah.

Voy a visitar a mi amiga en Miami.

See answers below.
23 Gramática en contexto

Leamos/Escribamos Completa las siguientes oraciones con la **a personal**. Algunas oraciones no necesitan nada.

1. Visitamos ＝＝＝＝ nuestros primos tres veces por mes.
2. Mario va a visitar ＝＝＝＝ el Museo de Antropología con su hermana.
3. Llamo ＝＝＝＝ mis abuelos todos los domingos.
4. Voy a visitar ＝＝＝＝ mis amigos en Colorado este verano.
5. Paula quiere conocer ＝＝＝＝ unos nuevos amigos este año.
6. Miro ＝＝＝＝ la televisión por la noche con mi familia.

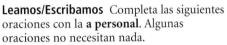

Make your Spanish real by connecting what you learn in class to people or events in your life. For example, as you're learning how to describe families, imagine talking to someone you know about his or her family. That person might be a new friend or even a coworker at your job. What kinds of questions would you want to ask? If you were living with a family in Venezuela, what do you think they'd like to know about your family in the United States?

Segundo paso

C A P Í T U L O   6

Presenting
Nota gramatical

Personal *a* Model the use of the personal **a** by using various people and objects in sentences. (**Veo la pizarra. También veo a Patricia.**) Then have one student close his or her eyes. Place a classroom object such as a book in front of the student. Ask him to open his eyes and say what he sees. (**Veo el libro.**) Then choose another student to close her eyes, and have a classmate stand silently at her desk. Have the first student open her eyes and say **Veo a...** Extension: ask other students **¿Qué ves...?** or **¿A quién ves...?**

Culture Note
The **a personal** is sometimes used with animals if they are treated as pets. (**Veo a mi perra Loli entre las flores.**)

Communication for All Students

Auditory Learners

22 In pairs, one student asks the other student one or two of the questions. The second student answers them. Then have students switch roles before proceeding to more items.

Additional Practice

24 Teach the words for street (**la calle**), avenue (**la avenida**), and boulevard (**el paseo**) so that students will be able to give their addresses when asked **¿Dónde vives?** Teach them to say the street name first and then the number. (**Vivo en la calle Real número 254.**)

Answers

23 1. a
2. nada
3. a
4. a
5. a
6. nada

Speaking Assessment

 25 You may wish to go over notes gathered from the interviews before students present their findings to the class. Encourage motivated students to use **Dice Que...** as introduced in **Tercer paso.** You may wish to evaluate their report using the following rubric.

Speaking Rubric	Points			
	4	3	2	1
Content (Complete–Incomplete)				
Comprehension (Total–Little)				
Comprehensibility (Comprehensible–Incomprehensible)				
Accuracy (Accurate–Seldom accurate)				
Fluency (Fluent–Not fluent)				

18–20: A	14–15: C	Under
16–17: B	12–13: D	12: F

Assess

▸ Testing Program, pp. 135–138
 Quiz 6-2A, Quiz 6-2B
 Audio CD 6, Tr. 19

▸ Student Make-Up Assignments, Chapter 6, Alternative Quiz

▸ Alternative Assessment Guide, p. 37

Answers

27 *Sample answer:*
—¿Por qué no hacemos algo juntos este fin de semana?
—Ay, no, papá. Pienso ir a la playa con mis amigos el sábado.
—Pero hija, nunca pasamos tiempo juntos.
—No es verdad, papi. Visitamos a nuestros primos casi todos los meses.
Endings will vary.

---

25 ## ¿Con qué frecuencia?

 Hablemos Use some of the following questions to interview a partner about his or her family, or about an imaginary family. Switch roles after four or five questions and be prepared to report your findings to the class.

1. ¿Dónde vives? ¿Quiénes viven contigo?
2. ¿Sales con tu familia los fines de semana? ¿Adónde van y qué hacen?
3. ¿Con quién vas a un centro comercial? ¿Cómo se llama el centro?
4. ¿Con qué frecuencia visitas a (tus abuelos, tus primos...)?
5. ¿A tu familia le gusta acampar, bucear o hacer esquí acuático?

26 ## La chica sándwich

Leamos/Hablemos Together with a partner, read the descriptions of **la hermana mayor, la chica sándwich,** and **la hermana menor.** Imagine that you're one of the three pictured and describe yourself to your partner. See if your partner can guess if you're the oldest, the youngest, or the middle child in the family.

TRES HERMANAS, TRES PERSONALIDADES

Retrato de "La mayor": Madura, responsable. Nadie tiene que decirle que estudie; saca muy buenas notas. Siempre está presentable. Se puede abrir su closet sin miedo de ser sepultada en vida.

Retrato de "la chica sándwich": Es el polo opuesto de sus hermanas, pero ¿es ésta su verdadera personalidad o nada contra la corriente? Más conocida como "La chica camaleón".

Retrato de "baby de la familia": Es simpática, alegre, el alma de la fiesta. ¿Responsabilidad? Y eso... ¿con qué se come? De todas formas, todos la adoran. Pero ¡qué insoportable!

27 ## Un conflicto See sample answer below.

 Escribamos Write a dialogue with six to nine sentences between a parent and a teenage son or daughter. The parent wants to do more things with the teenager as a family. The teenager feels that they already do too many things together. For example, will the teenager go with his or her parent to visit relatives this weekend, or go to the mall with friends? Follow these steps:

a. The parent asks to do something with the teenager.
b. The teenager objects, and tells what he or she really wants to do.
c. The parent says they never do things together.
d. The teenager says it's not true, and points out something they often do together.
e. Now create an ending! What do they end up doing?

Communication for All Students

Thinking Critically

26 **Drawing Inferences** Ask students to explain why they believe the expressions **la chica sándwich** and **el chico sándwich** are used.

Challenge

27 A more challenging option to this dialogue could be a persuasive argument. Have students imagine they are invited to spend a weekend with an out-of-town friend. The parent asks the student about plans for activities, distance, and other details. The parent may have other family plans and prefer that the student stay home, but the student must convince the parent to let him or her go on the trip.

CD 6
Trs. 7–10

¿Cuántas personas hay en tu familia?

In this chapter, we asked some people about their families and what they do to help around the house.

Pablo
Quito, Ecuador
CD 6 Tr. 8
"En mi familia hay cinco personas. Mi papá, mi mamá y mis dos hermanas. Yo lavo los platos, limpio la cocina,... arreglo mi cuarto y limpio mi baño".

Arantxa
Madrid, España
CD 6 Tr. 9
"Somos cinco... Tengo dos hermanos menores... Cuando se van mis padres, me quedo con ellos en casa... Tengo que ayudar en casa... Ayudo a mi madre a recoger la casa".

Brenda CD 6 Tr. 10
San Antonio, Texas
"Yo vivo en una familia de cinco... mi mamá es... muy protectiva... mi hermana es muy rebelde... mi hermano es como niño chiquito... y mi papá es... muy bueno... Mi hermano no hace muchas cosas; la que hace más soy yo, porque mi mamá va al trabajo todos los días y viene cansada. Soy yo, como soy la más grande de los niños, yo los cuido, hago los trastes *(dishes)*, trapeo *(mop)*".

Para pensar y hablar...

A. What responsibilities do you have? Are they similar to those mentioned above?

B. Many Hispanic families are large and close-knit. Family members spend a lot of time together and depend on each other for support. What advantages could this type of family offer?

> Cuaderno para hispanohablantes, pp. 29–30

Teaching Resources
p. 183

PRINT
▸ Video Guide, pp. 39–41, 44
▸ Cuaderno de actividades, p. 72
▸ Cuaderno para hispanohablantes, pp. 29–30

MEDIA
▸ One-Stop Planner
▸ Video Program, Videocassette 2, 44:38–47:34
▸ DVD Tutor, Disc 1
▸ Audio Compact Discs, CD 6, Trs. 7–10
▸ Interactive CD-ROM Tutor, Disc 2

Presenting
Panorama cultural

Have students read the captions or watch the video. How much do they identify with the interviewees with regard to family interdependence? If these issues seem too personal, have students discuss the ideal or typical family.

Preguntas

1. ¿Quiénes cuidan a sus hermanos menores? (Arantxa y Brenda)

2. ¿Cuántos chicos limpian sus cuartos? (uno)

3. ¿Quién hace la mayoría del trabajo en la casa de Brenda? (Brenda)

4. ¿Haces tú los mismos quehaceres que Pablo? (*Answers will vary.*)

5. ¿Qué chico tiene una familia como tu familia? ¿Por qué? (*Answers will vary.*)

Connections and Comparisons

Comparing and Contrasting
The number of family members may vary from one culture or region to the next. Have students talk about the potential advantages and disadvantages of having a large or small family regarding things such as finances, chores, and privacy. You might frame this discussion in the form of a debate, with different groups of students advocating large or small families.

Family Link
Ask students what they enjoy doing with their families. Would they like to spend more or less time with their families? Have students interview five relatives about what they consider to be the three most important aspects of family life. Students can synthesize their answers in a chart and compare their findings with the rest of the class.

Tercer paso
Objective Discussing problems and giving advice

Así se dice

Discussing problems and giving advice

To discuss a problem, say:

Tengo un problema. El profesor **dice**
que hablo **demasiado** en clase, pero
no es cierto.
. . . says that . . . too much . . . it's not true.

¿Qué debo hacer?
What should I do?

Your friend might answer:

Debes hablar **menos** en clase y
escuchar más.
You should . . . less . . .

Nota gramatical

The verb **deber** *(should, ought to)* is a
regular **-er** verb.

debo	debemos
debes	debéis
debe	deben

Cuaderno de actividades,
p. 68, Acts. 14–15

Más práctica gramatical,
pp. 192–193, Acts. 7–8

Cuaderno de gramática, p. 50, Acts. 11–12

---

 28 **Los problemas de Mónica**

Escuchemos Listen as Mónica describes
her family. Then match the pictures below
to the correct description you hear. One of
the people she describes isn't pictured.
Who is it? Scripts and answers on p. 167H.

CD 6
Tr. 11

1. Mónica
2. su mamá
3. su hermana menor
4. su tía

a.

b.

c.

 29 **Gramática en contexto**

Hablemos With a partner, look at the pictures above of Mónica's family. First state the
problem or situation and say what Mónica, her mother, and her younger sister should
do. Then create an original solution for each problem. Be prepared to present your ideas
to the class.

MODELO —**La madre de Mónica trabaja demasiado. Debe trabajar menos**
y descansar un poco más.

Connections and Comparisons

Language Note
Point out to students that in addition to the meanings *should* and *ought to,* **deber** also means *to*
owe. Combine the interrogative **¿Cuánto...?** to
model questions and answers relating to purchases,
and review some of the numbers as you elicit
responses: **Debes dieciséis dólares.** Ask students
if they can think of other meanings of *to owe* and
its uses in English: *To what do I owe . . . , You owe*

it to her to help her . . . If *owing to (due to)* is
mentioned, you may wish to expand vocabulary
terms to include **debido a,** or with exceptional
students, **se debe a:** *it's because of (due to).* These
same students may grasp the distinction between
debe + *infinitive* and **debe** + **de** + *infinitive*
(the first emphatic, the second speculative).

STANDARDS: 1.2, 1.3, 4.1

Los quehaceres domésticos *Household chores*

cortar el césped

trabajar en el jardín

hacer la cama

limpiar la cocina

pasar la aspiradora
en la sala

poner la mesa

cuidar al gato

planchar

> Cuaderno de gramática,
> p. 51, Acts. 13–15

Más práctica gramatical,
p. 193, Act. 8 →

CD-ROM 2
DVD 1

Nota gramatical

On page 180, you learned the verbs **hacer** and **salir**. The verb **poner** *(to put, to place)* is similiar in that it has **-go** in the **yo** form.

pongo	ponemos
pones	ponéis
pone	ponen

> Cuaderno de
> gramática,
> p. 52, Acts. 16–17

Más práctica gramatical,
p. 193, Act. 9 →

	pasar		
cenar		lavar	sacar
	preparar	poner	
deber			

30 Gramática en contexto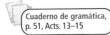

Leamos/Escribamos Ramón's mother is calling to see how he and his brothers and sister are coming with the housecleaning. Complete their conversation with the appropriate forms of verbs from the box. Not all of the verbs will be used. See answers below.

MAMÁ   Hola, mi hijo. Todavía estoy en el trabajo y tus tíos ___1___ con nosotros a las ocho. Ustedes ___2___ limpiar todo.

RAMÓN   Bueno, mamá, no te preocupes. Paco ___3___ la aspiradora en la sala, Laura y José ___4___ los platos y yo ___5___ la mesa.

MAMÁ   ¡Perfecto! Y yo les ___6___ algo delicioso.

Teaching Resources
pp. 184–187

PRINT 📖

▸ Lesson Planner, p. 31
▸ TPR Storytelling Book, pp. 23, 24
▸ Listening Activities, pp. 45, 49
▸ Activities for Communication, pp. 35–36, 102, 103–104, 147–148
▸ Cuaderno de gramática, pp. 50–52
▸ Grammar Tutor for Students of Spanish, Chapter 6
▸ Cuaderno de actividades, pp. 68–70
▸ Cuaderno para hispanohablantes, pp. 26–30
▸ Testing Program, pp. 139–142
▸ Alternative Assessment Guide, p. 37
▸ Student Make-Up Assignments, Chapter 6

MEDIA 📀📼

▸ One-Stop Planner
▸ Audio Compact Discs, CD 6, Trs. 11–16, 31–32, 20
▸ Teaching Transparencies 6-3, 6-C; **Más práctica gramatical** Answers; Cuaderno de gramática Answers
▸ Interactive CD-ROM Tutor, Disc 2

Answers

31 *Answers may vary.*
Pablo debe poner la mesa, no la cama.
Diana y Lola deben trabajar en el jardín, no en la sala.
Federico debe pasar la aspiradora en la casa, no en el jardín.
Miguelito debe sacar la basura, no poner la basura en el armario.
Frida debe darle de comer a un animal, no a la planta.

32 *Answers may vary.*
1. Mi hermana menor y yo cuidamos al perro.
2. Mis abuelos trabajan en el jardín.
3. Mi primo cuida a mis hermanitos.
4. Mi hermano mayor limpia la cocina y prepara la cena.
5. Yo paso la aspiradora.
6. Tú cortas el césped.

---

31 ¿Qué pasa aquí?

Hablemos/Escribamos Mira los dibujos y decide lo que deben o no deben hacer las personas.

 **Pablo**  **Diana y Lola**  **Federico** **Miguelito**  **Frida**

32 ¡Todo bajo control!

Leamos/Escribamos Assign everyone below a chore from the **Vocabulario** list on page 185. Try to assign each person the chore he or she likes. Some people may have more than one job.

1. A ti y a tu hermana menor les gustan los animales.
2. A tus abuelitos les gustan las plantas.
3. A tu primo le gusta pasar un rato con tus hermanos.
4. A tu hermano mayor le gusta preparar la cena.
5. A mí me gusta la sala limpia *(clean)*.
6. A ti te gusta estar afuera *(outside)* y te gustan las máquinas *(machines)*.

33 Querida Amalia

Leamos/Escribamos Completa la carta a Amalia con las formas correctas de las palabras en el cuadro.

	vivir		limpiar
ayudar		tener	
	mi		bonito
dicen		hacer	

Querida Amalia,

(Nosotros) __1__ en una casa muy __2__, pero nunca se ve bien porque __3__ hermanitos no limpian la casa. Yo no __4__ mucho tiempo libre. El problema es que mis padres __5__ que yo nunca __6__ en casa. ¿Qué debo __7__?

　　　Un cordial saludo de,

　　　La Trabajadora

34 ¡Una encuesta!

 Hablemos/Escribamos Take a survey of five classmates. Ask them what chores they do around the house. Using **dice que...**, write five sentences reporting what your classmates say. Be prepared to share your survey with the class.

Communication for All Students

Additional Practice

33 Write common problems on slips of paper. (**Tengo mucha tarea...**, **No me gusta la comida en la cafetería.**) Place the slips in a bag, a **bolsa de problemas.** Have each student draw a slip of paper and write some helpful advice to solve the problem.

Challenge

34 Have students, working in groups, come up with five chores they think are common. Then have groups survey other groups to determine which chore is the most common among them.

35  **Del colegio al trabajo**

Escribamos You work as an advice columnist. Take the role of Amalia and answer the letter from **La Trabajadora** in Activity 33. Use **Debes...** and **Necesitas...** with the verbs you know. Be prepared to present your solutions to the class. *See sample answer below.*

 36 **Problemas y más problemas**

Hablemos/Escribamos In small groups, get together and write a letter to an advice columnist. Your letter could be about housework, schoolwork, jobs, or friends. For additional vocabulary, see pages R5–R8. Exchange letters with another group and answer their letter.

 37 **En mi cuaderno** Answers will vary.

 Escribamos Write a description of two friends or family members from a TV series. Include their ages, where they live, and what they're like. Next, describe any problems they may have at home, such as household chores they don't like doing, or problems they have at work or school. Finally, give them some advice about what to do. Write at least ten sentences in your journal.

A lo nuestro

Spanish speakers often use special words when they are talking to someone they like a lot. These are called diminutives. For example, you could call your friend Juan **Juanito**, or your friend Rosa **Rosita**. You could call your grandmother **abuelita** and your father **papi**. Some other words adults often use to refer to people they care about are **mi cielo** or **mi vida** *(darling or dear)*. **Mi hijo/a** doesn't necessarily refer to an actual son or daughter, but to a young person the speaker is very fond of.

LETRA Y SONIDO

CD 6
Trs. 12–16

A. The **r** in Spanish does not sound like the *r* in English. English does have a sound that is similar, however. It's the sound made by quickly touching the tip of the tongue to the ridge behind the upper teeth, as in bu*tt*er, ba*tt*er, la*dd*er.

1. The **r** is pronounced this way between vowels.

   cariñoso   cara   moreno   favorito   pero

2. At the beginning of a word or after an **n** or **l**, the single **r** has a trilled or rolled sound. It is also trilled at the end of a word.

   rojo   rubio   enrojecer   Enrique   alrededor

3. The double **r** in Spanish always has a trilled or rolled sound.

   pelirrojo   perro   carro   correo

B. Dictado Script for Part B on p. 167H.

Listen to a TV ad that features a famous athlete, Rafael Ramírez. Write what you hear.

C. Trabalenguas

La rata roe la ropa del Rey de Roma.

Teacher to Teacher

Susan DiGiandomenico
Wellesley Middle School
Wellesley, Massachusetts

Susan takes her *Juegos Olímpicos* beyond the classroom
"I use this midwinter activity to unite the beginning Spanish classes for fun competition. Each teacher selects a chapter already taught and derives several challenges from it, to be combined onto a master list. They can be as routine as: 'Cuenta desde 10 hasta 100,' or as odd as: 'Baila la macarena mientras pronuncias el alfabeto.' The classes are recombined in groups of 10–12. Groups make introductions in Spanish, check the questions for understanding, then select a team member who can best answer. The games begin!"

 Portfolio

37 **Written** You may wish to suggest that students include this activity in their written Portfolio. For more Portfolio suggestions, see *Alternative Assessment Guide,* p. 23.

Auditory Learners

Ask students to record themselves reading the words in the **Letra y sonido** and the **Trabalenguas.** Ask pairs to listen to each other's recording and check each other's pronunciation. You might also play the **canción de cuna** *(lullaby)* on Audio CD 4, Track 30, and ask students to listen for **r** and **rr** sounds.

Assess

▸ Testing Program, pp. 139–142
  Quiz 6-3A, Quiz 6-3B
  Audio CD 6, Tr. 20

▸ Student Make-Up Assignments,
  Chapter 6, Alternative Quiz

▸ Alternative Assessment Guide,
  p. 37

 Answers

33 1. vivimos
2. bonita
3. mis
4. tengo
5. dicen
6. ayudo
7. hacer

35 *Sample answer:*
Querida Trabajadora,
Necesitas hablar con tu mamá sobre el problema. Ella puede hablar con tus hermanitos. Ellos pueden limpiar sus cuartos y poner sus juguetes en su lugar. Tú debes limpiar tu cuarto y ayudar en la cocina.
   Buena suerte,
   Amalia

CAPÍTULO 6

Teaching Resources
pp. 188–189

PRINT

▶ Lesson Planner, p. 31
▶ Cuaderno de actividades, p. 71
▶ Cuaderno para hispanohablantes, pp. 26–30
▶ Reading Strategies and Skills Handbook, Chapter 6
▶ ¡Lee conmigo! 1, Chapter 6
▶ Standardized Assessment Tutor, Chapter 6

MEDIA

▶ One-Stop Planner

Making Predictions

Have students skim the reading to find words they already know or cognates. **(parque, restaurante, chino, baile, frutas...)** Based on the words they identify, ask students to suggest a unifying theme for the reading selection, an alternative title, or a brief summary of any one of the parts.

Prereading
Activity A

Building on Previous Skills

After students have skimmed for the answers to ¡A comenzar! you might review vocabulary by asking **¿Te gusta la comida china? ¿Te gustan los restaurantes chinos? ¿Te gusta probar comida nueva? ¿Les gusta bailar? ¿Dónde bailan ustedes?**

Cinco cosas curiosas para hacer en la Pequeña Habana

Estrategia para leer

Before beginning to read, use the pictures, title, and subtitles to get a feeling for how the passage is organized. Knowing how the passage is organized will help you figure out what it's about. It can also help you hunt quickly through the passage to find a specific piece of information.

¡A comenzar!

A. This reading is from the **Guía oficial de la Pequeña Habana**, a guide for tourists in Miami. Skim it for one minute to find out which of these items are among the five suggestions.

- ⊙ buying fruit
- ⊙ watching a cultural dance
- · walking tours
- ⊙ playing dominoes
- ⊙ going to clubs
- · visiting museums
- ⊙ eating Chinese-Cuban food

Al grano

B. You have already studied two important ways to guess the meanings of words: using cognates and using context. Now you can combine these two skills to read more effectively.

Cognates. See if the unknown word looks like any English word. Does the English meaning you know make sense in context?

 ## Jugar dominó en el Parque del Dominó

Éste es un espectáculo que no tiene igual en todo los Estados Unidos. Los hombres se reúnen alrededor de las mesas de dominó y ajedrez para jugar. Aquí los hombres (no hay mujeres) juegan sin hablar casi. No se permite hablar ni de política. Sólo se interrumpe el juego para ir al cafetín de al lado y comprarse un guarapo o un fuerte café cubano.

 ## Ir a un restaurante chino-cubano y probar sus platos

Durante el siglo diecinueve muchos chinos llegaron a Cuba como esclavos y añadieron un sabor oriental a la cultura cubana. Sus descendientes mantuvieron las tradiciones culinarias chinas, y aquí en la Pequeña Habana se mantienen vivas en numerosos restaurantes.

Cultures and Communities

 ### Culture Note

Mambo, a Cuban dance with a beat derived from the African-rooted **rumba**, fascinated music fans in the U.S. during the 1940s. Cuban pianist Dámaso Pérez Prado had brought innovative rhythms to New York, and popularized the style with big band hits such as *Mambo Jambo* and *Voodoo Suite*. Credited with creating **mambo**, "Prez" influenced countless Hispanic musicians (Tito Puente, Arsenio Rodríguez, Xavier Cugat), and North American jazz artists (Perry Como, Dizzy Gillespie). With *Mambomania* and the popularity of Latin music came movie scores, dances, and TV creations such as Ricky Ricardo (Desi Arnaz), Cuban band leader and husband of Lucille Ball on the *I Love Lucy* show.

STANDARDS: 1.2, 2.2, 3.1

Ver un baile flamenco

Además de un baile, el flamenco es una expresión artística de pasión y rebeldía. Es un homenaje a la forma y movimientos del cuerpo humano. Tradicional en España, el flamenco es un espectáculo que se presenta diariamente en fabulosos restaurantes de la Pequeña Habana, como el Málaga.

Cabarets y discotecas

En un barrio donde predomina el español se encuentran los mejores clubes nocturnos de salsa, ritmo tropical y baladas. En lugares como "La Tranquera" se presentan artistas latinos de renombre.

Comprar diferentes variedades de frutas

Abundan mangos, papayas, mamey, coco, plátanos, bananas, naranjas, toronjas en diferentes tiendas y paradores.

Context. Look at all the words before and after the word you want to guess. Understanding the rest of the sentence will help you guess what the unknown word means.

C. Your family needs help reading the guide. Listed here are the words they're having trouble with. For each person the first two words are cognates. The third word you can guess through context. After you guess the meaning of a word, go back and make sure your guess makes sense in the rest of the sentence.

1. Your brother might like to try a game of dominoes. Help him with these words: **igual, política, cafetín** (**a.** caffeine **b.** game **c.** café)

2. Your mother is reading about the Chinese-Cuban restaurants, and these words are giving her trouble: **culinarias, numerosos, probar** (**a.** break **b.** prepare **c.** taste)

3. Your sister is deciding between watching a **flamenco** dance and going dancing. Help with these words: **pasión, movimientos, barrio** (**a.** bar **b.** language **c.** neighborhood)

4. You have decided to buy some fruit. Decide what these words mean: **variedades, coco, paradores** (**a.** roadside stands **b.** walls **c.** parades)

D. En español, escribe una lista de cinco cosas interesantes que puedes *(you can)* hacer en el lugar donde tú vives. Después, discute tus ideas con un/a compañero/a.

> Cuaderno para hispanohablantes, pp. 26–28

> Cuaderno de actividades, p. 71, Act. 19

Reading
Activities B and C

Using Context Clues
Have students do Activity B as individual work. If necessary, this may be assigned as homework. Emphasize the importance of testing a word in context, even if the word is a cognate. For example, many students may want to guess that **política** means *political,* but an adjective does not fit in the context of the sentence. Also, some students may guess that **coco** is *cacao,* which is not a fruit and would not make sense in context. Other words you may want your students to guess: **espectáculo, siglo, esclavos, sabor, rebeldía, homenaje, diariamente, baladas.**

Postreading
Activity D

Drawing on Your Experience
If your students have difficulty with the instructions to Activity D, go over the directions with them. The task itself may be challenging to some students, so you may choose to assign pairs so that one of each pair is able to help the other, if needed.

Group Work
As a longer project, have students construct a bulletin board about interesting things to do in your community. First, as a class, decide on five locations to highlight. Then assign students to groups and a location to each group. Each group prepares the Spanish description of a location and brings in photographs. You might display the bulletin board in the hall for other students and faculty to see.

Connections and Comparisons

Career Path
Ask students what they would do and see if they went to Florida. Write their responses on the board. Now ask the class to think about careers that are related to these activities and attractions. For example, a career in marine biology is related to the Miami Seaquarium; botany is related to the many tropical gardens in the area. You might ask students to research Florida Web sites or newspaper job listings that call for bilingual employees. Have them choose the listing that interests them the most and explain why to a partner. Visit the HRW Web site at **go.hrw.com**, keyword **WV3 FLORIDA-6,** for online resources and additional information about Florida.

For **Más práctica gramatical** Answer Transparencies, see the *Teaching Transparencies* binder.

Más práctica gramatical

CD-ROM2 DVD1

internet
go.hrw.com
MARCAR: go.hrw.com
PALABRA CLAVE: WV3 FLORIDA-6

Primer paso   **Objective** Describing a family

1 Usa los adjetivos posesivos **nuestro/a(s)** y **su/s** para escribir frases más cortas. (**p. 174**)

MODELO   la familia de Víctor → su familia

1. la casa de nosotros
2. el perro de Marcos y Verónica
3. los hermanos de Concha
4. el padre de Teresa
5. los tíos de Jaime
6. las abuelas de nosotros
7. la hermana de David
8. los gatos de nosotros

2 You and your friend Leonor are complete opposites. Explain how you differ by completing the statements below with the correct possessives and adjectives. (**p. 174**)

MODELO   *Mi* familia es pequeña. *Su* familia es *grande.*

1. ═══ padres son altos. ═══ padres son ═══.
2. ═══ perro es malo. ═══ perro es ═══.
3. ═══ hermano es rubio. ═══ hermano es ═══.
4. ═══ casa es pequeña. ═══ casa es ═══.
5. ═══ gatas son feas. ═══ gatas son ═══.
6. ═══ hermana mayor es antipática. ═══ hermana mayor es ═══.

Answers

1
1. nuestra casa
2. su perro
3. sus hermanos
4. su padre
5. sus tíos
6. nuestras abuelas
7. su hermana
8. nuestros gatos

2
1. Mis; Sus; bajos
2. Mi; Su; bueno
3. Mi; Su; moreno
4. Mi; Su; grande
5. Mis; Sus; bonitas
6. Mi; Su; simpática

Grammar Resources for Chapter 6

The **Más práctica gramatical** activities are designed as supplemental activities for the grammatical concepts presented in the chapter. You might use them as additional practice, for review, or for assessment.

For more grammar presentations, review, and practice refer to the following:
• Cuaderno de gramática
• Grammar Tutor for Students of Spanish

• Grammar Summary on pp. R9–R13
• Cuaderno de actividades
• Grammar and Vocabulary quizzes (Testing Program)
• Test Generator on the One-Stop Planner CD-ROM
• Interactive CD-ROM Tutor
• **Juegos interactivos** at <u>go.hrw.com</u>

3 Completa el siguiente párrafo con la forma correcta de **hacer**. (**p. 180**)

¿Cuándo y dónde ____1____ la tarea los estudiantes de la clase de español? ¡Depende! A veces, Olga y yo ____2____ la tarea en la biblioteca por la tarde. Pero si tengo clase de baile, entonces yo ____3____ la tarea por la noche, en casa. Beto ____4____ la tarea en casa también, porque le gusta escuchar música cuando estudia. ¿Y tú, Mercedes? Si hace sol, vas al parque y ____5____ la tarea allí, ¿verdad? A veces Martín y Gustavo ____6____ la tarea durante el almuerzo, en la cafetería. Y nadie ____7____ la tarea los viernes por la tarde.

4 Di a qué hora salen las siguientes personas de la escuela. (**p. 180**)

MODELO   tú (4:10)
Tú sales a las cuatro y diez de la tarde.

1. Maite (3:25)
2. Ricardo y yo (3:45)
3. Héctor (4:00)
4. Yoli y Sandra (4:15)
5. el profesor Cepeda (5:30)
6. yo (5:45)

5 Ahora di a qué hora hacen ejercicio. (**p. 180**)

MODELO   mi mamá (por la tarde)
Mi mamá hace ejercicio por la tarde.

1. Irina (los fines de semana)
2. yo (todos los días)
3. Luis y Javi (por la mañana)
4. tú (después de clases)
5. mis hermanos (los domingos)
6. todos nosotros (los sábados por la mañana)

Answers

3
1. hacen
2. hacemos
3. hago
4. hace
5. haces
6. hacen
7. hace

4
1. Maite sale a las tres y veinticinco.
2. Ricardo y yo salimos a las cuatro menos cuarto.
3. Héctor sale a las cuatro.
4. Yoli y Sandra salen a las cuatro y cuarto.
5. El profesor Cepeda sale a las cinco y media.
6. Yo salgo a las seis menos cuarto.

5
1. Irina hace ejercicio los fines de semana.
2. Yo hago ejercicio todos los días.
3. Luis y Javi hacen ejercicio por la mañana.
4. Tú haces ejercicio después de clases.
5. Mis hermanos hacen ejercicio los domingos.
6. Todos nosotros hacemos ejercicio los sábados por la mañana.

Communication for All Students

Additional Practice

3 Have students imagine that they are advising newcomers to their town on where to go to do certain activities. Have them create a dialogue which includes first the questions **¿Dónde hago ejercicio?** and **¿Dónde hacemos la tarea?**, followed by three questions using other verbs for other activities. Have them give at least two places for each activity, responding either in the **tú** form or the **ustedes** form of the verbs. In their answers, students should try to refer to real places around school or town. Encourage use of descriptive adjectives learned in this chapter.

Más práctica gramatical

WV3 FLORIDA-6

For **Más práctica gramatical**
Answer Transparencies, see the
Teaching Transparencies binder.

6 Raquel's cousin Marcos is coming to Miami for a visit. Complete their phone conversation by adding the personal "**a**" where necessary. If it's not necessary, don't write anything. (**p. 181**)

RAQUEL   Marcos, ¿quieres conocer ____1____ mi nuevo amigo, Armando? Es muy simpático.

MARCOS   Claro, y quiero visitar ____2____ todos los lugares de Miami: la playa, la Calle Ocho, el zoo, los museos…

RAQUEL   Muy bien. Y necesitamos ver ____3____ el nuevo parque de atracciones. ¡Es increíble!

MARCOS   ¿Y voy a ver ____4____ todos los primos?

RAQUEL   Bueno, no sé. Vas a ver ____5____ Chela, Nuria y Benjamín. ¿Y quieres visitar ____6____ Virginia y Chabeli?

MARCOS   Sí, si hay tiempo.

RAQUEL   Entonces, necesito llamar ____7____ tía Elena ahora para organizar todo. ¡Hasta el martes!

Tercer paso

Objective Discussing problems and giving advice

7 State what everyone should do to get the house ready for a family reunion. Use the correct form of **deber** in each sentence. (**p. 184**)

MODELO   el tío Lucho/poner más sillas en la sala
           El tío Lucho debe poner más sillas en la sala.

1. yo/limpiar la cocina
2. Raquel/pasar la aspiradora
3. Miguelito y Germán/organizar su cuarto
4. tú/poner la ropa en el armario
5. todos nosotros/preparar la comida
6. Papá/sacar la basura
7. Álvaro/cortar el césped
8. Mamá y yo/comprar los refrescos

Answers

6
1. a
2. —
3. —
4. a
5. a
6. a
7. a

7
1. Yo debo limpiar la cocina.
2. Raquel debe pasar la aspiradora.
3. Miguelito y Germán deben organizar su cuarto.
4. Tú debes poner la ropa en el armario.
5. Todos nosotros debemos preparar la comida.
6. Papá debe sacar la basura.
7. Álvaro debe cortar el césped.
8. Mamá y yo debemos comprar los refrescos.

Teacher to Teacher

Irene's students author their own booklets

Irene García
Austin High School
Austin, Texas

"I give students construction paper (for the cover) and five blank sheets of white paper (for the interleaf) stapled in the center to create vocabulary booklets. I have students decorate the booklet according to the theme of the chapter. They will add vocabulary learned through class discussions, readings, and activities as we progress through the chapter. Students write definitions, create sentences using the words and expressions, and draw pictures to help them remember the vocabulary. This is a good tool for vocabulary review before tests and the final exam since each student has a booklet for each chapter."

8 The following people have some problems and need your advice. Make suggestions using the correct form of **deber** and an expression from the box in each sentence. (pp. 184, 185)

> practicar el piano
>
> preparar la cena   limpiar la cocina
>
> cortar el césped
>
> hacer la tarea   ir al centro comercial

1. ¡Tengo un concierto de piano mañana y no estoy listo *(ready)*!
2. El césped de la casa del profesor Cortez está muy alto.
3. Nuestros amigos quieren cenar en nuestra casa, pero nosotros no tenemos comida preparada *(prepared)*.
4. Mañana hay una fiesta en la casa de Pepe. ¡Necesito comprar ropa nueva!
5. Su padre dice que ustedes necesitan estudiar más para la clase de matemáticas.
6. Sara prepara la cena y después la cocina es un desastre.

9 La mamá de Fede le dice que él necesita limpiar el cuarto. Completa lo que ella le dice con la forma correcta de **poner**. (p. 185)

Fede, eres un desastre. Siempre ___1___ tus cosas debajo de la cama. Debes ___2___ la tarea en el escritorio y los libros en tu mochila. Ahora yo ___3___ tus zapatos en el armario. Tus hermanas siempre ___4___ su ropa en el armario. Y tu hermano Nando nunca ___5___ sándwiches en su mochila como tú. ¿Y por qué ___6___ tu radio aquí, en la cama? Ahora yo ___7___ la radio en la mesita, al lado de tu lámpara. Bueno, ya está. Pues, vamos a la cocina y tú y yo ___8___ la mesa ahora, ¿está bien? Ven, cariño, necesito preparar la cena.

Answers

8 1. Debes practicar el piano.
2. Debe cortar el césped.
3. Deben preparar la cena.
4. Debes ir al centro comercial.
5. Debemos hacer la tarea.
6. Debe limpiar la cocina.

9 1. pones
2. poner
3. pongo
4. ponen
5. pone
6. pones
7. pongo
8. ponemos

Review and Assess

You may wish to assign the **Más práctica gramatical** activities as additional practice or homework after presenting material throughout the chapter. Assign Activities 1–2 after **Nota gramatical** (p. 174), Activities 3–5 after **Nota gramatical** (p. 180), Activity 6 after **Nota gramatical** (p. 181), Activities 7–8 after **Nota gramatical** (p. 184), and Activity 9 after **Nota** **gramatical** (p. 185). To prepare students for the **Paso** quizzes and Chapter Test, have them do the **Más práctica gramatical** activities in the following order: complete Activities 1–2 before taking Quiz 6-1A or 6-1B; Activities 3–6 before taking Quiz 6-2A or 6-2B; and Activities 7–9 before taking Quiz 6-3A or 6-3B.

Repaso

CAPÍTULO 6

The **Repaso** reviews and integrates all four skills and culture in preparation for the Chapter Test.

Teaching Resources
pp. 194–195

PRINT
▶ Lesson Planner, p. 32
▶ Listening Activities, p. 45
▶ Video Guide, pp. 39–41, 44
▶ Grammar Tutor for Students of Spanish, Chapter 6
▶ Cuaderno para hispanohablantes, pp. 26–30
▶ Standardized Assessment Tutor, Chapter 6

MEDIA
▶ One-Stop Planner
▶ Video Program, Videocassette 2, 47:35–48:08
▶ DVD Tutor, Disc 1
▶ Audio Compact Discs, CD 6, Tr. 17
▶ Interactive CD-ROM Tutor, Disc 2

Answers

2 *Possible answers:*
Sebastián no debe comer mucho.
La chica debe comprar una casa más grande para la Carlota.
Nacho y Duquesa deben jugar en el jardín, no en la casa.
Cervantes no debe leer el libro.

4
1. vivimos
2. ayudamos
3. corta
4. pasa
5. saca
6. limpio
7. visitamos a
8. caminamos
9. salgo
10. hacemos

Repaso

CD-ROM **2** DVD **1**

MARCAR: go.hrw.com
PALABRA CLAVE:
WV3 FLORIDA-6

1 First read the statements below about Marcos and his family. Then listen as Marcos describes his family in detail. Decide which family member matches each numbered item below.

CD 6
Tr. 17

1. Debe comer menos.
2. Trabaja demasiado.
3. Lee muchas novelas.
4. Tiene un cuarto muy organizado.
5. Le gusta tocar la guitarra.
6. No estudia mucho.

Script and answers on p. 167H.

2 Look at the four pictures of these kids and their pets. For each, use adjectives to describe the problem and **deber** to tell what should be done. See possible answers below.

Sebastián   Carlota   Nacho y Duquesa   Cervantes

3 Crea un diálogo en el cual Raquel y Armando hablan de lo que hacen con sus familias los fines de semana.

4 Imagine that you're going to study in Mexico next year and you've just received a letter from your host sister, Carolina. Complete her letter by filling in the correct form of the verbs in the box. See answers below.

hacer	limpiar	cortar	vivir
	visitar a	caminar	
ayudar	pasar	salir	sacar

¡Hola!

Me llamo Carolina. Mi familia y yo ___1___ en Cuernavaca. Mi casa es grande. Por eso los sábados todos ___2___ en casa. Primero todos nosotros hacemos las camas. Luego mi padre ___3___ el césped. Mi mamá ___4___ la aspiradora. Mi hermano ___5___ la basura, y yo ___6___ mi cuarto. Mi cuarto es muy desorganizado. Pero no sólo trabajamos. Por ejemplo, todos los sábados nosotros ___7___ mis abuelos. Después, nosotros ___8___ en el parque. Los sábados por la noche yo ___9___ con amigos. Y en verano, siempre ___10___ un viaje.

Recuerdos,
Carolina

Apply and Assess

Teaching Suggestions

2 Have students clip comic strips from the newspaper and cover the speech bubbles. Exchanging comics, students can then use Spanish to describe a problem and tell what should be done.

Slower Pace

3 To prepare for Activity 3, have students look at p. 185 and make a list of several chores they do on weekends. They might also list weekend leisure activities before they begin role-playing the dialogue.

5 Responde a las siguientes oraciones con **cierto** o **falso**. Corrige las oraciones falsas. Basa tus respuestas en las **Notas culturales**, el **Panorama cultural** y el **Encuentro cultural** de este capítulo. See answers below.

1. El compadrazgo ya no existe en Latinoamérica.
2. El concepto de la vida privada *(privacy)* es diferente en las culturas hispana y anglosajona.
3. La familia es muy importante para muchos hispanohablantes.
4. La relación que existe entre una persona y sus padrinos termina cuando el niño tiene veintiún años.
5. En las familias hispanohablantes es menos común pasar el tiempo solo.

Vamos a escribir

Laura, an exchange student from Chile, is coming to spend the year with your family. Write her a letter describing your family and mention several activities you do with them. Ask Laura about her family, too. Before you begin, make an outline.

Estrategia para escribir

Outlining will help you organize your topic. First put your ideas in related groups. Then put these groups in the order you want to write about them. Within each group, add subgroups to develop your ideas in more detail. In this case, the groups could be your family, your activities together, and some questions for Laura.

> I. Mi familia
>   A. Las personas en mi familia
>   1. nombres y edades
>   2. descripciones (apariencia, personalidad)
>   B. Las actividades que hacemos juntos
>   1. durante la semana
>   2. en los fines de semana
> II. Preguntas para Laura
>   A. ¿Cuántas personas hay en tu familia?
>   B. ¿Cómo es...?

Situación

a. You've just arrived at your host family's house in Bolivia. Your host introduces the family to you, and then asks about your family. With a partner, role-play the situation. Be sure to include all your family members, a description of each one, and what you and your family like to do together.

b. You're going to have a party at your house on Saturday night. Five of your friends volunteer to help you get the house ready for the party. Tell each of them what he or she should do.

> Cuaderno para hispanohablantes, p. 30

Apply and Assess

Process Writing

6 Before having students write their own outlines, create one as a class. Say that you plan to write about their love of basketball, and that you would like to create an outline. First, write **el baloncesto** on the board. Then have students brainstorm things they associate with basketball and might write about. As they call out ideas,

write them on the board in outline form. Some subtopics might include: where, with whom, and how often they play, a pro player they admire, the areas of their game in which they excel and those that need work. Leave the class outline on the board as students begin to work on their own.

Teaching Suggestions

5 After students complete the activity, have them write three true-or-false statements based on **Notas culturales, Panorama cultural,** and **Encuentro cultural.** Ask volunteers to read their best statements aloud for the class to respond to and correct.

6 As an option, have students give their letter to a partner. The partner in turn pretends to be Laura and responds to the letter he or she has read, coming up with imaginative answers to the questions.

Portfolio

6 **Written** You might suggest that students include this activity in the written Portfolio. For Portfolio information, see *Alternative Assessment Guide,* pp. iv–17.

7a As an extension to this theme, have students imagine their own families are being considered as hosts to visiting exchange students from Bolivia or elsewhere. The exchange program director interviews the prospective host about family members and routines to determine whether the family is a suitable match for a high school student from abroad.

Answers

5 1. Falso; El compadrazgo existe en Latinoamérica.
2. Cierto
3. Cierto
4. Falso; La relación que existe entre una persona y sus padrinos nunca termina.
5. Cierto

WV3 FLORIDA-6

Teaching Resources
p. 196

PRINT
▶ Grammar Tutor for Students of Spanish, Chapter 6

MEDIA
▶ Interactive CD-ROM Tutor, Disc 2
▶ Online self-test

🔵 **go.hrw.com**
WV3 FLORIDA-6

Teacher Note

This page is intended to help students prepare for the Chapter Test. It is designed for the students to work on their own initiative and consists of a brief checklist of the major points covered in the chapter. The students should be reminded that it is only a checklist and does not necessarily include everything that will appear on the Chapter Test.

Answers

3 Su abuelo tiene canas. Es viejo y delgado y es muy cariñoso.
Su mamá tiene pelo negro y trabaja en el jardín.
Toño tiene pelo negro y ojos de color café. Es cómico.
Óscar es moreno. Tiene pelo castaño y es travieso.

4 *Sample answer:*
Mi hermano tiene veinte años. Es alto y delgado con pelo rubio. Trabaja en una oficina. Como nosotros vivimos cerca de un parque, los fines de semana jugamos juntos allí.

5 *Answers may vary.*
1. Debe limpiar su cuarto.
2. No debe trabajar todo el tiempo.
3. Deben preparar la cena.
4. Debe estudiar más y hablar menos en clase.

Can you describe a family? p. 174

1 Can you tell Ramiro, a new student at your school, . . .? Answers will vary.
1. how many people there are in your family
2. how many brothers and sisters you have
3. what the names of your family members are
4. what they like to do in their free time

2 Can you complete each sentence with the correct family member?
1. La mamá de mi papá es mi ———. abuela
2. El hermano de mi mamá es mi ———. tío
3. La hija de mi tía es mi ———. prima
4. La hija de mis padres es mi ———. hermana
5. El hijo de mi padrastro es mi ———. hermanastro

Can you describe people? p. 178

3 Describe these members of Florencia's family. See answers below.

su abuelo   su mamá

su hermano, Toño   su hermano, Óscar

Can you discuss things a family does together? p. 180

4 Write one or two sentences about each member of your family or an imaginary family. Include age, physical description, where they live, and what you do with them. See sample answer below.

Can you discuss problems and give advice? p. 184

5 Paula and her family need help solving these problems. What should each person do? See possible answers below.
1. Her sister is disorganized and can't find any of her things.
2. Paula's brother works all the time and he's very tired.
3. It's six o'clock in the evening and everyone's hungry.
4. Paula's sister is in trouble at school because she talks too much in class.

Review and Assess

Slower Pace

2 Have students cut out magazine pictures that illustrate familial relationships. Then ask students to write on a piece of paper how they think the people are related. Tell students to exchange pictures with a partner and write what they think the relationship might be. Have partners compare their impressions and then describe the people's age and physical description.

Additional Practice

4 Have students bring in a photo of a family member and describe that person to the class, telling how the person is related, where he or she lives, giving a physical description, and explaining what the person likes to do. If possible, students could mount the photo and write a short paragraph on the same paper as an illustrated essay describing the person.

Primer paso

Describing a family

la abuela	grandmother	los hermanos	brothers, brothers and sisters	los padres	parents
el abuelo	grandfather			la prima	female cousin
los abuelos	grandparents			el primo	male cousin
la esposa	wife, spouse	la hija	daughter	los primos	cousins
el esposo	husband, spouse	el hijo	son	(ser) unido/a	(to be) close-knit
éstas	these (feminine)	los hijos	children	Somos cinco.	There are five of us.
éstos	these (masculine and feminine)	la madrastra	stepmother		
		la madre/mamá	mother/mom	su/sus	his, her, their, your (formal)
la familia	family	la media hermana	half sister		
el gato	cat	el medio hermano	half brother	la tía	aunt
la hermana	sister	mi/mis	my	el tío	uncle
la hermanastra	stepsister	nuestro/a	our	tu/tus	your (familiar)
el hermanastro	stepbrother	el padrastro	stepfather	vivir	to live
el hermano	brother	el padre/papá	father/dad	vuestro/a	your (pl. familiar Spain)

Segundo paso

Describing people

				Discussing things a family does together	
azul	blue	el pelo	hair	algo	something
cariñoso/a	affectionate	un poco gordo/a	a little overweight	casi siempre	almost always
de color café	brown	Se ve joven.	He/She looks young.	cenar	to eat dinner
¿De qué color es/son...?	What color is/ are...?	Tiene canas.	He/She has gray hair.	hacer un viaje	to take a trip
delgado/a	thin			¿Qué hacen ustedes?	What do you do?
listo/a	clever, smart	Tiene (los) ojos verdes/azules.	She/He has green/ blue eyes.	salir	to go out, to leave
mayor	older	travieso/a	mischievous		
menor	younger	verde	green	visitar	to visit
negro/a	black	viejo/a	old		
los ojos	eyes				
pelirrojo/a	redheaded				

Tercer paso

Discussing problems and giving advice

cortar el césped	to cut the grass	limpiar la cocina	to clean the kitchen	un problema	a problem
cuidar al gato	to take care of the cat	menos	less	¿Qué debo hacer?	What should I do?
		No es cierto.	It isn't true.	los quehaceres domésticos	household chores
deber	should, ought to	pasar la aspiradora	to vacuum	la sala	living room
Debes...	You should...			trabajar en el jardín	to work in the garden
demasiado	too much	planchar	to iron		
dice que	he/she says that	poner la mesa	to set the table		
hacer la cama	to make the bed				

Review and Assess

Circumlocution

Distribute slips of paper with the Spanish words for family members written on them. Have students form pairs or groups. Have members of each pair or group define his or her word to classmates without saying the word itself. Encourage them to use possessives in their definitions. **(Estas personas son los hijos de mis tíos. Answer: tus** **primos)** You might also consider playing a written version of this activity: have students write as many sentences as they can describing family members without naming the members. Recognize in some way the group that generates the most appropriate sentences.

Vocabulario

Teaching Suggestions

• To review the vocabulary in the **Primer paso,** you might wish to use the family tree on *Teaching Transparency 6-1* and ask students to identify the relationships.

• To review the vocabulary from each **Paso,** use pictures from magazines. Give groups one or two pictures each to describe. After they finish, groups can exchange pictures and describe the new ones.

Chapter 6 Assessment

▸ **Testing Program**
Chapter Test, pp. 143–148
 Audio Compact Discs, CD 6, Trs. 21–22

Speaking Test, p. 345

Midterm Exam, pp. 157–164
Score Sheet, pp. 165–167
Listening Scripts, pp. 168–169
Answers, p. 170
 Audio Compact Discs, CD 6, Trs. 23–26

▸ **Alternative Assessment Guide**
Performance Assessment, p. 37
Portfolio Assessment, p. 23
CD-ROM Assessment, p. 51

▸ **Interactive CD-ROM Tutor, Disc 2**
 ¡A hablar!
¡A escribir!

▸ **Standardized Assessment Tutor**
Chapter 6

▸ **One-Stop Planner, Disc 2**
Test Generator
Chapter 6

Teaching Resources
pp. 198–201

PRINT
▶ Lesson Planner, p. 32
▶ Video Guide, pp. 45–46

MEDIA
▶ One-Stop Planner
▶ Video Program:
  Videocassette 3, 0:57–3:24
▶ DVD Tutor, Disc 2
▶ Interactive CD-ROM Tutor, Disc 2
▶ Map Transparency 3

 go.hrw.com
WV3 ECUADOR

 Using the Almanac and Map

Terms in the Almanac

• **Gobierno:** Ecuador has been an independent republic since 1822. The people elect a president to one four-year term, and the president appoints a 15-member cabinet. The 121-member Chamber of Representatives is the country's lawmaking body.

• **Industrias: comestibles** *food products,* **productos de madera** *wood products,* **tejidos** *fabrics*

• **Minerales: cobre** *copper,* **hierro** *iron,* **plomo** *lead,* **plata** *silver,* **azufre** *sulphur*

• **Quechua:** The language of the former Incan Empire. It is now widely spoken throughout the Andes highlands from southern Colombia to Chile.

CAPÍTULOS 7 y 8

¡Ven conmigo a Ecuador!

Población: 12.646.000 (aproximadamente)

Área: 104.505 millas cuadradas (270.668 km²), similar en área al tamaño del estado de Colorado

Ubicación: En el noroeste de Sudamérica, con Colombia al norte, el Perú al sur y al este y el océano Pacífico al oeste

Capital: Quito, con una población de 1.500.000 (aproximadamente)

Gobierno: república federal

Industrias: comestibles, productos de madera, tejidos

Cosechas principales: plátanos, café, arroz, azúcar, maíz

Minerales: petróleo, cobre, hierro, plomo, plata, azufre

Unidad monetaria: el dólar

Idiomas: español (lengua oficial), quechua, quichua y otros idiomas indígenas

WV3 ECUADOR

Quito, la hermosa capital de Ecuador ▶

Cultures and Communities

 ### Culture Note

The Republic of Ecuador is divided into three regions with distinct cultures. The Coastal Lowlands (**la Costa**) are inhabited primarily by descendants of African slaves. The Andes Highlands (**la Sierra**) are home to many indigenous groups, including Otavalos, Salasacas, and descendants of the Puruhá. The Eastern Lowlands (**el Oriente**), which take up almost half the country, are mainly the home of indigenous Jívaro peoples. Quito is the capital and second-largest city in Ecuador. Set in the Quito Basin at the foot of the volcano Pichincha, at an altitude of 9,350 feet, Quito is the second-highest major city in Latin America. It is also the oldest capital city in South America.

STANDARDS: 2.2, 3.1, 5.1

MAPQUEST.COM

HRW Atlas Interactivo Mundial

Have students use the interactive atlas at go.hrw.com to find out more about the geography of Ecuador and complete the Map Activities below.

Map Activities

- Ask students to identify the two countries that border Ecuador. (Peru and Colombia)

- Ask students to point out the equator. Do they know what general characteristics equatorial countries have? (Most equatorial lowlands have heavy rains and average temperatures over 68°F.)

- Have students locate the Andes **(la Cordillera de los Andes)**. You may want to point out that they are the world's longest mountain chain. The Andes stretch over 4,500 miles, from Cape Horn at the tip of South America to Panama. Only the Himalayas of northern India and Tibet have higher peaks than the Andes.

CNNenEspañol.com

Have students check the **CNN en español** Web site for news on Ecuador. The **CNN en español** site is also a good source of timely, high-interest readings for Spanish students.

Connections and Comparisons

History Link

Quito, seat of the kingdom of **Quitu**, was named after the people who lived there before the arrival of the Spanish in 1534. From the 10th century to 1487 it was united with the Incan Empire. Quito remained the focal point of political, social, and economic affairs from the 16th to the 20th centuries, until economic dominance shifted to Guayaquil.

Geography Link

At 0° latitude, the **La Mitad del Mundo** monument lies just north of Quito. Here an 18th-century French expedition measured the equator, the imaginary 25,004-mile-long line dividing the Northern and Southern Hemispheres. A pebble strip marks where the equator crosses the site. Tourists enjoy standing with one foot in each hemisphere. Have students locate equatorial countries. See pp. xxiv–xxv.

Motivating Activity

Ask students if they have ever seen a 500-pound tortoise, a four-foot iguana, or a flightless cormorant. These animals are native to the Galapagos Islands. Have students describe the strangest animals or plants that they have ever seen. Discuss with students how these animals or plants have adapted to their environment or how environmental changes endanger their survival.

Using the Photo Essay

❶ Mujeres indígenas de compras There are many native ethnic groups in Ecuador, each of which considers itself a distinct nationality with its own language and culture. The most numerous **indígenas** are the Quechuas, who live mainly in the mountains of the Sierra. Among most groups are many **mestizos** (mix of European and indigenous races) and **zambos** (mix of African and indigenous races).

❷ La Catedral Nueva Many Ecuadoreans consider Cuenca to be the country's most beautiful city. Its colonial architecture stands beside new buildings built in a neocolonial style to complement the old. There are no skyscrapers to obscure the view of the surrounding mountains. Instead, the three domes of the **Catedral Nueva** dominate the skyline. Construction on the **Catedral Nueva** began in 1880.

❸ La música tradicional Traditional instruments of the highlands include the following: flutes (**flautas**), panpipes (**rondadores**), conch shells (**conchas**), and various percussion instruments (**instrumentos de percusión**). Also used are the **quena,** a notched bamboo recorder, and a smaller flute called a **pingullu,** which has three or four holes. The **charango** is a five-string guitar that is about two feet long.

Ecuador

Ecuador es una de las tres repúblicas andinas en donde casi la mitad de la población es indígena. Las otras dos son Perú y Bolivia. La cadena montañosa de los Andes divide a Ecuador en tres diferentes regiones geológicas, la costa fértil o la Costa, las montañas o la Sierra y la selva amazónica oriental llamada el Oriente. La cuarta región geológica de Ecuador es el famoso archipiélago Galápagos que se encuentra a 570 millas de la costa en el océano Pacífico.

📶 internet

MARCAR: go.hrw.com
PALABRA CLAVE:
WV3 ECUADOR

❶ Mujeres indígenas de compras
Aunque el español es la lengua oficial de Ecuador, un gran porcentaje de la población indígena es bilingüe. Muchos hablan el quechua, que es una de las lenguas nativas, así como el español.

❷ La Catedral Nueva
La arquitectura colonial de Ecuador es famosa en el mundo entero, y algunas de las nuevas estructuras reflejan el deseo por una unidad arquitectónica. La construcción neo-gótica de la Catedral Nueva de Cuenca comenzó en 1880 pero se interrumpió en 1967. Las cúpulas azules de la catedral miran hacia la plaza principal de Cuenca.

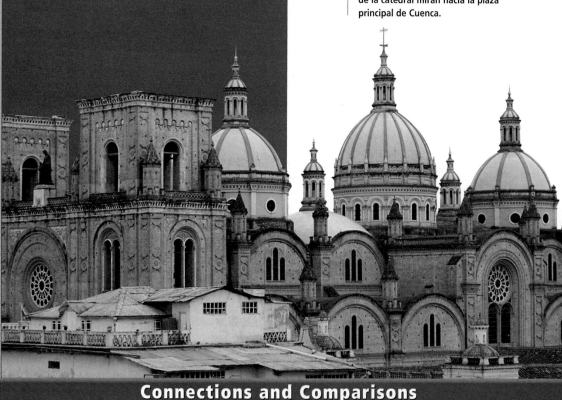

Connections and Comparisons

Biology Link

Have your students research an animal that is found on the Galapagos Islands. Suggest that they use books, magazines, and the World Wide Web to find pictures and other information describing their animal's characteristics, habitat, behaviors, and relationship to other animals. Have them make a poster that promotes the animal's protection.

Language Notes

- The word **galápago** means *giant tortoise* and refers primarily to the species *Geochelone elephantopus* found on the island.
- **Ecuador** is the Spanish word for *equator*.

3 La música tradicional
La música tradicional andina refleja una rica herencia cultural. Algunos instrumentos prehispánicos tales como la quena (un tipo de flauta) e instrumentos de percusión, se mezclan harmoniosamente con los instrumentos de cuerda traídos por los españoles.

4 Antonio José de Sucre (1795–1830)
Militar y estadista venezolano que luchó al lado de Simón Bolívar. Participó en la liberación del Ecuador y del Perú con las batallas de Pichincha y Ayacucho.

5 Las Islas Galápagos
Estas islas volcánicas fueron declaradas un parque nacional en 1959. Las islas tienen una extraordinaria variedad de aves (58 especies nativas) y algunas especies de animales poco comunes, tales como la iguana negra marina y la tortuga gigante.

En los capítulos 7 y 8,
vas a conocer a Carlos, Tomás y María, tres amigos que viven en Quito, Ecuador. El nombre "Ecuador" viene de la línea ecuatorial que cruza el país. Ecuador es rico en recursos naturales y está orgulloso de su cultura. Quito, la capital, es una ciudad maravillosa con miles de años de tradición cultural, desde antes de los incas hasta el presente.

4 Antonio José de Sucre At age 16, Sucre became a colonel in the army fighting for South American independence. A military genius, he assisted Simón Bolivar in liberating Colombia, Ecuador, and Perú from the Spanish. He later became the first president of Bolivia. In 1830, he headed the constitutional convention that tried to prevent Bolivar's Republic of Colombia from dissolving. The convention failed, Venezuela seceded, and Sucre was assassinated during his trip home to Quito.

5 Las Islas Galápagos
The Galapagos archipelago **(el Archipiélago de Colón)** is located in the Pacific Ocean, some 600 miles west of the coast of Ecuador. It consists of 13 major islands, six small islands, and 42 islets that are barely more than large rocks. All are of volcanic origin and total more than 23,000 square miles in area. In 1959, the Galapagos were declared a national park, and human settlement was restricted to areas that had already been developed. A Marine Resources Reserve was created in 1986, covering 19,300 square miles. Both the park and reserve are designed to protect the islands and to encourage scientific research. The islands are home to 58 bird species, various types of iguanas and other lizards, several species of giant tortoises, sea lions, dolphins, penguins, and many other forms of wildlife.

Cultures and Communities

Culture Note
The clothing of Otavalo closely resembles that of the Inca. Women of Otavalo wear skirt wraps called **anakus** and shoulder wraps called **fachalinas** that are made of handspun wool or cotton.

Music Link
Play a recording of Andean music or use the song **El cóndor pasa**, Audio CD 7, Tr. 29.

Additional Vocabulary
arpa criolla *Andean harp* **bombo** *Andean drum*
mandolina *mandolin* **maraca** *gourd rattle*
campana *bell*

Capítulo 7: ¿Qué te gustaría hacer?
Chapter Overview

De antemano pp. 204–206	¿Qué hacemos?

	FUNCTIONS	**GRAMMAR**	**VOCABULARY**	**RE-ENTRY**
Primer paso pp. 207–211	• Talking on the telephone, p. 207 • Extending and accepting invitations, p. 208	• e → ie stem-changing verbs, p. 209	Places and events, p. 210	• Invitations: **gustar** (**Capítulo 5**) • Days of the week (**Capítulo 4**)
Segundo paso pp. 212–216	• Making plans, p. 212 • Talking about getting ready, p. 214	• **pensar** and **ir + a +** infinitive, p. 212 • Reflexive verbs (infinitives only), p. 214	Personal items, p. 214	• Future expressions: **hoy, mañana,** etc. (**Capítulo 3**) • Expressions of frequency (**Capítulo 5**)
Tercer paso pp. 217–219	• Turning down an invitation and explaining why, p. 217	• Expressions with **tener**, p. 217	Expressions of apology, p. 217	• The verb **tener** (**Capítulo 2**)

Letra y sonido p. 219	**The letters *ll* and *y*** Audio CD 7, Track 12	**Dictado** Audio CD 7, Tracks 13–15

Vamos a leer pp. 220–221	**Caleidoscopio**	**Reading Strategy:** Previewing a passage

Más práctica gramatical	**pp. 222–225** **Primer paso,** p. 222	**Segundo paso,** pp. 223–224	**Tercer paso,** pp. 224–225

Review pp. 226–229	**Repaso:** pp. 226–227 **Vamos a escribir,** p. 227 Using connecting words	**A ver si puedo...,** p. 228	**Vocabulario,** p. 229

CULTURE

- **Realia,** Agenda, p. 211
- **Nota cultural,** Means of transportation, p. 213

- **Panorama cultural, ¿Qué haces para conocer a una persona?,** p. 216
- **A lo nuestro,** The several meanings of **ya,** p. 218

Capítulo 7: ¿Qué te gustaría hacer?
Chapter Resources

PRINT

Lesson Planning

One-Stop Planner

Lesson Planner with Substitute Teacher Lesson Plans, pp. 33–37, 71

Student Make-Up Assignments
- Make-Up Assignment Copying Masters, Chapter 7

Listening and Speaking

TPR Storytelling Book, pp. 25–28

Listening Activities
- Student Response Forms for Listening Activities, pp. 51–53
- Additional Listening Activities 7-1 to 7-6, pp. 55–57
- Additional Listening Activities (song), p. 58
- Scripts and Answers, pp. 132–136

Video Guide
- Teaching Suggestions, pp. 47–49
- Activity Masters, pp. 50–52
- Scripts and Answers, pp. 100–101, 116

Activities for Communication
- Communicative Activities, pp. 37–42
- Realia and Teaching Suggestions, pp. 105–109
- Situation Cards, pp. 149–150

Reading and Writing

Reading Strategies and Skills Handbook, Chapter 7

¡Lee conmigo! 1, Chapter 7
Cuaderno de actividades, pp. 73–84

Grammar

Cuaderno de gramática, pp. 53–60

Grammar Tutor for Students of Spanish, Chapter 7

Assessment

Testing Program
- Grammar and Vocabulary Quizzes, **Paso** Quizzes, and Chapter Test, pp. 171–188
- Score Sheet, Scripts and Answers, pp. 189–196

Alternative Assessment Guide
- Portfolio Assessment, p. 24
- Performance Assessment, p. 38
- CD-ROM Assessment, p. 52

Student Make-Up Assignments
- Alternative Quizzes, Chapter 7

Standardized Assessment Tutor
- Reading, pp. 27–29
- Writing, p. 30
- Math, pp. 51–52

Native Speakers

Cuaderno para hispanohablantes, pp. 31–35

MEDIA

 Online Activities
- Juegos interactivos
- Actividades Internet

 Video Program
- Videocassette 3
- Videocassette 5 (captioned version)

 Interactive CD-ROM Tutor, Disc 2
DVD Tutor, Disc 2

 Audio Compact Discs
- Textbook Listening Activities, CD 7, Tracks 1–17
- Additional Listening Activities, CD 7, Tracks 23–29
- Assessment Items, CD 7, Tracks 18–22

 Teaching Transparencies
- Situations 7-1 to 7-3
- Vocabulary 7-A
- **De antemano**
- **Más práctica gramatical** Answers
- **Cuaderno de gramática** Answers

 One-Stop Planner CD-ROM

Use the **One-Stop Planner CD-ROM with Test Generator** to aid in lesson planning and pacing.

For each chapter, the **One-Stop Planner** includes:
- Editable lesson plans with direct links to teaching resources
- Printable worksheets from resource books
- Direct launches to the HRW Internet activities
- Video and audio segments
- Test Generator
- Clip Art for vocabulary items

Capítulo 7: ¿Qué te gustaría hacer?

Projects

Guía de espectáculos

In this project students make an entertainment guide for their community. They create or research local events and write descriptions of them in Spanish. Students may get ideas for their projects from magazines, newspapers, brochures, or the Internet.

MATERIALS

✂ **Students may need**
- Paper
- Markers
- Magazines
- Entertainment section of newspaper
- Word processor or typewriter

SUGGESTED SEQUENCE

1. Students may work alone or in small groups to create their guides. The guides should include a short description of at least six events. If students work in small groups, each should create at least two events and descriptions. Each proofreads the group's work and makes sure that no one type of event appears too many times.

2. Show an example of an entertainment guide from a newspaper to explain the project. Students should use categories such as concerts, plays, movies, restaurants, museum or gallery exhibits, children's events, and sports. They may use the **Caleidoscopio** section as a guide (see pages 220–221).

3. Give students time in class to brainstorm and to check the local newspaper for material. Encourage students to create events on their own.

4. Students' guides should be in Spanish.

5. Set a due date for the entertainment guide.

6. Have students peer review rough drafts.

7. In the final draft, students may include photos from magazines illustrating the event described. The guide might be folded like a brochure, be a single-page poster, or like magazine pages.

GRADING THE PROJECT

Suggested point distribution: (total = 100 points)

Entertainment Guide
Vocabulary Use..40
Appearance 20
Creativity...20
Grammar and Clarity 20

Games

Adivinanza

This game allows students to apply the expressions and vocabulary from the chapter. It can be played with any number of students.

Preparation Supply things needed to get ready to go out. (brush, comb, washcloth, bar of soap, towel, razor, clothing)

Procedure One player leaves the room and the others choose an object for him or her to guess. Returning, he or she asks a question about the object with **¿cuándo? ¿por qué?** or **¿dónde?** (for example, **¿Dónde uso el objeto?**) Any member of the group may answer.

The player continues asking questions using the question words until he or she guesses the object. Someone else then leaves the room, and another object is chosen, then guessed, as before. Since the game uses circumlocution, you might write new or unfamiliar words on the board.

¿Quién habla?

In this game, students apply the expressions they know to create realistic telephone conversations.

Preparation Divide the class into pairs, allowing a trio if there is an odd number of students. Two to three telephones may be used as props.

Procedure Allow planning time for mini-dialogues to be presented to the class. A trio could have a three-party conference call or an operator-assisted call. Topics might be dialing a wrong number, ordering food delivery, or inviting someone to go out.

FAMILY LINK

Have some students go to one of the events in the guide with family or friends, then discuss the event with them. As they report to the class, see how their opinions differ from those reflected in the guide.

Storytelling

Mini-cuento

This story accompanies Teaching Transparency 7-2. The **mini-cuento** *can be told and retold in different formats, acted out, written, and read aloud to give students additional opportunities to practice all four skills. The following story tells of a Saturday night at the* **Casa de la familia Muñoz.**

Los señores Muñoz se preparan para una fiesta muy elegante y sus hijas Marcela y Nancy tienen planes también. Humberto Muñoz se baña, se afeita, se viste y se peina. Ahora se mira en el espejo y se cree muy guapo. Su esposa Marta no se cree guapa esta noche, y dice, "¡Ay! No me gusta cómo me veo!" No está lista. Lleva un vestido rojo muy elegante y zapatos de tacón alto pero necesita maquillarse todavía y eso le molesta mucho a Marcela. Marcela tiene una cita con su novio Tomás, el chico más guapo de su colegio. Acaba de hacer ejercicio y no tiene mucho tiempo para bañarse y prepararse. ¿Qué va a hacer? ¡No quiere llegar tarde! "Tengo que darme prisa," dice. Pero su hermanita Nancy está contenta. Nadie le hace caso, y puede comer paletas y mirar la televisión toda la noche. ¡Qué divertido!

Traditions

Arte

Otavalo, a town about 70 miles north of Quito, is world-renowned for its colorful and high-quality textiles. The Quichua-speaking indigenous peoples of this region, called **otavaleños,** have been using the loom to weave intricately designed clothing for over 3,000 years. These beautiful textiles have made them one of the wealthiest indigenous groups in Latin America. The **otavaleños** display their expertly woven ponchos, scarves, sweaters, blankets, and tapestries (**tapices**) at the Otavalo Market, around the Plaza de Ponchos. Have students research Ecuadorean weaving designs and patterns to create a **tapiz** on poster board representing their school's colors and mascot. You might set up a pretend market in which students take turns bargaining to buy their **tapices.** Then arrange to display students' work publicly in an appropriate area of the school.

Receta

Seafood dishes are typical of the coastal region of Ecuador. One of the most well-known is **ceviche,** *traditionally prepared with white fish, but shrimp, crab, or lobster may be used instead.* **Ceviche** *is a common dish in all Latin American Pacific coastal regions. To prepare* **ceviche,** *you must marinate the fish with plenty of citrus juice, onions, and garlic.* **Ceviche** *is also served with popcorn, potato chips, or sweet potatoes.*

EL CEVICHE ESTILO ECUATORIANO

para 4 personas

1 kilo de filete de pescado blanco

2 tazas de jugo de limón y naranja

2 cucharadas de vinagre

1 cebolla

1 ajo

sal y pimienta

Separe la piel del filete y córtelo en pequeños trozos. En una olla, coloque el pescado y vierta el jugo encima. Corte una cebolla y un ajo en pedacitos. Añada la sal, la pimienta y el vinagre con la cebolla y el ajo. Ponga la mezcla en el refrigerador por cinco o seis horas. Es buena idea mover la mezcla por lo menos tres veces para que quede bien escabechada.

Technology

DVD/Video

Videocassette 3, Videocassette 5 (captioned version)
DVD Tutor, Disc 2
See Video Guide, pages 47–52.

De antemano • ¿Qué hacemos?

Tomás tells his friend Carlos that he is in a bad mood because he is not invited to María's party. María calls Carlos to invite him, but he declines the invitation because he already has plans. María then calls Tomás's house and leaves a message inviting him also, but the message gets lost.

A continuación

María runs into Tomás and tells him about the party, so he and Carlos change their plans and decide to go the party after all. When Tomás and Carlos finally arrive at María's house, she realizes that she forgot to tell them that she postponed the party until next week. They all end up going out and spending the afternoon together.

¿Qué haces para conocer a una persona?

Students from Ecuador, Costa Rica, and Spain tell how they would ask someone out and who would pay for the date. In additional interviews, people from various Spanish-speaking countries talk about dating customs.

Videoclips

• **E.D.A.:** advertisement for a telephone company

Interactive CD-ROM Tutor

Activity	Activity Type	Pupil's Edition Page
En contexto	*Interactive conversation*	
1. Vocabulario	¡Super memoria!	p. 210
2. Gramática	¿Qué falta?	p. 209
3. Gramática	¡A escoger!	p. 212
4. Así se dice	¿Qué falta?	p. 214
5. Así se dice	¿Cuál es?	p. 217
6. Gramática	Imagen y sonido ¡Exploremos! Identifiquemos!	p. 217
Panorama cultural	¿Qué haces para conocer a una persona?	p. 216
¡A hablar!	*Guided recording*	pp. 226–227
¡A escribir!	*Guided writing*	p. 227

Teacher Management System

Launch the program, type "admin" in the password area, and press RETURN. Log on to **www.hrw.com/CDROMTUTOR** for a detailed explanation of the Teacher Management System.

DVD Tutor

The *DVD Tutor* contains all material from the *Video Program* as described above. Spanish captions are available for use at your discretion for all sections of the video. The *DVD Tutor* also provides a variety of video-based activities that assess students' understanding of the **De antemano, A continuación,** and **Panorama cultural.**

This part of the *DVD Tutor* may be used on any DVD video player connected to a television or video monitor.

In addition to the video material and the video-based comprehension activities, the *DVD Tutor* also contains the entire *Interactive CD-ROM Tutor* in DVD-ROM format. Each DVD disc contains the activities from all 12 chapters of the *Interactive CD-ROM Tutor.*

This part of the *DVD Tutor* may be used on a Macintosh® or Windows® computer with a DVD-ROM drive.

One-Stop Planner CD-ROM

To preview all resources available for this chapter, use the **One-Stop Planner CD-ROM**, Disc 2.

Internet Connection

MARCAR: go.hrw.com
PALABRA CLAVE:
WV3 ECUADOR-7

*Have students explore the **go.hrw.com** Web site for many online resources covering all chapters. All Chapter 7 resources are available under the keyword **WV3 ECUADOR-7**. Interactive games help students practice the material and provide them with immediate feedback. You will also find a printable worksheet that provides Internet activities that lead to a comprehensive online research project.*

Juegos interactivos

You can use the interactive activities in this chapter

- to practice grammar, vocabulary, and chapter functions
- as homework
- as an assessment option
- as a self-test
- to prepare for the Chapter Test

Actividades Internet

Students describe things they would like to do and see in a Latin American country. They describe activities they might do with different companions.

- To prepare students for the **Hoja de actividades,** have them review the chapter functions by viewing the dramatic episode on Videocassette 3.
- After students have completed the activity sheet, have them share the "rainy day" activities with a partner. Were any the same? Could students do any of those activities in their own city? Where?

Proyecto
Working in small groups, have students plan a group vacation to a city in the **Hoja de actividades**. They should find three or four activities that everyone in the group would like to do there. They then describe their group's vacation, including places they plan to visit. You might have them post the vacation itinerary, along with images from the city, on a personal Web site.

Primer paso

6   p. 207

1. — Aló.
— Buenas tardes, señorita. ¿Está Miguel, por favor?
— Sí, un momento. ¿De parte de quién?
— De parte de Roberto.

2. — Bueno, Silvia. Ya es tarde y necesito estudiar para el examen.
— Está bien. Hasta mañana, ¿eh?
— Sí, hasta mañana, Silvia. Chao.

3. — Bueno, Casa García a sus órdenes.
— Buenos días. ¿Está el señor Alejandro García, por favor?
— Lo siento mucho, pero el señor no está. ¿Quién habla?
— Soy Pedro Castillo.

4. — Aló. Colegio La Salle.
— Buenos días, señorita. ¿Está el señor Medina, por favor?
— Un momento, por favor. ¿Quién habla?
— Soy la doctora Isabel Martínez.
— Lo siento pero la línea está ocupada.
— Gracias.

5. — Bueno.
— Buenas noches, señora. ¿Está María en casa?
— ¿Eres tú, Alicia?
— Sí, señora. ¿Cómo está usted?
— Bien, gracias, pero María no está en casa.
— Bueno, señora, llamo más tarde.
— Adiós.

Answers to Activity 6
1. greeting someone
2. saying goodbye
3. unable to reach the person
4. unable to reach the person
5. greeting someone and unable to reach someone

9   p. 208

1. ¿Quieres jugar al tenis esta tarde?

2. ¿Quieres ir a cenar esta noche?

3. ¿Te gustaría ir al centro conmigo?

4. ¿Te gustaría estudiar con nosotras?

5. ¿Prefieres ir a la piscina el sábado?

6. ¿Prefieres la comida mexicana o la comida china?

7. ¿Te gustaría ir al cine conmigo esta tarde?

12   p. 210

MÓNICA	Oye, Carlos, ¿quieres hacer algo?
CARLOS	Claro que sí, Mónica.
MÓNICA	¿Qué prefieres hacer—ir al circo o ir al parque de atracciones?
CARLOS	Eh... no sé. Quiero ver la exhibición en el museo de antropología. ¿Quieres ir conmigo?
MÓNICA	Ay, Carlos, no me gustan los museos. Tengo otra idea. Hace buen tiempo hoy, ¿verdad? ¿Te gustaría ir al lago o al campo?
CARLOS	Prefiero ir al lago porque me gusta nadar.
MÓNICA	A mí también. Entonces, vamos a las diez y media, ¿no?

Answer to Activity 12
Deciden ir al lago.

Segundo paso

19   p. 214

1.	MAMÁ	Manuel, aquí viene el autobús.
	MANUEL	¡Ay, no! Mamá, todavía necesito lavarme los dientes.
	MAMÁ	Pues, ¡apúrate, hijo!
2.	MAMÁ	Gabi, ya son las ocho. Vas con tu novio a la fiesta de cumpleaños de Miguel a las ocho y media, ¿no? ¿Estás lista?
	GABI	No, mamá. Estoy un poco atrasada. Necesito maquillarme.
3.	MAMÁ	Armando, ¿estás listo para ir al circo con tus primos?
	ARMANDO	Sí...
	MAMÁ	Pero hijo, tu pelo es un desastre.
	ARMANDO	Ah, tienes razón, Mamá. Necesito peinarme.
4.	MAMÁ	¿Estás listo, querido? Tenemos que estar en el teatro en media hora.
	PAPÁ	Lo siento, mi amor. Todavía necesito afeitarme.
	MAMÁ	Está bien, pero apúrate, por favor.
5.	MAMÁ	Berta, hoy es la boda de tu amiga Verónica, ¿verdad?
	BERTA	Sí, mamá. A las tres. Hombre, son las dos y todavía necesito ducharme.

Answers to Activity 19
1. d   2. e   3. a   4. c   5. b

One-Stop Planner CD-ROM

To preview all resources available for this chapter, use the **One-Stop Planner CD-ROM**, Disc 2.

Tercer paso

24 p. 217

1. — Hola, Miguel. ¿Te gustaría ir con nosotros al partido de fútbol esta noche?
— Lo siento, pero tengo que estudiar.

2. — Hola, Gabriela. Este fin de semana vamos al lago. ¿Te gustaría ir con nosotros?
— ¡Qué lástima! Ya tengo planes para este fin de semana.

3. — Oye, Roberto, ¿te gustaría cenar con nosotros esta noche?
—¿Esta noche? Ay, tengo una cita esta noche.

4. — Mariana, ¿te gustaría tomar un refresco esta tarde?
— Estoy un poco cansada. Tal vez otro día, ¿eh?

Answers to Activity 24

1. c
2. d
3. a
4. b

LETRA Y SONIDO, P. 219

For the scripts for Parts A and C, see p. 219.
The script for Part B is below.

B. Dictado

¡Qué lástima! Lupita y Yolanda quieren ir al lago el lunes, pero ya tengo planes con Lorena. Yo no voy allí con ellas.

Repaso

1 p. 226

1. —¿Te gustaría ir al cine esta noche?
—Lo siento, pero estoy un poco enferma. Tengo que descansar.

2. —¿Te gustaría ir al museo el sábado?
—Me gustaría, pero ya tengo planes. Pienso ir al parque de atracciones.

3. —¿Quieres ir a caminar por la plaza?
—Me gustaría, pero necesito ducharme. Tal vez en dos horas.

4. —¿Quieres ir al partido de fútbol el domingo?
—Sí, me gustaría. ¿A qué hora es?

Answers to Repaso Activity 1

1. b
2. b
3. a
4. a

Capítulo 7: ¿Qué te gustaría hacer?
Suggested Lesson Plans *50-Minute Schedule*

Day 1

CHAPTER OPENER 5 min.
- Focusing on Outcomes, ATE, p. 203
- Photo Flash!, ATE, p. 203

DE ANTEMANO 40 min.
- Presenting **De antemano** and Preteaching Vocabulary, ATE, p. 204
- Present the Language Notes and follow the Group Work suggestion, ATE, p. 205.
- Activities 1–5, p. 206, and Comprehension Check, ATE, p. 206

Wrap-Up 5 min.
- Follow the suggested Challenge, ATE, p. 205, as a class.

Homework Options
Cuaderno de actividades, p. 73, Activities 1–2

Day 2

PRIMER PASO
Quick Review 5 min.
- Check homework.
- Bell Work, ATE, p. 207

Así se dice, p. 207 35 min.
- Presenting **Así se dice**, ATE, p. 207
- Present and practice **También se puede decir**, p. 207
- Do Activity 6, p. 207, with the Audio CD.
- Have students do Activity 7 individually, p. 208, then do Activity 8, p. 208, in pairs.
- Follow the Cooperative Learning Suggestion, ATE, p. 208.

Wrap-Up 10 min.
- Call on volunteers to perform their conversations from Activities 7 and 8, p. 208, for the class.

Homework Options
Cuaderno de actividades, pp. 74–75, Activities 3–4
Cuaderno de gramática, p. 53, Activities 1–2

Day 3

PRIMER PASO
Quick Review 5 min.
- Check homework.
- Review **Así se dice**, p. 207, by giving students a situation and having them respond with the appropriate expression.

Así se dice, p. 208 15 min.
- Presenting **Así se dice**, ATE, p. 208
- Do Activity 9, p. 208, with the Audio CD.

Gramática, p. 209 25 min.
- Presenting **Gramática**, ATE, p. 209
- Do **Más práctica gramatical**, Activities 1 and 2, p. 222.
- Have students do Activities 10 and 11, p. 209, individually. Ask volunteers to write their sentences for Activity 10 on the board for the class to check. Check Activity 11 orally.

Wrap-Up 5 min.
- Do Building on Previous Skills, ATE, p. 209.

Homework Options
Cuaderno de actividades, p. 75, Activity 5
Cuaderno de gramática, p. 54, Activities 3–4

Day 4

PRIMER PASO
Quick Review 5 min.
- Check homework.
- Review e→ie stem-changing verbs and **Así se dice**, p. 208.

Vocabulario, p. 210 25 min.
- Presenting **Vocabulario**, ATE, p. 210
- Present Additional Vocabulary, ATE, p. 210.
- Do Activity 12, p. 210, with the Audio CD.
- Have students do Activities 13 and 15, p. 211.
- Assign partners to do Activity 14, p. 211. Have them present one conversation tomorrow.

SEGUNDO PASO
Así se dice/Nota gramatical, p. 212 15 min.
- Presenting **Así se dice** and **Nota gramatical**, ATE, p. 212
- Have students do Activities 16–17, pp. 212–213.

Wrap-Up 5 min.
- Use Teaching Transparency 7-A. Point to a spot and have students say they plan to go there.

Homework Options
Practice conversations from Activity 14, p. 211.
Cuaderno de actividades, pp. 76–77, Activities 6–9
Cuaderno de gramática, pp. 55–57, Activities 5–8, 10

Day 5

PRIMER PASO
Quick Review 5 min.
- Check homework.
- Use Teaching Transparency 7-A to review **Vocabulario**, p. 210.

Así se dice/Gramática/Vocabulario, pp. 207–211 30 min.
- Give 2–3 minutes to practice conversations, Activity 14, p. 211. Have students perform for the class. See Speaking Rubric, pp. 3–9, Alternative Assessment Guide.

SEGUNDO PASO
Nota gramatical, p. 212 10 min.
- Have pairs do Activity 18, p. 213.
- Read **Nota cultural**, p. 213. Do Thinking Critically, ATE, p. 212.

Wrap-Up 5 min.
- Ask what students plan to do this weekend.
- Discuss the content and format of Quiz 7-1.

Homework Options
Study for Quiz 7-1.
Más práctica gramatical, pp. 223–224, Activities 3–5, Cuaderno de actividades, p. 78–79, Activities 10–11
Cuaderno de gramática, pp. 56–57, Activities 9, 11

Day 6

PRIMER PASO
Quick Review 5 min.
- Check homework.
- Quickly review the content of the **Primer paso**.

Quiz 20 min.
- Administer Quiz 7-1A, 7-1B, or a combination of the two.

SEGUNDO PASO
Así se dice/Nota gramatical, p. 214 20 min.
- Presenting **Así se dice** and **Nota gramatical**, ATE, p. 214
- Present Language-to-Language, ATE, p. 214.
- Present **Vocabulario adicional**, p. 214, using props for each vocabulary item. Then, ask students what they need in order to do one of the reflexive activities they just learned.
- Do Activity 19, p. 214, with the Audio CD.

Wrap-Up 5 min.
- Hold up a toiletry item or a photo of one. Have students say what it is and what it is used for.

Homework Options
Más práctica gramatical, p. 224, Activity 6
Cuaderno de actividades, p. 79, Activity 12
Cuaderno de gramática, p. 58, Activities 12–13

One-Stop Planner CD-ROM

For alternative lesson plans by chapter section, to create your own customized plans, or to preview all resources available for this chapter, use the **One-Stop Planner CD-ROM**, Disc 2.

 For additional homework suggestions, see activities accompanied by this symbol throughout the chapter.

Day 7

SEGUNDO PASO
Quick Review 5 min.
- Check homework.

Así se dice/Nota gramatical, p. 214–215 25 min.
- Have students do Activity 20, p. 214, in pairs, then do the Additional Practice activity, ATE, p. 215.
- Have students do Activity 21, p. 215. Check orally.
- Do Activity 22, p. 215.
- Have students do Activity 23, p. 215, in groups. Have groups report to the class.

PANORAMA CULTURAL 10 min.
- Presenting **Panorama cultural,** ATE, p. 216
- Follow the suggestion in the Language Note, ATE, p. 216.

Wrap-Up 10 min.
- Follow the suggestion in Thinking Critically, ATE, p. 216.
- Discuss the content and format of Quiz 7-2.

Homework Options
Study for Quiz 7-2.

Day 8

SEGUNDO PASO
Quick Review 5 min.
- Review the content of the **Segundo paso,** using Teaching Transparency 7-2.

Quiz 20 min.
- Administer Quiz 7-2A, 7-2B, or a combination of the two.

TERCER PASO
Así se dice/Nota gramatical, p. 217 20 min.
- Presenting **Así se dice** and **Nota gramatical,** ATE, p. 217
- Present **También se puede decir...** and the Language Note, ATE, p. 216
- Do Activity 24, p. 217, with Audio CD.

Wrap-Up 5 min.
- Have students invite a partner to do something. Partners respond stating why they cannot accept the invitation.

Homework Options
Cuaderno de actividades, pp. 80–81, Activities 13–15
Cuaderno de gramática, p. 59, Activities 14–15

Day 9

TERCER PASO
Quick Review 10 min.
- Check homework.
- Have students say how they feel using **tener** or **estar** + an adjective.

Así se dice/Nota gramatical, pp. 217–219 35 min.
- Activity 25, p. 218; check orally.
- Present **A lo nuestro,** p. 218.
- Have students do Activity 26, p. 218, in pairs.
- Do Activities 27–28, pp. 218–219.
- Activity 29, p. 219; exchange for peer-editing.
- Have students do Activity 30, p. 219, in pairs.

Wrap-Up 5 min.
- Have students invent an outrageous reason for not doing one activity from Activity 26, p. 218.

Homework Suggestions
Rewrite notes from Activity 29, p. 219.
Cuaderno de actividades, pp. 81–82
Cuaderno de gramática, p. 60, Activities 16–17

Day 10

TERCER PASO
Quick Review 5 min.
- Check homework.
- Collect the writing assignment (Activity 29, p. 219). You may wish to use the Writing Rubric, pp. 3–9 in the Alternative Assessment Guide, to grade the assignment.

Así se dice/Nota gramatical, pp. 217–219 15 min.
- **Más práctica gramatical,** p. 225, Activities 7–8
- Do Communicative Activity 7-3, pp. 41–42, in Activities for Communication.

VAMOS A LEER 20 min.
- Read the **Estrategia** and **¿Te acuerdas?,** p. 220, then do Activities A and B, pp. 220–221.
- Do Activities C and D, p. 221.
- Present and discuss the Culture Note and Language-to-Language, ATE, p. 221.

Wrap-Up 10 min.
- Do Thinking Critically, ATE, p. 220.
- Discuss the content and format of Quiz 7-3.

Homework Options
Study for Quiz 7-3.
Cuaderno de actividades, pp. 83–84, Activities 19–20

Day 11

TERCER PASO
Quick Review 5 min.
- Collect homework.
- Quickly review the content of the **Tercer paso.**

Quiz 20 min.
- Administer Quiz 7-3A, 7-3B, or a combination of the two.

Letra y sonido, p. 219 10 min.
- Present **Letra y sonido,** p. 219, using the Audio CD.

REPASO 10 min.
- Do Activity 1, p. 226, with the Audio CD.
- Do Activities 3–4, pp. 226–227.

Wrap-Up 5 min.
- Ask students to list the communicative skills and grammar they learned in this chapter.

Homework Options
Assign the **Vamos a escribir,** Activity 5, p. 227, as homework.
A ver si puedo..., p. 228

Day 12

REPASO 15 min.
- Have students do Activity 2, p. 226, in groups, and Activity 6, p. 227, in pairs.

Chapter Review 30 min.
- Review Chapter 7. Choose from **Más práctica gramatical,** Grammar Tutor for Students of Spanish, Activities for Communication, Listening Activities, Interactive CD-ROM Tutor, or **Juegos interactivos.**

Wrap-Up 5 min.
- Discuss the format of the Chapter 7 Test .

Homework Options
Study for the Chapter 7 Test.

Assessment

Quick Review 5 min.
- Answer any last-minute questions.

Test, Chapter 7 45 min.
- Administer Chapter 7 Test. Select from Testing Program, Alternative Assessment Guide, Test Generator, or Standardized Assessment Tutor.

Capítulo 7: ¿Qué te gustaría hacer?
Suggested Lesson Plans 90-Minute Block Schedule

Block 1

CHAPTER OPENER 5 min.
- Focusing on Outcomes, ATE, p. 203
- Photo Flash!, ATE, p. 203

DE ANTEMANO 40 min.
- Presenting **De antemano** and Preteaching Vocabulary, ATE, p. 204
- Present the Language Notes and follow the Group Work suggestion, ATE, p. 205.
- Activities 1–5, p. 206, and Comprehension Check, ATE, p. 206

Así se dice, p. 207 35 min.
- Presenting **Así se dice**, ATE, p. 207
- Present and practice **También se puede decir**, p. 207
- Do Activity 6, p. 207, with the Audio CD.
- Have students do Activity 7, p. 208, individually, then Activity 8, p. 208, in pairs.
- Follow the Cooperative Learning Suggestion, ATE, p. 208.

Wrap-Up 10 min.
- Call on volunteers to perform their conversations from Activities 7–8, p. 208, for the class.

Homework Options
Cuaderno de actividades, pp. 73–75, Activities 1–4
Cuaderno de gramática, p. 53, Activities 1–2

Block 2

PRIMER PASO
Quick Review 10 min.
- Check homework.
- Review **Así se dice**, p. 207, by giving students a situation and having them respond with the appropriate expression.

Así se dice, p. 208 15 min.
- Presenting **Así se dice**, ATE, p. 208
- Do Activity 9, p. 208, with the Audio CD.

Gramática, p. 209 25 min.
- Presenting **Gramática**, ATE, p. 209
- Do **Más práctica gramatical**, Activities 1–2, p. 222.
- Have students do Activities 10–11, p. 209, individually. Ask volunteers to write their sentences for Activity 10 on the board for the class to check. Check Activity 11 orally.

Vocabulario, p. 210 30 min.
- Presenting **Vocabulario**, ATE, p. 210
- Present Additional Vocabulary, ATE, p. 210.
- Do Activity 12, p. 210, with the Audio CD.
- Have students do Activities 13 and 15, p. 211.
- Assign students a partner to do Activity 14, p. 211. Have them practice both conversations so they may present one of them to the class tomorrow.

Wrap-Up 10 min.
- Do Building on Previous Skills, ATE, p. 209.
- Project Teaching Transparency 7-A, point to a location, and have students invite you to each place.

Homework Options
Have students practice conversations from Activity 14, p. 211.
Cuaderno de actividades, pp. 75–76, Activities 5–7
Cuaderno de gramática, pp. 54–55, Activities 3–7

Block 3

PRIMER PASO
Quick Review 10 min.
- Check homework.
- Review e→ie stem-changing verbs and expressions from **Así se dice**, p. 208, by asking students yes/no questions.
- Use Teaching Transparency 7-A to review **Vocabulario**, p. 210.

Así se dice/Gramática/Vocabulario, pp. 207–211 35 min.
- Give students 2–3 minutes to practice their conversations from Activity 14, p. 211. Then have students perform one of the two conversations for the class. You may wish to use the Speaking Rubric, pp. 3–9 in the Alternative Assessment Guide, to grade the assignment for students' oral portfolios.

SEGUNDO PASO
Así se dice/Nota gramatical, p. 212 35 min.
- Presenting **Así se dice** and **Nota gramatical**, ATE, p. 212
- Have students do Activities 16 and 17, pp. 212–213. Check orally.
- Have students do Activity 18, p. 213, in pairs, then follow the Additional Practice suggestion, ATE, p. 213.
- Read the **Nota cultural**, p. 213, with the class. Do the Thinking Critically activity, ATE, p. 212.

Wrap-Up 10 min.
- Ask individual students what they are going to do this weekend.
- Discuss the content and format of Quiz 7-1.

Homework Options
Study for Quiz 7-1.
Más práctica gramatical, pp. 223–224, Activities 3–5
Cuaderno de actividades, pp. 77–79, Activities 8–11
Cuaderno de gramática, pp. 56–57, Activities 8–11

One-Stop Planner CD-ROM

For alternative lesson plans by chapter section, to create your own customized plans, or to preview all resources available for this chapter, use the **One-Stop Planner CD-ROM**, Disc 2.

For additional homework suggestions, see activities accompanied by this symbol throughout the chapter.

Block 4

PRIMER PASO
Quick Review 10 min.
- Check homework.
- Quickly review the content of the **Primer paso**.

Quiz 20 min.
- Administer Quiz 7-1A, 7-1B, or a combination of the two.

SEGUNDO PASO
Así se dice/Nota gramatical, p. 214 45 min.
- Presenting **Así se dice** and **Nota gramatical**, ATE, p. 214
- Present Language-to-Language, ATE, p. 214.
- Do Activity 19, p. 214, with the Audio CD.
- Have students do Activity 20, p. 214, in pairs.
- Present **Vocabulario extra**, p. 214, using props for each vocabulary item. Then ask students what they need in order to do one of the reflexive activities they just learned.
- Have students do Activity 21, p. 215. Check orally.
- Do Activity 22, p. 215.
- Have students do Activity 23, p. 215, in groups.

PANORAMA CULTURAL 10 min.
- Presenting **Panorama cultural**, ATE, p. 216
- Follow the suggestion in the Language Note, ATE, p. 216.

Wrap-Up 5 min.
- Follow the suggestion in Thinking Critically, ATE, p. 216.
- Discuss the content and format of Quiz 7-2.

Homework Options
Study for Quiz 7-2.
Más práctica gramatical, p. 224, Activity 6
Cuaderno de actividades, p. 79, Activity 12
Cuaderno de gramática, p. 58, Activities 12–13

Block 5

SEGUNDO PASO
Quick Review 10 min.
- Check homework.
- Review **Segundo paso** by doing the Reteaching activity, p. 215, and asking students what the people in Teaching Transparency 7-2 are going to do. Follow up with questions to elicit all the reflexive pronouns.

Quiz 20 min.
- Administer Quiz 7-2A, 7-2B, or a combination of the two.

TERCER PASO
Así se dice/Nota gramatical, p. 217 30 min.
- Presenting **Así se dice** and **Nota gramatical**, ATE, p. 217
- Present **También se puede decir...**, p. 217.
- Do Activity 24, p. 217, with the Audio CD.
- Have students do Activity 25, p. 218. Check orally.
- Present **A lo nuestro**, p. 218.
- Have students do Activity 26, p. 218, in pairs.
- Do Activities 27–28, pp. 218–219.

VAMOS A LEER 20 min.
- Read the **Estrategia** and **¿Te acuerdas?**, p. 220, then do Activities A–B, pp. 220–221.
- Do Activities C and D, p. 221.
- Present and discuss the Culture Note and Language-to-Language, ATE, p. 221.

Wrap-Up 10 min.
- Do the Thinking Critically activity, ATE, p. 220.
- Have students invite a partner to do something. Partners respond stating why they cannot accept the invitation.
- Discuss the content and format of Quiz 7-3.

Homework Options
Study for Quiz 7-3.
Cuaderno de actividades, pp. 80–82, Activities 13–18
Cuaderno de gramática, pp. 59–60, Activities 14–17

Block 6

TERCER PASO
Quick Review 10 min.
- Check homework.

Así se dice/Nota gramatical, p. 217 35 min.
- Have students do Activity 29, p. 219, then exchange papers for peer-editing. Have students rewrite paragraphs to turn in to you. You may wish to use the Writing Rubric, pp. 3–9 in the Alternative Assessment Guide, to grade the assignment.
- Have students work in pairs to do Activity 30, p. 219.
- **Más práctica gramatical**, p. 225, Activities 7–8

Quiz 20 min.
- Administer Quiz 7-3A, 7-3B, or a combination of the two.

Letra y sonido, p. 219 10 min.
- Present **Letra y sonido**, p. 219, using the Audio CD.

REPASO 10 min.
- Do Activity 1, p. 226, with the Audio CD.
- Have students do Activity 2, p. 226, in groups.

Wrap-Up 5 min.
- Have students list the concepts they have studied in this chapter.
- Discuss the format of the Chapter 7 Test and provide sample questions.

Homework Options
Study for the Chapter 7 Test.
Assign Activity 5, p. 227, as homework.
A ver si puedo..., p. 228

Block 7

REPASO
Quick Review 10 min.
- Check homework.

Chapter Review 35 min.
- Review Chapter 7. Choose from **Más práctica gramatical**, Grammar Tutor for Students of Spanish, Activities for Communication, Listening Activities, Interactive CD-ROM Tutor, or **Juegos interactivos**.

Test, Chapter 7 45 min.
- Administer Chapter 7 Test. Select from Testing Program, Alternative Assessment Guide, Test Generator, or Standardized Assessment Tutor.

CAPÍTULO 7

Pacing Tips
The first two **Pasos** present important grammar points. Make sure the new grammar presentations leave time for the interactive speaking opportunities in this chapter. Emphasize cultural protocol in informal invitations and telephone conversations. For Lesson Plan and timing suggestions, see pp. 201I–201L.

Meeting the Standards

Communication
- Talking on the telephone, p. 207
- Extending and accepting invitations, p. 208
- Making plans, p. 212
- Talking about getting ready, p. 214
- Turning down an invitation and explaining why, p. 217

Cultures
- Nota cultural, p. 213
- Panorama cultural, p. 216
- Vamos a leer, pp. 220–221

Connections
- Multicultural Link, pp. 203
- Community Link, p. 210
- Multicultural Link, p. 213
- Culture Note, p. 221

Comparisons
- Language-to-Language, p. 214
- Native Speakers, p. 215
- A lo nuestro, p. 218
- Language-to-Language, p. 221

Communities
- Multicultural Link, p. 203
- Challenge, p. 207
- Native Speakers, p. 220

Communication for All Students

Challenge
Ask students what words or phrases they could use on the telephone. Remind them that they already know several words that can be put together to make such phrases. **(hola, buenos días, soy, está)** Have students work in pairs and come up with two or three phrases that they would use in a telephone conversation. You can use the students' phrases to make a word bank on the board or the overhead.

Auditory Learners
Have students work in pairs to role-play a situation in which one person makes an invitation **(¿Quieres ir al parque?)** and the other turns down the invitation with an explanation. **(No puedo. Tengo mucha tarea.)** Ask them to do as much of the role-play as possible in Spanish.

CAPÍTULO

7

¿Qué te gustaría hacer?

Objectives

In this chapter you will learn to

Primer paso

- talk on the telephone
- extend and accept invitations

Segundo paso

- make plans
- talk about getting ready

Tercer paso

- turn down an invitation and explain why

MARCAR: go.hrw.com
PALABRA CLAVE:
WV3 ECUADOR-7

◀ **Me gustaría caminar sobre la línea que divide al mundo.**

Connections and Comparisons

Multicultural Link

Have students research sporting events, movies, concerts, plays, or festivals in a Spanish-speaking city. Suggest that they search the World Wide Web, the public library, or bookstores for **guías de ocio**. A **guía de ocio** contains information about leisure activities. These guides are often sections of newspapers or magazines. Give students category ideas to get them started: the music scene in Quito, sporting events in Buenos Aires, movie showings in Bogota, festivals in Seville, and plays in Mexico City.

CAPÍTULO 7

Photo Flash!

Just twenty-four miles north of Quito near San Antonio de Pichincha, the monument **La Mitad del Mundo** marks the spot where an 18th-century French expedition scientifically measured the equator. As mentioned in the Geography Link on p. 199, it is now a popular tourist attraction, marking the imaginary line with a strip of white pebbles embedded in the ground.

Focusing on Outcomes

Have students describe the people in the photo. What plans might these friends be making? Ask students to imagine they are vacationing abroad with friends and are planning a day's activities. Ask them to make a list of things they would like to do with friends in different settings. Encourage use of vocabulary from past chapters. They might mention things such as **ir a un partido de fútbol, ir al cine, salir, caminar, bailar,** and **comer**. Tell students that in this chapter they will learn how to invite people to do things, to accept or turn down an invitation, to talk about future plans, and to talk about getting ready.

Teaching Resources
pp. 204–206

PRINT
▶ Lesson Planner, p. 32
▶ Video Guide, pp. 47–48, 50
▶ Cuaderno de actividades, p. 73

MEDIA
▶ One-Stop Planner
▶ Video Program
  De antemano
  Videocassette 3, 3:25–8:52
  Videocassette 5 (captioned version), 1:06:40–1:12:06
  A continuación
  Videocassette 3, 8:53–14:26
  Videocassette 5 (captioned version), 1:12:07–1:17:46
▶ DVD Tutor, Disc 2
▶ Audio Compact Discs, CD 7, Trs. 1–2
▶ **De antemano** Transparencies

Presenting
De antemano

While students read or watch the **fotonovela**, periodically stop to answer questions, such as those in the **Estrategia para comprender**. Then present the Preteaching Vocabulary. Follow-up by modeling pronunciation of the **fotonovela** dialogue and having students repeat after you. Have students guess meanings from context.

 De antemano Transparencies

DE ANTEMANO · *¿Qué hacemos?*

The **fotonovela** is an abridged version of the video episode.

CD 7 Trs. 1–2

Estrategia
para comprender
Look at the photos. What kind of mood is Tomás in? How is Carlos trying to help Tomás? Who is María and how is she involved? Read the story and see what happens.

Carlos   **María**   **Tomás**   **Sr. Ortiz**

1
Carlos: ¡Tomás! ¿Qué te pasa, Tomás? ¿Por qué estás de mal humor?
Tomás: María va a hacer una fiesta el sábado.
Carlos: ¿Y? Me parece super bien.
Tomás: Sí, pero no me invitó.
Carlos: ¡Qué lástima!

2
Carlos: Oye, ¿tienes prisa ahora? ¿Tienes que hacer algo?
Tomás: No, nada... ¿Por qué?
Carlos: ¿Quieres ver un video en mi casa?
Tomás: ¡Claro que sí! Vamos.

3
Carlos: Oye, Tomás. Tengo una idea. ¿Te gustaría hacer algo conmigo este sábado? No tengo planes.
Tomás: Sí, por qué no.
Carlos: Hombre, ¡qué entusiasmo! Bueno, ¿qué prefieres? ¿Salir o hacer algo en casa?

4
Tomás: En realidad, prefiero salir. Pero, ¿qué hacemos?
Carlos: Hay un concierto de guitarra en La Casa de la Cultura. ¿Tienes ganas de ir?
Tomás: Sí. ¡Buena idea!

Preteaching Vocabulary

Guessing Words from Context
Ask students what types of expressions they would expect to hear in a telephone conversation. (Hello., This is. . . speaking., May I please speak to. . . ?, Hold on. . .) Have students identify expressions in **De antemano** that they think would be categorized as telephone expressions. (**5** ¿Aló?, **5** Habla..., **6** ¿Está..., por favor?, **7** ¿De parte de quién?, **8** ¿Puedo dejar un recado?) Then have students order the expressions as they would appear in a phone conversation. Finally, have students think about the types of conversations they have with their friends. What do they think María and Carlos are talking about? What does María tell Sr. Ortiz?

5

Carlos: ¿Aló?

María: Hola, Carlos. Habla María.

Carlos: Ah... hola, María.

María: Carlos, ¿quieres venir a una fiesta este sábado? Es para un estudiante de intercambio de Estados Unidos.

6

Carlos: ¿Una fiesta? ¿El sábado? Eh... lo siento, María, pero no puedo. Ya tengo planes.

María: Ay... qué lástima. Bueno, tal vez otro día. Chao.

7

Sr. Ortiz: ¿Aló?

María: Buenas tardes, Sr. Ortiz. ¿Está Tomás, por favor?

Sr. Ortiz: ¿De parte de quién?

María: Habla María Pérez.

Sr. Ortiz: Hola, María... un momento. ¡Tomás! ¡Tomás! ¡Teléfono! Lo siento, María, pero no está.

8

María: ¿Puedo dejar un recado, por favor?

Sr. Ortiz: Claro que sí... pero un momento... Tengo que ponerme los lentes.

María: Voy a hacer una fiesta el sábado. Quiero invitar a Tomás.

Sr. Ortiz: A ver, María... fiesta... el sábado... Muy bien. Chao, María.

9

El señor Ortiz deja el recado para Tomás.

10

Pero... ¿lo va a recibir?

Cuaderno de actividades, p. 73, Acts. 1–2

Using the Captioned Video/DVD

Use Videocassette 5 to allow students to see the Spanish captions of *¿Qué hacemos?* Hearing the language and watching the story will reduce anxiety about the new language and facilitate comprehension. The reinforcement of seeing the written vocabulary words as they watch the gestures and actions will help prepare students to do the comprehension activities on p. 206. **NOTE:** The *DVD Tutor* contains captions for all sections of the *Video Program.*

Group Work

Divide students into groups of four. Assign each student the role of one of the persons in the **fotonovela**. Ask students to role-play the **fotonovela** with other members of their group, reading the various parts. You might have them change the ending and present their versions to the class.

Challenge

Ask students to create original endings for the story.

Language Notes

• **Los anteojos, los espejuelos,** and **las gafas** are some other common words for *eyeglasses.*

• **Chao,** an informal and popular way to say *goodbye,* comes from the Italian word *ciao.*

• Point out that the characters speak with a typical Ecuadorean accent and inflection.

A continuación

You may choose to continue with *¿Qué hacemos? (a continuación)* at this time or wait until later in the chapter. At this point, Tomás and Carlos change their weekend plans when they discover that they are both invited to María's party. They arrive for the party, but it has been rescheduled because the guest of honor will not arrive until Monday. You may wish to have students predict what will happen in the second part of the video.

CAPÍTULO 7

Teaching Suggestion

3 Once students have identified the Spanish expressions, have them practice them with a partner. If students have difficulty finding them, play the segment of the captioned video where these expressions are used, or have partners reread the **fotonovela**.

These activities check for comprehension only. Students should not yet be expected to produce language modeled in **De antemano**.

1 **¿Comprendes?** See answers below.

Contesta las preguntas sobre la fotonovela. Si no estás seguro/a, ¡adivina!

1. What are Tomás and Carlos talking about?
2. How does Tomás feel? Why does he feel that way?
3. What suggestion does Carlos make?
4. Why does María call Carlos? What is his reaction?
5. What happens when María calls Tomás's house? Will there be a problem?

2 **¿Cierto o falso?** See answers below.

Corrige *(Correct)* las oraciones falsas.

1. Tomás está de mal humor.
2. Carlos y Tomás deciden ir a un concierto el sábado.
3. María invita a Carlos, pero no a Tomás.
4. Carlos no acepta la invitación de María.
5. Tomás recibe el recado de María.

3 **¿Cómo se dice?** See answers below.

Find the words and phrases that . . .

1. Tomás uses to say what he prefers to do
2. Carlos uses to ask if Tomás has to do something
3. María uses to invite Carlos to her party
4. Carlos uses to turn down María's invitation
5. Sr. Ortiz uses to ask who's calling

4 **¡Qué lío!** *What a mess!*

Completa el párrafo de Tomás con palabras de la lista. Usa la fotonovela como guía.

> *el 16 de febrero*
>
> *Hoy, estoy de mal ___1___. No tengo invitación a la fiesta de María y me ___2___ mucho ir. ¡Qué ___3___! Carlos sí tiene invitación; pero es un buen amigo y dijo "Lo ___4___ pero no puedo. Ya tengo ___5___." Y ahora, si María me llama, no acepto. Ya no ___6___ ir. ___7___ ir al concierto con Carlos. ¡Qué lío!*

siento 4.	planes 5.	prisa	lástima 3.	prefiero 7.
prefieres		quiero 6.	quieres	humor 1. gustaría 2.

5 **¿Y tú?** Answers will vary.

Get together with a partner and discuss the following questions. Has something like Tomás's problem ever happened to you? What did you do? If something like this ever did happen to you, what would you do? What do you think Tomás is going to do?

Answers

1
1. They're talking about María's party.
2. Tomás is in a bad mood because María has not invited him to her party on Saturday.
3. He suggests they do something on Saturday.
4. María calls Carlos to invite him to her party. Carlos says he can't go because he has plans.
5. Tomás is not home, so María leaves a message for Tomás inviting him to the party. The message may get lost in other papers. Another problem is that now Tomás has plans with Carlos.

2
1. Cierto
2. Cierto
3. Falso; María invita a los dos muchachos.
4. Cierto
5. Falso; Tomás no recibe el recado de María.

3
1. Prefiero salir.
2. ¿Tienes que hacer algo?
3. ¿Quieres venir a una fiesta este sábado?
4. Lo siento, pero no puedo. Ya tengo planes.
5. ¿De parte de quién?

Comprehension Check

Slower Pace

1 Have students work in small groups to discuss the comprehension questions and look for answers in the **fotonovela**. They should see how many different ideas and opinions they have about what happens in the **fotonovela**.

Challenge

1 Ask students to close their books while you ask these questions in Spanish: **¿De qué hablan Tomás y Carlos? ¿Cómo se siente Tomás? ¿Por qué? ¿Por qué llama María a Carlos? ¿Cómo reacciona? ¿Qué pasa cuando María llama a la casa de Tomás? ¿Va a haber un problema?** Encourage students to take risks and use as much Spanish as possible in answering.

STANDARDS: 1.2

Así se dice

Talking on the telephone

If you called a friend who wasn't home, your conversation might go like this:

SEÑORA	**Aló.** *Hello.*
CARLOS	Buenos días, señora. ¿Está María, por favor?
SEÑORA	¿Quién habla?
CARLOS	Soy yo, Carlos.
SEÑORA	Ah, Carlos. ¿Cómo estás hoy?
CARLOS	Muy bien, ¿y usted?
SEÑORA	Muy bien. Pero María no está.
CARLOS	Bueno, **llamo más tarde.** *. . . I'll call later.*
SEÑORA	Adiós, Carlos.

If you needed to leave a message for someone, your conversation might go like this:

SECRETARIA	**Diga.** *Hello.*
TOMÁS	¿Está la señorita Álvarez, por favor?
SECRETARIA	**¿De parte de quién?** *Who's calling?*
TOMÁS	De parte de Tomás Ortiz.
SECRETARIA	**Un momento...** lo siento pero **la línea está ocupada.** *One moment . . . the line is busy.*
TOMÁS	Gracias. **¿Puedo dejar un recado?** *May I leave a message?*
SECRETARIA	**Está bien.** *All right.*

Cuaderno de actividades, p. 74, Acts. 3–4

Cuaderno de gramática, p. 53, Acts. 1–2

6 **Por teléfono** Scripts and answers on p. 201G.

 Escuchemos Listen to the following telephone calls. Decide if the caller is greeting someone, saying goodbye, or unable to reach the person.

CD 7 Tr. 3

También se puede decir...

A common telephone greeting in Mexico is **Bueno**. In some other countries you will hear **Hola, Dígame,** or **Pronto**.

Primer paso

CAPÍTULO 7

Teaching Resources
pp. 207–211

PRINT
▶ Lesson Planner, p. 33
▶ TPR Storytelling Book, pp. 25, 28
▶ Listening Activities, pp. 51–52, 55
▶ Activities for Communication, pp. 37–38, 105, 108–109, 149–150
▶ Cuaderno de gramática, pp. 53–55
▶ Grammar Tutor for Students of Spanish, Chapter 7
▶ Cuaderno de actividades, pp. 74–76
▶ Cuaderno para hispanohablantes, pp. 31–35
▶ Testing Program, pp. 171–174
▶ Alternative Assessment Guide, p. 38
▶ Student Make-Up Assignments, Chapter 7

MEDIA
▶ One-Stop Planner
▶ Audio Compact Discs, CD 7, Trs. 3–5, 23–24, 18
▶ Teaching Transparencies 7-1, 7-A; **Más práctica gramatical** Answers; Cuaderno de gramática Answers
▶ Interactive CD-ROM Tutor, Disc 2

Bell Work

Have students write out some phone numbers. Check to see if they expressed the last numbers two digits at a time. (555-1234 = **cinco, cincuenta y cinco, doce, treinta y cuatro**)

Communication for All Students

Challenge

Many U.S. companies use Spanish as an option for their calling customers. You may wish to have students ask their parents to use 1-800 numbers to contact credit card companies, long distance companies, or utilities companies and choose the Spanish option to hear prerecorded messages or instructions. Challenge students to think of where they have heard a Spanish option given, and assign a few of these calls as a listening exercise. Have students jot down what they hear, especially numbers, and report to the class. As an alternative, have them choose a local Spanish radio station and listen for advertisements in which phone numbers are given. Many stations give their call numbers as well. Have them report the company or station and give the number in Spanish.

Presenting
Así se dice

Have a student role-play the conversations with you, or use a puppet to "talk with" a partner. Have students practice, then switch roles. Then take the role of one of the participants and pick students to take the other role.

Teaching Resources
pp. 207–211

PRINT

▸ Lesson Planner, p. 33
▸ TPR Storytelling Book, pp. 25, 28
▸ Listening Activities, pp. 51–52, 55
▸ Activities for Communication, pp. 37–38, 105, 108–109, 149–150
▸ Cuaderno de gramática, pp. 53–55
▸ Grammar Tutor for Students of Spanish, Chapter 7
▸ Cuaderno de actividades, pp. 74–76
▸ Cuaderno para hispanohablantes, pp. 31–35
▸ Testing Program, pp. 171–174
▸ Alternative Assessment Guide, p. 38
▸ Student Make-Up Assignments, Chapter 7

MEDIA

▸ One-Stop Planner
▸ Audio Compact Discs, CD 7, Trs. 3–5, 23–24, 18
▸ Teaching Transparencies 7-1, 7-A; **Más práctica gramatical** Answers; Cuaderno de gramática Answers
▸ Interactive CD-ROM Tutor, Disc 2

Presenting
Así se dice

Ask volunteers to model the dialogues. Have groups practice the dialogues using variations such as **una fiesta** or **un baile**.

Answers
7 *Possible answer:*
1. —Aló. —Buenos días, señora. —¿Está Marta en casa? —No, Marta no está en casa. —Bueno, señora, llamo más tarde. —Está bien. —Adiós. —Adiós.

8 *Answers will vary.*

7 **Situaciones** Possible answer below.

Escribamos Escoge cuatro de las siguientes situaciones. Escribe una conversación telefónica para cada una. Incluye saludos y despedidas y deja un recado si es necesario.

1. You call your friend Marta, but she isn't at home. Her mother answers.
2. You call school to talk with Mrs. Castillo in the attendance office. The secretary in the office tells you that her line is busy.
3. You call Dr. Quintana, but the doctor is out.
4. You call your friend Benito and talk about school.
5. You call your mother or father at work. She/He is in a meeting and can't come to the phone.
6. You call your friend Pablo to ask him to play soccer.

8 **Hablamos por teléfono** See note below.

Hablemos Work with a partner to role-play the conversations you chose in Activity 7. The "caller" should work from the written conversation, but the "answerer" should role-play without the script. Then change roles.

Así se dice

Extending and accepting invitations

To invite a friend to do something, say:

¿Te gustaría ir al cine con nosotros? **Nos gustan** las películas de aventura y hay una a las nueve.
Would you like . . .? We like . . .

¿Quieres ir a comer el sábado? **Te invito.**
Do you want to . . .?It's my treat.

Your friend might answer:

Sí, **me gustaría** ir con ustedes.
. . . I would like . . .

¡Claro que sí! Gracias.
Of course!

9 **Planes**

Escuchemos Listen to the following questions. Do these sentences answer the questions you hear? If the sentence fits as a response, write **sí.** If it doesn't, write **no.**

CD 7
Tr. 4

1. Sí, me gusta mucho el tenis. sí
2. No me gustan los deportes. no
3. ¡Claro que sí! sí
4. ¡Claro que sí! La clase es muy difícil. sí
5. Sí, me gustaría ir al partido de fútbol. no
6. Prefiero comida china. sí
7. No, no me gustan las películas. sí

Communication for All Students

Cooperative Learning

Students form groups of three. One member asks the others **¿Cuántos minutos al día hablas por teléfono?** and **¿Cuántas llamadas haces?** The second adds up the totals of the group. The third reports the totals. **¿Qué grupo habla más por teléfono? ¿y menos? ¿Qué grupo hace más llamadas?**

Building on Previous Skills

On a transparency or on the board, write several names with phone numbers by them. (**Miguel— 42-58-74, Sara—27-64-31**) Ask students the number for each name. (**¿Cuál es el número de teléfono de Miguel?**) Students should answer by saying the numbers in pairs.

Gramática

e → ie stem-changing verbs

CD-ROM 2
DVD 2

1. In **e → ie** stem-changing verbs, the letter **e** in the stem changes to **ie** in all forms except the **nosotros** and **vosotros** forms.
   You've been working with an **e → ie** verb: **querer.**

Más práctica gramatical,
p. 222, Acts. 1–2

Cuaderno de gramática, p. 54, Acts. 3–4

quiero	queremos
quieres	queréis
quiere	quieren

Some other verbs that follow the same pattern are **preferir** *(to prefer)* and **empezar** *(to begin).*

2. Another **e → ie** stem-changing verb is **venir** *(to come).* It follows the same pattern as **tener.** Do you remember two other verbs with an irregular **-go** in the **yo** form?*

tengo	tienes	tiene	tenemos	tenéis	tienen
vengo	vienes	viene	venimos	venís	vienen

10 Gramática en contexto Possible answers below.

Escribamos ¿Cuántas oraciones puedes *(can you)* escribir? Usa una palabra o expresión de cada columna.

MODELO   Mi amiga prefiere ir a la fiesta de Miguel.

Yo	venir	ir al cine o al concierto
Tú	preferir	un examen mañana
Mi amiga	tener	a la fiesta de Miguel
Mi amigo y yo	querer	ir al baile el sábado contigo
Mis amigos		a nuestra casa para cenar
		¿?

11 Una fiesta [H] See answers below.

Escribamos ¿Qué pasa cuando Marta habla por teléfono con Luisa, la hermana de Paco? Usa las palabras de la lista para completar esta conversación.

empezar	fiesta	querer	preferir
venir	estar	sábado	hay

*Paco – Fiesta
sábado 8:30
casa de Marta*

LUISA   ¿Aló?

MARTA   Luisa, ¿qué tal? Habla Marta. Oye, ¿ __1__ Paco?

LUISA   Ay, no está. ¿ __2__ dejar un recado, o __3__ llamar más tarde?

MARTA   Pues, un recado. __4__ una __5__ en mi casa el __6__. __7__ a las ocho y media.

LUISA   Perfecto. Dime, ¿quiénes van?

MARTA   Uy, van a __8__ muchos amigos.

---

* **Hacer** and **salir** have irregular **yo** forms: **hago, salgo.**

Teacher to Teacher

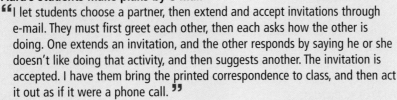

Aura's students make plans by e-mail

"I let students choose a partner, then extend and accept invitations through e-mail. They must first greet each other, then each asks how the other is doing. One extends an invitation, and the other responds by saying he or she doesn't like doing that activity, and then suggests another. The invitation is accepted. I have them bring the printed correspondence to class, and then act it out as if it were a phone call."

Aura Cole
Parkway Central Middle
School
Chesterfield, MO

Teaching Resources
pp. 207–211

PRINT
▶ Lesson Planner, p. 33
▶ TPR Storytelling Book, pp. 25, 28
▶ Listening Activities, pp. 51–52, 55
▶ Activities for Communication, pp. 37–38, 105, 108–109, 149–150
▶ Cuaderno de gramática, pp. 53–55
▶ Grammar Tutor for Students of Spanish, Chapter 7
▶ Cuaderno de actividades, pp. 74–76
▶ Cuaderno para hispanohablantes, pp. 31–35
▶ Testing Program, pp. 171–174
▶ Alternative Assessment Guide, p. 38
▶ Student Make-Up Assignments, Chapter 7

MEDIA
▶ One-Stop Planner
▶ Audio Compact Discs, CD 7, Trs. 3–5, 23–24, 18
▶ Teaching Transparencies 7-1, 7-A; **Más práctica gramatical** Answers; Cuaderno de gramática Answers
▶ Interactive CD-ROM Tutor, Disc 2

Additional Vocabulary
la tienda de discos *record store*
el centro juvenil *youth center*
el concierto de rock *rock concert*
la pista de patinaje *skating rink*

Presenting
Vocabulario
Have students look at the drawings and vocabulary words. Ask true/false questions about known locations. **La ciudad de Nueva York está en el campo, ¿verdad?** Then ask **¿Qué lugares están cerca de aquí? ¿de tu casa? ¿Cuáles están lejos?**

Vocabulario

Lugares *Places*

el acuario

el campo

el circo

la ciudad

el lago

el museo de antropología

el parque de atracciones

el teatro

el zoológico

Eventos *Events*

la fiesta de cumpleaños
de aniversario
de graduación
de sorpresa

la boda

Cuaderno de gramática, p. 55, Acts. 5–7

12 **Un sábado** Script and answer on p. 201G.

 Escuchemos It's Saturday morning and Mónica and Carlos are trying to figure out where to spend the day. Based on their conversation, where do they decide to go?

CD 7 Tr. 5

Cultures and Communities

Group Work
Have students converse in groups of three using the new vocabulary to say which places they like to visit with their families, which they prefer to go to with friends, and which they do not like. Have a member from each group report some of their findings to the class.

Community Link
Have students think about sections of their city and draw a map depicting well-known sites. Have them use the Additional Vocabulary on this page to label each site. Encourage use of dictionaries or previous knowledge of Spanish as you help them complete their maps. They may invent creative Spanish names for streets, stores, or parks. Display the maps around the classroom.

Invitación Answers will vary.

 Leamos/Escribamos Work with a partner. Look at the new vocabulary on page 210 and make a list of three places where you both want to go. Then take turns inviting each other and accepting each other's invitations.

 ¡Conversación! Possible answers below.

Hablemos Con un/a compañero/a escoge una de estas situaciones y crea una conversación.

1. a. *Call and greet the person who answers.*
   b. *Say who's calling and ask to speak to your friend.*
   c. *Your friend's not there, so leave a message.*
   d. *Say goodbye to each other.*
2. a. *Call and greet your friend who answers.*
   b. *Invite your friend to go someplace with you.*
   c. *Your friend accepts your invitation.*
   d. *Say goodbye to each other.*

 Un fin de semana en Quito See note below.

Escribamos Look at Cristina's schedule for the weekend. There are a lot of fun and interesting things to do in Ecuador. Write your weekend schedule modeled after Cristina's schedule. Include the times for each day. Then, compare your schedule with a partner's.

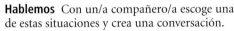

AGENDA

19	jueves	11:00 el museo 9:00 la fiesta de cumpleaños de Pablo
20	viernes	9:00 el zoológico 7:30 el teatro
21	sábado	10:00 el acuario 3:00 el parque de atracciones
22	domingo	12:00 el circo 4:00 el lago con Diego

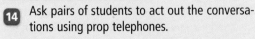

Communication for All Students

Kinesthetic Learners
14 Ask pairs of students to act out the conversations using prop telephones.

Slower Pace
15 Allow students time to prepare their schedules before getting together with a partner. Then have partners peer-edit each other's work.

Native Speakers
In their journals, have students list five Spanish words related to each of the vocabulary pictures. Then have them choose three words and create a short story. You might consider having students work in pairs to complete their stories.

Teaching Suggestion
14 Have students write some of the expressions they will need during the situation they choose.

Assess
▸ Testing Program, pp. 171–174
  Quiz 7-1A, Quiz 7-1B
  Audio CD 7, Tr. 18

▸ Student Make-Up Assignments, Chapter 7, Alternative Quiz

▸ Alternative Assessment Guide, p. 38

Answers
14 *Possible answer:*
1. —¿Bueno? —Buenos días, Sr. Montes. Soy yo, Margarita. ¿Está Eugenio? —Eugenio no está en casa. ¿Quieres dejar un recado? —Sí, por favor. Hay una fiesta en mi casa el sábado y quiero invitar a Eugenio. —Está bien. Adiós, Margarita. —Adiós, Sr. Montes.

15 *Answers will vary.* Students should include days, times, and location vocabulary. (**el teatro, el lago, el zoológico...**)

Bell Work

Write **¿En qué estación es el...?** and the dates **28 de diciembre, 5 de abril, 15 de julio, 3 de octubre,** and **16 de junio.**

Presenting
Así se dice

Ask comprehension questions about the cartoon.

Nota gramatical

Display the conjugation of **pensar.** Show the lack of stem change in **nosotros** and **vosotros** by drawing the "boot" around the other forms.

Segundo paso

Objectives Making plans; talking about getting ready

WV3 ECUADOR-7

Así se dice

Making plans

Pienso ir al zoológico hoy. **Voy a ver** muchos animales interesantes. ¿Te gustaría ir conmigo?

¡Cómo no! ¡Me gustan mucho los animales!

Nota gramatical

1. **Pensar** *(to think)* is another **e → ie** stem-changing verb.

   p**ie**nso, p**ie**nsas, p**ie**nsa, p**e**nsamos, p**e**nsáis, p**ie**nsan

   When followed by an infinitive, **pensar** means *to plan,* or *to intend* to do something.

   ¿Piensas jugar al tenis?
   Do you plan to play tennis?

2. You already know the verb **ir**. This verb can also be used to talk about the future, using the formula **ir + a +** infinitive.

   ¿Cuándo **vas a practicar** el piano?
   . . . are you going to practice . . .

   Voy a practicar mañana.
   I'm going to practice . . .

Cuaderno de gramática, pp. 56–57, Acts. 8–11

Cuaderno de actividades, pp. 77–78, Acts. 9–10

Más práctica gramatical, pp. 223–224, Acts. 3–5

---

16 **Gramática en contexto** Answers on p. 213.

Leamos/Escribamos There's a party tonight, but several people have other plans. Explain why they can't come by completing the passage with the correct forms of **pensar** or **ir**.

Pues, Manuel no puede ir porque ___1___ salir con unos amigos. Julio y yo ___2___ ir al museo. Lupe y Gabriel no van a ir porque ___3___ visitar el nuevo parque de atracciones. ¡Ellos ___4___ a pasar todo el día allí! Y Elisa ___5___ ir al teatro para ver un drama de Shakespeare. Y tú, ¿qué ___6___ a hacer?

Communication for All Students

Thinking Critically
Comparing and Contrasting Ask students to use what they already know about teens in Spanish-speaking countries to compare and contrast how the plans of such teens might be different from those of teenagers in the United States. Ask about part-time jobs, different sports, the use of an automobile, and so on.

Building on Previous Skills
Ask students to pick a destination in a Spanish-speaking country they have read about. Have them write a short paragraph in Spanish telling where they plan to go and at least three things that they would like to see there.

17 Gramática en contexto Possible answers below.

Escribamos ¿Qué vas a hacer? Escribe una frase para cada situación. Usa una forma de **ir** + **a** + el infinitivo del verbo.

1. Tienes un examen muy difícil mañana.
2. El próximo sábado hay una fiesta de cumpleaños para tu mejor amigo.
3. Quieres jugar al basquetbol pero no tienes zapatos.
4. Tus abuelos vienen a visitar y la casa está completamente desorganizada.
5. No hay comida en la casa.

 18 Y ustedes, ¿qué piensan hacer? Answers will vary.

Hablemos With a partner take turns asking each other what you and your friends plan to do at the times listed. Include where you're going to go or what you're going to do.

MODELO —¿Qué piensan hacer hoy?
—Hoy pensamos visitar el acuario.

hoy
este fin de semana

el sábado por la noche
el próximo (next) verano

el miércoles
el viernes por la mañana

mañana
el próximo domingo

Nota cultural

If you and a friend were making plans in Spain or Latin America, you probably would have to plan to get around without a car. There are several reasons for this. Cars are more expensive, so not all families have one. In some countries, you must be 18 years or older to get a driver's license. Finally, public transportation is inexpensive and convenient in most cities. In major cities, most people use the subway, taxis, buses, or **motos** (mopeds). Sometimes they just walk!

Segundo paso

CAPÍTULO 7

Slower Pace

18 If students have trouble recalling vocabulary, write some familiar activities on the board. (**esquiar, hacer ejercicios, leer, pescar, hacer un viaje, salir, visitar**) You might also have them work in groups to think about other words and phrases.

Additional Practice

18 After students have completed this activity, ask them to tell a partner how they plan to get to each of the activities they are planning. They might say **Pienso caminar a...** or **Pienso ir en el carro de mi amigo a...**

Answers
16 1. piensa
2. pensamos
3. piensan
4. van
5. piensa
6. vas

17 Possible answers:
1. Voy a estudiar esta noche.
2. Voy a asistir a la fiesta.
3. Voy a comprar unos zapatos.
4. Voy a organizar mi cuarto.
5. Voy a comprar comida.

Connections and Comparisons

Multicultural Link

Ask students to consider how the means of transportation in Spanish-speaking countries may have a connection to social life in these places. How many people are typically seen on the streets of the students' own town? Why do they think they are more likely to see people in the downtown areas than in suburbia? How does traveling alone by car rather than among other people on public transportation influence one's sociability positively or negatively? How might the means of transportation that one uses instill or detract from a distinct community awareness? Once ideas have been shared, have students write three ways their lives might be changed if they had access to public transportation. (more flexibility, easier to go places, less expensive)

Teaching Resources
pp. 212–215

PRINT 📖
▸ Lesson Planner, p. 34
▸ TPR Storytelling Book, pp. 26, 28
▸ Listening Activities, pp. 52, 56
▸ Activities for Communication, pp. 39–40, 106, 108–109, 149–150
▸ Cuaderno de gramática, pp. 56–58
▸ Grammar Tutor for Students of Spanish, Chapter 7
▸ Cuaderno de actividades, pp. 77–79
▸ Cuaderno para hispanohablantes, pp. 31–35
▸ Testing Program, pp. 175–178
▸ Alternative Assessment Guide, p. 38
▸ Student Make-Up Assignments, Chapter 7

MEDIA 💿📹🖼️
▸ One-Stop Planner
▸ Audio Compact Discs, CD 7, Trs. 6, 25–26, 19
▸ Teaching Transparencies 7-2; **Más práctica gramatical** Answers; Cuaderno de gramática Answers
▸ Interactive CD-ROM Tutor, Disc 2

Presenting
Así se dice,
Nota grammatical

Use props (comb, make-up, razor) to tell a story about what you and a friend need to do to get ready to go out. Have volunteers use the props to role-play the story as you repeat it.

Answers
20 *Answers will vary.* Students should include **necesito, todos los días, ¿a qué hora?, a veces, nunca,** days of the week, and other vocabulary learned so far.

Así se dice

Talking about getting ready

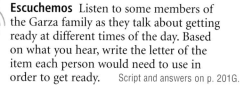

To ask if a friend is ready, say:

¿Estás listo/a?
Are you ready?

Your friend might answer:

No, **todavía necesito ducharme y afeitarme.**
. . . *I still need to shower and to shave.*

No, porque **necesito lavarme los dientes, peinarme** y **maquillarme.**
. . . *I need to brush my teeth, comb my hair, and put on makeup.*

No, **todavía necesito ponerme los zapatos.**
. . . *I still need to put on my shoes.*

Nota gramatical

A *reflexive verb* is a verb in which the action reflects back on the subject: *I bathe myself.* In Spanish, the infinitives of reflexive verbs have **se** attached to them (**afeitarse, ponerse**). The **se** changes according to the subject of the verb:

(Yo) necesito **ducharme.**
(Tú) necesitas **afeitarte.**
Juanito necesita **peinarse.**

Cuaderno de gramática, p. 58, Acts. 12–13

Más práctica gramatical, p. 224, Act. 6

19 **¿Todos listos?**

Escuchemos Listen to some members of the Garza family as they talk about getting ready at different times of the day. Based on what you hear, write the letter of the item each person would need to use in order to get ready. Script and answers on p. 201G.

CD 7 Tr. 6

a.  b.

c.  d.  e.

20 **Gramática en contexto** See note below.

 Escribamos/Hablemos Work with a partner. Each of you writes your daily routine, using **necesito** and the reflexive verbs you've just learned. Then ask each other questions about your daily routines. Include such phrases as **todos los días, ¿a qué hora?, a veces, nunca,** and days of the week.

MODELO Necesito peinarme.

Vocabulario extra

el cepillo	*brush*
el cepillo de dientes	*toothbrush*
el jabón	*soap*
el maquillaje	*makeup*
la navaja	*razor*
la pasta de dientes	*toothpaste*
el peine	*comb*

Connections and Comparisons

Language-to-Language

Point out that English uses reflexive pronouns much less frequently than Spanish. Write the following sentences on the board, and ask students to find two differences between the Spanish and English versions: **Sandra, ¿quieres lavarte el pelo?** *Sandra, do you want to wash your hair?* Students should point out that the Spanish reflexive pronoun has no equivalent in the English sentence, and that English uses a possessive with the body part, while Spanish uses the definite article.

21 **Gramática en contexto** Possible answers below.

Escribamos Escribe una oración para cada dibujo. Explica qué necesita hacer cada persona antes de salir.

el señor López

Ernesto

la señora López

Adela

22 **¡Vamos a celebrar!** See answers below.

Leamos/Escribamos Tonight's the big party! Read the invitation and answer the following questions. Then tell whether or not you would like to go and why or why not.

1. ¿Quién hace la fiesta?
2. ¿Dónde es?
3. ¿Dónde vive Ana?
4. ¿Cuál es la fecha de la fiesta?
5. ¿A qué hora empieza?
6. ¿Qué van a celebrar?
7. Son las cuatro de la tarde. ¿Qué vas a hacer antes de la fiesta? (ducharte, etc.)
8. ¿Qué piensas hacer en la fiesta?

Invitación para *Ana Macías Gómez*

Vamos a celebrar mi *cumpleaños*

con una fiesta en *mi casa*

el día *16* de *abril* a las *17h45*

calle *Independencia* número *35*

23 **¿Estás listo/a?**

Hablemos Work in a group of three. Discuss what you are going to do in order to get ready for each of the activities listed in the box.

una fiesta formal   las clases   ir al cine

ir al lago   un partido de fútbol   visitar a tus abuelos

salir con unos amigos   cenar en tu casa   un baile

una fiesta de cumpleaños

Communication for All Students

Native Speakers

Ask native speakers to work in a group to describe what they might do to get ready for a party. Have them compare and contrast their preparations for a formal party and a birthday party for a friend. You may wish to have students share the results of their discussion with the class.

Additional Practice

20 Ask students to tell their partner how their routine changes on Saturday and Sunday. **(Los sábados no tengo que maquillarme...)**

Answers

21 *Possible answers:*
El señor López necesita afeitarse.
Ernesto va a peinarse ahora.
La señora López necesita lavarse los dientes.
Adela va a maquillarse.

22 1. Ana Macías Gómez va a dar la fiesta.
2. Es en su casa.
3. Ana vive en la calle Independencia, número 35.
4. La fecha de la fiesta es el 16 de abril.
5. La fiesta empieza a las seis menos cuarto.
6. Van a celebrar su cumpleaños.
7. *Answers will vary.*
8. *Answers will vary.*

CAPÍTULO 7

Teaching Resources
p. 216

PRINT
▸ Video Guide, pp. 47–49, 52
▸ Cuaderno de actividades, p. 84
▸ Cuaderno para hispanohablantes, pp. 34–35

MEDIA
▸ One-Stop Planner
▸ Video Program, Videocassette 3, 14:27–17:10
▸ DVD Tutor, Disc 2
▸ Audio Compact Discs, CD 7, Trs. 7–10
▸ Interactive CD-ROM Tutor, Disc 2

Presenting
Panorama cultural

Show the video or play the audio, checking comprehension by asking the **Preguntas**. Students work in small groups to answer the questions in the **Para pensar y hablar...** section.

Preguntas

1. Cierto o falso: A Jessica le gusta llamar al chico primero. (falso)

2. Cierto o falso: A María Isabel le gustaría pagar la cita de vez en cuando. (cierto)

3. Cierto o falso: Rodrigo espera que sus amigos lo presenten a una chica. (falso)

4. ¿Qué les pide Rodrigo a las chicas? (su número telefónico)

5. Cierto o falso: A Jessica le gusta que sus amigas la presenten a un chico. (cierto)

6. Según las tres entrevistas, ¿quién paga la cita normalmente? (el chico)

CD 7
Trs. 7–10

¿Qué haces para conocer a una persona?

How would you ask someone out in a Spanish-speaking country? Who would pay for the date? We asked these students to tell us about dating customs in their countries.

CD 7 Tr. 8
Rodrigo
Quito, Ecuador
"Me le acerco, le pregunto su nombre, me presento y le pido su número telefónico, o algo así. Los hombres pagamos la cita en Ecuador".

Jessica CD 7 Tr. 9
San Miguel de Desamparados, Costa Rica
"Busco una persona amiga mía que me la presente. Él siempre paga la cita".

CD 7 Tr. 10
María Isabel
Sevilla, España
"Trato de que me lo presenten, y una vez que me lo presentan, pues trato de tener conversación con él. Me gusta que me inviten, pero yo también quiero; o sea, que me gusta invitar a mí también".

Para pensar y hablar...

A. In your opinion, which student has the best way of meeting someone new? Why? Who pays for dates according to these students? Why do you suppose that is, and how do you feel about it?

B. In small groups, talk about how you would meet someone you want to get to know. Compare what you would do to what these teens suggest, and write some similarities and differences between your ideas. Can you explain the differences? Be prepared to present your group's list to the class.

Cuaderno para hispanohablantes, pp. 34–35

Connections and Comparisons

Thinking Critically
Comparing and Contrasting Ask students to think about what the interviewees said about the males paying for the date. Do students imagine that customs vary by region? Who pays when they go out?

Language Note
Ask students to compare the interviewees' accents. What are some notable differences? Do they hear a unique sound in María Isabel's speech? (Her pronunciation of the **s** in **gusta** is unique to Seville.)

Así se dice

Turning down an invitation and explaining why

CD-ROM 2 / DVD 2

To find out if your friend would like to do something with you, say:

¿Te gustaría ir al museo de arte conmigo hoy?

Cuaderno de gramática, p. 59, Acts. 14–15

Your friend might say:

¡Qué lástima! Ya tengo planes. Tal vez otro día.
What a shame! I already have plans. Perhaps another day.

¿Hoy? **Lo siento,** pero no. Estoy **ocupado.** Tengo **una cita.**
I'm sorry . . . busy . . . a date (an appointment).

Lo siento hombre, pero **tengo prisa. Tengo que** trabajar.
. . . I'm in a hurry. I have to . . .

Me gustaría, pero no puedo. Estoy **cansado** y un poco **enfermo.**
I would like to, but I can't. . . . tired . . . sick.

También se puede decir...

Other words for **cansado** are **completamente muerto, agobiado, agotado, gastado,** and **rendido.**

24

¿Te gustaría...?

Escuchemos Listen as Margarita invites several friends to go with her to do some things. Match the name of the person with his or her explanation for not being able to go.

CD 7
Tr. 11

1. Miguel
2. Gabriela
3. Roberto
4. Mariana

a. Va a salir con otra persona.
b. Necesita descansar.
c. Necesita hacer sus lecciones.
d. Está ocupada este fin de semana.

Scripts and answers on p. 201H.

Nota gramatical

CD-ROM 2 / DVD 2

As you already know, **tener** means *to have.* But when used in certain phrases, it means *to be.* Do you remember **Tengo... años** (*I'm . . . years old*) from Chapter 1? Here are some expressions with **tener** you can use for excusing yourself.

tener ganas de + infinitive
to feel like (doing something)

tener prisa
to be in a hurry

tener que + infinitive
to have to (do something)

tener sueño
to be sleepy

Más práctica gramatical, p. 225, Acts. 7–8

Cuaderno de gramática, p. 60, Acts. 16–17

Cuaderno de actividades, pp. 81–82, Acts. 15–17

Teaching Resources
pp. 217–219

PRINT 📖

▸ Lesson Planner, p. 35
▸ TPR Storytelling Book, pp. 27, 28
▸ Listening Activities, pp. 53, 57
▸ Activities for Communication, pp. 41–42, 107, 108–109, 149–150
▸ Cuaderno de gramática, pp. 59–60
▸ Grammar Tutor for Students of Spanish, Chapter 7
▸ Cuaderno de actividades, pp. 80–82
▸ Cuaderno para hispanohablantes, pp. 31–35
▸ Testing Program, pp. 179–182
▸ Alternative Assessment Guide, p. 38
▸ Student Make-Up Assignments, Chapter 7

MEDIA 💿📹📼

▸ One-Stop Planner
▸ Audio Compact Discs, CD 7, Trs. 11–16, 27–28, 20
▸ Teaching Transparencies 7-3; **Más práctica gramatical** Answers; Cuaderno de gramática Answers
▸ Interactive CD-ROM Tutor, Disc 2

📁 Portfolio

26 Oral or Written Have students choose three of the activities and invent outrageous reasons for not doing them. Ask them to be creative. (**...voy a Japón, tengo que jugar con los Lakers de Los Ángeles...**) Have them enter these in their Portfolio as an oral or written entry. For Portfolio information, see *Alternative Assessment Guide,* pp. iv–17.

Additional Practice

26 Have students use the additional vocabulary on p. 186 and continue the activity.

---

25 Gramática en contexto Answers will vary. Possible answers in box.

Leamos/Escribamos Read the following conversations containing invitations. Complete the sentences with words or phrases from the box. Some blanks will have more than one correct answer.

— Hola, Paco, ¿ __1__ ir al cine esta noche?
— __2__ Roberto, pero __3__ . Tengo __4__ con Marilú.

— Marta, ¿ __5__ ir a comer esta tarde?
— Sí, __6__ . ¿A qué hora?

— Angélica, ¿ __7__ el tenis o el voleibol?
— Pues yo prefiero el voleibol.

— ¿ __8__ jugar el sábado?
— __9__ . Yo __10__ trabajar el sábado. Pero __11__ .

> quieres 1 5 8
> prefieres 7 · te gustaría 1 5 8
> Sí, muchísimas gracias 6
> ¡claro que sí! 6 · ¡qué lástima! 9
> lo siento pero no puedo 9
> me gustaría 2 · tal vez otro día 11
> una cita 4 · tengo que 10
> ¡cómo no! 6 · ya tengo planes 3 9

26 Gramática en contexto Answers will vary.

 Hablemos Imagine that you've been invited to do the following activities, but you don't want to do any of them. Take turns inviting your partner and declining the invitations. Offer a different explanation for each one, using an expression with **tener.**

1. ir al museo de historia
2. estudiar para el examen de álgebra
3. ir al concierto de violín
4. comer en la casa del profesor
5. ir a un partido de fútbol
6. estudiar en la biblioteca

> ### A lo nuestro
>
> **Ya** is usually translated as *already,* but it can mean several different things. If someone wants to say *I'm on my way,* they'd use **Ya voy.** If someone asks if you're ready, you can answer **ya** *(just a minute)* or **todavía no** *(not yet).* If you're being lectured and you're tired of listening, you might say **¡Ya, ya!** *(All right, already!)* or **¡Basta ya!** *(Enough!)*

27 Gracias, pero...

 Escribamos Sergio está muy ocupado y no tiene tiempo para pasar el rato con amigos. Escribe lo que dice en cada dibujo. Usa expresiones con **tener.**

a. Tengo prisa.

b. No tengo ganas de jugar.

c. Tengo que estudiar ahora.

Communication for All Students

Additional Practice

Have students complete **En contexto** for Chapter 7 on the *Interactive CD-ROM Program,* Disc 2. This activity provides further practice with many of the functions, grammar, and vocabulary in this chapter. In this simulated conversation, students help a teenager make plans for the weekend.

Challenge

27 Ask students to form pairs and create a brief but complete dialogue for one of the three scenes illustrated and present it to the class.

28 Pretextos

Escribamos/Hablemos Choose a picture from Activity 27 and create a conversation between Sergio and the other person in the picture. You might ask a classmate to help you present the conversation to the class.

29 En mi cuaderno See note below.

Escribamos You've just received an invitation from a friend to do something on Saturday night. Write a short reply in which you decline the invitation, give an explanation, and tell your friend what you plan to do instead. Use the **modelo** to help you get started.

MODELO

> Querido Julio,
> Gracias por la invitación, pero...

30

 **Del colegio al trabajo** Answers will vary.

Hablemos You work in a video store. You're scheduled to work on Sunday but you want to go to your sister's graduation party (**fiesta de graduación**) that day. With a partner role-play a conversation between you and the manager. Explain to your manager why you can't work that day. Your manager asks what other day(s) and times you can work that week. Together, come to an agreement on your schedule.

LETRA Y SONIDO

CD 7
Trs. 12–16

A. 1. The letters **ll** and **y** are usually pronounced alike. Their pronunciation in many Spanish-speaking countries is similar to the *y* in the English word *yes*.

yo	yate	yema	yugo	yerno
llamo	lleva	llora	maquillaje	toalla

2. The single **l** in Spanish is pronounced like the *l* in the English word *live*. Keep the tip of the tongue behind the upper teeth when pronouncing **l**.

zoológico	lavarse	levantarse	¡Qué lástima!
lo siento	el lago	Aló	línea

B. Dictado Script for Part B on page 201H.
Lalo is trying to make plans with his friends. Write what he says.

C. Trabalenguas
La nublada neblina lava las lomas de un lugar lejano.

Tercer paso

CAPÍTULO 7

Speaking Assessment
Before the students present Activity 30 to the class, have each group evaluate another. Explain the assessment mode before they act out their scenes. You may wish to evaluate their performance using the following rubric.

Speaking Rubric	Points			
	4	3	2	1
Content (Complete–Incomplete)				
Comprehension (Total–Little)				
Comprehensibility (Comprehensible–Incomprehensible)				
Accuracy (Accurate–Seldom accurate)				
Fluency (Fluent–Not fluent)				

18–20: A	14–15: C	Under
16–17: B	12–13: D	12: F

Assess
▶ Testing Program, pp. 179–182
Quiz 7-3A, Quiz 7-3B
Audio CD 7, Tr. 20

▶ Student Make-Up Assignments, Chapter 7, Alternative Quiz

▶ Alternative Assessment Guide, p. 38

Cultures and Communities

Language Note
Ya has several common and useful functions. **Ya no** is used to express an action that is no longer carried out: **Mario ya no mira dibujos animados.** Many native speakers say it to show that they have understood and agree with what someone has just said: **Ya, tienes razón.** Ya also serves to support what has been said in phrases like **Ya veo, ya entiendo.** It is also used to form

the conjunction **ya que**, meaning "because" or "since": **Ya que no tenemos el examen, podemos ir al cine.** Have pairs of students talk about things that they no longer do with **ya no**, and say why they do not, using **ya que.** They can respond to each other's explanations with **Ya, ya veo**, or **ya entiendo.** Have students present their dialogues to the class.

Answers
29 Answers should include **pero** + *explanation* and **pienso** + *infinitive.*

CAPÍTULO 7

Teaching Resources
pp. 220–221

PRINT
- Lesson Planner, p. 36
- Cuaderno de actividades, p. 83
- Cuaderno para hispanohablantes, pp. 31–32
- Reading Strategies and Skills Handbook, Chapter 7
- ¡Lee conmigo! 1, Chapter 7
- Standardized Assessment Tutor, Chapter 7

MEDIA
- One-Stop Planner

Prereading
Activity A

Making Predictions
Have students preview the readings. Then ask a few students to tell you briefly what they think the readings are about. Ask them how they figured this out. What clues did students get from prereading?

Answers

B 1. In El Cafélibro you can hear national music and poetry. There is also a drawing workshop for youths between 13 and 17 yrs. old.
2. In El Patio de Diversiones there is a mime performance. The marionetas ANGELONI are a puppet show with music and comedy.
3. In the Cafélibro you can listen to jazz. The latest concert in the Coliseo Rumiñahui with Miguel Bosé starts at 8:00 P.M. Concerts in the U.S. usually begin around 8:00 P.M.
4. In the Normandie Cocina they serve French food. In the Restaurante La Choza they serve Ecuadorean food. There is a buffet in the Restaurante Rincón La Ronda.

Vamos a leer

Caleidoscopio

Estrategia para leer
An important strategy is to preview a reading passage by using titles, subtitles, and pictures to tell what it is about. Previewing a passage will give you a feel for its purpose, form, and content.

¡A comenzar!
If you were in Quito making plans with your friends, chances are you'd want to find out what there is to do. But before planning anything, you'd need to know what is going on in the city.

A. Based on what you see, what do you think the **Caleidoscopio** section is?
   1. a concert program
   2. a listing of restaurant reviews
   3. a general entertainment guide
   4. a movie magazine with film reviews

¿Te acuerdas?
Scan for specific information

You have already studied scanning, an important way to find information. When you scan, look only for specific pieces of information. Look for one thing at a time, and don't concern yourself with the rest of the information.

Al grano See answers below.
B. Suppose you're in Quito with a group from your school. To find out what's going on, scan the **Caleidoscopio** section to answer these questions.

Caleidoscopio
DIVERSIONES

Circo Payaso
Un nuevo concepto en circo
lunes a viernes: 17h30 y 19h30
sábados: 15h00 - 17h30 y 19h30
domingos: 15h00 - 17h30 y 19h30
Avenida de la Independencia.

El Cafélibro
Peña cultural quiteña con anécdotas, música y poesía nacional. Participación espontánea de los asistentes.

En el Museo de Arte Moderno de la Casa de la Cultura Ecuatoriana
Se abrirá un taller juvenil de dibujo para chicos entre los 13 y los 17 años que se llevará a cabo de miércoles a viernes de 10h00 a 12h00.

TEATRO

Teatro República
presenta el gran espectáculo de teatro y marionetas ANGELONI CÓMICO, MUSICAL sábado y domingo 11:00 - 14:30 - 16:30 horas $ 3.00.

El mimo Pepe Velásquez
presenta su nueva obra "Risas y más" en el Patio de diversiones, de jueves a domingo, a las 20h00.

Communication for All Students

Native Speakers
Ask native speakers to gather information on a Hispanic singer or theater actor. Have them research individuals to find out where they are from, how they got started in their career, and what they do now. You might also ask students to find out whether the person they are researching is performing anywhere near them soon. Have them report what they find out to the class.

Thinking Critically
Drawing Inferences Ask students to compare and contrast the restaurant hours in Ecuador with those in the United States. What can they infer about when people eat in Ecuador? (They will learn more about this in Chapter 8.)

CONCIERTOS

Concierto de jazz
con Larry Salgado y su grupo.
Desde las 18h00 en el Cafélibro
(Almagro y Pradera).

Banda sinfónica municipal
Concierto de aniversario el jueves
a las 19h30 en el Teatro Nacional.

¡El concierto del año!
El viernes a las 20h00 en el
Coliseo Rumiñahui el cantante español,
Miguel Bosé.

RESTAURANTES

Restaurante La Choza,
El Palacio de la Cocina Ecuatoriana.
12 de Octubre No. 1955 y Cordero. Tels: 230-839
y 507-901 Quito. Atención de lunes a viernes de
12 p.m. a 3.30 p.m. y de 7 p.m. a 9.30 p.m. Sábados
y domingos de 12 p.m. a 4 p.m.

Normandie Cocina
francesa clásica. Lunes a viernes, almuerzo
12h30 a 14h30; y cena de 19h30 a 22h30. Sábados,
sólo cena de 19h30 a 22h30. Leónidas Plaza 1048
entre Baquerizo y García (atrás del teatro Fénix).
Tels: 233116, 507747 Quito

La Guarida del Coyote.
Antojitos mexicanos. Bar restaurante
mexicano. –Carrión 619 y Juan León Mera–Japón
542 y Naciones Unidas, Quito

Restaurante Rincón La Ronda.
La mejor comida nacional e internacional,
abierto los 365 días del año. Disfrute de nuestro
tradicional buffet familiar todos los domingos.
Belo Horizonte 400 y Almagro. Tels: 540459,
545176 Quito

---

1. Where can you hear national music and poetry? What's going on at the Museum of Modern Art?
2. Where can you see a mime perform? Which event is a musical comedy?
3. Where can you listen to jazz? Which concert begins the latest and when does it start? When do concerts in the U.S. usually begin?
4. Which restaurant serves French food? What kind of food is served in **Restaurante La Choza?** Which restaurant has a buffet?

C. Imagine you're standing in line at a tourist information desk in Quito. What do you think the clerk would suggest from the listings for each person or group? Explain why it would be appropriate. See answers below.
   1. a family that likes animals, clowns, etc.
   2. a young boy who enjoys puppet shows
   3. a family that wants to try typical Ecuadorean food
   4. a young woman who is interested in hearing Spanish music
   5. a woman who likes to draw and do artwork

D. Imagínate que estás en Quito con un grupo de turistas y ustedes tienen tres días libres. ¿Qué piensan hacer? Usa la guía para decidir qué lugares, restaurantes y atracciones piensan visitar. Invita a un compañero o compañera a algunos lugares que quieres visitar. Si quieres ir, acepta la invitación. Si no quieres ir, dale una excusa y dile qué prefieres hacer. Al final, hagan una lista de seis actividades que quieren hacer juntos.

Cuaderno para hispanohablantes, pp. 31–33

Cuaderno de actividades, p. 83, Act. 19

Connections and Comparisons

Language-to-Language
Point out that, as in English, many words in Spanish are derivatives of other words with similar meanings. For example, the word **asistente** comes from **asistir,** *to attend.* Knowing this, students may be able to deduce that **asistente** means *attendant.* Tell them that **cantante** comes from the verb **cantar** *(to sing)* and ask if they can deduce its meaning.

Culture Note
In Spain and many Latin American countries, the 24-hour clock is used for transportation timetables and entertainment listings. Ask students what time a movie starts if the 24-hour listing is 20h25. (las veinte y veinticinco, or 8:25 P.M.)

Reading
Activities B and C

Establishing a Purpose for Reading
Ask students to plan an extraordinary weekend for a friend who wants to experience as much as possible of Ecuadorean culture. Refer to the reading and have students write a letter to their friend telling him or her what they will be doing over the weekend, where they will go, and what time the events are.

Postreading
Activity D

Comparing and Contrasting
List some of the 24-hour times in the **Caleidoscopio** section on the board or a transparency. Ask students to give them in 12-hour times, referring to Chapter 3.

C 1. Circo Payaso. The circus usually has animals and clowns and is good family entertainment.
2. Teatro República. The marionette show is good for the young boy who likes puppet shows.
3. The Restaurante La Choza serves good Ecuadorean food.
4. El Coliseo Rumiñahui has Spanish music.
5. El Museo de Arte Moderno. Depending on her age, she may be able to participate in the workshop.

D *Answers will vary.*

Más práctica gramatical

CAPÍTULO 7

For **Más práctica gramatical**
Answer Transparencies, see the
Teaching Transparencies binder.

Más práctica gramatical

Primer paso

Objectives Talking on the telephone; extending and accepting invitations

1 Indica a qué hora todos vienen a la fiesta de sorpresa de Pedro. Usa la forma correcta de **venir**. (**p. 209**)

MODELO　　Felipe y Daniel/8:15
　　　　　　　Felipe y Daniel vienen a las ocho y cuarto.

1. Rebeca/8:00　　　　　　5. yo/7:50
2. ustedes/7:45　　　　　　6. Sonia y Yolanda/8:20
3. los padres de Pedro/8:10　　7. René/7:55
4. tú/8:05　　　　　　　　8. la abuela de Pedro/8:25

2 Tell what the following people like to do on vacation. Use the correct subject pronoun, the correct form of **preferir**, and the most logical expression from the box in each sentence. (**p. 209**)

MODELO　　A mis primos les gusta el baloncesto.
　　　　　　　Ellos prefieren ir al gimnasio.

ir a un concierto	comer en un restaurante	asistir a un partido
	nadar en la piscina	ir a la playa
ir al cine		
	dibujar en el parque	pasar el rato con sus amigos

1. A mi hermano le gusta bucear.
2. A mí me gusta la comida.
3. A todos nosotros nos gusta la música.
4. A mi padre le gusta el fútbol.
5. A mi hermana le gusta el arte.
6. A mis abuelos les gustan las películas.
7. A mis hermanas les gusta hablar.
8. A ti te gusta la natación.

Answers

1
1. Rebeca viene a las ocho.
2. Ustedes vienen a las ocho menos cuarto.
3. Los padres de Pedro vienen a las ocho y diez.
4. Tú vienes a las ocho y cinco.
5. Yo vengo a las ocho menos diez.
6. Sonia y Yolanda vienen a las ocho y veinte.
7. René viene a las ocho menos cinco.
8. La abuela de Pedro viene a las ocho y veinticinco.

2
1. Él prefiere ir a la playa.
2. Yo prefiero comer en un restaurante.
3. Nosotros preferimos ir a un concierto.
4. Él prefiere asistir a un partido.
5. Ella prefiere dibujar en el parque.
6. Ellos prefieren ir al cine.
7. Ellas prefieren pasar el rato con sus amigos.
8. Tú prefieres nadar en la piscina.

Grammar Resources for Chapter 7

The **Más práctica gramatical** activities are designed as supplemental activities for the grammatical concepts presented in the chapter. You might use them as additional practice, for review, or for assessment.

For more grammar presentations, review, and practice, refer to the following:
• Cuaderno de gramática
• Grammar Tutor for Students of Spanish

• Grammar Summary on pp. R9–R13
• Cuaderno de actividades
• Grammar and Vocabulary quizzes (Testing Program)
• Test Generator on the One-Stop Planner CD-ROM
• Interactive CD-ROM Tutor
• **Juegos interactivos** at **go.hrw.com.**

3   Pregunta o indica adónde piensan ir todos el sábado. Usa la forma correcta de **pensar** en cada oración. (**p. 212**)

MODELO   Alberto/lago
               Alberto piensa ir al lago.

1. mis primos y yo/parque de atracciones
2. Patricia y su familia/campo
3. David/acuario
4. ¿tú/playa?
5. yo/zoológico
6. ¿ustedes/restaurante chino?

4   Ask what the following people are going to do this weekend, based on their interests. Use the correct form of **ir + a** and an expression from the box in each question. (**p. 212**)

MODELO   Nélida y Luz bucean todos los fines de semana.
               ¿Ellas van a nadar en el lago?

asistir al teatro	visitar el acuario	ir al campo
ir al museo visitar el zoológico	nadar en el lago	

1. Olga tiene muchos peces.
2. Tu clase favorita es el arte, ¿verdad?
3. Carmelo quiere ser actor.
4. Iván y Julio quieren acampar este fin de semana.
5. A Paco y a Tere les gustan los animales.

Teacher to Teacher

Alisa Glick
Greenwich Country
Day School
Greenwich, Connecticut

Alisa's students use skills as exit passes
"As the students are leaving the classroom, ask them a question related to points covered in the **Pasos**. You might ask **¿Te gustaría ir al museo conmigo hoy?** Before being dismissed, the student must say **"Lo siento. Ya tengo planes,"** or another appropriate response. I change the question slightly with each exiting student to make sure that each has mastered the material and has been given individual attention. **"**

Answers

3   1. Mis primos y yo pensamos ir al parque de atracciones.
2. Patricia y su familia piensan ir al campo.
3. David piensa ir al acuario.
4. ¿Piensas ir a la playa?
5. Pienso ir al zoológico.
6. ¿Piensan Uds. ir al restaurante chino?

4   1. ¿Ella va a visitar el acuario?
2. ¿Vas a ir al museo?
3. ¿Él va a asistir al teatro?
4. ¿Ellos van a ir al campo?
5. ¿Ellos van a visitar el zoológico?

CAPÍTULO 7

For **Más práctica gramatical** Answer Transparencies, see the *Teaching Transparencies* binder.

5 Your cousin Joaquín has a full week planned during your visit at the beach. Use the calendar below to tell what you and Joaquín will do each day, and where you plan to go each evening. Use **ir** + **a** + infinitive and **pensar** + infinitive. (**p. 212**)

MODELO   El lunes, vamos a bucear. Por la noche, pensamos ir a la pizzería.

LUNES	MARTES	MIÉRCOLES	JUEVES	VIERNES	SÁBADO	DOMINGO
bucear	correr por la playa	jugar al voleibol	pescar	descansar	visitar el acuario	asistir al partido de fútbol
pizzería	parque de atracciones	concierto de salsa	restaurante mexicano	fiesta de cumpleaños	centro comercial	cine

1. El martes...   **4.** El viernes...

2. El miércoles...   **5.** El sábado...

3. El jueves...   **6.** El domingo...

6 Everyone prefers a different morning routine. State the sequence the following people prefer, using the correct form of **preferir** and the order listed in parentheses in each sentence. (**p. 214**)

MODELO   Emma (c, d, e)
Primero, Emma prefiere lavarse los dientes. Luego,
prefiere maquillarse y después peinarse.

a. ducharse   **b.** afeitarse   **c.** lavarse los dientes   **d.** maquillarse   **e.** peinarse

1. yo (a, c, e)   **3.** papá (a, b, e)

2. tú (c, a, b)   **4.** mamá (c, a, d)

Answers

5 1. El martes, vamos a correr por la playa. Por la noche, pensamos ir al parque de atracciones.
2. El miércoles, vamos a jugar al voleibol. Por la noche, pensamos ir a un concierto de salsa.
3. El jueves, vamos a pescar. Por la noche, pensamos ir a un restaurante mexicano.
4. El viernes, vamos a descansar. Por la noche, pensamos ir a una fiesta de cumpleaños.
5. El sábado, vamos a visitar el acuario. Por la noche, pensamos ir al centro comercial.
6. El domingo, vamos a asistir al partido de fútbol. Por la noche, pensamos ir al cine.

6 1. Primero, prefiero ducharme. Luego, prefiero lavarme los dientes y después peinarme.
2. Primero, prefieres lavarte los dientes. Luego, prefieres ducharte y después afeitarte.
3. Primero, papá prefiere ducharse. Luego, prefiere afeitarse y después peinarse.
4. Primero, mamá prefiere lavarse los dientes. Luego, prefiere ducharse y después maquillarse.

Communication for All Students

Slower Pace

6 Remind students that the pronouns **me, te,** and **se** are attached to the verb (**lavarme, ducharte, afeitarse**) and that these pronouns agree with the subject of the sentence. Review the sequencing words **primero, luego,** and **después.** Model examples such as **Primero, yo prefiero lavarme.** Have students work in pairs to read and explain their answers to each other.

Challenge

7 Have pairs of students create a brief dialogue indicating a need of some kind. —¿**Qué te pasa, Diego? —Pues, estoy muy cansado.** Students will say **Diego tiene que dormir más,** or any comment that expresses the need, using **tener que** + infinitive. The student who states the need then presents his or her dialogue with a partner for the class to solve.

Tercer paso

Objective Turning down an invitation and explaining why

7 Explica por qué algunos de los invitados a la fiesta de María no pueden ir. Usa la forma correcta de **tener que** + infinitivo en cada oración. (**p. 217**)

MODELO **Virginia/ir a una boda**
Virginia tiene que ir a una boda.

1. yo/visitar a mis tíos
2. Nelson y Sonia/trabajar
3. tú/cuidar a tu hermanita
4. Raúl/cenar en casa de sus abuelos
5. Santiago/jugar en un partido de fútbol
6. Emilia y yo/asistir a una clase de baile

8 It's a typical Saturday for the Aguilar family. Complete the description of their activities by filling in each blank with the correct form of a **tener** expression from the box. (**p. 217**)

MODELO **La ropa de Manolo está encima de su cama y hay muchos papeles y revistas en su cuarto.**
Manolo tiene que organizar su cuarto ahora.

tener ganas de	tener que
tener prisa	tener sueño

1. Isa y Lourdes leen el periódico para ver qué películas hay esta noche.
   Ellas ______ ir al cine.
2. El perro necesita salir.
   Nosotros ______ caminar con el perro ahora.
3. Son las diez de la noche. Papá quiere descansar en el sofá.
   Él ______.
4. Son las 4:10. Marta tiene una clase de ejercicios aeróbicos a las 4:15.
   Ella ______.
5. Lourdes y yo queremos cenar en un restaurante esta noche.
   No ______ preparar la cena.

Review and Assess

You may wish to assign the **Más práctica gramatical** activities as additional practice or homework after presenting material throughout the chapter. Assign Activities 1–2 after **Gramática** (p. 209), Activities 3–5 after **Nota gramatical** (p. 212), Activity 6 after **Nota gramatical** (p. 214), and Activities 7–8 after **Nota gramatical** (p. 217).

To prepare students for the **Paso** Quizzes and Chapter Test, have them do the **Más práctica gramatical** activities in the following order: complete Activities 1–2 before taking Quiz 7-1A or 7-1B; Activities 3–6 before taking Quiz 7-2A or 7-2B; and Activities 7–8 before taking Quiz 7-3A or 7-3B.

Más práctica gramatical

CAPÍTULO 7

Answers

7
1. Tengo que visitar a mis tíos.
2. Nelson y Sonia tienen que trabajar.
3. Tienes que cuidar a tu hermanita.
4. Raúl tiene que cenar en casa de sus abuelos.
5. Santiago tiene que jugar en un partido de fútbol.
6. Emilia y yo tenemos que asistir a una clase de baile.

8
1. tienen ganas de
2. tenemos que
3. tiene sueño
4. tiene prisa
5. tenemos ganas de

CAPÍTULO 7

The **Repaso** reviews all four skills and culture in preparation for the Chapter Test.

Teaching Resources
pp. 226–227

PRINT

▶ Lesson Planner, p. 36
▶ Listening Activities, p. 53
▶ Video Guide, pp. 47–49, 52
▶ Grammar Tutor for Students of Spanish, Chapter 7
▶ Cuaderno para hispanohablantes, pp. 31–35
▶ Standardized Assessment Tutor, Chapter 7

MEDIA

▶ One-Stop Planner
▶ Video Program, Videocassette 3, 17:11–17:57
▶ DVD Tutor, Disc 2
▶ Audio Compact Discs, CD 7, Tr. 17
▶ Interactive CD-ROM Tutor, Disc 2

MARCAR: go.hrw.com
PALABRA CLAVE:
WV3 ECUADOR-7

1 First read the following explanations. Then listen to the conversations and choose the sentence that best describes the response to each invitation. Script and answers on p. 201H.

CD 7
Tr. 17

1. **a.** No puede ir porque tiene que practicar el piano.
   b. No puede ir porque está enferma.

2. **a.** No puede ir al campo porque tiene otros planes.
   b. No puede ir al museo porque tiene otros planes.

3. **a.** Quiere ir a caminar más tarde.
   b. No quiere ir porque está cansado.

4. **a.** Tiene ganas de ir al partido de fútbol.
   b. No puede ir porque tiene una cita.

2 Working in groups of three, take turns looking at the picture and inviting your partners to go to the places shown. Each person should either accept the invitation or decline it. If you decline an invitation, you should explain why or tell what you prefer to do.

3 Responde a las siguientes oraciones con **cierto** o **falso**. Corrige las oraciones falsas.
1. En todos los países hispanohablantes, tienes que tener veintiún años para obtener una licencia de manejar.
2. Muchos jóvenes en los países en Latinoamérica tienen coches.
3. El transporte público es barato en España y en Latinoamérica.

Apply and Assess

Additional Practice

2 Have students write a paragraph describing what people in this town do in their free time. Include as much detail as possible, such as what they like and dislike doing, show times, the cost of tickets, where people go on dates, and how the weather affects people's plans.

Challenge

2 Have students suggest alternatives to the invitations they decline. They may offer alternate times or activities.

Answers

3 1. Falso; En algunos países hispano-hablantes hay que tener 18 años para obtener una licencia de manejar.
2. Falso; Muchas personas en los países de Latinoamérica no tienen carros porque son muy caros.
3. Cierto

STANDARDS: 1.1, 1.2, 1.3

4 La familia de Elena tiene que prepararse para salir. Lee la conversación y contesta las preguntas.

ELENA   A ver... Papá todavía necesita ducharse y afeitarse. Y después, yo tengo que ducharme. Susi, ¿piensas lavarte los dientes ahora o más tarde?

SUSI   Ahora. Y también necesito maquillarme.

ELENA   Ah, mira el pelo de Manolín. ¡Es un desastre! Debe peinarse ahora mismo.

1. ¿Quién necesita maquillarse?

2. ¿Qué tiene que hacer el padre de Elena?

3. ¿Cómo está el pelo de Manolín? ¿Qué necesita hacer?

4. ¿Quiénes tienen que ducharse?

Vamos a escribir

Write two paragraphs about your weekly activities. Use the art and **Vocabulario** on pages 210, 215, and 218 for ideas, and connect your ideas in chronological order.

> **Estrategia para escribir**
> Connecting words unify sentences in a paragraph by joining thoughts together in a logical way. For example, the words **primero, luego, antes (de), después (de),** and **por fin** help you describe a sequence of events that your reader can easily understand.

Primero, el lunes tengo que...
Luego necesito estudiar para un
* examen el miércoles.*
Por fin, el domingo me gustaría ir a...
Antes de ir quiero...

1. Make a list of the things you have to do during the week. Put them in order.

2. List some activities you'd like to do this weekend, and put them in order too.

3. Now combine the items on your list into a paragraph. Read your paragraph all the way through to make sure the ideas are in logical order, and that you've used the appropriate connecting words.

6 ## Situación

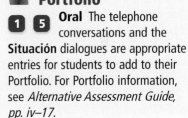

Your Great-Aunt Hortensia has invited you to an accordion concert (**concierto de acordeón**) this Saturday. You already have plans to go out with your friends, but you don't want to hurt her feelings. With a classmate, take turns role-playing a conversation between you and your **tía abuela** Hortensia. Politely turn down her invitation and explain why, but remember to thank her for inviting you.

Cuaderno para hispanohablantes, p. 35

Apply and Assess

Process Writing

5 • As a prewriting exercise, suggest that students diagram their list of activities on a horizontal timeline. Have them note on the timeline where they will use connecting words.

• Remind students that they can use many phrases to help them organize their paragraphs. For instance, **por la mañana** is useful, as are **a las diez de la mañana,** and **después de clase.**

Repaso

CAPÍTULO 7

Teacher Note
To reduce students' fears of speaking Spanish, illustrate that there are many ways to say the same thing. Write an English word on the board and draw a sun around it. Draw several rays coming from the sun. At the ends of the rays, write Spanish synonyms for the English word. For example, if the word you write in the center is TRUE, the Spanish words could include **verdad, cierto, preciso, correcto, verdadero.** You might make this a contest between groups to see who can come up with the most synonyms.

Portfolio

1 **5** **Oral** The telephone conversations and the **Situación** dialogues are appropriate entries for students to add to their Portfolio. For Portfolio information, see *Alternative Assessment Guide,* pp. iv–17.

Answers
4 1. Susi necesita maquillarse.
2. Tiene que ducharse y afeitarse.
3. Su pelo es un desastre. Tiene que peinarse.
4. Elena y su papá tienen que ducharse.

Teaching Resources
p. 228

PRINT
▶ Grammar Tutor for Students of Spanish, Chapter 7

MEDIA
▶ Interactive CD-ROM Tutor, Disc 2
▶ Online self-test

 go.hrw.com
WV3 ECUADOR–7

Teacher Note
This page is intended to prepare students for the Chapter Test. It is a brief checklist of the major points covered in the chapter. The students should be reminded that it is a checklist only and does not necessarily include everything that will appear on the Chapter Test.

Answers

1 *Possible answer:*
—Aló, buenas tardes.
—¿De parte de quién?
—Lo siento, está ocupada.
—Sí, cómo no.

2 *Possible answers:*
1. —¿Te gustaría ir conmigo al cine?
   —Sí, me gustaría ir contigo.
2. —¿Quieres salir con nosotros esta noche? —¡Claro que sí!
3. —¿Te gustaría ir a un restaurante conmigo? —Sí, me gustaría ir contigo.
4. —¿Le gustaría cenar con mi familia mañana? —¡Claro que sí!
5. —¿Te gustaría jugar al tenis con nosotros? —Sí, me gustaría jugar con ustedes.
6. —Te invito a la fiesta de cumpleaños de Luisa, ¿quieres ir? —Claro que sí.

5 *Possible answers:*
1. Me gustaría ir a la fiesta, pero no puedo. Estoy cansada.
2. Hoy no puedo ir. Tengo que hacer mi tarea.
3. ¡Qué lástima! Ya tenemos otros planes.

Can you talk on the telephone? p. 207

1 You're answering phones at the office at your school. What would you say in the following situation? See possible answer below.
El teléfono suena.

Tú ═══════
Sr. Gibson   Buenas tardes. ¿Está la profesora Margarita Gibson, por favor?
Tú ═══════
Sr. Gibson   De parte de su esposo.
Tú ═══════
Sr. Gibson   ¿Puedo dejar un recado?
Tú ═══════

Can you extend and accept invitations? p. 208

2 How would you invite the following people to do something with you? How might they accept your invitation? See possible answers below.
1. tu mejor amigo/a   3. uno de tus padres   5. tu primo/a
2. tu hermano/a   4. tu profesor/a   6. tu novio/a

Can you make plans? p. 212

3 What do you plan to do this weekend? Give specific days, times, and places you plan to go, people you plan to see, and things you plan to do. Answers will vary.

Can you talk about getting ready? p. 214

4 What do you usually need to do to get ready in these situations? Answers will vary.
1. para ir al colegio   4. para ir a una boda
2. para salir con amigos   5. para hacer un viaje al campo
3. para ir a una fiesta formal   6. para ir al teatro

Can you turn down an invitation and explain why? p. 217

5 How would you turn down the following invitations? See possible answers below.
1. your friend invites you to a surprise birthday party for his four-year-old brother
2. your parents invite you to go to the theater with them
3. your teacher invites you and your parents to go to the amusement park with him and his family

6 Regina is a new girl at school, and Samuel wants to get to know her better. Unfortunately, she has a different excuse for everything he asks her to do. What are some of her excuses? Answers will vary.
1. Regina, ¿quieres ir al partido de béisbol del colegio el viernes después de clase?
2. ¿Quieres ir al zoológico el sábado?
3. Entonces, ¿te gustaría estudiar juntos el domingo por la tarde?

Review and Assess

Challenge
5 Ask students to make a schedule of after-school and weekend activities using Spanish vocabulary they know. Have students work in pairs to invite each other to go to activities listed on the schedules. When one partner makes an invitation, the other will decline and refer to the activity in his or her schedule as an explanation. (—¿Quieres ir al cine el viernes? —Me gustaría ir, pero **voy a la fiesta de Pablo.**) For highly motivated learners, suggest that the after-school schedule include activities at a specific time of day. Students could also continue the conversation by offering to accept the invitation for another day or time. (**No puedo ir el viernes a las seis, pero me gustaría ir el sábado después de las siete.**)

Vocabulario

Primer paso

Talking on the telephone

Aló.	Hello.
¿De parte de quién?	Who's calling?
Diga.	Hello.
Está bien.	All right.
La línea está ocupada.	The line is busy.
Llamo más tarde.	I'll call later.
un momento	one moment
¿Puedo dejar un recado?	May I leave a message?

Extending and accepting invitations

el acuario	aquarium
la boda	wedding

el campo	country
el circo	circus
la ciudad	city
¡Claro que sí!	Of course!
empezar (ie)	to begin
el evento	event
la fiesta de...	anniversary party
aniversario	
de cumpleaños	birthday party
de graduación	graduation party
de sorpresa	surprise party
el lago	lake
el lugar	place
Me gustaría...	I would like . . .
el museo de antropología	anthropology museum

Nos gustan...	We like . . .
el parque de atracciones	amusement park
preferir (ie)	to prefer
¿Quieres + infinitive?	Do you want to . . .?
¿Te gustaría...?	Would you like . . .?
Te invito.	It's my treat.
el teatro	theater
venir (ie)	to come
el zoológico	zoo

Segundo paso

Making plans

¡Cómo no!	Of course!
ir + a + infinitive	to be going to (do something)
pensar (ie) + infinitive	to plan, to intend

Talking about getting ready

afeitarse	to shave
ducharse	to take a shower
estar listo/a	to be ready
lavarse los dientes	to brush your teeth

maquillarse	to put on makeup
peinarse	to comb your hair
ponerse	to put on (clothing)

Tercer paso

Turning down an invitation and explaining why

cansado/a	tired
una cita	a date, an appointment
enfermo/a	sick
Lo siento. No puedo.	I'm sorry. I can't.

ocupado/a	busy
¡Qué lástima!	What a shame!
tal vez otro día	perhaps another day
tener ganas de + infinitive	to feel like (doing something)

tener prisa	to be in a hurry
tener que + infinitive	to have to (do something)
tener sueño	to be sleepy
Ya tengo planes.	I already have plans.

Review and Assess

Game

La llamada Make an A set and a B set of cards, each with a telephone number written in numerals. Make a list of the numbers as well as one of major cities in Spain and Latin America. Divide the class into an A and B team, giving each member a card corresponding to his or her team. You will play the **operador/a** and call out a number from the list, to which the student with that card responds **Aló.** Then say **Tengo una llamada de...,** giving the name of a city on the list. The student responds **Está bien, una llamada de...,** repeating the city and adding the country. Team members get one point for recognizing their number and one for correctly identifying the country.

CAPÍTULO 7

 Circumlocution
Write the following phrases on the board: **hacer un viaje, escuchar música, hablar por teléfono, mirar la televisión, comer comida italiana.** Make a second column and write: **poner la mesa, limpiar la cocina, cuidar al gato, cortar el césped, organizar mi cuaderno.** Ask students to choose a phrase from the board and then describe it by using **tener ganas de** + infinitive and **tener que** + infinitive. They may not use any of the words from the phrase to communicate their ideas. For example, for **poner la mesa,** one could say **Tengo que encontrar los platos. Vamos a comer.** The class must guess what phrase each student is trying to communicate. You might offer a prize to the student with the most creative circumlocution. See page 167C for phrases students can use.

Teacher Note
Remind students of the Additional Vocabulary feature starting on page R5.

Chapter 7 Assessment

▶ **Testing Program**
Chapter Test, pp. 183–188
Audio Compact Discs, CD 7, Trs. 21–22
Speaking Test, p. 346

▶ **Alternative Assessment Guide**
Performance Assessment, p. 38
Portfolio Assessment, p. 24
CD-ROM Assessment, p. 52

▶ **Interactive CD-ROM Tutor, Disc 2**
 ¡A hablar!
¡A escribir!

▶ **Standardized Assessment Tutor**
Chapter 7

▶ **One-Stop Planner, Disc 2**
 Test Generator
Chapter 7

Capítulo 8: ¡A comer!
Chapter Overview

	FUNCTIONS	**GRAMMAR**	**VOCABULARY**	**RE-ENTRY**
Primer paso pp. 235–239	• Talking about meals and food, p. 235	• The verb **encantar** and indirect object pronouns, p. 236 • **o → ue** stem-changing verbs, p. 238	• Breakfast foods, p. 235 • Lunch foods, p. 237	• Expressing likes and dislikes (**Capítulo 3**) • **e → ie** stem-changing verbs (**Capítulo 7**)
Segundo paso pp. 240–243	• Commenting on food, p. 240	• Use of **estar** to talk about how things taste; **ser** to talk about generalizations, p. 240 • Expressions with **tener**, p. 241	• Commenting on food, p. 240 • Describing a restaurant, p. 242	• **ser, estar** (**Capítulo 3, Capítulo 4**) • Expressions with **tener** (**Capítulo 7**)
Tercer paso pp. 244–249	• Making polite requests, p. 244 • Ordering dinner in a restaurant, p. 246 • Asking for and paying the bill in a restaurant, p. 246	• **otro** and gender agreement, p. 244	• Tableware, p. 244 • Dinner foods, p. 245 • Numbers between 200–100,000, p. 247	• Question words ¿**qué?** and ¿**cuánto?** (**Capítulo 2**)

Letra y sonido p. 249	**Pronunciation of the letter c** Audio CD 8, Track 13	**Dictado** Audio CD 8, Tracks 14–16
Vamos a leer pp. 250–251	**Batidos y sorbetes**	**Reading Strategy:** Finding text organization
Más práctica gramatical	**pp. 252–255** **Primer paso,** pp. 252–253	**Segundo paso,** p. 254 **Tercer paso,** p. 255
Review pp. 256–259	**Repaso,** pp. 256–257 **Vamos a escribir,** p. 257 Finding good details	**A ver si puedo...,** p. 258 **Vocabulario,** p. 259

CULTURE

• **Nota cultural,** Breakfast, p. 237
• **Nota cultural,** Lunch, p. 238
• **Panorama cultural, ¿Cuál es un plato típico de tu país?,** p. 239
• **Nota cultural,** Common Andean dishes, p. 242

• **Encuentro cultural, La comida de las Américas,** p. 243
• **Nota cultural,** Dinner, p. 245
• **A lo nuestro,** Getting a waitperson's attention, p. 247
• **Nota cultural, tortillas,** p. 248
• **Nota cultural,** Table manners, p. 249

Capítulo 8: ¡A comer!
Chapter Resources

Lesson Planning

One-Stop Planner

Lesson Planner with Substitute Teacher Lesson Plans, pp. 38–42, 72

Student Make-Up Assignments
- Make-Up Assignment Copying Masters, Chapter 8

Listening and Speaking

TPR Storytelling Book, pp. 29–32

Listening Activities
- Student Response Forms for Listening Activities, pp. 59–61
- Additional Listening Activities 8-1 to 8-6, pp. 63–65
- Additional Listening Activities (song), p. 66
- Scripts and Answers, pp. 137–141

Video Guide
- Teaching Suggestions, pp. 53–55
- Activity Masters, pp. 56–58
- Scripts and Answers, pp. 102–104, 116

Activities for Communication
- Communicative Activities, pp. 43–48
- Realia and Teaching Suggestions, pp. 110–114
- Situation Cards, pp. 151–152

Reading and Writing

Reading Strategies and Skills Handbook, Chapter 8

¡Lee conmigo! 1, Chapter 8

Cuaderno de actividades, pp. 85–96

Grammar

Cuaderno de gramática, pp. 61–69

Grammar Tutor for Students of Spanish, Chapter 8

Assessment

Testing Program
- Grammar and Vocabulary Quizzes, **Paso** Quizzes, and Chapter Test, pp. 197–214
- Score Sheet, Scripts and Answers, pp. 215–222

Alternative Assessment Guide
- Portfolio Assessment, p. 25
- Performance Assessment, p. 39
- CD-ROM Assessment, p. 53

Student Make-Up Assignments
- Alternative Quizzes, Chapter 8

Standardized Assessment Tutor
- Reading, pp. 31–33
- Writing, p. 34
- Math, pp. 51–52

Native Speakers

Cuaderno para hispanohablantes, pp. 36–40

MEDIA

 Online Activities
- Juegos interactivos
- Actividades Internet

 Video Program
- Videocassette 3
- Videocassette 5 (captioned version)

 Interactive CD-ROM Tutor, Disc 2

 **DVD Tutor,** Disc 2

 Audio Compact Discs
- Textbook Listening Activities, CD 8, Tracks 1–18
- Additional Listening Activities, CD 8, Tracks 24–30
- Assessment Items, CD 8, Tracks 19–23

 Teaching Transparencies
- Situations 8-1 to 8-3
- Vocabulary 8-A to 8-D
- **De antemano**
- **Más práctica gramatical** Answers
- **Cuaderno de gramática** Answers

  One-Stop Planner CD-ROM

Use the **One-Stop Planner CD-ROM with Test Generator** to aid in lesson planning and pacing.

For each chapter, the **One-Stop Planner** includes:
- Editable lesson plans with direct links to teaching resources
- Printable worksheets from resource books
- Direct launches to the HRW Internet activities
- Video and audio segments
- Test Generator
- Clip Art for vocabulary items

Capítulo 8: ¡A comer!

Projects

Una fiesta internacional

In this project students plan a tasting party (una fiesta internacional) of everyday dishes from Spanish-speaking countries. They write invitations, accept invitations in role-played phone calls, cook, then sample dishes, converse in Spanish at the fiesta, and write thank-you notes.

MATERIALS

✄ **Students may need**
- Paper
- Markers
- Plates
- Drinking glasses
- Utensils
- Napkins

SUGGESTED SEQUENCE

1. Students work in groups of four. Each group selects a recipe to prepare. If students are unfamiliar with foods in Spanish-speaking countries, have them go to the library and research international cookbooks for recipe ideas. They could also search for ideas on the Internet.

2. Set a date for the **fiesta.**

3. Students divide the responsibilities for the preparation and decide how they will accomplish everything. Dishes are to be prepared outside of class. Students only need to prepare enough for everyone to have a taste.

4. Each student designs and writes an invitation in Spanish. Students exchange invitations with another group.

5. Pairs exchanging invitations act out calling each other to accept the invitation they have received. You might provide a series of questions or topics for students to discuss during the mock phone call. Their conversations might be recorded on audio or videotape for grading. Invitations are turned in.

6. At the **fiesta,** students sample the different items and use Spanish to converse and comment on the various dishes.

7. On the following day, students write a thank-you note in Spanish to the person who wrote to them.

GRADING THE PROJECT

Suggested point distribution: (total = 100 points)

Written invitation	10
Telephone conversation	20
Selecting recipe and preparing food	25
Using Spanish at fiesta	35
Thank-you note	10

Games

La vuelta al mundo

This is a fast vocabulary review game that is easy to set up and fun to play. It may be played after Primer paso or at the end of the chapter.

Preparation You will need picture flashcards of vocabulary items. Before the game begins, tell students that after the game, they will have to write down as many vocabulary words as they can remember. You may want to have students clear their desks so they will not be tempted to write the pool of words as the game proceeds. You may also want to ask for a volunteer to be the scorekeeper.

Procedure Divide the class into two teams. Representatives from each team stand side-by-side at a set location in the classroom. Hold up a flashcard so that all students can see it. The first of the contestants to name the picture in Spanish wins a point for his or her team. If neither of the contestants can identify the picture, neither team wins a point in that round.

Teammates are not allowed to call out the correct answer to each other; this behavior will reduce their team's score by one point. The round continues in this manner until each student has had a chance to play.

Play as many rounds as you like. When the game ends, have students write as many of the vocabulary words used in the game as they can remember. You might give a prize to the student who recalls the most vocabulary.

COMMUNITY LINK

If students know people from Spanish-speaking countries, they might obtain recipes from them to prepare. Invite native speakers to attend the fiesta and speak Spanish with students.

Storytelling

This story accompanies Teaching Transparency 8-3. The mini-cuento can be told and retold in different formats, acted out, written, and read aloud to give students additional opportunities to practice all four skills. The following story relates Rolando's difficult night working as a camarero at Café Cotopaxi.

Esta noche es difícil para Rolando. Toma la orden de una pareja simpática, pero no la oye bien. Un muchacho que come pastel le grita porque quiere helado también. Un grupo de clientes en otra mesa está furioso porque Rolando no tiene tiempo todavía de tomar su pedido. En otra mesa un grupo de muchachos hace mucho ruido y deja la mesa en desorden. Un chico deja caer utensilios y comida y deja sucio el piso. La chica derrama su leche. Todos quieren la atención del pobre Rolando, pero nadie lo ayuda a él.

Traditions

Música

The **quena,** or **kena,** is one of the most popular pre-Columbian instruments of the Andean countries. It is a kind of flute made of carved wood or bamboo and is generally accompanied by other instruments, including the **bombo** (a bass drum) and **charango** (a small stringed instrument). The ensemble of these instruments creates an extraordinary harmony of uniquely colloquial sounds. Play **El condor pasa** on Audio CD 7 for students to hear as an example of the **quena** and **charango**. Have students first describe the sounds of the two instruments and then compare them to the sounds of other instruments with which they may be familiar, such as the flute and guitar.

Receta

The **llapingacho** is an Ecuadorean and Peruvian potato cake with cheese, also referred to as a potato pancake, croquette, or **tortilla**. It is usually flavored with sauteed onions, **achiote** (annatto), and pork lard. **Llapingachos** may be topped with **salsa de maní** (a peanut sauce) and served with salad, fried eggs, and pork chops. The Andean varieties of potatoes will not be found in most of our supermarkets. Potatoes suitable for mashing, such as white or red potatoes, or creamy yellow-fleshed potatoes, if available, will make good substitutes.

LLAPINGACHOS

para 4 personas

4 libras de papas

2 tazas de queso blanco de crema, desmenuzado *(crumbled)*

1 cucharada de manteca o mantequilla

1 cucharada de achiote

sal y pimienta al gusto

Corte las papas en pedazos grandes y póngalas a hervir en una olla con agua y sal. Cuando estén blandas, sáquelas de la olla y guarde el agua. Pele las papas y aplástelas bien, agregando 1/2 taza del agua de la olla, y añada sal y pimienta al gusto. Amase la mezcla, formando bolas con un hueco en el centro. Rellénelas con queso y forme unas tortas de cuatro a cinco pulgadas de diámetro. Unte en un sartén la grasa y el achiote y fría las tortas a fuego lento hasta que se doren.

Capítulo 8: ¡A comer!
Technology

DVD/Video

Videocassette 1, Videocassette 5 (captioned version)
DVD Tutor, Disc 2
See Video Guide, pages 53–58.

De antemano • ¿Qué vas a pedir?
María, her brother Roberto, and Tomás take Hiroshi to a restaurant that serves typical Ecuadorean dishes. They describe the food to Hiroshi, who decides to order **locro**. After eating, they set off for **La Mitad del Mundo**. On their way, they suddenly have car trouble.

¿Cuál es un plato típico de tu país?
Three teenagers from Florida, Venezuela, and Ecuador tell about typical dishes from the regions where they live. In additional interviews, people from various Spanish-speaking countries tell us about dishes typical to their regions.

A continuación
A passerby helps the characters, and they are soon on their way to a market and to the **Monumento de la Mitad del Mundo**. They split up into two groups. While at an open-air market, Hiroshi and María bargain with vendors and buy traditional tapestries, sweaters, and gifts for Hiroshi and his family, as well as various other items. They return to the car and recount their experiences to Roberto and Tomás.

 Videoclips
- **Leche Ram®:** advertisement for milk
- **Néctares Dos Pinos®:** advertisement for juice
- **La Casera®:** advertisement for bottled water

Interactive CD-ROM Tutor

Activity	Activity Type	Pupil's Edition Page
En contexto	*Interactive conversation*	
1. Gramática	¿Qué falta?	p. 238
2. Vocabulario	¿Cuál es?	pp. 235, 237
3. Así se dice	Imagen y sonido ¡Exploremos! ¡Identifiquemos!	p. 240
4. Vocabulario	¡Super memoria!	p. 245
5. Vocabulario	¡A escoger!	p. 247
6. Así se dice	Patas arriba	pp. 244, 246
Panorama cultural	¿Cuál es un plato típico de tu país?	p. 239
¡A hablar!	*Guided recording*	pp. 256–257
¡A escribir!	*Guided writing*	pp. 256–257

Teacher Management System
Launch the program, type "admin" in the password area, and press RETURN. Log on to **www.hrw.com/CDROMTUTOR** for a detailed explanation of the Teacher Management System.

DVD Tutor

 The *DVD Tutor* contains all material from the *Video Program* as described above. Spanish captions are available for use at your discretion for all sections of the video. The *DVD Tutor* also provides a variety of video-based activities that assess students' understanding of the **De antemano, A continuación,** and **Panorama cultural.**

> This part of the *DVD Tutor* may be used on any DVD video player connected to a television or video monitor.

 In addition to the video material and the video-based comprehension activities, the *DVD Tutor* also contains the entire *Interactive CD-ROM Tutor* in DVD-ROM format. Each DVD disc contains the activities from all 12 chapters of the *Interactive CD-ROM Tutor.*

> This part of the *DVD Tutor* may be used on a Macintosh® or Windows® computer with a DVD-ROM drive.

One-Stop Planner CD-ROM

To preview all resources available for this chapter, use the **One-Stop Planner CD-ROM**, Disc 2.

Internet Connection ....

internet

MARCAR: go.hrw.com
PALABRA CLAVE:
WV3 ECUADOR-8

*Have students explore the **go.hrw.com** Web site for many online resources covering all chapters. All Chapter 8 resources are available under the keyword **WV3 ECUADOR-8**. Interactive games help students practice the material and provide them with immediate feedback. You will also find a printable worksheet that provides Internet activities that lead to a comprehensive online research project.*

Juegos interactivos

You can use the interactive activities in this chapter

- to practice grammar, vocabulary, and chapter functions
- as homework
- as an assessment option
- as a self-test
- to prepare for the Chapter Test

Actividades Internet

Students act as restaurant critics for a magazine. They evaluate restaurants they find on the Internet based on menu, price, and atmosphere.

- In preparation for the **Hoja de actividades,** have students complete the *Practice and Activity Book* activities from the **Segundo** and **Tercer pasos.**
- After students have completed the activity sheet, encourage them to record their restaurant critique. You might also have them share their critique as well as the restaurant's Web site with the class.

Proyecto

Have students create a Web site for restaurant critiques. Once they post the critique they wrote for the **Hoja de actividades** on their site, they should then post a "real" critique as well: the next time they eat at a local restaurant or the school cafeteria, ask students to take note of and critique the food, the service, and the atmosphere on their Web site.

Capítulo 8: ¡A comer!
Textbook Listening Activities Scripts

Primer paso

6   p. 236

MARCELA	¿Te gustan los huevos?
ROBERTO	Sí, me encantan los huevos revueltos con tocino.
MARCELA	A mí me encanta el pan dulce. ¿Y a ti?
ROBERTO	No, no me gusta para nada.
MARCELA	Bueno... a ver... ¿tomas café?
ROBERTO	Uy, no me gusta el café para nada. Es horrible.
MARCELA	Entonces, ¿qué prefieres tomar, jugo de naranja o leche?
ROBERTO	Prefiero tomar leche.
MARCELA	A mí me gusta más el jugo de naranja. Me encantan las frutas.
ROBERTO	A mí también. Especialmente los plátanos.

Answers to Activity 6
A Roberto le gustan los huevos revueltos con tocino,
la leche y las frutas, especialmente los plátanos.
A Marcela le gustan el pan dulce, el jugo de naranja y las frutas.

12   p. 238

ADELA	Pablo, quiero saber cómo son las comidas en los Estados Unidos. En general, ¿a qué hora desayunas?
PABLO	Bueno, en general desayunamos a las siete de la mañana.
ADELA	¿Y qué hay para el desayuno?
PABLO	Hay de todo. Muchas veces hay huevos, pan tostado, jugo de fruta y café.
ADELA	¿Y a qué hora almuerzan Uds.?
PABLO	Durante la semana, almorzamos a las doce.
ADELA	¿Y qué hay para el almuerzo?
PABLO	A veces hay sopa, sándwiches y leche.

Answers to Activity 12
el desayuno: a las siete de la mañana; come huevos,
        pan tostado, jugo de fruta y café
el almuerzo: a las doce; toma sopa, sándwiches y leche

Segundo paso

16   p. 240

1. Este pescado está muy rico. ¡Me encanta!
2. Esta sopa no me gusta. Está fría.
3. ¿Qué tal la ensalada? ¡Está deliciosa!, ¿no?
4. Esta carne está muy picante. ¡Necesito agua!
5. La sopa está muy salada. ¡Qué horrible!
6. La ensalada de frutas no está muy buena hoy.

Answers to Activity 16
1. pescado: sí
2. sopa: no
3. ensalada: sí
4. carne: no
5. sopa: no
6. ensalada de frutas: no

21   p. 241

DIEGO	¿Tienes hambre, Isabel?
ISABEL	No, Diego, no tengo mucha hambre, pero tengo sed.
DIEGO	¿Por qué no tomas una limonada?
ISABEL	Buena idea. Me encanta la limonada.
DIEGO	Estela, ¿qué quieres almorzar? ¿Tienes hambre?
ESTELA	Sí, sí, pero me gustaría desayunar. ¿Qué hay para el desayuno?
DIEGO	Sólo hay jugo de manzana y pan tostado. Yo voy a comer la sopa de legumbres. ¡Me encanta la sopa aquí! Y Rafael, ¿qué vas a almorzar tú?
RAFAEL	Nada. No tengo mucha hambre.

Answers to Activity 21
1. Estela
2. Isabel
3. Rafael e Isabel
4. Diego
5. jugo de manzana y pan tostado

⌁ One-Stop Planner CD-ROM

To preview all resources available for this chapter, use the **One-Stop Planner CD-ROM**, Disc 2.

Tercer paso

28 p. 245

1. —Voy a pedir una sopa de pollo, pescado, verduras y una ensalada, por favor.
—Muy bien, señorita.

2. —¿Me trae fruta, café y pan tostado, por favor?
—Sí, con mucho gusto.

3. —¿Nos trae café y un pastel, por favor?
—Claro que sí, señora.

4. —No tengo mucha hambre. Voy a pedir una sopa de pollo, pan y un refresco, nada más.
—Gracias, señor.

5. —Um, son las dos y media. Tengo mucha hambre. ¿Me trae la sopa de tomate, el bistec, papas fritas, zanahorias, una ensalada, pan y el postre, por favor? Y café más tarde. Gracias.
—Muy bien, señor.

6. —¿Nos trae huevos revueltos con jamón, pan tostado, jugo de naranja y café, por favor?
—Claro que sí.

7. —Voy a pedir una ensalada, arroz con pollo, postre y café.
—Muy bien, señora.

8. —¿Tiene pasteles, señor? ¿Me trae uno de chocolate? Y para mi amiga, uno de vainilla, por favor.
—Gracias, señoritas.

Answers to Activity 28

1. lunch or dinner	5. lunch
2. breakfast	6. breakfast
3. dessert	7. dinner or lunch
4. dinner or lunch	8. dessert

32 p. 247

1. tres mil quinientos pesos

2. cuatro mil doscientos cincuenta pesos

3. mil doscientos sesenta pesos

4. dos mil pesos

5. dos mil doscientos treinta pesos

6. cuatro mil setecientos cincuenta pesos

Answers to Activity 32

1. sancocho	4. ensalada mixta
2. ceviche de camarón	5. canoa de frutas
3. helado de naranjilla	6. arroz con pollo

LETRA Y SONIDO, P. 249

For the scripts for Parts A and C, see p. 249. The script for Part B is below.

B. Dictado

Para este pastel de chocolate, necesito harina, azúcar y huevos. También quiero poner coco y dos cucharadas de cacao.

Repaso

1 p. 256

No me gusta para nada el pescado, pero el pollo sí, me gusta mucho. Los frijoles no me gustan porque son muy salados. Me encantan las legumbres, pero la carne no me gusta mucho. Para el desayuno los huevos revueltos con queso son muy ricos.

Answers to Repaso Activity 1

Ángel likes:	*Ángel doesn't like:*
el pollo	el pescado
las legumbres	los frijoles
los huevos revueltos con queso	la carne

Capítulo 8: ¡A comer!
Suggested Lesson Plans 50-Minute Schedule

Day 1

CHAPTER OPENER 5 min.
- Focusing on Outcomes, ATE, p. 231
- Culture Note, ATE, p. 230

DE ANTEMANO 40 min.
- Presenting **De antemano** and Preteaching Vocabulary, ATE, p. 232
- Present the Language Notes, ATE, p. 233.
- Activities 1–5 and Comprehension Check, p. 234

Wrap-Up 5 min.
- Repeat Activity 5, p. 234, following the Challenge suggestion, ATE, p. 234.

Homework Options
Cuaderno de actividades, p. 85, Activities 1–2

Day 2

PRIMER PASO
Quick Review 5 min.
- Check homework.
- Bell Work, ATE, p. 235

Así se dice/Vocabulario, p. 235 25 min.
- Presenting **Así se dice** and **Vocabulario**, ATE, p. 235
- Have students do the Visual Learners suggestion, ATE, p. 235.
- Present **También se puede decir...**, p. 236.
- Do Activity 6, p. 236, with the Audio CD.

Gramática, p. 236 15 min.
- Presenting **Gramática**, ATE, p. 236
- Do Activity 7, p. 236.

Wrap-Up 5 min.
- Have students tell you one thing they love for breakfast and one thing they do not like.

Homework Options
Cuaderno de actividades, p. 86, Activities 3–4
Cuaderno de gramática, p. 61, Activities 1–2

Day 3

PRIMER PASO
Quick Review 10 min.
- Check homework.
- Use Teaching Transparency 8-A to review **Vocabulario**, p. 235, and **Gramática**, p. 236.

Gramática, p. 236 10 min.
- Do **Más práctica gramatical**, p. 252, Activity 1, orally with the class.
- Have students do Activity 8, p. 236.

Vocabulario, p. 237 25 min.
- Presenting **Vocabulario**, ATE, p. 237
- Present **También se puede decir...**, and the Language Notes, ATE, p. 237.
- Read the **Nota cultural**, p. 237.
- Do Activities 9–10, p. 237.
- Do Building on Previous Skills, ATE, p. 237, then have students do Activity 11, p. 237, in pairs.

Wrap-Up 5 min.
- Follow the Challenge suggestion, ATE, p. 236.

Homework Options
Más práctica gramatical, p. 252, Activity 2
Cuaderno de actividades, p. 87, Activities 5–6
Cuaderno de gramática, pp. 62–63, Activities 3–6

Day 4

PRIMER PASO
Quick Review 10 min.
- Check homework.
- Use Teaching Transparency 8-B to ask students if they like, love, or dislike the items pictured. Also ask students about what their classmates like to elicit other indirect object pronouns.

Gramática, p. 238 25 min.
- Presenting **Gramática**, ATE, p. 238
- Do Activity 12, p. 238, with the Audio CD.
- Do Activity 13, p. 238, orally with the class. Have students spell out conjugations.
- Have students do Activity 14, p. 238, in pairs, and Activity 15, p. 238, in groups.
- Read and discuss the **Nota cultural**, p. 238.

PANORAMA CULTURAL 10 min.
- Presenting **Panorama cultural**, ATE, p. 239
- Present the vocabulary in the Language Note, ATE, p. 239.

Wrap-Up 5 min.
- Follow the Thinking Critically suggestion, ATE, p. 239.

Homework Options
Cuaderno de actividades, p. 88, Activities 7–8
Cuaderno de gramática, p. 64, Activities 7–8

Day 5

PRIMER PASO
Quick Review 5 min.
- Check homework.

Gramática, p. 238 10 min.
- Review **almorzar** and **desayunar** using Teaching Transparency 8-1.
- **Más práctica gramatical**, p. 253, Activities 3–4

SEGUNDO PASO
Así se dice/Nota gramatical, p. 240 30 min.
- Presenting **Así se dice**, ATE, p. 240
- Read the **Nota gramatical**, p. 240.
- Do Activity 16, p. 240, with the Audio CD.
- Have students do Activities 17–18, pp. 240–241.
- Have students do Activity 19, p. 241, in pairs, and Activity 20, p. 241, in groups.

Wrap-Up 5 min.
- Have students describe a picture of a food and comment on eating that food.
- Discuss the content and format of Quiz 8-1.

Homework Options
Study for Quiz 8-1.
Cuaderno de actividades, pp. 89–90, Activities 9–11
Cuaderno de gramática, p. 65, Activities 9–10

Day 6

PRIMER PASO
Quick Review 10 min.
- Check homework.
- Quickly review the content of the **Primer paso**.

Quiz 20 min.
- Administer Quiz 8-1A, 8-1B, or a combination of the two.

SEGUNDO PASO
Nota gramatical, p. 240 5 min.
- Do **Más práctica gramatical**, p. 254, Activities 5–6, orally with the class.

Nota gramatical, p. 241 10 min.
- Presenting **Nota gramatical**, ATE, p. 241
- Present Language-to-Language, ATE, p. 241.
- Do Activity 21, p. 241, with the Audio CD.

Wrap-Up 5 min.
- Ask students what they eat or drink when they are hungry or thirsty.

Homework Options
Más práctica gramatical, p. 254, Activity 7
Cuaderno de gramática, p. 66, Activities 11–12

One-Stop Planner CD-ROM

For alternative lesson plans by chapter section, to create your own customized plans, or to preview all resources available for this chapter, use the **One-Stop Planner CD-ROM**, Disc 2.

 For additional homework suggestions, see activities accompanied by this symbol throughout the chapter.

Day 7

SEGUNDO PASO

Quick Review 5 min.
- Check homework.

Nota gramatical, p. 241 30 min.
- Have students complete Activity 22, p. 242, then share their preferences with the class.
- Have students do Activity 23, p. 242, in pairs, and Activity 24, p. 242, in groups.
- Read the **Nota cultural**, p. 242. Then describe an imaginary restaurant to present **Vocabulario extra**, p. 242. Incorporate the dishes from the **Nota cultural**, p. 242, in your presentation.
- Have students write Activity 25, p. 242, then exchange their reviews for peer-editing.

ENCUENTRO CULTURAL 10 min.
- Presenting **Encuentro cultural**, ATE, p. 243
- Do the **Vamos a comprenderlo** activity, p. 243.

Wrap-Up 5 min.
- Do the Thinking Critically activity, ATE, p. 243.
- Discuss the content and format of Quiz 8-2.

Homework Options
Study for Quiz 8-2.
Cuaderno de actividades, pp. 90–91, Activities 12–13

Day 8

SEGUNDO PASO

Quick Review 10 min.
- Check homework.
- Review the content of the **Segundo paso** using Teaching Transparency 8-2.

Quiz 20 min.
- Administer Quiz 8-2A, 8-2B, or a combination of the two.

TERCER PASO
Vocabulario, p. 245 15 min.
- Presenting **Vocabulario**, ATE, p. 245
- Read the **Nota cultural**, p. 245.

Wrap-Up 5 min.
- Project Teaching Transparency 8-D. Ask students whether they like the items pictured or not.

Homework Options
Cuaderno de gramática, p. 69, Activities 18–19

Day 9

TERCER PASO

Quick Review 5 min.
- Check homework.
- Bell Work, ATE, p. 244

Así se dice/Vocabulario, p. 244 25 min.
- Presenting **Así se dice** and **Vocabulario**, ATE, p. 244. Include vocabulary from **También se puede decir...**, p. 244, in your presentation.
- Present the **Nota gramatical**, p. 244. Practice agreement by calling out the singular and plural forms of the new vocabulary.
- Do Activities 26–27, pp. 244–245.
- Do Activity 28, p. 245, with the Audio CD.

Así se dice, p. 246 15 min.
- Presenting **Así se dice**, ATE, p. 246
- Do Activity 29, p. 246, orally with the class.
- Have students do Activity 30, p. 246, in groups.

Wrap-Up 5 min.
- Project Teaching Transparency 8-C. Point to an item and have students ask you to bring them that item.

Homework Options
Más práctica gramatical, p. 255, Activity 8
Cuaderno de actividades, pp. 92–93, Activities 14–16
Cuaderno de gramática, pp. 67–68, Activities 13–17

Day 10

TERCER PASO

Quick Review 5 min.
- Check homework.

Así se dice, p. 246 10 min.
- Presenting **Así se dice**, ATE, p. 246
- Present **A lo nuestro**, p. 247.

Vocabulario, p. 247 30 min.
- Presenting **Vocabulario**, ATE, p. 247
- Present the Culture Note, ATE, p. 247, and do Activity 31, p. 247.
- Do Activity 32, p. 247, with the Audio CD.
- Have students work with a partner to do Activities 33–34, p. 248.
- Read and discuss the **Notas culturales**, pp. 248 and 249. Present the Culture Note, ATE, p. 248.
- Have students do Activity 35, p. 249, in groups.

Wrap-Up 5 min.
- Discuss content and format of Quiz 8-3.

Homework Options
Study for Quiz 8-3.
Más práctica gramatical, p. 255, Activity 9
Cuaderno de actividades, p. 94, Activities 17–18
Cuaderno de gramática, p. 69, Activities 20–21

Day 11

TERCER PASO

Quick Review 5 min.
- Check homework.
- Quickly review the content of the **Tercer paso**.

Quiz 20 min.
- Administer Quiz 8-3A, 8-3B, or a combination of the two.

VAMOS A LEER 20 min.
- Discuss the **Estrategia para leer**, p. 250, then do Activity A, p. 250.
- Follow the Using Prior Knowledge suggestion, ATE, p. 250, then do Activity B, pp. 250–251.
- Do Activities C–D, p. 251.

Wrap-Up 5 min.
- Ask students to vote on which recipe is the best.

Homework Suggestions
Assign Activities 2, 4, and 5 of the **Repaso**, pp. 256–257, as homework.
A ver si puedo..., p. 258

Day 12

REPASO

Quick Review 5 min.
- Check homework and pick up students' display menus (Activity 5, p. 257).

Chapter Review 40 min.
- Review Chapter 8. Choose from **Más práctica gramatical**, Grammar Tutor for Students of Spanish, Activities for Communication, Listening Activities, Interactive CD-ROM Tutor, or **Juegos interactivos**.

Wrap-Up 5 min.
- Discuss the format of the Chapter 8 Test.

Homework Options
Study for the Chapter 8 test.

Assessment

Quick Review 5 min.
- Answer any last-minute questions.

Test, Chapter 8 45 min.
- Administer Chapter 8 Test. Select from Testing Program, Alternative Assessment Guide, Test Generator, or Standardized Assessment Tutor.

Capítulo 8: ¡A comer!
Suggested Lesson Plans 90-Minute Block Schedule

Block 1

CHAPTER OPENER 5 min.
- Focusing on Outcomes, ATE, p. 231
- Culture Note, ATE, p. 230

DE ANTEMANO 40 min.
- Presenting **De antemano** and Preteaching Vocabulary, ATE, p. 232
- Present the Language Notes, ATE, p. 233.
- Activities 1–5 and Comprehension Check, ATE, p. 234

Así se dice/Vocabulario, p. 235 25 min.
- Presenting **Así se dice** and **Vocabulario**, ATE, p. 235
- Have students do the Visual Learners suggestion, ATE, p. 235.
- Present **También se puede decir...**, p. 236.
- Do Activity 6, p. 236, with the Audio CD.

Gramática, p. 236 15 min.
Presenting **Gramática**, ATE, p. 236
Do Activity 7, p. 236.

Wrap-Up 5 min.
- Have students tell you one thing they love for breakfast and one thing they do not like.

Homework Options
Cuaderno de actividades, pp. 85–86, Activities 1–4
Cuaderno de gramática, p. 61, Activities 1–2

Block 2

PRIMER PASO
Quick Review 10 min.
- Check homework.
- Use Teaching Transparency 8-A to review **Así se dice** and **Vocabulario**, p. 235.

Gramática, p. 236 10 min.
- Do **Más práctica gramatical**, p. 252, Activity 1, orally with the class.
- Have students do Activity 8, p. 236.

Vocabulario, p. 237 25 min.
- Presenting **Vocabulario**, ATE, p. 237
- Present **También se puede decir...** and the Language Note, ATE, p. 237.
- Read the **Nota cultural**, p. 237. Ask students to compare what they eat for breakfast with what people in Spanish-speaking countries eat.
- Do Activities 9–10, p. 237.
- Do Building on Previous Skills, ATE, p. 237, then have students do Activity 11 in pairs.

Gramática, p. 238 25 min.
- Presenting **Gramática**, ATE, p. 238
- Do Activity 12, p. 238, with the Audio CD.
- Do Activity 13, p. 238, orally with the class. Have students spell out conjugations.
- Have students do Activity 14, p. 238, in pairs, and Activity 15, p. 238, in groups.
- Read and discuss the **Nota cultural**, p. 238.

PANORAMA CULTURAL 10 min.
- Presenting **Panorama cultural**, ATE, p. 239
- Present the vocabulary in the Language Note, ATE, p. 239.

Wrap-Up 10 min.
- Follow the Thinking Critically suggestion, ATE, p. 239.
- Use Teaching Transparency 8-1 to ask students questions about what the people pictured are eating. Then repeat some of the questions used in Presenting **Gramática**, ATE, p. 238.
- Discuss the content and format of Quiz 8-1.

Homework Options
Study for Quiz 8-1.
Cuaderno de actividades, pp. 87–88, Activities 5–8
Cuaderno de gramática, pp. 62–64, Activities 3–8

Block 3

PRIMER PASO
Quick Review 10 min.
- Check homework.

Así se dice/Vocabulario/Gramática, pp. 235–238 15 min.
- Review the vocabulary and **Así se dice** expressions from the **Primer paso**, using Teaching Transparencies 8-A and 8-B.
- Do **Más práctica gramatical**, pp. 252–253, Activities 2–4.

Quiz 20 min.
- Administer Quiz 8-1A, 8-1B, or a combination of the two.

SEGUNDO PASO
Así se dice/Nota gramatical, p. 240 30 min.
- Presenting **Así se dice**, ATE, p. 240
- Read the **Nota gramatical**, p. 240, with students.
- Do Activity 16, p. 240, with the Audio CD.
- Have students do Activities 17–18, pp. 240–241. Check orally.
- Have students do Activity 19, p. 241, in pairs, and Activity 20, p. 241, in groups.

Nota gramatical, p. 241 10 min.
- Presenting **Nota gramatical**, ATE, p. 241
- Present Language-to-Language, ATE, p. 241.
- Do Activity 21, p. 241, with the Audio CD.

Wrap-Up 5 min.
- Ask students what they eat or drink when they are hungry or thirsty.
- Hold up a picture of a food. Have students describe the food. Then have them imagine they are eating the food and comment on it.

Homework Options
Más práctica gramatical, p. 254, Activities 5–7
Cuaderno de actividades, pp. 89–90, Activities 9–11
Cuaderno de gramática, pp. 65–66, Activities 9–12

One-Stop Planner CD-ROM

For alternative lesson plans by chapter section, to create your own customized plans, or to preview all resources available for this chapter, use the **One-Stop Planner CD-ROM**, Disc 2.

 For additional homework suggestions, see activities accompanied by this symbol throughout the chapter.

Block 4

SEGUNDO PASO

Quick Review 10 min.
- Check homework.
- Describe several dishes and ask students to comment on them.

Nota gramatical, p. 241 30 min.
- Have students complete Activity 22, p. 242, then share their preferences with the class.
- Have students do Activity 23, p. 242, in pairs, and Activity 24, p. 242, in groups.
- Read the **Nota cultural**, p. 242. Then describe an imaginary restaurant to present **Vocabulario extra**. Incorporate the dishes from the **Nota cultural**, p. 242, in your presentation.
- Have students write Activity 25, p. 242, then exchange their reviews for peer-editing.

ENCUENTRO CULTURAL 15 min.
- Presenting **Encuentro cultural**, ATE, p. 243
- Do the **Vamos a comprenderlo** activity, p. 243.
- Do the Thinking Critically activity, ATE, p. 243.

TERCER PASO

Así se dice/Vocabulario, p. 244 25 min.
- Presenting **Así se dice** and **Vocabulario**, ATE, p. 244. Include vocabulary from **También se puede decir...**, p. 244, in your presentation.
- Present the **Nota gramatical**, p. 244. Practice agreement by calling out the singular and plural forms of the new vocabulary and having students give you the correct form of **otro**.
- Do Activities 26–27, pp. 244–245.

Wrap-Up 10 min.
- Project Teaching Transparency 8-C. Point to an item and have students ask you to bring them that item.
- Discuss the content and format of Quiz 8-2.

Homework Options
Study for Quiz 8-2.
Cuaderno de actividades, pp. 90–92, Activities 12–14
Cuaderno de gramática, pp. 67–68, Activities 13–17

Block 5

SEGUNDO PASO

Quick Review 10 min.
- Check homework.
- Review the content of the **Segundo paso** using Teaching Transparency 8-2.

Quiz 20 min.
- Administer Quiz 8-2A, 8-2B, or a combination of the two.

TERCER PASO

Vocabulario, p. 245 20 min.
- Presenting **Vocabulario**, ATE, p. 245
- Read the **Nota cultural**, p. 245.
- Do Activity 28, p. 245, with the Audio CD.

Así se dice, p. 246 15 min.
- Presenting **Así se dice**, ATE, p. 246
- Do Activity 29, p. 246, orally with the class.
- Have students do Activity 30, p. 246, in groups.

Así se dice, p. 246 10 min.
- Presenting **Así se dice**, ATE, p. 246
- Present **A lo nuestro**, p. 247.

Vocabulario, p. 247 10 min.
- Presenting **Vocabulario**, ATE, p. 247

Wrap-Up 5 min.
- Discuss content and format of Quiz 8-3.

Homework Options
Study for Quiz 8-3.
Más práctica gramatical, p. 255, Activities 8–9
Cuaderno de actividades, pp. 92–94, Activities 15–18
Cuaderno de gramática, p. 69, Activities 18–21

Block 6

TERCER PASO

Quick Review 10 min.
- Check homework.
- Use Teaching Transparencies 8-D and 8-3 to review **Vocabulario**, p. 245, and **Así se dice** expressions, p. 246.

Vocabulario, p. 247 30 min.
- Present Culture Note and do Activity 31, p. 247.
- Do Activity 32, p. 247, with the Audio CD.
- Do Activities 33–34, p. 248, in pairs.
- Read and discuss the **Notas culturales**, pp. 248 and 249. Present the Culture Note, ATE, p. 248.
- Have students do Activity 35, p. 249, in groups.

Quiz 20 min.
- Administer Quiz 8-3A, 8-3B, or a combination of the two.

VAMOS A LEER 20 min.
- Discuss the **Estrategia para leer**, p. 250, then do Activity A, p. 250.
- Follow the Using Prior Knowledge suggestion, ATE, p. 250, then do Activity B, pp. 250–251.
- Do Activities C–D, p. 251.

Wrap-Up 10 min.
- Ask students to vote on which recipe is the best.
- Have students list the main concepts of Chapter 8.
- Discuss the format of the Chapter 8 Test.

Homework Suggestions
Study for the Chapter 8 Test.
Assign Activities 2, 4, and 5 of the **Repaso**, pp. 256–257, as homework.
A ver si puedo..., p. 258

Block 7

REPASO

Quick Review 10 min.
- Check homework and pick up students' display menus (Activity 5, p. 257).

Chapter Review 35 min.
- Review Chapter 8. Choose from **Más práctica gramatical**, Grammar Tutor for Students of Spanish, Activities for Communication, Listening Activities, Interactive CD-ROM Tutor, or **Juegos interactivos**.

Test, Chapter 8 45 min.
- Administer Chapter 8 Test. Select from Testing Program, Alternative Assessment Guide, Test Generator, or Standardized Assessment Tutor.

CAPÍTULO 8

One-Stop Planner CD-ROM

For resource information, see the **One-Stop Planner**, Disc 2.

Pacing Tips
The first and third **Pasos** have more content to cover than the second. You might keep that in mind when planning your lessons, and make use of the cultural content in **Panorama cultural** and **Encuentro cultural,** both of which deal with varieties of food. For more tips on pacing, see Suggested Lesson Plans, pp. 229I–229L.

Meeting the Standards

Communication
- Talking about meals and food, p. 235
- Commenting on food, p. 240
- Making polite requests, p. 244
- Ordering dinner in a restaurant, p. 246
- Asking for and paying the bill in a restaurant, p. 246

Cultures
- Nota cultural, p. 237
- Nota cultural, p. 238
- Panorama cultural, p. 239

Connections
- Geography Link, p. 231
- Encuentro cultural, p. 243
- Math Link, p. 255

Comparisons
- Language-to-Language, p. 241
- Culture Note, p. 247
- A lo nuestro, p. 247
- Nota cultural, p. 248
- Nota cultural, p. 249

Communities
- Additional Practice, p. 243
- Community Link, p. 245
- Family Link, p. 256

Cultures and Communities

Culture Note
Soups and stews are very popular dishes in Ecuador. **Caldo de pollo** *(chicken soup)* is among the most popular. Other well-known soups and stews in Spain and Latin America include **gazpacho** *cold soup made with vegetables, oil, vinegar, and garlic;* **caldo de res** *beef broth;* **sopa de lentejas** *lentil soup;* **sopa de albóndigas** *meatball soup;* **menudo** (in Mexico; **mondongo** in Argentina) *tripe stew;* **sopa de tortilla** *tortilla soup;* **cocido madrileño** *stew made with chickpeas and various meats;* and **sopa de fideos** *noodle soup.*

CAPÍTULO

8

¡A comer!

Objectives

In this chapter you will learn to

Primer paso

• talk about meals and food

Segundo paso

• comment on food

Tercer paso

• make polite requests
• order dinner in a restaurant
• ask for and pay the bill in a restaurant

📶 internet

go.hrw.com   MARCAR: go.hrw.com
            PALABRA CLAVE:
                 WV3 ECUADOR-8

◀ ¡Me encanta la fruta del mercado en Otavalo!

Photo Flash!

Ask students to name the fruits they recognize in the photo. They might mention **plátano** *banana*, **piña** *pineapple*, **fresa** *strawberry*, and **coco** *coconut*. Ecuador also has many fruits students may not have tried, such as **maracuyás** *passion fruit*, **papayas**, **mangos,** and **naranjillas,** a fruit that tastes like a bitter orange.

Focusing on Outcomes

Point out to students that an important use of a language is talking about food. This includes being able to order and pay for meals and expressing preferences. By the end of the chapter, students will be able to participate in this important aspect of Spanish culture, whether in a Spanish-speaking country or at a local Hispanic restaurant.

Connections and Comparisons

Geography Link

Ecuador lies on the Earth's equator. Ask students what this means for Ecuador's climate and crops. (Ecuador has little change of climate throughout the year. For this reason, some fruits and vegetables are always in season.) Have students work in pairs to research which crops are grown year-round in Ecuador and which, if any, are seasonal. Have them report on what they find, using as much Spanish as possible. Some possible research tools are encyclopedias, travel guides, and Internet pages about Ecuador and the Andes. Visit the HRW Web site at **go.hrw.com**, Keyword **WV3 ECUADOR-8** for online resources and additional information about Ecuador.

Teaching Resources
pp. 232–234

PRINT
▸ Lesson Planner, p. 37
▸ Video Guide, pp. 53–54, 56
▸ Cuaderno de actividades, p. 85

MEDIA
▸ One-Stop Planner
▸ Video Program
  De antemano
  Videocassette 3, 18:10–24:29
  Videocassette 5 (captioned version), 1:17:47–1:24:06
  A continuación
  Videocassette 3, 24:30–30:45
  Videocassette 5 (captioned version), 1:24:07–1:30:26
▸ DVD Tutor, Disc 2
▸ Audio Compact Discs, CD 8, Trs. 1–2
▸ De antemano Transparencies

Presenting
De antemano

Have students predict the plot by reading and answering the questions in **Estrategia para comprender.** Play the video and check student comprehension. Have students try to guess meaning from context. Next, present the Preteaching Vocabulary. Follow up by modeling pronunciation of the **fotonovela** dialogue and having students repeat after you. Replay the video, then break the class into pairs for reading practice.

De antemano
Transparencies

DE ANTEMANO · ¿Qué vas a pedir?

The **fotonovela** is an abridged version of the video episode.

CD 8 Trs. 1–2

Estrategia para comprender

María, Roberto, Tomás, and Hiroshi stop for lunch on their way to the monument to the equator at **la Mitad del Mundo.** As you view the video, watch their gestures, particularly when they indicate that they like or dislike something. Who enjoys lunch the most?

① En camino...

María

Tomás

Hiroshi

Roberto

②
Hiroshi: Tengo mucha hambre. Ya es la una y media y por lo general almuerzo a las doce.
Tomás: No te preocupes. Vas a comer bien en el restaurante. Para el almuerzo hay platos especiales típicos de la región andina.

③
María: ¿Qué vas a pedir?
Hiroshi: Eh.... No sé... ¿qué van a pedir ustedes?
Tomás: Mm... creo que voy a pedir sancocho. Pero, el locro es delicioso aquí también.
Hiroshi: ¿Qué son ésos? ¿Son sopas?

④
Roberto: Sí, mira. El locro es una sopa de papa, aguacate y queso.
Tomás: Para mí, el sancocho, por favor.
María: El sancocho está bien, pero a mí me encantan las empanadas. Empanadas, por favor.
Tomás: No me gustan para nada las empanadas.

⑤
Roberto: ¿Me puede traer carne colorada con papas, por favor?
Camarero: Cómo no, señor. ¿Y para usted, joven?
Hiroshi: Eh... quisiera locro, por favor.
Roberto: ¿Y para tomar? ¿Nos trae cuatro aguas?

Preteaching Vocabulary

Guessing Words from Context

Have students guess the meaning of each of these new words or phrases based on related expressions that they already know and context clues.

frases nuevas
❷ tengo hambre/sed
❷ almorzar *(verb)*
❹ no me gusta para nada
❹ me encanta
❺ tomo *(un sándwich)*

frases familiares
tengo prisa/sueño
almuerzo *(noun)*
no me gusta
me gusta
tomo *(un refresco)*

STANDARDS: 1.2

6

Hiroshi: Saben, tengo mucha hambre.

María: ¡Cuidado Hiroshi, eso es ají! Es muy picante.

Hiroshi: ¡Está picante! En casa no como mucha comida picante. ¡Necesito agua!

María: Oh, aquí viene.

Tomás: El ají es un condimento con tomate, cebolla, chile. Puedes comer un poco de ají con pan, pero tienes que tener cuidado.

7

María: Hiroshi, ¿te gusta el locro?

Hiroshi: Sí, María, está muy rico. Por lo general como mucha sopa. Por eso me encanta.

8

María: ¿Cuánto es?

Roberto: A ver... son veintidós dólares con ochenta. Pero la propina es aparte. Yo los invito.

Todos: Gracias.

9

Después de comer

10

María: ¡Ay, no! Y ahora, ¿qué?

Cuaderno de actividades, p. 85, Acts. 1–2

¿Cómo van a llegar a la Mitad del Mundo?

11

Using the Captioned Video/DVD

As an alternative to reading the conversations in the book, you might want to show the captioned version of *¿Qué vas a pedir?* on Videocassette 5. As students hear the language and watch the story, anxiety about the new language will be reduced and comprehension

facilitated. The reinforcement of seeing the written words with the gestures and actions in context will help students do the comprehension activities on p. 234. **NOTE:** The *DVD Tutor* contains captions for all sections of the *Video Program*.

Language Notes

• **Carne colorada** is meat cooked with **achiote** *(annatto),* an orange spice that gives the cooked meat a reddish color and a special flavor. **Achiote** is made from the seeds of a shrub with decorative flowers that is grown in home gardens.

• **Empanadas** (also called **pasteles** or **hojaldres**) are small pies or turnovers, filled with seasoned meat or fish, vegetables, or sweets. They are popular in almost all Spanish-speaking countries. Small **empanadas** are served as hors d'oeuvres.

A continuación

You may choose to continue with *¿Qué vas a pedir? (a continuación)* at this time or wait until later in the chapter. At this point, the characters are helped with their car trouble by a passerby. They continue to **el Monumento de la Mitad del Mundo** where they buy traditional handicrafts from vendors in an open-air market. You may wish to have students write alternative versions of the second part of the video.

Teaching Suggestions

1 **2** **3** Have students work in pairs to do the first three activities: they should first answer the questions in Activity 1, then identify the functional expressions in Activity 2, and then tell who would make the statements in Activity 3. You might want to have student partners copy the expressions from the video that they identify in Activity 2.

4 Activity 4 can be done as a whole class activity, or you might want to set it up as a timed competition between small groups of students to see which group can put the sentences in the correct order first.

5 Have students do this activity as homework and go over it at the beginning of class the next day.

Answers

1 1. la Mitad del Mundo
2. no
3. He thinks it is very spicy.
4. He likes it.
5. They have car trouble.

2 1. ¿Qué vas a pedir?
2. Es una sopa de papa, aguacate y queso.
3. Me encantan las empanadas.
4. ¿Me puede traer carne colorada?
5. Está muy rico.
6. ¿Cuánto es?

These activities check for comprehension only. Students should not yet be expected to produce language modeled in **De antemano**.

1 **¿Comprendes?** See answers below.

Contesta las siguientes preguntas sobre la fotonovela. Si no estás seguro/a, ¡adivina!

1. ¿Adónde van Hiroshi, María, Tomás y Roberto?
2. ¿Conoce Hiroshi la comida del Ecuador?
3. ¿Qué pasa cuando Hiroshi prueba *(tastes)* el ají?
4. ¿Le gusta a Hiroshi la comida que pide?
5. ¿Qué pasa después de que el grupo sale del restaurante?

2 **¿Cómo se dice?** See answers below.

What phrases from the **fotonovela** can you use . . .?

1. to ask what someone will order
2. to explain what **locro** is
3. to say that you love **empanadas**
4. to ask a waiter to bring you **carne colorada**
5. to say that something is really good
6. to ask how much the bill is

3 **¿Quién lo diría?** *Who would say it?* Answers may vary.

1. Me encanta la comida de Ecuador. Hiroshi
2. ¿Empanadas? ¡Qué horribles! Tomás
3. Y usted, ¿qué va a pedir? el camarero
4. No quiero sancocho. Y no quiero empanadas. Roberto
5. ¿Empanadas? ¡Qué ricas! María

Los amigos y el camarero

4 **¡Qué lío!**

Con base en la fotonovela, pon las oraciones en el orden correcto.

4 **a.** Para Hiroshi, ¡el ají está muy picante!
6 **b.** Hay un problema con el carro.
2 **c.** Los amigos van a un restaurante que tiene comida típica de Ecuador.
5 **d.** A Hiroshi le encanta el locro. ¡Está muy rico!
3 **e.** Tomás quiere comer sancocho.
1 **f.** Hiroshi tiene mucha hambre.

5 **¿Y tú?** Answers will vary.

Contesta **cierto** si la oración es verdadera y **falso** si no lo es.

1. Generalmente como mucha sopa.
2. En casa no comemos comida picante.
3. Me encanta la sopa.
4. No me gustan para nada las empanadas.
5. Para tomar, prefiero el agua.
6. ¡Tengo hambre ahora!

Comprehension Check

Slower Pace

1 Have students first identify the frame or frames in the **fotonovela** where the answer for each question may be found. Then have them work in pairs comparing the frames they chose and checking the answers.

Challenge

5 Ask students to respond with an original statement to each of the **cierto** and **falso** statements. Have them use the expressions they have learned so far. Instead of saying **falso** for the first statement, encourage them to express likes, dislikes, and preferences. **(Generalmente no como muchas legumbres. No me gustan.)**

Así se dice

Talking about meals and food

To ask your friend about meals and food, say:

¿Qué tomas para el desayuno?
What do you have for breakfast?

¿...para el almuerzo?
. . . for lunch?

Tengo sed. ¿Qué hay para tomar?
I'm thirsty. What's there to drink?

Your friend might answer:

A veces tomo un vaso de jugo y un poco de pan. **¡No me gusta** el cereal **para nada!**
I don't like . . . at all!

Por lo general tomo un sándwich, una manzana y un vaso de leche.
Generally I have a sandwich, an apple, and a glass of milk.

Hay jugo, refrescos y agua. **¿Qué prefieres?**
What do you prefer?

Vocabulario

¡Me encanta el desayuno! *I love breakfast!*

un desayuno fuerte

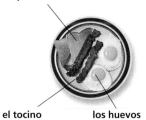

el pan tostado

el tocino   los huevos

un desayuno ecuatoriano

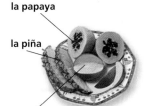

la papaya

la piña

el mango

el pan dulce

el plátano

un desayuno ligero

la toronja

la leche

el cereal

> Cuaderno de gramática, p. 61, Acts. 1–2

Communication for All Students

Visual Learners
Have students make vocabulary flashcards. Ask them to label the back of the cards with the Spanish definitions. They can use magazine pictures, newspaper grocery ads, or their own drawings on the front. For additional food-related vocabulary, refer them to pages 237, 244, 245, and R5.

Native Speakers
You might want to teach the word **blanquillos** for *eggs,* as some native speakers are familiar with the word **huevos** used in off-color, slang expressions.

Teaching Resources
pp. 235–238

PRINT
▸ Lesson Planner, p. 38
▸ TPR Storytelling Book, pp. 29, 32
▸ Listening Activities, pp. 59, 63
▸ Activities for Communication, pp. 43–44, 110, 113–114, 151–152
▸ Cuaderno de gramática, pp. 61–64
▸ Grammar Tutor for Students of Spanish, Chapter 8
▸ Cuaderno de actividades, pp. 86–88
▸ Cuaderno para hispanohablantes, pp. 36–40
▸ Testing Program, pp. 197–200
▸ Alternative Assessment Guide, p. 39
▸ Student Make-Up Assignments, Chapter 8

MEDIA
▸ One-Stop Planner
▸ Audio Compact Discs, CD 8, Trs. 3–4, 24–25, 19
▸ Teaching Transparencies 8-1, 8-A, 8-B; **Más práctica gramatical** Answers; Cuaderno de gramática Answers
▸ Interactive CD-ROM Tutor, Disc 2

Bell Work
Have students write three things they did before breakfast, and then three more things they did before coming to school. Have them read their sentences.

Presenting
Así se dice, Vocabulario

Model the phrases and vocabulary describing what you and others eat for breakfast and lunch. Ask **Así se dice** questions and have students refer to **Vocabulario** to answer.

Teaching Resources
pp. 235–238

PRINT 📖

▸ Lesson Planner, p. 38
▸ TPR Storytelling Book, pp. 29, 32
▸ Listening Activities, pp. 59, 63
▸ Activities for Communication, pp. 43–44, 110, 113–114, 151–152
▸ Cuaderno de gramática, pp. 61–64
▸ Grammar Tutor for Students of Spanish, Chapter 8
▸ Cuaderno de actividades, pp. 86–88
▸ Cuaderno para hispanohablantes, pp. 36–40
▸ Testing Program, pp. 197–200
▸ Alternative Assessment Guide, p. 39
▸ Student Make-Up Assignments, Chapter 8

MEDIA 💿📼

▸ One-Stop Planner
▸ Audio Compact Discs, CD 8, Trs. 3–4, 24–25, 19
▸ Teaching Transparencies 8-1, 8-A, 8-B; **Más práctica gramatical** Answers; Cuaderno de gramática Answers
▸ Interactive CD-ROM Tutor, Disc 2

Presenting
Gramática

The verb *encantar* and indirect object pronouns

Display *Teaching Transparencies 8-A* and *8-B* while modeling **gustar**, **encantar**, and indirect object pronouns. Ask students to say what they like to eat by using **gustar** and **encantar**. Then write two column heads on the board, **Me gusta/encanta** and **No me gusta**. Based on the transparency, have students go to the board and write one item in either column.

---

6 El desayuno

Escuchemos Listen as Marcela and Roberto discuss what foods they like and dislike. Write what each person likes for breakfast.
Scripts and answers on p. 229G.

CD 8
Tr. 3

> ### También se puede decir...
>
> Food vocabulary often varies widely from region to region, even within a particular Spanish-speaking country. Other common words for **el plátano** are **la banana**, **el banano**, and **el guineo**. **El jugo** is usually called **el zumo** in Spain.

Gramática

The verb *encantar* and indirect object pronouns

1. The verb **encantar** *(to really like; to love)* works just like the verb **gustar**.

   Me gusta la leche, pero **me encanta** el jugo de naranja.
   Nos encantan los plátanos.
   A Juan y a Sara **les encantan** los sándwiches.

2. The pronouns **me, te, le, nos, les** in front of the verbs above are called *indirect object pronouns*, which generally tell *to whom* or *for whom*. In this case, they tell *to whom* something is pleasing.

   Te gusta la leche, ¿verdad?   *Milk is pleasing to you, right?*

   You'll learn more about indirect object pronouns in Chapter 9.

3. Remember to use the definite article with **encantar** or **gustar** when you're saying that you like something in general.

   Me encanta **el** jugo de naranja.   *I love orange juice.*

Más práctica gramatical, p. 252, Acts. 1–2

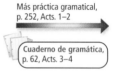

Cuaderno de gramática, p. 62, Acts. 3–4

7 Gramática en contexto

Escribamos ¿Qué les gusta comer a las personas que conoces? Completa las oraciones usando el pronombre de objeto indirecto y la forma correcta del verbo **encantar**.

1. A mi abuela ＝＝＝ ＝＝＝ la piña y los mangos. *le encantan*
2. A mis padres ＝＝＝ ＝＝＝ los desayunos fuertes. *les encantan*
3. A mí ＝＝＝ ＝＝＝ las ensaladas. *me encantan*
4. A mis primos ＝＝＝ ＝＝＝ la comida italiana. *les encanta*
5. A ti ＝＝＝ ＝＝＝ el helado de chocolate, ¿no? *te encanta*
6. A mi amiga y a mí ＝＝＝ ＝＝＝ tomar un refresco con el almuerzo. *nos encanta*

8 Gramática en contexto   Answers will vary.

Leamos/Escribamos Forma cuatro oraciones con los siguientes elementos. Usa las formas correctas de **gustar** o **encantar** con **me**, **te**, **le**, **nos** o **les**. Tus oraciones pueden ser negativas.

MODELO   A mi amigo le gusta el pan dulce.

A mí	A mi hermano/a	gustar
A nosotros/as	A mi amigo/a	encantar
A mis padres		

tomar el desayuno juntos/as	el jugo de toronja
los huevos	el pan dulce
tomar un café por la mañana	tomar leche
	el cereal

Communication for All Students

Native Speakers

8 Ask students to add a reason why they and their families like certain foods. **(Me encanta el jugo de naranja porque es dulce y muy rico.)** You might discuss what different kinds of foods people from different countries eat at each meal. For example, are foods that are normally eaten for breakfast in Ecuador or Mexico considered lunch items in the United States?

Challenge

10 Have students list some of the ingredients for several dishes as you call them out. **(ensalada de frutas, salsa de tomate, un sándwich de atún)**

Para almorzar...

la limonada — la sopa de pollo — el perro caliente — el té frío con azúcar

un sándwich de jamón

CD-ROM 2
DVD 2

la lechuga — el arroz — la manzana — las uvas — las papitas

el atún	*tuna*
la crema de maní y la jalea	*peanut butter and jelly*
el queso	*cheese*
la sopa de legumbres	*vegetable soup*

Cuaderno de actividades, p. 88, Act. 7

Cuaderno de gramática, p. 63, Acts. 5–6

También se puede decir...

Las legumbres are also called **los vegetales** or **las verduras**. Other words for **un sándwich** are **una torta** (Mexico) and **un bocadillo** (Spain).

El cacahuete and **el cacahuate** are other words for **el maní**.

Presenting
Vocabulario
Model pronunciation of these words using a tag question. Ask students if they like each item shown. (**Te gusta la limonada, ¿verdad?**) Elicit responses from several students for each question. Then ask if students can find cognates. Are there any false cognates? (**Sopa** does not mean *soap*.) Then ask students **¿Qué hay para almorzar?** They should answer with a new vocabulary word.

---

9 **¿Qué hay de comer?** Answers will vary.

Escribamos Prepara un menú para las siguientes comidas. Escribe las comidas y las bebidas apropiadas.

1. un desayuno fuerte
2. un almuerzo ligero
3. un desayuno ecuatoriano
4. un almuerzo vegetariano
5. un desayuno ligero

10 **¿Qué te gusta almorzar?** Answers will vary.

Escribamos Prepara una lista de comidas que puedes preparar con los siguientes ingredientes. Si necesitas más vocabulario, consulta la página R5.

1. queso	4. atún
2. legumbres	5. manzana
3. pollo	6. jamón

11 **Preguntas**

Hablemos Work with a partner. Pick three food items from the vocabulary or words you've learned before, but don't tell your partner what you've chosen. Using yes/no questions only, take turns trying to guess what your partner's choices are one by one.

Nota cultural

Breakfast in Spanish-speaking countries is usually eaten around 7:00 or 8:00 A.M. People often eat **un panecillo** (a plain or sweet roll) and a piece of fresh fruit, such as **papaya** or **piña** (*pineapple*). **Café con leche** (mostly warm milk with a little strong coffee), or **chocolate** (*hot chocolate*) are often served for breakfast.

Cuaderno de actividades, p. 96, Act. 20

Cultures and Communities

Culture Notes
• Explain to students that in Mexico and other Spanish-speaking countries, people often take a long lunch at midday. This means that schoolchildren often have at least an hour off for lunch, and some families can have their main meal together. In areas with oppressive midday heat, this break may include a **siesta**.

• At some restaurants in Spanish-speaking countries, an inexpensive lunch menu consists of only two or three complete meals for which substitutions cannot be made. These **menús del día**, or **comidas corrientes**, often include **una sopa**, **una ensalada**, **el primer plato**, **el segundo plato**, and **el postre**. The price of the meal usually includes bread and a beverage.

Building on Previous Skills

11 Remind students of adjectives they have learned in this and in previous chapters. Have them use these words in their questions to their partners about the foods. (**¿Es grande?, ¿Es para el desayuno?, ¿De qué color es?**)

Language Notes
• In Spanish, fast-food restaurants are called **restaurantes de comida al paso** or **de comida rápida**. Meals *to go* are **para llevar**.

• In addition to **sopa**, *soup* is also called **caldo** (or **locro**, in Ecuador, if corn is used). Stews are called **guisos**, or at times, **secos**, which means *dry*. Ask students why they think the word for *stew* is **seco**. (By comparison with soup, it is less liquid and "drier.")

• You may want to point out that Spanish often uses **de** followed by a noun to describe types of food: **ensalada de frutas, sándwich de jamón, caldo de pollo, jugo de naranja,** and so on.

Presenting
Gramática

o → ue stem-changing verbs Say **Yo almuerzo a las... Mis amigos Paco y Diana almuerzan sándwiches de...** Then ask students around the room **¿A qué hora almuerzas tú? ¿Qué almuerzan tú y tu familia? ¿A qué hora almorzamos nosotros en este colegio?** Students should respond using the appropriately conjugated verb. Continue the practice with **desayunar** and **cenar**.

Assess

▸ Testing Program, pp. 197–200
  Quiz 8-1A, Quiz 8-1B
  Audio CD 8, Tr. 19

▸ Student Make-Up Assignments, Chapter 8, Alternative Quiz

▸ Alternative Assessment Guide, p. 39

Answers

13
1. puede   4. almorzamos
2. almorzamos   5. Puedes
3. almuerzan   6. puedo

14 *Sample answer:*
Mi madre desayuna a las 7:30 y almuerza a las 2:00.

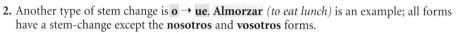

Gramática

o → ue stem-changing verbs

1. You've already learned about **e → ie** stem-changing verbs such as **querer**.

2. Another type of stem change is **o → ue**. **Almorzar** *(to eat lunch)* is an example; all forms have a stem-change except the **nosotros** and **vosotros** forms.

alm**ue**rzo	almorzamos
alm**ue**rzas	almorzáis
alm**ue**rza	alm**ue**rzan

> Cuaderno de actividades, p. 88, Act. 8

> Más práctica gramatical, p. 253, Acts. 3–4

3. Another **o → ue** stem-changing verb is **poder** *(can; to be able to)*.

> No **puedo** estudiar contigo esta noche porque tengo que trabajar.

> Cuaderno de gramática, p. 64, Acts. 7–8

---

12 **¿Qué hay de comer?**

Escuchemos/Escribamos Listen as an Ecuadorean student asks about meals in the United States. Write the time her friend says he eats each meal in the U.S., and what he eats. Scripts and answers on p. 229G.

13 **Gramática en contexto**

Leamos/Escribamos Dos amigos almuerzan juntos por primera vez. Completa su conversación con las formas correctas de **almorzar** o **poder**. See answers below.

—¡Qué lástima! Simón no ___1___ almorzar con nosotros hoy. En general, él y yo ___2___ juntos aquí los miércoles.

—Y los fines de semana, ¿a qué hora ___3___ Uds.?

—Nosotros siempre ___4___ a las dos de la tarde. ¿___5___ almorzar tú con Simón y conmigo este sábado a las dos?

—Este sábado yo no ___6___ porque tengo que trabajar. Tal vez otro día, ¿no?

—Sí, ¡cómo no!

14 **Horarios diferentes**

Escribamos/Hablemos Write three sentences saying at what time each member of your household eats breakfast and lunch. Give your partner 20 seconds to look at each sentence. Then read the sentences aloud without saying the person's name, and see if your partner can remember who it is you're talking about. Sample answer below.

15 **Y ustedes, ¿qué almuerzan?**

Hablemos Working in groups of four, take turns asking each other at what time you have breakfast and lunch, and what you usually eat for each meal. Write what each person says. Then report on those who eat meals at the same time or have similar foods for breakfast and lunch.

Nota cultural

In many Spanish-speaking countries, the main meal—called simply **la comida**—is usually eaten around two o'clock. It is typically a heavier meal than lunch in the U.S. It consists of soup, meat, or fish with rice and vegetables, followed by dessert and coffee. A typical Ecuadorean dish is **cazuela de mariscos**, a casserole prepared in a clay pot with seafood and **maní**. For many people, it is traditional to have a rest, or **siesta**, after the **comida**, and then go back to work until late evening. What advantages can you see in eating the main meal early in the day?

Communication for All Students

Tactile Learners

14 Have students write their three sentences onto strips of paper. Students should have their partner read the sentences. Then ask students to cut off each food word. Have each partner match the foods with the correct person. For a challenge, add foods that do not correspond to any family members.

Building on Previous Skills

15 Have each student invite the other three to lunch. The invitation should include the type of food and the time of day. (**¿Almuerzas conmigo en un restaurante italiano hoy a las 12:30?**) The students decline the invitation and explain why. (**No almuerzo comida italiana porque no me gusta.**) Then each student should restate the others' explanations.

CD 8 Trs. 5–8

¿Cuál es un plato típico de tu país?

There are as many different "typical" dishes in the Spanish-speaking world as there are countries and regions. In this chapter we asked people to tell us about the dishes typical to their areas.

Diana
Miami, Florida CD 8 Tr. 6

"Un plato típico… plátanos maduros con bistec empanizado… Tiene un bistec que está cocinado en pan, un poco de arroz y unos plátanos que están cocinados con azúcar".

Héctor
Valencia, Venezuela CD 8 Tr. 7

"El pabellón. Es un plato que contiene arroz, caraota, carne mechada y tajada. Es el plato típico de Venezuela".

Juan Fernando
Quito, Ecuador CD 8 Tr. 8

"El huevo frito con llapingachos y lechuga. Es uno de los platos más típicos que hay, que se inventó cuando vino la colonia española acá, ya que ellos no comían nada de lo preparado por los indígenas… Este plato lo comían los mineros en la época colonial. Llapingachos son tortillas de papa con queso".

Para pensar y hablar...

A. Do you think you would like the dishes that Diana, Héctor, and Juan Fernando describe? Which one would you most like to try? Which one least appeals to you? Why?

B. What characterizes a typical dish? List three things that could make a dish typical to a region. Then, using your list as a guide, answer the question **¿Cuál es un plato típico de tu país?** What would you suggest visitors try if they were in your area?

Cuaderno para hispanohablantes, pp. 39–40

Connections and Comparisons

Language Note

asado *grilled or roasted meat (usually beef)*
vacuno *pertaining to cattle*
pabellón *a regional dish with shredded beef, black beans, rice, and fried plantain*
caraota *bean*
carne mechada y tajada *shredded beef with fried plantain*
llapingacho *potato, egg, and cheese patty*

Thinking Critically

Drawing Conclusions Have students think about why those dishes are considered typical. Encourage students to consider geography, local agriculture, and the presence of immigrants or different ethnic groups.

CAPÍTULO 8

Teaching Resources
p. 239

PRINT
▸ Video Guide, pp. 53–55, 58
▸ Cuaderno de actividades, p. 96
▸ Cuaderno para hispanohablantes, pp. 29–30

MEDIA
▸ One-Stop Planner
▸ Video Program, Videocassette 3, 31:02–34:57
▸ DVD Tutor, Disc 2
▸ Audio Compact Discs, CD 8, Trs. 5–8
▸ Interactive CD-ROM Tutor, Disc 2

Presenting
Panorama cultural

Have students read the captions, then show the video. Discuss the questions in **Para pensar y hablar...** Play the video again and have students answer the **Preguntas.**

Preguntas

1. **¿Cuál es el plato típico de Miami, según Diana?** (plátanos con bistec)

2. **Según lo que dice Héctor, ¿qué plato es típico de Venezuela?** (el pabellón)

3. **Según Juan Fernando, ¿qué es un llapingacho?** (tortilla de papa con queso)

4. **¿Qué se come con los llapingachos?** (huevo frito y lechuga)

5. **¿Cuál es un plato típico de los Estados Unidos?** (*Answers will vary—apple pie, turkey, mashed potatoes*)

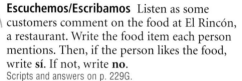
Bell Work
Have students choose items for breakfast from p. 235. Have them determine if their breakfasts are **fuertes, ligeros,** or **ecuatorianos.**

Presenting
Así se dice, Nota gramatical
Use **estar** with adjectives to describe foods. (**¿La sopa? — Está caliente.**) Elicit adjectives for the intrinsic quality of the food. (**La sopa es caliente.**) Then comment on how the food tastes. (**Hoy está fría.**)

Así se dice

Commenting on food

To find out how something tastes, ask:

¿Cómo está la sopa?
How is . . . ?

¿Y cómo están los frijoles?
And how do the beans taste?

¿Y cómo está el postre?
And how's the dessert?

Your friend might answer:

Está **deliciosa**. . . . *delicious.*
Está **fría** y **salada**. . . . *cold . . . salty.*
¡Está **caliente**! . . . *hot.*

Están muy **picantes** pero están **ricos.** . . . *spicy . . . delicious.*

¡Está muy **dulce**! *It's very sweet!*

Nota gramatical

The verb **estar** is often used to talk about how specific things taste, look, or feel. **Ser**, which also means *to be*, is used to tell what something is like, or to talk about the general nature of things. Look at the two sentences below. Which one is a general statement, and which is a comment about a particular dish?

Los camarones son ricos.
Shrimp are delicious.
Los camarones están ricos.
The shrimp are (taste) delicious.

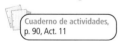

Cuaderno de actividades, p. 90, Act. 11

Cuaderno de gramática, p. 65, Acts. 9–10

Más práctica gramatical, p. 254, Acts. 5–6

16 ### Comentarios
Escuchemos/Escribamos Listen as some customers comment on the food at El Rincón, a restaurant. Write the food item each person mentions. Then, if the person likes the food, write **sí**. If not, write **no**.
Scripts and answers on p. 229G.

CD 8
Tr. 9

17 ### Gramática en contexto
Leamos Look at the Calvin and Hobbes comic strip and the statements below. Indicate whether each statement describes the opinion of Calvin or Hobbes.

1. Calvin
2. Hobbes
3. Calvin
4. Calvin
5. Hobbes

1. "Crispibombas de chocazúcar" es su cereal favorito.
2. Piensa que el cereal está demasiado dulce.
3. Piensa que el cereal no está bueno sin mucho azúcar.
4. Piensa que el cereal está delicioso.
5. Piensa que es difícil comer el cereal.

Communication for All Students

Building on Previous Skills
16 Have students make a list of three foods with descriptive adjectives. Encourage creativity. (**la sopa dulce, el sándwich congelado, el café frío**) Then have students form groups of three and ask classmates their likes and dislikes using **gustar**. Have students report on their classmates' answers. (**A Juan no le gustan las papas fritas pero a mí me gustan.**)

Visual Learners
18 Have students in groups of three or four look through magazines for depictions of food, then cut out photos or pictures they wish to describe. Have them cut and paste the images onto posterboard, adding labels describing the dish. You may wish to have them present the foods as dishes served at an elegant restaurant.

18 **Gramática en contexto**

Escribamos Write a short conversation between you and the person pictured in each drawing. Using the verb **estar,** first ask how the food tastes. Then write what the person would say as a response. Sample answer below.

Cristóbal — Leticia — Mariano — Gloria

 19 **Gramática en contexto**

Hablemos Work in pairs. Ask your partner to name a food with an unusual combination of qualities, such as **una sopa fría.** If your partner can name a food that fits in the category (such as **gazpacho,** a cold soup served in Spain), your partner wins a point. If you stump your partner, you win a point.

MODELO

—**Una ensalada dulce.**
—**La ensalada de frutas es dulce.**

comida	cualidades
sándwich	frío/a
sopa	picante
postre	dulce
ensalada	salado/a
¿?	caliente
	¿?

 20 **El menú del día**

Hablemos/Escribamos Imagine that you're planning daily menus at a local restaurant. You need to create different specials for the Monday through Friday lunch rushes. Be creative and come up with five tantalizing lunch specials. For additional food-related vocabulary, see page R5.

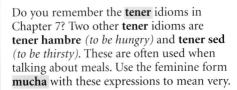

Nota gramatical

Do you remember the **tener** idioms in Chapter 7? Two other **tener** idioms are **tener hambre** (to be hungry) and **tener sed** (to be thirsty). These are often used when talking about meals. Use the feminine form **mucha** with these expressions to mean very.

Tengo mucha sed, pero no **tengo mucha** hambre.

 Cuaderno de gramática, p. 66, Acts. 11–12

Más práctica gramatical, pp. 254–255, Act. 7

 21 **Gramática en contexto**

 Escuchemos/Escribamos Cuatro amigos están en un café popular. Escucha mientras hablan de lo que van a comer. Luego contesta estas preguntas. Scripts and answers on p. 229G.

CD 8
Tr. 10

1. ¿Quién quiere desayunar?
2. ¿Quién tiene sed?
3. ¿Quién no tiene hambre?
4. ¿Quién va a comer sopa?
5. ¿Qué hay para el desayuno?

Native Speakers

19 Ask native speakers or students who have lived in or traveled to a Spanish-speaking country to help other students compile lists of "unusual" foods.

Visual Learners

19 Have students describe the foods illustrated in *Teaching Transparency 8-2,* based on each diner's reaction.

Additional Practice

20 Give each student a paper plate. Have students draw (or paste magazine pictures of) a meal on their plate. Then ask them to discuss their foods with a partner, using the vocabulary they have just learned. You might have students present their conversations to the class in pairs.

Presenting
Nota gramatical

Tener hambre, tener sed
Present students with situations to which they can respond, using an idiom with **tener.** For example, **Son las 12 del mediodía; _____. Susana quiere agua; _____.** Then have students write their own simple situation like one of these and have a partner complete it.

Connections and Comparisons

Language-to-Language
Point out that Spanish has many expressions in which the verb **tener** corresponds to the English *to be.* Ask students to recall the **tener** expressions they have learned so far (**tener años, tener prisa, tener sueño**) and their equivalents in English. Then ask students if this same correspondence is present in the **tener** expressions in the **Nota gramatical.** Point out that these expressions are formed with adjectives in English and with nouns (**hambre, sed, prisa, sueño**) in Spanish. Spanish therefore requires a form of the adjective **mucho,** and not the adverb **muy,** *very,* as would be used in English. Have students ask each other in what situations or at what time of day they are hungry, thirsty, sleepy, or in a hurry, and why.

Answers
18 *Sample answer:*
— Cristóbal, ¿cómo está la comida?
— ¡Está terrible!

Writing Assessment

25 Encourage use of varied vocabulary and grammar from this and previous chapters. Challenge students to use as many descriptive adjectives as possible in their restaurant reviews. Answer any questions, but explain that simple errors are expected and that risk-taking is rewarded. You may wish to assess the writing assignment using the following rubric.

Writing Rubric	Points			
	4	3	2	1
Content (Complete–Incomplete)				
Comprehensibility (Comprehensible–Incomprehensible)				
Accuracy (Accurate–Seldom accurate)				
Organization (Well organized–Poorly organized)				
Effort (Excellent–Minimal)				

18–20: A	14–15: C	Under
16–17: B	12–13: D	12: F

Assess

▸ Testing Program, pp. 201–204
Quiz 8-2A, Quiz 8-2B
Audio CD 8, Tr. 20

▸ Student Make-Up Assignments, Chapter 8, Alternative Quiz

▸ Alternative Assessment Guide, p. 39

---

22 **Gramática en contexto** Answers will vary.

Escribamos Completa las siguientes oraciones con tus preferencias personales.

1. Cuando tengo hambre, prefiero comer...
2. Cuando tengo sed, prefiero tomar...
3. En el verano cuando hace mucho calor me gusta comer...
4. En el invierno cuando hace frío me gusta comer... y tomar...
5. No me gusta(n) para nada...

23 **¿Te gustaría almorzar conmigo?**

Hablemos Inventa una conversación telefónica en que vas a invitar a tu compañero/a a almorzar contigo. Dile qué hay en el menú y a qué hora quieres ir. Si tu compañero/a acepta, decidan a qué hora van a ir. Si no acepta la invitación, pregúntale por qué no puede ir. ¡Sus explicaciones deben ser buenas!

¿Se te ha olvidado?
invitations
Consulta la página 208

24 **¿Qué vamos a almorzar?**

Hablemos You and your partner from the previous activity are at a local restaurant for lunch. Get together with another pair and imagine that you have all run into each other there. Talk abut the menu, whether or not you are really hungry and thirsty, and what you will order.

Nota cultural

Two common dishes in the Andes mountains are **sancocho** (a thick stew-like soup made of green plantains and corn) and **carne colorada**, (beef that has been prepared with **achiote**, or annatto, which gives it a characteristic red color). These dishes, like most Ecuadorean cuisine, are not spicy. **Ají**, a spicy condiment made of tomatoes, onions, and hot, red chili peppers, is placed on most tables at mealtime for added flavor.

ají

sancocho

25 **Mi restaurante favorito**

Escribamos What is your favorite restaurant? Write a brief review of one of your favorite places to eat. You could choose a fast-food place or an elegant restaurant. Comment on the service and the kind of food they serve. For more food-related vocabulary, turn to page R5.

Vocabulario extra	
abierto/a	*open*
el ambiente	*atmosphere*
cerrado/a	*closed*
la especialidad	*specialty*
exquisito/a	*exquisite*
el plato del día	*daily special*

Communication for All Students

Challenge

Use *Teaching Transparency 8-2* to review commenting on food and discussing preferences. Divide the class into groups of four, giving groups ten minutes to create a dialogue related to the characters in the transparency. Have them include the following elements: the location, a physical description of the people, a description of the meals being eaten, and how the people feel about their meals. Each group should also write three or four comprehension questions based on their dialogue. (**¿A Juanita le gusta la tortilla española?**) Then ask for volunteers to role-play their scene. After the role-playing, have students ask the class the comprehension questions.

La comida de las Américas

The Italians had no tomatoes for their sauce and the Irish didn't even know what a potato was until Europeans arrived in the Americas. Before that, Europeans had never eaten these foods, or peanuts, pineapples, turkey, chocolate, and squash. These foods were brought to Europe by Spanish explorers. The exchange went both ways. Many fruits, such as apples, plums, oranges, and limes, were brought from Europe or Asia and planted as seedlings in the Americas.

Para discutir... See answers below.

1. Which of the foods that you usually eat are native to the Americas?
2. Consider this typical school cafeteria menu in the United States: turkey, mashed potatoes, creamed corn, sliced tomatoes, and chocolate pudding. Which could have been eaten by Europeans before Columbus landed in the Americas in 1492?
3. Think of dishes or meals that combine food from both the Americas and Europe, and list the American and European ingredients. Example: beef tacos — beef (Europe), corn and tomato (Americas).

Vamos a comprenderlo See answers below.

Use the maps above to decide which of these foods could have been eaten by Native Americans and which by Spaniards before 1492.

french fries	hot cocoa	cornbread	roast turkey
bacon	hamburger	pork chops	ketchup
orange juice	popcorn	corn chips	steak
peanut butter	apple pie	fried squash	ice cream

Connections and Comparisons

Thinking Critically

Analyzing Ask students to consider how cuisines from around the world would be different if the early Spanish explorers had not carried foods back and forth between Europe and the Americas. (Perhaps there would be no famous Belgian chocolate, Italian tomato sauce, or German potato salad.)

Multicultural Link

The Pilgrims in Massachusetts were wary of the Native Americans' foods at first, but they soon came to cultivate and enjoy many of the same foods as their indigenous neighbors, such as corn and pumpkin. Ask students if they can think of any dishes that combine ingredients native to Europe and the Americas.

Encuentro cultural

Presenting
Encuentro cultural

After students have read **La comida de las Américas**, ask them to make a list of foods they eat frequently. Have them categorize each item under one of these headings: **de las Américas, de Europa,** or **una combinación de las dos.** Have them compare their list with a partner's. Does their partner agree that each food is placed in the correct category? Students may wish to refer to their list as they do the **Para discutir...** and **Vamos a comprenderlo** activities. You may wish to extend **Para discutir...** Activity 3 by asking students to write a breakfast, lunch, or dinner menu that contains foods from both Europe and the Americas.

Additional Practice

Have students research herbs and seasonings indigenous to Latin America and used in Latin American foods, such as **chiles, vainilla, achiote, epazote,** and **chocolate.** They may consult cookbooks, guidebooks, Web sites, and friends and family members of Latin American backgrounds. Ask students to find more information about the origin of these seasonings, as well as examples of dishes in which they are ingredients.

Answers
Para discutir
1. corn, tortillas, chocolate, potatoes . . .
2. none
3. *Answers will vary.*
Vamos a comprenderlo
Native American: french fries, peanut butter, hot cocoa, popcorn, cornbread, corn chips, fried squash, roast turkey, ketchup
European: bacon, orange juice, hamburger, apple pie, pork chops, steak, ice cream

Tercer paso

Objectives Making polite requests; ordering dinner; asking for and paying the bill in a restaurant

WV3 ECUADOR-8

Teaching Resources
pp. 244–249

PRINT 📖
▸ Lesson Planner, p. 41
▸ TPR Storytelling Book, pp. 31, 32
▸ Listening Activities, pp. 60–61, 65
▸ Activities for Communication, pp. 47–48, 112, 113–114, 151–152
▸ Cuaderno de gramática, pp. 67–69
▸ Grammar Tutor for Students of Spanish, Chapter 8
▸ Cuaderno de actividades, pp. 92–94
▸ Cuaderno para hispanohablantes, pp. 36–40
▸ Testing Program, pp. 205–208
▸ Alternative Assessment Guide, p. 39
▸ Student Make-Up Assignments, Chapter 8

MEDIA 💿📹
▸ One-Stop Planner
▸ Audio Compact Discs, CD 8, Trs. 11–17, 28–29, 21
▸ Teaching Transparencies 8-3, 8-C, 8-D; **Más práctica gramatical** Answers; Cuaderno de gramática Answers
▸ Interactive CD-ROM Tutor, Disc 2

 Bell Work
Have students list five items in a **comida ideal**. Ask them when they would eat this meal.

Presenting
Así se dice, Vocabulario Nota gramatical

Give pictures of items in the **Vocabulario** to a student. Have the student request another item. Next, prepare a table setting and invite a student to sit down with eyes closed. Remove an item and have the student ask for it.

Así se dice

Making polite requests

To ask the waitperson to bring you something, you might say:

Camarera, ¿nos puede traer el menú y unas servilletas, por favor?
Waitress, can you bring us the menu and some napkins, please?

Camarero, este plato está sucio. ¿Me puede traer un plato limpio?
Waiter, this plate is dirty. Can you bring me a clean plate?

¿Me trae un vaso de agua, **por favor?**
Will you bring me . . ., please?

También se puede decir...
Another word that you'll commonly hear in Mexico for **el camarero** or **la camarera** is **el mesero** or **la mesera**. Another word for **el menú** is **la carta**.

Vocabulario

Cuaderno de gramática, p. 67, Acts. 13–15

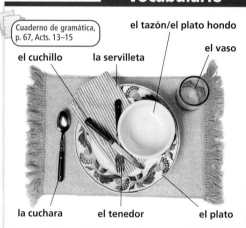

el tazón/el plato hondo
el vaso
el cuchillo
la servilleta
la cuchara
el tenedor
el plato

Nota gramatical

Otro means *other* or *another*. It agrees in gender and number with the noun it modifies.

otr**o** cuchill**o**   otr**a** servillet**a**
otr**os** plat**os**   otr**as** cuchar**as**

Cuaderno de gramática, p. 68, Acts. 16–17

Más práctica gramatical, p. 255, Act. 8

26 **Gramática en contexto** Answers on p. 245.

 Escribamos Look at the drawings and decide what each of the diners needs. Write a sentence in which each person asks the waitperson for what is needed.

1. los chicos

2. Claudia

3. Tanya

Communication for All Students

Native Speakers
Have students ask each other if they like each of the food items presented on p. 245 and why or why not. When, or for what meal, do they tend to eat these items and how do they like them to be prepared? Do students know how to prepare the items? Have students categorize the food regarding their nutritional or health value.

Kinesthetic Learners
27 Distribute a set of plastic cutlery, dishes, and bowls to pairs of students and have them hold up the appropriate utensil and dish as they give the answers. Add several items from the menu to continue the activity. You can also have them role-play a scene in a restaurant in which they ask the waitperson to bring them extra utensils and dishes.

Vocabulario

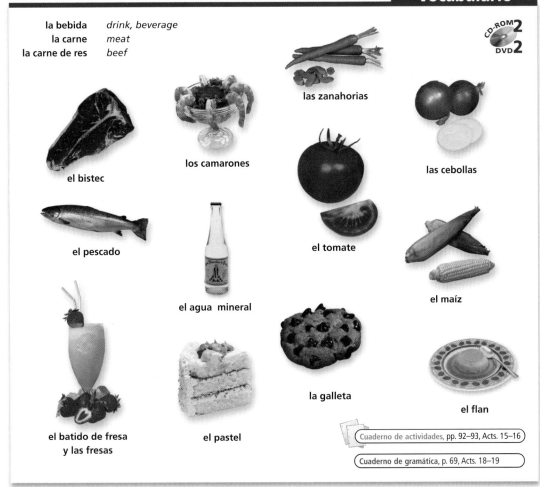

la bebida	drink, beverage
la carne	meat
la carne de res	beef

las zanahorias

los camarones

el bistec

las cebollas

el pescado

el tomate

el agua mineral

el maíz

el batido de fresa
y las fresas

el pastel

la galleta

el flan

CD-ROM 2
DVD 2

 Cuaderno de actividades, pp. 92–93, Acts. 15–16

Cuaderno de gramática, p. 69, Acts. 18–19

---

27 **Y para comer...** See answers below.

Escribamos Nombra todo lo que necesitas para comer lo siguiente. Usa el vocabulario en la página 244.

1. el helado
2. las legumbres
3. la ensalada
4. el arroz
5. los huevos
6. la sopa

28 **¿Me trae...?**

Escuchemos Imagine you're eating at Restaurante El Molino, a busy restaurant in Quito. Listen to these orders and decide whether each person is ordering breakfast, lunch, dinner, or dessert. Scripts and answers on p. 229H.

CD 8
Tr. 11

Nota cultural

In Spanish-speaking countries, **la cena** is a light meal, usually eaten around 8:00 P.M., sometimes as late as 10:00 P.M. (or even later) in Spain. People generally eat a snack (**una merienda**) around 5:00 P.M. In Ecuador, **la merienda** usually consists of tea or coffee with bread, or perhaps a bowl of soup.

Cultures and Communities

Community Link
If possible, plan a trip to a Spanish or to a Latin American restaurant. You might prearrange with the manager for Spanish-speaking employees to speak only Spanish with the students, if possible. Students should order their food in Spanish.

Career Path
Ask students to list food-related careers in which they can use Spanish. Many companies do international business; others have a growing Spanish-speaking clientele. Some ideas are: restaurants (server, chef, owner), retail companies (advertising, management), wholesale companies (international trade, market research), health fields (dietician, trainer), and science fields (food research).

Kinesthetic Learners
Have a student set a table (**poner la mesa**) according to your instructions. Using **Pon** and **No pongas** and the prepositions of place, tell the student what utensils and dishes to put on the table and where to put them. After students have mastered the vocabulary, ask one of them to give instructions while another sets the table. You might also do this activity with all of the students while they sit at their own desks and use plastic utensils.

Presenting
Vocabulario

To model pronunciation, tell students you are very hungry and say which things you would like to eat. Then ask students, **¿Qué te gusta cenar?** and **¿Qué hay para cenar?** Have them answer using the new vocabulary.

---

26 Answers
1. Por favor, ¿nos trae unas servilletas?
2. Por favor, ¿me puede traer un tenedor?
3. Por favor, ¿me trae un cuchillo?

27
1. la cuchara
2. el tenedor
3. el tenedor
4. el tenedor
5. el tenedor
6. la cuchara

Teaching Resources
pp. 244–249

PRINT 📖

▶ Lesson Planner, p. 40
▶ TPR Storytelling Book, pp. 31, 32
▶ Listening Activities, pp. 60–61, 65
▶ Activities for Communication, pp. 47–48, 112, 113–114, 151–152
▶ Cuaderno de gramática, pp. 67–69
▶ Grammar Tutor for Students of Spanish, Chapter 8
▶ Cuaderno de actividades, pp. 92–94
▶ Cuaderno para hispanohablantes, pp. 36–40
▶ Testing Program, pp. 205–208
▶ Alternative Assessment Guide, p. 39
▶ Student Make-Up Assignments, Chapter 8

MEDIA 💿📼

▶ One-Stop Planner
▶ Audio Compact Discs, CD 8, Trs. 11–17, 28–29, 21
▶ Teaching Transparencies 8-3, 8-C, 8-D; **Más práctica gramatical** Answers; Cuaderno de gramática Answers
▶ Interactive CD-ROM Tutor, Disc 2

Presenting
Así se dice

Model a restaurant scene by asking **¿Qué le puedo traer?** Students answer with **Me puede traer...** After students complete Activities 29 and 30, introduce the next **Así se dice** by replaying the **fotonovela** restaurant scene.

Answers

29 *Possible answers:*

1. la sopa del día, por favor
2. una legumbre, por favor
3. el maíz
4. una ensalada
5. tomar un refresco
6. No, gracias

Así se dice

Ordering dinner in a restaurant

To find out what a friend is going to order, ask:

¿Qué vas a pedir?
What are you going to order?

Your friend might say:

Voy a pedir los camarones.
I'm going to order . . .

The waitperson might ask:

¿Qué le puedo traer?
What can I bring you?

You might answer:

Yo quisiera el bistec.
I would like . . .

 Cuaderno de actividades, p. 94, Act. 17

---

29 **¿Qué vas a pedir?** See answers below.

Leamos/Escribamos Estás en un restaurante y el camarero va a tomar tu orden. Lee su parte del diálogo y completa tu parte pidiendo la comida. Usa el vocabulario que has aprendido. ¡No olvides ser cortés!

EL CAMARERO	TÚ
Buenas tardes. ¿Qué le puedo traer?	Buenas tardes, pues, ___1___.
Excelente. La sopa del día es sopa de legumbres.	Muy bien, y ___2___.
¿Prefiere las zanahorias o el maíz?	Prefiero ___3___.
¿Quiere una ensalada?	Sí, ___4___.
Y para tomar, ¿qué le puedo traer?	Me gustaría ___5___.
¿Algo más?	___6___.

30 **¿Qué van a pedir Uds.?**

 Escribamos/Hablemos Imagine that your favorite restaurant is offering you a day of free meals. Make a list of what you want to eat for breakfast, lunch, and dinner. Write when you want to eat each meal. Then ask your partners when they want to eat each meal, and what they're going to order. Decide which person has tastes most like yours.

Así se dice

Asking for and paying the bill in a restaurant

The waitperson may say:

¿Desean algo más?
Do you want anything else?

To ask the waitperson for the bill, say:

¿Nos puede traer la cuenta?
La cuenta, por favor.

To ask about the amount of the bill and the tip, say:

¿Cuánto es?
¿Está incluida la propina?
Is the tip included?

The waitperson might say:

Son veinte mil pesos.
No, no está incluida. **Es aparte.**
. . . It's separate.

Cuaderno de actividades, p. 94, Act. 18

Communication for All Students

Challenge

30 Have groups of three or four create a restaurant scene with a waiter or waitress and customers. Students should order using material from **Así se dice, Nota gramatical,** and **Vocabulario** pp. 244–246. What follows should be up to students: Have them act out reactions to problems with utensils and food, mixed up orders, improper billing, and so on. Encourage creativity.

Auditory Learners

31 Have two students come to the board to write out a simple math problem you dictate in Spanish. (**doscientos más treinta y tres**) They should solve the problem on the board, and then pronounce the answer clearly. (**Son doscientos treinta y tres.**) The first to do so remains at the board to face a new challenger and a new math problem. You may wish to vary the level of difficulty.

How do you get the attention of the waitperson in a crowded restaurant? Do you raise your hand? Do you call out loud? What is considered rude in one place may be perfectly acceptable somewhere else. In many Spanish-speaking countries, it's considered rude to raise your voice in a crowded room. In Spain, for example, people make the sound *tch-tch* to get the waitperson's attention; in Costa Rica it's *pfft*. In Colombia people clap or raise their hands.

Vocabulario

Los números del 200 al 100.000

200	doscientos/as	700	setecientos/as	10.000	diez mil
300	trescientos/as	800	ochocientos/as	45.000	cuarenta y cinco mil
400	cuatrocientos/as	900	novecientos/as	80.000	ochenta mil
500	quinientos/as	1.000	mil	100.000	cien mil
600	seiscientos/as				

1. When numbers 200 to 900 modify a noun, they agree with the gender of the noun.

seiscient**os** libr**os**   seiscient**as** cas**as**

2. Notice that in Spanish you can use a period instead of a comma when writing large numbers (one thousand or greater).

15.216   23.006   1.800   47.811   9.433

Más práctica gramatical, p. 255, Act. 9

Cuaderno de gramática, p. 69, Acts. 20–21

Presenting
Vocabulario

Make two sets of large flashcards: one with numbers from **Vocabulario** and one with pictures of vocabulary words. Begin by modeling pronunciation and having students read the explanation on gender agreement on this page. Then hold up one number card *(800)* and one picture card *(spoon)*. Say **ochocientas cucharas.** Then ask a student **¿Cuántas cucharas?** to elicit the answer. Continue with other pictures and numbers.

Culture Note
In many Spanish-speaking countries, it is important for travelers to know how to express large numbers. Sometimes local currency units are hundreds or even thousands to the U.S. dollar.

See answers below.

31 **¿Cómo se dicen?**

Hablemos ¿Cómo se dicen estos números en español?

1. 27.500
2. 3.609
3. 534
4. 94.800
5. 2.710
6. 615
7. 45.370
8. 8.112
9. 19.400
10. 100.000

32 **¿Cuánto es?** Scripts and answers on p. 229H.

Escuchemos Look at the menu and listen to the following prices in pesos. Match the price mentioned with the correct item on the menu.

CD 8 Tr. 12

Platos del día
Ensalada mixta $2.000
Ceviche de camarón $4.250
Sancocho $3.500
Arroz con pollo $4.750
Plato Vegetariano $3.800

Bebidas
Gaseosas $850
Té helado $550

Postres
Helado de naranjilla $1.260
Canoa de frutas $2.230

Teacher to Teacher

Bill Heller
Perry High School
Perry, New York

For Bill's students, learning is a numbers game

"After dividing my class into teams of ten, I prepare sets of large numerals 0–9 on 6" × 9" pieces of tagboard. I make each set using a different color, and add extra zeros to each set. Each student receives a card in his or her team's color. I call out a number once, and the students holding the digits in that number run to the front of the room and stand in the correct order. The first team to form the number gets a point. Then students return to their seats and a new number is called. Students shouting numbers in English disqualify their team. The first team to reach five points wins."

31 Answers
1. veintisiete mil quinientos
2. tres mil seiscientos nueve
3. quinientos treinta y cuatro
4. noventa y cuatro mil ochocientos
5. dos mil setecientos diez
6. seiscientos quince
7. cuarenta y cinco mil trescientos setenta
8. ocho mil ciento doce
9. diecinueve mil cuatrocientos
10. cien mil

Teaching Resources
pp. 244–249

PRINT

▸ Lesson Planner, p. 40
▸ TPR Storytelling Book, pp. 31, 32
▸ Listening Activities, pp. 60–61, 65
▸ Activities for Communication, pp. 47–48, 112, 113–114, 151–152
▸ Cuaderno de gramática, pp. 67–69
▸ Grammar Tutor for Students of Spanish, Chapter 8
▸ Cuaderno de actividades, pp. 92–94
▸ Cuaderno para hispanohablantes, pp. 36–40
▸ Testing Program, pp. 205–208
▸ Alternative Assessment Guide, p. 39
▸ Student Make-Up Assignments, Chapter 8

MEDIA

▸ One-Stop Planner
▸ Audio Compact Discs, CD 8, Trs. 11–17, 28–29, 21
▸ Teaching Transparencies 8-3, 8-C, 8-D; **Más práctica gramatical** Answers; Cuaderno de gramática Answers
▸ Interactive CD-ROM Tutor, Disc 2

TPR Use the recipes students collected for the Projects (p. 229C) to reinforce food vocabulary. Assign each student an ingredient from a recipe. Students should provide a visual representation of their ingredient. (Mount a magazine clipping of the ingredient on construction paper, or cut the shape out of poster board.) Collect the images, review them with the class, shuffle them, and hand one out to each student. Then give commands to make the various recipes. For example, if the recipe is **paella,** you might say **Arroz, ¡levántate! Camarones, ven acá. Pollo, ponte al lado de los camarones,** and so on.

---

 33 En mi cuaderno

Escribamos Write a dialogue in which you and a friend are customers in a restaurant. One of you has 12,000 pesos and wants to treat the other to dinner. Using the menu from Activity 32, discuss everything you want to order and the price of each item you choose. Add up the prices and be sure you have enough money to pay for your meal before you order.

34 La cuenta, por favor

Hablemos Work with a partner. Use these receipts to role-play scenes in a restaurant. One will take the role of the customer and ask for the bill. The other will take the role of the waitperson and add up the receipt. Switch roles and repeat the scene with the second receipt.

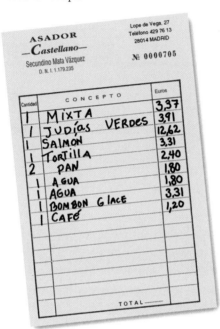

Nota cultural

tortilla española

In Spanish, as in English, a word can have more than one meaning. In Spain, a **tortilla** is a kind of omelet. The **tortilla española**, made of eggs, potatoes, onions, salt, and olive oil, is a popular dish for a light evening meal. In Mexico and Central America, a **tortilla** is made from cornmeal or flour, pressed into a flat round shape, and cooked on a griddle. These tortillas are the bread that goes with almost all meals. They are especially good when they're hot and fresh off the griddle.

Connections and Comparisons

 ### Culture Note

Tortillas are a staple in Mexico and some Central American countries. Supermarkets and restaurants make and sell them fresh every day. These are usually made in huge quantities in stores called **tortillerías.** However, many people still prefer to make them by hand. **Tortillas** are far less common in most of South America, except in Mexican restaurants. As a comparative project, you might have one group of students find a recipe for **tortilla española** on the Internet and another group use the recipe for corn **tortillas** on page 77D. They can make their dishes for the class and role-play a restaurant scene in which students order one dish or the other. Ask the class what other foods might go well with either type of **tortilla.**

Hablemos While spending the summer with a family in Miami, Florida, you get a job as a waitperson in an Ecuadorean restaurant. Two of your classmates are customers in your restaurant. Create a conversation that includes some small talk, a request for utensils and napkins, and information about dishes on the menu. The customers comment on the food while they are eating, and then ask you for the bill and pay it. Be prepared to present your scene to the class. Answers will vary.

Nota cultural

Did you know that if you order fruit for dessert in Spain or Latin America, it will be served on a plate with a knife and fork? Instead of switching the hand holding the fork after cutting, Spaniards and Latin Americans usually keep the knife in the right hand and the fork in the left. You may have been taught to put your free hand in your lap, but people in other countries often feel it's more polite to keep both hands on the table throughout the meal.

SUGERENCIA

Learning a foreign language is like any other long-term project, such as getting into shape or taking up a new sport: it may take some time to see the results you want. Don't get discouraged, and remember that you can learn Spanish! Keep yourself motivated by setting short-term, realistic goals. A simple goal could be learning five additional words this week or reading an interesting-looking article in a Spanish-language magazine. Once you've learned more Spanish, you could make a goal of going to a store or restaurant in a Spanish-speaking part of town and doing some shopping or ordering a meal entirely in Spanish.

LETRA Y SONIDO

CD 8
Trs. 13–17

A. The letter **c** before the vowels **e** and **i** is pronounced like **s**, as in **centro**, **cielo**. Before the vowels **a**, **o**, and **u** the letter **c** is pronounced like the *k* in the English word *kitchen*.

carne   rico   cuchara   delicioso   cebolla   dulce   camarero

To spell the *k* sound of the word *kitchen* before the vowels **e** and **i**, use the letters **qu**.

que   química   saque   quien   quinientos   queso

The pattern is similar to the one you learned for when the letters **g** and **j** sound alike.

B. Dictado Script for Part B on p. 229H.

Anita needs help with a cake recipe. Write what she says.

C. Trabalenguas

¿Quién quiere pastel de chocolate?

¿Cuánto queso cabe en la caja?

¿Cómo quiere que Queta conduzca el carro?

Communication for All Students

Native Speakers

In the *Native Speaker Activity Book,* Chapter 5, there is a discussion of the letters **c, s,** and **z**. Since all of these letters are pronounced [s] in various countries, native speakers may have developed erroneous spelling habits. The **Letra y sonido** reminds them that **c** followed by **i** or **e** is pronounced like **s** in the Americas. Have students review the lists of words they made in Activity 6 on p. 23. You might also consider having students listen to **Las mañanitas** on Audio CD 10, Tr. 29. Have them listen for words with the [s] sound, and then help them determine the proper spelling.

STANDARDS: 1.1, 3.2, 4.2, 5.1, 5.2

Tercer paso

Kinesthetic Learners

35 To heighten realism and facilitate role-play, provide two or three sets of props for students to use during this activity. Other groups may practice or work on written assignments while "waiting to be seated" at the "dining area."

Speaking Assessment

35 Before the students present Activity 35 to the class, have each group evaluate another. Explain the assessment mode before they act out their scenes. You may wish to evaluate their performance using the following rubric.

Speaking Rubric	Points			
	4	3	2	1
Content (Complete–Incomplete)				
Comprehension (Total–Little)				
Comprehensibility (Comprehensible–Incomprehensible)				
Accuracy (Accurate–Seldom accurate)				
Fluency (Fluent–Not fluent)				

18–20: A   14–15: C   Under
16–17: B   12–13: D   12: F

Assess

▸ Testing Program, pp. 205–208
  Quiz 8-3A, Quiz 8-3B
  Audio CD 8, Tr. 21

▸ Student Make-Up Assignments, Chapter 8, Alternative Quiz

▸ Alternative Assessment Guide, p. 39

Teaching Resources
pp. 250–251

PRINT
- Lesson Planner, p. 41
- Cuaderno de actividades, p. 95
- Cuaderno para hispanohablantes, pp. 36–38
- Reading Strategies and Skills Handbook, Chapter 8
- ¡Lee conmigo! 1, Chapter 8
- Standardized Assessment Tutor, Chapter 8

MEDIA
- One-Stop Planner

Prereading
Activity A

Paraphrasing
Have students paraphrase the title and subtitle of this essay in Spanish.

Using Prior Knowledge
Ask students to think about how recipes are organized. What typically appears first? What comes next? What sometimes accompanies recipes in cookbooks or magazines? List student responses on the board and then ask them if the recipes on pp. 250–251 appear to correspond to this typical organization. Remind them to keep this information in mind when doing Activities C and D.

Ask students to use their knowledge of the organization of recipes to create a mock-up of a recipe for a refreshing summer drink. Have them compare their mock-ups with one another and with the recipes in the text. What types of formats make recipes easy or difficult to follow?

Vamos a leer

Sorbetes y batidos

Estrategia para leer
Many articles have a clear organization, showing that the author probably followed an outline. If you can find the organization of a text, it will be easier to understand the main ideas, and you will know where to look for certain details. In this selection, the bold print and larger print will help you see some of the text's organization.

¡A comenzar!
Before you read the article, read the title, introduction, and subtitles to find out what this article is about.

A. Which of the following best expresses the meaning of the title and subtitles?
   1. Sorbets and milkshakes: Fruits, eggs, and milk make a healthy breakfast combination.
   2. Milkshakes: Fruits and milk are very healthy when combined.
   3. Sorbets and milkshakes: Fruits, ice, and milk can make a healthy and refreshing combination.

Al grano
B. The article "Sorbetes y batidos" is organized and easy to outline. Outlining is a great way to understand a reading, whether it be your social studies chapter or an article in Spanish like this one. On a piece of paper fill in the missing information.

por Bárbara Benavides

En junio, julio y agosto disfrutamos de unas combinaciones deliciosas, como los batidos y los sorbetes. Se puede combinar la leche, las frutas y un poco de hielo para producir una combinación refrescante.

Cuando hace mucho calor nos encantan siempre las bebidas frías. Una de las mejores maneras de disfrutar del verano es experimentar la increíble sensación de un buen refresco. Muchas veces tenemos ganas de tomar limonada o té helado o sólo agua fría. Pero a veces es más divertido preparar batidos y sorbetes.

Las frutas tropicales, como el plátano, la piña, la papaya y el mango, añaden un sabor exótico y son ideales para la creación de los batidos y los sorbetes. Existe una variedad enorme de frutas que se puede usar. También, tienen vitaminas y minerales importantes para la nutrición diaria.

LOS SORBETES

Sorbete de mango, pera y durazno (Sirve dos)
1 taza de pera
1 taza de mango
1 taza de durazno
2 vasos de jugo de naranja
1 taza de azúcar en polvo

Pele las frutas, quite las semillas y córtelas en pedacitos. Bata las frutas, el jugo de naranja y el azúcar en polvo en la licuadora. Ponga la mezcla en la sorbetera (máquina de hacer helado) o siga las instrucciones de la receta siguiente para hacer el sorbete en el congelador.

Sorbete de naranja (Sirve uno)
3 naranjas
1/2 limón
1/2 taza de azúcar en polvo

Exprima el limón y las naranjas. Agregue y disuelva bien el azúcar en polvo. Ponga los ingredientes en la sorbetera y siga las instrucciones para hacer el helado-sorbete. Si no tiene sorbetera, ponga la mezcla en las bandejitas del congelador. Cuando se formen cubitos de hielo, pase todo a la licuadora y haga un puré. Coloque en un recipiente de plástico y vuelva a congelar en seguida.

Connections and Comparisons

Health Link
Ask students why fruits are considered one of the most healthful foods in our diet. (They supply carbohydrates, essential vitamins, minerals, and fiber.) Have students choose a specific fruit and research its nutritional value and then report their findings using as much Spanish as possible.

Multicultural Link
Some tropical fruits popular in Latin America are also popular in Africa. These include oranges, bananas, pineapples, mangoes, papayas, soursop (**guanábana**), and sweetsop, or sugar apple. Have students research fruits native to Southeast Asia, Africa, and Australia. Ask them to report what they discover using as much Spanish as possible.

LOS BATIDOS

Los batidos se hacen con frutas combinadas con leche y hielo. Para darles una consistencia espesa, se necesita batir los ingredientes en una licuadora.

Batido de plátano con fresas (Sirve uno)

1/2 taza de plátanos
1/2 taza de fresas
1 vaso de leche
1/3 taza de hielo picado
azúcar al gusto

Mezcle en la licuadora y se sirve bien frío.

Batido de papaya (Sirve uno)

2 tazas de pulpa de papaya
1-1/2 taza de leche o agua
1/2 taza de azúcar
jugo de limón si se usa agua
hielo picado

Mezcle todos los ingredientes en la licuadora con leche o agua.

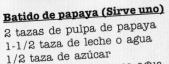

Batido de moras (Sirve uno)

1 vaso de leche
1 taza de moras (o fresas, frambuesas, o zarzamoras)
2 cucharadas de azúcar
hielo picado

Mezcle en la licuadora y se sirve bien frío.

Batidos y sorbetes

Title: _____

Author: _____ Bárbara Benavides

I. Introduction

   A. Frozen drinks are great in summer.

   B. Tropical fruits are ideal for these drinks.

II. Los sorbetes   Sorbete de mango, pera y durazno

   A. _____

   B. _____ Sorbete de naranja

III. _____

   A. _____ Los batidos

   B. Batido de papaya Batido de plátano con fresas

   C. _____ Batido de moras

¿Te acuerdas?

Scan to find specific information. Make a list of what you're looking for, and look for key words as you scan.

C. You'd like your school cafeteria to offer some of these delicious items. Your cafeteria director agrees, but has a few questions.

  1. What kinds of fruits are recommended (according to the introduction)? tropical fruits

  2. How many servings does the "Batido de papaya" make? 1

  3. What fruit, other than oranges, is in the "Sorbete de naranja"? lemon

D. ¡Ahora te toca a ti! Inventa una receta nueva para un batido o un sorbete. Si usas palabras y frases de estas recetas, puedes hacer todo en español. Answers will vary.

Cuaderno para hispanohablantes, pp. 36–38

Cuaderno de actividades, p. 95, Act. 19

Reading
Activities B and C

Using Text Structures

Al grano Have students read the passage and describe how it is organized. Once they recognize a rough outline, ask if they have any other ideas about how the author could have organized the essay. (recipes with orange first, recipes with other fruit second; discussion of tropical fruits first, recipes second)

Comparing and Contrasting

B. After students have finished adding the missing information to the outline, have them go back and reorganize a reading from a previous chapter.

C. Ask students to make up additional questions using more of the text.

Postreading
Activity D

Using Prior Knowledge

D. Have students come up with an original recipe. Have them use the various verbs and commands to write a recipe for a tropical fruit salad, a fruit-filled gelatin mold, or frozen fruit pops. You may wish to have students create an imaginary **batido** or **sorbete** using unlikely ingredients. Ask volunteers to read their recipes aloud and have the class vote on the ones they think would taste the best and the worst.

Communication for All Students

Native Speakers

Have your students bring in a family recipe or find one in a Spanish-language cookbook. Have them write out the instructions, then write a paragraph explaining why they chose that recipe. Is the recipe a personal favorite? Is this dish representative of their culture?

Additional Vocabulary

You might find the following phrases helpful:

un tercio de taza, la tercera parte de una taza *a third of a cup*
media taza *a half cup*
una taza y media *a cup and a half*
una cucharada *tablespoon*
batir *to beat*
picado *chopped, diced*

For **Más práctica gramatical** Answer Transparencies, see the *Teaching Transparencies* binder.

Más práctica gramatical

Primer paso   **Objective** Talking about meals and food

1 ¿Qué les encanta a estas personas para el desayuno? Usa el pronombre del complemento indirecto y la forma correcta del verbo **encantar** en cada oración. (**p. 236**)

> **MODELO**   **Mari/pan tostado**
> **A Mari le encanta el pan tostado.**

1. Félix/pan dulce
2. tú/huevos con tocino
3. yo/fruta
4. mis padres/café con leche
5. todos nosotros/jugo de naranja
6. Carolina/desayunos ligeros

2 You're planning what to serve at your party. Explain people's likes and dislikes, using the chart below and the verbs **encantar** and **gustar** in each sentence. (**p. 236**)

> **MODELO**   Norberto
> **A Norberto le encantan las empanadas. No le gustan las ensaladas.**

	SÍ	NO
Norberto	las empanadas	las ensaladas
1. yo	el jugo	los refrescos
2. todos nosotros	el helado de chocolate	el helado de piña
3. Marcela	la comida china	la comida mexicana
4. Carolina y Esteban	los sándwiches	las hamburguesas

Answers

1 1. A Félix le encanta el pan dulce.
2. A ti te encantan los huevos con tocino.
3. A mí me encanta la fruta.
4. A mis padres les encanta el café con leche.
5. A todos nosotros nos encanta el jugo de naranja.
6. A Carolina le encantan los desayunos ligeros.

2 1. A mí me encanta el jugo. No me gustan los refrescos.
2. A todos nosotros nos encanta el helado de chocolate. No nos gusta el helado de piña.
3. A Marcela le encanta la comida china. No le gusta la comida mexicana.
4. A Carolina y Esteban les encantan los sándwiches. No les gustan las hamburguesas.

Grammar Resources for Chapter 8

The **Más práctica gramatical** activities are designed as supplemental activities for the grammatical concepts presented in the chapter. You might use them as additional practice, for review, or for assessment.

For more grammar presentation, review, and practice, refer to the following:
- Cuaderno de gramática
- Grammar Tutor for Students of Spanish

- Grammar Summary on pp. R9–R13
- Cuaderno de actividades
- Grammar and Vocabulary quizzes (Testing Program)
- Test Generator on the One-Stop Planner CD-ROM
- Interactive CD-ROM Tutor
- **Juegos interactivos** at <u>go.hrw.com</u>

3 Decide what everyone is having for lunch. Use the subject pronoun, if needed; the correct form of **almorzar**; the correct indefinite article; and a food from the box in each sentence. (**p. 238**)

MODELO   A Sonia le encantan los mangos, las uvas y los plátanos.
          Ella almuerza una ensalada de frutas.

sopa de pollo   ensalada de frutas   ensalada
hamburguesa
pizza
sándwiches de crema de maní   tacos

1. A mí me encanta la comida italiana.
2. A Roberto y a Talía les encantan los sándwiches.
3. A Teodoro le encanta el pollo.
4. A ti te encanta la comida mexicana.
5. A nosotros nos encantan las legumbres.
6. A la profesora Benavides le encanta la carne *(meat)*.

4 Indica qué pueden preparar y comprar las siguientes personas para el picnic de la clase. Usa el verbo **poder** y la información en la lista de abajo. (**p. 238**)

MODELO   Celia puede preparar las hamburguesas. Y puede comprar
          la limonada también.

	PARA PREPARAR	PARA COMPRAR
Celia	hamburguesas	limonada
1. yo	ensalada de frutas	helado
2. Gilberto	sancocho	papitas
3. Ana y Gonzalo	empanadas	perros calientes
4. todos nosotros	sándwiches	refrescos

Answers

3
1. Almuerzo una pizza.
2. Ellos almuerzan unos sándwiches de crema de maní.
3. Él almuerza una sopa de pollo.
4. Almuerzas unos tacos.
5. Almorzamos una ensalada.
6. Ella almuerza una hamburguesa.

4
1. Yo puedo preparar la ensalada de frutas. Y puedo comprar el helado también.
2. Gilberto puede preparar el sancocho. Y puede comprar las papitas también.
3. Ana y Gonzalo pueden preparar las empanadas. Y pueden comprar los perros calientes también.
4. Todos nosotros podemos preparar los sándwiches. Y podemos comprar los refrescos también.

Communication for All Students

Visual Learners

3 Have students use magazine cutouts and markers to create and illustrate menus for an imaginary café. Have them give the café a name in Spanish, then assign categories for each type of food or drink served. Encourage creative dishes with descriptions. They may choose a currency from a Spanish-speaking country as they set prices, which they should write out. Display the completed menus.

Building on Previous Skills

4 Have students pretend to have a picnic. They will identify what each guest brings, and find out where the item is. Have them name five guests and the item(s) brought. (**¿Qué trae Juan?**) The answer should use a form of **ser**. (**Son papas.**) The next question elicits the location of the item(s). (**¿Y dónde están?**) Answers should include a prepositional phrase. (**Están al lado del flan.**)

Más práctica gramatical

CAPÍTULO 8

For **Más práctica gramatical**
Answer Transparencies, see the
Teaching Transparencies binder.

Más práctica gramatical

CD-ROM 2
DVD 2
WV3 ECUADOR-8

Segundo paso   Objective Commenting on food

5 Would you use **ser** or **estar** in the following situations? Indicate which verb is correct, then complete each statement or question by filling in each blank with the correct form of the verb. (**p. 240**)

1. to ask what sancocho is
   ¿Qué ════ el sancocho?

2. to say what your favorite fruit is
   La piña ════ mi fruta favorita.

3. to tell your aunt that the meal she prepared tastes great
   Tía, la comida ════ deliciosa.

4. to describe the food you generally have at home
   La comida que preparamos en casa ════ muy buena.

5. to tell your little brother to be careful because the soup is very hot
   ¡Cuidado! La sopa ════ muy caliente.

6. to say that Ecuadorean food is not spicy
   La comida ecuatoriana no ════ picante.

7. to compliment your family on your delicious birthday cake
   ¡El pastel ════ muy rico!

6 Completa los comentarios de María, Hiroshi, Tomás y Roberto. Usa la forma correcta de **ser** o **estar**. (**p. 240**)

1. ¡Qué calientes ════ las empanadas! Así me gustan.
2. El ají que prepara mi abuela siempre ════ muy rico, y no ════ muy picante.
3. El ají aquí ════ bastante picante hoy, pero me gusta así.
4. ¡Mmm! La carne colorada ════ deliciosa hoy. Hiroshi, ¿no quieres un poco?
5. Hiroshi, ¿cómo ════ un desayuno típico en tu país?
6. Pienso que los desayunos norteamericanos ════ más fuertes que los desayunos ecuatorianos.
7. Siempre tomo jugo para el desayuno. El jugo de piña ════ muy rico.
8. El sancocho ════ un poco salado, ¿verdad? ¿Quién quiere más agua?

7 Read what these people have to eat and drink, and then summarize each statement with the correct form of (**no**) **tener hambre** or (**no**) **tener sed**. (**p. 241**)

MODELO   ¡Chen quiere comer sancocho, empanadas y carne colorada!
              Tiene mucha hambre.

1. Hace mucho calor. Vamos a tomar un vaso de limonada grande.
2. Hoy Rafael almuerza sólo una manzana y un vaso de leche.
3. Después del partido de fútbol, Fabián come dos hamburguesas.

Answers

5 1. ser, es
   2. ser, es
   3. estar, está
   4. ser, es
   5. estar, está
   6. ser, es
   7. estar, está

6 1. están
   2. es, es
   3. está
   4. está
   5. es
   6. son
   7. es
   8. está

7 1. Tenemos mucha sed.
   2. No tiene hambre.
   3. Tiene mucha hambre.
   4. No tengo sed.
   5. No tiene hambre.
   6. Tenemos mucha hambre.
   7. No tienen hambre.
   8. Tienes mucha sed.

Teacher to Teacher

**Maritza and
Robert Furillo**
Franklin Alternative
Middle School
Columbus, Ohio

The Furillos' students aim high
❝We use a felt-face dart board with the numbers 100–100,000 and play money to teach numbers and purchasing food. 'Meals of the day,' labeled and priced, are displayed. We ask **¿Cuántos puntos ganaste?** each time a student throws a small Velcro® ball that sticks to the board. The student must reply correctly in order to get that amount of money. The money is used to purchase the different meals, but the student must order and pay for the chosen meal in Spanish. The student with the most meals wins some kind of prize.❞

4. No quiero más jugo, gracias.

5. Mamá no quiere cenar esta noche. Está un poco enferma y necesita descansar.

6. Cuando regresamos a casa después de clases, siempre preparamos unos sándwiches de crema de maní muy grandes.

7. Fátima y Alonso no desayunan esta mañana.

8. Tomas mucha agua durante tu clase de ejercicios aeróbicos, ¿verdad?

Tercer paso

Objectives Making polite requests; ordering dinner in a restaurant; asking for and paying the bill in a restaurant

8 How would you ask the waiter to bring you and your family another of the following things? (**p. 244**)

MODELO   yo/refresco
                ¿Me trae otro refresco, por favor?

1. nosotros/menú
2. nosotros/servilletas
3. yo/agua mineral
4. yo/cuchara
5. yo/plato
6. nosotros/vasos
7. yo/flan
8. yo/ensalada

9 Your friends from Colombia and Venezuela are explaining how much dishes cost at their favorite restaurants. Write what they say, spelling out all numbers. (**p. 247**)

MODELO   **arroz con pollo/5.300 pesos**
                El arroz con pollo cuesta (costs) **cinco mil trescientos pesos.**

En Colombia

1. ensalada mixta/1.750 pesos
2. empanadas de atún/3.200 pesos
3. sancocho/4.250 pesos
4. agua mineral/1.150 pesos
5. sopa de ajiaco/2.500 pesos

En Venezuela

6. pabellón/1.250 bolívares
7. carne colorada/1.325 bolívares
8. empanadas de papa y queso/ 950 bolívares
9. arroz con mariscos/1.630 bolívares
10. flan/575 bolívares

Review and Assess

You may wish to assign the **Más práctica gramatical** activities as additional practice or homework after presenting material throughout the chapter. Assign Activities 1–2 after **Gramática** (p. 236), Activities 3–4 after **Gramática** (p. 238), Activities 5–6 after **Nota gramatical** (p. 240), Activity 7 after **Nota gramatical** (p. 241), Activity 8 after **Nota gramatical** (p. 244), and Activity 9 after **Vocabulario** (p. 247). To prepare students for the **Paso** Quizzes and Chapter Test, have them do the **Más práctica gramatical** activities in the following order: complete Activities 1–4 before taking Quiz 8-1A or 8-1B; Activities 5–7 before taking Quiz 8-2A or 8-2B; and Activities 8–9 before taking Quiz 8-3A or 8-3B.

Math Link
Have students look up exchange rates for several currencies of Spanish-speaking countries and convert prices of some common things that they buy (CDs, fast food items, clothing) from dollars into **pesos, euros,** and so on. There are several national newspapers and Web sites that provide current international exchange rates.

Answers

8 *Answers may vary. Possible answers:*
1. ¿Nos trae otro menú, por favor?
2. ¿Nos trae otras servilletas, por favor?
3. ¿Me trae otra agua mineral, por favor?
4. ¿Me trae otra cuchara, por favor?
5. ¿Me trae otro plato, por favor?
6. Nos trae otros vasos, por favor?
7. ¿Me trae otro flan, por favor?
8. ¿Me trae otra ensalada, por favor?

9
1. La ensalada mixta cuesta mil setecientos cincuenta pesos.
2. Las empanadas de atún cuestan tres mil doscientos pesos.
3. El sancocho cuesta cuatro mil doscientos cincuenta pesos.
4. El agua mineral cuesta mil ciento cincuenta pesos.
5. La sopa de ajiaco cuesta dos mil quinientos pesos.
6. El pabellón cuesta mil doscientos cincuenta bolívares.
7. La carne colorada cuesta mil trescientos veinticinco bolívares.
8. Las empanadas de papa y queso cuestan novecientos cincuenta bolívares.
9. El arroz con mariscos cuesta mil seiscientos treinta bolívares.
10. El flan cuesta quinientos setenta y cinco bolívares.

MARCAR: go.hrw.com
PALABRA CLAVE:
WV3 ECUADOR-8

CAPÍTULO 8

The **Repaso** reviews all four skills and culture in preparation for the Chapter Test.

Teaching Resources
pp. 256–257

PRINT 📖
▸ Lesson Planner, p. 41
▸ Listening Activities, p. 61
▸ Video Guide, pp. 53–55, 58
▸ Grammar Tutor for Students of Spanish, Chapter 8
▸ Cuaderno para hispanohablantes, pp. 36–40
▸ Standardized Assessment Tutor, Chapter 8

MEDIA 💿📹🖥️
▸ One-Stop Planner
▸ Video Program, Videocassette 3, 34:58–36:45
▸ DVD Tutor, Disc 2
▸ Audio Compact Discs, CD 8, Tr. 18
▸ Interactive CD-ROM Tutor, Disc 2

Family Link

3 Encourage students to include foods their families eat for holidays and other special occasions. (religious holidays, birthdays, family reunions, Thanksgiving)

📁 Portfolio

3 **Written** Suggest that students include their menu in their written Portfolio. For Portfolio information, see *Alternative Assessment Guide*, pp. iv–17.

Answers

4 1. *Possible answers:* los llapingachos y el sancocho
2. en un plato con tenedor y cuchillo
3. el almuerzo
4. *Possible answer:* café, fruta y pan
5. un bistec cocinado en pan; Miami
6. Venezuela
7. una salsa de chile, tomate y cebolla; *Possible answer:* pico de gallo
8. La tortilla española se hace con huevos y patatas y es parecida a un *omelet.* La tortilla mexicana se hace con maíz o harina.

---

1 Listen as Ángel talks about some foods he likes and doesn't like. On a piece of paper make two columns, one for foods he likes, and the other for foods he doesn't like. Write the foods Ángel mentions in the correct columns. Script and answers on p. 229H.

CD 8 Tr. 18

2 Quieres hacer **empanadas** y **ensalada** para la Fiesta Internacional de tu colegio. Lee las recetas y prepara la lista de ingredientes necesarios antes de ir de compras.

Ingredientes

ENSALADA MIXTA
Tiempo: 15 minutos
Raciones: 6-8
1a lechuga grande
4 tomates
1a taza de arroz cocido
100 g atún de lata
1/2 zanahoria rallada
1/2 cebolla

Se limpian las legumbres y se cortan en trozos. Se mezcla todo junto y se sirve con aceite, vinagre, sal y pimienta.

Ingredientes

EMPANADAS DE QUESO
Tiempo: una hora
500 g de masa de maíz
2 tazas de queso blanco
2 huevos

Se baten la masa y los huevos. Se rellenan con el queso, se cierran y se fríen.

3 In groups of three or four, plan—in Spanish—a menu for a holiday meal. Include a soup, beverage, main course with meat or fish, vegetables, salad, and a dessert. Remember to compromise! As items are suggested, say whether you like them a lot, a little, or not at all. Suggest alternatives using **Prefiero**… Choose a member of your group to write your holiday menu. Be prepared to share your menu with the class.

4 Contesta las siguientes preguntas. Basa tus respuestas en las **Notas culturales** y el **Panorama cultural** de este capítulo. See answers below.

1. ¿Cuáles son dos platos típicos del Ecuador?
2. ¿Cómo se sirve la fruta en muchos restaurantes en Latinoamérica?
3. En los países hispanohablantes, ¿cuál es más fuerte, el almuerzo o la cena?
4. Describe un desayuno típico en un país hispanohablante.
5. ¿Qué es el bistec empanizado? ¿En dónde es un plato típico?
6. ¿Dónde se come el pabellón?
7. ¿Qué es el ají? ¿Se parece a algo que comes tú? ¿A qué?
8. ¿Cuáles son las diferencias entre la tortilla española y la tortilla mexicana?

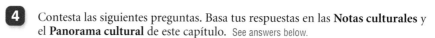

Apply and Assess

Building on Previous Skills

1 Have students compare the foods that Ángel likes and dislikes with their own preferences. (A Ángel le gusta el pollo, pero a mí no me gusta. A Ángel no le gusta el pescado y a mí no me gusta tampoco.)

Additional Practice

2 Have students alter these recipes to include ingredients that they especially like. What would they add to or leave out of the **ensalada**? How could they make a new kind of **empanada**?

5 Vamos a escribir

Imagine that you're going to open a restaurant. It can be an elegant restaurant, a 24-hour diner, or even a juice bar. You need to attract customers, so you want to create a display menu. List appetizers, entrées, beverages, and desserts, if appropriate. Also include some interesting details about each item, including the price.

Estrategia para escribir

Finding good details makes writing more interesting and lively. For example, menus and ads often have short phrases praising or describing each food entry, including its ingredients, flavors, and price. These details help customers decide what they want. To create your own menu, follow the steps below.

1. First, make a list of the items for your menu.
2. Describe each item. Use as many words and phrases to describe ingredients and flavors as you can.
3. Include the price for each item.

CHAS·ESKIMOS·JUGOS DE: VERDURAS DE: FRUTAS

¡Batidos y más!

Especiales del día:

Batido de fresa y naranja
Este batido es un buen desayuno ligero $3.50

Batido de manzana y plátano
Refresca y tiene muchas vitaminas $3.00

6 Situación

Get together with two classmates and create an original scene for one of the following situations. Role-play your scene for the class.

A. You and a friend have just finished eating lunch. The waitperson asks you if you want anything else and suggests a dessert. You politely decline and ask for the check. The waitperson tells you how much you owe. You pay the check and leave a tip.

B. You and your family are out for a nice dinner, but everything is going wrong! The waitperson forgets to give you the menu, the silverware is dirty, and when the food comes, it's cold and doesn't taste good. Point out the problems and politely request the things you need. Be creative, but mind your manners!

Cuaderno para hispanohablantes, p. 40

Apply and Assess

Process Writing

5 When students have finished a first draft of their menus, have them exchange papers for peer-editing and feedback. Help them make a checklist of things to look for as they edit their partner's paper: Does the restaurant sound like a place they would like to go? Are there enough details to give the reader a good idea of what kind of place it is? Do the details make sense? Does the menu sound appetizing? Students should also check spelling and grammar. After the peer-editing process is over, have volunteers read their menus aloud or display them around the room.

Visual Learners

5 Encourage students to decorate their menus as props for a television commercial. Each student can present the commercial to the class and should say where their restaurant is located and mention prices and ingredients of various dishes that are served.

Community Link

6 Before students begin their role-playing, have each group discuss their favorite restaurants: where the restaurants are located, when they go to these restaurants, what dish they usually order, its ingredients, and price. Then have groups of students pretend to be in one of their favorite restaurants as they do the **Situaciones**.

Multicultural Links

• Oranges have been cultivated in China since ancient times; they have been grown in Europe only since the 13th century. Oranges are also a popular fruit in the Caribbean, and in Puerto Rico they are usually called **chinas**. Similarly, *orange juice* is called **jugo de china**. Have students research the origins and uses of other foods, such as coffee, pasta, lemons, coriander, cinnamon, and rice, and share their findings with the class.

• In Southern China, people bring a small mandarin tree into their home for good luck during the Chinese New Year. Have students choose one country and research a custom from that country that includes food. Have them report what they found.

Teacher Note

This page is intended to prepare students for the Chapter Test. It is a brief checklist of the major points covered in the chapter. The students should be reminded that it is a checklist only and does not necessarily include everything that will appear on the Chapter Test.

Answers

1 *Sample answer:*
Para el desayuno, mis comidas favoritas son los huevos revueltos y el jugo de naranja. Normalmente, ¿qué te gusta desayunar? Los fines de semana como cereal con leche y plátanos para el desayuno.

4 *Possible answers:*
1. Por favor, ¿nos puede traer unas cucharas y tenedores?
2. ¿Me puede traer una servilleta, por favor?
3. ¿Nos puede traer otro menú, por favor?
4. Este vaso está sucio. ¿Me puede traer otro vaso?

5 *Possible answers:*
1. ¿Qué vas a pedir?
2. Me gustaría una ensalada, por favor.

A ver si puedo...

Can you talk about meals and food? p. 235

1 How would you tell a classmate what your favorite breakfast foods are? How would you ask what he or she usually eats for breakfast? How would you tell a classmate what you eat for breakfast . . .?
1. on weekends
2. when you're very hungry
3. when you're in a big hurry
4. when someone takes you out for breakfast
5. on school days
Sample answer below.

2 How would you tell a classmate what you have for lunch and ask what he or she has for lunch? Sample answers: Para almorzar tomo… ¿Qué tomas tú para el almuerzo.

Can you comment on food? p. 240

3 Look at the pictures below. Can you write a sentence describing how you think each dish tastes? Answers will vary.

a.

b.

c.

d.

Can you make polite requests? p. 244

4 You're eating with your family in a restaurant in Ecuador, and you're the only one who speaks Spanish. How would you ask the waitperson . . .? See answers below.
1. to bring forks and spoons for everyone
2. to bring you a napkin
3. to bring another menu
4. to bring you a clean glass

Can you order dinner in a restaurant? p. 246

5 Imagine you and a friend are at El Rancho Restaurant.
1. How would you ask your friend what he or she is going to order?
2. How would you tell the waitperson that you want to order a salad?
See answers below.

Can you ask for and pay the bill in a restaurant? p. 246

6 How would you ask the waitperson how much the meal is? How would you ask him or her to bring you the bill? Sample answer: ¿Cuánto es la comida? Camarera, la cuenta por favor.

Review and Assess

Tactile Learners

3 Create sets of numbered envelopes with the following sentences cut apart at each word. **La fruta está dulce y deliciosa. El pan está salado, por eso tengo sed. La sopa está caliente. El condimento está picante.** Give each pair of students one envelope. Students work together to create the sentences that match the photos in Activity 3.

Additional Practice

As a comprehensive review of the chapter vocabulary, functions, and grammar, have students write a conversation among two customers and a waitperson in a café using material from all three **Pasos**.

Talking about meals and food

almorzar (ue)	to eat lunch	las legumbres	vegetables	tomo...	eat/drink . . .
el arroz	rice	ligero/a	light	¿Qué prefieres?	What do you prefer?
el atún	tuna	la limonada	lemonade	¿Qué tomas para...?	What do you eat for . . .?
el azúcar	sugar	el mango	mango	el queso	cheese
el café con leche	coffee with milk	la manzana	apple	el sándwich	sandwich
el cereal	cereal	el pan dulce	sweet rolls	la sopa	soup
la crema de maní	peanut butter	el pan tostado	toast	el té frío	iced tea
el desayuno	breakfast	la papaya	papaya	Tengo sed. ¿Qué hay para tomar?	I'm thirsty. What is there to drink?
encantar	to really like, to love	las papitas	potato chips	el tocino	bacon
		para nada	at all	la toronja	grapefruit
fuerte	strong, heavy	el perro caliente	hot dog	las uvas	grapes
los huevos	eggs	la piña	pineapple	un vaso de leche	a glass of milk
la jalea	jelly	el plátano	banana		
el jamón	ham	poder (ue)	to be able; can		
el jugo de naranja	orange juice	el pollo	chicken		
la lechuga	lettuce	Por lo general	I generally		

Commenting on food

caliente	hot	frío/a	cold	salado/a	salty
delicioso/a	delicious	picante	spicy	tener (mucha) hambre	to be (really) hungry
dulce	sweet	el postre	dessert	tener (mucha) sed	to be (really) thirsty
los frijoles	beans	rico/a	rich, delicious		

Making polite requests

la camarera	waitress
el camarero	waiter
la cuchara	spoon
el cuchillo	knife
limpio/a	clean
¿Me puede traer...?	Can you bring me . . .?
el menú	menu
¿Nos puede traer...?	Can you bring us . . .?
otro/a	other, another
el plato	plate
el plato hondo	bowl
por favor	please
la servilleta	napkin
sucio/a	dirty
el tazón	bowl

Ordering dinner in a restaurant

el tenedor	fork
traer	to bring
el agua mineral	mineral water (fem.)
el batido	milkshake
la bebida	beverage, drink
el bistec	steak
los camarones	shrimp
la carne	meat
la carne de res	beef
la cebolla	onion
el flan	custard
la fresa	strawberry
la galleta	cookie
el maíz	corn
el pastel	cake
pedir (i)	to order, to ask for
el pescado	fish

¿Qué le puedo traer?	What can I bring you?
quisiera	I would like
el tomate	tomato
la zanahoria	carrot

Asking for and paying the bill in a restaurant

¿Cuánto es?	How much is it?
la cuenta	the bill
¿Desean algo más?	Would you like something else?
Es aparte.	It's separate.
¿Está incluida?	Is it included?
la propina	the tip

Numbers 200–100,000 See p. 247.

CAPÍTULO 8

Circumlocution
Write words for some popular snacks and drinks on the board: dill pickle, donut, Popsicle®, peanuts, corn chips, M&Ms®, hot apple cider. Ask student volunteers to describe these foods in Spanish without saying the actual name but using this chapter's vocabulary. You may want to put some of the phrases from ¿Cómo te diré? (p. 167C) on the board to help students complete their descriptions. The rest of the class tries to guess which food is being described.

Chapter 8 Assessment

▸ **Testing Program**
Chapter Test, pp. 209–214
Audio Compact Discs, CD 8, Trs. 22–23
Speaking Test, p. 346

▸ **Alternative Assessment Guide**
Performance Assessment, p. 39
Portfolio Assessment, p. 25
CD-ROM Assessment, p. 53

▸ **Interactive CD-ROM Tutor, Disc 2**

¡A hablar!
¡A escribir!

▸ **Standardized Assessment Tutor**
Chapter 8

▸ **One-Stop Planner, Disc 2**
Test Generator
Chapter 8

Review and Assess

Game
Tirar Palabras Bring in a foam ball. Call out a category based on the chapter vocabulary. **(frutas, comida para el desayuno, comida en general, utensilios)** As you name the category, toss the ball to a student. The student is to say a related vocabulary word and toss the ball to another student, who is to name a different item from that category. When a student cannot come up with a word, he or she is out of the game. The winners are the last ones remaining. You decide when a category has been exhausted. At that time, change the category and have all students resume play.

Teaching Resources
pp. 260–263

PRINT
▶ Lesson Planner, p. 42
▶ Video Guide, pp. 59–60

MEDIA
▶ One-Stop Planner
▶ Video Program
  Videocassette 3, 36:59–39:07
▶ DVD Tutor, Disc 2
▶ Interactive CD-ROM Tutor, Disc 3
▶ Map Transparency 6

go.hrw.com
WV3 TEXAS

 Using the Almanac and Map

Terms in the Almanac
- **Población:** Texas is the second most populous state after California. Houston, the largest city in Texas, is the fourth-largest city in the United States.
- **Clima:** The climate of Texas varies greatly. There may be blizzards in the northern plains, while winter temperatures in the Rio Grande Valley seldom dip below 60°F.
- **Historia:** Before the arrival of the Spanish explorer Alonso Álvarez de Piñeda in 1519, Texas was populated by the Caddos and other indigenous groups. The first Spanish missions were established in 1682. Texas gained independence from Spain in 1821 and from Mexico in 1836. The Republic of Texas became a U.S. state in 1845.

¡Ven conmigo a Texas!

Población: 20.851.820, de los cuales 6.669.666 son hispanos

Área: 266.807 millas cuadradas (691.030 km²)

Capital: Austin

Ciudades principales: Houston, Dallas, San Antonio, El Paso, Austin, Fort Worth

Clima: desde ligeramente templado en el noroeste hasta subtropical en la costa del sur

Economía: productos químicos, comestibles, equipos de transporte, equipos eléctricos, productos petroleros, computadoras, petróleo, gas natural, ganado, algodón, leche, frutas

Historia: Poblado por indígenas norteamericanos, entre ellos los Caddo, antes de la llegada del explorador español Álvarez de Piñeda en 1519. Primeras misiones españolas establecidas en 1682. Colonia francesa establecida en 1685. Independencia de España en 1821. Independencia de México en 1836. La República de Texas se hizo un estado de los Estados Unidos en 1845.

go.hrw.com
WV3 TEXAS
VIDEO
CD-ROM 3 / DVD 2

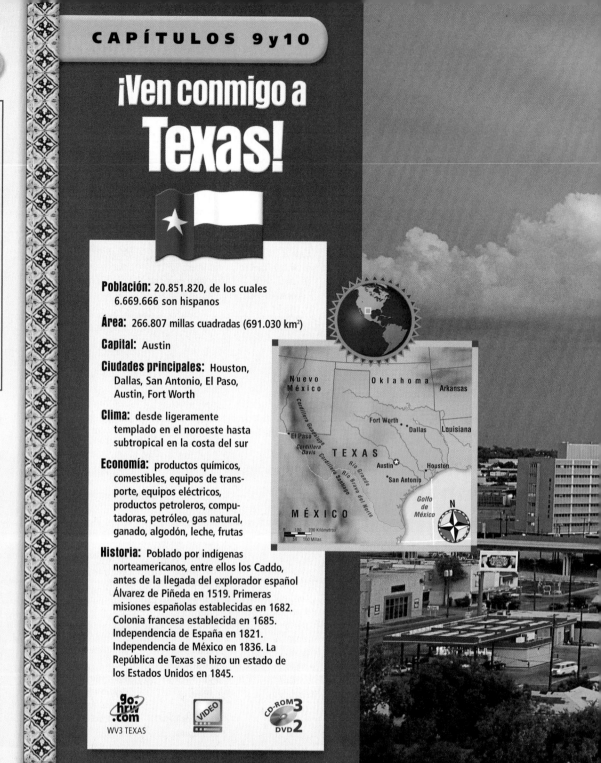

El centro de San Antonio, Texas ▶

Cultures and Communities

Background Information
Texas is the second largest state in the United States. Only Alaska is larger than Texas, but about 30 times as many people live in Texas as in Alaska. Six flags have flown over Texas—those of Spain, France, Mexico, the Republic of Texas, the Confederacy, and the United States. The Republic of Texas lasted from 1836 to 1845. Texas is often called the Lone Star State because of the single star on its flag (adopted in 1839 by the Republic). Austin has been the capital since 1845, when Texas joined the United States. Texas has been home to Spanish speakers since the 17th century, when the first permanent Spanish settlements were established.

Have students use the interactive atlas at go.hrw.com to find out more about the geography of Texas and to complete the Map Activities below.

Map Activities

- Have students name the U.S. states that border Texas. (Louisiana, Arkansas, Oklahoma, New Mexico)
- Tell students to find Houston, Dallas-Fort Worth, San Antonio, Austin, and El Paso. Ask students who have been to any of these cities to describe them to the class. Have students refer to the map on page xxviii and name the Mexican states that border Texas. (Chihuahua, Coahuila, Nuevo León, and Tamaulipas)

Connections and Comparisons

Social Studies Link

At least 30,000 indigenous people lived in what is today Texas when the first European settlers arrived. These indigenous groups, which varied widely in culture, technology, and language, included the Nacogdoches, Nasoni, Neche, Arkokisa, Attacapa, Darankawa, Comanche, Tonkawa, and Coahuiltec.

Divide the class into nine groups and assign each of them one of these indigenous groups to research. They should give a short oral presentation, including information about where and how the group lived. The students might also look on a map of Texas for place names derived from the name of their group.

Motivating Activity

Have students brainstorm about the ways various ethnic groups influence life in the United States. (music, art, literature, cooking) Look at the photos on pp. 262–263 and see if they confirm students' presuppositions.

Using the Photo Essay

❶ Un paseo en bote The San Antonio River winds through the heart of the city. Cobblestone walkways lead visitors to the river-level shops, restaurants, and an open-air amphitheater. The River Walk (**el Paseo del Río**) is the site of many of San Antonio's annual cultural events, such as art shows, **Fiesta Noche del Río**, and **Fiesta San Antonio**.

❷ De compras y de fiesta Market Square has been a shopping district since about 1840. It includes El Mercado, patterned after an authentic Mexican market.

❸ Un baile regional The **Fiesta San Antonio** tradition began in 1891 with a celebration on April 21, San Jacinto Day, in honor of the day on which Texas won its independence from Mexico. The Battle of Flowers Parade, which began around 1896, is an important part of the **Fiesta** tradition. The **Fiesta** features historic commemorations, art shows, festivals, band concerts, sporting events, fireworks, and coronations.

Texas

Texas fue por más tiempo parte de La Nueva España y de México que de los Estados Unidos. ¿Sabes que Texas fue una vez una nación independiente llamada la República de Texas? San Antonio es una de las ciudades más interesantes del mundo. Sus vínculos con México la hacen un lugar apasionante ahora que las economías de México y de los Estados Unidos son más interdependientes.

🖳 internet

MARCAR: go.hrw.com
PALABRA CLAVE:
WV3 TEXAS

❶ Un paseo en bote
El Paseo del Río atrae a millones de visitantes a sus cafés, restaurantes y tiendas. Los visitantes pueden tomar paseos en lancha por los canales del río.

❷ De compras y de fiesta
"El Mercado" es un lugar para divertirse todo el año. Su ambiente alegre incluye música tradicional mexicana, comida, arte y artesanías.

❸ Un baile regional
La fiesta de San Antonio es una celebración multicultural que se festeja cada abril. Esta celebración de diez días incluye desfiles, bailes folklóricos y conciertos de música.

Cultures and Communities

Music Link

The border region between Texas and Mexico has a culture that combines characteristics of both regions. By the early 20th century, **música norteña** had grown deep roots along the border. Have students research the music of a famous **tejano** artist. (Ramón Ayala, Paulino Bernal, Narciso Martínez)

Language Note

The name *Texas* is thought to come from the Spanish pronunciation of the Caddo word for *friend* or *ally*. The Caddos are Native Americans whose nation thrived in the area that is now Louisiana, Arkansas, and East Texas.

5 Las misiones
Las misiones españolas fueron la base de la ciudad de San Antonio. La majestuosa Misión Concepción se conserva igual desde hace 200 años.

4 La Torre de las Américas
Esta torre, que fue construida para la Feria Mundial de 1968, te da una vista panorámica de la ciudad de San Antonio. En un día claro, se pueden ver las colinas tejanas a 25 millas de distancia.

6 En familia
Texas es hogar de muchos mexicoamericanos.

 Culture Note
El Cinco de Mayo began as a commemoration of Mexico's liberation from France, but in Texas it has grown into a major celebration of Mexican American culture. The celebrations in San Antonio feature art exhibitions by Mexican artists as well as **tejano**, **conjunto**, and **mariachi** music. Performances of **baile folklórico** include dances from throughout Mexico, especially the **jarabe tapatío**.

4 La Torre de las Américas
The Tower of the Americas stands 750 feet tall from its base to the tip of the antenna. Its observation decks offer a panoramic view of San Antonio and the surrounding area. The tower was originally built for HemisFair '68, a world's fair celebrating the city's 250th anniversary.

5 Las misiones San Antonio's missions were part of the chain of Franciscan missions established early in the 18th century serving as churches, schools, Native American pueblos, military barracks, fortifications, and granaries. **Misión Concepción** is the oldest unrestored mission in Texas. It was established in 1731.

6 En familia The Mexican government sponsors the Mexican American Cultural Exchange Institute in San Antonio. It offers a program that includes art exhibits, lectures, workshops, movies, folk dancing, and concerts.

En los capítulos 9 y 10,
vas a conocer a Eva, Lisa y Gaby, tres amigas que viven en San Antonio, Texas, una de las diez ciudades más grandes de los Estados Unidos. San Antonio es famosa por su mezcla de culturas con un ambiente predominantemente tejano y mexicano. Como verás, las personas que viven en Texas tienen muchas cosas que hacer y lugares que visitar.

Connections and Comparisons

Literature Link

Texas has produced more contemporary Mexican American writers than any other state in the United States. Often **tejano** writers are closely linked to the South Texas communities in which they spent their youth, and the subject of their work is linked to **tejano** culture. In recent years, Chicano literature has gained a wider audience in the U.S., and works by **tejano** writers are increasingly available in bilingual or translated editions. Some **tejano** authors who have gained broader recognition are María Herrera-Sobek, Rolando Hinojosa, Ángela de Hoyos, Carmen Lomas Garza, Pat Mora, Tomás Rivera, Evangelina Vigil-Piñón, and Tino Villanueva.

Capítulo 9: ¡Vamos de compras!
Chapter Overview

De antemano pp. 266–268	¿Qué le compramos a Héctor?

	FUNCTIONS	GRAMMAR	VOCABULARY	RE-ENTRY
Primer paso pp. 269–273	• Discussing gift suggestions, p. 269 • Asking for and giving directions downtown, p. 271	• Indirect object pronouns, p. 270	• Gift items, p. 269 • Store names, p. 271	• ir + a + infinitive for planning (**Capítulo 7**) • Describing family (**Capítulo 6**) • Talking about locations (**Capítulo 4**) • Talking about where things are (**Capítulo 4**)
Segundo paso pp. 274–278	• Commenting on clothes, p. 274 • Making comparisons, p. 277	• es/son + de + material or pattern, p. 275 • Making comparisons: **más...que, menos...que, tan...como,** p. 277	• Clothing, p. 274	• Present tense of **ser** for description (**Capítulo 3**)
Tercer paso pp. 279–281	• Expressing preferences, p. 279 • Asking about prices and paying for something, p. 280	• Using the demonstrative adjectives **este** and **ese**, p. 279	• Expressions related to cost, p. 280	• Numbers 0 to 100,000 (**Capítulo 8**)

Letra y sonido p. 281	**Pronouncing the letters *s, z,* and *c*** Audio CD 9, Track 12	**Dictado** Audio CD 9, Tracks 13–15

Vamos a leer pp. 282–283	**San Antonio**	**Reading Strategy:** Scanning for specific information

Más práctica gramatical	**pp. 284–287** **Primer paso,** pp. 284–285	**Segundo paso,** pp. 285–286	**Tercer paso,** pp. 286–287

Review pp. 288–291	**Repaso,** pp. 288–289 **Vamos a escribir,** p. 289 Writing a snappy introduction	**A ver si puedo...,** p. 290	**Vocabulario,** p. 291

CULTURE

- **Nota cultural,** Specialty stores in Spain, p. 272
- **Panorama cultural, ¿Estás a la moda?,** p. 273
- Fine Art, *Tamalada,* 1987, by Carmen Lomas Garza, p. 276
- **Realia,** Catalog page with clothing, p. 278
- **Realia,** Currencies in Spanish-speaking countries, p. 280
- **A lo nuestro,** Compliments, p. 281

Capítulo 9: ¡Vamos de compras!
Chapter Resources

 **PRINT**

Lesson Planning

 One-Stop Planner

**Lesson Planner with Substitute Teacher
Lesson Plans,** pp. 43–47, 73

Student Make-Up Assignments

- Make-Up Assignment Copying Masters, Chapter 9

Listening and Speaking

TPR Storytelling Book, pp. 33–36

Listening Activities

- Student Response Forms for Listening Activities, pp. 67–69
- Additional Listening Activities 9-1 to 9-6, pp. 71–73
- Additional Listening Activities (song), p. 74
- Scripts and Answers, pp. 142–146

Video Guide

- Teaching Suggestions, pp. 61–63
- Activity Masters, pp. 64–66
- Scripts and Answers, pp. 104–106, 117

Activities for Communication

- Communicative Activities, pp. 49–54
- Realia and Teaching Suggestions, pp. 115–119
- Situation Cards, pp. 153–154

Reading and Writing

Reading Strategies and Skills Handbook, Chapter 9

¡Lee conmigo! 1, Chapter 9

Cuaderno de actividades, pp. 97–108

Grammar

Cuaderno de gramática, pp. 70–78

Grammar Tutor for Students of Spanish, Chapter 9

Assessment

Testing Program

- Grammar and Vocabulary Quizzes, **Paso** Quizzes, and Chapter Test, pp. 223–240
- Score Sheet, Scripts and Answers, pp. 241–248

Alternative Assessment Guide

- Portfolio Assessment, p. 26
- Performance Assessment, p. 40
- CD-ROM Assessment, p. 54

Student Make-Up Assignments

- Alternative Quizzes, Chapter 9

Standardized Assessment Tutor

- Reading, pp. 35–37
- Writing, p. 38
- Math, pp. 51–52

Native Speakers

Cuaderno para hispanohablantes, pp. 41–45

 **MEDIA**

 Online Activities

- Juegos interactivos
- Actividades Internet

 Video Program

- Videocassette 3
- Videocassette 5 (captioned version)

 Interactive CD-ROM Tutor, Disc 3

DVD Tutor, Disc 2

 Audio Compact Discs

- Textbook Listening Activities, CD 9, Tracks 1–17
- Additional Listening Activities, CD 9, Tracks 23–29
- Assessment Items, CD 9, Tracks 18–22

 Teaching Transparencies

- Situations 9-1 to 9-3
- Vocabulary 9-A to 9-D
- **De antemano**
- **Más práctica gramatical** Answers
- **Cuaderno de gramática** Answers

 One-Stop Planner CD-ROM

Use the **One-Stop Planner CD-ROM with Test Generator** to aid in lesson planning and pacing.

For each chapter, the **One-Stop Planner** includes:

- Editable lesson plans with direct links to teaching resources
- Printable worksheets from resource books
- Direct launches to the HRW Internet activities
- Video and audio segments
- Test Generator
- Clip Art for vocabulary items

Capítulo 9: ¡Vamos de compras!

Projects

La ropa tradicional

Students will research traditional indigenous clothing. For a multicultural approach, allow them to choose articles of clothing from any indigenous group in the world, or any clothing that has become popular worldwide. You may have students compare styles, materials, dyes, embroidery, weaving techniques, and other aspects of clothing manufacturing across cultures. They create a poster and present it to the class.

MATERIALS

✂ **Students may need**

- Library resources
- Markers or colored pencils
- Scissors
- Posterboard
- Glue or tape
- Magazines

SUGGESTED SEQUENCE

1. Students conduct library research to select a type of clothing and obtain information on it. Types of clothing might include **gauchos, huipiles,** and **sarapes.**

2. Students prepare a presentation in Spanish on the item of clothing, its origin, its material, and why it is worn. (climate, natural resources, aesthetics, to show marital status or origin)

3. Students create posters, using magazine pictures or original personal drawings of the clothing. They may bring in authentic costumes or fabrics.

4. Students present their information to the class. When the project is completed, display the posters around the room.

GRADING THE PROJECT

Suggested point distribution: (total = 100 points)
Accuracy of information 40
Poster 20
Presentation to class 40

Games

Los cognados

This game reminds students of the influence of Spanish on English in the U.S. and helps them increase their vocabulary in both languages.

Materials Index cards

Preparation On one side of the cards write these definitions (do not include the answers in parentheses). On the other side write the word's point value (10, 20, or 50) in large print.

10 points

Prairie wolf (coyote)	Helena is the capital (Montana)
Rope used by cowboys (lariat or lasso)	Largest city in California (Los Angeles)
Bothersome insect (mosquito)	Denver is the capital (Colorado)
Texas cattle farm (ranch)	Tallahassee is the capital (Florida)
Village square (plaza)	City featured in this chapter (San Antonio)
Carson City is the capital (Nevada)	Corn (maize)

20 points

Wild horse (bronco)	Red fruit we think of as a vegetable (tomato)
Type of warfare (guerrilla)	
Cloak or rain garment (poncho)	View (vista)
Cowboy contest (rodeo)	Deep valley (canyon)

50 points

Building material used in the Southwest (adobe)	Very masculine (macho)
Tavern (cantina)	Mountain range (sierra)
Group formed to rule (junta)	

Procedure Place 10-point cards in one stack, those worth 20 in a second, and those worth 50 in a third. Form two teams, having a player from Team A choose a stack, draw the top card, and read the definition aloud. If he or she can give the defined word within 10 seconds, his or her team receives the card's point value. If not, a Team B player gets a chance. If he or she is successful, half the points on the card are awarded. The second player on Team B follows the same procedure. When all cards in one stack are used, the teams draw from the remaining stacks—cards are not reused. Continue until all cards are drawn, or until your time limit is reached. High score wins.

NATIVE SPEAKERS

Have native speakers help by contributing words of their own.

Storytelling

Mini-cuento

This story accompanies Teaching Transparency 9-1. The
mini-cuento *can be told and retold in different formats, acted*
out, written, and read aloud, to give students additional
opportunities to practice all four skills. The following story
tells about shopping in traditional stores and in an open-air
market in a Latin American or Spanish town.

A mucha gente le gusta ir de compras, especialmente los
fines de semana. María está enamorada y va al mercado
porque le quiere regalar a su novio unas flores. Elena va a
la Zapatería Mely porque ella quiere darle unas zapatillas
rojas a su amiga Gloria. Jorge quiere comprar un disco
compacto. Él busca la tienda Mundo de Música en un mapa.
María y Margarita piensan preparar una comida vegetariana
esta noche y necesitan comprar muchas frutas y legumbres.
José compró pasteles y está esperando el autobús en la
esquina donde está el Almacén Princesa. Siempre es más
interesante ir de compras a las pequeñas tiendas y al
mercado al aire libre.

Traditions

Música

Texas was settled by Spain in the late seventeenth century
and has always been influenced by Mexican culture and
music. In the mid-nineteenth century, German, Polish, and
Czech immigrants to Texas brought their own styles of
music, such as the waltz and the polka, which would eventu-
ally fuse with traditional Mexican and Spanish styles to
create a new sound, **tejano** music. The traditional Spanish
guitar joined the European accordion in a uniquely Texan
way, giving rise to a lively, festive sound. There are now
many **tejano** radio stations, some of which transmit via

the Internet. Have students compare a sample of **tejano**
music to their favorite types of music. Ask them to research
styles of music influenced by other countries and cultures.

Receta

Texas chili encompasses a wide variety of meat and vegetable
stews spiced with several peppers. There are vegetarian
versions, which can include an assortment of beans; however,
ground beef with bean chili is probably the best known com-
bination. There are recipes for chicken, pork, and venison
chili. These hearty stews were touted as good meals for the
cattle trails and are part of the rugged cowboy culture. This
recipe can be modified to adjust the degree of spiciness.

CHILI ESTILO TEXAS

para 6 personas

2 libras de carne de res molida	1 cucharadita de comino molido
2 latas de frijoles	1 cucharadita de hojitas de orégano
6–8 chiles jalapeños o *anaheim* (cortados en trocitos)	1 cucharada de azúcar
1 cebolla grande (cortada en rebanadas)	1 cucharadita de pimienta
2 tomates medianos (cortados en trozos)	2 cucharadas de maicena
6–8 dientes de ajos, en pedacitos	sal al gusto
1 1/4 taza de agua	
1/4 taza de aceite vegetal	
4 cucharadas de chile en polvo	

En una cacerola, dore la carne. En otra, vierta
la grasa vegetal con los pedazos de ajo, cebolla
y chile. Remuévalos por dos minutos. Después
añada los frijoles junto con una taza de agua, el
tomate, el chile en polvo, el comino, el orégano, la
sal, el azúcar y la pimienta. Cuando la carne esté
cocida, agréguela a la segunda cacerola. Hierva la
mezcla y después cocínela a fuego lento por 30
minutos. Haga una pasta con la maicena y 1/4 de
taza de agua. Añada la pasta y cocine por cinco
minutos más.

Capítulo 9: ¡Vamos de compras!
Technology

Videocassette 3, Videocassette 5 (captioned version)
DVD Tutor, Disc 2
See Video Guide, pages 61–66.

DVD/Video

De antemano • ¿Qué le compramos a Héctor?

Eva, Lisa, and Gabi go shopping for graduation presents for Héctor. They take a few moments to look at some clothing for themselves. Finally they decide to split up and shop separately and meet back together in half an hour. Without knowing, each of the girls buys Hector exactly the same poster as a gift.

A continuación

When Eva, Lisa, and Gabi get back together, they walk around San Antonio and listen to a **mariachi** band. When they realize that they all have the same gift, Eva and Gabi decide to return theirs for a CD and a different poster.

¿Estás a la moda?

People from Spain, Venezuela, and Costa Rica tell about what they think is in style and what is not. In additional interviews, people from various Spanish-speaking countries tell us their opinions about fashion.

Videoclips

2x1: advertisement for a department store

Interactive CD-ROM Tutor

Activity	Activity Type	Pupil's Edition Page
En contexto	*Interactive Conversation*	
1. Vocabulario	¡Super memoria!	p. 269
2. Así se dice	Patas arriba	p. 269
3. Gramática	¡A escoger!	p. 277
4. Vocabulario	Imagen y sonido ¡Exploremos! ¡Identifiquemos!	p. 274
5. Así se dice	¿Cuál es?	pp. 279–280
6. Gramática	¡A escoger!	p. 279
Panorama cultural	¿Estás a la moda? ¡A escoger!	p. 273
¡A hablar!	*Guided recording*	pp. 288–289
¡A escribir!	*Guided writing*	pp. 288–289

Teacher Management System

Launch the program, type "admin" in the password area, and press RETURN. Log on to **www.hrw.com/CDROMTUTOR** for a detailed explanation of the Teacher Management System.

DVD Tutor

The *DVD Tutor* contains all material from the *Video Program* as described above. Spanish captions are available for use at your discretion for all sections of the video.

The *DVD Tutor* also provides a variety of video-based activities that assess students' understanding of the **De antemano, A continuación,** and **Panorama cultural.**

This part of the *DVD Tutor* may be used on any DVD video player connected to a television or video monitor.

In addition to the video material and the video-based comprehension activities, the *DVD Tutor* also contains the entire *Interactive CD-ROM Tutor* in DVD-ROM format. Each DVD disc contains the activities from all 12 chapters of the *Interactive CD-ROM Tutor.*

This part of the *DVD Tutor* may be used on a Macintosh® or Windows® computer with a DVD-ROM drive.

One-Stop Planner CD-ROM

To preview all resources available for this chapter, use the **One-Stop Planner CD-ROM**, Disc 3.

Internet Connection

MARCAR: go.hrw.com
PALABRA CLAVE:
WV3 TEXAS-9

*Have students explore the **go.hrw.com** Web site for many online resources covering all chapters. All Chapter 9 resources are available under the keyword **WV3 TEXAS-9**. Interactive games help students practice the material and provide them with immediate feedback. You will also find a printable worksheet that provides Internet activities that lead to a comprehensive online research project.*

Juegos interactivos

You can use the interactive activities in this chapter

- to practice grammar, vocabulary, and chapter functions
- as homework
- as an assessment option
- as a self-test
- to prepare for the Chapter Test

Actividades Internet

Students use Web sites that sell clothes to choose and then describe various items of clothing they like.

- To prepare students for the **Hoja de actividades,** have them review the vocabulary from the **Segundo paso** by completing the related activities in the *Cuaderno de gramática.*
- After students have completed the **Hoja de actividades,** encourage them to work with a partner and ask that partner about his or her favorite clothes. Why do they like those clothes? Do they choose clothing because of comfort? style? fabric?

Proyecto

High-fashion designers often create ridiculous combinations of style, colors, and fabrics. Have students find a fashion **(moda)** Web site. Ask them to choose two or three articles of clothing pictured on the site. Have them first describe each article of clothing in as much detail as they can, then critique each of them. You might have students download free images and include the images with their descriptions.

Capítulo 9: ¡Vamos de compras!
Textbook Listening Activities Scripts

Primer paso

6 p. 269

a. A mi padre le encanta escuchar la música.

b. A mi madre le gusta mirar películas en casa.

c. A mi hermano Santiago le gustaría tocar un instrumento musical.

d. A mi hermana Eva le gusta practicar deportes.

e. A mi abuelo le encantan los animales.

f. A mi hermana Silvia le encanta decorar su cuarto con fotos grandes.

Answers to Activity 6
1. Los carteles son para su hermana Silvia.
2. El perro es para su abuelo.
3. Los zapatos de tenis son para su hermana Eva.
4. La radio es para su papá.
5. La guitarra es para su hermano Santiago.
6. Los videos son para su madre.

11 p. 272

1. Necesito comprar unas galletas y un pastel para el cumpleaños de mi hermanito.

2. Me gustaría comprar unos aretes para mi amiga.

3. Necesito comprar un juego de mesa para mi primo Luis.

4. Busco sandalias para la playa.

5. Busco una camisa elegante para llevar a la fiesta de Enrique este sábado.

6. Quiero comprar plantas para mi casa.

7. Voy a comprar pan dulce para la fiesta de mi papá.

Answers to Activity 11
1. d
2. c
3. e
4. a
5. g
6. f
7. b

Segundo paso

15 p. 275

CARLOS — Necesito comprar unos bluejeans, una camiseta y unos zapatos de tenis.

ELENITA — Quiero buscar un traje de baño porque hace mucho calor.

SERGIO — Necesito unas camisetas, unos pantalones cortos y unos zapatos de tenis.

TERESA — Necesito pantalones y una blusa de rayas. También necesito zapatos cafés.

LUIS — Yo busco una camisa blanca, una corbata, calcetines y zapatos negros.

Answers to Activity 15
Possible answers:
Carlos—clases
Elenita—ir a la piscina
Sergio—jugar al tenis
Teresa—trabajar en la oficina/un baile
Luis—trabajar en la oficina/un baile

24 p. 278

1. La corbata de seda es más bonita que la corbata de lana.

2. ¡El perro es más gordo que el gato! ¡Necesita ponerse a dieta!

3. La falda negra es más corta que la falda amarilla.

4. Este vestido caro es más bonito que ese vestido barato.

Answers to Activity 24
1. d
2. a
3. c
4. b
Sample answer: El perro es más gordo que el gato.

One-Stop Planner CD-ROM

To preview all resources available for this chapter, use the **One-Stop Planner CD-ROM**, Disc 3.

Tercer paso

29 p. 280

1. — Perdón, señorita. ¿Cuánto cuesta esta blusa?
— ¿La roja? El precio es $58.00.
— ¡Qué cara!

2. — Bueno, me gustaría comprar esta camisa.
— ¿La blanca?
— Sí. ¿Cuánto cuesta?
— Son ocho dólares con cincuenta y cinco centavos.
— ¡Qué ganga!

3. — ¿Cuánto cuestan estas sandalias amarillas?
— Son $27.00.
— Creo que prefiero esas sandalias pardas.
— Las pardas son más baratas. Sólo $18.00.

4. — Señorita, ¿cuánto es el pastel de chocolate?
— Este es nuestro especial del día. Sólo cuesta $4.00.
— ¡Qué barato!

5. — Perdón, señor. Necesito unos bluejeans.
— Usted tiene suerte, señor. Aquí tenemos unos baratos.
— ¿Sólo $17.00? ¡Qué baratos!

6. — Señorita, busco un vestido elegante para un baile.
— Tenemos varios. Este azul, por ejemplo. O si prefiere otro color, lo tenemos también en rojo y en negro.
— ¿Cuánto cuesta el vestido rojo?
— Sólo $760.00.
— ¡Ay, qué caro!

7. — Busco unos zapatos negros.
— Aquí tenemos varios estilos. Éstos, por ejemplo, cuestan sólo $189.00.
— ¡$189.00! ¡Qué caros! Gracias, pero no.

Answers to Activity 29
1. blusa roja: $58.00
2. camisa blanca: $8.55
3. sandalias amarillas: $27.00, sandalias pardas: $18.00
4. pastel de chocolate: $4.00
5. bluejeans: $17.00
6. vestido rojo: $760.00
7. zapatos negros: $189.00

LETRA Y SONIDO, P. 249

For the scripts for Parts A and C, see p. 249.
The script for Part B is below.

B. Dictado

Para tía Silvia una blusa de seda.
Para César un suéter azul.
Para Simón unas sandalias.
Y para Celia unos zapatos.

Repaso

1 p. 288

SARA Ana, mañana es la fiesta de Lisa. ¿Ya tienes tu ropa?

ANA Sí, voy de King Kong. ¿De qué vas tú?

SARA Voy de payaso, pero todavía tengo que comprar mi ropa. ¿Me acompañas?

ANA Cómo no.

SARA Necesito una corbata bastante fea.

ANA Ay, sí. Compra una corbata de los años setenta.

SARA Ja, ja, ja. Oye, ¿qué te parece si vamos a una tienda ahora?

ANA Sí, perfecto. ¿Qué más necesitas?

SARA Bueno, una camisa de cuadros, unos zapatos grandes y unos pantalones grandes.

ANA ¿Sabes qué? Mi hermano tiene unos pantalones viejos que puedes usar.

SARA ¡Fantástico!

Answers to Repaso Activity 1
una corbata fea, unos pantalones grandes

Capítulo 9: ¡Vamos de compras!
Suggested Lesson Plans *50-Minute Schedule*

Day 1

CHAPTER OPENER 5 min.
- Focusing on Outcomes, ATE, p. 265
- Culture Notes, ATE, p. 264
- Language Note, ATE, p. 265

DE ANTEMANO 40 min.
- Presenting **De antemano** and Preteaching Vocabulary, ATE, p. 266
- Do the Thinking Critically activity, ATE, p. 267.
- Activities 1–5, p. 268, and Comprehension Check, ATE, p. 268

Wrap-Up 5 min.
- Call on students to share their responses to Activity 5, p. 268.

Homework Options
Cuaderno de actividades, p. 97, Activities 1–2

Day 2

PRIMER PASO
Quick Review 5 min.
- Check homework.
- Bell Work, ATE, p. 269

Así se dice/Vocabulario, p. 269 25 min.
- Presenting **Así se dice** and **Vocabulario**, ATE, p. 269
- Present **También se puede decir...**, p. 269
- Do Activity 6, p. 269, with the Audio CD.
- Do Activity 7, p. 270.

Gramática, p. 270 15 min.
- Presenting **Gramática**, ATE, p. 270
- Present Language-to-Language, ATE, p. 270.
- Do Activity 8, p. 270, with the class.
- Have students write **Más práctica gramatical**, p. 284, Activity 2. Check orally.

Wrap-Up 5 min.
- Point to an item on Teaching Transparency 9-A and ask students what they are going to give different individuals in the class.

Homework Options
Más práctica gramatical, p. 284, Activity 1
Cuaderno de actividades, pp. 98–99, Activities 3–4
Cuaderno de gramática, p. 70, Activities 1–2

Day 3

PRIMER PASO
Quick Review 5 min.
- Check homework.

Gramática, p. 270 15 min.
- Do Cuaderno de gramática, Activities 3 and 4, p. 71, with the class.
- Have students do Activity 9, p. 270, in pairs. Follow the Teaching Suggestion, ATE, p. 270.

Vocabulario/Así se dice, p. 271 25 min.
- Presenting **Así se dice/Vocabulario**, ATE, p. 271
- Read **¿Te acuerdas?** and review prepositions of location, p. 271.
- Present the Language Note, ATE, p. 271.
- Have students do Activity 10, p. 271, in pairs.

Wrap-Up 5 min.
- Project Teaching Transparency 9-1. Describe the location of something in the transparency and have students guess what it is.

Homework Options
Cuaderno de actividades, pp. 99–100, Activities 5–6
Cuaderno de gramática, pp. 72–73, Activities 5–8

Day 4

PRIMER PASO
Quick Review 10 min.
- Check homework.
- Review **Vocabulario** and **Así se dice** expressions, p. 271, using Teaching Transparency 9-B.

Vocabulario/Así se dice, p. 271 25 min.
- Follow the Photo Flash! suggestion, ATE, p. 272, then do Activity 11, p. 272, with the Audio CD.
- Read the **Nota cultural**, p. 272.
- Have students do Activity 12, p. 272, in pairs, and Activity 13, p. 272, in groups.
- Have students write Activity 14, p. 272, then peer-edit papers.

PANORAMA CULTURAL 10 min.
- Presenting **Panorama cultural**, ATE, p. 273
- Present the Language Note, ATE, p. 273.

Wrap-Up 5 min.
- Have students share reasons why people should or should not follow **la moda** from **Para pensar y hablar...**, p. 273.
- Discuss the content and format of Quiz 9-1.

Homework Options
Study for Quiz 9-1.

Day 5

PRIMER PASO
Quick Review 5 min.
- Review the content of the **Primer paso**.

Quiz 20 min.
- Administer Quiz 9-1A, 9-1B, or a combination of the two.

SEGUNDO PASO
Así se dice/Vocabulario, p. 274 20 min.
- Presenting **Así se dice** and **Vocabulario**, ATE, p. 274
- Do Activity 15, p. 275, with the Audio CD.

Wrap-Up 5 min.
- Ask students the color of different articles of clothing they are wearing.

Homework Options
Cuaderno de actividades, p. 101, Activity 7
Cuaderno de gramática, p. 74, Activities 9–10

Day 6

SEGUNDO PASO
Quick Review 5 min.
- Check homework.
- Ask students what the people are wearing in Teaching Transparency 9-C.

Así se dice/Vocabulario, p. 274 20 min.
- Have students do Activity 16, p. 275, and share answers with the class.
- Have students do Activities 17–18, p. 275.

Vocabulario/Nota gramatical, p. 275 20 min.
- Presenting **Vocabulario** and **Nota gramatical**, ATE p. 275
- Have students do Activity 19, p. 276, with a partner. Have pairs write their descriptions on the board. Have the class decide who was described.
- Present the Background Information, ATE, p. 276.

Wrap-Up 5 min.
- Do the Communication for all Students activities, ATE, p. 275.

Homework Options
Más práctica gramatical, p. 285, Activities 3–4
Cuaderno de actividades, pp. 101–102, Activity 8
Cuaderno de gramática, p. 75, Activities 11–12

One-Stop Planner CD-ROM

For alternative lesson plans by chapter section, to create your own customized plans, or to preview all resources available for this chapter, use the **One-Stop Planner CD-ROM**, Disc 3.

 For additional homework suggestions, see activities accompanied by this symbol throughout the chapter.

Day 7

SEGUNDO PASO

Quick Review 5 min.
- Check homework.
- Ask students what their classmates are wearing.

Vocabulario extra, p. 276 20 min.
- Present **Vocabulario extra** holding up articles of clothing and having students repeat the vocabulary words. Ask students when they would wear each article of clothing.
- Have students do Activity 20, p. 276, then peer-edit papers.
- Have students do Activity 21, p. 277, in groups.

Así se dice/Gramática, p. 277 20 min.
- Presenting **Así se dice/Gramática**, ATE, p. 277
- Have students do Activity 23, p. 277.
- Present the Culture Note, ATE, p. 276.

Wrap-Up 5 min.
- Hold up photos of or actual articles of clothing. Have students compare two items.

Homework Options
Activity 22, p. 277 (done as a writing activity)
Cuaderno de actividades, pp. 102–103, Activities 9–10
Cuaderno de gramática, p. 76, Activities 13–14

Day 8

SEGUNDO PASO

Quick Review 5 min.
- Check Activity 22, p. 277 assignment. You may wish to use the Writing Rubric, pp. 3–9, in the Alternative Assessment Guide to grade the assignment.

Así se dice/Gramática, p. 277 20 min.
- Do **Más práctica gramatical**, Activity 5, p. 286, with the class.
- Do Activity 24, p. 278, with the Audio CD.
- Have students do Activity 25, p. 278.
- Do the Math Link activity, ATE, p. 278.

TERCER PASO

Así se dice/Nota gramatical, p. 279 20 min.
- Presenting **Así se dice** and **Nota gramatical**, ATE, p. 279
- Do Activity 26, p. 279. Check orally.
- Have students do Activity 27, p. 279, in pairs.

Wrap-Up 5 min.
- Hold up two items found in the classroom and ask students to compare them.
- Discuss the content and format of Quiz 9-2.

Homework Options
Study for Quiz 9-2.
Cuaderno de gramática, p. 77, Activities 15–16

Day 9

SEGUNDO PASO

Quick Review 10 min.
- Check homework.
- Review the content of the **Segundo paso**.

Quiz 20 min.
- Administer Quiz 9-2A, 9-2B, or a combination of the two.

TERCER PASO

Así se dice/Nota gramatical, p. 279 15 min.
- Do **Más práctica gramatical**, Activities 6 and 7, pp. 286–287, with the class.
- Have students do Activity 28, p. 279, in groups.

Wrap-Up 5 min.
- Call on groups to present their opinions from Activity 28, p. 279, to the class.

Homework Options
Cuaderno de actividades, pp. 104–105, Activities 12–13

Day 10

TERCER PASO

Quick Review 5 min.
- Check homework and review numbers.

Así se dice/Vocabulario, p. 280 30 min.
- Presenting **Así se dice/Vocabulario**, ATE, p. 280
- Do Activity 29, p. 280, with the Audio CD. Then do Activity 30, p. 281, with the class.
- Present **Nota cultural**, p. 280, then do Additional Practice, ATE, p. 280.
- Present **A lo nuestro**, p. 281, then have students do Activity 31, p. 281, in pairs.
- Have partners write Activity 32, p. 281.

Letra y sonido, p. 281 10 min.
- Present **Letra y sonido**, p. 281, using the Audio CD.

Wrap-Up 5 min.
- Have students name and react to the cost of items on Teaching Transparency 9-3.
- Discuss the content and format of Quiz 9-3.

Homework Options
Study for Quiz 9-3.
Más práctica gramatical, p. 287, Activity 8
Cuaderno de actividades, pp. 104–106, Activities 11–15
Cuaderno de gramática, p. 78, Activities 17–19

Day 11

TERCER PASO

Quick Review 5 min.
- Check homework.
- Quickly review the content of the **Tercer paso**.

Quiz 20 min.
- Administer Quiz 9-3A, 9-3B, or a combination of the two.

VAMOS A LEER 20 min.
- Do Activities A and B, p. 282.
- Do Activities C and D, p. 283.

Wrap-Up 5 min.
- Do the Group Work activity, ATE, p. 282.

Homework Options
Cuaderno de actividades, pp. 107–108, Activities 16–18
Assign Activities 2 and 4–6 of the Repaso, pp. 288–289, as homework.
A ver si puedo..., p. 290

Day 12

REPASO

Quick Review 10 min.
- Check homework.

Chapter Review 35 min.
- Review Chapter 9. Choose from **Más práctica gramatical**, Grammar Tutor for Students of Spanish, Activities for Communication, Listening Activities, Interactive CD-ROM Tutor, or **Juegos interactivos**.

Wrap-Up 5 min.
- Discuss the format of the Chapter 9 Test.

Homework Options
Study for the Chapter 9 Test.

Assessment

Quick Review 5 min.
- Answer any last-minute questions.

Test, Chapter 9 45 min.
- Administer Chapter 9 Test. Select from Testing Program, Alternative Assessment Guide, Test Generator, or Standardized Assessment Tutor.

Capítulo 9: ¡Vamos de compras!
Suggested Lesson Plans 90-Minute Block Schedule

Block 1

CHAPTER OPENER 5 min.
- Focusing on Outcomes, ATE, p. 265
- Culture Notes, ATE, p. 264
- Language Note, ATE, p. 265

DE ANTEMANO 40 min.
- Presenting **De antemano** and Preteaching Vocabulary, ATE, p. 266
- Do the Thinking Critically activity, ATE, p. 267.
- Activities 1–5, p. 268, and Comprehension Check, ATE, p. 268

PRIMER PASO
Así se dice/Vocabulario, p. 269 25 min.
- Presenting **Así se dice** and **Vocabulario**, ATE, p. 269
- Present **También se puede decir...**, p. 269.
- Do Activity 6, p. 269, with the Audio CD.
- Do Activity 7, p. 270.

Gramática, p. 270 15 min.
- Presenting **Gramática**, ATE, p. 270
- Present Language-to-Language, ATE, p. 270.
- Do Activity 8, p. 270, with the class.
- Have students write **Más práctica gramatical**, p. 284, Activity 2. Check orally.

Wrap-Up 5 min.
- Point to an item on Teaching Transparency 9-A and ask students what they are going to give different individuals in the class.

Homework Options
Más práctica gramatical, p. 284, Activity 1
Cuaderno de actividades, pp. 97–99, Activities 1–4
Cuaderno de gramática, p. 70, Activities 1–2

Block 2

PRIMER PASO
Quick Review 10 min.
- Check homework.
- Review **Así se dice** expressions and **Vocabulario**, p. 269, using Teaching Transparency 9-A.

Gramática, p. 270 15 min.
- Do Cuaderno de gramática, Activities 3 and 4, p. 71, with the class.
- Have students do Activity 9, p. 270, in pairs.

Vocabulario/Así se dice, p. 271 50 min.
- Presenting **Vocabulario**, ATE, p. 271
- Read **¿Te acuerdas?** and review prepositions of location.
- Presenting **Así se dice**, ATE, p. 271
- Present the Language Note, ATE, p. 271.
- Have students do Activity 10, p. 271, in pairs.
- Follow the Photo Flash! suggestion, ATE, p. 272, then do Activity 11, p. 272, with the Audio CD.
- Read the **Nota cultural**, p. 272.
- Have students do Activity 12, p. 272, in pairs, and Activity 13, p. 272, in groups.
- Have students write Activity 14, p. 272, then exchange papers with a partner for peer-editing.

PANORAMA CULTURAL 10 min.
- Presenting **Panorama cultural**, ATE, p. 273
- Present the vocabulary in the Language Note, ATE, p. 273.

Wrap-Up 5 min.
- Describe the location of something in Teaching Transparency 9-1 and have students guess what it is.
- Discuss the content and format of Quiz 9-1.

Homework Options
Study for Quiz 9-1.
Cuaderno de actividades, pp. 99–100, Activities 5–6
Cuaderno de gramática, pp. 72–73, Activities 5–8

Block 3

PRIMER PASO
Quick Review 10 min.
- Check homework.
- Use Teaching Transparency 9-1 and 9-A to review the content of the **Primer paso**.

Quiz 20 min.
- Administer Quiz 9-1A, 9-1B, or a combination of the two.

SEGUNDO PASO
Así se dice/Vocabulario, p. 274 40 min.
- Presenting **Así se dice** and **Vocabulario**, p. 274
- Do Activity 15, p. 275, with the Audio CD.
- Have students do Activity 16, p. 275. Ask students to share their answers with the class.
- Have students do Activities 17 and 18, p. 275, in pairs. Follow the Kinesthetic Learners suggestion, ATE, p. 275.

Vocabulario/Nota gramatical, p. 275 15 min.
- Presenting **Vocabulario** and **Nota gramatical**, ATE, p. 275
- Have students do Activity 19, p. 276, with a partner. Present the Background Information, ATE, p. 276.

Wrap-Up 5 min.
- Call on pairs to write one of their descriptions from Activity 19, p. 276, on the board. Have the class decide who in the painting was described.

Homework Options
Más práctica gramatical, p. 285, Activities 3–4
Cuaderno de actividades, pp. 101–102, Activities 7–8
Cuaderno de gramática, pp. 74–75, Activities 9–12

One-Stop Planner CD-ROM

For alternative lesson plans by chapter section, to create your own customized plans, or to preview all resources available for this chapter, use the **One-Stop Planner CD-ROM**, Disc 3.

 For additional homework suggestions, see activities accompanied by this symbol throughout the chapter.

Block 4

SEGUNDO PASO

Quick Review 10 min.
- Check homework.
- Have students describe what people are wearing in Teaching Transparency 9-2.

Vocabulario extra, p. 276 20 min.
- Present **Vocabulario extra** by holding up articles of clothing or pictures of them and having students repeat the vocabulary words after you. Then ask students when they would wear each article of clothing.
- Have students do Activity 20, p. 276, then exchange papers for peer-editing.
- Have students do Activity 21, p. 277, in groups.

Así se dice/Gramática, p. 277 40 min.
- Presenting **Así se dice** and **Gramática**, ATE, p. 277
- Do Activity 23, p. 277, with the class.
- Present the activity for Visual Learners, ATE, p. 277.
- Do Activity 24, p. 278, with the Audio CD.
- Have students write **Más práctica gramatical**, Activity 5, p. 286. Check answers orally.
- Have students do Activity 25, p. 278. Have students correct each other's work in groups.
- Do the Math Link activity, ATE, p. 278.

Letra y sonido, p. 281 10 min.
- Present **Letra y sonido**, p. 281, using the Audio CD.

Wrap-Up 10 min.
- Hold up photos of or actual articles of clothing. Ask students questions that call for them to compare the two items.
- Discuss the content and format of Quiz 9-2.

Homework Options
Assign Activity 22, p. 277, as a writing activity. You may wish to have students include some comparisons in their essays.
Study for Quiz 9-2.
Cuaderno de actividades, pp. 102–103, Activities 9–10
Cuaderno de gramática, p. 76, Activities 13–14

Block 5

SEGUNDO PASO

Quick Review 10 min.
- Check homework.
- Pick up the assignment from Activity 22, p. 277, while students review for Quiz 9-2. You may wish to use the Writing Rubric, pp. 3–9, in the Alternative Assessment Guide to grade the assignment.

Quiz 20 min.
- Administer Quiz 9-2A, 9-2B, or a combination of the two.

TERCER PASO

Así se dice/Nota gramatical, p. 279 35 min.
- Presenting **Así se dice** and **Nota gramatical**, ATE, p. 279
- Do Activity 26, p. 279.
- Have students do Activity 27, p. 279, in pairs and Activity 28, p. 279, in groups.
- Do **Más práctica gramatical**, Activities 6 and 7, pp. 286–287, with the class.

Así se dice/Vocabulario, p. 280 20 min.
- Quickly review numbers by writing a number on the board and having students read it aloud.
- Presenting **Así se dice** and **Vocabulario**, ATE, p. 280
- Do Activity 29, p. 280, with the Audio CD. Then do Activity 30, p. 281, with the class.
- Read and discuss the **Nota cultural**, p. 280.

Wrap-Up 5 min.
- Ask students how much different items cost in Teaching Transparency 9-3, then have them react to the cost.
- Discuss the content and format of Quiz 9-3.

Homework Options
Study for Quiz 9-3.
Cuaderno de actividades, 104–106, Activities 11–15
Cuaderno de gramática, pp. 77–78, Activities 15–19

Block 6

TERCER PASO

Quick Review 10 min.
- Check homework.
- Hold up different articles or pictures of clothing with price tags. Ask students which items they prefer and how much they cost.

Así se dice/Vocabulario, p. 280 15 min.
- Do **Más práctica gramatical**, Activity 8, p. 287.
- Present the expressions in **A lo nuestro**, p. 281, then have students do Activity 31, p. 281, in pairs.
- Have students work with a partner to write Activity 32, p. 281.

Quiz 20 min.
- Administer Quiz 9-3A, 9-3B, or a combination of the two.

VAMOS A LEER 20 min.
- Do Activities A and B, p. 282.
- Do Activities C and D, p. 283.

REPASO 20 min.
- Do Activity 1, p. 288, with the Audio CD.
- Have students do Activities 2, 4, and 5, pp. 288–289, individually, then check orally with the class.
- Have students do Activity 3, p. 288 in groups.

Wrap-Up 5 min.
- Discuss the format of the Chapter 9 test and provide sample questions.

Homework Options
Assign Activity 6, p. 289, as homework.
Assign groups to prepare Activity 7, p. 289.
Study for the Chapter 9 test.
A ver si puedo..., p. 290

Block 7

REPASO

Quick Review 10 min.
- Have students practice their situations from Activity 7, p. 289, while you check homework.

Chapter Review 35 min.
- Review Chapter 9. Choose from **Más práctica gramatical**, Grammar Tutor for Students of Spanish, Activities for Communication, Listening Activities, Interactive CD-ROM Tutor, or **Juegos interactivos**.

Test, Chapter 9 45 min.
- Administer Chapter 9 Test. Select from Testing Program, Alternative Assessment Guide, Test Generator, or Standardized Assessment Tutor.

Chapter Opener

CAPÍTULO 9

One-Stop Planner CD-ROM

For resource information, see the **One-Stop Planner**, Disc 3.

Pacing Tips
Important new grammar functions are found in the first **Paso**, while the next two **Pasos** introduce many new vocabulary terms. Make sure to leave sufficient time for spoken activities which will help students acquire the new terms. For lesson plan and timing ideas, see pp. 263I–263L.

Meeting the Standards
Communication
- Discussing gift suggestions, p. 269
- Asking for and giving directions downtown, p. 271
- Commenting on clothes, p. 274
- Making comparisons, p. 277
- Expressing preferences, p. 279
- Asking about prices and paying for something, p. 280

Cultures
- Nota cultural, p. 272
- Panorama cultural, p. 273
- Background Information, p. 276
- Vamos a leer, pp. 282–283

Connections
- Language Note, p. 265
- Math Link, p. 278
- Culture Note, p. 283

Comparisons
- Culture Notes, p. 264
- Language-to-Language, p. 270
- Additional Practice, p. 280

Communities
- Sugerencia, p. 278
- Native Speakers, p. 282
- Multicultural Link, p. 283

Cultures and Communities

Culture Notes
- Spanish and Mexican heritages influence San Antonio's history, culture, and cuisine. There is an abundance of hand-crafted gifts from Mexico in the shops of El Mercado. Galleries and museums in the city are known for both folk art and fine art inspired by the traditions of the Southwest.

- Ask students on what occasions they give or receive gifts. (Christmas, Hanukkah, Valentine's Day, birthday) In Latin America and Spain, children often are given gifts on both their birthday and their saint's day.

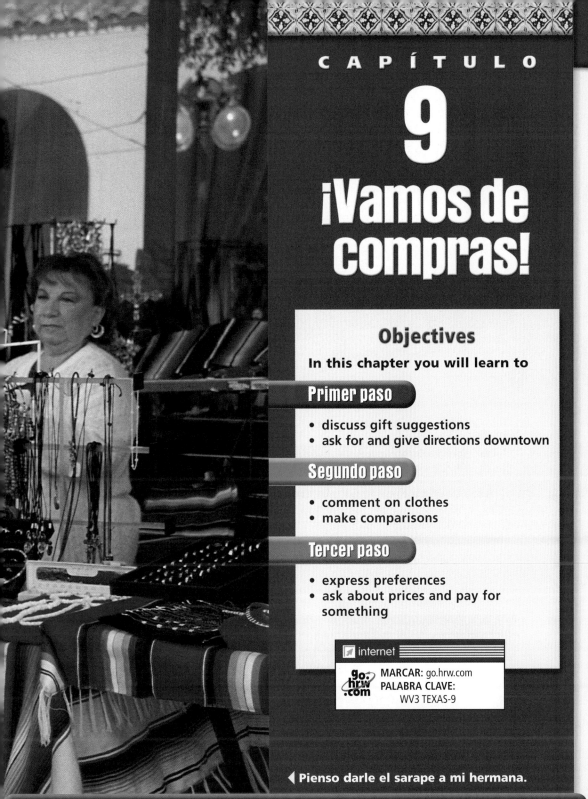

CAPÍTULO

9
¡Vamos de compras!

Objectives

In this chapter you will learn to

Primer paso

- discuss gift suggestions
- ask for and give directions downtown

Segundo paso

- comment on clothes
- make comparisons

Tercer paso

- express preferences
- ask about prices and pay for something

📶 internet

MARCAR: go.hrw.com
PALABRA CLAVE:
WV3 TEXAS-9

◀ **Pienso darle el sarape a mi hermana.**

Photo Flash!

El Mercado near downtown San Antonio is a popular shopping site among San Antonians and tourists. Its open-air walkways lead shoppers to restaurants, clothing and authentic Mexican and Mexican-American handicrafts stores. One can relax after shopping in the outside **cafés**, where **mariachis** often entertain.

Focusing on Outcomes

An important use of language is talking about clothing or other things that students buy for themselves or others. Point out to students that describing the price and quality of things they buy is an important skill. By the end of the chapter, students will be able to identify various stores, compare products, and ask how much things cost.

Chapter Sequence

Connections and Comparisons

Language Note

The word *blanket* has several different translations in Spanish. **Manta, cobija,** and **frazada** are all used, depending on the region. Students might like to know that a *wet blanket* is **un(a) aguafiestas** in Spanish. Have students describe the personality of an **aguafiestas.**

Multicultural Link

Markets are an important part of life in Spanish-speaking countries, especially in smaller communities. In these traditional markets, haggling over prices is often accepted and expected. Ask students when it is appropriate to haggle, or **regatear,** in the United States. Do students feel comfortable doing this?

Teaching Resources
pp. 266–268

PRINT
▸ Lesson Planner, p. 42
▸ Video Guide, pp. 61–62, 64
▸ Cuaderno de actividades, p. 97

MEDIA
▸ One-Stop Planner
▸ Video Program
  De antemano
  Videocassette 3, 39:08–43:08
  Videocassette 5 (captioned version), 1:30:27–1:34:28
  A continuación
  Videocassette 3, 43:09–47:17
  Videocassette 5 (captioned version), 1:34:29–1:38:40
▸ DVD Tutor, Disc 2
▸ Audio Compact Discs, CD 9, Trs. 1–2
▸ **De antemano** Transparencies

Presenting
De antemano

While students read or view the **fotonovela**, periodically stop to answer questions, such as those in the **Estrategia para comprender.** Then present the Preteaching Vocabulary. Follow up by modeling pronunciation of the **fotonovela** dialogue and having students repeat after you. Have students predict meanings from context.

De antemano Transparencies

DE ANTEMANO · *¿Qué le compramos a Héctor?*

The **fotonovela** is an abridged version of the video episode.

CD 9 Trs. 1–2

Estrategia para comprender
Eva's brother, Héctor, is graduating from high school. Eva, Lisa, and Gabi are downtown shopping for a graduation gift and doing some window shopping as well. Why do you think the girls will be surprised when each sees what the others have bought?

Eva   **Lisa**   **Gabi**

Lisa: Bueno, ¿qué le van a comprar a Héctor para su graduación?
Eva: No sé, tal vez unos discos compactos de Gloria Estefan.
Gabi: Me gustaría regalarle algo divertido.
Lisa: Gabi, yo también quiero regalarle algo divertido.

①

Eva: ¿Por qué no le compran regalos divertidos las dos? Pero tenemos que encontrarlos hoy... ¡su fiesta de graduación es el viernes!
Lisa: ¿Quieren entrar en esta tienda de ropa? Para mirar, nada más. Y después, vamos a la papelería para comprarle a Héctor las tarjetas.

②

Eva: ¿Cuál prefieren, la blusa roja o la de rayas?
Gabi: Yo prefiero la roja. ¿Cuánto cuesta?
Eva: Uy, cuarenta dólares. Es cara.
Lisa: ¿Qué les parecen estos pantalones cortos?
Gabi: Eh... de verdad, Lisa, no me gustan para nada los cuadros.

③

Preteaching Vocabulary

Guessing Words from Context
First ask students to predict the context of **De antemano.** (shopping for gifts) Then have them identify words or phrases that indicate what is happening. They should first find words that give them information about shopping or gift-giving. (❶comprar, ❶regalarle, ❸¿Cuánto cuesta?) They should then look for words that describe gifts. (❶divertido, ❸cara, ❹bonita) Can students identify three phrases that tell about the price of the items? (❸Es cara, ❹¡Qué barata!, ❹¡Es una ganga!) What words or phrases in frames support that conclusion? (❸cuarenta dólares, ❹12 dólares)

4

Gabi: ¿Qué tal esta falda?
Eva: Es bonita.
Lisa: Y es de algodón...
Eva: Y sólo cuesta 12 dólares. ¡Qué barata!
Gabi: Sí, ¡es una ganga!

Thinking Critically
Drawing Inferences Ask students to point out the various expressions in which **le** is used, and to infer what it means by the context of the expressions.

Challenge
Ask the students to draw another frame for the fotonovela in which they include the conversation between Eva, Lisa, and Gabi when they meet each other after buying their gifts.

5

Lisa: Bueno, ¿qué le compramos a Héctor?
Eva: Uf... es difícil. No sé... le interesan los libros, ¿tal vez un libro? Hay una librería al lado de la zapatería.
Gabi: No, eso no, prefiero regalarle algo divertido.

6

Lisa: Vamos a ver quién le compra el regalo más divertido. ¿Por qué no vas a buscar algo, y yo voy también? Y nos vemos aquí en... ¿media hora?
Eva: Y yo voy a buscar algo también. Muy bien, hasta luego... aquí en media hora.

7

Primero Lisa...

8

...luego Gabi...

9

...y después Eva...

Pero, ¿qué hacen en la misma tienda?

Cuaderno de actividades, p. 97, Acts. 1–2

A continuación

You may choose to continue with *¿Qué le compramos a Héctor? (a continuación)* at this time or wait until later in the chapter. At this point, Eva, Lisa, and Gabi meet after shopping for Hector's gifts. They discover that they have all purchased the same gift. You may wish to have students discuss what they would do in a situation similar to that described in the second part of the video.

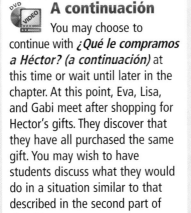

Using the Captioned Video/DVD

As an alternative to having students read the conversations in the book, you might want to show the captioned version of *¿Qué le compramos a Héctor?* on Videocassette 5. As students hear the language and watch the story, anxiety about the new language will be reduced and comprehension facilitated. The reinforcement of seeing the written words with the gestures and actions in context will help students to do the comprehension activities on p. 268. **NOTE:** The *DVD Tutor* contains captions for all sections of the *Video Program*.

Slower Pace

1 Before having students begin this activity, write on a transparency or on the board the Spanish question words in one column and their English glosses in another. Have students match each English meaning with its Spanish counterpart and make up questions in Spanish using the question words. Then have them do the activity in the text.

Teaching Suggestion

4 After they answer the questions, have students look again at the **fotonovela** on pp. 266–267 and justify their answers based on what each character says.

These activities check for comprehension only. Students should not yet be expected to produce language modeled in **De antemano**.

1 **¿Comprendes?** See answers below.

Contesta las preguntas. Acuérdate *(Remember)*... si no sabes, puedes adivinar.

1. ¿Para quién compran Eva, Lisa y Gabi los regalos?
2. ¿Por qué van a comprar los regalos?
3. ¿Adónde van primero? ¿Qué miran allí?
4. ¿Qué tipo de regalo quieren comprar Lisa y Gabi?
5. ¿Qué pasa cuando las chicas van solas a buscar sus regalos?

2 **¿Cierto o falso?** See answers below.

Indica si cada oración es cierta o falsa. Corrige las oraciones falsas.

1. Las chicas le compran regalos a Héctor.
2. Van a la zapatería para comprar tarjetas.
3. Gabi prefiere la blusa azul.
4. La falda es de algodón.
5. A Héctor no le interesan los libros.
6. Las chicas compran tres regalos diferentes.

3 **¿Cómo se dice?** See answers below.

Imagine that you're a friend of Héctor's. Find the phrases you could use . . .

1. to say you'd like to buy him something fun
2. to ask how much something costs
3. to say that something is made out of cotton
4. to ask "What should we buy him?"
5. to say he is interested in books

4 **¿Quién lo diría?** *Who might say it?*

Identifica al personaje que dice algo similar a lo siguiente.

Eva   Lisa   Gabi

1. A Héctor le interesan los deportes—el fútbol, el basquetbol... Eva
2. Me gustaría mirar la ropa en esta tienda. Lisa
3. Necesito unos nuevos pantalones cortos. Lisa
4. La falda no cuesta mucho—¡sólo veinte dólares! Eva
5. La librería está cerca de la zapatería. Eva

5 **¿Y tú?** Answers will vary.

Completa las siguientes oraciones con referencia a un amigo o una amiga.

1. Su fiesta de cumpleaños es...
2. Me gustaría comprarle...
3. No le gusta(n) para nada...

Answers

1
1. Héctor
2. para su graduación
3. a una tienda de ropa, blusas y pantalones cortos
4. algo divertido
5. compran el mismo cartel

2
1. cierto
2. falso; Van a una papelería para comprar las tarjetas.
3. falso; Gabi prefiere la blusa roja.
4. cierto
5. falso; A Héctor le interesan los libros.
6. falso; Las chicas compran el mismo regalo.

3
1. Me gustaría comprarle algo divertido.
2. ¿Cuánto cuesta?
3. Es de algodón.
4. ¿Qué le compramos a él?
5. Le interesan los libros.

Comprehension Check

Additional Practice

2 After students complete the activity, have them close their books as you read aloud the statements with slight modifications (changing nouns, adding **no**) to which the class responds true or false. Ask students to correct any false statements.

5 Have pairs of students think of a mutual friend and role-play a scene in a store in which they try to find a gift for that person. A third student can play the part of the clerk. Have volunteers present their scenes in front of the class.

Objectives Discussing gift suggestions; asking for and giving directions downtown

go. hrw .com
WV3 TEXAS-9

Así se dice

Discussing gift suggestions

To find out what gift a friend has in mind for someone, ask:

¿Qué piensas regalarle a tu hermano?
What are you planning on giving (as a gift) to . . .?

¿Para quién es el regalo?
Who is the gift for?

¿Qué tipo de regalo buscas?
What kind of gift are you looking for?

Your friend might answer:

Le voy a dar unas camisetas.
I'm going to give him some T-shirts.

El regalo **es para** mi novia.

Busco unos pantalones para mi primo.
I'm looking for some pants for my cousin.

CD-ROM 3
DVD 2

Cuaderno de actividades, p. 98, Act. 3

---

6 **Los regalos** Scripts and answers on p. 263G.

Escuchemos/Escribamos Listen and take notes as Rodolfo tells you what his family members like. Then, answer the questions.

CD 9 Tr. 3

1. ¿Para quién son los carteles?
2. ¿Para quién es el perro?
3. ¿Para quién son los zapatos de tenis?
4. ¿Para quién es la radio?
5. ¿Para quién es la guitarra?
6. ¿Para quién son los videos?

También se puede decir...

In some Spanish-speaking countries you will also hear **los pendientes** or **los aros** for *earrings*. Other words for *wallet* include **la billetera**, which is used more widely. **Cartera** is used to mean *purse* in many countries. In Costa Rica, **los confites** is used for *candy*, and in Argentina and Cuba you will hear **los caramelos**.

Vocabulario

 CD-ROM 3 DVD 2

un disco compacto

unos aretes y un collar

una cartera

unas corbatas

unos dulces

unas flores

un juego de mesa

unos juguetes

una planta

una tarjeta

Cuaderno de gramática, p. 70, Acts. 1–2

Más práctica gramatical, p. 284, Acts. 1–2 →

Communication for All Students

Visual Learners
Display *Teaching Transparency 9-1* and ask students which of the gifts is the best, worst, and most interesting. What gift would they give to a friend? a family member? As students give their opinions, write the Spanish words for the items on the board.

Tactile/Kinesthetic Learners
Ask students to write the word for a gift from **Vocabulario** on a note card. Also have them write their names and **(No) me gusta(n)... Le voy a dar este regalo a...** Students then deliver the "gifts." After repeating the process several times, ask them about their gift preferences.

STANDARDS: 1.2

Teaching Resources
pp. 269–272

PRINT
- Lesson Planner, p. 43
- TPR Storytelling Book, pp. 33, 36
- Listening Activities, pp. 67, 71
- Activities for Communication, pp. 49–50, 115, 118–119, 153–154
- Cuaderno de gramática, pp. 70–73
- Grammar Tutor for Students of Spanish, Chapter 9
- Cuaderno de actividades, pp. 98–100
- Cuaderno para hispanohablantes, pp. 41–45
- Testing Program, pp. 223–226
- Alternative Assessment Guide, p. 40
- Student Make-Up Assignments, Chapter 9

MEDIA
- One-Stop Planner
- Audio Compact Discs, CD 9, Trs. 3–4
- Teaching Transparencies 9-1, 9-A, 9-B; **Más práctica gramatical** Answers; Cuaderno de gramática Answers
- Interactive CD-ROM Tutor, Disc 3

Presenting
Gramática

Indirect object pronouns
Remind students they have used the indirect object pronouns with **gustar**. Write the following sentences on the board or on a transparency: **Le doy unos aretes a mamá. Pablo quiere regalarte unas flores a ti.** Point out the indirect objects. Remind students of the meanings of **le** and **les** and how **a** + pronoun or **a** + noun is used.

---

7 Regalos para todos

Escribamos Using the gift items in the vocabulary list on page 269, write sentences telling what you'll buy these people. Base your choices on what they like. Possible answers on p. 271.

1. A tu hermano le gusta jugar en casa.
2. A tu hermana le encantan las joyas *(jewelry)*.
3. A tu mejor amigo/a le gusta escuchar música.
4. A tu padre le gusta vestirse bien *(dress well)*.
5. A tus abuelos les encanta su jardín.
6. A tu profesor/a le encanta el chocolate.

¿Se te ha olvidado? **indirect object pronouns** Consulta la página 236

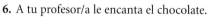

Gramática

Indirect object pronouns

Indirect objects tell *to whom* or *for whom* something is intended.

1. Indirect object pronouns either precede a conjugated verb or may be attached to an infinitive.
   Le quiero regalar algo divertido a Héctor.
   Quiero regalar**le** algo divertido a Héctor.
   I want to give something fun to Hector (to him).

2. **Le** can mean *to him, to her,* or *to you* (singular). **Les** can mean *to them* or *to you* (plural). To clarify **le** or **les**, you can add the phrase **a** + *pronoun* or **a** + *noun*.
   ¿Qué **le** compramos **a Héctor**?
   Les voy a regalar unos juguetes **a ellos**.

Más práctica gramatical, p. 284, Acts. 1–2

Cuaderno de actividades, p. 98, Act. 4   Cuaderno de gramática, pp. 71–72, Acts. 3–5

---

8 Gramática en contexto

Leamos/Escribamos Completa el párrafo con **me, te, le, nos** o **les**.

¡Qué divertido ir de compras! A mi hermana Teresa ____1____ voy a regalar un collar y a mi hermano ____2____ doy una camiseta. A mamá y a papá ____3____ regalo un video de su película favorita. ____4____ voy a regalar aretes a mi abuelita y a mi abuelito ____5____ quiero regalar una corbata. ¿Qué crees que voy a regalar ____6____ a ti? ¡Es una sorpresa! ¿Qué crees que Roberto ____7____ va a regalar a mí? Mis papás ____8____ van a regalar boletos para el concierto a mí y a mi hermano. ¿Qué te parece?
1. le; 2. le; 3. les; 4. Le; 5. le; 6. te; 7. me; 8. nos

9 Gramática en contexto

Hablemos Work in pairs. Decide which gifts each of you will give to the people listed in the last box. Be sure to include **le** or **les** in your sentences. Answers will vary.

MODELO   **Le voy a regalar un disco compacto a mi hermano para su graduación.**

voy a	dar	unas flores	un juego de mesa	a mi hermano
quiero	regalar	un cartel	una planta	a mis padres
prefiero	comprar	una bicicleta	¿?	a mi hermana
				a mis amigos
				a mi abuelo
				a ¿?

Connections and Comparisons

Language-to-Language
Point out to students that Spanish and English express indirect objects in more than one way. Write on the board **A su mamá le da flores** and **Le da flores a su mamá.** Ask students to identify the 'receiver' of the direct object in each example. Then ask what the difference is between the sentences and if the meaning is different. (placement of **a su mamá;** no) Then write *He gives his mom flowers* and *He gives flowers to his mom.* In Spanish, the preposition **a** identifies an indirect object and may precede or follow the noun. In English the indirect object can go between the verb and the direct object or after a preposition.

Así se dice

Asking for and giving directions downtown

To find out where a shop is located, ask:

Perdón, ¿dónde está el almacén?
Excuse me, where is the department store?

¿Me puede decir dónde queda la joyería?
Can you tell me where the jewelry store is?

Some responses might be:

Está a dos cuadras de aquí.
It's two blocks from here.

Queda al lado de la zapatería.
It's next to the shoe store.

10 En las tiendas

Hablemos Working with a partner, look at the drawing of downtown Río Blanco and take turns asking and answering where each store is. Use **estar** + **lejos de**, **al lado de**, and **cerca de** in your sentences.
Sample answer below.

Modelo La zapatería está al lado de la dulcería.

¿Te acuerdas?

You've already learned to say where someone or something is located using **estar** + *location*. If you've forgotten the prepositions of location, see page 119.

Cuaderno de gramática, p. 72, Act. 6

Vocabulario

Cuaderno de actividades, pp. 99–100, Acts. 5–6

Cuaderno de gramática, p. 73, Acts. 7–8

Communication for All Students

Challenge
Copy the map on p. 71 of the *Listening Activities* book and distribute. Have students imagine they are race directors designing a 3.1-mile course. Each **cuadra** is 0.2 miles. Have them determine the start, the route, and the finish. Have them explain to the runners where to go. The 3.1-mile race must start or end in the middle of a block.

Kinesthetic Learners
Arrange several of the students' desks to form a downtown area, placing a sign with the name of a store on each desk. One student asks directions and a second student answers. The first student then walks to the desired location. You might change the signs around to provide additional practice.

Photo Flash!

On the board, write these phrases one might see on a bakery window. Ask students to guess their meanings: **pan caliente** *hot bread*, **hornada de tarde** *batch of bread baked in the afternoon*. Explain that window-shopping is a favorite pastime in Spanish-speaking countries, and that even stores selling hardware or pots and pans generally have eye-catching displays.

Speaking Assessment

Students preparing a dialogue for Activity 12 should practice in front of another pair of students for peer-editing before presenting to the class. You may wish to use the following

Speaking Rubric	Points			
	4	3	2	1
Content (Complete–Incomplete)				
Comprehension (Total–Little)				
Comprehensibility (Comprehensible–Incomprehensible)				
Accuracy (Accurate–Seldom accurate)				
Fluency (Fluent–Not fluent)				

18–20: A   14–15: C   Under
16–17: B   12–13: D   12: F

Assess

▶ Testing Program, pp. 223–226
Quiz 9-1A, Quiz 9-1B
Audio CD 9, Tr. 18

▶ Student Make-Up Assignments, Chapter 9, Alternative Quiz

▶ Alternative Assessment Guide, p. 40

11 **De compras** Scripts and answers on p. 263G.

Escuchemos Where is Eva going to shop? Listen as she talks about what she's going to buy. Match each item with the correct store.

CD 9
Tr. 4

1. pastel
2. aretes
3. juego de mesa
4. sandalias
5. camisa
6. plantas
7. pan dulce

a. Zapatería Monterrey
b. Panadería El Molino
c. Joyería Central
d. Pastelería Río Grande
e. Juguetería de San Antonio
f. Florería Martínez
g. Almacén Vargas

12 **¿Dónde está?** Answers will vary.

Hablemos Imagine that you and your partner are in Río Blanco with this shopping list. Using the drawing on page 271, take turns deciding where you have to go to buy each item.

MODELO   —Tengo que comprar un collar.
          ¿Sabes dónde está la joyería?
          —Sí. Queda al lado de la zapatería.

13 **Las tiendas**

Escribamos/Hablemos Get together with two or three classmates and write a list of four items you buy frequently, such as clothing, food, compact discs, and books. Then ask each other for the names of stores in your city or town where you can buy the different items you've listed. Include where the stores are located. Be sure to take notes and be ready to report to the class.

14 **Amigos y familiares** Answers will vary.

Escribamos Indica la edad de las personas y lo que les gusta y no les gusta hacer. Escoge un regalo para cada una.

1. your best friend
2. three family members
3. an elderly person you know

Nota cultural

Although people in the U.S. are likely to buy groceries in large supermarkets, many people in Spanish-speaking countries still shop at smaller stores that specialize in one kind of item, such as bread, meat, or vegetables. Shoppers in Madrid or Mexico City might go to a supermarket occasionally, but they would probably prefer to shop in smaller stores, buying only what is needed for a day or two at a time. That way the food in the kitchen is always fresh and a person has a chance to meet and chat with acquaintances in the neighborhood.

Cuaderno de actividades, p. 108, Act. 18

collar
sandalias
flores
juguetes
zapatos de tenis
pan
galletas
corbata

Communication for All Students

Challenge

Teach students **doble a la derecha** *(turn right)*, **doble a la izquierda** *(turn left)*, and **siga derecho** *(continue straight ahead)*. Students can then give more elaborate directions for a downtown area, using either a map of your town or the student desks (see Kinesthetic Learners, p. 271).

Circumlocution

Display *Teaching Transparency 9-B*. Ask students to explain what each store is without using its root word. If you point to the **zapatería**, a student may not use the word **zapato** to describe it. She might say **En esta tienda puedo comprar cosas para caminar.**

CD 9
Trs. 5–8

¿Estás a la moda?

Hispanic teens usually try to look as fashionable as they possibly can. Much of what is popular in the United States is also in style in Spain and Latin America. But what counts is quality, not quantity. Here are some comments from teenagers about what is usually **de moda** *(in style)* for parties and what's definitely not.

Pablo CD 9 Tr. 8
San Vito, Costa Rica

"A como amerite, si es en el campo, vamos de esport, y si es algo ya normal nos ponemos traje... Claro que sí, [estar a la moda] es andar en la actualidad con todos, ¿verdad? No quedarse atrás".

Gisela CD 9 Tr. 7
Caracas, Venezuela

"Depende de la fiesta, pero una fiesta de mis amigos normalmente como estoy ahorita, ¿no? Un vestido, blue jeans... No es tan importante [estar a la moda], es más la ropa que me guste, más que la moda. No toda la moda me queda bien".

Soledad
Madrid, España

"Yo cuando voy a una fiesta me pongo un vestido... Lo importante es uno mismo, y uno mismo nunca pasará de moda".

Para pensar y hablar...

A. In small groups, discuss what is fashionable. Make a list of the things that one group member is wearing and present it to the group.

B. With a classmate, suggest five reasons why people should or should not be concerned about being in style.

Cuaderno para hispanohablantes, pp. 44–45

Connections and Comparisons

Language Note

uno mismo *oneself*
pasar de moda *to go out of style*
a como amerite *it depends* (**ameritar** *to merit, to value*)
esport *casual, sporty*
andar en la actualidad *to be up to date*
quedarse atrás *to be behind the times*

Thinking Critically

Ask students to look at the clothing of teenagers in photos throughout this book and in Spanish-language magazines and to compare it with the clothing they like to wear. Ask them to identify clothing styles that are popular both with them and the Spanish-speaking teenagers. Do they notice any differences?

Teaching Resources
p. 273

PRINT
▸ Video Guide, pp. 61–63, 66
▸ Cuaderno de actividades, p. 108
▸ Cuaderno para hispanohablantes, pp. 44–45

MEDIA
▸ One-Stop Planner
▸ Video Program, Videocassette 3, 47:18–50:41
▸ DVD Tutor, Disc 2
▸ Audio Compact Discs, CD 9, Trs. 5–8
▸ Interactive CD-ROM Tutor, Disc 3

Presenting
Panorama cultural

Have students listen to the audio recording or watch the video. Ask for volunteers to read one of the interviews aloud for pronunciation practice. Then have students answer the **Preguntas** to check comprehension.

Preguntas

1. ¿Quién es de España? ¿de Costa Rica? ¿de Venezuela? (Soledad, Pablo, Gisela)
2. A Soledad, ¿qué le gusta llevar a una fiesta? (un vestido)
3. Según Gisela, ¿es importante llevar ropa elegante a las fiestas? (no)¿Por qué? (Depende de la fiesta.)
4. ¿A Pablo le importa estar a la moda? ¿por qué? (Sí, porque le gusta andar en la actualidad.)

Objectives Commenting on clothes; making comparisons

go.hrw.com
WV3 TEXAS-9

Teaching Resources
pp. 274–278

PRINT
▸ Lesson Planner, p. 44
▸ TPR Storytelling Book, pp. 34, 36
▸ Listening Activities, pp. 68, 72
▸ Activities for Communication, pp. 51–52, 116, 118–119, 153–154
▸ Cuaderno de gramática, pp. 74–76
▸ Grammar Tutor for Students of Spanish, Chapter 9
▸ Cuaderno de actividades, pp. 68, 72
▸ Cuaderno para hispanohablantes, pp. 41–45
▸ Testing Program, pp. 227–230
▸ Alternative Assessment Guide, p. 40
▸ Student Make-Up Assignments, Chapter 9

MEDIA
▸ One-Stop Planner
▸ Audio Compact Discs, CD 9, Trs. 9–10
▸ Teaching Transparencies 9-2, 9-C, 9-D; **Más práctica gramatical** Answers; Cuaderno de gramática Answers
▸ Interactive CD-ROM Tutor, Disc 3

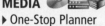

Bell Work
Display a list of local stores and have students say what kind each one is. (Smith's Bakery—**panadería**)

Presenting
Así se dice, Vocabulario
Model **Así se dice** phrases. Call on students to practice the first question and answer with books open and then closed. Incorporate **Vocabulario** filling a bag with clothes and having students ask each other **Así se dice** questions about clothes taken from the bag.

Así se dice

Commenting on clothes

To find out what someone is going to wear, ask:

¿Qué ropa vas a llevar a la fiesta?
What are you going to wear . . .?

¿No tienes algo más formal?
Don't you have something more formal?

Your friend might say:

¡Lo de siempre! Una camiseta con bluejeans.
The usual!

Sí, pero **prefiero llevar ropa cómoda**.
. . . I prefer to wear comfortable clothes.

Vocabulario

una camisa blanca
una chaqueta gris
una blusa amarilla
unas botas negras
un traje de baño morado
una camiseta blanca
unos bluejeans
una falda parda
un traje de baño rojo
unos pantalones cortos anaranjados
unos calcetines azules
unas sandalias pardas

CD-ROM 3
DVD 2

Cuaderno de gramática, p. 74, Acts. 9–10

Más práctica gramatical, p. 285, Act. 3

Teacher to Teacher

Paula Bernard
Sandy Creek High School
Fayette County, GA

Paula packs her bags for class
"I bring to class a suitcase packed with clothing items from the vocabulary and I unpack it, naming each item in Spanish. Students repeat the words. After completely unpacking, I randomly choose items of clothing and have students identify them. Finally, I repack, having students help me as I ask for the items in Spanish. You may vary this by packing unusual items, putting on some clothing, or asking what things may be missing."

15 **¿Qué necesitas llevar?** Scripts and answers on p. 263G.

CD 9 Tr. 9

Escuchemos Listen as various people talk about clothing they need for certain occasions. Choose an event for which the clothing would be appropriate.

Eventos: un baile, clases, jugar al tenis, ir a la piscina, trabajar en la oficina

16 **Mis preferencias** Possible answers below.

Escribamos Completa las oraciones con tus preferencias personales.

1. Cuando hace calor, me gusta llevar...
2. En el invierno, cuando hace mucho frío, llevo...
3. Cuando voy al colegio, en general llevo...
4. Cuando salgo con mis amigos, llevo...
5. Cuando voy a una fiesta, me gusta llevar...
6. Me gusta jugar a los deportes. En general llevo...
7. Voy a ir a un picnic. Voy a llevar...
8. En la primavera, me encanta llevar...
9. Tan pronto como tenga el dinero (*As soon as I have the money*), voy a comprar...

17 **¿Cómo es su ropa?**

Hablemos Work with a partner. Describe the clothing someone in your class is wearing. See if your partner can guess whom you're describing.

18 **El fin de semana**

Hablemos Working in pairs, tell your partner three or four places you'll be going this weekend. Then take turns suggesting what each of you should wear.

MODELO   —Voy al cine y al centro comercial.
—Para ir al cine debes llevar bluejeans y una camiseta.

Presenting
Vocabulario, Nota gramatical

Hold up photos of people wearing the new articles of clothing. Point them out to the students and model the vocabulary, having students repeat after you. Then shuffle the photos and ask, **¿Qué lleva ____?** Have them include vocabulary from page 274. Have students say what each item of clothing is made of using ____ **es/son de** ____. If time permits, you may want to include vocabulary from **Vocabulario extra** on page 276.

Nota gramatical

In earlier lessons you've used **ser** to describe people and things and to tell where someone is from. The formula **es/son** + **de** + *material* or *pattern* is used to tell what something is made of.

El suéter es de lana.
¿Son de cuero tus botas?

Cuaderno de gramática, p. 75, Acts. 11–12

Más práctica gramatical, p. 285, Act. 4

Vocabulario

un vestido de algodón
una chaqueta
de rayas
un traje de seda
un cinturón de cuero
de cuadros
un suéter de lana
unos pantalones largos
unos zapatos

Más práctica gramatical, p. 285, Acts. 3–4

Cuaderno de actividades, p. 101, Acts. 7–8

Communication for All Students

Visual Learners

16 Ask students **¿Qué llevan los muchachos que juegan al baloncesto?** Then you might ask **¿Qué llevas tú cuando juegas al baloncesto?** Show students other pictures of sporting events and ask questions about clothing preferences during different times of the year and for various activities.

Tactile Learners

18 Review the color words by giving students pieces of cotton, wool, silk, leather, striped cloth, and plaid cloth. Let students hold the materials as you teach the **Vocabulario**. Have each student describe the color and material of the clothing that he suggests to his partner.

Answers

16 *Possible answers:*
1. los pantalones cortos y una camiseta
2. una chaqueta de lana y unas botas
3. unos bluejeans y una camiseta
4. los bluejeans y una camisa
5. un vestido y un suéter
6. los pantalones cortos y zapatillas de tenis
7. el traje de baño y unos pantalones cortos
8. las sandalias
9. una chaqueta de cuero

Teaching Resources
pp. 274–278

PRINT
▸ Lesson Planner, p. 44
▸ TPR Storytelling Book, pp. 34, 36
▸ Listening Activities, pp. 68, 72
▸ Activities for Communication, pp. 51–52, 116, 118–119, 153–154
▸ Cuaderno de gramática, pp. 74–76
▸ Grammar Tutor for Students of Spanish, Chapter 9
▸ Cuaderno de actividades, pp. 101–103
▸ Cuaderno para hispanohablantes, pp. 41–45
▸ Testing Program, pp. 227–230
▸ Alternative Assessment Guide, p. 40
▸ Student Make-Up Assignments, Chapter 9

MEDIA
▸ One-Stop Planner
▸ Audio Compact Discs, CD 9, Trs. 9–10
▸ Teaching Transparencies 9-2, 9-C, 9-D; **Más práctica gramatical** Answers; Cuaderno de gramática Answers
▸ Interactive CD-ROM Tutor, Disc 3

Answers

Possible answer:

19 El hombre lleva anteojos, un suéter pardo y una camisa. La niña lleva un vestido de algodón, unos calcetines y unos zapatos grises.

20 *Possible answers:*
1. Lleva un traje de baño. Debe llevar una chaqueta, pantalones y botas.
2. Lleva una chaqueta formal con pantalones cortos. Debe llevar pantalones largos.
3. No lleva zapatos. Debe llevar las botas.
4. Lleva pantalones largos y un suéter. Debe llevar un traje de baño.

---

19 Gramática en contexto

Hablemos Look at the picture and describe at least four different outfits. Include colors and materials in your descriptions. What do you think these people are doing? Possible answer below.

Carmen Lomas Garza, *Tamalada*, 1987, Gouache on paper. 20" × 27".

20 ¡Qué ropa tan rara!

Escribamos Look at these drawings of different people in different situations. What do you think is wrong in each drawing? Write a sentence telling what the people are wearing. Then write a sentence telling what you think they should be wearing instead. For additional clothing vocabulary, see page R8. Possible answers below.

Vocabulario extra	
el abrigo	*coat*
la bolsa	*purse*
la gorra	*cap*
los guantes	*gloves*
el impermeable	*raincoat*
las medias	*stockings*
el paraguas	*umbrella*
el sombrero	*hat*

1.   2.   3.   4.

Cultures and Communities

Background Information

19 The artist Carmen Lomas Garza paints about her life as a Mexican American growing up in Kingsville, Texas. She captures the magic of daily events such as gathering cactus during Lent (**Cuaresma**), or making **tamales** during the Christmas season (**las Navidades**) depicted here in *Tamalada*.

Culture Note

Sizes for clothes in Spain and Latin America are different from those in the U. S. Women's size 10 pants in the U.S. are size 42 in Spain and Latin America. Men's size 32 pants are European size 81. Have students look for clothing with European sizes when they go shopping and report their findings.

21 **Una encuesta**

Hablemos/Escribamos Working in groups of three or four, take a survey of clothing preferences for the situations listed. Make a chart of what each person prefers and report to the class.

1. to wear to school
3. in the summer
5. to go to a formal dance
2. to wear on a date
4. to go to the park
6. to play tennis

22 **Me gustaría comprarle...** Possible answers below.

Hablemos You've just won a $500 gift certificate for your favorite department store. Say what you'd like to buy for your friends and family. Be sure to describe colors, patterns, and material.

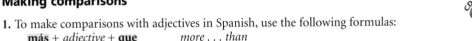
Así se dice

Making comparisons

To compare things, you might ask:

¿Cuál es más barato — el reloj o el disco compacto?
Which is cheaper . . .?

¿Son los carteles tan caros como el juguete?
Are the posters as expensive as the toy?

Some responses might be:

El disco compacto **cuesta menos.** El reloj es **más caro.**
. . . costs less . . . more expensive.

Sí. **Son del mismo precio.**
They're the same price.

Gramática

Making comparisons

1. To make comparisons with adjectives in Spanish, use the following formulas:

más + *adjective* + **que**	*more . . . than*
menos + *adjective* + **que**	*less . . . than*
tan + *adjective* + **como**	*as . . . as*

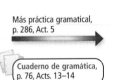

2. The adjective agrees in gender and number with the item it describes.
La camisa blanca es **más bonita que** el vestido azul.
Las sandalias son **menos cómodas que** los zapatos de tenis.
El cinturón es **tan barato como** la corbata.

Más práctica gramatical, p. 286, Act. 5

Cuaderno de gramática, p. 76, Acts. 13–14

23 **Gramática en contexto** Possible answers below.

Hablemos Antonio is unfamiliar with U.S. prices and products and wants your advice on what to buy. Tell him how the items listed compare to one another.

MODELO zapatos de tenis (− formal)/corbatas
Los zapatos de tenis son menos formales que las corbatas.

1. cartel (− interesante)/disco compacto
3. camisetas (+ barato)/suéteres
2. aretes (= caro)/collar
4. cinturón de cuero (= bonito)/ camisa de seda

Communication for All Students

Native Speakers

Have students role-play a scene in their favorite store between a difficult customer and a pushy clerk. Using comparisons, the clerk should make suggestions about various pieces of clothing to the customer, who always prefers something larger, more comfortable, and so on.

Visual Learners

Have students form a circle. One student will stand in the middle and quickly look at what everyone is wearing. That student will then close his or her eyes, and another student will ask a question like **¿Quién lleva una camiseta roja?** The student being questioned will then try, without looking, to name someone wearing that item of clothing. If no one is wearing such an item, the students answers **nadie.**

Teaching Suggestion

21 You might provide each group with a transparency for their chart. Compile the data onto one transparency and make generalizations about class preferences. Have a simple discussion about **la ropa favorita.** (Los jóvenes prefieren los bluejeans, zapatos de tenis, camisas de rayas o de cuadros. Para un baile las chicas prefieren vestidos elegantes.)

Presenting
Así se dice, Gramática

Making comparisons Write the formulas from **Gramática** on the board or on a transparency. Then use each formula in a sentence. Next divide the class into groups of three. Give each group an envelope containing components of sentences written on slips of paper. For example, on six slips of paper, write **Rosa/es/más/alta/que/Raúl.** Have the groups arrange the words to form a sentence.

Answers

22 *Possible answer:*
Me gustaría comprar un vestido de seda. También necesito unos zapatos de cuero. Voy a comprar suéteres de lana para el invierno. También voy a comprar un abrigo de cuero y lana que cuesta $300.

23 *Possible answers:*
1. El cartel es menos interesante que el disco compacto.
2. Los aretes son tan caros como el collar.
3. Las camisetas son más baratas que los suéteres.
4. El cinturón de cuero es tan bonito como la camisa de seda.

Slower Pace

24 Have students describe the items pictured to each other before listening to the audio recording.

Additional Practice

25 To give students additional practice with comparisons and to review the food vocabulary from Chapter 8, bring in food store ads from newspapers. Ask each pair of students to make at least five price comparisons. Then have two or three students share their comparisons with the rest of the class.

Teaching Suggestion

Walk around the classroom and ask the class about the material in the clothing of various students. (**¿De qué es el suéter de Stephen?**) After you have done this, ask students to work in pairs. They are to tell their partner what they are wearing, and then say what color their clothing is and what material it is made of. How are their clothing choices affected by the seasons?

Assess

▶ Testing Program, pp. 227–230
Quiz 9-2A, Quiz 9-2B
Audio CD 9, Tr. 19

▶ Student Make-Up Assignments, Chapter 9, Alternative Quiz

▶ Alternative Assessment Guide, p. 40

24 **¿Cómo son?** Scripts and answers on p. 263G.

Escuchemos/Escribamos Look at the drawings. Listen and match what you hear to the correct pair of items. When you're finished, write sentences to compare each pair of items using the adjectives you've learned.

CD 9
Tr. 10

a.   b.   c.   d.

25 **Regalos y más regalos**

Escribamos You need to buy gifts for your family and friends. Look at the catalog page and decide what to buy for each person. Be sure to say what each person needs. Use comparisons in deciding upon which item to buy.

MODELO   Mi hermana necesita ropa nueva. Quiero comprarle una blusa porque es más barata que un vestido. Los vestidos son caros.

MÁS POR MENOS   **MODA**   ¡Ropa en especial!

blusa punto de seda (15,00€)

chaqueta nylon (42,00€)

vestido lino-viscosa (24,00€)

falda viscosa (18,00€)

pantalones canvas (18,00€)

camisa popelín (18,00€)

camiseta algodón (6,00€)

zapatos nobuck (18,00€)

Abrimos sábados • aceptamos tarjetas de crédito
Sierra de Guadarrama, 12 (Torres Bellas)
Telf. 612 72 53   Alcorcón, Madrid

SUGERENCIA

Sometimes you don't know the exact word for something even in your native language. Remember that one way you can still get your message across is by describing what you can't remember. Use a phrase like **Es una cosa que...** and then tell what it does, how it's used, or where it is. As practice, look around your room or classroom and pick three things you don't know how to say in Spanish. How could you describe them so a Spanish speaker would understand? Test your skills on a classmate! Look at these four drawings. Can you describe these items to a friend?

Connections and Comparisons

Career Path

Divide students into groups to discuss clothes worn by people in diverse professions. Cut out magazine pictures of people in work clothes for each group. Have students determine each person's profession. Ask a student from each group to use the vocabulary on p. 291 to describe the clothes of the person in the picture.

Math Link

Ask students how much they can save on clothing items on sale. Write the following on the board or the overhead:

Precios reducidos:	Antes	Ahora
Trajes de seda	$225.00	$189.95
Camisas de algodón	$25.95	$18.00
Zapatos de cuero	$63.00	$49.98

Así se dice

Expressing preferences

To find out which item a friend prefers, ask:

¿Cuál de estos trajes prefieres?
Which of these suits do you prefer?

¿Qué camisa te gusta más? ¿La verde o la amarilla? *Which shirt do you like more? The green one or the yellow one?*

Your friend might say:

Prefiero el azul.
I prefer the blue one.

La verde. **Además, te queda muy bien.**
Besides, it fits you very well.

Más práctica gramatical, p. 286, Act. 6

Nota gramatical

Demonstrative adjectives point out people and things. Like other adjectives, they agree in gender and number with the noun they modify.

CD-ROM **3**
DVD **2**

MASCULINE

este vestido	**estos** vestidos
this . . .	*these . . .*
ese vestido	**esos** vestidos
that . . .	*those . . .*

FEMININE

esta falda	**estas** faldas
esa falda	**esas** faldas

Cuaderno de gramática, p. 77, Acts. 15–16

Más práctica gramatical, p. 287, Act. 7

Cuaderno de actividades, pp. 104–105, Acts. 11–13

---

26 Gramática en contexto

Escribamos Alicia y su hermana Mónica están de compras. Escribe los comentarios de Alicia. See sample answers below.

MODELO blusa/feo
—Oye, Mónica. Esta blusa es fea, ¿no?

1. camisa/caro
2. botas/feo
3. suéter/pequeño
4. zapatos/barato
5. falda/grande
6. cinturón/bonito
7. chaqueta/barato
8. vestido/caro

Sample answers
1. Esta camisa es cara, ¿no?
2. Estas botas son feas, ¿no?

---

27 Gramática en contexto

Hablemos Now it's Mónica's turn! Work with a partner. Using your sentences from Activity 26, take turns giving Mónica's responses to Alicia's comments. Answers will vary.

MODELO
—Oye, Mónica. Esta blusa es fea, ¿no?
—No, Alicia, esa blusa no es fea. Es bonita.

28 Preferencias

Hablemos Work in groups of three. Look at the pictures of clothing throughout this chapter. What are your tastes in clothing? Tell which items you like and don't like. Use demonstrative adjectives when giving your opinion.

Communication for All Students

Slower Pace

Hold up two magazine pictures showing different articles of clothing. Model a question and answer about the appropriateness of the articles of clothing in certain situations (**¿Cuál de estas camisas prefieres llevar cuando juegas al fútbol? Yo prefiero la roja.**) Show different clothing items to practice gender and number of demonstrative adjectives in **Nota gramatical.**

Kinesthetic Learners

Bring in a collection of old clothing (or have students do so) and set up a pretend **mercado** in the classroom. Have five or six students role-play the vendors and set up around the room with several items to sell. Students should use demonstrative adjectives as they discuss the clothes and haggle with the vendors.

Teaching Resources
pp. 279–281

PRINT
▶ Lesson Planner, p. 45
▶ TPR Storytelling Book, pp. 35, 36
▶ Listening Activities, pp. 69, 73
▶ Activities for Communication, pp. 53–54, 117, 118–119, 153–154
▶ Cuaderno de gramática, pp. 77–78
▶ Grammar Tutor for Students of Spanish, Chapter 9
▶ Cuaderno de actividades, pp. 104–106
▶ Cuaderno para hispanohablantes, pp. 41–45
▶ Testing Program, pp. 231–234
▶ Alternative Assessment Guide, p. 40
▶ Student Make-Up Assignments, Chapter 9

MEDIA
▶ One-Stop Planner
▶ Audio Compact Discs, CD 9, Trs. 11–16
▶ Teaching Transparencies 9-3; **Más práctica gramatical** Answers; Cuaderno de gramática Answers
▶ Interactive CD-ROM Tutor, Disc 3

Bell Work

Have students write the answers to: **¿Qué ropa llevas hoy? ¿Te gusta llevar ropa elegante? ¿Qué lleva tu amigo/a?**

Presenting
Así se dice, Nota gramatical
Show pictures of people in varied clothing to introduce expressing preferences. Show contrasting men's and women's clothing to present **Nota gramatical.** To contrast forms of **este** and **ese,** hang some pictures close to students and others farther away.

Teaching Resources
pp. 279–281

PRINT
▸ Lesson Planner, p. 45
▸ TPR Storytelling Book, pp. 35, 36
▸ Listening Activities, pp. 69, 73
▸ Activities for Communication, pp. 53–54, 117, 118–119, 153–154
▸ Cuaderno de gramática, pp. 77–78
▸ Grammar Tutor for Students of Spanish, Chapter 9
▸ Cuaderno de actividades, pp. 104–106
▸ Cuaderno para hispanohablantes, pp. 41–45
▸ Testing Program, pp. 231–234
▸ Alternative Assessment Guide, p. 40
▸ Student Make-Up Assignments, Chapter 9

MEDIA
▸ One-Stop Planner
▸ Audio Compact Discs, CD 9, Trs. 11–16
▸ Teaching Transparencies 9-3; **Más práctica gramatical** Answers; Cuaderno de gramática Answers
▸ Interactive CD-ROM Tutor, Disc 3

Presenting
Así se dice, Vocabulario

To introduce talking about prices, put large, legible price tags on various articles of clothing. Then ask questions about the prices. Include expressions from **Vocabulario**. (**¿Cuánto cuesta esta corbata? Cuesta treinta dólares. ¡Es un robo!**) Hold up items and ask individual students **¿Cuánto cuesta(n) _____?** Each student should give a price and use an expression from **Vocabulario**.

Así se dice

Asking about prices and paying for something

To ask how much one item costs, say:

¿Cuánto cuesta esta chaqueta?
How much does . . . cost?

To ask how much two or more items cost, say:

¿Cuánto cuestan...?
How much do . . . cost?

Some responses might be:

Cuesta 90 dólares.

Cuestan 30 euros.

Más práctica gramatical, p. 287, Act. 8

Cuaderno de gramática, p. 78, Acts. 17–18

29 **¡Qué caro!**

Escuchemos Listen to conversations between a clerk and some customers. Write the name, price, and color of the items mentioned.
Scripts and answers on p. 263H.

CD 9
Tr. 11

Nota cultural

Have you ever wondered what kind of money is used in other countries? Sometimes currency is named after a person: Colón, Balboa, Bolívar, Sucre.

Argentina el peso	**Guatemala** el quetzal
Colombia el peso	**México** el nuevo peso
Costa Rica el colón	**Panamá** el balboa
Ecuador el dólar estadounidense	**Puerto Rico** el dólar
(antes del 2000, el sucre)	**Venezuela** el bolívar

España el euro (antes del 2002 la peseta)

During the 1980s, the countries of the European Union, including Spain, made a commitment to use a single currency: the **euro**. Since 1999, banks, companies, and stock markets have been trading in **euros**. Spaniards were able to use both **pesetas** and **euros** until 2002. Now the **euro** is Spain's only currency. Bills are issued in 5, 10, 20, 50, 100, 200, and 500 **euro** denominations. **Euro** coins have a common symbol on one face, and unique symbols representing each country on the other. The **euro** is intended to strengthen Europe economically. It also makes it easier for countries around the world to do business with the European Union. Can you think of some ways it might affect travel, tourism, and banking if several countries in the Western Hemisphere decided to use a common currency? What might such a currency be called?

Cuaderno de actividades, p. 108, Act. 17

Vocabulario

¡Es un robo!	*It's a rip-off!*
¡Qué barato!	*How cheap!*
¡Qué caro!	*How expensive!*
¡Qué ganga!	*What a bargain!*

Cuaderno de gramática, p. 78, Act. 19

Cultures and Communities

Additional Practice

Have students find the current exchange rates for three countries listed. Post the exchange rates of the board or a transparency. Give students advertising sections from newspapers that list products they would probably like to buy. (clothing, DVDs, CDs, electronics) Ask each student to pick two items he or she would like to buy and convert the price from dollars into the currencies of three different countries. Check the exchange rates in two or three weeks and have students recalculate the prices of the items to see how the new rates impact their spending power. Ask students to report their findings using forms of the verb **costar**.

30 ¡Qué precios! See answers below.

Escribamos Complete various shoppers' comments with the correct demonstrative adjective, **cuesta** or **cuestan**, and the most logical expression from the **Vocabulario**.

1. ═══ blusas de nylon ═══ ochenta y cinco dólares. ¡Qué ═══!
2. ═══ chaqueta de cuero ═══ diez dólares. ¡Qué ═══!
3. ═══ bluejeans ═══ doscientos dólares. ¡Es ═══!
4. ═══ vestido de algodón ═══ noventa y ocho dólares. ¡Qué ═══!
5. ═══ pantalones ═══ dieciocho dólares. ¡Qué ═══!
6. ═══ traje de seda ═══ seiscientos dólares. ¡Es ═══!

 31  **Del colegio al trabajo** Answers will vary.

Hablemos With a partner, role-play a conversation between a customer and a store clerk. The customer should ask about the material, colors, and prices of two items of clothing, and the clerk should answer. The customer and clerk then discuss how the items fit, their cost, and which one the customer will buy.

32 En mi cuaderno Possible answer below.

Escribamos Write a dialogue in which you are a clerk who tries to talk a customer out of buying clothing that doesn't match. Convince the customer that the colors and patterns don't look good together, and that the clothes are out of fashion. Then, compare the customer's choices with clothing that does look good.

> **A lo nuestro**
>
> To tell a friend he or she looks good today, you can say **¡Qué bien te ves!** or **¡Qué guapo/a estás!** (You look great!). To compliment someone on an outfit, say **Estás a la última** (You're stylish). To say something doesn't match, say **No hace juego**.

LETRA Y SONIDO

 CD 9 Trs. 12–16

A. 1. s: The letter **s** in Spanish is pronounced like the *s* in the English word *pass*.

camiseta   flores   pastelería   gris   suéter   seda

2. z: In Latin America, the letter **z** is also pronounced like the *s* in the English word *pass*.

azul   zapatos   zanahoria   zarzuela   zapatería

However, in Spain, the letter **z** is pronounced much like the *th* in the English word *think*.

3. c: In Latin America, the letter **c** before the vowels **e** and **i** is also pronounced like an *s*.

almacén   dulces   dulcería   calcetines   cinturón

In Spain, the letter **c** before the vowels **e** and **i** is also pronounced like the *th* in English.

B. Dictado Script for Part B on p. 263H.

Selena wants to go to the store for some gifts. Write everything she says.

C. Trabalenguas

La señora Sánchez sazona la sopa con sal y sasafrás.
César y Cecilia cocinan cinco cebollas con cilantro a las once.

Communication for All Students

Visual Learners

Review material from this **Paso** with *Teaching Transparency 9-3*. Have students describe the clothing tried on and bought, tell how the clothing fits the customers, and say how much it will cost. Ask students to create dialogues among the people depicted or to make suggestions regarding what the customers should buy.

Challenge

Have a few students bring items of clothing to class and wear an odd array of loose articles over school clothes. Have them model outfits, which may be **a la última,** ill fitting, or mismatched. Have the class describe each one, then suggest how each model might improve the look. Models leave class, put on new outfits, and return to elicit more comments.

Additional Practice
Use *Teaching Transparency 9-3* to review the material from this **Paso** with students. If time permits, use *Teaching Transparencies 9-1* and *9-2* for a comprehensive review.

Assess

▸ Testing Program, pp. 231–234
Quiz 9-3A, Quiz 9-3B
Audio CD 9, Tr. 20

▸ Student Make-Up Assignments, Chapter 9, Alternative Quiz

▸ Alternative Assessment Guide, p. 40

Answers

30 1. Estas; cuestan; *Answer will vary.*
2. Esta; cuesta; *Answer will vary.*
3. Estos; cuestan; *Answer will vary.*
4. Este; cuesta; *Answer will vary.*
5. Estos; cuestan; *Answer will vary.*
6. Este; cuesta; *Answer will vary.*

32 *Possible answer:*
Lo siento, señor, pero este traje no le va muy bien. La camisa no queda muy bien con la chaqueta anaranjada. Y creo que la corbata de cuadros amarillos no hace juego con los pantalones rojos. Sinceramente, este traje no está de moda. ¿Por qué no se pone el traje azul con la camisa blanca? Sí, esta ropa es mucho mejor.

Vamos a leer

San Antonio

Teaching Resources
pp. 282–283

PRINT
▶ Lesson Planner, p. 46
▶ Cuaderno de actividades, p. 107
▶ Cuaderno para hispanohablantes, pp. 41–43
▶ Reading Strategies and Skills Handbook, Chapter 9
▶ ¡Lee conmigo! 1, Chapter 9
▶ Standardized Assessment Tutor, Chapter 9

MEDIA
▶ One-Stop Planner

Prereading
Activities A and B

Using Prior Knowledge
Ask students what they know about San Antonio. Have they ever visited the city, read about it, or seen anything about it on TV? Do they know anything about San Antonio's festivals? If so, ask them to share their knowledge with the class.

Drawing Inferences
In Spanish, read aloud descriptions of the five activities in the reading as a listening comprehension activity. Students are to respond with the name of the corresponding activity.

San Antonio

Estrategia para leer
Scanning for specific information means looking for one thing at a time, without concerning yourself with the rest of the information. Some examples of scanning are looking up the spelling of a word in a dictionary or hunting through the TV listing to see what time a certain show comes on.

¡A comenzar!
Let's look at the pictures and sub-titles in this brochure about San Antonio.

A. Using pictures only, determine which of these topics are addressed in the article.
1. sports
2. a zoo
③ eating
4. police protection
⑤ shopping
6. nightclubs
⑦ holiday activities
⑧ a river near the city
⑨ an old Spanish building

B. Suppose you're in a hurry and don't have time to read every section. Look only at subtitles to determine where you could read about the following. Write the appropriate subtitle.
1. where the good shopping is
2. the river that runs through the city
3. churches
4. where to have dinner
5. what to do on holidays
   See answers below.

---

ofrece generosas porciones de su vida cosmopolita, incluyendo finos restaurantes, vida nocturna, deportes profesionales y bellas artes. Nuestros grupos étnicos añaden su propio sabor.

Restaurantes.
Nuestra herencia multicultural hace posible que usted pueda escoger entre muchos restaurantes, desde parrilladas de estilo tejano y picantes platillos mexicanos hasta la cocina continental, oriental y "alta americana".

Compras.
¿Listo para ir de compras? Tome un taxi acuático al refrescante centro comercial al lado del Paseo del Río. Encuentre tesoros deslumbrantes en los centros comerciales de la ciudad. Disfrute de las artesanías de La Villita y El Mercado.

Communication for All Students

Native Speakers
Ask native speakers to choose a local establishment or event that shows Latino influence, such as a grocery store, restaurant, or festival. Have them imagine that they are going to describe this place or event in a city tourism guide. Before they begin writing, have them brainstorm aspects of the place or event they would like to highlight. Suggest that they include the paragraph in their journals.

Group Work
Have each student write one question about each section of the reading. Have students ask these aloud in small groups and see which group member can correctly answer first.

Answers
 B 1. Compras
2. Río San Antonio
3. Las misiones
4. Restaurantes
5. Festivales

Río San Antonio.

Absorba las vistas de nuestro Paseo del Río, con sus tiendas, galerías y cafés al aire libre. Es una gran introducción al encanto y romance de nuestra ciudad.

Las Misiones.

Parte del sistema de parques nacionales es el conjunto más completo de misiones españolas en los Estados Unidos. Cada una de las cuatro misiones hermanas del Álamo tiene una historia fascinante que contar. No deje de asistir a la Misa de los Mariachis los domingos en la Misión San José. Es un recuerdo inolvidable.

Festivales.

En abril hay desfiles y fiestas en la calle. En febrero tenemos la Muestra Ganadera y el Rodeo. En agosto, se celebra la herencia multicultural de Texas en el Festival "Texas Folklife".

¿Te acuerdas?

Use pictures, titles, and subtitles first.

- It will make understanding easier.
- It will save you time.

Sometimes you're only interested in one small part of an article.

Al grano See answers below.

From the pictures and subtitles you got a general overview of this article about San Antonio. You know what areas are mentioned, and you should be able to locate important details very quickly.

C. Imagine that you work for the San Antonio Chamber of Commerce. Answer the tourists' questions, using the information in the brochure. You already know where to look for the answers, but you will have to read the descriptions thoroughly to find out the details.

1. Are there any Chinese or Japanese restaurants in town?
2. The riverfront shopping district is surrounded by water. How do I get there?
3. What's the name of the riverfront area that has stores, galleries, and cafés?
4. In which mission does the Mariachi Mass take place?
5. In what month does the **Muestra Ganadera** festival occur?

D. Además de responder a las preguntas, otra de tus tareas en la Cámara de Comercio es la de hacer itinerarios de muestra (sample) para los turistas. Crea tu propio folleto en el que describes tres cosas que se pueden hacer en San Antonio en un día. Las tres actividades deben basarse en la lectura.

Cuaderno para hispanohablantes, pp. 41–43

Cuaderno de actividades, p. 107, Act. 16

Reading
Activity C

Paraphrasing

Students might also develop a telephone conversation between an employee of the San Antonio Chamber of Commerce and a prospective visitor to the city.

Postreading
Activity D

Summarizing

Have students do class presentations on some aspect of San Antonio. Cultural and historical information is readily available on the Internet, and travel guides with information about restaurants and shopping are in many libraries. Visit the HRW Web site at **go.hrw.com** keyword **WV3 TEXAS** for online resources and information about San Antonio. You might also create a bulletin board about San Antonio by having students bring in pictures or drawings and then write Spanish captions.

Cultures and Communities

Multicultural Link

Texas is rich in various cultural heritages, including Mexican, German, Polish, Scottish, and Czech. You might have students research a Texas ethnic group and give a report to the class. The University of Texas Institute of Texan Cultures in San Antonio is a source of information students might contact or research on the Internet.

Culture Note

There are five Spanish missions along the San Antonio River: **San Antonio de Valero** (the Alamo), **San Juan, San José, Concepción,** and **Espada.** The missions were built early in the eighteenth century. Have students research and report on the role of the missions in Texan history and their status today.

Answers

C 1. yes
2. by water taxi
3. El Paseo del Río
4. Misión San José
5. February

Más práctica gramatical

CAPÍTULO 9

For **Más práctica gramatical** Answer Transparencies, see the *Teaching Transparencies* binder.

Más práctica gramatical

CD-ROM 3
DVD 2

internet

MARCAR: go.hrw.com
PALABRA CLAVE:
WV3 TEXAS-9

Primer paso **Objectives** Discussing gift suggestions; asking for and giving directions downtown

1 Tu amigo Luis necesita escoger regalos para su familia. Sugiérele un regalo diferente para cada persona. (**pp. 269–270**)

MODELO   —A mi abuela le encanta leer.
—Debes regalarle una novela.

> cartel   aretes   disco compacto   dulces
> planta   novela
> cartera   juego de mesa
> corbatas

1. A mi tía le encanta trabajar en el jardín.
2. A mi primo le gusta la música.
3. A mi hermano mayor le encanta la ropa elegante.
4. A mi hermanita le encanta jugar en casa.
5. A mi mamá le encantan las joyas.
6. A mi hermana le gusta el arte.
7. A mi primito le encanta comer.
8. A mi padre le gustan los regalos prácticos *(practical)*.

2 Below is Manuela's gift list. Tell what she is planning to give everyone, using the indirect object pronoun **le** or **les** in each sentence. (**pp. 269–270**)

MODELO   Su perro Max
Piensa regalarle (Le piensa regalar) su comida favorita a su perro Max.

Max	su comida favorita
los abuelos	libro
el tío Fernando	corbata
Chela y Nuria	collares
mamá	planta
Micha	juguete
los primos	camisetas
papá	disco compacto

Grammar Resources for Chapter 9

The **Más práctica gramatical** activities are designed as supplemental activities for the grammatical concepts presented in the chapter. You might use them as additional practice, for review, or for assessment.

For more grammar presentation, review, and practice, refer to the following:

• Cuaderno de gramática
• Grammar Tutor for Students of Spanish

• Grammar Summary on pp. R9–R13
• Cuaderno de actividades
• Grammar and Vocabulary Quizzes (Testing Program)
• Test Generator on the One-Stop Planner CD-ROM
• Interactive CD-ROM Tutor
• DVD Tutor
• **Juegos interactivos** at **go.hrw.com**

Answers

1
1. Debes regalarle una planta.
2. Debes regalarle un disco compacto.
3. Debes regalarle unas corbatas.
4. Debes regalarle un juego de mesa.
5. Debes regalarle unos aretes.
6. Debes regalarle un cartel.
7. Debes regalarle unos dulces.
8. Debes regalarle una cartera.

1. Sus abuelos
2. Su tío Fernando
3. Sus hermanas Chela y Nuria
4. Su mamá
5. Su gata Micha
6. Sus primos
7. Su papá

Segundo paso

Objectives Commenting on clothes; making comparisons

3 Completa las oraciones lógicamente. Indica qué ropa lleva la gente en diferentes situaciones. (pp. 274, 275)

1. Cuando hace calor, prefiero llevar (un suéter/unos pantalones cortos).
2. Para ir a su clase de ejercicio, mi hermana lleva (sandalias/zapatos de tenis).
3. Cuando hace fresco, Juan Pablo lleva una (chaqueta/camiseta).
4. Para ir a esquiar, necesitamos llevar suéteres (de lana/de algodón).
5. Cuando voy al lago, llevo un traje (de baño/de seda).
6. Para ir a trabajar en el banco, papá lleva un (traje/vestido) muy elegante.
7. Cuando nieva, mamá prefiere llevar (sandalias/botas).
8. Para jugar al tenis, Rebeca necesita buscar sus (calcetines/cinturones) blancos.

4 Trabajas en la sección de ropa en un almacén. Explica a tus clientes de qué están hechos los siguientes artículos. (p. 275)

MODELO   blusas/*silk*
Las blusas son de seda.

1. camisas/*cotton*
2. corbatas/*silk*
3. suéteres para niños/*wool*
4. trajes para señoras/*silk*
5. camisetas/*cotton*
6. cinturones/*leather*
7. suéteres para hombres/*cotton*
8. trajes para hombres/*wool*
9. botas/*leather*
10. vestidos/*cotton*

Teacher to Teacher

Jean Schuster
Eagan High School
Eagan, MN

TPRS helps Jean's students find ways to tell a story
"I have students take about 3 minutes at the end of our TPRS time to write the story for me. They switch papers then and edit each other's stories. The students' computers allow them to download stories to my computer. For oral proficiency evaluation, I have students record the story at our tape station for me to review later. On a test I give them ten verbs in the infinitive with a picture and have them create their own story. The more I use TPRS, the easier they find the writing and oral sections of my tests."

Answers

2
1. Piensa regalarles (Les piensa regalar) un libro a sus abuelos.
2. Piensa regalarle (Le piensa regalar) una corbata a su tío Fernando.
3. Piensa regalarles (Les piensa regalar) unos collares a sus hermanas Chela y Nuria.
4. Piensa regalarle (Le piensa regalar) una planta a su mamá.
5. Piensa regalarle (Le piensa regalar) un juguete a su gata Micha.
6. Piensa regalarles (Les piensa regalar) unas camisetas a sus primos.
7. Piensa regalarle (Le piensa regalar) un disco compacto a su papá.

3
1. unos pantalones cortos
2. zapatos de tenis
3. chaqueta
4. de lana
5. de baño
6. traje
7. botas
8. calcetines

4
1. Las camisas son de algodón.
2. Las corbatas son de seda.
3. Los suéteres para niños son de lana.
4. Los trajes para señoras son de seda.
5. Las camisetas son de algodón.
6. Los cinturones son de cuero.
7. Los suéteres para hombres son de algodón.
8. Los trajes para hombres son de lana.
9. Las botas son de cuero.
10. Los vestidos son de algodón.

For **Más práctica gramatical** Answer Transparencies, see the *Teaching Transparencies* binder.

Más práctica gramatical

WV3 TEXAS-9

5 You've just won a free room decoration from a local store. Decide what to get by comparing the things listed below. In each sentence, use the correct form of the adjective and a comparative expression: more . . . than (+), less . . . than (−), or as . . . as (=). (**p. 277**)

MODELO la lámpara negra/(+ grande)/la lámpara verde
La lámpara negra es más grande que la verde.

1. la alfombra azul/(+ bonito)/la alfombra parda
2. el televisor blanco/(= caro)/el televisor negro
3. los carteles de fútbol/(− interesante)/los carteles de animales
4. la radio azul/(+ pequeño)/la radio roja
5. el teléfono morado/(= feo)/el teléfono anaranjado
6. los peces/(− aburrido)/las plantas
7. la silla grande/(+ cómodo)/la silla pequeña

Tercer paso

Objectives Expressing preferences; asking about prices and paying for something

6 You're being interviewed by a fashion designer who wants to know about the latest trends in clothing. Complete your conversation by filling in each blank with the correct definite article: **el, la, los,** or **las**. (**p. 279**)

DISEÑADOR ¿Qué camisa te gusta más?
Tú Me gusta más ___1___ roja.
DISEÑADOR Y, ¿qué pantalones prefieres, ___2___ de cuadros?
Tú No, prefiero ___3___ de rayas.
DISEÑADOR ¿Qué abrigo te gusta más?
Tú Me gusta más ___4___ de cuero.
DISEÑADOR Y para una fiesta, ¿qué zapatos prefieres ponerte?
Tú Prefiero ponerme ___5___ negros, por supuesto.
DISEÑADOR En tu opinión, ¿cuál es el color más popular? ¿___6___ amarillo?
Tú No, el color más popular es ___7___ morado.

Answers

5 1. La alfombra azul es más bonita que la parda.
2. El televisor blanco es tan caro como el negro.
3. Los carteles de fútbol son menos interesantes que los de animales.
4. La radio azul es más pequeña que la roja.
5. El teléfono morado es tan feo como el anaranjado.
6. Los peces son menos aburridos que las plantas.
7. La silla grande es más cómoda que la pequeña.

6 1. la
2. los
3. los
4. el
5. los
6. el
7. el

Communication for All Students

Additional Practice

5 Bring in a collection of pairs of different articles of clothing or gather common objects (two ties, two pairs of shoes, two pencils). Give each student a pair of items to compare. Using demonstrative adjectives, each student asks a partner **¿Qué piensas de estas corbatas?** The partner then compares the items using different adjectives. Students exchange the items and find a new partner.

6 Have students repeat the dialogue using real objects as suggested in the previous activity. You might distribute the items around the classroom and have pairs of students circulate throughout the room, asking each other questions like the ones in the dialogue.

7 Le estás ayudando a Graciela a hacer la maleta para su viaje. Pregúntale qué ropa prefiere llevar. Usa adjetivos demostrativos en tus preguntas. (**p. 279**)

MODELO   **falda negra/vestido azul**
¿Prefieres esta falda negra o ese vestido azul?

1. camisa de algodón/blusa de seda
2. sandalias/zapatos de tenis
3. pantalones grises/bluejeans negros
4. camiseta de rayas/blusa morada
5. botas pardas/zapatos negros
6. pantalones cortos rojos/falda de rayas
7. suéter de algodón/camisa blanca

8 You're doing the inventory for a department store. Write how many of each item there are, and the price for each. Spell out all numbers. (**p. 280**)

MODELO   **Hay setecientas sesenta camisetas. Cuestan doce dólares cada una.**

1. corbatas   5. vestidos
2. chaquetas   6. blusas
3. cinturones   7. faldas
4. trajes de baño

ROPA PARA CHICOS		
ARTÍCULO	CANTIDAD	PRECIO C/U
camisetas	760	$12.00
corbatas	312	$25.00
chaquetas	197	$58.00
cinturones	52	$21.00

ROPA PARA CHICAS		
ARTÍCULO	CANTIDAD	PRECIO C/U
trajes de baño	548	$62.00
vestidos	630	$88.00
blusas	329	$36.00
faldas	177	$49.00

Answers

7 1. ¿Prefieres esta camisa de algodón o esa blusa de seda?
2. ¿Prefieres estas sandalias o esos zapatos de tenis?
3. ¿Prefieres estos pantalones grises o esos bluejeans negros?
4. ¿Prefieres esta camiseta de rayas o esa blusa morada?
5. ¿Prefieres estas botas pardas o esos zapatos negros?
6. ¿Prefieres estos pantalones cortos rojos o esa falda de rayas?
7. ¿Prefieres este suéter de algodón o esa camisa blanca?

8 1. Hay trescientas doce corbatas. Cuestan veinticinco dólares cada una.
2. Hay ciento noventa y siete chaquetas. Cuestan cincuenta y ocho dólares cada una.
3. Hay cincuenta y dos cinturones. Cuestan veintiún dólares cada uno.
4. Hay quinientos cuarenta y ocho trajes de baño. Cuestan sesenta y dos dólares cada uno.
5. Hay seiscientos treinta vestidos. Cuestan ochenta y ocho dólares cada uno.
6. Hay trescientas veintinueve blusas. Cuestan treinta y seis dólares cada una.
7. Hay ciento setenta y siete faldas. Cuestan cuarenta y nueve dólares cada una.

Review and Assess

You may wish to assign the **Más práctica gramatical** activities as additional practice or homework after presenting material throughout the chapter. Assign Activity 1 after **Vocabulario** (p. 269), Activity 2 after **Gramática** (p. 270), Activities 3–4 after **Vocabulario** (p. 274–275), Activity 5 after **Gramática** (p. 277), Activity 6 after **Así se dice** (p. 279), Activity 7 after **Nota gramatical** (p. 279), and Activity 8 after **Así se dice** (p. 280).

To prepare students for the **Paso** Quizzes and Chapter Test, have them do the **Más práctica gramatical** activities in the following order: Complete Activities 1–2 before taking Quizzes 9-1A or 9-1B; Activities 3–5 before taking Quizzes 9-2A or 9-2B; and Activities 6–8 before taking Quizzes 9-3A or 9-3B.

The **Repaso** reviews all four skills and culture in preparation for the Chapter Test.

Teaching Resources
pp. 288–289

PRINT
▶ Lesson Planner, p. 46
▶ Listening Activities, p. 77
▶ Video Guide, pp. 61–63, 66
▶ Grammar Tutor for Students of Spanish, Chapter 9
▶ Cuaderno para hispanohablantes, pp. 41–45
▶ Standardized Assessment Tutor, Chapter 9

MEDIA
▶ One-Stop Planner
▶ Video Program, Videocassette 3, 46:57–1:00:05
▶ DVD Tutor, Disc 2
▶ Audio Compact Discs, CD 9, Tr. 17
▶ Interactive CD-ROM Tutor, Disc 3

Reteaching
Expressing preferences
Hold up two magazine or catalogue photos of clothing and tell the class which you prefer. Repeat with several pairs of pictures. Then show two pictures of the same item and ask **¿Cuál de estos/as _____ prefieres?** or **¿Qué _____ te gusta más?** Have students answer. Pass out catalogues or photos and have students continue this activity in small groups.

Teaching Suggestion
2 **3** You may wish to have students use these activities for oral practice.

Answers
2 1. *Possible answers:* camisa, flores, disco compacto
2. regalarle el mismo disco compacto
3. el cinturón
4. rosas; sí
5. azul; de seda; bonita

Repaso

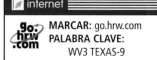

MARCAR: go.hrw.com
PALABRA CLAVE: WV3 TEXAS-9

1 Listen as Sara and Ana talk about what Sara needs for the costume party (**fiesta de disfraces**). Choose the items she mentions. Not all will be used. *Script and answers on p. 263H.*

CD 9 Tr. 17

2 Marisa recibió muchos regalos maravillosos para su cumpleaños. Lee la carta de agradecimiento a sus abuelos y contesta las preguntas. *See answers below.*

> Queridos abuelo y abuelita,
>
> Les escribo para decir que me encantan todos los regalos. Esta camisa azul de seda es más bonita que las otras camisas que tengo. ¡Y me encanta el disco compacto! Voy a regalarle el mismo disco compacto a mi amiga Gloria. Estas flores son increíbles. Me gustan mucho las rosas. ¡Qué bonitas! Y el cinturón de cuero me queda muy bien. Me gusta mucho. En fin, ustedes son super generosos. Muchísimas gracias por todo.
>
> Un abrazo muy fuerte,
>
> Marisa

1. Menciona tres regalos que los abuelos de Marisa le dan para su cumpleaños.
2. ¿Qué piensa hacer Marisa para su amiga Gloria?
3. ¿Qué le queda bien a Marisa?
4. ¿Qué tipo de flores tiene Marisa? ¿Le gustan las flores?
5. Describe la nueva camisa de Marisa.

3 Work in groups of three or four to discuss your tastes in clothing, where you prefer to shop, and which local stores have the best prices. Be sure to include colors, styles, and materials. Make a list for a new student of the best places to shop. Take notes and be prepared to present the information to the class.

Apply and Assess

Slower Pace
1 Before students listen to the audio recording, have them ask a partner if he or she likes the items pictured, using demonstrative adjectives. Students should tell why they do or do not like the articles and explain their preferences. Remind students to make adjectives agree in gender and number with the modified noun.

Additional Practice
2 Have pairs of students play the role of Marisa's grandparents as they try to decide what to buy for her birthday. They should take into account her likes and dislikes, as well as the things she already has. Students should eventually choose to purchase the things that Marisa mentions in her letter.

4 Compare how teenagers in the United States feel about fashion compared with how teenagers in Spanish-speaking countries feel. Possible answers below.

5 How would you tell a friend that you are going to give these items to various relatives for their birthdays? Possible answer below.

a. mi papá   b. mi hermana   c. mi tía   d. mis primos

6

Vamos a escribir

Your shop is having a big seasonal clothing sale. Write a newspaper advertisement announcing the sale. Include different clothing items, colors, materials, and prices, and think of a snappy introduction that will make people want to read your ad.

Estrategia para escribir

A snappy introduction will get your reader's attention immediately. You might begin with a question or exclamation to arouse the reader's curiosity. Another way to begin is by highlighting what you think is most important or interesting to your readers.

¡Qué barato! ¡Ponte a la moda! ¡Qué ganga!

1. First think of a name for your store. Then decide which adjectives or expressions you'll use to describe three or four pieces of clothing. Don't forget to mention the prices.

MODELO   **Camisetas de algodón de muchos colores.**
           Originalmente a $26.00 y ahora a $18.00.

2. Write the rest of the ad, using the descriptions you listed in Step 1. You might want to illustrate your ad with drawings or photos clipped from magazines.

7

Situación

Create a store within your classroom. Gather materials to "sell," choose clerks, make signs and price tags, and set up a cashier's station. Then use the vocabulary and grammar from this chapter to "buy and sell" the merchandise.

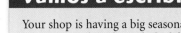

Cuaderno para hispanohablantes, p. 45

Apply and Assess

Process Writing

6 Bring in advertisements from Spanish or English language newspapers. Divide the class into small groups and give each group an advertisement. Have them look for different styles of advertising: snappy introductions, product descriptions, calling attention to low prices or sales. Once they have discussed the ads with their groups, have them begin creating an advertisement on their own. Set clear guidelines for evaluation: Let students know that you will assess their work based on adjective agreement and use of chapter vocabulary.

Teaching Suggestion

7 Explain that in many stores in Spanish-speaking countries customers pay at the cashier's booth, where they are given a receipt stamped **cancelado** or **pagado**. They then return to the checkout counter, where the clerk delivers the merchandise and gives them another receipt. Have students price the items using one of the currencies in **Nota cultural,** page 280.

 Portfolio

3 **Oral** Suggest that students include portions of their discussions in their oral portfolios.

6 **Written** Students may want to include notes and advertisement ideas from Activity 6 in their written portfolios. For portfolio suggestions, see *Alternative Assessment Guide,* p. 26.

Answers

4 *Possible answer:*
Teenagers in all countries want to wear the most up-to-date styles. Quality is often more important than quantity.

5 a. Le voy a dar una corbata a mi papá.
b. Le voy a regalar un reloj a mi hermana.
c. Le voy a dar una planta a mi tía.
d. Les voy a regalar unos juguetes a mis primos.

A ver si puedo

Teacher Note

This page is intended to help students prepare for the Chapter Test. It is designed for the students to work on their own initiative and consists of a brief checklist of the major points covered in the chapter. The students should be reminded that it is a checklist only and not necessarily everything that will appear on the test. Remind students that cultural information is included in the Chapter Test.

Answers

1 *Sample answer:*
—¿Qué le regalamos a la profesora?
—Vamos a comprarle chocolates porque (a ella) le encantan los dulces.

2 *Answers may vary.*
—¿Dónde está la librería?
—Está a dos cuadras de aquí.
—¿Me puede decir dónde queda la panadería?
—Queda al lado de la zapatería.

4 *Answers may vary.* a. El collar es más caro que los aretes. b. La chaqueta de cuero es más formal que la chaqueta de cuadros. c. El zapato negro es más bonito que la sandalia.

6 a. ¿Cuánto cuesta la blusa amarilla de algodón?
b. ¿Cuánto cuesta la corbata de seda?
c. ¿Cuánto cuestan estos dulces?
d. ¿Cuánto cuesta esta tarjeta?

A ver si puedo...

WV3 TEXAS-9

Can you discuss gift suggestions? p. 269

1 You and a friend are shopping for a birthday gift for your Spanish teacher. How would you ask your friend about what you should get for your teacher? How might he or she make a suggestion? See sample answer below.

Can you ask for and give directions downtown? p. 271

2 You're at the supermarket on this map. Can you ask someone where the restaurant and the hospital are? How would he or she answer? See possible answers below.

Can you comment on clothes? p. 274

3 How would you describe the clothes you're wearing right now? Describe the color, pattern, and material of each item. Answers will vary.

Can you make comparisons? p. 277

4 How would you compare the two items in each drawing? Possible answers below.

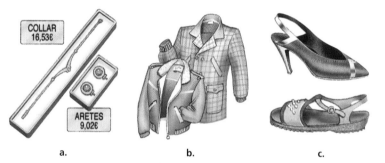

a.   b.   c.

Can you express preferences? p. 279

5 Look at the pictures in Activity 4. For each pair of items, tell which one you prefer and why. Answers will vary.

Can you ask about prices and pay for something? p. 280

6 You're in a shopping center in Mexico and the salesclerk doesn't speak English. How would you ask the prices of the following items? How might the clerk answer? See answers below.

a. a yellow cotton blouse
b. a silk tie
c. chocolate candies
d. a greeting card

Review and Assess

Cooperative Learning

Tell students that you are having a party for a popular teacher or other person at your school. Tape to the board magazine pictures of possible gift items from the chapter vocabulary. Label each picture with a price. Divide the class into groups of four and give each group an amount of money they may spend on gifts. Explain that they may give more than one gift, but that they may not exceed the total amount allotted. A member from each group writes which item(s) to buy and at what stores they could buy each one. Then each group chooses a spokesperson to explain their group's decisions.

Primer paso

Discussing gift suggestions

el arete	earring	les	to/for them, you (pl.)	la dulcería	candy store
buscar	to look for	me	to/for me	la florería	flower shop
la camiseta	T-shirt	nos	to/for us	la joyería	jewelry store
la cartera	wallet	los pantalones	pants	la juguetería	toy store
el collar	necklace	¿Para quién...?	For whom . . .?	¿Me puede	Can you tell me . . .?
la corbata	tie	la planta	plant	decir...?	
dar	to give	regalar	to give (as a gift)	la panadería	bakery
el disco compacto	compact disc	el regalo	gift	la pastelería	pastry shop; sweet
los dulces	candy	la tarjeta	greeting card		shop
las flores	flowers	te	to/for you		
el juego de mesa	(board) game			Perdón.	Excuse me.
los juguetes	toys	**Asking for and giving**		el precio	price
le	to/for her, him,	**directions downtown**		quedar	to be (situated)
	you			la tienda de	grocery store
		el almacén	department store	comestibles	
		la cuadra	city block	la zapatería	shoe store

Segundo paso

Commenting on clothes

de algodón	(made of) cotton	formal	formal	el traje	suit
amarillo/a	yellow	gris	gray	el traje de baño	bathing suit
anaranjado/a	orange	de lana	(made of) wool	el vestido	dress
blanco/a	white	largo	long	los zapatos	shoes
los bluejeans	bluejeans	llevar	to wear		
la blusa	blouse	¡Lo de siempre!	The usual!	**Making comparisons**	
las botas	boots	morado/a	purple		
los calcetines	socks	los pantalones	shorts	barato/a	cheap
la camisa	shirt	cortos		cuesta	costs
la chaqueta	jacket	pardo/a	brown	caro/a	expensive
el cinturón	belt	de rayas	striped	más ... que	more . . . than
cómodo/a	comfortable	rojo/a	red	menos ... que	less . . . than
de cuadros	plaid	las sandalias	sandals	Son del mismo	They're the same
de cuero	(made of) leather	de seda	(made of) silk	precio.	price.
la falda	skirt	el suéter	sweater	tan ... como	as . . . as

Tercer paso

Expressing preferences

además	besides
esa, ese	that
esas, esos	those
esta, este	this
estas, estos	these
Te queda muy bien.	It fits you very well.

Asking about prices and paying for something

¿Cuánto cuesta...?	How much does . . . cost?	¡Es un robo!	It's a rip-off!
		¡Qué barato!	How cheap!
¿Cuánto cuestan...?	How much do . . . cost?	¡Qué caro!	How expensive!
		¡Qué ganga!	What a bargain!

Review and Assess

? Circumlocution

Divide students into two teams. Write on the board several nouns and an adjective for each. (**chaqueta marrón, camisa blanca,** etc.) Give each item a price. Have teams play a circumlocution game. One student picks an item and whispers it to you. The other student tries to find out what it is. His or her team may help by raising hands to suggest questions. Neither student may say the word or its root. Both students must circumlocute as they ask and answer questions. (—**¿Es ropa?** —**Sí.** —**¿Qué tipo de ropa es?** —**Es ropa para el otoño.** —**¿De qué color es?** —**Es de un color oscuro.** —**¿Es una chaqueta marrón?** —**Sí.**)

CAPÍTULO 9

Game

Regalos Give each student an index card on which a word for a gift is written or a picture of a gift is pasted or drawn. Be sure to give yourself a card also. Put the following questions on the board or on a transparency to practice the vocabulary and the indirect object pronouns: **¿Qué le vas a regalar a ____? ¿Qué me vas a regalar a mí? ¿Qué te voy a regalar a ti? ¿Qué les vas a regalar a ____ y a ____?** Students will answer with the item they have on their card. Practice placing the pronoun before the verb, then expand by attaching the pronoun to the infinitive.

Chapter 9 Assessment

▸ **Testing Program**
Chapter Test, pp. 235–240
Audio Compact Discs, CD 9, Trs. 21–22
Speaking Test, p. 347

▸ **Alternative Assessment Guide**
Performance Assessment, p. 40
Portfolio Assessment, p. 26
CD-ROM Assessment, p. 54

▸ **Interactive CD-ROM Tutor, Disc 3**

CD-ROM 3 ¡A hablar!
DVD 2 ¡A escribir!

▸ **Standardized Assessment Tutor**
Chapter 9

▸ **One-Stop Planner, Disc 3**
Test Generator
Chapter 9

Capítulo 10: Celebraciones
Chapter Overview

De antemano pp. 294–296	¡Felicidades, Héctor!

	FUNCTIONS	GRAMMAR	VOCABULARY	RE-ENTRY
Primer paso pp. 297–301	• Talking about what you're doing right now, p. 298 • Asking for and giving an opinion, p. 300	• Present progressive, p. 299	• Holidays, p. 297	• estar (Capítulo 4) • Dates, months, seasons (Capítulo 5) • Extending, accepting, and turning down invitations (Capítulo 7)
Segundo paso pp. 302–306	• Asking for help and responding to requests, p. 302 • Telling a friend what to do, p. 304	• Informal commands, p. 304	• Party expressions, p. 302	• tú versus usted (Capítulo 4) • Household chores (Capítulo 6)
Tercer paso pp. 307–311	• Talking about past events, p. 307	• Preterite tense of regular -ar verbs, p. 307 • Direct object pronouns lo and la, p. 310	• Time expressions, p. 307	• Days of the week (Capítulo 4) • ¿quién?, ¿quiénes? (Capítulo 4) • Activities and places (Capítulo 4)

Letra y sonido p. 311	**Listening for Spanish syllables** Audio CD 10, Track 12	**Dictado** Audio CD 10, Tracks 13–15

Vamos a leer pp. 312–313	**Festivales del mundo hispanohablante**	**Reading Strategy:** Making comparisons

Más práctica gramatical	**pp. 314–317** **Primer paso,** pp. 314–315	**Segundo paso,** pp. 315–316	**Tercer paso,** pp. 316–317

Review pp. 318–321	**Repaso,** pp. 318–319 **Vamos a escribir,** p. 319 Combining sentences	**A ver si puedo...,** p. 320	**Vocabulario,** p. 321

CULTURE

- **Nota cultural, El quinceañero,** p. 296
- **A lo nuestro,** Expressions using **feliz,** p. 297
- **Nota cultural, Día del santo,** p. 298
- **Panorama cultural, ¿Qué hacen ustedes para celebrar?,** p. 301
- **Encuentro cultural, ¿Cómo se celebra una boda?,** p. 306
- **Realia, Las piñatas,** p. 309

Capítulo 10: Celebraciones
Chapter Resources

Lesson Planning

One-Stop Planner

**Lesson Planner with Substitute Teacher
Lesson Plans,** pp. 48–52, 74

Student Make-Up Assignments
- Make-Up Assignment Copying Masters, Chapter 10

Listening and Speaking

TPR Storytelling Book, pp. 37–40

Listening Activities
- Student Response Forms for Listening Activities, pp. 75–77
- Additional Listening Activities 10-1 to 10-6, pp. 79–81
- Additional Listening Activities (song), p. 82
- Scripts and Answers, pp. 147–151

Video Guide
- Teaching Suggestions, pp. 67–69
- Activity Masters, pp. 70–72
- Scripts and Answers, pp. 106–108, 117

Activities for Communication
- Communicative Activities, pp. 55–60
- Realia and Teaching Suggestions, pp. 120–124
- Situation Cards, pp. 155–156

Reading and Writing

Reading Strategies and Skills Handbook, Chapter 10

¡Lee conmigo! 1, Chapter 10
Cuaderno de actividades, pp. 109–120

Grammar

Cuaderno de gramática, pp. 79–88
Grammar Tutor for Students of Spanish, Chapter 10

Assessment

Testing Program
- Grammar and Vocabulary Quizzes, **Paso** Quizzes, and Chapter Test, pp. 249–266
- Score Sheet, Scripts and Answers, pp. 267–274

Alternative Assessment Guide
- Portfolio Assessment, p. 27
- Performance Assessment, p. 41
- CD-ROM Assessment, p. 55

Student Make-Up Assignments
- Alternative Quizzes, Chapter 10

Standardized Assessment Tutor
- Reading, pp. 39–41
- Writing, p. 42
- Math, pp. 51–52

Native Speakers

Cuaderno para hispanohablantes, pp. 46–50

 Online Activities
- Juegos interactivos
- Actividades Internet

 Video Program
- Videocassette 4
- Videocassette 5 (captioned version)

 Interactive CD-ROM Tutor, Disc 3
DVD Tutor, Disc 2

 Audio Compact Discs
- Textbook Listening Activities, CD 10, Tracks 1–17
- Additional Listening Activities, CD 10, Tracks 23–29
- Assessment Items, CD 10, Tracks 18–22

 Teaching Transparencies
- Situations 10-1 to 10-3
- Vocabulary 10-A to 10-B
- **De antemano**
- **Más práctica gramatical** Answers
- **Cuaderno de gramática** Answers

  One-Stop Planner CD-ROM

Use the **One-Stop Planner CD-ROM with Test Generator** to aid in lesson planning and pacing.

For each chapter, the **One-Stop Planner** includes:
- Editable lesson plans with direct links to teaching resources
- Printable worksheets from resource books
- Direct launches to the HRW Internet activities
- Video and audio segments
- Test Generator
- Clip Art for vocabulary items

Capítulo 10: Celebraciones

Projects ··········

Teatro guiñol

In this project students work in groups to create puppet shows about holiday celebrations. Each group researches the history, customs, and cultural importance of a different holiday. They then produce a brief puppet show that tells a story of the celebration. Students gather information together and use all four language skills as they write, practice, and present their shows.

MATERIALS

✂ **Students may need**

- Materials for making puppets (socks, bags, cloth)
- Glue
- Markers
- A table as a stage
- A sheet to cover the front and sides of the table
- Audio or video recording equipment (optional)

SUGGESTED SEQUENCE

1. Explain the project and set due dates for research, a written script, and the show.

2. Divide the students into groups of four or five. Students decide on the holiday they would like to learn more about in groups. Assist groups having trouble.

3. Allow time for research and script writing. Remind them to use Spanish they know and allow dictionary use.

4. Have students turn in rough draft scripts. Review, then return the scripts.

5. Make puppets in class. Students bring usable materials. (socks, yarn, string, buttons) Have them look up the Spanish for the materials and list them.

6. Allow students time to rehearse the shows in class or as groups outside of class.

7. Groups turn in a copy of their script and (optional) a short paragraph giving information about the celebration they researched.

8. Students present their shows to the class.

GRADING THE PROJECT

Suggested point distribution: (total = 100 points)
Cultural research	20
Accurate Spanish in script	25
Creativity in script	10
Accurate Spanish in show	25
Creativity in show	10
Individual contributions	10

Games ··········

Un año de celebraciones

This game provides practice with the preterite and naming holidays. It serves as a chapter review.

Preparation On index cards, have students write verbs associated with activities or celebrations. (**acampar, ayudar, bailar, bucear, cenar, comprar, cortar, cuidar, decorar, descansar, escuchar, inflar, llevar, tomar**) Place the pile face down so students may draw from it. Write the 12 months in order on the board. Have them name one holiday per month. Accept birthdays or special school days.

Procedure 1 The object is for each of two teams to go through the year and "celebrate" each holiday. Teams "celebrate" a **día festivo** when a player uses a preterite verb correctly in a sentence about the holiday. The first team's player starts with **enero,** for which the class has assigned **el Día de los Reyes Magos,** for example. He or she picks a card (**caminar**), and must build a sentence about the holiday using the verb in the preterite. (**Los reyes caminaron por los pueblos.**)

If the student succeeds, Team 1 advances to **febrero** and play goes to Team 2. If not, play goes to Team 2, and Team 1 does not advance. The first team to celebrate all 12 holidays wins.

For longer sentences, or for a larger class, try this variation:

Procedure 2 Several small teams simultaneously build a sentence for the same holiday, but each team has a different verb. Set time limits and rules about looking up words.

When time is up, one player from each team reads the group's sentence. Groups whose sentences pass advance to the next month and make a new sentence about the new holiday. Groups whose sentences do not pass draw another verb, making a new sentence about the same holiday. The first team to celebrate all 12 holidays wins.

COMMUNITY LINK

To create interest in other cultures and help students decide on celebrations they would like to research, invite a person from a Spanish-speaking country to speak to the class about holidays in his or her country. The guest might be asked to bring and show realia unique to the culture.

Storytelling

Mini-cuento

This story accompanies Teaching Transparency 10-3. The **mini-cuento** *can be told and retold in different formats, acted out, written, and read aloud to give students additional opportunities to practice all four skills. The following story relates what happened yesterday at Kara's party.*

Anoche Kara celebró su cumpleaños y organizó una fiesta muy divertida. Todos los invitados lo pasaron muy bien. Por ejemplo, Kim tocó la guitarra y cantó para Rosalinda, pero Rosalinda sólo habló, habló y habló. A Manuel le gustan mucho los deportes y habló con María sobre el partido de béisbol del domingo pasado. Al mismo tiempo Manuel comió muchas hamburguesas. Jorge pasó el rato en la cocina con Pedro y Susana y preparó el ponche de frutas. Rosa, Calvin y Fernando bailaron salsa y merengue toda la noche hasta que se cansaron. Kara habló con Cristina sobre sus discos compactos. Al final de la fiesta todos los amigos de Kara le cantaron "Las mañanitas". Ella trabajó mucho para organizar una fiesta de cumpleaños maravillosa.

Traditions

Festivales

Six flags (of Spain, France, Mexico, the Republic of Texas, the Confederacy, the United States) have flown over Texas, representing its complicated and fascinating history. Many other groups, however, have helped to shape the multi-cultural state that Texas is today. Festivals throughout the state celebrate the cultures, music, and food of the Mexican, German, Polish, Scottish, and Czech communities. Ennis, Texas, hosts the National Polka Festival, which highlights traditional Czech music, while the town of New Braunfels sponsors the Wurstfest, with German food and music.

Houston is home to the popular International Festival. Have students log on to **go.hrw.com** and enter the keyword **WV3 TEXAS** to find out more about the six flags of Texas and the diverse ethnic groups that form the basis of Texan history and culture. Have students research and share with the class the significance of the flag and the ethnic and cultural makeup of their own state. Are there any local or state festivals that celebrate the region's history or ethnic groups?

Receta

Tex-Mex cooking is prevalent in Texas. It is the result of a blending of cuisines of various Texan cultures from the years before statehood. At social gatherings and restaurants, Tex-Mex dips and **salsas** *are popular snacks and appetizers. The main ingredients are tomatoes, chili peppers, avocados, cheese, and beans, which are relatively inexpensive and require little or no cooking. The following cheese dip requires stovetop cooking and is especially delicious!*

CHILE CON QUESO

para 10 personas

16 onzas de chorizo (opcional)

2 libras de queso del tipo Velveeta®

1 cebolla mediana-grande

2–4 chiles jalapeños (al gusto)

2 tomates grandes o medianos

En una sartén, fría el chorizo. Si no quiere usar chorizo, caliente grasa vegetal en una sartén y fría los ingredientes en ella. Pique la cebolla y los jalapeños. Cuando el chorizo esté dorado, deje escurrir la grasa. Agregue la cebolla y revuélvala con el chorizo. Cuando la cebolla esté transparente, agregue el chile jalapeño y vuelva a removerlo todo. Baje el fuego. Corte y agregue el tomate. Corte el queso en tajaditas de 1/4 de pulgada y colóquelas encima de la mezcla en la sartén. Cuando se derrita el queso puede vertirlo todo en un recipiente y servirlo con tostadas.

Capítulo 10: Celebraciones
Technology

Videocassette 4, Videocassette 5 (captioned version)
DVD Tutor, Disc 2
See Video Guide, pages 67–74.

DVD/Video ....

De antemano • ¡Felicidades, Héctor!
The Villarreal family is preparing for Héctor's graduation party. While making **tamales,** Héctor's grandmother tells Lisa, Eva, and Gabi about holidays in Mexico. At the end of the episode, Héctor's father discovers that he has forgotten to send out the invitations to the party, which is set to begin in two hours.

A continuación
Héctor's mother calls all the guests on the telephone and invites them to the party. Eva, Lisa, and Gabi go to the bakery to pick up the cake and mistakenly bring back the wrong one. Fortunately, they have just enough time to exchange the cake and return before Héctor gets home. In the end, the party is a success.

¿Qué hacen ustedes para celebrar?
Spanish-speakers from Texas, Spain, and Venezuela tell about holidays and celebrations where they live. In additional interviews, people from various Spanish-speaking countries tell us about their favorite celebrations and holidays.

Videoclips
• **Idea:** public service announcement concerning Christmas holidays

Interactive CD-ROM Tutor ....

Activity	Activity Type	Pupil's Edition Page
En contexto	*Interactive conversation*	
1. Vocabulario	¡Super memoria!	p. 297
2. Gramática	¿Qué falta?	p. 299
3. Gramática	¡A escoger!	p. 304
4. Vocabulario	¿Cuál es?	p. 302
5. Gramática	¿Qué falta?	p. 307
6. Gramática	¡A escoger!	p. 310
Panorama cultural	¿Qué hacen ustedes para celebrar?	p. 301
¡A hablar!	*Guided recording*	pp. 318–319
¡A escribir!	*Guided writing*	pp. 318–319

Teacher Management System
Launch the program, type "admin" in the password area and press RETURN. Log on to **www.hrw.com/CDROMTUTOR** for a detailed explanation of the Teacher Management System.

DVD Tutor ....

The *DVD Tutor* contains all material from the *Video Program* as described above. Spanish captions are available for use at your discretion for all sections of the video. The *DVD Tutor* also provides a variety of video-based activities that assess students' understanding of the **De antemano, A continuación,** and **Panorama cultural.**

This part of the *DVD Tutor* may be used on any DVD video player connected to a television or video monitor.

In addition to the video material and the video-based comprehension activities, the *DVD Tutor* also contains the entire *Interactive CD-ROM Tutor* in DVD-ROM format. Each DVD disc contains the activities from all 12 chapters of the *Interactive CD-ROM Tutor.*

This part of the *DVD Tutor* may be used on a Macintosh® or Windows® computer with a DVD-ROM drive.

Internet Connection

*Have students explore the **go.hrw.com** Web site for many online resources covering all chapters. All Chapter 10 resources are available under the keyword **WV3 TEXAS-10**. Interactive games help students practice the material and provide them with immediate feedback. You will also find a printable worksheet that provides Internet activities that lead to a comprehensive online research project.*

Juegos interactivos

You can use the interactive activities in this chapter

- to practice grammar, vocabulary, and chapter functions
- as homework
- as an assessment option
- as a self-test
- to prepare for the Chapter Test

Actividades Internet

Students research holidays in Spanish-speaking countries on the Internet. They choose a holiday to celebrate, describe how to prepare for the celebration, and say how their party turned out.

- In preparation for the **Hoja de actividades,** have students watch the dramatic episode and the **Panorama cultural** on Videocassette 4.

- After students have completed the activity sheet, have them compare their celebration with that of a classmate who chose a different holiday, preferably in a different country. Which customs are similar? Which are different?

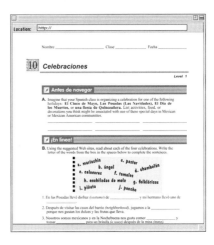

Proyecto

Have students choose a celebration they learned about from their own research or a classmate's in the **Hoja de actividades.** Ask them to use the Internet to research how, if at all, that holiday has been adapted by immigrants from that country whose descendents make their home in the United States.

Capítulo 10: Celebraciones
Textbook Listening Activities Scripts

Primer paso

7 p. 298

1. Me llamo Rolando. Vivo en Miami. Nosotros celebramos el Día de Acción de Gracias, pero como todas las familias, nuestra cena tiene cosas especiales de nuestra tradición cubana. Servimos pavo, pero también servimos arroz con frijoles negros.

2. Soy Marta. Vivo en San Antonio. Mi día favorito es el Día de los Enamorados que celebramos en febrero. Mando tarjetas a mis amigos y mi novio siempre me regala chocolates, flores o algo especial.

3. Soy Daniela. En mi familia nuestra fiesta favorita es la Navidad. Toda la familia va a la casa de mis abuelos. Vamos a misa a las doce de la noche y luego regresamos a casa para una cena fabulosa.

4. Yo me llamo Bernardo. Tengo seis años. Mi día favorito es mi cumpleaños. Este año mi mamá me va a llevar al zoológico. Luego vamos al cine y después voy a tener una fiesta.

Answers to Activity 7
1. d
2. a
3. c
4. b

9 p. 299

Esta tarde va a haber una fiesta estupenda en nuestra casa. Es el cumpleaños de mi abuelo y mi familia y yo vamos a hacer una fiesta para él. Pero hay muchas cosas que tenemos que hacer antes de la fiesta. Julia está limpiando la cocina. Mi tía Rosita está preparando una cena muy especial para mi abuelo. Mi hermana Sarita está en el patio. Ella está poniendo la mesa. Mis primos Teresa y Mauricio están lavando los platos. Roberto está decorando la sala. Y yo, ¿qué estoy haciendo yo? Bueno, yo estoy organizando mi cuarto. ¡Es un desastre!

Answers to Activity 9
1. Sarita, e
2. Guadalupe, d
3. Roberto, a
4. Rosita, b
5. Teresa y Mauricio, f
6. Julia, c

Segundo paso

18 p. 303

1. Roberto, ¿me puedes ayudar a decorar la sala?

2. Elenita, ¿me haces el favor de llamar a Gregorio? Toca muy bien la guitarra.

3. Oye, ¿quién me ayuda con las decoraciones?

4. Jaime, ¿me haces el favor de ir a la pastelería?

5. Laura, ¿quiénes van a traer la música para bailar?

6. Mamá, ¿me ayudas a preparar los sándwiches?

7. ¿Me traes una silla, por favor?

Answers to Activity 18
1. no
2. sí
3. sí
4. no
5. sí
6. sí
7. no

22 p. 304

1. —Buenos días. Habla Nicolás. ¿Qué necesitan para la fiesta?
—Este... trae unos refrescos, por favor.

2. —Hola, soy Soledad. ¿Qué hago para la fiesta?
—A ver... eh... ve al supermercado y compra helado, por favor.

3. —¿Qué tal? Habla Gustavo. ¿Qué puedo traer a la fiesta?
—Trae unos discos compactos, por favor.

4. —Buenas tardes. Habla Verónica. ¿Ya está todo listo para la fiesta? ¿Puedo preparar algo especial?
—A ver... prepara una ensalada de frutas, por favor.

5. —¿Qué tal? Habla Gloria. ¿Qué puedo hacer para la fiesta?
—Bueno... Tú tienes una cámara, ¿verdad? Saca fotos de todos, por favor.

6. —Hola, soy Cristóbal. ¿Necesitan algo para la fiesta?
—Sí, Cristóbal. Compra los globos, por favor.

Answers to Activity 22
1. a
2. b
3. d
4. c
5. f
6. e

One-Stop Planner CD-ROM

To preview all resources available for this chapter, use the **One-Stop Planner CD-ROM**, Disc 3.

Tercer paso

28 p. 308

1. Raquel y Gloria jugaron a las cartas con Felipe y su hermano Guillermo.

2. Un amigo mío, Shoji, cantó unas canciones en español y Kerry tocó la guitarra.

3. Bárbara bailó con su novio, Miguel. Ellos bailaron en la fiesta toda la noche.

4. Pablo miró la televisión. ¡A él no le gustan las fiestas para nada!

5. Patricia preparó un postre muy rico para la fiesta anoche.

6. Gracie y Kim jugaron a los videojuegos.

7. Andrés y Valerie escucharon música.

8. Y Francisco, ¡a él le encanta nadar! Nadó mucho en nuestra piscina.

Answers to Activity 28
1. a
2. c
3. b
4. d
5. g
6. e
7. h
8. f

LETRA Y SONIDO, P. 311

For the scripts for Parts A and C, see p. 311.
The script for Part B is below.

B. Dictado

Bueno, primero tengo que ayudar a lavar la ropa. Después, a las seis, voy a comprar unas zapatillas nuevas. Y luego, a las ocho, voy a ver una película con unos amigos.

Repaso

1 p. 318

Me llamo Mariana y vivo en San Antonio. En diciembre viajamos a Monterrey para celebrar las fiestas de Navidad con mis abuelos. ¡Qué viaje más fantástico! Mi abuela preparó unas decoraciones bonitas. Todos mis primos llegaron de Guadalajara y preparamos una cena maravillosa de pavo, enchiladas, bacalao y ensalada de Nochebuena. Cenamos a las ocho. Después bailamos, cantamos y hablamos toda la noche. La Navidad es mi día festivo favorito porque siempre la pasamos en México con mis abuelos.

Answers to Activity 1
1. Monterrey
2. para celebrar la Navidad con sus abuelos
3. diciembre
4. decoraciones bonitas
5. bailaron, cantaron y hablaron toda la noche
6. la pasan en México con sus abuelos

Capítulo 10: Celebraciones
Suggested Lesson Plans 50-Minute Schedule

Day 1

CHAPTER OPENER 5 min.
- Focusing on Outcomes, ATE, p. 293
- Do the Multicultural Link suggestion, ATE, p. 292.

DE ANTEMANO 40 min.
- Presenting **De antemano** and Preteaching Vocabulary, ATE, p. 294
- Activities 1–5, p. 296, and Comprehension Check, ATE, p. 296
- Read the **Nota cultural**, p. 296.

Wrap-Up 5 min.
- Have students share their responses from Activity 5, p. 296.
- Ask students what the equivalent to a **quinceañera** is in their culture.

Homework Options
Cuaderno de actividades, p. 109, Activities 1–2

Day 2

PRIMER PASO
Quick Review 5 min.
- Check homework.
- Bell Work, ATE, p. 297

Vocabulario, p. 297 30 min.
- Presenting **Vocabulario**, ATE, p. 297
- Present **A lo nuestro**, p. 297.
- Have students do Activity 6, p. 297, individually. List student answers on the board.
- Do Activity 7, p. 298, with the Audio CD.
- Read and discuss the **Nota cultural**, p. 298.
- Have students do Activity 8, p. 298, in pairs.

Así se dice, p. 298 10 min.
- Presenting **Así se dice**, ATE, p. 298

Wrap-Up 5 min.
- Mime a series of activities that you would do to get ready for a particular holiday. Have students guess the holiday.

Homework Options
Más práctica gramatical, p. 314, Activity 1
Cuaderno de actividades, p. 110, Activity 3
Cuaderno de gramática, p. 79, Activity 1

Day 3

PRIMER PASO
Quick Review 5 min.
- Check homework.
- Ask students yes/no questions about what people are doing in the class.

Gramática, p. 299 25 min.
- Presenting **Gramática**, ATE, p. 299
- Do Activity 9, p. 299, with the Audio CD.
- Have students do Activity 2 in **Más práctica gramatical**, p. 314. Check orally.
- Have students do Activity 10, p. 299, in pairs, then Activity 11, p. 299, individually.
- Have students do Activity 12, p. 300, in pairs.

Así se dice, p. 300 15 min.
- Presenting **Así se dice**, ATE, p. 300
- Have students do Activities 13–14, p. 300, in pairs.

Wrap-Up 5 min.
- Ask students what the people are doing in Teaching Transparency 10-1.

Homework Options
Más práctica gramatical, p. 315, Activity 3
Cuaderno de actividades, pp. 110–111, Activities 4–6
Cuaderno de gramática, pp. 80–81, Activities 2–4

Day 4

PRIMER PASO
Quick Review 5 min.
- Check homework.

Así se dice, p. 300 10 min.
- Have students do Activity 15, p. 300, in groups. Call on groups to report their plans to the class.

PANORAMA CULTURAL 10 min.
- Presenting **Panorama cultural**, ATE, p. 301
- Discuss questions from **Para pensar y hablar...**, Activity A, p. 301.

SEGUNDO PASO
Así se dice/Vocabulario, p. 302 20 min.
- Presenting **Así se dice** and **Vocabulario**, ATE, p. 302
- Do Activity 17, p. 302, with the class.
- Do Activity 18, p. 303, with the Audio CD.

Wrap-Up 5 min.
Give students a situation and have them ask for help, or respond to a request.
Discuss the content and format of Quiz 10-1.

Homework Options
Study for Quiz 10-1.
Assign Activity 16, p. 300, as homework.
Cuaderno de actividades, p. 112, Activities 7–8
Cuaderno de gramática, p. 81, Activities 5–6

Day 5

PRIMER PASO
Quick Review 10 min.
- Check homework. Check Activity 16, p. 300, for completion.
- Review the content of the **Primer paso**.

Quiz 20 min.
- Administer Quiz 10-1A, 10-1B, or a combination of the two.

SEGUNDO PASO
Así se dice/Vocabulario, p. 302 15 min.
- Follow the Teaching Suggestion, p. 303, ATE, to do Activity 19, p. 303.
- Have students do Activity 20, p. 303, then work in pairs to do Activity 21, p. 303.

Wrap-Up 5 min.
- Point to someone in Teaching Transparency 10-2. Have students pretend they are that person and ask for help. Then call on a student to respond to the request.

Homework Options
Más práctica gramatical, p. 315, Activity 4
Cuaderno de actividades, p. 113, p. 9
Cuaderno de gramática, p. 82, Activities 7–8

Day 6

SEGUNDO PASO
Quick Review 5 min.
- Check homework.

Así se dice/Nota gramatical, p. 304 30 min.
- Presenting **Así se dice** and **Nota gramatical**, ATE, p. 304
- Do Activity 22, p. 304, with the Audio CD.
- Have students do Activity 23, p. 304.
- Have students do Activity 24, p. 305, in pairs. You may wish them to follow the Slower Pace suggestion, ATE, p. 305.
- Have students do Activities 25–26, p. 305.

ENCUENTRO CULTURAL 10 min.
- Discuss the **Encuentro cultural**, p. 306.
- Present the Culture Note, ATE, p. 306, and the Additional Vocabulary, ATE, p. 306.

Wrap-Up 5 min.
- Have volunteers act out commands.
- Discuss the content and format of Quiz 10-2.

Homework Options
Study for Quiz 10-2.
Más práctica gramatical, p. 316, Activity 5
Cuaderno de actividades, pp. 114–115, Activities 10–12
Cuaderno de gramática, pp. 83–84, Activities 9–12

One-Stop Planner CD-ROM

For alternative lesson plans by chapter section, to create your own customized plans, or to preview all resources available for this chapter, use the **One-Stop Planner CD-ROM**, Disc 3.

 For additional homework suggestions, see activities accompanied by this symbol throughout the chapter.

Day 7

SEGUNDO PASO
Quick Review 10 min.
- Check homework.
- Review the content of the **Segundo paso.**

Quiz 20 min.
- Administer Quiz 10-2A, 10-2B, or a combination of the two.

TERCER PASO
Así se dice/Nota gramatical/Vocabulario, p. 307 15 min.
- Presenting **Así se dice** and **Nota gramatical,** ATE, p. 307
- Presenting **Vocabulario,** ATE, p. 307

Wrap-Up 5 min.
- List several **-ar** verbs on the board. Ask students to name something they did yesterday, the day before yesterday, or last Saturday. Then ask other students to report what their classmates did.

Homework Options
Cuaderno de actividades, p. 116, Activities 13–14
Cuaderno de gramática, p. 85, Activities 13–14

Day 8

TERCER PASO
Quick Review 5 min.
- Check homework.
- Ask students to tell a partner two things they did yesterday. Have partners report to the class.

Así se dice/Nota gramatical/Vocabulario, pp. 308–309 35 min.
- Do Activity 27, p. 307, with the class.
- Do Activity 28, p. 308, with the Audio CD. Do the Additional Practice activity, p. 308.
- Have students do Activity 29, p. 308, in pairs.
- Have students do Activities 30, 31, and 32, pp. 308–309. Discuss possible answers.
- Have students read the article on **piñatas,** then do Activity 33, p. 309, in pairs. Discuss with the class. Present the Culture Note, ATE, p. 309.

Wrap-Up 10 min.
- Do the Additional Practice suggestion, ATE, p. 309.

Homework Options
Más práctica gramatical, pp. 316–317, Activities 6–7
Cuaderno de actividades, p. 117, Activity 15
Cuaderno de gramática, p. 86, Activities 15–17

Day 9

TERCER PASO
Quick Review 5 min.
- Check homework.

Nota gramatical, p. 310 40 min.
- Presenting **Nota gramatical,** ATE, p. 310
- Present Language-to-Language, ATE, p. 310.
- Do Activity 8 from **Más práctica gramatical,** p. 317, with the class.
- Have students do Activity 34, p. 310, in groups. Discuss Language-to-Language, ATE, p. 310.
- Have students do Actvitiy 35, p. 310. Check orally with the class.
- Have students do Activities 36–37, pp. 310–311, in pairs.
- Have students do Activity 38, p. 311. Have students exchange papers for peer-editing.

Wrap-Up 5 min.
- Ask students yes/no questions that call for them to substitute **lo, la, los,** or **las** for a direct object pronoun.

Homework Suggestions
Cuaderno de actividades, pp. 117–118, Activities 16–17
Cuaderno de gramática, p. 87, Activities 18–19

Day 10

TERCER PASO
Quick Review 5 min.
- Check homework.

Así se dice/Vocabulario/Notas gramaticales, pp. 307–311 10 min.
- Do Activities 20–21, p. 88 in the Cuaderno de gramática.
- Have students do Activity 10-3, pp. 59–60, in Activities for Communication.

Letra y sonido 10 min.
- Present **Letra y sonido,** p. 311, with the Audio CD.

VAMOS A LEER 20 min.
- Do Activities A and B, pp. 312–313.
- Do Activities C and D, p. 313.
- Have students do Additional Practice, ATE, p. 313.

Wrap-Up 5 min.
- Ask students to compare one of the festivals from the reading with a festival in their area.
- Discuss the content and format of Quiz 10-3.

Homework Options
Study for Quiz 10-3.
Cuaderno de actividades, pp. 119–120, Activities 18–19

Day 11

TERCER PASO
Quick Review 5 min.
- Check homework.
- Review the content of the **Tercer paso.**

Quiz 20 min.
- Administer Quiz 10-3A, 10-3B, or a combination of the two.

REPASO 20 min.
- Do Activity 1, p. 318, with the Audio CD.
- Have students do Activities 2 and 5, pp. 318–319, individually. Check orally.
- Have students do Activity 3, p. 318, in pairs.
- Do Activity 4, p. 318.
- Discuss the strategy for Activity 6, p. 319. Have students do the Prewriting component.

Wrap-Up 5 min.
- Discuss and compare the three verb tenses students learned in this chapter. Have students list the communicative skills and some of the expressions they learned to carry out those skills.

Homework Options
Have students finish Activity 6, p. 319, for homework.
A ver si puedo..., p. 320

Day 12

REPASO
Quick Review 5 min.
- Check **A ver si puedo...,** p. 320.

Chapter Review 40 min.
- Review Chapter 10. Choose from **Más práctica gramatical,** Grammar Tutor for Students of Spanish, Activities for Communication, Listening Activities, Interactive CD-ROM Tutor, or **Juegos interactivos.**

Wrap-Up 5 min.
- Discuss the format of the Chapter 10 test.

Homework Options
Study for the Chapter 10 Test.

Assessment

Quick Review 5 min.
- Answer any last-minute questions.

Test, Chapter 10 45 min.
- Administer Chapter 10 Test. Select from Testing Program, Alternative Assessment Guide, Test Generator, or Standardized Assessment Tutor.

Capítulo 10: Celebraciones
Suggested Lesson Plans 90-Minute Block Schedule

Block 1

CHAPTER OPENER 5 min.
- Focusing on Outcomes, ATE, p. 293
- Culture Note, ATE, p. 293

DE ANTEMANO 40 min.
- Presenting **De antemano** and Preteaching Vocabulary, ATE, p. 294
- Activities 1–5, p. 296, and Comprehension Check, ATE, p. 296
- Read the **Nota cultural**, p. 296.

Vocabulario, p. 297 30 min.
- Presenting **Vocabulario**, ATE, p. 297
- Present **A lo nuestro**, p. 297.
- Have students do Activity 6, p. 297, individually. Write student answers on the board.
- Do Activity 7, p. 298, with the Audio CD.
- Read and discuss the **Nota cultural**, p. 298.
- Have students do Activity 8, p. 298, in pairs.

Así se dice, p. 298 10 min.
- Presenting **Así se dice**, ATE, p. 298

Wrap-Up 5 min.
- Mime a series of activities that you would do to get ready for a particular holiday. Tell students what you are doing in Spanish and have them guess the holiday.

Homework Options
Más práctica gramatical, p. 314, Activity 1
Cuaderno de actividades, pp. 109–110, Activities 1–3
Cuaderno de gramática, p. 79, Activity 1

Block 2

PRIMER PASO
Quick Review 10 min.
- Check homework.
- Ask students which holiday is represented in each photo on Transparency 10-A. Next, ask students yes/no questions about what the people are doing in the photos.

Gramática, p. 299 25 min.
- Presenting **Gramática**, ATE, p. 299
- Do Activity 9, p. 299, with the Audio CD.
- Have students do Activity 2 in **Más práctica gramatical**, p. 314. Check orally.
- Have students do Activity 10, p. 299, in pairs, then Activity 11, p. 299, individually. Have students exchange papers for peer-editing.
- Have students do Activity 12, p. 300, in pairs.

Así se dice, p. 300 35 min.
- Presenting **Así se dice**, ATE, p. 300
- Have students do Activities 13–14, p. 300, in pairs.
- Have students do Activity 15, p. 300, in groups. Call on groups to report their plans to the class.
- Have students work with a partner to write Activity 16, p. 300. Call on a few volunteers to read their essays to the class.

PANORAMA CULTURAL 10 min.
- Presenting **Panorama cultural**, ATE, p. 301
- Discuss questions from **Para pensar y hablar...**, Activity A, p. 301.

Wrap-Up 10 min.
- Ask students what the people are doing in Teaching Transparency 10-1, then have students imagine they are participating in the celebration. Ask them what they are doing. Follow up with questions to the class to elicit all conjugations of the present progressive. Finally, ask students their opinions regarding the celebration pictured.
- Discuss the content and format of Quiz 10-1.

Homework Options
Study for Quiz 10-1.
Más práctica gramatical, p. 315, Activity 3
Cuaderno de actividades, pp. 110–112, Activities 4–8
Cuaderno de gramática, pp. 80–81, Activities 2–6

Block 3

PRIMER PASO
Quick Review 10 min.
- Check homework.
- Quickly review the content of the **Primer paso**.

Quiz 20 min.
- Administer Quiz 10-1A, 10-1B, or a combination of the two.

SEGUNDO PASO
Así se dice/Vocabulario, p. 302 35 min.
- Presenting **Así se dice** and **Vocabulario**, ATE, p. 302
- Do Activity 17, p. 302, with the class.
- Do Activity 18, p. 303, with the Audio CD.
- Have students follow the Teaching Suggestion, ATE, p. 303, to do Activity 19, p. 303.
- Have students do Activity 20, p. 303, then work in pairs to do Activity 21, p. 303.

Así se dice/Nota gramatical, p. 304 20 min.
- Presenting **Así se dice** and **Nota gramatical**, ATE, p. 304
- Do Activity 22, p. 304, with the Audio CD.
- Have students do Activity 23, p. 304, individually. Call on volunteers to write the answers on the board.

Wrap-Up 5 min.
- Give students a situation. Have them ask for help, tell someone what to do, or respond to a request.

Homework Options
Más práctica gramatical, p. 315, Activity 4
Cuaderno de actividades, pp. 113–115, Activities 9–12
Cuaderno de gramática, pp. 82–84, Activities 7–12

One-Stop Planner CD-ROM

For alternative lesson plans by chapter section, to create your own customized plans, or to preview all resources available for this chapter, use the **One-Stop Planner CD-ROM**, Disc 3.

For additional homework suggestions, see activities accompanied by this symbol throughout the chapter.

Block 4

SEGUNDO PASO

Quick Review 10 min.
- Check homework.
- Point to someone in Teaching Transparency 10-2. Have students pretend they are that person and ask for help. Then call on a student to respond to the request.

Así se dice/Vocabulario, pp. 304–305 20 min.
- **Más práctica gramatical**, Activity 5, p. 316
- Have students do Activity 24, p. 305, in pairs.
- Have students do Activities 25–26, p. 305. You may wish to have them follow the Slower Pace suggestion, ATE, p. 305.

ENCUENTRO CULTURAL 10 min.
- Read and discuss the **Encuentro cultural**, p. 306.
- Present the Culture Note, ATE, p. 306, and the Additional Vocabulary, ATE, p. 306.

TERCER PASO

Así se dice/Nota gramatical/Vocabulario, p. 307 40 min.
- Presenting **Así se dice** and **Nota gramatical**, ATE, p. 307
- Presenting **Vocabulario**, ATE, p. 307
- Do Activity 27, p. 307, with the class.
- Do Activity 28, p. 308, with the Audio CD. Do the Additional Practice activity, ATE, p. 308.
- Have students do Activity 29, p. 308, in pairs, then Activity 30, p. 308, individually.
- Discuss possible answers to Activity 30.

Wrap-Up 10 min.
- List several **-ar** verbs on the board. Ask students to name something they did yesterday, the day before yesterday, or last Saturday. Then ask other students to report what their classmates did.
- Discuss the content and format of Quiz 10-2.

Homework Options
Study for Quiz 10-2.
Cuaderno de actividades, pp. 116–117, Activities 13–15
Cuaderno de gramática, pp. 85–86, Activities 13–17

Block 5

SEGUNDO PASO

Quick Review 10 min.
- Check homework.
- Review the content of the **Segundo paso.**

Quiz 20 min.
- Administer Quiz 10-2A, 10-2B, or a combination of the two.

TERCER PASO

Así se dice/Nota gramatical/Vocabulario, p. 309 25 min.
- Have students do the Additional Practice suggestion, ATE, p. 309.
- **Más práctica gramatical**, Activities 6–7, pp. 316–317
- Have students do Activities 31–32, p. 309. Discuss possible answers with the class.
- Have students read the article on **piñatas**, then do Activity 33, p. 309, in pairs. Discuss with the class. Present the Culture Note, ATE, p. 309.

Nota gramatical, p. 310 30 min.
- Presenting **Nota gramatical**, ATE, p. 310
- Present Language-to-Language, ATE, p. 310.
- Do Activity 8 from **Más práctica gramatical**, p. 317, with the class.
- Have students do Activity 34, p. 310, in groups.
- Have students do Actvitiy 35, p. 310. Check orally with the class.
- Have students do Activity 36, p. 310, in pairs.

Wrap-Up 5 min.
- Ask students yes/no questions that call for them to substitute **lo, la, los,** or **las** for a direct object.
- Discuss the content and format of Quiz 10-3.

Homework Options
Study for Quiz 10-3.
Cuaderno de actividades, pp. 117–118, Activities 16–17
Cuaderno de gramática, pp. 87–88, Activities 18–21

Block 6

TERCER PASO

Quick Review 5 min.
- Check homework.

Nota gramatical, p. 311 15 min.
- Have students do Activity 37, p. 311, in pairs.
- Have students do Activity 38, p. 311. Have students exchange papers for peer-editing.

Quiz 20 min.
- Administer Quiz 10-3A, 10-3B, or a combination of the two.

Letra y sonido 10 min.
- Present **Letra y sonido,** p. 311, with the Audio CD.

VAMOS A LEER 20 min.
- Do Activities A and B, pp. 312–313. Follow the Using Prior Knowledge suggestion, ATE, p. 312.
- Do Activities C and D, p. 313.
- Present the Culture Notes, ATE, p. 312.

REPASO 15 min.
- Do Activity 1, p. 318, with the Audio CD.
- Have students do Activities 2 and 5, pp. 318–319, individually. Check orally.
- Have students do Activity 3, p. 318, in pairs.

Wrap-Up 5 min.
- Discuss and compare the three verb tenses students learned in this chapter.
- Discuss the format of the Chapter 10 Test.

Homework Options
Study for the Chapter 10 Test.
Assign Activity 4, p. 318, and Activity 6, p. 319, for homework.
A ver si puedo..., p. 320

Block 7

REPASO

Quick Review 5 min.
- Check **A ver si puedo...,** p. 320, and content of Activity 4, p. 318.

Chapter Review 40 min.
- Review Chapter 10. Choose from **Más práctica gramatical**, Grammar Tutor for Students of Spanish, Activities for Communication, Listening Activities, Interactive CD-ROM Tutor, or **Juegos interactivos.**

Test, Chapter 10 45 min.
- Administer Chapter 10 Test. Select from Testing Program, Alternative Assessment Guide, Test Generator, or Standardized Assessment Tutor.

One-Stop Planner CD-ROM

For resource information, see the **One-Stop Planner,** Disc 3.

 Pacing Tips
This chapter includes grammar presentations which lend themselves to interactive practice. As you introduce the grammar in **Segundo** and **Tercer Pasos,** make sure to provide time for speaking activities. For Lesson Plan and timing suggestions, see pages 291I–291L.

Meeting the Standards

Communication
- Talking about what you're doing right now, p. 298
- Asking for and giving an opinion, p. 300
- Asking for help and responding to requests, p. 302
- Telling a friend what to do, p. 304
- Talking about past events, p. 307

Cultures
- Culture Note, p. 295
- Nota cultural, p. 296
- Nota cultural, p. 298

Connections
- Culture Note, p. 293
- Culture Notes, p. 312

Comparisons
- Panorama cultural, p. 301
- Culture Note, p. 306
- Language-to-Language, p. 310

Communities
- Challenge, p. 305
- Sugerencia, p. 305
- Career Path, p. 306

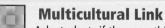

Connections and Comparisons

Multicultural Link
Ask students if they can think of any traditions from Spanish-speaking countries that have been adopted by people in the United States who are not Hispanic. (They might mention **piñatas, luminarias,** and **poinsettias,** all of which have come to the United States from Mexico.) Ask students to research a holiday in the United States that originated in Europe, Asia, or Africa. Have them report on what they find.

Building on Previous Skills
Ask students to think back to Chapter 8, **¡A comer!,** and recall what they learned about foods in Spanish-speaking countries. What are some typical dishes in various countries?

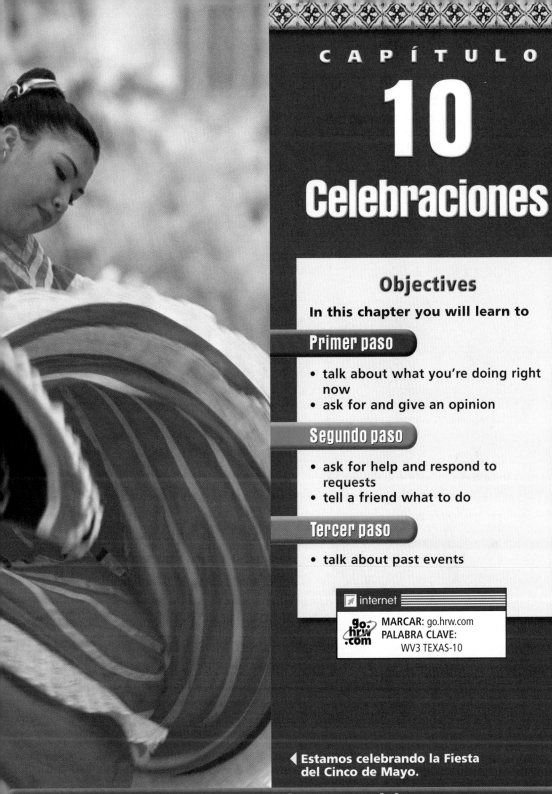

CAPÍTULO
10
Celebraciones

Objectives

In this chapter you will learn to

Primer paso

- talk about what you're doing right now
- ask for and give an opinion

Segundo paso

- ask for help and respond to requests
- tell a friend what to do

Tercer paso

- talk about past events

internet

MARCAR: go.hrw.com
PALABRA CLAVE:
WV3 TEXAS-10

◄ Estamos celebrando la Fiesta del Cinco de Mayo.

Photo Flash!

Hispanic communities in the U.S. celebrate many Mexican holidays, as these festive dancers from Phoenix illustrate. Phoenix, as well as many communities throughout the United States with sizable populations of Mexican descent, celebrates its **Cinco de Mayo** Festival commemorating General Zaragoza's victory over the French in the **Batalla de Puebla** in 1862.

Focusing on Outcomes

Planning celebrations requires the use of a variety of language functions and skills. Point out to students that they will need to be able to ask for and give opinions, ask others for help, respond to requests for help, and tell others what to do. By the end of the chapter, students will be able to explain what they are doing now and what they have already done to prepare for their celebrations.

Chapter Sequence

Cultures and Communities

Culture Note

El Cinco de Mayo is a holiday celebrated by both Mexicans and Mexican-Americans. It commemorates the Mexican victory at the Battle of Puebla, 1862, between the army led by President Benito Juárez and an invading army sent from France by Napoleon III. Although the French later defeated the Mexicans and installed Maximilian as emperor of Mexico, the Mexicans eventually expelled the French in 1867. Maximilian was executed and Juárez was restored as president. The battle of Puebla is considered the first and most symbolic victory of the war. While in power, Maximilian ordered the construction of what is today the **Paseo de la Reforma,** Mexico City's most elegant boulevard.

Teaching Resources
pp. 294–296

PRINT 📖
▶ Lesson Planner, p. 47
▶ Video Guide, pp. 67–68, 70
▶ Cuaderno de actividades, p. 109

MEDIA 💿📼🎞
▶ One-Stop Planner
▶ Video Program
  De antemano
  Videocassette 4, 1:15–5:21
  Videocassette 5 (captioned version), 1:38:41–1:42:47
  A continuación
  Videocassette 4, 5:22–10:54
  Videocassette 5 (captioned version), 1:42:48–1:48:23
▶ DVD Tutor, Disc 2
▶ Audio Compact Discs, CD 10, Trs. 1–2
▶ **De antemano** Transparencies

Presenting
De antemano

Have students read and answer the questions in **Estrategia para comprender.** Then play the video once. Next, present Preteaching Vocabulary. Follow up by modeling pronunciation of the **fotonovela** dialogue and having students repeat after you. Discuss each picture. Ask students what Héctor's family did to get ready for the party. What do they need to do? How will the family solve the problem?

De antemano Transparencies

DE ANTEMANO ▪ *¡Felicidades, Héctor!*

The **fotonovela** is an abridged version of the video episode.

CD 10 Trs. 1–2

Estrategia
para comprender
Lots of things are going on at once in the Villarreal house. They're getting ready for a really big celebration! Look at the photos to see what they're doing. Has something been forgotten?

Tío Tomás, Tía Marcela y Juan

Rebeca y Manuel

Eva

Lisa

Gabi

Abuela

❶
Tía Marcela: ¡Tomás! Mira... ¿Qué te parece?
Tío Tomás: Perfecto. Oye, Marcela, ¿dónde están los globos?
Tía Marcela: No sé... pregúntale a Juan.
Tío Tomás: ¡Juan! ¿Tienes los globos?

❷
Juan: Aquí están.
Tío Tomás: ¿Me ayudas a inflar los globos?
Juan: ¡Claro que sí, papá! ¿Qué tal si usamos de todos los colores? Hay de violeta, rojo, azul, verde...

❸
Manuel: Sí, sí... el apellido es Villarreal, Manuel Villarreal... es un pastel para mi hijo Héctor... es para su graduación de la escuela secundaria... sí, de chocolate. Ah, muy bien. ¿Cómo? Mmmm... un momento... ¡Rebeca! Estoy hablando con un empleado de la pastelería. ¿Qué escribimos en el pastel?

❹
Rebeca: ¿Cuántas palabras podemos escribir?
Manuel: ¿Cuántas palabras pueden escribir? Ajá... un momento, por favor. Es un pastel bastante grande. Pueden escribir muchas.
Rebeca: Entonces, pon "¡Felicidades en el día de tu graduación, Héctor!"

Preteaching Vocabulary

Recognizing Cognates
De antemano contains several words that students will be able to recognize as cognates. Have students find these words and guess what is happening in the story.

❷ colores
❷ violeta
❸ graduación
❸ chocolate
❻ diciembre
❻ tradición

❻ cultura
❻ mexicana
❼ Independencia
❼ septiembre
❾ invitaciones

5

Abuela: Eva, ¿me pasas las hojas? Gracias.

Eva: Preparar tamales es mucho trabajo, ¿no?

Abuela: Pero es la comida favorita de Héctor. Generalmente, sólo preparamos muchos tamales en diciembre para la Navidad. Es una tradición de la cultura mexicana.

6

Lisa: ¿Hay tradiciones mexicanas para otros días festivos también?

Abuela: Claro que sí, hay muchas. Durante las Pascuas, sobre todo en Semana Santa, hay desfiles... el Día de la Independencia, que es el 16 de septiembre, hay fuegos artificiales. Pero mi día festivo favorito es el Día de los Muertos. Me acuerdo de un año en particular...

7

Eva: ¿Qué hiciste, Abuela?

Abuela: Pues, lo de siempre. Mi mamá preparó comida para llevar a la tumba de la familia. Yo ayudé también. Ese año, yo compré comida en la pequeña tienda cerca de la casa. Pero pasó algo especial...

8

Tío Tomás: Manuel... ¡Manuel! ¿Qué son éstos, hermano?

Manuel: ¿Mmmm? Ah... son las invitaciones.

9

Manuel: ¿Las invitaciones? ¡No mandé las invitaciones!

> Cuaderno de actividades, p. 109, Acts. 1–2

Using the Captioned Video/DVD

You may wish to use Videocassette 5 to allow students to see the Spanish captions for *¡Felicidades, Héctor!* Hearing the language and watching the story will reduce anxiety about the new language and facilitate comprehension.

The reinforcement of seeing the written vocabulary words with the gestures and actions will help prepare students to do the comprehension activities on p. 296. **NOTE:** The *DVD Tutor* contains captions for all sections of the *Video Program*.

DE ANTEMANO

CAPÍTULO 10

Culture Note

Tamales, a popular food throughout Mexico, Central America, and parts of the United States, are less common in South America. Generally served on festive occasions, they may differ from place to place, and may be spicy or sweet. They are made with cornmeal dough spread on cornhusks or leaves, stuffed with fillings, and steamed. In **Yucatán** and Central America, they are made with plantain leaves. In Honduras, a **nacatamal** is a meat **tamal** while a **tamal** is without meat. In Venezuela, **tamales** are called **hallacas.**

Language Note

The Spanish word **tamal** (plural **tamales**) comes from the Nahuatl word **tamalli,** which was a food staple of the Aztec empire.

A continuación

You may choose to continue with *¡Felicidades, Héctor! (a continuación)* at this time or wait until later in the chapter. At this point, Héctor's mother begins to call everyone who was supposed to be invited so that they know about the party. Eva has to make two trips to the bakery because the first time they gave her the wrong cake. You may wish to have students compare their celebrations to the celebration depicted in the video.

CAPÍTULO 10

Multicultural Link
Ask students to find out about coming-of-age celebrations in a culture or religion different from their own, such as Jewish bar mitzvah and bat mitzvah celebrations when a boy or girl turns thirteen.

Answers

1.
1. la familia Villarreal
2. una fiesta de graduación para Héctor
3. a la pastelería para pedir el pastel
4. preparan tamales; abuela Dolores
5. que no mandó las invitaciones
6. *Sample answer:* Debe llamar a los invitados.

2.
1. Tía Marcela ayuda con las decoraciones.
2. Juan y su papá inflan los globos.
3. Manuel Villarreal llama a la pastelería.
4. Abuela Dolores explica unas tradiciones mexicanas.
5. Tío Tomás pregunta sobre las invitaciones.

3.
1. ¿Me ayudas a inflar los globos?
2. No mandé las invitaciones.
3. Que pongan "Felicidades" en el pastel.
4. ¿Qué te parece la música?
5. Estoy hablando con la pastelería.

4.
¿Quién va a comprar la comida?
¿Quién va a preparar la comida?
¿Quién va a inflar los globos?
¿Quién va a mandar las invitaciones?
¿Quién va a comprar el pastel?
¿Quién va a comprar un regalo?

These activities check for comprehension only. Students should not yet be expected to produce language modeled in **De antemano.**

1 **¿Comprendes?**
¿Comprendes lo que pasa en la fotonovela? Contesta las preguntas. Si no estás seguro/a, adivina. See answers below.
1. ¿Quiénes son las personas en la fotonovela?
2. ¿Qué tipo de fiesta preparan? ¿Para quién es la fiesta?
3. ¿A quién llama Manuel? ¿Por qué?
4. ¿Qué hacen Eva, Lisa y Gabi? ¿Quién les ayuda?
5. ¿Qué descubre Manuel al final?
6. ¿Qué crees que Manuel debe hacer en esta situación?

2 **Ordena las oraciones** See answers below.
Con base en la fotonovela, pon estas oraciones en el orden correcto.

Manuel Villarreal llama a la pastelería.	Tía Marcela ayuda con las decoraciones.	Abuela Dolores explica unas tradiciones mexicanas.	Juan y su papá inflan los globos.	Tío Tomás pregunta sobre las invitaciones.
a.	b.	c.	d.	e.

3 **¿Cómo dirías?** See answers below.
If you were having a party, what words and phrases from the **fotonovela** might you use . . .?
1. to ask for help with the balloons
2. to say that you didn't send the invitations
3. to tell the bakery to put "Congratulations" on the cake
4. to ask someone what they think of the music
5. to say "I'm talking with the bakery"

4 **Una fiesta bien organizada**

Aquí tienes una lista de cosas necesarias para una fiesta de cumpleaños. Pregúntale a tu compañero/a quién va a hacer estos preparativos. See answers below.

comprar la comida	mandar las invitaciones
preparar la comida	comprar el pastel
inflar los globos	comprar un regalo

5 **¿Y tú?** Answers will vary.
Nombra (*Name*) una cosa que corresponde a cada categoría.
1. un plato tradicional de los días de fiesta
2. un baile típico de tu cultura
3. la celebración más importante de tu vida
4. la fiesta que más le gusta a tu familia

Nota cultural
The fifteenth birthday for many Hispanic girls is a coming-of-age celebration with a party at home. This party is called **una fiesta de quinceañera** and can range from a small, informal gathering to a large party resembling a wedding celebration. In most cases a local **conjunto** (*group of musicians*) plays. It is customary for the **padrino** or **madrina** to present the honoree with a special gift.

Comprehension Check

Building on Previous Skills
Ask students to write a paragraph about a male and a female in the **fotonovela**. They should describe what each is wearing and what each looks like, including color of hair and eyes and height. You might ask students also to imagine what the two people are like—what they like to do and where they like to go.

Additional Practice
Assign the role of each of the persons in the video to a student in the class. Ask the students to act out the video, and to begin by introducing themselves as they appear in the first three photos. Continue with the photos that follow, asking each student to read his or her lines.

Vocabulario

Los días festivos

CD-ROM **3**
DVD **2**

la Nochevieja y el Año Nuevo

la Nochebuena y la Navidad

las Pascuas

el Día de los Enamorados

el Día de Acción de Gracias

el Día de las Madres

el Día del Padre

el Día de la Independencia

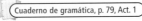
Cuaderno de gramática, p. 79, Act. 1

Más práctica gramatical, p. 314, Act. 1

---

6 **Los días de fiesta**

Escribamos Choose four holidays from the list above. List at least four things you associate with each holiday. For additional words and phrases you might want to use, see page R5. Answers will vary.

MODELO el Día de la Independencia en los Estados Unidos: Un picnic con la familia, el béisbol, el mes de julio, hace mucho calor...

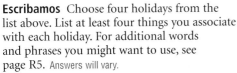
A lo nuestro

Feliz *(happy)* turns up in many expressions used during holidays and celebrations. On your birthday, a friend will say **Feliz cumpleaños. Feliz Navidad** means *Merry Christmas.* What do you think **Feliz Año Nuevo** and **Feliz aniversario** mean? To congratulate someone, you say **Felicidades** or **Te felicito.**

Teaching Resources
pp. 297–300

PRINT
▸ Lesson Planner, p. 48
▸ TPR Storytelling Book, pp. 37, 40
▸ Listening Activities, pp. 75, 79
▸ Activities for Communication, pp. 55–56, 120, 123–124, 155–156
▸ Cuaderno de gramática, pp. 79–81
▸ Grammar Tutor for Students of Spanish, Chapter 10
▸ Cuaderno de actividades, pp. 110–112
▸ Cuaderno para hispanohablantes, pp. 46–50
▸ Testing Program, pp. 249–252
▸ Alternative Assessment Guide, p. 41
▸ Student Make-Up Assignments, Chapter 10

MEDIA
▸ One-Stop Planner
▸ Audio Compact Discs, CD 10, Trs. 3–4, 23–24, 18
▸ Teaching Transparencies 10-1, 10-A; **Más práctica gramatical** Answers; Cuaderno de gramática Answers
▸ Interactive CD-ROM Tutor, Disc 3

Presenting
Así se dice

Model the dialogue between Lisa and her friend, using gestures to clarify meaning. Ask **Lisa, ¿qué estás haciendo?** Pretend to hang decorations as you answer **Estoy colgando decoraciones.** Continue to model by describing your actions: **Estoy caminando. Estoy escribiendo. Estoy limpiando la clase.** Then ask **¿Estás escuchando/pensando?** to elicit appropriate responses such as **Sí, estoy escuchando.**

---

7 **¡De fiesta!**

Escuchemos You'll hear four conversations, each about a different holiday. Match each conversation with the most appropriate greeting card. Scripts and answers on p. 291G.

CD 10
Tr. 3

a. 2

b. 4

c. 3

d. 1

Nota cultural

In small towns and cities throughout the Spanish-speaking world, there are special celebrations for all kinds of occasions. You've already learned that in Spanish-speaking countries many people celebrate not only their birthday, but also their **Día del santo.** Many cities and countries have saints' days which they often celebrate as holidays. Spain's patron saint, for example, is Santiago. July 25 is the Feast of Santiago and is an important holiday in Spain. Since Juan Carlos, the king of Spain, has his saint's day on June 24, **el Día de San Juan** is a national holiday.

Cuaderno de actividades, p. 120, Act. 19

8 **¿Cuál es tu día festivo favorito?**

Hablemos Pregúntale a un/a compañero/a sobre sus días festivos favoritos y qué hace para celebrarlos. Hay preguntas en el cuadro para ayudarte a comenzar.
Answers will vary.

> ¿Miras un partido en la televisión?
> ¿Con quién(es) pasas el día? ¿Adónde vas?
> ¿Comes algo en especial? ¿Cantas o bailas?

Así se dice

Talking about what you're doing right now

To find out what someone is doing right now, ask:

Lisa, **¿qué estás haciendo?**
   . . . what are you doing?

¿Y tu hermano?

¿Todos **están decorando** la casa?
   Are you all decorating . . .?

He or she might say:

Estoy colgando las decoraciones.
   I'm hanging the decorations.

Él **está limpiando** la sala.
   He is cleaning . . .

Sí, **estamos decorando** la casa.
   . . . we are decorating . . .

Teacher to Teacher

Carolyn Ostermann-Healy
Oakton High School
Vienna, Virginia

Verb forms are a hands-down cinch to Carolyn's students

"I have students prepare flashcards with the infinitive of a verb on one side and its present participle on the other. In groups of three, students place one set of ten cards, participle side up, on the desk. Two students face each other, while the third is the caller. The caller calls out an infinitive, and the first of the other two to pronounce the participle and slap the correct card keeps it. The student with the most cards after three minutes wins. I then have the winners become callers. This game can be altered to provide practice with vocabulary, or other verb forms"

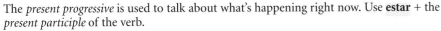

Present progressive

The *present progressive* is used to talk about what's happening right now. Use **estar** + the *present participle* of the verb.

- For **-ar** verbs, add **-ando** to the stem:
  Estoy bailando.   No **están cantando.**
- For **-er** and **-ir** verbs, add **-iendo** to the stem:
  ¿Qué **están comiendo** Uds.?   Enrique **está escribiendo** las invitaciones.

  Más práctica gramatical, pp. 314–315, Acts. 2–3

- If the stem ends in a vowel, the **-iendo** changes to **-yendo:**
  ¿**Estás leyendo** el periódico?

  Cuaderno de gramática, pp. 80–81, Acts. 2–6

9 **Un día especial** Scripts and answers on p. 291G.

Escuchemos What are these people doing right now? Listen to Guadalupe's statements and match the person or persons with the correct picture.

CD 10
Tr. 4

1. Sarita e
2. Guadalupe d
3. Roberto a
4. Rosita b
5. Teresa y Mauricio f
6. Julia c

a.

b.

c.

d.

e.

f.

10 **Gramática en contexto**

Hablemos Pregúntale a tu compañero/a qué están haciendo tres de las personas en las fotos en la Actividad 9. Después, contesta las preguntas de tu compañero/a sobre las otras tres personas en las fotos.

11 **Gramática en contexto**

Escribamos Write a short paragraph about what each person in Activity 9 is doing. Give a different reason why each person is doing what he or she is doing to get ready for the party.

MODELO   A Julia le encanta limpiar todo.
            Por eso ella está limpiando la cocina.

Presenting Gramática

Present progressive Model several sentences using the present progressive, referring to the explanation on this page. Have students turn to pages 294–295 of their texts. Discuss what is happening in each photo by asking students questions: **En la foto 2, ¿quiénes están inflando los globos?** As students show comprehension, switch to questions that require students to produce the present progressive in their answers: **¿Qué está haciendo la tía Marcela en la foto 1?**

Assessment

You might have students invent their own anecdotes about preparing for a party. Provide your own sequential pictures to customize the assignment. You may wish to use the following rubric in assessing this or other writing activities.

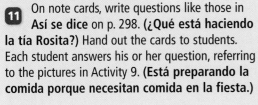

Writing Rubric	Points			
	4	3	2	1
Content (Complete– Incomplete)				
Comprehensibility (Comprehensible– Incomprehensible)				
Accuracy (Accurate– Seldom accurate)				
Organization (Well organized– Poorly organized)				
Effort (Excellent–Minimal)				

18–20: A   14–15: C   Under
16–17: B   12–13: D   12: F

Teaching Suggestion

12 Assign the following to each pair and allow students three to five minutes to prepare. One will determine the type of celebration and kinds of preparation going on, and the other will come up with a list of questions to be asked.

Presenting
Así se dice

Model the expressions for correct pronunciation and intonation. Then ask a student one of the questions and have him or her respond with an appropriate answer. Call on individuals to give their opinions on original questions. (**¿Crees que pasamos bastante tiempo en las clases? ¿Qué te parece la clase de ciencias naturales? ¿Qué te parece si asistimos al colegio durante el verano?**)

Teaching Suggestion

13 This activity may be done as an individual assignment with answers discussed by the entire class.

Assess

▸ Testing Program, pp. 249–252
  Quiz 10-1A, Quiz 10-1B
  Audio CD 10, Tr. 18

▸ Student Make-Up Assignments, Chapter 10, Alternative Quiz

▸ Alternative Assessment Guide, p. 41

---

12 **Todos están ocupados**

Hablemos Work in pairs. Imagine that one of your friends calls while you and your family are in the middle of getting ready for a big celebration. Your friend wants to know what you're doing to prepare for it. Take turns asking and answering questions about what's going on and what each person is doing to help.

Así se dice

Asking for and giving an opinion

To find out what a friend thinks about something, ask:

¿Crees que hay **bastante** comida para la fiesta?
  Do you think that . . . enough . . .?

¿Qué te parece si llamamos a Eva?
  How do you feel about . . .?

Your friend might say:

Creo que sí.
Creo que no.

Me parece bien.
Perfecto.
Buena idea.

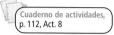
Cuaderno de actividades, p. 112, Act. 8

---

13 **Compramos regalos** Answers will vary.

Leamos/Hablemos Tú y tu compañero/a van a comprar regalos de cumpleaños para varios amigos. Lee las oraciones y piensa en un buen regalo. Den sugerencias y expresen sus reacciones a cada sugerencia. Intercambien papeles.

> **MODELO**   A Teresa le encanta la música.
> — ¿Qué te parece si le regalamos un disco compacto a Teresa?
> — Me parece bien.

1. A Carolina le gusta mucho el arte.
2. A Ricardo le encanta cocinar.
3. A Marcos le gustan todos los deportes.
4. A Patricia le encantan las joyas.
5. A Malena le gusta leer.
6. A Ángela le encanta sacar fotos.

14 **Y tú, ¿qué crees?**

Hablemos Pregúntale a tu compañero/a qué piensa de los días festivos. Pregúntale por qué algunos le gustan y otros no. Después, contesta las preguntas de tu compañero/a. Usa **Creo que es..., Me parece...** y **porque...** en las respuestas.

15 **¡Vamos a la fiesta!**

Hablemos Work with two or three classmates to plan a celebration for a holiday of your choice. Plan who will attend, the food you would like to serve, and what kinds of activities there will be. When your partners say what they want to do, give your opinion. Appoint a spokesperson to report your plans to the class. Use **Nos parece** to tell about an opinion you all have.

16 **Una celebración diferente**

Escribamos Having a celebration doesn't necessarily mean having a party. Choose a holiday or event you would like to add to the calendar. Write two paragraphs in Spanish explaining why and how we should celebrate it.

Communication for All Students

Building on Previous Skills

Write several holidays and their dates on the board or on a transparency. Then ask the class to imagine today is that holiday. Have a student choose one of the dates you have written and answer **¿Con quién pasas el día?** The student should answer appropriately. (**Paso el Día de las Madres con mi madre y mi abuela.**) Vary the questions for each student. Ask them what colors are traditionally associated with each holiday and what the weather is typically like on that day. Since some students may not want to discuss personal holidays, you could ask **¿Cómo celebra mucha gente este día festivo?**

STANDARDS: 1.1, 1.3, 3.1, 5.1, 5.2

CD 10
Trs. 5–8

¿Qué hacen ustedes para celebrar?

Festivals are a very important part of life in Spanish-speaking countries. Often the whole community participates. Here is how some people celebrate.

CD 10 Tr. 7
Sra. Pardo
La Coruña, España

"Es la fiesta de la Virgen del Rosario. Es una fiesta eminentemente religiosa. Bueno, la música tradicional es,… hay bailes típicos gallegos, como la muñeira y luego canciones, música popular gallega de origen celta fundamentalmente…"

CD 10 Tr. 8
Angélica
Caracas, Venezuela

"El 5 de julio se celebra la batalla de Carabobo. Eso se celebra en Los Próceres, que es un parque que queda cerca… Todos los militares salen a desfilar, sale la armada, la aviación, el ejército y la guardia. Eso fue por… la independencia de Carabobo, del estado de Carabobo".

CD 10 Tr. 6
Verónica
San Antonio, Texas

"El 16 de septiembre significa la independencia de México… En Laredo tenemos como un baile… o tenemos una celebración… Si México no hubiera ganado su independencia de España, nunca estuviéramos nosotros aquí, los hispanos, aquí donde estamos hoy".

Para pensar y hablar...

A. Are any of the holidays mentioned by the interviewees similar to holidays you're familiar with? Which ones? How are they similar? How are they different?

B. Choose your favorite holiday and write a description in Spanish of the way you usually celebrate it. Then find out how a classmate celebrates the same holiday. Are there any differences? If so, what might explain them?

Cuaderno para hispanohablantes, pp. 49–50

Teaching Resources
p. 301

PRINT
▸ Video Guide, pp. 67–69, 72
▸ Cuaderno de actividades, p. 120
▸ Cuaderno para hispanohablantes, pp. 49–50

MEDIA
▸ One-Stop Planner
▸ Video Program, Videocassette 4, 11:17–15:00
▸ DVD Tutor, Disc 2
▸ Audio Compact Discs, CD 10, Trs. 5–8
▸ Interactive CD-ROM Tutor, Disc 3

History Link
Point out to your students that on July 5, 1811, Venezuela declared its independence from Spain. The Battle of Carabobo was actually fought between the forces of Simón Bolívar and Spain on June 24, 1821. The country celebrates its Independence Day on July 5.

Presenting
Panorama cultural

Read the interviews as a class or play the audio or video and ask students to take notes on the key points that each interviewee makes. Then ask students to compare notes with a partner and to discuss the interviews.

Cultures and Communities

Multicultural Link
Ask students how many of them celebrate national holidays like the Fourth of July and Memorial Day. What events are celebrated on these holidays? Have students research similar holidays of historic importance in other countries. How do people in different cultures celebrate their national history?

Native Speakers
Ask students from Spanish-speaking families whether they observe any holiday customs that originated in Hispanic countries. Students might be interested in researching how a particular holiday is celebrated in their family's country of origin and telling the class about it.

Segundo paso

Objectives Asking for help and responding to requests; telling a friend what to do

WV3 TEXAS-10

Teaching Resources
pp. 302–305

PRINT
- Lesson Planner, p. 49
- TPR Storytelling Book, pp. 38, 40
- Listening Activities, pp. 76, 80
- Activities for Communication, pp. 57–58, 121, 123–124, 155–156
- Cuaderno de gramática, pp. 82–84
- Grammar Tutor for Students of Spanish, Chapter 10
- Cuaderno de actividades, pp. 113–115
- Cuaderno para hispanohablantes, pp. 46–50
- Testing Program, pp. 253–256
- Alternative Assessment Guide, p. 41
- Student Make-Up Assignments, Chapter 10

MEDIA
- One-Stop Planner
- Audio Compact Discs, CD 10, Trs. 9–10, 25–26, 19
- Teaching Transparencies 10-2, 10-B; **Más práctica gramatical** Answers; Cuaderno de gramática Answers
- Interactive CD-ROM Tutor, Disc 3

Bell Work
On a transparency display **REGALO,** with space between each letter. Under the **R** write **Radio.** Have students think of five ideas for birthday gifts using the remaining letters.

Presenting
Así se dice, Vocabulario

Have students practice asking for help and responding. Have each student create three requests, using indirect objects. Other students should respond with an **Así se dice** expression.

Así se dice

Asking for help and responding to requests

To ask for help, say:

¿Me haces el favor de llamar a Gabi?
Can you do me the favor of . . .?
¿Me ayudas a decorar la sala?
¿Me traes una silla, por favor?
¿Me pasas el helado?

To agree to help, say:

Claro que sí.
Cómo no.
¡Con mucho gusto! *Sure!*
Un momentito. *Just a second.*

To politely refuse to help, say:

Lo siento, pero en este momento estoy ocupado/a.
I'm sorry, but right now . . .
Perdóname, pero no puedo.
Excuse me, but . . .

Más práctica gramatical, p. 315, Act. 4 →

Cuaderno de actividades, p. 113, Act. 9

Vocabulario

inflar los globos
llamar a los invitados

colgar las decoraciones
decorar la casa

mandar las invitaciones

recibir regalos
abrir los regalos

CD-ROM 3
DVD 2

Cuaderno de gramática, p. 82, Acts. 7–8

---

 17 **Las fiestas** Possible answers on p. 303.

Escribamos Read the following scenarios and look at the drawings above. How would each person ask you to help with what he or she is doing? How would you respond?

1. Jorge needs help blowing up balloons.
2. Rebeca doesn't have time to mail out the invitations.
3. Sonia needs help decorating the house.
4. Grandmother wants you to open some of her gifts.
5. Consuelo wants help calling the guests.

Communication for All Students

Tactile Learners

17 Give students objects representing the actions in **Vocabulario** (decorations, phone list, envelopes), but not enough objects for everyone. Have students ask each other to help with their activity. (**¿Me ayudas a decorar la casa?**) If the other person has an object, he or she refuses and gives an excuse. (**Lo siento, pero estoy** **inflando los globos.**) If the other person does not have one, he or she agrees to help. Have students switch items to vary the exchanges.

Language Note
Your students may be interested to know that the word **globo** can mean *balloon, globe,* or *hot air balloon,* depending on the context.

18 ¿Me ayudas? Script and answers on p. 291G.

CD 10
Tr. 9

Escuchemos Listen as various people help each other get ready for the upcoming party. For each request, decide if the response given is logical (**sí**) or illogical (**no**).

1. Sí, cómo no. Él canta y baila también.
2. Sí. ¿Necesitas algo más?
3. Todos te ayudamos, Hilda.
4. Sí. ¿Dónde pongo los globos?
5. Creo que todos van a traer música.
6. En este momento no puedo, pero más tarde, sí, te ayudo con los sándwiches.
7. Sí. ¿Dónde está? ¿En el centro?

19 ¿Necesitas ayuda? Answers will vary.

Escribamos Look at the drawings of Fernando getting ready for his party tonight. He forgot to do a lot of things, and now he needs some help. Create mini-conversations for each picture. Fernando asks for assistance and the other person agrees or refuses to help. Be creative!

a.

b.

c.

d.

20 ¿Me puedes ayudar?

Escribamos Imagina que vas a dar una fiesta en tu casa la semana que viene. Haz una lista de seis preguntas, solicitando ayuda con los preparativos. Incluye preguntas sobre la comida, las decoraciones y las invitaciones. Sample questions below.

21 ¡Claro que sí!

Hablemos Now get together with a partner and ask for help with the preparations on your list from Activity 20. Your partner agrees to help, politely refuses, or suggests someone else who can do the job. Take turns asking questions.

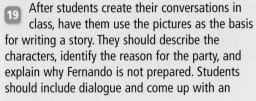

Communication for All Students

Challenge

19 After students create their conversations in class, have them use the pictures as the basis for writing a story. They should describe the characters, identify the reason for the party, and explain why Fernando is not prepared. Students should include dialogue and come up with an original ending to the story, telling how the party goes, who comes, and what they do. You might ask students to illustrate a scene from the party on a transparency to show as volunteers read their stories to the class. Have students vote on the most original ending and illustration.

Additional Practice

18 Play the audio recording again and ask students to come up with original responses to the questions that the characters ask. You might ask students to come up with original questions.

Teaching Suggestion

19 Have students work in pairs to create these conversations. Ask them to present them to the class and have the class guess which picture corresponds to their conversation.

Slower Pace

21 Have students work in pairs to list the things they need to prepare for the party. Together, pairs create the questions asking for help with each thing.

Answers

17 *Possible answers:*
1. ¿Me ayudas a inflar los globos, por favor?; Sí, Jorge, cómo no.
2. ¿Me haces el favor de mandar las invitaciones?; Claro que sí, Rebeca.
3. ¿Puedes decorar la casa, por favor?; Lo siento, Sonia, pero en este momento estoy ocupada.
4. ¿Me abres unos regalos, por favor?; ¡Con mucho gusto, abuela!
5. ¿Me ayudas a llamar a los invitados?; Un momentito, Consuelo.

20 *Sample questions:*
Anita, ¿puedes traer algo especial para decorar la casa?
Pedro, ¿me ayudas a colgar las decoraciones, por favor?
Philip, ¿me haces el favor de llamar a los invitados?

Teaching Resources
pp. 302–305

PRINT
▶ Lesson Planner, p. 49
▶ TPR Storytelling Book, pp. 38, 40
▶ Listening Activities, pp. 76, 80
▶ Activities for Communication, pp. 57–58, 121, 123–124, 155–156
▶ Cuaderno de gramática, pp. 82–84
▶ Grammar Tutor for Students of Spanish, Chapter 10
▶ Cuaderno de actividades, pp. 113–115
▶ Cuaderno para hispanohablantes, pp. 46–50
▶ Testing Program, pp. 253–256
▶ Alternative Assessment Guide, p. 41
▶ Student Make-Up Assignments, Chapter 10

MEDIA
▶ One-Stop Planner
▶ Audio Compact Discs, CD 10, Trs. 9–10, 25–26, 19
▶ Teaching Transparencies 10-2, 10-B; **Más práctica gramatical** Answers; Cuaderno de gramática Answers
▶ Interactive CD-ROM Tutor, Disc 3

Presenting
Así se dice, Nota gramatical

Distribute props such as a broom, balloons, and a phone. Give commands (**cuelga los globos**), miming the action. Have students act out a response. Write **tú** commands on the board and have volunteers give and act out their own commands.
Ask individual students to comply with a command by moving around the room. (**ven acá, escribe en la pizarra**)

Así se dice

Telling a friend what to do

To tell a friend what to do, say:

Prepara la ensalada y **limpia** la cocina, **¿quieres?**
  Prepare . . . clean . . . will you?

Por favor, **decora** la sala y **llama** a los invitados.
  . . . decorate . . . call . . .

Your friend might say:

De acuerdo. *Agreed.*

Está bien. *OK.*

Nota gramatical

Informal commands are used with people you would address as **tú**. To state an informal command in Spanish, take the second person singular of the verb and drop the **-s.** For example:

cantas minus **s** = **canta** (*sing!*)

Several command forms are irregular and should be memorized because they don't follow a single pattern. A few of these are:

haz	*do, make!*	**pon**	*put, place!*
ve	*go!*	**ven**	*come!*
vete	*go away!*		

Cuaderno de actividades, pp. 114–115, Acts. 10–12

Cuaderno de gramática, pp. 83–84, Acts. 9–12

Más práctica gramatical, p. 316, Act. 5

CD 10 Tr. 10

22 Preparativos

Escuchemos Listen as several people call the Villarreal house to ask what they can do to help with the preparations for Héctor's graduation party. Match each person with the correct task. Scripts and answers on p. 291G.

1. Gustavo
2. Soledad
3. Cristóbal
4. Verónica
5. Nicolás
6. Gloria

a. trae unos discos
b. ve al supermercado
c. prepara la ensalada
d. compra los globos
e. saca las fotos
f. trae unos refrescos

---

23 Gramática en contexto See answers on p. 305.

Escribamos Imagine that you're at Héctor's graduation party and Mr. Villarreal wants everyone to have a good time. How would he tell each person to do the following things?

1. María/sacar unas fotos del grupo
2. Guillermo/comer más tamales
3. Mercedes/bailar con Héctor
4. Gabi/cantar canciones populares
5. Eva/tocar la guitarra para Gabi
6. Lisa/poner la música

Communication for All Students

Additional Practice

22 Play the audio recording again. For each request, ask students to write a response in which they say they cannot bring the item asked for while offering a reason for not bringing the item or an alternative. (**—Buenos días. Habla** Nicolás. ¿Qué necesitan para la fiesta? **—Trae unos tamales, por favor. —Lo siento. No puedo traer tamales. ¿Qué te parece si traigo unos refrescos?**)

---

24 Gramática en contexto See sample answers below.

 Hablemos You're having a party and your partner is helping you get ready. You've already done some of the preparations, but you still have some things left to do. Take turns telling each other to do the items left on the list. Don't forget to be polite!

comprar los refrescos
preparar la comida

decorar la sala
inflar los globos

limpiar la sala
llamar a nuestros amigos

 25 Antes...

 Escribamos ¡Qué fiesta! Ya es hora de limpiar todo el desorden de la fiesta de anoche. Mira el dibujo y prepara una lista de todas las cosas que hay que hacer para poner la casa en orden.

 26 ...y después

 Hablemos Work with a partner. Using the lists you made in Activity 25, take turns telling your partner what he or she can do to help you get the house together. Don't forget—you also promised your parents that you would wash the clothes, walk the dog, and cut the grass!

SUGERENCIA

When you learn new material, add what you're learning to what you already know, and think about how to use it in a conversation. For example, instead of just making a list of informal commands (like **haz, ven,** and **pon**), put them into a context by thinking of sentences that go with each one (like **¡Haz la tarea!, ¡Ven conmigo!,** and **¡Pon la mesa!**). When you learn a new word, make up sentences about your own life for each of the new vocabulary items.

Cultures and Communities

History Link

Have students research New Year celebrations in other countries where the holiday may be celebrated on different dates (China, Iran, parts of India) and report findings in Spanish. How was the year celebrated by the Aztecs according to their calendar? You may wish to treat this as a written assignment.

Challenge

Have students find an advertisement in Spanish that uses commands. They might look in magazines, on TV, or on the Internet. In their journals, have students write why the commands are formal or informal. (product, target audience, and so on) Then have them create their own ad using informal commands.

Slower Pace

25 Use the illustration to review home-related vocabulary before students do Activity 25.

Challenge

25 Have students write a paragraph describing the house and what must be done.

Group Work

26 Ask students to work in groups of four or five as they role-play the following conversation: After a party, the host or hostess asks friends to help out by doing specific things to clean up the mess. Some friends respond affirmatively; others politely refuse and explain why. (—¿Me ayudas a lavar los platos? —Lo siento, pero tengo que caminar con el perro. —¿Me haces el favor de pasar la aspiradora? —Cómo no.) Have group members take turns playing the host or hostess. You might have groups present their conversations to the class.

Assess

▸ Testing Program, pp. 253–256
   Quiz 10-2A, Quiz 10-2B
   Audio CD 10, Tr. 19

▸ Student Make-Up Assignments, Chapter 10, Alternative Quiz

▸ Alternative Assessment Guide, p. 41

Answers

23 1. María, saca unas fotos del grupo.
   2. Guillermo, come más tamales.
   3. Mercedes, baila con Héctor.
   4. Gabi, canta canciones populares.
   5. Eva, toca la guitarra para Gabi.
   6. Lisa, pon la música.

24 *Sample answers:* Compra los refrescos, por favor. Me haces el favor de preparar la comida?

Presenting
Encuentro cultural

Ask students what types of food and clothing they associate with weddings. Do students enjoy going to weddings? Why or why not? Have students describe some of the events that occurred during the last wedding they attended.

Additional Vocabulary

madrina *maid of honor*
damas de boda *bridesmaids*
padrino de boda *best man*
chambelanes *groomsmen*

Answers

27 *Possible answers:*
1. Probablemente Pilar pasó la aspiradora, limpió la cocina y lavó los platos anoche.
2. Probablemente Luis compró los ingredientes, cocinó la comida y preparó los platos anoche.
3. Probablemente Liliana no miró el partido ni escuchó la radio ni habló con sus amigos anoche.
4. Probablemente Federico no miró la televisión anoche pero estudió mucho y no habló por teléfono con amigos.
5. Probablemente Marta y Patricia caminaron mucho, trabajaron hasta muy tarde y regresaron a casa tarde anoche.
6. Probablemente Bernardo viajó el año pasado a Santo Domingo donde nadó y esquió en el agua.

Encuentro cultural

¿Cómo se celebra una boda?

GUADALUPE	¿Quieres ir conmigo esta tarde? Mi hermana Clara y su novio, Simón, se van a casar.
CHARLIE	¿Hoy?
GUADALUPE	Sí, la ceremonia no dura mucho tiempo. Estoy segura de que tenemos suficiente tiempo para ir al museo.
CHARLIE	Pero, tus padres están en Nueva York, ¿no? ¿No van a asistir a la boda?
GUADALUPE	¡Claro que sí! Regresan el jueves antes de la boda.
CHARLIE	Pero... la boda es hoy, ¿verdad?
GUADALUPE	Sí, pero es la ceremonia civil, nada más.
CHARLIE	Entonces, ¿la boda es el domingo? ¡No entiendo!

Para discutir...

1. Why does Charlie seem so surprised that Guadalupe's sister is getting married today without her parents being present?
2. Why are Clara and Simón having two different wedding ceremonies?

Vamos a comprenderlo

In Latin American countries, many couples participate in two ceremonies. For most, the civil ceremony is just a formality, similiar to getting a marriage license. The religious ceremony is the important one for the family and the one after which all the festivities occur. Although the civil ceremony is fully legal and binding, family and friends often don't consider the couple married until after the ceremony in church.

Cultures and Communities

Culture Note
A typical wedding party in Mexico includes several pairs of **padrinos** *(godparents)* who help pay for the costs of the wedding and reception. Wedding receptions are usually held in a **salón de baile,** and last until late in the evening or until dawn. For entertainment, there is dancing and music, often with **mariachis.**

Career Path
Have students imagine that they are in charge of coordinating a wedding. Whom would they call to help organize the event? (caterers, musicians, photographers, florists) Have students explain how knowledge of Spanish could give them an advantage in any of the above careers.

Tercer paso

Objective Talking about past events

WV3 TEXAS-10

Así se dice

Talking about past events

To find out what a friend did, ask:

¿Qué hiciste anoche en la fiesta?
What did you do last night . . .?

¿Qué hizo Kathy **ayer?**
What did . . . do yesterday?

¿Lo pasaron bien la semana pasada?
Did you have a good time last week?

Your friend might answer:

Bailé un poco y **hablé** con Lisa.
I danced . . . I talked . . .

Cantó unas canciones. *She sang . . .*

Sí, **lo pasamos bien.**

Vocabulario

anteayer	*day before yesterday*
el año pasado	*last year*
el sábado pasado	*last Saturday*
el verano pasado	*last summer*

Cuaderno de actividades, p. 118, Act. 17

Cuaderno de gramática, p. 86, Acts. 16–17

27 Gramática en contexto Answers on p. 306.

Leamos/Escribamos ¿Qué crees tú que hizo o no hizo cada persona según el contexto? Sigue el modelo.

MODELO Raúl no tiene mucha hambre a la hora del desayuno. (tomar helado, cenar tarde) Probablemente tomó helado y cenó tarde anoche.

1. La casa de Pilar está muy limpia. (pasar la aspiradora, limpiar la cocina, lavar los platos)

2. La comida para la fiesta de Luis está lista. (comprar los ingredientes, cocinar la comida, preparar los platos)

3. Liliana no sabe los resultados del gran partido de fútbol. (mirar el partido, escuchar la radio, hablar con sus amigos)

4. Federico sabe todas las respuestas para el examen de hoy. (mirar la televisión, estudiar mucho, hablar por teléfono con amigos)

5. Marta y Patricia están muy cansadas hoy. (caminar mucho, trabajar muy tarde, regresar a casa tarde)

6. Bernardo está aburrido con sus vacaciones este verano. (viajar a Santo Domingo, nadar, esquiar en el agua)

Nota gramatical

Use the preterite tense to talk about events completed sometime in the past. The preterite endings for **trabajar,** a regular **-ar** verb, are:

trabaj**é**	trabaj**amos**
trabaj**aste**	trabaj**asteis**
trabaj**ó**	trabaj**aron**

Notice the accent marks and how they affect pronunciation in the **yo** and the **él/ella/usted** forms.

Cuaderno de actividades, pp. 116–117, Acts. 13–14

Cuaderno de gramática, pp. 85–86, Acts. 13–15

Más práctica gramatical, pp. 316–317, Acts. 6–7

Communication for All Students

Visual Learners

Write six expressions on the board with infinitives of -ar verbs. (**bailar anoche, estudiar ayer**) Have students draw three columns labeled: **Actividad, Sí, No.** Tell them to write the phrases under **Actividad.** Then have them ask classmates questions with the **tú** form of the preterite. (**¿Estudiaste ayer?**) The person asked responds in the **yo** form and signs the chart. Ask students to find someone who did each activity.

Teaching Resources
pp. 307–311

PRINT
- Lesson Planner, p. 50
- TPR Storytelling Book, pp. 39, 40
- Listening Activities, pp. 77, 81
- Activities for Communication, pp. 59–60, 122, 123–124, 155–156
- Cuaderno de gramática, pp. 85–88
- Grammar Tutor for Students of Spanish, Chapter 10
- Cuaderno de actividades, pp. 116–118
- Cuaderno para hispanohablantes, pp. 46–50
- Testing Program, pp. 257–260
- Alternative Assessment Guide, p. 41
- Student Make-Up Assignments, Chapter 10

MEDIA
- One-Stop Planner
- Audio Compact Discs, CD 10, Trs. 11–16, 27–28, 20
- Teaching Transparencies 10-3; **Más práctica gramatical** Answers; Cuaderno de gramática Answers
- Interactive CD-ROM Tutor, Disc 3

Bell Work
Write the following on the board: **Hay un gran baile este sábado. Todos se visten muy de moda. ¿Qué vas a llevar tú?**

Presenting
Así se dice, Nota gramatical, Vocabulario

Model the **Así se dice** phrases before students read the **Nota gramatical.** Have students use the **Vocabulario** to practice the preterite.

Teaching Resources
pp. 307–311

PRINT 📖

▸ Lesson Planner, p. 50
▸ TPR Storytelling Book, pp. 39, 40
▸ Listening Activities, pp. 77, 81
▸ Activities for Communication, pp. 59–60, 122, 123–124, 155–156
▸ Cuaderno de gramática, pp. 85–88
▸ Grammar Tutor for Students of Spanish, Chapter 10
▸ Cuaderno de actividades, pp. 116–118
▸ Cuaderno para hispanohablantes, pp. 46–50
▸ Testing Program, pp. 257–260
▸ Alternative Assessment Guide, p. 41
▸ Student Make-Up Assignments, Chapter 10

MEDIA 💿📼

▸ One-Stop Planner
▸ Audio Compact Discs, CD 10, Trs. 11–16, 27–28, 20
▸ Teaching Transparencies 10-3; **Más práctica gramatical** Answers; Cuaderno de gramática Answers
▸ Interactive CD-ROM Tutor, Disc 3

Additional Practice

28 After doing this activity as a listening comprehension exercise, call on several students and ask questions about the characters on the audio recording. (**¿Qué hicieron Andrés y Valerie?**) Students should answer appropriately, according to the answers given in the listening activity. You might have students ask their classmates questions.

---

28 **La fiesta de Abby** Scripts and answers on p. 291H.

CD 10
Tr. 11

Escuchemos Abby's party was great! Listen as she tells her parents about what some of her friends did at her party last night. Match the name(s) of the person(s) to the correct drawing.

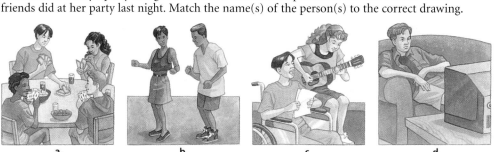

a.   b.   c.   d.

e.   f.   g.   h.

1. Raquel y Gloria a
2. Kerry y Shoji c
3. Bárbara y Miguel b
4. Pablo d
5. Patricia g
6. Gracie y Kim e
7. Andrés y Valerie h
8. Francisco f

29 **La semana pasada**

 Hablemos Trabaja con un compañero o una compañera. Pregúntale si hizo las siguientes actividades la semana pasada. Incluye dónde, en qué día y con quién las hizo. Luego, contesta sus preguntas.

1. hablar por teléfono
2. nadar
3. escuchar música
4. caminar con el perro
5. tomar helado
6. estudiar
7. montar en bicicleta
8. mirar la televisión
9. desayunar
10. trabajar

30 **¿Qué hicieron todos?**

 Escribamos Imagina que tú y tus amigos pasaron un día magnífico en el campo. Escribe un párrafo sobre las cosas divertidas que todos hicieron allí, contestando las siguientes preguntas. ¡Sé creativo/a!

1. ¿A qué hora llegaron?
2. ¿Quiénes montaron a caballo?
3. ¿Nadaron todos?
4. ¿Quién pescó?
5. ¿Quiénes jugaron al voleibol?
6. ¿Quién no hizo nada?

Communication for All Students

Cooperative Learning

29 Divide students into groups of three. On the board or on a transparency write: **comprar un regalo, escuchar la radio, acampar el verano pasado,** and **caminar mucho ayer.** Have one student ask another if he or she did one of these things. The second student answers, and a third student tells what was said.

Slower Pace

30 Present an outline for the paragraph on the board or the overhead. Model an introductory sentence, sentences for the body of the paragraph, and a concluding sentence. You may wish to have students work in pairs to peer-edit each other's paragraphs.

31 **¿Qué pasó aquí?** Possible answers below.

Escribamos Look at the two drawings. What makes the room look so different? Describe at least five changes that family members made.

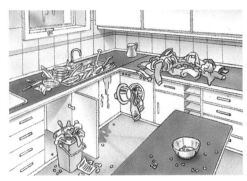
antes

después

32 **¿Quién hizo qué?**

Escribamos Mira los dibujos de arriba. Indica qué hizo cada miembro de la familia para ayudar a limpiar.

1. tú
2. tú y tu hermana
3. la abuela
4. los padres

33 **Las piñatas**

Leamos/Hablemos Después de leer el artículo sobre las piñatas, trabaja con un compañero o una compañera y contesta las preguntas.

1. Según el artículo, ¿quién introdujo *(introduced)* las piñatas a Europa?
2. ¿Quiénes las usaron en las Américas?
3. Para ellos, ¿qué significado espiritual tenían *(had)* las piñatas?
4. ¿Con qué se rellenan *(are filled)* las piñatas? ¿Qué es "la trampa" de las piñatas?
5. ¿Cómo se rompen *(are broken)* las piñatas?
6. ¿Participas tú en alguna celebración con piñatas? Describe esa fiesta.

Se cree que fue Marco Polo quien llevó las piñatas del Oriente a Italia en el siglo XIII. En las Américas las piñatas se usaron para motivar a la gente a ir a las ceremonias religiosas. Los frailes españoles les enseñaron a los indígenas mexicanos el cristianismo usando las piñatas como símbolo de las tres virtudes cristianas: la fe porque vamos con los ojos vendados, la espe-ranza porque miramos al cielo y la caridad porque rompemos el pecado y alcanzamos los regalos que deseamos.

Hoy en día las piñatas no tienen ningún significado religioso y se usan en todo tipo de fiesta. Las piñatas clásicas tienen forma de estrellas, animales, frutas y flores; se llenan de frutas o dulces aunque también existen las piñatas "trampas",  rellenas de harina o confeti. Las personas que van a romper la piñata deben tener cubiertos los ojos, dar vueltas y luego intentar romperla con un palo.

Cultures and Communities

Culture Note
Historically, **piñatas** have represented different things for different cultures. Traditional **piñatas** were in animal shapes that were used to celebrate agricultural prosperity. Later, **piñatas** became popular elsewhere in Europe and in the Americas.

History Link
Marco Polo's travels in China were described in his book, *Il milione,* which influenced and inspired explorers such as Christopher Columbus. Based upon miscalculations and Marco Polo's geography, Columbus believed he would reach Asia at approximately the point where he actually made his first landfall.

Additional Practice

31 Have students work with a partner to come up with five sentences about the picture labeled **después.** They should write sentences in the preterite tense explaining what was done to clean up the room. (**Alguien lavó los platos.**) You might have students share their sentences with the class. An alternative is to have students make up a story. (like *Goldilocks*— **el padre lavó los platos, la madre recogió...**)

Visual Learners

31 After students have done this activity, ask them to look closely at both pictures and memorize as many details as they can. Then have them close their books and recall the pictures without looking at them. See how many differences between the pictures the class can remember.

Slower Pace

33 Have students work together in groups, first brainstorming about what the questions are asking, then finding phrases in the **piñata** article that will help them answer questions 1–6. To read the questions, they might identify key words and familiar constructions, and decide which chapters they have to go to for a review. For instance, the **Nota gramatical** on page 146 of Chapter 5 discusses questions with **¿quién?** and **¿quiénes?** Having students decide what needs to be reviewed helps them control their own learning and teaches them to work together to solve a common problem.

31 *Possible answers:*
Mamá compró una planta. Papá lavó la ropa. Él sacó la basura. Ella organizó la ropa. Todos limpiamos la cocina.

Teaching Resources
pp. 307–311

PRINT

▶ Lesson Planner, p. 50
▶ TPR Storytelling Book, pp. 39, 40
▶ Listening Activities, pp. 77, 81
▶ Activities for Communication, pp. 59–60, 122, 123–124, 155–156
▶ Cuaderno de gramática, pp. 85–88
▶ Grammar Tutor for Students of Spanish, Chapter 10
▶ Cuaderno de actividades, pp. 116–118
▶ Cuaderno para hispanohablantes, pp. 46–50
▶ Testing Program, pp. 257–260
▶ Alternative Assessment Guide, p. 41
▶ Student Make-Up Assignments, Chapter 10

MEDIA

▶ One-Stop Planner
▶ Audio Compact Discs, CD 10, Trs. 11–16, 27–28, 20
▶ Teaching Transparencies 10-3; **Más práctica gramatical** Answers; Cuaderno de gramática Answers
▶ Interactive CD-ROM Tutor, Disc 3

Presenting
Nota gramatical

First have students read the explanation. Then ask questions to which students respond using a direct object pronoun. (**¿Estudias el español todos los días?**)

Teaching Suggestion

 Ask students who at their house did each of the tasks the last time it was done. Ask them to use direct object pronouns. Remind them that they may give imaginary "facts" about their families.

Nota gramatical

Just as we use subject pronouns to avoid repetition of names, we can use *direct object pronouns* to refer to someone or something already mentioned. The singular forms of these pronouns are:

lo *him, it, you (formal)*
la *her, it, you (formal)*

The pronoun agrees in gender with the noun replaced and comes right before the verb.

Sarita compró **el regalo** ayer.
Sarita **lo** compró ayer.

Daniel, ¿lavaste **la ropa** anoche?
Sí, ya **la** lavé anoche.

Cuaderno de actividades, pp. 117–118, Act. 16

Cuaderno de gramática, pp. 87–88, Acts. 18–21

Más práctica gramatical, p. 317, Act. 8

---

35 ¿Todo listo? See answers on p. 311.

 Leamos/Escribamos Mr. Villarreal wants to make sure that everything is ready for Héctor's graduation party. How would the following people answer his questions? Be sure to use the correct direct object pronoun in your answers.

MODELO —Rebeca, ¿ya compraste el pastel? **(no)**
—No, no lo compré.

1. Eva, ¿ya invitaste al profesor de Héctor? (no)
2. Gabi y Lisa, ¿ya limpiaron la casa? (sí)
3. Lisa, ¿ya decoraste el patio? (no)
4. Abuela, ¿ya preparaste la comida? (no)

36 ¿Y qué hizo...?

 Escribamos Averigua al menos una cosa que tu compañero/a de clase y sus amigos o parientes hicieron...

1. el año pasado
2. el domingo pasado
3. anteayer
4. ayer por la mañana
5. ayer a las doce
6. hoy antes de llegar al colegio

---

34 Gramática en contexto

 **Hablemos** Take turns asking each other if you do these activities during the week. Include when and how often you do each activity. Use the correct direct object pronoun.

MODELO —¿Cuándo lees el periódico?
—Lo leo todos los días.

1. hacer la cama
2. practicar la guitarra
3. preparar el almuerzo
4. mirar la televisión
5. llamar a tu mejor amigo/a
6. limpiar el cuarto
7. estudiar español (o álgebra,...)
8. lavar la ropa o lavar el carro
9. hacer la tarea
10. poner la mesa

5. Chicos, ¿ya compraron el regalo? (sí)
6. Marcela, ¿ya llamaste a Victoria? (sí)
7. Aníbal, ¿ya ayudaste a tu papá? (sí)
8. Gabi y Eva, ¿ya compraron el helado? (no)

¿Se te ha olvidado?

activities

Consulta la página 113

Connections and Comparisons

Language-to-Language

In English, a pronoun's sentence placement is the same as the noun it substitutes: *John bought the gift yesterday. / John bought it yesterday.* Using Spanish pronouns may be difficult for students at first, since they have to remember to put them before the verb: **Juan compró el *regalo* ayer. Juan *lo* compró ayer.** To reinforce the information in the **Nota gramatical,** write the first Spanish sentence on the board, and ask students to help you replace **el regalo** with its pronoun, **lo**. Erase **el regalo** and draw an arrow to the position before the verb; then insert **lo**. This visual representation should help students remember where to put Spanish direct object pronouns when they speak and write.

37 Del colegio al trabajo

 Escribamos You are a reporter working for a local television station and are responsible for presenting news about the festival held in your school last weekend. Combine these expressions to write your report about what happened. Answers will vary.

MODELO los chicos (jugar con los globos)
—Los chicos jugaron con los globos.

los profesores	decorar el patio
los chicos	limpiar el gimnasio
la familia Sánchez	preparar comida muy rica
los jóvenes	tocar música tradicional
el director	probar platos típicos
la gente	bailar
todo el mundo	jugar con los globos
los estudiantes	pasarlo bien

38 En mi cuaderno

 Escribamos Create a journal entry telling what you did each day last week. Tell about the activities you participated in each day. Use the verbs you've worked with so far in the preterite. For the preterite forms of other verbs, see page R13. Answers will vary.

LETRA Y SONIDO

CD 10
Trs. 12–16

A. You may sometimes feel that Spanish is spoken very fast. This is because Spanish divides the chain of speech into even syllables. It does not mark word boundaries. Here are some guidelines to help you.

 1. Two vowels that come together are joined and are not separated even if they are part of different words.

   él va‿a‿hablar   entra‿en la casa
   lo‿encuentro   hablo‿inglés

 2. If a word ends in a consonant and the next one begins with a vowel, the preceding consonant begins the new syllable.

   Daniel‿es‿inteligente.
   Tiene los‿ojos‿azules.

 3. Identical vowels and consonants are reduced to a slightly longer single sound.

   ¿Tienes‿soda? Sus hijos‿son‿nuestros amigos.
   Quieren‿nadar.

B. **Dictado** Script for Part B on p. 291H.

Listen as Ricardo tells you what he's going to do tonight. Write what you hear.

C. Trabalenguas

Abre, cierra, saca afuera.
No tires chicle en la acera.

Tercer paso

CAPÍTULO 10

Assess
▸ Testing Program, pp. 257–260
Quiz 10-3A, Quiz 10-3B
Audio CD 10, Tr. 20

▸ Student Make-Up Assignments, Chapter 10, Alternative Quiz

▸ Alternative Assessment Guide, p. 41

Answers
35 1. No, no lo invité todavía.
2. Sí, ya la limpiamos.
3. No, no lo decoré todavía.
4. No, no la preparé todavía.
5. Sí, ya lo compramos.
6. Sí, ya la llamé.
7. Sí, ya lo ayudé.
8. No, no lo compramos todavía.

Vamos a leer

Festivales del mundo hispanohablante

Festivales
del mundo hispanohablante

Teaching Resources
pp. 312–313

PRINT
▶ Lesson Planner, p. 51
▶ Cuaderno de actividades, p. 119
▶ Cuaderno para hispanohablantes, pp. 46–48
▶ Reading Strategies and Skills Handbook, Chapter 10
▶ ¡Lee conmigo! 1, Chapter 10
▶ Standardized Assessment Tutor, Chapter 10

MEDIA
▶ One-Stop Planner

Prereading
Activity A

Using Prior Knowledge
Have students take a few moments to look at the pictures on these pages. Ask them to call out adjectives these pictures bring to mind. Have a volunteer write the adjectives on the board. Then divide the class into groups of three or four to complete Activity A.

Reading
Activities B and C

Using Context Clues
Ask students to use other reading strategies they have learned to help them to understand these passages. Ask students to point out cognates, skim for main ideas, and make an outline of each of the festivals described here.

Estrategia para leer

Make comparisons
When you read an article that discusses a topic from different points of view, it's logical to make comparisons. You can either make comparisons in your head, or you can write them. You'll remember more if you write your comparisons as you read.

¡A comenzar!
This reading passage is about festivals in the Spanish-speaking world. As you read, you'll be able to make some comparisons with local and national festivals in the United States.

¿Te acuerdas?
Use your background knowledge before you read in depth.

A Work with two or three other students to complete these statements about festivals where you live. Not every item will apply to your hometown. Answers will vary.

In our town people celebrate by . . .

1. wearing masks and costumes during ———.
2. having parades during ———.
3. honoring religious occasions such as ———.
4. sharing the harvest during ———.
5. enjoying European foods and traditions such as ———.

LAS fiestas del mundo hispanohablante tienen sus raíces en las culturas europeas, indígenas y africanas. Con el tiempo, estas celebraciones están cambiando y se van enriqueciendo con los aportes de cada comunidad.

Muchas de las fiestas son de carácter festivo o religioso, mientras que otras combinan la espiritualidad y la sana diversión. La mayoría de las fiestas religiosas son cristianas, pero también se celebran festivales judíos como el Hánukkah, fiestas musulmanas como el Ramadán y varias fiestas de otras religiones.

LA fiesta de Las Turas, de origen indígena, se celebra el 23 y 24 de septiembre en el estado Falcón en Venezuela. El festival da las gracias por una cosecha buena. Los participantes llevan maíz y caña de azúcar y lo dejan al pie del "árbol de la basura". El nombre de la fiesta viene de unos instrumentos llamados turas, hechos de tallos de bambú y cráneo de venado.

LA Fiesta de la Calle Ocho celebra la herencia latina de Miami cada marzo. En Miami la cultura hispana y el idioma español dominan la atmósfera de esta ciudad diariamente. Los cubano americanos forman el grupo hispano más grande. Durante las últimas dos décadas con la llegada de inmigrantes nicaragüenses, colombianos, hondureños, peruanos y dominicanos la población latina de la ciudad está cambiando. En el año 1997 la Fiesta de la Calle Ocho tuvo como tema "El Festival de las Américas" por la gran diversidad de los grupos latinos que ahora residen en Miami.

Cultures and Communities

 Culture Notes
• **El Día de los Inocentes** is celebrated in December in Hatillo, Puerto Rico. People wearing African masks gather in the town square for festivities. In other Latin American countries **El Día de los Inocentes** is celebrated like April Fool's Day.

• **La Fiesta de las Turas** is a harvest festival much like Thanksgiving. Participants leave shucked corn under the **árbol de la basura**, a specially chosen tree. The corn kernels then protect the harvest. Of indigenous origin, the festival is celebrated during the feast days of the **Virgen de las Mercedes** in September due to European influence, but is considered a harvest festival.

UN festival importante de raíces africanas se celebra en Puerto Rico en el pueblo de Hatillo. Es el Festival de las Máscaras. Los puertorriqueños lo celebran el 28 de diciembre en conjunto con la fiesta cristiana del Día de los Inocentes. En el festival hay desfiles de gente con máscaras y disfraces coloridos.

EL Carnaval se celebra por todo el mundo hispanohablante un lunes y martes en febrero o marzo, cuarenta días antes de las Pascuas. En el Ecuador lo celebran con mucho entusiasmo, tirando globos llenos de agua a las personas en las calles. En Argentina las personas se disfrazan y celebran el Carnaval con desfiles en las calles y plazas.

ESTOS cuatro festivales son un pequeño ejemplo de las numerosas fiestas celebradas en el mundo hispano. Representan los aportes indígenas, africanos y europeos a nuestra cultura actual.

6. enjoying Native American foods, music, and traditions including _____.

7. enjoying African American foods, music, and traditions including _____.

See answers to part B below. Answers to parts C and D will vary.

Al grano

B As you read this article about cultural holidays, keep in mind what holidays are like where you live. Answer the following questions:

1. What are two different ways that **Carnaval** is celebrated?

2. What are some things you may see at the **Festival de las Máscaras** in Puerto Rico?

3. Why do people bring things to **el árbol de la basura**?

C Now answer the questions to help you figure out if there are any similarities or differences between these holidays and holidays in your hometown.

1. Is **Carnaval** celebrated where you live? How? If not, do any of your holidays reflect similar customs or traditions? Explain what is similar.

2. Is **Calle Ocho** similar to any other holiday you know about? Which one(s)?

3. What holiday does **Las Turas** remind you of? Why?

D Imagínate que tú puedes participar en uno de estos festivales. ¿Por qué te parece divertido o interesante? Haz una lista de tus razones *(reasons)*. Después, reúnete con dos compañeros de clase para decidir qué festival quieren celebrar. ¡Todos deben estar de acuerdo!

Cuaderno para hispanohablantes, pp. 46–48

Cuaderno de actividades, p. 119, Act. 18

Postreading
Activities C and D

Comparing and Contrasting

• Ask students to write about one of the festivals on pages 312–313 that has aspects similar to a holiday or festival that they celebrate. Write on the board several of the festivities seen here to help students get started. **(desfiles, disfraces, gente y música en las calles)**

• Have students prepare an oral presentation highlighting the music, dances, and traditional costumes of a Spanish-speaking country or region. A few suggestions: **la zarzuela** and **el flamenco** of Spain; **la jota** of Aragón, Spain; **el baile folklórico (el jarabe tapatío)** of Mexico; **el merengue** of the Dominican Republic; **el tango** of Argentina.

Communication for All Students

Additional Practice
Have students write which festival they would most like to attend and why. You might have students work with a partner to discuss what is attractive about the festival they have selected. Pairs could then write paragraphs cooperatively.

Native Speakers
Ask native speakers to tell the class about their favorite holidays. Ask them which celebrations or activities are most important to them and why. Then ask all students if they think there are common aspects to celebrations around the world. (time with family and friends, special foods, costumes) As a variation, have students write a description of their favorite holiday.

Answers
B 1. disfraces, desfiles
2. desfiles, máscaras, disfraces
3. para dar las gracias por una cosecha buena

For **Más práctica gramatical** Answer Transparencies, see the *Teaching Transparencies* binder.

Más práctica gramatical

internet

MARCAR: go.hrw.com
PALABRA CLAVE:
WV3 TEXAS-10

Primer paso

Objectives Talking about what you're doing right now; asking for and giving an opinion

1 Carlitos is three years old and is always asking when the next celebration is. Tell him when the following holidays take place this year, using the dates from the box. **(p. 297)**

> **MODELO** **¿Cuándo es la Nochebuena?**
> **La Nochebuena es el 24 de diciembre.**

> 14 de febrero 12 de mayo
> 25 de diciembre
> 4 de julio 15 de junio
> 12 de abril
> 25 de noviembre 31 de diciembre

1. ¿Cuándo es el Día de Acción de Gracias?
2. ¿Cuándo son las Pascuas?
3. ¿Cuándo es el Día de las Madres?
4. ¿Cuándo es el Día de la Independencia?
5. ¿Cuándo es la Navidad?
6. ¿Cuándo es el Día de los Enamorados?
7. ¿Cuándo es el Día del Padre?
8. ¿Cuándo es la Nochevieja?

2 Es día festivo para las siguientes personas. Completa las oraciones e indica qué están haciendo en este momento, con las formas correctas del presente progresivo. Después de cada oración, indica qué día festivo están celebrando. **(pp. 297, 299)**

> **MODELO** **Yo ═══ (pintar) huevos y Nélida ═══ (comer) dulces de chocolate.**
> **Yo *estoy pintando* huevos y Nélida *está comiendo* dulces de chocolate. *Son las Pascuas.***

1. Los niños ═══ (jugar) con sus regalos y nosotros ═══ (cantar).
2. Gabi les ═══ (dibujar) tarjetas para todos sus amigos, y Leo le ═══ (dar) flores a su novia.
3. Papá ═══ (leer) una tarjeta de todos los niños.
4. Todos nosotros ═══ (hacer) una cena muy especial para mamá.
5. Raquel y su familia ═══ (comer) hamburguesas, perros calientes y papitas en el patio.
6. Todos los invitados ═══ (llevar) sombreros muy cómicos.
7. Mamá ═══ (preparar) una cena muy grande y nosotros ═══ (poner) la mesa.

Answers

1 1. El Día de Acción de Gracias es el 25 de noviembre.
2. Las Pascuas son el 12 de abril.
3. El Día de las Madres es el 12 de mayo.
4. El Día de la Independencia es el 4 de julio.
5. La Navidad es el 25 de diciembre.
6. El Día de los Enamorados es el 14 de febrero.
7. El Día del Padre es el 15 de junio.
8. La Nochevieja es el 31 de diciembre.

2 1. están jugando; estamos cantando; Es la Navidad.
2. está dibujando; está dando; Es el Día de los Enamorados.
3. está leyendo; Es el Día del Padre.
4. estamos haciendo; Es el Día de las Madres.
5. están comiendo; Es el Día de la Independencia.
6. están llevando; Es la Nochevieja.
7. está preparando; estamos poniendo. Es el Día de Acción de Gracias.

Grammar Resources for Chapter 10

The **Más práctica gramatical** activities are designed as supplemental activities for the grammatical concepts presented in the chapter. You might use them as additional practice, for review, or for assessment.

For more grammar presentation, review, and practice, refer to the following:

• Cuaderno de gramática
• Grammar Tutor for Students of Spanish

• Grammar Summary on pp. R9–R13
• Cuaderno de actividades
• Grammar and Vocabulary quizzes (Testing Program)
• Test Generator on the One-Stop Planner CD-ROM
• Interactive CD-ROM Tutor
• DVD Tutor
• **Juegos interactivos** at <u>go.hrw.com</u>

3 La señora Mercado está hablando con su hija por teléfono para preguntar cómo van los preparativos de la fiesta de sorpresa del señor Mercado. Completa su conversación con las formas correctas del presente progresivo. No uses ningún verbo más de una vez. (**p. 299**)

pasar	decorar	salir	descansar	ayudar
comprar	limpiar	preparar	colgar	hacer

SRA. MERCADO Paula, hola, soy yo. ¿Cómo va todo? ¿Qué ___1___ tú ahora?

PAULA Hola, mami. Todo va bien. Yo ___2___ la cocina.

SRA. MERCADO ¿Y tu abuela? ¿___3___ en su cuarto?

PAULA No, no. Ella está aquí conmigo. Ella y Margarita ___4___ las empanadas.

SRA. MERCADO Qué bueno. ¿Y ___5___ Tomás con las empanadas también?

PAULA No, Tomás está en el supermercado. ___6___ las bebidas y el hielo.

SRA. MERCADO ¿Y las decoraciones?

PAULA Tranquila, mami. Tío Mario e Inés ___7___ los globos ahora. Y Tía Cristina ___8___ el pastel.

SRA. MERCADO ¿Y van a limpiar la sala después?

PAULA Pues, Marta ___9___ la aspiradora en la sala ahora.

SRA. MERCADO Veo que todo está bajo control. Bueno, yo ___10___ del trabajo ahora. Nos vemos pronto.

Segundo paso

Objectives Asking for help and responding to requests; telling a friend what to do.

4 You're running into some problems getting ready for a party. Ask for help with each problem, using a different expression from the box in each sentence. (**p. 302**)

MODELO Hay muchos platos en la cocina.
¿Me ayudas a lavar los platos, por favor?

pasar la aspiradora	llamar a los amigos	colgar las decoraciones
poner la comida en el refrigerador	organizar el cuarto	preparar más comida
	sacar la basura	lavar los platos

1. Tu cuarto está muy desordenado.
2. Hay mucha basura en la cocina.
3. Mamá regresa ahora del supermercado con toda la comida.
4. Unos amigos no saben todavía a qué hora es la fiesta.
5. La alfombra de la sala está muy sucia.
6. No hay decoraciones en el patio todavía.
7. Vienen muchos invitados, y no hay mucha comida.

Teacher to Teacher

Sarah Voorhees
Saratoga High School
Saratoga, California

Sarah's students reap sweet spoils

"To practice familiar commands, I have each student first hide a piece of candy somewhere on campus before coming to class the next day. Students may hide candy near lockers, outside the building, near the cafeteria or auditorium, or in another teacher's classroom. In class I have them write commands as clues to find the hidden candy. They give the clues to another student who has to go find the candy. The students can't believe that I am permitting them to leave the classroom!"

Answers

3 1. estás haciendo
2. estoy limpiando
3. Está descansando
4. están preparando
5. está ayudando
6. Está comprando
7. están colgando
8. está decorando
9. está pasando
10. estoy saliendo

4 1. ¿Me ayudas a organizar el cuarto, por favor?
2. ¿Me ayudas a sacar la basura, por favor?
3. ¿Me ayudas a poner la comida en el refrigerador, por favor?
4. ¿Me ayudas a llamar a los amigos, por favor?
5. ¿Me ayudas a pasar la aspiradora, por favor?
6. ¿Me ayudas a colgar las decoraciones, por favor?
7. ¿Me ayudas a preparar más comida, por favor?

Más práctica gramatical

WV3 TEXAS-10

For **Más práctica gramatical** Answer Transparencies, see the *Teaching Transparencies* binder.

5 Algunos amigos llegaron temprano a tu fiesta para ayudarte a prepararla. Dile a cada uno qué hacer. Usa la lista de tareas de abajo con mandatos informales. (p. 304)

MODELO   Emiliano/traer más sillas
               Emiliano, trae más sillas, por favor.

PERSONA	TAREA
1. **Alida**	ir al supermercado
2. **Sebastián**	inflar los globos
3. **Ricardo**	poner la mesa
4. **Catalina**	hacer los sándwiches
5. **Iñigo**	colgar las decoraciones
6. **Luz**	organizar los discos compactos
7. **Wilfredo**	limpiar la sala
8. **Belén**	llamar a la pastelería

Tercer paso

Objective Talking about past events

6 Gabi y Luisa están hablando por teléfono para saber qué pasó durante el fin de semana. Completa su conversación. Usa la forma correcta del verbo en el pretérito. (p. 307)

LUISA   Gabi, hola. ¿Cómo estás? ¿Qué ___1___ (hacer) tú el fin de semana?

GABI   Pues, Susana me ___2___ (invitar) a su fiesta el sábado. ¿Y tú?

LUISA   ___3___ (Visitar) a unos primos en San Antonio. Pero cuéntame… ¿qué ___4___ (pasar) en la fiesta?

GABI   Bueno, Maripili y Francisco ___5___ (llegar) juntos. Y Pedro ___6___ (bailar) muchísimo con Bárbara. Yo ___7___ (hablar) con el primo de Rosaura toda la noche. Fue una fiesta excelente. ¿Y qué tal con tus primos en San Antonio? ¿Lo ___8___ (pasar) bien ustedes?

LUISA   Sí, muy bien. Mis primos y yo ___9___ (caminar) por el centro de la ciudad, ___10___ (sacar) muchas fotos y ___11___ (visitar) El Mercado. Yo ___12___ (comprar) muchos regalos allí.

GABI   ¿Y cuándo ___13___ (regresar) a casa?

LUISA   El domingo.

Answers

5
1. Alida, ve al supermercado, por favor.
2. Sebastián, infla los globos, por favor.
3. Ricardo, pon la mesa, por favor.
4. Catalina, haz los sándwiches, por favor.
5. Iñigo, cuelga las decoraciones, por favor.
6. Luz, organiza los discos compactos, por favor.
7. Wilfredo, limpia la sala, por favor.
8. Belén, llama a la pastelería, por favor.

6
1. hiciste
2. invitó
3. Visité
4. pasó
5. llegaron
6. bailó
7. hablé
8. pasaron
9. caminamos
10. sacamos
11. visitamos
12. compré
13. regresaste

Communication for All Students

Kinesthetic Learners

7 Have groups of eight students list typical weekend activities, each expressing one in the preterite using **yo.** Have the group stand forming a circle. Have one student announce the activity **(Yo corté el césped.)** as you hand him or her a ball of yarn. Holding on to a strand, the student passes the ball to a classmate, who includes the previous activity and a new one in a sentence. **(Después de cortar el césped, miré la tele.)** Each passes the yarn holding on to a strand, until an eight-verb sentence is formed in the same manner. The crisscrossed strands are unraveled as they recount the events backwards, using **antes de** and the infinitive.

7 When was the last time the following people did these things? Use the correct preterite form of each verb to form sentences telling what they did and when. (**p. 307**)

MODELO   **Carla/organizar el cuarto/anoche**
                Carla organizó el cuarto anoche.

1. Maripili/limpiar la casa/ayer
2. La familia Benavides/preparar la cena/anoche
3. Nuestros amigos/decorar la sala para la fiesta/el sábado pasado
4. Alfredo/cortar el césped en casa de su abuela/anteayer
5. Yo/cuidar al gato de Carlos/el verano pasado
6. Tú/llamar a Pedro/anoche
7. Nosotros/escuchar la música rock/el fin de semana pasado
8. Cristina y su hermana Alex/mirar la televisión/ayer

8 Dolores's family is having a Mother's Day celebration. Write Dolores's answers to questions about who is doing what to prepare for the festivities. Use a direct object pronoun in each sentence. (**p. 310**)

MODELO   —**¿Quién compra la comida? (Andrés)**
               —**Andrés la compra.**

1. ¿Quién compra el helado? (yo)
2. ¿Quién decora el pastel? (Juanita)
3. ¿Quién saca la basura? (Andrés)
4. ¿Quién llama a Tío Martín? (yo)
5. ¿Quién dibuja la tarjeta? (Juanita)
6. ¿Quién prepara la cena? (tú y yo)
7. ¿Quién lleva a mamá al parque durante las preparaciones? (tú)

Answers

7
1. Maripili limpió la casa ayer.
2. La familia Benavides preparó la cena anoche.
3. Nuestros amigos decoraron la sala para la fiesta el sábado pasado.
4. Alfredo cortó el césped en casa de su abuela anteayer.
5. Yo cuidé al gato de Carlos el verano pasado.
6. Tú llamaste a Pedro anoche.
7. Nosotros escuchamos la música rock el fin de semana pasado.
8. Cristina y su hermana Alex miraron la televisión ayer.

8
1. Yo lo compro.
2. Juanita lo decora.
3. Andrés la saca.
4. Yo lo llamo.
5. Juanita la dibuja.
6. Tú y yo la preparamos.
7. Tú la llevas.

Review and Assess

You may wish to assign the **Más práctica gramatical** activities as additional practice or homework after presenting material throughout the chapter. Assign Activity 1 after **Vocabulario** (p. 297), Activities 2–3 after **Vocabulario** (p. 297) and **Gramática** (p. 299), Activity 4 after **Vocabulario** (p. 302), Activity 5 after **Nota gramatical** (p. 304), Activities 6–7 after **Nota Gramatical** (p. 307), and

Activity 8 after **Nota gramatical** (p. 310). To prepare students for the **Paso** Quizzes and Chapter Test, have them do the **Más práctica gramatical** activities in the following order: complete Activities 1–3 before taking Quiz 10-1A or 10-1B; Activities 4–5 before taking Quiz 10-2A or 10-2B; and Activities 6–8 before taking Quiz 10-3A or 10-3B.

Repaso

CAPÍTULO 10

The **Repaso** reviews all four skills and culture in preparation for the Chapter Test.

Repaso

internet

MARCAR: go.hrw.com
PALABRA CLAVE:
WV3 TEXAS-10

Teaching Resources
pp. 318–319

PRINT
▶ Lesson Planner, p. 52
▶ Listening Activities, p. 77
▶ Video Guide, pp. 67–69, 72
▶ Grammar Tutor for Students of Spanish, Chapter 10
▶ Cuaderno para hispanohablantes, pp. 46–50
▶ Standardized Assessment Tutor, Chapter 10

MEDIA
▶ One-Stop Planner
▶ Video Program, Videocassette 4, 15:01–15:36
▶ DVD Tutor, Disc 2
▶ Audio Compact Discs, CD 10, Tr. 17
▶ Interactive CD-ROM Tutor, Disc 3

Portfolio

4 **Written** Ask students to write a letter to a friend or relative who will be coming home to celebrate a special family holiday. Students should tell what each person is doing now to prepare for the occasion and ask the person's opinion about a special gift for someone in the family. For Portfolio information, see *Alternative Assessment Guide*, pp. iv–17.

---

1 Listen to Mariana tell about her favorite holiday. Write the information requested for each question. Script and answers on p. 291H.

CD 10
Tr. 17

1. ¿Adónde viajaron Mariana y su familia?
2. ¿Por qué viajaron allí?
3. ¿En qué mes viajaron?
4. ¿Qué preparó la abuela?
5. Después de la cena, ¿qué hicieron todos?
6. ¿Por qué es la Navidad su fiesta favorita?

2 Completa cada oración usando el presente progresivo para decir qué están haciendo en este momento las siguientes personas. See sample answer below.

MODELO   Adela toca muchos instrumentos y ahora *está tocando* la guitarra.

1. Graciela come muchas ensaladas pero ahora ══════ una hamburguesa.
2. Nosotros leemos mucho y ahora ══════ una novela popular.
3. Limpio la casa con frecuencia y ahora ══════ la sala.
4. Ellos escriben muchas cartas pero ahora ══════ una composición.
5. A Mildred y a Ivonne les gusta comprar muchas cosas y ahora ══════ regalos para sus amigos.
6. Mamá necesita decorar la casa para la fiesta y ahora ella ══════ la sala.
7. Tú y yo ayudamos en casa mucho y ahora ══════ a papá.

3 Look at the pictures and create a conversation with a partner. Take turns telling each other what to do to help and responding to the request.

a.

b.

c.

4 Write a short paragraph about what you learned about celebrations in Spanish-speaking countries. In your paragraph, compare these celebrations to those in the United States. State three differences and three similarities in the way in which celebrations are observed. If you and your family or friends celebrate one of the holidays mentioned in the chapter, include how you celebrate it and what you like about it.

Apply and Assess

Slower Pace

2 Divide the class into pairs. Ask students to identify the verb(s) and subject(s) in each sentence. Have one student write the infinitive of the verb that will be conjugated. The other student should conjugate the verb using the present progressive. Then have students switch roles.

Challenge

3 Ask students to come up with as many combinations of commands, requests, and responses as they can for these pictures, based on what they have learned in the chapter. Encourage students to be imaginative.

Answers

2 *Answers will vary. Students should use the present progressive in their answers. Sample answer:* Todos están esperando a Héctor. La abuela está hablando con dos invitados.

5 Read Alicia's note about Jaime's birthday party in the park last Saturday, and then answer the questions. Be sure to use the preterite and direct object pronouns. See answers below.

> Para la fiesta de Jaime, yo preparé un flan y Yoli hizo una tortilla española deliciosa. Fede y Luisa compraron el helado. Todos llegamos al parque a las once de la mañana. Chela y yo le compramos un cartel y Javier le regaló un disco compacto. Después, Chela y yo tocamos la guitarra y Fede sacó unas fotos de todo el grupo. Más tarde, nosotros jugamos al béisbol y al voleibol.

1. ¿Quién preparó el flan?
2. ¿Quién preparó la tortilla?
3. ¿Compró Chela el helado?
4. ¿Quién compró el cartel para Jaime?
5. ¿Tocaron todos la guitarra?
6. ¿Quién sacó la foto del grupo?

6 Vamos a escribir

Write a conversation between two friends who are planning a surprise party. Combine your sentences to make the conversation sound natural.

Estrategia para escribir

Combining sentences will improve your writing. Short, choppy sentences tend to break up the reader's thoughts. If you use words like *y, o,* or *pero,* your ideas will flow more naturally. For example, *A Ana le gusta el chocolate pero no le gustan los pasteles* sounds more natural than *A Ana le gusta el chocolate. No le gustan los pasteles.*

Prewriting

Brainstorm and list what needs to be done to create a successful surprise party. Decide on two characters and list the tasks. Include what each person already has done, what both still need to do, and a few tasks they will ask each other to do.

Writing

Write the conversation. Combine your ideas so they flow naturally.

MODELO
— Bueno, ya preparé el pastel pero no decoré la sala.
— Yo estoy decorando la sala. Compra las bebidas, ¿quieres?

Revising

Read your dialogue to a classmate, making sure your ideas are in a logical order and that the conversation flows naturally. Correct errors and prepare a final draft.

7 Situación

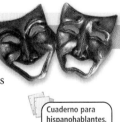

You're on a committee to plan the end-of-the-year dance, but your class doesn't have enough money. Work with three or four classmates to discuss a solution. Give your opinion about affordable food and music and a low-cost location. Suggest ways to earn money for the project. Be prepared to present your conversation to the class.

> Cuaderno para hispanohablantes, p. 50

Apply and Assess

Slower Pace

5 Have students answer the questions in two steps, first looking for the correct response. Then ask them to reread the question and identify the direct object. Have students come to the board and incorporate the answer and the correct direct object pronoun in a sentence. (**Alicia lo preparó.**)

6 Suggest that students review the **Panorama cultural** and **De antemano** in Chapter 10 to find examples of smoothly connected sentences and natural conversation. Students might refer to these examples as they make up their own conversations.

Answers
5 1. Alicia lo preparó.
2. Yoli la preparó. (Yoli la hizo.)
3. No; lo compraron Fede y Luisa.
4. Chela y Alicia lo compraron.
5. No, Chela y Alicia la tocaron.
6. Fede la sacó.

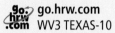
Teacher Note
This page is intended to help students prepare independently for the Chapter Test. It is a brief checklist of the major points covered in the chapter. The students should be reminded that it is only a checklist and does not necessarily include everything that will appear on the Chapter Test.

Answers

2 1. Héctor está abriendo regalos.
2. Manuel está comprando el pastel.
3. Rebeca está llamando a los invitados.
4. Mario y Juan están decorando la sala.
5. La abuela está preparando los tamales.
6. Todos estamos comiendo y bebiendo.
7. Aníbal está hablando por teléfono.
8. Eva está inflando los globos.

3 *Answers may vary.*
1. ¿Qué piensas de la fiesta?
2. ¿Qué piensas de la comida?
3. ¿Qué te parece la música?
4. ¿Te gusta el postre?

5 1. Estudia más.
2. Haz tu tarea.
3. Organiza tu cuarto.
4. Lee tu libro.
5. Come más vegetales.
6. Haz ejercicios.
7. Asiste a clase todos los días.
8. Ayuda en casa.

6 *Sample answer:* **a.** Mis abuelos miraron su programa favorito en la televisión anoche.

Can you talk about what you're doing right now? p. 298

1 Imagine that today is one of the following holidays. How would you tell a friend on the phone what you're doing right now? Answers will vary.

1. la Navidad
2. el Día de Acción de Gracias

2 How would you say that . . .?

1. Héctor is opening gifts
2. Manuel is buying the cake
3. Rebeca is calling the guests
4. Mario and Juan are decorating the living room
5. Grandmother is preparing the tamales
6. We are all eating and drinking
7. Aníbal is talking on the phone
8. Eva is blowing up balloons
See answers below.

Can you ask for and give an opinion? p. 300

3 How would you ask a guest what she or he thinks of . . .?

1. the party
2. the food
3. the music
4. the dessert
See answers below.

Can you ask for help and respond to requests? p. 302

4 The Spanish Club is planning an end-of-the-year party. Can you write notes to five club members asking for their help in completing the preparations?

Can you tell a friend what to do? p. 304

5 How would you tell a friend to do the following things?

1. study more
2. do your homework
3. organize your room
4. read your book
5. eat more vegetables
6. do exercises
7. attend class every day
8. help at home
See answers below.

Can you talk about past events? p. 307

6 Can you write a sentence for each drawing saying what these people did last night? Use your imagination and create a name for each person.
See sample answer below.

a. b. c.

d. e. f.

Review and Assess

Building on Previous Skills
Have students invent and name an imaginary holiday. **(El día de la Película)** Ask them to come up with a date for their new holiday and to decide who celebrates it. (their town, the country) They should write a brief description of their holiday, including what it celebrates and how it is celebrated. (movies; free tickets and popcorn are given away) Once students have written about their holidays individually, divide the class into pairs to describe their holidays to each other. Ask for volunteers to explain their partner's holiday to the rest of the class.

Vocabulario

Primer paso

Talking about what you're doing right now

el Año Nuevo	New Year's Day
colgar (ue) las	to hang
decoraciones	decorations
decorar	to decorate
el Día de Acción	Thanksgiving
de Gracias	
el Día de la	Independence Day
Independencia	
el Día de las	Mother's Day
Madres	

el Día de los	Valentine's Day
Enamorados	
el Día del Padre	Father's Day
los días festivos	holidays
la Navidad	Christmas
la Nochebuena	Christmas Eve
la Nochevieja	New Year's Eve
las Pascuas	Easter
¿Qué estás	What are you
haciendo?	doing?

Asking for and giving an opinion

Buena idea.	Good idea.
creer	to believe, to think
¿Crees que...?	Do you think
	that . . . ?
Creo que no.	I don't think so.
Creo que sí.	I think so.
Me parece bien.	It seems fine
	to me.
Perfecto.	Perfect.
¿Qué te parece	How do you feel
si...?	about . . . ?

Segundo paso

Asking for help and responding to requests

abrir los regalos	to open gifts
Claro que sí.	Of course.
¡Con mucho	Sure!
gusto!	
inflar los globos	to blow up
	balloons
llamar a los	to call the guests
invitados	
Lo siento, pero en	I'm sorry, but right
este momento...	now . . .

mandar las	to send invitations
invitaciones	
¿Me ayudas a...?	Can you help
	me to . . . ?
¿Me haces el	Can you do me the
favor de...?	favor of . . . ?
¿Me pasas...?	Can you pass
	me . . . ?
¿Me traes...?	Can you
	bring me . . . ?
Perdóname.	Excuse me.
recibir regalos	to receive gifts
Un momentito.	Just a second.

Telling a friend what to do

De acuerdo.	Agreed.
Está bien.	OK.
Haz...	Do/Make . . .
Pon...	Put/Place . . .
Ve...	Go . . .
Ven...	Come . . .
Vete...	Go away . . .

Tercer paso

Talking about past events

anoche	last night
anteayer	day before
	yesterday
el año pasado	last year
ayer	yesterday

la	it/her/you (formal)
lo	it/him/you (formal)
pasarlo bien	to have a good
	time
¿Qué hiciste?	What did you do?

¿Qué hizo?	What did
	he/she/you do?
el sábado pasado	last Saturday
la semana pasada	last week
el verano pasado	last summer

Review and Assess

Circumlocution

Make cards with one vocabulary word on each card. Divide the class into two teams and set up a desk at the front of the classroom with two chairs facing each other. A student from each team plays in turn. One student is the reader (**lector/a**) and the other is the guesser (**adivinador/a**). Give the reader five cards and tell him or her not to look at them yet. Set a time limit of one minute.

When you say **¡Empieza!,** the reader looks at the first card. He or she gives the guesser verbal clues without saying the word on the card or a derivative of it. Neither student may use gestures. If the guesser gets the word right, the reader moves on to the next card. The team gets one point for each word the guesser gets in one minute.

Game

Treinta segundos Prepare a list of questions to ask what people are doing at that moment. (**¿Qué está haciendo el profesor de matemáticas? ¿Qué están haciendo tus amigos?**) Divide the class into two teams. Each team receives one point per logical answer given in 30 seconds. (**El profesor está escribiendo en la pizarra.**) As a variation, ask students what people did in the past, using **-ar** verbs. (**¿Qué compraste ayer?**)

Chapter 10 Assessment

▶ **Testing Program**
Chapter Test, pp. 261–266

Audio Compact Discs,
CD 10, Trs. 21–22

Speaking Test, p. 347

▶ **Alternative Assessment Guide**
Performance Assessment, p. 41
Portfolio Assessment, p. 27
CD-ROM Assessment, p. 55

▶ **Interactive CD-ROM Tutor, Disc 3**

CD-ROM 3 ¡A hablar!
DVD 2 ¡A escribir!

▶ **Standardized Assessment Tutor**
Chapter 10

▶ **One-Stop Planner, Disc 3**
Test Generator
Chapter 10

Teaching Resources
pp. 322–325

PRINT
▶ Lesson Planner, pp. 52, 75
▶ Video Guide, pp. 73–74

MEDIA
▶ One-Stop Planner
▶ Video Program,
  Videocassette 3, 15:01–18:11
▶ DVD Tutor, Disc 2
▶ Interactive CD-ROM Tutor, Disc 3
▶ Map Transparency 4

 go.hrw.com
WV3 PUERTO RICO

 Using the Almanac and Map

Terms in the Almanac

- **Gobierno:** Since 1952 Puerto Rico has been a commonwealth of the U.S., or **estado libre asociado.** While living on the island, Puerto Ricans cannot vote in presidential elections and do not pay federal income tax, although they do have full U.S. citizenship. If they move to the U.S. mainland, they may vote, and they must also pay federal taxes.

- **Minerales: arcilla** *clay;* **caliza** *limestone;* **cobalto** *cobalt;* **cobre** *copper;* **hierro** *iron;* **níquel** *nickel*

- **Unidad monetaria:** Puerto Rico uses U.S. currency, but the names of units may be different. A *dollar* is sometimes called a **peso.** The *half-dollar* is called **medio peso,** a *quarter* is a **peseta,** a *nickel* is a **níquel** or **vellón,** and a *penny* is a **chavo** or **centavo.** As in English, a ten-cent coin is pronounced *dime.*

- **Idiomas:** On January 28, 1993, Governor Pedro Rosselló of Puerto Rico declared Spanish and English joint official languages of the island.

¡Ven conmigo a Puerto Rico!

Población: 3.808.610 (el 99.9% habla español, pero la mayoría habla inglés también)

Área: 9.104 km² (3.515 millas cuadradas)

Ubicación: una isla entre el océano Atlántico al norte y el mar Caribe al sur

Capital: San Juan, con una población de más de un millón (área metropolitana)

Gobierno: estado libre asociado

Industrias: la pesca, productos farmacéuticos, maquinarias y metales, turismo

Cosechas principales: azúcar, café, piña, plátanos, vegetales

Minerales: arcilla, caliza, cobalto, cobre, hierro, níquel

Unidad monetaria: el dólar

Idiomas: español, inglés

 WV3 PUERTO RICO

San Juan, la hermosa capital de Puerto Rico ▶

Connections and Comparisons

Geography Link
Puerto Rico, the smallest of the Greater Antilles Islands, is 100 miles long and 35 miles wide. The first known inhabitants of Puerto Rico, the Taíno, were there when Columbus and the Spanish settlers arrived in 1493. During the first three centuries of the Spanish colonial period, the settlers often battled the Dutch and English for control of the island.

Language Note
The Taíno people called Puerto Rico *Borinquén,* or "Island of the Brave Lord." Today, many Puerto Ricans still refer to themselves as **boricuas.** The Taíno feared and respected the god Juracán who lived on Borinquén's highest peak and was responsible for the weather.

STANDARDS: 2.2, 3.1, 5.1

MAPQUEST.COM

**HRW
Atlas Interactivo
Mundial**

Have students use the interactive atlas at **go.hrw.com** to find out more about the geography of Puerto Rico and complete the Map Activities below.

Map Activities

You may direct students to use the map in the *Pupil's Edition*, p. xxvii.

• Ask students to point out the West Indies archipelago. (Greater Antilles, Lesser Antilles, Bahama Islands)

• Have students locate the islands that constitute the Greater Antilles archipelago. (Cuba; Jamaica; Hispaniola, which includes Haiti and the Dominican Republic)

• Ask students to identify the bodies of water that surround Puerto Rico. (Atlantic Ocean and Caribbean Sea) You may want to tell students that it only takes about six hours to drive around the island.

CNNenEspañol.com

Have students check the **CNN en español** Web site for news on Puerto Rico. The **CNN en español** site is also a good source of timely, high interest readings for Spanish students.

Cultures and Communities

Culture Notes

• At midnight on June 23, the eve of **el Día de San Juan Bautista** (*the day of Saint John,* patron saint of San Juan), **los sanjuaneros** (*people from San Juan*) traditionally walk into the sea backward three times for good luck for the coming year. Throughout the island, there are many festivals that celebrate this event.

• The Taíno cultivated corn (**maíz**), peanuts (**maní**), yams (**ñame**), taro (**yautía**), and cassava (**yuca**). Fruits such as guava (**guayaba**), pineapple (**piña**), and sea grapes (**uvas playeras**) grew wild. These foods are all still popular in Puerto Rico today. The Taíno also grew arrowroot (**arrurruz**), which they called *aru-aru,* meaning "meal of meals."

Motivating Activity

Ask students to name a territory in the Caribbean that is associated with the United States. (Puerto Rico, U.S. Virgin Islands) Ask them what they already know about Puerto Rico. Ask who has been there to describe it, or have students tell what they think it may be like.

Using the Photo Essay

1 Una bonita playa Hotels and high-rise condominiums along the shore of Isla Verde were built within the last 30 years. Today, Isla Verde is one of San Juan's top tourist centers, with miles of beaches, hotels, restaurants, and boutiques. Puerto Rico has 280 miles of shoreline dotted with popular resorts, including Luquillo, Condado, Miramar, and Ocean Park.

2 La Alcadía de San Juan The City Hall (la Alcaldía) was built in stages from 1602 to 1789. It is one of the government buildings surrounding the **Plaza de Armas**, so named for the drills carried out by the city's inhabitants in preparation for attack by pirates. Planned in the 16th century as San Juan's main square, the **Plaza de Armas** later became a social gathering place.

Puerto Rico

Puerto Rico es una de las islas más hermosas del Caribe. La isla es en su mayor parte montañosa, con un clima tropical y pintorescas playas. La vida cultural de Puerto Rico tiene una mezcla de influencias antillanas, africanas, españolas y norteamericanas.

internet

MARCAR: go.hrw.com
PALABRA CLAVE:
WV3 PUERTO RICO

1 Una bonita playa
Puerto Rico tiene magníficas playas con cientos de millas de línea costera. Esto hace a la isla un lugar ideal para que los puertorriqueños y visitantes internacionales practiquen los deportes acuáticos.

2 La Alcaldía de San Juan
La histórica Alcaldía *(City Hall)* se fundó en 1604. Aquí se encuentra el gobierno local y algunos negocios pequeños. La Plaza de Armas al lado sirvió de campo de entrenamiento para los soldados españoles que defendieron la isla.

Connections and Comparisons

Language Note

Puerto Rican speech varies across the island. In Mayagüez the **r** is pronounced similarly to the uvular [r], as in French. In other areas, the syllable-final **r** may be pronounced as **l** *(pol favol)*. As is common in the Caribbean, Central America, coastal Mexico, Colombia, and Venezuela, the **d** between vowels can be silent *(pescao, lao)*. The **s** or **z** at the end of syllables is often aspirated, like the English *h*. *(¿Cómo ehtah tú? arroh con pollo).* People from Jayuya in the central Cordillera tend to "close" final vowels. (**Leche** would be pronounced *lechi.*) The **ll** and **y** may be pronounced like the *s* in *leisure* (**El Yunque** pronounced *El zhunque*), as is also common in Argentina.

❸ De compras en la Calle del Cristo
La avenida principal para ir de compras en el Viejo San Juan es la Calle del Cristo. Muchas personas visitan sus estrechas calles de adoquines día y noche.

❸ De compras en la Calle del Cristo This street in Old San Juan is the home of the **Centro Nacional de Artes Populares y Artesanías** of the Institute of Puerto Rican Culture. Nearby is the **Casa del Libro,** a collection of rare books, some pre–16th century. At the end of the street is the **Capilla de Cristo,** a chapel with a small silver altar.

❹ Pescado y frutas frescas
En todo Puerto Rico vas a encontrar deliciosas comidas, con una gran variedad de mariscos y deliciosas frutas tropicales.

❹ Pescado y frutas frescas Some typical Puerto Rican dishes include deep-fried **tostones,** made from sliced plantains or breadfruit (**pana**). Pork dishes include fried rinds (**chicharrón**), a tripe stew (**mondongo**), and **gandinga,** made from minced liver, heart, and kidney. Bananas are often fried to make a sweet dessert. Another popular food is **pastel,** which is not a dessert but a **tamal** made with meat, olives, onions, and plantain flour.

> **En los capítulos 11 y 12,**
> vas a conocer a Ben y a su hermana, Carmen, dos neo-yorquinos que están visitando a parientes en Puerto Rico. Ellos, con su mamá y su abue-lo, visitan algunos de los fascinantes lugares en la isla de Puerto Rico. ¿Cómo te gustaría pasar dos semanas en una isla?

❺ El Castillo de San Felipe del Morro is the oldest and most strategic fort in San Juan. Its six levels rise more than 140 feet and dominate the harbor entrance. It was originally named **San Felipe del Morro,** in honor of King Philip III of Spain. A deep moat surrounds its 20-foot-thick walls, and it is equipped with barracks, wells, supply rooms, dungeons, a chapel, and an armory.

❺ El Castillo de San Felipe del Morro
Los españoles comenzaron a construir El Morro en 1540. Desde esa fecha el fuerte sirvió como guarnición de muchas batallas, incluso el ataque de Sir Francis Drake en 1595 y también durante la guerra de España contra los Estados Unidos. El Morro se utilizó estratégicamente y por última vez como puesto de observación durante la Segunda Guerra Mundial.

❻ Listas para el festival Puerto Ricans celebrate many national festivals and traditional holidays. Among them are the **Parrandas**, or Christmas carols, **Carnaval**, which is especially popular in Arecibo, and the **Fiesta de las Máscaras**, which takes place every year on December 28th in Hatillo.

❻ Listas para el festival
Casi cada día festivo es una ocasión para tener una celebración en Puerto Rico.

Cultures and Communities

Culture Note
Puerto Rico is known for **la música salsa** which is derived from the **rumba,** a dance music of Afro-Cuban origin. The instruments normally used for **salsa** are the piano, trumpet, saxophone, and percussion instruments like the conga drums and the **güiro,** first used by the indigenous Taíno people. The lyrics of **salsa** often combine poetry and politics. **Salsa** was introduced in the 1930s in the dance halls of New York City, where it became very popular. Since then, legendary **salseros** Willie Colón, Celia Cruz, Rubén Blades, Hector Lavoe and Tito Puente have popularized **salsa** throughout the Spanish-speaking world and beyond.

Capítulo 11: Para vivir bien
Chapter Overview

De antemano pp. 328–330	*Un recorrido por San Juan*

	FUNCTIONS	GRAMMAR	VOCABULARY	RE-ENTRY
Primer paso pp. 331–333	• Making suggestions and expressing feelings, p. 331	• Present tense of the verb **sentirse**, p. 331	• Keeping fit, p. 332	• **e** to **ie** stem-changing verbs (**Capítulo 7**) • Food vocabulary (**Capítulo 8**) • Expressions of frequency (**Capítulo 5**)
Segundo paso pp. 334–339	• Talking about moods and physical condition, p. 334	• The verb **doler** with **me**, **te**, **le**, p. 336	• Physical conditions, p. 334 • Parts of the body, p. 335	• Definite articles (**Capítulo 1, Capítulo 3**) • **estar** (**Capítulo 8**) • **o** to **ue** stem-changing verbs (**Capítulo 8**)
Tercer paso pp. 340–345	• Saying what you did, p. 340 • Talking about where you went and when, p. 342	• The verb **jugar** in the preterite, p. 340 • The verb **ir** in the preterite, p. 342	• Expressions for the past, p. 342 • Different sports fields, p. 343	• Use of preterite tense to discuss past events (**Capítulo 10**) • Sports (**Capítulo 3**)

Letra y sonido p. 344	**Strong vowels and weak vowels** Audio CD 11, Track 11	**Dictado** Audio CD 11, Tracks 12–14

Vamos a leer pp. 346–347	**Para estar en forma**	**Reading Strategy:** Using background knowledge

Más práctica gramatical	**pp. 348–351**		
	Primer paso, pp. 348–349	**Segundo paso**, p. 349	**Tercer paso**, pp. 350–351

Review pp. 352–355	**Repaso**, pp. 352–353 **Vamos a escribir**, p. 353 Using dialogue	**A ver si puedo...**, p. 354	**Vocabulario**, p. 355

CULTURE

- **A lo nuestro**, Body parts in expressions, p. 335
- **Realia, 7 claves para manejar el estrés**, p. 337
- **Nota cultural**, Hispanic athletes in U.S. athletic teams, p. 338
- **Panorama cultural, ¿Qué deporte practicas?**, p. 339
- **Nota cultural**, Common sports in Spanish-speaking countries, p. 341
- **Encuentro cultural, Remedios caseros**, p. 345

Capítulo 11: Para vivir bien
Chapter Resources

 **PRINT**

Lesson Planning

One-Stop Planner

Lesson Planner with Substitute Teacher Lesson Plans, pp. 53–57, 75

Student Make-Up Assignments
- Make-Up Assignment Copying Masters, Chapter 11

Listening and Speaking

TPR Storytelling Book, pp. 41–44

Listening Activities
- Student Response Forms for Listening Activities, pp. 83–85
- Additional Listening Activities 11-1 to 11-6, pp. 87–89
- Additional Listening Activities (song), p. 90
- Scripts and Answers, pp. 152–156

Video Guide
- Teaching Suggestions, pp. 75–77
- Activity Masters, pp. 78–80
- Scripts and Answers, pp. 108–111, 118

Activities for Communication
- Communicative Activities, pp. 61–66
- Realia and Teaching Suggestions, pp. 125–129
- Situation Cards, pp. 157–158

Reading and Writing

Reading Strategies and Skills Handbook, Chapter 11

¡Lee conmigo! 1, Chapter 11

Cuaderno de actividades, pp. 121–132

Grammar

Cuaderno de gramática, pp. 89–96

Grammar Tutor for Students of Spanish, Chapter 11

Assessment

Testing Program
- Grammar and Vocabulary Quizzes, **Paso** Quizzes, and Chapter Test, pp. 275–292
- Score Sheet, Scripts, and Answers, pp. 293–300

Alternative Assessment Guide
- Portfolio Assessment, p. 28
- Performance Assessment, p. 42
- CD-ROM Assessment, p. 56

Student Make-Up Assignments
- Alternative Quizzes, Chapter 11

Standardized Assessment Tutor
- Reading, pp. 43–45
- Writing, p. 46
- Math, pp. 51–52

Native Speakers

Cuaderno para hispanohablantes, pp. 51–55

 **MEDIA**

 Online Activities
- Juegos interactivos
- Actividades Internet

 Video Program
- Videocassette 4
- Videocassette 5 (captioned version)

 Interactive CD-ROM Tutor, Disc 3

DVD Tutor, Disc 2

 Audio Compact Discs
- Textbook Listening Activities, CD 11, Tracks 1–16
- Additional Listening Activities, CD 11, Tracks 22–28
- Assessment Items, CD 11, Tracks 17–21

 Teaching Transparencies
- Situations 11-1 to 11-3
- Vocabulary 11-A to 11-D
- De antemano
- Más práctica gramatical Answers
- Cuaderno de gramática Answers

 One-Stop Planner CD-ROM

Use the **One-Stop Planner CD-ROM with Test Generator** to aid in lesson planning and pacing.

For each chapter, the **One-Stop Planner** includes:
- Editable lesson plans with direct links to teaching resources
- Printable worksheets from resource books
- Direct launches to the HRW Internet activities
- Video and audio segments
- Test Generator
- Clip Art for vocabulary items

Capítulo 11: Para vivir bien

Projects

Refranes interpretados

In this activity, groups of students will translate a Spanish **refrán** *(proverb) and make a poster to illustrate it.*

> **MATERIALS**
>
> ✂ **Students may need**
> - Poster board
> - Pens and markers
> - Magazines
> - Scissors
> - Glue
> - Bilingual dictionary

REFRANES

(Give students only the Spanish proverbs, not the English.)

Más vale pájaro en mano que cien volando. A bird in the hand is worth two in the bush.

Hijo no tenemos y nombre le ponemos. Don't count your chickens before they're hatched.

El hábito no hace al monje. Clothes don't make the man.

Ojos que no ven, corazón que no siente. Out of sight, out of mind.

Cara vemos, corazón no sabemos. You can't judge a book by its cover.

Donde una puerta se cierra, otra se abre. Every cloud has a silver lining.

En boca cerrada no entran moscas. Silence is golden.

Dime con quién andas y te diré quién eres. Birds of a feather flock together.

SUGGESTED SEQUENCE

1. Assign one **refrán** to each group. Have students look up the words and write a literal translation. They then add an English proverb with the same meaning to their translation.

2. Students make a poster in which they write and illustrate the **refrán,** and then present their posters to the class.

GRADING THE PROJECT

The same grade should be given to all members of each group.

Suggested point distribution: (total = 100 points)
Literal translation (accuracy)	30
Equivalent English proverb	20
Poster (content, design)	20
Oral presentation (grammar, vocabulary)	30

Games

Béisbol con las palabras

With this game students will practice the new chapter vocabulary words and expressions and review previously learned vocabulary. It may be played at the end of the chapter.

Preparation Develop a list of questions whose answers require the students to use words and phrases from this and previous chapters. (Examples: **Para evitar el estrés yo practico _____. Para tener músculos grandes hay que levantar _____. Debes dormir para no estar _____. Antes de hacer ejercicio hay que _____.**)

Procedure Divide the class into two teams. Assign a student scorekeeper. Draw a baseball diamond with bases on the board. Set a number of innings for playing.

The batter is the first player on Team A. You serve as the pitcher and ask the batter a question. If the batter gives a correct answer, he or she moves to first base. The scorekeeper places a mark on first base. If the batter cannot answer, he or she is out. You then ask a question of the second batter on Team A. If the second batter answers correctly, he or she goes to first base. If there is a player on first base, he or she advances to second base and the scorekeeper places a mark on second base.

A team scores a run by advancing a player to home plate. Team A continues batting until it has three outs. Then Team B goes to bat. When Team B has three outs, the first inning is over. Teams get one point for each run, and the team with the most points wins.

> **FAMILY LINK**
>
> **If students are not familiar with an English proverb that has the same meaning as the refrán assigned to their group, they might ask their parents or grandparents if they know one.**

Storytelling

Mini-cuento

This story accompanies Teaching Transparency 11-2. The mini-cuento can be told and retold in different formats, acted out, written as dictation, and read aloud to give students additional opportunities to practice all four skills. The following story tells what happened to the people who are waiting in a clinic to see the doctor.

Hoy todo el mundo está enfermo. La Sra. Muñoz llevó a su hijo Luisito porque tiene mucha tos. José acompañó a su hermana Graciela porque ella no se siente bien. Ella está resfriada y le duelen la garganta y la cabeza. La semana pasada Lolita jugó al fútbol y se lastimó la pierna. Por eso, hoy tiene una cita con la doctora Arroyo. El Sr. Abundi es una persona muy ocupada; no le gusta esperar y tiene mucho estrés. Él tiene una cita con el doctor Rojas pero el doctor todavía no llega. El Sr. Abundi está preocupado porque no quiere llegar tarde a su trabajo. ¿Qué le pasa a Nara? Ella tiene gripe y un poco de fiebre. Su papá está muy triste porque ella está enferma. Manuel no se siente bien y le duele el estómago. Él fue a visitar a la doctora Fuentes y ahora tiene que pagar por la consulta.

¡Qué día más ocupado para los doctores!

Traditions

Festivales

New Year's Eve and Day are important holidays for families in Puerto Rico. Some people spend December 31 cleaning the house and yard in preparation for the coming year. If all is in order as the new year begins, one hopes that things will stay that way for the next 12 months. At midnight on New Year's Eve, Puerto Ricans traditionally practice the Spanish custom of eating 12 grapes, one with each stroke of the clock, to bring them good luck. Have students research New Year's celebrations around the world and compare the traditions with their own.

Receta

Flan has become an international dessert. It is a custard-like dish with many regional variations. Puerto Rican flans include cream cheese, coconut, pineapple, pumpkin, or a combination of these ingredients.

FLAN DE COCO
para 4–6 personas

3 cucharadas de azúcar
  (para el caramelo)

2 cucharadas de agua
  (para el caramelo)

1 taza de leche condensada

1 taza de leche evaporada

1 taza de crema de coco

3 huevos

1 cucharadita de vainilla

Para preparar el caramelo, caliente el azúcar y el agua en una sartén a fuego moderado. Revuelva el azúcar hasta que se derrita y quede de un color dorado claro. Inmediatamente vierta el caramelo en un molde hasta que cubra el fondo y los lados. En una licuadora mezcle los demás ingredientes. Vierta la mezcla en el molde y colóquelo al baño María (un recipiente con agua). Cocine el flan a 350° por 45 minutos o hasta que se pueda insertar un palillo y éste salga limpio. Déjelo enfriar a temperatura ambiente antes de meterlo al refrigerador.

Capítulo 11: Para vivir bien
Technology

Videocassette 4, Videocassette 5 (captioned version)
DVD Tutor, Disc 2
See Video Guide, pages 75–80.

DVD/Video

De antemano • Un recorrido por San Juan

Ben, Carmen, and their mother are visiting family in Puerto Rico. Ben and Carmen go sightseeing, but they need to meet their mother at 3:00. In a park they meet Pedro, who takes them on a tour of the city. Later, Ben realizes that it is 2:55, and they must hurry.

A continuación

Ben, Carmen, and Pedro hurry to **la Plaza de Hostos** and make it in time to meet their mother. Ben and Carmen introduce Pedro to their mother, who realizes that Pedro is actually Ben and Carmen's cousin. Later that day they all go to watch Pedro, Ben, and Carmen's uncle play baseball.

¿Qué deporte practicas?

Teens from Mexico, Spain, and Florida tell what sports they like to play and why. In other interviews, people from various countries talk about their favorite sports.

Videoclips

• **Happydent®**: advertisement for sugarless chewing gum

Interactive CD-ROM Tutor

Activity	Activity Type	Pupil's Edition Page
En contexto	*Interactive conversation*	
1. Gramática	¿Qué falta?	p. 331
2. Vocabulario	¿Cuál es?	p. 332
3. Vocabulario	¡Super memoria!	p. 334
4. Vocabulario	Imagen y sonido ¡Exploremos! ¡Identifiquemos! *Interactive image*	p. 335
5. Así se dice	¡A escoger!	p. 340
6. Gramática	¿Qué falta?	p. 340
Panorama cultural	¿Qué deporte practicas? ¡A escoger!	p. 339
¡A hablar!	*Guided recording*	pp. 352–353
¡A escribir!	*Guided writing*	pp. 352–353

Teacher Management System

Launch the program, type "admin" in the password area, and press RETURN. Log on to **www.hrw.com/CDROMTUTOR** for a detailed explanation of the Teacher Management System.

DVD Tutor

The *DVD Tutor* contains all material from the *Video Program* as described above. Spanish captions are available for use at your discretion for all sections of the video. The *DVD Tutor* also provides a variety of video-based activities that assess students' understanding of the **De antemano, A continuación,** and **Panorama cultural.**

This part of the *DVD Tutor* may be used on any DVD video player connected to a television or video monitor.

In addition to the video material and the video-based comprehension activities, the *DVD Tutor* also contains the entire *Interactive CD-ROM Tutor* in DVD-ROM format. Each DVD disc contains the activities from all 12 chapters of the *Interactive CD-ROM Tutor.*

This part of the *DVD Tutor* may be used on a Macintosh® or Windows® computer with a DVD-ROM drive.

One-Stop Planner CD-ROM

To preview all resources available for this chapter, use the **One-Stop Planner CD-ROM**, Disc 3.

Internet Connection

MARCAR: go.hrw.com
PALABRA CLAVE:
WV3 PUERTO RICO-11

*Have students explore the **go.hrw.com** Web site for many online resources covering all chapters. All Chapter 11 resources are available under the keyword WV3 PUERTO RICO-11. Interactive games help students practice the material and provide them with immediate feedback. You will also find a printable worksheet that provides Internet activities that lead to a comprehensive online research project.*

Juegos interactivos

You can use the interactive games in this chapter

- to practice grammar, vocabulary, and chapter functions
- as homework
- as an assessment option
- as a self-test
- to prepare for the Chapter Test

Actividades Internet

Students research nutrition and healthy living habits on the Internet. They determine which parts of the body benefit most from the various good foods and exercise routines.

- As preparation for the **Hoja de actividades,** have students review the *Cuaderno de gramática* for the **Segundo paso.** You may also want to have them view the dramatic episode on Videocassette 4.

- After students complete the activity sheet, have them compare wellness plans with a partner. Ask pairs to think critically about which foods and exercises may or may not be good for people with special needs or other health issues.

Proyecto

Have students create a Web site devoted to healthy living. Have them give recommendations on their site about what foods to eat and what exercises and activities are best for different types of people. Have them suggest, if they can, activities that are designed to have specific outcomes: giving people more energy, relieving stress, or building strength, for example.

Primer paso

6 p. 331

1. No sé qué me pasa. Siempre me siento muy cansada. ¿Qué hago?

2. Bueno, me gusta mucho mirar la televisión. No hago mucho ejercicio pero quiero empezar a hacerlo.

3. No me gusta para nada la leche. Prefiero tomar refrescos.

4. Yo trabajo día y noche. Siempre estoy aquí en la oficina.

5. Me encanta comer pizza, hamburguesas y papas fritas.

6. No me siento bien porque casi siempre estoy en casa. Debo salir más.

Answers to Activity 6
Sample answer: 1. Natalia

Segundo paso

13 p. 334

1. ¡Uy! ¡Me siento muy mal! Tengo una fiebre de 102 grados.

2. ¡Hombre! No sé qué hacer. Hoy tengo un examen muy difícil en la clase de álgebra.

3. Esta noche voy a cantar por primera vez en un concierto y no estoy preparado.

4. ¡Qué lástima! No puedo pasar las vacaciones con mi tía en Puerto Rico.

5. Ay, mi hermanita es terrible. Siempre quiere llevar mis camisas y mis suéteres.

6. Aquí estoy en el restaurante con mi novia. No tengo el dinero para pagar la cena. ¿Qué voy a hacer?

7. No me siento bien. No puedo asistir a clases hoy.

8. Todo el mundo está enfermo. Yo también.

Answers to Activity 13
1. 6
2. 2, 5
3. 2, 5
4. 4
5. 3
6. 2, 5
7. 1, 6, 7, 8
8. 1, 6, 7, 8

17 p. 336

1. —¿Qué te pasa, Gregorio?
   —No puedo más. ¡Treinta kilómetros en bicicleta ya es suficiente!

2. —Flor, ¿no vas a terminar la tarea?
   —Lo siento, profesora, pero no puedo escribir más.

3. —¿Qué pasa, Félix, te sientes mal?
   —¡Ay! Tomé dos batidos y cuatro hamburguesas.

4. —¿No vas al gimnasio hoy, Betty?
   —No. Normalmente levanto pesas todos los días, pero hoy no puedo.

5. —¿Qué síntomas tiene, señorita?
   —Estoy resfriada, doctor, y no puedo hablar.

6. —¿Por qué estás sentado allí?
   —No puedo correr más. Mis nuevas zapatillas no me quedan bien. Son horribles.

7. —¿Quieres ir al cine con nosotros?
   —No, pasé cinco horas en la biblioteca hoy.

Answers to Activity 17
1. d
2. e
3. g
4. a
5. f
6. c
7. b

To preview all resources available for this chapter, use the **One-Stop Planner CD-ROM**, Disc 3.

Tercer paso

33 p. 343

1. Ricardo y Miguel fueron al estadio a desayunar.
2. Angélica y Marta fueron a la cancha de tenis a bailar con Roberto y Sergio.
3. Gabriel fue a la piscina a nadar.
4. Yo fui a la pista de correr a hacer yoga.
5. María y Pablo fueron a la biblioteca a escuchar el concierto.
6. Mi hermano fue al gimnasio a levantar pesas.
7. Mis padres fueron al estadio a ver un partido de fútbol.
8. Mis hermanos y yo fuimos al cine a jugar al basquetbol con nuestros primos.

Answers to Activity 33
1. no; Fueron al estadio a ver un partido de béisbol.
2. no; Fueron a la cancha de tenis a jugar al tenis con Roberto y Sergio.
3. sí
4. no; Fui a la pista de correr a hacer ejercicio.
5. no; Fueron a la biblioteca a leer.
6. sí
7. sí
8. no; Fuimos al cine y vimos una película muy buena.

LETRA Y SONIDO, P. 344

For the scripts for Parts A and C, see p. 304.
The script for Part B is below.

B. Dictado

Mi horario no es fácil. Estudio geometría, historia y física. Me gusta estudiar por la tarde y ver televisión por la noche.

Repaso

4 p. 353

RAFI   Ay, Sara. Estoy muy triste. El lunes regresamos a casa y yo quiero quedarme en Puerto Rico.

SARA   Yo también, Rafi. Pero estoy muy contenta porque pasamos unas vacaciones maravillosas con nuestra familia. Visitamos muchos lugares en Puerto Rico.

RAFI   Me gustaría regresar a El Yunque. ¡Qué interesante! Y ¡qué hermoso! Las flores, los pájaros, todo.

SARA   También me gustó mucho El Yunque. Pero a mí me gusta más pasar todo el día en la playa, como la semana pasada. Nadamos, llevamos comida, jugamos al voleibol y cantamos. Ay, qué bien lo pasé.

RAFI   Me gustó mucho el museo y también me gustaron los cuentos del abuelo.

SARA   Sí, éstas fueron unas vacaciones maravillosas.

Answers to Repaso Activity 4
1. Rafi está muy triste.
2. Sara está triste pero también contenta.
3. Rafi quiere regresar a El Yunque. Sara quiere pasar el día en la playa.
4. A Sara le gustaron El Yunque y la playa.
5. A Rafi le gustó el museo y también le gustaron los cuentos del abuelo.

Capítulo 11: Para vivir bien
Suggested Lesson Plans 50-Minute Schedule

Day 1

CHAPTER OPENER 5 min.
- Focusing on Outcomes, ATE, p. 327
- Thinking Critically, ATE, p. 326

DE ANTEMANO 40 min.
- Presenting **De antemano** and Preteaching Vocabulary, ATE, p. 328
- Present Background Information, ATE, p. 329
- Activities 1–5, p. 330, and Comprehension Check, ATE, p. 330
- Present the Biology Link and Language Note, ATE, p. 330.

Wrap-Up 5 min.
- Discuss the questions from Activity 5, p. 330.

Homework Options
Cuaderno de actividades, p. 121, Activities 1–2

Day 2

PRIMER PASO
Quick Review 5 min.
- Check homework.
- Bell Work, ATE, p. 331

Así se dice/Nota gramatical, p. 331 25 min.
- Presenting **Así se dice** and **Nota gramatical**, ATE, p. 331
- **Más práctica gramatical**, p. 348, Activity 1
- Do Activity 6, p. 331, with the Audio CD.
- Do Activity 7, p. 332, orally with the class.

Vocabulario, p. 332 15 min.
- Presenting **Vocabulario**, ATE, p. 332
- Present the Language Notes, ATE, p. 332.
- Do Activity 9, p. 332, with the class.
- Have students do Activity 8, p. 332, and the Additional Practice, ATE, p. 333.

Wrap-Up 5 min.
- Ask students what the people in Transparency 11-A are doing and how they feel in different situations.

Homework Options
Cuaderno de actividades, pp. 122–123, Activities 3–5
Cuaderno de gramática, pp. 89–90, Activities 1–4

Day 3

PRIMER PASO
Quick Review 5 min.
- Check homework.

Vocabulario, p. 332 40 min.
- Do Activities 2 and 3, p. 348, in **Más práctica gramatical**.
- Have students do Activity 10, p. 333, individually, then do Activity 11, p. 333, in groups. Call on groups to share their suggestions with the class.
- Have students do Activity 12, p. 333, then exchange papers for peer editing. Ask volunteers to share their papers with the class.
- Have students do Communicative Activity 11-1, pp. 61–62, in Activities for Communication.

Wrap-Up 5 min.
- Have students ask partners if they would like to do one of the activities from **Vocabulario**, p. 332. Partners respond with one of the expressions from **Así se dice**, p. 331.
- Discuss the content and format for Quiz 11-1.

Homework Options
Study for Quiz 11-1.
Cuaderno de actividades, p. 124, Activity 6

Day 4

PRIMER PASO
Quick Review 5 min.
- Check homework.
- Quickly review the content of the **Primer paso**.

Quiz 20 min.
- Administer Quiz 11-1A, 11-1B, or a combination of the two.

SEGUNDO PASO
Así se dice/Vocabulario, p. 334 20 min.
- Presenting **Así se dice** and **Vocabulario**, ATE, p. 334
- Present **También se puede decir...**, p. 334.
- Do Activity 13, p. 334, with the Audio CD.
- Do Activity 14, p. 335.

Wrap-Up 5 min.
- Act out the conditions from **Vocabulario**, p. 334, and have students tell how you feel.

Homework Options
Cuaderno de actividades, pp. 125–126, Activities 7–8
Cuaderno de gramática, pp. 91–92, Activities 5–7

Day 5

SEGUNDO PASO
Quick Review 5 min.
- Check homework.
- Ask students what is wrong with the people in Teaching Transparency 11-B.

Vocabulario, p. 335 25 min.
- Presenting **Vocabulario**, ATE, p. 335
- Present Language-to-Language and Language Note, ATE, p. 335.
- Present **A lo nuestro**, p. 335, and practice expressions with students.
- Have students do Activities 15 and 16, p. 335, in groups.

Nota gramatical, p. 336 15 min.
- Presenting **Nota gramatical**, ATE, p. 336
- Do Activity 17, p. 336, with the Audio CD.
- Do Activity 18, p. 336.

Wrap-Up 5 min.
- Indicate a body part and have students say that it is hurting them.

Homework Options
Cuaderno de actividades, pp. 126–127, Activities 9–10
Cuaderno de gramática, pp. 92–93, Activities 8–11
Más práctica gramatical, p. 349, Activities 4–5

Day 6

SEGUNDO PASO
Quick Review 5 min.
- Check homework.

Nota gramatical, p. 336 40 min.
- Have students do Activities 19 and 20, pp. 336–337, in pairs.
- Have students do Activities 21 and 22, p. 337. Call on volunteers to share their answers with the class.
- Read and discuss the **Nota cultural**, p. 338.
- Have students do Activity 23, p. 338, in pairs and Activity 24, p. 338, in groups.
- Have students work with a partner to prepare the dialogue for the Performance Assessment, p. 42, in the Alternative Assessment Guide.

Wrap-Up 5 min.
- List the health conditions of several imaginary people and have students describe how they feel.

Homework Options
Have students finish writing their dialogues for the Performance Assessment.
Assign Activity 25, p. 338, as homework.

One-Stop Planner CD-ROM

For alternative lesson plans by chapter section, to create your own customized plans, or to preview all resources available for this chapter, use the **One-Stop Planner CD-ROM**, Disc 3.

 For additional homework suggestions, see activities accompanied by this symbol throughout the chapter.

Day 7

SEGUNDO PASO
Quick Review 10 min.
- Check the writing assignment from Activity 25, p. 338, for completion.
- Allow students to rehearse their dialogues for the Performance Assessment.

Así se dice/Vocabulario/Nota gramatical, pp. 334, 336 30 min.
- Have students perform their dialogues for the Performance Assessment, p. 42, in the Alternative Assessment Guide. You may wish to grade both the written dialogues and oral presentations using the Writing and Speaking Rubrics on pages 3–9 in the Alternative Assessment Guide.

Wrap-Up 10 min.
- Have students tell how the people in Teaching Transparency 11-2 are feeling and what hurts them.
- Discuss the format and content of Quiz 11-2.

Homework Options
Study for Quiz 11-2.

Day 8

SEGUNDO PASO
Quick Review 5 min.
- Review the contents of the **Segundo paso**.

PANORAMA CULTURAL 10 min.
- Presenting **Panorama cultural**, ATE, p. 339

Quiz 20 min.
- Administer Quiz 11-2A, 11-2B, or a combination of the two.

TERCER PASO
Así se dice/Nota gramatical, p. 340 10 min.
- Presenting **Así se dice** and **Nota gramatical**, ATE, p. 340

Wrap-Up 5 min.
- Mime a sport and have students respond that different people in the class played that sport yesterday.

Homework Options
Cuaderno de gramática, p. 94, Activities 12–13
Cuaderno de actividades, p. 128, Activity 11
Más práctica gramatical, p. 350, Activity 6

Day 9

TERCER PASO
Quick Review 5 min.
- Check homework.
- Have students write Activity 26, p. 340. Check.

Así se dice/Nota gramatical, p. 340 20 min.
- Have students do Activity 27, p. 340, in pairs and Activity 28, p. 341, in groups.
- Read and discuss the **Nota cultural**, p. 341, and the Culture Note, ATE, p. 341.
- Have students do Activity 29, p. 341, individually, then do Activity 30, p. 341, in pairs.

Así se dice/Nota gramatical, p. 342 20 min.
- Presenting **Así se dice** and **Nota gramatical**, ATE, p. 342
- Do Activity 31, p. 342.
- Have students do Activity 32, p. 343, in groups. Call on groups to report to the class.

Wrap-Up 5 min.
- Use the preterite of **ir** to review names of stores from p. 217.

Homework Options
Más práctica gramatical, p. 350, Activity 7
Cuaderno de actividades, p. 129, Activity 12
Cuaderno de gramática, p. 95, Activities 14–16

Day 10

TERCER PASO
Quick Review 5 min.
- Check homework.
- Ask students where they went yesterday.

Vocabulario, p. 343 20 min.
- Presenting **Vocabulario**, ATE, p. 343
- Do Activity 33, p. 343, with the Audio CD.
- Do Activity 34, p. 343, following the Game suggestion, ATE, p. 343.
- Have students do Activity 35, p. 344.

Letra y sonido, p. 344 10 min.
- Present **Letra y sonido**, p. 344, using the Audio CD.

ENCUENTRO CULTURAL 10 min.
- Presenting **Encuentro cultural**, ATE, p. 345
- Do the Thinking Critically activity, ATE, p. 345.

Wrap-Up 5 min.
- Ask where people went and what they played in Teaching Transparency 11-3
- Discuss the content and format of Quiz 11-3.

Homework Options
Cuaderno de actividades, p. 130, Activities 13–14
Cuaderno de gramática, p. 96, Activities 17–18
Más práctica gramatical, p. 351, Activities 8–9

Day 11

TERCER PASO
Quick Review 5 min.
- Check homework.
- Quickly review the content of the **Tercer paso**.

Quiz 20 min.
- Administer Quiz 11-3A, 11-3B, or a combination of the two.

VAMOS A LEER 20 min.
- Have students read the **Estrategia para leer**, p. 346, and do Activity A, p. 346.
- Have students do Activities B, C, and D, pp. 346–347.

Wrap-Up 5 min.
- Ask students what kind of background knowledge was necessary to understand the reading.
- Do the Visual/Auditory Learners activity, ATE, p. 347.

Homework Options
Assign Activities 2, 3, and 5 of the Repaso, pp. 352–353, as homework.
Cuaderno de actividades, pp. 131–132, Activities 15–17
A ver si puedo..., p. 354

Day 12

REPASO
Quick Review 5 min.
- Check homework. Check Activity 5, p. 353, for completion.

Chapter Review 40 min.
- Review Chapter 11. Choose from **Más práctica gramatical**, Grammar Tutor for Students of Spanish, Activities for Communication, Listening Activities, Interactive CD-ROM Tutor, or **Juegos interactivos**.

Wrap-Up 5 min.
- Discuss the format of the Chapter 11 Test.

Homework Options
Study for the Chapter 11 test.

Assessment

Quick Review 5 min.
- Answer any last-minute questions.

Test, Chapter 11 45 min.
- Administer Chapter 11 Test. Select from Testing Program, Alternative Assessment Guide, Test Generator, or Standardized Assessment Tutor.

Capítulo 11: Para vivir bien
Suggested Lesson Plans *90-Minute Block Schedule*

Block 1

CHAPTER OPENER 5 min.
- Focusing on Outcomes, ATE, p. 327
- Thinking Critically, ATE, pp. 326–327

DE ANTEMANO 40 min.
- Presenting **De antemano** and Preteaching Vocabulary, ATE, p. 328
- Present Background Information, ATE, p. 329
- Activities 1–5 p. 330, and Comprehension Check, ATE, p. 330
- Present the Biology Link and Language Note, ATE, p. 330.

Así se dice/Nota gramatical, p. 331 25 min.
- Presenting **Así se dice** and **Nota gramatical**, ATE, p. 331
- **Más práctica gramatical**, p. 348, Activity 1
- Do Activity 6, p. 331, with the Audio CD.
- Do Activity 7, p. 332, orally with the class.

Vocabulario, p. 332 15 min.
- Presenting **Vocabulario**, ATE, p. 332
- Present the Language Notes, ATE, p. 332.
- Do Activity 9, p. 332, with the class.
- Have students do Activity 8, p. 332, in pairs.

Wrap-Up 5 min.
- Ask students what the people in Transparency 11-A are doing. Then ask students how they or the people in the transparency feel in different situations.

Homework Options
Cuaderno de actividades, pp. 121–123, Activities 1–5
Cuaderno de gramática, pp. 89–90, Activities 1–4

Block 2

PRIMER PASO
Quick Review 10 min.
- Check homework.
- Mime an activity from **Vocabulario**, p. 332. Have students name the activity, then have them imagine they just finished the activity and say how they feel.

Vocabulario, p. 332 30 min.
- Do Activities 2 and 3, p. 348, in **Más practica gramatical**.
- Have students do Activity 10, p. 333, individually, then do Activity 11, p. 333, in groups. Call on groups to share their suggestions with the class.
- Have students do Activity 12, p. 333, then exchange papers for peer editing. Call on a few volunteers to share their papers with the class.

SEGUNDO PASO
Así se dice/Vocabulario, p. 334 20 min.
- Presenting **Así se dice** and **Vocabulario**, ATE, p. 334
- Present **También se puede decir...**, p. 334.
- Do Activity 13, p. 334, with the Audio CD.
- Do Activity 14, p. 335.

Vocabulario, p. 335 25 min.
- Presenting **Vocabulario**, ATE, p. 335
- Present Language-to-Language and Language Note, ATE, p. 335.
- Present **A lo nuestro**, p. 335, and practice expressions with students.
- Have students do Activities 15 and 16, p. 335, in groups.

Wrap-Up 5 min.
- Act out the conditions from **Vocabulario**, p. 334, and have students tell how you feel.
- Discuss the content and format for Quiz 11-1.

Homework Options
Study for Quiz 11-1.
Cuaderno de actividades, pp. 124–126, Activities 6–9
Cuaderno de gramática, pp. 91–92, Activities 5–9

Block 3

PRIMER PASO
Quick Review 10 min.
- Check homework.
- Quickly review the content of the **Primer paso**, using Teaching Transparency 11-1.

Quiz 20 min.
- Administer Quiz 11-1A, 11-1B, or a combination of the two.

SEGUNDO PASO
Nota gramatical, p. 336 55 min.
- Play **Simón dice** to review body parts.
- Presenting **Nota gramatical**, ATE, p. 336
- Do Activity 17, p. 336, with the Audio CD.
- Do Activity 18, p. 336.
- Have students do Activities 19 and 20, pp. 336–337, in pairs.
- Have students do Activities 21 and 22, p. 337. Call on volunteers to share their answers with the class.
- Read and discuss the **Nota cultural**, p. 338.
- Have students do Activity 23, p. 338, in pairs and Activity 24, p. 338, in groups.
- Have students work with a partner to prepare the dialogue for the Performance Assessment, p. 42, in the Alternative Assessment Guide.

Wrap-Up 5 min.
- Do Activity 25, p. 338, as a whole class activity.

Homework Options
Have students finish writing their dialogues for the Performance Assessment.
Más práctica gramatical, p. 349, Activities 4–5
Cuaderno de gramática, p. 93, Activities 10–11
Cuaderno de actividades, p. 127, Activity 10

One-Stop Planner CD-ROM

For alternative lesson plans by chapter section, to create your own customized plans, or to preview all resources available for this chapter, use the **One-Stop Planner CD-ROM**, Disc 3.

For additional homework suggestions, see activities accompanied by this symbol throughout the chapter.

Block 4

SEGUNDO PASO

Quick Review 10 min.
- Check homework.
- Allow students to rehearse their dialogues for the Performance Assessment.

Así se dice/Vocabulario/Nota gramatical, pp. 334, 336 30 min.
- Have students perform their dialogues for the Performance Assessment, p. 42, in the Alternative Assessment Guide. You may wish to grade both the written dialogues and oral presentations using the Writing and Speaking Rubrics on pages 3–9 in the Alternative Assessment Guides.

PANORAMA CULTURAL 10 min.
- Presenting **Panorama cultural**, ATE, p. 339

TERCER PASO

Así se dice/Nota gramatical, p. 340 30 min.
- Presenting **Así se dice** and **Nota gramatical**, ATE, p. 340
- Have students write Activity 26, p. 340. Check.
- Have students do Activity 27, p. 340, in pairs and Activity 28, p. 341, in groups.
- Read and discuss the **Nota cultural**, p. 341, and the Culture Note, ATE, p. 341.
- Have students do Activity 29, p. 341, individually, then do Activity 30, p. 341, in pairs.

Wrap-Up 10 min.
- Tell students to imagine that the activities pictured in Teaching Transparency 11-3 happened yesterday. Ask them what sport the people played and how they feel today as a result.
- Discuss the format and content of Quiz 11-2.

Homework Options
Study for Quiz 11-2.
Más práctica gramatical, p. 350, Activity 6
Cuaderno de actividades, p. 128, Activity 11
Cuaderno de gramática, p. 94, Activities 12–13

Block 5

SEGUNDO PASO

Quick Review 5 min.
- Check homework.
- Quickly review the content of the **Segundo paso**.

Quiz 20 min.
- Administer Quiz 11-2A, 11-2B, or a combination of the two.

TERCER PASO

Así se dice/Nota gramatical, p. 342 20 min.
- Presenting **Así se dice** and **Nota gramatical**, ATE, p. 342
- Do Activity 31, p. 342.
- Have students do Activity 32, p. 343, in groups. Call on groups to report their activities to the class.

Vocabulario, p. 343 20 min.
- Presenting **Vocabulario**, ATE, p. 343
- Do Activity 33, p. 343, with the Audio CD.
- Do Activity 34, p. 343, following the Game suggestion, ATE, p. 343.
- Have students do Activity 35, p. 344.

Letra y sonido, p. 344 10 min.
- Present **Letra y sonido**, p. 344, using the Audio CD.

ENCUENTRO CULTURAL 10 min.
- Presenting **Encuentro cultural**, ATE, p. 345
- Discuss the Thinking Critically activity, ATE, p. 345.

Wrap-Up 5 min.
- Ask students where the people went in Teaching Transparency 11-3 and what sport they played there.
- Discuss the content and format of Quiz 11-3.

Homework Options
Study for Quiz 11-3.
Cuaderno de actividades, pp. 129–130, Activities 12–14.
Cuaderno de gramática, pp. 95–96, Activities 14–18
Más práctica gramatical, pp. 350–351, Activities 7–9

Block 6

TERCER PASO

Quick Review 10 min.
- Check homework.
- Review the content of the **Tercer paso**.

Quiz 20 min.
- Administer Quiz 11-3A, 11-3B, or a combination of the two.

VAMOS A LEER 20 min.
- Have students read the **Estrategia para leer**, p. 346, and do Activity A, p. 346.
- Have students do Activities B, C, and D, pp. 346–347.

REPASO 35 min.
- Have students do Activity 1, p. 352, in pairs.
- Have students do Activities 2 and 3, p. 352, individually. Check.
- Do Activity 4, p. 353, with the Audio CD.
- Have students do Activity 6, p. 353, in groups.
- Have students begin writing Activity 5, p. 353.

Wrap-Up 5 min.
- Discuss the format of the Chapter 11 test and provide sample questions.

Homework Options
Study for the Chapter 11 test.
Finish the writing assignment from Activity 6, p. 353.
A ver si puedo..., p. 354

Block 7

REPASO

Quick Review 10 min.
- Check homework. Check Activity 6, p. 353, for completion.

Chapter Review 35 min.
- Review Chapter 11. Choose from **Más práctica gramatical**, Grammar Tutor for Students of Spanish, Activities for Communication, Listening Activities, Interactive CD-ROM Tutor, or **Juegos interactivos**.

Test, Chapter 11 45 min.
- Administer Chapter 11 Test. Select from Testing Program, Alternative Assessment Guide, Test Generator, or Standardized Assessment Tutor.

Chapter Opener

One-Stop Planner CD-ROM

For resource information, see the **One-Stop Planner**, Disc 3.

Pacing Tips

The first two **Pasos** combine pronominal concepts with feelings and health themes. Make sure to take advantage of the opportunities for student interaction with regard to these themes, while still leaving time for the new preterite uses in the **Tercer Paso.** For more pacing tips, see pp. 325I–325L.

Meeting the Standards

Communication
- Making suggestions and expressing feelings, p. 331
- Talking about moods and physical condition, p. 334
- Saying what you did, p. 340
- Talking about where you went and when, p. 342

Cultures
- Culture Note, p. 327
- Nota cultural, p. 338
- Panorama cultural, p. 339
- Culture Note, p. 341
- Encuentro cultural, p. 345

Connections
- Health Link, p. 326
- Biology Link, p. 330
- Music Link, p. 344
- Science Link, p. 345
- Vamos a leer, p. 346

Comparisons
- Language-to-Language, p. 335
- A lo nuestro, p. 335
- Nota cultural, p. 341
- Sugerencia, p. 342

Communities
- Career Path, p. 336
- Native Speakers, p. 346

Connections and Comparisons

Health Link
Adequate exercise is important for good health. However, it is also vital that participants use safety equipment, warm-up before exercise, and stay well-hydrated. Point out to students that the young people in the picture are wearing helmets and pads. They are also taking a break to get a drink. Have students discuss the safety equipment and precautions they use for sports or exercise.

Thinking Critically
Analyzing Ask students to discuss the following questions. Do moods and feelings affect one physically? If so, how? Does a smile or a frown always mean the same thing? If not, what are possible reasons for differences?

CAPÍTULO 11
Para vivir bien

Objectives

In this chapter you will learn to

Primer paso

- make suggestions and express feelings

Segundo paso

- talk about moods and physical condition

Tercer paso

- say what you did
- talk about where you went and when

 internet

go.hrw.com
MARCAR: go.hrw.com
PALABRA CLAVE:
  WV3 PUERTO RICO-11

◀ Fuimos a patinar sobre ruedas y nos divertimos mucho.

Photo Flash!
In-line-skating (**patinar en línea**) is a very popular sport in Puerto Rico. Ice-skating (**patinar sobre hielo**) is also popular. San Juan has ice-skating and roller-skating rinks that are open until late at night.

Focusing on Outcomes
- Have students consider the photo and caption and imagine a possible conversation among the skaters. How might the objectives topics be represented in the conversation? Perhaps students can suggest other situations in which the same topics might be discussed.
- Ask students why it is important to describe moods, feelings, and physical conditions. How would they feel if they were unable to express such things?

Chapter Sequence

Cultures and Communities

Building on Previous Skills
Review the vocabulary for the different sports that the students have worked with in past chapters and the verbs **jugar, mirar, gustar,** and **encantar.** Have students interview a partner in Spanish, asking which sports they like to play and which ones they like to watch. Students should take notes (**tomar apuntes**) on what their partner says, so they can report the conversation to the class.

Culture Note
Puerto Rico has all types of water sports, golf, tennis, hiking, horse racing, basketball, and boxing. With the island's temperate climate, most sports can be enjoyed year-round. Other activities enjoyed by many Puerto Ricans are **jugar paleta** (*playing a type of sand-tennis*) and **escalar El Yunque** (*climbing the peaks of El Yunque*).

Teaching Resources
pp. 328–330

PRINT
▸ Lesson Planner, p. 52
▸ Video Guide, pp. 75–76, 78
▸ Cuaderno de actividades, p. 121

MEDIA
▸ One-Stop Planner
▸ Video Program
  De antemano
  Videocassette 4, 18:12–25:45
  Videocassette 5 (captioned version), 1:48:24–1:55:56
  A continuación
  Videocassette 4, 25:46–32:37
  Videocassette 5 (captioned version), 1:55:57–2:02:53
▸ DVD Tutor, Disc 2
▸ Audio Compact Discs, CD 11, Trs. 1–2
▸ **De antemano** Transparencies

Presenting
De antemano

From the questions in **Estrategia para comprender** and from visual clues in the **fotonovela,** have students predict what will happen in the scene. Then play the Audio CD. Have students form groups of four to practice reading the roles of the characters. Next, present the Preteaching Vocabulary to check for comprehension.

De antemano Transparencies

DE ANTEMANO · *Un recorrido por San Juan*

The **fotonovela** is an abridged version of the video episode.

CD 11 Trs. 1–2

> **Estrategia**
> **para comprender**
> Ben and Carmen have taken time to do some exploring in San Juan, Puerto Rico. Read the **fotonovela** to find out what they see and who they meet. Why might Ben and Carmen get into trouble at the end of the episode?

Benjamín   Carmen   Sra. Corredor   Pedro

1
Sra. Corredor: Bueno, hijos... a las tres paso por Uds. por la Plaza de Hostos. Y después, vamos al partido de béisbol de su tío. ¿De acuerdo?
Benjamín: Sí. Te esperamos en la Plaza de Hostos a las tres. ¡Adiós!

2
Carmen: Vamos, tenemos todo el día para explorar el Viejo San Juan. ¿Tienes ganas de caminar?

Dos horas más tarde...

3
Carmen: Ben, me duelen los pies... estoy cansada. ¿Podemos descansar? Caminamos mucho.
Benjamín: Claro, Carmen. A mí me duelen los pies. ¿Por qué no descansamos en esta banca?

4
Carmen: ¡Hola! ¿Eres de San Juan?
Pedro: Sí. Y ustedes no son de aquí, ¿verdad?
Carmen: ¡Somos de Nueva York!
Benjamín: Estamos en Puerto Rico de vacaciones. Estamos visitando a nuestra familia de aquí.
Pedro: Me llamo Pedro Méndez.
Benjamín: Yo soy Benjamín. Y ésta es mi hermana Carmen.

Preteaching Vocabulary

Activating Prior Knowledge
Point out that the setting for this **fotonovela** is exploring a city. What kinds of statements might the characters be making, or what kinds of questions might they be asking? Based on Spanish expressions students already know (**estoy bien, estoy listo, estoy atrasado**), can they guess what ❸**estoy cansada** means? Ask students how they feel after a long walk. What does Carmen mean when she says ❸**Me duelen los pies?** Ben and Pedro talk about what they like to do. Ben points to a man who is skating and says ❻**...me gusta patinar sobre ruedas.** What do students think ❼**patinas sobre hielo** means?

Background Information
Pablo (Pau) Casals (1876–1973), was born in Vendrell, Cataluña, and died in Río Piedras, Puerto Rico. Casals was an outspoken opponent of fascism who lived most of his life in exile. He moved to Puerto Rico in 1956, where he continued his personal musical crusade for peace. At the **Museo Pablo Casals** in Old San Juan, one can see his cello and other memorabilia. Casals is honored by Puerto Ricans at an annual festival in mid-June in San Juan.

⑥

Pedro: ¿Juegan mucho al béisbol en Nueva York?

Benjamín: Sí, pero a mí me gusta patinar sobre ruedas, como ese muchacho que va por allí.

⑤

Pedro: ¿Adónde van ahora?

Benjamín: Bueno, ya fuimos a la puerta de San Juan y al Museo Pablo Casals.

Carmen: Yo tengo ganas de ver el Castillo del Morro. ¿Podemos?

Pedro: ¿Qué tal si yo los acompaño?

⑦

Pedro: Ah, ¿patinas sobre hielo también?

Carmen: Yo sí, pero no me gusta el frío. Cuando hace frío me duele la nariz y también me duelen las orejas.

⑧

Pedro: Oye, Carmen... ¡Corres mucho! ¿Siempre haces tanto ejercicio?

Carmen: ¡Sí! Mamá y yo hacemos mucho ejercicio. Hago aeróbicos todas las mañanas con mi mamá.

⑨

Pedro: Bueno, ¿tienen ganas de ir a otra parte? ¿Ya fueron a la Plaza de Hostos?

Benjamín: No... ¡La Plaza de Hostos! ¡Ay, no! Carmen, si son las tres menos cinco! ¡Mamá nos espera en la Plaza de Hostos a las tres!

Cuaderno de actividades, p. 121, Acts. 1–2

A continuación

You may choose to continue with *Un recorrido por San Juan (a continuación)* at this time or wait until later in the chapter. At this point, the children rush to meet Ben and Carmen's mother, but they find she has not arrived. When she arrives, they discover that Pedro is Ben and Carmen's cousin. Later, they all attend a baseball game. Have students discuss the importance of sports or sporting events in their vacation plans.

Using the Captioned Video/DVD

As an alternative to reading the conversations in the book, you might want to show the captioned version of *Un recorrido por San Juan* on Videocassette 5. As students hear the language and watch the story, anxiety about the new language will be reduced and comprehension facilitated. The reinforcement of seeing the written words with the gestures and actions in context will help students do the comprehension activities on p. 330. **NOTE:** The *DVD Tutor* contains captions for all sections of the *Video Program*.

DE ANTEMANO

CAPÍTULO 11

Teaching Suggestion
Ask students to write a caption for this photo which señora Corredor put in the family album after they returned to New York from Puerto Rico.

Captioned Video
1 To help students answer these questions, you may want to play **Un recorrido por San Juan** with captions on Videocassette 5. Stop the tape at relevant points to give students a chance to answer.

Biology Link
In the video, Carmen orders a **batida de guanábana** *(custard apple or soursop milkshake)* from a vendor in Old San Juan. The **guanábana** is a sweet, acidic fruit from the **guanábano** tree of the *Annona* genus that is native to the Caribbean. Have students look up information about other trees that are native to the Americas. (guavas, papayas)

Language Note
You might point out that **batido** is another common word for *milkshake*. The feminine form **batida** is most often used in Puerto Rico.

Answers
1 1. in Puerto Rico on vacation and visiting relatives
2. walking around Old San Juan and visiting different places
3. Pedro from Puerto Rico
4. baseball and skating
5. It is almost 3:00 and they are not at the **Plaza de Hostos** where their mother is waiting to meet them.
6. *Answers will vary.*

2 1. ¿Qué tal si yo lo/la acompaño?
2. Me duelen los pies.
3. ¿Tienes ganas de caminar?
4. Ya fuimos al museo.
5. Mi amigo y yo hacemos mucho ejercicio.
6. Hago ejercicio aeróbico.
7. Un amigo me está esperando en la plaza.

4 *Sample answer:* Ben y Carmen son de Nueva York. Son hermanos. Tienen familia en Puerto Rico.

These activities check for comprehension only. Students should not yet be expected to produce language modeled in **De antemano**.

1 **¿Comprendes?** See answers below.
Contesta las preguntas para ver si entiendes lo que pasa en la fotonovela.
1. Where are Ben and Carmen, and why?
2. What are they doing today?
3. Who do they meet, and where is that person from?
4. What do Ben and Pedro talk about?
5. Why is Ben upset at the end of the story?
6. What do you think they'll do? What would you do?

2 **¿Cómo se dice?** See answers below.
¿Qué frases de la fotonovela puedes usar para expresar estos conceptos?
1. to suggest that you go with a friend
2. to say that your feet hurt
3. to ask if someone feels like walking
4. to say you've already been to the museum
5. to say you and a friend exercise a lot
6. to say you do aerobics
7. to say that a friend is waiting for you in the plaza

3 **¿Quién lo diría?**
Con base en la fotonovela, ¿quién diría lo siguiente?
1. ¡Patinar sobre ruedas es mi deporte favorito! Ben
2. Son las tres. ¿Qué están haciendo mis hijos? Sra. Corredor
3. A mí me gustaría visitar Nueva York. Pedro
4. ¡No quiero caminar más! Tengo ganas de descansar. Carmen
5. Yo voy con ustedes al Castillo del Morro. Pedro
6. Me encanta hacer ejercicios aeróbicos. Carmen

4 **¡Escribamos!** See sample answer below.
¿Qué sabes de *(What do you know about)* Ben, Carmen y Pedro? Escribe tres oraciones sobre cada persona, con base en lo que hace o dice en la fotonovela.

5 **¿Y tu ciudad?**
If this story happened in a tourist spot in or near your hometown, how would the story be different? What places would Ben and Carmen go to and what kind of people might they meet?

Comprehension Check

Thinking Critically
3 **Analyzing** Ask students to explain how they decided on their answers. What cues did they identify in the **fotonovela**?

Slower Pace
4 Before students write their sentences, have the class suggest adjectives describing the characters and opinions about the possible **gustos** of each, based on what was stated in the **De antemano** video or on impressions students got from the viewing. Arrange the answers in a grid on the board to serve as an easy guide.

Así se dice

Making suggestions and expressing feelings

To suggest something to a friend, say:

¿Qué tal si montamos a caballo?
What if we ride horses?

¿Por qué no vamos mañana?
Why don't . . .?

Your friend might answer:

Gracias, pero no quiero.
¡Magnífico!
Great!
No, en realidad **no tengo ganas.**

To ask how a friend is feeling, say:

¿Qué tienes? ¿Te sientes mal?
What's the matter? Do you feel bad?

No, **me siento bien.**
. . . I feel fine.

Estoy un poco cansado,
nada más. *. . . that's all.*

Más práctica gramatical,
p. 348, Act. 3

Cuaderno de actividades,
p. 122, Act. 4

6 Régimen de salud

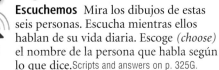

Escuchemos Mira los dibujos de estas seis personas. Escucha mientras ellos hablan de su vida diaria. Escoge *(choose)* el nombre de la persona que habla según lo que dice. Scripts and answers on p. 325G.

CD 11
Tr. 3

Nota gramatical

Sentirse (ie) is a reflexive verb.
yo **me siento**
tú **te sientes**
él/ella/usted **se siente**
nosotros **nos sentimos**
vosotros **os sentís**
ellos/ellas/ustedes **se sienten**

Más práctica gramatical,
p. 348, Acts. 1–2

Cuaderno de gramática,
p. 89, Acts. 1–2

Adriana

Raúl

Daniel

Fernando

Natalia

Soledad

Communication for All Students

Challenge

Have groups of three act out visits to the **consultorio.** One student plays the role of a doctor giving advice to each patient regarding his or her lifestyle. Have students use the pictures from the **Paso** as ideas. Patients may have health concerns or be seeking a checkup. Allow time for practice, then have groups act out the scenes for the class.

Building on Previous Skills

Ask **¿Cómo te sientes?** After the student replies, ask another student to report how the first one feels. (**Miguel, ¿cómo se siente Susana?**) Finally, have pairs practice the **Así se dice** dialogue, substituting other adjectives they know. (**estupendo/a, magnífico/a, triste, feliz**)

Teaching Resources
pp. 331–333

PRINT
- Lesson Planner, p. 53
- TPR Storytelling Book, pp. 41, 44
- Listening Activities, pp. 83, 87
- Activities for Communication, pp. 61–62, 125, 128–129, 157–158
- Cuaderno de gramática, pp. 89–90
- Grammar Tutor for Students of Spanish, Chapter 11
- Cuaderno de actividades, pp. 122–124
- Cuaderno para hispanohablantes, pp. 51–55
- Testing Program, pp. 275–278
- Alternative Assessment Guide, p. 42
- Student Make-Up Assignments, Chapter 11

MEDIA
- One-Stop Planner
- Audio Compact Discs, CD 11, Trs. 3, 22–23, 17
- Teaching Transparencies 11-1, 11-A; **Más práctica gramatical** Answers; Cuaderno de gramática Answers
- Interactive CD-ROM Tutor, Disc 3

Bell Work

Ask students to write an antonym (**antónimo**) for each of the following: **bajo, aquí, tarde, nada, debajo de, antes, frío, viejo.**

Presenting
Así se dice, Nota gramatical

Model both sides of the conversation in **Así se dice.** Explain that **sentirse** means *to feel,* while **sentir** means *to regret* or *to be sorry.* Next, have students answer your questions.

Teaching Resources
pp. 331–333

PRINT 📖
▶ Lesson Planner, p. 53
▶ TPR Storytelling Book, pp. 41, 44
▶ Listening Activities, pp. 83, 87
▶ Activities for Communication, pp. 61–62, 125, 128–129, 157–158
▶ Cuaderno de gramática, pp. 89–90
▶ Grammar Tutor for Students of Spanish, Chapter 11
▶ Cuaderno de actividades, pp. 122–124
▶ Cuaderno para hispanohablantes, pp. 51–55
▶ Testing Program, pp. 275–278
▶ Alternative Assessment Guide, p. 42
▶ Student Make-Up Assignments, Chapter 11

MEDIA 📀
▶ One-Stop Planner
▶ Audio Compact Discs, CD 11, Trs. 3, 22–23, 17
▶ Teaching Transparencies 11-1, 11-A; **Más práctica gramatical** Answers; Cuaderno de gramática Answers
▶ Interactive CD-ROM Tutor, Disc 3

Presenting
Vocabulario

Display *Teaching Transparency 11-A* and label each person on the transparency. Have students practice vocabulary by playing Jeopardy®. For example, one student says **Se estira.** Another responds **¿Quién es Felipe?**

---

9 *Answers may vary.*
1. necesitas estirarte
2. 10 minutos
3. debes levantar pesas
4. puedes asistir a una clase de yoga
5. Empieza a las 7:00 todos los días.
6. ¡Sí! ¿Quieres empezar hoy?

---

7 **Gramática en contexto** Answers will vary.

Hablemos Mira de nuevo los dibujos de la Actividad 6. Indica qué tienen y cómo se sienten las personas. Después di cómo se sienten tú y tus amigos en las siguientes situaciones. Usa las frases de **Así se dice.**

1. los lunes por la mañana
2. antes de un examen
3. durante las vacaciones
4. después de hacer ejercicio

Vocabulario

Para llevar una vida sana

patinar sobre ruedas · hacer yoga · levantar pesas · estirarse

Cuaderno de gramática, p. 90, Acts. 3–4

Más práctica gramatical, pp. 348–349, Acts. 3–4

---

8 **Y a ti, ¿qué te gusta?**

Hablemos ¿Cuáles de las actividades en el dibujo te gustan? Pregúntale a un compañero o una compañera sobre su rutina y compartan *(share)* sus ideas con el resto de la clase.

9 **Una nueva rutina** 🅷 See answers below.

Leamos/Escribamos You've just joined a health club but you're not sure how to get started. Complete the dialogue between you and Jill, your personal trainer for the day.

Tú	Quiero cambiar mi rutina pero no sé qué hacer. ¿Me ayudas?	JILL	Con mucho gusto. Primero, _____.
Tú	¿Estirarme? ¿Por cuántos minutos?	JILL	_____. Entonces, _____.
Tú	Ay, pero no me gusta levantar pesas.	JILL	Bueno, _____.
Tú	Muy bien. ¿A qué hora empieza la clase?	JILL	_____.
Tú	¡Dios mío! ¿Tan temprano?	JILL	_____.

Cultures and Communities

Multicultural Link
Yoga is a Hindu system of breathing and stretching exercises to promote control of the body and mind. Many non-Hindus in Western countries practice forms of yoga in hopes of improving their physical and mental health. Have students discuss the sports they do or are familiar with. Do they help both mind and body?

Language Notes
• The word *yoga* means *yoking* or *uniting* in Sanskrit, the classical language of India.
• While *to roller-skate* is **patinar sobre ruedas** in Spanish, *skating* in general may be called **el patinaje.** This may include *ice skating* (**patinar sobre hielo**) as well. The verb **patinarse** by itself means *to skid* or *to slide.*

10 **Un cuestionario**

Leamos/Escribamos Complete this questionnaire about your health habits by choosing the correct letters for each question. Then write your answers to the last two questions. Answers will vary.

Cuestionario SOBRE LA SALUD

 1 ¿Cuántas veces a la semana tomas...?

a. café	**d.** jugo de fruta
b. agua	**e.** té con cafeína
c. refrescos	**f.** vitaminas

 2 ¿Cuántas veces a la semana comes...?

a. pizza	**d.** carne
b. verduras	**e.** papas fritas
c. hamburguesas	**f.** pescado

 3 ¿Cuántas veces a la semana...?

a. duermes por la tarde	**d.** corres o caminas
b. montas en bicicleta	**e.** hablas por teléfono por dos horas o más
c. miras la televisión por tres horas o más	**f.** haces ejercicio

Cuenta el número de cada letra que tienes.

☐ Si tienes más de cuatro **a, c,** o **e,** ¡debes tratar de llevar una vida un poco más sana!

☐ Si sólo tienes uno o dos de **a, c,** o **e,** ya estás viviendo bastante bien.

Más para pensar:

☐ ¿Cuántas horas duermes cada noche? ¿Te gustaría dormir más? ¿Por qué sí o por qué no?

☐ En general, ¿crees que llevas una vida sana? ¿Por qué sí o por qué no?

 11 **Una vida diferente**

 Hablemos Get together with three classmates and compare your answers from Activity 10. Make suggestions about how each person in your group can improve her or his weekly routine. Be prepared to share your suggestions with the class.

 12 **Cómo cambiar mi rutina** See sample answer below.

 Escribamos Con base en la conversación con tus compañeros en la Actividad 11, escribe un párrafo sobre tus planes para tratar de mejorar tu rutina la próxima semana.

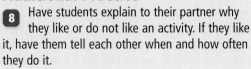 **Communication for All Students**

Additional Practice

8 Have students explain to their partner why they like or do not like an activity. If they like it, have them tell each other when and how often they do it.

Building on Previous Skills

Have groups of students come up with an hour-by-hour schedule for a typical day for Juana Sana, a very healthy and active person. Students should specify what time she begins her day, what she has for breakfast, lunch, and dinner, what physical activity she does during the day, and so on until bedtime. Have volunteers present their schedules to the class, including times and places.

Primer paso

CAPÍTULO 11

Assess

▶ Testing Program, pp. 275–278
Quiz 11-1A, Quiz 11-1B
Audio CD 11, Tr. 17

▶ Student Make-Up Assignments, Chapter 11, Alternative Quiz

▶ Alternative Assessment Guide, p. 42

Answers

 12 *Sample answer:*
Para llevar una vida más sana, voy a hacer ejercicio tres veces a la semana. Voy a beber ocho vasos de agua cada día. No voy a mirar tanta televisión por la noche. Voy a dormir ocho horas cada noche.

Bell Work
Have students write answers to these questions: ¿**Levantas pesas?** ¿**Te gusta hacer yoga?** ¿**Cuántas veces a la semana te estiras?** ¿**Cómo te sientes hoy?**

Presenting
Así se dice, Vocabulario
Present new phrases by building backward upon syllables.
(-pe, -gripe, -er gripe, tener gripe) To elicit new vocabulary, ask ¿**Cómo te sientes?**, ¿**Cómo estás?**, and ¿**Qué tienes?**

Segundo paso

Así se dice

Talking about moods and physical condition

To find out what kind of mood or condition a friend is in, ask:

¿**Cómo estás?**

¿**Cómo te sientes?**

¿**Qué le pasa a** Roberto?
What's wrong with . . .?

Your friend might say:

Estoy nervioso/a. Tengo un examen hoy.

Estoy mal. Tengo gripe.

No sé, pero me parece que **está preocupado por algo.**

Vocabulario

1. estar resfriado/a   2. estar nervioso/a   3. estar enojado/a   4. estar triste

5. estar preocupado/a   6. tener fiebre   7. tener tos   8. tener gripe

Cuaderno de actividades, pp. 125–126, Acts. 7–8   Cuaderno de gramática, pp. 91–92, Acts. 5–7

13 ¿**Cómo te sientes hoy?**

Escuchemos Listen to these people talk about how they feel today. Using the drawings in the vocabulary box above, write the correct number/numbers that correspond(s) to each description. Scripts and answers on p. 325G.
CD 11 Tr. 4

También se puede decir…
Another expression for **estar resfriado** is **tener catarro.** Another way to say **tener fiebre** is **tener calentura.**

Communication for All Students

Visual Learners
Have students create sentences using the eight vocabulary illustrations, using names of acquaintances as subjects. Have half the class follow each statement with **por eso...** and a reason for the condition. (**Ana va al dentista; por eso está nerviosa.**) Have the other half provide **porque** phrases. (**Paco está resfriado porque no lleva una vida sana.**)

Native Speakers
Encourage native speakers to list and share with the class regional vocabulary variations for expressions related to how one is feeling: **tener resfrío** *(to have a cold);* **tener ansias, estar comiendo ansias** *(to feel anxious);* **tener calambre** *(to have a cramp);* **tener náuseas, estar nauseabundo** *(to feel nauseated, to be sick to one's stomach).*

14 Dificultades See possible answers below.

 Escribamos Escribe unas oraciones para explicar cómo te sientes en estas situaciones.

1. Estás en un restaurante con unos amigos. Necesitas pagar la cuenta pero no tienes dinero.
2. Tienes tres exámenes muy importantes hoy y necesitas sacar buenas notas.
3. Tu hermanito acaba de romper *(has just broken)* el televisor y no puedes ver tu programa favorito.
4. Estás haciendo la tarea en la computadora cuando de repente *(suddenly)* no hay electricidad.
5. Tu mejor amigo va a vivir en otra ciudad.
6. Mañana vas a empezar un trabajo nuevo.
7. Hace mucho frío y no te sientes bien.

Vocabulario

El cuerpo humano

- la cabeza
- el oído
- la oreja
- la boca
- la garganta
- el pelo
- el ojo
- la nariz
- el cuello
- la mano
- los dedos
- el brazo
- el estómago
- la espalda
- la pierna
- el pie
- los dedos

Cuaderno de gramática, p. 92, Acts. 8–9

Más práctica gramatical, p. 349, Act. 5 →

15 ¿Para qué sirve?

 Hablemos ¿Qué parte o partes del cuerpo usamos en las siguientes situaciones? Cada persona debe mencionar una parte diferente.
See possible answers below.

1. para hablar por teléfono
2. para escuchar música rock
3. para correr por el parque
4. para maquillarte o afeitarte
5. para hacer ejercicios aeróbicos
6. para tocar el piano
7. para escribir una carta
8. para levantar *(to lift)* cosas
9. para montar en bicicleta

16 Simón dice...

 Hablemos Work in groups of four to play **Simón dice.** Take turns being leader and practice the words in the **Vocabulario.** Here are some commands you may need:

Levanta	**Cierra**	**Abre**
Lift	*Close*	*Open*

Toca	**Indica**
Touch	*Point*

A lo nuestro

Parts of the body are used in many common expressions in Spanish.

¡Ojo! *Pay attention!* or *Watch out!*
Él es muy **codo.** He's really *stingy.* (**Codo** means *elbow.*)
Cuesta **un ojo de la cara**. It's *very expensive.*
¿Me estás tomando el pelo?
Are you pulling my leg?

Connections and Comparisons

Language-to-Language

To help students learn the Spanish words for body parts, encourage the use of mnemonic aids. Point out that many of the **Vocabulario** terms share roots with related English words. Write these questions on the board: On what part of your body do you wear a <u>cap</u>? What part of your body touches your <u>collar</u>? Where do you wear a <u>bracelet</u>? Ask students to find the answers in **Vocabulario** and to explain how the English and Spanish words are alike. (Answers: **la cabeza, el cuello, el brazo**)

Slower Pace

14 Go over the sentences with the class before having students answer them. Ask them to give as many alternative answers as possible.

Presenting
Vocabulario

Pronounce new words as you point to the correct part of the body. Teach parts of the body by using TPR and playing **Simón dice.** (See Preliminary Chapter, page 8.) After a few rounds of play, have a student be **Simón.**

Kinesthetic/ Tactile Learners

15 Have students write a sentence telling of an action requiring a part of the body. Make sure they include the body parts in the sentence. (**Leo un libro con los ojos y las manos.**) Then have them act out their sentences. You may wish to have teams compete by naming both the action and the parts of the body involved.

Language Note

La oreja is the term for the *outer ear,* while **el oído** means *inner ear* and refers to the hearing apparatus.

Answers

14 *Possible answers:*
1. Estoy muy preocupado/a.
2. Estoy nervioso/a.
3. Estoy enojado/a.
4. Estoy enojado/a.
5. Estoy triste.
6. Estoy contento/a.
7. Tengo gripe.

15 *Possible answers:*
1. los oídos, la boca
2. los oídos
3. las piernas, los pies
4. el brazo, los dedos
5. los brazos, las piernas, los pies
6. los dedos, los oídos, los pies
7. el brazo, los ojos
8. la espalda, las piernas, los brazos
9. las piernas, los brazos

Teaching Resources
pp. 334–338

PRINT
- Lesson Planner, p. 54
- TPR Storytelling Book, pp. 42, 44
- Listening Activities, pp. 84, 88
- Activities for Communication, pp. 63–64, 126, 128–129, 157–158
- Cuaderno de gramática, pp. 91–93
- Grammar Tutor for Students of Spanish, Chapter 11
- Cuaderno de actividades, pp. 125–127
- Cuaderno para hispanohablantes, pp. 51–55
- Testing Program, pp. 279–282
- Alternative Assessment Guide, p. 42
- Student Make-Up Assignments, Chapter 11

MEDIA
- One-Stop Planner
- Audio Compact Discs, CD 11, Trs. 4–5, 24–25, 18
- Teaching Transparencies 11-2, 11-C; **Más práctica gramatical** Answers; Cuaderno de gramática Answers
- Interactive CD-ROM Tutor, Disc 3

Presenting
Nota gramatical

Review the use of **gustar.** Explain the similar use of **doler (ue).** Have volunteers use gestures to pretend that body part hurt. Ask comprehension questions. **(¿A Ana le duele el pie?)**

Answers

18 1. me duelen los ojos.
2. le duelen las piernas.
3. me duele el estómago.
4. me duele la boca.
5. le duelen los brazos.
6. me duele la garganta.

---

17 Quejas

Escuchemos Listen to several people tell how they feel. Match each person's complaint with the correct symptom. Scripts and answers on p. 325G.

CD 11
Tr. 5

1. Gregorio
2. Flor
3. Félix
4. Betty
5. Laura
6. Roberto
7. Cecilia

a. Me duelen los brazos.
b. Me duelen los ojos.
c. Me duelen los pies.
d. Me duelen las piernas.
e. Me duele la mano.
f. Me duele la garganta.
g. Me duele el estómago.

18 Gramática en contexto See answers below.

Escribamos Completa las oraciones con la forma apropiada del verbo **doler** y las partes del cuerpo que correspondan.

1. Cuando leo demasiado...
2. Cuando mi papá corre mucho...
3. Si como helado muy rápido...
4. Cuando voy al dentista...
5. Cuando Brenda levanta pesas...
6. Cuando estoy resfriado/a...

19 Gramática en contexto Answers will vary.

Hablemos Look at the drawings. With a partner, take turns saying what you think is wrong with each person. Then tell each person what he or she should do to feel better.

Midori

Linda

Joe

Deidre

Conchita

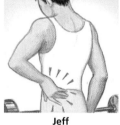
Jeff

Laura

Benito

*The definite article, rather than a possessive, is used with body parts in Spanish.

Nota gramatical

Doler *(to hurt, ache)* is an **o** to **ue** stem-changing verb. Like **gustar, doler** is used with indirect object pronouns and can be singular or plural. Do you notice anything special about how you refer to body parts?*

Me duele el estómago.
¿Te duele la garganta?
Le duele la cabeza.
Me duelen los pies.
Te duelen las piernas.
¿Le duelen los brazos?

Cuaderno de gramática, p. 93, Acts. 10–11

Más práctica gramatical, p. 350, Act. 6

Connections and Comparisons

Career Path

Ask students to list health and fitness-related careers. For example, they might think of becoming a doctor, nurse, physical therapist, personal trainer, massage therapist, or nutritionist. Have students choose one of the careers they have listed and imagine that it is their first day on the job. They have many Spanish-speaking clients. What Spanish words and phrases would students need to perform their job? You might have pairs collaborate and write a short dialogue based on this scenario and present it to the class.

20 **¡Un día fatal!**

Hablemos ¿Cómo te sientes cuando tienes un mal día? Intercambia papeles con tu compañero/a preguntando y contestando las preguntas.

MODELO —¿Cómo te sientes?
—Me duele la cabeza y no tengo ganas de estudiar.

1. ¿Qué te pasa?
2. ¿Cómo te sientes?
3. ¿Te gustaría estudiar conmigo?
4. ¿Qué tal si tomamos un refresco?
5. ¿Te duele la cabeza?
6. ¿Por qué no descansas un poco?

21 **Para sentirse mejor**

Hablemos ¿Qué haces para sentirte mejor cuando...

1. estás muy nervioso/a?
2. te duele mucho el estómago?
3. estás triste y te sientes solo/a?
4. tienes gripe?
5. estás enojado/a con tu mejor amigo/a?
6. tienes fiebre?

22 **¿Qué haces para manejar el estrés?**

Leamos/Escribamos Lee el artículo, piensa en tus hábitos y contesta las siguientes preguntas.

7 Claves para manejar el **ESTRÉS**

1. Comer por lo menos una comida balanceada al día. La nutrición es esencial para una buena salud y proporciona defensas contra el estrés.

2. Dormir por lo menos 8 horas cada noche. Un sueño apropiado puede añadir años de vida. Trate de acostarse y levantarse a la misma hora.

3. Hacer ejercicio, por lo menos 3 veces por semana. Busque una actividad divertida, como montar en bicicleta, caminar o nadar.

4. No debe tomar demasiada cafeína. Puede producir irritabilidad, dolor de cabeza, ansiedad y depresión.

5. Salir y cultivar sus amistades. Tener amigos ayuda a mantener en alto la auto-estima.

6. Organizar su tiempo. Planee su uso y empléelo.

7. Conservar una actitud positiva: las personas optimistas tienen menos problemas mentales y físicos.

1. ¿Comes por lo menos una comida balanceada al día? ¿En qué consiste?
2. ¿Cuántas horas duermes cada noche?
3. ¿Cuántas veces a la semana haces ejercicio? ¿Qué te gusta hacer?
4. ¿Tomas muchos refrescos?
5. ¿Sales con frecuencia con tus amigos?
6. ¿Tienes un buen amigo o una buena amiga a quien le puedes contar tus cosas?
7. ¿Organizas bien tu tiempo?
8. ¿Eres optimista o pesimista?

Assess

▶ Testing Program, pp. 279–282
Quiz 11-2A, Quiz 11-2B
Audio CD 11, Tr. 18

▶ Student Make-Up Assignments, Chapter 11, Alternative Quiz

▶ Alternative Assessment Guide, p. 42

Nota cultural

Athletes from Spanish-speaking countries are important to the success of U.S. teams in many different sports, but nowhere is this more visible than in baseball. Since 1911, more than 500 Spanish-speaking athletes from Puerto Rico, Colombia, Cuba, the Dominican Republic, Mexico, Nicaragua, Panama, and Venezuela have made it into baseball's major leagues. The Baseball Hall of Fame currently honors seven acclaimed Hispanic players: Puerto Rico's Orlando Cepeda and Roberto Clemente, Martín Dihigo and Tony Perez of Cuba, the Dominican Republic's Juan Marichal, Luis Aparicio of Venezuela, and Rod Carew of Panama.

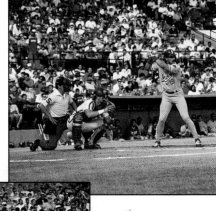

Cuaderno de actividades, p. 132, Act. 17

23 **El estrés**

Hablemos Many professional athletes must deal with a lot of stress. Imagine that you are your favorite athlete. With a partner, use the suggestions included in Activity 22 and take turns suggesting to each other what you can do to relieve stress.

24 **¡Qué problemas tengo yo!**

Hablemos Form a group of three. For each of the following situations, one of you will role-play the situation and the other two will make suggestions on how the person can relieve stress in his or her life. Take turns acting out these situations, and then each of you create your own.

1. Quieres ir al gimnasio con tus amigos esta noche, pero tienes dos exámenes mañana y mucha tarea y no tienes tiempo para hacer todo.

2. Pasas todas las tardes y los fines de semana en las actividades del colegio. Nunca tienes tiempo para salir con tus amigos.

3. Trabajas diez horas cada día en una oficina muy ocupada. Muchas veces no tienes tiempo ni para desayunar ni almorzar. Siempre estás muy cansado/a.

25 **Una semana sin estrés** See sample answer below.

Escribamos ¿Puedes reducir el estrés por una semana? Escribe un párrafo de seis oraciones en que describes con detalles las cosas que puedes hacer durante la próxima semana para reducir (reduce) el estrés.

Answers

25 *Sample answer:*
Para reducir el estrés, necesito dormir 8 horas cada noche. No debo tomar muchos refrescos con cafeína. Debo hacer ejercicio tres veces a la semana y tener una dieta sana con muchas frutas y legumbres. Necesito organizar bien mi tiempo y debo ser optimista.

Communication for All Students

Auditory Learners

Have students role-play the following situation. A local Spanish-speaking television station has a call-in health program that answers viewers' questions. Ask one student to serve as the television counselor (**consejero/a**) and the others to call in with questions. If a student is able to stump the counselor, that student becomes the new counselor.

Additional Practice

Have students give each person in *Teaching Transparency 11-B* a name. Then ask students what is wrong with each person. (**¿Qué le pasa a...?**) Have them name symptoms that each person may have. (**¿Qué le duele a...?**)

CD 11
Trs. 6–9

CD-ROM 3
DVD 2

¿Qué deporte practicas?

Although some sports, like soccer or baseball, are perceived to be more popular in Spanish-speaking countries, there are other sports that many people play. In this chapter, we asked some people what sport they play and why.

Víctor CD 11 Tr. 7
Ciudad de México

"Yo practico la charrería *(Mexican rodeo)*, que es el deporte nacional, es el deporte mexicano... [Son] suertes a caballo. Es... como en Estados Unidos los "cowboys", aquí son los charros... Mi abuelo fue charro y mi padre fue charro y... por seguir la tradición".

CD 11 Tr. 8

Manoli
Sevilla, España

"Practico piragüismo... Esto es un K-1 [ca-uno] ... en inglés, "kayak", por eso le decimos K-1 nosotros. Ésta es una pala... Me gusta porque el agua me encanta y me gusta estar aquí... en el río".

Raquel CD 11 Tr. 9
Managua, Nicaragua

"Me gusta el voleibol... Es bonito jugarlo, es un deporte muy femenino, no es tan masculino como el "softball" o el fútbol "soccer".

Para pensar y hablar

A. With a classmate, make a list of five reasons why you like a particular sport. Present your list to the class.

B. In small groups, make a list of your favorite sports players. Then, choose the two most popular players and discuss why you like them.

Cuaderno para hispanohablantes, pp. 54–55

CAPÍTULO 11

Teaching Resources
p. 339

PRINT
▶ Video Guide, pp. 75–77
▶ Cuaderno de actividades, p. 132
▶ Cuaderno para hispanohablantes, pp. 54–55

MEDIA
▶ One-Stop Planner
▶ Video Program, Videocassette 4, 32:38–35:42
▶ DVD Tutor, Disc 2
▶ Audio Compact Discs, CD 11, Trs. 6–9
▶ Interactive CD-ROM Tutor, Disc 3

Presenting
Panorama cultural

Ask students **¿Qué deporte practica Manoli? ¿Raquel?** After asking several comprehension questions, ask a student **¿Qué deportes practicas tú?** Next, have students ask each other what sports they play and why.

Preguntas

1. **¿Qué se necesita para practicar el piragüismo?** (un bote y una pala)

2. **Según Víctor, ¿cuál es el deporte nacional de México?** (la charrería)

3. **¿Por qué practica Víctor la charrería?** (para seguir la tradición de su familia)

4. **¿Por qué dice Raquel que el voleibol es un deporte femenino?** (Es bonito jugarlo. No es tan masculino como el "softball" o el fútbol.) **¿Estás de acuerdo con ella?** *(Answers will vary.)*

Teaching Resources
pp. 340–344

PRINT
▸ Lesson Planner, p. 55
▸ TPR Storytelling Book, pp. 43, 44
▸ Listening Activities, pp. 85, 89
▸ Activities for Communication, pp. 65–66, 127, 128–129, 157–158
▸ Cuaderno de gramática, pp. 94–96
▸ Grammar Tutor for Students of Spanish, Chapter 11
▸ Cuaderno de actividades, pp. 128–130
▸ Cuaderno para hispanohablantes, pp. 51–55
▸ Testing Program, pp. 283–286
▸ Alternative Assessment Guide, p. 42
▸ Student Make-Up Assignments, Chapter 11

MEDIA
▸ One-Stop Planner
▸ Audio Compact Discs, CD 11, Trs. 10–15, 26–27, 19
▸ Teaching Transparencies 11-3, 11-D; **Más práctica gramatical** Answers; Cuaderno de gramática Answers
▸ Interactive CD-ROM Tutor, Disc 3

Bell Work
Have students illustrate the following expressions: **estar resfriado/a, estar enojado/a, estar triste, estar preocupado/a, estar bien.**

Presenting
Así se dice, Nota gramatical

Model the preterite beginning with **¿Qué hiciste ayer?**, then vary the subject asking others to recall **¿Qué hizo ___ ayer?** With questions using **jugar**, have students name sports and activities. Correct errors, then review the preterite of **jugar.**

Tercer paso

Objectives Saying what you did; talking about where you went and when

WV3 PUERTO RICO-11

Tercer paso

Así se dice

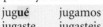

Saying what you did

To find out what a friend did last night, ask:

¿Qué hiciste anoche?
What did you do . . .?

¿Ganaste?
Did you win?

Your friend might say:

Jugué al tenis.
I played . . .

No. Mi prima ganó. **Jugó** muy bien.
. . . She played . . .

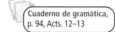

Nota gramatical

In the preterite, **jugar** *(to play)* has a regular conjugation in all forms except the **yo** form.

jug**ué**	jugamos
jugaste	jugasteis
jugó	jugaron

Cuaderno de gramática, p. 94, Acts. 12–13

Más práctica gramatical, p. 350, Act. 7

Answers:
jugamos, jugaron, jugué, jugó, Jugaste

26 ## Gramática en contexto

Leamos/Escribamos Mira el dibujo y completa el párrafo con formas del verbo **jugar** en el pretérito.

El sábado pasado todos nosotros ===== algún deporte en el parque. Mis padres ===== al tenis. Yo ===== al basquetbol con unos amigos. Marcos ===== con el perro. ¿Y tú? ¿ ===== un deporte el sábado?

mis padres

Marcela

mi hermano

27 ## ¿Qué hicieron?

Hablemos Mira el dibujo otra vez. Ahora dile a un compañero/a qué más hicieron Marcela y su familia el fin de semana pasado.

Communication for All Students

Native Speakers
Have native speakers imagine they visited Puerto Rico recently. As a diary entry in their journals, have students express their feelings about what they saw and did, and where they went and when. They may read the Location Opener on pages 322–325 for information or they may search the Internet, using "Puerto Rico" as a keyword. Visit the HRW Web site at **www.go.hrw.com**, keyword **WV3 PUERTO RICO** for online resources and additional information about Puerto Rico.

28 Una semana llena de actividades

Hablemos/Escribamos Trabaja en un grupo de cuatro. Describe a tus compañeros lo que hicieron los miembros de tu familia durante la semana pasada. Uno de Uds. debe tomar apuntes *(to take notes)* y todos necesitan describir las actividades de la semana. Incluye los días de la semana, adónde fueron y a qué hora hicieron cada actividad.

Nota cultural

In general, the majority of sports played in the United States are also very popular in Spanish-speaking countries. The one exception is American football. While it's often played on an informal basis, it's only beginning to gain official status in a few Spanish-speaking countries. When Spanish speakers talk about **el fútbol**, they're referring to the game that North Americans call *soccer*. On the other hand, a game that originated in the Basque country of Spain, **jai alai** (sometimes known as **pelota**), is not widely played in the United States.

Additional Practice
Have students practice asking each other questions about what they did and answering them with **jugar**. You might wish to introduce the Additional Vocabulary on pages R5–R8.

Additional Vocabulary
las cartas *playing cards*
el dominó *dominoes*
el crucigrama *crossword puzzle*
el rompecabezas *jigsaw puzzle*
el ajedrez *chess*
las damas *checkers*

29 ¿Qué hiciste durante la semana? Answers will vary.

  Escribamos Escribe un párrafo en español que incluya siete cosas que hiciste durante la semana pasada. Incluye cuándo, con quién y dónde hiciste cada actividad. Aquí hay unas sugerencias:

escuchar música   lavar platos   estudiar para mis clases

preparar la cena   mirar la televisión   hablar por teléfono

jugar al...   levantar pesas   limpiar el cuarto

30 Te toca a ti

  Hablemos Work with a partner and share information from Activity 29 about what you did last week. As you ask about your partner's activities, check off in your paragraph those activities that match. How many of the same things did you do?

Cultures and Communities

 Culture Note
Jai alai is a fast and exciting game that resembles handball. Players use a narrow wicker basket to throw a hard ball against the front wall of a court. The basket, called a **cesta**, has a glove on one end that fits the player's hand. The other end is used for catching and throwing the ball. The **pelota** is slightly smaller than a baseball. **Jai alai** is played on a walled court called a **cancha**. Spectators watch the game through a clear, protective screen. **Jai alai** originated from a game played in the Basque regions of Spain and France during the 1600s. Ask students if they have ever seen or played **jai alai**.

Teaching Resources
pp. 340–344

PRINT
▸ Lesson Planner, p. 55
▸ TPR Storytelling Book, pp. 43, 44
▸ Listening Activities, pp. 85, 89
▸ Activities for Communication, pp. 65–66, 127, 128–129, 157–158
▸ Cuaderno de gramática, pp. 94–96
▸ Grammar Tutor for Students of Spanish, Chapter 11
▸ Cuaderno de actividades, pp. 128–130
▸ Cuaderno para hispanohablantes, pp. 51–55
▸ Testing Program, pp. 283–286
▸ Alternative Assessment Guide, p. 42
▸ Student Make-Up Assignments, Chapter 11

MEDIA
▸ One-Stop Planner
▸ Audio Compact Discs, CD 11, Trs. 10–15, 26–27, 19
▸ Teaching Transparencies 11-3, 11-D; **Más práctica gramatical** Answers; Cuaderno de gramática Answers
▸ Interactive CD-ROM Tutor, Disc 3

Presenting
Así se dice, Nota gramatical

Model **Así se dice,** then ask students **¿Adónde fuiste?** As you vary the subject, use more time references. (**anoche,** etc.) Explain the distinction between **¿dónde?** and **¿adónde?** Have students practice asking where others went and when.

Answers

31 *Sample answer:*
a. Fue al centro comercial. Compró muchos regalos para su hijo.

Así se dice

Talking about where you went and when

To ask where someone went, say:

¿Adónde fuiste anoche?
Where did you go . . .?

Your friend might answer:

Anoche **fui** al parque con mi familia.

To talk about different times in the past, you might say:

¿Adónde fuiste anteayer?
anteanoche? *(night before last)*
la semana pasada?
antes de regresar a casa?

Anteayer **fui** a la piscina.

Nota gramatical

The verb **ir** has an irregular conjugation in the preterite.

fui	fuimos
fuiste	fuisteis
fue	fueron

Más práctica gramatical, p. 351, Act. 8

Cuaderno de actividades, pp. 128–129, Acts. 11–12

Cuaderno de gramática, p. 95, Acts. 14–16

SUGERENCIA

When you know an English word and want to find its Spanish equivalent, look up the English word in an English-Spanish dictionary. Make sure you read *all* of the meanings, since most words can mean several different things. For example, you can cut down trees with a *saw* or talk about a movie you *saw*. To choose the right meaning, think about how you're going to use the Spanish word.

---

31 **Gramática en contexto** See sample answer below.

Escribamos Look at each of the drawings. Create two sentences for each drawing telling where the people went and what they did there. Add any other details that you might find interesting. Use your imagination.

a. Sergio

b. nosotros

c. los Arroyo

d. don Felipe

e. Ana y Ramón

f. yo

g. mis amigos

h. tú

Teacher to Teacher

Jeanne's students summarize the day's events from home.

Jeanne Jendrzejewski
LSU Lab School,
Baton Rouge, LA

"I have my students e-mail me from home with comments about how their day went. They can say how they felt, what they did at school, and what they did after school using the preterite. So they don't feel they're being graded, I simply answer the questions using correctly whatever form they're having trouble with. (*Student writes:* **Yo** *tiene* **que trabajar.** *I answer:* **Yo tuve que trabajar también.**)"

32 Gramática en contexto

Hablemos/Escribamos Júntate con dos o tres compañeros y averigua adónde ellos y sus amigos fueron la semana pasada. Toma apuntes y presenta la información a la clase. Indica qué grupo fue el más activo.

Vocabulario

la cancha de fútbol

la cancha de tenis

el estadio

la pista de correr

Cuaderno de gramática, p. 96, Acts. 17–18

Más práctica gramatical, p. 351, Act. 8

33 ¿Adónde fuiste?

 Escuchemos Listen as people talk about where they went last weekend. When they mention what they did there, write **sí** if it's logical and **no** if it isn't. If it isn't logical, write an activity or two that you might do at the place mentioned.

34 En mi cuaderno

 Escribamos Write about your sports and fitness routine in your journal. First explain what sports you usually play, where you go to exercise, and how you feel afterward. Then describe what sports you played last week or weekend, where you went to play, and who won. You may want to use the expressions below.

jugar al...	la cancha	jugué (con)...
me siento...	la pista de correr	fuimos a...
estirarse	el estadio	gané...
me duele...	el gimnasio	fui a...

Communication for All Students

 Game

34 Divide the class into two teams. On the board or a transparency, draw a tic-tac-toe grid. In each square, write either an expression, a verb, or a vocabulary word from Activity 34. Have Team 1 choose a square. Then have every member of both teams write a sentence using the word in the square. After a previously-stated amount of time (1 minute), call on a member of Team 1 to read his or her sentence aloud. If the sentence is correct, that team gets an **X** or an **O** in the square. If not, call on a member of Team 2. Repeat, alternating teams, until one team wins.

Letra y sonido Ask the students to look at the **Vocabulario** on page 355 to see if they can find additional examples of diphthongs.

Music Link

Play the song **De colores,** from Chapter 2. (Audio CD 2, Tr. 28) Provide students with the lyrics *(Listening Activities,* p. 18) and have them listen for combinations of a strong vowel and a weak vowel, or of two weak vowels. Examples from the song are: **vienen, afuera, polluelos, diamante, quiero.** Remind students that some vowels are silent (as is the **u** in **quiero**).

Assess

▸ Testing Program, pp. 283–286 Quiz 11-3A, Quiz 11-3B Audio CD 11, Tr. 19

▸ Student Make-Up Assignments, Chapter 11, Alternative Quiz

▸ Alternative Assessment Guide, p. 42

---

35 **Una excursión de los amigos** See sample answer below.

Escribamos/Hablemos Mira las fotos de Ben, Carmen y Pedro. Escribe lo que pasó durante su día en San Juan y compara tu descripción con la de un compañero/a.

1.　　　　　　2.　　　　　　3.　　　　　　4.

36  **Del colegio al trabajo**

Hablemos You are a personal trainer with a client who is out of shape. Ask what activities he or she did recently and how he or she feels. Give advice about staying healthy by eating well, avoiding stress, and keeping fit. Use **sentirse,** and vocabulary and expressions learned in this chapter.

MODELO	Tú	—¿Qué actividades hiciste la semana pasada?
	Tu compañero/a	—Hice ejercicio en el gimnasio.
	Tú	—¿Cómo te sientes ahora?
	Tu compañero/a	—Me siento mal y me duelen los brazos.

Hice...	Limpié...	Fui a...	¿Cómo estás?
Miré...	Jugué...	Me duele(n) ...	¿Qué tienes?

LETRA Y SONIDO

CD 11
Trs. 11–15

A. In Spanish the vowels **a, e,** and **o** are called strong vowels and **i** and **u** weak vowels.

1. Two strong vowels together are pronounced as separate syllables:

   peor　　oeste　　rodeo　　correo　　Rafael

2. A strong vowel and a weak vowel or two weak vowels combine into one syllable called a *diphthong.* When the weak vowel comes first in this combination, the **i** is pronounced like the *y* in *yet* and the **u** is pronounced like the *w* in *wet:*

   familia　　pie　　adiós　　ciudad

   cuando　　bueno　　Europa　　fui

3. An accent mark over a weak vowel keeps it from combining into one syllable with another vowel:

   tía　　día　　período　　baúl　　aúlla

B. Dictado

You're going to hear Rafael describe a typical day in his life. Write what he says.

C. Trabalenguas Script for Part B on p. 325H.

Bueno es el aire suave cuando sueño da, pero el fuerte viento despierto nos mantiene ya.

Communication for All Students

Challenge

Have students imagine they took a Caribbean cruise (**un crucero por el mar Caribe**) as a class. The ship (**barco**) offered an array of recreational facilities. (**pista para correr, cancha de tenis, pista de baile, cafés, piscinas**) They also toured Puerto Rico, sightseeing and visiting friends. Have each student say what he or she did, what they did as a group, and what friends did, and when. You may wish to have students divide the tasks and present the material orally in groups, or assign this as individual written reports.

Answers
35 *Sample answer:*
1. Ben y Carmen fueron a la playa.

Remedios caseros

LAURA ¡Cómo me duele la cabeza!

ALICIA ¿De veras? ¿Por qué no descansas un ratito?

LAURA Buena idea, pero primero voy a tomar un vaso de agua fría. Tengo mucho calor.

ALICIA ¿Tienes fiebre? No debes tomar nada frío. No es bueno para el cuerpo.

LAURA No tengo fiebre. Sólo un dolor de cabeza.

ALICIA De todos modos, debes tomar algo. Tal vez una limonada tibia y dos aspirinas.

LAURA ¡Una limonada tibia! Tengo ganas de tomar agua fría.

ALICIA El frío te da un dolor de cabeza y también te puede dar un resfriado.

LAURA ¿El agua fría me puede dar un resfriado? ¿Cómo?

Para discutir...

1. Why do you think Alicia doesn't want Laura to drink cold water? What is strange about what she suggests Laura drink instead?

2. Have you heard of other remedies that might be considered unusual? Get in groups of four and discuss them. Be prepared to share your findings with the class.

Vamos a comprenderlo

Many Latin Americans don't drink very cold drinks and tend not to put ice in lemonade, water, and soft drinks. Like Alicia, many Latin Americans consider cold drinks to be harmful to the body.

Connections and Comparisons

Science Link
Have students research a home remedy, finding procedures and ingredients as well as its cultural origin. Then elicit help from a science teacher in determining whether the remedy has been proven effective. This may be done as a cooperative assignment between two classes.

Thinking Critically
Evaluating Ask students why they think Laura recommends warm lemonade for her friend's headache. (Some people believe that warm fluids are less apt to cause changes in body temperature, while cold fluids will initially cool your body, but then make you feel even warmer.)

Teaching Resources
pp. 346–347

PRINT
▸ Lesson Planner, p. 53
▸ Cuaderno de actividades, p. 131
▸ Cuaderno para hispanohablantes, pp. 51–53
▸ Reading Strategies and Skills Handbook, Chapter 11
▸ ¡Lee conmigo! 1, Chapter 11
▸ Standardized Assessment Tutor, Chapter 11

MEDIA
▸ One-Stop Planner

Prereading
Activity A

Using Prior Knowledge
• Have students look at the reading to identify words that are similar to English expressions used to describe exercises.

• In small groups, students compare and discuss their answers to **¡A comenzar!** before you go over the correct answers. Once students have completed this section, remind them of how using background knowledge helped.

Answers

A 1. *(simple exercises)* ejercicios simples
2. *(maintain muscles)* mantener los músculos
3. *(eliminate stiffness)* eliminar tensión

B Answers will vary. Sample answer:
Client 1
Using background knowledge: Low-impact exercises are less likely to cause pain or injury; calisthenics and stretching improve circulation and flexibility and can help to prevent back problems.
Using the article: The section "Músculos en forma" has some information. There are other exercises demonstrated in the photos on page 346.

Vamos a leer

Para estar en forma

Estrategia para leer
You learned about background knowledge in Chapter 3. Background knowledge is what you already know about a subject. Before you read something, take a minute to remember what you already know about that topic. Doing this will make it easier to guess the meanings of difficult words or phrases.

¡A comenzar! See answers below.
A. Look at the pictures, title, and subtitles first. Then, complete the following statements:
1. Both of these readings are about ══════.
2. In Reading A, the goal of doing those activities is to ══════.
3. In Reading B, the goal of doing those activities is to ══════.

Compare your answers with at least two classmates.

Al grano See answers below.
B. Imagine that you work as a personal trainer at a gym. Your clients often ask your advice about their exercise programs. To answer their questions, use your background knowledge about exercise, as well as information from the article. Follow the steps outlined below.

Client 1: "High-impact aerobics classes are not for me! Those classes hurt my legs and back. What other sorts of exercises can I do instead?"

A
MÚSCULOS EN FORMA PARA UNA FIGURA SENSACIONAL

Hacer ejercicio al aire libre es ideal cuando vacacionamos en la playa o en el bosque. Lo importante es comenzar con los ejercicios simples, similares a los que hacemos día a día pero de una manera constante. No se trata de saltar de un lado para otro, sino de hacer movimientos suaves, continuos y lentos, especialmente diseñados para ejercitar todos los músculos del cuerpo.

1. Con los antebrazos y las rodillas en el suelo, levanta una pierna, flexionándola con el pie en punta. Repite diez veces con cada pierna y fortalece tus músculos.

2. Recostado, flexiona una pierna hasta que puedas sujetar el pie con la mano; luego, estira la pierna. Repite diez veces con cada pierna.

3. Acostada pero con los hombros levantados, flexiona las piernas. Repite diez veces para endurecer el abdomen y las piernas.

Connections and Comparisons

Native Speakers
Encourage native speakers to look in Spanish-language magazines for creative suggestions and additional information about exercise. Have students write a paragraph describing an exercise that interests them. Ask students to provide some background knowledge for their readers about the exercise and explain why they chose it. Students can use **Vamos a leer** as a guide.

Kinesthetic Learners
The Hokey Pokey is a dance in which individual body parts are named as part of the dance. The song can be translated and taught in Spanish, or can be sung and danced to in English with only the body parts named in Spanish.

STANDARDS: 1.2, 3.1

B

DILE ADIÓS A LAS TENSIONES... ¡CON EJERCICIOS!

Aprende a eliminar la tensión muscular sin moverte de tu asiento. Las personas que pasan mucho tiempo en sillas — en la escuela o en la oficina — frecuentemente sufren de dolores de cabeza, en el cuello, en la barbilla, en los hombros y en la espalda. Para eliminar esas desagradables tensiones, aquí tienes ejercicios sencillos y fáciles de realizar, que te ayudarán muchísimo.

4. Para los hombros y la espalda: Cruza los brazos poniendo las palmas encima de los hombros (como si te estuvieras abrazando). Respira profundamente y ve girando tu cuerpo (de la cintura hacia arriba) todo lo que puedas de izquierda a derecha y en dirección contraria. Suelta el aire cuando estés en el centro. De tu cintura hacia abajo nada debe moverse.

5. Para la espalda y el cuello: Levanta los brazos en forma recta. Luego déjalos caer poco a poco hasta tocar el piso con las manos, doblando también tu cintura, el cuello y la cabeza.

Using background knowledge: What do you know about low-impact exercises, calisthenics, and stretching?

Using the article: Where in the article can you find more information about this sort of exercise? Use reading strategies such as scanning and looking at pictures to help you.

Client 2: "I spend all day at my computer, and get very stiff and tense. What can I do to feel better?"

Using background knowledge: What parts of your body become tired or tense from sitting and working at the computer?

Using the article: Where in the article can you find information about this topic? Remember that reading strategies such as using context and cognates can help you guess the meaning of unknown vocabulary.

Now you're ready to answer your clients' questions. Combine what you already know about these topics with what you've learned from this article, and write some advice for each client. Use informal commands and **(No) debes...** + *infinitive* in your answers.

C. Form groups of two or three students. Choose one of the five exercises. While one person reads the description, listen and try to act it out. Try this with all five exercises. Take turns reading and acting out the exercises.

D. Inventa un ejercicio nuevo de tres pasos. Escribe las instrucciones en español. Luego, júntate con un compañero o una compañera de clase. Lee tu ejercicio en voz alta y verifica si tu compañero/a puede seguir las instrucciones.

Cuaderno para hispanohablantes, pp. 51–53

Cuaderno de actividades, p. 131, Act. 15

Reading
Activities B and C

Making Inferences
Observing Ask students which body parts will be toned or relaxed in each of the exercises.

Additional Practice
B. Have one student express to a partner in Spanish a different problem or question. The partner then gives advice with **(No) debes...** Have volunteers present their queries to the class to get other students' advice.

Postreading
Activity D

Monitoring Comprehension
Ask students to imagine that they did not understand the directions for an exercise. Have them work with a partner and write an additional question about each exercise. Then have students exchange questions with a partner and see if they can answer their partner's questions.

Communication for All Students

Slower Pace
Explain that in order to find the information in the article, students will need a combination of strategies in addition to their background knowledge. Briefly review how to scan, use pictures, guess from context, and use cognates to understand a reading. Work as a class to answer the first question. Have students work individually to answer the second question.

Visual/Auditory Learners
Hold up pictures of three different exercises. Give oral directions for one of the three exercises. The class is to guess which one you described.

Más práctica gramatical

CAPÍTULO 11

For **Más práctica gramatical**
Answer Transparencies, see the
Teaching Transparencies binder.

Más práctica gramatical

Primer paso

Objective Making suggestions and expressing feelings

1 Explica cómo se sienten todos después de la feria de deportes del colegio. Usa la forma correcta de **sentirse**. (**p. 331**)

1. el profesor Santana/cansado
2. yo/bien
3. Rogelio/horrible
4. Sandra y Claudia/excelente
5. tú/muy mal
6. nosotros/muy bien
7. Perico y Javi/mal

2 You're the coach of your school's soccer team and tomorrow is the big championship game. Write sentences with **sentirse**, saying how each of the following people feel before the big game. (**p. 331**)

MODELO   María/feliz
            María se siente feliz.

1. Yo/nervioso
2. Ustedes/muy bien
3. Rogelio/muy mal
5. Humberto y María/cansados
6. Luis y yo/preocupados

3 Read what your friends say about sports. Then suggest an activity for each friend, using **¿Qué tal si...?** or **¿Por qué no...?** and an expression from the box. (**pp. 331, 332**)

MODELO   —Me encanta el fútbol.
            —**¿Qué tal si/Por qué no asistes a un partido?**

patinar sobre ruedas	hacer yoga	estirarse un poco antes
asistir a un partido	levantar pesas	ir al lago	ir al gimnasio

1. —Me gustaría ser muy fuerte.
   —¿▦▦▦?
2. —Me encanta nadar.
   —¿▦▦▦?
3. —A mí me gustan las clases de ejercicios aeróbicos.
   —¿▦▦▦?
4. —Quiero practicar un deporte nuevo y divertido.
   —¿▦▦▦?
5. —Siempre me siento mal cuando hago ejercicio.
   —¿▦▦▦?
6. —Hace mucho calor, y no tengo ganas de correr en el parque.
   —¿▦▦▦?

Answers

1 1. El profesor Santana se siente cansado.
2. Yo me siento bien.
3. Rogelio se siente horrible.
4. Ellas se sienten excelentes.
5. Tú te sientes muy mal.
6. Nosotros nos sentimos muy bien.
7. Ellos se sienten mal.

2 1. Yo me siento nervioso.
2. Ustedes se sienten muy bien.
3. Rogelio se siente muy mal.
4. Humberto y María se sienten cansados.
5. Luis y yo nos sentimos preocupados.

3 1. ¿Qué tal si/Por qué no levantas pesas?
2. ¿Qué tal si/Por qué no vas al lago?
3. ¿Qué tal si/Por qué no vas al gimnasio?
4. ¿Qué tal si/Por qué no patinas sobre ruedas?
5. ¿Qué tal si/Por qué no te estiras un poco antes?
6. ¿Qué tal si/Por qué no haces yoga?

Grammar Resources for Chapter 11

The **Más práctica gramatical** activities are designed as supplemental activities for the grammatical concepts presented in the chapter. You might use them as additional practice, for review, or for assessment.

For more grammar presentation, review, and practice, refer to the following:
• Cuaderno de gramática
• Grammar Tutor for Students of Spanish

• Grammar Summary on pp. R9–R13
• Cuaderno de actividades
• Grammar and Vocabulary quizzes (Testing Program)
• Test Generator on the One-Stop Planner CD-ROM
• Interactive CD-ROM Tutor
• DVD Tutor
• **Juegos interactivos** at **go.hrw.com**

4 It's Saturday morning, and everyone is getting exercise. Complete the description of what's going on at the fitness center by filling in each blank with the correct present tense form of a verb from the box. (**p. 332**)

patinar	tomar	hacer	correr
levantar	jugar	nadar	estirarse

Hay muchas personas en el club deportivo esta mañana. En la piscina, unos chicos
____1____ muy rápido y al lado, unas señoras ____2____ una clase de aeróbicos en el agua.
Arriba, en el salón grande, Celia ____3____ y después ____4____ yoga con Felicia. Óscar
quiere ser más fuerte, y por eso él ____5____ pesas con unos amigos. En el gimnasio,
Lorenzo ____6____ al baloncesto. Afuera Alonso y Guille ____7____ sobre ruedas mientras
Julia ____8____ con su perro.

Segundo paso

Objective Talking about moods and physical condition

5 Indica qué parte del cuerpo se asocia con las siguientes cosas y actividades. Cada parte del cuerpo se usa solamente una vez. (**p. 335**)

1. las flores
2. escuchar la radio
3. un sombrero
4. levantar pesas
5. las corbatas
6. tener hambre
7. patinar sobre ruedas
8. los zapatos

a. las piernas
b. el cuello
c. la cabeza
d. los oídos
e. la nariz
f. los pies
g. los brazos
h. el estómago

Answers

4 1. nadan
2. toman
3. se estira
4. hace
5. levanta
6. juega
7. patinan
8. corre

5 1. e
2. d
3. c
4. g
5. b
6. h
7. a
8. f

Teacher to Teacher

Carol Chadwick
Taipei American School,
Taipei, Taiwan

Sharp eyes help sharpen skills in Carol's class.
"Before the students enter the room, I tape 20 small pictures of different parts of the body around the room, numbered 1–20, visible but not too obvious. The first five students to write down all 20 correctly get a small prize or extra points. This totally engages the students!"

Más práctica gramatical

WV3 PUERTO RICO-11

6 What these people did yesterday is causing them aches and pains today. Write what is bothering them, using the correct form of **doler** and a different expression from the box in each sentence. (**p. 336**)

MODELO   Cristóbal estudió por cuatro horas ayer.
   Le duelen los ojos.

> los brazos   los oídos   los dedos   la espalda
>
> las piernas   la garganta   el estómago

1. Irina tocó la guitarra toda la tarde ayer.
2. Humberto y Luisa bailaron mucho en la fiesta anoche.
3. Marisa y Silvia levantaron pesas ayer.
4. Tú cantaste con el coro en un concierto anoche.
5. Por la mañana, ayudé a papá a poner muchas cosas en el garaje.
6. Samuel y yo escuchamos música rock toda la noche.
7. Joselito tomó ocho vasos de limonada ayer.

Tercer paso

Objectives Saying what you did; talking about where you went and when

7 Todos en tu familia lo pasaron bien este fin de semana. Explica qué hizo cada persona, usando la forma correcta de **jugar** en el pretérito. (**p. 340**)

MODELO   Mis primos/baloncesto
   Mis primos jugaron al baloncesto.

1. mi abuelo/dominó
2. mi hermana menor/con sus amigos
3. yo/voleibol
4. mi mamá y mi tía/tenis
5. mis hermanos y yo/béisbol
6. mi papá/fútbol
7. mi perro/con el gato

Answers

6 1. Le duelen los dedos.
2. Les duelen las piernas.
3. Les duelen los brazos.
4. Te duele la garganta.
5. Me duele la espalda.
6. Nos duelen los oídos.
7. Le duele el estómago.

7 1. Mi abuelo jugó al dominó.
2. Mi hermana menor jugó con sus amigos.
3. Yo jugué al voleibol.
4. Mamá y mi tía jugaron al tenis.
5. Mis hermanos y yo jugamos al béisbol.
6. Papá jugó al fútbol.
7. El perro jugó con el gato.

Communication for All Students

Building on Previous Skills

7 As students respond to questions about sports activities using the preterite, have them then respond to questions using **ganar**. (**¿Quién ganó? ¿Quiénes ganaron?**) This may elicit responses in other verbal persons. (**Nosotros ganamos. Ellos ganaron. Yo gané.**) Next, challenge students to tell the more specific results (el resultado), or score (el marcador). Write the final scores of the game on the board as you review the numbers. You may have them tell recent scores from local or well-known professional teams. (**Los Toros les ganaron a los Leones ochenta y tres a setenta y cinco.**)

8 Complete the sentences about where everyone went this weekend using the correct preterite form of **ir** in each blank. Then tell what everyone did, using **jugar** in the preterite and a different expression from the box in each sentence. (**pp. 342, 343**)

MODELO Tere ═══ a la playa con sus amigos.
Tere *fue* a la playa con sus amigos. *Jugaron al voleibol.*

dominó	tenis	unos videojuegos	fútbol
un nuevo juego de mesa		baloncesto	béisbol

1. Fede ═══ a la cancha de fútbol.
2. Marcia y Daniel ═══ al centro comercial.
3. Roberto y Felipe ═══ al estadio.
4. Yo ═══ a la cancha de tenis.
5. Carlota y yo ═══ al gimnasio.
6. Abuelo y tío Antón ═══ al parque.
7. Manolito ═══ a la casa de su amigo.

9 Complete the following paragraph using the preterite to tell what Jorge and his friends did last week after school. (**pp. 340, 342**)

Mis amigos y yo ___1___ (practicar) muchos deportes la semana pasada. El lunes yo ___2___ (jugar) al fútbol con Carlos y María. El martes mis amigos José, Kara y yo ___3___ (ir) a la pista de correr. El miércoles y el jueves Pedro y Lola ___4___ (levantar) pesas en el gimnasio. El sábado yo ___5___ (ir) a la cancha de fútbol con Milagros. Milagros ___6___ (jugar) muy bien.

Answers

8 *Answers may vary.*
1. fue. Jugó al fútbol.
2. fueron. Jugaron unos videojuegos nuevos.
3. fueron. Jugaron al béisbol.
4. fui. Jugué al tenis.
5. fuimos. Jugamos al basquetbol.
6. fueron. Jugaron al dominó.
7. fue. Jugó un nuevo juego de mesa.

9 1. practicamos
2. jugué
3. fuimos
4. levantaron
5. fui
6. jugó

Review and Assess

You may wish to assign the **Más práctica gramatical** activities as additional practice or homework after presenting material throughout the chapter. Assign Activities 1–2 after **Nota gramatical** (p. 331), Activity 3 after **Así se dice** (p. 331) and **Vocabulario** (p. 332), Activity 4 after **Vocabulario** (p. 332), Activity 5 after **Vocabulario** (p. 335), Activity 6 after **Nota gramatical** (p. 336), Activity 7 after **Nota gramatical** (p. 340), Activity 8 after **Nota gramatical** (p. 340) and **Vocabulario** (p. 343), and Activity 9 after **Nota gramatical** (pp. 340, 342). To prepare students for the **Paso** Quizzes and Chapter Test, have them do the **Más práctica gramatical** activities in the following order: complete Activities 1–4 before taking Quiz 11-1A or 11-1B; Activities 5–6 before taking Quiz 11-2A or 11-2B; and Activities 7–9 before taking Quiz 11-3A or 11-3B.

The **Repaso** reviews all four skills and culture in preparation for the Chapter Test.

Teaching Resources
pp. 352–353

PRINT

▶ Lesson Planner, p. 56
▶ Listening Activities, p. 85
▶ Video Guide, pp. 75–77, 80
▶ Grammar Tutor for Students of Spanish, Chapter 11
▶ Cuaderno para hispanohablantes, pp. 51–55
▶ Standardized Assessment Tutor, Chapter 11

MEDIA

▶ One-Stop Planner
▶ Video Program, Videocassette 4, 18:31–23:03
▶ DVD Tutor, Disc 2
▶ Audio Compact Discs, CD 11, Tr. 16
▶ Interactive CD-ROM Tutor, Disc 3

Answers

1 Ray—Estoy resfriado.
Bernardo—Tengo fiebre.
Lu—Me duele la cabeza.
Bonita—Me duele el brazo.
Lupita—Me duele el estómago.
Mickey—Me duele el oído.

2 *Possible answers:*
1. Roberto Clemente, Rod Carew
2. like a rodeo competition, Mexico
3. Football

3 1. cierto
2. cierto
3. falso; Los dos asistieron a clases.
4. falso; Los dos evitaron la grasa.

Repaso

internet

MARCAR: go.hrw.com
PALABRA CLAVE:
WV3 PUERTO RICO-11

1 Look at the drawing of Dra. Demora's waiting room. What would each patient say to tell the doctor how he or she feels? See answers below.

Ray   Bernardo   Lu   Bonita   Lupita   Mickey

2 Use the **Notas culturales** and the **Panorama cultural** in this chapter to answer the following questions. See possible answers below.
1. Name two Hispanic players in the Baseball Hall of Fame.
2. What kind of sport is **la charrería?** Which country claims it as a national sport?
3. Name a popular North-American sport that is not widely played in Spanish-speaking countries.

3 Lee el artículo sobre los dos atletas. Decide si las oraciones que siguen son **ciertas** o **falsas**. Si la oración es falsa, cámbiala. See answers below.

¿Cómo fue el día para estos dos campeones? Alejandra Villarreal, campeona de tenis, y Martín Reyes, campeón de natación, se entrenaron y prepararon para sus competencias.

Ayer Alejandra se levantó a las cinco y media y pasó una hora haciendo yoga y montando en bicicleta estacionaria antes de desayunar. Después de las clases, fue a la cancha de tenis donde practicó por dos horas. Martín se levantó a la seis y se estiró antes de levantar pesas por una hora. A las tres de la tarde fue a la piscina y practicó por

dos horas. Los dos dicen que comieron muchas frutas e hidratos de carbono, evitaron las grasas y el estrés, bebieron mucha agua y se acostaron temprano. Para ser campeón o campeona es necesario tener mucha disciplina y dedicación. Gracias a su preparación, los dos ganaron sus competencias.

1. Los dos practicaron sus deportes el día antes de la competencia.
2. Alejandra y Martín se levantaron y se acostaron temprano ayer.
3. Ninguno fue a las clases ese día.
4. Ellos comieron bien pero también comieron mucha grasa.

Apply and Assess

Challenge
2 Ask students to work in pairs. Have them create two more questions using the **Notas culturales** and the **Panorama cultural.** Then have the class trade questions and try to answer them.

Auditory Learners
3 Have students read the article aloud, pausing when they think they have reached a false statement. Ask them to keep a numbered list of false statements that they can correct later.

Slower Pace
Use pictures clipped from magazines to review the various expressions and vocabulary in this chapter.

4 Listen as Rafi and Sara talk about their last weekend in Puerto Rico. Answer the questions in Spanish. Script and answers on p. 325H.

CD 11
Tr. 16

1. ¿Cómo se siente Rafi?
2. ¿Cómo se siente Sara?
3. ¿Qué quieren hacer ellos?
4. ¿Qué le gustó a Sara?
5. ¿Qué le gustó a Rafi?

5 ## Vamos a escribir

Imagine you're a reporter. Write up an interview you conducted with Benjamín and his mother about their recent vacation in Puerto Rico. Introduce your subjects, then include some of your conversation along with your narrative.

Estrategia para escribir
Using dialogue is a good way to make your writing more lively and vivid. When writing a dialogue, consider who your characters are and make their style of speaking appropriate for their personalities and ages.

Prewriting

1. Write a list of adjectives to describe Benjamín and his mother. Choose three adjectives that you think best describe the personality of each.

2. Think of four questions you want to ask Ben and his mother about their recent vacation. Put these in logical order.

Writing

1. Write a two-to-three-sentence introduction, telling your readers what the interview is about.

2. Write a question for either Ben or his mother.

3. Give the answer, based on what they did on their vacation. Remember to write each answer from either Ben's or his mother's point of view.

4. Repeat with the rest of the interview questions. Be sure to include as many details as you can, and keep Ben's and his mother's personalities in mind.

Revising

Work with a partner to look for the strengths and weaknesses of your dialogue. Are the questions and responses clear? Are the ideas well organized? Check spelling and adjective agreement, too. Make all necessary changes to your interview.

 Re-entry
Have students look back to the Location Opener on pages 322–325 or to the Chapter Opener on pages 326–327 for ideas to support the **Situación.**

 Portfolio

5 **Written** Suggest that students write their interviews in their written Portfolio. For Portfolio information, see *Alternative Assessment Guide,* pp. iv–17.

6 ### Situación

Work with three or four classmates. Invite each other to go to the variety of places in San Juan you learned about. Turn down some invitations and make suggestions of other places to go. In the end, decide on an activity. Present the scene to the class.

Cuaderno para hispanohablantes, p. 55

Apply and Assess

Process Writing

5 You might want to show *Un recorrido por San Juan* on video to remind students how the characters speak to one another. (Ben speaks more informally than his mother.) What surprising things happened to Ben and his mother during their vacation in Puerto Rico? What did they learn? Did they have a good time?

A ver si puedo

Teaching Resources
p. 354

PRINT
▸ Grammar Tutor for Students of Spanish, Chapter 11

MEDIA
▸ Interactive CD-ROM Tutor, Disc 3
▸ Online self-test

go.hrw.com
WV3 PUERTO RICO-11

Teacher Note
This page is intended to help students prepare for the Chapter Test. It is designed for the students to work on their own initiative and consists of a brief checklist of the major points covered in the chapter. The students should be reminded that this is only a checklist and does not necessarily include everything that will appear on the Chapter Test.

Answers

1 Cristóbal levanta pesas.
Dolores hace yoga.
Adriana monta a caballo.

2 *Sample answer:*
1. No deben trabajar tanto.

3 *Sample answer:*
1. Estoy cansada y me duelen las piernas.

5 *Answers may vary.*
1. Roberto nadó en la piscina.
2. Silvia y Sofía jugaron al tenis en la cancha de tenis.
3. La familia Pérez miró el partido en la cancha de fútbol.
4. Mi hermana y yo compramos discos compactos en la tienda de discos.
5. Tú jugaste al fútbol americano en el estadio.
6. Mónica y Gabi estudiaron en la biblioteca.
7. Federico y sus padres caminaron en el parque.
8. Yo hice ejercicio en el gimnasio.

A ver si puedo...

Can you make suggestions and express feelings? p. 331

1 Look at the drawings. Can you tell what each person does to lead a healthy life? See answers below.

Cristóbal

Dolores

Adriana

2 What would you suggest to the following people who want to live a healthy life? See sample answer below.
1. tus padres
2. tu mejor amigo/a
3. tu profesor(a)
4. tu hermano/a
5. tu novio/a
6. tu primo/a

Can you talk about moods and physical condition? p. 334

3 Write a sentence telling how you feel in these situations. See sample answer below.
1. cuando corres mucho
2. cuando comes muy rápido
3. cuando trabajas demasiado
4. cuando lees mucho
5. cuando estudias seis horas
6. cuando recibes una mala nota
7. cuando tienes tos
8. cuando hace mucho frío
9. cuando escribes exámenes todo el día
10. cuando no estudias para un examen

4 What parts of the body do you use in these activities? Answers will vary.
1. patinar
2. preparar la cena
3. bailar
4. dibujar
5. hablar por teléfono
6. nadar
7. cantar
8. esquiar
9. escuchar música
10. leer

Can you say what you did and talk about where you went and when? pp. 340, 342

5 For each combination below, write a sentence telling where the person or persons went and what they did at each location. See answers below.
1. Roberto/la piscina
2. Silvia y Sofía/la cancha de tenis
3. La familia Pérez/la cancha de fútbol
4. Mi hermana y yo/la tienda de discos
5. Tú/el estadio
6. Mónica y Gabi/la biblioteca
7. Federico y sus padres/el parque
8. Yo/el gimnasio

Communication for All Students

Additional Practice

3 On the board or a transparency, write several sentences that describe a physcial or emotional condition. (**A Jorge le duelen las piernas. Miguel está preocupado.**) Ask students to offer explanations for how each person feels. (**A Jorge le duelen las piernas porque fue al gimnasio ayer. Miguel está preocupado porque no terminó la tarea anoche.**) Encourage students to use the preterite tense in their explanations.

5 Ask students to pick an item from the activity and write about where that person or persons went and what they did for an entire day.

Primer paso

Making suggestions and expressing feelings

estirarse	to stretch	montar a caballo	to ride a horse	¿Qué tienes?	What's the matter?
hacer yoga	to do yoga	nada más	that's all	sano/a	healthy
levantar pesas	to lift weights	patinar sobre ruedas	to roller skate	sentirse (ie)	to feel
llevar una vida sana	to lead a healthy life	¿Por qué no...?	Why don't . . .?	¿Te sientes mal?	Do you feel bad?
¡Magnífico!	Great!	¿Qué tal si...?	What if . . .?	la vida	life

Segundo paso

Talking about moods and physical condition

la boca	mouth	la espalda	back	el pie	foot
el brazo	arm	estar mal	to feel poorly	la pierna	leg
la cabeza	head	estar resfriado/a	to have a cold	preocupado/a por algo	worried about something
¿Cómo te sientes?	How are you feeling?	el estómago	stomach	¿Qué le pasa a...?	What's wrong with . . .?
el cuello	neck	la garganta	throat		
el cuerpo	body	la mano	hand	tener fiebre	to have a fever
el dedo	finger, toe	la nariz	nose	tener gripe	to have the flu
doler (ue)	to hurt, to ache	nervioso/a	nervous	tener tos	to have a cough
enojado/a	angry	el oído	ear	triste	sad
		la oreja	earlobe		

Tercer paso

Saying what you did and talking about where you went and when

¿Adónde fuiste?	Where did you go?	la cancha (de fútbol)	(soccer) field	ganar	to win, to earn
anteanoche	the night before last	la cancha de tenis	tennis court	la pista de correr	running track
		el estadio	stadium		

Review and Assess

 Game

The Rose technique is a fun, useful way to practice vocabulary. Ask students to draw a monster using the body parts in the **Vocabulario**. (with two heads, three arms, etc.) Tell them not to let other students see what they draw. Then have them describe their monster to a partner, holding the drawing so the partner cannot see it. The student draws the monster his or her partner describes. They should then compare the two monsters and evaluate description, comprehension, and creative interpretation. You may wish to display students' artwork.

Vocabulario

CAPÍTULO 11

Teacher Note

The active vocabulary list in this chapter is intentionally light to allow your class more time for end-of-the-year wrap-up activities, such as oral interviews or completion of long-term projects.

Circumlocution

Have the class play ¿**Cómo te diré?** (p. 167C) to practice vocabulary for body parts. Ask students to describe parts of the body not included in Chapter 11. Some suggestions are **la frente** *forehead*, **la mandíbula** *jaw*, **la cintura** *waist*, **el diente** *tooth*, **el antebrazo** *forearm*, **la lengua** *tongue*. You might ask students what words in English remind them of these words. Refer to the Language-to-Language note on page 335.

Chapter 11 Assessment

▶ **Testing Program**
Chapter Test, pp. 287–292
Audio Compact Discs, CD 11, Trs. 20–21
Speaking Test, p. 348

▶ **Alternative Assessment Guide**
Performance Assessment, p. 42
Portfolio Assessment, p. 28
CD-ROM Assessment, p. 56

▶ **Interactive CD-ROM Tutor, Disc 3**
 ¡A hablar!
¡A escribir!

▶ **Standardized Assessment Tutor**
Chapter 11

▶ **One-Stop Planner, Disc 3**
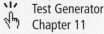 Test Generator
Chapter 11

Capítulo 12: Las vacaciones ideales

Chapter Overview

De antemano pp. 358–360	*Unas vacaciones ideales*

	FUNCTIONS	GRAMMAR	VOCABULARY	RE-ENTRY
Primer paso pp. 361–364	• Talking about what you do and like to do every day, p. 361 • Making future plans, p. 362	• Stem-changing verbs: e→ie and o→ue, p. 362 • Verbs followed by an infinitive, p. 363	• Vacation items, p. 363	• Chapter 12 is a global review of Chapters 1–11.
Segundo paso pp. 366–370	• Discussing what you would like to do on vacation, p. 367	• Uses of **ser** and **estar**, p. 369	• Vacation activities, p. 370	• Chapter 12 is a global review of Chapters 1–11.
Tercer paso pp. 371–373	• Saying where you went and what you did on vacation, p. 371	• The preterite of -**ar** and **ir** verbs, p. 371	• Countries, p. 372	• Chapter 12 is a global review of Chapters 1–11.

Letra y sonido p. 373	**The letters *p, t,* and *k*** Audio CD 12, Track 10	**Dictado** Audio CD 12, Tracks 11–13
Vamos a leer pp. 374–375	**¿Cuáles son las vacaciones ideales para ti?**	**Reading Strategy:** Recognizing text organization
Más práctica gramatical	**pp. 376–379** **Primer paso,** pp. 376–377	**Segundo paso,** p. 378 **Tercer paso,** p. 379
Review pp. 380–383	**Repaso,** pp. 380–381 **Vamos a escribir,** p. 381 Writing good conclusions	**A ver si puedo...,** p. 382 **Vocabulario,** p. 383

CULTURE

- **Panorama cultural, ¿Adónde vas y qué haces en las vacaciones?,** p. 365
- **Realia,** Ad for Puerto Rican resort, p. 368
- **Nota cultural,** Spain's **paradores,** p. 370
- **A lo nuestro,** Spanish colloquialisms, p. 372

Capítulo 12: Las vacaciones ideales

Chapter Resources

PRINT 📖

Lesson Planning

\|/ **One-Stop Planner**

🖐 **Lesson Planner with Substitute Teacher Lesson Plans,** pp. 58–62, 76

Student Make-Up Assignments

- Make-Up Assignment Copying Masters, Chapter 12

Listening and Speaking

TPR Storytelling Book, pp. 45–48

Listening Activities

- Student Response Forms for Listening Activities, pp. 91–93
- Additional Listening Activities 12-1 to 12-6, pp. 95–97
- Additional Listening Activities (song), p. 98
- Scripts and Answers, pp. 157–161

Video Guide

- Teaching Suggestions, pp. 81–83
- Activity Masters, pp. 84–86
- Scripts and Answers, pp. 111–112, 118

Activities for Communication

- Communicative Activities, pp. 67–72
- Realia and Teaching Suggestions, pp. 130–134
- Situation Cards, pp. 159–160

Reading and Writing

Reading Strategies and Skills Handbook, Chapter 12

¡Lee conmigo! 1, Chapter 12

Cuaderno de actividades, pp. 133–144

Grammar

Cuaderno de gramática, pp. 97–107

Grammar Tutor for Students of Spanish, Chapter 12

Assessment

Testing Program

- Grammar and Vocabulary Quizzes, **Paso** Quizzes, and Chapter Test, pp. 301–318
- Score Sheet, Scripts and Answers, pp. 319–326

- Final Exam, pp. 327–334
- Score Sheet, Scripts, and Answers, pp. 335–340

Alternative Assessment Guide

- Portfolio Assessment, p. 29
- Performance Assessment, p. 43
- CD-ROM Assessment, p. 57

Student Make-Up Assignments

- Alternative Quizzes, Chapter 12

Standardized Assessment Tutor

- Reading, pp. 47–49
- Writing, p. 50
- Math, pp. 51–52

Native Speakers

Cuaderno para hispanohablantes, pp. 56–60

MEDIA 💿📹📚

 **Online Activities**

- Juegos interactivos
- Actividades Internet

 Video Program

- Videocassette 4
- Videocassette 5 (captioned version)

 Interactive CD-ROM Tutor, Disc 3

DVD Tutor, Disc 2

 Audio Compact Discs

- Textbook Listening Activities, CD 12, Tracks 1–15
- Additional Listening Activities, CD 12, Tracks 25–31
- Assessment Items, CD 12, Tracks 16–24

 Teaching Transparencies

- Situations 12-1 to 12-3
- Vocabulary 12-A
- **De antemano**
- **Más práctica gramatical** Answers
- **Cuaderno de gramática** Answers

 \|/ **One-Stop** Planner CD-ROM

Use the **One-Stop Planner CD-ROM with Test Generator** to aid in lesson planning and pacing.

For each chapter, the **One-Stop Planner** includes:

- Editable lesson plans with direct links to teaching resources
- Printable worksheets from resource books
- Direct launches to the HRW Internet activities
- Video and audio segments
- Test Generator
- Clip Art for vocabulary items

Projects ·····················

Collage de fotos

In this activity students describe their ideal vacation spot and make collages to enhance their presentation.

> **MATERIALS**
>
> ✂ **Students may need**
> - Poster board
> - Magazines
> - Crayons or markers
> - Scissors
> - Glue or tape
> - Index cards

SUGGESTED SEQUENCE

1. Assign as group or individual work, depending on class size and time available.

2. Students decide on a vacation spot to illustrate.

3. Ask students to search for information in the school or public library, using almanacs, reference books, and magazines, or to contact local travel agencies for more information. You may also have them search Web sites for information.

4. Have students gather drawings, photographs, magazine images, or small objects for their collages. Allow dictionaries, but require that all text be in Spanish.

5. Have students make temporary layouts of collages until they decide on the final design. Then they can affix materials to poster board.

6. Have students outline their plan for presentation with suggestions from you. They may peer-edit their work.

7. Have students practice presentations in pairs, working on not reading verbatim.

8. Students present projects and posters are displayed.

GRADING THE PROJECT

Each member of a group receives the same grade.
Suggested point distribution: (total = 100 points)

Collage
Creativity...20
Labels and explanations 10
Neatness 10
Oral presentation
Content 20
Vocabulary and grammar 30
Oral presentation skills 10

Games ·····················

Las vacaciones ideales

In this game, students learn the location and pronunciation of various cities. You can use this game at any time.

Materials One index card with the names of two Spanish-speaking cities for each student. Tape a large world map (or map of Latin America) on the board. Cut string long enough to reach across the map.

Procedure Divide the class into two teams. Give the first player on Team A a card. The player is to say **Vivo en** (first city on card) y **voy a** (second city on card) **para las vacaciones.** If the player can locate and connect the two cities with the string, his or her team gets one point. The string and a new card then go to the first player on Team B. Follow the same procedure until all cards have been used. The team with the highest score wins.

Variation Instead of Spanish-speaking cities, write the names in Spanish of any two countries in the world and ask students to connect them. Refer students to the world map on pages T72–T73 and tell them that the names of most places will be similar to their English forms.

Busca a alguien

Students will enjoy reviewing vocabulary with this game.

Procedure Divide the class into groups of four. A group must find someone who fits a description below. The students have a minute to walk around the room asking questions in Spanish to find at least one person who fits each description. A group gets one point if it succeeds. You may choose to give bonus points for the more exotic items listed. Follow the same procedure with each group. The group with the highest score wins.

Busca a alguien. Esta persona...

- lleva chancletas
- quiere viajar a Inglaterra, Francia, Egipto...
- quiere saltar en paracaídas
- quiere tomar el sol en la China, en Cancún...
- quiere explorar la selva o usa el bloqueador en el verano o lleva lentes (de sol)
- tiene una cámara buena, una bicicleta...
- tiene un traje de baño verde
- bajó un río en canoa
- fue de vela el verano pasado

Storytelling

Mini-cuento

This story accompanies Teaching Transparency 12-2. The mini-cuento can be told and retold in different formats, acted out, written, and read aloud to give students additional opportunities to practice all four skills. The following story relates what people plan to do during summer vacation.

Las vacaciones ideales

No falta mucho para el verano y los estudiantes del Colegio Lomas Verdes están hablando sobre las cosas que les gustaría hacer en las vacaciones. El maestro Godínez les dice que hay una fantástica isla en el Pacífico que se llama Paraíso. Así que los estudiantes dicen lo que les gustaría hacer en la isla. Josefina dice que le gustaría leer y tomar el sol todo el día. Manuel piensa saltar en paracaídas. A María y a Raúl les gusta caminar por el bosque y escalar montañas. Lola tiene ganas de bajar el río en canoa. A Efrén y a Marta les gusta hacer turismo tomando fotos. Miguel todavía es muy chico y sólo quiere acampar. A Fernando le gustan las plantas y los animales y dice que piensa explorar la selva. A Luis le gustaría ir de vela y pasar todo el verano en la isla.

¿Qué te gustaría hacer este verano?

Traditions

Arte

Puerto Rican folk art represents a colorful blend of cultures. The **vejigantes,** with roots in medieval Spain, are brightly decorated masks of animals and monsters with jagged teeth and horns. They are traditionally made out of dried coconut shells or papier-mâché, and are especially associated with **carnaval** in the towns of Ponce and Loíza. Have students research this tradition and make their own **vejigante**s, perhaps representing their school mascot and colors.

Receta

Arroz con gandules *(rice with pigeon peas) is a popular dish made with typical Puerto Rican ingredients.*

ARROZ CON GANDULES

para 6 personas

1 pimiento dulce	2 tazas de aceitunas verdes, cortadas a la mitad
1 tomate	
2 dientes de ajo	4 tazas de agua caliente
1 cebolla pequeña	4 ajíes
1 cucharadita de pimienta negra	6 ramitas enteras de cilantro (culantro)
2 onzas de salsa de tomate enlatado	4 cucharadas de aceite de achiote
2 tazas de gandules cocidos (se puede usar garbanzos)	1 cucharada de hojitas de orégano seco
2 tazas de arroz	sal al gusto

Lave, pele, y corte todo, excepto la salsa de tomate, los gandules, el arroz y las aceitunas. No olvide quitar las semillas de los chiles y del pimiento. Mezcle los ingredientes en una licuadora hasta que se haga un puré. Caliente el aceite en una olla gruesa a fuego mediano. Vierta el puré en la olla y cocínelo, removiendo por 5 minutos. Agregue los gandules y después el arroz. Cocine y remueva hasta cubrir el arroz con el aceite. Añada la salsa de tomate, las aceitunas y la sal. Después agregue el agua y caliéntelo hasta que hierva. Después baje la llama hasta que el agua se evapore. Voltee una o dos veces el arroz. Cúbralo y cocínelo a fuego lento por 30 minutos.

Technology

Videocassette 4, Videocassette 5 (captioned version)
DVD Tutor, Disc 2
See Video Guide, pages 81–86.

DVD/Video

De antemano • Unas vacaciones ideales

Ben and Carmen are bored, so their grandfather asks them what they would do on their ideal vacation. Ben says that he would travel down the Amazon in a canoe and explore the jungles of South America. Carmen says that she would sail the Pacific and find a deserted island. Then Ben and Carmen's mother comes in and tells them that they are going to take a short trip, but she won't tell them where.

¿Adónde vas y qué haces en las vacaciones?

Teenagers from Argentina, Puerto Rico, and Venezuela talk about what they do and where they go during their vacations. In additional interviews, people from various Spanish-speaking countries tell us about their vacations.

A continuación

Ben and Carmen's mother surprises them by taking them to El Yunque National Park, where Ben finds an orchid and they hear a coquí. The next day they go to the beach for a picnic. With these two trips, Ben and Carmen feel they have experienced their ideal vacation.

Videoclips

- Los parques acuáticos: informational report about water parks in Spain

Interactive CD-ROM Tutor

Activity	Activity Type	Pupil's Edition Page
En contexto	*Interactive conversation*	
1. Vocabulario	¡Super memoria!	p. 363
2. Gramática	¿Qué falta?	p. 362
3. Vocabulario	¿Cuál es?	p. 366
4. Gramática	¡A escoger!	p. 369
5. Así se dice	Patas arriba	p. 371
6. Gramática	¿Qué falta?	p. 371
Panorama cultural	¿Adónde vas y qué haces en las vacaciones?	p. 365
¡A hablar!	*Guided recording*	pp. 376–377
¡A escribir!	*Guided writing*	pp. 376–377

Teacher Management System

Launch the program, type "admin" in the password area, and press RETURN. Log on to **www.hrw.com/CDROMTUTOR** for a detailed explanation of the Teacher Management System.

DVD Tutor

The *DVD Tutor* contains all material from the *Video Program* as described above. Spanish captions are available for use at your discretion for all sections of the video. The *DVD Tutor* also provides a variety of video-based activities that assess students' understanding of the **De antemano, A continuación,** and **Panorama cultural.**

This part of the *DVD Tutor* may be used on any DVD video player connected to a television or video monitor.

In addition to the video material and the video-based comprehension activities, the *DVD Tutor* also contains the entire *Interactive CD-ROM Tutor* in DVD-ROM format. Each DVD disc contains the activities from all 12 chapters of the *Interactive CD-ROM Tutor.*

This part of the *DVD Tutor* may be used on a Macintosh® or Windows® computer with a DVD-ROM drive.

Internet Connection ....

One-Stop Planner CD-ROM

To preview all resources available for this chapter, use the **One-Stop Planner CD-ROM**, Disc 3.

internet

go.hrw.com

MARCAR: go.hrw.com
PALABRA CLAVE:
WV3 PUERTO RICO-12

*Have students explore the **go.hrw.com** Web site for many online resources covering all chapters. All Chapter 12 resources are available under the keyword WV3 PUERTO RICO-12. Interactive games help students practice the material and provide them with immediate feedback. You will also find a printable worksheet that provides Internet activities that lead to a comprehensive online research project.*

Juegos interactivos

You can use the interactive activities in this chapter

- to practice grammar, vocabulary, and chapter functions
- as homework
- as an assessment option
- as a self-test
- to prepare for the Chapter Test

Actividades Internet

Students choose a place they would like to visit on a fantasy vacation. They then research the destination on the Internet and write about what activities they would do there.

- To prepare students for the **Hoja de actividades**, encourage them to list their criteria for a perfect vacation. If they do not know how to express an idea in Spanish, have them look it up in a dictionary before searching the Internet.

- After completing the activity sheet, have students review the **Panorama cultural** on page 365. Do any of those teenagers do the things they like to do on vacation? Ask them to choose one person and research the place he or she mentions.

Proyecto

Travel writing is a popular genre. Good travel writers not only describe facts, but they include how a place makes them feel and what beauty and humor they find there. Ask students to describe a recent vacation, either a real trip or the "perfect" one they took in the **Hoja de actividades**. Encourage them to describe their experience in as much detail as possible.

Primer paso

 10 p. 363

1. — ¡Ay, las montañas de Colorado! Me encanta esquiar.
— Sí, pero debes tener cuidado.

2. — Es el viaje de mis sueños—una semana en Cancún.
— ¡Qué maravilla! Voy a pasar todos los días en la playa.

3. — ¡Dos semanas en el Caribe! Pensamos acampar, estar lejos de todo, sin trabajar ni estudiar.
— Y espero dar muchos paseos. Va a ser fantástico.
— A propósito, ¿tienes la cámara?

Answers to Activity 10
1. a
2. c
3. b

Segundo paso

20 p. 368

SARA Me llamo Sara Mercado y vivo en San Juan, Puerto Rico. A mí me gustaría viajar a España porque quiero ver el país de mis abuelos. En España hay muchas cosas interesantes, sobre todo las montañas y los castillos hermosos. Quiero quedarme en España durante todo el verano. Pienso viajar con mis primos que viven en Nueva York.

DAVID Soy David Álvarez Medellín y vivo en Guadalajara. A mí me gustaría ver las Islas Galápagos. Quiero ir de excursión a las Galápagos porque tengo muchas ganas de ver los animales que viven allí. Es que hay muchos que no existen en otras partes del mundo. Me gustaría viajar a las Galápagos en dos años, al terminar mi colegio. Tengo tres amigos que también quieren viajar conmigo.

MARTÍN Me llamo Martín Valerio y vivo en Los Ángeles. Tengo muchas ganas de viajar a la Argentina. Quiero ver la capital, Buenos Aires, y los gauchos y las pampas. También me gustaría esquiar y escalar una montaña en los Andes. La Argentina es un país muy interesante. Espero ir allí con unos amigos, pero no sé cuándo.

Answers to Activity 20

SARA MERCADO:	San Juan, Puerto Rico, España, quedarse todo el verano
DAVID ÁLVAREZ MEDELLÍN:	Guadalajara, las Galápagos, ver los animales allí
MARTÍN VALERIO:	Los Ángeles, la Argentina, ver Buenos Aires, los gauchos y las pampas, y esquiar y escalar una montaña

The following scripts are for the listening activities found in the *Pupil's Edition*. For Student Response Forms, see *Listening Activites*, pages 91–93. To provide students with additional listening practice, see *Listening Activities*, pages 95–98.

To preview all resources available for this chapter, use the **One-Stop Planner CD-ROM**, Disc 3.

Tercer paso

29 p. 371

CARLOS	¡Qué divertido el viaje!
YOLANDA	Sí, tienes razón. Me gustó mucho el día en que fuimos a la playa con la prima Mari y preparamos una comida.
CARLOS	Sí, tomamos el sol, hablamos con Mari y luego jugamos al voleibol. ¿Te gustó el partido?
YOLANDA	Sí, muchísimo.
CARLOS	Y a mí me gustó mucho ver El Yunque. Cuando pienso en Puerto Rico, voy a pensar en las flores y la selva.
YOLANDA	Sí, es muy bonito. Caminamos mucho ese día, ¿no?
CARLOS	Sí, y sacamos muchas fotos.
YOLANDA	¿Te acuerdas de la fiesta con los amigos de Miguel?
CARLOS	¡Claro que sí! Lo pasé muy bien. Voy a escribir cartas a todos ellos.
YOLANDA	La visita a los abuelos también fue muy bonita. Su vida es muy diferente de nuestra vida en Nueva York, pero me encantó.
CARLOS	Sí, a mí también.

Answers to Activity 29
1. b
2. a
3. d
4. c

LETRA Y SONIDO, P. 373

For the scripts for Parts A and C, see p. 373. The script for Part B is below.

B. Dictado

Hola, Pablo, habla Pedro. Hoy tenemos que preparar la cena para papá. Voy a comprar la comida en la tienda. Tú necesitas poner las papas en el horno a las cinco. Hasta entonces.

Repaso

1 p. 380

1.	MARTA	Espero ir de vacaciones en julio. Este verano pienso ir con mi mejor amiga al norte de California para saltar en paracaídas.
2.	FRANCISCO	Voy a pasar mis vacaciones en Colorado, en las montañas. Ahí pienso acampar, pescar y dar caminatas por el bosque. Por eso necesito comprar una tienda de camping.
3.	JUAN	Yo no voy a ningún lugar. Pienso quedarme en casa y pasar el verano con mi mejor amigo.
4.	ROSARIO	A mí me gusta mucho el océano. Por eso me gustaría ir de vela este verano con mi perro. A él también le gusta.
5.	SILVIO	Para mí no hay nada mejor que tomar el sol con unos buenos libros. Por eso me gustaría pasar una semana en la playa.
6.	LETICIA	Espero ir a México este verano. Quiero escalar unas montañas con mi padre.

Answers to Repaso Activity 1
1. a
2. b
3. f
4. e
5. d
6. c

Capítulo 12: Las vacaciones ideales
Review Chapter
Suggested Lesson Plans 50-*Minute Schedule*

Day 1

CHAPTER OPENER 5 min.
- Focusing on Outcomes, ATE, p. 357
- Culture Note, ATE, p. 357

DE ANTEMANO 40 min.
- Presenting **De antemano** and Preteaching Vocabulary, ATE, p. 358
- Activities 1–5, p. 360, and Comprehension Check, ATE, p. 360
- Follow the Teaching Suggestion, ATE, p. 359.

Wrap-Up 5 min.
- Do the Using Background Knowledge activity, ATE, p. 360.

Homework Options
Cuaderno de actividades, p. 133, Activity 1

Day 2

PRIMER PASO
Quick Review 5 min.
- Check homework.
- Bell Work, ATE, p. 361

Así se dice, p. 361 15 min.
- Presenting **Así se dice**, ATE, p. 361
- Do Activity 6, p. 361.

Gramática/Así se dice, p. 362 25 min.
- Presenting **Gramática** and **Así se dice**, ATE, p. 362
- Have pairs do Activity 7, p. 362. Ask individuals the questions. Have the class report what students said.
- Have students do Activity 8, p. 362, in pairs and Activity 9, p. 362, in groups.
- Do Activities 1–3 from **Más práctica gramatical**, p. 376.

Wrap-Up 5 min.
- Have students tell a partner three things they do daily after school. Call on students to tell the class what their partner said.

Homework Options
Cuaderno de actividades, p. 134, Activities 2–3
Cuaderno de gramática, pp. 97–98, Activities 1–3

Day 3

PRIMER PASO
Quick Review 5 min.
- Check homework.
- Ask students how often they do different activities. Use stem-changing verbs and verbs ending in **–go** in the first person singular.

Así se dice, p. 362 10 min.
- Presenting **Así se dice**, ATE, p. 362

Vocabulario, p. 363 20 min.
- Presenting **Vocabulario**, ATE, p. 363
- Present **También se puede decir...**, p. 363, and the Language Note, ATE, p. 363.
- Do Activity 10, p. 363, with the Audio CD.
- Have students do Activity 11, p. 363, in pairs.

Gramática, p. 363 10 min.
- Presenting **Gramática**, ATE, p. 363
- Do Activity 12, p. 363, with the class.

Wrap-Up 5 min.
- Assign each student a destination. Have them say what they will do there and what they need to bring.

Homework Options
Más práctica gramatical, p. 377, Activities 4–5
Cuaderno de actividades, pp. 135–136, Activities 4–6
Cuaderno de gramática, pp. 99–100, Activities 4–7

Day 4

PRIMER PASO
Quick Review 10 min.
- Check homework.
- Review the **Vocabulario**, p. 363, using Teaching Transparency 12-A.

Vocabulario/Gramática, p. 363 25 min.
- Have students do Activities 13 and 14, p. 364, in pairs.
- Do the Math Link, ATE, p. 364. Then do Activity 15, p. 364, with the class.
- Have pairs do Activity 16, p. 364. Have volunteers role-play the situation.

PANORAMA CULTURAL 10 min.
- Presenting **Panorama cultural**, ATE, p. 365
- Present the Culture Note, ATE, p. 365.

Wrap-Up 5 min.
- Have students share their answers to question A from **Para pensar y hablar...**, p. 365.
- Discuss the content and format of Quiz 12-1.

Homework Options
Study for Quiz 12-1.
Cuaderno de gramática, pp. 101–102, Activities 8–11

Day 5

PRIMER PASO
Quick Review 5 min.
- Check homework.
- Quickly review the content of the **Primer paso.**

Quiz 20 min.
- Administer Quiz 12-1A, 12-1B, or a combination of the two.

SEGUNDO PASO
Vocabulario, p. 366 20 min.
- Presenting **Vocabulario**, ATE, p. 366
- Present **También se puede decir...**, p. 366.
- Do Activity 17, p. 367, with the class.

Wrap-Up 5 min.
- Do the Biology Link or Social Studies Link activity, ATE, p. 366.

Homework Options
Cuaderno de actividades, p. 137, Activity 7
Cuaderno de gramática, p. 103, Activity 12

Day 6

SEGUNDO PASO
Quick Review 10 min.
- Check homework.
- Have students write Activity 18, p. 367. Have volunteers write answers on board.

Así se dice, p. 367 35 min.
- Presenting **Así se dice**, ATE, p. 367
- Have students do Activity 19, p. 367, in pairs.
- Do Activity 20, p. 368, with the Audio CD.
- Do Activity 21, p. 368, with the class.
- Follow the Teaching Suggestion, ATE, p. 368; have pairs do Activity 22, p. 368.
- Have students work in groups to do Activity 23, p. 368 for a completion grade.

Wrap-Up 5 min.
- Ask students to name two things they would like to do while on vacation.

Homework Options
Más práctica gramatical, p. 378, Activity 6
Cuaderno de actividades, p. 137, Activity 8

One-Stop Planner CD-ROM

For alternative lesson plans by chapter section, to create your own customized plans, or to preview all resources available for this chapter, use the **One-Stop Planner CD-ROM**, Disc 3.

 For additional homework suggestions, see activities accompanied by this symbol throughout the chapter.

Day 7

SEGUNDO PASO

Quick Review 5 min.
- Check homework.
- Ask students if they would like to do the activities on Teaching Transparency 12-2.

Gramática, p. 369 40 min.
- Presenting **Gramática**, ATE, p. 369
- Present Language-to-Language, ATE, p. 369.
- Do Activities 24 and 25, p. 369.
- Do Activities 7–8, p. 378, **Más práctica gramatical.**
- Have students do Activity 26, p. 370. Give sample sentences for each location.
- Read **Nota cultural,** p. 370, then present Culture Notes, ATE, p. 370.

Wrap-Up 5 min.
- Give statements with *to be*. Have students tell whether **ser** or **estar** would be used in Spanish. As a challenge, have students translate the statements.

Homework Options
Cuaderno de actividades, pp. 138–139, Activities 9–11
Cuaderno de gramática, pp. 104–105, Activities 13–16

Day 8

SEGUNDO PASO

Quick Review 5 min.
- Check homework.

Vocabulario/Así se dice/Gramática, pp. 366–370 15 min.
- Have students do Activity 28, p. 370, then exchange paragraphs for peer-editing.
- Have students do Activity 27, p. 370, in pairs.

TERCER PASO

Así se dice/Gramática, p. 371 25 min.
- Presenting **Así se dice/Gramática**, ATE, p. 371
- Present **También se puede decir...,** p. 371.
- Do Activity 29, p. 371, with the Audio CD.
- Have students do Activity 30, p. 372. Have volunteers write their sentences on the board.
- Have students do Activity 31, p. 372, in pairs.

Wrap-Up 5 min.
- Write two locations on the board. Tell students to choose one, and to say where they went and tell what they did there.
- Discuss the content and format of Quiz 12-2.

Homework Options
Cuaderno de actividades, pp. 139–140, Activities 12–14
Cuaderno de gramática, p. 106, Activities 17–18

Day 9

SEGUNDO PASO

Quick Review 5 min.
- Check homework.
- Quickly review the content of the **Segundo paso**.

Quiz 20 min.
- Administer Quiz 12-2A, 12-2B, or a combination of the two.

TERCER PASO

Vocabulario, p. 372 20 min.
- Presenting **Vocabulario**, ATE, p. 372
- Do the Geography Link, ATE, p. 373.
- Do Activity 32, p. 373.
- Present **A lo nuestro,** p. 372, then have students do Activity 33, p. 373, in pairs.

Wrap-Up 5 min.
- Point to a location on Teaching Transparency 12-3, then ask students where different people went and what they did there.

Homework Options
Assign Activity 34, p. 373, as homework.
Cuaderno de actividades, pp. 141–142, Activities 15–16
Cuaderno de gramática, p. 107, Activities 19–20

Day 10

TERCER PASO

Quick Review 5 min.
- Check homework and collect the writing assignment for Activity 34, p. 373.

Así se dice/Gramática/Vocabulario, pp. 371–373 10 min.
- Using a map of the world, quickly review the countries from **Vocabulario**, p. 372.
- Do Communicative Activity 12-3, pp. 71–72, Activities for Communication.

Letra y sonido, p. 373 10 min.
- Present **Letra y sonido**, p. 373, using the Audio CD.

VAMOS A LEER 20 min.
- Read the **Estrategia**, p. 374, then do Using Background Information, ATE, p. 374.
- Do Activities A, B, C, and D, pp. 374–375.

Wrap-Up 5 min.
- Ask students where on the map on pp. 374–375 they would like to go and why.
- Discuss the content and format of Quiz 12-3.

Homework Options
Study for Quiz 12-3.
Cuaderno de actividades, pp. 143–144, Activities 17–19

Day 11

TERCER PASO

Quick Review 5 min.
- Check homework.
- Quickly review the content of the **Tercer paso.**

Quiz 20 min.
- Administer Quiz 12-3A, 12-3B, or a combination of the two.

REPASO 20 min.
- Do Activity 1, p. 380, with the Audio CD.
- Do Activity 2, p. 380.
- Have students do Activity 3, p. 380, in groups.

Wrap-Up 5 min.
- Review the concepts and functions of the chapter. Have students give examples of each concept or function.

Homework Options
Assign Activity 4, p. 381, to be written as homework. Have students prepare the situation in Activity 5, p. 381.
A ver si puedo..., p. 382

Day 12

REPASO

Quick Review 10 min.
- Check homework as students do the situation from Activity 5, p. 381.

Chapter Review 35 min.
- Review Chapter 12. Choose from **Más práctica gramatical,** Grammar Tutor for Students of Spanish, Activities for Communication, Listening Activities, Interactive CD-ROM Tutor, or **Juegos interactivos.**

Wrap-up 5 min.
- Discuss the format of the Chapter 12 Test.

Homework Options
Study for the Chapter 12 test.

Assessment

Quick Review 5 min.
- Answer any last-minute questions.

Test, Chapter 12 45 min.
- Administer Chapter 12 Test. Select from Testing Program, Alternative Assessment Guide, Test Generator, or Standardized Assessment Tutor.

Block 1

CHAPTER OPENER 5 min.
- Focusing on Outcomes, ATE, p. 357
- Culture Note, ATE, p. 357

DE ANTEMANO 40 min.
- Presenting **De antemano** and Preteaching Vocabulary, ATE, p. 358
- Activities 1–5, p. 360, and Comprehension Check, ATE, p. 360
- Do the Building on Previous Skills activity, ATE, p. 361.

Así se dice, p. 361 15 min.
- Presenting **Así se dice**, ATE, p. 361
- Do Activity 6, p. 361.

Gramática, p. 362 25 min.
- Presenting **Gramática**, ATE, p. 362
- Have students do Activity 7, p. 362, in pairs, then ask individual students the questions. Have the class report what students said.
- Have students do Activity 8, p. 362, in pairs and Activity 9, p. 362, in groups.
- Do Activities 1–3 from **Más práctica gramatical**, p. 376.

Wrap-Up 5 min.
- Ask students to tell a partner three things they do every day after school. Call on students to tell the class what their partner said.

Homework Options
Cuaderno de actividades, pp. 133–134, Activities 1–3
Cuaderno de gramática, pp. 97–98, Activities 1–3

Block 2

PRIMER PASO
Quick Review 10 min.
- Check homework.
- Ask students how often they do different activities. Incorporate stem-changing verbs and verbs ending in **-go** in the first person singular.

Así se dice, p. 362 10 min.
- Presenting **Así se dice**, ATE, p. 362

Vocabulario, p. 363 20 min.
- Presenting **Vocabulario**, ATE, p. 363
- Present **También se puede decir...**, p. 363, and the Language Note, ATE, p. 363.
- Do Activity 10, p. 363, with the Audio CD.
- Have students do Activity 11, p. 363, in pairs.

Gramática, p. 363 35 min.
- Presenting **Gramática**, ATE, p. 363
- Do Activity 12, p. 363, with the class.
- Have students do Activities 13 and 14, p. 364, in pairs.
- Do the Math Link, ATE, p. 364. Then do Activity 15, p. 364, with the class.
- Have students do Activity 16, p. 364, in pairs. Call on volunteers to role-play the situation for the class.

PANORAMA CULTURAL 10 min.
- Presenting **Panorama cultural**, ATE, p. 365
- Present the Culture Note, ATE, p. 365.

Wrap-Up 5 min.
- Tell students they will be travelling to a destination you've written on the board. Have students say what they plan to do there and what they need to bring.
- Discuss the content and format of Quiz 12-1.

Homework Options
Study for Quiz 12-1.
Cuaderno de actividades, pp. 135–136, Activities 4–6
Cuaderno de gramática, pp. 99–102, Activities 4–11

Block 3

PRIMER PASO
Quick Review 10 min.
- Check homework.

Así se dice/Gramática/Vocabulario, pp. 361–364 10 min.
- Review the **Vocabulario**, p. 363, and **Así se dice** expressions, pp. 361 and 362, using Teaching Transparency 12-A.
- **Más práctica gramatical**, p. 377, Activities 4–5

Quiz 20 min.
- Administer Quiz 12-1A, 12-1B, or a combination of the two.

SEGUNDO PASO
Vocabulario, p. 366 25 min.
- Presenting **Vocabulario**, ATE, p. 366
- Present **También se puede decir...**, p. 366.
- Do Activity 17, p. 367, with the class.
- Have students write Activity 18, p. 367. Call on volunteers to write their answers on the board.

Así se dice, p. 367 20 min.
- Presenting **Así se dice**, ATE, p. 367
- Have students do Activity 19, p. 367, in pairs.
- Do Activity 20, p. 368, with the Audio CD.

Wrap-Up 5 min.
- Mime an activity from **Vocabulario**, p. 366, and ask students if they would like to do that while on vacation.

Homework Options
Cuaderno de actividades, p. 137, Activities 7–8
Cuaderno de gramática, p. 103, Activity 12
Más práctica gramatical, p. 378, Activity 6

One-Stop Planner CD-ROM

For alternative lesson plans by chapter section, to create your own customized plans, or to preview all resources available for this chapter, use the **One-Stop Planner CD-ROM**, Disc 3.

 For additional homework suggestions, see activities accompanied by this symbol throughout the chapter.

Block 4

SEGUNDO PASO

Quick Review 10 min.
- Check homework.
- Ask students what the people are doing in Teaching Transparency 12-2 and if they would like to do those things this summer.

Así se dice, p. 367 20 min.
- Do Activity 21, p. 368, with the class.
- Follow the Teaching Suggestion, ATE, p. 368, then have student pairs do Activity 22, p. 368.
- Have students do Activity 23, p. 368 in groups, and turn in work for a completion grade.

Gramática, p. 369 55 min.
- Presenting **Gramática**, ATE, p. 369
- Present Language-to-Language, ATE, p. 369.
- Do Activities 24 and 25, p. 369.
- Do Activities 7–8, p. 378, **Más práctica gramatical.**
- Have students write Activity 26, p. 370. Ask students to provide sample sentences for each location and write them on the board.
- Read the **Nota cultural**, p. 370, then present Culture Notes, ATE, p. 370.
- Have students do Activity 27, p. 370, in pairs.
- Have students do Activity 28, p. 370, then exchange paragraphs for peer-editing.

Wrap-Up 5 min.
- Make a series of statements using the verb *to be*. Have students tell whether **ser** or **estar** would be used. As a challenge, have students translate the statements.
- Discuss the content and format of Quiz 12-2.

Homework Options
Study for Quiz 12-2.
Cuaderno de actividades, pp. 138–139, Activities 9–12
Cuaderno de gramática, pp. 104–105, Activities 13–16

Block 5

SEGUNDO PASO

Quick Review 10 min.
- Check homework.
- Quickly review the content of the **Segundo paso.**

Quiz 20 min.
- Administer Quiz 12-2A, 12-2B, or a combination of the two.

TERCER PASO

Así se dice/Gramática, p. 371 25 min.
- Presenting **Así se dice** and **Gramática**, ATE, p. 371
- Present **También se puede decir...**, p. 371.
- Do Activity 29, p. 371, with the Audio CD.
- Have students do Activity 30, p. 372. Have volunteers write sentences on the board for the class to correct.
- Have students do Activity 31, p. 372, in pairs.

Vocabulario, p. 372 20 min.
- Presenting **Vocabulario**, ATE, p. 372
- Do the Geography Link, ATE, p. 373.
- Do Activity 32, p. 373.
- Present **A lo nuestro**, p. 372, then have students do Activity 33, p. 373, in pairs.

Letra y sonido, p. 373 10 min.
- Present **Letra y sonido, p. 373,** using the Audio CD.

Wrap-Up 5 min.
- Have students choose a country from the **Vocabulario**, p. 372. Then ask students where they went and what they did in that country.
- Discuss the content and format of Quiz 12-3.

Homework Options
Assign Activity 34, p. 373, as homework.
Cuaderno de actividades, pp. 140–142, Activities 13–16
Cuaderno de gramática, p. 106–107, Activities 17–20

Block 6

TERCER PASO

Quick Review 10 min.
- Check homework and collect writing assignment from Activity 34, p. 373. You may wish to use the Writing Rubric on pages 3–9 of the Alternative Assessment Guide to assess work.

Así se dice/Gramática/Vocabulario, pp. 371–373 15 min.
- Point to a location on Teaching Transparency 12-3. Ask students where certain people went and what they did there. Continue with personal questions to practice **-ar** verbs.
- Communicative Activity 12-3, pp. 71–72, Activities for Communication

Quiz 20 min.
- Administer Quiz 12-3A, 12-3B, or a combination of the two.

VAMOS A LEER 20 min.
- Read the **Estrategia,** p. 374, then do Using Background Information, ATE, p. 374.
- Do Activities A, B, C, and D, pp. 374–375.

REPASO 20 min.
- Do Activity 1, p. 380, with the Audio CD.
- Do Activity 2, p. 380.
- Have students do Activity 3, p. 380, in groups.

Wrap-Up 5 min.
- Review the concepts and functions of the chapter. Have students give examples of each.
- Discuss the format of the Chapter 12 test.

Homework Options
Study for the Chapter 12 test.
Assign Activity 4, p. 381, as homework.
Have students prepare Activity 5, p. 381.
A ver si puedo..., p. 382

Block 7

REPASO

Quick Review 10 min.
- Check homework for completion as students do the situation from Activity 5, p. 381.

Chapter Review 35 min.
- Review Chapter 12. Choose from **Más práctica gramatical,** Grammar Tutor for Students of Spanish, Activities for Communication, Listening Activities, Interactive CD-ROM Tutor, or **Juegos interactivos.**

Test, Chapter 12 45 min.
- Administer Chapter 12 Test. Select from Testing Program, Alternative Assessment Guide, Test Generator, or Standardized Assessment Tutor.

One-Stop Planner CD-ROM

For resource information, see the **One-Stop Planner**, Disc 3.

Pacing Tip
While all three **Pasos** allow for student conjecture and personalized responses, the last two encourage recall of cultural information and use of previous skills as well. Allow time for activities in the last two **Pasos**, since they may set the tone for a semester review. For more pacing suggestions, see the Lesson Plans on pp. 355I–355L.

Meeting the Standards
Communication
- Talking about what you do and like to do every day, p. 361
- Making future plans, p. 362
- Discussing what you would like to do on vacation, p. 367
- Saying where you went and what you did on vacation, p. 371

Cultures
- Culture Note, p. 357
- Photo Flash, p. 357
- Panorama cultural, p. 365
- Nota cultural, p. 370

Connections
- History Link, p. 356
- Architectural Link, p. 356
- Math Link, p. 364

Comparisons
- Social Studies Link, p. 366
- Language-to-Language, p. 369

Communities
- Community Link, p. 363
- Challenge, p. 374
- Community Link, p. 375
- Family Link, p. 375

Connections and Comparisons

History Link
Old San Juan is home to some of the oldest buildings in Puerto Rico. **La Fortaleza** is one of the oldest governor's mansions still in use in the Western Hemisphere. Ask students to describe historic buildings in their area. Are these structures still being used for their original purpose or have they been turned into museums or tourist attractions?

Architectural Link
Front balconies, inside patios, and high ceilings are features of Spanish architecture in Puerto Rico. The layout of Old San Juan reflects its role as a military stronghold under Spanish rule. Nowadays its charm attracts artists, businesses, and tourists while serving as a center for cultural events. Ask students how environment and history shape a city's infrastructure.

CAPÍTULO

12
Las vacaciones ideales

Objectives

In this chapter you will learn to

Primer paso

- talk about what you do and like to do every day
- make future plans

Segundo paso

- discuss what you would like to do on vacation

Tercer paso

- say where you went and what you did on vacation

 internet

MARCAR: go.hrw.com
PALABRA CLAVE:
WV3 PUERTO RICO-12

◀ En México, D.F. visitamos La Zona Rosa.

Photo Flash!
Sightseeing in Latin American cities on foot, by bus, or by metro is an activity enjoyed by locals as well as tourists. Here students get to know Mexico City's **Zona Rosa** with the help of a **plano de la ciudad**. In this chapter characters from **De antemano** tour Old San Juan on foot.

Focusing on Outcomes
An important use of language is talking about things you like to do and future plans. Point out to students that making plans is an important skill as they discuss what they would like to do on their vacations. By the end of the chapter, students will be able to tell others what they plan for their vacations, as well as describe where they have gone and what they have done on previous vacations.

Cultures and Communities

Culture Note
Although Puerto Rico is well known for singers (Ricky Martin and Jennifer López) and athletes (Iván "Pudge" Rodríguez and Feliz "Tito" Trinidad), the island is also the home of numerous aritists and writers. Famous Puerto Rican painters include Luis Alonzo, Cecilio Colón, Carlos Irizarry, and Antonio Martorell. Playwright and novelist Luis Rafael Sánchez is known throughout Latin America, and Rosario Ferré was nominated for a National Book Award in 1995 for her novel *House on the Lagoon*.

Teaching Resources
pp. 358–360

PRINT
▶ Lesson Planner, p. 57
▶ Video Guide, pp. 81–82, 84
▶ Cuaderno de actividades, p. 133

MEDIA
▶ One-Stop Planner
▶ Video Program
  De antemano
  Videocassette 4, 36:55–41:10
  Videocassette 5 (captioned version), 2:02:54–2:07:08
  A continuación
  Videocassette 4, 41:11–47:28
  Videocassette 5 (captioned version), 2:07:09–2:13:26
▶ DVD Tutor, Disc 2
▶ Audio Compact Discs, CD 12, Trs. 1–2
▶ **De antemano** Transparencies

Presenting
De antemano

Have students answer the questions in the **Estrategia para comprender**. Play the video. Ask groups of three or four to practice reading the roles of the characters. Then present the Preteaching Vocabulary.

De antemano Transparencies

DE ANTEMANO ▪ *Unas vacaciones ideales*

The **fotonovela** is an abridged version of the video episode.

CD 12 Trs. 1–2

Estrategia
para comprender
Can you imagine being bored on a trip to a tropical island? Ben and Carmen were, at least for a while! Read the **fotonovela** to find out what their ideal vacations are.

Benjamín **Carmen** **Abuelo** **Sra. Corredor**

①

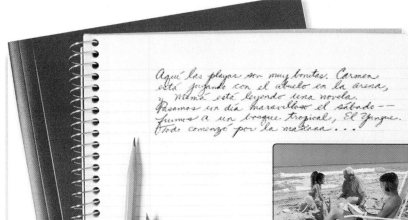

②
Abuelo: ¿Qué hacen aquí en la casa? Hace mucho sol. ¿Por qué no juegan afuera? ¿Por qué no dan un paseo?
Benjamín: Ay, abuelo... Carmen y yo dimos un paseo anoche.

③
Abuelo: ¿Por qué no visitan a los vecinos?
Benjamín: Yo visité a los vecinos ayer. No hay nada interesante que hacer, abuelo.
Abuelo: ¿Cómo que no hay nada interesante que hacer? Están en una isla, hace un tiempo maravilloso y están de vacaciones. Díganme, entonces... ¿qué les gustaría hacer? En su opinión, ¿qué son las vacaciones ideales?

Preteaching Vocabulary

Guessing Words from Context
Ask students what their ideal vacation would be. Have students identify expressions in **De antemano** that they think would be categorized as a part of a dream vacation. (❹ **viajar a una selva**, ❹ **bajar un río en canoa**, ❹ **acampar**, ❹ **pescar, explorar**, ❺ **ir de vela**, ❺ **navegar por el océano**, ❺ **descubrir una isla desierta**) Have students use the images and cognates to figure out the meaning of some of the new expressions.

4 **Benjamín:** ¿Las vacaciones ideales...? ¡Yo sé! A mí me gustaría viajar a una selva y bajar el río en canoa. Me gustaría acampar en la selva, pescar, y explorar... Sí, algún día espero explorar todo el río Amazonas.

5 **Carmen:** A mí me gustaría ir de vela, navegar por el océano Pacífico en un barco de vela antiguo... ¡Pienso descubrir una isla desierta!

6 **Sra. Corredor:** ¿De qué hablan?
Abuelo: Los muchachos están aburridos.
Sra. Corredor: ¿Aburridos? ¿En una isla tropical? Puerto Rico es una maravilla. Y hoy vamos a hacer un pequeño viaje.

7 **Carmen:** ¿Un viaje? ¿Adónde vamos?
Benjamín: ¿Y qué hacemos?
Sra. Corredor: Ya verán, ya verán... ¡es una sorpresa!

8 **Unas horas después...**

VEREDA
⬆ EL YUNQUE ⬆
EL YUNQUE TRAIL
Ⓤ🅢 BOSQUE NACIONAL
DEL CARIBE

Cuaderno de actividades, p. 133, Act. 1

Using the Captioned Video/DVD

As an alternative to reading the conversations in the book, you might want to show the captioned version of *Unas vacaciones ideales* on Videocassette 5. Hearing the language and watching the story will reduce anxiety about the new language and facilitate comprehension. The reinforcement of seeing the written words with the gestures and actions in context will help students do the comprehension activities on p. 360.

NOTE: The *DVD Tutor* contains captions for all sections of the *Video Program*.

Teaching Suggestion
Have students tell partners whether they would prefer Ben's ideal vacation, Carmen's, or neither. Students should explain why or why not. Those who would prefer neither should then describe their own ideal vacation. Have the others discuss where they would have to go to visit their relatives or a famous person they admire in another state or country.

Background Information
In the second act of the video, the characters visit El Yunque, a tropical rain forest that supports many different trees, vines, and tropical flowers. More than 200 species of birds live there. It is the only tropical rain forest managed by the U.S. Forest Service.

A continuación
You may choose to continue with *Unas vacaciones ideales (a continuación)* at this time or wait until later in the chapter. At this point, Sra. Corredor tells Ben and Carmen what they will need for their trip. They visit **El Yunque** and end the day having a picnic supper on the beach. You may wish to have students write an alternative script for the second half of the video that includes their ideas about what makes an ideal vacation.

Native Speakers

Ask native speakers to write a journal entry about a trip, real or imaginary, that they made to visit a friend or relative. Or, have them interview an older friend or relative about a trip he or she has made, and write about it. Review any spelling and writing skills you have targeted with your native speakers over the course of the school year, and ask them to incorporate these skills in their reports.

Answers

1 1. Están en casa del abuelo en Puerto Rico.
2. porque no hay nada interesante que hacer
3. ¿Qué les gustaría hacer? ¿Cómo son unas vacaciones ideales?
4. Benjamín sueña con unas vacaciones en la selva amazónica. Carmen sueña con navegar por el océano Pacífico en un barco de vela antiguo.
5. que van a hacer un viaje

2 1. Cierto
2. Falso: Están aburridos porque no hay nada interesante que hacer.
3. Falso: A Ben le gustaría bajar el río Amazonas en canoa, acampar en la selva y explorar.
4. Cierto
5. Falso: Van a hacer un viaje.

3 1. Fui a una selva tropical.
2. ¿Qué hace aquí en la casa?
3. Hace un tiempo maravilloso.
4. Me gustaría explorar un río en canoa.
5. Pienso descubrir una isla desierta.

4 1. Ben or Carmen
2. señora Corredor
3. Carmen
4. Abuelo
5. Ben

These activities check for comprehension only. Students should not yet be expected to produce language modeled in **De antemano**.

1 ¿Comprendes?

¿Comprendes lo que pasa en la fotonovela? Contesta las preguntas. Si es necesario, adivina. See answers below.

1. ¿Dónde están Benjamín y su familia, y por qué?
2. ¿Por qué están tristes Carmen y Benjamín en la segunda foto?
3. ¿Qué les pregunta su abuelo en la tercera foto?
4. ¿Con qué sueñan (dream) Benjamín y Carmen?
5. ¿Qué les menciona su mamá que los anima (cheers them up)?

2 ¿Cierto o falso? See answers below.

Decide si las oraciones son ciertas o falsas. Si son falsas, corrígelas.

1. Ben escribe en su diario sobre sus vacaciones en Puerto Rico.
2. Ben y Carmen están aburridos porque hace mal tiempo.
3. Las vacaciones ideales de Ben consisten en ir a la playa y nadar.
4. Las vacaciones ideales de Carmen consisten en navegar en barco de vela.
5. Ben y Carmen no van a hacer nada interesante hoy.

3 ¿Cómo se dice? See answers below.

Find the words and phrases in the **fotonovela** that you could use to . . .

1. say that you went to a tropical forest
2. ask what someone is doing in the house
3. say that the weather is great
4. say that you'd like to explore a river in a canoe
5. say that you plan on discovering a desert island

4 ¿Quién lo diría? See answers below.

Según la fotonovela, ¿quién diría lo siguiente?

Ben   **Carmen**   **Abuelo**   **Sra. Corredor**

1. Estoy muy aburrido, abuelo.
2. Vamos a ir a un lugar muy interesante, hijos.
3. Los barcos de vela me encantan.
4. ¡Hoy es un día muy bonito!
5. ¡Me gustaría ir a la selva amazónica!

5 ¿Y tú?

 Imagina que estás en las vacaciones ideales y que estás escribiendo en tu diario. Escribe tres actividades que puedes hacer durante las vacaciones. Usa la fotonovela si necesitas ideas. Possible answers: pasar el día en la playa, nadar y tomar el sol, ir de vela

Comprehension Check

Slower Pace

3 Once students have located the Spanish expressions, have them practice saying them with a partner. If they have difficulty identifying the phrases, play the segment of the audio recording or videocassette where these expressions are used.

Using Background Knowledge

After students have watched the video and completed Activities 1–5, ask them to make two packing lists in Spanish: one for the things Ben would need to pack for his ideal vacation, and another for Carmen. Have students compare their list with a partner's to see if they have forgotten anything.

Así se dice

Talking about what you do and like to do every day

To find out what someone does on a regular basis, ask:

Bueno, ¿qué haces tú **todos los días?**

Your friend might answer:

Primero voy a la escuela, y **después** regreso a casa y hago mi tarea. Ceno con la familia a las seis y **luego** miro la televisión.

To ask about someone's routine, say:

¿Con qué frecuencia sales con tus amigos?

¿Qué te gusta hacer **después de clases?**

Your friend might answer:

Pues, salgo **todos los viernes.**

Me gusta escuchar música en casa. También me gusta jugar al basquetbol.

---

6 **¿Qué hacen los demás?** Answers will vary.

Hablemos/Escribamos Describe las rutinas de las personas en el dibujo. Explica dónde están, qué hacen y con qué frecuencia hacen estas actividades.

Mamá   Papá   Marcos

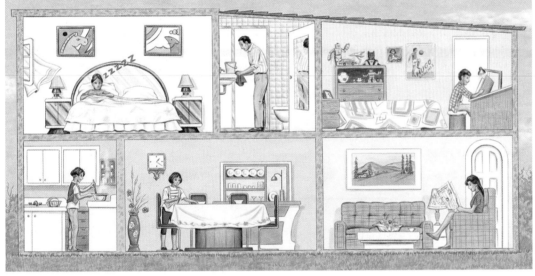

Claudia   Marcia   María

Communication for All Students

Additional Practice

As an extension, have students respond to **¿Qué haces todos los días?** Their responses should include **primero, después,** and **luego.** Have them then distinguish between what they enjoy doing and what they do only because of obligations.

Building on Previous Skills

Review vocabulary for free-time activities from previous chapters. Have students interview a partner in Spanish, asking what he or she does and likes to do every day. They should take notes on what their partner says to report his or her answers to the class.

Teaching Resources
pp. 361–364

PRINT
- Lesson Planner, p. 58
- TPR Storytelling Book, pp. 45, 48
- Listening Activities, pp. 91, 95
- Activities for Communication, pp. 67–68, 130, 133–134, 159–160
- Cuaderno de gramática, pp. 97–102
- Grammar Tutor for Students of Spanish, Chapter 12
- Cuaderno de actividades, pp. 134–136
- Cuaderno para hispanohablantes, pp. 56–60
- Testing Program, pp. 301–304
- Alternative Assessment Guide, p. 43
- Student Make-Up Assignments, Chapter 12

MEDIA
- One-Stop Planner
- Audio Compact Discs, CD 12, Trs. 3, 25–26, 16
- Teaching Transparencies 12-1, 12-A; **Más práctica gramatical** Answers; Cuaderno de gramática Answers
- Interactive CD-ROM Tutor, Disc 3

Bell Work
Scramble the verbs **jugar, visitar, viajar, acampar, navegar,** and **descubrir** on the board. Have students unscramble them.

Presenting
Así se dice

Present **Así se dice** by telling a story, using Activity 6 family names. Then ask students about the family's activities. **¿Qué hace María después de clases?** (Lee el periódico en la sala después de clases.)

Teaching Resources
pp. 361–364

PRINT
▸ Lesson Planner, p. 58
▸ TPR Storytelling Book, pp. 45, 48
▸ Listening Activities, pp. 91, 95
▸ Activities for Communication, pp. 67–68, 130, 133–134, 159–160
▸ Cuaderno de gramática, pp. 97–102
▸ Grammar Tutor for Students of Spanish, Chapter 12
▸ Cuaderno de actividades, pp. 134–136
▸ Cuaderno para hispanohablantes, pp. 56–60
▸ Testing Program, pp. 301–304
▸ Alternative Assessment Guide, p. 43
▸ Student Make-Up Assignments, Chapter 12

MEDIA
▸ One-Stop Planner
▸ Audio Compact Discs, CD 12, Trs. 3, 25–26, 16
▸ Teaching Transparencies 12-1, 12-A; **Más práctica gramatical** Answers; Cuaderno de gramática Answers
▸ Interactive CD-ROM Tutor, Disc 3

Presenting
Gramática,
Así se dice

List infinitives of stem-changing verbs on the board. (**e → ie** and **o → ue**) Then do a rapid-response activity with a foam ball. Toss the ball to a student while saying an infinitive and a subject pronoun. The student conjugates the verb, then tosses the ball to another student, giving the classmate a new verb and subject pronoun. This activity may also be used to practice **Así se dice**. To extend the activity, modify the questions with future time expressions.

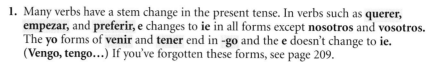

Gramática

Stem–changing verbs

1. Many verbs have a stem change in the present tense. In verbs such as **querer, empezar,** and **preferir, e** changes to **ie** in all forms except **nosotros** and **vosotros**. The **yo** forms of **venir** and **tener** end in **-go** and the **e** doesn't change to **ie**. (**Vengo, tengo...**) If you've forgotten these forms, see page 209.

2. Other verbs, including **poder** and **almorzar,** have **o** to **ue** stem changes. If you've forgotten these forms, see page 238.

Cuaderno de gramática, pp. 97–98, Acts. 1–3

Más práctica gramatical, pp. 376–377, Acts. 1–4

7 ### Gramática en contexto

Leamos/Escribamos Contesta las siguientes preguntas sobre lo que hacen tú y tus amigos en la escuela.

1. ¿Prefieres tomar clases por la mañana o por la tarde?
2. ¿Quiénes almuerzan en la cafetería?
3. ¿Quiénes saben hablar español?
4. ¿Tus amigos quieren estudiar matemáticas o español?
5. ¿A qué hora empiezan tus clases los lunes?

¿Se te ha olvidado?
gustar and encantar
Consulta la página 236

8 ### ¿Qué le gusta hacer? Answers will vary.

Hablemos Pregúntale a tu compañero/a si va a estos lugares durante el año escolar o cuando está de vacaciones. Pregúntale también con qué frecuencia va a estos lugares.

1. la piscina
2. la cafetería
3. la playa
4. el cine
5. el colegio
6. el centro comercial
7. el gimnasio
8. el parque

9 ### ¿Por qué no vamos a...?

Hablemos/Escribamos Work in groups of three. You have some time after school and the three of you would like to get together. Find out what everyone in your group likes so you can decide where to go and what to do. Make a list of your first, second, and third choices.

Así se dice

Making future plans

To ask what a friend is planning to do, say:

¿Adónde **piensas** viajar algún día?

¿**Quieres** viajar a México?

¿**Qué vas a hacer** este verano?

Your friend might answer:

A Europa, si (*if*) puedo.

No, pero **espero** hacer un viaje a Guatemala.
. . . *I hope* . . .

Voy al Perú.

Communication for All Students

Visual Learners

8 Use photos of the places mentioned to elicit answers from the entire class or to expand on this activity.

Additional Practice

To practice stem-changing verbs and vocabulary, have students sit in a circle and ask one to say what he or she has and wants: **Tengo una mochila y quiero una guitarra.** The next person says what the first person has and wants and then makes a statement for him or herself. Each succeeding student must state what all the preceding students have said.

la chaqueta
la bufanda
los esquís

hacer la maleta
la cámara
el boleto

los lentes de sol
la toalla
el traje de baño
el bloqueador
las chancletas

CD-ROM 3
DVD 2

a.   b.   c.

Cuaderno de actividades, p. 136, Act. 6   Cuaderno de gramática, pp. 99–100, Acts. 4–7

Presenting
Vocabulario

Bring the objects listed in the vocabulary to class in a suitcase. Role-play a vacationer unpacking the bag. Say the name of each thing as you remove it from the suitcase, and ask students to repeat after you. At the end of the chapter, you can use the suitcase and its contents to review vocabulary.

Gramática

Verbs + infinitives Say the infinitives aloud, modeling the correct pronunciation of each. Read the example sentences in the **Gramática**. You may want to add some of your own. **(Ella espera nadar en el mar Caribe. Usted puede llamarme por teléfono.)** Then model sentences using **ir a** and **tener que** + infinitive. **(Tengo que organizar mi maleta. Ellos van a nadar.)** If you are able to display CD-ROM activities on a large screen, you might use **¿Qué falta?** (Activity 2, Chapter 12, Disc 3) as a class presentation.

10 De vacaciones

Escuchemos Mira los dibujos y escucha las conversaciones. Decide qué conversación corresponde a cada dibujo. Scripts and answers on p. 355G.

CD 12
Tr. 3

11 ¿Qué necesito?

Escribamos/Hablemos Pick a place where you'd like to travel and make a list of things you'd need to bring with you. With a partner, ask each other a series of yes/no questions to guess where you're going to go on vacation. You might ask: **¿Traes un/a…? ¿Vas a llevar…?**

También se puede decir...

En España se dice **el billete** por **el boleto**. En México, por **la chaqueta** muchas personas dicen también **la chamarra.**

Gramática

Verbs + infinitives

1. You've learned a number of verbs that may be followed by an infinitive and others that require **a** or **que** before the infinitive.

> querer
> necesitar
> pensar   } + infinitive
> deber
> esperar
> poder

> ir a
> tener que } + infinitive

2. Remember to conjugate only the first verb:

> **Pienso pasear** en bicicleta.
> **¿Quieres venir** conmigo?

Cuaderno de gramática, pp. 101–102, Acts. 8–10   Más práctica gramatical, p. 377, Act. 5

12 Gramática en contexto See sample answer below.

Hablemos Mira los dibujos en el **Vocabulario**. Menciona tres cosas que cada persona piensa hacer durante sus vacaciones. Usa los verbos en la **Gramática.**

Cultures and Communities

Community Link

11 Have students investigate vacation activities in Puerto Rico by contacting local travel agents to request brochures. Ask students to list in Spanish the total estimated cost and the items they would need in order to participate in each activity. You may also wish to have students request brochures about other Caribbean destinations in order to make comparisons.

Language Note

Point out to students some words that vary regionally. (**espejuelos, anteojos,** or **gafas** for **lentes;** and **sandalias** for **chancletas**) You might also tell them that **bloqueador** means specifically *sunscreen* or *sunblock,* whereas *suntan lotion* is **bronceador.**

Answers
12 *Sample answer:*
  a. Piensan esquiar en las montañas. Quieren patinar sobre hielo. Pueden hacer un hombre de nieve.

Math Link

15 Note that the temperature in the drawing is in degrees Fahrenheit, although Celsius is the standard in many Spanish-speaking countries. Ask students to convert the current temperature from Fahrenheit to Celsius. (subtract 32 degrees, multiply by 5, and divide by 9)

Assess

▶ Testing Program, pp. 301–304
Quiz 12-1A, Quiz 12-1B
Audio CD 12, Tr. 16

▶ Student Make-Up Assignments, Chapter 12, Alternative Quiz

▶ Alternative Assessment Guide, p. 43

Answers

15 *Answers may vary.*
a. Hace frío. Es invierno.
b. Hace mucho viento. Es otoño.
c. Hace sol y mucho calor. Es verano.
d. Hace buen tiempo. Es primavera.
e. Llueve. Es primavera.
f. Nieva. Es invierno.

16 *Possible answers:*
1. Nueva Zelanda o la Argentina
2. el Caribe, México, Hawaii
3. Nueva York, San Francisco, Londres, París
4. parques nacionales en Colorado y Nuevo México
5. México, Guatemala, Grecia
6. África

---

13 **Gramática en contexto**

Hablemos Planea unas vacaciones ideales con tu compañero/a. Decidan...
1. adónde quieren ir
2. cuándo esperan salir
3. cómo quieren viajar (en coche, por avión...)
4. qué necesitan llevar
5. cuánto tiempo piensan quedarse *(to stay)*

14 **¿Por qué no te quedas?** *Why don't you stay?*

Escribamos/Hablemos Make a list of five fun things that you can do in your community during vacation. Then try to convince your partner to stay home by telling him or her what you plan to do during vacation. Answers will vary.

15 **¿Qué tiempo hace en...?** See answers below.

Hablemos ¿Qué estación del año representan los siguientes dibujos? ¿Qué tiempo hace?

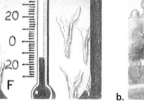
a.

b.

c.

d.

e.

f.

¿Se te ha olvidado?
weather
Consulta la página 156

Cuaderno de gramática, p. 102, Act. 11

---

16 Del colegio al trabajo → See possible answers below.

Leamos/Hablemos In your summer job as an assistant in a travel agency, one task is to give advice to customers. How would you respond to the following questions and comments? Role-play the activity with a partner and take turns playing the assistant and the customer.

1. Tengo vacaciones en julio y quiero esquiar. ¿Adónde puedo viajar?
2. Quiero pasar dos semanas en una playa tropical. ¿Adónde puedo ir?
3. Me gustan las ciudades grandes, el teatro, los museos y los conciertos.
4. No tengo mucho dinero. Quiero viajar con unos amigos a las montañas.
5. Me encantan las ruinas arqueológicas. ¿Adónde puedo viajar?
6. Nos gusta mucho la aventura y ver cosas diferentes.

Communication for All Students

Slower Pace

Tell students you vacationed in a given area. **(Viajé a Puerto Rico. Visité San Antonio.)** Have them ask you **¿Qué tiempo hizo en ——?** When you respond with a weather expression **(Hizo frío en San Antonio)**, the students should guess the time of year you visited. **(Ud. visitó San Antonio en invierno, ¿no?)** Give some destinations in the southern hemisphere for more varied answers.

Challenge

16 Have students develop a follow-up conversation in which the assistant and the customer discuss the date and time the customer can leave, the cost of the trip, and what the customer will need to take.

¿Adónde vas y qué haces en las vacaciones?

If you lived in a Spanish-speaking country, what would you look forward to doing on your vacation? The answer would depend on where you lived. We asked these teenagers in Spanish-speaking countries what they do and where they go during their vacations.

CAPÍTULO 12

Teaching Resources
p. 365

PRINT
▸ Video Guide, pp. 81–83
▸ Cuaderno de actividades, p. 144
▸ Cuaderno para hispanohablantes, pp. 59–60

MEDIA
▸ One-Stop Planner
▸ Video Program, Videocassette 4, 47:47–50:00
▸ DVD Tutor, Disc 2
▸ Audio Compact Discs, CD 12, Trs. 4–7
▸ Interactive CD-ROM Tutor, Disc 3

CD 12 Tr. 7

José Luis
Valencia, Venezuela

"Generalmente también voy para la playa, a Puerto Cabello, puede ser desde un mes hasta los dos meses completos de las vacaciones de agosto. Con toda mi familia".

Jaharlyn CD 12 Tr. 6
Ponce, Puerto Rico

"Me dan dos meses en verano y tres semanas en Navidad. No más lo que hago es que voy a la playa, al río, veo televisión y duermo mucho".

Camila CD 12 Tr. 5
Buenos Aires, Argentina

"Voy con mi familia a Pinamar y a Uruguay. Estamos en la playa y recorremos un poco el lugar".

Presenting
Panorama cultural

Ask **¿Adónde va Camila? ¿Jaharlyn?** After you have received answers for several questions, ask a student **¿Adónde vas tú?** Then have students ask each other where they go and what they do on vacation. Play the audio or video and have students answer the **Preguntas.**

Para pensar y hablar...

A. Which of the interviewees' vacation trips do you find most appealing? Why?

B. You've won a trip to the Spanish-speaking country of your choice! In small groups, discuss which country you would most like to visit. Why did you choose that particular country? What things do you already know about it? Which places would you most want to see? Why?

Cuaderno para hispanohablantes, pp. 59–60

Preguntas

1. **¿Con quién viaja Camila?** (con su familia)

2. **¿Cuántos meses de vacaciones tiene José Luis? ¿Jaharlyn?** (dos meses; dos meses en el verano y tres semanas en Navidad)

3. **¿Quién va a Puerto Cabello?** (José Luis)

4. **¿A quién le gusta dormir mucho?** (a Jaharlyn)

5. **En tu opinión, ¿cuáles son las playas más bonitas de los Estados Unidos?** (*Answers will vary.*)

Cultures and Communities

Culture Note
• Locations such as **Pinamar** are popular among Argentines, who often return to the same vacation spot each year. Which attractions in the United States would the class recommend to students from a Spanish-speaking country and why? Ask students if their families return to any of these vacation spots each year.

• Have groups of students research the interviewees' hometowns (Buenos Aires, Ponce, and Valencia) and find out what these places have to offer tourists. The groups can then create a travel brochure or poster for one of the cities.

Segundo paso

Objective Discussing what you would like to do on vacation

WV3 PUERTO RICO-12

Teaching Resources
pp. 366–370

PRINT
▸ Lesson Planner, p. 59
▸ TPR Storytelling Book, pp. 46, 48
▸ Listening Activities, pp. 92, 96
▸ Activities for Communication, pp. 69–70, 131, 133–134, 159–160
▸ Cuaderno de gramática, pp. 103–105
▸ Grammar Tutor for Students of Spanish, Chapter 12
▸ Cuaderno de actividades, pp. 137–139
▸ Cuaderno para hispanohablantes, pp. 56–60
▸ Testing Program, pp. 305–308
▸ Alternative Assessment Guide, p. 43
▸ Student Make-Up Assignments, Chapter 12

MEDIA
▸ One-Stop Planner
▸ Audio Compact Discs, CD 12, Trs. 8, 27–28, 17
▸ Teaching Transparencies 12-2; **Más práctica gramatical** Answers; Cuaderno de gramática Answers
▸ Interactive CD-ROM Tutor, Disc 3

Bell Work
On the board or on a transparency write the following words: **playa, ciudad, campo, montaña.** Students write as many associated words as they can for each.

Vocabulario

La Isla del Paraíso

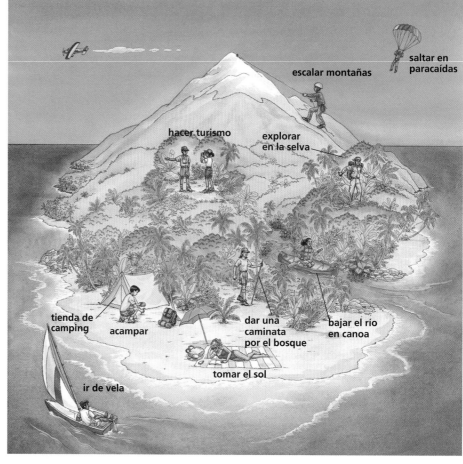

saltar en paracaídas
escalar montañas
hacer turismo
explorar en la selva
tienda de camping
acampar
dar una caminata por el bosque
bajar el río en canoa
tomar el sol
ir de vela

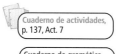
Cuaderno de actividades, p. 137, Act. 7

Cuaderno de gramática, p. 103, Act. 12

Más práctica gramatical, p. 378, Act. 6

También se puede decir...
Por **acampar,** también se dice **hacer camping.** Por **hacer turismo** también se puede decir **ir de excursión** o **hacer un recorrido.** En vez de **dar una caminata,** muchas personas dicen **andar** o **caminar.**

Presenting
Vocabulario
Give a "tour" of **La Isla del Paraíso,** talking about the activities shown as students point to each activity you mention. Then have them repeat the words after you, using backward buildup. **(-mo, -ismo, turismo)**

Connections and Comparisons

Social Studies Link
Tourism is a significant part of the economy of Puerto Rico. Are there similar tropical or sub-tropical locations in the United States where tourism plays a significant role in the economy? (Florida Keys, Florida; South Padre Island, Texas; Honolulu, Hawaii) Ask students to investigate and compare the geography, climate, and economies of other tropical or sub-tropical locations in the United States.

Biology Link
Ask students if they know the location of other tropical forests besides El Yunque. (Central America, Amazon River Basin of South America, Congo River Basin of Africa, Southeast Asia) Discuss the environmental consequences of the destruction of the world's rain forests. (disruption of weather patterns, plant and animal extinction, land erosion)

¿Qué pueden hacer? See answers below.

Leamos/Escribamos ¿Qué pueden hacer estas personas en sus vacaciones? Completa cada oración con una o más frases del **Vocabulario** en la página 366.

1. Benjamín y Carmen van a pasar sus vacaciones en Texas, en la costa del golfo de México. Allí pueden ══════.

2. Margarita y sus padres piensan ir a los Andes de Chile. Ellos pueden ══════.

3. Elizabeth va a pasar una semana en Madrid. Ella quiere ══════.

4. Roberto y Carlos esperan ir a Puerto Rico en verano. Ellos van a ══════.

5. Voy a Miami, Florida porque quiero ══════.

6. Luz María y su familia piensan ir a las montañas en agosto para ══════. Por eso necesitan comprar una nueva ══════.

18 ¿Qué están haciendo?

Escribamos Mira el dibujo de la Isla del Paraíso en la página 366. Escribe lo que está haciendo cada persona en este momento.

¿Se te ha olvidado?
present progressive
Consulta la página 299

Así se dice

Discussing what you would like to do on vacation

Más práctica gramatical, p. 378, Act. 6

To find out what a friend would like to do, ask:

¿Qué te gustaría hacer este verano?

¿Adónde te gustaría ir este verano?

¡Qué aburrido estoy! Y tú, **¿qué tienes ganas de hacer?**

Your friend might answer:

Pues, a mí **me gustaría** ir a las playas en México. Dicen que son fantásticas.

A mí **me gustaría** escalar montañas en Colorado porque son muy bonitas.

Tengo ganas de dar una caminata en el bosque. ¿Vamos?

 19 Destinos

Hablemos You and your partner look at the list below and each choose three places you'd like to go. Don't tell each other which places you chose. Then, take turns asking each other what you'd like to do in each place. Can you guess each other's **destinos?**

1. Cuenca, Ecuador
2. Madrid, España
3. Cancún, México
4. San Juan, Puerto Rico
5. San Antonio, Texas
6. el Parque Nacional de Yellowstone
7. México, D.F., México
8. El Yunque, Puerto Rico
9. Cuernavaca, México
10. Los Ángeles, California

Communication for All Students

Kinesthetic Learners

Have students find old outdoor or travel magazines and try to find pictures that depict some of the activities pictured in the **Segundo paso** in different regions. For activities other than those pictured, have them use dictionaries or other sources to label the illustration. Have them use no fewer than four illustrations to design a poster entitled **¿Qué te gustaría hacer durante las vacaciones?**

Slower Pace

17 19 If students are having difficulty, have them look up the locations on the map. Discuss the topography of each place and what activities might be best suited to the climate and geographical features. Provide examples of how the new vocabulary can be associated with one or two destinations.

Presenting
Así se dice

Write the words from **Vocabulario** on page 366 on index cards. Then, call on students to take a card and, without telling the others what is on the card, act out the activity. When a student knows what activity is being mimed, he or she responds, using a phrase from **Así se dice**. (Tengo ganas de acampar.)

Group Work

19 List the Activity 19 destinations on the left column of grids and distribute. In groups of three, students determine three travelers' names and write them across the top in any order so that each appears at least three times. In the intersecting space, each student writes what his traveler did at three places. By asking questions, students determine what was done by whom at each destination.

Answers

17 *Possible answers:*
1. tomar el sol y nadar
2. escalar montañas
3. hacer turismo
4. acampar y tomar el sol
5. hacer turismo e ir de vela
6. acampar; tienda de camping

Segundo paso

Teaching Resources
pp. 366–370

PRINT

▶ Lesson Planner, p. 59
▶ TPR Storytelling Book, pp. 46, 48
▶ Listening Activities, pp. 92, 96
▶ Activities for Communication, pp. 69–70, 131, 133–134, 159–160
▶ Cuaderno de gramática, pp. 103–105
▶ Grammar Tutor for Students of Spanish, Chapter 12
▶ Cuaderno de actividades, pp. 137–139
▶ Cuaderno para hispanohablantes, pp. 56–60
▶ Testing Program, pp. 305–308
▶ Alternative Assessment Guide, p. 43
▶ Student Make-Up Assignments, Chapter 12

MEDIA

▶ One-Stop Planner
▶ Audio Compact Discs, CD 12, Trs. 8, 27–28, 17
▶ Teaching Transparencies 12-2; **Más práctica gramatical** Answers; Cuaderno de gramática Answers
▶ Interactive CD-ROM Tutor, Disc 3

Teaching Suggestion

22 Have students use the maps on pages xxiii–xxix to choose their destinations and plan their trips before getting together with their partner.

Answers

21 1. Rincón, Puerto Rico
2. tranquilo
3. surfing
4. *Answers will vary.*
5. *Answers will vary.*

23 *Sample answer:*
Deben pasar las vacaciones en la Isla del Paraíso. Es un verdadero paraíso. Hay playas hermosas con arena blanca y fina. Pueden nadar, tomar el sol, jugar en la playa e ir de vela. También pueden bucear en el mar y ver los peces fantásticos.

---

 20 **Me gustaría...** Scripts and answers on p. 355G.

 Escuchemos/Escribamos Sara, David y Martín dicen todo lo que les gustaría hacer durante sus vacaciones. Escribe los siguientes datos para cada persona:

CD 12
Tr. 8

> Nombre
> Vive en
> Le gustaría ir a
> Quiere

21 **¡En la playa... en Puerto Rico!** See answers below.

Leamos/Escribamos Lee este anuncio de un parador puertorriqueño y contesta las preguntas que siguen.

1. ¿Dónde se encuentra *(is located)* el Parador Villa Antonio?
2. Según el anuncio, ¿cómo es el Parador Villa Antonio?
3. ¿Las playas del Parador Villa Antonio son ideales para qué deporte?
4. ¿A ti te gustaría quedarte en este parador? ¿Por qué?
5. ¿Qué te gustaría hacer en este lugar?

 22 **¡Pongámonos de acuerdo!** *Let's come to an agreement!*

Hablemos You and your partner have each just won a trip together to anywhere in Latin America. Each of you will choose a different destination. Try to convince each other that your own choice is better. Describe the place and say what you can do if you go there.

 23 **¡Ven a la Isla del Paraíso!** See sample answer below.

Hablemos/Escribamos Work with two or three other students to write a short ad convincing people to spend their vacation on la **Isla del Paraíso** on page 366. Describe the setting, say what there is on the island, and tell people what they can do there.

Cultures and Communities

Additional Practice

20 Have groups of three students pretend to be each of the speakers and introduce themselves with as many details from the audio recording as they can remember.

Challenge

21 Have small groups of students create an advertisement for their school to interest international students in studying there. They should tell what the surrounding area and campus facilities are like, what classes and extracurricular activities are offered, and why international students would like to enroll in the school.

Gramática

ser and estar

You've learned to use **ser** and **estar,** the two Spanish verbs for *to be.*

Use **ser** . . .

1. to say what someone or something is like:
   ¿Cómo **es** Juanita?   **Es** simpática y muy lista.

2. to say where someone or something is from:
   ¿De dónde **son** Uds.?   **Somos** de Guadalajara.

3. to define something or someone:
   ¿Quién **es** la chica?   **Es** mi amiga Marta. **Es** estudiante.

4. to say what something is made of:
   ¿De qué **son** tus calcetines?   **Son** de algodón.

5. to give the date or the time:
   ¿Qué hora **es**?   **Son** las dos menos cuarto.

Use **estar** . . .

1. to talk about states and conditions:
   ¿Cómo **está** Rogelio hoy?   ¡Uy! **Está** de mal humor.

2. to talk about location:
   ¿Dónde **está** mi libro de álgebra?   **Está** debajo de tu cama.

3. with the present participle, to talk about what is happening right now:
   ¿Qué **están** haciendo Ana Clara y Meme?   **Están** jugando al voleibol en la playa.

> Cuaderno de gramática,
> pp. 104–105, Acts. 13–16

> Más práctica gramatical,
> p. 378, Acts. 7–8

---

24 ### Gramática en contexto  See answers below.

Leamos/Escribamos Rubén y su hermano Marcos tienen que salir inmediatamente para el aeropuerto. Completa su diálogo con la forma apropiada de **ser** o **estar.**

RUBÉN   ¡Marcos! ¿Por qué no ___1___ (tú) listo?

MARCOS   Es que todavía ___2___ haciendo la maleta.

RUBÉN   ¡Ay, Marcos! ¡(Tú) ___3___ un desastre! No vas a cambiar nunca.

MARCOS   Ayúdame a encontrar mi camiseta favorita. ___4___ roja y ___5___ de algodón.

RUBÉN   ¿Por qué no sabes dónde ___6___?

MARCOS   ¿Por qué ___7___ (tú) de tan mal humor? Hombre, en tres horas vamos a ___8___ en las playas de Puerto Rico. ¡Qué bien!

RUBÉN   Ya sé, pero el avión sale a las tres. Mira, ya ___9___ las dos.

MARCOS   Mira, ¡aquí tengo mi camiseta! Ahora, ¿dónde ___10___ mis zapatos de tenis?

25 ### ¡Unas vacaciones fantásticas!

Hablemos/Escribamos Estás de vacaciones en Puerto Rico y llamas a tu amigo por teléfono en Chile. Describe y compara el clima y las actividades en cada lugar.

Communication for All Students

Slower Pace

Ser y estar Have students turn to the **fotonovela** on pages 358–359, and allow them two to three minutes to find all the examples of the verbs **ser** and **estar.** Call for volunteers to write these excerpts on the board. As a class, read the **Gramática** on page 369. Ask students to identify which usage of **ser** or **estar** each excerpt

represents. (**Están en una isla** represents talking about location.) For usages not represented in the **fotonovela,** ask students to create sentences. (For **estar** with the present progressive, students might say **Ben y Carmen están hablando con su abuelo.**)

Language Note

27 Another way to say **cada cual a su gusto** *(to each his own)* is **cada uno a lo suyo.**

Writing Assessment

Have students imagine they are visiting a foreign country and that a friend from that country is visiting their country. They write a post card to the friend asking about what sights to see and what to do. Students from one class will receive post cards from another class and write back with suggestions. You may wish to use the following rubric for assessment.

Writing Rubric	Points			
	4	3	2	1
Content (Complete–Incomplete)				
Comprehensibility (Comprehensible–Incomprehensible)				
Accuracy (Accurate–Seldom accurate)				
Organization (Well organized–Poorly organized)				
Effort (Excellent–Minimal)				

18–20: A   14–15: C   Under
16–17: B   12–13: D   12: F

Assess

▶ Testing Program, pp. 305–308
  Quiz 12-2A, Quiz 12-2B
  Audio CD 12, Tr. 17

▶ Student Make-Up Assignments, Chapter 12, Alternative Quiz

▶ Alternative Assessment Guide, p. 43

---

26 **Gramática en contexto** Answers will vary.

Escribamos Imagínate que estás de vacaciones en uno de estos lugares. Escribe una tarjeta postal a tu mejor amigo/a. Dile la fecha, dónde estás y cómo es el lugar. Menciona también cómo estás y lo que estás haciendo. Usa un mínimo de tres adjetivos para describir el lugar y menciona tres actividades en que estás participando.

México, D.F.

Ponce, Puerto Rico

27 **Cada cual a su gusto**
To each his own

 Hablemos Entrevista a un compañero/a sobre lo que le gustaría hacer en sus vacaciones. Luego sugiere adónde debe ir de vacaciones con las frases **¿Por qué no vas a...?** y **Debes ir a...**

Toledo, España

Los Andes

28 **Quedarse en casa** Answers will vary.

 Escribamos Muchas personas pasan las vacaciones en casa. Escribe un párrafo que explica qué vas a hacer en casa este verano.

MODELO   Me gustaría ir a Barcelona, pero no puedo. Tengo que trabajar. Voy a...

Nota cultural

Vista de Toledo, España desde el Parador Conde de Orgaz.

Several Spanish-speaking countries offer fascinating **paradores,** or inns, for travelers to stay overnight. In Spain, many **paradores** are in old castles, palaces, convents, and monasteries. In the **Parador de Zafra,** for example, you can sleep in the same castle where Hernán Cortés stayed before setting out for the New World. You could stay in a room at the **Parador Reyes Católicos** in Santiago de Compostela, founded by King Ferdinand and Queen Isabella. And if you get a room at the **Parador de Alarcón,** you'll sleep in a castle built in the eighth century by Moors from North Africa!

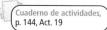
Cuaderno de actividades, p. 144, Act. 19

Cultures and Communities

 Culture Notes

• Puerto Rico has a number of **paradores** patterned after the **paradores nacionales** in Spain. Some are guest houses; others are tourist villas and small hotels. Operated by the government, the **paradores** in Puerto Rico are situated where the traveler can experience the natural beauty of the island.

• Tell students that all over the world old buildings are sometimes used for purposes other than those for which they were built. (a mansion made into a museum) Have students ever visited a historical building that has been converted in such a way?

Así se dice

Saying where you went and what you did on vacation

To find out about a friend's vacation, ask:

¿Adónde viajaste el verano pasado?

¿Adónde fueron tú y tu familia durante las vacaciones?

¿Qué hiciste cuando fuiste a Buenos Aires?

Your friend might answer:

Yo **no fui a ningún lugar.**
I didn't go anywhere (lit., nowhere).

Fuimos a Puerto Rico.

En Buenos Aires, **visité** la Plaza de Mayo.

Cuaderno de actividades, p. 141, Act. 15

También se puede decir...
Por **ningún lugar** (*nowhere, not anywhere*) también se dice **ninguna parte** o **ningún lado**, como en **No fuimos a ningún lado.**

29 **¡Qué divertido!**

CD 12
Tr. 9

Escuchemos Carlos and Yolanda have just returned from their trip to Puerto Rico. Listen to them tell about it. Place the pictures in the correct order, according to what they say.
Scripts and answers on p. 355H.

a.

b.

c.

d.

Gramática

Preterite tense

To talk about what happened in the past, use the preterite tense. All regular **-ar** verbs follow the same pattern as **trabajar.** The verb **ir** is irregular in the preterite.

trabajar		ir	
trabaj**é**	trabaj**amos**	**fui**	**fuimos**
trabaj**aste**	trabaj**asteis**	**fuiste**	**fuisteis**
trabaj**ó**	trabaj**aron**	**fue**	**fueron**

Cuaderno de actividades, p. 140, Acts. 13–14

Cuaderno de gramática, p. 106, Acts. 17–18

Más práctica gramatical, p. 379, Act. 9

Communication for All Students

Additional Practice

Have students write the name of a vacation spot. Ask them **¿Adónde fuiste?** and have them answer, using what they wrote. Incorporate questions with plural forms **¿Fueron ustedes a _____ este año?** To practice preterite verb forms, ask students what they did while on vacation.

Challenge

Sometimes vacation plans go wrong. Have students write a paragraph about an imaginary vacation that runs into difficulty because of weather (rain at the beach, warm weather at the ski resort), travel difficulties (arriving late, running out of gas), disagreements (everyone wants to do something different), or other problems.

Teaching Resources
pp. 371–373

PRINT
- Lesson Planner, pp. 61, 76
- TPR Storytelling Book, pp. 47, 48
- Listening Activities, pp. 92, 97
- Activities for Communication, pp. 71–72, 132, 133–134, 159–160
- Cuaderno de gramática, pp. 106–107
- Grammar Tutor for Students of Spanish, Chapter 12
- Cuaderno de actividades, pp. 140–142
- Cuaderno para hispanohablantes, pp. 56–60
- Testing Program, pp. 309–312
- Alternative Assessment Guide, p. 43
- Student Make-Up Assignments, Chapter 12

MEDIA
- One-Stop Planner
- Audio Compact Discs, CD 12, Trs. 9–14, 29–30, 18
- Teaching Transparencies 12-3; **Más práctica gramatical** Answers; Cuaderno de gramática Answers
- Interactive CD-ROM Tutor, Disc 3

 Bell Work
Display two columns, one with verbs in preterite, the other with predicate phrases. Have students copy, then connect the logical phrase with the verb.

Presenting
Así se dice, Gramática
Use preterite forms of **ir** to say where you went on a vacation. Next, write some regular **-ar** verbs on the board and tell what you did. Ask students if they did these things as well. Gradually incorporate questions about classmates: **¿Qué hizo Allen?**

Teaching Resources
pp. 371–373

PRINT
▶ Lesson Planner, p. 60
▶ TPR Storytelling Book, pp. 47, 48
▶ Listening Activities, pp. 92, 97
▶ Activities for Communication, pp. 71–72, 132, 133–134, 159–160
▶ Cuaderno de gramática, pp. 106–107
▶ Grammar Tutor for Students of Spanish, Chapter 12
▶ Cuaderno de actividades, pp. 140–142
▶ Cuaderno para hispanohablantes, pp. 56–60
▶ Testing Program, pp. 309–312
▶ Alternative Assessment Guide, p. 43
▶ Student Make-Up Assignments, Chapter 12

MEDIA
▶ One-Stop Planner
▶ Audio Compact Discs, CD 12, Trs. 9–14, 29–30, 18
▶ Teaching Transparencies 12-3; **Más práctica gramatical** Answers; Cuaderno de gramática Answers
▶ Interactive CD-ROM Tutor, Disc 3

Presenting
Vocabulario

After students have practiced the pronunciation of the countries, have them consult a world map. They are to list the countries in the order of closest to farthest from where they live. Then have them list the countries in order from the one they would most like to visit to the one they are least interested in visiting.

Answers

30 *Sample answer:* Fuimos al partido de béisbol. Fue muy divertido porque el equipo de tío Juan ganó.

30 **Gramática en contexto** See sample answer below.

Escribamos Carmen and Benjamín are sorting out their pictures from their trip to Puerto Rico. Help them by writing two sentences for each picture about what they did and where they went.

31 **Gramática en contexto**

Escribamos/Hablemos Escribe una lista de diez cosas que llevaste en un viaje pasado. Tu compañero/a tiene que hacerte preguntas del tipo sí/no para averiguar qué llevaste y para adivinar dónde pasaste tus vacaciones.

MODELO —¿Llevaste una cámara?
—Sí, llevé una cámara.

Vocabulario

Alemania (f.)	*Germany*
China (f.)	*China*
Egipto (m.)	*Egypt*
Francia (f.)	*France*
Inglaterra (f.)	*England*
Italia (f.)	*Italy*

Cuaderno de gramática, p. 107, Acts. 19–20

A lo nuestro

A common way to say you had a great time in Spanish is **Lo pasé muy bien** or **fenomenal**. There are different expressions in different countries. In Costa Rica you'll hear **Lo pasé pura vida**. The most common way to say that you had a bad time is **Lo pasé mal**, but you could also say **Lo pasé fatal**.

Teacher to Teacher

Kim Peters
Mooresville High School,
Mooresville, Indiana

Kim's students make the rounds as they review.

" *Alrededor del mundo* is similar to the basketball game where players compete against each other, shooting baskets. In a Spanish vocabulary version, one student stands next to a seated student. I show an English flashcard. The first student to give the Spanish translation continues by moving to the next desk/student. A student is declared the winner when he or she goes through one row. The last student to lose to the winner then stands up to try to win against the next row. This can work with verb conjugations as well. "

32 **De viaje en el Caribe**

Leamos/Escribamos Imagine that your Spanish class went to Puerto Rico and met Ben and his family. Create six sentences about what people did and where they went by combining the items in the boxes.

MODELO mis compañeros y yo/jugar/en el agua
Mis compañeros y yo jugamos en el agua.

yo Benjamín y Carmen tú la señora Corredor mis compañeros y yo el profesor/la profesora	ir a explorar visitar nadar caminar por jugar tomar	el Yunque el sol el Museo Pablo Casals el Morro muchas fotos un partido de béisbol la playa al voleibol en el agua

33 **Una entrevista**

Hablemos/Escribamos Interview a classmate who has taken a trip. In Spanish, find out where he or she went, what he or she did, and so on. Ask as many questions as you can. Take notes in order to be able to report to the class.

¿Adónde viajaste/fuiste...?	en tu viaje
¿Qué hiciste...?	durante las vacaciones
¿Qué llevaste...?	cuando fuiste a

34 **En mi cuaderno** See sample answer below.

Escribamos Escribe en un párrafo cinco oraciones para explicar a qué lugar esperas viajar algún día y por qué. Incluye qué quieres hacer allí y qué tiempo hace típicamente.

LETRA Y SONIDO

CD 12
Trs. 10–14

A. In English we pronounce *p*, *t*, and *k* (as in *pin*, *tin*, and *kin*) with a puff of air. This puff of air does not happen in Spanish. Practice saying these words without releasing that puff of air.

hotel papa paracaídas caminata canoa toalla

In addition, the letter **t** in Spanish is pronounced with the tongue against the upper teeth, not against the area immediately above the teeth known as the alveolar ridge.

tienda carta tiempo hasta tractor tanto

B. Dictado Scripts for Part B on p. 355H.

Listen to the answering machine and take down the message you hear word for word.

C. Trabalenguas

Paco Pérez pone poco papel en el pupitre.
Carla quiere cantar en el coro con Claudia Cortés.

Communication for All Students

Visual Learners
Have students create a photo album with vacation pictures clipped from magazines. Tell them to write a brief description under each picture, explaining what they did and where they went.

Additional Practice
Give each student a small piece of paper with the name of a country on it, and tell the students to imagine that they have just returned from a trip there. Students are to tell a partner where they went, who they went with, what they took with them, what they did there, and whether or not they had a good time.

Tercer paso

CAPÍTULO 12

Geography Link
Point out to students that the world map on pages xxiv–xxv shows the names in Spanish of most of the world's countries and capital cities. Consider giving students extra credit on the Chapter Test or Final Exam if they can name cities and countries in the Spanish-speaking world.

33 Have a few pairs of students perform the interview in front of the class for a speaking grade. You may wish to use the following rubric to assess performance.

Speaking Rubric	Points			
	4	3	2	1
Content (Complete– Incomplete)				
Comprehension (Total–Little)				
Comprehensibility (Comprehensible– Incomprehensible)				
Accuracy (Accurate– Seldom accurate)				
Fluency (Fluent–Not fluent)				

18–20: A	14–15: C	Under
16–17: B	12–13: D	12: F

Assess
▸ Testing Program, pp. 309–312
  Quiz 12-3A, Quiz 12-3B
  Audio CD 12, Tr. 18

▸ Student Make-Up Assignments,
  Chapter 12, Alternative Quiz

▸ Alternative Assessment Guide,
  p. 43

Answers
34 *Sample answer:*
Un día espero viajar a Alaska. Me gustaría hacer un viaje en un barco de lujo para ver de cerca los glaciares y las ballenas. Hace mucho frío en invierno y hace fresco en verano. Quiero ir en verano.

Vamos a leer

Teaching Resources
pp. 374–375

PRINT
▶ Lesson Planner, p. 61
▶ Cuaderno de actividades, p. 143
▶ Cuaderno para hispanohablantes, pp. 56–58
▶ Reading Strategies and Skills Handbook, Chapter 12
▶ ¡Lee conmigo! 1, Chapter 12
▶ Standardized Assessment Tutor, Chapter 12

MEDIA
▶ One-Stop Planner

Prereading
Activity A

Drawing on Your Experience
Ask students to list five things they would like to do on an ideal vacation. Do they know of an ideal spot where they could do all five things?

Reading
Activities B and C

Monitoring Reading
Observing To help them understand as they read, ask students to name as many of the items in the illustration as they can.

Using Background Information
This would be a good time to discuss the locations mentioned in this reading, especially the ones outside the United States. Ask what students know about these locations, and try to point out some common background knowledge prior to reading in detail.

Answers
B Berta:
1. falso
2. cierto
3. cierto
4. falso

Matías:
1. falso
2. falso
3. cierto
4. falso

¿Cuáles son las vacaciones ideales para ti?

Estrategia para leer
Before reading a passage in detail, you should try to recognize how it is organized. This helps you follow along more easily, and can save you time if you need to look only for a certain piece of information.

¡A comenzar!

A. The reading on these pages is about how to choose the vacation that is best for you. Take a minute or two and see if you can determine how it is organized. Doing this will help you enjoy it more. Be sure to look at the following hints.

1. **¿Te gusta mucho el sol?** is the beginning.
2. Notice the footprints, and think about their purpose. Write your answer, then discuss it with at least two classmates. Make sure that you all agree about how this text is organized.

Al grano

B. Suppose that there will be two Costa Rican exchange students in your school next year, Matías and Berta. You can find out a little about them by seeing what choices they made on the flow chart. Matías' path is blue, and Berta's is red. Read through all their choices, then see how well you know them. Answer *true* or *false*. See answers below.

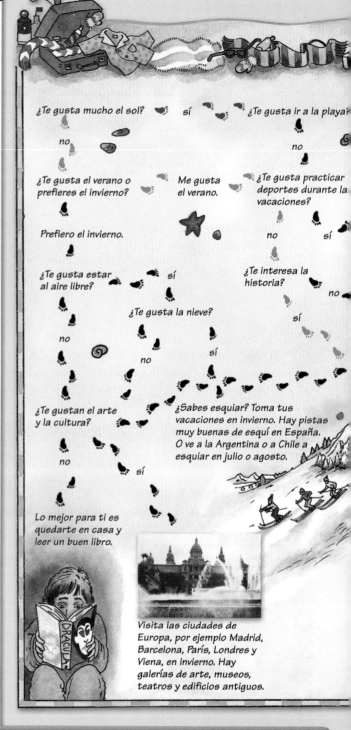

¿Te gusta mucho el sol? sí ¿Te gusta ir a la playa?
no no
¿Te gusta el verano o prefieres el invierno? Me gusta el verano. ¿Te gusta practicar deportes durante las vacaciones?
Prefiero el invierno. no sí
¿Te gusta estar al aire libre? sí ¿Te interesa la historia?
no
¿Te gusta la nieve? no
no sí
¿Te gustan el arte y la cultura? ¿Sabes esquiar? Toma tus vacaciones en invierno. Hay pistas muy buenas de esquí en España. O ve a la Argentina o a Chile a esquiar en julio o agosto.
no sí
Lo mejor para ti es quedarte en casa y leer un buen libro.

Visita las ciudades de Europa, por ejemplo Madrid, Barcelona, París, Londres y Viena, en invierno. Hay galerías de arte, museos, teatros y edificios antiguos.

Communication for All Students

Challenge
Ask students to make up a country. They should think of a name, and provide a description of its topography, climate, economy, population, and perhaps even its history. The description should be detailed enough to convince a tourist that it is a good place to visit. Students might also draw a map or create a three-dimensional model.

Native Speakers
Have native speakers write in their journals about their favorite and least favorite vacations. Students can describe a vacation they really took or they may choose to make up a story. What happened and when? Who was there? What made the trip good or bad?

¿Sabes nadar? → sí → ¿Te gustan los deportes acuáticos, por ejemplo el windsurf, el esquí acuático o la vela?

no

¿Te gusta aprender cosas nuevas? no → sí

no → sí → Hay sitios ideales para practicar deportes acuáticos en España, en las Canarias, y en el Caribe.

¿Te gusta charlar con los amigos, tomar el sol e ir a bailar por la tarde?

sí

...a ti son ideales unas ...aciones en Acapulco, México, o el Caribe, en ...rto Rico o en la ...pública Dominicana.

Busca un campamento de verano donde puedes practicar deportes, tocar un instrumento musical o aprender a pintar.

...ta México. Es un país tan ... en cultura antigua como ...oto. Visita las pirámides. ... fascinantes.

Berta . . .

1. doesn't like the beach.
2. thinks dancing is fun.
3. likes the sun.
4. is a great swimmer.

Matías . . .

1. loves wintertime.
2. really likes sports.
3. is interested in history.
4. likes the sun.

C. Imagine that you're a travel agent and several people come to you for advice about where to spend their vacation. According to the map, which of the seven destinations would you recommend for a person who . . .?

1. likes the sun, the beach, and learning new things, but can't swim
2. likes being indoors and likes art and culture
3. doesn't like talking with friends, dancing, art, or culture
4. likes the beach, but not swimming or doing new things
5. doesn't like to play sports, but does like history

See answers below.

D. Mira el mapa una vez más y decide dónde quieres pasar tus vacaciones. Sigue las instrucciones y contesta cada pregunta con cuidado. Piensa en los lugares que recomienda el mapa y decide qué lugares prefieres para tus vacaciones ideales. Escribe un párrafo breve y explica adónde quieres ir y por qué. Puedes usar las siguientes frases: **Quiero ir a... porque...**
Answers will vary.

Cuaderno para hispanohablantes, pp. 56–58

Cuaderno de actividades, p. 143, Act. 17

Postreading
Activity D

Using Text Organizers
To extend Activity D, have students make oral presentations. Ask them to choose one place they would like to visit and to prepare a brief oral description of that location. Suggest they use visuals with their presentations to facilitate listening comprehension.

Drawing on Your Experience
In the Chapter Opener, it was suggested that students put a note on a wall map showing their ideal vacation spot. Based on what they have learned in this chapter, would students change their ideal vacation destination?

Connections and Comparisons

Community Link
Have students investigate the cost of their ideal vacation by checking the travel section of their local paper. How expensive is their ideal compared to others listed? How could students modify their ideal vacation to make it more affordable?

Family Link
Ask students to interview family members to find out what factors influence vacation plans and choices. (personal interests, proximity, cost, climate) Have students write the results of their interview in their journals.

Answers
C 1. un campamento
2. quedarte en casa y leer un buen libro
3. visitar las ciudades de Europa
4. ir a Acapulco, el Caribe, Puerto Rico o la República Dominicana
5. visitar las pirámides de México

Más práctica gramatical

CAPÍTULO 12

For **Más práctica gramatical** Answer Transparencies, see the *Teaching Transparencies* binder.

Más práctica gramatical

Primer paso

Objectives Talking about what you do and like to do every day; making future plans

1 Cada persona tiene una rutina diferente. Di cómo llegan al colegio las siguientes personas, usando las formas correctas de **venir. (p. 362)**

MODELO   El profesor Vargas/en coche
El profesor Vargas viene en coche.

1. Norberto/en autobús
2. Tú/en bicicleta
3. Teresa y Rafi/caminando
4. Yo/en el coche de mi hermano

2 Explica qué come la gente para el almuerzo. Usa las formas correctas de **almorzar. (p. 362)**

MODELO   Javi/perros calientes y papitas
Javi almuerza perros calientes y papitas.

1. Nosotros/sándwiches de jamón y queso
2. Tú/hamburguesas
3. Roque y Alma/ensaladas
4. Yo/pizza

3 ¿Cuándo comienzan a hacer la tarea las siguientes personas? Usa las formas correctas de **empezar. (p. 362)**

MODELO   Adrián/7:00
Adrián empieza la tarea a las siete.

1. Marilú/7:30
2. Clara y yo/8:15
3. Jaime y Laura/5:00
4. Tú/6:30

Answers

1 1. Norberto viene en autobús.
2. Tú vienes en bicicleta.
3. Teresa y Rafi vienen caminando.
4. Yo vengo en el coche de mi hermano.

2 1. Nosotros almorzamos sándwiches de jamón y queso.
2. Tú almuerzas hamburguesas.
3. Roque y Alma almuerzan ensaladas.
4. Yo almuerzo pizza.

3 1. Marilú empieza la tarea a las siete y media.
2. Clara y yo empezamos la tarea a las ocho y cuarto.
3. Jaime y Laura empiezan la tarea a las cinco.
4. Tú empiezas la tarea a las seis y media.

Grammar Resources for Chapter 12

The **Más práctica gramatical** activities are designed as supplemental activities for the grammatical concepts presented in the chapter. You might use them as additional practice, for review, or for assessment.

For more grammar presentation, review, and practice, refer to the following:
• Cuaderno de gramática
• Grammar Tutor for Students of Spanish

• Grammar Summary on pp. R9–R13
• Cuaderno de actividades
• Grammar and Vocabulary quizzes (Testing Program)
• Test Generator on the One-Stop Planner CD-ROM
• Interactive CD-ROM Tutor
• DVD Tutor
• **Juegos interactivos** at <u>go.hrw.com</u>

4 Carmiña y Felipe están organizando una excursión para su clase. Completa su conversación con la forma correcta de los verbos, en el tiempo presente. (p. 362)

CARMIÑA   Felipe, ¿tú __1__ (tener) la lista de estudiantes? Yo __2__ (querer) verla.

FELIPE   Aquí está. Me parece que unos estudiantes no __3__ (poder) venir.

CARMIÑA   ¿Por qué no __4__ (venir) Esteban y Adriana?

FELIPE   Pues, Esteban no __5__ (poder), porque __6__ (empezar) su nuevo trabajo este fin de semana. Y yo __7__ (pensar) que Adriana __8__ (tener) que visitar a sus tíos el sábado.

CARMIÑA   ¿Y Marcela?

FELIPE   Ella __9__ (querer) venir, pero todavía no está segura si __10__ (poder) o no.

CARMIÑA   Pues, ¿tú __11__ (querer) llamarla ahora? Mañana nosotros __12__ (tener) que hacer las reservaciones, y yo __13__ (preferir) organizar todo hoy.

FELIPE   De acuerdo.

5 You took a poll on people's summer plans. Now report where the following people are going to go, what they want to do, and what they have to do this summer. Use information from the poll below. (p. 363)

MODELO   **Alonso va a ir a Puerto Rico. Quiere ver El Yunque y San Juan, pero tiene que cuidar a su hermana.**

PERSONA	¿ADÓNDE VA?	¿QUÉ QUIERE HACER?	¿QUÉ TIENE QUE HACER?
Alonso	Puerto Rico	ver El Yunque y San Juan	cuidar a su hermana
el profesor Sastre	España	descansar y viajar	escribir un libro
yo	la casa de los abuelos	ir al cine mucho	tomar una clase
Nieves	el campo	acampar y leer novelas	trabajar en un hospital
Patricio y Efraín	el lago	nadar y jugar al tenis	trabajar en un restaurante
mis amigos y yo	la playa	bucear y salir a comer	ayudar en casa

1. El profesor Sastre
2. Yo
3. Nieves
4. Patricio y Efraín
5. Mis amigos y yo

Answers

4
1. tienes
2. quiero
3. pueden
4. vienen
5. puede
6. empieza
7. pienso
8. tiene
9. quiere
10. puede
11. quieres
12. tenemos
13. prefiero

5
1. El profesor Sastre va a ir a España. Quiere descansar y viajar, pero tiene que escribir un libro.
2. Yo voy a ir a casa de los abuelos. Quiero ir al cine mucho, pero tengo que tomar una clase.
3. Nieves va a ir al campo. Quiere acampar y leer novelas, pero tiene que trabajar en un hospital.
4. Patricio y Efraín van a ir al lago. Quieren nadar y jugar al tenis, pero tienen que trabajar en un restaurante.
5. Mis amigos y yo vamos a la playa. Queremos bucear y salir a comer, pero tenemos que ayudar en casa.

For **Más práctica gramatical**
Answer Transparencies, see the
Teaching Transparencies binder.

Más práctica gramatical

Segundo paso   **Objective** Discussing what you would like to do on vacation

6 Create sentences about what the following people would like to do on a dream vacation to **la Isla del Paraíso.** Use **gustaría** and the correct indirect object pronoun in each sentence. (**pp. 366, 367**)

> **MODELO**   Linda/bajar el río en canoa
> **A Linda le gustaría bajar el río en canoa.**

1. ¿tú/saltar en paracaídas?
2. nosotros/dar una caminata por el bosque
3. Roberto y Guille/ir de vela
4. ¿Isa/escalar montañas?
5. yo/acampar
6. ¿ustedes/tomar el sol?

7 Estás en el aeropuerto y escuchas los comentarios de otras personas. Completa sus comentarios con la forma correcta de **ser** o **estar.** (**p. 369**)

1. Esa maleta parda no ===== de nosotros. Todas nuestras maletas ===== negras.
2. ¿Dónde ===== los pasaportes y los boletos?
3. ¿Qué hora =====? ¿Hay tiempo para tomar un refresco?
4. Yo ===== de Miami. ¿De dónde ===== usted?
5. ¡La comida en la cafetería aquí ===== horrible!
6. Señorita, necesito un boleto a Caracas, Venezuela. ¿Cuánto =====?
7. Julia y Toño ===== en la librería. Creo que ===== comprando revistas.
8. No me siento bien. ===== un poco nervioso y me duele el estómago.

8 José Luis está de vacaciones en la Isla del Paraíso. Completa lo que escribe en su diario con la forma correcta de **ser** o **estar.** (**p. 369**)

¡Qué divertida __1__ la Isla del Paraíso! Yo __2__ aquí de vacaciones con unos amigos. __3__ aquí conmigo Pablo, Delia y Pilar. La isla __4__ grande y bonita, y hay muchas cosas que hacer. Pablo __5__ muy contento porque a él le encantan los deportes acuáticos. Él __6__ buceando ahora, y más tarde va a ir de vela. Delia y Pilar __7__ muy atléticas, y van a escalar montañas esta tarde. Yo __8__ un poco cansado hoy, y por eso no voy con ellas. Pienso tomar el sol en la playa que __9__ cerca del río. Pero ahora __10__ las nueve, y voy a dar una caminata. ¡Hasta luego!

Answers

6
1. ¿A ti te gustaría saltar en paracaídas?
2. A nosotros nos gustaría dar una caminata por el bosque.
3. A Roberto y Guille les gustaría ir de vela.
4. ¿A Isa le gustaría escalar montañas?
5. A mí me gustaría acampar.
6. ¿A ustedes les gustaría tomar el sol?

7
1. es, son
2. están
3. es
4. soy, es
5. es
6. es
7. están, están
8. Estoy

8
1. es
2. estoy
3. Están
4. es
5. está
6. está
7. son
8. estoy
9. está
10. son

Communication for All Students

Additional Practice

6 Have students ask a partner questions about what different friends and relatives would like to do. (**¿A tus abuelos les gustaría asistir a un concierto de rock?**) The partner answers, giving a brief explanation of the response.

8 Have pairs of students choose a person, place, or thing, and write six descriptive sentences about it, three with **estar** and three with **ser.** Students can then read their sentences to the class, which will guess what is being described.

9 Using the preterite form of the verbs in parentheses, complete each sentence about what the following people did on vacation. Then tell where they went by creating sentences with the preterite form of **ir** and the places in the box. (**p. 371**)

MODELO   Yolanda (hacer) recorridos por Madrid, Sevilla y Barcelona.
Yolanda *hizo* recorridos por Madrid, Sevilla y Barcelona. *Ella fue a España.*

México   Egipto   Alemania

Ecuador   España   Francia

Puerto Rico   Italia

1. Yo (acampar) en El Yunque y (tomar) el sol en la playa.
2. Fernando (escalar) montañas en las Alpes y (estudiar) alemán.
3. Alicia y Martín (sacar) muchas fotos de las pirámides y (montar) en camello.
4. Margarita y su familia (visitar) a unos primos en París.
5. Gianna y yo (practicar) el italiano y (comprar) muchas pizzas.
6. Tú (esquiar) en los Andes y (pasar) tiempo en Cuenca.
7. Gonzalo y su hermano (viajar) a la Península de Yucatán y (nadar) en la playa en Cancún.

Review and Assess

You may wish to assign the **Más práctica gramatical** activities as additional practice or homework after presenting material throughout the chapter. Assign Activities 1–4 after **Gramática** (p. 362), Activity 5 after **Gramática** (p. 363), Activity 6 after **Vocabulario** (p. 366) and **Así se dice** (p. 367), Activities 7–8 after **Gramática** (p. 369), and Activity 9 after **Gramática** (p. 371).

To prepare students for the **Paso** quizzes and Chapter Test, have them do the **Más práctica gramatical** activities in the following order: complete Activities 1–5 before taking Quiz 12-1A or 12-1B; Activities 6–8 before taking Quiz 12-2A or 12-2B; and Activity 9 before taking Quiz 12-3A or 12-3B.

Answers

9 1. acampé, tomé; Fui a Puerto Rico.
2. escaló, estudió; Fue a Alemania.
3. sacaron, montaron; Fueron a Egipto.
4. visitaron; Fueron a Francia.
5. practicamos, compramos; Fuimos a Italia.
6. esquiaste, pasaste. Fuiste a Ecuador.
7. viajaron, nadaron. Fueron a México.

CD-ROM3
DVD2

☑ internet
MARCAR: go.hrw.com
PALABRA CLAVE:
WV3 PUERTO RICO-12

Teacher Note
The **Repaso** reviews and integrates all four skills and culture in preparation for the Chapter Test.

Teaching Resources
pp. 380–381

PRINT 📖
▸ Lesson Planner, p. 61
▸ Listening Activities, p. 93
▸ Video Guide, pp. 81–83, 86
▸ Grammar Tutor for Students of Spanish, Chapter 12
▸ Cuaderno para hispanohablantes, pp. 56–60
▸ Standardized Assessment Tutor, Chapter 12

MEDIA 💿📼
▸ One-Stop Planner
▸ Video Program, Videocassette 4, 50:01–51:58
▸ DVD Tutor, Disc 2
▸ Audio Compact Discs, CD 12, Tr. 15
▸ Interactive CD-ROM Tutor, Disc 3

1 Las siguientes personas describen sus planes para las vacaciones. Para cada descripción que oyes, indica el dibujo correspondiente. Scripts and answers on p. 355H.

CD 12
Tr. 15

a.   b.   c.

d.   e.   f.

2 Lee el artículo y contesta las preguntas. See answers below.

De viaje

*E*ntre la gente de los países hispanohablantes es muy popular viajar. Algunos de los destinos más preferidos por los turistas son los paradores. Estos son hoteles en castillos antiguos, palacios, conventos y monasterios.

Muchos paradores ofrecen vistas espectaculares del lugar, actividades para los turistas y hasta deportes acuáticos en las playas de la zona.

1. Según el artículo, ¿qué les gusta a muchos turistas de los países hispanohablantes? ¿Por qué?
2. ¿Qué son los paradores?
3. ¿Qué puede hacer un turista en un parador?

3 Work with two or three classmates to plan a group trip. Decide when and where you will go and what you will need. Talk about the clothing you must take, the weather, and what you will see. Also agree on at least three activities you would like to do and how long you would like to stay. Be ready to present your itinerary to the class.

Slower Pace
1 Before they listen to the CD, ask students to identify a specific word or phrase in each picture. By listening for that phrase, they can identify the drawing more easily.

Group Work
3 Have each group develop its discussion and itinerary into a skit. Then have them present it to the class. If time permits, ask the class to vote on the trip that they would most like to take.

Answers
2 1. Viajar; porque les gusta visitar los paradores
2. Son hoteles en castillos antiguos, palacios, conventos y monasterios.
3. mirar vistas espectaculares del lugar, hacer diferentes actividades y practicar deportes acuáticos en las playas de la zona

Apply and Assess

Cooperative Learning
On the board or a transparency write the following: **Quiero... Necesitan... ¿Piensas...? Debemos... Mi amigo/a espera... ustedes pueden... Vamos a... Tengo que...** Divide the class into groups of three. Ask each group to complete the sentences with an infinitive and any other needed words. All sentences should relate to a class trip the students are planning. Group members assume the roles of discussion leader, writer, and reporter. The discussion leader steers the discussion as members build the sentences. The writer records the sentences. The reporter reads the completed sentences to the class. Call on different groups until you have two or three sentences for each verb. To help visual learners, have a student write the sentences on the board or on a transparency as they are read.

4 Vamos a escribir

Write an article for the Spanish class yearbook. Describe some events you participated in this year, such as games, concerts, or trips. Conclude by summarizing the year with a short description.

Estrategia para escribir

Writing good conclusions will help tie your ideas together. You might review the highlights of the school year. A conclusion is also a good place to evaluate the positive and negative aspects of your topic.

Prewriting

1. List several highlights of the year and note some facts about each, such as what happened and when, what you did, and where you went.

2. Choose which events to include, and organize them with a cluster diagram or an outline.

Writing

For your first draft, use some writing strategies you've practiced this year:

- Think about the grammar and vocabulary you'll need. Review preterite forms and words for school and free time activities.

- Get your reader's attention with a snappy introduction—perhaps a question or an exclamation about the school year.

- Don't forget that connectors such as **y, también,** and **pero** will make your sentences flow more smoothly and logically.

Revising

1. Switch papers with a classmate, and check to see that she or he included several events and supporting details about each. Then read the conclusion. Does it review or summarize the main ideas? Check for spelling and grammar errors too.

2. Write a final draft of your article, making any changes and corrections.

5 Situación

Imagine that you're on a bus from San Juan to Ponce, and you strike up a conversation with the person sitting next to you. With a partner, role-play a scene in which you find out your fellow passenger's name and age, and where he or she is from. Then ask where your new friend is going and what he or she plans to do there. Also find out where your new friend has already gone in Puerto Rico and what he or she did there.
Your partner should also ask you the same questions.
Be prepared to present your scene to the class.

Cuaderno para hispanohablantes, p. 60

CAPÍTULO 12

Portfolio

3 **Oral** You might recommend that students record their conversation for their oral Portfolio. For Portfolio information, see *Alternative Assessment Guide,* pp. iv–17.

Teaching Suggestion

5 After partners have completed their scenes, put two pairs of students together and have each student introduce his or her new friend to the other pair, summarizing what has been learned about that person. The other pair should ask questions to get more information.

Apply and Assess

Process Writing

4 Encourage students to give some thought to writing a strong conclusion. A good ending restates the main themes of the article, and gives some sort of resolution. You might teach students concluding phrases, such as **en conclusión, para resumir,** and **en resumen.** Remind students that they can consult pages R9–R13 and pages R41–44 to review grammar points they have learned throughout the year. You might also give some guidelines for peer-editing. Stress the importance of constructive criticism and specificity.

Teaching Resources
p. 382

PRINT
▸ Grammar Tutor for Students of Spanish, Chapter 12

MEDIA
▸ Interactive CD-ROM Tutor, Disc 3
▸ Online self-test

go.hrw.com
WV3 PUERTO RICO-12

Teacher Note

This page is intended to help prepare students for the Chapter Test. It is a brief checklist of the major points covered in the chapter. The students should be reminded that this is only a checklist and does not necessarily include everything that will appear on the Chapter Test.

Answers

1
1. ¿Qué haces todos los días?
2. ¿Qué haces todos los días?
3. ¿Qué haces todos los días?
4. ¿Qué haces todos los días?
5. ¿Qué hacen todos los días?
6. ¿Qué hace todos los días?

2 *Answers may vary.*
a. ¿Te gustaría saltar en paracaídas?
b. ¿Te gustaría bajar el río en canoa?
c. ¿Te gustaría hacer caminatas en la montaña?
d. ¿Te gustaría tomar el sol en la playa?

3
1. ¿Qué vas a hacer mañana?
2. ¿Qué piensas hacer este verano?
3. ¿Qué esperas hacer en el futuro?

7
1. Fui a Egipto el verano pasado.
2. Mi familia y yo hicimos un viaje a la ciudad de México.
3. Fuimos a Nueva York.

8
1. Mis padres visitaron a parientes en Chicago.
2. Mi hermana y yo no fuimos a ningún lugar y trabajamos todo el verano.

Can you talk about what you do and like to do every day? p. 361

1 How would you ask the following people what they do every day?
1. your best friend
2. a new student in your class
3. your cousin
4. your brother or sister
5. a group of friends
6. your teacher
See answers below.

Can you make future plans? p. 362

2 How do you ask someone . . .?
1. what he or she is going to do tomorrow
2. what he or she plans to do this summer
3. what he or she hopes to do in the future
See answers below.

3 Tell a friend about a future trip to Mexico. Say what you plan and hope to do. Use these cues:
1. ir a México, D.F., este verano
2. hacer turismo
3. practicar el español
4. visitar las pirámides
5. sacar fotos
6. explorar la selva

Can you discuss what you would like to do on vacation? p. 367

4 How would you ask someone if he or she would like to do the following?
See answers below.

a.   b.   c.   d.

5 How would you answer if someone asked you the following questions?
1. ¿Qué te gustaría hacer hoy?
2. ¿Adónde te gustaría viajar?
Answers will vary.

6 How would you ask a friend on vacation . . .?
1. where he or she is
2. what it's like there
3. what the people are like
4. what she or he is doing right now
Answers will vary.

Can you say where you went and what you did on vacation? p. 371

7 How would you tell your friend that . . .?
1. you went to Egypt last summer
2. you and your family took a trip to Mexico City
3. you and your friends went to New York
See answers below.

8 How would you tell someone that . . .?
1. your parents visited relatives in Chicago
2. you and your sister didn't go anywhere and worked all summer
See answers below.

Review and Assess

Additional Practice

1 3 Have students use the answers from these activities to interview each other to find out what they do every day, what they are going to do tomorrow, what they plan to do this summer, and what they hope to do in the future.

Visual Learners

4 Ask students to imagine that they could extend their vacation to Spain or elsewhere in Latin America. Have students use the maps on pages xxiii–xxviii to point out the places they would go as they tell each other what they would do in each place. You may wish to have them refer back to the Location Openers in Chapters 1, 3, 7, or 11 for ideas about places to visit.

Primer paso

Making future plans

el bloqueador	sunscreen	las chancletas	sandals, slippers	los lentes de sol	sunglasses
el boleto	ticket	esperar	to hope	la toalla	towel
la bufanda	scarf	los esquís	skis		
la cámara	camera	hacer la maleta	to pack the suitcase		

Segundo paso

Discussing what you would like to do on vacation

bajar el río en canoa	to go canoeing	explorar	to explore	la selva	jungle
el bosque	forest	hacer turismo	to go sightseeing	la tienda de camping	camping tent
dar una caminata	to go hiking	ir de vela	to go sailing	tomar el sol	to sunbathe
escalar montañas	to go mountain climbing	la isla	island		
		el paraíso	paradise		
		saltar en paracaídas	to go skydiving		

Tercer paso

Saying where you went and what you did on vacation

Alemania (fem.)	Germany	**Francia** (fem.)	France	**Italia** (fem.)	Italy
China (fem.)	China	**Inglaterra** (fem.)	England	**ningún lugar**	nowhere, not anywhere
Egipto (masc.)	Egypt				

Review and Assess

? Circumlocution

Ask students to explain the function of each vocabulary word from the **Primer paso,** using the phrase **Se usa(n) para...** *(It is/They are used for . . .)* For example, to describe **las chancletas,** students may say **Se usan para andar por la playa.** Remind students that they may use other

expressions listed on page 147J and that they may not say the word itself. You may provide additional related words such as **la sombrilla** *beach umbrella,* **la pelota de playa** *beach ball,* **las raquetas de nieve** *snow shoes,* **gafas de esquiar** *ski goggles,* etc.

CAPÍTULO 12

Visual Learners
Create scrambled versions of vocabulary to be reviewed. For example, you could make a list of scrambled words for vacation activities. **(rache mosritu** for **hacer turismo.)** Give each student a copy of the scrambled activities and have the students unscramble them.

Chapter 12 Assessment

▶ **Testing Program**
Chapter Test, pp. 313–318
 Audio Compact Discs, CD 12, Trs. 19–20
Speaking Test, p. 348

Final Exam, pp. 327–334
Score Sheet, pp. 335–337
Listening Scripts, pp. 338–339
Answers, p. 340
 Audio Compact Discs, CD 12, Trs. 21–24

▶ **Alternative Assessment Guide**
Performance Assessment, p. 43
Portfolio Assessment, p. 29
CD-ROM Assessment, p. 57

▶ **Interactive CD-ROM Tutor, Disc 3**
 CD-ROM **3** ¡A hablar!
DVD **2** ¡A escribir!

▶ **Standardized Assessment Tutor**
Chapter 12

▶ **One-Stop Planner, Disc 3**
Test Generator
Chapter 12

Reference Section

Functions are probably best defined as the ways in which you use a language for particular purposes. When you find yourself in specific situations, such as in a restaurant, in a grocery store, or at a school, you will want to communicate with those around you. In order to do that, you have to "function" in Spanish: you place an order, make a purchase, or talk about your class schedule.

Such functions form the core of this book. They are easily identified by the boxes in each chapter that are labeled **Así se dice**. These functional phrases are the building blocks you need to become a speaker of Spanish. All the other features in the chapter—the grammar, the vocabulary, even the culture notes—are there to support the functions you are learning.

Here is a list of the functions presented in this book and the Spanish expressions you'll need in order to communicate in a wide range of situations. Following each function is the chapter and page number where it was introduced.

Socializing

Saying hello
Ch. 1, p. 21
Buenos días.   Buenas noches.
Buenas tardes.   Hola.

Saying goodbye
Ch. 1, p. 21
Adiós.   Hasta luego.
Bueno, tengo clase.   Hasta mañana.
Chao.   Tengo que irme.

Introducing people and responding to an introduction
Ch. 1, p. 22
Me llamo...   Ésta es mi amiga...
Soy...   Se llama...
¿Cómo te llamas?   ¡Mucho gusto!
Éste es mi amigo...   Encantado/a.
                         Igualmente.

Asking how someone is and saying how you are
Ch. 1, p. 24
¿Cómo estás?   Estupendo/a.
¿Y tú?   Excelente.
¿Qué tal?   Regular.
Estoy (bastante)   Más o menos.
  bien, gracias.   (Muy) mal.
Yo también.   ¡Horrible!

Talking on the telephone
Ch. 7, p. 207
Aló.   ¿De parte de quién?
Diga.   La línea está ocupada.
¿Quién habla?   ¿Puedo dejar un recado?
¿Está ..., por favor?   Un momento...
                         Llamo más tarde.

Extending and accepting invitations
Ch. 7, p. 208
¿Te gustaría...?   ¿Quieres...?
Sí, me gustaría...   Te invito.
Nos gustan...   ¡Claro que sí!

Making plans
Ch. 7, p. 212
¿Qué piensas   Pienso...
  hacer hoy?   ¿Piensas...?

Talking about getting ready
Ch. 7, p. 214
¿Estás listo/a?   No, porque necesito...
No, todavía
  necesito...

Turning down an invitation and explaining why
Ch. 7, p. 217
¡Qué lástima!   Tengo una cita.
Ya tengo planes.   Tengo que...
Tal vez otro día.   Me gustaría, pero no puedo.
Lo siento, pero no.   Estoy cansado/a y un poco
Estoy ocupado/a.   enfermo/a.

Exchanging Information

Asking and saying how old someone is
Ch. 1, p. 27
¿Cuántos años   ¿Cuántos años tiene?
  tienes?   Tiene ... años.
Tengo ... años.

Asking where someone is from and saying where you're from
Ch. 1, p. 28
¿De dónde eres?   ¿De dónde es...?
Soy de...   Es de...

Talking about what you want and need
Ch. 2, p. 52

¿Qué quieres?	Necesito...
Quiero...	¿Qué necesita?
Quiere...	Ya tengo...
¿Qué necesitas?	Necesita...
¿Necesitas...?	

Describing the contents of your room
Ch. 2, p. 57

¿Qué hay en tu cuarto?	Hay ... en su cuarto.
(No)tengo... en mi cuarto.	¿Tienes...?
¿Qué tiene ... en su cuarto?	
¿Qué hay en el cuarto de...?	Tiene ... en su cuarto.

Talking about what you need and want to do
Ch. 2, p. 60

¿Qué necesitas hacer?	¿Qué quieres hacer?
Necesito...	¿Qué quiere hacer...?
¿Qué necesita hacer...?	No sé, pero no quiero...
Necesita...	Quiere...

Talking about classes and sequencing events
Ch. 3, p. 84

¿Qué clases tienes este semestre?	Primero tengo..., después... y luego...
Tengo...	¿Y cuándo tienes un día libre?
¿Qué clases tienes hoy?	Mañana, por fin…

Telling time
Ch. 3, p. 85

¿Qué hora es?	Son las...
Es la una.	Son las ... y media.
Es la una y cuarto.	¿Ya son las...?
	Es tarde.

Telling at what time something happens
Ch. 3, p. 88

¿A qué hora es...?	¡Es ahora!
(Es) a las ... de la tarde.	En punto.

Talking about being late or in a hurry
Ch. 3, p. 90

Estoy atrasado/a.	Tengo prisa.
Está atrasado/a.	¡Date prisa!

Describing people and things
Ch. 3, p. 92

¿Cómo es...?	¿Cómo son...?
Es...	Son...
	No son...

Discussing what you and others do during free time
Ch. 4, p. 114

¿Qué haces después de clases?
Antes de regresar a casa...
En el tiempo libre...
¡Descanso!
Toco la guitarra.
Jugamos al...

Telling where people and things are
Ch. 4, p. 118

¿Dónde estás?	¿No está en...?
Estoy en...	No, no está aquí. Está en...

Talking about where you and others go during free time
Ch. 4, p. 123

¿Adónde vas?	
Voy a...	Va al...
¿Adónde va...?	

Discussing how often you do things
Ch. 5, p. 145

¿Con qué frecuencia...?	¿Todavía...?
Todos los días...	Durante la semana...
Siempre...	A veces...
Nunca...	Muchas veces...
	Sólo cuando...

Talking about what you do during a typical week
Ch. 5, p. 151

¿Qué haces típicamente durante el día?
¿ ... por la mañana?
¿ ... por la tarde?
¿ ... por la noche?

Giving today's date
Ch. 5, p. 154

¿Cuál es la fecha?
¿Qué fecha es hoy?
Hoy es el primero de...
Es el ... de...
El cuatro de este mes hay...

Talking about the weather
Ch. 5, p. 156

¿Qué tiempo hace?
Hace buen tiempo.
Hace muy mal tiempo hoy.

Describing a family
Ch. 6, p. 174

¿Cuántas personas hay en tu familia?	Somos cinco.
	¿Cómo es tu familia?
Hay ... en mi familia.	Tenemos...
	Somos muy unidos.

Describing people
Ch. 6, p. 178

¿Cómo es...?   ¿De qué color es...?
Tiene...   ¿De qué color son...?

Discussing things a family does together
Ch. 6, p. 180

¿Qué hacen ustedes los fines de semana?
¿Hacen ustedes algo durante el verano?

Talking about meals and food
Ch. 8, p. 235

¿Qué tomas para el desayuno?   No me gusta ... para nada.
¿Qué tomas para el almuerzo?   Tengo sed. ¿Qué hay para tomar?
A veces tomo...   ¿Qué prefieres?
    Por lo general tomo...

Ordering dinner in a restaurant
Ch. 8, p. 246

¿Qué vas a pedir?   ¿Qué le puedo traer?
Voy a pedir...   Yo quisiera...

Asking for and paying the bill in a restaurant
Ch. 8, p. 246

¿Nos puede traer la cuenta?   ¿Cuánto es?
La cuenta, por favor.   ¿Está incluida la propina?
¿Desean algo más?   No, no está incluida. Es aparte.

Discussing gift suggestions
Ch. 9, p. 269

¿Qué piensas regalarle a...?   El regalo es para...
Le voy a dar...   ¿Qué tipo de regalo buscas?
¿Para quién es el regalo?   Busco...

Asking for and giving directions downtown
Ch. 9, p. 271

Perdón, ¿dónde está...?
Está a ... cuadras de aquí.
¿Me puede decir dónde queda...?
Queda al lado de...

Making comparisons
Ch. 9, p. 277

¿Cuál es más barato?
El ... cuesta menos. El ... es más caro.
¿Son los ... tan caros como el...?
Son del mismo precio.

Asking about prices and paying for something
Ch. 9, p. 280

¿Cuánto cuesta...?   ¿Cuánto cuestan...?
Cuesta...   Cuestan...

Talking about what you're doing right now
Ch. 10, p. 298

¿Qué estás haciendo?
Estoy colgando las decoraciones.
Él está limpiando la sala.
¿Todos están decorando la casa?
Sí, estamos decorando la casa.

Talking about past events
Ch. 10, p. 307

¿Qué hiciste anoche?   ¿Lo pasaron bien la semana pasada?
Bailé y hablé con...   Sí, lo pasamos bien.
¿Qué hizo ... ayer?   Cantó...

Saying what you did
Ch. 11, p. 340

¿Qué hiciste anoche?   Jugué...
¿Ganaste?   Jugó...

Talking about where you went and when
Ch. 11, p. 342

¿Adónde fuiste anteayer?
¿Adónde fuiste anteanoche?
Anoche fui...

Talking about what you do and like to do every day
Ch. 12, p. 361

¿Qué haces todos los días?   ¿Con qué frecuencia...?
Primero...   ¿Qué te gusta hacer después de clases?
Después...   Me gusta...
Y luego...   Pues ... todos los viernes.

Making future plans
Ch. 12, p. 362

¿Adónde piensas viajar algún día?
¿Quieres viajar a...?
No, pero espero hacer un viaje a...
¿Qué vas a hacer este verano?

Saying where you went and what you did on vacation
Ch. 12, p. 371

¿Adónde viajaste el verano pasado?
No fui a ningún lugar.
¿Adónde fueron durante las vacaciones?
Fuimos a...
¿Qué hiciste cuando fuiste a...?

Expressing Attitudes and Opinions

Talking about things you like and explaining why
Ch. 3, p. 95

¿Te gustan...?   Sí, a ella le gustan mucho.
Sí, me gustan.   ¿Por qué?
¿Cuál es...?   Porque...
¿A ella le gustan...?

Talking about what you like to do
Ch. 4, p. 113

¿Qué te gusta   ¿A quién le gusta...?
  hacer?   A mí me gusta...
Me gusta...   Por eso, me gustan...
¿A él le gusta...?
No, no le gusta...,
  pero le gusta...

Talking about what you and your friends like to do together
Ch. 5, p. 148

¿Qué les gusta   ¿Les gusta ... juntos?
  hacer?   Especialmente durante las
Nos gusta...   vacaciones...

Discussing problems and giving advice
Ch. 6, p. 184

Tengo un problema.   ¿Qué debo hacer?
Dice que ..., pero no   Debes ... menos.
  es cierto.

Commenting on food
Ch. 8, p. 240

¿Cómo está...?   ¿Cómo están...?
Está...   Están...

Commenting on clothes
Ch. 9, p. 274

¿Qué ropa vas   ¿No tienes algo más
  a llevar?   formal?
¡Lo de siempre!   Sí, pero prefiero llevar...

Expressing preferences
Ch. 9, p. 279

¿Cuál de estos ... prefieres?
Prefiero el azul.
¿Qué camisa te gusta más? ¿La verde o la
  amarilla?
La verde. Además, te queda muy bien.

Asking for and giving an opinion
Ch. 10, p. 300

¿Crees que...?   Me parece bien.
Creo que sí.   Perfecto.
¿Qué te parece   Buena idea.
  si...?   Creo que no.

Discussing what you would like to do on vacation
Ch. 12, p. 367

¿Qué te gustaría hacer este verano?
A mí me gustaría...
¿Adónde te gustaría ir este verano?
¿Qué tienes ganas de hacer?
Tengo ganas de...

Expressing Feelings and Emotions

Talking about likes and dislikes
Ch. 1, p. 32

¿Qué te gusta?   Me gusta (más)...
¿Te gusta...?   No me gusta...

Making suggestions and expressing feelings
Ch. 11, p. 331

¿Qué tal si...?   ¿Qué tienes?
¿Por qué no...?   ¿Te sientes mal?
Gracias, pero no   No me siento bien.
  quiero.   Estoy un poco cansado/a,
En realidad no   nada más.
  tengo ganas.

Talking about moods and physical condition
Ch. 11, p. 334

¿Cómo estás?   Tengo gripe.
Estoy...   ¿Qué le pasa a...?
¿Cómo te sientes?   Está preocupado/a
       por algo.

Persuading

Making polite requests
Ch. 8, p. 244

Camarero/a, ¿nos puede traer..., por favor?
¿Me puede traer..., por favor?

Asking for help and responding to requests
Ch. 10, p. 302

¿Me haces el   ¡Con mucho gusto!
  favor de...?   Un momentito.
Claro que sí.   Me pasas...
¿Me ayudas a...?   Lo siento, pero en este mo-
Cómo no.   mento estoy ocupado/a.
¿Me traes...?   Perdóname, pero...

Telling a friend what to do
Ch. 10, p. 304

Prepara ... y limpia..., ¿quieres?
De acuerdo.
Por favor, decora ... y llama...
Está bien.

This list includes additional vocabulary that you may want to use to personalize activities. If you can't find a word you need here, try the Spanish-English and English-Spanish vocabulary sections, beginning on page R15.

Asignaturas *(School Subjects)*

el cálculo	*calculus*
la contabilidad	*accounting*
la física	*physics*
la geometría	*geometry*
el latín	*Latin*
la mecanografía	*typing*
el ruso	*Russian*

Celebraciones *(Celebrations)*

el bautizo	*baptism*
la canción	*song*
el Día de la Raza	*Columbus Day*
los fuegos artificiales	*fireworks*
la Pascua Florida	*Easter*
la piñata	*piñata*
la Semana Santa	*Holy Week*
la vela	*candle*
Rosh Hashaná	*Rosh Hashanah*
Hanukah	*Hanukkah*
el Ramadán	*Ramadan*

Comida *(Food)*

el aguacate	*avocado*
las arvejas	*peas*
el bróculi	*broccoli*
la carne asada	*roast beef*
la cereza	*cherry*
la coliflor	*cauliflower*
el champiñón	*mushroom*
la chuleta de cerdo	*pork chop*
las espinacas	*spinach*
los fideos	*noodles*
el filete de pescado	*fish fillet*
la mayonesa	*mayonnaise*
el melón	*cantaloupe*
la mostaza	*mustard*
la pimienta	*pepper*
la sal	*salt*
el yogur	*yogurt*

De compras *(Shopping)*

ahorrar	*to save*
el/la dependiente	*clerk*
el descuento	*discount*
dinero en efectivo	*cash*
en venta	*for sale*
gastar	*to spend*
hacer cola	*to stand in line*
hacer una pregunta	*to ask a question*
la rebaja	*discount*
regatear	*to bargain*
el vendedor, la vendedora	*salesperson*

Computadoras *(Computers)*

la computadora, el ordenador

la unidad de CD-ROM

el CD-ROM

el teclado

el ratón

la búsqueda; buscar	*search; to search*
comenzar la sesión	*to log on*
la contraseña, el código	*password*
el disco duro	*hard drive*
en línea	*online*
grabar	*to save*
la impresora; imprimir	*printer; to print*
Internet	*Internet*
el marcapáginas, el separador	*bookmark*
los multimedios	*multimedia*

navegar (por la Red)	to surf (the Net)
la página Web inicial	homepage
la tecla de aceptación	return key
la tecla de borrar, la tecla correctora	delete key
terminar la sesión	to log off
el Web, la Telaraña Mundial	World Wide Web

Deportes y pasatiempos
(Sports and Hobbies)

el anuario	yearbook
las artes marciales	martial arts
la banda	band
el boxeo	boxing
coleccionar sellos	to collect stamp
coser	to sew
el drama	drama
la fotografía	photography
la gimnasia	gymnastics
jugar al ajedrez	to play chess
jugar a las cartas	to play cards
la lucha libre	wrestling
la orquesta	orchestra
patinar sobre hielo	to ice skate

En el zoológico (In the Zoo)

las aves	birds
el canguro	kangaroo
la cebra	zebra
el cocodrilo	crocodile
el delfín	dolfin
el elefante	elephant
el gorila	gorilla
el hipopótamo	hippopotamus
la jirafa	giraffe
el león	lion
la foca	seal
el mono	monkey
el oso	bear
el oso blanco	polar bear
el pingüino	penguin
la serpiente	snake
el tigre	tiger

En la casa (Around the House)

la alcoba	bedroom
la alfombra	rug, carpet
el balcón	balcony
el comedor	dining room

las cortinas	curtains
el cuarto de baño	bathroom
el despertador	alarm clock
las escaleras	stairs
el escritorio	desk
el espejo	mirror
el estante	bookcase
el garaje	garage
la lavadora	washing machine
la mesita de noche	nightstand
los muebles	furniture
el patio	patio
el refrigerador	refrigerator
la secadora	dryer
el sillón	easy chair
el sofá	couch
el sótano	basement
el timbre	doorbell
el tocador	dresser

En la ciudad (In the City)

el aeropuerto	airport
la agencia de viajes	travel agency
la autopista	highway
el banco	bank
el edificio	building
la esquina	corner
la fábrica	factory
la farmacia	pharmacy
el hospital	hospital
la iglesia	church
la mezquita	mosque

la oficina	office
la parada de autobuses	bus stop
la peluquería	barber shop
el puente	bridge
el rascacielos	skyscraper
el salón de belleza	beauty salon
el semáforo	traffic light
el templo	temple

Instrumentos musicales
(Musical Instruments)

el acordeón	accordion
la armónica	harmonica
el bajo	bass
la batería	drum set
el clarinete	clarinet
la mandolina	mandolin
el oboe	oboe
el saxofón	saxophone
el sintetizador	synthesizer
el tambor	drum
el trombón	trombone
la trompeta	trumpet
la tuba	tuba
la viola	viola
el violín	violin

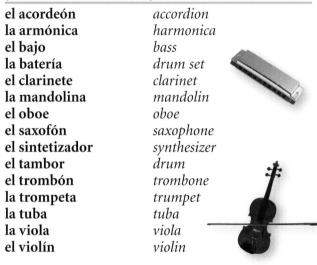

Números ordinales *(Ordinal Numbers)*

primero/a	first
segundo/a	second
tercero/a	third
cuarto/a	fourth
quinto/a	fifth
sexto/a	sixth
séptimo/a	seventh
octavo/a	eighth
noveno/a	ninth
décimo/a	tenth

Palabras descriptivas
(Descriptive Words)

amistoso/a	friendly
bien educado/a	polite
gracioso/a	funny
llevar gafas	to wear glasses
las pecas	freckles
el pelo lacio	straight hair
el pelo rizado	curly hair
ser calvo/a	to be bald
tener barba	to have a beard
tener bigote	to have a moustache

Refranes *(Proverbs)*

Más vale pájaro en mano que cien volando.
A bird in the hand is worth two in the bush.
Hijo no tenemos y nombre le ponemos.
Don't count your chickens before they're hatched.
Quien primero viene, primero tiene.
The early bird catches the worm.
Más vale tarde que nunca.
Better late than never.
El hábito no hace al monje.
Clothes don't make the man.
Más ven cuatro ojos que dos.
Two heads are better than one.
Querer es poder.
Where there's a will, there's a way.
Ojos que no ven, corazón que no siente.
Out of sight, out of mind.
No todo lo que brilla es oro.
All that glitters is not gold.
Caras vemos, corazones no sabemos.
Appearances are deceiving.
Donde una puerta se cierra, otra se abre.
Every cloud has a silver lining.
En boca cerrada no entran moscas.
Silence is golden.
Dime con quién andas y te diré quién eres.
Birds of a feather flock together.
A mal tiempo buena cara.
When life gives you lemons, make lemonade.

Regalos *(Gifts)*

la agenda	agenda, daily planner
el álbum	album
el anillo	ring
el animal de peluche	stuffed animal
el calendario	calendar
la cámara	camera
el certificado de compra	gift certificate
la colonia	cologne

el llavero	key chain
el perfume	perfume
la pulsera	bracelet
el rompecabezas	puzzle
las rosas	roses

Ropa *(Clothes)*

la bata	robe
el chaleco	vest

el jersey	sweater
las medias	stockings, nylons
el paraguas	umbrella
las pijamas	pajamas
la ropa interior	underwear
el saco	blazer, sports jacket
los tacones	high heels

Temas de actualidad *(Current Issues)*

el bosque tropical	rain forest
la contaminación	pollution
el crimen	crime
los derechos humanos	human rights
la educación	education
el medio ambiente	the environment

las noticias	news
la política	politics
la salud	health
el SIDA	AIDS
la tecnología	technology
la violencia	violence

Vacaciones *(Vacation)*

la aduana	customs
el aeropuerto	airport

el avión	airplane
los cheques de viajero	traveler's checks
el equipaje	luggage
hacer una reservación	to make a reservation
el hotel	hotel
la llegada	arrival
el mar	sea
el pasaporte	passport
la salida	departure
el tren	train
visitar los lugares de interés	to sightsee
volar (ue)	to fly

NOUNS AND ARTICLES

GENDER OF NOUNS

In Spanish, nouns (words that name a person, place, or thing) are grouped into two classes or genders: masculine and feminine. All nouns, both persons and objects, fall into one of these groups. Most nouns that end in **-o** are masculine, and most nouns that end in **-a**, **-ción**, **-tad**, and **-dad** are feminine.

Masculine Nouns	Feminine Nouns
libro	casa
chico	universidad
cuaderno	situación
bolígrafo	mesa
vestido	libertad

FORMATION OF PLURAL NOUNS

Add **-s** to nouns that end in a vowel.		Add **-es** to nouns that end in a consonant.		With nouns that end in **-z**, the **-z** changes to a **-c**.	
SINGULAR	PLURAL	SINGULAR	PLURAL	SINGULAR	PLURAL
libro	libros	profesor	profesores	vez	veces
casa	casas	papel	papeles	lápiz	lápices

DEFINITE ARTICLES

There are words that signal the class of the noun. One of these is the definite article. In English there is one definite article: *the.* In Spanish, there are four: **el, la, los, las**.

SUMMARY OF DEFINITE ARTICLES

	Masculine	Feminine
Singular	**el** chico	**la** chica
Plural	**los** chicos	**las** chicas

CONTRACTIONS

a + el → **al**
de + el → **del**

INDEFINITE ARTICLES

Another group of words that are used with nouns is the *indefinite article:* **un, una,** (*a* or *an*) and **unos, unas** (*some* or *a few*).

SUMMARY OF INDEFINITE ARTICLES

	Masculine	Feminine
Singular	**un** chico	**una** chica
Plural	**unos** chicos	**unas** chicas

PRONOUNS

Subject Pronouns	Direct Object Pronouns	Indirect Object Pronouns	Objects of Prepositions
yo	me	me	mí
tú	te	te	ti
él, ella, usted	lo, la	le	él, ella, usted
nosotros, nosotras	nos	nos	nosotros, nosotras
vosotros, vosotras	os	os	vosotros, vosotras
ellos, ellas, ustedes	los, las	les	ellos, ellas, ustedes

ADJECTIVES

Adjectives are words that describe nouns. The adjective must agree in gender (masculine or feminine) and number (singular or plural) with the noun it modifies. Adjectives that end in -**e** or a consonant only agree in number.

		Masculine	Feminine
Adjectives that end in -**o**	Singular Plural	chico alt**o** chicos alt**os**	chica alt**a** chicas alt**as**
Adjectives that end in -**e**	Singular Plural	chico inteligent**e** chicos inteligent**es**	chica inteligent**e** chicas inteligent**es**
Adjectives that end in a consonant	Singular Plural	examen difícil exámenes difícil**es**	clase difícil clases difícil**es**

DEMONSTRATIVE ADJECTIVES

	Masculine	Feminine		Masculine	Feminine
Singular Plural	**este** chico **estos** chicos	**esta** chica **estas** chicas	Singular Plural	**ese** chico **esos** chicos	**esa** chica **esas** chicas

When demonstratives are used as pronouns, they match the gender and number of the noun they replace and are written with an accent mark: **éste, éstos, ésta, éstas, ése, ésos, ésa, ésas**.

POSSESSIVE ADJECTIVES

These words also modify nouns and tell you *whose* object or person is being referred to (*my* car, *his* book, *her* mother).

SINGULAR		PLURAL	
Masculine	**Feminine**	**Masculine**	**Feminine**
mi libro	**mi** casa	**mis** libros	**mis** casas
tu libro	**tu** casa	**tus** libros	**tus** casas
su libro	**su** casa	**sus** libros	**sus** casas
nuestro libro	**nuestra** casa	**nuestros** libros	**nuestras** casas
vuestro libro	**vuestra** casa	**vuestros** libros	**vuestras** casas

AFFIRMATIVE AND NEGATIVE EXPRESSIONS

Affirmative	Negative
algo	nada
alguien	nadie
alguno (algún), -a	ninguno (ningún), -a
o ... o	ni ... ni
siempre	nunca

INTERROGATIVE WORDS

¿Adónde?	¿Cuánto(a)?	¿Por qué?
¿Cómo?	¿Cuántos(as)?	¿Qué?
¿Cuál(es)?	¿De dónde?	¿Quién(es)?
¿Cuándo?	¿Dónde?	

COMPARATIVES

Comparatives are used to compare people or things. With comparisons of inequality, the same structure is used with adjectives, adverbs, or nouns. With comparisons of equality, **tan** is used with adjectives and adverbs, and **tanto/a/os/as** with nouns.

COMPARATIVE OF INEQUALITY

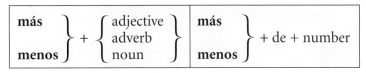

COMPARATIVE OF EQUALITY

tan + adjective or adverb + **como**
tanto/a/os/as + noun + **como**

VERBS

REGULAR VERBS

In Spanish we use a formula to conjugate regular verbs. The endings change in each person, but the stem of the verb remains the same.

PRESENT TENSE OF REGULAR VERBS

Infinitive	Present	
hablar	hablo	hablamos
	hablas	habláis
	habla	hablan
comer	como	comemos
	comes	coméis
	come	comen
escribir	escribo	escribimos
	escribes	escribís
	escribe	escriben

VERBS WITH IRREGULAR *YO* FORMS

hacer		poner		saber		salir		traer	
hago	hacemos	**pongo**	ponemos	**sé**	sabemos	**salgo**	salimos	**traigo**	traemos
haces	hacéis	pones	ponéis	sabes	sabéis	sales	salís	traes	traéis
hace	hacen	pone	ponen	sabe	saben	sale	salen	trae	traen

VERBS WITH IRREGULAR FORMS

ser		estar		ir	
soy	somos	estoy	estamos	voy	vamos
eres	sois	estás	estáis	vas	vais
es	son	está	están	va	van

PRESENT PROGRESSIVE

The present progressive in English is formed by using the verb *to be* plus the *-ing* form of another verb. In Spanish, the present progressive is formed by using the verb **estar** plus the **-ndo** form of another verb.

-ar verbs	**-er** and **-ir** verbs	For **-er** and **-ir** verbs with a stem that ends in a vowel, the **-iendo** changes to **-yendo**:
hablar → estoy habl**ando** trabajar → trabaj**ando**	comer → com**iendo** escribir → escrib**iendo**	leer → le**yendo**

STEM-CHANGING VERBS

In Spanish, some verbs have an irregular stem in the present tense. The final vowel of the stem changes from **e → ie** and **o → ue** in all forms except **nosotros** and **vosotros**.

e → ie		o → ue		u → ue	
preferir		**poder**		**jugar**	
prefiero	preferimos	puedo	podemos	juego	jugamos
prefieres	preferís	puedes	podéis	juegas	jugáis
prefiere	prefieren	puede	pueden	juega	juegan

The following is a list of some **e → ie** stem-changing verbs:	The following is a list of some **o → ue** stem-changing verbs:
empezar **pensar** **querer**	**almorzar** **doler** **encontrar**

THE VERBS *GUSTAR* AND *ENCANTAR*

To express likes and dislikes, the verb **gustar** is used in Spanish. The verb **encantar** is used to talk about things you really like or love. The verb endings for **gustar** and **encantar** always agree with what is liked or loved. The indirect object pronouns always precede the verb forms.

gustar		encantar	
If one thing is liked:	If more than one thing is liked:	If one thing is really liked:	If more than one thing is really liked:
me te le } gusta nos les	me te le } gustan nos les	me te le } encanta nos les	me te le } encantan nos les

PRETERITE OF REGULAR VERBS

Infinitive	Preterite of Regular Verbs	
hablar	hablé hablaste habló	hablamos hablasteis hablaron
comer	comí comiste comió	comimos comisteis comieron
escribir	escribí escribiste escribió	escribimos escribisteis escribieron

PRETERITE OF *HACER, IR, SER,* AND *VER*

hacer	ir	ser	ver
hice	fui	fui	vi
hiciste	fuiste	fuiste	viste
hizo	fue	fue	vio
hicimos	fuimos	fuimos	vimos
hicisteis	fuisteis	fuisteis	visteis
hicieron	fueron	fueron	vieron

This vocabulary includes almost all words in the textbook, both active (for production) and passive (for recognition only). Active words and phrases are practiced in the chapter and are listed on the **Vocabulario** page at the end of each chapter. You are expected to know and be able to use active vocabulary. An entry in black, heavy type indicates that the word or phrase is active. All other words—some in the opening dialogues, in exercises, in optional and visual material, in **Panorama cultural**, **Encuentro cultural**, **A lo nuestro**, **También se puede decir**, **Vamos a leer**, and **A ver si puedo...** —are for recognition only. The meaning of these words and phrases can usually be understood from the context or may be looked up in this vocabulary index.

Nouns are listed with definite article and plural form, when applicable. The number after each entry refers to the chapter where the word or phrase first appears or where it becomes an active vocabulary word. Vocabulary from the preliminary chapter is followed by the letter "P".

Although the **Real Academia** has recently deleted the letters **ch** and **ll** from the alphabet, many dictionaries still have separate entries for these letters. This end-of-book vocabulary follows the new rules, with **ch** and **ll** in the same sequence as in English.

Stem changes are indicated in parentheses after the verb: **poder** (**ue**).

a   *to, at*, 5
a comenzar   *let's begin*, 1
a ellas   *to them*, 5
a ellos   *to them*, 5
a lo largo de   *along*, 10
a lo nuestro   *our way*, 3
A mí me gusta + infinitive   *I (emphatic) like (to) ...*, 4
a principios de   *at the beginning of*, 10
¿A qué hora...?   *At what time . . .?*, 3
¿A quién le gusta...?   *Who likes . . .?*, 4
A ti, ¿qué te gusta hacer?   *What do you* (emphatic) *like to do?*, 4
a todo color   *in full color*, 2
a Uds. (ustedes)   *to you*, (pl.), 5
a veces   *sometimes*, 5
a ver si puedo   *let's see if I can*, 1
abajo   *down*, 11
el abdomen   *abdomen*, 11
abierto   *open*, 7
el abrazo   *hug*, 1
el abrigo   *coat*
abril (m.)   *April*, 5
abrir   *to open*, 10; **abrir los regalos**   *to open gifts*, 10
la abuela   *grandmother*, 6
el abuelo   *grandfather*, 6
los abuelos   *grandparents*, 6
la abundancia   *abundance; plenty*, 2
abundar   *to abound*, 6
aburrido/a   *boring*, 3
acabemos   *let's finish*, 5

acampar   *to camp*, 5
el acceso   *access*, 4
el aceite   *oil*, 8
el acento   *accent mark*, P
aceptar   *to accept*, 7
acercarse   *to approach; me le acerco I approach him/her*, 7
el acero   *steel*
el achiote   *annatto*, 8
acompañar   *to accompany*, 4
el acontecimiento   *event*, 5
acordarse (ue)   *to remember*, 10
acostado/a   *lying down*, 11
acostarse (ue)   *to go to bed, to lie down*, 11; *me acuesto   I go to bed*, 3
la actitud   *attitude*, 3
la actividad   *activity*, 5
activo/a   *active*, 11
el actor   *actor* (male); *mi actor favorito es   my favorite actor is*, P
la actriz   *actress; mi actriz favorita es my favorite actress is*, P
el acuario   *aquarium*, 7
acuático/a   *aquatic*, 12
el acuerdo   *agreement*, 10; **De acuerdo.**   *Agreed.*, 10
adelante   *let's get started*, P
además   *besides*, 9
el adiestramiento   *teaching, training, instruction*, 2
Adiós.   *Goodbye.*, 1
adivinar   *to guess*, 6; *adivina   guess* (command), 5
el adjetivo posesivo   *possessive adjective*, 6
¿adónde?   *to where?*, 4   **¿Adónde**

fuiste?   *Where did you go?*, 11
Adonde fueres haz lo que vieres.   *Wherever you go, do as you see.*, 1
el adoquín, los adoquines   *cobblestone*, 11
adorar   *to adore*, 6
aeróbico/a   *aerobic;* **una clase de ejercicios aeróbicos**   *aerobics class*, 5
el aeropuerto   *airport*, 12
afeitarse   *to shave*, 7
el afiche   *poster*, 2
africano/a   *African*, 11
afuera   *outside*, 12
la agencia   *agency*, 5
agitar   *to agitate, to stir up*, 3
agobiado/a   *tired*, 7
agosto (m.)   *August*, 5
agotado/a   *tired*, 7
agotar   *to use up, to exhaust*, 3
el agradecimiento   *gratitude, thanks, appreciation*, 9
agregar   *to add*, 8
agresivo/a   *aggressive*, 6
agrícola   *agricultural*, 7
el agua (f.) *water*, 5 (pl. las aguas); **el agua mineral** *mineral water*, 8
el águila (f.) *eagle*, P (pl. las águilas)
ahí   *there*, 3
ahijado, -a (m./f.)   *godchild*, 6
ahora   *now*, 3
el aire   *air; al aire libre   outdoors*, 11
el ajedrez   *chess*, 6
el ají   *spicy condiment made of tomatoes, onions, and hot, red chili peppers*, 8

el ajiaco *sauce or stew made with ají, a type of chili pepper*, 8
al (a + el) *to the*, 4
al ajillo *cooked with garlic*, 8
al final *finally*, 7
al grano *to the point*; Vamos al grano. *Let's get to the point.*, 1
al gusto *to your liking*, 8
al lado de *next to*, 4
al menos *at least*, 10
al principio *at first, in the beginning*, 10
la alberca *swimming pool*, 4
el álbum *album*, 4
el alcalde *mayor*, 10
alcanzar *to reach*, 11
alegre *happy*, 10
el alemán *German*, 3
Alemania (f.) *Germany*, 12
el alfabeto *alphabet*, P
el alfarero *pottery maker*
la alfombra *rug*, 2
el álgebra *algebra*, 3
algo *something*, 6; algo así *something like that*, 7; **¿Desean algo más?** *Would you like something else?*, 8; **preocupado/a por algo** *worried about something*, 11
el algodón *cotton*, 9; **de algodón** *(made of) cotton*, 9
alguno/a (masc. sing. algún) *some, any*; alguna parte *someplace*; alguna vez *sometime*, 6
allá *there*, 4
el almacén *department store*, 9
el almendro *almond tree*, 12
el almíbar *syrup*, 8
almorzar (ue) *to eat lunch*, 8
el almuerzo *lunch*, 3
Aló. *Hello.*, 7
alquilar *to rent*, 5
alrededor de *around*, 6
alto/a *tall*, 3
la amalgama *amalgamation, blend*, 10
amarillo/a *yellow*, 9
amazónico/a *of the Amazon*, 12
el ambiente *atmosphere*
americano/a *American*, 1; **el fútbol norteamericano** *football*, 1
las Américas *North, Central, and South America*, 8
la amiga *friend* (female), 1; **Ésta es mi amiga.** *This is my* (female) *friend.*, 1
el amigo *friend* (male), 1; amigo/a por correspondencia *pen pal*, 4; amigos hispanos *Hispanic friends*, 1; **Éste es mi amigo.** *This is my* (male) *friend.*, 1; **nuevos amigos** *new friends*, 2; **pasar el rato con amigos** *to spend time with friends*, 4
la amistad *friendship*, 1
anaranjado/a *orange*, 9
andaluz *Andalusian*
andar *to walk*, 12; **¡Ándale!** *Hurry up!*, 3; andar en bicicleta *to ride a bike*, 4
andino/a *Andean*, 8
la anécdota *anecdote*, 7
el anfibio *amphibian*, 2
la anfitriona *hostess*, 10
el ángulo *angle*, 3
el animal *animal*, 2; el animal doméstico *pet*
el aniversario *anniversary*; **una fiesta de aniversario** *anniversary party*, 7; ¡Feliz aniversario! *Happy anniversary!*, 10
anoche *last night*, 10
la ansiedad *anxiety*, 11
anteanoche *the night before last*, 11
anteayer *day before yesterday*, 10
el antebrazo *forearm*, 11
anterior *earlier*, 8
antes de *before*, 4
antiguo/a *old, ancient*, 12
antillano/a *Antillean*, 11
antinarcótico/a *antidrug*, 3
antipático/a *disagreeable*, 3
los antojitos *appetizers*, 8
la antropología *anthropology*, 7; **el museo de antropología** *anthropology museum*, 7
el anuncio *advertisement*, 12; los anuncios personales *personal ads*, 4
añadir *to add*, 8
el año *year*, 5; **el Año Nuevo** *New Year's Day*, 10; **el año pasado** *last year*, 10; ¡Feliz Año Nuevo! *Happy New Year!*, 10; **¿Cuántos años tiene?** *How old is (she/he)?*, 1; **¿Cuántos años tienes?** *How old are you?*, 1; **Tengo ... años.** *I'm . . . years old.*, 1; **Tiene ... años.** *She/He is . . . years old.*, 1
el apartado postal *post office box*, 4
aparte *separate*; **Es aparte.** *It's separate.*, 8
apasionante *passionate, exciting*, 9
el apellido *last name*, 1
aprender *to learn*, 12
apropiado/a *appropriate*, 8
aproximadamente *approximately*
los apuntes *notes*, 11
¡Apúrate! *Hurry up!*, 3
apurarse *to hurry up*, 12
aquí *here*, 4
el archipiélago *archipelago*
la arcilla *clay*
el área (f.) *area*
el arete *earring*, 9
la Argelia *Algeria*, 1
la armada *navy*, 10
el armario *closet*, 2
la armonía *harmony*, 7
los aros *earrings*, 9
la arqueología *archeology*, 1
arquitectónico/a *architectural*
la arquitectura *architecture*, 7
el arrecife de coral *coral reef*
arreglar *to fix, to arrange*, 6

arriba *up*, 11
arrojar *to throw (out)*, 10
el arroz *rice*, 8
el arte (f.) *art* (pl. **las artes**), 3
la artesanía *handicrafts*, 9
el artículo *article; item*, 9
el artista *artist (male)*, 6
la artista *artist (female)*, 6
artístico/a *artistic*, 6
asado/a *roasted*, 6
asegurarse *to be sure*, 10
así *thus, in this way*, 6; así se dice *here's how you say it*, 1
el asiento *seat*, 11
la asignatura *subject*, 3
los asistentes *participants*, 7
asistir a *to attend*, 5
asociado/a *associated*; asociado, -a (m./f.) *member of an association*
la aspiradora *vacuum cleaner*; **pasar la aspiradora** *to vacuum*, 6
el astronauta, la astronauta *astronaut*, 1
el ataque *attack*, 11
el atleta, la atleta *athlete*, 11
atlético/a *athletic*, 6
la atmósfera *atmosphere; ambience*, 9
la atracción *attraction*; **el parque de atracciones** *amusement park*, 7
atractivo/a *attractive*, 2
atraer *to attract*, 9
atrasado/a *late*; **Está atrasado/a.** *He/She is late.*, 3; **Estoy atrasado/a.** *I'm late.*, 3
el atún *tuna*, 8
el auditorio *auditorium*, 10
aúlla *he/she howls*, 11
el auto *car*, 4
aun *even, still*, 8
aunque *although*, 7
el autobús *bus*; **tomar el autobús** *to take the bus*, 5
auxiliar *auxiliary; assistant*, 1
la avenida *avenue*, 4
las aventuras *adventures*, 2
averiguar *to find out, to investigate*, 10
las aves *birds*, 2
la aviación *air force*, 10
el aviso *notice, advertisement*, 6
ayer *yesterday*, 10
ayudar *to help*; **ayudar en casa** *to help at home*, 5; **¿Me ayudas a...?** *Can you help me . . .?*, 10
el azúcar *sugar*, 8, el azúcar en polvo *powdered sugar*, 8
el azufre *sulfur*
azul *blue*, 6

bailando *dancing*, 10
bailar *to dance*, 4

el **baile** *dance*, 3
bajar *to descend, to go down*; **bajar el río en canoa** *to go canoeing*, 12
bajo/a *short*, 3
la balada *ballad*, 6
balanceado/a *balanced*, 11
el balcón *balcony*, 2
el balneario *beach resort*, 12
el baloncesto *basketball*, 1
la banca *bench*, 11
el banco *bank*, 2
la banda sinfónica *symphonic band*, 7
la bandeja *tray*, 8; la bandejita de hielo *ice tray*, 8
bañarse *to take a bath*, 5
el baño *bath*; **el traje de baño** *bathing suit*, 9
las barajas *card games, decks of cards*, 3
barato/a *cheap*, 9; **¡Qué barato/a!** *How cheap!*, 9
la barbacoa *barbecue*, 6
la barbilla *chin*, 11
el barco *boat, ship, vessel*, 5
el barrio *district, quarter, neighborhood*, 6
basado en *based on*, 2
el básquet *basketball*, 1
el basquetbol *basketball*, 1
¡Basta ya! *Enough!*, 7
bastante *quite, pretty, enough*, 10; **Estoy (bastante) bien, gracias.** *I am (pretty) well thanks.*, 1; ¿Hay bastante comida? *Is there enough food?*, 10
la basura *garbage, trash*; **sacar la basura** *to take out the garbage*, 4
la batalla *battle*, 10
la batería *drum set*, 4
el batido *milkshake*, 8
la batidora *beater*, 10
batir *to beat*, 8
el baúl *trunk for storage*, 11
beber *to drink*, 5
la bebida *beverage*, 8
el béisbol *baseball*, 1
las bellas artes *fine arts*, 9
la biblioteca *library*, 4
la bicicleta *bicycle*; andar en bicicleta, *to ride a bicycle*, 4; dar un paseo en bicicleta *to ride a bicycle*, 4; **montar en bicicleta** *to ride a bicycle*, 4; pasear en bicicleta *to ride a bicycle*, 3
bien *good, well*; **Está bien.** *All right.*, 7; **Estoy (bastante) bien, gracias.** *I'm (pretty) well, thanks.*, 1; Lo pasé muy bien. *I had a great time.*, 12; **Me parece bien.** *It seems fine to me.*, 10; ¡Qué bien te ves! *You look great!*, 9
bienvenido/a *welcome*
bilingüe *bilingual*, 1
el billete *ticket*, 12
la billetera *wallet*, 9
la biología *biology*, 3
el bistec *steak*, 8

blanco/a *white*, 9
el **bloqueador** *sunscreen*, 12
los **bluejeans** *bluejeans*, 9
la blusa *blouse*, 9
la boca *mouth*, 11
el bocadillo *sandwich (Spain)*, 8
la boda *wedding*, 7
el boleto *ticket*, 12
el bolígrafo *ballpoint pen*, 2
el bolívar *domestic currency in Venezuela*, 9
la bolsa *bag, purse*, 10; la bolsa de plástico *plastic bag*, 10
bonito/a *pretty*, 3
borrar *to erase*, **goma de borrar** *eraser*, 2
el bosque *forest*, 12
las botas *boots*, 9
bote *ship, boat*, 9
el **brazo** *arm*, 11
breve *short, brief*, 1
bucear *to scuba dive*, 5
Bueno... *Well...*, 2; Bueno. *Hello.* (telephone greeting in Mexico), 7; **Bueno, tengo clase.** *Well, I have class (now).*, 1
bueno/a *good*, 3; **Buenos días.** *Good morning.*, 1; **Buena idea.** *Good idea.*, 10; **Buenas noches.** *Good night.*, 1; **Buenas tardes.** *Good afternoon.*, 1
la bufanda *scarf*, 12
el bulevar *boulevard*, 10
la burla *joke; ridicule*, 2
el burro *donkey*, P
buscar *to look for*, 9

el caballo *horse*, 10; **montar a caballo** *to ride a horse*, 11
la cabeza *head*, 11
el cacahuate (cacahuete) *peanut*, 8
cada *each*, 2; cada cual *each one, each person*, 12
la cadena *chain*, 7
caer *to fall*, 11
el café *coffee*; **café con leche** *coffee with milk*, 8; **de color café** *brown*, 6
la cafeína *caffeine*, 11
la cafetería *cafeteria*, 1
el cafetín *cafeteria*, 6
la caja *box*, 8
los **calcetines** *socks*, 9
la calculadora *calculator*, 2
el caleidoscopio *kaleidoscope*, 7
el calendario *calendar*, 5
la calentura *fever*; tener calentura *to have a fever*, 11
caliente *hot*, 8; **el perro caliente** *hot dog*, 8
la calificación *grade*, 3

la caliza *limestone*
la calle *lane* (in a swimming pool), 5; *street*, 9
callejero/a *street* (adj.), *in the street*, 10
el calor *heat*; **Hace calor.** *It's hot.*, 5; Hace un calor tremendo. *It's really hot.*, 5
la cama *bed*, 2; **hacer la cama** *to make the bed*, 6
la cámara *camera*, 12
la camarera *waitress*, 8
el camarero *waiter*, 8
los **camarones** *shrimp*, 8
cambiar *to change*, 12; cambia *change* (command), 1
el cambio *change*, 4
caminar *to walk*; **caminar con el perro** *to walk the dog*, 4
la caminata *stroll, walk*; **dar una caminata** *to go hiking*, 12
el camino *way*; en camino *on the way*, 8
la camisa *shirt*, 9
la camiseta *T-shirt*, 9
la campana *bell*, 3
el camping *camping*; hacer camping *to camp*, 12; **la tienda de camping** *tent*, 12
el campo *country*, 7; *field*
las canas *gray hair*; **Tiene canas.** *He/She has gray hair.*, 6
la cancha *playing court*; **la cancha de fútbol** *soccer field*, 11; **la cancha de tenis** *tennis court*, 11
la canoa *canoe*; **bajar el río en canoa** *to go canoeing*, 12
cansado/a *tired*, 7
cantando *singing*, 10
cantante (m./f.) *singer*, 7
cantar *to sing*, 4
el cántaro *pitcher*; llover a cántaros *to pour, to rain cats and dogs*, 5
la caña de azúcar *sugarcane*
la capital *capital city*, 3
el capítulo *chapter*, 1
la cara *face*, 11; Cuesta un ojo de la cara. *It's very expensive.*, 11
el caramelo *candy*, 9
la caraota *kidney bean*, 8
el carbón *charcoal*, 8
cariñoso/a *affectionate*, 6
el carnaval *carnival*, 10
la carne *meat*, 8; la carne colorada *red meat, an Andean dish*, 8; **la carne de res** *beef*, 8; la carne mechada *shredded meat*, 8
caro/a *expensive*, 9; **¡Qué caro!** *How expensive!*, 9
la carpeta *folder*, 2
el carro *car*, 4; **lavar el carro** *to wash the car*, 4
la carta *letter*, 5; la carta de amor *love letter*, 5
la carta *menu*, 8
el cartel *poster*, 2
la cartera *wallet*, 9

la cartuchera *pencil case*, 2
la casa *house, home*, 4
casarse *to get married*, 10
casi *almost*; **casi siempre** *almost always*, 6
castaño/a *brown, chestnut-colored*, 6
las castañuelas *castanets*, P
el castellano *Spanish language*, 2
el castillo *fortress, castle*, 11
la casualidad *coincidence*; ¡Qué casualidad! *What a coincidence!*, 5
el catarro *cold*; tener catarro *to have a cold*, 11
la catedral *cathedral*, 7
la categoría *category*, 1
catorce *fourteen*, 1
el caucho *rubber*
el cayo *key, small island*
el cazador *hunter*, 2
la cazuela *casserole*; cazuela de marisco *Ecuadorean casserole dish with seafood and peanuts*, 8
la cebolla *onion*, 8
ceder *to cede, to give up (territory)*
la cédula *certificate*, 1
la celebración *celebration*, 10
celebrar *to celebrate*, 10; celebrarse *to be celebrated*, 10
la cena *dinner*, 4; **preparar la cena** *to prepare dinner*, 4
cenar *to eat dinner*, 6
el censo *census*
el centro *downtown*, 4
el centro comercial *shopping mall*, 2; **ir al centro comercial** *to go to the mall*, 2
cerca de *near*, 4
cercano/a *near, nearby (adj.)*, 11
el cerdo *pig*, 2
el cereal *cereal*, 8
la ceremonia *ceremony*, 10
cero *zero*, 1
cerrar (ie) *to close*, 11
el césped *grass*; **cortar el césped** *to cut the grass*, 6
el ceviche *raw seafood marinated in lemon juice*, 8
el chaleco *vest*, P
chamaco,-a (m./f.) *friend*, 4
la chamarra *jacket*, 12
las chancletas *sandals, slippers*, 12
Chao. *'Bye.*, 1
la chaqueta *jacket*, 9
la charla *chat*, 1
charlar *to chat*, 12
las charreadas *rodeo festivities*
la charrería *Mexican rodeo*, 11
la charra *Mexican cowgirl*, 11
el charro *Mexican cowboy*, 11
chavo,-a (m./f.) *friend*, 4
la chica *girl*, 5
el chico *boy*, 5
el chile *chili pepper*, 8
China (f.) *China*, 12
chino/a *Chinese*, 6; **la comida china** *Chinese food*, 1

chiquito/a *very small, very young*, 6
el chiste *joke*, 2
el chocolate *chocolate*, 1; el chocolate *hot chocolate*, 8
la choza *hut, shanty*, 7
el ciclismo *cycling*, P
cien, ciento/a *one hundred*, 2
la ciencia ficción *science fiction*, 6
las ciencias *science*, 3; **las ciencias sociales** *social studies*, 3
cierto *true*, 1; **No es cierto.** *It isn't true.*, 6
el cilantro *cilantro, coriander*, 9
cinco *five*, 1
cincuenta *fifty*, 2
el cine *movie theater*, 4
la cintura *waist*, 11
el cinturón *belt*, 9
el circo *circus*, 7
una cita *date, appointment*, 7
cítrico/a *citrus*
la ciudad *city*, 7
la ciudadanía *citizenship*, 1
el ciudadano *citizen*, 1
civil *civil*, 10
la civilización *civilization*
el civismo *civics*, 3
el clarinete *clarinet*, 4
¡Claro que sí! *Of course!*, 7
la clase *class, classroom*, 1; **Bueno, tengo clase.** *Well, I have class (now).*, 1; **la clase de baile** *dance class*, 5; **una clase de ejercicios aeróbicos** *aerobics class*, 5; **la clase de inglés** *English class*, 1; ¿Qué clases tiene? *What classes do you/does he/she have?*, 2; **¿Qué haces después de clase?** *What do you do after school?*, 4
clásico/a *classical*, 1
la clave *key*, 11
el cliente, la cliente *client*, 9
el clima *climate*
el club *club*; el club campeón *champion club, first-ranked club*, 4; el club deportivo *sports club, gym*, 5; el club nocturno *nightclub*, 6
el cobalto *cobalt*
el cobre *copper*
el coche *car*, 4
la cocina *kitchen*; cocina francesa clásica *classical French cooking*, 7; **limpiar la cocina** *to clean the kitchen*, 6
cocinado/a *cooked*, 8
el coco *coconut*, 6
codo/a *stingy*; ser muy codo/a *to be really stingy*, 11
el cognado *cognate*, 1
el cohete *rocket*, 1
coleccionar *to collect, to form a collection*, 4
el colegio *high school*, 2
la colina *hill*, 9
colgar (ue) *to hang up*, 10; **colgar (ue) las decoraciones** *to hang*

decorations, 10
el coliseo *coliseum*, 7
el collar *necklace*, 9
colocar *to put, to place*, 8; colocarse *to be put, to be placed*, 10
el colón *currency in Costa Rica*, 9
la colonia *colony*
colonial *colonial*
el color *color*, 6; **de color café** brown, 6; **¿De qué color es/son...?** *What color is/are ...?*, 6
colorido/a *colored*, 10
la combinación *combination*, 8
combinar *to combine*, 8; combina *combine* (command), 4
combustible *combustible*, 1
la comedia *comedy*, 3
el comentario *comment*, 8
comenzar (ie) *to begin*, 11
comenzó *he/she/it began*
comer *to eat*, 5
el comercial *commercial*
comestible *related to food; edible*
los comestibles, *groceries*; **la tienda de comestibles** *grocery store*, 9
cómico/a *comical, funny*, 3
la comida *food, meal*, (Mex.) *lunch*; **la comida italiana/ china/mexicana** *Italian/ Chinese/Mexican food*, 1
comiendo *eating*, 10
el comienzo *beginning*, 1
como *like, as*; **tan ... como** *as ... as*, 9
¿Cómo? *How?, What?*; **¿Cómo es...?** *What's ... like?*, 3; **¿Cómo estás?** *How are you?* (to ask a friend), 1; ¿Cómo se escribe? *How do you write (spell) it?* P; **¿Cómo son...?** *What are ... like?*, 3; **¿Cómo te llamas?** *What's your name?*, 1; **¿Cómo te sientes?** *How are you feeling?*, 11
¡Cómo no! *Of course!*, 7
cómodo/a *comfortable*, 9
compacto/a *compact*; **el disco compacto** *compact disc*, 9
el compadrazgo *relationship between parents and godparents of a child*, 6
el compadre *friend* (male), 4
la compañera *friend, pal* (female), 3
el compañero *friend, pal* (male), 3
la compañía *company*, 10; la compañía de balet *ballet company*, 2
la comparación *comparison*, 2
compartir *to share*, 11
el complemento *complement, object pronoun*, 8
completa *complete* (command), 1
completar *to complete*, 8
completo/a *complete*, 2
comprar *to buy*, 2
comprender *to understand*, 1
compuesto/a *composed*, 2
la computación *computer science*, 3
la computadora *computer*, 2
común *common* (pl. comunes), P

con *with*, 4; **conmigo** *with me*, 4; **contigo** *with you*, 4
con base en *based on*, 1
con frecuencia *often*, 5; **¿Con qué frecuencia?** *How often?*, 5
¡Con mucho gusto! *Sure!*, 10
el concepto *concept*, 7
el concierto *concert*, 3
el concurso *game, competition, contest*, 3
el condimento *condiment*, 8
el conejo *rabbit*
confirmar *to confirm*, 4
el confite *candy*, 9
la confitería *sweetshop*, 9
el conflicto *conflict*, 6
el congelador *freezer*, 8
el conjunto *group, collection; band*, 9
conmigo *with me*, 4
conocer *to be familiar or acquainted with*, 2; **conocer a** *to get to know (someone)*, 2
conocido/a *known* (adj.), 10
los conocimientos *information; knowledge*, 2
el consejo *advice*, 6
conservar *to conserve*, 11
la consistencia *consistency*, 8
consistir en *to consist of*, 8
constante *constant*, 11
la constitución *constitution*, 4
la construcción *construction*, 1
construido/a *built, constructed*, 9
construir *to build*, 11
consultar *to consult*, 8
el contado *cash*, 8
contar (ue) *to say, to tell*, 9
contener (ie) *to contain*, 8
contesta *answer* (command), 5
contestar *to answer*, 12
el contexto *context*, 10
contigo *with you*, 4
continuo/a *continuous*, 11
contra *against*, 11
controlar *to control*, 5
el convento *convent*, 12
la conversación *conversation*, 1
convertirse (ie) *to change*, 10
el corazón *heart*, 10
la corbata *tie*, 9
la cordillera *mountain range*, 1
el coro *choir*, 3
la coronación *coronation*, 10
correcto/a *correct*, 5
corregir (i) *to correct*, 3
el correo *post office*, 4
correr *to run*, 5; **¡Córrele!** *Hurry up!, Run along!*, 3; **la pista de correr** *running track*, 11
la correspondencia *mail*, 4
corresponder *to correspond*, 6
la corriente: contra la corriente *against the flow*, 6
corrige *correct* (command), 9
cortar *to cut;* **cortar el césped** *to cut the grass*, 6
cortés *polite, courteous*, 8

corto/a *short* (to describe length); **los pantalones cortos** *short pants*, 9
la cosa *thing*, 2
la cosecha *crop*
cosmopolita *cosmopolitan*, 9
la costa *coast*
costar (ue) *to cost;* **¿Cuánto cuesta...?** *How much does . . . cost?*, 9; **¿Cuánto cuestan...?** *How much do . . . cost?*, 9
costero/a *coastal*
crea *create* (command), 7
la creación *creation*, 8
crear *to create*, 7
creativo/a *creative*, 6
creer *to believe, to think*, 10; **¿Crees que...?** *Do you think that . . .?*, 10; **Creo que no.** *I don't think so.*, 10; **Creo que sí.** *I think so.*, 10
la crema de maní *peanut butter*, 8
la cruz *cross*, 2; las cruces *crosses*, 2
cruzar *to cross*, 11
el cuaderno *notebook*, 2
la cuadra *city block*, 9
cuadrado/a *square*
el cuadro *square*, 4; **de cuadros** *plaid*, 9
cual, cuales *which*
¿Cuál? *which?*, 3; **¿Cuál es la fecha?** *What is today's date?*, 5; **¿Cuál es tu clase favorita?** *Which is your favorite class?*, 3
cuando *when*, 5; **sólo cuando** *only when*, 5
¿cuándo? *when?*, 3
¿cuánto/a? *how much?*, 2; **¿Cuántas personas hay en tu familia?** *How many people are there in your family?*, 6; **¿Cuánto cuesta...?** *How much does . . . cost?*, 9; **¿Cuánto cuestan...?** *How much do . . . cost?*, 9; **¿cuántos/as?** *how many?*, 2; **¿Cuánto es?** *How much is it?*, 8; **¿Cuántos años tiene?** *How old is (she/he)?*, 1; **¿Cuántos años tienes?** *How old are you?*, 1
cuarenta *forty*, 2
cuarto *quarter, fourth;* **menos cuarto** *quarter to (the hour)*, 3
el cuarto *room*, 2
cuarto/a *fourth*
el cuate *friend* (slang), 4
cuatro *four*, 1
cuatrocientos/as *four hundred*, 8
cubano/a *Cuban*, 6
el cubo *cube;* cubo de hielo *ice cube*, 8
la cuchara *spoon*, 8
la cucharada *tablespoon*, 8
el cuchillo *knife*, 8
el cuello *neck*, 11
la cuenta *bill*, 8
cuéntame *tell me*, 1
el cuento *story, tale*, 3
la cuerda *string*, 7
el cuero *leather;* **de cuero** *(made of) leather*, 9

el cuerpo *body*, 11
Cuesta un ojo de la cara. *It's very expensive.*, 11
la cuestión *question*, 1
el cuestionario *questionnaire*, 6
cuidar *to take care of;* **cuidar al gato** *to take care of the cat*, 6; **cuidar a tu hermano/a** *to take care of your brother/sister*, 4
la culebra *snake*
culinario/a *culinary*, 6
culminar *to culminate*, 10
cultivar *to farm, to cultivate*, 7
el cultivo *farming, cultivation*
la cultura *culture*, 12
cultural *cultural*
el cumpleaños *birthday;* ¡Feliz cumpleaños! *Happy birthday!*, 10; **una fiesta de cumpleaños** *birthday party*, 7
la cúpula *cupola*, 7
curioso/a *curious, strange*, 6

los dados *dice*, 2
la danza *dance*, 3
dar *to give*, 9; **dar una caminata** *to go hiking*, 12; dar un paseo en bicicleta *to ride a bike*, 4
¡Date prisa! *Hurry up!*, 3
los datos *information*, 12; los datos personales *personal information*, 6
de *of, from, made of, in*, 1; **de algodón** *(made of) cotton*, 9; de antemano *beforehand;* **de color café** *brown*, 6; **de cuadros** *plaid*, 9; **de cuero** *(made of) leather*, 9; **¿De dónde eres?** *Where are you from?*, 1; **¿De dónde es?** *Where is she/he from?*, 1; **de la mañana** *in the morning* (A.M.), 3; **de lana** *(made of) wool*, 9; **de la noche** *in the evening* (P.M.), 3; **de la tarde** *in the afternoon* (P.M.), 3; **¿De parte de quién?** *Who's calling?*, 7; **¿De qué color es/son...?** *What color is/are . . .?*, 6; **de rayas** *striped*, 9; **de seda** *(made of) silk*, 9
De acuerdo. *Agreed.*, 10
de compras *shopping*, 8
de modo que *in such a way that*, 10
de nuevo *again*, 1
de todos modos *by all means, anyway*, 11
de vacaciones *on vacation*, 5
de visita *on a visit*, 3
debajo de *under, beneath*, 4
el debate *debate*, 1
deber *should, ought to*, 6

decidan   *decide* (command), 8
decidir   *to decide*, 6
decir   *to say*; **Dice que...**   *She/He says that . . .*, 6; **Diga.**   *Hello.* (to answer the phone), 7; **¿Me puede decir...?**   *Can you tell me . . .?*, 9
declarado/a   *declared*
declarar   *to declare*, 7
la decoración   *decoration*, 10; **colgar (ue) las decoraciones**   *to hang decorations*, 10
decorar   *to decorate*, 10
el dedo   *finger, toe*, 11
defender   *to defend*, 11
defendieron   *you* (pl.)/*they defended*
deja   *leave* (command), 7
dejar   *to leave behind*, 7; dejar de   *to stop*, 9; **¿Puedo dejar un recado?**   *May I leave a message?*, 7
del (de + el)   *of the, from the*, 3
deletrea   *spell out* (command), 5
delgado/a   *thin*, 6
delicioso/a   *delicious*, 8
demasiado/a   *too much*, 6
demostrativo/a   *demonstrative*, 9
den   *give* (command), 10
dentro   *inside, within*, 8
depender (de)   *to depend (on)*, 1
los deportes   *sports*, 3
deportivo/a   *having to do with sports*, 10
el depósito   *deposit*, 1
la derecha   *right hand*, 11
el derecho   *right*, 1
desagradable   *unpleasant*, 11
el desastre   *disaster*, 2
desayunar   *to eat breakfast*, 5
el desayuno   *breakfast*, 8
descansar   *to rest*; **descansar en el parque**   *to rest in the park*, 4
el descanso   *recess, break*, 3
el descendiente   *descendant*, 6
describe   *describe* (command), 3
la descripción   *description*, 3
el descubrimiento   *discovery*, 2
descubrir   *to discover*, 10
desde   *since*, 7
¿Desean algo más?   *Would you like something else?*, 8
el deseo   *desire*
el desfile   *parade*, 10
el desierto   *desert*; la isla desierta   *desert island*, 12
deslumbrante   *dazzling*, 9
el desorden   *disarray, disorder, mess*, 10
desorganizado/a   *disorganized*, 6
la despedida   *farewell, goodbye, leave-taking*, 1
después   *after*, 3; **después de**   *after*, 4
el destino   *destination*, 12
el detalle   *detail*, 11
determinar   *to determine*, 4
di   *tell* (command), 11
el día   *day*, 4; **Buenos días.**   *Good morning.* 1; cada día   *each day*, 5; día a día   *day by day*, 11; **el Día de**

Acción de Gracias   *Thanksgiving*, 10; **el Día de la Independencia**   *Independence Day*, 10; **el Día de las Madres**   *Mother's Day*, 10; **el Día de los Enamorados**   *Valentine's Day*, 10; **el Día del Padre**   *Father's Day*, 10; día de santo   *saint's day*, 1; **los días festivos**   *holidays*, 10; **un día libre**   *a free day*, 3; **tal vez otro día**   *perhaps another day*, 7; **todos los días**   *every day*, 5
el diálogo   *dialogue*, 1
diariamente   *daily*, 6
diario/a   *daily*, 8
el diario   *diary, journal*, 12
dibujar   *to draw*, 4
el dibujo   *drawing*; dibujos animados   *animated cartoons*, 2
el diccionario   *dictionary*, 2
dice   *he/she says*, 2
diciembre (m.)   *December*, 5
el dictado   *dictation*, 1
diecinueve   *nineteen*, 1
dieciocho   *eighteen*, 1
diecciséis   *sixteen*, 1
diecisiete   *seventeen*, 1
el diente   *tooth*; **lavarse los dientes**   *to brush one's teeth*, 7
la dieta   *diet*; estar a dieta   *to be on a diet*, 5
diez   *ten*, 1
diferente   *different*, 8
difícil   *difficult*, 3
la dificultad   *difficulty*, 11
Diga.   *Hello.* (to answer the phone), 7; Dígame.   *Hello.* (telephone greeting), 7
dile   *tell him/her* (command), 8; dime   *tell me*, 2
el dineral   *large sum of money*, 2
el dinero   *money*, 2
el dinosaurio   *dinosaur*, 2
la dirección   *address*, 4
directo/a   *direct*, 4
diría   *would say*, 11
el disco   *phonograph record*; **el disco compacto**   *compact disc*, 9
discutir   *to argue, to discuss*, 1
diseñado/a   *designed*, 11
el diseño   *design*, 2
el disfraz   *costume*, 10
disfrutar   *to enjoy*, 8
el disgusto   *distaste*, 1
disolver (ue)   *to dissolve*, 8
la distancia   *distance*; distancia social   *interpersonal distance*, 1
el distrito   *district*
la diversión   *diversion, fun*, 10
divertido/a   *amusing, fun*, 3
dividido/a   *divided*, 5
doblado/a   *dubbed*, 2
doblar (una película)   *to dub (a film)*, 2
doce   *twelve*, 1
el dólar   *dollar*, 2
doler (ue)   *to hurt, to ache*, 11
el dolor de cabeza   *headache*, 11; el

dolor de espalda   *backache*, 11
doméstico/a   *household*; **los quehaceres domésticos**   *household chores*, 6
el domicilio   *residence*, 1
el domingo   *Sunday*, 4
el dominó   *dominoes*, 6
donde   *where*; **¿Adónde?**   *Where (to)?*, 4; **¿De dónde eres?**   *Where are you from?*, 1; **¿De dónde es?**   *Where is she/he from?*, 1; **¿dónde?**   *where?*, 4; ¿Dónde te gustaría estudiar?   *Where would you like to study?*, 3
dos   *two*, 1
doscientos/as   *two hundred*, 8
ducharse   *to take a shower*, 7
dulce   *sweet*, 8; **el pan dulce**   *sweet rolls*, 8
la dulcería   *candy store*, 9
los dulces   *candy*, 9
la duración   *length, duration*, 2
durante   *during*, 5
durar   *to last*, 10
el durazno   *peach*, 8

la ecología   *ecology*, 1
la edad   *age*, 1
la edición   *edition*, 2
el edificio   *building*, 12
la educación   *education*, 3
la educación física   *physical education*, 3
educar   *to educate*, 2
Egipto (m.)   *Egypt*, 12
egoísta   *selfish*, 6
el ejercicio   *exercise*, 5; **una clase de ejercicios aeróbicos**   *aerobics class*, 5; **hacer ejercicio**   *to exercise*, 5; hacer ejercicios aeróbicos   *to do aerobics*, 4
ejercitar   *to exercise*, 11
el ejército   *army*, 10
el   *the*, 1
él   *he*, 2; **Él es...**   *He is . . .*, 3
el electrodoméstico   *electrical appliance*
la electrónica   *electronics*
eliminar   *to eliminate*, 11
ella   *she*, 2; **Ella es...**   *She is . . .*, 3
ellas   *they* (f.), 3; **a ellas**   *to them*, 5; **Ellas son...**   *They are . . .*, 3
ellos   *they*, 3; **a ellos**   *to them*, 5; **Ellos son...**   *They are . . .*, 3
la empanada   *turnover-like pastry*, 8
empanizado/a   *breaded*, 8
empezar (ie)   *to begin*, 7
en forma   *in shape*, 11
en   *in, on*, 3; **en punto**   *on the dot*, 3
en punta: con el pie en punta   *with*

the foot extended, 11
en punto *on the dot*, 3
en seguida *immediately*, 8
en voz alta *aloud*, 11
Encantado/a. *Delighted to meet you.*, 1
encantar *to really like, to love*, 8
el encanto *delight, pleasure, enchantment, charm*, 9
la enciclopedia *encyclopedia*, 2
encima de *on top of*, 4
encontrar (ue) *to find*, 2; se encuentra *is found*
el encuadre *framing*, 3
el encuentro *encounter, meeting*, 1; encuentro cultural *cultural encounter*
la encuesta *survey*, 1
endurecer *to strengthen*, 11
enero (m.) *January*, 5
enfermo/a *sick*, 7
enojado/a *angry*, 11
enorme *enormous, large*, 8
la ensalada *salad*, 1
entero/a *entire, whole*, 10
entonces *then*, 12
la entrada *entrance*, 7
entre *among, between*, 8
el entrenador, la entrenadora *coach*, 11
el entrenamiento *training*
el entretenimiento *entertainment*, 10
la entrevista *interview*, 1
entrevistar *to interview*, 5
enviarse *to be sent*, 10
la época *time, epoch*, 8
el equilibrio *equilibrium*, 5
el equipo de transporte *transportation equipment*
la equivocación *mistake*, 5
erigirse *to be built, to be erected*, 10
Es aparte. *It's separate.*, 8
es de... *he/she/it is from . . .*, 1; **es de** + material/pattern *it is made of . . .*, 9
Es el ... de ... *It's the (date) of (month).*, 5
Es la una. *It's one o'clock.*, 3
¡Es un robo! *It's a rip-off!*, 9
esa, ese *that*, 9
esas, esos *those* (adj), 9
escalar *to climb*; **escalar montañas** *to go mountain climbing*, 12
el escándalo *scandal*, 6
el esclavo *slave*, 6
escoge *choose* (command), 7
escoger *to choose*, 9
escolar *school* (adj.), 3
escribamos *let's write*, P
escribe *write* (command), 1
escribiendo *writing*, 10
escribir *to write*, 5
el escritorio *desk*, 2
escuchar *to listen*, 4; escuchar la radio *listen to the radio*, 4; **escuchar música** *to listen to*

music, 4; para escuchar *for listening*, P
escuchemos *let's listen*, P
la escuela *school*, 2; escuela secundaria *secondary school*, 2
esencial *essential*, 11
eso/a *that*; **por eso** *that's why*, 4
el espacio *space*, 1
la espalda *back*, 11
España (f.) *Spain*
el español *Spanish*, 1
especial (adj.) *special*, 3
la especialidad *specialty*
especialmente *especially*, 5
la especie *species*, 7
el espectáculo *show*, 7
esperar *to wait, to hope for*, 12
espeso/a *thick*, 8
espontáneo/a *spontaneous*, 7
la esposa *wife*, 6
el esposo *husband*, 6
el esqueleto *skeleton*, 1
el esquema *scheme*, 2
esquiar *to ski*, 5
los esquís *skis*, 12
esta, este *this*, 9
ésta, éste *this* (pron.), 1
Ésta es mi amiga. *This is my friend (female).*, 1
establecido/a *established*
las estaciones *seasons*, 5
el estadio *stadium*, 11
el estadista, la estadista *statesperson*
la estadística *statistic*, 2
el estado *state*
las estampillas *stamps*, 4
el estante *bookcase*, 2
estar de acuerdo *to agree, to be in agreement*, 10
estar *to be*, 4; **¿Cómo estás?** *How are you?*, 1; **Está atrasado/a.** *He/She is late.*, 3; **Está bien.** *She/He is okay.*, 7; **Está bien.** *All right.*, 7; **¿Está incluida?** *Is it included?*, 8; **Está lloviendo.** *It's raining.*, 5; Está lloviendo a cántaros. *It's raining cats and dogs*, 5; **Está nevando.** *It's snowing.*, 5; **Está nublado.** *It's cloudy.*, 5; estar en forma *to be in shape*, 11; **estar listo/a** *to be ready*, 7; **estar mal** *to feel poorly*, 11; **estar resfriado/a** *to have a cold*, 11; Estás a la última. *You're stylish.*, 9; **Estoy atrasado/a.** *I'm late.*, 3; **Estoy (bastante) bien, gracias.** *I'm (quite) well, thanks.*, 1; **La línea está ocupada.** *The line is busy.*, 7
estás ayudando *you are helping*, 9
estas, estos *these* (adj.), 9
éstas, éstos *these* (pron.), 6
la estatura *height*, 1
Éste es mi amigo. *This is my friend (male).*, 1
el estéreo *stereo*, 2
el estilo *style*, 1; el estilo personal

personal style, 1
la estima *esteem; respect*, 11
estirarse *to stretch*, 11
el estómago *stomach*, 11
Estoy atrasado/a. *I'm late.*, 3
la estrategia *strategy*, 1
estratégicamente *strategically*
estrecho/a *narrow*, 11
la estrella *star*, 10
el estrés *stress*, 11
estricto/a *strict*, 3
la estructura *structures*
estudiante (m./f.) *student*, 3; estudiante de intercambio (m./f.) *exchange student*, 7
la estudiantina *strolling student band*, 10
estudiar *to study*, 4
Estupendo/a. *Great./Marvelous.*, 1
estuviéramos *we might be, we would be*, 10
estuvieras: como si estuvieras... *as if you were . . .*, 11
la etiqueta *label*, 1
étnico/a *ethnic*, 9
Europa *Europe*, 1
el evento *event*, 7
la exageración *exaggeration*, 2
el examen *exam* (pl. **los exámenes**), 3
Excelente. *Great./Excellent.*, 1
excepto *except*, 10
la excursión *excursion*; ir de excursión *to go sightseeing*, 12
la exhibición *exhibition*, 10
exótico/a *exotic*, 8
la experiencia *experience*, 5
experimentar *to experience*, 8
explica *explain* (command), 7
la explicación *explanation*, 4
explicar *to explain*, 12
el explorador *explorer*
explorar *to explore*, 12
la exposición *exhibition*, 3
expresar *to express*, 10; expresen *express* (command), 10
la expresión *expression*, 1
exprimir *to squeeze*, 8
exquisito/a *exquisite*
externo *external; outside*, 1
extraordinario/a *extraordinary*, 7

fácil *easy*, 3
la falda *skirt*, 9
las Fallas *spring festival in Valencia, Spain*, 10
falso/a *false*, 1
la falta de asistencia *absence (from class)*, 3
la familia extensa *extended family*, 6
la familia *family*, 6; **¿Cuántas**

personas hay en tu familia? *How many people are there in your family?*, 6

la **familia nuclear** *nuclear family, immediate family*, 6

familiar *family member*, 9

famoso/a *famous*, 4

el **fanático** *fan*, 5

fantástico/a *fantastic*, 3

farmacéutico/a *pharmaceutical*

fascinante *fascinating*, 12

fascinar *to fascinate, captivate*, 1

favor *favor*; **¿Me haces el favor de...?** *Can you do me the favor of . . .?*, 10; **por favor** *please*, 8

favorito/a *favorite*, 3

febrero (m.) *February*, 5

la **fecha** *date*, 5; **¿Cuál es la fecha?** *What is today's date?*, 5; **¿Qué fecha es hoy?** *What's today's date?*, 5

felicitar *to congratulate*; Te felicito. *Congratulations.*, 10

feliz *happy*, 10; ¡Feliz aniversario! *Happy anniversary!*, 10; ¡Feliz Año Nuevo! *Happy New Year!*, 10; ¡Feliz cumpleaños! *Happy birthday!*, 10; ¡Feliz Navidad! *Merry Christmas!*, 10

¡Felicidades! *Congratulations!*, 10

fenomenal *phenomenal*, 6

el **fenómeno** *phenomenon*, 2

feo/a *ugly*, 3

la **feria** *fair*, 10

fértil *fertile*, 7

festejar *to celebrate*, 10

el **festival** *festival*, 10

festivo/a *festive*; **los días festivos** *holidays*, 10

la **fiebre** *fever*, 11; **tener fiebre** *to have a fever*, 11

la **fiesta** *party*, 3; **una fiesta de aniversario** *anniversary party*, 7; **una fiesta de cumpleaños** *birthday party*, 7; **una fiesta de graduación** *graduation party*, 7; **una fiesta de sorpresa** *surprise party*, 7

la **figura** *figure*, 10

filmado/a *filmed*, 2

la **filosofía** *philosophy*, 2

el **fin** *end*, 4; **el fin de semana** *weekend*, 4

la **firma** *signature*, 1

la **física** *physics*, 3

flamenco *flamenco (music, singing, dancing)*, 6

el **flan** *custard*, 8

la **flauta** *flute*, 4

flexionar *to flex*, 11

la **florería** *flower shop*, 9

las **flores** *flowers*, 9

folklórico/a *folkloric*

el **folleto** *pamphlet*, 9

la **forma negativa** *the negative form*, 4

formal *formal*, 9

formar *to form*, 9

fortalecer *to strengthen*; fortalece *strengthen, fortify* (command), 11

la **foto** *photo*, 10

la **fotografía** *photograph*, 1

la **fotonovela** *illustrated story*, 1

la **frambuesa** *raspberry*, 8

el **francés** *French*, 3

Francia (f.) *France*, 12

la **frase** *sentence, phrase*, P

la **frecuencia** *frequency*, 6; **¿Con qué frecuencia?** *How often?*, 5

freír *to fry*, 8

la **fresa** *strawberry*, 8

fresco/a *fresh*; **Hace fresco.** *It's cool.*, 5

los **frijoles** *beans*, 8

frío/a (adj.) *cold*, 8

el **frío** *cold*, 8; **Hace frío.** *It's cold.*, 5; Hace un frío tremendo. *It's really cold.*, 7

la **fruta** *fruit*, 1

los **fuegos artificiales** *fireworks*, 10

fueron *you* (pl.)/*they were*; *you* (pl.)/*they went*

fuerte *strong, heavy*, 8

el **fuerte** *fortress*, 11

la **fundación** *founding*, 10

fundado/a *founded*, 2

fundar *to found*, 12; se fundó *was founded*

el **fútbol** *soccer*, 1; **la cancha de fútbol** *soccer field*, 11; **el fútbol norteamericano** *football*, 1

el **futuro** *future*, 2

la **galería** *gallery*, 9

gallego/a *Galician*, 3

la **galleta** *cookie*, 8

la **gana** *desire*; **tener ganas de** (+ infinitive) *to feel like (doing something)*, 7

ganadero/a *having to do with livestock*, 9

el **ganado** *livestock*

ganar *to win, to earn*, 11

la **ganga** *bargain*; **¡Qué ganga!** *What a bargain!*, 9

la **garganta** *throat*, 11

la **gaseosa** (Col.) *soda pop, carbonated beverage*, 8

gastado/a *tired*, 7

el **gato** *cat*, 6; **cuidar al gato** *to take care of the cat*, 6

el **gazpacho** *cold soup served in Spain*, 8

general *general*; por lo general *in general*, 4

generalmente *generally*, 8

generoso/a *generous*, 6

¡Genial! *Great!*, 2

la **gente** *people*; gente famosa *famous people*, 1

la **geografía** *geography*, 3

geológico/a *geological*, 7

gigante *giant*

el **gimnasio** *gym*, 4

girar *to turn around, to rotate*, 11

el **globo** *balloon*; **inflar los globos** *to blow up balloons*, 10

el **gobierno** *government*

la **goma de borrar** *eraser*, 2

gordo/a *overweight*; **un poco gordo/a** *a little overweight*, 6

la **gorra** *cap*

Gracias. *Thanks.*, 1; **el Día de Acción de Gracias** *Thanksgiving Day*, 10

la **graduación** *graduation*; **una fiesta de graduación** *graduation party*, 7

la **gramática** *grammar*, 2

grande *big*, 3; **gran** *great*, 3

el **grano** *grain*; al grano *to the point.*

la **gripe** *flu*; **tener gripe** *to have the flu*, 11

gris *gray*, 9

el **grupo** *group*, 1

los **guantes** *gloves*

guapo/a *good-looking, handsome, pretty*, 3; ¡Qué guapo/a estás! *You look great!*, 9

el **guarapo** *sugarcane juice*, 6

la **guarida** *den, lair*, 7

la **guarnición** *garrison*, 11

la **guerra** *war*, 11

la **guía** *guide*, 2

el **guineo** *banana*, 8

la **guitarra** *guitar*, 4

gustar *to like (someone/something)*; **A mí me gusta** + infinitive *I (emphatic) like to . . .*, 4; **¿A quién le gusta...?** *Who likes . . .?*, 4; **le gustan** *she/he likes*, 3; **les gusta** *they like*, 5; **Me gusta...** *I like . . .*, 1; **Me gusta más...** *I like . . . better*, 1; **Me gustan...** *I like . . .*, 3; **Me gustaría...** *I would like . . .*, 7; **No me gusta...** *I don't like . . .*, 1; **nos gusta** *we like*, 5; **Nos gustan...** *We like . . .*, 7; **¿Qué te gusta?** *What do you like?*, 1; **¿Qué te gusta hacer?** *What do you like to do?*, 4; **Sí, me gusta.** *Yes, I like it.*, 1; **¿Te gusta...?** *Do you like . . .?*, 1; **Te gustan...** *You like . . .*, 3; **¿Te gustaría...?** *Would you like . . .?*, 7

el **gusto** *taste, pleasure*, 9; **¡Con mucho gusto!** *Sure!*, 10; gustos personales *personal tastes*, 1; **Mucho gusto.** *Nice to meet you.*, 1

H

la habitación *room*, 12
el habitante *inhabitant*
hablando *speaking*, 2
hablar *to speak, to talk*; **hablar por teléfono** *to talk on the phone*, 4
hablemos *let's speak; let's talk*, P
hacer *to do, to make*, 2; **Hace buen tiempo.** *The weather is nice.*, 5; **Hace calor.** *It's hot.*, 5; **Hace fresco.** *It's cool.*, 5; **Hace mal tiempo.** *The weather is bad.*, 5; **Hace (mucho) frío.** *It's (very) cold.*, 5; **Hace sol.** *It's sunny.*, 5; **Hace viento.** *It's windy.*, 5; **hacer ejercicio** *to exercise*, 5; **hacer la cama** *to make the bed*, 6; **hacer la maleta** *to pack the suitcase*, 12; **hacer turismo** *to go sightseeing*, 12; **hacer un viaje** *to take a trip*, 6; **hacer yoga** *to do yoga*, 11; **haz** *do, make*, 10; **¿Me haces el favor de...?** *Can you do me the favor of . . .?*, 10; **¿Qué debo hacer?** *What should I do?*, 6; **¿Qué estás haciendo?** *What are you doing?*, 10; **¿Qué hacen ustedes los fines de semana?** *What do you do on weekends?*, 6; **¿Qué tiempo hace?** *What's the weather like?*, 5
hacia abajo *downward*, 11
hacia arriba *upward*, 11
el hado *destiny, fate*, 2
hagan una lista *make a list* (command), 7
el hambre (f.) *hunger*; **tener (mucha) hambre** *to be (really) hungry*, 8
la hamburguesa *hamburger*, 5
ha sido *he/she/it has been*, 9
hasta *until*; **Hasta luego.** *See you later.*, 1; **Hasta mañana.** *See you tomorrow.*, 1
hay *there is, there are*, 2; **¿Cuántas personas hay en tu familia?** *How many people are there in your family?*, 6
haz *do, make* (command), 10
hecho/a *made, done*, 9; hecho/a a mano *handmade*, 10
el helado *ice cream*, 4; **tomar un helado** *to eat ice cream*, 4
el helicóptero *helicopter*, P
la herencia *heritage*, 9
la hermana *sister*, 6; **la media hermana** *half sister*, 6
la hermanastra *stepsister*, 6
el hermanastro *stepbrother*, 6
el hermano *brother*, 6; **el medio hermano** *half brother*, 6
los hermanos *brothers, brothers and sisters*, 6
hermoso/a *beautiful*, 11

el héroe *hero*, 3
hicieron *they did, they made*, 11
hiciste *you did, you made*, 10
el hielo *ice*, 8
el hierro *iron*
la hija *daughter*, 6
el hijo *son*, 6
los hijos *children*, 6
hispano/a *Hispanic*
hispanohablante *Spanish-speaking*, 8
la historia *history*, 3
histórico/a *historic*, 10
hizo *he/she/it did, made*, 10
el hogar *home*, 9
¡Hola! *Hello!*, 1; ¡Hola, pata! *Hello friend!* (slang), 4
el hombre *man*, 10
el hombro *shoulder*, 11
el homenaje *homage*, 6
la hora *hour, time*; **¿A qué hora...?** *At what time . . .?*, 3; la hora latina *Latin time*, 3; **¿Qué hora es?** *What time is it?*, 3
la hora local *local time*, 3
el horario *schedule*, 3; horario escolar *school schedule*, 3
Horrible. *Horrible.*, 1; ¡Qué horrible! *How terrible!*, 2
hoy *today*, 3; **¿Qué fecha es hoy?** *What's today's date?*, 5
hubiera ganado *would have won*, 10
los huevos *eggs*, 8
humanístico/a: lo humanístico *the humanities*, 3
el humano *human*, 1
el humor *humor*, 1; de mal humor *in a bad mood*, 7

I

la idea *idea*, 10; **Buena idea.** *Good idea.*, 10
ideal *ideal*, 8
identificar *to identify*, 9
el idioma *language*
la iglesia *church*, 6
igual *equal*, 6
Igualmente. *Same here.*, 1
la iguana *iguana*, 7
iluminar *to illuminate, to light up*, 10
ilustrado/a *illustrated*, 2
imaginar *to imagine*, 10
el impermeable *raincoat*, 10
el importe *amount*, 8
imposible *impossible*, 3
el impuesto *tax*, 3
los incas *the Incas*
incluir *to include*, 8; **¿Está incluida?** *Is it included?*, 8

incluso *including*
incluye *include* (command), 6; *he/she/it includes*, 10
¡Increíble! *Incredible!*, 2
la independencia *independence*; **el Día de la Independencia** *Independence Day*, 10
independiente *independent*, 6
indica *state, indicate* (command), 1
la indicación *suggestion*, 11
indicar *to point, to show, to indicate*, 2
el índice *index; index finger*, 2
indígena *indigenous, native*
indirecto/a *indirect*, 8
la individualidad *individuality*, 10
la industria *industry*; las industrias extractivas *mining industries*, 3
infantil *for children*, 3
el infinitivo *infinitive*, 11
inflar *to blow up, to inflate*, 10; **inflar los globos** *to blow up balloons*, 10
la influencia *influence*, 10
la información *the information*, 8
informal *informal*, 10
la informática *computer science*, 3
la ingeniería *engineering*, 3
el ingenio *cleverness*, 1
ingenioso/a *ingenious; witty*, 2
Inglaterra (f.) *England*, 12
inglés *English*; **la clase de inglés** *English class*, 1
los ingredientes *ingredients*, 8
ingresar *to enter*, 1
el inicio *beginning*, 10
inocente *innocent*, 10
inolvidable *unforgettable*, 9
insoportable *unbearable*, 6
la instalación *installation, facility*, 1
el instituto *institute*, 3
las instrucciones *instructions*, 8
el instrumento *(musical) instrument*; **tocar un instrumento** *to play an instrument*, 4
inteligente *intelligent*, 3
intentar *to try*, 12
intercambiar *to exchange*, 3; intercambiar papeles *to exchange roles*, 3
el intercambio *exchange*; estudiante de intercambio (m./f.) *exchange student*, 7
interdependiente *interdependent*, 9
interesante *interesting*, 3
interesarse *to be interested*, 12
internacional *international*, 7
interrumpirse *to interrupt*, 6; se interrumpió *was interrupted*
intocable *untouchable*, 3
la intriga *intrigue*, 3
inventa *invent* (command), 8
inventar *to invent, to make up*, 7
el invierno *winter*, 5
la invitación *invitation*; **mandar las invitaciones** *to send the invitations*, 10

invitado,-a (m./f.)   *guest*; **llamar a los invitados**   *to call the guests*, 10
invitar   *to invite*, 7; **Te invito.**   *It's my treat.*, 7
ir   *to go*, 2; **ir + a + infinitive**   *to be going to (do something)*, 7; **ir al centro comercial**   *to go to the mall*, 2; **ir de vela**   *to go sailing*, 12; **¡Ve!**   *Go!*, 10; **¡Vete!**   *Go away!*, 10
la **irritabilidad**   *irritability*, 11
la **isla**   *island*, 2
Italia (f.)   *Italy*, 12
italiano/a   *Italian*; **la comida italiana**   *Italian food*, 1
el **itinerario**   *itinerary, route taken on a trip*, 9
izquierdo/a   *left*, 11

J

el **jabón**   *soap*, P
el **jai alai**   *Basque ball game*, 11
el **jamón**   *ham*, 8
el **jardín**   *garden*, 6; **trabajar en el jardín**   *to work in the garden*, 6
el **jazz**   *jazz*, 1
joven (pl. **jóvenes**)   *young*, 6; **Se ve joven.**   *He/She looks young.*, 6
el **joven**, la **joven**   *young man, young woman*, 1
las **joyas**   *jewelry*, 9
la **joyería**   *jewelry store*, 9
el **juego**   *game*, 3; **juego de ingenio**   *guessing game*, 1; **el juego de mesa**   *board game*, 9; **el videojuego**   *videogame*, 3
el **jueves**   *Thursday*, 4
jugar (ue)   *to play*, 4; **jugar al tenis**   *to play tennis*, 4
el **jugo**   *juice*, 5; **jugo de naranja**   *orange juice*, 8
la **juguetería**   *toy store*, 9
los **juguetes**   *toys*, 9
julio (m.)   *July*, 5
junio (m.)   *June*, 5
juntar   *to get together*, 11
juntos/as   *together*, 5
juvenil   *juvenile*, 7
la **juventud**   *youth*, 3

K

el **kilómetro**   *kilometer*, P

L

la   *the*, 1; *it/her*, 10
el **lado**   *side*; **al lado de**   *next to*, 4
el **lago**   *lake*, 7
la **lámpara**   *lamp*, 2
la **lana**   *wool*; **de lana**   *(made of) wool*, 9
la **lancha**   *boat*, 5
la **lapicera**   *pencil holder*, 2
el **lápiz**   *pencil*, (pl. **los lápices**) 2; lápiz de color   *colored pencil*, 2
largo/a   *long*, 5
las   *the*, 3
lástima   *shame*; **¡Qué lástima!**   *What a shame!*, 7
la **lata**   *can*, 8
el **latín**   *Latin*, 3
lavar   *to wash*; **lavar el carro**   *to wash the car*, 4; **lavar la ropa**   *to wash clothes*, 4
lavarse   *to wash oneself*; **lavarse los dientes**   *to brush your teeth*, 7
le   *to/for him, her, you*, 9
Le pido su número.   *I ask him/ her for his/her number.*, 7
leal   *loyal*, 6
leamos   *let's read*, P
las **lecciones**   *lessons*, 5; tomar lecciones   *to take lessons*, 5
la **leche**   *milk*; **el café con leche**   *coffee with milk*, 8; **un vaso de leche**   *a glass of milk*, 8
la **lechuga**   *lettuce*, 8
la **lectura**   *reading passage*, 10
lee   *read* (command), 7
leer   *to read*, 5
legal   *legal*, 1
las **legumbres**   *vegetables*, 8
lejano/a   *far away*, 7
lejos   *far*, 4; **lejos de**   *far from*, 4
la **lengua**   *language*; la lengua extranjera   *foreign language*, 3
los **lentes**   *contact lenses, glasses*; **los lentes de sol**   *sunglasses*, 12; ponerse los lentes   *to put on one's glasses*, 7
lento/a   *slow*, 11
les   *to/for them, you* (pl.), 8; **Les gusta...**   *They/You like...*, 5
la **letra**   *letter*, 1; letra y sonido   *letter and sound*
levantado/a   *raised*, 11
levantar   *to lift, to raise*, 11; **levantar pesas**   *to lift weights*, 11
la **ley**   *law*, 3
leyendo   *reading*, 10
la **liberación**   *liberation*
libre   *free*; **un día libre**   *a free day*, 3
la **librería**   *bookstore*, 2
el **libro**   *book*, 2
el **liceo**   *school*, 2
la **licuadora**   *blender*, 8
ligeramente   *lightly*

ligero/a   *light*, 8
el **limón**   *lemon*, 8
la **limonada**   *lemonade*, 8
limpiar   *to clean*, 6; **limpiar la cocina**   *to clean the kitchen*, 6
limpio/a   *clean*, 8
la **línea**   *line*; **La línea está ocupada.**   *The line is busy.*, 7; línea ecuatorial   *equator*, 7
el **lío**   *mess*, 7
la **lista**   *the list*, 8
listo/a   *clever, smart* (with **ser**), 6; **estar listo/a**   *to be ready* (with **estar**), 7
la **literatura**   *literature*, 3
llamado/a   *called, named*, 9
llamar   *to call, name*; Me llamo...   *My name is...*, P; Mi amigo/a se llama...   *My friend's name is...*, P
llamar   *to call, to phone*; **llamar a los invitados**   *to call the guests*, 10; **Llamo más tarde.**   *I'll call later.*, 7
llamarse   *to be named*, 1; **¿Cómo te llamas?**   *What's your name?*, 1; **Me llamo...**   *My name is...*, 1; **Se llama...**   *Her/His name is...*, 1
la **llanta**   *tire*, P
el **llapingacho**   *potato cake with cheese*, 8
la **llegada**   *arrival*
llegué   *I arrived*, 3
llenar   *to fill*, 10
llenarse   *to be filled*, 10
llevar   *to wear*, 9; *to carry, to lead*; **llevar una vida sana**   *to lead a healthy life*, 11
¡Llévatelo!   *Take it away!*, 3
llora   *he/she cries*, 7
llover (ue)   *to rain*; 5; **Está lloviendo.**   *It's raining.*, 5; Está lloviendo a cántaros.   *It's raining cats and dogs.*, 5; **Llueve.**   *It's raining.*, 5
lo   *it, him, you*, 10; **Lo de siempre.**   *The usual.*, 9; lo mejor   *the best thing*, 12; lo que   *what, that which*, 6; **Lo siento. No puedo.**   *I'm sorry. I can't.*, 7; lo siguiente   *the following*, 11
el **lobo**   *wolf*, 4
local   *local*
el **locro**   *stew containing meat, beans, and vegetables*, 8
lógicamente   *logically*, 9
lógico/a   *logical*, 6
la **loma**   *small hill, slope*, 7
el **lomo**   *loin*, 8
los **demás**   *the others, the rest*, 12
los   *the* (pl.), 3
las **luces**   *lights*, 2
luchó   *he/she fought*
luego   *then, later*, 3; **Hasta luego.**   *See you later.*, 1
el **lugar**   *place*, 7; **ningún lugar**   *nowhere, not anywhere*, 12
el **lunes**   *Monday*, 4
la **luz**   *light*, 2

la madera *wood*

la madrastra *stepmother*, 6

la madre/mamá *mother/mom*, 6; **el Día de las Madres** *Mother's Day*, 10

la madrileña *resident of Madrid (female)*, 1

el madrileño *resident of Madrid, (male)*, 1

la madrina *godmother*, 6

los maduros *plantains*, 6

maduro/a *mature*, 6

la maestra *teacher (female)*, 3

el maestro *teacher (male)*, 3

magníficamente *magnificently*, 2

¡Magnífico! *Great!*, 11

el maíz *corn*, 8

majestuoso/a *majestic*, 9

mal *bad*, 1; **Hace mal tiempo.** *The weather is bad.*, 5; Lo pasé mal. *I had a bad time.*, 12; No está mal. *It's not bad.*, 2

la maleta *suitcase*, 12; **hacer la maleta** *to pack the suitcase*, 12

malo/a *bad*, 3; Es un perro malo. *It is a bad dog.*, 3

la mamá *mom*, 6

el mamey *mamey (fruit)*, 6

el mamífero *mammal*, 2

la mañana *morning*; **de la mañana** *in the morning (A.M.)*, 3; **por la mañana** *in the morning*, 5

mañana *tomorrow*, 3; **¡Hasta mañana!** *See you tomorrow!*, 1

mandar *to send, to order*, 10; **mandar las invitaciones** *to send invitations*, 10

el mandato *mandate; command, order*, 10

manejar *to manage*, 11

la manera *way*, 8

el mango *mango*, 8

el maní *peanut*; la crema de maní *peanut butter*, 8

la mano *hand*, 11

'mano,-a *friend* (short for hermano,-a), 4

mantener (ie) *to maintain*, 6

la mantequilla *butter*, 8

mantuvieron *they maintained*, 6

la manufactura *manufacturing*

la manzana *apple*, 8

el mapa *map*, 2

el maquillaje *makeup*, 7

maquillarse *to put on makeup*, 7

la máquina *machine*, 2; la máquina del tiempo *time machine*, 2

la maquinaria *machinery*

el mar Mediterráneo *Mediterranean Sea*, P

la maravilla *marvel*, 12

maravilloso/a *great, marvelous*, 3

el marcador *marker*, 2

el mariachi *mariachi*, 10

marino/a *marine*, 7

la marioneta *marionette*, 7

los mariscos *shellfish*, 8

marrón *brown*, 6

el martes *Tuesday*, 4

marzo (m.) *March*, 5

más *more*, 1; **Llamo más tarde.** *I'll call later.*, 7; **Más o menos.** *So-so.*, 1; **más ... que** *more ... than*, 9; **nada más** *that's all*, 11

la masa *dough*, 8

la máscara *mask*, 10

la mascota *pet*, 6

las matemáticas *mathematics*, 3

la materia *subject*, 3

la matrícula *enrollment*, 3

mayo (m.) *May*, 5

mayor *older*, 6; *greater*

la mayoría *majority; largest part*

me *to/for me*, 9; me acuesto *I go to bed*, 3; **¿Me ayudas a...?** *Can you help me to . . .?*, 10; **Me gusta...** *I like . . .*, 1; **Me gusta más...** *I like . . . better*, 1; **Me gustan...** *I like . . .*, 3; **Me gustaría...** *I would like . . .*, 7; **¿Me haces el favor de...?** *Can you do me the favor of . . .?*, 10; me le acerco *I approach him/her*, 7; **Me llamo...** *My name is . . .*, 1; **Me parece bien.** *It seems fine with me.*, 10; **¿Me pasas...?** *Can you pass me . . .?*, 10; me pongo: Me pongo a estudiar *I start studying.*, 3; me presento *I introduce myself*, 7; **¿Me puede decir...?** *Can you tell me . . .?*, 9; **¿Me puede traer...?** *Can you bring me . . .?*, 8; me quedo con *I stay with*, 6; **¿Me traes...?** *Can you (familiar) bring me . . .?*, 10

el mecanismo *mechanism*, 1

mediante *through*, 11

las medias *stockings*

medio/a *half*; **media hermana** *half sister*, 6; **medio hermano** *half brother*, 6; **y media** *half past (the hour)*, 3

mejor *best; better*, 5

mejorar *to improve*, 11

mencionar *to mention*, 12

menor *younger*, 6

menos *less*, 6; **Más o menos.** *So-so.*, 1; **menos cuarto** *quarter to (the hour)*, 3; **menos... que** *less ... than*, 9

el menú *menu*, 8

menudo/a *minute, small*; a menudo *often*, 5

la merienda *snack served around 5:00 P.M.*, 8

la mermelada *jam*, 8

el mes *month*, 5; **El ... de este mes...** *On the (date) of this month . . .*, 5

la mesa *table*, 2; **el juego de mesa** *board game*, 9; **poner la mesa** *to set the table*, 6

la mesera *waitress*, 8

el mesero *waiter*, 8

la meseta *plateau*, 1

el meteorólogo *weather forecaster*(male), 5

la meteoróloga *weather forecaster*(female), 5

la mezcla *mixture*, 8

mezclar *to mix*, 8

mi/mis *my*, 2, 6

mí *me* (emphatic); **A mí me gusta** + infinitive *I (emphatic) like to . . .*, 4

el miembro *member*, 10

el miércoles *Wednesday*, 4

mil *one thousand*, 8

el militar *soldier*, 10

la milla *mile*, 5; las millas por hora *miles per hour*, 5

el millón, los millones *million*, 9

el mimo *mime*, 7

los minerales *minerals*, 8

minero, -a (m./f.) *miner*, 8

mirar *to watch, to look*; ¡Mira! *Look!*, 1; **mirar la televisión** *to watch television*, 4; mirar hacia *to overlook; to face; to look toward*, 7

la misa *mass*, 9

las misiones *missions*, 9

mismo/a *same*; **Son del mismo precio.** *They're the same price.*, 9

el misterio *mystery*, 1

la mitad *half*, 7

mixto/a *mixed*, 8

la mochila *book bag, backpack*, 2

el modelo *model, example*, 1

el modo *way, mode*, 2

el momento *moment*, 7; **Lo siento, pero en este momento...** *I'm sorry, but right now . . .*, 10; **Un momentito.** *Just a second.*, 10; **un momento** *one moment*, 7

el monasterio *monastery*, 12

la montaña *mountain*; **escalar montañas** *to go mountain climbing*, 12

montañoso/a *mountainous*

montar *to ride*; **montar a caballo** *to ride a horse*, 11; **montar en bicicleta** *to ride a bike*, 4

la mora *blackberry*, 8

morado/a *purple*, 9

la moral *morale*, 11

moreno/a *dark-haired, dark-skinned*, 3

mostrar (ue) *to show, to exhibit*, 10

la moto *moped*, 7

el motoesquí *jet-ski*, 5

el motor *motor*, 1

moverse (ue) *to move*, 5

el movimiento *movement*, 6

la muchacha *girl*, 3

el muchacho *boy*, 3

mucho *a lot*, 1

mucho/a *a lot (of)*, 2; **¡Con mucho**

gusto! *Sure!*, 10; **Mucho gusto.** *Nice to meet you.*, 1

muchos/as *many, a lot of*, 2; **muchas veces** *often*, 5

muerto/a *dead*; **completamente muerto/a** *dead tired* (slang), 7

muestra *show* (command), 4

la **muestra** *display, sample*, 9

la **mujer** *woman*, 10

multicultural *multicultural*, 10

mundial *worldly, of the world*, 9

el **mundo** *world*, 2

la **muñeira** *traditional Galician dance*, 10

municipal *municipal, city* (adj.), 4

el **músculo** *muscle*, 11

el **museo** *museum*, 7; **el museo de antropología** *anthropology museum*, 7

la **música** *music*, 1; **escuchar música** *to listen to music*, 4; **la música clásica/pop/rock** *classical/pop/rock music*, 1; **la música de...** *music by . . .*, 1; la música folklórica *folkloric music*, 10

muy *very*, 1; **muy bien** *very well*, 1; **(muy) mal** *(very) bad*, 1

nacido/a en *born in*, 1

nacional *national*

nada *nothing*, 5; **nada más** *that's all*, 11; **para nada** *at all*, 8

nadar *to swim*, 4

nadie *nobody*, 5

la **naranja** *orange*, 8; **el jugo de naranja** *orange juice*, 8

la **nariz** *nose*, 11

la **natación** *swimming*, 1

nativo/a *native*, 7

la **natura** *nature*, 1

naturalmente *naturally*, 5

náutico/a *aquatic*; el club náutico *sailing club*, 5

natural *natural*, 7

la **navaja** *razor*

la **Navidad** *Christmas*, 10; ¡Feliz Navidad! *Merry Christmas!*, 10

la **neblina** *fog*, 7

necesario/a *necessary*, 7

necesitar *to need*, 2; **Necesita** *She/He needs*, 2; **Necesitas** *You need*, 2; **Necesito** *I need*, 2

negativo/a *negative*, 4

el **negocio** *business*, 11

negro/a *black*, 6

neo-gótico/a *neo-Gothic*

neoyorquino/a *New Yorker*, 11

nervioso/a *nervous*, 11

nevar (ie) *to snow*; **Está nevando.** *It's snowing.*, 5; **Nieva.** *It's snowing.*, 5

ni *nor*; ni... ni... *neither . . . nor . . .*, 6

el **nido** *nest*, 2

la **nieve** *snow*, 12

ningún/ninguna *none, not any*, 12; **ninguna parte** *nowhere, not anywhere*, 12; ningún lado *nowhere, not anywhere*, 12; **ningún lugar** *nowhere, not anywhere*, 12

el **níquel** *nickel*

no *no*, 1; **¿no?** *isn't it?/right?*, 3; **No es cierto.** *It isn't true.*, 6; **No me gusta.** *I don't like it.*, 1; **No me gusta el/la...** *I don't like . . .*, 1; No nos dejan pagar. *They don't let us pay.*, 7; **No puedo.** *I can't.*, 7; **No sé.** *I don't know.*, 2; **No te preocupes.** *Don't worry.*, 3

la **noche** *night*; **Buenas noches.** *Good night.*, 1; **de la noche** *in the evening* (P.M.), 3; **por la noche** *at night*, 5

la **Nochebuena** *Christmas Eve*, 10

la **Nochevieja** *New Year's Eve*, 10

nombra *name* (command), 8

nombrar *to name*, 4

el **nombre** *name*, P; el nombre completo *full name*, 6; nombres comunes *common names*, P

el **noreste** *northeast*, 10

normal *normal*, 5

normalmente *normally*, 3

el **noroeste** *northwest*

norteamericano/a *North American*, 11

nos *to/for us*, 9; **Nos gusta...** *We like . . .*, 5; **Nos gustan...** *We like . . .*, 7; **Nos gusta** + infinitive *We like + infinitive* 5; **¿Nos puede traer...?** *Can you bring us . . .?*, 8

nosotros/as *we*, 4

la **nota** *note*, 8

las **noticias** *news*, 5

notificar *to notify*, 1

la **novela** *novel*, 3

noventa *ninety*, 2

la **novia** *girlfriend, fiancée*, 10

noviembre (m.) *November*, 5

el **novio** *boyfriend, fiancé*, 10

nublado/a *cloudy*, 5; **Está nublado.** *It's cloudy.*, 5

nuestro/a(s) *our*, 6

nueve *nine*, 1

nuevo/a *new*, 3; el Año Nuevo *New Year's Day*, 10; **nuevos amigos** *new friends*, 2

el **número** *number*, 1; el número secreto *secret number*, 1

numeroso *numerous*, 6

nunca *never, not ever*, 5

la **nutrición** *nutrition*, 8

o *or*; **Más o menos.** *So-so.*, 1; o sea... *or else . . .*; *I mean . . .*, 7

la **obra** *work*, 7

la **observación** *observation*

la **ocasión** *occasion*, 11

el **oceanario** *oceanographic institute*, 2

el **océano** *ocean*, 5; el océano Atlántico *Atlantic Ocean*, P; el océano Índico *Indian Ocean*, P; el océano Pacífico *Pacific Ocean*, P

ochenta *eighty*, 2

ocho *eight*, 1

ochocientos/as *eight hundred*, 8

octubre (m.) *October*, 5

ocupado/a *busy*, 7; **La línea está ocupada.** *The line is busy.*, 7

oficial *official*, 7

ofrecer *to offer*, 9

el **oído** *inner ear*, 11

oír *to hear, to listen to*, 4; ¡Oye! *Listen!, Hey!*, 3

los **ojos** *eyes*, 6; ¡Ojo! *Pay attention! Watch out!*, 11; **Tiene (los) ojos verdes/azules.** *He/She has green/blue eyes.*, 6

la **ola** *wave*, 5

olímpico/a *Olympic*, 5

once *eleven*, 1

operar *to operate*, 5

la **opinión** *opinion*, 12

la **oración** *sentence*, 1

orbital *orbital*, 1

el **orden** *order*, 6

la **oreja** *(outer) ear*, 11

organizar *to organize*, 2; organizar mi cuarto *organize my room*, 2

el **orgullo** *pride*, 3

orgulloso/a *proud*

las **órdenes** *orders*; a sus órdenes *at your service*, 5

oriental *Eastern*

el **origen** *origin*

originario/a de *from, originating from, native to*

el **oso** *bear*, P

el **otoño** *fall*, 5

otro/a *other, another*, 8; **tal vez otro día** *perhaps another day*, 7

¡Oye! *Listen!*, 3

el **pabellón** *typical dish of Venezuela*, 8

el **padrastro** *stepfather*, 6

el **padre/papá** *father*, 6; **el Día del Padre** *Father's Day*, 10 los **padres** *parents*, 6

el **padrino** *godfather*, 6

Pagamos la cita. *We pay for the date.*, 7

la **página** *page*, P

el **país** *country*, 4

el **pájaro** *bird*

la **pala** *paddle*, 11

la **palabra** *word*, 1

el **palacio** *palace*

las **palmas** *palms*, 11

el **pan** *bread*; **el pan dulce** *sweet rolls*, 8; **el pan tostado** *toast*, 8

la **panadería** *bakery*, 9

el **panecillo** *plain or sweet roll*, 8

el **panorama** *panorama*, 1; panorama cultural *cultural panorama*

los **pantalones** *pants*, 9; los **pantalones cortos** *shorts*, 9

la **pantomima** *pantomime*, 10

la **papa** *potato*; **las papas fritas** *french fries*, 5

el **papá** *dad*, 6

la **papaya** *papaya*, 8

el **papel** *paper*, 2

la **papelería** *stationery store*, 1

las **papitas** *potato chips*, 8

para *for, to*, 9; **para** + infinitive *in order to*, 4; **para nada** *at all*, 8; **¿Para quién...?** *For whom . . .?*, 9

el **paracaídas** *parachute*; **saltar en paracaídas** *to go skydiving*, 12

el **parador** *inn*, 12; *roadside stand*, 6

el **paraguas** *umbrella*, 10

el **paraíso** *paradise*, 12

pardo/a *brown*, 9

parecer *to give the impression of, to seem*; **Me parece bien.** *It seems fine to me.*, 10; **¿Qué te parece si...?** *How do you feel about . . .?*, 10

la **pared** *wall*, 2

el **pariente** *relative*, 6

el **parking** *parking lot or parking garage* (Spain), 4

el **parque** *park*, 4; **descansar en el parque** *to rest in the park*, 4; **el parque de atracciones** *amusement park*, 7

el **párrafo** *paragraph*, 3

la **parrilla** *grill*, 9; la **parrillada** *barbecue*, 9

la **parte** *part*; **¿De parte de quién?** *Who's calling?*, 7; ninguna parte *nowhere, not anywhere*, 12

la **participación** *participation*, 7

participar *to participate*, 5

participó *he/she participated*

el **partido de...** *game of . . . (sport)*, 3

pasado/a *past, last* (with time), 10; **el año pasado** *last year*, 10; **el sábado pasado** *last Saturday*, 10; **la semana pasada** *last week*, 10; **el verano pasado** *last summer*, 10

el **pasaje** *passage; excerpt; fare*, 1

pasar *to pass, to spend time*; **¿Me pasas...?** *Can you pass me . . .?*, 10; **pasar el rato con amigos** *to spend time with friends*, 4; **pasar la aspiradora** *to vacuum*, 6; **pasarlo bien** *to have a good time*, 10; **¿Qué le pasa a...?** *What's wrong with . . .?*, 11

el **pasatiempo** *hobby*, 1

las **Pascuas** *Easter*, 10

paseante (m./f.) *passerby*, 10

pasear *to go for a stroll*, 4; pasear en bicicleta *to ride a bicycle*, 4

el **paseo** *stroll*, 4

la **pasión** *passion*, 6

el **paso** *step*, 1

el **pastel** *cake*, 8

la **pastelería** *pastry shop, sweet shop*, 9

patinar *to skate*; **patinar sobre ruedas** *to roller skate*, 11

el **patio** *patio*, 7

el **payaso** *clown*, 7

la **pecera** *fishbowl*, 2

los **peces** *fish*, 2

el **pedacito** *small piece*, 8

el **pedazo** *piece*, 8

el **pedido** *order* (in a restaurant), 8

pedir (i) *to order, to ask for*, 8

peinarse *to comb your hair*, 7

pelar *to peel*, 8

la **película** *movie, film*, 4; **ver una película** *to see a movie*, 4

pelirrojo/a *redheaded*, 6

el **pelo** *hair*, 6

la **peña** *South American musical event or club*, 7

los **pendientes** *earrings*, 9

pensar (ie) *to think*; **pensar** + infinitive *to plan, to intend*, 7

pequeño/a *small*, 3

la **pera** *pear*, 8

la **percusión** *drums*, 7

la **pérdida** *loss*, 1

Perdón. *Excuse me.*, 9; **Perdóname.** *Excuse me.*, 10

perezoso/a *lazy*, 6

Perfecto. *Perfect.*, 10

el **periódico** *newspaper*, 5

el **período** *period*, 11

el **permiso** *permission, permit*, P

pero *but*, 1

el **perro** *dog*; **caminar con el perro** *to walk the dog*, 4; **el perro caliente** *hot dog*, 8

la **persona** *person*, 3; **¿Cuántas personas hay en tu familia?** *How many people are there in your family?*, 6

el **personaje** *character*, 6

personal *personal*, 2; anuncios personales *personal ads*, 4; estilo personal *personal style*, 2

la **personalidad** *personality*, 1

pesado/a *heavy*, 2

las **pesas** *weights*, 11; **levantar pesas** *to lift weights*, 11

la **pesca** *fishing*

el **pescado** *fish*, 8

pescar *to fish*, 5

la **peseta** *unit of currency in Spain*, 9

¡Pésimo! *Terrible!*, 2

el **peso** *currency in Colombia, Argentina, and Mexico*, 9

el **petróleo** *petroleum*

el **pez** (pl. los **peces**) *fish*, 2; el pez dorado *goldfish*

el **piano** *piano*, 4

picado *chopped, crushed*, 8

picante *spicy*, 8

el **picnic** *picnic*, 8

el **pie** *foot*, 11

pienso *I think*, 4

la **pierna** *leg*, 11

la **pileta** *swimming pool*, 4

el **piloto** *pilot*, 5

el **pincel** *paintbrush*, 2

pintar *to paint*, 4

pintoresco/a *picturesque*, 11

la **pintura** *paint, painting*, 2

la **piña** *pineapple*, 8

la **piñata** *hanging ornament filled with fruits and candies*, 10

el **piragüismo** *canoeing*, 11

la **pirámide** *pyramid*, 12

los **Pirineos** *Pyrenees*, 1

la **piscina** *swimming pool*, 4

el **piso** *apartment*, 2

la **pista** *track*; **la pista de correr** *running track*, 11; la pista de esquí *ski slope*, 12

la **pizza** *pizza*, 1

la **pizzería** *pizzeria*, 1

la **placa** *license plate*, P

el **plan** *plan*, 7; **Ya tengo planes.** *I already have plans.*, 7

planchar *to iron*, 6

la **planta** *plant*, 9

el **plástico** *plastic*, 8

la **plata** *silver*

el **plátano** *banana*, 8

el **plato** *plate*, 8

el **plato del día** *daily special*

el **plato hondo** *bowl*, 8

los **platos** *dishes*, 6; lavar los platos *to wash the dishes*, 6

la **playa** *beach*, 5; **por la playa** *along the beach*, 5

la **plaza** *square*

Plaza de Armas *Military Square*, 11

el **plomo** *lead*

la **pluma** *ballpoint pen*, 2

la **población** *population*

poblado/a *populated*

poco, un *a little*; **un poco gordo/a** *a little overweight*, 6

poder (ue) *to be able, can*, 8; **¿Me puede decir...?** *Can you tell me . . .?*, 9; **¿Me puede traer...?** *Can you bring me . . .?*, 8; **No puedo.** *I can't.*, 7; **¿Puedo dejar un recado?** *May I leave a message?*, 7

la **poesía** *poetry*, 7

policíaco/a *police* (adj.), *detective* (adj.), 3

la **política** *politics*, 6

el **pollo** *chicken*, 8; el pollo asado *roasted chicken*, 6

el polo opuesto *opposite pole*, 6
el polvo *powder*, 8
 poner *to put, to place*, 2; **pon** *put, place*, 10; **poner la mesa** *to set the table*, 6; me pongo: Me pongo a estudiar *I start studying.*, 3; ponerse de acuerdo *to come to an agreement*, 12; ponerse los lentes *to put on one's glasses*, 7
 ponerse *to put on (clothing)*, 7
 por *at*, 3; *by*, 5; *for*, 12; *in, around*, 4; por ejemplo *for example*, 12; **por eso** *that's why*, 4; **por favor** *please*, 8; **por fin** *at last*, 3; **por la mañana** *in the morning*, 5; **por la noche** *at night, in the evening*, 5; **por la playa** *along the beach*, 5; **por la tarde** *in the afternoon*, 5; **Por lo general tomo...** *I generally eat/drink . . .*, 8; por teléfono *by telephone*, 7
el porcentaje *percentage*
 ¿Por qué? *Why?*, 3; **¿Por qué no...?** *Why don't . . .?*, 11
 porque *because*, 3
la portada *cover* (of a book or magazine), 2
 posible *possible*, 5
el póster *poster*, 2
 el postre *dessert*, 8
el porcentaje *percentage*, 7
 practicar *to practice*, 4; practicar deportes *to play sports*, 4
 practiquen *you* (pl.)*/they practice* (subjunctive mood)
 el precio *price*, 9; **Son del mismo precio.** *They're the same price.*, 9
 predominar *to predominate, to be most important*, 6
 preferido/a *favorite*, 3
 preferir (ie) *to prefer*, 7
 pregunta *ask* (command), 7
la pregunta *question*, 5
 pregúntale *ask him/her* (command), 8
 preguntar *to ask*, 11
 prehispánico/a *pre-Hispanic*, 7
 preliminar *preliminary*, P
el premio *prize, award*, 4; Premio Nóbel *Nobel Prize*, 3
 preocupado/a por algo *worried about something*, 11
 preocuparse *to worry*, **No te preocupes.** *Don't worry.*, 3
 preparado/a *prepared, cooked*, 8
 preparar *to prepare*, 4; prepararse *to prepare oneself*, 7; prepara *prepare* (command), 8
el preparativo *preparation*, 10
 preparatorio/a *preparatory*, 3
 presentable *presentable, well dressed*, 6
la presentación *introduction*, 1
 presentar *to present*, 11
 presentarse *to be introduced, to be presented*, 10; me presento *I introduce myself*, 7

el presente *the present*; el presente progresivo *the present progressive*, 10
el pretérito *the preterite (tense)*, 10
la prima *cousin* (female), 6
la primavera *spring*, 5
 primero/a *first*, 3
el primero *the first (of the month)*, 5
el primo *cousin* (male), 6
 principal *principal*, 1
la prisa *hurry*; **tener prisa** *to be in a hurry*, 7; **Tengo prisa.** *I'm in a hurry.*, 3
 prisionero, -a (m./f.) *prisoner*, 3
 probar (ue) *to try, to taste*, 6
 el problema *problem*, 6
la procesión *procession*, 10
 producir *to produce*, 8
el producto petrolero *petroleum product*
 el profesor *teacher* (male), 3
 la profesora *teacher* (female), 3
 profundamente *deeply*, 11
el programa *program*, 3; el programa de televisión *television program*, 3
el pronombre *pronoun*, 5
el pronóstico *forecast*, 5; el pronóstico del tiempo *weather report*, 5
 Pronto. *Hello.* (telephone greeting), 7; pronto *soon*, 8
 la propina *tip*, 8
 propio/a *own*, 9
 proporcionar *to supply*, 11
el propósito *purpose*, 10
el protagonista *protagonist, main character*, 2
 protectivo/a *protective*, 6
la proteína *protein*, 7
 provenir *to come from*, 9
 ptas. *abbreviation of* **pesetas**, *currency of Spain*, 2
 pueden *you* (pl.) *can*, 3
 puedo *I can*, 2; **¿Puedo dejar un recado?** *May I leave a message?*, 7
 la puerta *door*, 2
 puertorriqueño/a *Puerto Rican*, 11
 pues *well*, 2
el puesto *place, position*; el puesto *stand*, 10
 punto *point, dot*; **en punto** *on the dot*, 3
el pupitre *student desk*, 2
el puré *purée*, 8

 que *that, which, who*, 4; **Dice que...** *She/He says that . . .*, 6; lo que *what, that which*, 6
 ¿Qué? *What?*, 3; **¿Qué debo hacer?** *What should I do?*, 6; **¿Qué estás haciendo?** *What are you doing?*,

10; **¿Qué fecha es hoy?** *What's today's date?*, 5; **¿Qué haces despues de clases?** *What do you do after school?*, 4; **¿Qué hay?** *What's up?*, 1; **¿Qué hay en...?** *What's in . . .?*, 2; **¿Qué hay para tomar?** *What is there to drink?*, 8; **¿Qué hiciste?** *What did you do?*, 10; **¿Qué hizo?** *What did he/she/you do?*, 10; **¿Qué hora es?** *What time is it?*, 3; ¿Qué hubo? *What's up?*, 1; **¿Qué le pasa a...?** *What's wrong with . . .?*, 11; ¿Qué onda? *What's up?*, 1; ¿Qué pasa? *What's happening?*, 1; **¿Qué prefieres?** *What do you prefer?*, 8; **¿Qué tal?** *How's it going?*, 1; ¿Qué tal? *What's up?*, 1; **¿Qué tal si...?** *What if . . .?*, 11; **¿Qué te gusta?** *What do you like?*, 1; **¿Qué te gusta hacer?** *What do you like to do?*, 4; **¿Qué te parece si...?** *How do you feel about . . .?*, 10; **¿Qué tiempo hace?** *What's the weather like?*, 5; **¿Qué tienes?** *What's the matter?*, 11; **¿Qué tipo de...?** *What kind of . . .?*, 9
 ¡Qué barato/a! *How cheap!*, 9
 ¡Qué caro/a! *How expensive!*, 9
 ¡Qué ganga! *What a bargain!*, 9
 ¡Qué lástima! *What a shame!*, 7
 ¡Qué lío! *What a mess!*, 3
 ¡Qué padre! *How cool!*, 2
 ¡Qué pesado/a! *How annoying!*, 2
 quechua, quichua *Quechua* (adj. & noun), *indigenous Andean people*
 quedar *to be (situated)*, 9; **Te queda muy bien.** *It fits you very well.*, 9
 quedarse *to stay, to remain*, 12
 los quehaceres *chores*, 6; **los quehaceres domésticos** *household chores*, 6
la queja *complaint*, 11
 quemado *burned* (past participle), 10
 quemar *to set on fire*, 10
la quena *reed flute used in Andean music*
 querer (ie) *to want*, 2; **Quiere...** *He/She wants . . .*, 2; quiere decir *means*, 4; **Quieres...** *You want . . .*, 2; **¿Quieres...?** *Do you want to . . .?*, 7; **Quiero...** *I want . . .*, 2; **quisiera** *I would like*, 8
 querido/a *dear*, 1
 el queso *cheese*, 8
el quetzal *Guatemalan bird; Guatemalan currency*, P
 ¿quién? *who?*, 4; **¿De parte de quién?** *Who's calling?*, 7; **Para quién?** *For whom?*, 9; **¿quiénes?** *who?*, 5
la química *chemistry*, 3
 químico/a *chemical*
 quince *fifteen*, 1
la quinceañera *girl celebrating her fifteenth birthday*, 10

quinientos/as *five hundred*, 8
la quinoa *quinoa (plant with edible spinach-like leaves and edible seeds)*
quisiera *I would like*, 8
quitar *to remove, to take out*, 8
quiteño/a *from Quito*, 7

la ración *serving portion*, 8
el racismo *racism*, 1
la radio *radio*, 2
la raíz *root*, 10
rallado/a *grated*, 8
el rancho *ranch*, 8
los rápidos *rapids*
ratito *short while*, 11
el ratón *mouse*
la raya *stripe*; **de rayas** *striped*, 9
la reacción *reaction*, 10
real *royal*, 1
la realeza *royalty*, 10
la realidad *reality*, 7
realizar *to carry out, to perform*, 11
rebelde *rebellious*, 6
la rebeldía *rebelliousness*, 6
el recado *message*; **¿Puedo dejar un recado?** *May I leave a message?*, 7
la recepción *reception*, 1
la receta *recipe*, 8
recibió *he/she received*, 9
recibir *to receive*, 5; **recibir regalos** *to receive gifts*, 10
el recipiente de plástico *plastic container, receptacle*, 8
recoger la casa *to clean and straighten up the house*, 6
recorrer *to travel around*, 12
el recorrido *trip, journey*, 11; hacer un recorrido *to go sightseeing*, 12
recostar (ue) *to recline, to lean back*, 11
recto/a *straight*, 11
el recuerdo *souvenir, remembrance*, 9
el recurso *resource*, 7
reducir *to reduce*, 11
la referencia *reference*, 9
referirse (a) *to refer to*, 4
reflejar *to reflect*, 7
refrescante *refreshing*, 8
el refresco *soft drink*; **tomar un refresco** *to drink a soft drink*, 4
regalar *to give (as a gift)*, 9
el regalo *gift*, 9; **abrir regalos** *to open gifts*, 10; **recibir regalos** *to receive gifts*, 10
la región *region*, 8
regional *regional*
la regla *ruler*, 2
regresar *to return*, 4
Regular. *Okay.*, 1
la reina *queen*, P

el relajamiento *relaxation*, 12
el relato *story*, 7
la religión *religion*, 3
el reloj *clock, watch*, 2
la remembranza *memory, remembrance*, 10
el remo *paddle, oar*, 5
rendido/a *tired*, 7
el renombre: de renombre *famous, renowned*, 6
repasar *to review*, 12
el repaso *review*, 1
repetir (i) *to repeat*, 11
el reportaje *report*, 2
los reptiles *reptiles*, 2
la república *republic*, 1
la res *head of cattle*; **la carne de res** *beef*, 8
el resfriado *cold*; resfriado/a *congested*; **estar resfriado/a** *to have a cold*, 11
respirar *to breathe*, 11
responder *to answer*, 8
responsable *responsible*, 6
la respuesta *answer; response*, 2
el restaurante *restaurant*, 4
el resto *rest, remainder*, 11
el retrato *portrait*, 6
la reunión *meeting, reunion*, 6
reunirse *to gather, to join together*, 6
la revista *magazine*, 2
rico/a *rich, delicious*, 8
el río *river*, 12; **bajar el río en canoa** *to go canoeing*, 12; el río Amazonas *Amazon River*, 12
el ritmo *rhythm*, 6
el robo *rip-off*; **¡Es un robo!** *It's a rip-off!*, 9
la rodilla *knee*, 11
rojo/a *red*, 9
romántico/a *romantic*, 4
la ropa *clothing*, 2; **lavar la ropa** *to wash the clothes*, 4
rosado/a *pink*, P
rubio/a *blond*, 3
la rueda *wheel*; **patinar sobre ruedas** *to roller skate*, 11
la ruina *ruin*
la rutina *routine*, 7

el sábado *Saturday*, 4; **el sábado pasado** *last Saturday*, 10
saber *to know (information)*; **No sé.** *I don't know.*, 2; **Sé.** *I know.*, 2; ¿Sabías? *Did you (fam.) know?*, P
el sabor *flavor, taste*, 8
sacar buenas/malas notas *to get good/bad grades*, 6
sacar *to take out*; **sacar la basura** *to take out the trash*, 4

la sala *living room*, 6
la sala de clase *classroom*, 2
salado/a *salty*, 8
salgo *I go out*, 5
salir *to go out, to leave*, 6
la salsa *salsa music*, 6
saltar *to jump*; **saltar en paracaídas** *to go skydiving*, 12
la salud *health*, 11
el saludo *greeting*, 1
salvar *to save*, 2
el salvavidas *life jacket*, P
el sancocho *soup made of green plantains, corn, and carne colorada*, 8
las sandalias *sandals*, 9
el sándwich *sandwich*, 5
sano/a *healthy*, 11; **llevar una vida sana** *to lead a healthy life*, 11
el sasafrás *sassafras*, 9
el saxofón *saxophone*, 4
sazonar *to season, to add seasoning*, 9
Se llama... *Her/His name is . . .*, 1
Se ve joven. *She/He looks young.*, 6
Sé. *I know.*; **No sé.** *I don't know.*, 2
sé (command) *be*; Sé cortés. *Be polite.*, 10
la sección *section, department*, 9
el secreto *secret*, 1
la sed *thirst*; **tener (mucha) sed** *to be (really) thirsty*, 8
la seda *silk*; **de seda** *(made of) silk*, 9
el segmento *segment*, 5
seguir (i) *to follow*, 8; *to continue*, 12
según *according to*, 10
segundo/a *second*
seguro/a *sure, certain*, 5
seis *six*, 1
seiscientos/as *six hundred*, 8
la selva *jungle*, 12
el semáforo *traffic signal*, 5
la semana *week*, 4; **el fin de semana** *weekend*, 4; **la semana pasada** *last week*, 10
el semestre *semester*, 3
las semillas *seeds*, 8
las señales *distinguishing marks*, 1
sencillo/a *simple*, 11
señor *sir, Mr.*, 1
señora *ma'am, Mrs.*, 1
señorita *miss*, 1
la sensación *sensation*, 8
el sentido *sense, faculty of sensation*, 5
sentir (ie) *to regret*; **Lo siento.** *I'm sorry.*, 7; **Lo siento. No puedo.** *I'm sorry but I can't.*, 7; **Lo siento, pero en este momento...** *I'm sorry, but right now . . .*, 10
sentirse (ie) *to feel*, 11; **¿Cómo te sientes?** *How are you feeling?*, 11
septiembre (m.) *September*, 5
sepultado/a en vida *buried alive*, 6
ser *to be*, 1; **¿Cómo es...?** *What's he/she/it like . . .?*, 3; **¿Cómo son...?** *What are . . . like?*, 3; **¿De dónde**

eres? *Where are you from?*, 1; **eres** *you are*, 3; **es** *he/she/it is*, 3; **Es aparte.** *It's separate.* 8; **Es de...** *He/She/It is from . . .*, 1; **Es la una.** *It's one o'clock.*, 3; **¡Es un robo!** *It's a rip-off!*, 9; **No es cierto.** *It isn't true.*, 6; **son** *they are, you are* (pl.), 3; **Son las...** *It's . . . o'clock.*, 3; **soy** *I am*, 1; **Soy de...** *I'm from . . .*, 1

serio/a *serious*, 5

el servicio *service*, 1

la servilleta *napkin*, 8

servir *to serve*, 8

sesenta *sixty*, 2

la sesión *session*, 4

setecientos/as *seven hundred*, 8

setenta *seventy*, 2

la sevillana *folk dance of Seville*, 10

sevillano/a *from Seville, Spain*, 10

el sexismo *sexism*, 1

si *if*; **¿Qué tal si...?** *What if . . .?*, 11

sí *yes*, 1; **¡Claro que sí!** *Of course!*, 7

la sicología *psychology*, 1

siempre *always*, 5; **casi siempre** *almost always*, 6; **¡Lo de siempre!** *The usual!*, 9

siento *I regret*; **Lo siento. No puedo.** *I'm sorry. I can't.*, 7

la sierra *mountain range*, 7

la siesta *nap, afternoon rest*, 8

siete *seven*, 1

siga las instrucciones *follow the instructions*, 8

el siglo *century*, 6

significar *to mean*, 10

siguiente *following*, 3

la silla *chair*, 2

simpático/a *nice*, 3

sinfónico/a *symphonic*, 7

sino *but rather*, 11

el sintetizador *synthesizer*, 4

síquico/a *mental*, 11

sirve *he/she/it serves*, 11

sirvió *he/she/it served*

el sistema *system*, 9

la situación *situation*, 1

sobre *about, on*, 4

social *social*, 1

socio, -a (m./f.) *member*, 1

la sociología *sociology*, 1

sol *sun*; **los lentes de sol** *sunglasses*, 12; **tomar el sol** *to sunbathe*, 12; **Hace sol.** *It's sunny.*, 5

el soldado, la mujer soldado *soldier*, 11

sólo *only*; **sólo cuando** *only when*, 5

solo/a *alone*, 9

soltar (ue) *to let go, to let out*, 11

el sombrero *hat*

son *they are, you are* (pl.) 3; **¿Cómo son...?** *What are . . . like?*, 3; **Son del mismo precio.** *They're the same price.*, 9; **Son las...** *It's . . . o'clock.*, 3

el sonido *sound*, 1

la sopa *soup*, 8

el soporte *support*, 11

el sorbete *sherbet*, 8

la sorbetera *ice cream/sherbet maker*, 8

la sorpresa *surprise*; **la fiesta de sorpresa** *surprise party*, 7

soy *I am*, 1; **Soy de...** *I'm from . . .*, 1

su/sus *his, her, its, their, your* (formal), 2, 6

suave *soft*, 11

subir *to go up, to move up*, 11

sucio/a *dirty*, 8

el sucre *domestic currency in Ecuador*, 9

Sudamérica *South America*

el suelo *floor, ground*, 11

suelta el aire *let your breath out* (command), 11

el sueño *dream*; **tener sueño** *to be sleepy*, 7

la suerte *skillful maneuver*; suertes a caballo *skillful maneuver riding a horse*, 11

el suéter *sweater*, 9

suficiente *sufficient, enough*, 10

sufrir *to suffer*, 11

la sugerencia *suggestion*, 11

sugerir (ie) *to suggest*, 12

sugiérele *suggest to him/her*, 9

sujetar *to fasten, to hold*, 11

el supermercado *supermarket*, 4

el surtido *assortment*, 8

la tajada *slice of fried plantain*, 8

tal: **¿Qué tal?** *How's it going?*, 1

tales como *such as*

tal vez *maybe, perhaps*; **tal vez otro día** *perhaps another day*, 7

el taller *workshop*, 7

la tamalada *party at which tamales are made or served*, 9

el tamaño *size*, 5

también *too, also*; También se puede decir. . . *You can also say. . .*; **Yo también.** *Me too.*, 1

tampoco *neither, nor, not either*

tan... como *as . . . as*, 9

la taquilla *ticket office*, 4

la tarde *afternoon*, 3; **Buenas tardes.** *Good afternoon.*, 1; **de la tarde** *in the afternoon (P.M.)*, 3; **por la tarde** *in the afternoon*, 5

tarde *late*, 3; **Llamo más tarde.** *I'll call later.*, 7

la tarea *homework*, 1; *task, chore*, 10

la tarjeta de crédito *credit card*, 9

la tarjeta *greeting card*, 9; **la tarjeta**

postal *postcard*, 5

la taza *cup*, 8

el tazón *bowl*, 8

¿Te acuerdas? *Do you remember?*, 5

te *to/for you*, 9; **No te preocupes.** *Don't worry.*, 3; **¿Te gusta...?** *Do you like . . .?*, 1; **Te gustan...** *You like . . .*, 3; **Te felicito.** *Congratulations.*, 9 **¿Te gustaría...?** *Would you like . . .?*, 7; **Te invito.** *It's my treat.*, 7; **Te queda muy bien.** *It fits you very well.*, 9; **¿Te sientes mal?** *Do you feel bad?*, 11; Te toca a ti. *It's your turn.*, 11

el té *tea*; **el té frío** *iced tea*, 8

el teatro *theater*, 7

el techo *ceiling, roof*, 6

la tecnología *technology*, 1

tecnológico/a *technological*, 3

el tejido *cloth*

la tele *TV*, 5

telefónico/a *by phone*, 7

el teléfono *telephone*, 7; **hablar por teléfono** *to talk on the phone*, 7; los números de teléfono *telephone numbers*, 10

la telenovela *soap opera*, 3

la televisión *television*, 4; **mirar la televisión** *to watch television*, 4; el programa de televisión *television program*, 3

el televisor *television set*, 2

templado/a *temperate, mild*

el tenedor *fork*, 8

tener (ie) *to have*, 2; **Bueno, tengo clase.** *Well, I have class.*, 1; **¿Cuántos años tiene?** *How old is (she/he)?*, 1; **¿Cuántos años tienes?** *How old are you?*, 1; **¿Qué tienes?** *What's the matter?*, 11; **tener fiebre** *to have a fever*, 11; **tener ganas de** + infinitive *to feel like (doing something)*, 7; **tener gripe** *to have the flu*, 11; **tener (mucha) hambre** *to be (really) hungry*, 8; **tener (mucha) sed** *to be (really) thirsty*, 8; **tener prisa** *to be in a hurry*, 7; **tener que** + infinitive *to have to (do something)*, 7; **tener sueño** *to be sleepy*, 7; **tener tos** *to have a cough*, 11; tener lugar *to take place*, 5; **Tengo ... años.** *I'm . . . years old.*, 1; **Tengo prisa.** *I'm in a hurry.*, 3; **Tengo que irme.** *I have to go.*, 1; **Tiene ... años.** *She/He is . . . years old.*, 1; **Tiene canas.** *He/She has gray hair.*, 6; **Ya tengo planes.** *I already have plans.*, 7

el tenis *tennis*, 1; **la cancha de tenis** *tennis court*, 11; **las zapatillas de tenis** *tennis shoes* (Spain), 2

la tensión *tension*, 11

tercer (o/a) *third*

terminar *to end, to finish*, 5

el territorio *territory*

el terror *terror*, 2

los tesoros *treasures*, 9

el textil *textile*

la tía *aunt*, 6

tibio/a *lukewarm*, 11

el tiempo *weather; time; verb tense;*
Hace buen tiempo. *The weather is nice.*, 5; **Hace mal tiempo.** *The weather is bad.*, 5; Hace un tiempo precioso. *It's a beautiful day.*, 5; pronóstico del tiempo *weather report*, 5; **¿Qué tiempo hace?** *What's the weather like?*, 5; **el tiempo libre** *free time*, 4

la tienda *store*, 4; **la tienda de camping** *camping tent*, 12; **la tienda de comestibles** *grocery store*, 9

tiene *he/she/it has*, 2; **Tiene … años.** *He/She/It is … years old.*, 1; **Tiene canas.** *He/She has gray hair.*, 6

tienes *you have*, 2; **¿Cuántos años tienes?** *How old are you?*, 1; **¿Qué tienes?** *What's the matter?*, 11

la Tierra *Earth*, 2

las tierras pantanosas *swamplands, wetlands*

tímido/a *shy*, 6

el tío *uncle*, 6

típicamente *typically*, 5

típico/a *typical*, 3

el tipo *type, kind*, 1

las tiras cómicas *comics*, 5

la toalla *towel*, 12

el tocador de discos compactos *compact disc player*, 2

tocar *to touch, to play;* **tocar** (un instrumento) *to play (an instrument)*, 4

el tocino *bacon*, 8

todavía *still, yet*, 5; todavía no *not yet*, 7

todo *everything*, 8; todos/as *everyone*, 7

todo/a *all, every;* todo el tiempo *all the time*, 5; **todos los días** *every day*, 5

tomar apuntes *to take notes*, 11

tomar *to drink, to take*, 4; **tomar el autobús** *to take the bus*, 5; tomarle el pelo *to pull someone's leg*, 11; **tomar el sol** *to sunbathe*, 12; tomar fotos *to take pictures*, 12; **tomar un refresco** *to drink a soft drink*, 4

el tomate *tomato*, 8

el tomo *volume (in a series of books)*, 2

el toro *bull*, 10

la toronja *grapefruit*, 8

la torre *tower*, 9

la torta *sandwich*, 8

la tortilla *tortilla, omelet*, 8; tortilla española *omelet with potatoes, onions, and olive oil*, 8

la tortuga *turtle*

la tos *cough;* **tener tos** *to have a cough*, 11

tostado/a *toasted;* **el pan tostado** *toast*, 8

los tostones *fried plantains*, 6

trabajador,-a *hard-working*, 6

trabajar *to work*, 4; **trabajar en el jardín** *to work in the garden*, 6

el trabajo *work, job*, 4

el trabalenguas *tongue twister*, 2

tradicional *traditional*, 6

las tradiciones *traditions*, 6

traer *to bring*, 8; **¿Me puede traer...?** *Can you bring me …?*, 8; **¿Me traes...?** *Can you (informal) bring me …?*, 10

traído/a *brought*

el traje *suit*, 9; **el traje de baño** *bathing suit*, 9

tranquilo/a *tranquil; calm*, 11

transportado/a *transported, carried away*, 2

el transporte *transportation*, 1

tras *after*, 7

tratar de + infinitive *to try to*, 11

tratarse de *to be a question of*, 11

travieso/a *mischievous*, 6

trece *thirteen*, 1

treinta *thirty*, 1

tremendo/a *tremendous*, 5

tres *three*, 1

trescientos/as *three hundred*, 8

el trigo *wheat*

triste *sad*, 11

la trivia *trivia*, 1

la trompeta *trumpet*, 4

tropical *tropical*, 8

el trozo *piece, bit, fragment*, 8

tú *you*, 1

tu/tus *your (informal)*, 2, 6; Tu ropa hace juego. *Your clothes go well together.*, 9

la tumba *tomb, grave*, 10

el turismo *tourism;* **hacer turismo** *to go sightseeing*, 12

el turista *tourist*, 7

tuve *I had*, 2

la ubicación *location*

último/a *last;* Estás a la última. *You're stylish.*, 9

un *a, an*, 2; **Un momentito.** *Just a second.* 10; **un momento** *one moment*, 7; **un poco gordo/a** *a little over weight*, 6; un poco más *a little more*

una *a, an*, 2

los unicornios *unicorns*, 4

la unidad monetaria *monetary unit*

unido/a *close-knit*, 6

el uniforme *school uniform*, 2

uno *one*, 1

unos/as *some, a few*, 2

usa *use (command)*, 7

usar *to use*, 5; no uses *don't use (command)*, 10

usted *you*, 4

ustedes *you (pl.)*, 4,; **a ustedes** *to you (pl.)*, 5

útil (m./f.) *useful*, P

la utilidad *utility, use*, 2

la utilización *use, utilization*, 1

utilizar *to use*, 6

las uvas *grapes*, 8

vacacionar *to vacation*, 11

las vacaciones *vacation*, 5

valiente *valient*, 1

valioso/a *valuable, worthwhile*, 11

vamos a... *let's …;* Vamos a comprenderlo. *Let's understand (it).*, 1; Vamos a leer. *Let's read.*, 1; **¡Vamos!** *Let's go!*, 3; **vamos** *we go*, 3

variar *to vary*, 3

la variedad *variety*, 8

varios/varias *various, several*, 3

el vaso *glass;* **un vaso de leche** *a glass of milk*, 8

ve *go*, 10; **vete** *go away*, 10

veces: a veces *sometimes*, 5; **muchas veces** *often*, 5

el vecino *neighbor*, 12

vegetal *vegetable (adj.)*, 8

los vegetales *vegetables*, 8

vegetariano/a *vegetarian*, 8

el vehículo *vehicle*, 1

veinte *twenty*, 1

vejigante (m./f.) *reveler*, 10

la vela *sail;* **ir de vela** *to go sailing*, 12

el velero *sailboat*, 5

la velocidad *velocity, speed*, 5

venir *to come*, 7; **ven** *come*, 10; ven conmigo *come with me, come along*

la ventaja *advantage*, 8

la ventana *window*, 2

ver *to watch, to see*, 4; **ver una película** *to see a movie*, 4; ya verán *they'll see, you'll see (pl.)*, 12

el verano *summer*, 5; **el verano pasado** *last summer*, 10

verazmente *truly*, 12

el verbo *verb*, 8

¿verdad? *don't you?, right?*, 3

verdadero/a *true, real, genuine*, 1

verde *green*, 6

las verduras *greens, vegetables*, 8

la vereda *trail*, 12

verificar *to verify, to confirm*, 11

el vertebrado *vertebrate*, 2
el vestido *dress*, 9
la vez *time, turn, occasion, occurrence;*
a veces *sometimes*, 5; de vez en
cuando *once in a while*, 5;
muchas veces *often*, 5; otra vez
again, 8; **tal vez otro día** *perhaps
another day*, 7; una vez *once*, 5
¡vete! *go away!*, 10
viajar *to travel*, 12
el viaje *trip;* **hacer un viaje** *to take a
trip*, 6
la vida *life*, 11; **llevar una vida sana**
to lead a healthy life, 11; Lo pasé
pura vida. *I had a great time.*, 12;
la vida nocturna *night life*, 9
el video *video*, 1
la videocasetera *VCR*, 2
videojuego *video game*, 3
viejo/a *old*, 6
el viejo amigo *old friend, long-time
friend*, 5
el viento *wind* **Hace (mucho)
viento.** *It's (very) windy.*, 5
el viernes *Friday*, 4
vigilar *to watch over*, 6
la villa *village*
el vinagre *vinegar*, 8
el vínculo *bond, tie, link, connection*, 9

el violín *violin*, 4
visitante (m./f.) *visitor*, 7
visitar *to visit*, 6
la vista *view*, 12
la vitamina *vitamin*, 8
vivir *to live*, 6
vivo/a *alive*, 6
el vocabulario *vocabulary, glossary*, 1
volcánico/a *volcanic*
el voleibol *volleyball*, 1
volver (ue) *to return*, 8
vosotros/as *you* (pl.), 4
vuelvo *I return, I go back*, 5
vuestro/a (s) *your*, 6

y *and*, 1; **y media** *half past (the
hour)*, 3; **¿Y tú?** *And you?*, 1
ya *already*, 2; **Ya tengo planes.**
I already have plans., 7; ya verán
you'll/they'll see, 12; Ya voy. *I'm
on my way.*, 7; ¡Ya, ya! *Enough!*, 7
el yahuarlocro *Andean dish*, 8

el yate *yacht*, P
la yema *yolk*, 7
el yerno *son-in-law*, 7
yo *I*, 1; **Yo también.** *Me too.*, 1
yoga *yoga;* **hacer yoga** *to do yoga*,
11
el yugo *yoke*, 7

Z

la **zanahoria** *carrot*, 8
la **zapatería** *shoe store*, 9
las **zapatillas de tenis** *tennis shoes*
(Spain), 2
los **zapatos** *shoes*, 9
la zarzamora *blackberry*, 8
la zarzuela *light opera*, 9
la zona *zone*
la zoología *zoology*, 1
el zoológico *zoo*, 7
el zumo *juice*, 8

This vocabulary includes all of the words presented in the **Vocabulario** sections of the chapters. These words are considered active—you are expected to know them and be able to use them. Expressions are listed under the English word you would be most likely to look up.

Spanish nouns are listed with the definite article and plural forms, when applicable. If a Spanish verb is stem-changing, the change is indicated in parentheses after the verb: **dormir (ue)**. The number after each entry refers to the chapter in which the word or phrase is introduced.

To be sure you are using Spanish words and phrases in their correct context, refer to the chapters listed. You may also want to look up Spanish phrases in the Summary of Functions, pp. R1–R4.

a/an *un, una,* 2
a few *unos, unas,* 2
a little *un poco,* 6
a lot *mucho,* 1
a lot of; a lot *mucho/a, muchos/as,* 2
ache, to *doler (ue),* 11
aerobics class *una clase de ejercicios aeróbicos,* 5
affectionate *cariñoso/a ,* 6
after *después,* 3; *después de,* 4
afternoon *la tarde,* 3; **in the afternoon** *de la tarde,* 3; *por la tarde,* 5
afterward *después,* 3
agreed *de acuerdo,* 10
all *todo/a, todos/as,* 5
all right *está bien,* 7
almost *casi,* 6; **almost always** *casi siempre,* 6
along *por,* 5; **along the beach** *por la playa,* 5
already *ya,* 2
also *también,* 2
always *siempre,* 5
American *americano/a,* 1; *norteamericano/a,* 1; **American football** *el fútbol norteamericano,* 1
amusement park *el parque de atracciones,* 7
amusing *divertido/a,* 3
and *y,* 1; **And you?** *¿Y tú?,* 1
angry *enojado/a,* 11
anniversary *el aniversario,* 7; **anniversary party** *la fiesta de aniversario,* 7

another *otro/a,* 8
anthropology *la antropología,* 7
apple *la manzana,* 8
appointment *la cita,* 7
April *abril* (m.), 5
aquarium *el acuario,* 7
arm *el brazo,* 11
art *el arte, las artes* (pl.), 3;
as ... as ... *tan... como...,* 9
ask for, to *pedir (i),* 8
at *a, por,* 3; **at all** *para nada,* 8; **at last** *por fin,* 3; **at night** *por la noche, en la noche,* 5; **At what time ...?** *¿A qué hora...?,* 3
attend, to *asistir a,* 5
attraction *la atracción,* 7
August *agosto* (m.), 5
aunt *la tía,* 6
autumn *el otoño,* 5

back *la espalda,* 11
backpack *la mochila,* 2
bacon *el tocino,* 8
bad *mal,* 1; *malo/a,* 3; **to feel bad** *(estar) mal,* 1; *sentirse mal,* 11
bakery *la panadería,* 9
balloons *los globos,* 10
ballpoint pen *el bolígrafo,* 2
banana *el plátano,* 8
bargain *la ganga,* 9; **What a bargain!** *¡Qué ganga!,* 9
baseball *el béisbol,* 1
basketball *el baloncesto, el basquetbol,* 1
bathing suit *el traje de baño,* 9
be, to *ser,* 1; *estar,* 4; **to be**

able *poder (ue),* 8; **to be hungry** *tener hambre,* 8; **to be in a hurry** *tener prisa,* 3; **to be ready** *estar listo/a,* 7; **to be situated** *quedar,* 9; **to be sleepy** *tener sueño,* 7; **to be thirsty** *tener sed,* 8; **to be ... years old** *tener... años,* 1
beach *la playa,* 5
beans *los frijoles,* 8
because *porque,* 3
bed *la cama,* 2
beef *la carne de res,* 8
before *antes de,* 4
begin, to *empezar (ie),* 7
believe, to *creer,* 10
belt *el cinturón,* 9
beneath *debajo de,* 4
besides *además,* 9
beverage *la bebida,* 8
bicycle *la bicicleta,* 4
big *grande,* 3
bill *la cuenta,* 8
birthday *el cumpleaños,* 7; **birthday party** *una fiesta de cumpleaños,* 7
black *negro/a,* 6
block, city *la cuadra,* 9
blond *rubio/a,* 3
blouse *la blusa,* 9
blow up balloons, to *inflar los globos,* 10
blue *azul,* 6
bluejeans *los bluejeans,* 9
board game *el juego de mesa,* 9
body *el cuerpo,* 11
book *el libro,* 2
book bag *la mochila,* 2
bookstore *la librería,* 2
boots *las botas,* 9
boring *aburrido/a,* 3
bowl *el plato hondo, el tazón,* 8

boy   *el chico,* 5
bread   *el pan,* 8
break   *el descanso,* 3
breakfast   *el desayuno,* 8
bring, to   *traer,* 8
brother   *el hermano,* 6; **brothers and sisters**   *los hermanos,* 6
brown   *de color café,* 6; *pardo/a,* 9
brunette   *moreno/a,* 3
brush one's teeth, to   *lavarse los dientes,* 7
bus   *el autobús,* 5
busy   *ocupado/a,* 7; **the line is busy**   *la línea está ocupada,* 7
but   *pero,* 1
buy, to   *comprar,* 2
by   *por,* 5
'bye   *chao,* 1

C

cafeteria   *la cafetería,* 1
cake   *el pastel,* 8
calculator   *la calculadora,* 2
call, to   *llamar,* 7; **to call the guests**   *llamar a los invitados,* 10
camera   *la cámara,* 12
camp, to   *acampar,* 5
Can you bring me …?   *¿Me puede* (formal) *traer...?,* 8; *¿Me traes* (familiar)*...?,* 7; **Can you do me the favor of …?**   *¿Me haces el favor de...?,* 10; **Can you give me …?**   *¿Me das...?,* 10; **Can you help me …?**   *¿Me ayudas a...?,* 10; **Can you pass me …?**   *¿Me pasas...?,* 10; **Can you tell me …?**   *¿Me puede decir...?,* 9
candy   *los dulces,* 9; **candy store**   *la dulcería,* 9
canoe   *la canoa,* 12; **to go canoeing**   *bajar el río en canoa,* 12
can't, I   *No puedo,* 7
car   *el carro,* 4
card   *la tarjeta,* 9
carrot   *la zanahoria,* 8
cat   *el gato, la gata* 6; **to take care of the cat**   *cuidar al gato,* 6
cereal   *el cereal,* 8
chair   *la silla,* 2
cheap   *barato/a,* 9
cheese   *el queso,* 8
chicken   *el pollo,* 8
children   *los hijos,* 6
China   *China* (f.), 12
Chinese food   *la comida china,* 1
chocolate   *el chocolate,* 1
chores   *los quehaceres domésticos,* 6
Christmas   *la Navidad,* 10; **Christmas Eve**   *la Nochebuena,* 10
circus   *el circo,* 7

city   *la ciudad,* 7
city block   *la cuadra,* 9
class   *la clase,* 1
classical music   *la música clásica,* 1
classmate   *el compañero* (male)*, la compañera* (female) *de clase,* 3
clean   *limpio/a,* 8
clean, to   *limpiar,* 6; **to clean the kitchen**   *limpiar la cocina,* 6
clever   *listo/a,* 6
climb, to   *escalar,* 12
clock   *el reloj,* 2
close-knit   *unido/a,* 6
closet   *el armario,* 2
clothes/clothing   *la ropa,* 2
cloudy   *nublado,* 5; **It's cloudy.**   *Está nublado.,* 5
coffee   *el café,* 8; **coffee with milk**   *el café con leche,* 8
cold   *frío,* 8; **It's cold.**   *Hace frío.,* 5; **to have a cold**   *estar resfriado/a,* 11
color   *el color,* 6
comb your hair, to   *peinarse,* 7
come, to   *venir (ie),* 7; **Come!**   *¡Ven!,* 10
comfortable   *cómodo/a,* 9
comical   *cómico/a,* 3
comics   *las tiras cómicas,* 5
compact disc   *el disco compacto,* 9
computer science   *la computación,* 3
concert   *el concierto,* 3
congested   *resfriado/a,* 11
cookie   *la galleta,* 8
corn   *el maíz,* 8
cost, to   *costar(ue),* 9
cotton   *el algodón,* 9; **(made of) cotton**   *de algodón,* 9
cough   *la tos,* 11
country   *el campo,* 7
court (playing)   *la cancha,* 11
cousin   *el primo* (male)*, la prima* (female)*,* 6
custard   *el flan,* 8
cut, to   *cortar,* 6; **to cut the grass**   *cortar el césped,* 6

D

dad   *el papá,* 6
dance   *el baile,* 3
dance, to   *bailar,* 4
dark-haired, dark-skinned   *moreno/a,* 3
date   *la fecha,* 5; *la cita,* 7
daughter   *la hija,* 6
day   *el día,* 4; **day before yesterday**   *anteayer,* 10; **every day**   *todos los días,* 5; **free day**   *día libre,* 3
December   *diciembre* (m.), 5
decorate, to   *decorar,* 10

decorations   *las decoraciones,* 10
delicious   *delicioso/a,* 8; *rico/a,* 8
delighted   *encantado/a,* 1
department store   *el almacén,* 9
desk   *el escritorio,* 2
dessert   *el postre,* 8
dictionary   *el diccionario,* 2
diet   *la dieta,* 8
difficult   *difícil,* 3
dinner   *la cena,* 4
dirty   *sucio/a,* 8
disagreeable   *antipático/a,* 3
do, to   *hacer,* 2; **Do!**   *¡Haz!,* 10; **Don't worry!**   *¡No te preocupes!,* 3; **to do yoga**   *hacer yoga,* 11
dog   *el perro,* 4; **to walk the dog**   *caminar con el perro,* 4
dollar   *el dólar,* 2
door   *la puerta,* 2
downtown   *el centro,* 4
draw, to   *dibujar,* 4
dress   *el vestido,* 9
drink, to   *tomar,* 4; *beber,* 5
during   *durante,* 5

E

ear (inner)   *el oído,* 11; **(outer) ear**   *la oreja,* 11
earring   *el arete,* 9
Easter   *las Pascuas,* 10
easy   *fácil,* 3
eat, to   *comer,* 5; **to eat breakfast**   *desayunar,* 5; **to eat dinner**   *cenar,* 6; **to eat lunch**   *almorzar (ue),* 8
education   *la educación,* 3; **physical education**   *la educación física,* 3
eggs   *los huevos,* 8
Egypt   *Egipto* (m.), 12
eight   *ocho,* 1
eighteen   *dieciocho,* 1
eight hundred   *ochocientos/as,* 8
eighty   *ochenta,* 2
eleven   *once,* 1
end   *el fin,* 4
England   *Inglaterra* (f.), 12
English class   *la clase de inglés,* 1
enough   *bastante,* 6
erase, to   *borrar,* 2
eraser   *la goma de borrar,* 2
especially   *especialmente,* 5
evening   *la noche,* 5; **in the evening** (P.M.)   *de la noche,* 3; *por la noche,* 5
event   *el evento,* 7
every   *todo/a, todos/as;* **every day**   *todos los días,* 5
exam   *el examen* (pl. *los exámenes*), 3
excellent   *excelente,* 1
Excuse me.   *Perdón.,* 9; *Perdóname.,* 10

exercise *el ejercicio*, 5; **to exercise** *hacer ejercicio*, 5
expensive *caro/a*, 9
explore, to *explorar*, 12
eyes *los ojos*, 6

F

fall *el otoño*, 5
family *la familia*, 6
family member *familiar*, 9
fantastic *fantástico/a*, 3
far *lejos*, 4; **far from** *lejos de*, 4
father *el padre*, 6; **Father's Day** *el Día del Padre*, 10
favorite *favorito/a*, 3
February *febrero* (m.), 5
feel, to *sentirse (ie)*, 11; **to feel like (doing something)** *tener ganas de* + infinitive, 7
fever *la fiebre*, 11; **to have a fever** *tener fiebre*, 11
few, a *unos/as*, 2
field, playing *la cancha*, 11
fifteen *quince*, 1
fifty *cincuenta*, 2
find, to *encontrar (ue)*, 2
finger *el dedo*, 11
first *primero*, 2
fish *el pescado*, 8
fish, to *pescar*, 5
fit, to *quedar*, 9; **It fits you very well.** *Te queda muy bien.*, 9
five *cinco*, 1
five hundred *quinientos/as*, 8
flower shop *la florería*, 9
flowers *las flores*, 9
flu *la gripe*, 11
folder *la carpeta*, 2
food *la comida*, 6
foot *el pie*, 11
football *el fútbol norteamericano*, 1
for *para*, 9; **For whom?** *¿Para quién?*, 9
forest *el bosque*, 12
fork *el tenedor*, 8
formal *formal*, 9
forty *cuarenta*, 2
four *cuatro*, 1
four hundred *cuatrocientos/as*, 8
fourteen *catorce*, 1
France *Francia* (f.), 12
free day *el día libre*, 3
free time *el tiempo libre*, 4
French *el francés*, 3
french fries *las papas fritas*, 5
Friday *el viernes*, 4
friend *el amigo* (male), *la amiga* (female), 1; *el compañero* (male), *la compañera* (female), 3
from *de*, 1
fruit *la fruta*, 1

fun *divertido/a*, 3
funny *cómico/a*, 3

G

game *el juego*, 9; **game of . . . (sport)** *el partido de...*, 3
garbage *la basura*, 4
garden *el jardín*, 6
geography *la geografía*, 3
Germany *Alemania* (f.), 12
get to know someone, to *conocer a*, 2
gift *el regalo*, 9; **to open gifts** *abrir los regalos*, 10; **to receive gifts** *recibir regalos*, 10
girl *la chica*, 5
give, to *dar*; **to give a gift** *regalar*, 9
Gladly! *¡Con mucho gusto!*, 10
glass *el vaso*, 8
go, to *ir*, 2; **Go!** *¡Ve!*, 10; **Go away!** *¡Vete!*, 10; **going to (do something)** *ir* + *a* + infinitive, 7; **to go canoeing** *bajar el río en canoa*, 12; **to go down** *bajar*, 12; **to go hiking** *dar una caminata*, 12; **to go mountain climbing** *escalar montañas*, 12; **to go out** *salir*, 6; **to go sailing** *ir de vela*, 12; **to go sightseeing** *hacer turismo*, 12; **to go skydiving** *saltar en paracaídas*, 12; **to go to the mall** *ir al centro comercial*, 2
good *bueno/a*, 3; **Good afternoon.** *Buenas tardes.*, 1; **Good evening.** *Buenas noches.*, 1; **Good idea.** *Buena idea.*, 10; **Good morning.** *Buenos días.*, 1; **Good night.** *Buenas noches.*, 1
Goodbye. *Adiós.*, 1
good-looking *guapo/a*, 3
graduation *la graduación*, 7; **graduation party** *la fiesta de graduación*, 7
grandfather *el abuelo*, 6
grandmother *la abuela*, 6
grandparents *los abuelos*, 6
grapefruit *la toronja*, 8
grapes *las uvas*, 8
grass *el césped*, 6
gray *gris*, 9; **gray hair** *las canas*, 6
great *excelente*, 1; *estupendo/a*, 1; *¡Magnífico!*, 11
green *verde*, 6
greeting card *la tarjeta*, 9
grocery store *la tienda de comestibles*, 9
guests *los invitados*, 10
guitar *la guitarra*, 4
gym *el gimnasio*, 4

H

hair *el pelo*, 6; **He/she has gray hair.** *Tiene canas.*, 6
half brother *el medio hermano*, 6
half past (the hour) *y media*, 3
half sister *la media hermana*, 6
ham *el jamón*, 8
hamburger *la hamburguesa*, 5
hang up, to *colgar (ue)*, 10
have, to *tener (ie)*, 2; **to have a cold** *estar resfriado/a*, 11; **to have a cough** *tener tos*, 11; **to have a fever** *tener fiebre*, 11; **to have breakfast** *desayunar*, 5; **to have the flu** *tener gripe*, 11; **to have to (do something)** *tener que* + infinitive, 7; **to have to go** *tener que irse*, 1
he *él*, 2
head *la cabeza*, 11
healthy *sano/a*, 11
heat *el calor*, 5
heavy (meal) *fuerte*, 8
Hello. *Aló.*, 7; *Diga.*, 7; *¡Hola!*, 1 (telephone greetings)
help *ayudar*, 5; **Can you help me . . . ?** *¿Me ayudas a...*, 10; **to help at home** *ayudar en casa*, 5
her *la*, 10; **to/for her** *le*, 9
her *su(s)*, 2
here *aquí*, 4
high school *el colegio*, 2
him *lo*, 10; **to/for him** *le*, 9
his *su(s)*, 2
holidays *los días festivos*, 10
home *la casa*, 4; **at home** *en casa*, 4
homework *la tarea*, 1
horrible *horrible*, 1
hot *caliente*, 8; **to be hot** *hacer calor*, 4
hot dog *el perro caliente*, 8
hour *la hora*, 3
house *la casa*, 4
how? *¿cómo?*, 1; **How are you?** *¿Cómo estás?*, 1
How cheap! *¡Qué barato/a!*, 9
How do you feel about . . . ? *¿Qué te parece si...?*, 10
How expensive! *¡Qué caro/a!*, 9
how many? *¿cuántos?*, *¿cuántas?*, 2
how much? *¿cuánto/a?*, 2; **How much do . . . cost?** *¿Cuánto cuestan...?*, 9; **How much does . . . cost?** *¿Cuánto cuesta...?*, 9; **How much is it?** *¿Cuánto es?*, 8
how often? *¿con qué frecuencia?*, 5
How old are you? *¿Cuántos años tienes?*, 1; **How old is (she/he)?** *¿Cuántos años tiene?*, 1
How's it going? *¿Qué tal?*, 1
hundred *cien*, *ciento*, 2
hungry, to be *tener hambre*, 8

hurry *la prisa;* **Hurry up!** *¡Date prisa!,* 3; **I'm in a hurry.** *Tengo prisa.,* 3
hurt, to *doler (ue),* 11
husband *el esposo,* 6

I *yo,* 1
I would like *quisiera,* 8
ice cream *el helado,* 4; **to eat ice cream** *tomar un helado,* 4
iced tea *el té frío,* 8
idea *la idea,* 10
if *si,* 11
I'm sorry. *Lo siento.,* 7
in *en, por, de,* 4; **in order to … ** *para + infinitive,* 4; **in the afternoon** (P.M.) *de la tarde,* 3; *por la tarde,* 5; **in the evening** (P.M.) *de la noche,* 3; *por la noche,* 5; **in the morning** (A.M.) *de la mañana,* 3; *por la mañana,* 5
included *incluido/a,* 8 **Is it included?** *¿Está incluido/a?,* 8
Independence Day *el Día de la Independencia,* 10
inflate, to *inflar,* 10
intelligent *inteligente,* 3
intend, to *pensar + infinitive,* 7
interesting *interesante,* 3
invitation *la invitación,* 10
invite, to *invitar,* 7; **It's my treat.** *Te invito.,* 7
iron, to *planchar,* 6
island *la isla,* 12
isn't it? *¿no?,* 3
it *la, lo,* 10
Italian food *la comida italiana,* 1
Italy *Italia* (f.), 12
It's a rip-off! *¡Es un robo!,* 9
It's cloudy. *Está nublado.,* 5
It's cold. *Hace frío.,* 5
It's cool. *Hace fresco.,* 5
It's hot. *Hace calor.,* 5
It's raining. *Está lloviendo.,* 5; *Llueve.,* 5
It's snowing. *Está nevando.,* 5; *Nieva.,* 5
It's sunny. *Hace sol.,* 5
It's (very) windy. *Hace (mucho) viento.,* 5

jacket *la chaqueta,* 9
January *enero* (m.), 5

jazz *el jazz,* 1
jewelry store *la joyería,* 9
job *el trabajo,* 4
juice *el jugo,* 5; **orange juice** *el jugo de naranja,* 8
July *julio* (m.), 5
June *junio* (m.), 5
jungle *la selva,* 12

kitchen *la cocina,* 6
knife *el cuchillo,* 8
know, to *saber,* 2; *conocer,* 2

lake *el lago,* 7
lamp *la lámpara,* 2
last *pasado/a,* 10; **last night** *anoche,* 10; **last Saturday** *el sábado pasado,* 10; **last summer** *el verano pasado,* 10; **last week** *la semana pasada,* 10; **last year** *el año pasado,* 10
late *atrasado/a, tarde,* 3; **It is late.** *Es tarde.;* **to be late** *estar atrasado/a,* 3
later *más tarde,* 7
lead, to *llevar,* 11; **to lead a healthy life** *llevar una vida sana,* 11
leather (made of) *de cuero,* 9
leave, to *salir,* 6; **to leave a message** *dejar un recado,* 7
leg *la pierna,* 11
lemonade *la limonada,* 8
less *menos,* 6; **less … than** *menos... que,* 9
letter *la carta,* 5
lettuce *la lechuga,* 8
library *la biblioteca,* 4
life *la vida,* 11
lift, to *levantar,* 11; **to lift weights** *levantar pesas,* 11
light *ligero/a,* 8
like, as *como;* **as … as** *tan... como,* 9
like, to *gustar,* 1; **to really like** *encantar,* 8; **I (emphatic) like to …** *A mí me gusta + infinitive,* 4
likewise *igualmente,* 1
line *la línea,* 7; **The line is busy.** *La línea está ocupada.,* 7
listen to, to *escuchar,* 4; **to listen to music** *escuchar música,* 4
little, a *un poco,* 6

live, to *vivir,* 6
living room *la sala,* 6
look at, to *mirar,* 4; **Look!** *¡Mira!,* 4
look for, to *buscar,* 9
look young, to *verse joven,* 6
lot, a *mucho,* 1; *mucho/a,* 2
love, to *encantar,* 8
lunch *el almuerzo,* 3

ma'am *señora,* 1
made of *de,* 3
magazine *la revista,* 2
make, to *hacer,* 2
make the bed, to *hacer la cama,* 6
makeup, to put on *maquillarse,* 7
mall *el centro comercial,* 2
mango *el mango,* 8
many *muchos/as,* 2
March *marzo* (m.), 5
mathematics *las matemáticas,* 3
May *mayo* (m.), 5
maybe *tal vez,* 7
me too *yo también,* 1
meat *la carne,* 8
menu *el menú,* 8
message *el recado,* 7; **May I leave a message?** *¿Puedo dejar un recado?,* 7
Mexican food *la comida mexicana,* 1
mile *la milla,* 5
milk *la leche,* 8
milkshake *el batido,* 8
mineral water *el agua mineral,* 8
mischievous *travieso/a,* 6
miss *señorita,* 1
moment *el momento,* 7
Monday *el lunes,* 4
money *el dinero,* 2
month *el mes,* 5
more *más,* 1; **more … than** *más... que,* 9
morning *la mañana,* 5; **in the morning** (A.M.) *de la mañana,* 3; *por la mañana,* 5
mother/mom *la madre/mamá,* 6; **Mother's Day** *el Día de las Madres,* 10
mountain *la montaña,* 12; **to go mountain climbing** *escalar montañas,* 12
mouth *la boca,* 11
movie *la película,* 4
movie theater *el cine,* 4
Mr. *señor,* 1
Mrs. *señora,* 1
museum *el museo,* 7
music *la música,* 1; **classical music** *la música clásica,* 1; **music**

by... *la música de...*, 1; **pop music** *la música pop*, 1; **rock music** *la música rock*, 1
my *mi*, 2; *mis*, 6

named, to be *llamarse*, 1; **My name is...** *Me llamo...*, 1
napkin *la servilleta*, 8
near *cerca de*, 4
neck *el cuello*, 11
necklace *el collar*, 9
need, to *necesitar*, 2
nervous *nervioso/a*, 11
never *nunca*, 5
new *nuevo/a*, 3; **new friends** *los nuevos amigos*, 2; **New Year's Day** *el Año Nuevo*, 10; **New Year's Eve** *la Nochevieja*, 10
newspaper *el periódico*, 5
next to *al lado de*, 4
nice *simpático/a*, 3
Nice to meet you. *Mucho gusto.*, 1
night *la noche*, 1; **Good night.** *Buenas noches.*, 1; **last night** *anoche*, 10; **the night before last** *anteanoche*, 11
nine *nueve*, 1
nine hundred *novecientos/as*, 8
nineteen *diecinueve*, 1
ninety *noventa*, 2
no *no*, 1
nobody *nadie*, 5
nor *ni*, 6
nose *la nariz*, 11
not *no*, 1
notebook *el cuaderno*, 2
nothing *nada*, 5
novel *la novela*, 3
November *noviembre* (m.), 5
now *ahora*, 3
nowhere *ningún lugar*, 12
number *el número*, P

October *octubre* (m.), 5
of *de*, 3
Of course! *¡Claro que sí!*, 7; *¡Cómo no!*, 7
often *con frecuencia*, 5; *muchas veces*, 5
okay *regular*, 1
old *viejo/a*, 6; **older** *mayor*, 6
on *en*, 3; **on the dot** *en punto*, 3; **on top of** *encima de*, 4

one *uno*, 1; **one moment** *un momento*, 7
one hundred *cien, ciento/a*, 2
one thousand *mil*, 8
onion *la cebolla*, 8
only *sólo*, 5; **only when** *sólo cuando*, 5
open, to *abrir*, 10; **to open gifts** *abrir regalos*, 10
orange *anaranjado/a*, 9
orange *la naranja*, 8; **orange juice** *el jugo de naranja*, 8
order, to *pedir* (i), 8
organize, to *organizar*, 2
other *otro/a*, 8
ought to, should *deber*, 6
our *nuestro/a*, 6
overweight *gordo/a*; **a little overweight** *un poco gordo/a*, 6

pack the suitcase, to *hacer la maleta*, 12
paint, to *pintar*, 4
pal *el compañero* (male), *la compañera* (female), 3
pants *los pantalones*, 9
papaya *la papaya*, 8
paper *el papel*, 2
paradise *el paraíso*, 12
parents *los padres*, 6
park *el parque*, 4; **amusement park** *el parque de atracciones*, 7
party *la fiesta*, 3
pastry shop *la pastelería*, 9
peanut butter *la crema de maní*, 8
pencil *el lápiz* (pl. *los lápices*), 2
perfect *perfecto/a*, 10
perhaps *tal vez*, 7; **perhaps another day** *tal vez otro día*, 7
physical education *la educación física*, 3
piano *el piano*, 4
pineapple *la piña*, 8
pizza *la pizza*, 1
pizzeria *la pizzería*, 2
place *el lugar*, 7
place, to *poner*, 2; **Place!** *¡Pon!*, 10
plaid *de cuadros*, 9
plan *el plan*, 7; **I already have plans.** *Ya tengo planes.*, 7
plan, to *pensar* + infinitive, 7
plant *la planta*, 9
plate *el plato*, 8
play an instrument, to *tocar un instrumento*, 4
playing court *la cancha*, 11
please *por favor*, 8
pop music *la música pop*, 1
post office *el correo*, 4

postcards *las tarjetas postales*, 5
poster *el cartel*, 2
potato *la papa*, 5
potato chips *las papitas*, 8
practice, to *practicar*, 4
prefer, to *preferir* (ie), 7
prepare, to *preparar*, 4
pretty *bonito/a*, 3
price *el precio*, 9; **They're the same price.** *Son del mismo precio.*, 9
problem *el problema*, 6
purple *morado/a*, 9
put on makeup, to *maquillarse*, 7
put, to *poner*, 2; **Put!** *¡Pon!*, 10

quarter to (the hour) *menos cuarto*, 3
quite *bastante*, 6

radio *la radio*, 2
rain, to *llover*, 5
read, to *leer*, 5
ready *listo/a*, 7
receive, to *recibir*, 5; **to receive gifts** *recibir regalos*, 10; **to receive letters** *recibir cartas*, 5
recess *el descanso*, 3
red *rojo/a*, 9
redheaded *pelirrojo/a*, 6
rest, to *descansar*, 4; **to rest in the park** *descansar en el parque*, 4
restaurant *el restaurante*, 4
return, to *regresar*, 4
rice *el arroz*, 8
ride, to *montar*, 4; **to ride a bike** *montar en bicicleta*, 4; **to ride a horse** *montar a caballo*, 11
right? *¿verdad?*, 3
rip-off *el robo*, 9; **It's a rip-off!** *¡Es un robo!*, 9
river *el río*, 12
rock music *la música rock*, 1
roller skate, to *patinar sobre ruedas*, 11
room *el cuarto*, 2
ruler *la regla*, 2
run, to *correr*, 5
running track *la pista de correr*, 11

S

sad *triste*, 11
salad *la ensalada*, 1
salty *salado/a*, 8
same *mismo/a*, 9
Same here. *Igualmente.*, 1
sandals *las sandalias*, 9; *las chancletas*, 12
sandwich *el sándwich*, 5
Saturday *el sábado*, 4
say, to *decir*, 6
scarf *la bufanda*, 12
science *las ciencias*, 3
scuba dive, to *bucear*, 5
seasons *las estaciones*, 5
see, to *ver*, 7; **to see a movie** *ver una película*, 4
See you later. *Hasta luego.*, 1
See you tomorrow. *Hasta mañana.*, 1
seem, to *parecer*, 10; **It seems fine to me.** *Me parece bien.*, 10
semester *el semestre*, 3
send, to *mandar*, 10; **to send invitations** *mandar las invitaciones*, 10
separate *aparte*, 8; **It's separate.** *Es aparte.*, 8
September *septiembre* (m.), 5
set the table, to *poner la mesa*, 6
seven *siete*, 1
seven hundred *setecientos/as*, 8
seventeen *diecisiete*, 1
seventy *setenta*, 2
shave, to *afeitarse*, 7
she *ella*, 2
shirt *la camisa*, 9
shoe *el zapato*, 9
shoe store *la zapatería*, 9
shopping mall *el centro comercial*, 2
short (to describe people) *bajo/a*, 3; (to describe length) *corto/a*, 9
shorts *los pantalones cortos*, 9
should *deber*, 6
shrimp *los camarones*, 8
sick *enfermo/a*, 7
silk (made of) *de seda*, 9
sing, to *cantar*, 4
sir *señor*, 1
sister *la hermana*, 6
six *seis*, 1
six hundred *seiscientos/as*, 8
sixteen *dieciséis*, 1
sixty *sesenta*, 2
skate, to *patinar*, 11
ski, to *esquiar*, 5
skirt *la falda*, 9
skis *los esquís*, 12
sleepy, to be *tener sueño*, 7
slippers *las chancletas*, 12
small *pequeño/a*, 3

smart *listo/a*, 6
snow *la nieve*, 5; **It's snowing.** *Nieva.*, 5
soccer *el fútbol*, 1; **soccer field** *la cancha de fútbol*, 11
social studies *las ciencias sociales*, 3
socks *los calcetines*, 9
soft drink *el refresco*, 4
some *unos/as*, 2
something *algo*, 6
sometimes *a veces*, 5
son *el hijo*, 6
so-so *más o menos*, 1
sorry, I'm *Lo siento*, 7
soup *la sopa*, 8
Spanish *el español*, 1
speak, to *hablar*, 4
spend time with friends, to *pasar el rato con amigos*, 4
spicy *picante*, 8
spoon *la cuchara*, 8
sports *los deportes*, 3
spouse *la esposa* (wife), *el esposo* (husband), 6
spring *la primavera*, 5
stadium *el estadio*, 11
stay, to *quedarse*, 12
steak *el bistec*, 8
stepbrother *el hermanastro*, 6
stepfather *el padrastro*, 6
stepmother *la madrastra*, 6
stepsister *la hermanastra*, 6
still *todavía*, 5
stomach *el estómago*, 11
store *la tienda*, 4
strawberry *la fresa*, 8
stretch, to *estirarse*, 11
strict *estricto/a*, 3
striped *de rayas*, 9
stroll *el paseo*, 4; **to go hiking** *dar una caminata*, 12
strong *fuerte*, 8
student *el/la estudiante*, 3
study, to *estudiar*, 4
subject *la materia*, 3
sugar *el azúcar*, 8
suit *el traje*, 9; **bathing suit** *el traje de baño*, 9
suitcase *la maleta*, 12; **to pack the suitcase** *hacer la maleta*, 12
summer *el verano*, 5
sunbathe, to *tomar el sol*, 12
Sunday *el domingo*, 4
sunglasses *los lentes de sol*, 12
sunscreen *el bloqueador*, 12
supermarket *el supermercado*, 4
Sure! *¡Con mucho gusto!*, 10
surprise *la sorpresa*, 7; **surprise party** *la fiesta de sorpresa*, 7
sweater *el suéter*, 9
sweet *dulce*, 8
sweet rolls *el pan dulce*, 8
sweet shop *la pastelería*, 9
swim, to *nadar*, 4
swimming *la natación*, 1
swimming pool *la piscina*, 4

T

T-shirt *la camiseta*, 9
table *la mesa*, 2
take, to *tomar*, 4
take a shower, to *ducharse*, 7
take a trip, to *hacer un viaje*, 6
take care of, to *cuidar*, 4; **to take care of your brother/sister** *cuidar a tu hermano/a*, 4
take out the trash, to *sacar la basura*, 4
take the bus, to *tomar el autobús*, 5
talk, to *hablar*, 4; **to talk on the phone** *hablar por teléfono*, 4
tall *alto/a*, 3
tea *el té*, 8; **iced tea** *el té frío*, 8
teacher *el profesor* (male), *la profesora* (female), 3
teeth *los dientes*, 7; **to brush one's teeth** *lavarse los dientes*, 7
telephone *el teléfono*, 4
television *la televisión*, 4; **television set** *el televisor*, 2
tell, to *decir*, 6
ten *diez*, 1
tennis *el tenis*, 1; **tennis court** *la cancha de tenis*, 11; **tennis shoes** *las zapatillas de tenis* (Spain), 2
tent *la tienda de camping*, 12
Thanks. *Gracias.*, 1
Thanksgiving *el Día de Acción de Gracias*, 10
that *esa, ese*, 9
that *que*, 4
that's all *nada más*, 11
that's why *por eso*, 4
the *el, la*, 1; *los, las*, 3
theater *el teatro*, 7
their *su(s)*, 6
them *ellas/ellos*, 4; **to/for them** *les*, 9
then *luego*, 3
there *allá*, 4
there is, there are *hay*, 2
these (adj.) *estas, estos*, 9; (pron.) *éstas, éstos*, 6
they *ellas, ellos*, 3
thin *delgado/a*, 6
thing *la cosa*, 2
think, to *creer*, 10; *pensar (ie)*, 7
thirsty, to be *tener sed*, 8
thirteen *trece*, 1
thirty *treinta*, 1
this *esta, este*, 9; *ésta, éste*, 1
those *esas, esos*, 9
thousand *mil*, 8
three *tres*, 1
three hundred *trescientos/as*, 8
throat *la garganta*, 11
Thursday *el jueves*, 4
ticket *el boleto*, 12
tie *la corbata*, 9

time   la hora, 3; **to spend time with friends**   pasar el rato con amigos, 4
tip   la propina, 8
tired   cansado/a, 7
to   a, 4; **to the**   al (a + el), a la, 4; para, 9
to/for her, him, you   le, 9; **to/for me**   me, 9; **to/for them, you (pl.)**   les, 9; **to/for us**   nos, 9; **to/for you**   te, 9
toast   el pan tostado, 8
today   hoy, 3
toe   el dedo, 11
together   juntos/as, 5
tomato   el tomate, 8
tomorrow   mañana, 3
too   también, 1
too much   demasiado/a, 6
towel   la toalla, 12
toys   los juguetes, 9
toy store   la juguetería, 9
trash   la basura, 4
trip   el viaje, 6; **to take a trip**   hacer un viaje, 6
true   cierto, 6; verdad, 3
Tuesday   el martes, 4
tuna   el atún, 8
twelve   doce, 1
twenty   veinte, 1
two   dos, 1
two hundred   doscientos/as, 8
typically   típicamente, 5

ugly   feo/a, 3
uncle   el tío, 6
under   debajo de, 4
usual   lo de siempre, 9

vacation   las vacaciones, 5; **on vacation**   de vacaciones, 12
vacuum cleaner   la aspiradora, 6; **to vacuum**   pasar la aspiradora, 6
Valentine's Day   el Día de los Enamorados, 10
vegetables   las legumbres, 8
very   muy, 1; **very bad**   muy mal, 1; **very well**   muy bien, 1
video game   el videojuego, 3
visit, to   visitar, 6
volleyball   el voleibol, 1

waiter   el camarero, 8
waitress   la camarera, 8
walk   la caminata, 12
walk, to   caminar, 4; **to walk the dog**   caminar con el perro, 4
wallet   la cartera, 9
want, to   querer (ie), 2
wash, to   lavar, 4; **to wash the car**   lavar el coche, 4; **to wash oneself**   lavarse, 7
watch   el reloj, 2
watch, to   mirar, 4; **to watch TV**   mirar la televisión, 4
water   el agua (pl. las aguas), 5; **mineral water**   el agua mineral, 8
we   nosotros/as, 4
wear, to   llevar, 9
weather   el tiempo, 5; **The weather is bad.**   Hace mal tiempo., 5; **The weather is nice.**   Hace buen tiempo., 5; **What's the weather like?**   ¿Qué tiempo hace?, 5
wedding   la boda, 7
Wednesday   el miércoles, 4
week   la semana, 4
weekend   el fin de semana, 4
weights   las pesas, 11
well   bien, 1; **I'm (pretty) well, thanks.**   Estoy (bastante) bien, gracias., 1
Well, . . .   Bueno..., 2
what?   ¿cuál?, 3; ¿qué?, 3
What a bargain!   ¡Qué ganga!, 9
What are . . . like?   ¿Cómo son...?, 3
What a shame!   ¡Qué lástima!, 7
What color is . . .?   ¿De qué color es...?, 6
What did you do?   ¿Qué hiciste?, 10
What do you like?   ¿Qué te gusta?, 1
What do you like to do?   ¿Qué te gusta hacer?, 4
What if . . .?   ¿Qué tal si...?, 11
What is today's date?   ¿Cuál es la fecha?, 5; ¿Qué fecha es hoy?, 5
What's . . . like?   ¿Cómo es...?, 3
What's the matter?   ¿Qué tienes?, 11
What's wrong with . . .?   ¿Qué le pasa a...?, 11
What's your name?   ¿Cómo te llamas?, 1
What should I do?   ¿Qué debo hacer?, 6
What time is it?   ¿Qué hora es?, 3
when   cuando, 5
when?   ¿cuándo?, 3
where   donde, 1
where?   ¿dónde?, 4; **Where are you from?**   ¿De dónde eres?, 1
where (to)?   ¿adónde?, 4
which   que, 4

which?   ¿cuál?, 3; ¿qué?, 1
white   blanco/a, 9
who   que, 4
who?   ¿quién?, 4; ¿quiénes?, 5; **Who likes . . .?**   ¿A quién le gusta...?, 4; **Who's calling?**   ¿De parte de quién?, 7
why?   ¿por qué?, 3; **Why don't you . . .?**   ¿Por qué no...?, 11
wife   la esposa, 6
win, to   ganar, 11
window   la ventana, 2
winter   el invierno, 5
wish, to   querer (ie), 2
with   con, 4; **with me**   conmigo, 4; **with you**   contigo, 4
wool (made of)   de lana, 9
work   el trabajo, 4
work, to   trabajar, 4; **to work in the garden**   trabajar en el jardín, 6
worried about something   preocupado/a por algo, 11
worry, to   preocuparse, 3; **Don't worry!**   ¡No te preocupes!, 3
Would you like . . .?   ¿Te gustaría...?, 7; **I would like . . .**   Me gustaría..., 7; Quisiera..., 8
write, to   escribir, 5

year   el año, 5; **last year**   el año pasado, 10; **How old is (she/he)?**, ¿Cuántos años tiene?, 1; **I'm . . . years old.**   Tengo... años, 1
yellow   amarillo/a, 9
yes   sí, 1
yesterday   ayer, 10
yet   todavía, 5; **not yet**   todavía no, 5
yoga   la yoga, 11; **to do yoga**   hacer yoga, 11
you   tú, vosotros/as (informal), 4
you   usted, ustedes, 4
young   joven, 6; **She/He looks young.**   Se ve joven., 6
younger   menor, 6
your   tu, 2; tus, 6; su, 2; sus 6; vuestro/a(s), 6

zero   cero, 1
zoo   el zoológico, 7

Page numbers in boldface type refer to **Gramática** and **Nota gramatical** presentations. Other page numbers refer to grammar structures presented in the **Así se dice, Nota cultural, Vocabulario,** and **A lo nuestro** sections. Page numbers beginning with R refer to the Grammar Summary in this Reference Section (pages R9–R13).

A

a: **149**, 269, 334; see also prepositions

accent marks: 5, **23**

adjectives: agreement—masculine and feminine **93**; agreement—singular and plural **58, 93**, R10; demonstrative adjectives all forms **279**, R10; possessive adjectives all forms **174**, R10

adónde: **123**, R11; see also question words

adverbs: adverbs of frequency—**siempre, sólo cuando, nunca, todavía, todos los días, muchas veces** 145; **una vez, de vez en cuando, todo el tiempo, cada día, a menudo** 151; adverbs of sequence—**primero, después, luego** 84, 361; adverbs of time—**de la mañana, de la tarde, de la noche** 88; **por la mañana, por la tarde, por la noche** 151; **anoche, ayer, la semana pasada** 307

affirmative expressions: **algo** 180, 246, 274, 334, R11; **alguien** R11; **alguno (algún), alguna,** R11; **o ... o** R11; **sí** 32, 85; **siempre** 145, 180, R11; **ya** 52, 85, 217

al: contraction of **a + el 114,** 123, R9; see also prepositions

algo: 180, 246, 274, 334, R11

almorzar: 238, 362, R12; see also verbs

-ando: 299

-ar verbs: regular tense **114,** R11; preterite tense **307, 371,** R13; see also verbs

articles: **el, la** 33, R9; **los, las** 83, R9; **un, una 51, 53,** R9; **unos, unas** 53, R9

C

calendar expressions: dates **154**; days of the week 124

commands (imperatives): 90, 92; introduction to informal commands **304**

cómo: 30, 92, 178, R11; see also question words

comparisons: with adjectives using **más ... que, menos ... que, tan ... como** 277, R11; all comparatives, including **tanto/a/os/as ... como** R11

con: **116**; see also prepositions

conjunctions: **pero** 32, 217; **y** 217; **o** 148, 277, 279; **porque** 95; subordinating conjunction: **que** 184

conmigo: **116**

contigo: **116**

contractions: **al 114,** 123, R9; **del 89**

cuál: 95, 154, 277, 279, R11; see also question words

cuando: 145

cuándo: 84, R11; see also question words

cuánto: agreement with nouns **58, 174;** used as a question word 246, 280; see also question words

D

dates (calendar): **154**

days of the week: **124**

de: used in showing possession **89**; used with color 178; used with material or pattern **275**; used as a preposition 114, 119; see also prepositions

deber: all present tense forms **184**

definite articles: **el, la** 33, R9; **los, las** 83, R9

del: contraction of **de + el 89**

demonstrative adjectives: all forms **279**, R10

demonstrative pronouns: **ésta** and **éste** 22; see also pronouns

diminutives: 187

direct object pronouns: **lo, la 310**, R10; see also pronouns

doler: with parts of the body **336**; all present tense forms R12

dónde: 28, 30, 118, 271, R11; see also question words

durante: 145; see also prepositions

E

e → ie stem-changing verbs: **querer, empezar, preferir, tener, venir 209, 362,** R12; **pensar 212,** R12; see also verbs

el: **33,** R9; see also definite articles

empezar: **209, 362,** R12; see also verbs

en: as "on" 88; as "at" 145; see also prepositions

encantar: **236,** R13

-er verbs: regular tense **150,** R11; see also verbs

estar: all present tense forms **118**; to ask how someone is and say how you are 24; to tell where people and things are located **118**; to talk about how things taste, look, or feel 240; contrasted with **ser** 240, 369; **estar** + present participle **299**

F

frequency: adverbs of—**siempre, sólo cuando, nunca, todavía, todos los días, muchas veces** 145; **una vez, de vez en cuando, todo el tiempo, cada día, a menudo** 151

future plans: expressions in the present tense 362

ACKNOWLEDGMENTS

For permission to reprint copyrighted material, grateful acknowledgment is made to the following sources:

Banco Central de Cuenca: Excerpts and illustrations from "Calendario de Eventos" from *60 Aniversario de la Fundación del Banco Central de Cuenca, Antiguo Hospital San Vicente de Paul,* June–July 1988.

Cafélibro, Ecuador: Advertisement for "Cafélibro" from the "Caleidoscopio" section from *El Comercio,* September 4, 1993.

Casa de la Cultura Ecuatoriana: Advertisement for "En el Museo de Arte Moderno de la Casa de la Cultura Ecuatoriana" from the "Registro Cultural" section from *El Comercio,* September 6, 1993.

La Choza: Advertisement for "La Choza: El palacio de la comida ecuatoriana" from brochure, *Viajes y entretenimientos guía de establecimientos Diners Club del Ecuador.*

Cines Lumiere: Advertisement for "Cines Lumiere" from *Guía El País,* no. 57, December 27, 1990.

Club de Tenis Las Lomas: Advertisement for "Club de Tenis Las Lomas" from *Guía El País,* no. 57, December 27, 1990.

Colsanitas: Adaptation from "17 Claves para manejar el Estrés" (retitled "7 Claves para manejar el Estrés") from *Bienestar,* no. 9. Copyright © by Colsanitas.

Compañía de Turismo, Estado Libre Asociado de Puerto Rico: Excerpts and symbols from brochure, "Descubre los Paradores de Puerto Rico."

Diario Hoy: Advertisement for "El Cafélibro" from the "Ruta del lector" section from *Hoy,* February 11, 1994.

Editorial Atlántida, S.A.: Front cover from video, *Billiken presenta: Mundo Marino.* Copyright © 1992 by Editorial Atlántida, S.A. Excerpt from "Deportes en el agua" by Alejandra Becco from *Billiken,* no. 3762, February 17, 1992. Copyright © 1992 by Editorial Atlántida, S.A. "El esqueleto" and text from front cover of *Billiken,* no. 3767, March 23, 1992. Copyright © 1992 by Editorial Atlántida, S.A. Spaceship drawing and text from "El transbordador espacial" from *Billiken,* no. 3791, September 7, 1992. Copyright © 1992 by Editorial Atlántida, S.A.

Editorial Televisa: Text from front cover of *GeoMundo,* año XXI, no. 6, 1997. Copyright © 1997 by Editorial Televisa. From "Dile adiós a las tensiones... ¡Con ejercicios!" from the "Consejos" section from *Tú Internacional,* año 11, no. 5, May 1990. Copyright © 1990 by Editorial Televisa. Header and adaptation of excerpts from "línea directa" from *Tú Internacional,* año 13, no. 11, November 1992. Copyright © 1992 by Editorial Televisa. From "La Chica Sandwich" from *Tú Internacional,* año 14, no. 1, January 1993. Copyright © 1993 by Editorial Televisa. Header and adaptation of excerpts from "línea directa" from *Tú Internacional,* año 14, no. 6, June 1993. Copyright © 1993 by Editorial Televisa.

Editorial Televisión, S.A. de C.V.: Excerpts adapted from *Tele*Guía,* año 42, no. 2159, December 25-31, 1993. Copyright © 1993 by Editorial Televisión, S.A. de C.V.

Fortín Salteño: Restaurant receipt from Fortín Salteño.

La Guarida del Coyote: Advertisement for "La Guarida del Coyote" from brochure, *Viajes y entretenimientos guía de establecimientos Diners Club del Ecuador.*

Hotel Tryp María Pita: Advertisement for "Hotel Tryp María Pita."

Instituto Municipal de Deportes, Ayuntamiento de Madrid: Advertisement for "Piscina Municipal Aluche" from the "En Forma" section from *Guía El País,* no. 57, December 27, 1990.

Mango: Photographs, descriptive labels, and prices from *Suplemento Mango,* Summer 1992. Photographs, descriptive labels, and prices from Mango, Winter 1992–1993.

Normandie: Advertisement for "Normandie: Cocina Francesa Clásica" from brochure, *Viajes y entretenimientos guía de establecimientos Diners Club del Ecuador.*

The Quintus Communications Group: Excerpts from "Diez cosas curiosas para hacer en la Pequeña Habana" (retitled "Cinco cosas curiosas para hacer en la Pequeña Habana") from *Miami Mensual,* año 13, no. 3, March 1993. Copyright © 1993 by The Quintus Communications Group.

Rincón la Ronda Restaurante: Advertisement for "Rincón la Ronda Restaurante" from brochure, *Viajes y entretenimientos guía de establecimientos Diners Club del Ecuador.*

San Antonio Convention Center and Visitors Bureau: "San Antonio" design, text and photograph from "1: Rio San Antonio," text and photograph from "16: Las Misiones," text from "San Antonio ofrece generosas porciones de su vida cosmopolita..., añaden su sabor propio," text and photographs from "Festivales," text and photographs from "Restaurantes," and text and photographs from "Compras" from *San Antonio...Guía de visitantes y mapa* by the Oficina de Convenciones y Visitantes de San Antonio.

Scholastic, Inc.: Adapted text, photographs, and illustrations from "¿Cuáles son las vacaciones ideales para ti?" from *¿Qué tal?,* vol. 24, no. 6, April–May 1990. Copyright © 1990 by Scholastic, Inc.

Teatro República: Advertisement for "Teatro República" from the "Deportes" section from *El Comercio,* August 22, 1993.

PHOTOGRAPHY CREDITS

Abbreviations used: (t) top, (b) bottom, (c) center, (l) left, (r) right, (bkgd) background.

All photographs belong to Holt, Rinehart and Winston by Marty Granger/Edge Video Productions except:

Page ix (br) John Langford/HRW; xii (b) Robert Frerck/Odyssey/Chicago; xvi (b) Sam Dudgeon/HRW; xvii (t) Joe Viesti/Viesti Collection; xix (t) Michael Heron/Corbis Stock Market; xix (b) Comstock; xx (t) Suzanne L. Murphy/DDB Stock; 2 (tl) Univision; (br) Michelle Bridwell/Frontera Fotos; (tr) Christine Galida/HRW; (cl) Digital imagery (c) copyright 2003 PhotoDisc, Inc.; (bl) Christine Galida/HRW; 4 (cr) Christie's Images/SuperStock; (tl) Christie's Image/SuperStock; (cl) SuperStock; (bl) Culver Pictures, Inc.; (br) Laurie Platt Winfrey, Inc.; Sor Juana Inés del la Cruz (detail); oil; Miranda; 1651; University of Mexico City.; (tr) Jonathan Daniel/Allsport; 6 (B, J, CH, D, F, G, L, LL,) Sam Dudgeon/HRW; (A, C, I, K) Digital imagery (c) copyright 2003 PhotoDisc, Inc.; (H) Corbis Images; 7 (M, N, Ñ, P, S, U, V, Z) Sam Dudgeon/HRW (O, RR, T, W) Digital imagery (c) copyright 2003 PhotoDisc, Inc.; (Q) Michael Fogden/Animals, Animals/Earth Scenes; (R) C. Prescott-Allen/Animals, Animals/Earth Scenes; (RR) Digital imagery (c) copyright 2003 PhotoDisc, Inc.; (X) Victoria Smith/HRW; (Y) Corbis Images; 8 (all) EyeWire, Inc.; 9 (all) Michelle Bridwell/Frontera Fotos; 11 (all) Victoria Smith/HRW; 12 (border) Joe Viesti/Viesti Collection, Inc.; 12–13 (all) Dallas & John Heaton/ Westlight; 14 (cr) Zygmont Nowak Solins/Tony Stone Images; (tr) Danilo Boschung/Leo de Wys; (l) Steve Vidler/Leo de Wys; 14–15 (c) Latin Focus/HRW; 15 (t) David R. Frazier Photolibrary; (cr) Steve Vidler /Leo de Wys; (br) Mike Busselle/Leo de Wys; 26 (tr) David R. Frazier Photolibrary; 27 (1, 9) Mavournea Hay/Frontera Fotos; (10) Michelle Bridwell/Frontera Fotos; (all others) Sam Dudgeon/HRW; 29 (cr) AP/Wide World Photos/Daniel Maurer; (bl, br) Michelle Bridwell/ Frontera Fotos; 34 (tr) John Langford/HRW; (br) Steve Powell/Allsport; (cr, bl) John Langford/HRW; (cl) UPPER DECK and the Upper Deck logo are trademarks of The Upper Deck Company, LLC. (c) 2000 The Upper Deck Company, LLC. All rights reserved. Used with permission.; (cl) SuperStock; 36 (tr) Samivel–Rapho/ Gamma Liaison; (br) Billiken, no. 3767, March 23, 1992. Copyright (c) 1992 by Editorial Atlántida, S.A.; 37 (tl) Billiken, no. 3791, September 7, 1992. Copyright (c) 1992 by Editorial Atlántida, S.A.; (b) John Cancalosi/Stock Boston; 43 (br) Michelle Bridwell/Frontera Fotos; 47 (border) Joe Viesti/Viesti Collection, Inc.; 48 (cr) Sam Dudgeon/HRW; 49 (tl, tr, cr) Sam Dudgeon/HRW; 57 (br) John Langford/HRW; 58 (tr) Michelle Bridwell/ Frontera Fotos; 59 (all) Michelle Bridwell/Frontera Fotos; 61 (all) Michelle Bridwell/Frontera Fotos; 64 (tl) Temas de Hoy: Front cover of book, Nutrición y Salud by Francisco Grande Covian. (c) by Temas de Hoy.; (cl) Emecé Editores, S.A.: Front cover from 50 cosas que los niûos pueden hacer para salvar la tierra by The Earth Works Group; (br) Editorial de Vecchi, S.A.: Front cover from Guía completa para el adiestramiento del perro by Vittoria Rossi; 65 (cr) Penguin photo by Sergio Fitch; (br) Billiken presenta: Mundo Marino Copyright (c) 1992 by Editorial Atlántida, S.A.; 67 (cr) Scott Van Osdol/HRW; 70 (all) Sam Dudgeon/HRW; 71 (all) Michelle Bridwell/Frontera Fotos; 74 (border) Robert Frerck/Odyssey/Chicago; 74–75 (all) Peter Gridley/FPG International; 75 (tr) Marie Ueda /Leo de Wys; 76 (cr) Chip & Rosa María de la Cueva Peterson; (b) Randy Faris/Westlight; 77 (cl) Jorge Núñez/Latin Focus; (tl) SuperStock; (tr) Randy J. Faris/Westlight; (b) Melinda Berge/Bruce Coleman, Inc.; 85 (a, d, f, h) Sam Dudgeon/HRW; (b, e) Richard Haynes/HRW; (c) Ken Lax/HRW; (g) Richard Haynes/HRW; 86 (tr) Chip & Rosa María de la Cueva Peterson; 91 (r) Michelle Bridwell/Frontera Fotos; 100 (c) Sam Dudgeon/HRW; 101 (tr) Chip & Rosa María de la Cueva Peterson; 106 (cl) John Langford/HRW; (l) Michelle Bridwell/Frontera Fotos; (r) Charles Palek/Animals, Animals/Earth Scenes; (tl) Sam Dudgeon/HRW; (tcl) Richard Haynes/HRW; (tr) Eric Beggs/HRW; 109 (border) Robert Frerck/Odyssey/ Chicago; 113 (tl) David Young-Wolff/PhotoEdit; (tr, bl, br) Michelle Bridwell/Frontera Fotos; 115 (tc) Index Stock Photography, Inc.; (cl, cr) Peter Van Steen/HRW; (tl) Robert Frerck/Woodfin Camp & Associates, Inc.; (tr, br) Michelle Bridwell/Frontera Fotos; (bl) Bob Daemmrich Photography; 134 (tr) Sam Dudgeon/HRW; 136 (border) Christine Galida/HRW; 136–137 (all) SuperStock; 138 (cr) Stephen Frink/The Stock Market; (bl) Fritz Polking/Peter Arnold, Inc.; 139 (tl) José Fernández/ Woodfin Camp & Associates, Inc.; (br) Tony Arruza/ Bruce Coleman, Inc.; (bl) David Phillips/HRW; 140–41 (all) Robert Frerck/Odyssey/Chicago; 147 (b) Universal Press Syndicate; 148 (cr) Michelle Bridwell/Frontera Fotos; (bl) Michelle Bridwell/Frontera Fotos; (bc) Michelle Bridwell/Frontera Fotos; (bc) Michelle Bridwell/Frontera Fotos; (br) Michelle Bridwell/Frontera Fotos; 149 (tl) Mark Richards/PhotoEdit; (all others) Michelle Bridwell/Frontera Fotos; 150 (bl) Stuart Cohen/

Comstock; 151 (tl) D. L. Baldwin/Index Stock; (t, tr, c, cr) Michelle Bridwell/Frontera Fotos; (cl) John Langford/ HRW; 158 (tr) Michelle Bridwell/Frontera Fotos; (cr) Bob Martin/Allsport; 159 (t, cl) Comstock; (bc) Peter Grumann/Image Bank; 160 (c) Sam Dudgeon/HRW; 164 (tl) David Young–Wolff/PhotoEdit; (tr) Susan Van Etten/ PhotoEdit; (cl) SuperStock; (cr) Michelle Bridwell/ Frontera Fotos; 169 (border) Christine Galida/HRW; 173 (tl, tr) Michelle Bridwell/Frontera Fotos; (cl) Index Stock; (br) David Young–Wolff/PhotoEdit; 177 (all) Michelle Bridwell/Frontera Fotos; 178 (bc) John Langford/HRW; 180 (bl, cl) Michelle Bridwell/Frontera Fotos; (cr) HRW Photo; (br) Robert Frerck/Woodfin Camp & Associates, Inc.; 181 (bl) Comstock; 182 (all) Sam Dudgeon/HRW; 184 (all) Michelle Bridwell/Frontera Fotos; 188 (all) Michelle Bridwell/Frontera Fotos; 189 (tl) Michelle Bridwell/Frontera Fotos; (t) Bob Thomason/Tony Stone Images; (cl, bl, br) Michelle Bridwell/Frontera Fotos; 196 (all) Natasha Lane/HRW; 198–199 (all) R. Smith/Leo de Wys; 200 (b) Suzanne L. Murphy/DDB Stock; (tr) Suzanne L. Murphy/DDB Stock; 201 (t) Suzanne L. Murphy/FPG International; (bl) Kevin Schafer/Peter Arnold, Inc.; (cr) The Art Archive/Catholic University Quito Ecuador/Dagli Orti; 202–203 (all) Martha Granger Photography/HRW; 204 (all) Martha Granger Photography/ HRW; 205 (all) Martha Granger Photography/HRW; 207 (c) Comstock; (br) Stuart Cohen/Comstock; 208 (br) David Young Wolff/Tony Stone Images; 213 (bl) David Phillips/Words & Images; (cr) Chip & Rosa María de la Cueva Peterson; 214 (all) Sam Dudgeon/HRW; 217 (tl) David Phillips/HRW; 220 (tl) Metaphoto/HRW; (cr, bl) Digital imagery (c) copyright 2003 PhotoDisc, Inc.; (c) Corbis Images; 221 (tl) Digital imagery (c) copyright 2003 PhotoDisc, Inc.; (tr) EyeWire, Inc., Image Club Graphics (c) 1998 Adobe Systems, Inc.; 224 (c) Michelle Bridwell/ Frontera Fotos; 232 (all) Martha Granger Photography/ HRW; 233 (all) Martha Granger Photography/HRW; 235 (all) Sam Dudgeon/HRW; 236 (all) Sam Dudgeon/HRW; 237 (tl) Corbis Images; (tl, tc) Sam Dudgeon/HRW; (c, cr, cl) Digital imagery (c) copyright 2003 PhotoDisc, Inc.; (tr) Sam Dudgeon/HRW; (tc, r, cl) Corbis Images; 240 (b) Universal Press Syndicate; 242 (cl) Martha Granger Photography/HRW; (cr) Martha Granger Photography/ HRW; 244 (cl) Sam Dudgeon/HRW; 245 (flan) Michelle Bridwell/HRW; (camarones) Michelle Bridwell/HRW; (agua) Sam Dudgeon/HRW; (all others) Digital imagery (c) copyright 2003 PhotoDisc, Inc.; 250 (cr) Sam Dudgeon/HRW; 251 (bl) Sam Dudgeon/HRW; 258

(cl, cr, br) Sam Dudgeon/HRW; (bl) Michelle Bridwell/Frontera Fotos; 260–261(all) Sanford/Richard Stockton; 262 (l) C.H. Chryslin/Tony Stone Images; (tr) Courtesy Texas Highways Magazine; (br) Courtesy Texas Highways Magazine; 263 (bl) Stephanie Maize/HBJ Photo; (tl) Michail Schneps/Image Bank; (cr) Bullaty Lomeo/Image Bank; 264–265 (all) Sam Dudgeon/ HRW; 269 (all) Sam Dudgeon/HRW; 276 (t) Carmen Lomas Garza/Wolfgang Dietze; 278 (cr) Digital imagery (c) copyright 2003 PhotoDisc, Inc.; (bc, br) Sam Dudgeon/HRW; (bl) Corbis Images; 279 (cr) Michelle Bridwell/Frontera Fotos; 282 (tc, bc) Courtesy of Adkins Agency, San Antonio, Texas; 283 (tl, c, bl) Courtesy of Adkins Agency, San Antonio, Texas; 284 (c) Michelle Bridwell/Frontera Fotos; 285 (c) Michelle Bridwell/ Frontera Fotos; 288 (all) Sam Dudgeon/HRW; 289 (tr) Digital imagery (c) copyright 2003 PhotoDisc, Inc.; 292–293 (all) Joe Viesti/Viesti Collection, Inc.; (all others) Sam Dudgeon/HRW; 297 (tl) Christine Galida/HRW; 297 (tcr) Pascuas John Neuauer/PhotoEdit; (br) Bob Daemmrich Photography; (tcl) Steven D. Elmore/The Stock Market; (tr) Chip & Rosa María de la Cueva Peterson; (bl) Bob Daemmrich/Tony Stone Images; (bcl, bcr) Michelle Bridwell/Frontera Fotos; 299 (all) David Phillips/Words & Images; 306 (tc) Ramey/Woodfin Camp & Associates, Inc.; 308 (br) John Feingersch/The Stock Market; 309 (br) Rob Gage/FPG International; 312 (cr) Fundación de Etnomusicología y Folklore; (bl) Jack Messler/DDB Stock; 313 (t) Héctor Méndez Caratini; (b) Joe Viesti/Viesti Collection; 318 (all) David Phillips/ Words & Images; 322 (border) Suzanne Murphy-Larronde; 322–323 (all) Ben Simmons/The Stock Market; 324 (tr) SuperStock; (b) Wolfgang Kaehler Photography; 325 (tl, br) DDB Stock/Suzanne Murphy-Larronde; (cr, c) David R. Frazier Photolibrary; (cl) Ira Block/Image Bank; 337 (c) Comstock; 341 (cr) Josy Sturino/Allsport; (cl) Dave Cannon/Tony Stone Images; 343 (tl, cl) Peter Van Steen/HRW; (tr, cr, tr) Michelle Bridwell/Frontera Fotos; 346 (all) Michelle Bridwell/Frontera Fotos; 347 (cl) Michelle Bridwell/Frontera Fotos; 349 (tl) Michelle Bridwell/Frontera Fotos; 351(bc) Daniel J. Schaefer; 352 (cl) Jim Cummins/FPG International; (br) Richard Martin Vandystadt/Allsport; 356 (border) Suzanne Murphy-Larronde; 356–357 (all) Michael Heron/Corbis Stock Market; 359 (tl) Dan Morrison; 368 (tr) David R. Frazier Photolibrary; 370 (cl) John Heaton/Westlight; (cr) Art Wolfe/AllStock; 379 (bc) FPG International.

ILLUSTRATIONS AND CARTOGRAPHY CREDITS

Abbreviations used : (t) top; (b) bottom; (l) left; (r) right; (c) center.

All art, unless otherwise noted, by Holt, Rinehart & Winston.

FRONT MATTER: Page xxiii, MapQuest.com; xxiv–xxv, MapQuest.com; xxvi, MapQuest.com; xxvii, MapQuest.com; xxviii, MapQuest.com; xxix, MapQuest.com.

PRELIMINARY CHAPTER: Page xxx–1, MapQuest.com; 3, MapQuest.com; 9, Precision Graphics; 10, Precision Graphics.

CHAPTER ONE: Page 12, MapQuest.com; 22, Edson Campos; 25, Edson Campos; 28, Manuel García/Richard Salzman; 32, Edson Campos; 40, MapQuest.com.

CHAPTER TWO: Page 51, Edson Campos; 53, Mauro Mistiano; 54, Edson Campos; 56, Antonio Castro; 72, Eva Vagretti Cockrille.

CHAPTER THREE: Page 74, MapQuest.com; 83, Holly Cooper; 86, Precision Graphics; 92, Holly Copper; 94, Antonio Castro; 95, Holly Cooper; 104, Precision Graphics.

CHAPTER FOUR: Page 111, Eva Vagretti Cockrille; 118, Ignacio Gomez/Carol Chislovsky Design, Inc.; 119, Eva Vagretti Cockrille; 120, Gary Undercuffler; 122, MapQuest.com.

CHAPTER FIVE: Page 136, MapQuest.com; 147, Edson Campos; 152, Edson Campos; 154, Eva Vagretti Cockrille; 155, Edson Campos; 156, Precision Graphics; 165, Precision Graphics.

CHAPTER SIX: Page 175, Reggie Holladay; 179, Meryl Henderson; 185, Ignacio Gomez/Carol Chislovsky Design, Inc.; 186, Fian Arroyo/Dick Washington; 192, Fian Arroyo/Dick Washington; 194, Fian Arroyo/Dick Washington.

CHAPTER SEVEN: Page 198, MapQuest.com; 210, Edson Campos; 212, Reggie Holladay; 215, Meryl Henderson; 218, Edson Campos; 226, Eva Vagretti Cockrille.

CHAPTER EIGHT: Page 241, Fian Arroyo/Dick Washington; 243, Precision Graphics.

CHAPTER NINE: Page 260, MapQuest.com; 271, Eva Vagretti Cockrille; 274, Edson Campos; 276, Fian Arroyo/Dick Washington; 278, Mauro Mistiano; 290 (tc), Precision Graphics; 290 (c), Mauro Mistiano.

CHAPTER TEN: Page 298, Holly Cooper; 302, Ignacio Gomez/Carol Chislovsky Design, Inc.; 305, Fian Arroyo/Dick Washington; 308, Meryl Henderson; 309, Mauro Mistiano; 303, Fian Arrayo/Dick Washington; 317, Meryl Henderson; 320, Meryl Henderson.

CHAPTER ELEVEN: Page 322, MapQuest.com; 331, Fian Arroyo/Dick Washington; 332, Edson Campos; 334, Bob McMahon; 335, Fian Arroyo/Dick Washington; 336, Edson Campos; 340, Edson Campos; 342, Ignacio Gomez/Carol Chislovsky Design, Inc.; 352, Fian Arroyo/Dick Washington; 354, Meryl Henderson.

CHAPTER TWELVE: Page 361, José Luis Briseño; 363, Ignacio Gomez/Carol Chislovsky Design, Inc.; 364, Ignacio Gomez/Carol Chislovsky Design, Inc.; 366, Holly Cooper; 371, Ignacio Gomez/Carol Chislovsky Design, Inc.; 374–375, Holly Cooper; 376, Edson Campos; 380, Bob McMahon; 382, Meryl Henderson.